HUMAN RESOURCE MANAGEMENT

CONTENTS

PART 1 RECRUITMENT AND PLACEMENT 74

CHAPTER 3

JOB ANALYSIS 76

CHAPTER 4

PERSONNEL PLANNING AND RECRUITING 107

CHAPTER 5

EMPLOYEE TESTING AND SELECTION 153

CHAPTER 9

MANAGING QUALITY AND PRODUCTIVITY 299

CHAPTER 10

CHAPTER 11

CHAPTER 12

CHAPTER 13

PAY-FOR-PERFORMANCE AND FINANCIAL INCENTIVES 454

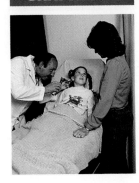

PART 4 LABOR RELATIONS 526

CHAPTER 15

BASICS OF LABOR RELATIONS 528

CHAPTER 16

COLLECTIVE BARGAINING 565

CHAPTER 17

CHAPTER 18

NOTICE
THE FOLLOWING PERSONAL PROTECTIVE EQUIPMENT IS REQUIRED ON THIS PROPERTY
HARD HAT
SAFETY GLASSES
SAFETY SHOES

PREFACE

Human Resource Management provides students in human resource/personnel management courses and practicing managers with a complete, comprehensive review of essential personnel management concepts and techniques in a highly readable and understandable form.

This Sixth Edition has several distinguishing characteristics. While it again focuses almost entirely on essential personnel management topics like job analysis, testing, compensation, and appraisal, *fostering employee commitment* is used as an integrating theme. Practical applications—such as how to appraise performance, how to establish pay plans, and how to handle grievances—are used throughout to provide students with important personnel management skills. Because all managers have personnel-related responsibilities, *Human Resource Management* is aimed at all students of management, not just those who will some day carry the title Human Resource Manager. The legal environment of personnel management—equal employment, labor relations, and occupational safety—is covered fully. A complete instructor's manual and computerized test bank are available, as is a new computer simulation package and several other supplements (described below). A continuing case that runs through each chapter provides vignettes that illustrate the front-line supervisor's role in personnel management.

Many important changes have been made in this sixth edition. Every chapter has been updated to include the latest material on topics such as the Family and Medical Leave Act of 1993, the Civil Rights Act of 1991, controlling benefit costs due to AIDS, wrongful discharge, substance abuse, and health insurance cost containment. As this sixth edition goes to press, I feel even more strongly than I did when the first edition was published that all managers—not just human resource/personnel managers—need a strong foundation in personnel management concepts and techniques to do their jobs. I have, therefore, increased the practical techniques contained in this book by adding more "how-to" topics such as how to deal with substance abusers and how to avoid wrongful dismissal charges.

Adopters of the previous edition will also find several other *major changes* to this edition, including the following:

- The chapter sequence has been revised, in response to adopters' and reviewers' recommendations. Chapter 2 (Equal Employment Opportunity and the Law) is no longer part of the Recruitment and Placement chapters; it is now grouped with Chapter 1, to underscore the impact Equal Employment legislation has on all the personnel/human resource management activities. Similarly,
- The chapter on Performance Appraisal (which followed the Compensation chapters in the fifth edition) has been repositioned to the section on Training and Development, so that it now precedes the Compensation chapters. Similarly,

- The Career Management chapter (which was toward the end of the book in the fifth edition) has been repositioned; it is now grouped with the Training and Development chapters that immediately precede the Compensation chapters.
- Part V of the book (which was titled "The Legal Environment of Personnel Management" in the fifth edition) has been retitled "Labor-Management Relations."
- The Fundamentals of Motivation chapter has been replaced by a new chapter on "Guaranteed Fair Treatment." This new chapter includes all the material on discipline and dismissals (including separations and layoffs), plus material on employee job security and techniques for improving communications in an organization so that employees are, indeed, "guaranteed" fair treatment by the organization and its management.
- The chapter on Non-Financial Incentives (which was at the end of the Compensation chapters in the fifth edition) has been thoroughly refocused and rewritten. In its place, in the section on Training and Development, you'll find a chapter on Managing Quality and Productivity, which stresses total quality management and productivity-improving techniques.
- A new theme—specifically, *how personnel/human resource management policies and practices can help build employee commitment*—has been added to the sixth edition. With flatter hierarchies, wider spans of control, many more service jobs, and an emphasis on quality and flexible manufacturing, companies today must increasingly rely on committed employees, people who do their jobs "as if they own the company." Human resource management practices can play a role in building such commitment, and I've tried to illustrate throughout this book how personnel practices from testing and selection to compensation and grievance procedures can and do help to build commitment. Practical, hands-on illustrations are used to show how companies actually do this.
- The information on validity and relativity has been expanded substantially.
- This edition represents a major rewrite of the previous edition. Every sentence was reviewed and (where necessary) pruned, and most tables and figures and case incidents were updated. In addition, we have continued or expanded the following features:

COMPUTER APPLICATIONS IN PERSONNEL

Many illustrations of how computers are used in personnel/HR management are included. First, there are computer applications illustrations in many chapters—for example, describing how computers are used to link performance appraisal with merit pay. Second, to underscore the computer's use in personnel, "computer boxes" in most chapters highlight computer applications appropriate to each chapter's material, such as utilization analysis in the equal employment chapter and computerized interactive performance tests in the testing chapter. An all-new computerized simulation has also been produced. Used with the textbook, this simulation lets students gain practical HR experience solving realistic HR problems.

INTERNATIONAL ASPECTS OF PERSONNEL

In addition to international applications illustrations in many chapters, there is a comprehensive appendix on "International Issues in Human Resource Management." This appendix covers topics such as international aspects of human resource selection, training, and compensation management, as well as managing intercountry differences in personnel-related laws and requirements.

SMALL BUSINESS APPLICATIONS

At least two-thirds of the jobs opening up any year in the United States are in small businesses. In addition, many students will end up running their own businesses. A continuing feature of this edition is, therefore, the inclusion of a number of concrete, practical small-business applications that show how smaller businesses with limited resources and limited time can implement improved human resource management procedures. In Chapter 3, for instance, you'll find an example of how to use the widely available *Dictionary of Occupational Titles* to do a job analysis, complete with special client-tested forms. Other examples include procedures for setting up a training program in a small business, incentive hints for smaller employers, and developing a workable pay plan for smaller businesses.

QUALITY IMPROVEMENT IN SERVICE ORGANIZATIONS

The Sixth Edition contains increased coverage of quality management and total quality management programs, as well as on the human resource manager's role in setting up and running quality improvement programs, particularly in service enterprises. Included again is an example of the program used by Florida Power & Light Company, the first employer outside of Japan to win the Deming Prize for quality.

ABC NEWS/PRENTICE HALL VIDEOS

To underscore the practical, real-world orientation of this book, we again include a customized video library available for class use. Taken from such ABC news shows as *World News Tonight* and *Business World*, these videos deal with relevant topics such as occupational safety, worker pensions, and team training. Part-opener minicases are keyed to these videos, which you may use to focus and summarize the chapters in each part of the book.

ACKNOWLEDGMENTS

While I am of course solely responsible for the contents in *Human Resource Management*, I want to thank several people for their professional assistance. This includes the following reviewers: Augustus B. Colangelo, Pennsylvania State University; Dennis Dossett, University of Missouri, St. Louis; Craig Tunwall, Ithaca College; Roger D. Weikle, Winthrop University; Robert S. Bulls, J. Sargeant Reynolds College; Wallace L. Duvall, Wayland Baptist University; Mark Wesolowski, Miami University and Robert A. Figler, University of Akron.

I would also like to thank the following people for their work on the supplementary package under the direction of Maureen Hull: Karen Dill Bowerman, Ken York, Thomas W. Lloyd and Ann Schwartz.

Professor Hrach Bedrosian of New York University's Stern School of Business shared his impressions of the fifth edition and its supplements with me. I am sincerely grateful to Professor Enzo Valenzi who developed additional material on validity and reliability for Chapter 5. At Prentice Hall the dedicated efforts of Garret White, Valerie Ashton, Natalie Anderson, Steven Rigolosi, Diane Peirano, and my production editor, Edie Pullman, helped immeasurably and I am very grateful for their help.

My son, Derek, was always a source of encouragement and useful advice, as was my wife Claudia.

Gary Dessler

INTRODUCTION TO PERSONNEL/HUMAN RESOURCE MANAGEMENT: PHILOSOPHY AND PLAN

CHAPTER 1

OVERVIEW

In this chapter we see that human resource management—activities like recruiting, hiring, training, appraising, and paying employees—is both a part of every manager's job and a separate staff function, one through which the personnel director assists all managers in important ways. We also explain some factors that affect a philosophy of personnel management and explain how personnel activities can affect productivity and performance at work. Finally, we emphasize the importance of employee commitment, and how winning commitment is used as a theme throughout this book. When you finish studying this chapter, you should be able to explain what personnel management is and the role it plays in the management process; cite the personnel management responsibilities of line managers and staff (personnel) managers; discuss the factors that influence one's personnel management philosophy; and explain some HR policies and practices that foster employee commitment.

▶ PERSONNEL MANAGEMENT AT WORK

WHAT IS PERSONNEL MANAGEMENT?

To understand what personnel management is, we have to first ask what managers do. Most experts agree that there are five basic functions all managers perform: planning, organizing, staffing, leading, and controlling. In total, these functions represent what is often called the **management process.**[1] Some of the specific activities involved in each function include:

management process The five basic functions of planning, organizing, staffing, leading, and controlling.

Planning: Establishing goals and standards; developing rules and procedures; developing plans and forecasting—predicting or projecting some future occurrence.

Organizing: Giving each subordinate a specific task; establishing departments; delegating authority to subordinates; establishing channels of authority and communication; coordinating the work of subordinates.

Staffing: Deciding what type of people should be hired; recruiting prospective employees; selecting employees; setting performance standards; compensating employees; evaluating performance; counseling employees; training and developing employees.

Leading: Getting others to get the job done; maintaining morale; motivating subordinates.

Controlling: Setting standards such as sales quotas, quality standards, or production levels; checking to see how actual performance compares with these standards; taking corrective action as needed.

In this book, we are going to focus on one of these functions, the *staffing* or **personnel management function. Personnel management** (usually known today as human resource management (HRM), or as personnel, human resource, or simply HR management in this text) refers to the concepts and techniques you need to carry out the *people* or *personnel* aspects of your management job. These include:

personnel management The concepts and techniques one needs to carry out the "people" or human resource aspects of a management position, including recruiting, screening, training, rewarding, and appraising.

Job analysis (determining the nature of each employee's job)
Planning labor needs and *recruiting* job candidates
Selecting job candidates
Orienting and *training* new employees
Wage and salary management (how to *compensate* employees)
Providing *incentives* and *benefits*
Appraising performance
Communicating (interviewing, counseling, disciplining)
Training and developing
Building employee commitment

And what a manager should know about:

Equal opportunity and affirmative action
Employee health and safety
Handling grievances and labor relations

WHY IS PERSONNEL/HR MANAGEMENT IMPORTANT TO ALL MANAGERS?

Why are these concepts and techniques important to all managers? Perhaps it's easier to answer this by listing some of the personnel mistakes you *don't* want to make while managing. For example, *you don't want:*

To hire the wrong person for the job

High turnover

Your people not doing their best

To waste time with useless interviews

To have your company taken to court because of your discriminatory actions

To have your company cited under federal occupational safety laws for unsafe practices.

To have some of your employees think their salaries are unfair and inequitable relative to others in the organization

A lack of training undermining your department's effectiveness

To commit any unfair labor practices

Carefully studying this book can help you avoid mistakes like these. More important, it can help ensure that you get results—through others. Remember that you could do everything else right as a manager—lay brilliant plans, draw clear organization charts, set up modern assembly lines, and use sophisticated accounting controls—and yet still fail as a manager (by hiring the wrong people or by not motivating subordinates, for instance). On the other hand, many managers—whether presidents, generals, governors, or supervisors—have been successful even with inadequate plans, organization, or controls. They were successful because they had the knack for hiring the right people for the right jobs and motivating, appraising, and developing them. Remember as you read this book that *getting results* is the bottom line of managing and that, as a manager, you will have to get these results through people. As one company president summed up:

Many studies have shown that people are more committed to their jobs when their participation is valued and encouraged. Here, a group of assembly-line workers in a Tokyo Nissan factory participate in a worker productivity session attended by managers and supervisors.

> For many years it has been said that capital is the bottleneck for a developing industry. I don't think this any longer holds true. I think it's the work force and the company's inability to recruit and maintain a good work force that does constitute the bottleneck for production. I don't know of any major project backed by good ideas, vigor, and enthusiasm that has been stopped by a shortage of cash. I do know of industries whose growth has been partly stopped or hampered because they can't maintain an efficient and enthusiastic labor force, and I think this will hold true even more in the future. . . .[2]

At no time in our history has that statement been more true than it is today. As we'll see in a moment, intensified global competition, deregulation, and technical advances have triggered an avalanche of change, one that many firms have not survived. In this environment, the future belongs to those managers who can best manage change; but to manage change they must have committed employees, employees who do their jobs as if they own the company. In this book we'll see that human resource management practices and policies can play a crucial role in fostering such employee commitment.

▸ LINE AND STAFF ASPECTS OF PERSONNEL/HRM

All managers are, in a sense, personnel managers, since they all get involved in activities like recruiting, interviewing, selecting, and training. Yet most firms also have a Human Resource Department with its own human resource manager. How do the duties of this HR manager and his or her staff relate to "line" managers' human resource duties? Let's answer this question, starting with a short definition of "line" versus "staff" authority.

LINE VERSUS STAFF AUTHORITY

authority
The right to make decisions, direct others' work, and give orders.

line manager
A manager who is authorized to direct the work of subordinates and responsible for accomplishing the organization's goals.

staff manager
A manager who assists and advises line managers.

Authority is the right to make decisions, to direct the work of others, and to give orders. In management, we usually distinguish between line authority and staff authority.

Line managers are authorized to direct the work of subordinates—they're always someone's boss. In addition, line managers are in charge of accomplishing the organization's basic goals. (Hotel managers and sales managers are almost always line managers, for example.) **Staff managers**, on the other hand, are authorized to *assist and advise* line managers in accomplishing these basic goals. These ideas are illustrated in Figure 1.1. Here (as is usually the case) the human resource manager is a *staff manager.* He or she is responsible for advising line managers (like those for production and marketing) in areas like recruiting, hiring, and compensation. The managers for production and marketing are *line managers.* They have direct responsibility for accomplishing the organization's basic goals. They also have the authority to direct the work of their subordinates.

LINE MANAGERS' HUMAN RESOURCE MANAGEMENT RESPONSIBILITIES

According to one expert, "The direct handling of people is, and always has been, an integral part of every line manager's responsibility, from president down to the lowest level supervisor."[3]

For example, one major company outlines its line supervisor's responsibilities for effective human resource management under the following general headings:

1. *Placing* the right person on the right job
2. *Starting* new employees in the organization (orientation)
3. *Training* employees for jobs that are new to them
4. *Improving job performance* of each person
5. *Gaining creative cooperation* and developing smooth working relationships
6. *Interpreting* the company policies and procedures
7. *Controlling labor costs*
8. *Developing* abilities of each person
9. *Creating and maintaining departmental morale*
10. *Protecting* employees' health and physical condition

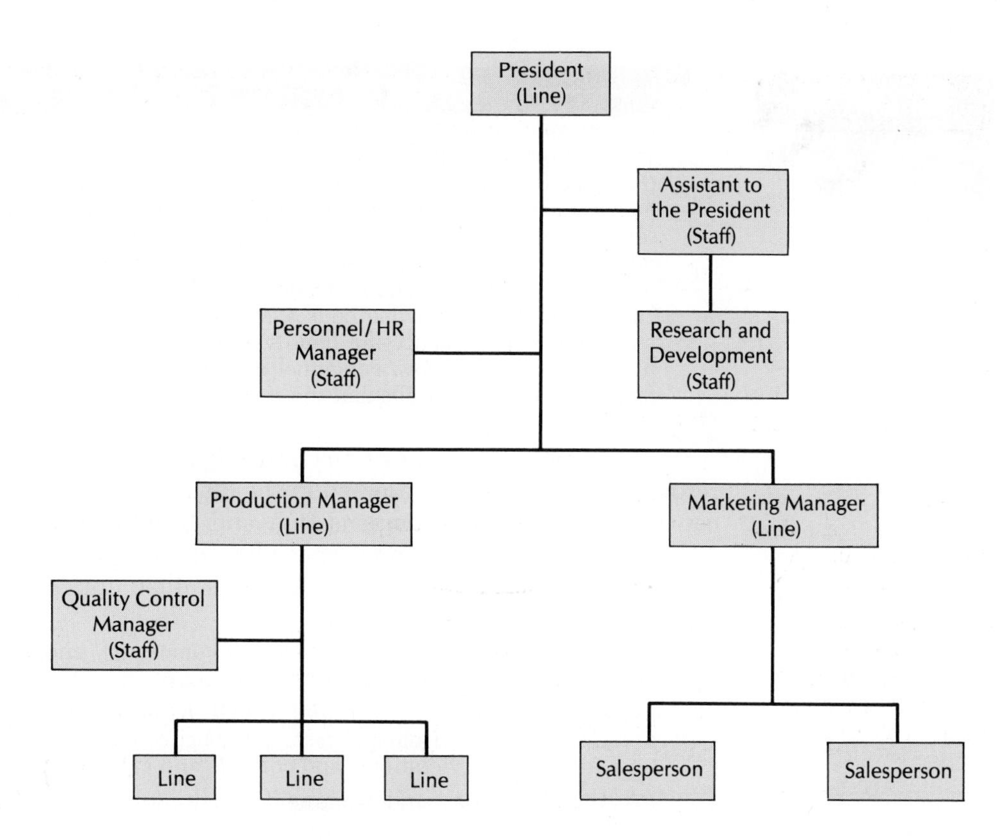

FIGURE 1.1
Line and Staff Authority

In small organizations, line managers may carry out all these personnel duties unassisted. But as the organization grows, they need the assistance, specialized knowledge, and advice of a separate human resource staff.[4]

PERSONNEL/HR DEPARTMENT STAFF'S PERSONNEL MANAGEMENT RESPONSIBILITIES

The personnel (or human resource) department provides this specialized assistance.[5] In doing so, the personnel manager carries out three distinct functions:

implied authority
The authority exerted by a personnel manager by virtue of others' knowledge that he or she has access to top management (in areas like testing and affirmative action).

functional control
The authority exerted by a personnel manager as coordinator of personnel activities.

1. *A line function.* First, the personnel HR/manager performs a *line* function by directing the activities of the people in his or her own department and in service areas (like the plant cafeteria). In other words, he or she exerts *line authority* within the personnel department. Personnel managers are also likely to exert **implied authority**. This is because line managers know the personnel director often has access to top management in personnel areas like testing and affirmative action. As a result, personnel directors' "suggestions" are often viewed as "orders from topside." This implied authority often carries even more weight with supervisors troubled with human resource/personnel problems.
2. *A coordinative function.* Personnel managers also function as coordinators of personnel activities, a duty often referred to as **functional control**. Here the personnel director and department act as "the right arm of the top executive to assure him that personnel objectives, policies, and procedures (concerning, for example, occupational safety and health) which have been approved and adopted are being consistently carried out by line managers."[6]

staff (service) function The function of a personnel manager in assisting and advising line management.

3. *Staff (service) functions.* **Staff (service) functions**—in other words, serving and assisting line managers—is the "bread and butter" of the personnel manager's job. For example, personnel *assists* in the hiring, training, evaluating, rewarding, counseling, promoting, and firing of employees. It also *administers* the various benefit programs (health and accident insurance, retirement, vacation, etc.). It *assists* line managers in their attempts to comply with equal employment and occupational safety laws. And it plays an important role with respect to grievances and labor relations.[7] As part of these service activities, the personnel managers (and department) also carries out an "innovator" role by providing "up to date information on current trends and new methods of solving problems."[8] For example, there is today much interest in instituting quality improvement teams and in providing career planning for employees. Personnel managers stay on top of such trends and help their organizations implement the required programs.

A summary of the positions you might find in a large company's human resource department is presented in the organization chart in Figure 1.2. As you can see, they include compensation and benefits manager, employment and recruiting supervisor, training specialist, employee relations executive, safety supervisor, and industrial nurse. Examples of job duties here include:

Recruiters: Maintain contact within the community and may travel extensively to search for qualified job applicants.

Equal Employment Opportunity (EEO) Representatives or Affirmative Action Coordinators: Investigate and resolve EEO grievances, examine organizational practices for potential violations, and compile and submit EEO reports.

Job Analysts: Collect and examine detailed information about job duties to prepare job descriptions.

Compensation Managers: Develop compensation plans and handle the employee benefits program.

Training Specialists: Responsible for planning, organizing, and directing training activities.

Labor Relations Specialists: Advise management on all aspects of union-management relations.[9]

COOPERATIVE LINE AND STAFF HUMAN RESOURCE MANAGEMENT: AN EXAMPLE

Exactly what personnel management activities are carried out by line managers and staff managers? There's no single division of line and staff responsibility that could be applied across the board in all organizations. But to show you what such a division might look like, we've presented an example in Figure 1.3[10] This shows some personnel/HR responsibilities of line managers and staff managers in four areas: *recruitment and selection, training and development, compensation, labor relations*, and *employee security and safety.*

For example, in the area of *recruiting and hiring* it's the line manager's responsibility to specify the qualifications of employees needed to fill specific positions. Then the personnel/HR department takes over. They develop sources of qualified applicants and conduct initial screening interviews. They administer the appropriate tests. Then they refer the best applicants to the supervisor (line manager) who interviews and selects the ones he or she wants. A similar division of duties between line and staff is presented (in Figure 1.3) for the *training, compensation, labor relations,* and *security and safety* areas.

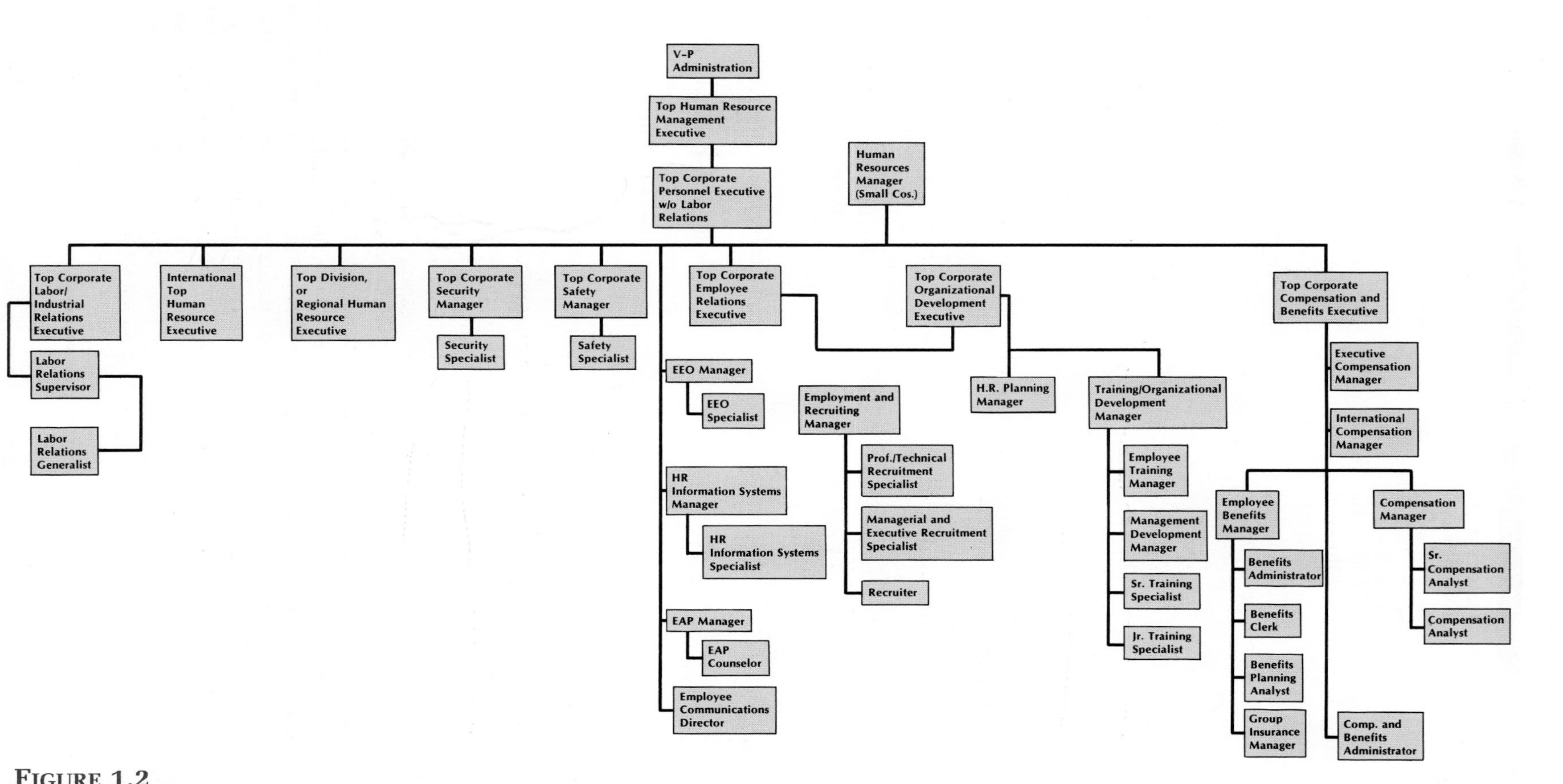

FIGURE 1.2

Positions Often Found Within a Large Personnel/Human Resource Department

Source: Adapted from Bureau of National Affairs, *Datagraph,* August 6, 1992, pp. 244–245.

Selected Activities Illustrating Division of Personnel/HR Responsibility Between Line and Staff

	DEPARTMENT SUPERVISORS' (LINE) ACTIVITIES	PERSONNEL/HR SPECIALISTS' (STAFF) ACTIVITIES
I Recruitment and Selection	Assist job analyst by listing the specific duties and responsibilities of the job in question. Explain to personnel/HR future staffing needs and the sorts of people needed to be hired. Describe "human requirements" of the job so personnel/HR can develop appropriate selection tests. Interview candidates and make final selection decisions.	Write job description and job specification based on input from department supervisor. Develop personnel plans showing promotable employees. Develop sources of qualified applicants and engage in recruiting activities aimed at developing a pool of qualified applicants. Conduct initial screening interviews of job candidates and refer feasible candidates to department supervisor.
II Training and Development	Orient employees with details regarding the company and the job and instruct and train new employees. Evaluate and recommend managers for developmental activities. Provide the leadership and empowerment that builds effective work teams. Use the firm's appraisal forms to appraise employee performance. Assess subordinates' career progress and advise them regarding their career possibilities.	Prepare training materials and orientation documents and outlines. Advise CEO regarding development plan for managers based on CEO's stated vision of firm's future needs. Serve as resource for providing information regarding how to institute and operate quality improvement programs and team building efforts. Develop performance appraisal tools and maintain records of appraisals. Develop career planning and promotion system including promotion from within procedures, career advisement tools, and records for monitoring employees' career progress.
III Compensation	Assist personnel/HR by providing information regarding the nature and relative worth of each job, to serve as the basis for compensation decisions. Appraise employee's performance for the purpose of awarding raises and merit increases. Make the decisions regarding the nature and amounts of incentives to be paid to subordinates. Decide on the package of benefits and services the firm is to pay.	Conduct job evaluation procedures aimed at determining relative worth of each job in the firm. Conduct salary surveys to determine how other firms are paying the same or similar positions. Serve as a resource in advising line management regarding financial incentives, alternatives, and pay plan alternatives. Develop, in consultation with line management, the firm's benefits and services packages including health care options and pensions. Monitor the firm's unemployment tax rate and workers' compensation performance and advise line management regarding the steps needed to reduce both costs.

IV Labor Relations	Establish the day-to-day climate of mutual respect and trust needed to maintain healthy labor-management relations. Consistently apply the terms of the labor agreement. Ensure that the firm's grievance process is functioning in a manner consistent with the labor agreement and make final decisions on grievances after investigating same. Work with personnel/HR in negotiating the collective bargaining agreement.	Diagnose underlying causes of labor discontent with an eye toward anticipating the sorts of morale and other problems that may lead to unionization efforts. Conduct the research needed to prepare for negotiations regarding the labor contract, in particular researching matters such as cost of union demands, popularity of various union terms, and what comparable firms are doing. Train line managers regarding the interpretation of contract terms and the legal pitfalls to be avoided during the union organizing effort. Advise managers regarding how to handle grievances and assist all parties in reaching agreements regarding grievances. Maintain contacts with union officials.
V Employee Security and Safety	Keep the lines of communication open between employees and managers so that employees are continually kept abreast of important company matters and that employees have a variety of vehicles they can use to express concerns and gripes up the chain of command. Make sure that employees are guaranteed fair treatment as it relates to discipline, dismissals, and job security. Continually direct employees in the consistent application of safe work habits. Recognize and reward employees for safe behavior at work. Prepare accident reports promptly and accurately. Develop a strategic, long-term plan for the firm in order to provide guidance for departments (including personnel/HR) regarding the types and numbers of employees to hire, the appropriateness of various types of compensation plans, and so on.	Advise line management regarding the communication techniques that can be used to encourage both upward and downward communication. Develop a guaranteed fair treatment process and train line managers in its use. Analyze jobs to develop safe practice rules and to advise on design of safety apparatus such as machinery guards. Promptly investigate accidents, analyze causes, make recommendations for accident prevention and submit necessary forms to Occupational Safety and Health Administration. Study workers' compensation law and work with insurance carrier and if necessary attorneys to manage workers' compensation cases.

In summary, you should see that personnel management is an integral part of *every* manager's job. Whether you're a first-line supervisor, middle manager, or president, whether you're a production manager, sales manager, office manager, hospital administrator, county manager (or personnel manager!), getting results through people is the name of the game. And to do this, a good working knowledge of the personnel concepts and techniques in this book is vital.

THE CHANGING ENVIRONMENT OF PERSONNEL

As important as personnel has been in the past, its importance will grow in the future. This is because changes are occurring today in the environment of personnel management, changes that are requiring Personnel to play an evermore crucial role in organizations. For example, more service-type jobs will demand more care in selecting and training courteous employees, while a diminishing supply of employees will make recruiting more difficult than ever.

SERVICE ECONOMY TRENDS IMPACTING PERSONNEL

Fast-food restaurants sell both food and fast service. Because of the intense competition in the fast-food industry, courteous service with a smile is an extremely important ingredient in getting customers to return, and this requires employee commitment.

A dramatic shift from manufacturing to services has taken place in North America and Western Europe. Today, for example, nearly two-thirds of the U.S. work force is employed in producing and delivering services: In fact, the manufacturing work force declined over 12% during the 1980s. And of all the 21 million or so new jobs added by the U.S. economy in the 1990s, virtually all will be in services, in industries like fast foods, retailing, consulting, teaching, and legal work.

To see why this change is important for personnel, you needn't look further than your local fast-food, clothing, or dry cleaning store. In their book *Service America!*, Karl Albrecht and Ron Zemke point out that in service businesses "critical incidents can make you or break you" and that what they call "the last four feet" can mean success or failure for your firm. In discussing a retail furniture chain, for instance, they relate how "much of the enormous advertising investment evaporated at the moment when a customer walked into the store and encountered a nonsupportive psychological environment."[11] All of those thousands of dollars spent on advertising were effective, in terms of getting the customers to walk in the front door. But once they're in the door, "it's up to the people in the store to take over at the last four feet." And here, if your customer is confronted by a salesperson who is tactless, or unprepared to discuss the pros and cons of your different products, or (even worse) downright discourteous, all your other efforts will have been for naught. Service organizations have little to sell but their service, and that makes them uniquely dependent on their employees' aptitudes and motivation.

Personnel/HR management therefore plays a crucial role in service companies. Specific examples include:

Service and quality of work life. Getting the best from your employees requires that the culture, morale, and psychological environment of the company be positive, and one barometer of this is the overall *quality of work life* of the workplace itself. Quality of work life can be defined as the degree to which employees can satisfy their important personal needs at work. It involves, according to one expert, at least the following factors:[12]

1. A job worth doing
2. Safe and secure working conditions
3. Adequate pay and benefits
4. Job security
5. Competent supervision

6. Feedback on job performance
7. Opportunities to learn and grow in the job
8. A chance to get ahead on merit
9. Positive social climate
10. Justice and fair play

As explained in later chapters, the human resource manager is normally charged with designing and implementing the systems to improve many of these factors. For example, job design (explained in Chapters 3 and 9) helps ensure that the job is worth doing, and employee safety and health programs (Chapter 18) are aimed at ensuring safe and secure working conditions. Similarly, pay and benefits (Chapters 12 through 14), promotions based on merit (Chapter 11), and feedback on job performance (performance appraisal, Chapter 10) are all essentially personnel/HR responsibilities. An effective human resource management department thus helps to create the overall fabric—the quality of work life—within which service employees can be motivated to do their jobs.

Service and selection. In many respects effective selection is the first line of defense for service companies. It has been noted, for instance, that there are "quite a few who lack the temperament, maturity, social skills, and tolerance for frequent human contact" and that the first step in avoiding this problem is screening and selection.[13] Yet, ironically, many of the front-line jobs in service firms are often minimum wage positions with relatively little career potential. As a result, the selection job is complicated by the fact that there is often a relatively limited work history to go by when hiring into these entry-level positions. The sorts of personnel screening and testing techniques discussed in Chapter 3 thus take on a critical importance in service firms.

Service and training. Poorly trained or untrained front-line service people usually have no choice but to improvise whatever methods they can in order to help them do their jobs; this can in turn have a corrosive effect on service performance.[14] Many employees in service firms are front-line employees who deal with customers every day. Unlike errors made by some "back office" or production workers, errors made on the front line normally can't be easily detected by inspectors. As a result, the sorts of training and development techniques explained in Chapters 7 and 8 are important ones for service companies.

Service and performance measurement and feedback. The fact that front-line service employees often fill positions that aren't subject to traditional types of "inspection" demands an effective way to measure and evaluate their performance. Techniques like those explained in Chapter 10 (performance appraisal) are therefore important here.

While other examples could be cited, the basic point is that in today's economy, personnel is more important than ever. The vast majority of employees today are in service jobs, working for service organizations that range from colleges to florists to zoos. (Even among manufacturing firms, companies find that their competitive advantage lies not just in their products but in the quality of the accompanying service that they provide.) In an economy like ours, which relies so heavily on committed front-line people, the concepts and techniques of personnel/HR management take on a new significance.

Demographic Trends Impacting Personnel

Just when it is becoming more important to hire and train an effective front-line work force, the rate of growth of the nation's work force is projected to drop over

the next few years. For example, the nation's labor force will expand by about 21 million people (or 18%) in the 1990s. This marks a dramatic slowdown in labor-force growth, which between 1972 and 1986 grew by almost 31 million people, or 35%. This will make the HR manager's job more difficult in terms of recruiting, screening, and training employees.

At the same time, the composition of the work force will change dramatically. For one thing, it will include more minorities and women. For example, between now and the year 2000, the white labor force is projected to increase less than 15%, while the black labor force will grow by nearly 29%, and the Hispanic labor force by more than 74%. Also, women are projected to account for about 64% of the net increase in the labor force in the 1990s. Related to this, about two-thirds of all single mothers (separated, divorced, widowed, or never married) are in the labor force today, as are almost 45% of mothers with children under three. The human resource department will increasingly be called upon to help companies accommodate these new employees, with new child care and maternity leave provisions, for example, and with basic skills training where such training is required.

Along with the shift from manufacturing to services, five occupational groups are projected to expand faster than average over the next 10 years. Technicians, service workers, professional workers, sales workers, and executive and management employees will all experience faster than average employment growth between now and the year 2000. Increasingly, jobs will require at least one year of college, while the share of jobs requiring high school completion as the predominant educational level will decline slightly. There will be a sharp decline in the share of jobs for which less than a high school education is sufficient to perform the job. New jobs will thus increasingly require a higher level of education, while the workers available for these jobs will increasingly come from minority groups who are less likely to have the requisite skills and education. Basic skills training, selection on the basis of training potential, and programs to encourage continuing education will thus take on added importance over the next few years.

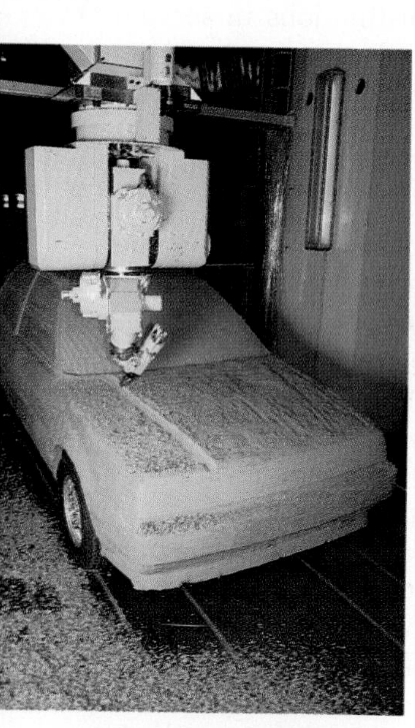

Computer-aided design and computer-aided engineering are revolutionizing manufacturing processes. Sophisticated computer programs can be used to create a design prototype, either on screen or on the shop floor. In turn, such techniques require more trained and committed employees.

Technological Trends Impacting Personnel

At the same time, technological advances will continue to shift employment from some occupations to others while contributing to a gradual rise in productivity. For example, telecommunicating already makes it relatively easy for many workers to work at home. Computer-aided design/computer-aided manufacturing systems plus robotics will also increase rapidly. In 1990, for instance, General Motors had about 14,000 robots building automobiles (compared to about 1,000 in 1984); researchers at Carnegie Mellon University estimated that there were between 100,000 and 200,000 robots in the United States in 1990. Manufacturing advances like these will eliminate many blue-collar jobs, replacing them with fewer but more highly skilled jobs.

Similar changes are taking place in office automation, where personal computers, word processing, and management information systems continue to change the face of office work.

The skills required to operate these new technologies will obviously have major effects on all levels of organizational functioning. Labor-intensive blue-collar and clerical functions will decrease while technical, managerial, and professional functions will increase. Here, again, therefore, the nature of work will change and with it the nature of the work force with which HRM must cope. Jobs and organizations' structures will have to be redesigned, new incentive and compensation plans instituted, new job descriptions written, and new employee selection, evaluation, and training programs instituted. These trends, too, will therefore influence personnel management.

Competitive and Managerial Trends Impacting Personnel

Increasing global and domestic pressures will also continue to shape organizations. The increasing internationalization of business and intensified competition mean that downsizing is now a continuing corporate activity. At the same time, increased competition and shorter product life cycles are creating the need for more flexible, adaptable companies, ones that are more decentralized and participative and that rely on cooperative project teams to "intrapreneur" new products and fulfill customers' needs. HR management will be in the vanguard helping companies make the required changes, in activities ranging from writing new job descriptions to hiring new international managers to building better communications.

Other Factors Impacting Personnel

Other social, economic, and political trends are shaping personnel/HR management. For example, only a fraction of the jobs in the United States require more than a high school education, yet an increasing number of workers have college degrees. As the supply of college graduates outstrips demand, more graduates will find themselves in jobs for which they are overqualified. Dealing with the resultant dissatisfaction and learning how to motivate a better-educated work force will therefore become critical personnel issues in the future.

Some also feel that basic work values are changing. Years ago, it was assumed that a "work ethic" motivated workers to work hard and do their best. Today, some feel this commitment to work is on the decline; if so, motivating employees may become a more difficult task.

Related to this, men and women of all ages (but particularly the young) often seem more interested in choosing a life-style and career than just a job. Therefore, career development and adapting work to workers' flexible life-styles and changing interests will become more important.

Also, as we will see in this book, many laws continue to be passed, laws which constrain the managers' actions. For example, equal employment opportunity laws bar discrimination on the basis of race, age, disability, religion, sex, or national origin. As a result, all managers are now legally bound to uncover and correct instances of discrimination. Mandated health benefits represent another example: In some states employers are already legally bound to provide health benefits to employees. And other laws—for example, covering occupational safety and health or labor relations—are among the other legal constraints managers will have to deal with.

In summary, several trends—including the emergence of a service economy, demographic trends, technological trends, competitive/managerial trends, and political/legal trends—are molding the way that firms do business, and (more particularly) the role played by Personnel. Personnel/HR activities will thus become more crucial in the years ahead, both because of these trends and one other factor: the need to improve performance at work.

There are many ways to improve performance at work. For example, many legislative factors may inhibit productivity (such as required pollution control equipment and occupational safety equipment). Yet many believe that reducing or eliminating legislative controls would actually have an adverse effect on society. In any case, this is not a factor over which an individual manager usually has much control. Worker productivity could also be increased by investing more heavily in more modern equipment—whether robots on an assembly line or word processors for secretaries. While useful, though, this is only part of the solution since, ultimately, virtually all service and manufacturing activities (no matter how automated) rely on human beings. Even in the most automated auto assembly plants, for example, poor employee attendance, resistant employee attitudes, and worker sabotage can drastically curtail productivity. And, in service industries, this is especially the case.

Another way to improve productivity and performance (and the one focused on in this book) is to improve human behavior at work through the application of modern human resource management concepts and techniques. There are, in other words, human resource management concepts and techniques that are being used today in organizations that have been shown to be effective for improving the commitment and performance of employees, and explaining how to use them is one purpose of this book. We explain, for example: how to use interviewing and other selection techniques to hire high performers; how to train and motivate employees; and how to use incentives, benefits, and commitment-building practices to improve performance at work.

Productivity and Human Resource Management

Can human resource management techniques really impact a firm's bottom line? Here the answer is a definite "yes."[15] As one writer says, "productivity is the problem—and personnel is definitely part of the solution."[16] In the U.S. government, for example, researchers found that using a personnel screening test to choose high-potential computer programmers could result in savings of millions of dollars per year. As another example, R. J. Reynolds invested $2.5 million in a company-sponsored health maintenance organization (HMO). (An HMO is an alternative to a traditional health care insurance plan. With an HMO the company contracts with a group of doctors and other health professionals to service all the firm's employees, usually at company expense.) Reynolds found that under the HMO, employee hospitalization declined 52%. Savings for 30,000 employees, as compared with their conventional plan, permitted payback of the investment in 24 months, plus the gains enjoyed from increased productivity.[17]

A dominant trend in personnel management over the next few years will be to keep labor costs down, and companies will do this in three main ways. According to a study by Hewitt Associates, "The first line of attack on this problem in most businesses is to institute tough headcount controls that go beyond temporary expedients like hiring freezes." To do this, companies are finding ways to operate permanently with fewer employees. This is particularly affecting salaried professionals: Companies are reducing the number of staff jobs compared to line and reducing the number of line managers per production worker, for instance. Massive layoffs have been taking place, as evidenced by the widely publicized release by firms like IBM and Northwest Air of tens of thousands of employees.

After headcount control, the next step in labor cost control is limiting compensation gains, both pay and employee benefits. By the early 1990s, for instance, annual salary increases had dropped to about 5% from a peak of 10% in 1981, in part due to reduced inflation rates. Furthermore, companies are finding ways to increase pay without adding to their salary bases. For example, lump-sum (one-time) bonus payments are being used and use of individual and group incentives is spreading. This reinforces the concept of "pay for performance" and helps relate compensation costs to the firms' well-being. By making lump-sum awards, employers also avoid building up base salaries, as would occur if raises were awarded as salary increases every year.

Employers are also reducing labor costs by controlling medical benefits. They are doing this by changing their medical plans, for instance, by forcing employees to pay part of their medical expenses. There is also more use of deductibles for hospital benefits.[18]

Other examples could be cited. Productivity incentives like *Scanlon plans* can boost performance. *Occupational safety and health programs* can reduce costs for lost-time accidents and illnesses. *Methods-improvement training* can improve employee efficiency. Even in relatively "hard-nosed" industries like steel, managers see that human resource techniques like *quality circles*, in which employees are asked to identify performance bottlenecks and suggest solutions, can boost performance.[19] In fact virtually every topic in this book—job analysis, interviewing, testing, training, incentives, and appraisal, for instance—can and will have a measurable impact on productivity and performance. #7

How This Book Will Help You

All managers will need good human resource management skills to deal with an increasingly sophisticated work force and changing job demands. In light of this, how exactly can studying this book help you? In five ways. First, it will increase your *knowledge of human resource management concepts and techniques* and will provide you with the personnel vocabulary supervisors need on the job. Supervisors must understand the meaning of terms like *unfair labor practices, job evaluation,* and *adverse impact.* At a minimum, studying this book will familiarize you with these terms.

Second, studying this book can provide you with the basis of important human resource *management skills.* In other words, you should not only learn the meaning of terms like *performance appraisal, interviewing,* and *job analysis,* you should be well on your way to understanding how to use and apply these techniques on the job. This should help you and your subordinates perform better and help you avoid the sorts of errors we alluded to earlier.

Third, even if you don't have plans to go into personnel management yourself, companies are increasingly promoting their best people up *through* personnel. Delta Airlines and Eli Lilly are among the firms that do this. Even if you have no current plans for going into personnel, the "people" aspects of business have become so important that you have to assume that you may do a stint in personnel on your way to the top; carefully studying this book should give you a big jump on preparing for that job.

Fourth, if you *are* interested in personnel management as a career, you'll get the basic foundation that you'll need here to begin your work—or update your knowledge and skills—in this exciting and fast-moving field: You'll learn the latest fair employment laws, for instance, and the most modern appraisal and compensation techniques as well.

Should you consider human resource management as a career? The answer, of course, depends on your aptitudes, interests, and skills; after all, you want to spend your career doing something that you like and that you're good at. But your decision regarding a career will also depend in part on how attractive personnel management is as a career, and here the prospects seem to be good indeed. The change from a production- to a service-centered (and, thus, more people-oriented) society, the increased education of workers, new laws, and the emerging interest in quality improvement and commitment at work all suggest that human resource management will be a vital and growing career in the years ahead.

Finally, studying this book could also sensitize you to employees' needs and perhaps *change your attitudes, values, and assumptions,* and thereby your behavior toward the people you deal with at work. Studying what this book has to say about activities like appraising, interviewing, disciplining, and compensating employees can, in other words, help to shape your *philosophy of human resource management*, a subject to which we turn now.

DEVELOPING YOUR HUMAN RESOURCE MANAGEMENT PHILOSOPHY

People's actions are always based in part on the basic assumptions they make, and this is especially true with regard to human resource management. The basic assumptions you make about people, such as whether they can be trusted, whether they dislike work, whether they can be creative, why they act as they do, and how they should be treated, comprise your philosophy of human resource management. And every personnel decision you make—the people you hire, the training you provide, the benefits you offer—reflects (for better or worse) this basic philosophy.

How do you go about developing such a philosophy? To some extent, it is preordained. There is no doubt that a person brings to a job an initial philosophy based on his or her experiences, education, and background. But this philosophy doesn't have to be set in stone. It should and will continually evolve as the person accumulates new knowledge and experiences. Let's therefore discuss some of the factors that will influence your own evolving philosophy.

Influence of Top Management's Philosophy

One of the things molding your personnel philosophy will be that of your employer's top management. While top management's philosophy may or may not be stated, it will usually be communicated by their actions and permeate every level and department in the organization. For example, here is part of the personnel philosophy of Edwin Land, founder and former chief executive officer of the Polaroid Corporation:

> to give everyone working for the company a personal opportunity within the company for full exercise of his talents—to express his opinions, to share in the

progress of the company as far as his capacity permits, and to earn enough money so that the need for earning more will not always be the first thing on his mind. The opportunity, in short, to make his work here a fully rewarding and important part of his life.[20]

What sort of impact does a philosophy like this have? For one thing, all personnel policies and actions at Polaroid flow directly or indirectly from Land's basic aims. For example, there is a top-level human resource policy committee. This consists of top corporate officers and is chaired by a senior vice-president, and members of the human resource department serve as staff, providing advice to the committee. The existence of this high-powered committee reflects the company's commitment to Land's personnel philosophy. And its existence helps ensure that all Polaroid human resource policies and practices—such as in the areas of training, promotions, and layoffs—also reflect this basic philosophy.

Influence of Your Own Basic Assumptions About People

Theory X
The set of assumptions which holds that workers cannot be trusted and must be coerced into doing their jobs.

Theory Y
McGregor's alternative theory that people do *not* have an aversion to work and are capable of self-control in the work situation.

Your personnel management philosophy will also be influenced by the basic assumptions you make about people. For example, Douglas McGregor distinguished between two sets of assumptions that he classified as **Theory X** and **Theory Y.** He says that the Theory X assumptions hold that:

1. The average human being has an inherent dislike of work and will avoid it if he or she can.
2. Because of this human characteristic of dislike of work, most people must be coerced, controlled, directed, and threatened with punishment to get them to put forth adequate effort.
3. The average human being prefers to be directed and wishes to avoid responsibility.

At the other extreme, some managers' actions reflect a set of Theory Y assumptions. These hold that:

1. The average human being does not inherently dislike work.
2. External control and the threat of punishment are not the only means for bringing about effort toward organizational objectives.
3. People are motivated best by satisfying their higher-order needs for achievement, esteem, and self-actualization.
4. The average human being learns, under proper conditions, not only to accept but also to seek responsibilities.
5. The capacity to exercise a relatively high degree of imagination, ingenuity, and creativity in the solution of organizational problems is widely, not narrowly, distributed in the population.[21]

System I
The organizational system, described by Rensis Likert, in which managers mistrust subordinates and thus feel compelled to coerce them to work. (Corresponds to Theory X.)

System IV
Likert's alternative system in which managers have confidence in workers and purposely involve them in decision-making processes. (Corresponds to Theory Y.)

Rensis Likert says that assumptions like these manifest themselves in two basic types or systems of organizations, which he calls **System I** and **System IV.** In System I organizations, he says:

1. Management is seen as having no confidence or trust in subordinates.
2. The bulk of decisions and the goal setting of the organization are made at the top.
3. Subordinates are forced to work with fear, threats, and punishment.
4. Control is highly concentrated in top management.

In their place, Likert proposes System IV, an organization built on Theory Y-type assumptions. In System IV organizations:

1. Management is seen as having complete confidence and trust in subordinates.
2. Decision making is widely dispersed and decentralized.
3. Workers are motivated by participation and involvement in decision making.
4. There is extensive, friendly superior-subordinate interaction.
5. There is widespread responsibility for control, with the lower echelon fully involved.[22]

In addition to factors like top management's philosophy and your own values and assumptions, there is another—*the need to win your employees' commitment*—that will affect your personnel philosophy, and gaining commitment is so important today that it is a central theme of this book.

BUILDING EMPLOYEE COMMITMENT

An Overview

The Need for Commitment

For managers, as we've seen, intensified global competition, deregulation, and technical advances have triggered an avalanche of change.[23] Bank failures skyrocketed from single digits in the 1970s to almost 200 annually in the early 1980s; in the past 10 years three U.S. airlines—Eastern, Peoples' Express, and Braniff—have closed, while others, including Pan Am and U.S. Air, were either taken over or had to sell substantial shares; still others, including TWA, Northwest, and Continental, are barely holding on; major currency prices—once stable—now swing as much as 60% per year; and in the United States, cutthroat competition has been fed by deregulation, the increasingly global nature of competition, and a tapering off in population trends.

In this environment, success goes to those managers who can best manage change; but managing change usually requires having committed employees. That's why many firms such as Delta Airlines, Toyota Motor Manufacturing, U.S.A., Saturn, and Federal Express have survived—and often thrived—by knowing that under conditions of rapid change *committed employees* were their most important competitive edge. As the vice-president of human resources at Toyota Motor Manufacturing in Georgetown, Kentucky, put it:

> People are behind our success. Machines don't have new ideas, solve problems, or grasp opportunities. Only people who are involved and thinking can make a difference . . . every auto plant in the U.S. has basically the same machinery. But how people are utilized and involved varies widely from one company to another. The work force gives any company its true competitive edge.[24]

In a study of several manufacturers, the authors of *Made in America* similarly argue that "In successful firms, the role of the production worker is shifting from one of passive performance of narrow jobs to active collaboration in production." These firms therefore promote participation, teamwork, flatter hierarchies, and much broader responsibilities for their workers. As a result, "Best practice firms have recognized that quality and flexibility improvements require levels of commitment, responsibility, and knowledge that cannot be obtained by compulsion or cosmetic improvements in human resource policies."[25]

Yet just as the need for commitment is on the rise, employee commitment is growing more elusive. Several things account for this, but perhaps the most serious threat is what one expert calls "The rash of corporate downsizings and restructurings that have seen tens of thousands of employees terminated in the last few years."[26] As he says, "The resulting message to chief executives is that if the firm is free to sack its managers and downsize at will, it can no longer expect the same levels of commitment, involvement and caring from its own employees."[27] Firms therefore need commitment as never before but creating it, ironically, is more difficult, too.

A firm's human resource management system can play a central role in fostering employee commitment and in many of America's best-known firms, it does. Studies in firms like Federal Express, JC Penney, Saturn, and Toyota, U.S.A., suggest some of the HR practices that can help foster employee commitment, including the following:

People-First Values

people-first values
Values that emphasize putting employees first in all decisions because it is believed that employees are the firm's most important assets and deserve respect and trust.

As we mentioned earlier in this chapter, a person's actions are usually in large part a product of his or her values. The U.S. Military Academy at West Point therefore works hard to mold values like duty, honor, and country because it knows that these values will then be the guideposts for its graduates both on and off the battlefield.

Companies like Federal Express, Delta, and Saturn build employee commitment on a firm foundation of what might be called people-first values. As one Fed Ex executive put it, "You start the process of boosting employee commitment by making sure you know how you and your top managers really feel about people."[28] What this means is that firms like these know that they must be willing to commit to the idea that their employees are their most important assets and that they can be trusted, treated with respect, involved in making on-the-job decisions, and encouraged to grow and reach their full potential. These firms, in other words, tend to adhere closely to the sorts of "people" assumptions that McGregor described as Theory Y: People deserve to be respected, can be trusted, and want to do a good job and are capable of creativity and initiative.

Federal Express has built its business on a firm commitment to its people. In turn, its employees are known for their commitment to the organization.

Fed Ex's Chairman Fred Smith has been quoted as saying that "Every company says it's a people company, but consistently keeping people first is hard work."[29] "Furthermore, putting people first in every action, every planning process, every business decision requires an extraordinary commitment from every manager and every employee . . . putting that somewhat ideal philosophy into practice means we must look for a multitude of ways to replace talk with action."[30]

There are several specific Personnel steps employers can take to "replace talk with action." Doing so begins with *knowing what you want.* That's why the Fed Ex executive said "You start the process of boosting employee commitment by making sure you know how you and your top managers really feel about people." Next, *put your people-first values in writing.* Continually "talk up" the fact that you are committed to the ideal of "putting your people first" by putting that fact in writing—like the employee manual, in company memos, and in other company documents. At Saturn Corp., for instance, employees carry a card that lists Saturn's values. One of these values is

> Trust and respect for the individual: we have nothing of greater value than our people. We believe that demonstrating respect for the uniqueness of every individual builds a team of confident, creative members possessing a high degree of initiative, self-respect, and self-discipline.

Companies like these also know that operationalizing people-first values depends on *hiring people* who have people-first values from the start. For example, here's how one officer at JC Penney describes its management selection process:

One Golden Rule of human-resource management at the J.C. Penney's chain is "Do right by your people." The company has built on this image with a recently-launched advertising campaign that stresses the courtesy of its employees, courtesy that results, in part, from Penney's commitment to its people.

> Mr. Penney's Golden Rule means do right by your people, and all of us work hard to maintain that philosophy. All Penney's people are therefore nice people—they have a heart and you would relate to them. If they're not nice, they'll be filtered out in the hiring and evaluation process. For example, we have a process called certified interviewing in which candidates are evaluated on, amongst other things, their leadership qualities and their sensitivity to the needs of others and on how they influence and deal with people and work with people to get the work done. (From a personal interview by the author at JC Penney in December, 1991.)

Similarly, Federal Express is very careful about whom it promotes to manager. All aspiring Fed Ex supervisory candidates must take the firm's multistep leadership evaluation program to prove they have the values and skills to be Fed Ex managers. About 20% fall out after the first "Is management for me?" phase, a one-day session that familiarizes them with the manager's job. This is followed by about three months of both self- and supervisory evaluations of the candidate's values and skills. Management training courses in the firm's leadership institute then use lectures and exercises to reinforce the firm's people-first values and indoctrinate the new managers in the values of the firm.

Firms like these also "walk the talk" in many other ways. For example, they

- Continually remind their supervisors that employees come first and that every action they take must be based on that standard
- Eliminate symbols like time clocks that say "I don't trust you"
- Monitor each group's reactions to its supervisor's actions
- Maintain open and honest communications with their people.

Policies and practices like these are the foundations of employee commitment, reflecting as they do the firm's sincere commitment to people-first values. Here's how one Toyota U.S.A. general manager put it:

> In all my thirty years in this business, I've never seen anything like the sort of total commitment to its people that Toyota top managers live every day. That is probably the single biggest difference between Toyota and GM: here our people *are* the company—Toyota makes you feel that you are part of the company and virtually every one of us sees Toyota's long-term success inseparable from ours. (From a personal interview by the author at Toyota U.S.A. in March, 1992.)

We've discussed people-first values at length because of the role they play as the foundation for all the other HR policies and practices that help foster and win employees' commitment. Some of the other policies and practices—most of which we'll discuss in more detail at the appropriate points in this book—include the following:

Two-Way Communications/ Guaranteed Fair Treatment

Managers of high-commitment firms seem to know that commitment is built on trust, and that trust requires floods of two-way communications.[31] We'll see in Chapter 17 that firms therefore establish programs that guarantee such communication. These programs include *guaranteed fair treatment* programs. These are basically "super" grievance procedures that guarantee fair treatment of all employees in all grievance and disciplinary matters.

Creation of a Sense of Community Among Employees

Firms such as Delta, Saturn, Toyota, and Federal Express also work hard to create a strong "we-feeling," a sense that "we are all in this together." Firms do this in part through what we call "value-based hiring" (see Chapter 5). This means they select people whose values (excellence, teamwork, quality, for instance) fit their firm's value system. They also tend to eliminate unnecessary status differences (such as executive parking spots and executive lunch rooms). As explained in Chapters 12-14 they also institute profit- and risk-sharing plans to further evoke the sense of sharing—the sense that all employees are "partners" in the firm. And as we'll see in Chapter 9 they also encourage joint effort and communal work, for instance, by organizing around small work teams and using job rotation to encourage employees to learn each other's jobs.

value-based hiring An exhaustive selection process that seeks to match not only the person's skills with the job but also his or her values with those of the company.

Exhaustive "Value-Based Hiring"

Companies that have high-commitment employees also seem to know that the time to start building commitment is before—not after—employees are hired. They are therefore very careful about whom they hire and use "value-based" hiring practices. They try to get a sense of the person and his or her personal qualities and values. They then design employee screening tools such as carefully structured interviews to help ensure that applicants' values (such as dedication to quality) fit the firm's.

Employee Security

Companies like these also emphasize employee security, by practicing what we might call "lifetime employment without guarantees." As we'll see in Chapter 17, these firms work hard to protect their employees' job security. They do this, for example, by instituting compensation plans that place a substantial portion of each employee's salary "at risk," with yearly bonuses that shrink in hard economic times; and they use large numbers of temporary or part-time employees. We'll see that there are usually no guarantees: Employees can (and sometimes do) get laid off. But generally speaking firms that want to win their employees' commitment work hard to show that they are committed to protecting their employees' jobs.

Rewards

As we'll see in Chapters 12-14, companies like Delta and Toyota also offer packages of above-average pay combined with incentives and extensive benefits. Overall, they all tend to build pay plans that encourage employees to think of themselves as partners. This means employees should have a healthy share of profits in good years and share in the downturn during bad times.

Employee Self-actualization

self-actualization The full utilization of one's skills to become "all that one can be."

In Part II of this book we'll see that high-commitment firms tend to engage in "actualizing" practices, practices that aim to ensure that their employees have every opportunity to fully use all their skills and gifts at work and become all they can be. Companies do this because they know that few needs are as strong as the need to fulfill one's dreams, to become all one is capable of becoming. Firms therefore use orientation, training, development, team building, performance appraisal, and career management to make sure that each employee can say "The best I can be is what I can be here." For example, work is "enriched" so that employees can use all their skills and gifts on the job; employees receive extensive training and development; and comprehensive promotion from within and career progress programs are used to make sure that employees can "be all they can be."

THE PLAN OF THIS BOOK

This book is built around two themes. First, we assume that personnel/HR management is the responsibility of *every* manager—not just of those in the human resource department. Throughout this book, you'll therefore find an emphasis on practical material that you as a manager will need in carrying out your day-to-day management responsibilities. The second theme is that winning employee commitment is a basic cornerstone of a sound personnel/HR management philosophy. Here is a brief overview of the chapters to come.

Chapter 2: Equal Opportunity and the Law (What you'll need to know about equal opportunity laws as they relate to human resource management activities such as interviewing, selecting employees, and performance appraisal.)

Part I: Recruitment and Placement

Chapter 3: Job Analysis (How to analyze a job; how to determine the "human" requirements of the job, as well as its specific duties and responsibilities.)

Chapter 4: Personnel Planning and Recruiting (Determining what sorts of people need to be hired; recruiting them.)

Chapter 5: Employee Testing and Selection (Techniques—like testing—you can use to ensure that you're hiring the right people.)

Chapter 6: Interviewing Job Candidates (How to interview candidates to help ensure that you hire the right person for the right job.)

Part II: Training and Development

Chapter 7: Orientation and Training (Providing the training necessary to ensure that your employees have the knowledge and skills needed to accomplish their tasks.)

Chapter 8: Developing Managers (Concepts and techniques for developing more capable employees, managers, and organizations.)

Chapter 9: Managing Quality and Productivity (Techniques such as quality improvement programs and team building that firms use to help them manage quality and productivity.)

Chapter 10: Appraising Performance (Techniques for appraising performance.)

Chapter 11: Managing Careers (Techniques such as career planning and promotion from within that firms use to help ensure that employees can "be all that they can be.")

Part III: Compensation

Chapter 12: Establishing Pay Plans (How to develop equitable pay plans for your employees.)

Chapter 13: Financial Incentives (Pay for performance plans such as financial incentives, merit pay, and incentives that help tie performance to pay.)

Chapter 14: Benefits and Services (Providing benefits that make it clear that the firms view their employees as long-term investments and that the firm is concerned with their welfare—such as stock ownership plans, pensions, and above-average health plans.)

Part IV: Labor Relations

Chapter 15: Basics of Labor Relations (Concepts and techniques concerning the relations between unions and management, including the union organizing campaign.)

Chapter 16: Collective Bargaining (Negotiating and agreeing upon a collective bargaining agreement between the union and the employer, and then managing the agreement via the grievance process.)

Part V: Employee Security and Safety

Chapter 17: Guaranteed Fair Treatment (Ensuring floods of two-way communication within the organization, as well as guaranteed fair treatment as it relates to discipline, dismissals, and employee job security.)

Chapter 18: Employee Safety and Health (The causes of accidents, how to make the workplace safe, and laws governing your responsibilities in regard to employee safety and health.)

Chapter 19: Strategic Issues in Personnel/Human Resource Management (The role that personnel plays in the employer's strategic planning process and a summary of trends influencing HR in the years immediately ahead. Included is an appendix on the international aspects of human resource management.)

Chapter Review

SUMMARY

1. There are certain basic functions all managers perform: planning, organizing, staffing, leading, and controlling. These represent what is often called the *management process.*
2. Staffing—or personnel management—is the function focused on in this book. It includes activities like recruiting, selecting, training, compensating, appraising, and developing. Today it's usually called human resource management.
3. Several trends—including the emergence of a service economy, demographic trends, technological trends, competitive/managerial trends, and political-legal trends—are all contributing to the way that organizations do business, and (more particularly) to the role played in companies by personnel.

4. All managers are authorized to direct the work of subordinates—they are always someone's boss. Line managers also have direct responsibility for accomplishing the basic goals of the organization. Staff managers are authorized to assist and advise line managers in accomplishing these basic goals.
5. Personnel/HR management is very much a part of *every* line manager's responsibility. These personnel management responsibilities include placing the right person on the right job, orienting, training, and working to improve his or her job performance.
6. The human resource manager (and his or her department) carry out three main functions. First, he or she exerts *line authority* in his or her own unit and implied authority elsewhere in the organization. He or she exerts a *coordinative function* to ensure that the personnel objectives and policies of the organization are coordinated and carried out. And he or she provides various *staff services* to line management; for example, the personnel manager or department assists in the hiring, training, evaluation, rewarding, promotion, and disciplining of employees at all levels.
7. Peoples' actions are always based in part on the basic assumptions they make, and this is why it is important to develop an overall guiding philosophy of personnel/HR management. Factors that will influence your own personnel management philosophy include prior experiences, education, and background; top management's philosophy; your basic assumptions about people; and the need to win your subordinates' commitment and improve performance at work.

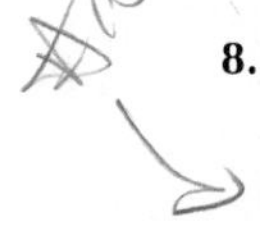

8. Because winning employee commitment is so important, it is emphasized as a theme throughout this book. HR policies and practices that foster employee commitment include people-first values, floods of two-way communication, fostering a sense of community, providing employee security, value-based hiring, the firm's reward system, and "actualizing" employees.

KEY TERMS

management process
personnel (or human resource) management
authority
line manager
staff manager
implied authority
functional control
staff (service) function
Theory X
Theory Y
System I
System IV
people-first values
value-based hiring
self-actualization

DISCUSSION QUESTIONS

1. Explain what personnel management is and how it relates to the management process.
2. Give several examples of how personnel management concepts and techniques can be of use to all managers.
3. Compare and contrast the work of line and staff managers; give examples of each.
4. What do we mean by a "personnel management philosophy"? What factors influence it? Why is it important?
5. Compare and contrast Theory X and Theory Y management assumptions.
6. Explain some HR policies and practices that foster commitment.

▶ APPLICATION EXERCISES

RUNNING CASE

CARTER CLEANING COMPANY

Introduction

The main theme of this book is that personnel management—activities like recruiting, selecting, training, and rewarding employees—is not just the job of some central personnel group but rather a job in which every manager must engage. Perhaps nowhere is this more apparent than in the typical small service business. Here the owner/manager usually has no personnel staff to rely on. However, the success of his or her enterprise (not to mention his or her family's peace of mind) often depends largely on the effectiveness through which workers are recruited, hired, trained, evaluated, and rewarded. Therefore, to help illustrate and emphasize the front-line manager's personnel role we will use, throughout this book, a continuing case based on an actual small business in the southeastern United States. Each chapter's segment of the case will illustrate how the case's main player—owner/manager Jennifer Carter—confronts and solves personnel problems each day at work by applying the concepts and techniques of that particular chapter. Here is some background information you will need to answer questions that arise in subsequent chapters. (A second, unrelated case incident will also be presented in each chapter.)

Carter Cleaning Centers

Jennifer Carter graduated from State University in June 1984, and after considering several job offers decided to do what she really always planned to do—go into business with her father Jack Carter.

Jack Carter opened his first laundromat in 1970 and his second in 1972. The main attraction to him of these coin laundry businesses was that they were capital rather than labor intensive; thus, once the investment in machinery was made, the stores could be run with just one unskilled attendant and none of the labor problems one normally expects from being in the retail service business.

The attractiveness of operating with virtually no skilled labor notwithstanding, Jack had decided by 1974 to expand the services in each of his stores to include the dry cleaning and pressing of clothes. He embarked, in other words, on a strategy of related diversification in that he added new services that were related to and consistent with his existing coin laundry activities. He added these new services in part because he wanted to better utilize the unused space in the rather large stores he currently had under lease and partly because he was, as he put it, "tired of sending out the dry cleaning and pressing work that came in from our coin laundry clients to a dry cleaner five miles away who then took most of what should have been our profits." To reflect the new expanded line of services he renamed each of his two stores "Carter Cleaning Centers" and was sufficiently satisfied with their performance to open four more of the same type of stores over the next five years. Each store had its own on-site manager and, on average, about seven employees and annual revenues of about $300,000. It was this six-store chain of cleaning centers that Jennifer joined upon graduating from State University.

Her understanding with her father was that she would serve as a troubleshooter/consultant to the elder Carter with the aim of both learning the business and bringing to it modern management concepts and techniques for solving the business's problems and facilitating its growth.

CASE INCIDENT *Jack Nelson's Problem*

As a new member of the board of directors for a local savings and loan association, Jack Nelson was being introduced to all the employees in the home office. When he was introduced to Ruth, he was curious about her work and asked her what her machine did. Ruth replied that she really did not know what the machine was called or what it did. She explained that she had only been work-

NO TRAINING

ing there for two months. She did, however, know precisely how to operate the machine and, according to her supervisor, she was an excellent employee.

At one of the branch offices, the supervisor in charge spoke to Mr. Nelson quite confidentially, telling him that "something was wrong" but she didn't know what. For one thing, she explained, employee turnover was too high and no sooner had one employee been put on a job, when another one resigned. With customers to see and loans to be made, she explained that she had little time to work with the new employees as they came and went.

All branch supervisors hired their own employees with no communications with the home office or other branches. When an opening developed, the supervisor tried to find a suitable employee to replace the worker who quit.

After touring the 22 branches and finding similar problems in many of them, Mr. Nelson wondered what the home office should do or what action he should take. The savings and loan firm was generally regarded as a well run institution that had grown from 27 to 191 employees during the past eight years. The more he thought about the matter, the more puzzled Mr. Nelson became. He couldn't quite put his finger on the problem, and he didn't know whether or not to report his findings to the president.

Questions

1. What do you think was causing some of the problems in the savings and loan home office and branches?
2. Do you think setting up a personnel unit in the main office would help?
3. What functions should it carry out, specifically? What personnel functions would then be carried out by supervisors and other line managers?

Source: Claude S. George, Jr., *Supervision in Action,* 4th ed. pp. 307–8. © 1985. Reprinted by permission of Prentice Hall, Englewood Cliffs, New Jersey.

HUMAN RESOURCE MANAGEMENT SIMULATION

One of the ancillary manuals available with this text is the *Human Resources Management Simulation* by Smith and Golden. Unlike some exercises, a simulation provides students with the opportunity to practice managing an organization's human-resources functions. With a simulation, students have the opportunity to make decisions, see the effects of those decisions, and then try again. In other words, players get "hands-on" experience with manipulating key human resources variables in a dynamic setting.

Simulation techniques have been used for some time to create business models that can help to explain the real world. Smith and Golden computer simulation attempts to combine the human-resources elements found in the HR world with the business environment found in each situation. Student teams manage the HR department of a medium-size organization that will be competing with other teams and organizations (up to 20). The simulation can be programmed to simulate a profit or nonprofit organization in a manufacturing or service industry. Teams are expected to establish objectives, plan their strategy, and make the decisions dictated by these plans. Decisions are submitted to the instructor periodically. Each decision "set" represents a quarter of a year (three months). These decisions are entered into the computer, which simulates the reaction of the firm and the labor market and produces a report for each team. This is done for several iterations. All teams will make a few mistakes throughout the simulation, so do not allow a few setbacks to affect your play—mistakes happen in the real world too. Keep your spirits up and good luck!

NOTES

1. This discussion is based on Gary Dessler, *Management Fundamentals* (Reston, VA: Reston, 1977), p. 2; William Berliner and William McClarney, *Management Practice and Training* (Homewood, IL: Irwin, 1974), p. 11.
2. Quoted in Fred K. Foulkes, "The Expanding Role of the Personnel Function," *Harvard Business Review* (March– April 1975), pp. 71–84.
3. The remainder of this section is based largely on Robert Saltonstall, "Who's Who in Personnel Administration," *Harvard Business Review,* Vol. 33 (July–August 1955), pp. 75–83, reprinted in Paul Pigors, Charles Meyers, and F. P. Malm, *Management of Human Resources* (New York: McGraw-Hill, 1969), pp. 61–73.
4. Saltonstall, "Who's Who," p. 63.
5. For a detailed discussion of the responsibilities and duties of the human resource department, see Mary Zippo, "Personal Activities: Where the Dollars Went in 1979," *Personnel,* Vol. 57 (March–April 1980), pp. 61–67; and "ASPABNA Survey No. 49, Personnel Activities, Budgets, and Staffs: 1985–1986," *BNA Bulletin to Management,* June 5, 1986.
6. Saltonstall, "Who's Who," p. 65.
7. Fred K. Foulkes and Henry Morgan, "Organizing and Staffing the Personnel Function," *Harvard Business Review,* Vol. 56 (May–June 1977), p. 146.
8. Ibid., p. 149.
9. U.S. Department of Labor, Bureau of Labor Statistics, *Occupational Outlook Handbook,* Bulletin 2250, 1986–1987 Edition, pp. 45–47.
10. Saltonstall, "Who's Who," pp. 68–69.
11. Karl Albrecht and Ron Zemke, *Service America!* (Homewood, IL: Dow Jones-Irwin, 1985), pp. 96–117.
12. Karl Albrecht, *At America's Service* (Homewood, IL: Dow Jones-Irwin, 1988), p. 169.
13. Albrecht and Zemke, *Service America!,* p. 101.
14. Based on ibid., p. 99.
15. See, for example, Wayne F. Cascio, *Costing Human Resources: The Financial Impact of Behavior in Organizations* (Boston: Kent, 1982).
16. Lawrence Baytos, "Nine Strategies for Productivity Improvement," *Personnel Journal,* Vol. 58 (July 1979), pp. 446–449.
17. Ibid., p. 454.
18. Thomas Paine, "Outlook for Compensation and Benefits: 1986 and Beyond," Hewitt Associates, October 30, 1985.
19. "Steel Seeks Higher Output via Workplace Reform," *Business Week,* August 18, 1980, p. 98.
20. Quoted in Foulkes and Morgan, "Organizing and Staffing the Personnel Function," p. 144.
21. Douglas McGregor, *The Human Side of Enterprise* (New York: McGraw-Hill, 1960), pp. 16–18, quoted in Daniel Wren, *The Evolution of Management Thought* (New York: Ronald Press, 1972), pp. 449–450.
22. Based on Paul Hersey and Kenneth Blanchard, *Management of Organizational Behavior* (Englewood Cliffs, NJ: Prentice Hall, 1969), pp. 52–56.
23. Except as noted, this section is based on Gary Dessler, *Winning Commitment* (New York: McGraw-Hill Book Co., 1993).
24. Commerce Clearing House, "HR Role: Maximize the Competitive Advantage of People," *Ideas and Trends in Personnel,* August 5, 1992, p. 121.
25. Michael L. Detouzas, et al., *Made in America,* (Cambridge, MA, The MIT Press, 1989) p. 137.
26. Paul Hirsch, *Pack Your Own Parachute* (Reading, MA: Addison-Wesley, Inc., 1987).
27. Ibid., p. 17.
28. Personal interview.
29. *Blueprints for Quality,* AMA.
30. Ibid.
31. This section of the chapter is based on Dessler, *Winning Commitment.*

CHAPTER 2

EQUAL OPPORTUNITY AND THE LAW

OVERVIEW

The purpose of this chapter is to provide the knowledge you need to deal effectively with equal employment opportunity questions on the job. Some employment discrimination laws are reviewed first, including Title VII of the 1964 Civil Rights Act and Equal Employment Opportunity Commission (EEOC) guidelines. Next is a discussion of some specific discriminatory personnel management practices—in recruitment, selection, promotion, transfers, layoffs, and pay. Also explained are the two basic defenses to be used in the event of a discriminatory practice allegation: business necessity and bona fide occupational qualification. When you finish studying this chapter you should be able to discuss major pieces of equal employment opportunity legislation from 1964 to the present; explain the main defenses against discriminatory practice allegations; list examples of discriminatory employment practices; describe the EEOC enforcement process.

▸ EQUAL EMPLOYMENT OPPORTUNITY LEGISLATION

In 1992 State Farm Insurance Companies agreed to pay $157 million to 814 women who were unlawfully denied entry-level sales agents positions by the company between 1974 and 1987.[1] This was the largest civil rights settlement in history.

State Farm's alleged errors help to illustrate the personnel problems equal employment opportunity laws were designed to prevent. The basic problem in this case was that decisions about hiring women as State Farm sales agents were not based on whether or not they could perform the sales agent jobs; instead, various untested standards were applied. For example, some women were told they needed a four-year degree, although some male agents had no degree. Others were told that it might be unsafe for women to make sales calls at night, although the evidence showed that women could do the job. The managers doing the hiring, in other words, were not asking, "Can these women do the job?" Instead, they were applying subjective criteria unrelated to job performance, criteria that let them illegally reject women applicants for jobs for which they were actually qualified. On the following pages we'll look more closely at the equal employment opportunity laws with which employers are required to comply.

SOME BACKGROUND

Legislation barring discrimination against members of minority groups in the United States is certainly nothing new. For example, the Fifth Amendment to the U.S. Constitution (ratified in 1791) states that "no person shall . . . be deprived of life, liberty, or property, without due process of the law." The Thirteenth Amendment (ratified in 1865) outlawed slavery and has been held by the courts to bar racial discrimination. The Fourteenth Amendment (ratified in 1868) makes it illegal for any state to "make or enforce any law which shall abridge the privileges and immunities of citizens of the United States," and the courts have generally viewed this law as barring discrimination on the basis of sex or national origin, as well as race. Section 1981 of Title 42 of the U.S. Code, passed over 100 years ago as the Civil Rights Act of 1866, gives all persons within the jurisdiction of the United States the same right to make and enforce contracts and benefit from the laws of the land; as we'll see, this has recently become an important legal basis for attacking discrimination.[2] Other laws as well as various court decisions made discrimination against minorities illegal as early as the turn of the century—at least in theory.[3]

But as a practical matter, Congress and various presidents were reluctant to take dramatic action on equal employment issues until the early 1960s. At that point, "they were finally prompted to act primarily as a result of civil unrest among the minorities and women" who eventually became protected by the new equal rights legislation and the agencies created to implement and enforce it.[4]

▸ EQUAL EMPLOYMENT OPPORTUNITY 1964–1989

TITLE VII OF THE 1964 CIVIL RIGHTS ACT

What the Law Says

Title VII of the 1964 Civil Rights Act
The section of the act that says you cannot discriminate on the basis of race, color, religion, sex, or national origin with respect to employment.

One of the first of these new laws was **Title VII of the 1964 Civil Rights Act**. Title VII (as amended by the 1972 Equal Employment Opportunity Act) states that an employer cannot discriminate on the basis of race, color, religion, sex, or national origin. Specifically, it states that it shall be an unlawful employment practice for an employer:[5]

1. *To fail or refuse to hire or to discharge an individual* or otherwise to discriminate against any individual with respect to his/her compensation, terms, conditions, or privileges of employment, because of such individual's race, color, religion, sex, or national origin.
2. To *limit, segregate, or classify his/her employees or applicants for employment* in any way that would deprive or tend to deprive any individual of employment opportunities or otherwise adversely affect his/her status as an employee, because of such individual's race, color, religion, sex, or national origin.[6]

Who Does Title VII Cover?

Title VII of the Civil Rights Act bars discrimination on the part of all public or private employers of 15 or more persons. In addition, it covers all private and public educational institutions, the federal government, and state and local governments. Public and private employment agencies are also barred from failing or refusing to refer for employment any individual because of race, color, religion, sex, or national origin. Labor unions with 15 or more members are barred from excluding, expelling, or classifying their membership because of race, color, religion, sex, or national origin. Joint labor-management committees established for selecting workers for apprenticeships and training similarly cannot discriminate against individuals.

The EEOC

Equal Employment Opportunity Commission (EEOC)
The commission, created by Title VII, is empowered to investigate job discrimination complaints and sue on behalf of complainants.

EEOC stands for **Equal Employment Opportunity Commission**, which was instituted by Title VII. The EEOC consists of five members who are appointed by the president with the advice and consent of the Senate; each member serves a term of five years.

The establishment of the EEOC greatly enhanced the federal government's ability to enforce equal employment opportunity laws. Its basic procedure is as follows: The EEOC receives and investigates job discrimination complaints from aggrieved individuals. When it finds reasonable cause that the charges are justified, it attempts (through conciliation) to reach an agreement eliminating all aspects of the discrimination. If this conciliation fails, the EEOC has the power to go directly to court to enforce the law. Under the Equal Employment Opportunity Act of 1972, discrimination charges may be filed by EEOC *on behalf of* an aggrieved individual, as well as by the individuals themselves. This procedure is explained in more detail later in this chapter.

EXECUTIVE ORDERS

Under **executive orders** issued by former President Johnson, employers who do business with the U.S. government have an obligation beyond that imposed by Title VII to refrain from employment discrimination.

These orders prohibit employment discrimination by employers with federal contracts of more than $10,000 (and by their subcontractors), and by contractors and subcontractors in federally assisted construction projects. In addition, Executive Order 11246 (as amended by Executive Order 11375) imposes three other obligations on federal contractors. First, unlike Title VII, the executive orders require that contractors take **affirmative action** to ensure equal employment opportunity (we will explain affirmative action later). All firms with contracts over $50,000 and 50 or more employees must develop and implement such programs. Second, the orders state a policy against employment discrimination based on *age or physical handicap,* in addition to race, color, religion, sex, or national origin. Finally, these orders also established the **Office of Federal Contract Compliance Programs (OFCCP).** It is responsible for implementing the executive orders and ensuring the compliance of federal contractors.

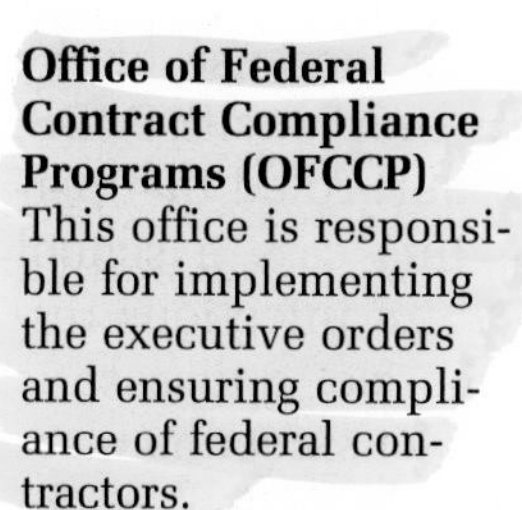

Office of Federal Contract Compliance Programs (OFCCP) This office is responsible for implementing the executive orders and ensuring compliance of federal contractors.

EQUAL PAY ACT OF 1963

Equal Pay Act of 1963 The act requiring equal pay for equal work, regardless of sex.

The **Equal Pay Act of 1963** (amended in 1972) made it unlawful to discriminate in pay on the basis of sex when jobs require equal work—equivalent skills, effort, and responsibility—and are performed under similar working conditions. However, differences in pay do not violate the act if the difference is based on a seniority system; a merit system; a system that measures earnings by quantity or quality of production; or a differential based on any factor other than sex.

AGE DISCRIMINATION IN EMPLOYMENT ACT OF 1967

Age Discrimination in Employment Act of 1967 The act prohibiting arbitrary age discrimination and specifically protecting individuals over 40 years old.

The **Age Discrimination in Employment Act of 1967 (ADEA)** made it unlawful to discriminate against employees or applicants for employment who are between 40 and 65 years of age. As amended by Congress in 1978 the act extended protection to age 70 for most workers and without upper limit for employees of the federal government.

A 1973 Supreme Court ruling held that most states and local agencies when acting in the role of employer must also adhere to provisions of the act that protect workers from age discrimination. Subsequent actions by Congress have eliminated the age cap of 70, effectively ending most mandatory retirement.

One-fifth of the court actions filed by the EEOC recently were ADEA cases. (Another 30% were sex discrimination cases.) This act is a "favored statute" among employees and lawyers because it allows jury trials and double damages to those proving "willful" discrimination.[7]

VOCATIONAL REHABILITATION ACT OF 1973

Vocational Rehabilitation Act of 1973
The act requiring certain federal contractors to take affirmative action for disabled persons.

The **Vocational Rehabilitation Act of 1973** required employers with federal contracts over $2,500 to take affirmative action for the employment of handicapped persons. The act does not require that an unqualified person be hired, but it does require that an employer take steps to accommodate a handicapped worker unless doing so imposes an undue hardship on the employer.[8] A federal district court recently held that compensatory damages are available under the 1973 rehabilitation act.[9]

Legal Aspects of AIDS at Work

School Board of Nassau County* v. *Arline
U.S. Supreme Court ruling that persons with contagious diseases are covered by the Vocational Rehabilitation Act of 1973.

The Vocational Rehabilitation Act took on added prominence because of the likelihood it could be used to prohibit discrimination against people with AIDS. In ***School Board of Nassau County* v. *Arline***, the Supreme Court ruled that persons with contagious diseases are covered by the act. In this case a school teacher (Arline) was dismissed because she had tuberculosis, an infectious respiratory disease.[10] In *Arline*, the Supreme Court held that the fact a disease is contagious can place an employee under the protection of the act since the mere fear of the disease (rather than its actual likelihood of being transmitted) might cause employers to discriminate against the ailing persons.[11] In any case, the EEOC's position today is that the new Americans with Disabilities Act (discussed later) prohibits discriminating against people with AIDS. Furthermore, numerous state laws now protect people with AIDS from discrimination. The guidelines issued by the Labor Department's Office of Federal Contract Compliance Programs also require that AIDS-type diseases be treated according to the provisions of the Rehabilitation Act.[12] The bottom line is that for most employers discriminating against people with AIDS would be viewed as unlawful.[13] In one recent situation, for instance, Delta Airlines was sued by a former Pan Am worker who said Delta refused to hire him because he was gay and HIV positive. Delta settled the claim, which was brought by New York City's Human Rights Commission.[14]

VIETNAM ERA VETERANS' READJUSTMENT ASSISTANCE ACT OF 1974

The provisions of the **Vietnam Era Veterans' Readjustment Act of 1974** require that employers with government contracts of $10,000 or more take affirmative action to employ and advance disabled veterans and qualified veterans of the Vietnam era. The act is administered by the OFCCP.[15]

PREGNANCY DISCRIMINATION ACT OF 1978

Pregnancy Discrimination Act (PDA)
An amendment to Title VII of the Civil Rights Act that prohibits sex discrimination based on "pregnancy, childbirth, or related medical conditions."

In 1978, Congress passed the **Pregnancy Discrimination Act (PDA)** as an amendment to the Civil Rights Act of 1964, Title VII. The act broadened the definition of sex discrimination to encompass pregnancy, childbirth, or related medical conditions. It prohibits using these factors for discrimination in hiring, promotion, suspension or discharge, or any other term or condition of employment.[16] Basically, the act says that if an employer offers its employees disability coverage, pregnancy and childbirth must be treated like any other disability and must be included in the plan as a covered condition.[17] The U.S. Supreme Court ruled in ***California Federal Savings and Loan Association* v. *Guerra*** that if an employer offers no disability leave to any of its employees it *can* (but need not necessarily) grant pregnancy leave to a woman who requests it when disabled for pregnancy, childbirth, or a related medical condition, although men get no comparable benefits.[18]

FEDERAL AGENCY GUIDELINES

federal agency guidelines
Guidelines issued by federal agencies charged with ensuring compliance with equal employment federal legislation that explain recommended employer procedures in detail.

The federal agencies charged with ensuring compliance with the aforementioned laws and executive orders issue their own guidelines on these matters. The overall purpose of these **federal agency guidelines** is to explain in detail the procedures these agencies recommend employers follow in complying with the equal opportunity laws.

Uniform Guidelines on Employee Selection Procedures

For example, detailed guidelines to be used by employers were approved by the EEOC, Civil Service Commission, Department of Labor, and Department of Justice.[19] These uniform guidelines supersede earlier guidelines developed by the EEOC alone. They set forth "highly recommended" procedures regarding such matters as employee selection, record-keeping, preemployment inquiries, and affirmative action programs. As an example, the guidelines specify that any employment selection devices (including but not limited to written tests) that screen out disproportionate numbers of women or minorities must be *validated.* The guidelines also explain in detail *how* an employer can validate a selection device. (This procedure will be explained in Chapter 5.) For its part, the OFCCP has its own *Manual of Guidelines.*[20]

The American Psychological Association has published the latest *Standards for Educational Psychological Testing,* and many experts expect that this document, which represents a consensus among testing authorities "will be used in court to help judges resolve disagreements about the quality of . . . validity studies that arise during litigation."[21]

EEOC Guidelines

The EEOC and other agencies also issue updated guidelines clarifying and revising their positions regarding matters such as *national origin discrimination, age,* and *sexual harassment.*[22] In the first quarter of 1992 alone, federal agencies issued several sets of regulations and guidelines: The EEOC issued guidelines on the 1991 Civil Rights Act and the Americans with Disabilities Act; the Department of Labor issued guidelines on immigration; and the Office of Federal Contract Compliance Programs issued a compliance manual dealing in part with "glass ceiling" audits—audits of firms that have subtle barriers to promotion for minorities.[23]

Historically, these guidelines have fleshed out the procedures to be used in complying with equal employment laws. For example, the EEOC published guidelines that further explained and revised the agency's position on age discrimination.[24] Recall that the Age Discrimination in Employment Act of 1967 (as amended) prohibited employers from discrimination against persons over 40 years of age merely because of age. Subsequent EEOC guidelines stated that it was unlawful to discriminate in hiring (or in any way) by giving preference because of age to individuals *within* the 40-plus age bracket. Thus, if two people apply for the same job, and one is 45 and the other is 55, you may not lawfully turn down the 55-year-old candidate because of his or her age and expect to defend yourself by saying that you hired someone over 40—in this case someone 45 years of age.[25]

SEXUAL HARASSMENT

sexual harassment Harassment, on the basis of sex, that has the purpose or effect of substantially interfering with a person's work performance or creating an intimidating, hostile, or offensive work environment.

The 1991 Judge Clarence Thomas hearings drew wide public attention to the question of sexual harassment and may trigger an increase in harassment suits; firms are now doubly advised to guard against the situations that spawn charges of sexual harassment.[26] In fact, the EEOC experienced a 41% increase in sexual harassment claims filed in the first quarter of 1992 relative to the same quarter the year before; it has begun a study to determine the industries in which sexual harassment is most prevalent.[27]

The EEOC had earlier issued interpretive guidelines on **sexual harassment**. These guidelines state that employers have an affirmative duty to maintain a workplace free of sexual harassment and intimidation.[28] These and related guidelines state that harassment on the basis of sex is a violation of Title VII when such conduct has the purpose or effect of substantially interfering with a person's work performance or creating an intimidating, hostile, or offensive work environment. The Civil Rights Act of 1991 (discussed later) added teeth to this by permitting victims of intentional discrimination, including sexual harassment, to have jury trials and to collect compensatory damages for pain and suffering and punitive damages in cases in which the employer acted with "malice or reckless indifference" to the individual's rights.[29]

Although sexual harassment in the workplace has occurred for decades, the issue came to the forefront of public awareness in 1991 when Professor Anita Hill testified that she had been sexually harassed by Supreme Court nominee Clarence Thomas.

The EEOC guidelines define sexual harassment as "unwelcome sexual advances, requests for sexual favors, and other verbal or physical conduct of a sexual nature that takes place under any of the following conditions".[30]

1. Submission to such conduct is made either explicitly or implicitly a term or condition of an individual's employment.
2. Submission to or rejection of such conduct by an individual is used as the basis for employment decisions affecting such individual.
3. Such conduct has the purpose or effect of unreasonably interfering with an individual's work performance or creating an intimidating, hostile, or offensive work environment.

Experts suggest that the EEOC and the courts will ask two basic questions when determining whether or not a company is liable for sexual harassment:

1. Did the company know or should it have known that harassment was taking place?
2. Did the company take any action to stop the harassment.?[31]

There are three main ways an employee can prove sexual harassment.

Quid pro quo. The most direct is to prove that rejecting a supervisor's advances adversely affected the employee's tangible benefits, like raises or promotions. For example, in one case the employee was able to show that continued job success and advancement were dependent on her agreeing to the sexual demands of her supervisors. And she showed that after an initial complaint to her employer she was subjected to adverse performance evaluations, disciplinary layoffs, and other adverse actions.[32]

Hostile environment created by supervisors. It is not always necessary to show that the harassment had tangible consequences such as a demotion or termination. For example, in one case the court found that a male supervisor's sexual harassment had substantially affected a female employee's emotional and psychological ability to the point that she felt she had to quit her job. Therefore, even though no direct threats or promises were made in exchange for sexual advances, the fact that the advances interfered with the woman's performance and created an offensive work environment were enough to prove that sexual harassment had occurred. On the other hand, the courts will not interpret as sexual harassment any sexual relationships that arise during the course of employment but that do not have substantial effect on that employment.[33]

Hostile environment created by coworkers or nonemployees. To qualify as sexual harassment, the advances do not have to be made by the person's supervisor: an employee's coworkers (or even the employer's customers) can cause the employer to be held responsible for sexual harassment. In one case the court held that a sexually provocative uniform that the employer required resulted in lewd comments and innuendos by customers toward the employee; when she complained that she would no longer wear the uniform, she was fired. Since the employer could not show that there was a job-related necessity for requiring such a uniform (and because the uniform was required only for female employees), the court ruled that the employer, in effect, was responsible for the sexually harassing behavior. The EEOC guidelines also state that an employer is liable for the sexually harassing acts of its nonsupervisory employees if the employer knew or should have known of the harassing conduct.

Meritor Savings Bank, FSB* v. *Vinson U.S. Supreme Court's first decision on sexual harassment. Held that existence of a hostile environment even without economic hardship is sufficient to prove harassment, even if participation was voluntary.

The U.S. Supreme Court's first decision on sexual harassment was ***Meritor Savings Bank, FSB* v. *Vinson***, decided in June 1986. In this case there were three sexual harassment issues before the Court:

> (1) Whether a hostile work environment (where hostility is due to the victim's sex) in which the victim does not suffer any economic injury violates Title VII, (2) whether an employee's voluntary participation in sexual acts with a manager constitutes a valid defense for an employer to a Title VII complaint, and (3) whether an employer is liable for the conduct of supervisors or coworkers when the employer is unaware of that conduct.[34]

The Court's ruling broadly endorsed the EEOC guidelines (issues 1 and 2), but the majority on a 5-to-4 split vote declined to issue a definitive ruling on employers' automatic liability (issue 3). However, the clear message of the decision is that employers should establish accessible and meaningful complaint procedures for employee claims of sexual harassment.

What the Employer Should Do

Employers can take steps to minimize liability if a sexual harassment claim is filed against the organization and to prevent such claims arising in the first place:

1. First, all complaints about harassment must be taken seriously. As one sexual harassment manual for managers and supervisors advises, "When confronted with sexual harassment complaints or when sexual conduct is observed in the workplace, the best reaction is to address the complaint or stop the conduct."[35]
2. Issue a strong policy statement condemning such behavior. The policy should include a workable definition of sexual harassment, spell out possible actions against those who harass others, and make it clear that retaliatory action against an employee who makes charges will not be tolerated. An example, presented in Figure 2.1, states, for example, that "such behavior may result in . . . dismissal".
3. Inform all employees about the policy prohibiting sexual harassment and of their rights under the policy.
4. Develop a complaint procedure.
5. Establish a management response system that includes an immediate reaction and investigation by senior management.
6. Begin management training sessions with supervisors and managers to increase their own awareness of the issues.
7. Discipline managers and employees involved in sexual harassment.
8. Keep thorough records of complaints, investigations, and actions taken.
9. Conduct exit interviews that uncover any complaints and that acknowledge by signature the reasons for leaving.
10. Republish the sexual harassment policy periodically.
11. Encourage upward communication through periodic written attitude surveys, hot lines, suggestion boxes, and other feedback procedures to discover employees' feelings concerning any evidence of sexual harassment and to keep management informed.[36]

FIGURE 2.1
Sample Sexual Harassment Policy

Source: Adapted from *Sexual Harassment Manual for Managers and Supervisors*, Commerce Clearing House, Inc., October 1991, p. 46.

The company's position is that sexual harassment is a form of misconduct that undermines the integrity of the employment relationship. No employee—either male or female—should be subject to unsolicited and unwelcome sexual overtures or conduct, either verbal or physical. Sexual harassment does not refer to occasional compliments of a socially accepted nature. It refers to behavior that is not welcome, that is personally offensive, that debilitates morale, and that, therefore, interferes with work effectiveness. Such behavior may result in disciplinary action up to and including dismissal.

What the Individual Can Do

An employee—either male or female—who believes he or she has been sexually harassed can also take several steps to eliminate the problem. The first step should be a verbal request to the harasser and his or her boss that the unwanted overtures cease because the conduct is unwelcome. The next step is for the offended person to write a letter to the accused. This should be a polite, low-key letter written in three parts. The first part should be a detailed statement of facts as the writer sees them: "This is what I think happened . . ." (include all facts and relevant dates). In the second part of the letter, the writer should describe his or her feelings and what damage the writer thinks has been done (e.g., "Your action made me feel terrible"; "I'm deeply embarrassed . . ."). Here mention any perceived or actual cost and damages along with feelings of dismay, distrust, and so on. Next, the accuser should state what he or she would like to have happen next. For example, "I ask that our relationship from now on be on a purely professional basis." The accuser should, according to one expert, deliver the letter in person if possible, to ensure that it arrived and when it arrived; if necessary, a witness should accompany the writer to be present when the letter is delivered. Finally, the individual should report the unwelcome conduct and unsuccessful efforts to get it to stop to the harasser's manager or to the human resource director (or both) verbally and in writing. This will leave no doubt that the employer has notice of the unwelcome nature of the conduct and create an obligation on the part of the employer to investigate and take warranted corrective action. If the letter and appeals to the employer do not suffice, the accuser should turn to the local office of the EEOC to file the necessary claim.[37] The individual can also consult an attorney about suing the harasser for assault and battery, intentional infliction of emotional distress, and injunctive relief and to recover compensatory and punitive damages if the harassment is of a serious nature.

SELECTED EARLY COURT DECISIONS REGARDING EQUAL EMPLOYMENT OPPORTUNITY

Griggs* v. *The Duke Power Company
Case heard by the Supreme Court in which the plaintiff argued that his employer's requirement that coal handlers be high school graduates was unfairly discriminatory. In finding for the plaintiff, the Court ruled that discrimination need not be overt to be illegal, that employment practices must be related to job performance, and that the burden of proof is on the employer to show that hiring standards are job related.

Griggs v. *Duke Power Company*

Griggs was a landmark case, since the Supreme Court used it to define unfair discrimination. In this case, a suit was brought against the Duke Power Company on behalf of Willie Griggs, an applicant for a job as a coal handler. The company required its coal handlers to be high school graduates. Griggs claimed this requirement was illegally discriminatory because it wasn't related to success on the job (wasn't *valid*) and because it resulted in more blacks than whites being rejected for these jobs.

The company lost the case. The decision of the Court was unanimous, and in his written opinion Chief Justice Burger laid out three crucial guidelines affecting equal employment legislation. First, the Court ruled that discrimination on the part of the employer *need not be overt*; in other words, the employer does not have to be shown to have intentionally discriminated against the employee or applicant—it need only be shown that discrimination did take place. Second, the court held that an employment practice (in this case requiring the high school degree) must be shown to be *job related* if it has an unequal (disparate) impact on members of a protected class. In the words of Justice Burger,

> The act proscribes not only overt discrimination but also practices that are fair in form, but discriminatory in operation. The touchstone is business necessity. If an employment practice which operates to exclude Negroes cannot be shown to be related to job performance the practice is prohibited.[38]

Chief Justice Burger's opinion also *clearly placed the burden of proof on the employer to show that the hiring practice is job related*. Thus, the *employer* must show that the employment practice (in this case, requiring a high school degree) is needed to perform the job satisfactorily if it has disparate impact on (unintentionally discriminates against) members of a protected class.

Albemarle Paper Company* v. *Moody
Supreme Court case in which it was ruled that the validity of job tests must be documented and that employee performance standards must be unambiguous.

Albemarle Paper Company v. *Moody*

In the *Albemarle* case,[39] the Supreme Court addressed the issue of how to validate an employment practice like a selection test. In the *Griggs* case, the Supreme Court had decided a screening tool (like a test) had to be job related or *valid*, in that performance on the test must be related to performance on the job. The *Albemarle* case is important because here the Court provided more details regarding how an employer should validate its screening tools—in other words, how it should prove that the test or other screening tools are related to or *predict* performance on the job. In the *Albemarle* case the Court emphasized that if a test is to be used to screen candidates for a job, then the nature of that job—its specific duties and responsibilities—must first be carefully analyzed and documented. Similarly, the Court ruled that the performance standards for employees on the job in question should be clear and unambiguous, so the employer could intelligently identify which employees were performing better than others.

In arriving at its decision, the Court also cited the EEOC guidelines concerning acceptable selection procedures and made these guidelines the "law of the land."[40] Specifically, the Court's ruling had the effect of establishing the detailed EEOC (now federal) guidelines on validation as the procedures for validating employment practices.[41]

EQUAL EMPLOYMENT OPPORTUNITY 1989–1991

A SHIFTING SUPREME COURT

Introduction

After more or less championing the cause of minorities and women in the workplace for three decades, a series of decisions by the Supreme Court in 1989 signaled a shift toward narrowing the scope of civil rights protection. Several factors (including the addition of several legal conservatives to the Supreme Court) caused the change. However, whatever the factors were, the results were quite dramatic. For example, in one case (*Wards Cove* v. *Atonio*) the Court ruled, 5 to 4, that an employer does *not* have to prove that a particular business practice such as a test was necessary to run the business, or valid, even if that practice is apparently discriminatory based on statistics. Instead the *plaintiff* (the applicant or employee claiming discrimination) has to prove that only illegal discrimination could have caused the disparity. The decisions in these cases are so fundamental to equal employment opportunity practice that we should review them in some detail.

Price Waterhouse v. *Hopkins*

The background of this case was as follows:[42] In 1982, the plaintiff, a woman, was proposed for partnership in the accounting firm she worked for. At the time, the firm had 662 partners, of whom 7 were women. In 1982, 88 candidates were proposed for partnership, but only 1—the employee who sued—was a woman. Of the 88, 47 became partners, 21 were rejected, and 20 were "held" for further consideration the following year. The employee who sued had brought $25 million in business with the State Department into the firm—but her promotion was held for further consideration. She responded by resigning and bringing suit under Title VII.

At the trial, it was found that both unlawful and lawful factors had contributed to her being passed over. She showed that her sex had been an unlawful factor in her denial of promotion, while the employer showed that "abrasiveness" had been a lawful factor. She won her case and won on appeal, but the U.S. Supreme Court eventually (on May 1, 1989) reversed the U.S. Court of Appeals for the District of Columbia Circuit. The Supreme Court found she would have been passed over anyway due to her abrasiveness.[43]

Wards Cove v. _Atonio_ U.S. Supreme Court decision that makes it difficult to prove a case of unlawful discrimination against an employer.

disparate impact Means there is an unintentional disparity between the proportion of a protected group applying for a position and the proportion getting the job.

disparate treatment Means there is an intentional disparity between the proportion of a protected group and the proportion getting the job.

Wards Cove Packing Company v. *Atonio*

The *Wards Cove* case is important because the Supreme Court's decision made it more difficult to prove a case of unlawful (disparate impact) discrimination against an employer. (**Disparate impact** means there is an unintentional disparity between the proportion of a protected group applying for a position and the proportion getting the job. In **disparate treatment** the disparity is allegedly intentional.)

The Supreme Court acted in a 15-year-old case of alleged racial discrimination in Alaskan salmon canneries.[44] The facts of the case were as follows: Unskilled jobs in the canneries are held mostly by nonwhite Alaskans of Japanese, Filipino, Chinese, and Alaskan native descent. Higher-paid noncannery jobs (carpenters, accountants, etc.) are mostly held by white employees who are recruited in the Seattle area. Cannery and noncannery workers at Wards Cove Packing Company are housed and fed separately. The predominantly white noncannery workers are assigned to more desirable, better insulated bunkhouses. The racial minorities at the canneries sued, claiming that the employment practices at the canneries discriminated and also had the effect of blocking them from getting the higher-paying jobs. Decisions at the lower courts were mixed; the U.S. Supreme Court's ruling favored the employer.

To understand the importance of the Supreme Court's *Ward Cove* decision, we have to step back several years. In the Civil Rights Act of 1964 (as explained earlier) Congress said that an employer may not discriminate on the basis of race, color, religion, sex, or national origin. In *Griggs* v. *Duke Power Company* (also discussed earlier), the Supreme Court defined what was meant by unfair discrimination and placed the burden of proof on the employer to show that the hiring practice in question is job related *when it has disparate impact on members of a protected class.* In the *Griggs* case the court also defined disparate impact, holding that it occurs when an employer has a policy or practice that appears to be neutral (such as the requirement in *Griggs* that all employees have a high school diploma), but that is, in practice, discriminatory.[45] After the *Griggs* case, proving that you were illegally discriminated against thus often just involved showing statistically that a biased situation existed. For example, the applicant or employee might simply have to show that one classification of jobs was primarily held by whites while a second less attractive classification was held by blacks. Having made his or her statistical case, the burden of proof then shifted to the employer to prove that its employment practices served a necessary business purpose—a defense that became known as the *business necessity defense.* Mounting a defense in such a case was often so expensive that many employers didn't try.

Wards Cove basically changed all that. Under *Griggs*, once bias was shown by the employee, it was up to the employer to demonstrate that its practices were justified by reasonable business necessity.[46] Under *Wards Cove*, statistical imbalances themselves no longer demonstrated disparate impact: Instead the employee/applicant had to prove that the statistical imbalances were caused by an employment policy or practice of the employer.[47]

Patterson v. *McLean Credit Union*

The Supreme Court's decision in *Patterson* further weakened the rights of minorities and women. The basic facts of the case were as follows: The employee testified that her supervisor periodically stared at her for several minutes at a time, gave her too many tasks, caused her to complain that she was under too much pressure, and gave her tasks that included sweeping and dusting which were not jobs given to white employees. On one occasion, she testified that her supervisor told her that blacks are known to work slower than whites. She also alleged that her supervisor criticized her in staff meetings while not similarly criticizing white employees.

The main issue in *Patterson* involved permissible use of Section 1981 of the Civil Rights Act of 1866. In particular, Section 1981 (rather than the more recent Title VII) was used increasingly in the late 1970s and early 1980s to attack racial discrimination in employment because the section permits the plaintiff to seek compensatory and punitive damages (in addition to back pay), covers all employers irrespective of the number of employees they have, and provides for a jury trial which is not available under Title VII.

In *Patterson* the Supreme Court said the plaintiff could not use Section 1981. It held that Section 1981 of the Civil Rights Act of 1866 could be used by minorities and women if their complaint involved either a refusal to make a contract or the impairment of the person's ability to enforce her established contract rights, neither of which, said the Court, applied in this case.[48]

Martin v. *Wilks*

The *Wilks* case began in 1974 and was decided by the U.S. Supreme Court on June 12, 1989. The case began when the NAACP and seven black firefighters sued the city of Birmingham, Alabama, for practicing racial discrimination. A settlement was worked out in which the city agreed to promote one black for every white it promoted. This resulted in a consent decree in which the courts allowed both parties to the suit to settle their disagreement as they had agreed. A group of white firefighters subsequently sued the city to try and stop the decree from being implemented; they said the decree would have the effect of discriminating against white firefighters. This case involves the issue of affirmative action, which, as we'll see later in this chapter, means efforts made by employers that are designed to eliminate the present effects of past discrimination.

Settlements like the one reached between the NAACP and the black firefighters under the supervision of the court meant, up until *Wilks*, that the employer was protected (under a court consent decree) from lawsuits by disgruntled white males. White males, for instance, couldn't sue employers who, when operating under such consent decrees, agreed to promote a certain proportion of blacks. One could reasonably assume that if employers no longer believed they were protected from such suits by white males, they might be very reluctant to enter into such affirmative action settlements. It is exactly this protection that the *Wilks* decision strips from employers. The court, on a 5-to-4 vote, agreed that one who is not a party to the original court proceedings that led to a consent decree, or who did not agree to the original decree, is not bound by the decree and can sue on a claim of reverse discrimination. The *Wilks* decision is therefore a change in the prevailing law; up until the *Wilks* decision most federal appeals courts had held that consent decrees could not be attacked once they took affect.[49]

Mixed Signals: The Supreme Court's 1991 Title VII Decisions

In March 1991 the U.S. Supreme Court issued two decisions regarding the 1964 Civil Rights Act. To some extent the decisions sent mixed signals to experts regarding the Supreme Court's intentions with regard to protecting the rights of employees. One of the decisions—*Johnson Controls, Inc.*—supported employees' rights, while the other—*Arabian American Oil Company, et al.*—seemed to restrict employees' rights.[50]

In *Johnson Controls, Inc.*, the Supreme Court basically held that Title VII prohibits all gender-specific fetal protection policies that companies might try to promulgate. In this particular case, Johnson Controls manufactures automobile batteries. Since lead is a main ingredient in battery manufacturing, the amount of airborne lead in Johnson Controls's workplace is often very high. Thus in 1982 Johnson Controls implemented a workplace "fetal protection policy." It forbade all women "capable of bearing children" from jobs involving exposure to airborne lead. In 1984 a group of workers at Johnson Controls challenged the policy, and the Supreme Court eventually decided in their favor, outlawing the Johnson Controls's fetal protection policy.

In the second, the *Arabian American Oil Company* case, the Court held that Title VII protections against discrimination do not extend to the foreign operations of American companies. In this case, the plaintiff Ali Boureslan was a naturalized citizen of the United States who was hired by a Houston subsidiary of Aramco as a cost engineer. A year later he requested a transfer to a position with Aramco in Saudi Arabia, where he remained until his discharge in 1984. He subsequently claimed under Title VII that he was harassed and ultimately discharged on account of his race, religion, and national origin. The U.S. Supreme Court eventually held that Congress has authority to enforce its laws extraterritorially, but that Congress could not have intended Title VII to apply abroad because the statute provides no mechanisms for overseas enforcement. At that point, employees of U.S. firms stationed overseas were no longer covered by Title VII.

▶ EQUAL EMPLOYMENT OPPURTUNITY 1991–PRESENT

THE CIVIL RIGHTS ACT OF 1991

Civil Rights Act of 1991 (CRA 1991)
It places burden of proof back on employers and permits compensatory and punitive damages.

Supreme Court rulings such as *Wards Cove* and *Patterson* had the effect of limiting the protection of women and minority groups under equal employment laws, and this prompted Congress to pass a new Civil Rights Act in 1991. The **Civil Rights Act of 1991 (CRA 1991)** was then signed into law by President Bush in November 1991. The basic effect of CRA 1991 is to reverse several U.S. Supreme Court decisions (including *Wards Cove, Patterson, Price-Waterhouse, Martin* v.

Wilkes, and *Arabian American Oil Company*). Further, as we'll see, the effect is not just to roll back the clock to where it stood prior to these Supreme Court decisions. The effect is to add additional legislation that makes it even more important that employers and their managers and supervisors adhere to both the spirit and the letter of EEO law. We can summarize the act's main provisions as follows.

Burden of Proof (*Wards Cove*). Prior to *Wards Cove* the equal employment litigation process basically went like this: The plaintiff (say, a rejected applicant) had to demonstrate that an employment practice (such as a test) had a disparate impact on a particular group. For example, a requirement that employees be able to lift heavy weights might unintentionally discriminate against women.[51] Then, once the plaintiff showed such disparate impact, the *employer* had to show that the challenged practice was job related for the position in question. For example, the employer had to show that the "lift heavy weights" requirement was actually required for the position in question, and that the business could not run efficiently without the requirement. In *Wards Cove*, the Supreme Court said that the burden of proof was no longer on the employer to prove that the requirement (lifting heavy weights) was a business necessity. The employer just had to show a business justification and then the burden shifted back to the plaintiff. The latter then had to prove that the requirement was put in to intentionally discriminate against the members of his or her minority group. This was difficult for plaintiffs to do.

The Civil Rights Act of 1991 rejects the Court's position and basically turns the EEO clock back to where it was prior to *Wards Cove* with respect to this matter. With the passage of CRA 1991, the burden is once again on the employer to demonstrate business necessity, not merely business justification.

Money Damages. Section 102 of the new Civil Rights Act provides that an employee who is claiming *intentional discrimination* can ask for (1) compensatory damages (a payment for "future pecuniary losses, emotional pain, suffering, inconvenience, mental anguish, loss of enjoyment of life, and other nonpecuniary losses"); and (2) punitive damages, if it can be shown the employer engaged in discrimination "with malice or reckless indifference to the federally protected rights of an aggrieved individual."[52]

This is a marked change from the conditions that prevailed up until 1991. Until that time, victims of intentional discrimination who had not suffered financial loss and who sued under Title VII could not sue for compensatory or punitive damages. All they could expect was to have their jobs reinstated (or be awarded a particular job). They were also eligible for back pay, attorney's fees, and court costs. Now, victims of illegal discrimination, including sexual harassment, can also sue for compensatory and punitive damages. This of course raises the stakes for employers. It may make it more likely that many employers will be more inclined to settle discrimination claims out of court. And it should certainly make it more likely that employers will be more conscientious about avoiding the conditions that prompt such claims.

Hiring and promotion under the Civil Rights Act of 1866 (*Patterson*). As previously explained, there are some advantages to suing under the Civil Rights Act of 1866, Section 1981. In the *Patterson* case, the U.S. Supreme Court held that that law didn't protect employees who, once hired, were discriminated against, for instance, in promotions or discharges. The Civil Rights Act of 1991 reverses the *Patterson* decision and explicitly states that Section 1981 applies to all instances of workplace racial and ethnic discrimination, even if they occur after hiring.[53]

MIXED MOTIVES (*PRICE-WATERHOUSE*). In the *Price-Waterhouse* case, the Supreme Court ruled that if a personnel decision would have been taken anyway, based on nondiscriminatory reasons, the fact that there was also a discriminatory reason for the decision was not enough to prove discrimination. The Civil Rights Act of 1991, on the other hand, states that

> An unlawful employment practice is established when the complaining party demonstrates that race, color, religion, sex, or national origin was a motivating factor for any employment practice, even though other factors also motivated the practice.[54]

In other words, under the new Civil Rights Act, an employer can no longer avoid liability by proving it would have taken the same action even without the discriminatory motive.[55]

CONSENT DECREES (*MARTIN* V. *WILKES*). The effect of *Martin* was to permit individuals who had not been involved in an affirmative action consent decree to subsequently sue the employer for reverse discrimination. CRA 1991 reverses that decision. Specifically, individuals who had actual notice of the consent decree at the time (or who had a reasonable opportunity to present objections or to be represented by someone whose interests were similar to theirs at the time) cannot come back years later to attack the consent decree. In other words, subsequent objections to consent decrees—decrees often used to institute affirmative action programs—will again be difficult to raise, as they were before *Martin* v. *Wilkes*.

OVERSEAS EMPLOYMENT (*ARABIAN AMERICAN OIL COMPANY*). Recall that in this case the Supreme Court ruled that the Civil Rights Act of 1964 didn't apply outside the United States. CRA 1991 says that it does. Specifically, it now applies to employees of American firms in foreign countries when such individuals are citizens of the United States.

OTHER SECTIONS OF CRA 1991. This new Civil Rights Act contains two more sections that will impact employment law. First, Section 107 of this act could actually make it a bit more difficult for minorities to prove discrimination. This section says that test scores cannot be "adjusted" to "alter the results of employment related tests on the basis of race, color, religion, sex, or national origin." Up to now, some employers might have allowed minority applicants who scored, say, 80 on a test to be employed, while nonminority applicants had to score 90. Such adjustments are no longer permitted under CRA 1991.[56]

Finally, CRA 1991 may turn out to be the first big shot in the war to break through the "glass ceiling" that inhibits women and minorities from getting ahead on the job. The glass ceiling is the collection of subtle and perhaps unintentional and invisible barriers that often prevent women and minorities from advancing at work. Glass ceiling barriers might include, for example, golf club memberships and trips to football games by male managers from which women

and minorities are often unofficially banned. The Civil Rights Act of 1991 does not outlaw such glass ceilings. However, it does set up a commission to study the issue.

THE AMERICANS WITH DISABILITIES ACT

Americans with Disabilities Act (ADA) The act requiring employers to make reasonable accommodations for disabled employees, it prohibits discrimination against disabled persons.

In July 1990 President Bush signed into law the **Americans with Disabilities Act (ADA)**. Title I of the act prohibits employment discrimination against the disabled.[57] The employment provisions of the ADA went into effect in July 1992. From that time employers with 25 or more workers are prohibited from discriminating against qualified individuals with disabilities with regard to applications, hiring, discharge, compensation, advancement, training, or other terms, conditions, or privileges of employment.[58] As of July 1994, the act covers employers with only 15 or more employees.

The Americans with Disabilities Act was enacted to reduce or eliminate serious problems of discrimination against disabled individuals. The Senate Committee on Labor and Human Resources had estimated that 43 million Americans have some type of disability and that two-thirds of those between the ages of 16 and 64 are unemployed although they want to work. Testimonials like those of a severely arthritic woman who was refused employment by a college because a trustee thought "normal students shouldn't see her" and a blind Harvard law school student who was rejected for employment three different times from each of 600 corporations convinced lawmakers of the need for ADA.[59]

Being disabled does not disqualify a person for a job. Indeed, advantages in technology have enabled many people with disabilities to enter the workforce and work productively. Here, telephone operator Nancy Thibeault uses specially designed equipment in her job as telephone operator and receptionist at PAC Corporation.

The act prohibits employers from discriminating against qualified disabled individuals. It also says employers must make "reasonable accommodations" for physical or mental limitations unless doing so imposed an "undue hardship" on the business.

The definitions of the act's pivotal terms are important in understanding its impact. For example, specific disabilities aren't listed; instead, the EEOC's implementing regulations regarding ADA provide that an individual is disabled when he or she has a physical or mental impairment that substantially limits one or more major life activities. They also provide that an impairment includes any physiological disorder or condition, cosmetic disfigurement, or anatomical loss affecting one or more of several body systems, or any mental or psychological disorder.[60] On the other hand, the act does set forth certain conditions that are not to be regarded as disabilities, including homosexuality, bisexuality, voyeurism, compulsive gambling, pyromania, and certain disorders resulting from the current illegal use of drugs.[61]

Simply being disabled doesn't qualify someone for a job, of course. Instead, the act prohibits discrimination against qualified individuals, in other words, those who, with (or without) a reasonable accommodation, can carry out the essential functions of the job. That means that the individual must have the requisite skills, educational background, and experience to do the essential functions of the position. A job function is essential when, for instance, it is the reason the position exists, or because the function is so highly specialized that the person doing the job is hired for his or her expertise or ability to perform that particular function.

If the individual can't perform the job as currently structured, the employer is required to make a "reasonable accommodation" unless doing so would present an "undue hardship." Reasonable accommodation might include redesigning the job, modifying work schedules, or modifying or acquiring equipment or other devices to assist the person in performing the job.

The ADA imposes certain legal obligations on employers:[62]

1. An employer must not deny a job to a disabled individual if the person is qualified and able to perform the essential functions of the job; if the person is otherwise qualified but unable to perform an essential function the employer must make a reasonable accommodation unless doing so would result in undue hardship. One expert says that cases in which handicapped individuals are denied employment because of risk of future injury will represent the largest category of suits under ADA. He says firms must make decisions on a situation-by-situation basis and not make blanket rules excluding all persons with specific disabilities.[63]
2. Employers are not required to lower existing performance standards for a job as long as those standards are job related and uniformly applied to all employees and candidates for that job; tests or other qualification standards that may tend to screen out an individual on the basis of disability must be job related and consistent with business necessity.
3. Employers may not make preemployment inquiries about a person's disability. However, employers may ask questions about the person's ability to perform specific job functions; similarly, preemployment medical exams or medical histories may not be required, but employers may condition job offers on the results of a post-offer medical exam.
4. Employers should review job application forms, interview procedures, and job descriptions. For example, employers may not ask applicants questions about their health, disabilities, medical histories, or previous worker's compensation claims.[64]
5. The ADA does not require employers to have job descriptions but it's probably advisable to do so. As one expert writes: "In virtually any ADA legal action, a critical question will be, what are the essential functions of the position involved? . . . If, for example, a disabled employee is terminated because he or she cannot perform a particular function, in the absence of a job description that includes such function it will be difficult to convince a court that the function truly was an essential part of the job."[65]

STATE AND LOCAL EQUAL EMPLOYMENT OPPORTUNITY LAWS

In addition to the federal laws, all states and many local governments also prohibit employment discrimination.

In most cases the effect of the state and local laws is to further restrict employers regarding their treatment of job applicants and employees. In many cases, state equal employment opportunity laws cover employers (like those with fewer than 15 employees) who are not covered by federal legislation.[66] Similarly, some local governments extend the protection of age discrimination laws to young people as well, barring discrimination not only of those over 40, but those over 17 as well; here, for instance, it would be illegal to advertise for "mature" applicants since that might discourage some teenagers from applying. The point is that a wide range of actions by many employers that might be legal under federal laws are illegal under state and local laws.[67]

State and local equal employment opportunity agencies (often called Human Resources Commissions, Commissions on Human Relations, or Fair Employment Commissions) play a role in the equal employment compliance process. When the EEOC receives a discrimination charge, it usually defers it for a limited time to the state and local agencies that have comparable jurisdiction. Then, if satisfactory remedies are not achieved, the charges are referred back to the EEOC for resolution.

SUMMARY

Selected equal employment opportunity legislation, executive orders, and agency guidelines are summarized in Table 2.1.

▶ DEFENSES AGAINST DISCRIMINATION ALLEGATIONS

WHAT IS ADVERSE IMPACT

adverse impact
The overall impact of employer practices that result in significantly higher percentages of members of minorities and other protected groups being rejected for employment, placement, or promotion.

Adverse impact plays a central role in discriminatory practice allegations. Today, under the Civil Rights Act of 1991 (and pre-*Wards Cove* laws), a person who believes he or she has been unintentionally discriminated against need only establish a prima facie case of discrimination: This means showing that the employer's selection procedures had an **adverse impact** on a protected minority group. Adverse impact "refers to the total employment process that results in a significantly higher percentage of a protected group in the candidate population being rejected for employment, placement, or promotion."[68]

What does this mean? If a minority (protected group) applicant for the job feels he's been discriminated against, he need only show that your selection procedures resulted in an adverse impact on his minority group. (For example, if 80% of the white applicants passed the test, but only 20% of the black applicants passed, a black applicant had a prima facie case proving adverse impact.) *Then, once the employee had proved his point, the burden of proof shifted to you, the employer.* It became *your* task to prove that your test, application blank, interview, or the like, was a valid predictor of performance on the job (and that it was applied fairly and equitably to both minorities and nonminorities).

HOW CAN ADVERSE IMPACT BE PROVED?

It is actually not too difficult for an applicant to show that one of your personnel procedures (such as a selection test) had an adverse impact on a protected group. Four basic approaches can be used.

disparate rejection rates
One test for adverse impact, in which it can be demonstrated that there is a discrepancy between rates of rejection of members of a protected group and of others.

1. *Disparate Rejection Rates.* This involves comparing the rejection rates between a minority group and another group (usually the remaining nonminority applicants). For example, ask, "Is there a disparity between the percentage of blacks among those *applying* for a particular position and the percentage of blacks among those *hired* for the position?" Or, "Do proportionately more blacks than whites fail the written examination you give to all applicants?" If the answer to either question is yes, you and your firm could be faced with a lawsuit.

Federal agencies adopted a formula to determine when disparate rejection rates actually exist. Their guidelines state that "a selection rate for any racial, ethnic or sex group which is less than 4/5 or 80% of the rate for the group with the highest rate will generally be regarded as evidence of adverse impact, while a greater than 4/5 rate will generally not be regarded as evidence of adverse

TABLE 2.1 Summary of Important Equal Employment Opportunity Actions

ACTION	WHAT IT DOES
Title VII of 1964 Civil Rights Act, as amended	Bars discrimination because of race, color, religion, sex, or national origin; instituted EEOC
Executive orders	Prohibit employment discrimination by employers with federal contracts of more than $10,000 (and their subcontractors); establish office of federal compliance; require affirmative action programs
Federal agency guidelines	Indicate policy covering discrimination based on sex, national origin, and religion, as well as employee selection procedures; for example, require validation of tests
Supreme court decisions: *Griggs* v. *Duke Power Co.*, *Albemarle* v. *Moody*	Ruled that job requirements must be related to job success; that discrimination need not be overt to be proved; that the burden of proof is on the employer to prove the qualification is valid
Equal Pay Act of 1963	Requires equal pay for men and women for performing similar work
Age Discrimination in Employment Act of 1967	Prohibits discriminating against a person 40 or over in any area of employment because of age
State and local laws	Often cover organizations too small to be covered by federal laws
Vocational Rehabilitation Act of 1973	Requires affirmative action to employ and promote qualified handicapped persons and prohibits discrimination against handicapped persons
Pregnancy Discrimination Act of 1978	Prohibits discrimination in employment against pregnant women, or related conditions
Vietnam Era Veterans' Readjustment Assistance Act of 1974	Requires affirmative action in employment for veterans of the Vietnam war era
Wards Cove v. *Atonio*, *Patterson v. McLean Credit Union*	These Supreme Court decisions made it more difficult to prove a case of unlawful discrimination against an employer
Morton v. *Wilks*	This case allowed consent degrees to be attacked and could have had a chilling effect on certain affirmative action programs
Americans with Disabilities Act of 1990	Strengthens the need for most employers to make reasonable accommodations for disabled employees at work; prohibits discrimination
Civil Rights Act of 1991	Reverses *Wards Cove*, *Patterson*, and *Martin* decisions; places burden of proof back on employer and permits compensatory and punitive money damages for discrimination

impact." For example, suppose 90% of male applicants are hired, but only 60% of female applicants are hired. Then, since 60% is less than four-fifths of 90%, adverse impact exists as far as these federal agencies are concerned.[69]

restricted policy
Another test for adverse impact, involving demonstration that an employer's hiring practices exclude a protected group, whether intentionally or not.

2. *Restricted Policy.* The **restricted policy** approach means demonstrating that the employer has (intentionally *or* unintentionally) been using a hiring policy to exclude members of a protected group. Here the problem is usually obvious. For example, policies have been unearthed against hiring bartenders under six feet tall. Evidence of restricted policies such as these (against women) is enough to prove adverse impact and open you to litigation.

3. *Population Comparisons.* This approach involves comparing the percentage of a firm's minority group employees and the percentage of that minority in the general population in the surrounding community.[70] This approach can be complicated to use in practice. For some jobs (such as manual laborer or secretary), it makes sense to compare the percentage of minority employees with the percentage of minorities in the surrounding community, since these employees will in fact be drawn from the surrounding community. However, for some jobs—such as engineers—the surrounding community may not be the relevant labor market, since these people may have to be recruited nationwide. Determining whether an employer has enough black engineers might thus involve determining the number of black engineers available nationwide rather than just in the surrounding community. Defining the *relevant labor market* is thus a crucial task here.

4. *McDonnell-Douglas Test.* This approach (which grew out of a case at the McDonnell-Douglas Corporation) involves showing that the applicant was qualified but was rejected by the employer who continued seeking applicants for the position. It is used in situations of (intentional) disparate *treatment* rather than (unintentional) disparate *impact* (for which approaches 1-3 are used). Here the rejected protected class candidate uses the following guidelines as set forth by the U.S. Supreme Court: (a) that he or she belongs to a protected class; (b) that he or she applied and was qualified for a job in which the employer was seeking applicants; (c) that, despite this qualification, he or she was rejected; and (d) that, after his or her rejection, the position remained open and the employer continued to seek applications from persons of complainant's qualifications. If all these conditions are met, then a prima facie case of disparate treatment is established. At that point the employer is required to articulate a legitimate nondiscriminatory reason for its action and produce evidence but not prove that it acted on the basis of such a reason. If it meets this relatively easy standard, the plaintiff then has the burden of proving that the employer's articulated reason is merely a pretext for engaging in unlawful discrimination.

Bringing a Case of Discrimination: Summary

Assume that you turn down a member of a protected group for a job based on a test score (although it could have been some other employment practice such as interview questions or application blank responses). Further assume that the person believes that he or she was discriminated against due to being in a protected class and decides to sue your company.

All he or she basically has to do is show that your test had an *adverse impact* on members of his or her minority group, and there are four approaches that could be used to show that such adverse impact exists: disparate rejection rates, restricted policy, population comparisons, and the McDonnell-Douglas test. Once the person has shown the existence of adverse impact to the satisfaction of the court, the burden of proof shifts to you, the employer. You then have to defend yourself against the charges of discrimination.

In this regard, there are basically two defenses that the employer can use: the *bona fide occupational qualification (BFOQ)* defense and the *business necessity* defense. Either can be used to *justify* an employment practice that has been shown to have an adverse impact on the members of some minority group.[71]

BONA FIDE OCCUPATIONAL QUALIFICATION

bona fide occupational qualification (BFOQ)
Requirement that an employee be of a certain religion, sex, or national origin where that is reasonably necessary to the organization's normal operation. Specified by the 1964 Civil Rights Act.

One approach an employer can use to defend itself against charges of discrimination is to claim that the employment practice is a **bona fide occupational qualification** for performing the job. Specifically, Title VII provides that "it should not be an unlawful employment practice for an employer to hire an employee . . . on the basis of religion, sex, or national origin *in those certain instances where religion, sex, or national origin is a bona fide occupational qualification* reasonably necessary to the normal operation of that particular business or enterprise." BFOQ is a statutory exception to the equal employment opportunity laws. It is an exception that is written into the laws and that allows employers to discriminate in certain very specific instances. The BFOQ exception is usually interpreted narrowly by the courts. As a practical matter, it is used primarily (but not exclusively) as a defense against charges of intentional discrimination based on age. BFOQ is essentially a defense to a disparate treatment case based upon direct evidence of intentional discrimination and not to disparate (unintentional) impact discrimination.

Age as a BFOQ

The Age Discrimination in Employment Act (ADEA) does permit disparate treatment in those instances when age is a BFOQ. For example, age is a BFOQ when federal requirements impose a compulsory age limit, such as when the Federal Aviation Agency sets a ceiling of age 64 for pilots. Actors required for youthful or elderly roles or persons used to advertise or promote the sales of products designed for youthful or elderly consumers are other instances when age may be a BFOQ. As another example, a bus line's maximum-age hiring policy for bus drivers has been held to be a BFOQ by the courts. The court said that the essence of the business was safe transportation of passengers and that as such the employer could strive to employ the most qualified persons available.[72] Yet Supreme Court decisions such as *Western Airlines, Inc.* v. *Criswell* seem to be narrowing BFOQ exceptions under ADEA. In this case the Court held that the airline could not impose a mandatory retirement age (of 60) for flight engineers, even though they could for pilots. Similarly, in *Johnson* v. *Mayor and City Council of Baltimore*, the Court held that the city of Baltimore could not require its firefighters to retire at age 55.

Some employers historically used "overqualification" as a tactic for rejecting older candidates, but today there is a great risk that a jury will find such an approach to be illegal.[73] In another case, a radio station changed its format from "beautiful music" featuring violin-driven instrumentals to a more upbeat "easy listening" style and fired all its over-40 DJs on the assumption they didn't fit the new style. The U.S. Court of Appeals in Chicago ruled in the DJs' favor, saying they should have been auditioned and given a chance to change their style.[74]

There has been a dramatic increase in the number of employment-related age discrimination complaints filed with state and federal agencies over the past few years. There are several reasons for this, including increasing numbers of older workers, increasingly militant older workers, corporate downsizings, and the prospect of collecting double damages (as plaintiffs can under the Age Discrimination in Employment Act).[75]

Employer defenses against such ADEA claims usually fall into one of two categories: BFOQ or FOA (Factors Other than Age). Employers using the BFOQ defense admit their personnel decisions were based on age but seek to justify them by showing that the decisions were reasonably necessary to normal business operations. (Here, for example, an airline might insist that a pilot maximum-age requirement is necessary for the safe transportation of its passengers.) An employer who raises the FOA defense generally argues that its actions were "reasonable" based on some business factor other than age, such as the terminated person's poor performance.

Religion as a BFOQ

Religion may be a BFOQ in the case of religious organizations or societies that require employees to share their particular religion. For example, religion may be a BFOQ when hiring persons to teach in a denominational school. Similarly, practices such as Saturday work rules that adversely affect certain religious groups are excusable if the employer "is unable to reasonably accommodate . . . without undue hardship."[76] In this and in all cases, however, the BFOQ defense is construed very narrowly by the courts.

Sex as a BFOQ

It is difficult today to claim that sex is a BFOQ for most jobs for which you are recruiting. For example, sex is not accepted as a BFOQ for positions just because they require overtime or the lifting of heavy objects. Sex is not a BFOQ for parole and probation officers, nor, of course, is sex a BFOQ for flight attendants.[77] Courts have said that it is illegal to apply a "no marriage" rule to stewardesses (and not to male employees) even though one airline claimed the rule was justified as a BFOQ due to customer preference. On the other hand, sex may be a BFOQ for positions requiring specific physical characteristics necessarily possessed by one sex. These include positions like actor, model, and restroom attendant.

National Origin as a BFOQ

In some cases a person's country of national origin may be a BFOQ. For example, an employer who is running the Chinese pavilion at a fair might claim that Chinese heritage is a BFOQ for persons to be selected as pavilion employees to deal with the public.

BUSINESS NECESSITY

business necessity Justification for an otherwise discriminatory employment practice, provided there is an overriding legitimate business purpose.

The **business necessity** defense basically involves showing that there is an overriding business purpose for the discriminatory practice and that the practice is therefore acceptable.

It's not easy proving that a practice is required for "business necessity."[78] The Supreme Court has made it clear that business necessity does not encompass such matters as inconvenience, annoyance, or expense to the employer. The

Second Circuit Court of Appeals held that business necessity means an "irresistible demand" and that to be retained the practice "must not only directly foster safety and efficiency" but also be essential to these goals.[79] Similarly, another court held that

> the test is whether there exists an overriding legitimate business purpose such that the practice is necessary to the safe and efficient operation of a business; thus, the business purpose must be sufficiently compelling to override any racial impact; and the challenged practice must effectively carry out the business purpose it is alleged to serve.[80]

Thus, to repeat, it is not easy to prove that a practice is required for business necessity. For example, an employer cannot generally discharge employees whose wages have been garnished merely because garnishment creates an inconvenience for the employer. On the other hand, the business necessity defense has been used successfully by many employers. Thus, in *Spurlock* v. *United Airlines*, a minority candidate sued United Airlines, stating that its requirements that pilot candidates have 500 flight hours and college degrees were unfairly discriminatory. The court agreed that these requirements did have an adverse impact on members of the person's minority group. However, the court held that in light of the cost of the training program and the tremendous human and economic risks involved in hiring unqualified candidates, the selection standards were required by business necessity and were job related.[81] In general, when a job requires a small amount of skill and training, the courts scrutinize closely any preemployment standards or criteria that discriminate against minorities. The employer in such instances has a heavy burden to demonstrate that the practices are job related. However, there is a correspondingly lighter burden when the job requires a high degree of skill and when the economic and human risks in hiring an unqualified applicant are great.[82]

Attempts by employers to show that their selection tests (or other employment practices) are valid represent one example of the business-necessity defense. Here the employer is required to show that the test or other practice is job related—in other words, that it is a valid predictor of performance on the job. Where such validity can be established, the courts have often supported the use of the test or other employment practice as a business necessity. Used in this context, the word *validity* basically means the degree to which the test or other employment practice is related to or predicts performance on the job; validation will be discussed in Chapter 5.

OTHER CONSIDERATIONS IN DISCRIMINATORY PRACTICE DEFENSES

There are three other points to stress in regard to defending yourself against charges of discrimination. First, *good intentions* on your part are no excuse. As the Supreme Court held in the *Griggs* case,

> Good intent or absence of discriminatory intent does not redeem procedures or testing mechanisms that operate as built-in headwinds for minority groups and are unrelated to measuring job capability.[83]

Second, employers cannot count on hiding behind collective bargaining agreements (for instance, by claiming that the discriminatory practice is required by a union agreement). Courts have often held that equal employment opportunity laws take precedence over the rights embodied in a labor contract. However, in a related matter, the U.S. Supreme Court, in its *Stotts* decision, did recently hold that a court cannot require retention of black employees hired under a consent decree in preference to white employees with greater seniority who were protected by a bona fide seniority system. There is disagreement regarding whether this decision also extends to hiring, recruitment, promotions, transfers, and layoffs not governed by seniority systems.[84]

Finally, remember that although a defense is often the most sensible response to charges of discrimination, it is not the only response. When confronted with the fact that one or more of your personnel practices is discriminatory, you can react by agreeing to eliminate the illegal practice and (when required) by compensating the people you discriminated against.

ILLUSTRATIVE DISCRIMINATORY EMPLOYMENT PRACTICES

A NOTE ON WHAT YOU CAN AND CANNOT DO

Before proceeding it is important to clarify what federal fair employment laws allow (and do not allow) you to say and do. Federal laws like Title VII usually do *not* expressly ban preemployment questions about an applicant's race, color, religion, sex, or national origin. In other words, "with the exception of personnel policies calling for outright discrimination against the members of some protected group, it is not really the intrinsic nature of an employer's personnel policies or practices that the courts object to. Instead, it is the *result* of applying a policy or practice in a particular way or in a particular context that leads to an *adverse impact* on some protected group."[85] For example, it is not illegal to ask a job candidate about her marital status (although at first glance such a question might seem discriminatory). In reality, you can *ask* such a question as long as you can show either that you do not discriminate or that the practice can be defended as a BFOQ or business necessity.

But, in practice, there are two good reasons why most employers avoid using such questionable practices. First, although federal law may not bar asking such questions, many state and local laws do. Second, the EEOC has said that it will *disapprove* of such practices (as asking women their marital status or applicants their age). Therefore, just asking such questions may raise a red flag that draws the attention of the EEOC and other regulatory agencies. Employers who use such practices will thus increase their chances of having to defend themselves against charges of discriminatory employment practices.

In summary, inquiries and practices like those summarized on the next few pages are not illegal per se. They are "problem questions" that *may* be potentially illegal. They are problem questions because they tend to identify an applicant as a member of a protected group or to adversely affect members of a protected group. However, they become *illegal* questions *if it can be shown that the questions as used do screen out a greater proportion of a protected group's applicants and that the employer cannot prove the practice is required as a*

BFOQ or a business necessity. Thus, if you are sure that your hiring practices do not adversely affect the members of a protected group—that, for example, you hire the same proportion of female applicants as male—then you may choose to continue asking such problem questions. Similarly, if you are convinced that an employment practice (such as a question about age) is required as a BFOQ or business necessity, you may choose to continue using it. However, these questions will draw the attention of regulatory agencies. Therefore, most employers do eliminate them, or at least delay asking them until after the applicant has been hired, when the questions might be useful for, say, insurance purposes. (Furthermore, local laws may bar such questions.)

We can now turn to a listing of some of the specific discriminatory personnel management practices you should avoid.[86]

RECRUITMENT

Word of Mouth

You cannot rely upon word-of-mouth dissemination of information about work opportunities when your work force is all or substantially all white or all members of som other class such as all female, all Hispanic, and so on.

Misleading Information

It is unlawful to give false or misleading information to members of any group or to fail or refuse to advise them of work opportunities and the procedures for obtaining them.

Help Wanted Ads

"Help wanted—male" and "Help wanted—female" advertising classifications are violations of laws forbidding sex discrimination in employment unless sex is a bona fide occupational qualification for the job advertised.[87] Also, you cannot advertise in any way that suggests that applicants are being discriminated against because of their age. For example, you cannot advertise for a "young" man or woman.

SELECTION STANDARDS

Educational Requirements

An educational requirement may be held illegal when (1) it can be shown that minority groups are less likely to possess the educational qualifications (such as a high school degree), and (2) such qualifications are also not job related. For example, in the *Griggs* v. *Duke Power* case, a high school diploma was found *both* unnecessary for job performance *and* discriminatory against blacks. In other cases, a public school board was found to have unlawfully discriminated against blacks by requiring a master's degree (and specific scores on Graduate Record Examinations) *that had not been validated* as predictors of job performance. A requirement for a college degree for management trainee positions was found to be unfairly discriminatory against blacks in another case.

Tests

According to former Chief Justice Burger,

> Nothing in the [Title VII] act precludes the use of testing or measuring procedures; obviously they are useful. What Congress has forbidden is giving these devices and mechanisms controlling force *unless they are demonstrating a reasonable measure of job performance.*

Tests that disproportionately screen out minorities or women *and* are not job related are deemed unlawful by the courts. But remember that the fact that a test (or other selection standard) that screens out a disproportionate number of minorities or women in not *by itself* sufficient to prove that the test *unfairly* discriminates. To do this, it must also be shown that the tests (or other screening devices) are not job related

Preference to Relatives

You cannot give preference to relatives of your current employees with respect to employment opportunities if your current employees are substantially nonminority.

Height, Weight, and Physical Characteristics

Physical characteristics (such as height and weight) that can have an adverse impact upon certain ethnic groups or women are unlawful unless they can be shown to be job related. For example, one company required that a person weigh a minimum of 150 pounds for positions on its assembly lines. This requirement was held to discriminate unfairly against women. Under the Americans with Disabilities Act, you cannot ask applicants about physical (or mental) disabilities.

Arrest Records

You cannot ask about or use a person's arrest record to disqualify him or her automatically for a position since there is always a presumption of innocence until proven guilty. In addition, (1) arrest records in general have not been shown valid for predicting job performance and (2) a higher proportion of blacks than whites have been arrested. Thus, disqualifying applicants based on arrest records automatically has an adverse impact on blacks. Therefore, unless security clearance is necessary, you cannot ask an applicant whether he or she has ever been arrested or spent time in jail. However, you can ask about *conviction* records and then determine on a case-by-case basis if the facts concerning any conviction justify refusal to employ an applicant in a particular position.

Discharge Due to Garnishment

A disproportionately higher number of minorities are subjected to garnishment procedures. (Here creditors make a claim to a portion of the person's wages.) Therefore, firing a minority whose salary has been garnished is illegal, unless you can show some overriding business necessity.

SAMPLE DISCRIMINATORY PROMOTION, TRANSFER, AND LAYOFF PRACTICES

Fair employment laws protect not just job *applicants* but *current employees* as well.[88] The Equal Pay Act requires that equal wages be paid for substantially similar work performed by men and women. Similarly, Title VII prohibits discrimination in compensation regardless of race, national origin, religion, or sex. With respect to promotions, terminations, and disciplinary actions, standards for determining when a person will be promoted, terminated, or disciplined should also be the same for all employees. Therefore, any employment practices regarding pay, promotion, termination, discipline, or benefits which (1) are applied differently to different classes of persons; (2) have the effect of adversely affecting members of a protected group; and (3) cannot be shown to be required as a BFOQ or business necessity may be held to be illegally discriminatory.

Personal Appearance Regulations and Title VII

Employees have filed suits against employers' dress and appearance codes under Title VII, usually claiming sex discrimination but sometimes claiming racial discrimination as well. A sampling of what has been ruled to be acceptable or unacceptable personal appearance codes follow.[89]

Dress. In general, employers do not violate Title VII's ban on sex bias by requiring all employees to dress conservatively. For example, a supervisor's suggestion that a female attorney tone down her attire was permissible when the firm consistently sought to maintain a conservative dress style and men were also counseled on the conservativeness of their dress.

Grooming. Minor gender-related differences in personal appearance are also usually deemed lawful when they reflect customary codes of grooming. For example, short hair requirements for men but not for women probably wouldn't constitute sex bias under Title VII, nor would letting women but not men wear earrings.

Hair. Hair styles, beards, sideburns, and mustaches have also come in for scrutiny by the courts. Here again the courts usually rule in favor of the employers. For example, employer rules against facial hair do not constitute sex discrimination because they discriminate only between clean-shaven and bearded men, a type of discrimination not qualified as sex bias under Title VII. In many cases courts have also rejected arguments that grooming regulations such as prohibitions against cornrow hair styles are racially biased in that they infringe on black employees' expression of cultural identification. In one case involving American Airlines, for example, the court decided that an all-braided hair style is a characteristic easily changed and not worn exclusively or even predominantly by black people. The U.S. Court of Appeals at St. Louis recently held that courts should intervene in personal grooming cases only when government-imposed grooming codes are "irrational." The county in this case, for hygienic reasons, had fired three ambulance service employees who had refused to remove their beards; the court sided with the county.[90]

UNIFORMS. When it comes to discriminatory uniforms and suggestive attire, however, courts have frequently sided with the employee. For example, a bank's dress policy requiring female employees to wear prescribed uniforms consisting of five basic color-coordinated items but requiring male employees only to wear "appropriate business attire" is an example of a discriminatory policy. Similarly, requiring female salesclerks to wear smocks, while male clerks were allowed to wear business attire, or hospitals requiring female technologists to wear white or pastel colored uniforms while male technologists could wear white lab coats over street clothing was ruled discriminatory. And requiring female employees (such as waitresses) to wear sexually suggestive attire as a condition of employment also has been ruled as violating Title VII in many cases.[91]

THE EEOC ENFORCEMENT PROCESS

PROCESSING A CHARGE

There are several factors involved in filing and processing an employment discrimination charge with the EEOC.[92] Under CRA 1991, the charge itself must generally be filed within two years after the alleged unlawful practice took place. This charge must be filed in writing and under oath by (or on behalf of) either the person claiming to be aggrieved or a member of the EEOC who has reasonable cause to believe that a violation occurred. In practice, the Supreme Court has approved the EEOC's practice of accepting a charge, orally referring it to the state or local agency on behalf of the charging party, and then, if the matter has not been cleared up, beginning to process it upon the expiration of a deferral period without requiring the filing of a new charge.[93] In practice, then, a person's charge to the EEOC is often first deferred to the relevant state or local regulatory agency; if the latter waives jurisdiction or cannot obtain a satisfactory solution to the charge, it is referred back to the EEOC. (Note that if the EEOC does not sue on behalf of the charging party it must issue that person a Notice of Right to Sue irrespective of whether it finds "cause" or "no cause" to believe that unlawful discrimination occurred. The charging party must file a lawsuit in federal district court within 90 days of receipt of that Notice of Right to Sue.)

After a charge is filed (or the state or local deferral period is ended), the EEOC must serve notice of the charge on the employer within 10 days. The EEOC then investigates the charge to determine if there is reasonable cause to believe it is true; it is expected to make this determination within 120 days. If no reasonable cause is found, the EEOC must dismiss the charge, in which case the person who filed the charge has 90 days to file a suit on his or her own behalf. If reasonable cause for the charge *is* found, the EEOC must attempt to conciliate. If this conciliation is not satisfactory, it may bring a civil suit in a federal district court, or issue a Notice of Right to Sue to the person who filed the charge. Figure 2.2 summarizes some important questions an employer should ask after receiving notice from the EEOC that a bias complaint has been filed. Note that the questions include, for example, "To what protected group does the worker belong?" and "Is the employee protected by more than one statute?"[94] As we'll discuss further in Chapter 6, the EEOC has recently begun to approve the use of "testers"—individuals who pose as applicants to test a firm's equal employment procedures. Employers thus must be even more diligent in devising interview procedures and training recruiters.[95]

1. To what protected group does the worker belong? Is the employee protected by more than one statute?
2. Would the action complained of have been taken if the worker were not a member of a protected group? Is the action having an adverse impact on other members of a protected group?
3. Is the employee's charge of discrimination subject to attack because it was not filed on time, according to the applicable law?
4. In the case of a sexual harassment claim, are there offensive posters or calendars on display in the workplace?
5. Do the employees' personnel records demonstrate discriminatory treatment in the form of unjustified warnings and reprimands?
6. In reviewing the nature of the action complained of, can it be characterized as disparate impact or disparate treatment? Can it be characterized as an individual complaint or a class action?
7. What are the company's probable defenses and rebuttal?
8. Who are the decision makers involved in the employment action, and what would be their effectiveness as potential witnesses?
9. What are the prospects for a settlement of the case that would be satisfactory to all involved?

FIGURE 2.2
Questions to Ask When an Employer Receives Notice That a Bias Complaint Has Been Filed

Source: Gail J. Wright, assistant counsel for the NAACP's Legal Defense and Education Fund, quoted in Bureau of National Affairs, Fair Employment Practices, January 7, 1988, p. 3.

CONCILIATION PROCEEDINGS

Under Title VII, the EEOC is allowed 30 days to work out a conciliation agreement between the parties before a suit is brought. The EEOC conciliator first meets with the employee to determine what remedy would be satisfactory and then tries to persuade the employer to accept the remedy. If accepted by both parties, a conciliation agreement is reached, signed, and submitted to the EEOC for approval. Finally (if the EEOC is unable to obtain an acceptable conciliation agreement within 30 days after a finding of reasonable cause to believe that discrimination occurred), it may sue the employer in a federal district court. The EEOC is now also experimenting with using outside mediators to settle claims in selected cities.[96]

HOW TO RESPOND TO EMPLOYMENT DISCRIMINATION CHARGES

There are several things to keep in mind when confronted by a charge of illegal employment discrimination; some of the more important can be summarized as follows:[97]

Investigating the Charge

First, remember that the EEOC investigators are not judges and are not empowered to act as courts; they cannot make findings of discrimination on their own, but can merely make recommendations. If the EEOC eventually determines that an employer may be in violation of a law, its only recourse is to file a suit or issue a Notice of Right to Sue to the person who filed the charge.

As far as documents are concerned, it may often be in your employer's best interests to cooperate (or appear cooperative). However, remember that the EEOC can only ask for, not demand, the submission of documents.[98] The EEOC can *ask* employers to submit documents and *ask* for the appearance and testimony of witnesses under oath. However, it cannot compel employers to do so. If your employer feels that the EEOC has overstepped its authority and refuses to cooperate, the commission's only recourse is to obtain a court subpoena.

It may also be in your employer's best interest to submit to the EEOC a position statement based on your own investigation of the matter. One congressional investigation found, at least in the Chicago office of the EEOC, that EEOC investigators were writing up cases based solely on the position statement filed by the employer because the EEOC is under such internal pressure to resolve cases. According to one management attorney, your position statements should contain words to the effect that "We understand that a charge of discrimination has been filed against this establishment and this statement is to inform the agency that the company has a policy against discrimination and would not discriminate in the manner charged in the complaint." The statement should be supported by some statistical analysis of the work force, copies of any documents that support your employer's position, or an explanation of any legitimate business justification for the employment decision that is the subject of the complaint.[99]

Computer Application in Equal Employment: Utilization Analysis

Companies and universities that have grants or contracts with the federal government periodically are required to complete utilization analyses, which are then submitted to the Department of Labor's Office of Contract Compliance Programs (OFCCP). The basis of comparison may be the most recently completed census on a valid industry survey. The comparison is made between (1) company employees in various EEO categories or subgroups (women, blacks, etc.) and (2) the number of people in the recruitment area who state that they have comparable skills in response to census or employment service requests for information.

A report format, called the Availability Analysis, accepted by OFCCP allows the employer to assign appropriate weights to the following eight factors which are incorporated into the report: (1) general population, but including only those subgroups who are seeking employment; (2) % unemployment; (3) % work force; (4) requisite skills available in the immediate area; (5) requisite skills available in the recruitment area; (6) feeder jobs from which internal employees may be promoted or transferred; (7) training institutions in recruitment area; and (8) internal training available. In other words, this is the employer's opportunity to show the effect on hiring of certain ingredients in the internal and external environments for that specific company. Thus, if there is no adequate training facility for crafts in the area, that factor may have no value (zero) in addressing recruitment needs for Category 5; Skilled Crafts. On the other hand, the company might hire plumbers helpers and, over a period of three years, train those helpers both on-the-job and in the classroom so that the employers can sit for the licensing exam. In this case, internal training would account for a significant portion of individuals placed into the position of plumber. The company could examine the percentage hired versus the percentage promoted over the last few years to appropriately balance the weights. The usual goal for any given category is for the labor force of the company to approximate the general population's availability of that skill level.

Spreadsheets can easily accommodate these comparisons through user-friendly formulas which calculate weights, percentages, sums, and complicated "if-then" statements. Employees are roughly divided into approximately seven categories which differentiate between sales, clerical, crafts, technical, supervisors, professionals, and executives. These main groups are then subdivided by salary ranges. Within each group, the employees are counted according to race and sex. When a spreadsheet has been established, the count in each category (black male, black female, etc.) may be manually entered along with the number of vacancies that were filled the previous year. All of the other data are then completed by the spreadsheet as your formulas pull from the few entries you have made.

The population of the labor area usually changes only with the census. The percentage of unemployment, which is calculated by the state employment service, changes monthly. The weight that you assign each factor should change infrequently, unless there has been a significant change in one of the factors, such as the unemployment rate. After the formulas have been established and the raw data entered, the spreadsheet will compare availability with actual current utilization. If underutilization exists, the spreadsheet is able to calculate the percentage of underutilization, how many hires/transfers are needed to overcome the underutilization, and how many need to be hired in the current year. The OFCCP report must be calculated for the major minorities (such as black and Hispanic, or whatever protected groups represent more than 10%-12% of the labor force in your immediate geographical area) and females.

The reason that this information should be built into a spreadsheet is so that goals for the given year may be available to recruiters and hiring supervisors at the beginning of the measured year. Although affirmative action does not require the company to favor protected groups (assuming there is no court order to require partiality), significant underutilization in a particular group strongly suggests that the recruitment techniques need to be examined.

If a predetermination settlement isn't reached, the EEOC will make a complete investigation of the charge, and here there are three major principles your employer should follow. First, your employer should ensure that there is information in the EEOC's file demonstrating *lack of merit* of the charge; often, the best way to do that is by *not* answering the EEOC's questionnaire, but by providing a detailed statement describing your defense in its best and most persuasive light.

Second, your employer *should* limit the information supplied as narrowly as possible to only those issues raised in the charge itself. For example, if the charge only alleges sex discrimination, do not respond unwittingly to the EEOC's request for a breakdown of your employees by age and sex. Finally, seek *as much information* as you can about the charging party's claim in order to ensure you understand it and its ramifications.

The Fact-Finding Conference

You should also be aware of the problems that can arise in the EEOC's "fact-finding conferences." According to the commission, these conferences are supposed to be informal meetings held early in the investigatory process aimed at defining issues and determining if there's a basis for negotiation. According to one expert, though, the EEOC's emphasis here is often on settlement. Its investigators therefore use the conferences to find weak spots in each party's respective position so that they can use this information as leverage to push for a settlement.

If your employer wants a settlement, the fact-finding conference can be a good forum at which to negotiate, but there are three big problems to watch out for. First, the only official record maintained is the notes taken by the EEOC investigator, and the parties cannot have access to them to rectify mistakes or clarify facts. Second, although your employer can bring an attorney, the EEOC often "seems to go out of its way to tell employers that an attorney's presence is unnecessary."[100] Finally, these conferences are often arranged soon after a charge is filed, before your employer has been fully informed of the charges and facts of the case.

An employer should thoroughly prepare witnesses who are going to testify at a fact-finding conference, especially supervisors, because their statements can be considered admissions against the employer's interest. Therefore, before appearing, they need to be aware of the legal significance of the facts they will present and the possible claims that may be made by the charging party and other witnesses.

THE EEOC'S DETERMINATION AND THE ATTEMPTED CONCILIATION

If the fact-finding conference does not solve the matter, the EEOC's investigator will determine whether there is reason to believe ("cause") or not to believe ("no cause") that discrimination may have taken place, and there are several things to keep in mind here. First, the investigator's recommendation is often the determining factor in whether the EEOC finds cause, so it is usually best to be courteous and cooperative (within limits). Second, if there is a finding of cause, review the finding very carefully; make sure that inaccuracies are pointed out in writing to the EEOC. Use this letter to again try to convince the EEOC, the charging party, and the charging party's attorney that the charge is without merit, in spite of the finding. Finally, keep in mind that even with a no cause finding, the charging party will still be issued a right to sue letter by the EEOC and will then be allowed 90 days (from receipt of the letter) to bring a private lawsuit.

If the EEOC issues a cause finding, it will ask you to conciliate. However, some experts argue against conciliating at this point, for several reasons. First, the EEOC often views conciliation not as a compromise but as complete relief to the charging party. Second, "if you have properly investigated and evaluated the case previously, there may be no real advantage in settling at this stage. It is more than likely (based on the statistics) that no suit will be filed by the EEOC."[101] Furthermore, even if a lawsuit is later filed by either the EEOC or the charging party, the employer can consider settling after receiving the complaint.

AVOIDING DISCRIMINATION LAWSUITS

Employment discrimination claims constitute the largest number of civil suits filed annually in federal courts. As a result, some companies are setting up internal dispute resolution procedures similar to the following one at Aetna Life and Casualty Company:

Step 1.

First the employee discusses the problem with a supervisor, who may consult other members of the management team who might have handled similar problems.

Step 2.

Here the employee may contact a divisional personnel consultant for a case review if he or she is dissatisfied with the results of the first step. The employee is then informed and advised on plausible alternatives.

Step 3.

If the employee believes that company policy is not being followed, he or she may then request a corporate level review of the case and a corporate consultant will review the case with management. The employee is then notified of the decision in writing.

Step 4.

Finally, a senior management review committee may be asked to review the case. The committee itself is comprised of the senior vice-president of the employees' division as well as the vice-presidents of corporate personnel and corporate public involvement.[102]

AFFIRMATIVE ACTION PROGRAMS

EQUAL EMPLOYMENT OPPORTUNITY VERSUS AFFIRMATIVE ACTION

Equal employment opportunity aims to ensure that anyone regardless of race, color, sex, religion, national origin, or age has an equal chance for a job based on his or her qualifications.

affirmative action Steps that are taken for the purpose of eliminating the present effects of past discrimination.

Affirmative action goes beyond equal employment opportunity. It requires the employer to make an **extra effort** to hire and promote those in the protected group. Affirmative action thus includes specific actions (in recruitment, hiring, promotions, and compensation) that are designed to eliminate the present effects of past discrimination. According to the EEOC, the most important measure of an affirmative action program is its results. The program should result in "measurable, yearly improvements in hiring, training, and promotion of minorities and females" in all parts of your organization.

STEPS IN AN AFFIRMATIVE ACTION PROGRAM

According to the EEOC, in an affirmative action program the employer ideally takes eight steps:

1. Issues a written equal employment policy indicating that it is an equal employment opportunity employer, as well as a statement indicating the employer's commitment to affirmative action.
2. Appoints a top official with responsibility and authority to direct and implement the program.
3. Publicizes the equal employment policy and affirmative action commitment.
4. Surveys present minority and female employment by department and job classification to determine locations where affirmative action programs are especially desirable. (See Fig. 2.3.)
5. Develops goals and timetables to improve utilization of minorities, males, and females in each area where utilization has been identified.
6. Develops and implements specific programs to achieve these goals. According to the EEOC, this is the heart of the affirmative action program. Here the employer has to review its entire personnel management system (including recruitment, selection, promotion, compensation, and disciplining) to identify barriers to equal employment opportunity and to make needed changes.
7. Establishes an internal audit and reporting system to monitor and evaluate progress in each aspect of the program.
8. Develops support for the affirmative action program, both inside the company (among supervisors, for instance) and outside the company, in the community.[103]

AFFIRMATIVE ACTION: TWO BASIC STRATEGIES

good faith effort strategy Employment strategy aimed at changing practices that have contributed in the past to excluding or underutilizing protected groups.

quota strategy Employment strategy aimed at mandating the same results as the good faith effort strategy through specific hiring and promotion restrictions.

When designing an affirmative action plan, your employer can choose either of two basic strategies to pursue—the **good faith effort strategy** or the **quota strategy**—each with its own risks.[104] The first emphasizes identifying and eliminating the obstacles to hiring and promoting women and minorities, on the assumption that eliminating these obstacles will result in increased utilization of women and minorities. The quota strategy, on the other hand, mandates bottom-line results by instituting hiring and promotion restrictions.

Good Faith Effort Strategy

This strategy is aimed at changing the practices that have contributed to the exclusion or underutilization of minority groups or females. Specific actions here might include placing advertisements where they can reach target groups, supporting day care services and flexible working hours for women with small children, and establishing a training program to enable minority group members to better compete for entry-level jobs. The basic assumption is that if existing obstacles are identified and eliminated, the desired results (improved utilization of minority members and women) will follow.

The basic risk here is that if the desired results are *not* achieved (in terms of hiring or promoting more minorities or women), then your employer must convince the EEO that (1) a reasonable effort to hire or promote more protected individuals has taken place and (2) that failure to do so resulted from factors outside the employer's control. Should management fail to convince the EEOC,

FIGURE 2.3
Sample Affirmative Action Report. EEO Category: Technical/Paraprofessional

Job Group 47	TOTAL							Asian		Black		Hispanics		American Indian		White	
	Incumb	Males		Female		Minority											
Title	#	#	%	#	%	#	%	#	%	#	%	#	%	#	%	#	%
Data Pro. Control Spec.	2			2	100.00	1	50.00					1	50.00			1	50.00
Computer Operator	5	5	100.00			4	80.00	1	20.00	2	40.00	1	20.00			1	20.00
Computer Repair Tech.	1	1	100.00			1	100.00					1	100.00				
Computer Programmer	2			2	100.00	1	50.00					1	50.00			1	50.00
Photographer	3	2	66.67	1	33.33	1	33.33					1	33.33			2	66.67
Graphic Artist	2	2	100.00			2	100.00					2	100.00				
Library Tech. Asst.	11	2	18.18	9	81.82	9	81.82			3	27.27	6	54.55			2	18.18.
Laboratory Technician	1			1	100.00	1	100.00					1	100.00				
TOTALS	27	12	44.44	15	55.56	20	74.07	1	3.70	5	18.52	14	51.85			7	25.95

Date of Survey *1991–1992*

it may then find itself in an unenviable negotiating position. The EEOC compliance officer has considerable leverage in the form of economic sanctions (through possible federal contract termination) and through legal action. In the absence of results, the employer may find it has little power to resist any recommendations the compliance officer might make.

Quota Strategy

Whereas the good faith strategy attempts to get results by eliminating obstacles, the quota strategy aims at mandating results through hiring and promotion restrictions. With the quota strategy, "desirable" hiring goals are operationally treated as required employment quotas.

reverse discrimination Claim that due to affirmative action quota systems, white males are discriminated against.

The courts have been grappling with the role of quotas in hiring, and particularly with claims by white males of **reverse discrimination**. A series of cases has addressed these issues without a uniform answer emerging. In *Bakke* v. *The Regents of the University of California* (1978), white student Allen Bakke had been denied admission to the University of California at Davis Medical School, allegedly because of the school's affirmative action quota system, which required that a specific number of openings go to minority applicants. In a 5-to-4 vote, the Court struck down the school's policy that made race the only factor in considering applications for a certain number of class openings and thus allowed Bakke to be admitted.

United Steel Workers of America* v. *Weber Supreme Court case in which the plaintiff claimed being a victim of reverse discrimination.

In ***United Steelworkers of America* v. *Weber*** (1979) involving Kaiser Aluminum and Chemical Company, the Supreme Court found for the company. By a 5-to-2 vote, the Court rejected the complaint of Brian Weber, a white employee of the company. Weber, a 32-year-old lab technician, had claimed that a union-management plan that reserved 50% of certain training positions for minority workers violated the antidiscrimination provisions of the Civil Rights Act of 1964 by discriminating against white males. In its opinion, the Court specifically avoided detailing "the line of demarcation between permissible and impermissible affirmative action plans." The justices avoided, in other words, clarifying the elements of an acceptable or unacceptable affirmative action plan, focusing instead on the unique characteristics of the Kaiser situation. In its majority opinion, however, the Court did state that Title VII was not intended to forbid all race-related affirmative action. The effect of the Court decision was to permit Kaiser to continue letting minorities and women with less seniority than Weber (and other white males) to be admitted to the training program. Again, however, the Court's decision is a narrow one, stating only that Kaiser's plan at that specific plant was permissible. The questions of (1) when preferential treatment becomes discrimination and (2) under what circumstances discrimination will be temporarily permitted were not fully clarified in *Bakke* or *Weber*.

However, subsequent U.S. Supreme court cases have continued to address those issues and clarify more specifically the scope and intent of affirmative action:

Firefighters Local No. 1784 v. *Stotts* (1984): The Court ruled that Title VII prohibits courts from requiring racial preferences as a remedy for prior discrimination unless the preference benefits only those individuals who were the actual victims of discrimination.[105]

Wygant v. *Jackson Board of Education* (1986): The Court struck down a mechanism in a collective bargaining agreement that gave preferential treatment to minority teachers in the event of a layoff.[106]

Local 28 Sheet Metal Workers v. *EEOC* (1986): The Court ruled that Title VII empowers a court to order a union to use quotas to overcome "egregious discrimination" and that the quota may benefit individuals who are not themselves victims of past unlawful union discrimination.[107]

International Association of Firefighters v. *The City of Cleveland* (1986): The Court upheld a consent decree that reserved a specific number of promotions for minority firefighters and established percentage goals for minority promotions.[108]

U.S. v. *Paradise* (1987): The Court ruled that the courts can impose racial quotas to address the most serious cases of racial discrimination.[109]

Johnson v. *Transportation Agency, Santa Clara County* (1987): Public and private employers may voluntarily adopt hiring and promotion goals to benefit minorities and women. This ruling will limit claims of reverse discrimination by white males.[110]

Martin v. *Wilks* (1989): An employer who has signed a consent decree requiring affirmative action under court supervision can be sued for reverse discrimination provided the person (or persons) bringing suit was not a party to the original consent decree. CRA 1991 reverses this decision.

As a good-faith affirmative action policy, some firms offer special summer programs to train high school students in an industry-specific trade. Here, students from a South Carolina high school learn the ins and outs of food preparation at a local restaurant.

A Practical Approach

According to one writer, these legal uncertainties suggest that the good faith effort strategy is often preferable to the quota strategy.[111] An employer might reasonably ask, therefore, "What specific actions should I take to be able to show that I have in fact made a good faith effort?"

One study helps answer this question. Questionnaires were sent to EEOC compliance officers who were asked to rate about 30 possible actions on their importance in evaluating the compliance effort of a hypothetical company. This company was described as having determined that minorities were underutilized in several blue-collar and white-collar jobs. The compliance officers were asked to indicate the possible tactics or actions they thought the employer could take in order to show evidence of an acceptable good faith effort affirmative action program.

As summarized in Table 2.2, the results of this study showed that there were six main areas for action:

1. Increasing the minority female applicant flow.
2. Demonstrating top management support for the equal employment policy.
3. Demonstrating equal employment commitment to the community.
4. Keeping employees informed.
5. Broadening the work skills of incumbent employees.
6. Internalizing the equal employment policy to encourage supervisors' support of it.

Some of the possible tactics or actions that the compliance officers felt would reflect a good faith effort on the part of the employer are also summarized in Table 2.2. For example, a good faith effort aimed at increasing the minority female applicant flow might involve actions like "include minority colleges and

TABLE 2.2 Specific Actions in a "Good Faith Effort" Strategy

AREAS FOR ACTION	OVERALL OBJECTIVES	POSSIBLE TACTICS
1. Increasing minority and female applicant flow	To ensure that minorities and females are not systematically excluded and to encourage those individuals to apply	1. Include minority colleges and universities in campus recruitment programs 2. Place employment advertising in minority-oriented print and broadcast media 3. Retain applications of unhired minority female applicants to be reviewed as vacancies occur
2. Demonstrating top-management support for EEO policy	To indicate to all employees that top management considers affirmative action and equal employment opportunity important	1. Prepare written reports evaluating progress toward affirmative action goals as frequently as other management control reports are prepared 2. Involve the line supervisors in the establishment of the affirmative action hiring goals 3. Appoint an EEO coordinator who is both highly visible within the facility and from a department other than personnel
3. Demonstrating EEO commitment to the local community	To indicate to the public and local labor market management's concern for equal employment opportunity	1. Appoint key management personnel to serve on community relations board or similar organizations 2. Establish a formal EEO complaint procedure within the facility 3. Establish an on-the-job training program at the facility 4. Establish or support existing child-care facilities

continued

TABLE 2.2 (continued)

AREAS FOR ACTION	OVERALL OBJECTIVES	POSSIBLE TACTICS
4. Keeping employees informed	To communicate to employees the specifics of the affirmative action programs, including their rights, benefits, and opportunities	1. Discuss EEO matters, such as program success and new program efforts, in internal newsletter 2. Display EEO policy statement in work areas 3. Explain the EEO policy, job posting procedures, tuition refund programs, and so on, during the new employee orientation procedure
5. Broadening skills of incumbent employees	To increase the advancement opportunities and potential of employees	1. Provide tuition refund benefits to all employees 2. Institute a job rotation program within work groups
6. Internalizing the EEO policy	To encourage adherence to the EEO policy through modification of the organization's control, communication, and reward systems	1. Incorporate affirmative action progress into the performance evaluations of line supervisors 2. Directly notify eligible employees of advancement and training opportunities as vacancies occur 3. Formalize and communicate sanctions for violations of EEO policy

universities in campus recruitment programs" and "retain applications of unhired minority and female applicants to be reviewed as vacancies occur." Actions like these, this writer concludes, can help to ensure that the employer's good faith effort is an effective one, both in improving the employer's utilization of minorities and women and in convincing the EEOC that a good faith effort to do so was made.

CHAPTER REVIEW

SUMMARY

1. Legislation barring discrimination is nothing new. For example, the Fifth Amendment to the U.S. Constitution (ratified in 1791) states that no person shall be deprived of life, liberty, or property without due process of law.
2. As a reaction to changing values in America, new legislation barring employment discrimination was passed. This included Title VII of the 1964 Civil Rights Act (as amended) (which bars discrimination because of race, color, religion, sex, or

national origin), various executive orders, federal guidelines (covering procedures for validating employee selection tools, etc.), the Equal Pay Act of 1963, and the Age Discrimination in Employment Act of 1967. In addition, various court decisions (such as *Griggs* v. *Duke Power Company*) and state and local laws bar various aspects of discrimination.

3. The EEOC was created by title VII of the Civil Rights Act. It is empowered to try conciliating discrimination complaints, but if this fails, the EEOC has the power to go directly to court to enforce the law.
4. The Civil Rights Act of 1991 had the effect of revising several Supreme Court equal employment decisions and "rolling back the clock." It placed the burden of proof back on employers, said postemployment decisions were covered by the 1866 Civil Rights Act, held that a nondiscriminatory reason was insufficient to let an employer avoid liability for an action that also had a discriminatory motive, and said that Title VII applied to U.S. employees of U.S. firms overseas. It also now permits compensatory and punitive damages, as well as jury trials.
5. The Americans with Disabilities Act prohibits employment discrimination against the disabled. Specifically, qualified persons can't be discriminated against if the firm can make reasonable accommodations without undue hardship on the business.
6. A person who feels he or she has been discriminated against by a personnel procedure or decision must prove either that he or she was subjected to unlawful disparate treatment (intentional discrimination) or that the procedure in question has a disparate impact upon members of his or her protected class. Disparate treatment can be proven under the *McDonnell-Douglas* standards, while disparate impact proof can involve disparate rejection rates, restrictive policies, or population comparisons. Once a *prima facie* case of disparate *treatment* is established, an employer must produce evidence that its decision was based upon legitimate nondiscriminatory reasons. If the employer does that, the person claiming discrimination must prove the employer's reasons are pretextual. Once a *prima facie* case of disparate *impact* is established, the employer must produce evidence that the allegedly discriminatory practice or procedure is job related and is based upon a not insubstantial business reason. If it does so, the employee must prove a less discriminatory alternative existed that would have been equally effective in achieving the employer's legitimate objectives or disprove the employer's justification for disparate impact.
7. Various specific discriminatory human resource management practices that an employer should avoid were discussed.
   a. *In recruitment.* An employer usually should not rely on word-of-mouth advertising or give false or misleading information to minority group members. Also (usually), do not specify the desired sex in advertising or in any way suggest that applicants might be discriminated against.
   b. *In selection.* Avoid using any educational or other requirements where (1) it can be shown that minority group members are less likely to possess the qualification and (2) such requirement is also not job related. Tests that disproportionately screen out minorities and women *and that are not job related* are deemed unlawful by the courts. Do not give preference to relatives of current employees (when most are nonminority) or specify physical characteristics unless it can be proved they are needed for job performance. Similarly, a person's arrest record should not be used to disqualify him or her automatically for a position, nor should a person be fired whose salary has been garnished. Remember that you *can* use various tests and standards, but must prove that they are job related or show that they are not used to discriminate against protected groups.
8. In practice, a person's charge to the EEOC is often first referred to a local agency. When it does proceed, and if it finds reasonable cause to believe that discrimination occurred, EEOC has 30 days to try to work out a conciliation. Important points for the employer to remember include (a) EEOC investigators can only make recommendations, (b) you can't be compelled to submit documents without a court order, and (c) limit the information you do submit. Also, make sure you clearly document your position (as the employer).

9. There are two basic defenses an employer can use in the event of a discriminatory practice allegation. One is *business necessity*. Attempts to show that tests (or other selection standards) are valid is one example of this defense. *Bona fide occupational qualification* is the second defense. This is applied when, for example, religion, national origin, or sex is a bona fide requirement of the job (such as for actors or actresses). An employer's "good intentions" and/or a collective bargaining agreement are not defenses. (A third defense is that the decision was made on the basis of legitimate nondiscriminatory reasons [such as poor performance] having nothing to do with the prohibited discrimination alleged.)
10. Eight steps in an affirmative action program (based on suggestions from the EEOC) are (a) issue a written equal employment *policy*, (b) *appoint* a top official, (c) *publicize* policy, (d) *survey* present minority and female employment, (e) *develop* goals and timetables, (f) develop and implement *specific programs* to achieve goals, (g) establish an *internal audit* and reporting system, and (h) *develop support* of in-house and community programs.

KEY TERMS

- Title VII of the 1964 Civil Rights Act
- Equal Employment Opportunity Commission (EEOC)
- Executive orders
- Office of Federal Contract Compliance Programs (OFCCP)
- Equal Pay Act of 1963
- Age Discrimination in Employment Act of 1967
- Vocational Rehabilitation Act of 1973
- *Arline* v. *School Board of Nassau County*
- Americans with Disabilities Act
- Vietnam Era Veterans' Readjustment Assistance Act of 1974
- Pregnancy Discrimination Act (PDA)
- *California Federal Savings and Loan Association* v. *Guerra*
- Federal agency guidelines
- Sexual harassment
- *Meritor Savings Bank, FSB* v. *Vinson*
- *Griggs* v. *Duke Power Company*
- *Albemarle Paper Company* v. *Moody*
- *Wards Cove* v. *Atonio*
- Disparate impact
- Disparate treatment
- Civil Rights Act of 1991
- Adverse impact
- Disparate rejection rates
- Restricted policy
- Bona fide occupational qualification (BFOQ)
- Business necessity
- Validity
- Affirmative action
- Extra effort
- Good faith effort strategy
- Quota strategy
- Reverse discrimination
- *United Steelworkers of America* v. *Weber*

DISCUSSION QUESTIONS

1. What is Title VII? What does it say?
2. What important precedents were set by the *Griggs* v. *Duke Power Company* case? The *Albemarle* v. *Moody* case?
3. What is adverse impact? How can it be proven?
4. Assume you are a supervisor on an assembly line; you are responsible for hiring subordinates, supervising them, and recommending them for promotion. Compile a list of discriminatory management practices you should avoid.
5. Explain the defenses and exceptions to discriminatory practice allegations.
6. What is the difference between affirmative action and equal employment opportunity? Explain how you would set up an affirmative action program.
7. Compare and contrast the issues presented in *Bakke* and *Weber* with new court rulings on affirmative action. What is the current direction of affirmative action as a policy in light of the *Johnson* ruling?
8. Explain how the Civil Rights Act of 1991 "turned back the clock" on equal employment Supreme Court cases decided in 1989–1991.

▶ APPLICATION EXERCISES

RUNNING CASE

CARTER CLEANING COMPANY

A Question of Discrimination

One of the first problems Jennifer faced at her father's Carter Cleaning Centers concerned the inadequacies of the firm's current personnel management practices and procedures.

One problem that particularly concerned her was the lack of attention to equal employment matters. Virtually all hiring was handled independently by each store manager, and the managers themselves had received no training regarding such fundamental matters as the types of questions that should not be asked of job applicants. It was therefore not unusual—in fact it was even routine—for female applicants to be asked questions such as "Who's going to take care of your children while you are at work?" and for minority applicants to be asked questions about arrest records and credit histories. Nonminority applicants—three store managers were white males and three were white females, by the way—were not asked these questions, as Jennifer discerned from her interviews with the managers.

Based on discussions with her father, Jennifer deduced that part of the reason for the laid-back attitude toward equal employment stemmed from (1) her father's lack of sophistication regarding the legal requirements and (2) the fact that, as Jack Carter put it, "Virtually all our workers are women or minority members anyway, so no one can really come in here and accuse us of being discriminatory, can they?"

Jennifer decided to mull that question over, but before she could, she was faced with two serious equal rights problems. Two women in one of her stores privately confided to her that their manager was making unwelcome sexual advances toward them, and one claimed he had threatened to fire her unless she "socialized" with him after hours. And on a fact-finding trip to another store, an elderly gentleman—he was 73 years old—complained of that fact that although he had almost 50 years of experience in the business, he was being paid less than people half his age who were doing the very same job. Her review of the stores resulted in the following questions.

Questions

1. Is it true, as Jack Carter claims, that "we can't be accused of being discriminatory because we hire mostly women and minorities anyway"?
2. How should Jennifer and her company address the sexual harassment charges and problems?
3. How should she and her company address the possible problems of age discrimination?
4. Given the fact that each of its stores has only a handful of employees, is her company in fact covered by equal rights legislation?
5. And finally, aside from the specific problems, what other personnel management matters (application forms, training, etc.) have to be reviewed given the need to bring them into compliance with equal rights laws?

CASE INCIDENT *Eliminating the Effects of Past Discrimination*

The Swormsville Company has a job career ladder that starts at job class 1, the lowest paid, and ends at job class 24, the highest. Normally one moves up the ladder, from job class to job class, with the worker who has had the job longest in any one job class being given preference whenever there is a vacancy in the next higher job class. In the past, however, there was one major exception: no African-American could be promoted above job class 5.

Assuming this discriminatory provision is eliminated, what should the rights be of Mr. X, an African-American with 24 years' departmental seniority, who is still in job class 5 while whites with equal seniority are now in job class 15? Three possibilities have been suggested:

1. Mr. X moves immediately to job 15, even though this means displacing someone currently on the job and even though he does not have the training and experience to handle the job.
2. Mr. X will be given special training and he will be moved upward from job to job as fast as his abilities permit him, in each case having first priority for any vacancy, but not displacing anyone from a job.
3. As the longest-service man in job class 5, Mr. X can move to job class 6 when there is a vacancy, but he can't move to job class 7 until all those currently in job class 6 are promoted.

Questions

1. Which of these alternatives seems most fair? Can you devise a fairer one?
2. Would the nature of the jobs make any difference in your answer?

HUMAN RESOURCE MANAGEMENT SIMULATION

Affirmative Action is one of the key elements in the simulation. The firm currently has fewer female and minority workers, percentage-wise, than the local working population. Hiring has been generally done on a "walk-in" basis and there is no formal plan to increase the number of women and minorities in the firm. Your team must decide if it wants to establish a formal affirmative action program or simply stress hiring more women and minorities in its hiring program. In addition, you will be asked to decide what percentage of women and minorities you want to hire each decision period. If you do not set a goal that is high enough, you may be charged with discrimination. If the goal is too high, your current workforce may conclude there is reverse discrimination. Your status report will indicate the demographic composition of your workforce each quarter so you can track your progress.

If your team is to be successful, it is extremely important that you obtain all the information available to you in the simulation. Each decision period you will have the opportunity to purchase industry research that will aid you in the decision-making process. The surveys available are: (1) industry average quality, morale, grievances, and absenteeism; (2) industry average and local comparable wage rates; (3) average industry training, safety, and quality budgets; and (4) the number of firms with employee participation programs.

▶ NOTES

1. Commerce Clearing House, *Ideas and Trends in Personnel*, May 13, 1992, p. 73.
2. "Section 1981 Covers Racial Discrimination in Hiring and Promotions—But No Other Situations," Commerce Clearing House, *Human Resources Management*, June 28, 1989, p. 116.
3. Portions of this chapter are based on or quoted from *Principles of Employment Discrimination Law*, International Association of Official Human Rights Agencies, Washington, DC. In addition, see W. Clay Hamner and Frank Schmidt, *Contemporary Problems in Personnel*, rev. ed. (Chicago: St. Clair Press, 1977), Chapter 3. Employment discrimination law is a changing field, and the appropriateness of the rules, guidelines, and conclusions in this book may also be affected by factors unique to an employer's operation. They should, therefore, be reviewed by the employer's attorney before implementation.
4. James Higgins, 'A Manager's Guide to the Equal Employment Opportunity Laws,' *Personnel Journal*,

Vol. 55, no. 8 (August 1976), p. 406.

5. The Equal Employment Opportunity Act of 1972, Sub-Committee on Labor or the Committee of Labor and Public Welfare, United States Senate (March 1972), p. 3. In general, it is not discrimination, but *unfair* discrimination against a person merely because of that person's race, age, sex, national origin, or religion, that is forbidden by federal statutes. In the federal government's *Uniform Employee Selection Guidelines*, "unfair" discrimination is defined as follows: "unfairness is demonstrated through a showing that members of a particular interest group perform better or poorer on the job than their scores on the selection procedure (test, etc.) would indicate through comparison with how members of the other groups performed. . . ." For a discussion of the meaning of fairness, see James Ledvinka, "The Statistical Definition of Fairness in the Federal Selection Guidelines and Its Implications for Minority Employment," *Personnel Psychology*, Vol. 32 (August 1979), pp. 551–562. In summary, a selection device (like a test) *may* discriminate—say between low and high performers. However, it is *unfair* discrimination that is illegal, discrimination that is based solely on the person's race, age, sex, national origin, or religion.
6. A growing issue today is whether homosexuals are due equal protection from discrimination. Initially attempts to assert that discrimination based on sexual orientation was illegal were unsuccessful, and even the EEOC was unsympathetic. However, a recent case (*Watkins* v. *U.S. Army*, F.2d 1428, 1429, 9th Cir. 1988) involving an army sergeant forced to resign after 14 years, notable service may possibly open the door to successful suits by identifying homosexuals as a "suspect class that deserve special protection against discrimination." Sabrina Wrenn, "Gay Rights and Workplace Discrimination," *Personnel Journal*, Vol. 67, no. 10 (October 1988), p. 94.
7. Bureau of National Affairs, *Fair Employment Practices*, October 8, 1992, p. 117.
8. Note that under the Rehabilitation Act, the law strictly speaking applied only to a particular "program" of the employer. In March 1988 Congress passed the Civil Rights Restoration Act of 1987, overturning this interpretation. Now, with few exceptions, any institution, organization, corporation, state agency, or municipality using federal funding in any of its programs must abide by the section of the act prohibiting discriminating against handicapped individuals. See Bureau of National Affairs, "Federal Law Mandates Affirmative Action for Handicapped," *Fair Employment Practices*, March 30, 1989, p. 42.
9. *Tanberg* v. *Weld County Sheriff*, USDA Colo, No. 91-B-248, 3/18/92.
10. Steven Fox, "Employment Provisions of the Rehabilitation Act," *Personnel Journal*, Vol. 66, no. 10 (October 1987), p. 140.
11. Commerce Clearing House, "Is AIDS a Protected Handicap?" *Human Resource Management Ideas and Trends*, March 20, 1987, p. 46.
12. Bureau of National Affairs, "Guidelines on AIDS," *Fair Employment Practices*, March 30, 1989, p. 39.
13. David B. Ritter and Ronald Turner, "AIDS: Employer Concerns and Options," *Labor Law Journal*, Vol. 38, no. 2 (February 1987), pp. 67–83.
14. Bureau of National Affairs, *Fair Employment Practices*, August 27, 1992, p. 102.
15. Howard J. Anderson and Michael D. Levin-Epstein, *Primer of Equal Employment Opportunity*, 2nd ed. (Washington, DC: Bureau of National Affairs, 1982), pp. 5–7; and Commerce Clearing House, "Federal Contractors Must File VETS-100 by March 31," *Ideas and Trends*, February 23, 1988, p. 32.
16. Ann Harriman, *Women/Men Management* (New York: Praeger, 1985), pp. 66–68.
17. Commerce Clearing House, "Pregnancy Leave," *Ideas and Trends*, January 23, 1987, p. 10.
18. Bureau of National Affairs, "High Court Upholds Pregnancy Law," *Fair Employment Practices*, January 22, 1987, p. 7; Betty Sonthard Murphy, Wayne E. Barlow, and D. Diane Hatch, "Manager's Newsfront: U.S. Supreme Court Approves Preferential Treatment for Pregnancy," *Personnel Journal*, Vol. 66, no. 3 (March 1987), p. 18.
19. Thomas Dhanens, "Implications of the New EEOC Guidelines," *Personnel*, Vol. 56 (September–October 1979), pp. 32–39.
20. Bureau of National Affairs, "First Two Chapters of Long-Awaited Manual Released by OFCCP," *Fair Employment Practices*, January 5, 1989, p. 6.
21. Lawrence S. Kleiman and Robert Faley, "The Applications of Professional and Legal Guidelines for Court Decisions Involving Criterion-Related Validity: A Review and Analysis," *Personnel Psychology*, Vol. 38, no. 4 (Winter 1985), pp. 803–833.
22. Oscar A. Ornati and Margaret J. Eisen, "Are You Complying with EEOC's New Rules on National Origin Discrimination?" *Personnel*, Vol. 58 (March–April 1981), pp. 12–20; Paul S. Greenlaw and John P. Kohl, "National Origin Discrimination and the New EEOC Guidelines," *Personnel Journal*, Vol. 60, no. 8 (August 1981), pp. 634–636.
23. Barbara Berish Brown, "Guidance and Regs from EEOC, OFCCP, and INS," *Employment Relations Today* (Spring 1992), pp. 81–86.
24. Paul S. Greenlaw and John P. Kohl, "Age Discrimination and Employment Guidelines," *Personnel Journal*, Vol. 61, no. 3 (March 1982), pp. 224–228.
25. 29 CFR 1625.2(a) quoted in Greenlaw and Kohl, "Age Discrimination."
26. Charles Mishkind, "Sexual Harassment Hostile Work Environment Class Actions: Is There Cause for Concern?" *Employee Relations Law Journal*, Vol. 18, no. 2 (Summer 1992).
27. Bureau of National Affairs, *Fair Employment Practices*, April 23, 1992, p. 47.
28. Patricia Linenberger and Timothy Keaveny, "Sexual Harassment: The Employer's Legal Obligations," *Personnel*, Vol. 58 (November–December 1981), pp. 60–68.
29. Milton Zall, "What to Expect from the Civil Rights Act," *Personnel Journal*, Vol. 71, no. 3 (March 1992), p. 50.
30. Mary Rowe, "Dealing with Sexual Harassment," *Harvard Business Review*, Vol. 61 (May–June 1981), pp. 42–46.
31. Commerce Clearing House, *Sexual Harassment Manual for Managers and Supervisors* (Chicago, IL: Commerce Clearing House, Inc., 1991), pp. 28–29.
32. Robert H. Faley, "Sexual Harassment: Critical Review of Legal Cases with General Principles and Preventive Measures," *Personnel Psychology*, Vol. 35, no. 3 (Autumn 1982), pp. 590–591; Bureau of National Affairs, "In Terms of Sexual Harassment, What Makes an Environment 'Hostile'?" *Fair Employment Practices*, June 1988, p. 78.
33. Linenberger and Keaveny, "Sexual Harassment," p. 64.
34. Michael W. Sculnick, "The Supreme Court 1985–86 EEO Decisions: A Review," *Employment Relations Today*, Vol. 13, no. 3 (Fall 1986), pp. 197–206; *Brown* v. *City of Guthrie*, 22FEP Cases 1627, 1980.
35. Commerce Clearing House, *Sexual Harassment Manual*, p. 8.

36. Frederick L. Sullivan, "Sexual Harassment: The Supreme Court Ruling," *Personnel*, Vol. 65, no. 12 (December 1986), pp. 42–44. Also see the following for additional information on sexual harassment: Jonathan S. Monat and Angel Gomez, "Decisional Standards Used by Arbitrators in Sexual Harassment Cases," *Labor Law Journal*, Vol. 37, no. 10 (October 1986), pp. 712–718; George M. Sullivan and William H. Nowlin, "Critical New Aspects of Sexual Harassment Law," *Labor Law Journal*, Vol. 37, no. 9 (September 1986), pp. 617–623.
37. Rowe, "Dealing with Sexual Harassment."
38. *Griggs* v. *Duke Power Company*, 3FEP Cases 175.
39. James Ledvinka, *Federal Regulation of Personnel and Human Resource Management* (Boston: Kent, 1982), p. 41.
40. 10FEP cases 1181.
41. James Ledvinka and Lyle Schoenfeldt, "Legal Development in Employment Testing: Albemarle and Beyond," *Personnel Psychology*, Vol. 31, no. 1 (Spring 1978), pp. 1–13. It should be noted that the Court, in its *Albemarle* opinion, made one important modification regarding the EEOC guidelines. The guidelines required that employers using tests that screened out disproportionate numbers of minorities or women had to validate those tests—prove that they did in fact predict performance on the job—*and further had to prove that there was no other alternative screening device the employer could use that did not screen out disproportionate numbers of minorities and women.* This second requirement proved a virtually impossible burden for employers. Up through the *Griggs* decision, it was not enough to just validate the test; instead, the employer also had to show that some other tests or screening tools were not available that were (1) also valid but that (2) did not screen out a disproportionate number of minorities or women. In the *Albemarle* case the Court held that the burden of proof was no longer on the employer to show that there was no suitable alternative screening device available. Instead, the burden for that was now on the charging party (the person allegedly discriminated against) to show that a suitable alternative is available. Ledvinka and Schoenfeldt, "Legal Development," p. 4; Gary Lubben, Dwayne Thompson, and Charles Klasson, "Performance Appraisal: The Legal Implications of Title VII," *Personnel* (May–June 1980), pp. 11–21.
42. This was quoted from Commerce Clearing House, "Supreme Court Releases First 'Mixed Motives' Decision Under Title VII," *Ideas and Trends*, May 17, 1989, p. 82.
43. Ibid., p. 82.
44. "High Court Makes Race, Sex Bias in Work Place Tougher to Prove," *The Miami Herald*, June 6, 1989, p. 4A.
45. Commerce Clearing House, "The Supreme Court Explains How Statistics Are to Be Used in Fair Employment Suits," *Ideas and Trends*, June 14, 1989, p. 109.
46. These are based on Ibid., p. 101.
47. Based on Ibid.
48. *Patterson* v. *McLean Credit Union*, Docket no. 87–107, June 15, 1989, p. 11.
49. Commerce Clearing House, "Those Who Played No Role in Original Consent Decree Can Sue for Reverse Discrimination," *Ideas and Trends*, June 28, 1989, p. 115.
50. Howard A. Simon, "Mixed Signals: The Supreme Court's 1991 Title VII Decisions," *Employee Relations*, Vol. 17, no. 2 (Autumn 1991), pp. 207–223.
51. See Zall, "What to Expect from the Civil Rights Act," pp. 46–50.
52. Commerce Clearing House, "House and Senate Pass Civil Rights Compromise by Wide Margin," *Ideas and Trends in Personnel*, November 13, 1991, p. 179.
53. Zall, "What to Expect from the Civil Rights Act," p. 50.
54. Commerce Clearing House, "House and Senate Pass Civil Rights Compromise," p. 182.
55. Mark Kobata, "The Civil Rights Act of 1991," *Personnel Journal* (March 1992), p. 48.
56. For a discussion, see Commerce Clearing House, *Ideas and Trends in Personnel*, November 13, 1991, p. 182.
57. Elliot H. Shaller and Dean Rosen, "A Guide to the EEOC's Final Regulations on the Americans with Disabilities Act," *Employee Relations*, Vol. 17, no. 3 (Winter 1991–92), pp. 405–430.
58. Bureau of National Affairs, "ADA—Simple Common Sense Principles," *Fair Employment Practices*, June 4, 1992, p. 63.
59. Karen Simpkins and Rochelle Kaplan, "Fair Play for Disabled Persons: Responsibilities Under the Americans with Disabilities Act," *Journal of Career Planning and Employment*, Vol. 51, no. 2 (January 1991), p. 41.
60. Shaller and Rosen, "A Guide to the EEOC's Final Regulations," p. 408.
61. Ibid., p. 409.
62. These are adapted from Wayne Barlow and Edward Hane, "A Practical Guide to the Americans with Disabilities Act," *Personnel Journal*, Vol. 72 (June 1992), p. 59.
63. James Frierson, "An Analysis of ADA Provisions on Denying Employment Because of a Risk of Future Injury," *Employee Relations Law Journal*, Vol. 17, no. 4 (Spring 1992).
64. Elliot Shaller, "Reasonable Accommodation Under the Americans with Disabilities Act—What Does It Mean?" *Employee Relations Law Journal*, Vol. 16, no. 4 (Spring 1991), pp. 445–446.
65. Ibid., p. 446.
66. James Ledvinka and Robert Gatewood, "EEO Issues with Preemployment Inquiries," *Personnel Administrator*, Vol. 22, no. 2 (February 1977), pp. 22–26.
67. These are based on Bureau of National Affairs, "A Wrap-up of State Legislation: 1988 Anti-bias Laws Focus on AIDS," *Fair Employment Practices*, January 5, 1989, pp. 3–4.
68. John Klinfelter and James Thompkins, "Adverse Impact in Employment Selection," *Public Personnel Management* (May–June 1976), pp. 199–204.
69. H. John Bernardin, Richard Beatty, and Walter Jensin, "The New Uniform Guidelines on Employee Selection Procedures in the Context of University Personnel Decisions," *Personnel Psychology*, Vol. 33 (Summer 1980), pp. 301–316.
70. See Howard Bloch and Robert Pennington, "Labor Market Analysis as a Test of Discrimination," *Personnel Journal*, Vol. 59, no. 8 (August 19809), pp. 649–652.
71. International Association of Official Human Rights Agencies, *Principles of Employment Discrimination Law*; James M. Higgins, "A Manager's Guide to the Equal Opportunity Laws," *Personnel*, Vol. 55 (August 1976); James Ledvinka, *Federal Regulation.*
72. *Usery* v. *Tamiami Trail Tours*, 12FEP cases 1233; see also Anderson and Levine-Epstein, *Primer of Equal Employment Opportunity*, p. 57.
73. William Kandel, "'Overqualified' or 'Appropriately Qualified': New ADEA Risks," *Employee Relations Law Journal*, Vol. 17, no. 2 (Autumn 1991), pp. 287–306.
74. *EEOC* v. *Century Broadcasting*, CA 7, 1992, 58 FEP cases 696.
75. *Benjamin* v. *United Merchants and Manufacturers*, CA2, 1989, 49FEP cases 1020, discussed in Bureau of National Affairs, *Fair Employment Practices*, May 25, 1989, p. 61; Bureau of National Affairs, *Fair Employment Practices*,

February 18, 1988, p. 19.

76. Ledvinka, *Federal Regulation*, p. 82. For a further discussion of religious and other types of accommodation and what they involve see, for example, Bureau of National Affairs, *Fair Employment Practices*, January 21, 1988, pp. 9–10; Bureau of National Affairs, *Fair Employment Practices*, April 14, 1988, pp. 45–46; and James G. Frierson, "Religion in the Work Place," *Personnel Journal*, Vol. 67, no. 7 (July 1988), pp. 60–67.
77. Ledvinka, *Federal Regulation*.
78. Anderson and Levin-Epstein, *Primer of Equal Employment Opportunity*, pp. 13–14.
79. *U.S.* v. *Bethlehem Steel Company*, 3FEP cases 589.
80. *Robinson* v. *Lorillard Corporation*, 3FEP cases 653.
81. *Spurlock* v. *United Airlines*, 5FEP cases 17.
82. Anderson and Levin-Epstein, *Primer of Equal Employment Opportunity*, p. 14.
83. Quoted in Wayne Cascio, *Applied Psychology in Personnel Management* (Reston, VA: Reston, 1978), p. 25.
84. *Firefighters Local 1784* v. *Stotts* (BNA, April 14, 1985).
85. Ledvinka and Gatewood, "EEO Issues with Preemployment Inquiries," pp. 22–26.
86. Ibid.
87. Anderson and Levin-Epstein, *Primer of Equal Opportunity* p. 28.
88. This is based on Anderson, Ibid., pp. 93–97.
89. This is based on Bureau of National Affairs, *Fair Employment Practices*, April 13, 1989, pp. 45–47.
90. *Hottinger* v. *Pope County, Ark*, CA 8, No. 91-3633, June 27, 1992.
91. Eric Matusewitch, "Tailor Your Dress Codes," *Personnel Journal*, Vol. 68, no. 2 (February 19898), pp. 86–91.
92. Even during President Reagan's administration—often viewed as a not particularly supportive period for equal rights enforcement in the United States—an EEOC press release dated June 13, 1988 says it filed 527 court actions during fiscal year 1987, "setting an agency record for legal activity and maintaining its high level of enforcement on behalf of persons discriminated against in the work place." The release continues: "A record high 430 lawsuits were filed on the merits of discrimination charges in fiscal 1987, topping the previous record of 427 direct suits and interventions filed in fiscal 1986. Cases filed under Title VII of the 1964 Civil Rights Act totaled 69 and 12 filings, respectively. Twenty-nine cases were filed concurrently under Title VII and ADEA or Title VII and EPA. Agency investigative subpoena enforcement actions totaled 97, slightly below the 99 filed in fiscal 1986." Furthermore, in fiscal 1987, "The commission resolved more cases of discrimination through litigation than ever before: 460 as compared to 386 in fiscal 1986, the previous record number of resolutions. Direct suits and interventions accounted for 357 of the resolutions and there were 103 subpoena enforcement actions." EEOC news release dated June 13, 1988, and titled "EEOC Continues Record Enforcement Pace in Fiscal Year 1987." Quoted in Commerce Clearing House, *Ideas and Trends*, June 28, 1988, pp. 101–102.
93. If the charge was filed initially with a state or local agency within 180 days after the alleged unlawful practice occurred, the charge may then be filed with the EEOC within 30 days after the practice occurred or within 30 days after the person received notice that the state or local agency has ended its proceedings.
94. Paul S. Greenlaw, "Reverse Discrimination: The Supreme Court's Dilemma, *Personnel Journal*, Vol. 67, no. 1 (January 1988), pp. 84–89.
95. John Wymer III and Deborah Sudbury, "Employment Discrimination 'Testers'—Will Your Hiring Practices 'Pass'?" *Employee Relations Law Journal*, Vol. 17, no. 4 (Spring 1992), pp. 623–633.
96. Bureau of National Affairs, *Fair Employment Practices*, May 21, 1992, p. 59.
97. Robert H. Sheahan, "Responding to Employment Discrimination Charges," *Personnel Journal*, Vol. 60, no. 3 (March 1981), pp. 217–220; Wayne Baham, "Learn to Deal with Agency Investigations," *Personnel Journal*, Vol. 67, no 9 (September 1988), pp. 104–107.
98. Note, however, that there are certain general guidelines regarding the archival data your firm must periodically compile. See E. Bryan Kennedy, "Archival Data Must Be Accurate," *Personnel Journal*, Vol. 6, no. 11 (November 1988), pp. 108–111.
99. Based on Commerce Clearing House, *Ideas and Trends*, January 23, 1987, pp. 14–15.
100. Ibid., p. 219.
101. Ibid., p. 220.
102. Quoted from Bureau of National Affairs, *Fair Employment Practices*, February 9, 1984, p. 4.
103. U.S. Equal Employment Opportunity Commission, *Affirmative Action and Equal Employment* (Washington, DC: January 1974); Antonio Handler Chayes, "Make Your Equal Opportunity Program Court Proof," *Harvard Business Review* (September 1974), pp. 81–89.
104. This discussion is based on Kenneth Marino, "Conducting an Internal Compliance Review of Affirmative Action," *Personnel*, Vol. 59 (March–April 1980), pp. 24–34.
105. See James R. Redeker, "The Supreme Court on Affirmative Action: Conflicting Opinions," *Personnel*, Vol. 65, no. 10 (October 1986).
106. See Michael W. Sculnick, "The Supreme Court 1985–86 EEO Decisions: A Review," *Employment Relations Today*, Vol. 13, no. 3 (Fall 1986).
107. Ibid.
108. Ibid.
109. Ibid.
110. Aric Press and Ann McDaniel, "A Woman's Day in Court," *Newsweek*, April 6, 1987, pp. 58–59.
111. Marino, "Conducting an Internal Compliance Review": Lawrence Kleiman and Robert Faley, "Voluntary Affirmative Action and Preferential Treatment: Legal and Research Implications," *Personnel Psychology*, Vol. 42, no. 3 (Autumn 1988), pp. 481–496.

PART 1

Recruitment and Placement

VIDEO CASE 1
—Introduction—

WOMEN IN THE WORK FORCE

from "Business World," ABC News, February 23, 1992

Part 1 introduces the topics of recruitment and placement, which represent the oldest and most crucial categories of the personnel manager's job. Recruiting, selecting, and placing employees have always been central to personnel's role. If anything, this role is more important today than ever before. When jobs are primarily of the routine, assembly-line variety and there is an abundance of candidates for these jobs, the tasks of recruiting, selecting, and placing employees are relatively easy. But in today's competitive world, in which jobs increasingly demand high levels of worker commitment and in which quality, service, and flexibility are required for a firm's survival, hiring people who are capable of a committed effort can be a much greater challenge. The specific topics we'll discuss in this part of the book include:

Chapter 3: Job Analysis

Chapter 4: Personnel Planning and Recruiting

Chapter 5: Employee Testing and Selection

Chapter 6: Interviewing Candidates and Building a Total Selection Program

The video that accompanies Part 1 describes one very important aspect of recruitment and placement—namely, the issue of discrimination at work. In Chapter 2 we discussed a number of important antidiscrimination laws. While these laws impact every aspect of personnel management—from compensation to performance appraisal to training—their impact is most apparent in the areas of recruiting and selecting employees. To many of us, discrimination is something that happens only to "someone else." But, as the video shows, women—who comprise about half the population—are often discriminated against in the workplace.

As you read Chapters 3 through 6, ask yourself the following questions, all of which are addressed in the video.

1. In explaining why it can be difficult for companies to reduce discriminatory acts, one manager says: "It's one thing to pass a policy, but what we're really talking about is changing a culture and that isn't going to be quick and easy." What does she mean by this statement?
2. If you were asked to set up an employee testing and selection process, what testing and selection devices would you use?
3. What factors would you have to consider in developing a selection and testing process?

CHAPTER 3

JOB ANALYSIS

OVERVIEW

In this chapter we first explain job analysis, which means determining what the job entails and what kind of people should be hired for it. We also discuss several techniques for analyzing jobs and for writing job descriptions. When you finish studying this chapter you should be able to: Explain why job analysis is important; discuss the main techniques used to collect job analysis information; write a job description.

THE NATURE OF JOB ANALYSIS

JOB ANALYSIS DEFINED

job analysis
The procedure for determining the duties and skill requirements of a job and the kind of person who should be hired for it.

job description
A list of a job's duties, responsibilities, reporting relationships, working conditions, and supervisory responsibilities—one product of a job analysis.

job specification
A list of a job's "human requirements," that is, the requisite education, skills, personality, and so on—another product of a job analysis.

Developing an organization results in jobs that have to be staffed. **Job analysis** is the procedure through which you determine the duties and nature of the jobs and the kinds of people (in terms of skills and experience) who should be hired for them.[1] It provides data on job requirements, which are then used for developing **job descriptions** (what the job entails) and **job specifications** (what kind of people to hire for the job).

As a supervisor or personnel specialist, you will normally aim to collect one or more of the following types of information by doing the job analysis.[2]

Job activities. First, information is usually collected on the *actual work activities* performed, such as cleaning, sewing, galvanizing, coding, or painting. Sometimes such a list of activities indicates how, why, and when a worker performs each activity.

Human behaviors. Information on *human behaviors* like sensing, communicating, decision making, and writing may also be compiled. Included here would be information regarding personal job demands in terms of human energy expenditure, walking long distances, and so on.

Machines, tools, equipment, and work aids used. Included here would be information regarding products made, materials processed, knowledge dealt with or applied (such as physics or law), and services rendered (such as counseling or repairing).

Performance standards. Information is also collected regarding the performance standards (in terms of quantity, quality, or time taken for each aspect of the job, for instance), standards by which an employee in this job will be evaluated.

Job context. Here you would include information concerning such matters as physical working conditions, work schedule, and the organizational and social context—for instance, in terms of people with whom the employee would normally be expected to interact. Also included here might be information regarding financial and nonfinancial incentives the job entails.

Human requirements. Finally, information is usually compiled regarding such human requirements of the job as job-related knowledge or skills (education, training, work experience, etc.) and personal attributes (aptitudes, physical characteristics, personality, interests, etc.) required.

USES OF JOB ANALYSIS INFORMATION

As summarized in Figure 3.1, the information produced by the job analysis is used as a basis for several interrelated personnel management activities.

Recruitment and Selection

Job analysis provides you with information on what the job entails and what human requirements are required to carry out these activities. This job description and job specification information is the basis on which you decide what sort of people to recruit and hire.

Compensation

You also need a clear understanding of what each job entails to estimate the value and appropriate compensation for each job. This is because compensation

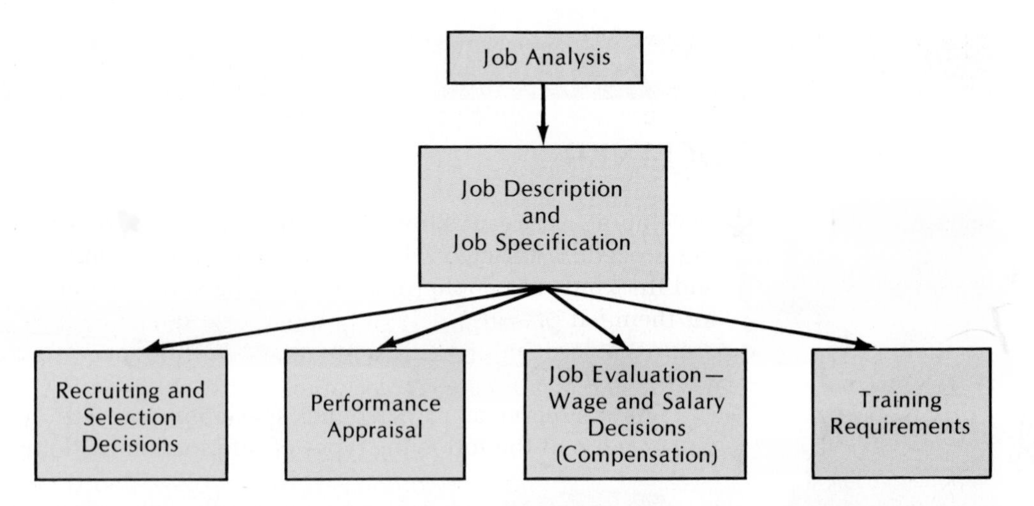

FIGURE 3.1
Uses of Job Analysis Information

(such as salary and bonus) is usually tied to the job's required skills, education level, safety hazards, and so on—all factors that are identified through job analysis. We'll also see that many employers classify jobs into categories (like Secretary III and IV), and job analysis provides data for determining the relative worth of each job so that each job can be classified.

Performance Appraisal

Performance appraisal involves comparing each employee's actual performance with his or her desired performance. It is often through job analysis that industrial engineers and other experts determine standards to be achieved and specific activities to be performed.

Training

You will also use job analysis information for designing training and development programs because the job analysis and resulting job description show what sorts of skills—and therefore training—are required.

Ensure Complete Assignment of Duties

The job analysis is also useful for ensuring that all the duties that have to be done are in fact assigned to particular positions. For example, in analyzing the current job of your company's production manager, you may find she reports herself as being responsible for two dozen or so specific duties including planning weekly production schedules, purchasing raw materials, and supervising the daily activities of each of her first-line supervisors. Missing, however, is any reference to managing raw material or finished goods inventories. On further investigation you find that none of the other people in manufacturing is responsible for inventory management either. Your job analysis (based as it is not just on what these employees report as their duties, but on your knowledge of what these jobs should entail) has identified a missing duty that must be assigned. Missing duties like this are often uncovered through job analysis. As a result, job analysis plays a role in remedying problems of the sort that would arise if, for example, there was no one assigned to manage inventories.

STEPS IN JOB ANALYSIS

The six steps in doing a job analysis are as follows.

Step 1.

Determine the use of the job analysis information. Start by identifying the use to which the information will be put, since this will determine the types of data you collect and the technique you use to collect them. Some techniques—like interviewing the employee and asking what the job entails and what his responsibilities are—are good for writing job descriptions and selecting employees for the job. Other job analysis techniques (like the position analysis questionnaire described below) do not provide descriptive information for job descriptions, but *do* provide numerical ratings for each job; these can be used to compare jobs to one another for compensation purposes. Your first step should therefore be to determine the use of the job analysis information. Then you can decide how to collect the information.

Step 2.

Collect background information. Next, review available background information such as organization charts, process charts, and job descriptions.[3] *Organization charts* show you how the job in question relates to other jobs and where it fits in the overall organization. The organization chart should identify the title of each position and, by means of its interconnecting lines, show who reports to whom and with whom the job incumbent is expected to communicate.

A *process chart* provides a more detailed understanding of the flow of work than you can obtain from the organization chart alone. In its simplest form, a process chart like the one in Figure 3.2 shows the flow of inputs to and outputs from the job under study. In this case, for instance, the inventory control clerk is expected to receive inventory from suppliers; take requests for inventory from the two plant managers; provide requested inventory to these managers; and give information to these managers on the status of in-stock inventories. Finally, the existing *job description,* if there is one, can provide a good starting point from which to build your revised job description.

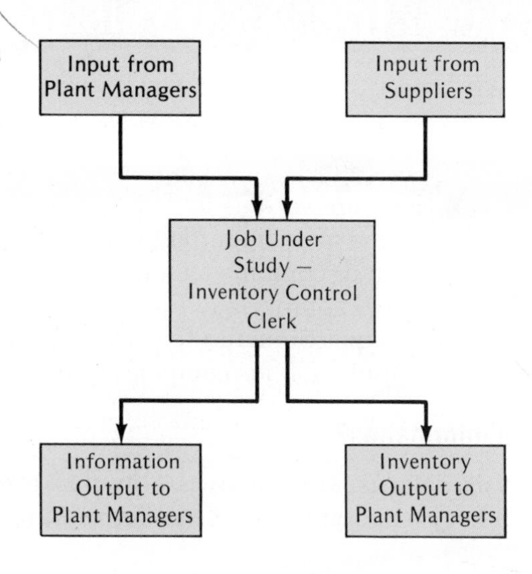

FIGURE 3.2 Process Chart for Analyzing a Job's Work Flow

Source: Richard I. Henderson, *Compensation Management: Rewarding Performance,* 2nd ed., copyright 1985, p. 158. Reprinted by permission of Prentice-Hall, Englewood Cliffs, NJ.

Step 3.

Select representative positions to be analyzed. This is necessary when many similar jobs are to be analyzed and it is too time-consuming to analyze, say, the jobs of all assembly workers.

Step 4.

Collect job analysis information. Your next step is to actually analyze the job by collecting data on job activities, required employee behaviors, working conditions, and human requirements (like the traits and abilities needed to perform the job). For this, you would use one or more of the job analysis techniques explained in the remainder of this chapter.

Step 5.

Review the information with the participants. The job analysis provides information on the nature and functions of the job. This information should be verified with the worker performing the job and the person's immediate supervisor. Verifying the information will help to determine if it is factually correct, complete, and easily understood by all concerned. This "review" step can also help gain the person's acceptance of the job analysis data you collected by giving that person a chance to modify your description of the activities he or she performs.

Step 6.

Develop a job description, and job specification. In most cases, a job description and a job specification are two concrete outcomes of the job analysis. The *job description* (to repeat) is a written statement that describes the activities and responsibilities of the job, as well as important features of the job such as working conditions and safety hazards. The *job specification* summarizes the personal qualities, traits, skills, and background required for getting the job done. It may be either a separate document or on the same document as the job description.

METHODS OF COLLECTING JOB ANALYSIS INFORMATION

INTRODUCTION

Your next step is actually to collect information on the duties, responsibilities, and activities of the job. There are various techniques you can use for collecting these data, and we'll discuss the most important ones in this section. In practice, you could use any one of them or combine techniques that best fit your purpose. Thus, an interview might be appropriate for developing a job description, whereas the position analysis questionnaire that we'll discuss is more appropriate for determining the worth of a job for compensation purposes.

Who Collects the Job Information?

Collecting job analysis data usually involves a human resource specialist, the worker, and the worker's supervisor. The human resource specialist (like the human resource manager, job analyst, or consultant) may be asked to observe and analyze the work being done and then develop a job description and specification. The supervisor and worker will also get involved, perhaps by filling out questionnaires listing the subordinate's activities. Both the supervisor and worker may then be asked to review and verify the job analyst's conclusions regarding the job's activities and duties. Job analysis thus usually involves an integrated effort among the specialist, the supervisor, and the worker.

Job Analysis and Equal Employment Opportunity

Job analysis plays a crucial role in employers' attempts to comply with equal employment opportunity legislation.[4] Federal guidelines and court decisions admonish an employer to do a thorough job analysis before using a screening tool (like a test) for predicting job performance. The main reason is that an employer must be able to show that its screening tools and performance appraisals are actually related to performance on the job in question. To do this, a competent job analysis describing the nature of the job is required.[5] Popular methods for collecting job analysis information are discussed next.

THE INTERVIEW

There are three types of interviews used to collect job analysis data: individual interviews with each employee; group interviews with groups of employees having the same job; and supervisor interviews with one or more supervisors who are thoroughly knowledgeable about the job being analyzed. The group interview is used when a large number of employees are performing similar or identical work, since this can be a quick and inexpensive way of learning about the job. As a rule, the worker's immediate supervisor would attend the group session; if not, you should interview the supervisor separately to get that person's perspective on the duties and responsibilities of the job.

Whichever interview you use, it is important that the interviewee fully understands the reason for the interview, since there's a tendency for interviews like these to be misconstrued as "efficiency evaluations." When they are, interviewees may not be willing to describe their jobs or those of their subordinates accurately.

Pros and Cons

The interview is probably the most widely used method for determining the duties and responsibilities of a job, and its wide use reflects its advantages. Most important, interviewing the worker allows that person to report activities and behavior that might not otherwise come to light. For example, important activities that occur only occasionally or informal communication (between, say, a production supervisor and the sales manager) that would not appear on the organization chart could be unearthed by a skilled interviewer. In addition, an interview can provide an opportunity to explain the need for and functions of the job analysis. It can also allow the interviewee to vent frustrations or views that might otherwise go unnoticed by management. An interview is also a relatively simple and quick way of collecting information.

The major problem with this technique is distortion of information, whether due to outright falsification or an honest misunderstanding.[6] A job analysis is often used as a prelude to changing a job's pay rate. Employees, therefore (to repeat), sometimes view it as an efficiency evaluation that may (and often will) affect their pay. Employees thus tend to exaggerate certain responsibilities while minimizing others. Obtaining valid information can thus be a slow and painstaking process.

Typical Questions

Despite their drawbacks, interviews are widely used. Some typical interview questions follow.

What is the job being performed?
What are the major duties of your position? What exactly do you do?
What different physical locations do you work in?
What are the education, experience, skill, and (where applicable) certification and licensing requirements?
What activities do you participate in?
What are the responsibilities and duties of the job?
What are the basic accountabilities or performance standards that typify your work?
What exactly do the activities you participate in involve?
What are your responsibilities? What are the environmental and working conditions involved?
What are the physical demands of the job? The emotional and mental demands?
What are the health and safety conditions?
Are there any hazards or unusual working conditions you are exposed to?

Job analysis at a bread company can even mean checking out roll production.

These questions notwithstanding, it is generally agreed that the most fruitful interviews follow a structured or checklist format. One such *job analysis questionnaire* is presented in Figure 3.3 on page 84–85. It includes a series of detailed questions regarding such matters as the general purpose of the job; supervisory responsibilities, job duties; and education, experience, and skills required. A form like this can also be used by a job analyst for collecting information by *observing* the work being done or by administering a *questionnaire*, two methods that will be explained shortly.[7]

Interview Guidelines

There are several things to keep in mind when conducting a job analysis interview. First, if you are doing the job analysis, you and the supervisor should work together. Identify the workers who know most about the job, as well as workers who might be expected to be the most objective in describing their duties and responsibilities.

Second, you must establish rapport quickly with the interviewee, by knowing the person's name, speaking in easily understood language, briefly reviewing the purpose of the interview, and explaining how the person came to be chosen for the interview.

Third, you should follow a structured guide or checklist, one that lists questions and provides space for answers. This ensures that you'll identify crucial questions ahead of time and that all interviewers (if there are more than one) cover all the required questions. However, make sure to also give the worker some leeway in answering questions and provide some open-ended questions like "Was there anything we didn't cover with our questions?"

Fourth, when duties are not performed in a regular manner—for instance, when the worker doesn't perform the same job over and over again many times a day—you should ask the worker to list his or her duties *in order of importance* and *frequency* of occurrence. This will ensure that crucial activities that occur infrequently—like a nurse's occasional emergency room duties—aren't overlooked.

Finally, after completing the interview, review and verify the data. This is normally done by reviewing the information with the worker's immediate supervisor and with the interviewee himself or herself.

QUESTIONNAIRES

Having employees fill out questionnaires in which they describe their job-related duties and responsibilities is another good method for obtaining job analysis information.

The main thing to decide here is how structured the questionnaire should be and what questions to include. At one extreme, some questionnaires are very structured checklists. Each employee is presented with an inventory of perhaps hundreds of specific duties or tasks (such as "change and splice wire"). He or she is asked to indicate whether or not he or she performs each task and, if so, how much time is normally spent on each. At the other extreme, the questionnaire can be open ended and simply ask the employee to "describe the major duties of your job." In practice, the best questionnaire often falls between these two extremes. As illustrated in Figure 3.3 a typical job analysis questionnaire might have several open-ended questions (such as "state your main job duties") as well as structured questions (concerning, for instance, previous experience required).

Whether structured or unstructured, any questionnaire has advantages and disadvantages. A questionnaire is, first, a quick and efficient way of obtaining information from a large number of employees; it's less costly than interviewing hundreds of workers, for instance. On the other hand, developing the questionnaire and testing it (perhaps by making sure the workers understand the questions) can be an expensive and time-consuming process. Therefore, the potentially higher development costs have to be weighed against the time and expense you'll save by not having to interview as many workers.

OBSERVATION

Direct observation is especially useful in jobs that consist mainly of observable physical activity. Jobs like those of janitor, assembly-line worker, and accounting clerk are examples. On the other hand, observation is usually not appropriate when the job entails a lot of unmeasurable mental activity (lawyer, design engineer). Nor is it useful if the employee engages in important activities that might occur only occasionally, such as a nurse who handles emergencies.

Direct observation is often used in conjunction with interviewing. One approach is to observe the worker on the job during a complete work cycle. (The cycle is the time it takes to complete the job; it could be a minute for an assembly-line worker or an hour, a day, or more for complex jobs.) Here you take notes of all the job activities you observe. Then, after accumulating as much

FIGURE 3.3
Job Analysis Questionnaire for Developing Job Descriptions

Source: Douglas Bartley, *Job Evaluation: Wage and Salary Administration* (Reading, MA: Addison-Wesley Publishing Company, 1981) pp. 101–103.

JOB QUESTIONNAIRE
KANE MANUFACTURING COMPANY

NAME ______________________ JOB TITLE ______________________

DEPARTMENT ______________________ JOB NUMBER ______________________

SUPERVISOR'S NAME ______________________ SUPERVISOR'S TITLE ______________________

1. *SUMMARY OF DUTIES:* State in your own words briefly your main duties. If you are responsible for filling out reports/records, also complete Section 8.

2. *SPECIAL QUALIFICATIONS:* List any licenses, permits, certifications, etc. required to perform duties assigned to your position.

3. *EQUIPMENT:* List any equipment, machines, or tools (e.g., typewriter, calculator, motor vehicles, lathes, fork lifts, drill presses, etc.) you normally operate as a part of your position's duties.

   MACHINE *AVERAGE NO. HOURS PER WEEK*

4. *REGULAR DUTIES:* In general terms, describe duties you regularly perform. Please list these duties in descending order of importance and percent of time spent on them per month. List as many duties as possible and attach additional sheets, if necessary.

5. *CONTACTS:* Does your job require any contacts with other department personnel, other departments, outside companies or agencies. If yes, please define the duties requiring contacts and *how often.*

6. *SUPERVISION:* Does your position have supervisory responsibilities? ( ) Yes ( ) No. If yes, please fill out a *Supplemental Position Description Questionnaire for Supervisors* and attach it to this form. If you have responsibility for the work of others but do not directly supervise them, please explain.

7. *DECISION MAKING:* Please explain the decisions you make while performing the regular duties of your job.

FIGURE 3.3
(continued)

(a) What would be the probable result of your making (a) poor judgment(s) or decision(s), or (b) improper actions?

____

____

8. *RESPONSIBILITY FOR RECORDS:* List the reports and files you are required to prepare or maintain. State, in general, for whom each report is intended.

   (a) *REPORT* *INTENDED FOR*

   ____

   ____

   ____

   (b) *FILES MAINTAINED*

   ____

   ____

9. *FREQUENCY OF SUPERVISION:* How frequently must you confer with your supervisor or other personnel in making decisions or in determining the proper course of action to be taken?

   ( ) Frequently ( ) Occasionally ( ) Seldom ( ) Never

10. *WORKING CONDITIONS:* Please describe the conditions under which you work—inside, outside, air conditioned area, etc. Be sure to list any disagreeable or unusual working conditions.

    ____

    ____

11. *JOB REQUIREMENTS:* Please indicate the minimum requirements you believe are necessary to perform satisfactorily in your position.

    (a) Education:
    Minimum schooling ____________________
    Number of years ____________________
    Specialization or major ____________________

    (b) Experience:
    Type ____________________
    Number of years ____________________

    (c) Special training:

    TYPE *NUMBER OF YEARS*

    ____

    ____

    (d) Special Skills:
    Typing: ____________ w.p.m. Shorthand ____________ w.p.m.
    Other: ____________________

12. *ADDITIONAL INFORMATION:* Please provide additional information, not included in any of the previous items, which you feel would be important in a description of your position.

    ____

    ____

    ____

EMPLOYEE'S SIGNATURE ____________________ DATE: __________

information as possible, you interview the worker; the person is encouraged to clarify points not understood and explain what additional activities he or she performs that you didn't observe. Another approach is to observe and interview simultaneously, while the worker performs his or her task. It's often best to withhold questions until after observations are made, however, since this gives you more chance to unobtrusively observe the employee. This in turn helps reduce the chance that the employee will become anxious or in some way distort his or her usual routine.

PARTICIPANT DIARY/LOGS

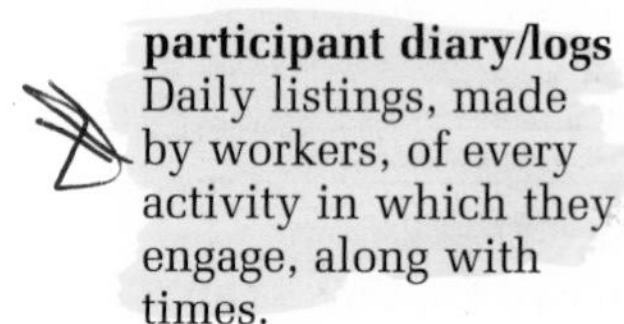

participant diary/logs Daily listings, made by workers, of every activity in which they engage, along with times.

Workers can be asked to keep daily **participant diary/logs** or lists of things they do during the day. For every activity he or she engages in, the employee records the activity (along with the time) in a log. This can provide you with a very complete picture of the job, especially when it's supplemented with subsequent interviews with the worker and his or her supervisor. The employee might, of course, try to exaggerate some activities and underplay others. However, the detailed, chronological nature of the log tends to mediate against this.

In summary, interviews, questionnaires, observations, and diary/logs are the most popular methods for gathering job analysis data. They all provide realistic information about what job incumbents actually do. They can thus be used for developing job descriptions and job specifications.

U.S. CIVIL SERVICE PROCEDURE

The U.S. Civil Service Commission has developed a job analysis technique that aims to provide a standardized procedure by which different jobs can be compared and classified. With this method the information is compiled on a "job analysis record sheet." Here, as illustrated in Figure 3.4, identifying information (like job title) and a brief summary of the job are listed first. Next, the specialist lists the job's specific tasks in order of importance. Then, *for each task,* the analyst specifies the

1. Knowledge required (for example, the facts or principles the worker must be acquainted with to do his or her job).
2. Skills required (for example, the skills needed to operate machines or vehicles).
3. Abilities required (for example, mathematical, reasoning, problem solving, or interpersonal abilities).
4. Physical activities involved (for example, pulling, pushing, or carrying).
5. Any special environmental conditions (cramped quarters, vibration, inadequate ventilation, or moving objects).
6. Typical work incidents (for example, performing under stress in emergencies, working with people beyond giving and receiving instructions, or performing repetitive work).
7. Worker interests areas (the preference the worker should have for activities dealing with "things and objects," or the "communication of data," or "dealing with people," for example).[8]

This is illustrated in Figure 3.4. In this case the first task listed for a"welfare eligibility examiner" is to "decide (determine) eligibility of applicant in

FIGURE 3.4
Portion of a Completed Civil Service Job Analysis Record Sheet

JOB ANALYSIS RECORD SHEET

IDENTIFYING INFORMATION

Name of Incumbent:	A. Adler
Organization/Unit:	Welfare Services
Title:	Welfare Eligibility Examiner
Date:	11/12/92
Interviewer:	E. Jones

BRIEF SUMMARY OF JOB

Conducts interviews, completes applications, determines eligibility, provides information to community sources regarding food stamp program; refers noneligible food stamp applicants to other applicable community resource agencies.

TASKS*

1. Decides (determines) eligibility of applicant in order to complete client's application for food stamps using regulatory policies as guide.

   Knowledge Required
   —Knowledge of contents and meaning of items on standard application form
   —Knowledge of Social-Health Services food stamp regulatory policies
   —Knowledge of statues relating to Social-Health Services food stamp program

   Skills Required
   —None

   Abilities Required
   —Ability to read and understand complex instructions such as regulatory policies
   —Ability to read and understand a variety of procedural instructions, written and oral, and convert these to proper actions
   —Ability to use simple arithmetic: addition and subtraction
   —Ability to translate requirements into language appropriate to laymen

   Physical Activities
   —Sedentary

   Environmental Conditions
   —None

   Typical Work Incidents
   —Working with people beyond giving and receiving instructions

   Interest Areas
   —Communication of data
   —Business contact with people
   —Working for the presumed good of people

2. Decides upon, describes, and explains other agencies available for client to contact in order to assist and refer client to appropriate community resource using worker's knowledge of resources available and knowledge of client's needs.

   Knowledge Required
   —Knowledge of functions of various assistance agencies
   —Knowledge of community resources available and their locations
   —Knowledge of referral procedures

   Skills Required
   —None

   Abilities Required
   —Ability to extract (discern) persons' needs from oral discussion
   —Ability to give simple oral and written instructions to persons

   Physical Activities
   —Sedentary

   Environmental Conditions
   —None

   Typical Work Incidents
   —Working with people beyond giving and receiving instructions

   Interest Areas
   —Communication of data
   —Business contact with people
   —Abstract and creative problem solving
   —Working for presumed good of people

*This job might typically involve five or six tasks. For *each* task, list the knowledge, skills, abilities, physical activities, environmental conditions, typical work incidents, and interest areas.

order to complete client's application for food stamps using regulatory policies as guide." Beneath this task are listed the analyst's conclusions concerning the *knowledge* a welfare eligibility examiner is required to have; any *special skills* or abilities; types of *physical activities* involved in this task; special *environmental conditions;* typical *work incidents;* and the sorts of *interests* that would correspond to this task. An analyst would typically apply his or her own knowledge of the job as well as information obtained through interviews, observations, logs, or questionnaires in completing the job analysis record sheet. Virtually any job can be broken into its component tasks, each of which is then analyzed in terms of knowledge required, skills required, and so forth. Thus, the Civil Service procedure provides a standardized method by which different jobs can be compared, contrasted, and classified. (In other words, the knowledge, skills, and abilities required to perform, say, an assistant fire chief's job can be contrasted with the knowledge, skills, and abilities required to perform a librarian's job. If the requirements are similar the jobs can be classified together for pay purposes.)

QUANTITATIVE JOB ANALYSIS TECHNIQUES

Although most employers use interviews, questionnaires, observations, or diary/logs for collecting job analysis data, there are many times when these narrative approaches are not appropriate. For example, when your aim is to assign a quantitative value to each job, so the jobs can be compared for pay purposes, a more *quantitative* job analysis approach may be best. Three popular quantitative methods are the *position analysis questionnaire,* the *Department of Labor approach,* and *functional job analysis.*

Position Analysis Questionnaire

position analysis questionnaire (PAQ) A questionnaire used to collect quantifiable data concerning the duties and responsibilities of various jobs.

The **position analysis questionnaire (PAQ)** is a very structured job analysis questionnaire.[9] The PAQ itself is filled in by a job analyst, a person who should already be acquainted with the particular job to be analyzed. The PAQ contains 194 items. As in Figure 3.5, each of these 194 items (such as "written materials") *represents a basic item that may or may not play an important role on the job.* The job analyst decides if the item plays a role on the job and, if so, to what extent. In Figure 3.5, for example, "written materials" received a rating of 4, indicating that written materials (like books, reports, office notes, etc.) play a *considerable* role on the job.

The advantage of the PAQ is that it provides a quantitative score or profile of any job in terms of how that job rates on five basic dimensions: (1) having decision-making/communications/social responsibilities, (2) performing skilled activities, (3) being physically active, (4) operating vehicles/equipment, and (5) processing information. As a result, the PAQ's real strength is in classifying jobs. In other words, the PAQ allows you to assign a quantitative score to each job based on its decision-making, skilled activities, physical activity, vehicle/equipment, operation, and information-processing characteristics. You can therefore use the results of the PAQ to compare jobs to one another and to decide, for instance, which jobs are more challenging;[10] this information can then be used to determine salary or wage levels for each job.[11]

Computer Application in Job Analysis and Staffing: Skills Inventory

Most managers lack complete, accurate information about their employees' capabilities. Furthermore, when vacancies occur, either due to attrition or to new opportunities, simply posting the opening on a company bulletin board does not guarantee that every employee will see the posting or will interpret the information appropriately. One way to improve the likelihood that qualified internal candidates will be introduced into the selection process is to have a skills inventory completed and updated regularly by employees.

Both the development of the inventory content and the updating of inventories requires significant input from employees. They must believe in the validity of the inventory, and this will happen only if they participate in the development process. If employees have ready access to computers, the inventory can be developed and updated from their workstations. Otherwise, hard copy memos should invite every employee to describe him or herself in terms of the range of skills to be listed, the standards that differentiate various skill levels, and how skills should be categorized.

Inventories should be regularly updated when an employee has completed a course, seminar, workshop, or assignment that is applcable. If computers are not generally available, employees should be allowed time (20 to 30 minutes) each quarter to update the inventory. Time spent on the updating may be minimized by periodically providing each employee with a hard copy of his or her inventory to mark up before the actual data entry. Skills should be reassessed at least annually at the time of performance appraisals. If an employee has questions about interpretations of skill levels or categories, supervisors or HRM personnel should offer assistance. Periodic review of the inventory and the process should occur, and all employees should receive regular training to maintain the validity of the system.

When a vacancy occurs, interviewers (either in HRM or, in small businesses, managers) would specify the parameters of the job in terms of the skill categories and levels. (This would be based on the job analysis.) The computer program would then produce a list of employees who qualify according to these parameters. This list would be modified based on other factors, such as attendance, quality of performance, time in position, or interest of the candidate. Employees otherwise qualified could receive a letter informing them of the opening and inviting them to apply if interested, with a copy to the employee's supervisor.

Expressing interest in a position that offers greater responsibility should be encouraged by a company that is interested in retention. Employees who see company behaviors that encourage growth and development are more likely to stay with the company. Developing a skills inventory system with significant employee input, active encouragement to update, and results that keep employees informed of promotional possibilities will enhance retention.

Another aspect of developing a skills inventory process as previously described is straightforward communication with employees. If an employee is otherwise qualified, is invited to apply, does so, and is then found to have either performance or attendance problems, those hindrances to promotion will be addressed because the process encourages informational supervision. Most employees accept constructive criticism if it is offered in a manner designed to help them progress. Further, with employee participation in establishing the content and standards of the inventory, employees should have a better understanding of what is expected of them in order to qualify at specified levels and should be able to provide valuable job analysis data based on what they actually know about their jobs.

INFORMATION INPUT

1 INFORMATION INPUT

1.1 Sources of Job Information

Rate each of the following items in terms of the extent to which it is used by the worker as a source of information in performing his job.

	Extent of Use (U)
NA	Does not apply
1	Nominal/very infrequent
2	Occasional
3	Moderate
4	Considerable
5	Very substantial

1.1.1 Visual Sources of Job Information

1 4 Written materials (books, reports, office notes, articles, job instructions, signs, etc.)

2 2 Quantitative materials (materials which deal with quantities or amounts, such as graphs, accounts, specifications, tables of numbers, etc.)

3 1 Pictorial materials (pictures or picturelike materials used as *sources* of information, for example, drawings, blueprints, diagrams, maps, tracings, photographic films, x-ray films, TV pictures, etc.)

4 1 Patterns/related devices (templates, stencils, patterns, etc., used as *sources* of information when *observed* during use; do *not* include here materials described in item 3 above)

5 2 Visual displays (dials, gauges, signal lights, radarscopes, speedometers, clocks, etc.)

6 5 Measuring devices (rulers, calipers, tire pressure gauges, scales, thickness gauges, pipettes, thermometers, protractors, etc., used to obtain visual information about physical measurements; do *not* include here devices described in item 5 above)

7 4 Mechanical devices (tools, equipment, machinery, and other mechanical devices which are *sources* of information when *observed* during use or operation)

8 3 Materials in process (parts, materials, objects, etc., which are *sources* of information when being modified, worked on, or otherwise processed, such as bread dough being mixed, workpiece being turned in a lathe, fabric being cut, shoe being resoled, etc.)

9 4 Materials *not* in process (parts, materials, objects, etc., not in the process of being changed or modified, which are *sources* of information when being inspected, handled, packaged, distributed, or selected, etc., such as items or materials in inventory, storage, or distribution channels, items being inspected, etc.)

10 3 Features of nature (landscapes, fields, geological samples, vegetation, cloud formations, and other features of nature which are observed or inspected to provide information)

11 2 Man-made features of environment (structures, buildings, dams, highways, bridges, docks, railroads, and other "man-made" or altered aspects of the indoor or outdoor environment which are *observed* or *inspected* to provide job information; do not consider equipment, machines, etc., that an individual uses in his work, as covered by item 7).

Note: This exhibits 11 of the "information input" questions or elements. Other PAQ pages contain questions regarding mental processes, work output, relationships with others, job context, and other job characteristics.

FIGURE 3.5
Portions of a Completed Page from the Position Analysis Questionnaire

Source: E. J. McCormick, P. R. Jeanneret, and R. D. Mecham, *Position Analysis Questionnaire.* Copyright 1989 by *Purdue Research Foundation, West Lafayette, Ind.* Reprinted with permission.

Department of Labor (DOL) Procedure

The U.S. Department of Labor (DOL) procedure also aims to provide a standardized method by which different jobs can be quantitatively rated, classified, and

Department of Labor job analysis Standardized method for rating, classifying, and comparing virtually every kind of job based on data, people, and things.

compared. The heart of this **Department of Labor job analysis** involves rating each job in terms of what an employee does with respect to *data, people,* and *things.*

The basic procedure is as follows. As illustrated in Table 3.1, a set of basic activities "worker functions" describes what a worker can do with respect to data, people, and things. With respect to *data,* for instance, the basic functions include synthesizing, coordinating, and copying. With respect to *people*, they include mentoring, negotiating, and supervising. With respect to *things,* the basic functions include manipulating, tending, and handling. Note also that each worker function has been assigned an importance level. Thus, "coordinating" is 1, while copying is 5. If you were analyzing the job of a receptionist/clerk, for example, you might label the job 5, 6, 7, which would represent copying data, speaking-signaling people, and handling things. On the other hand, a psychiatric aide in a hospital might be coded 1, 7, 5 in relation to data, people, and things. In practice, *each task* that the worker performed would be analyzed in terms of data, people, and things. Then the highest combination (say, 4, 6, 5) would be used to identify the job, since this is the highest level that a job incumbent would be expected to attain.

Before writing a Help Wanted ad, a company should conduct a job analysis to identify the task and human requirements of the job.

As illustrated in Figure 3.6, the summary sheet produced from the DOL procedure contains several types of information. Listed first is the job title, in this case dough mixer in a bakery. Also listed are the industry in which this job is found and the industry's standard industrial classification code. There is also a brief one- or two-sentence summary of the job and the worker function ratings (in this case 5, 6, 2) for data, people, and things. This indicates that in terms of difficulty level, a dough mixer in a bakery is expected to copy data, speak-signal with people, and operate-control with respect to things. Finally, you would also specify the human requirements of the job in question, for instance, in terms of training time required, aptitudes, and temperaments. As you can see, each job analyzed in this way gets a numerical score (such as 5, 6, 2), and so all jobs with similar scores can be grouped together and paid the same, even though one job might be dough mixer and another mechanics helper.

Functional Job Analysis

This method is based on the DOL approach but provides additional information regarding the job's tasks, objectives, and training requirements.[12]

TABLE 3.1 Basic Department of Labor Worker Functions

	DATA	PEOPLE	THINGS
Basic Activities	0 Synthesizing 1 Coordinating 2 Analyzing 3 Compiling 4 Computing 5 Copying 6 Comparing	0 Mentoring 1 Negotiating 2 Instructing 3 Supervising 4 Diverting 5 Persuading 6 Speaking–signaling 7 Serving 8 Taking instructions–helping	0 Setting up 1 Precision working 2 Operating–controlling 3 Driving–operating 4 Manipulating 5 Tending 6 Feeding–offbearing 7 Handling

Note: Determine employee's job "score" on data, people, and things by observing his or her job and determining, for each of the three categories, which of the basic functions illustrates the person's job. "0" is high, "6," "8," and "7" are lows in each column.

Sample of the End Result of Using the Department of Labor Job Analysis Technique.

JOB ANALYSIS SCHEDULE

1. Established Job Title DOUGH MIXER

2. Ind. Assign (bake prod.)

3. SIC Code(s) and Title(s) 2051 Bread and other bakery products

4. JOB SUMMARY:

Operates mixing machine to mix ingredients for straight and sponge (yeast) doughs according to established formulas, directs other workers in fermentation of dough, and curls dough into pieces with hand cutter.

5. WORK PERFORMED RATINGS: (From Exhibit 3.9)

	D	P	(T)
Worker Functions	Data	People	Things
	5	6	2

Work Field Cooking, Food Preparing

6. WORKER TRAITS RATINGS: (To be filled in by analyst)

Training time required

Aptitudes

Temperaments

Interests

Physical Demands

Environment Conditions

FIGURE 3.6 Sample Report Based on Department of Labor Job Analysis Technique

functional job analysis A method for classifying jobs similar to the Department of Labor job analysis, but additionally taking into account the extent to which instructions, reasoning, judgment, and verbal facility are necessary for performing job tasks.

Functional job analysis differs from the DOL approach in two ways. First, functional job analysis rates the job not only on data, people, and things, but also on the following four dimensions: the extent to which specific *instructions* are necessary to perform the task, the extent to which *reasoning* and *judgment* are required to perform the task, the *mathematical ability* required to perform the task; and the verbal and *language facilities* required to perform the task. Second, functional job analysis also identifies performance standards and training requirements. Performing a job analysis using functional job analysis therefore allows you to answer the question, "To do this task and meet these new standards, what training does the worker require?"

An example of a completed functional job analysis summary sheet is presented in Figure 3.7. In this case the job is that of grader (a type of heavy equipment operator involved in road building). As illustrated, the functional job analysis provides information on things, data, people, instructions, reasoning,

TASK CODE: GR-08

WORKER FUNCTION AND ORIENTATION						WORKER INSTRUCTIONS	GENERAL EDUCATIONAL DEVELOPMENT		
THINGS	%	DATA	%	PEOPLE	%		REASONING	MATH	LANGUAGE
3	65	3	25	1	10	3	2	1	3

GOAL:	OBJECTIVE:
Operates Grader—Output Basic	Backfilling, scarifying, windrowing, cutting firebreak, maintaining haul road, snow removal

TASK: Operates grader manipulating controls to travel forward/back, turn, raise/lower blade, position wheels and blade at correct angles; follows work order, drawing on knowledge and experience, monitoring the performance of the equipment and adapting to the changing situation, constantly alert to the presence and safety of other workers/equipment, in order to perform routine grader tasks such as backfilling, haul road maintenance, snow removal.

(To Perform This Task)

PERFORMANCE STANDARDS	TRAINING CONTENT
DESCRIPTIVE: – Operates equipment properly. – Is alert and attentive.	FUNCTIONAL: – How to operate grader. – How to do routine grader tasks, such as backfilling, scarifying, windrowing, cutting firebreak, maintaining road, snow removal.
NUMERICAL: – All work meets work order requirements. – No accidents/damage due to improper operating techniques.	SPECIFIC: – Knowledge of specific grader. – Knowledge of work requirements. – Knowledge of specific job site (i.e., layout, soil condition, environment).
(To These Standards)	*(Worker Needs This Training)*

FIGURE 3.7 Functional Job Analysis Task Statement

Source: Howard Olson, Sidney A. Fine, David C. Myers, and Margarette C. Jennings, "The Use of Functional Job Analysis in Establishing Performance for Heavy Equipment Operators," *Personnel Psychology,* Summer 1981, p. 354.

math, and language. All this is quantitatively rated. Also, the summary sheet lists the main tasks involved in the job, performance standards, and training required.

▸ WRITING JOB DESCRIPTIONS

A job description is a written statement of *what* the jobholder actually does, *how* he or she does it, and under *what conditions* the job is performed. This information is in turn used to write a *job specification.* This lists the knowledge, abilities, and skills needed to perform the job satisfactorily.

Although there is no standard format you must use in writing a job description, most descriptions contain sections on:

1. Job identification
2. Job summary
3. Relationships, responsibilities, and duties
4. Authority
5. Standards of performance
6. Working conditions
7. Job specifications

An example of a job description is presented in Figure 3.8.

JOB IDENTIFICATION

The *job identification* section contains, as in Figure 3.8, several types of information.[13] The *job title* specifies the title of the job, such as supervisor of data processing operations, sales manager, or inventory control clerk. (Like the job description itself, you should keep job titles current, and the Department of Labor's *Dictionary of Occupational Titles* can be useful in this regard. It lists titles for thousands of jobs as well as descriptions of typical job duties for each.) The *job status* section of the job description permits quick identification of the exempt or nonexempt status of the job. (Under the Fair Labor Standards Act certain positions, primarily administrative and professional, are exempt from the act's overtime and minimum wage provisions.) The *job code* permits easy referencing of all jobs: Each job in the organization should be identified with a code; these codes represent important characteristics of the job, such as the wage class to which it belongs. The *date* refers to the date the job description was actually written, and *written by* indicates the person who wrote it. There is also space to indicate who the description was *approved by* and space that indicates the location of the job in terms of its *plant/division* and *department/section.* The *title of the immediate supervisor* is also shown in the identification section.

The job identification section also often contains information regarding the job's salary and/or pay scale. The space *grade/level* indicates the grade or level of the job if there is such a category; for example, a firm may classify secretaries as secretary II, secretary III, and so on. Finally, the *pay* range space provides for the specific pay or pay range of the job.

JOB SUMMARY

The *job summary* should describe the general nature of the job, listing only its major functions or activities. Thus (as in Figure 3.8) the supervisor of data processing "directs the operation of all data processing, data control, and data preparation requirements." For the job of materials manager, the summary might state that "the materials manager purchases economically, regulates deliveries of, stores, and distributes all material necessary on the production line." For the job of mailroom supervisor, "the mailroom supervisor receives, sorts, and delivers all incoming mail properly, and he or she handles all outgoing mail including the accurate and timely posting of such mail."[14]

Try to avoid including a general statement like "performs other assignments as required." Including such a statement can give supervisors more flexi-

SAMPLE JOB DESCRIPTION

Supervisor of Data Processing Operations Job Title	*Exempt* Status	*012.168* Job Code
July 3, 1993 Date		*Olympia, Inc. - Main Office* Plant/Division
Arthur Allen Written By		*Information Data Processing - Systems* Department/Section
Juanita Montgomery Approved By		*12* Grade/Level *736* Points
Manager of Information Systems Title of Immediate Supervisor		*14,800 - Mid 17,760 - 20,720* Pay Range

SUMMARY

Directs the operation of all data processing, data control, and data preparation requirements.

JOB DUTIES*

1. Follows broadly-based directives.
   (a). Operates Independently.
   (b). Informs Manager of Information Systems of activities through weekly, monthly, and/or quarterly schedules.
2. Selects, trains, and develops subordinate personnel.
   (a). Develops spirit of cooperation and understanding among work group members.
   (b). Ensures that work group members receive specialized training as necessary in the proper functioning or execution of machines, equipment, systems, procedures, processes, and/or methods.
   (c). Directs training involving teaching, demonstrating, and/or advising users in productive work methods and effective communications with data processing.
3. Reads and analyzes wide variety of instructional and training information.
   (a). Applies latest concepts and ideas to changing organizational requirements.
   (b). Assists in developing and/or updating manuals, procedures, specifications, etc., relative to organizational requirements and needs.
   (c). Assists in the preparation of specifications and related evaluations of supporting software and hardware.
4. Plans, directs, and controls a wide variety of operational assignments by 5 to 7 subordinates; works closely with other managers, specialists, and technicians within Information Systems as well as with managers in other departments with data needs and with vendors.
   (a). Receives, interprets, develops, and distributes directives ranging from the very simple to the highly complex and technological in nature.
   (b). Establishes and implements annual budget for department.
5. Interacts and communicates with people representing a wide variety of units and organizations.
   (a). Communicates both personally and impersonally, through oral or written directives and memoranda, with all involved parties.
   (b). Attends local meetings of professional organizations in the field of data processing.

*This section should also include description of uncomfortable, dirty, or dangerous assignments.

FIGURE 3.8 Sample Job Description

Source: Richard I. Henderson, *Compensation Management: Rewarding Performance,* 4th ed., copyright 1985, p. 176. Reprinted by permission of Prentice-Hall, Inc., Englewood Cliffs, N.J.

bility in assigning duties. However, some experts state unequivocally that "one item frequently found that should *never* be included in a job description is a "cop-out clause" like 'other duties, as assigned,'"[15] since this leaves open the nature of the job—and the people needed to staff it.

RELATIONSHIPS

The *relationships* statement shows the jobholder's relationships with others inside and outside the organization and might look like this for a human resource manager:[16]

Reports to: vice-president of employee relations.

Supervises: human resource clerk, test administrator, labor relations director, and one secretary.

Works with: all department managers and executive management.

Outside the company: employment agencies, executive recruiting firms, union representatives, state and federal employment offices, and various vendors.[17]

RESPONSIBILITIES AND DUTIES

Another section should be used to present a detailed list of the actual responsibilities and duties of the job. As in Figure 3.8, each of the job's major duties should be listed separately, with one or two sentences used for describing each. In the figure, for instance, the duty "selects, trains, and develops subordinate personnel" is further defined as follows: "develops spirit of cooperation and understanding...," "ensures that work group members receive specialized training as necessary...," and "directs training involving teaching, demonstrating, and/or advising...." Other typical duties for different jobs might include maintaining balanced and controlled inventories, accurate posting of accounts payable, maintaining favorable purchase price variances, and repairing production line tools and equipment.

You can use the Department of Labor's *Dictionary of Occupational Titles* here for itemizing the job's duties and responsibilities. As shown in Figure 3.9, for example, the dictionary lists a human resource manager's specific duties and responsibilities, including "plans and carries out policies relating to all phases of personnel activity," "recruits, interviews, and selects employees to fill vacant positions," and "conducts wage survey within labor market to determine competitive wage rate."

AUTHORITY

Another section should define the limits of the jobholder's authority, including his or her decision-making limitations, direct supervision of other personnel, and budgetary limitations. For example, the jobholder might have authority to approve purchase requests up to $500, grant time off or leaves of absence, discipline department personnel, recommend salary increases, and interview and hire new employees.[18]

FIGURE 3.9
"Personnel Manager" Description from *Dictionary of Occupational Titles*

Source: *Dictionary of Occupational Titles,* 4th ed. (Washington, DC: U.S. Department of Labor, Employment Training Administration, U.S. Employment Service, 1991).

166.117–018 MANAGER, PERSONNEL (profess. & kin.) alternate titles: manager, human resources

Plans and carries out policies relating to all phases of personnel activity: Recruits, interviews, and selects employees to fill vacant positions. Plans and conducts new employee orientation to foster positive attitude toward company goals. Keeps record of insurance coverage, pension plan, and personnel transactions, such as hires, promotions, transfers, and terminations. Investigates accidents and prepares reports for insurance carrier. Conducts wage survey within labor market to determine competitive wage rate. Prepares budget of personnel operations. Meets with shop stewards and supervisors to resolve grievances. Writes separation notices for employees separating with cause and conducts exit interviews to determine reasons behind separations. Prepares reports and recommends procedures to reduce absenteeism and turnover. Represents company at personnel-related hearings and investigations. Contracts with outside suppliers to provide employee services, such as canteen, transportation, or relocation service. May prepare budget of personnel operations, using computer terminal. May administer manual and dexterity tests to applicants. May supervise clerical workers. May keep records of hired employee characteristics for governmental reporting purposes. May negotiate collective bargaining agreement with BUSINESS REPRESENTATIVE, LABOR UNION (profess & kin.) 187.167–018. *GOE: 11.05.02 STRENGTH: S GED: R5 M5 L5 SVP: 8 DLU: 88*

STANDARDS OF PERFORMANCE

Some job descriptions also contain a *standards of performance* section. This states the standards the employee is expected to achieve in each of the job descriptions' main duties and responsibilities.

Setting standards is never an easy matter. However, most managers soon learn that just telling subordinates to "do their best" doesn't provide enough guidance to ensure top performance. One straightforward way of setting standards is to finish the statement: "I will be completely satisfied with your work when..." This sentence, if completed for each responsibility listed in the job description, should result in a usable set of performance standards.[19] Some examples would include the following:

DUTY: ACCURATE POSTING OF ACCOUNTS PAYABLE

1. All invoices received are posted within the same working day.
2. All invoices are routed to proper department managers for approval no later than the day following receipt.
3. An average of no more than three posting errors per month occurs.
4. Posting ledger is balanced by the end of the third working day of each month.

DUTY: MEETING DAILY PRODUCTION SCHEDULE

1. Work group produces no less than 426 units per working day.
2. No more than an average of 2% of units is rejected at the next workstation.
3. Work is completed with no more than an average of 5% overtime per week.

WORKING CONDITIONS AND PHYSICAL ENVIRONMENT

The job description will also list the general *working conditions* involved on the job. These might include things like noise level, hazardous conditions, or heat.

JOB DESCRIPTION GUIDELINES

Here are some hints for writing up your job descriptions:[20]

Be clear. The job description should portray the work of the position so well that the duties are clear without reference to other job descriptions.

Indicate scope. In defining the position, be sure to indicate the scope and nature of the work by using phrases such as "for the department" or "as requested by the manager." Include all important relationships.

Be specific. Select the most specific words to show (1) the kind of work, (2) the degree of complexity, (3) the degree of skill required, (4) the extent to which problems are standardized, (5) the extent of the worker's responsibility for each phase of the work, and (6) the degree and type of accountability. Use action words such as *analyze, gather, assemble, plan, devise, infer, deliver, transmit, maintain, supervise,* and *recommend.* Positions at the lower levels of organization generally have the most detailed duties or tasks, while higher-level positions deal with broader aspects.

Be brief. Brief accurate statements usually best accomplish the purpose.

Recheck. Finally, to check whether the description fulfills the basic requirements, ask yourself, "Will a new employee understand the job if he or she reads the job description?"

Small Business Applications

A Practical Approach

Without the benefit of their own job analysts or (in many cases) their own human resource managers, many small business owners face two hurdles when conducting job analyses and writing job descriptions. First (given their need to concentrate on other pressing matters), they often need a more streamlined approach than those provided by questionnaires like the one shown in Figure 3.3. Second, there is always the reasonable fear that in writing up their job descriptions they will inadvertently overlook duties that should be assigned to subordinates or assign duties to positions that are usually not associated with such positions. What they need here is a sort of encyclopedia listing all the possible positions they might encounter, including a detailed listing of the duties normally assigned to these positions. Such an "encyclopedia" exists, of course, and is the *Dictionary of Occupational Titles* briefly mentioned earlier. The *Practical Approach to Job Analysis for Small Businesspeople* presented next is built around this invaluable device and involves the following steps:

Step 1. Decide on a Plan

The development of at least the broad guidelines of a plan should precede your writing of an organization chart or job descriptions. What do you expect your sales revenue to be next year and in the next few years? What products do you intend to emphasize? What areas or departments in your company do you think will have to be expanded, reduced, or consolidated given where you plan to go with your firm over the next few years? What kinds of new positions do you think you'll need to be able to accomplish your strategic plans? These are the sorts of questions you should ask before proceeding.

Step 2. Develop an Organization Chart

Your next step should be to develop an organization chart for your firm. To do this, draw a chart showing who reports to the president and to each of his or her subordinates. Then complete the chart by showing who reports to each of the other managers and supervisors in the firm. Start by drawing up the organization chart as it is now. Then, depending upon how far in advance you're planning, produce a chart showing how you'd like your chart to look in the immediate future (say, in two months) and perhaps two or three other charts showing how you'd like your organization to evolve over the next two or three years.

Step 3. Use Job Analysis/Description Questionnaire

Next, use a job analysis questionnaire to determine what the job entails. You can use one of the more comprehensive job analysis questionnaires (like the one in Figure 3.3, for instance) to collect job analysis data. A simpler and often satisfactory alternative is to use the job description questionnaire presented in Figure 3.10. You can do this by filling in the information called for (using the procedure outlined shortly) and by asking your supervisors or the employees them-

Background Data for Job Description

Job Title ______________________ Department ______________________

Job Number ______________________ Written by ______________________

Today's Date ______________________ Applicable DOT codes ______________________

I. Applicable DOT Definition(s):

II. Job Summary:
(List the more important or regularly performed tasks)

III. Reports to: ______________________

IV. Supervises: ______________________

V. Job Duties:
(Briefly describe, for each duty, what *employee does and, if possible,* how *employee does it. Show in parentheses at end of each duty the approximate percentage of time devoted to duty.)*

A. Daily Duties:

B. Periodic Duties:
(Indicate whether weekly, monthly, quarterly, etc.)

C. Duties Performed at Irregular Intervals:

FIGURE 3.10
Job Description Questionnaire

selves to list their job duties (on the bottom of the page), breaking them into daily duties, periodic duties, and duties performed at irregular intervals. A sample of how one of these duties should be described (Figure 3.11) can be distributed to supervisors and/or employees.

Example of Job Title: Customer Service Clerk

Example of Job Summary: Answers inquiries and gives directions to customers, authorizes cashing of customers' checks, records and returns lost charge cards, sorts and reviews new credit applications, work at customer service desk in department store.

Example of One Job Duty: Authorizes cashing of checks: Authorizes cashing of personal or payroll checks (up to a specified amount) by customers desiring to make payment by check. Requests identification, such as driver's license, from customers, and examines check to verify date, amount, signature, and endorsement. Initials check, and sends customer to cashier.

FIGURE 3.11
Background Data For Examples

Step 4. Obtain the *Dictionary of Occupational Titles*

Your next step is to obtain standardized examples of the job descriptions you will need from the *Dictionary of Occupational Titles* (DOT).

The best way to learn how to use the *Dictionary of Occupational Titles* is to buy yourself a copy and begin using it. The *Dictionary* and its one supplement are available for $37.50 from the Superintendent of Documents, Government Printing Office, Washington, DC 20402–9325. You can call the order and information desk at 202/783–3238 to verify prices and order your manuals over the phone.

Step 5. Choose Appropriate Definitions and Put on Index Cards

Next, for each of your departments choose, from the DOT, job titles and job descriptions that you believe might be appropriate for your own enterprise. For example, suppose you want to develop job descriptions for your employees in the retail sales department of your store.

You leaf through occupational code numbers in the DOT starting with 0, 1, or 2 (since these include all professional, technical, and managerial occupations as well as clerical and sales occupations). On page 134 (see Figure 3.12) you find that category 185 refers to "Wholesale and Retail Trade Managers and Officials," and you find here "Manager, Department Store" (185.117–010) and "Fashion Coordinator" (185.157–010). Moving on, on page 208 you find that category 261 refers to "Sales Occupations—Apparel" and here you find "Salesperson, Children's Wear," (261.357–046), "Salesperson, Men's Clothing" (261.357–050), and "Salesperson, Women's Wear" (261.357–038). On the off chance that you may have inadvertently left out some titles that might be appropriate, you leaf through the alphabetical index of occupational titles under "Retail Trade Industry" occupations toward the back of the manual and stumble across "Assistant Buyer, Retail Trade" (162.157–022). You decide you should pick up several aspects of this job's duties as well. Make copies of each of the pertinent descriptions and glue them to index cards. You now have a comprehensive set of the management-related jobs typically found in a retail sales department and can rearrange them on your chart and consolidate positions until you have a division of work that you believe will work for you. Having this array of jobs on cards will help to ensure that you have considered the full range of retail sales management jobs that might be pertinent for your enterprise. It also helps to ensure that no important retail–management duties are inadvertently left out.

lizing knowledge of railroad maintenance regulations: Analyzes production reports, work schedules, and freight car repair list to determine efficient utilization of human resources, and recommends to superiors increasing, reducing, or shifting human resources as necessary to complete work requirements. Fills out daily worksheets identifying defective freight cars, necessary repairs, and priority of repairs for use of subordinate supervisors. Notifies YARD MANAGER (r.r. trans.) 184.167-278 to close tracks on which freight trains are being inspected to other rail traffic. Coordinates dispatching of wreck crews and heavy equipment to wreck site within yard or assigned geographic area. Contacts private contractors to rent equipment needed at wreck site. Informs consignees of damaged freight cars and obtains permission to transfer loads when necessary. Observes work in yard and repair shop to determine that areas are clean and free of hazards. Serves on committees to investigate causes of wrecks. Conducts investigations to determine cause of accidental worker injuries. Submits written reports of findings to superiors.
GOE: 05.02.02 STRENGTH: L GED: R4 M3 L3 SVP: 7 DLU: 86

184.167-290 SUPERVISOR, COMMUNICATIONS-AND-SIGNALS (r.r. trans.)
Directs and coordinates, through subordinate supervisory personnel, activities of workers engaged in installing, maintaining, and testing communications and signalling equipment within specified jurisdiction of railroad: Reviews reports that describe handling of communications and signal irregularities to discern whether deployment of personnel and maintenance procedures followed administrative and labor regulations. Discusses causes of irregularities with supervisor who directed repairs to suggest changes in inspection or maintenance techniques that would prevent recurrence of irregularities, utilizing knowledge of communication and signal functioning. Writes summary of reports indicating worker overtime involved and nature of equipment malfunctions and routes reports to superior. Confers with company engineers regarding major repairs or installation projects in communication and signal system to stay apprised of changes within system. Confers with supervisors throughout projects to provide technical assistance and to ensure availability of equipment needed to complete project.
GOE: 11.11.03 STRENGTH: L GED: R4 M4 L4 SVP: 8 DLU: 86

184.167-294 SUPERVISOR, TRAIN OPERATIONS (r.r. trans.)
Directs and coordinates activities of personnel engaged in scheduling and routing trains and engines in specified railroad territory: Observes record entries and monitors railroad radio communications and lights on train location panelboard to oversee train and engine movements along specified territory of railroad. Confers with railroad dispatchers to determine scheduling of trains and engines. Directs delays of train departures upon notification of substandard track conditions. Coordinates train movements to utilize train crews efficiently to schedule engines to arrive at service locations when due for maintenance and to maximize use of local trains versus special work trains. Scrutinizes train schedules and advises specified personnel of availability of tracks for scheduled repair and maintenance. Issues directives to subordinates to coordinate movement of expedited, late, or special railroad trains, using information received through railroad information network.
GOE: 05.02.02 STRENGTH: L GED: R4 M3 L4 SVP: 8 DLU: 86

184.267-010 FREIGHT-TRAFFIC CONSULTANT (business ser.) alternate titles: transportation consultant
Advises industries, business firms, and individuals concerning methods of preparation of freight for shipment, rates to be applied, and mode of transportation to be used: Consults with client regarding packing procedures and inspects packed or crated goods for conformance to shipping specifications to prevent damage, delay, or penalties. Selects mode of transportation, such as air, water, railroad, or truck without regard to higher rates when speed is necessary. Confers with shipping brokers concerning export and import papers, docking facilities, or packing and marking procedures. Files claims with insurance company for losses, damages, and overcharges of freight shipments.
GOE: 11.05.02 STRENGTH: S GED: R5 M4 L4 SVP: 8 DLU: 77

184.387-010 WHARFINGER (water trans.)
Compiles reports, such as dockage, demurrage, wharfage, and storage, to ensure that shipping companies are assessed specified harbor fees: Compares information on statements, records, and reports with ship's manifest to determine that weight, measurement, and classification of commodities are in accordance with tariff. Calculates tariff assessment from ship's manifest to ensure that charges are correct. Prepares and submits reports. Inspects sheds and wharves to determine need for repair. Arranges for temporary connection of water and electrical services from wharves. Reads service meters to determine charges to be made.
GOE: 07.02.04 STRENGTH: L GED: R3 M3 L2 SVP: 5 DLU: 77

185 WHOLESALE AND RETAIL TRADE MANAGERS AND OFFICIALS

This group includes managerial occupations concerned with selling merchandise to retailers; to industrial, commercial, institutional or professional users; or to other wholesalers; or acting as agents in buying merchandise for or selling merchandise to such persons or companies.

185.117-010 MANAGER, DEPARTMENT STORE (retail trade)
Directs and coordinates, through subordinate managerial personnel, activities of department store selling lines of merchandise in specialized departments: Formulates pricing policies for sale of merchandise, or implements policies set forth by merchandising board. Coordinates activities of nonmerchandising departments, as purchasing, credit, accounting, and advertising with merchandising departments to obtain optimum efficiency of operations with minimum costs in order to maximize profits. Develops and implements, through subordinate managerial personnel, policies and procedures for store and departmental operations and customer personnel and community relations. Negotiates or approves contracts negotiated with suppliers of merchandise, or with other establishments providing security, maintenance, or cleaning services. Reviews operating and financial statements and departmental sales records to determine merchandising activities that require additional sales promotion, clearance sales, or other sales procedures in order to turn over merchandise and achieve profitability of store operations and merchandising objectives.
GOE: 11.05.02 STRENGTH: S GED: R5 M4 L5 SVP: 8 DLU: 77

185.117-014 AREA SUPERVISOR, RETAIL CHAIN STORE (retail trade) alternate titles: operations manager
Directs and coordinates activities of subordinate managerial personnel involved in operating retail chain stores in assigned area: Interviews and selects individuals to fill managerial vacancies. Maintains employment records for each manager. Terminates employment of store managers whose performance does not meet company standards. Directs, through subordinate managerial personnel, compliance of workers with established company policies, procedures, and standards, such as safekeeping of company funds and property, personnel and grievance practices, and adherence to policies governing acceptance and processing of customer credit card charges. Inspects premises of assigned area stores to ensure that adequate security exists and that physical facilities comply with safety and environmental codes and ordinances. Reviews operational records and reports of store managers to project sales and to determine store profitability. Coordinates sales and promotional activities of store managers. Analyzes marketing potential of new and existing store locations and recommends additional sites or deletion of existing area stores. Negotiates with vendors to enter into contracts for merchandise and determines allocations to each store manager.
GOE: 11.11.05 STRENGTH: L GED: R4 M3 L4 SVP: 7 DLU: 86

185.137-010 MANAGER, FAST FOOD SERVICES (retail trade; wholesale tr.)
Manages franchised or independent fast food or wholesale prepared food establishment: Directs, coordinates, and participates in preparation of, and cooking, wrapping or packing types of food served or prepared by establishment, collecting of monies from in-house or take-out customers, or assembling food orders for wholesale customers. Coordinates activities of workers engaged in keeping business records, collecting and paying accounts, ordering or purchasing supplies, and delivery of foodstuffs to wholesale or retail customers. Interviews, hires, and trains personnel. May contact prospective wholesale customers, such as mobile food vendors, vending machine operators, bar and tavern owners, and institutional personnel, to promote sale of prepared foods, such as doughnuts, sandwiches, and specialty food items. May establish delivery routes and schedules for supplying wholesale customers. Workers may be known according to type or name of franchised establishment or type of prepared foodstuff retailed or wholesaled.
GOE: 11.11.04 STRENGTH: L GED: R4 M4 L4 SVP: 5 DLU: 81

185.157-010 FASHION COORDINATOR (retail trade) alternate titles: fashion stylist
Promotes new fashions and coordinates promotional activities, such as fashion shows, to induce consumer acceptance: Studies fashion and trade journals, travels to garment centers, attends fashion shows, and visits manufacturers and merchandise markets to obtain information on fashion trends. Consults with buying personnel to gain advice regarding type of fashions store will purchase and feature for season. Advises publicity and display departments of merchandise to be publicized. Selects garments and accessories to be shown at fashion shows. Provides information on current fashions, style trends, and use of accessories. May contract with models, musicians, caterers, and other personnel to manage staging of shows. May conduct teenage fashion shows and direct activities of store-sponsored club for teenage girls.
GOE: 11.09.01 STRENGTH: L GED: R5 M4 L5 SVP: 7 DLU: 77

185.157-014 SUPERVISOR OF SALES (business ser.)
Coordinates and publicizes tobacco marketing activities within specified area: Visits tobacco growers, buyers, and auction warehouses to cultivate interest and goodwill. Develops publicity for tobacco industry. Investigates and confirms eligibility of buyers. Collects membership dues for tobacco Board of Trade. Schedules tobacco auction dates. Records quantity and purchase price of tobacco sold daily, and prepares reports specified by board. May prepare report of marketing activities for state and federal agencies. May review and verify reports for individual warehouses. May examine quality and growth of tobacco in fields of individual growers and inform buyers of results.
GOE: 11.09.01 STRENGTH: L GED: R4 M4 L4 SVP: 7 DLU: 77

185.157-018 WHOLESALER II (wholesale tr.)
Exports domestic merchandise to foreign merchants and consumers and imports foreign merchandise for sale to domestic merchants or consumers: Arranges for purchase and transportation of imports through company representatives abroad and sells imports to local customers. Sells domestic goods, materials, or products to representatives of foreign companies. May be required

FIGURE 3.12 Page from *Dictionary of Occupational Titles*
Source: *Dictionary of Occupational Titles* (Washington, DC: U.S. Department of Labor, 1991), p. 134.

The job specification for already-trained candidates such as the financial analysts here at IBM, should indicate clearly that computer literacy is a requirement.

Step 6. Put Appropriate DOT Summaries on the Top of Your Job Description Form

Next, write a job description for the job you want done. To facilitate this, write the corresponding DOT codes and DOT definitions under "Applicable DOT Definitions" in the Job Description Form in Figure 3.10. Particularly when (as is usually the case) only one or two DOT definitions apply to the job description you are writing, the DOT definition will give your own definition a firm foundation. It will provide a standardized list of duties and will serve as a constant reminder of the specific duties that should be included in your own definition. Including the DOT codes and definitions will also facilitate your conversations with the state job service should you use them to help you find employees for your open positions.

Step 7. Complete Your Job Description

Finally, in Figure 3.10, write a job summary that is appropriate for the job under consideration. Then use the job analysis information you obtained in step 3 together with the information you gleaned from the DOT to develop a complete listing of the tasks and duties of each of your jobs.

WRITING JOB SPECIFICATIONS

The job specification takes the job description and answers the question, "What human traits and experience are necessary to do this job well?" It shows you what kind of person to recruit for and for what qualities that person should be tested. The job specification may be a separate section on the job description or a separate document entirely; often it is presented on the back of the job description.[21]

SPECIFICATIONS FOR TRAINED VERSUS UNTRAINED PERSONNEL

Suppose you were looking for a trained bookkeeper (or trained counselor or auto mechanic). In cases like these your job specifications would probably focus on things like length of previous service, quality of any relevant training, and so forth. Thus, it's usually not too difficult to determine the human requirements for placing *already trained* people on a job.

But the problems are more complex when you're seeking *untrained* people for your jobs (probably with the intention of training them on the job). Here you need to specify qualities such as physical traits, personality, interests, or sensory skills that imply some potential for performing the job or for having the ability to be trained for the job. For example, suppose the job requires detailed manipulation on an electronic assembly line. Then, you might want to ensure the person scores high on a test of finger dexterity. Your goal is thus to identify those personal traits—those human requirements—that validly predict which candidate would do well on the job and which would not. Identifying these human requirements for a job is accomplished either through a subjective, judgmental approach or through statistical analysis.

JOB SPECIFICATIONS BASED ON JUDGMENT

The judgmental approach involves developing your job specification based on the educated guesses of people like supervisors and human resource managers. The basic procedure here is to ask: "What does it take in terms of education, intelligence, training, and the like to do this job well?"

One of the most extensive judgmental approaches to developing job specifications is contained in the *Dictionary of Occupational Titles.* For jobs in the dictionary, judgments have been made by job analysts and vocational counselors regarding each job's human requirements. Each of these human requirements or traits has been assigned a letter, as follows: G (intelligence), V (verbal), N (numerical), S (spatial), P (perception), Q (clerical perception), K (motor coordination), F (finger dexterity), M (manual dexterity), E (eye–hand–foot coordination), and C (color dissemination). These ratings reflect the amount of each trait or ability possessed by people with different performance levels currently working on the job.

JOB SPECIFICATIONS BASED ON STATISTICAL ANALYSIS

Basing your job specifications on statistical analysis is the most defensible approach, but is also more difficult. Basically, what you do here is (statistically) determine the relationship between (1) some *predictor* or human trait such as height, intelligence, or finger dexterity and (2) some indicator or *criterion* of job effectiveness (such as performance as rated by the supervisor). The basic process involves five steps: (1) analyze the job and decide how to measure job performance, (2) select personal traits like finger dexterity that you believe should predict successful performance, (3) test job candidates for these traits, (4) measure these candidates' subsequent job performance, and (5) statistically analyze the relationship between the human trait (finger dexterity) and job performance. Your objective is to determine whether the former predicts the latter. In this way the human requirements for performing the job can be statistically ascertained.

This method, to repeat, is more defensible than is the judgmental approach. Specifically, equal rights legislation forbids using traits that you can't *prove* distinguish between high and low job performers. Standards that directly or indirectly discriminate on the basis of sex, race, religion, national origin, or age may have to be shown (by you) to be good predictors, and this generally requires a statistical validation study.

▶ CHAPTER REVIEW

SUMMARY

1. Developing an organization structure results in jobs that have to be staffed. Job analysis is the procedure through which you find out (1) what the job entails, and (2) what kinds of people should be hired for the job. It involves six steps: (1) Determine the use of the job analysis information, (2) collect background informa-

tion, (3) select the positions to be analyzed, (4) collect job analysis data, (5) review information with participants, and (6) develop a job description and job specification.

2. There are five *basic techniques* one can use to gather job analysis data: interviews, direct observation, a questionnaire, participant logs, and the U.S. Civil Service Procedure. These are good for developing job descriptions and specifications. The *Department of Labor, functional job analysis,* and *PAQ* approaches result in quantitative ratings of each job and are therefore useful for classifying jobs for pay purposes.
3. The job description should portray the work of the position so well that the duties are clear without reference to other job descriptions. Always ask, "Will the new employee understand the job if he or she reads the job description?"
4. The job specification takes the job description and answers the question, "What human traits and experience are necessary to do this job well?" It tells what kind of person to recruit for and for what qualities that person should be tested. Job specifications are usually based on the educated guesses of managers; however, a more accurate statistical approach to developing job specifications can also be used.
5. Job analysis is in many ways the first personnel activity that affects commitment. Most people can't perform a job when they don't have the ability and skills to do the job. It is through job analysis that you determine what the job entails and what skills and abilities you should look for in job candidates.
6. You can use the *Dictionary of Occupational Titles* to help you write your job descriptions. Find and reproduce the DOT descriptions that relate to the job you're describing. Then use those DOT descriptions to "anchor" your own description and particularly to suggest duties to be included.

KEY TERMS

job analysis
job description
job specifications
participant diary/logs
position analysis
questionnaire (PAQ)
Department of Labor job
analysis
functional job analysis

DISCUSSION QUESTIONS

1. What items are typically included in the job description? What items are not shown?
2. What is job analysis? How can you make use of the information it provides?
3. We discussed several methods for collecting job analysis data—questionnaires, the position analysis questionnaire, and so on. Compare and contrast these methods, explaining what each is useful for and listing the pros and cons of each.
4. Describe the types of information typically found in a job specification.
5. Explain how you would conduct a job analysis.

APPLICATION EXERCISES

RUNNING CASE

CARTER CLEANING COMPANY

The Job Description

Based on her review of the stores, Jennifer concluded that one of the first matters she had to attend to involved developing job descriptions for her store managers.

As Jennifer tells it, her lessons regarding job descriptions in her basic management and personnel management courses were by themselves insufficient to fully convince her of the pivotal role job descriptions played in the smooth functioning of an enterprise. Many times during her first few weeks on the job, Jennifer found herself asking one of her store managers why he was violating what she knew to be recommended company policies and procedures. Repeatedly the answers were either "Because I didn't know it was my job" or "Because I didn't know that was the way we were supposed to do it." Jennifer knew that a job description, along with a set of standards and procedures that specified what was to be done and how to do it, would go a long way toward alleviating this problem.

In general, the store manager is responsible for directing all store activities in such a way that quality work is produced, customer relations and sales are maximized, and profitability is maintained through effective control of labor, supply, and energy costs. In accomplishing that general aim, specific store manager's duties and responsibilities include quality control, store appearance and cleanliness, customer relations, bookkeeping and cash management, cost control and productivity, damage control, pricing, inventory control, spotting and cleaning, machine maintenance, employee safety, hazardous waste removal, human resource administration, and pest control.

The questions that Jennifer had to address follow.

Questions

1. What should be the format and final form of the store manager's job description?
2. Was it practical to specify standards and procedures in the body of the job description, or should these be kept separate?
3. How should Jennifer go about collecting the information required for the standards, procedures, and job description?

CASE INCIDENT *Hurricane Andrew*

In August 1992 Hurricane Andrew hit South Florida and the Optima Air Filter Company. Many employees' homes were devastated and the firm found that it had to hire almost three completely new crews, one for each of its shifts. The problem was that the "old timers" had known their jobs so well that no one had ever bothered to draw up job descriptions for them. When about 30 new employees began taking their posts there was general confusion about what they should do and how they should do it.

The hurricane quickly became old news to the firm's out-of-state customers who wanted filters, not excuses. Phil Mann, the firm's president, was at his wit's end. He had about 30 new employees, 10 old timers, and his original factory supervisor, Maybelline. He decided to meet with Linda Lowe, a consultant from the local university's business school who immediately had the old timers fill out a job questionnaire which listed all their duties. Arguments ensued almost at once because both Phil and Maybelline thought the old timers were exaggerating to make themselves look more important while the old timers insisted that the list faithfully reflected their duties. Meanwhile the customers clammered for their filters.

Questions

1. Should Phil and Linda ignore the old timers' protests and write up the job descriptions as they see fit? Why? Why not? How would you go about resolving the differences?
2. How would you have conducted the job analysis?

HUMAN RESOURCE MANAGEMENT SIMULATION

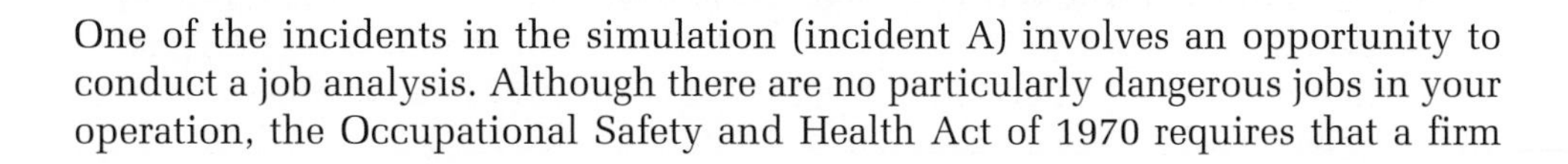

One of the incidents in the simulation (incident A) involves an opportunity to conduct a job analysis. Although there are no particularly dangerous jobs in your operation, the Occupational Safety and Health Act of 1970 requires that a firm specify "elements of the job that endanger health, or are to be considered unsatisfactory or distasteful to the majority of the population." Providing a job description to employees is a good defense against possible legal actions. Because the firm does not have the personnel or in-house expertise to conduct such an analysis, you will need to decide which consultant should do the work. The proposals range from a complete organization-wide analysis to training your staff to do the analysis in-house. You may also decide that other programs should take precedence and delay this decision.

Notes

1. Wayne Cascio, *Applied Psychology in Personnel Management* (Reston, VA: Reston, 1978), p. 132.
2. Ernest J. McCormick, "Job and Task Analysis," in Marvin D. Dunnette, ed., *Handbook of Industrial and Organizational Psychology* (Chicago: Rand McNally, 1976), pp. 651–696.
3. Richard Henderson, *Compensation Management: Rewarding Performance,* 2nd ed. (Reston, VA: Reston, 1979), pp. 139–150. See also Patrick W. Wright and Kenneth Wexley, "How to Choose the Kind of Job Analysis You Really Need," *Personnel,* Vol. 62, no. 5 (May 1985), pp. 51–55; C. J. Cranny and Michael E. Doherty, "Importance Ratings in Job Analysis: Note on the Misinterpretation of Factor Analyses," *Journal of Applied Psychology* (May 1988), pp. 320–322.
4. See, for example, Ernest McCormick, James Shaw, and Angelo DeNisi, "Use of the Position Analysis Questionnaire for Establishing the Job Component Validity of a Test," *Journal of Applied Psychology,* Vol. 64, no. 1 (1979), pp. 51–56; Marvin Tratner, "Task Analysis In the Design of Three Concurrent Validity Studies of the Professional and Administrative Career Examination," *Personnel Psychology,* Vol. 32 (Spring 1979), pp. 109–119.
5. Ibid.
6. Cascio, *Applied Psychology,* p. 140.
7. The appendixes from Henderson, *Compensation Management,* pp. 148–152.
8. A complete explanation and definition of each of these seven attributes (knowledge, skills, abilities, etc.) can be found in U.S. Civil Service Commission, *Job Analysis* (Washington, DC: U.S. Government Printing Office, December 1976).
9. Note that the PAQ (and other quantitative techniques) can also be used for job evaluation, which is explained in Chapter 12.
10. Again, we will see that *job evaluation* is the process through which jobs are compared to one another and their values determined. Although usually viewed as a job analysis technique, the PAQ is, in practice, actually as much or more of a job evaluation technique and could therefore be discussed in either this chapter or in Chapter 12. For a discussion of how to use PAQ for classifying jobs, see Edwin Cornelius III, Theodore Carron, and Marianne Collins, "Job Analysis Models and Job Classifications," *Personnel Psychology,* Vol. 32 (Winter 1979), pp. 693–708. See also Edwin Cornelius III, Frank Schmidt, and Theodore Carron, "Job Classification Approaches and the Implementation of Validity Generalization Results," *Personnel Psychology,* Vol. 37, no. 2 (Summer 1984), pp. 247–260.
11. Jack Smith and Milton Hakel, "Comparisons Among Data Sources, Response Bias, and Reliability and Validity of a Structured Job Analysis Questionnaire," *Personnel Psychology,* Vol. 32 (Winter 1979), pp. 677–692. See also Edwin Cornelius III, Angelo Denisi, and Allyn Blencoe, "Expert and Naive Raters Using the PAQ: Does It Matter?" *Personnel Psychology,* Vol. 37, no. 3 (Autumn 1984), pp. 453–464; Lee Friedman and Robert Harvey, "Can Raters with Reduced Job Description Information Provide Accurate Position Analysis Questionnaire (PAQ) Ratings?" *Personnel Psychology,* Vol. 34 (Winter 1986), pp. 779–789; and Robert J. Harvey et al., "Dimensionality of the Job Element Inventory, A Simplified Worker-Oriented Job Analysis Questionnaire," *Journal of Applied Psychology* (November 1988), pp. 639–646; Stephanie Butler and Robert Harvey, "A Comparison of Holistic Versus Decomposed Rating of Position Analysis Questionnaire Work Dimensions," *Personnel Psychology* (Winter 1988), pp. 761–772.
12. This discussion is based on Howard Olson et al., "The Use of Functional Job Analysis in Establishing Performance Standards for Heavy Equipment Operators," *Personnel Psychology,* Vol. 34 (Summer 1981), pp. 351–364.
13. Regarding this discussion, see Henderson, *Compensation Management,* pp. 175–184.
14. James Evered, "How to Write a Good Job Description," *Supervisory Management* (April 1981), pp. 14–19; Roger J. Plachy, "Writing Job Descriptions That Get Results," *Personnel* (October 1987), pp. 56–58.
15. Ibid., p. 16.
16. This discussion is based on Ibid.
17. Ibid., p. 16.
18. Ibid., p. 17.
19. Ibid., p. 18.
20. Ernest Dale, *Organizations* (New York: American Management Association, 1967).
21. The remainder of this chapter, except as noted, is based on Ernest J. McCormick and Joseph Tiffin, *Industrial Psychology* (Englewood Cliffs, NJ: Prentice Hall, 1974), pp. 56–61.

PERSONNEL PLANNING AND RECRUITING

CHAPTER 4

OVERVIEW

Once you define the jobs in your organization (Chapter 3) you must plan for job openings and decide how you will fill them. In this chapter we first discuss personnel planning and forecasting, which involve projecting personnel requirements and supply. Next, you must develop a pool of qualified candidates for the jobs, candidates who have the skills and ability to do them successfully. We explain how to develop that pool of viable job candidates, discuss developing and using application forms, and explain a technique for using application forms to predict success on the job. When you finish studying this chapter, you should be able to explain how to forecast personnel requirements; discuss the role of promotion from within in fostering commitment; explain the pros and cons of the main sources of applicants; and develop an application form for a position.

▶ PERSONNEL PLANNING AND FORECASTING

How do you plan for the openings that inevitably develop in your organization? You could choose to wait for the opening to develop and then try to fill it as best you can. Most managers use this approach and it is probably effective enough for small organizations. But for larger firms (and for managers who want to avoid last-minute scurrying and mistakes), some forecasting and planning are worthwhile.

To be worthwhile personnel planning has to be *integrated* both internally and externally. This is summarized in Figure 4.1. *Internally*, plans for recruitment, selection, placement, training, and appraisal should be developed in such a way that, for instance, the organization's training plans reflect its plans for recruiting and selecting new employees. *Externally*, personnel plans should be part of the organization's overall planning process, since plans to enter (or not enter) new businesses, to build (or not build) new plants, or to reduce the level of activities have significant labor implications—in terms of recruiting, and training, for instance.[1]

Personnel plans (like any good plans) are built on premises—basic assumptions about the future. The purpose of *forecasting* is to develop these basic premises. If it is *personnel* requirements you are planning for, you'll usually need three sets of forecasts: one for your *personnel requirements*, one for the *supply of outside candidates*, and one for your *available internal candidates*.

FIGURE 4.1
How All Personnel Functions Impact Personnel Planning

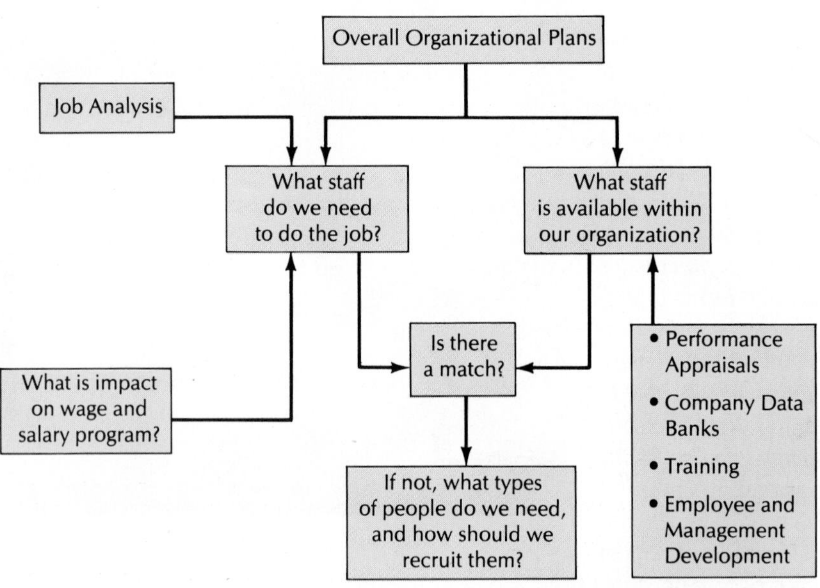

Note: Personnel planning should be integrated externally and internally. *Externally*, it should be integrated with the organization's overall plans. For example, opening new plants, building a new hospital wing, or reducing operations due to an impending recession all have staffing implications. *Internally*, staff planning should be integrated in that planning for all the personnel functions—such as recruiting, training, job analysis, and development—should be integrated or coordinated. For example, hiring 50 new employees means they must be trained, and their wages budgeted for.

FORECASTING PERSONNEL REQUIREMENTS

FACTORS IN FORECASTING PERSONNEL REQUIREMENTS

Managers should consider several factors when forecasting personnel requirements.[2] From a practical point of view, *the demand for your product or service* is paramount.[3] Thus, in a manufacturing firm, sales are projected first. Then the volume of production required to meet these sales requirements is determined. Finally, the staff needed to maintain this volume of output is estimated. In addition to production or sales demand, you will also have to consider several other factors:

1. *Projected turnover* (as a result of resignations or terminations).
2. *Quality and nature* of your employees (in relation to what you see as the changing needs of your organization).
3. *Decisions* to upgrade the quality of products or services or enter into new markets.
4. *Technological and administrative changes* resulting in increased productivity.
5. The *financial resources* available to your department.

Specific techniques for determining human resource requirements include trend analysis, ratio analysis, scatter plot analysis, and computerized forecasting.[4]

Trend Analysis

trend analysis
Study of a firm's past employment needs over a period of years to predict future needs.

Trend analysis means studying your firm's employment trends over the last five years or so to predict future needs. For example, you might compute the number of employees in your firm at the end of each of the last five years, or perhaps the number in each subgroup (like salespeople, production people, secretarial, and administrative) at the end of each of those years. The purpose is to identify employment trends that you think might continue into the future.

Trend analysis is valuable as an initial estimate, since employment levels rarely depend solely on the passage of time. Other factors (like changes in sales volume and productivity) will also affect your future staffing needs.

Ratio Analysis

ratio analysis
A forecasting technique for determining future staff needs by using ratios between sales volume and number of employees needed.

Another forecasting approach, **ratio analysis**, depends on the *ratio* between (1) some causal factor (like sales volume) and (2) number of employees required (for instance, number of salespeople). For example, suppose you find that a salesperson traditionally generates $500,000 in sales and that in each of the last two years you required ten salespeople to generate $5 million in sales. Also assume that your plans call for increasing your firm's sales to $8 million next year and to $10 million two years hence. Then, if the sales revenue–salespeople ratio remains the same, you would require six new salespeople next year (each of whom produces an extra $500,000 in sales). In the following year you would need an additional four salespeople to generate the extra $2 million in sales (between next year's $8 million and the following year's $10 million in sales).

You can also use ratio analysis to help forecast your other employee requirements. For example, you can compute a salesperson–secretary ratio and thereby determine how many new secretaries will be needed to support the extra sales staff.

As with trend analysis, ratio analysis assumes that productivity remains about the same—for instance that each salesperson can't be motivated to produce much more than $500,000 in sales each. If sales productivity *were* to increase or decrease, then the ratio of sales to salespeople would change. A forecast based on historical ratios would then no longer be as accurate.

The Scatter Plot

scatter plot
A graphical method used to help identify the relationship between two variables.

In the case of forecasting your personnel requirements, using scatter plots involves determining whether two factors—a measure of business activity and your staffing levels—are related. If they are, then if you can forecast the measure of business activity, you should also be able to estimate your personnel requirements.

Here is an example.[5] A 500-bed hospital in Chicago expects to expand to 1,200 beds over the next five years. The director of nursing and the human resource director want to forecast the requirement for registered nurses. The human resource director therefore decides to determine the relationship between size of hospital (in terms of number of beds) and number of nurses required. She calls five similar hospitals of various sizes and gets the following figures:

SIZE OF HOSPITAL (NUMBER OF BEDS)	NUMBER OF REGISTERED NURSES
200	240
300	260
400	470
500	500
600	620
700	660
800	820
900	860

One way to determine the relationship between size of hospital and nurses would be to draw a scatter plot as illustrated in Figure 4.2. *Hospital size* is shown on the horizontal axis. *Number of nurses* is shown on the vertical axis. If the two factors are related, then the points will tend to fall along a straight line, as in Figure 4.2. If you then carefully draw in a line in such a way as to minimize the distances between the line and each one of the plotted points, you will be able to estimate the number of nurses that will be needed for each given hospital size. Thus, for a 1,200-bed hospital, the human resource director would assume she needs about 1,210 nurses.

Using Computers to Forecast Personnel Requirements

computerized forecast
The determination of future staff needs by projecting a firm's sales, volume of production, and personnel required to maintain this volume of output, with computers and software packages.

Some employers use computerized systems for developing personnel requirement forecasts. With such a system, a personnel specialist, working with line managers, compiles the information needed to develop a **computerized forecast** of personnel requirements.[6] Typical data needed include direct labor hours needed to produce one unit of product (a measure of productivity), and three

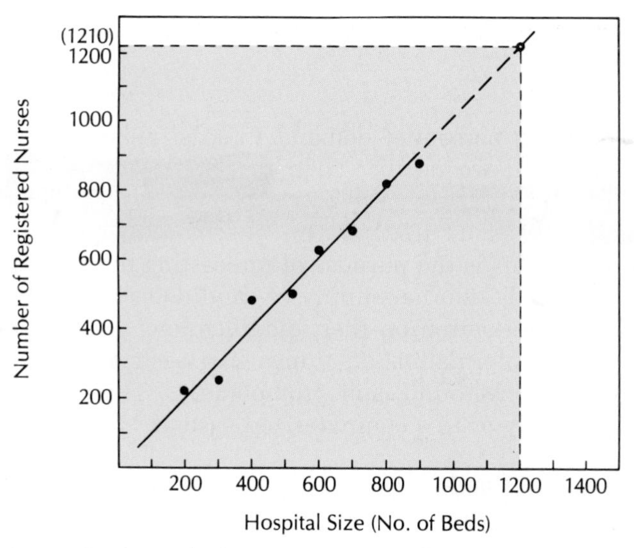

Note: After fitting the line, you can extrapolate—project—how many employees you'll need, given your projected volume.

FIGURE 4.2
Determining the Relationship Between Hospital Size and Number of Nurses

sales projections—minimum, maximum, and probable—for the product line in question. Based on such data, a typical program generates figures on "average staff levels required to meet product demands," as well as separate forecasts for direct labor (such as assembly workers), indirect staff (such as secretaries), and exempt staff (such as executives).

With such a system, an employer can quickly translate estimates of projected productivity and sales levels into forecasts of personnel needs and can estimate the effects of *various* levels of productivity and sales on personnel requirements.[7]

Managerial Judgment

Whichever forecasting approach you use, *managerial judgment* will play a big role. It's rare that any historical trend, ratio, or relationship will continue unchanged into the future. Judgment is thus needed to modify the forecast based on factors you believe will change in the future. Important factors that may modify your initial forecast of personnel requirements include the following:

1. Decisions to upgrade the quality of products or services or enter into new markets. These have implications for the nature of the employees you'll require. Ask, for instance, whether the skills of current employees fit with your organization's new products or services.
2. Technological and administrative changes resulting in increased productivity. Increased efficiency (in terms of output per hour) could reduce personnel needs. It might come about through installing new equipment or a new financial incentive plan, for instance.
3. The financial resources available. For example, a larger budget lets you hire more people and pay higher wages. Conversely, a projected budget crunch could mean fewer positions and lower salary offers.

FORECASTING THE SUPPLY OF INSIDE CANDIDATES

The preceding personnel demand forecast answers the question: "How many employees will we need?" Then, before determining how many new outside candidates to hire, you must know how many candidates for your projected job openings will come from within your organization, from the existing ranks. Determining this is the purpose of forecasting the supply of inside candidates.

To tap this internal supply of candidates you will first need some way of compiling information on their qualifications. These **qualifications inventories** will contain information on things like each employee's performance record, educational background, and promotability. This information can be compiled either manually or in a computerized system.

qualifications inventories Systematic records, either manual or computerized, listing employees' education, career and development interests, languages, special skills, etc., to be used in forecasting inside candidates for promotion.

Manual Systems and Replacement Charts

There are several types of manual systems used to keep track of employees' qualifications. In the *personnel inventory and development record* shown in Figure 4.3, information is compiled on each employee and then recorded on the inventory. The information includes education, company-sponsored courses taken, career and development interests, languages, and skills. Information like this can then be used to determine which current employees are available for promotion or transfer to projected open positions.

Some employers use **personnel replacement charts** (Figure 4.4) to keep track of inside candidates for their most important positions. These show the present performance and promotability for each potential replacement for your employer's important positions. As an alternative, you can develop a **position replacement card**. Here you make up a card for each position, showing possible replacements as well as present performance, promotion potential, and training required by each possible candidate.

personnel replacement charts Company records showing present performance and promotability of inside candidates for the most important positions.

position replacement card A card prepared for each position in a company to show possible replacement candidates and their qualifications.

Computerized Information Systems

Particularly for large employers, maintaining qualifications inventories on hundreds or thousands of employees can't be adequately managed manually. Many firms have thus computerized this information, and a number of packaged systems are now available for accomplishing this computerization.[8]

In one such system, employees fill out a 12-page booklet, in which they describe their background and experience. All this information is stored on the computer. When a manager needs a qualified person to fill a position, he or she describes the position (for instance, in terms of the education and skills it entails) and then enters this information into the computer. After scanning its bank of possible candidates, the program presents the manager with a computer printout of qualified candidates.

According to one expert the basic ingredients of such a computerized human resource skills inventory should include the following:

> *Work experience codes.* A list of work experience descriptors, titles, or codes that describe jobs within the company so that the individual's present, previous, and desired jobs can be coded.

PERSONNEL INVENTORY AND DEVELOPMENT RECORD | Date: month, year

Department	Area or sub-department	Branch or section	Location

Company service date (month, day, year)	Birthdate (month, day, year)	Marital status	Job title

Education — Degree, year obtained, college, and major field of study

Grade school 6 7 8 | High school 9 10 11 12 13
College 1 2 3 4 5

Courses (company sponsored)

Type of course	Subject or course	Year	Type of course	Subject or course	Year

Career and development interests

Are you interested in an alternative type of work? Yes ☐ No ☐ | Would you accept transfer to another division? Yes ☐ No ☐ | Would you accept lateral moves for further development? Yes ☐ No ☐

If yes, specifically what type? | Comment on any qualifying circumstances | Photo

What type of training do you believe you require to:
A) Improve your skills and performance in your present position
B) Improve your experience and abilities for advancement.

Last name | First name | Middle name | SS Number

What other assignments do you believe you are qualified to perform now?

Languages	Written		Spoken	
	☐	☐	☐	☐
	☐	☐	☐	☐

Societies and organizations — Memberships in community organizations, etc., within last five years, indicate name of association and office held, if any

Skills

Type of skill	Certification, if any	Type of skill	Certification, if any

Other significant work experience, and/or military service. (Omit repetitive experiences)

	Location	From yr.	To yr.

Comments: Other significant experience, recreational activities, hobbies, interests, or personal data.

FIGURE 4.3
Personnel Inventory Form Appropriate for Manual Storage and Retrieval

Product knowledge. The employee's level of familiarity with the employer's product lines or services as an indication of where the person might be transferred or promoted.

Industry experience. The person's industry experiences should be coded, since for certain positions the employee's knowledge of key related industries is very useful.

Formal education. Here enter the name of each postsecondary educational institution attended, the field of study, degree granted, and year granted.

Training courses. Indicate here training courses conducted by the employee and, possibly, training courses taught by outside agents like the American Management Association.

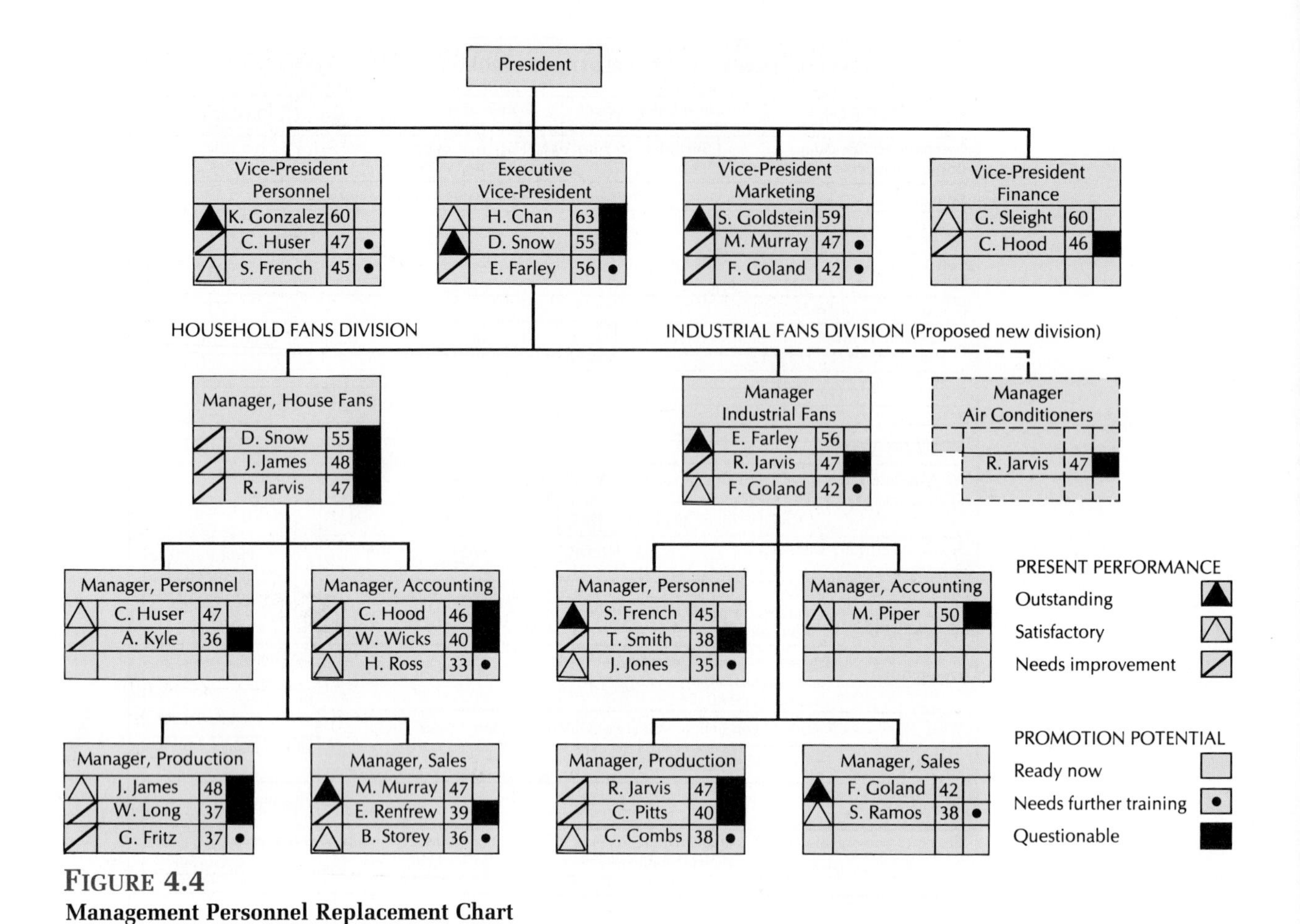

FIGURE 4.4
Management Personnel Replacement Chart

Foreign language skills. Here include a degree of proficiency as well as whether the foreign language is the employee's native tongue.

Relocation limitations. Compile information regarding the employee's willingness to relocate and the locales to which the person would prefer to be relocated.

Career interests. Using the same work experience codes as before, the employee should indicate what he or she would like to be doing for the employer in the future. Space can be provided for a brief priority of choices, and a code should be included indicating whether the employee's main qualification for the work he or she wants to do is experience, knowledge, or interests.

Performance appraisals. These should be entered into the employee's skill bank and updated periodically to indicate the employee's achievement on each dimension (leadership ability, motivation, communication skills, etc.) appraised, along with a summary of the employee's strengths and deficiencies.[9]

In fact the typical data elements in a human resources information system could number 100 or more. For example, one major vendor of a mainframe personnel/payroll package reportedly used by over 2,000 companies suggests the 140 elements shown in Table 4.1. Notice that these elements range from home address to driver's license number, employee weight, organizational property,

TABLE 4.1 Typical Data Elements in a Human Resources Information System

Address (work)	Garnishments	Salary change type
Address (home	Grievance (type)	Salary
Birthdate	Grievance (outcome)	Salary range
Birthplace	Grievance (filing date)	Schools attended
Child support deductions	Handicap status	Service date
Citizenship	Health plan coverage	Service branch
Claim pending (description)	Health plan (no. dependents)	Service discharge type
Claim pending (outcome)		Service ending rank
Claim pending (court)	Injury date	Service discharge date
Claim pending (date)	Injury type	Sex
Date on current job	Job location	Sick leave used
Department	Job preference	Sick leave available
Dependent (sex)	Job position number	Skill function (type)
Dependent (number of)	Job title	Skill sub-function (type)
Dependent (relationship)	Job location	Skill (number of years)
Dependent (birthdate)	Leave of absence start date	Skill (proficiency level)
Dependent (name)	Leave of absence end date	Skill (date last used)
Discipline (appeal date)	Leave of absence type	Skill (location)
Discipline (type of charge)	Life insurance coverage	Skill (supervisory)
Discipline (appeal outcome)	Marital status	Social Security number
Discipline (date of charge)	Marriage date	Spouse's employment
Discipline (outcome)	Medical exam (date)	Spouse's date of death
Discipline (hearing date)	Medical exam (restrictions)	Spouse's name
Division	Medical exam (blood type)	Spouse's birthdate
Driver's license (number)	Medical exam (outcome)	Spouse's sex
Driver's license (state)	Miscellaneous deductions	Spouse's Social Security number
Driver's license (exp. date)	Name	
Education in progress (date)	Organizational property	Start date
Education in progress (type)	Pay status	Stock plan membership
Educational degree (date)	Pension plan membership	Supervisor's name
Educational degree (type)	Performance rating	Supervisor's work address
Educational minor (minor)	Performance increase ($)	Supervisor's work phone
Educational level attained	Performance increase (%)	Supervisor's title
Educational field (major)	Phone number (work)	Termination date
EEO-1 code	Phone number (home)	Termination reason
Emergency contact (phone)	Prior service (term. date)	Training schools attended
Emergency contact (name)	Prior service (hire date)	Training schools (date)
Emergency contact (relation)	Prior service (term. reason)	Training schools (field)
Emergency contact (address)	Professional license (type)	Training schools completed
Employee weight	Professional license (date)	Transfer date
Employee number	Race	Transfer reason
Employee code	Rehire code	Union code
Employee status	Religious preference	Union deductions
Employee height	Salary points	United Way deductions
Employee date of death	Salary (previous)	Vacation leave available
Federal job code	Salary change date	Vacation leave used
Full-time/part-time code	Salary change reason	Veteran status

Source: Donald Harris, "A Matter of Privacy: Managing Personal Data in Company Computers," *Personnel* (February 1987), p. 37.

salary, sick leave used, skill (type), to veteran status.[10] Note that *skills* are often included in these types of data banks. Including "training courses completed" might only show what the employee is trained to do, not what he or she has actually shown he or she can do. Including skills such as "remove boiler casings and doors" (number of times performed, date last performed, time spent) lets you use your computer to zero in on which employees are competent to accomplish the task that must be done. Here you can even include a skill level in the data bank, perhaps ranging from skill level 1 (can lead or instruct others) down to 2 (can perform the job with minimum supervision), 3 (has some experience: can assist experienced workers), to 4 (has not had opportunity to work on this job).[11]

The Matter of Privacy

Several developments have intensified the human resource manager's need to create better ways to actually control the personnel data that are stored in the organization's data banks. First, there is now, as you can see in Table 4.1, a great deal of information about employees in most employer's data banks. Second, the expansion of end-user computing capabilities offers more opportunities for more people to have access to this data.[12] Related to this, it's become much more difficult for the personnel department to review and approve each request for information. And, finally, under certain legislation (such as the Federal Privacy Act of 1974 and the New York Personal Privacy Protection Act of 1985), employees may have legal rights regarding who has access to information about their work history and job performance.

Balancing the employer's legitimate right to make this information available to those in the organization who need it with the employees' rights to privacy isn't easy. One approach is to use the *access matrices* incorporated in the software of many data base management systems. Basically, these matrices define the rights of users (specified by name, rank, or functional identification) to have various kinds of access (such as "read only" or "write only") to each data element contained in the data base. Thus the computer programmers who are charged with the job of inputting data regarding employees might be authorized only to "write" information into the data base, while those in accounting are authorized to "read" a limited range of information such as the person's address, phone number, Social Security number, and pension status. The human resource director, on the other hand, might be authorized to both "read and write" all items when interacting with the data base.

INTERNAL SOURCES OF CANDIDATES

Although *recruiting* often brings to mind employment agencies and classified ads, *current employees* are often your largest source of recruits. Some surveys even indicated that up to 90% of all management positions are filled internally.[13]

Filling open positions with inside candidates has several benefits. Employees see that competence is rewarded and morale and performance may

Job posting can be an effective way of spreading the word about job opportunities to existing employees.

thus be enhanced. Inside candidates (having already been with your firm for some time) may be more committed to its goals and less likely to leave. Promotion from within can also boost employee commitment and provide a longer-term perspective when making managerial decisions. It may also be safer to promote employees from within, since you're more likely to have a more accurate assessment of the person's skills than you would otherwise. Inside candidates may also require less orientation and training than outsiders.

Yet promotion from within can also backfire. Employees who apply for jobs and don't get them may become discontented; informing unsuccessful applicants as to why they were rejected and what remedial actions they might take to be more successful in the future is thus essential.[14] Similarly, many employers require managers to post job openings and interview all inside candidates. Yet the manager often knows ahead of time exactly whom he or she wants to hire, and requiring the person to interview a stream of unsuspecting inside candidates is therefore a waste of time for all concerned. Groups may also not be as satisfied when their new boss is appointed from within their own ranks as when he or she is a newcomer; sometimes, for instance, it is difficult for the newly chosen leader to shake off the reputation of being "one of the gang."[15]

Perhaps the biggest drawback, though, is inbreeding. When an entire management team has been brought up through the ranks, there may be a tendency to make decisions "by the book" and to maintain the status quo, when an innovative and new direction is what's called for. Balancing the benefits of morale and loyalty with the drawback of inbreeding is thus a problem.

job posting
Posting notices of job openings on company bulletin boards is an effective recruiting method.

Promotion from within, to be effective, requires using job posting, personnel records, and skill banks.[16] **Job posting** means posting the open job and listing its attributes like qualifications, supervisor, working schedule, and pay rate (as in Figure 4.5). Some union contracts require job posting to ensure that union members get first choice of new and better positions. Yet job posting can also be a good practice even in nonunion firms, if it facilitates the transfer and promotion of your qualified inside candidates. Posting is usually not used when promotion to a supervisory position is involved, since management often prefers to select personnel itself for promotion to management levels.[17] *Personnel records* are also useful here. Examining personnel records (including application blanks) may uncover employees who are working in jobs below their educational or skill levels. It may also reveal persons who have potential for further training or those who already have the right background for the open jobs in question. Computerized systems, discussed previously, can help to ensure that qualified inside candidates are identified and considered for the opening. Some firms also develop *skill banks* that list current employees who have specific skills. For example, under "aerospace engineers," the names of all persons with this experience or training are listed. If you need an engineer in unit A, and the skill bank shows a person with those skills in unit B, that person may be approached about transferring to unit A although he or she is not now using the aerospace skills.

A statement of one firm's job posting policies is presented in Figure 4.6. As you can see, important guiding policies include "All permanent employees . . . are eligible to use the open position listing policy . . . to request consideration for a position," and "A list of open positions will be communicated to all employees in all facilities."

FIGURE 4.5
Job Posting Form

Source: Bureau of National Affairs, Inc. *Recruiting and Selection Procedures* (Washington, D.C., 1988), p. 35.

NO. ____

POSTED: ________
CLOSING: ________

____

There is a full-time position available for a __________________ in the
____________________ Department. This position is/is not open to outside candidates.

PAY SCALE

	Minimum	Midpoint	Maximum
	$______	$______	$______

or
SALARIED

DUTIES
See attached job description.

REQUIRED SKILLS AND ABILITIES
(Must possess all the following skills and abilities to be considered for this position.)

1. Demonstrated successful performance at past/present positions including:
   - ability to perform tasks in a complete and accurate manner
   - demonstrated timeliness and follow-through on duties and assignments
   - ability to work well with other people
   - ability to communicate effectively
   - reliability and good attendance
   - good organizational skills
   - problem solving attitude and approach
   - positive work attitude: enthusiastic, confident, outgoing, helpful, committed
2.

DESIRED SKILLS AND ABILITIES
(These skills and abilities will make a candidate more competitive.)

Application procedure FOR EMPLOYEES is as follows:

1. Apply by phoning ______________________, on ext.____, by 3:00 p.m. ______________
2. Ensure that a completed Internal Job Application and up-to-date resume/application is delivered to ____________________ by the same date.

Applicants will be pre-screened according to the above qualifications.
Selection will be made by the ______________________.
is an equal opportunity employer.
0255M/1

BUILDING EMPLOYEE COMMITMENT

Promotion from Within

Employees tend to be committed to firms that are committed to them. We'll see that two-way communications, guaranteed fair treatment, and job security are some of the things a firm's HR system can provide to show that the firm is indeed committed to its employees. But many employees will ultimately measure their firm's commitment by the degree to which they were able to achieve their career goals. We'll discuss promotion from within systems in more detail in Chapter 11 (Managing Careers). However at this point it's useful to emphasize

ELIGIBILITY

- All permanent employees who have completed their probationary period are eligible to use the open position listing policy in order to request consideration for a position that would constitute a growth opportunity.
- Employees who have been promoted or transferred, or who have changed jobs for any reason, must wait a six-month period before applying for a different position.

POLICY

- A list of open positions will be communicated to all employees in all facilities. Notices will include information on job title, salary grade, department, supervisor's name and title, location, brief description of the job content, qualifications, and instructions concerning whether or not candidates will be expected to demonstrate their skills during the interview process.
- Basic job qualifications and experience needed to fill the job will be listed on the sheet. Employees should consult with the human resource department if there are questions concerning the promotional opportunities associated with the job.
- Open position lists will remain on bulletin boards for five working days.
- Forms for use in requesting consideration for an open position may be obtained from the human resource department.
- The human resource department will review requests to substantiate the employee's qualifications for the position.
- The hiring manager will review requests for employees inside the company before going outside the company to fill the position.
- It is the responsibility of the employees to notify their managers of their intent to interview for an open position.
- The hiring manager makes the final decision when filling the position; however, the guidelines for filling any open position are based on the employees' ability, qualifications, experience, background, and the skills they possess that will allow them to carry out the job successfully. It is the responsibility of the hiring manager to notify the previous manager of the intent to hire the employee.
- Employees who are aware of a pending opening, and who will be on vacation when the opening occurs, may leave a request with the human resource department for consideration.
- It is the manager's responsibility to ensure that the human resource department has notified all internal applicants that they did or did not get the job before general announcement by the manager of the person who did get the job.
- "Blanket" applications will not be accepted. Employees should apply each time a position they are interested in becomes available.
- Since preselection often occurs, employees should be planning for their career growth by scheduling time with potential managers before posting, to become acquainted with them, and to secure developmental information to be used in acquiring appropriate skills for future consideration.
- There are occasions when jobs will not be listed. Two such examples might be (1) when a job can be filled best by natural progression or is a logical career path for an employee, and (2) when a job is created to provide a development opportunity for a specific high-performance employee.
- In keeping with this policy, managers are encouraged to work with employees in career development in order to assist them in pursuing upward movement in a particular career path or job ladder.

FIGURE 4.6
One Firm's Job Posting Policies
Source: From the book, *Human Resource Director's Handbook* by Mary F. Cook © 1984. Used by permission of the publisher, Prentice-Hall, Inc., Englewood Cliffs, N.J.

the fact that internal recruiting and job posting can be central to a firm's efforts to boost employee commitment.

Many high commitment-oriented firms therefore have comprehensive promotion from within programs.[18] Certainly, firms often associated with committed employees—firms like Delta Airlines and Federal Express—have promotion from within *policies*. At Federal Express, for instance, "open positions are filled, whenever possible, by qualified candidates from the within the existing workforce."[19] But there's much more to a successful promotion from within program than just a strong statement of policy. As we'll see in Chapter 11, promotion from within is aided first by careful employee selection. As one Delta manager explained: "First of all, we hire for the future . . . the employment process favors applicants who have the potential for promotion." That helps explain how Chairman Allen climbed the ranks at Delta from an entry-level position, to head of Personnel and then to CEO and Chairman. Effective promotion from within also depends on providing the education and training needed to help employees identify and develop their promotion potential. These firms also provide career-oriented appraisals: The supervisor and the employee are charged with linking the latter's past performance, career preferences, and developmental needs in a formal career plan. Finally, commitment-oriented internal recruiting requires a coordinated system for accessing career records and posting job openings, one that guarantees all eligible employees will be informed of openings and considered for them. For example, Federal Express has a job posting/career coordination system called JCATS (Job Change Applicant Tracking System). Announcements of new job openings via this electronic system usually take place each Friday. All employees applying for the position get numerical scores based on job performance and length of service. They are then advised as to whether they were chosen as candidates. Internal recruiting and promotion from within can thus be a force for creating employee commitment. However, a simple job posting policy alone will not do it.

Delta Airlines CEO R. W. Allen is a product of the company's strong commitment to promotion from within.

FORECASTING THE SUPPLY OF OUTSIDE CANDIDATES

Assuming that there are not enough inside candidates to fill your positions, you will probably next focus on outside candidates—those not currently employed by your organization. Forecasting the supply of outside candidates will involve forecasting *general economic* conditions, *local market* conditions, and *occupational market* conditions.

General Economic Conditions

The first step is to forecast **general economic conditions** and the expected prevailing rate of unemployment. Usually, the lower the rate of unemployment, the lower the labor supply and the more difficult it will be to recruit personnel.

There is a wealth of published information you can use to develop economic forecasts. In December of each year, *Business Week* magazine presents its economic forecast for the following year; each week it presents a snapshot of the economy on its *outlook* page. *Fortune* magazine has a monthly forecast of the business outlook that is usually buttressed in its January issue with a forecast for the coming year. *Forbes* magazine has regular articles on business trends both domestic and foreign. Many banks, such as New York's Citibank, Manufacturers Hanover Trust, and Chase Manhattan, publish periodic analyses and forecasts of the economy. Each December the Prudential Insurance Company publishes an economic forecast for the coming year.

Several agencies of the federal government also provide economic forecast information. The U.S. Council of Economic Advisors prepares *Economic Indicators* each month that shows the trend to date of various economic indicators. The regional branches of the Federal Reserve also publish economic reports monthly. The Federal Reserve Bank of St. Louis publishes a monthly summary that reports on various economic indicators.

Local Market Conditions

Projected **local labor conditions** are also important. For example, the phasing down of defense programs resulted in relatively high unemployment in cities like Seattle, quite aside from general economic conditions in the country.

occupational market conditions
The Bureau of Labor Statistics of the U.S. Department of Labor publishes projections of labor supply and demand for various occupations, as do other agencies.

Occupational Market Conditions

Finally, you may want to forecast the availability of potential job candidates in specific occupations (engineers, drill press operators, accountants, etc.) for which you will be recruiting. Recently, for instance, there has been an undersupply of accountants and nurses.

Forecasts of available labor in different occupations are available from various sources. For example, the Bureau of Labor Statistics of the U.S. Department of Labor publishes projections in the *Monthly Labor Review*. The National Science Foundation regularly forecasts labor market conditions in the science and technology fields. Other agencies providing occupational forecasts include the Public Health Service, the U.S. Employment Service, and the Office of Education.

▸ RECRUITING JOB CANDIDATES

INTRODUCTION

Once you have decided to fill a position (and have received permission to do so), the next step is to develop a pool of applicants. For this, you will use one or more of the recruitment sources described next. Recruiting is an important activity, because the higher the number of applicants the more selective you can be in your hiring. If only two candidates appear for two openings, you may have little choice but to hire them. But if 10 or 20 applicants appear, then you can employ techniques like interviews and tests to screen out all but the best.

Some employers use a *recruiting yield pyramid* to determine the number of applicants they must generate to hire the required number of new employees. As illustrated in Figure 4.7, the pyramid graphically displays the number of new leads you must generate through your recruiting efforts to hire the required number of new employees. In this case, the company knows it must hire 50 new entry-level accountants next year. From its experience, it also knows that the ratio of offers made to actual new hires is 2 to 1; about half the people they make offers to accept those offers. Similarly, the firm knows that the ratio of candidates interviewed to offers made is 3 to 2, while the ratio of candidates invited

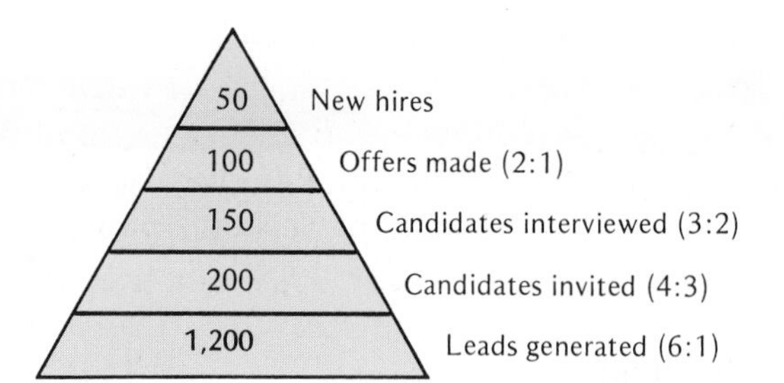

FIGURE 4.7
Recruiting Yield Pyramid

for interviews to candidates actually interviewed has been 4 to 3. Finally, the firm knows that the ratio of new leads generated to candidates actually invited has been 6 to 1; in other words, of six leads that come in from the firm's advertising, college recruiting, and other recruiting efforts, only one lead in six typically gets an invitation to come in for an interview. Given these ratios, the firm knows it must generate 1,200 leads to be able to invite 200 viable candidates to its offices for interviews. It will then get to interview about 150 of those it invites, and from these it will make 100 offers. Of those 100 offers, half (or 50 new CPAs) will be hired.

College recruiting efforts are more successful when the recruiters themselves are carefully chosen and trained. Here, an IRS recruiter participates in a job fair on the campus of Southwest Texas State University in San Marcos, Texas.

However, it's not just recruiting but effective recruiting that is important. For example, consider the results of a recent study of college recruiters.[20] Subjects were 41 graduating students from four colleges (arts and sciences, engineering, industrial relations, and business) of a university in the Northeast. The students were questioned twice during their spring semester, once just after they'd had their first round of interviews with employers, and once after their second round of interviews.

It was apparent that the quality of a firm's recruiting process had a big impact on what candidates thought of the firm. For example, when asked after the initial job interview why they thought a particular company might be a good fit, all 41 mentioned the nature of the job; however, 12 also mentioned the impression made by the recruiters themselves and 9 said the comments of friends and acquaintances affected their impressions. Unfortunately, the reverse was also true. When asked why they judged some firms as bad fits, 39 mentioned the nature of the job, but 23 said they'd been turned off by ineffectual recruiters. For example, some were dressed sloppily; others were "barely literate"; some were rude; and some made offensively sexist comments. All these recruiters, needless to say, were ineffectual representatives of their firms.

Recruitment is one area in which line and staff cooperation is essential. The human resource specialist who recruits and does the initial screening for the vacant job is seldom the one responsible for supervising its performance. He or she must therefore have as clear a picture as possible of what the job entails, and this, in turn, means speaking with the supervisor involved. For example, the human resource specialist might want to know something about the behavioral style of the supervisor and the members of the work group. Is it a "tough" group to get along with, for instance? The human resource specialist might also want to visit the work site and review the job description with the supervisor to ensure that the job has not changed since the description was written. Furthermore, the supervisor may be able to supply additional insight into the skills and talents the new worker will need. Personnel planning in general—and recruitment in particular—thus requires close cooperation between line and staff personnel.

ADVERTISING AS A SOURCE OF CANDIDATES

For help wanted ads to bring results, there are two issues you have to address: the media to be used and the construction of the ad.[21] The selection of the best medium—be it the local paper, the *Wall Street Journal*, or a technical journal—depends on the type of positions for which you're recruiting. Your local newspaper is usually the best source of blue-collar help, clerical employees, and lower-level administrative employees. For specialized employees, you can advertise in trade and professional journals like the *American Psychologist, Sales Management, Chemical Engineering*, and *Electronics News*. And there are publications like *Travel Trade, Women's Wear Daily, American Banker, Hospital Administration*, and the *Chronicle of Higher Education* in which you would most likely place your ads for professionals like bankers, hospital administrators, or educators. One drawback to this type of trade paper advertising is the long lead time that is usually required; there may be a month or more between insertion of the ad and publication of the journal or specialized paper, for instance. Yet ads remain good sources, and so ads like that in Figure 4.8 continue to appear.

Placing help wanted ads in papers like the *Wall Street Journal* can be good sources of middle or senior management personnel. The *Wall Street Journal*, for instance, has several regional editions so that either the entire country or the appropriate geographic area can be targeted for coverage.

Most firms use newspaper ads, but other media are used too. Table 4.2 summarizes when to use each. For example, magazines are best when special-

TABLE 4.2 Advantages and Disadvantages of some Major Types of Media

TYPE OF MEDIUM	ADVANTAGES	DISADVANTAGES	WHEN TO USE
Newspapers	Short deadlines. Ad size flexibility. Circulation concentrated in specific geographic areas. Classified sections well organized for easy access by active job seekers.	Easy for prospects to ignore. Considerable competitive clutter. Circulation not specialized—you must pay for great amount of unwanted readers. Poor printing quality.	When you want to limit recruiting to a specific area. When sufficient numbers of prospects are clustered in a specific area. When enough prospects are reading help wanted ads to fill hiring needs.
Magazines	Specialized magazines reach pinpointed occupation categories. Ad size flexibility. High-quality printing. Prestigious editorial environment. Long life—prospects keep magazines and reread them.	Wide geographic circulation—usually cannot be used to limit recruiting to specific area. Long lead time for ad placement.	When job is specialized. When time and geographic limitations are not of utmost importance. When involved in ongoing recruiting programs.

(continued)

TABLE 4.2 (Continued)

TYPE OF MEDIUM	ADVANTAGES	DISADVANTAGES	WHEN TO USE
Radio and television	Difficult to ignore. Can reach prospects who are not actively looking for a job better than newspapers and magazines. Can be limited to specific geographic areas. Creatively flexible. Can dramatize employment story more effectively than printed ads. Little competitive recruitment clutter.	Only brief, uncomplicated messages are possible. Lack of permanence; prospect cannot refer back to it. (Repeated airings necessary to make impression.) Creation and production of commercials—particularly TV—can be time-consuming and costly. Lack of special interest selectivity; paying for waste circulation.	In competitive situations when not enough prospects are reading your printed ads. When there are multiple job openings and there are enough prospects in specific geographic area. When a large impact is needed quickly. A "blitz" campaign can saturate an area in two weeks or less. Useful to call attention to printed ads.
"Point-of-purchase" (promotional materials at recruiting location).	Calls attention to employment story at time when prospects can take some type of immediate action. Creative flexibility.	Limited usefulness; prospects must visit a recruiting location before it can be effective.	Posters, banners, brochures, audiovisual presentations at special events such as job fairs, open houses, conventions, as part of an employee referral program, at placement offices, or whenever prospects visit at organization facilities.

Source: Adapted from Bernard S. Hodes, "Planning for Recruitment Advertising: Part II," *Personnel Journal*, Vol. 28, no. 5 (June 1983), p. 499. Reprinted with the permission of *Personnel Journal*, Costa Mesa, CA.

ized jobs are involved, such as using a computer engineering magazine to reach computer engineers.

Principles of Help Wanted Advertising

In addition to the media to be used, the construction of the ad is important.

Experienced advertisers use a four-point guide called AIDA to construct their ads. First, you must attract *attention* to the ad. Figure 4.9 shows a page from one paper's classified section. Which ads attract attention? Note that closely printed ads are lost while those using wide borders or a lot of empty space stand out. For the same reason, key positions are often advertised in display ads, where they don't get lost in the columns of classified ads.

Introduce Yourself to an Industry Leader.

SUPERIOR PRODUCTS, INNOVATIVE MARKETING PROGRAMS AND UNPARALLELED CUSTOMER SERVICE HELP MAKE FIDELITY INVESTMENTS® ONE OF THE NATION'S TOP FINANCIAL SERVICES ORGANIZATIONS. BEHIND OUR SUCCESS ARE HIGHLY-SKILLED AND COMMITTED INDIVIDUALS WHOSE EXPERTISE AND DRIVE ARE POSITIONING FIDELITY FOR UNPRECEDENTED GROWTH IN THE 1990S. IF YOU SHARE OUR ETHIC AND VISION, PLEASE CONSIDER THE FOLLOWING OPENING:

HOW TO GET YOUR CAREER OUT OF THE BOX

Introduce Yourself to Fidelity.

WRITE. NOW.

SENIOR STAFFING MANAGER

Fidelity Investments has an opening for an experienced staffing specialist to manage the employment function for the Fidelity Institutional and Brokerage businesses. Responsibilities include working with H.R. generalists and business managers to identify future staffing needs, develop candidate pools and creative sourcing strategies, and filling varied professional openings. Candidates must have at least 10 years' responsible business and/or H.R. experience with a focus on high volume, professional-level recruiting and experience in the brokerage and/or mutual fund/institutional financial services industries.

Fidelity offers exceptional benefits for exceptional people, including health/dental insurance, tuition reimbursement, profit sharing and a 401(k) plan. Send your resume to:

FIDELITY INVESTMENTS, HUMAN RESOURCES,
82 DEVONSHIRE ST., DEPT. SSM, MAIL ZONE I7A, BOSTON, MA 02109
An equal opportunity employer, M/F/D/V.

FIGURE 4.8
Managerial Help Wanted Ad

Next, develop *interest* in the job. As in Figure 4.10, interest may be created by the nature of the job itself, such as "you'll thrive on challenging work." Sometimes, other aspects of the job, such as its location, can be used to create interest.

Accountant

ch, multi-plant manu-
r with home offices
heast NJ seeks an ag-
e Sr. Accountant to
ır expanding team.
sibilities include
ıtion of income & bal-
sheet statements,
s of divisional & cor-
financial reports,
preparation, capital
s & developing ac-
g methods. The suc-
candidate will pos-
ᐳA, Accounting or Fi-
Degree, 5-8 years ex-
:e in a manufacturing
ıment with strong
ound in cost account-
:nowledge of DP sys-
Supervisory experi-
; strongly preferred.
ırn we offer a dy-
results-oriented envi-
ıt with compensation
e designed to attract
onal talent. Send re-
in complete confi-
o:
ȝ210, Wall Street Journal
l opportunity employer m/f

ERCIAL MORTGAGE
OAN OFFICER

of America, a $9.1 bil-
ift, is accepting re-
r the position of Com-
Mortgage Loan Officer
Hudson Valley/NYC
adquartered in White
Requirements incld 3-5
nercial lending exp in
on and underwriting,
to analyze financial
ıts, good oral and writ-
nunication skills. Pre-
d in Hudson Valley/
kt. Finance/Real Es-
gree desired. Travel
ubmit resume WITH
REQUIREMENTS to:
Karen Solenick
E OF AMERICA F.S.B.
8 East Post Road
te Plains, NY 10601
ual Oppty Employer
M/F/V/HC

Stock/Commodity.

ACCOUNTING

AUDIT & TAX PROFESSIONALS

Opportunities in Atlanta and the Southeast

Touche Ross, a leading Big Eight firm, is experiencing substantial growth.
We are a leader in micro-computer applications, innovative in the development of new product lines, and we challenge our professionals early with exposure to our clients' senior management.
This emphasis on the highest quality of service and close client relationships provides the best environment for rapid professional growth—yours and ours. Our offices operate with a high degree of autonomy, but you have available the full resources of our national organization. Advancement can be rapid—partnership opportunities are based on performance. And you'll find we have a real interest in helping you advance.
Other advantages include an excellent compensation package and the professional prestige of the Touche Ross name.
Opportunities are now available in Atlanta and other southeast locations.
If you have two to seven years of current or recent experience with a national or major regional public accounting firm and a drive to reach the top of the profession, we'd like to hear from you.
To find out more, direct a summary of your experience and salary history to:

Shelley Hanke
TOUCHE ROSS
225 Peachtree St., N.E.
Suite 1400
Atlanta, GA 30043
An Equal Opportunity Employer M/F/H

Touche Ross

$100,000+++COMM/YR
CLOSER
Mature-Exp

Nat'l auto aftermarket co. seeks Super Sales Pro who can come aboard by next week. You will avg $2000. comm per sale and receive 15 double confirmed leads per week. If you can't document 50K past income, don't call. Ideal candidate will have sold franchises, pools, home improvements or

Eastcoast importer & national distributor of high quality conventional machine tools has a requirement for an experienced machine tool salesperson familiar with turning & milling. The successful candidate will be responsible for all aspects of marketing established machine tools in the United States, as well as expanding imported products.
Experience in working with distributors & a successful sales record are requirements for

THE MART CONTINUED ON FOLLOWING

FIGURE 4.9 A Help Wanted Ad That Draws Attention

Next, create *desire* by amplifying on the interest factors plus the extras of the job in terms of job satisfaction, career development, travel, or similar advantages. Here it is important to write the ad with the target audience in mind. For example, tuition refund and nearby graduate schools appeal to engineers and professional people.

Finally, the ad should instigate *action*. Pick up almost any ad, and you'll find some statement like "call today," "write today for more information," or "go to your nearest travel agent and sign up for the trip." The help wanted ad shown in Figure 4.11 is a good example of this.

The increased internationalization of the U.S. economy has created many opportunities for positions with multinational firms. Figure 4.12 gives you an example of the use of ads for these broader opportunities.

Finally, even though most employers today know that discriminatory recruitment advertising is generally illegal, one study found that while not blatant, such illegal or questionable advertising still exists.[22] As you know, ads that are sex specific (calling for "man," "woman," "girl Friday," and so forth) are usually discriminatory, as are sex-related gender terms like "yard man," "repair man," or ads implying a certain age (such as "student," "recent grad," or "retiree"). Similarly, terms like "bilingual required," or "Japanese," are also questionable. As we explained in Chapter 2, employers using ads

FIGURE 4.10
A Help Wanted Ad That Creates Interest

Group Health Underwriters

WE NEED AN UNDERWRITER WHO'S AN OVERACHIEVER.

To keep pace with our rapidly expanding account base, we're looking for ambitious self starters to join the Employee Benefit Group in our Orinda office. The kind of pro's with proven records and super analytical skills.

If this sounds like you, consider joining The Travelers, a $46 billion insurance and financial services leader.

To qualify, you need at least 3 years of group health underwriting experience where you've gained a solid knowledge of employee benefits coverages. You must also have excellent communications and interpersonal skills.

In return, you'll thrive on challenging work in a dynamic environment. We've recently combined our New Business and Customer Relations Groups, creating a leaner, more aggressive force. As part of this new unit, you'll have broad exposure and career growth opportunities. Plus receive a highly competitive salary and benefits package.

So, if you're an overachiever, join The Travelers. And enjoy a career that's a cut above the rest.

Send your resume, with salary requirements, to: Sonia Mielnik, The Travelers Companies, 30-CR, SF426L1, One Tower Square, Hartford, CT 06183-7060.

Home Office: The Travelers Companies, Hartford, Connecticut. An Equal Opportunity Employer.

We Can Take You Places.

Kaiser Permanente Medical Care Program is one of the largest Health Maintenance Organizations in the nation. We offer highly skilled professionals who are committed to those in need of quality medical care to consider these excellent opportunities and experience health care at its best.

We reward our people with competitive salaries, comprehensive benefits, educational programs and the ability to transfer between facilities without losing seniority. Kaiser Permanente is proud to be an equal opportunity employer.

Hayward

For these positions in our Hayward Medical Center please apply Monday-Thursday, 10am-1pm to **Personnel Department, 27400 Hesperian Blvd., Hayward, CA 94545** or call **Ellen Gutstadt at (415) 784-4258.**

Staff Nurses

ER: Nights & On-Call
ICU/CCU: Evenings & Nights
L&D: Nights
Med/Surg: Nights
ICN: All shifts available
Float: All shifts available

Employee Health Service Nurse Practitioner: Requires 5 years of adult practitioner experience and a Master's degree.

Adult Nurse Practitioner: Requires 2 years of experience and a Master's degree.

OB Supervisor: A Bachelors degree, strong clinical and management skills combined with a clinical speciality are necessary to supervise our active tertiary, L&D, Gyn and perinatal units. RN licensure and 3 years of labor and delivery are required. MS degree preferred.

Advice Nurse: Two years of recent Med/Surg experience. Part-time and on-call positions available.

OR Nurses: Day and evening positions available with 6 months experience and a current CA RN license.

Night Shift Supervisor: To work 3 nights per week, Bachelors degree preferred.

We are also accepting applications for:
New Graduate Program: Deadline May 11th, 1987.
Re-entry Program: Deadline May 4th, 1987.

KAISER PERMANENTE
Medical Care Program

FIGURE 4.11
A Help Wanted Ad with a Call to Action
Source: BSA Advertising, San Mateo, CA.

like these usually place themselves in the position of possibly having to defend their rationale for limiting their search to the type of person called for in the ad.

INTERNATIONAL OPERATIONS MANAGEMENT TRAINEES

Tokyo, London, Zurich or Frankfurt

Salomon Brothers Inc, a major force in the international investment banking community, has excellent, entry level opportunities for hardworking, energetic individuals to join our International Operations Management Trainee Program. This program is designed to give candidates with little or no previous industry experience both product knowledge and operational management skills.

During this one year training program in our New York City headquarters, you will rotate through various operations areas and participate in a variety of special projects and assignments. The object is to develop a working knowledge of many areas through hands-on experience and participative observation. After your training is complete, you will be assigned to one of our Branch Offices in Japan, London, Zurich or Frankfort.

This position demands an independent thinker who is flexible and capable of demonstrating a high level of initiative. Your ability to develop a management perspective and demonstrate skill in performing many job functions will be important. Excellent communications skills and some fluency in Japanese, French, or German is essential. You must be able to relocate abroad.

We offer an excellent starting salary and a comprehensive benefits program, along with a unique opportunity for career growth. If you have a solid commitment to success and are ready for the challenge, send your resume, including salary history and a cover letter, in complete confidence to: **Management Trainee Recruiter, Salomon Brothers Inc, One New York Plaza, New York, N.Y. 10004.**

We are an Equal Opportunity Employer M/F

Salomon Brothers Inc

FIGURE 4.12
A Help Wanted Ad in International Management

EMPLOYMENT AGENCIES AS A SOURCE OF CANDIDATES

There are three basic types of employment agencies: (1) those operated by federal, state, or local governments; (2) those associated with nonprofit organizations; and (3) privately owned agencies.[23]

Public state employment service agencies exist in every state. They are aided and coordinated by the United States Employment Service of the U.S. Department of Labor. The service also maintains a nationwide computerized job bank to which all state employment offices are connected. Using the computer-listed job information, an agency interviewer is better able to counsel job applicants concerning available jobs in their own and other geographical areas.

Public agencies are a major source of both blue-collar and white-collar workers, but the experience of some employers with these agencies has been mixed. Applicants for unemployment insurance are required to register with these agencies. They must make themselves available for job interviews to collect their unemployment payments. Some of these people are not interested in getting back to work, and employers can end up with applicants who have little or no real desire to obtain immediate employment.

Other employment agencies are associated with nonprofit organizations. For example, most professional and technical societies have units that help their members find jobs. Similarly, many public welfare agencies try to place people who are in special categories, such as those who are physically disabled or are Vietnam veterans.

Private employment agencies are important sources of clerical, white-collar, and managerial personnel. Such agencies charge fees for each applicant they place. These fees are usually set by state law and are posted in their offices. Whether the employer or the candidate pays the fee is mostly determined by market conditions, although the trend in the last few years has been toward "fee-paid jobs." Here the employer and not the candidate pays the fees. The assumption is that the most qualified candidates are presently employed and would not be as willing to switch jobs if they had to pay the fees themselves. Many private agencies now offer (or specialize in) temporary help service and provide secretarial, clerical, or semiskilled labor on a per diem basis. These agencies can be useful in helping you cope with peak loads and fill in for vacationing employees.

There are several reasons to use an employment agency for some or all of your recruiting needs.[24] Employment agencies' ads in the *Wall Street Journal* list advantages like "cut down on your interviews," "interview only the right people," and "have recruiting specialists save you time by finding, interviewing, and selecting only the most qualified candidates for your final hiring process." Some specific situations in which you might want to turn to an agency include the following:

1. Your employer does not have its own human resource department and is therefore not geared up to do the necessary recruiting and screening.
2. Your employer has found it difficult in the past to generate a pool of qualified applicants.
3. A particular opening must be filled quickly.
4. There is a perceived need to attract a greater number of minority or female applicants.
5. The recruitment effort is aimed at reaching individuals who are currently employed and who might therefore feel more comfortable answering ads from and dealing with employment agencies rather than competing companies.

One of the main advantages of an employment agency is that it pre-screens applicants for your job, but this advantage can also backfire.[25] For example, the employment agency's screening may allow poor applicants to bypass the preliminary stages of your own selection process. Unqualified applicants may thus be sent directly to the supervisors responsible for the hiring, who may in turn naively hire them. Such errors may in turn show up in high turnover and absenteeism rates, morale problems, and low quality and productivity. Similarly, successful applicants may be blocked from entering your applicant pool by improper testing and screening at the employment agency. To help avoid such problems, two experts suggest the following:

1. **Give the agency an accurate and complete job description.** The better the employment agency understands the job or jobs to be filled, the greater the likelihood that a reasonable pool of applicants will be generated.
2. **Specify the devices or tools that the employment agency should use in screening potential applicants.** Tests, application blanks, and interviews should be a proven part of the employer's selection process. At the very least, you should know which devices the agency uses and consider their relevance to the selection process. Of particular concern would be any subjective decision-making procedures used by the agency.
3. **Where possible, periodically review data on accepted or rejected candidates.** This will serve as a check on the screening process and provide valuable information if there is a legal challenge to the fairness of the selection process.
4. **If feasible, develop a long-term relationship with one or two agencies.** It may also be advantageous to designate one person to serve as the liaison between the employer and agency. Similarly, try to have a specific contact on the agency's staff to coordinate your recruiting needs.

There are several things you can do to select the best agency for your needs. Checking with other managers or human resource people will reveal the agencies that have proved to be the most effective at filling the sorts of positions you want to have filled. Another approach is to review seven or eight back issues of the Sunday classified ads in your library to find the agencies that consistently handle the positions you want. This will help narrow the field.

Once you've narrowed the field, there are several questions you should ask to decide which agency is best for your firm: What is the background of the agency's staff? What are the levels of their education and experience and their ages? Do they have the qualifications to understand the sorts of jobs for which you are recruiting? And what is their reputation in the community and with the Better Business Bureau?

Temporary Help Agencies

Temporary help agencies (mentioned earlier) are today an increasingly important type of employment agency. One survey reported that over 84% of the questioned employers make use of such agencies and their use seems to be on the rise.[26] Most of the part-time employees hired through these agencies are used for either office/clerical or production/service jobs. The reason most often cited (by 78% of the firms) for calling in agency temporaries was to fill in for absent employees. Other important reasons are to staff short-term projects, to fill vacancies until regular employees are hired, and to fill a need for a specialized skill on a short-term basis. Among firms reporting an increase in agency temporaries, many said that labor shortages had prompted the increase, and this is a need that will probably increase over the next few years. One problem more employers will have to grapple with in the 1990s, as explained in Chapter One, may be a diminishing supply of labor. Temporary help agencies can help fill the gap by offering employees who are, for one reason or another, not interested in making long-term commitments to single employers.

Maintaining a satisfactory relationship with one of these agencies requires, first, putting time and effort into meeting with several and choosing the one that's best for you. Next, you must ensure that basic policy and procedures questions are answered. Plan on asking about or giving answers to the following:[27]

Invoicing. Get a sample copy of the company's invoice: Make sure you understand the invoicing procedure and that it fits your company's needs.

Time Sheets. Also get a sample time sheet. With temps, the time sheet that is signed by the worker's supervisor is usually in effect an agreement rather than simply a verification of hours worked.

Temp-to-Perm Policy. Specifically, what is the policy if the client wants to hire permanently one of the service's temps? Most services prefer to keep the temp on their payroll for a specific waiting period before moving (at no extra cost) the person to the client's payroll.

Recruitment of and Benefits for Temp Employees. Find out how the temp service plans to recruit employees and what sorts of benefits they pay.

Inside Staff. Learn as much as you can about how the temp service's staff (such as the people who interview applicants) match skills to position requirements and place and dispatch the temp work force.

Dress Code. Make it clear what is appropriate attire at each of your offices or plants.

Equal Employment Opportunity Statement. You should get a document from the temp service stating that it is not discriminating when filling temp orders.

Job Description Information. Set up a procedure whereby you can be reasonably sure that the temp service understands completely the nature of the job to be filled and the sort of person, in terms of skills and so forth, you want to fill it.

EXECUTIVE RECRUITERS AS A SOURCE OF CANDIDATES

Executive Recruiters (also known as "head hunters") are retained by employers to seek out top management talent for their clients. They fill jobs in the $40,000 and up category, although $50,000 is often the lower limit. The percentage of your firm's positions filled by these services might be small. However, these jobs would include your most crucial executive and technical positions. For your executive positions, head hunters may be your *only* source. Their fees are always paid by the employer.

These firms can be very useful. They have many contacts and are especially adept at contacting qualified candidates who are employed and not actively looking to change jobs. They can also keep your firm's name confidential until late into the search process. The recruiter can also save top management time by doing the preliminary work of advertising for the position and screening what could turn out to be hundreds of applicants. The recruiter's fee could actually turn out to be insignificant compared to the cost of the executive time he or she saves.

But there are some pitfalls. As an employer, it is essential to explain completely what sort of candidate is required—and why. Some recruiters are also more salespeople than professionals. They may be more interested in persuading you to hire a candidate than finding one that will really do the job. Recruiters also claim that what their client *says* he or she wants is often not really what is wanted. Therefore, be prepared for some in-depth dissecting of your request. In choosing a recruiter, one expert suggests following these guidelines:[28]

1. *Make sure the firm you choose is capable of conducting a thorough search.* Under the code of the Association of Executive Recruiting Consultants, a head hunter cannot approach the executive talent of a former client for a vacancy with a new client for a period of two years after completing a search for the former client. Former clients are thus off limits to the recruiter for a period of two years, and the recruiter must thus make his or her search from a constantly diminishing market. Particularly for the largest executive recruiting firms, it could turn out to be very difficult to deliver a top-notch candidate, since the best potential candidates may already be working for the recruiter's former clients, from which he or she is barred for two years.
2. *Ask to meet the individual who will be handling your assignment.* The person handling your search will determine the fate of the search. If this person hasn't the ability to seek out top-notch candidates aggressively and sell them on your firm, it is unlikely you will get to see the best candidates. Beware of the fact that in wooing a new client the search firm will send along its best salesperson, someone with a record of successfully signing new clients. However, this is usually not the person who will be doing the actual search.
3. *Ask how much the search firm charges.* There are several things to keep in mind here. Search firm fees range from 25% to 35% of the guaranteed annual income attaching to the position being filled. They are often payable one-third as a retainer at the outset, one-third at the end of 30 days, and one-third after 60 days and are not necessarily only paid on a contingency basis. Often, a fee is payable whether or not the search is terminated for any reason. The out-of-pocket expenses are extra and could run up to 10% to 20% of the fee itself, and sometimes more.
4. *Choose a recruiter you can trust.* This is essential because this person will not only find your firm's strengths, but its weaknesses too. It is therefore important that you find someone you can trust with what may be privileged information.
5. *Talk to a couple of their clients.* Finally, ask to be given the names of two or three companies for whom the search firm has recently completed assignments. Then, ask such questions as: Did their appraisal of the candidate seem accurate? Did they really conduct a search, or was the job simply filled from their files? And were time and care taken in developing the job specifications?[29]

As a job candidate there are several things to keep in mind when dealing with executive search firms. First, most of these firms pay little heed to unsolicited resumes, preferring instead to ferret out their own candidates. Some firms have also been known to present an unpromising candidate to a client simply to make their other one or two proposed candidates look that much better. Some eager clients may also jump the gun, checking your references and thereby undermining your present position prematurely. Also, keep in mind that executive recruiters and their clients are usually much more impressed with candidates who are obviously "not looking" for a job and that eagerness to take the job has been the downfall of many candidates.[30]

COLLEGE RECRUITING AS A SOURCE OF CANDIDATES

Many promotable candidates are originally hired through *college recruiting.* This is therefore an important source of management trainees, as well as of professional and technical employees.

There are two main problems with on-campus recruiting. First, it is usually expensive and time-consuming for the people doing the recruiting. To be done right, schedules must be set well in advance, company brochures printed, records of interviews kept, and much recruiting time spent on campus. Second, recruiters themselves are sometimes ineffective (or worse). Some recruiters are unprepared, show little interest in the candidate, and act superior. Similarly, many recruiters don't effectively screen their student candidates. For example, students' physical attractiveness often outweighs other, more valid traits and skills.[31] Some recruiters also tend to assign females to "female-type" jobs and males to "male-type" jobs.[32] One suggestion is to train recruiters before sending them to the college campus.[33]

You have two main goals as a campus recruiter. Your main function is screening and is aimed at determining whether a candidate is worthy of further consideration. Exactly which traits you look for will depend on your specific recruiting needs. However, the checklist presented in Figure 4.13 is typical. Traits to look for include motivation, communication skills, and education, appearance, and attitude.[34]

While your main function is to find and screen good candidates, your other aim is to *attract* them to your firm. Keeping the student at ease, a sincere and informal attitude, respect for the applicant as an individual and quickly sending follow-up letters can help you to sell the employer to the interviewee.

As summarized in Table 4.3, employers choose their college recruiters largely on the basis of who can do the best job of identifying good applicants and filling all vacancies. Factors in selecting schools in which to recruit include (see Table 4.4) reputation and performance of previous hires from the school.

Applicants who favorably impress recruiters are generally invited to the employer's office or plant for an on-site visit. To make sure this visit is fruitful, there are several things you can do.[35] The letter of invitation should be warm and friendly, but businesslike, and the person should be given a choice of dates to visit the company. Somebody should be assigned to meet the applicant and

TABLE 4.3 Factors in Selecting College Recruiters

RECRUITING ASPECT	STRENGTH (1–7)
Identification of high-quality applicants	5.8
Professionalism of recruiters	5.6
Filling all vacancies	5.5
Generating the right number of applicants	5.5
High performance of new recruits	5.4
High retention of new recruits	5.3
High job acceptance rates	5.0
Administrative procedures	4.7
Turn-around times	4.5
Planning and goal setting	4.5
Meeting EEO/AA targets	4.4
Program evaluation	4.3
Cost control	4.2

Source: Reprinted with permission from the March 1987 issue of *Personnel Administrator*. Copyright 1987, The American Society for Personnel Administration, 606 North Washington Street, Alexandria, VA 22314.

CAMPUS INTERVIEW REPORT

Name ________________ Anticipated Graduation Date ________

Current Address ________________
If different than placement form

Position Applied For ________________

If Applicable (Use Comment section if necessary)

Drivers License Yes ____ No ____

Any special considerations affecting your availability for relocation?

Are you willing to travel? ____ If so, what % of time ______

EVALUATION	Outstanding	Above Average	Average	Below Average
Education: Courses relevant to job? Does performance in class indicate good potential for work?				
Appearance: Was applicant neat and dressed appropriately?				
Communication Skills: Was applicant mentally alert? Did he or she express ideas clearly?				
Motivation: Does applicant have high energy level? Are his or her interests compatible with job?				
Attitude: Did applicant appear to be pleasant, people-oriented?				

COMMENTS (Use back of sheet if necessary)

Given Application Yes ____ No ____ Received Transcript Release Authorization ____

Recommendations Invite ____ Reject ____

Interviewed by: ________________ Date: ________

Campus ________________

A one-page report of an individual interview on campus. A decision to invite the student to the company for further interviewing is made as a result of this report.

FIGURE 4.13
Campus Applicant Interview Report
Source: Adapted from Joseph J. Famularo, *Handbook of Personnel Forms, Records, and Reports,* (New York: McGraw-Hill Book Company, 1982), pp. 70.

act as his or her host, preferably meeting the person at the airport or at his or her hotel. A package describing the applicant's schedule as well as other information regarding the employer—such as annual reports and description of benefits—should be waiting for the applicant at the hotel. The interviews should be carefully planned and the scheduled adhered to as closely as possible. Interruptions should be avoided; the candidate should have the undivided atten-

TABLE 4.4 Factors in Selecting Schools in Which to Recruit

TOPIC	IMPORTANCE (1–7)
Reputation in critical skill areas	6.5
General school reputation	5.8
Performance of previous hires from the school	5.7
Location	5.1
Reputation of faculty in critical skill areas	5.1
Previous job offer and acceptance rates	4.6
Past practice	4.5
Number of potential recruits	4.5
Ability to meet EEO targets	4.3
Cost	3.9
Familiarity with faculty members	3.8
SAT or GRE scores	3.0
Alma mater of CEO or other executives	3.0

7 is high; 1 is low.

Source: Reprinted with permission from the March 1987 issue of *Personnel Administrator*. Copyright 1987, The American Society for Personnel Administration, 606 North Washington Street, Alexandria, VA 22314.

tion of each person with whom he or she interviews. Luncheon should be arranged at the plant or at a nearby restaurant or club, preferably hosted by one or more other recently hired graduates with whom the applicant may feel more at ease. An offer, if any, should be made as soon as possible, preferably at the time of visit. If this is not possible, the candidate should be told when he or she can expect a decision. If an offer is made, keep in mind that the applicant may have other offers too. Frequent follow-ups to "find out how the decision process is going" or to "ask if there are any other questions" may help to tilt the applicant in your favor.

REFERRALS AND WALK-INS AS A SOURCE OF CANDIDATES

Particularly for hourly workers, "walk-ins"—direct application at your office—are a major source of applicants.[36] Some organizations encourage such applicants by mounting an "employee referrals" campaign. Announcements of openings and requests for referrals are made in the organization's bulletin and posted on bulletin boards. Prizes are offered for referrals that culminate in hirings. This sort of campaign can cut recruiting costs by eliminating advertising and agency fees. It can also result in higher quality candidates (since many people are reluctant to refer less qualified candidates). But the success of the campaign depends largely on the morale of your employees.[37] And the campaign can backfire if an employee's referral is rejected and the employee becomes dissatisfied. Using referrals exclusively may also be judged to be discriminatory when most of your current employees are either white or male.

Forty percent of the firms responding to one survey said they use some sort of employee referral system and actually hire about 15% of their people directly through such referrals by current workers. A cash award for referring candidates who are hired is the most common type of referral incentive. Naturally, the total amount a firm spends on its referral program will depend on its size. Large firms reportedly spent about $34,000 on their referral programs (including cash payments for candidates), medium companies spent about $17,000, and small ones with fewer than 500 employees, about $3,600. The cost per hire, though, is the important consideration and was uniformly low, with average per hire expenses of only $388—far below the comparable cost of an employment service.[38]

Particularly for hourly workers, walk-ins are a major source of applicants, and there are also several things to keep in mind here. As a rule, all walk-ins should be treated courteously and diplomatically since the employer's reputation in the community—not to mention the applicant's self-esteem—often rides on such diplomatic treatment. Similarly, many employers ensure that every walk-in gets a brief interview with someone in the human resource office, even if it is only to compile information on the applicant "in case a position should open in the future." Good business practice also requires that all letters of inquiry from applicants be answered promptly and courteously.

EMPLOYEE DATA BASES

Employers are increasingly turning to computerized resume registries to identify candidates. Several of these computerized registries are now functioning, but the nature of one of the first—Career Placement Registry, Inc. (CPR), of Alexandria, Virginia—provides an illustration of how they work. CPR is not an employment agency, but rather a company that compiles a data base of resumes from people who are looking for jobs. That data base is then available on-line to all businesses, service organizations, and government agencies that subscribe to DIALOG INFORMATION SERVICES, INC., a large computerized information network. (Companies that do not subscribe to DIALOG can have a resume search done by CPR at a cost of about $50 for 12 CPR-registered resumes. Any employer that is aware of CPR can thus have access to its data base of resumes, with or without subscribing to the DIALOG data base.)

CPR compiles resume data bases for both students and recent graduates, and for experienced job seekers. Each fills out data entry forms covering items such as name, address, career objectives (accounting, administration, advertising—52 in all), work experience, type of position desired, and educational background. Along with the "personal summary of qualifications," the form presents a fairly complete picture of each candidate's qualifications, occupational preferences, and desired salary range. The form is then returned to CPR along with a check for the registration fee: Students pay $12 to register, while experienced job seekers pay $25 to $45, depending upon desired salary level. Resumes remain in the CPR data base for six months, and are available to employers 24 hours a day, seven days a week. Candidates can also specify their desired geographic areas.

Employers get a manual explaining how to access the data base and can customize their search based on the skills and experience required as well as preferred geographic areas. Employers pay no subscription fee—just the cost of being on-line with DIALOG (about $95 per hour) plus a print charge of $1 per resume. The average cost to search CPR is about $20, according to the company. This particular system is available to the approximately 50,000 employers that subscribe to DIALOG INFORMATION SERVICES, INC. (it is also available through many university libraries).[39]

OLDER WORKERS AS A SOURCE OF CANDIDATES

There are fewer 18- to 25-year-olds entering the work force than there were in 1979; this has caused many employers to begin looking into alternative sources to help meet their employment needs.[40] For many employers this means "harnessing America's gray power," either by encouraging current retirement-age employees to remain with the company or actively recruiting for employees who are at or near (or beyond) retirement age.[41] Is it practical in terms of productivity to keep older workers on? Here the answer seems to be unequivocably "yes."[42] For example, age-related changes in physical ability, cognitive performance, and personality have little effect on worker's output except in the most physically demanding tasks.[43] Similarly, creative and intellectual achievements do not decline with age, absenteeism drops as age increases, older workers usually display more company loyalty than youthful workers, older workers tend to be more satisfied with their jobs and supervision, and older people can be trained or retrained as effectively as anyone.

Recruiting and attracting older workers involves any or all the sources described earlier (advertising, employment agencies, and so forth), but with one big difference. Recruiting and attracting older workers generally requires a concerted effort before the recruiting begins. The aim is to make the company an attractive place in which the older worker can work. Specifically:

Examine your personnel policies. Check to make sure your policies and procedures do not discourage recruitment of seniors or encourage valuable older people to leave. For example, employer policies like paying limited or no benefits to part-time workers, promoting early retirement, or offering no flexible work schedules will impede the recruitment and/or retention of valued older workers.

Develop flexible work options. Develop flexible work options including part-time, less than 30-hour-per-week work weeks; consulting or seasonal work; reduced hours with reduced pay; and flextime (building the workday around a core of required hours like 11 to 3, but letting workers otherwise come and go as they please). For example, at Wrigley Company, workers over 65 can progressively shorten their work schedules; another company uses "minishifts" to accommodate those interested in working less than full time.[44]

Create or redesign suitable jobs. At Xerox, unionized hourly workers over 55 with 15 years of service and those over 50 with 20 years of service can bid on jobs at lower stress and lower pay levels if they so desire.

Offer flexible benefit plans. Allowing employees to pick and choose among benefit options can be attractive to older (as well as younger) employees. For example, older employees may put added emphasis on longer vacations or on continued accrual of pension credits than do younger workers.

As one expert puts it,

> To recruit older workers, the message must be tailored to their way of thinking. Appealing to job qualities they value will attract attention. These include flexible hours, flexible benefits, autonomy, opportunity to meet new friends, and working with people their own age. You might also stress that you value their maturity and experience.[45]

SOME OTHER RECRUITING SOURCES

As the pool of viable candidates has dried up in some geographic areas, more and more employers are turning to relatively nontraditional sources of appli-

Computer Applications in Planning and Recruiting: Recruitment Sources

As companies strive to increase the usefulness of each dollar, it is important for HRM managers to investigate the return earned for recruitment costs. To facilitate this, each employment application should ask how the applicant heard of the company/position. The answers can then be coded for easy data entry. (If a computerized application is used, the applicant would choose from a list of codes.) The usual sources include a relative/friend who is already employed, newspaper, state employment service, employment agency, magazine, or radio/TV ad. If more than one newspaper is used, then use a different code for each.

Analysis of the data may show you that different types of positions are filled from different sources. If quality applicants for certain classifications (such as clerical help) come from a particular source, that is where funds should be spent for those vacancies. If few or no quality applicants come from a given source, then review the reasons for using that source. (For example, a commitment to increasing the applicant pool of minorities may be a justification for placing an ad in a paper designed for a given ethnic group, even if most quality applicants from that group are found through traditional newspapers.)

General ads, which use the company logo and an appropriate slogan, may be more cost-effective than ads that list job titles and specifications if the company has a wide variety of positions available. The comparison can be tested by asking applicants which ad brought them in.

It is also possible to retain the dates of the application so that different types of ads may be evaluated. It is expensive to place an ad with a border, for example, but in a city where there is a lot of competition for the same type of employee, the border may be necessary to emphasize the ad. Only an analysis of who responded to which ads combined with an evaluation of the quality of the applicants will determine whether or not that was money well spent. In addition, the comparative costs of the various media should be factored into the analysis. This type of analysis should be reviewed at least quarterly, so that seasonal differences may also be observed.

Research often shows that the best source of quality applicants is current employees. If your analysis agrees, this suggests the importance of keeping your employees informed of vacancies as well as the benefits of working for your company. The effectiveness of your efforts should be evaluated regularly. One way to accomplish this is to computerize a survey listing all vacancies and have it available on a portable computer at various locations. Employees should be able to step up to the screen and complete the survey (listing friends to contact) anonymously within a few minutes. Some surveys include a brief computer game at the end of the survey as a reward. This works well in locations where there are many computer-literate employees.

Whenever a company spends money, it should analyze the return from comparative sources. The computer facilitates this analysis.

cants. For example, *displaced homemakers* are women who reenter the work force after a long period out of work, or those who are forced to work due to hardship.[46] The Displaced Homemakers Network (202-628-6767) assists these individuals in obtaining training and placement. *Moonlighters* have often been avoided by employers on the assumption that employees with full-time jobs at other firms might not have the required commitment to a second employer to do their jobs responsibly. Yet more employers are finding that moonlighters usually take second jobs because they need to, and that their commitment to their second employer is certainly high enough to do their jobs well. Advertising aimed at groups such as teachers, police officers, retail clerks, and firefighters can be a good source of such employees, particularly if you can provide flexible work hours.

Other nontraditional sources are being increasingly tapped today. For example, *retired or exiting military personnel* often bring with them excellent skills. Testimonials from former military personnel who have joined your firm and ads with slogans such as "Join Our Team" can help attract these individuals. *Disabled individuals* are a most underused pool of labor. State rehabilitation agencies, Projects With Industry (write the U.S. Department of Education, 330 C Street, S.W., Switzer Building, Washington, DC, 20202), and the U.S. Veterans' Administration can be helpful in identifying such candidates.

RECRUITING METHODS USED

Some sources are more appropriate for recruiting for some types of jobs than are others. For managerial positions, 80% of the companies in one survey used newspaper ads, 75% used private employment agencies, and 65% relied on employee referrals. For professional and technical jobs, 75% used college recruiting, 75% also used ads in newspapers and technical journals, and 70% used private employment agencies. For recruiting sales personnel, 80% of the firms used newspaper ads, 75% used referrals, and 65% also used private employment agencies. For office and plant personnel, on the other hand, referrals and walk-ins were relied on by 90% of the firms, while 80% of the firms used newspaper ads and 70% used public employment agencies.[48]

GLOBAL HRM

The Global Talent Search

As companies expand their operations across national borders, it becomes increasingly important for them to tap overseas recruiting sources.[47] Gillette International, for example, has an international graduate training program aimed at identifying and developing foreign nationals for positions with the firm. Gillette subsidiaries overseas hire outstanding business students from top local universities. These foreign nationals are then trained for six months at the Gillette facility in their home countries. Some are then selected to spend 18 months being trained at the firm's Boston headquarters in areas such as finance and marketing. Those who pass muster are offered entry-level management positions at Gillette facilities in their home countries.

Coca-Cola also actively recruits foreign nationals. In addition to recruiting students abroad, it looks for foreign students studying in well-known international business programs like those at the University of South Carolina, UCLA, and the American Graduate School of International Management in Arizona.

Small Business Applications

There comes a time in the life of most small businesses when it dawns on the owner that the managers he or she has in-house are not up to the task of taking the company into the realm of expanded sales. It is then that a decision must be made regarding what kinds of people must be hired from outside and how this hiring should take place.

Should the owner decide the type of person required and recruit this person himself or herself? Or should some outside expert be brought in to help with the search?

USING EXECUTIVE RECRUITERS

The heads of most large firms often won't think twice about retaining executive search firms to conduct their search. However, small companies' owners (with their relatively limited funds) will hesitate before committing to a fee that could reach $20,000 to $30,000 (with expenses) for a $60,000 to $70,000 marketing manager. As a small business owner, however, you should keep in mind that this sort of thinking can be short sighted when you consider what your options actually are.

Engaging in a search like this by yourself is not at all like looking for secretaries, supervisors, or data entry clerks. Recruiting lower-level employees can usually be accomplished quite easily by using the techniques described earlier, for instance, by placing ads, using (relatively low-cost) employment agencies, or even by placing "help wanted" signs in your front windows. However, executive recruiting is different, and if you haven't engaged in a search like this yourself, consider what you're doing carefully before you do it. When you're hiring (or looking to hire) a key executive to help you run your firm, chances are you are not going to find the person you want by placing ads or using most of the other traditional approaches. For one thing, the person you want (or should want) is probably already employed and is probably not reading the want ads. If she does happen to glance at the ads, chances are she is happy enough where she is now not to take the effort to embark on a job search with you.

In other words, what you'll find you end up with is a drawer full of resumes of people who are, for one reason or another, out of work, or unhappy with their work, or unsuited for your job (based on the ad that you placed). It is then going to fall to you to try to find several gems in this group of resumes. You are then going to have to interview and assess these applicants yourself. This is hardly an attractive proposition, unless you happen to be an expert at interviewing and checking backgrounds (and have nothing else to do).

There are thus two problems with conducting these kinds of executive searches yourself. First, as a nonexpert, you will basically not even know where to begin: You won't know where to place or how to write the ads; you won't know where to search or who to contact; you won't know how to do the sort of job that needs to be done to interview this person in order to screen out the laggards and misfits that may well appear on the surface to be viable candidates; you also won't know enough to really do the kind of background checking that a position at this level calls for. The second big problem is that this process is going to be extremely time-consuming and will divert your attention from other duties. Many business owners find that when they consider the opportunity costs involved with doing their own searches, they are not saving any money at all. For example, the money they lose by having to manage executive recruiting costs them X number of sales calls, so that their company actually comes out behind, financially speaking. Instead of being able to assess the chemistry between yourself and three carefully screened candidates from an executive recruiter, in other words, you'll find yourself plodding through resumes and interviews with perhaps 20 or 30 possible candidates. Often, in other words, the question is not whether you can afford to use an executive recruiter, but can you afford not to?

In any event, if you do decide to do the job yourself, consider retaining the services of an industrial psychologist (ask your friends for some references, or look some up in the Yellow Pages). He or she will be able to spend four or five hours assessing the problem-solving ability, personality, interests, and energy level of the two or three candidates in which you are most interested. Although you certainly don't want the psychologist to make the decision for you, the input itself can provide an additional perspective on your candidates.

USING THE STATE JOB SERVICES

If you contact your local job service office they'll probably send a representative/counselor to discuss your staffing needs. They may even draw up short job descriptions that they'll key to the DOT and use in their recruiting efforts. Many of these job service offices are also linked with various governmental agencies that will arrange to subsidize the first three or four months of wages for certain (usually disadvantaged) groups of employees. The job service agencies are also a good source of information on prevailing wages for different classifications of jobs. In any event, if you're thinking of recruiting, it certainly pays to spend an hour or so discussing your needs with one of their counselors.

DEVELOPING AND USING APPLICATION FORMS

PURPOSE OF APPLICATION FORMS

application form The application that provides information on education, prior work record, and skills.

Once you have a pool of applicants, you can begin the process of screening and selecting the person you want to hire. For most employers the **application form** is the first step in the selection process. (Some firms first require a brief, prescreening interview.) The application form is a good means of quickly collecting verifiable and therefore fairly accurate historical data from the candidate. It usually includes information on such things as education, prior work history, and hobbies.

A filled-in form can give you four types of information.[49] First, you can make judgments on substantive matters, such as "Does the applicant have the education and experience to do the job?" Second, you can draw conclusions about the applicant's previous progress and growth, a trait that is especially important for management candidates. Third, you can also draw some tentative conclusions regarding the applicant's stability based on the person's previous

work record. (Here, however, you have to be careful not to assume that an unusual number of job changes necessarily reflects on the applicant's ability; for example, the person's last two employers may have had to lay off large numbers of employees.) Fourth, you may be able to use the data in the application to predict which candidates will succeed on the job and which will not, a point we return to later.

In practice, most organizations use several application forms. For technical and managerial personnel, for example, the form may require detailed answers to questions concerning the applicant's education and so on. The form for hourly factory workers might focus on the tools and equipment the applicant has used and the like.

EQUAL OPPORTUNITY AND APPLICATION FORMS

The Equal Employment Laws explained in Chapter 2 have particular relevance for application forms. Questions concerning race, religion, age, sex, or national origin are generally not illegal per se under federal laws although they are under some state laws. However, they *are* viewed with disfavor by the EEOC, and the burden of proof will always be on you to prove that the potentially discriminatory items are *both* related to success or failure on the job and not unfairly discriminatory. Thus, you generally can request photographs prior to employment, and even ask such potentially discriminatory questions as, "Have you ever been arrested?" The problem is that an unsuccessful applicant might establish a prima facie case of discrimination by demonstrating that the item produces an adverse impact. Having so demonstrated, the burden of proof would then shift to you to show that the item is a valid predictor of job performance and that it is applied fairly to all applicants—that, for instance, the employer checks arrest records of all applicants, not just minority applicants.

A study of 50 application forms revealed 17 types of questions that contained possible violations of federal regulations.[50] Many of the items should probably have been left out. These included questions regarding maiden name or name used previously, height and weight, age, religion, race or color, national origin, and sex. In addition, several more subtle types of potentially discriminatory questions often crept into the forms:

Education. One common violation on many of the applications was a question on the dates of attendance and graduation from various schools—academic, vocational, or professional. This question may be illegal in that it may reflect the applicant's age.

Military background. Questions concerning what branch of the armed forces the applicant served in and type of discharge are usually considered unlawful.

Arrest records. The courts have usually held that employers violate Title VII by disqualifying applicants from employment because of an arrest record. This item has an adverse impact on minorities and in most cases cannot be shown to be justified by business necessity.

Relatives. Although legal for an applicant who is a minor, it is generally not acceptable to ask questions about an applicant's relatives when the applicant is an adult because it can provide a window on the applicant's religion, race, or national origin. However, an employer can ask about any relatives who are currently employed by the employer.

Notify in case of emergency. It is generally legal to require the name, address, and phone number of a person who can be notified in case of emergency. However, asking the relationship of this person could indicate the applicant's marital status or lineage. In any event, information such as this can just as well be requested *after* the offer has been made and accepted.

Membership in organizations. Many forms ask the applicant to list memberships in clubs, organizations, or societies along with offices held. However, employers should add instructions not to include organizations that would reveal race, religion, physical handicaps, marital status, or ancestry. Those not adding such a clause may be indirectly asking for the applicant's race or religion, for instance, and thus be guilty of making an unlawful inquiry.

Physical handicaps. It is usually illegal to require the listing of an applicant's physical handicaps, defects, or past illnesses unless the application blank specifically asks only for those that "may interfere with your job performance." Similarly, it is generally illegal to ask whether the applicant has ever received worker's compensation for previous injury or illness.

Marital status. In general, the application should not ask whether an applicant is single, married, divorced, separated, or living with anyone, or the names and ages of the applicant's spouse or children. Similarly, it may be shown to be discriminatory to ask a woman for her husband's occupation and then reject the woman because, say, her husband is in the military and therefore subject to frequent relocation.

Housing. Asking whether an applicant owns, rents, or leases a house may also be discriminatory. It can adversely impact minority groups and is difficult to explain on grounds of business necessity.

One employer's approach to collecting application form information is presented in Figure 4.14. Some employers require applicants to complete two separate forms. One form contains information deemed necessary for evaluating the person's future performance, information regarding, for instance, education and work history. The second (Figure 4.15) contains information compiled and used solely by the employer for its Equal Employment and Affirmative Action Reports. (These reports are required of most employers to monitor and demonstrate compliance with equal employment opportunity law.) This form contains information on age, religion, national origin, and so forth. Note that the form in Figure 4.15 includes a cover letter. This letter makes it clear that although the applicant must complete both forms, the information on the second is used solely for EEO reporting purposes and will not be used for screening applicants.

USING APPLICATION FORMS TO PREDICT JOB PERFORMANCE

Some firms conduct statistical studies to find the relationship between (1) responses on the application form and (2) measures of success on the job. Then they use each person's application form to predict which candidates will be successful and which will not, in much the same way that employers use personnel tests for screening. Some examples follow.

Using Application Forms to Predict Job Tenure

One study was aimed at reducing turnover at a large insurance company. At the time of the study the company was experiencing a 48% turnover rate among its clerical personnel. This meant that for every two employees hired at the same time, there was about a 50–50 chance that one of the two would not remain with the company 12 months or longer.

FIGURE 4.14 Example of Application Form

EMPLOYMENT APPLICATION

As an equal opportunity employer, the firm does not discriminate in hiring or in terms and conditions of employment because of an individual's race, creed, color, sex, age, religion, disability or natural origin. The firm only hires individuals authorized for employment in the United States.

Position Applying for: ______________________

Schedule Desired: ( ) Full time ( ) Temporary ( ) Part time

___ / ___ / ___
Date of Application

PERSONAL INFORMATION

Last Name	First Name	Middle Name	Are you authorized for employment in the U.S.? [ ] Yes [ ] No
Present Street Address	City State Zip		How long have you lived there? Yrs. Mo.
Previous Street Address	City State Zip		How long did you live there? Yrs. Mo.
Home Phone Number	Social Security Number	If you are under 18 years of age, state your age:	

EDUCATION

Type of School	Name and Location of School	Degree/Area of Study	Number of Years Attended	Graduated (Check One)
HIGH SCHOOL	Name City State			Yes ☐ No ☐
JUNIOR COLLEGE	Name City State			Yes ☐ No ☐
COLLEGE	Name City State			Yes ☐ No ☐
GRADUATE SCHOOL	Name City State			Yes ☐ No ☐
OTHER	Name City State			Yes ☐ No ☐

ACADEMIC AND PROFESSIONAL ACTIVITIES AND ACHIEVEMENTS

Academic and Professional Activities and Achievements, Awards, Publications or Technical-Professional Societies. Indicate type or name. Exclude organizations which indicate race, creed, color, sex, age, religion, handicap or national origin of its members.	Date Awarded

SKILLS

Skills applicable to position applied for

PERSON TO CONTACT IN CASE OF EMERGENCY

This information is to facilitate contact in the event of an emergency and is not used in the selection process.

Full Name	Address	Phone	Relationship to you?
Place of Employment	Address	Phone	

15-10-22227 Rev. 5/92 GC 7520

(continued)

FIGURE 4.14 (continued)

EMPLOYMENT HISTORY

List employment starting with your most recent position. Account for any time during this period that you were unemployed by stating the nature of your activities. If you have less than four places of employment, include personal references to be contacted. May we contact your present employer?
[ ] Yes [ ] No

DATES	NAME AND ADDRESS OF EMPLOYER	POSITION HELD AND SUPERVISOR	LIST MAJOR DUTIES	WAGES	REASON FOR LEAVING
FROM: / MO. YR.	NAME	YOUR JOB TITLE		STARTING	
	ADDRESS				
TO: / MO. YR.		SUPERVISOR		FINAL	
	PHONE				
FROM: / MO. YR.	NAME	YOUR JOB TITLE		STARTING	
	ADDRESS				
TO: / MO. YR.		SUPERVISOR		FINAL	
	PHONE				
FROM: / MO. YR.	NAME	YOUR JOB TITLE		STARTING	
	ADDRESS				
TO: / MO. YR.		SUPERVISOR		FINAL	
	PHONE				
FROM: / MO. YR.	NAME	YOUR JOB TITLE		STARTING	
	ADDRESS				
TO: / MO. YR.		SUPERVISOR		FINAL	
	PHONE				

MISCELLANEOUS

Is there any additional information involving a change of your name or assumed name that will permit us to check your work record? If yes, please explain.

Have you ever been employed by The Firm or any of its divisions or subsidiaries before? ☐ Yes ☐ No

If yes, Please Indicate: When | Where | Position

List Names of Friends or Relatives now employed by The Firm.

Have you ever been convicted of a crime? ☐ Yes ☐ No If yes, please explain:

PLEASE READ THIS STATEMENT CAREFULLY

I hereby affirm that the information given by me on this application for employment is complete and accurate. I understand that any falsification or ommission will be immediate grounds for dismissal. I authorize a thorough investigation to be made in connection with this application concerning my character, general reputation, employment and education background, and criminal record, whichever may be applicable. I understand what this investigation may include and I hereby authorize the release of documents, and personal interviews with third parties, such as prior employers, family members, business associates, financial sources, friends, neighbors or others with whom I am acquainted. I further understand that I have the right to make a written request within a reasonable period of time for a complete and accurate disclosure of the nature and scope of the investigation.

It is understood that, as a condition of initial or continued employment, I agree to submit to such lawful examinations, medical, substance abuse, or other, as may be required by the company. The company will pay the reasonable cost of any such examination which may be required.

If I am hired, I agree that my employment and compensation can be terminated with or without cause and without notice, at any time, at the option of the firm or myself. I understand that no store manager or other representative of the firm other than a Vice-President, and in writing, has the authority to enter into any agreement for employment for any specified period of time, or to make any agreement contrary to the foregoing.

I have read and affirm as my own the above statements.

Signature Date

APPLICANTS IN THE STATE OF MARYLAND ONLY

Under Maryland law an employer may not require or demand any applicant for employment or prospective employment or any employee to submit to or take a polygraph, lie detector or similar test or examination as a condition of employment or continued employment. Any employer who violates this provision is guilty of a misdemeanor and subject to a fine not to exceed $100.

Signature Date

APPLICANTS IN THE STATE OF MASSACHUSETTS ONLY

It is unlawful in Massachusetts to require or administer a lie detector test as a condition of employment or continued employment. An employer who violates this law shall be subject to criminal penalties and civil liability.

Signature Date

EQUAL OPPORTUNITY INFORMATION

The information on the reverse side of this form is requested as part of the affirmative action program and to provide statistical information in compliance with Federal and State regulations. Your response is strictly voluntary and will not result in any adverse treatment.

(reverse side of form)

EQUAL OPPORTUNITY INFORMATION

Date of Birth ____________________ Social Security Number ____________________

Racial/Ethnic Data:

☐ Black (Non-Hispanic) ☐ Native American Indian or Alaskan ☐ Asian/Pacific Islander

☐ Hispanic ☐ White (Non-Hispanic)

Sex:

☐ Female ☐ Male

Do you have any disabling or handicapping conditions: ☐ Yes ☐ No If yes, please describe: ____________________

If a handicap has been identified, please describe any accommodations needed to assist you. ____________________

Position(s) applied for:

____________ ____________ ____________

____________ ____________ ____________

FIGURE 4.15
Equal Employment Opportunity Disclaimer Letter for Applicants

This study was done as follows: The researcher obtained the application forms of about 160 clerical employees of the company from the firm's personnel files. The researcher then split the application forms into two categories: long-tenure and short-tenure employees. He then found that some responses on the application form were highly related to job tenure. He was thereby able to use the company's application forms to predict which of the firm's new applicants would stay on the job and which would not.

The study helped the firm comply with its equal employment opportunity responsibilities. For example, some of the items on the application form (like marital status) could be viewed as potentially discriminatory. In this case the researcher was able to prove that these items did predict success or failure on the job (long tenure versus short tenure). There was thus a business necessity reason for asking them.[51]

Using Application Forms to Predict Employee Theft

Employee theft and pilferage is a serious problem, one that employers find difficult to deal with. Employee shoplifting, pilferage, and theft losses range up to $16 billion per year. Yet useful tests aimed at predicting stealing tend to be in-depth tests of personality and are difficult and time-consuming to administer and evaluate.

A possible solution is to use the application form to predict which applicants have a higher likelihood of stealing. One researcher carried out studies for both a mass merchandiser and a supermarket in Detroit. He found that responses to some application form items (like "does not own automobile" and "not living with parents") were highly related to whether or not the employee was subsequently caught stealing. He was therefore able to identify potential thieves early, before they were hired.[52]

▶ CHAPTER REVIEW

SUMMARY

1. Developing personnel plans requires three forecasts: one for personnel *requirements*, one for the *supply of outside candidates*, and one for the *supply of inside candidates*. To predict the need for personnel, first project the demand for the product or service ("sales"). Next, project the volume of production required to meet these sales estimates; finally, relate personnel needs to these production estimates.
2. Once personnel needs are projected, the next step is to build up a pool of qualified applicants. We discussed several sources of candidates, including internal sources (or promotion from within), advertising, employment agencies, executive recruiters, college recruiting, and referrals and walk-ins. Remember that it is unlawful to discriminate against any individual with respect to employment because of race, color, religion, sex, national origin, or age (unless religion, sex, or origin are bona fide occupational qualifications).
3. The initial selection screening in most organizations begins with an application form. Most managers just use these to obtain background data. However, you can use application form data to make *predictions* about the applicant's future performance. For example, application forms have been used to predict job tenure, job success, and employee theft.
4. Personnel planning and recruiting directly affect employee commitment because commitment depends on hiring employees who have the potential to develop. And the more qualified applicants you have, the higher your selection standards can be. Then, once a pool of qualified applicants is available, you can turn to selecting the best. This process usually begins with effective testing and interviewing, to which we now turn.

KEY TERMS

trend analysis
ratio analysis
scatter plot
computerized forecast
qualifications inventories
personnel replacement charts
position replacement cards
job posting
general economic conditions
local market conditions
occupational market conditions
application form

DISCUSSION QUESTIONS

1. Compare and contrast at least five sources of job candidates.
2. What types of information can an application form provide you with?
3. Discuss some of the ways in which equal rights legislation limits what you can do in recruiting.

APPLICATION EXERCISES

RUNNING CASE

Carter Cleaning Company

Getting Better Applicants

If you were to ask Jennifer and her father what the main problem was in running their firm, their answer would be quick and short: hiring good people. Originally begun as a string of coin-operated laundromats requiring virtually no skilled help, the chain grew to six stores, each heavily dependent on skilled managers, cleaner–spotters, and pressers. Employees generally have no more than a high school education (often less), and the market for them is very competitive. Over a typical weekend literally dozens of want ads for experienced pressers or cleaner–spotters can be found in area newspapers. All these people are usually paid around $6.00 per hour, and they change jobs frequently. Jennifer and her father are thus faced with the continuing task of recruiting and hiring qualified workers out of a pool of individuals they feel are almost nomadic in their propensity to move from area to area and job to job. Turnover in their stores (as in the stores of many of their competitors) often approaches 400%. "Don't talk to me about human resources planning and trend analysis," says Jennifer. "We're fighting an economic war and I'm happy just to be able to round up enough live applicants to be able to keep my trenches fully manned."

In light of this problem, Jennifer's father asked her to answer the following questions:

Questions

1. First, how would you recommend we go about reducing the turnover in our stores?
2. Provide a detailed list of recommendations concerning how we should go about increasing our pool of acceptable job applicants so we are no longer faced with the need of hiring almost anyone who walks in the door. (Your recommendations regarding the latter should include completely worded advertisements and recommendations regarding any other recruiting strategies you would suggest we use.)

CASE INCIDENT *Only Asians Wanted Here*

It was certainly a human resource manager's nightmare. IBM Japan Limited, the firm's Japanese subsidiary, seemed to have been recruiting in Japanese magazines in the United States in a discriminatory fashion. Although IBM Japan insists they never instructed their employment agency to screen out white people and black people in favor of Asians, it does seem that some discriminatory actions actually might have taken place.

The problem revolves around the employment agencies owned by a Japanese firm called Recruit. According to allegations made by Recruit USA's former staffers, Recruit USA had actually set up a fairly formal system to see to it that only Asians were hired for the IBM Japan jobs. According to one memo submitted by a former staffer to the EEOC, Recruit officials summarized the hiring policy as: "Foreigners, no good—IBM current rule . . . white people, black people—no, but second generation Japanese or others of Asian descent o.k." Another Recruit agency in the United States allegedly set up a system of code words to discriminate against people they didn't want to hire. For example, if the job order said "see Adam," it meant the client only wanted a male employee. If the job order said "talk to Haruo," it meant the client only wanted a Japanese worker. The whole story first broke when former Recruit employees described their allegation to the *San Francisco Chronicle*. Then, the EEOC got involved and more allegations were unearthed. Japanese firms and other multinationals are therefore learning the truth of the old saying, "When in Rome, do as the Romans." But in this case it means that when you're doing business in a country, you'd better know and follow the laws of the land.

Questions

1. Do you think a client (in this case IBM Japan) should be held responsible for the actions of an independent employment agency that it hires? Why or why not?
2. Do you think it would be right for a company hiring people in the United States for work overseas to discriminate, since it's not hiring people to work in the United States? Why or why not?
3. If you were the human resource manager of a company using an employment agency, how would you avoid the sort of discrimination problem described in this case?

HUMAN RESOURCE MANAGEMENT SIMULATION

Personnel planning and forecasting are key elements of the simulation. You will be furnished with the total number of operations/production employees needed each quarter and an estimate of how many employees may quit during the quarter. You will then need to hire and/or promote employees to fill jobs at all levels. If you do not hire enough people, the firm will need to schedule overtime work to fill production quotas and your team will be charged for this extra expense. Due to the nature of the work and lower-than-local wage rates, your organization has fairly high turnover when the simulation begins. Your team will need to discuss ways of decreasing this costly turnover rate.

Also, one of the incidents (C) involves recruiting for temporary positions. Because temporary employees can be a good source of permanent employees, your decisions in this regard will be important.

NOTES

1. Wayne Cascio, *Applied Psychology in Personnel Management* (Reston, VA: Reston, 1978), p. 158. See also Ernest C. Miller, "Strategic Planning Pays Off," *Personnel Journal* (April 1989), pp. 127–132; Jim Bindl, "Align Plans with Data," *Personnel Journal* (May 1989), pp. 64–71.
2. Herbert G. Heneman, Jr., and George Seitzer, "Manpower Planning and Forecasting in the Firm: An Exploratory Probe," in Elmer Burack and James Walker, *Manpower Planning and Programming* (Boston: Allyn & Bacon, 1972), pp. 102–120; Sheldon Zedeck and Milton Blood, "Selection and Placement," from *Foundations of Behavioral Science Research in Organizations* (Monterey, CA: Brooks/Cole, 1974), in J. Richard Hackman, Edward Lawler III, and Lyman Porter, *Perspectives on Behavior in Organizations* (New York: McGraw-Hill, 1977), pp. 103–119. For a discussion of equal employment implications of work force planning, see James Ledvinka, "Technical Implications of Equal Employment Law for Manpower Planning," *Personnel Psychology*, Vol. 28 (Autumn 1975).
3. Roger Hawk, *The Recruitment Function* (New York: American Management Association, 1967). See also Paul

Pakchar, "Effective Manpower Planning," *Personnel Journal*, Vol. 62, no. 10 (October 1983), pp. 826–830.
4. Richard B. Frantzreb, "Human Resource Planning: Forecasting Manpower Needs," *Personnel Journal*, Vol. 60, no. 11 (November 1981), pp. 850–857. See also John Gridley, "Who Will Be Where When? Forecast the Easy Way," *Personnel Journal*, Vol. 65 (May 1986), pp. 50–58.
5. Based on an idea in Elmer H. Burack and Robert D. Smith, *Personnel Management: A Human Resource Systems Approach* (St. Paul, MN: West, 1977), pp. 134–135. Reprinted by permission. Copyright 1977 by West Publishing Co. All rights reserved.
6. Glenn Bassett, "Elements of Manpower Forecasting and Scheduling," *Human Resource Management*, Vol. 12, no. 3 (Fall 1973), pp. 35–43, reprinted in Richard Peterson, Lane Tracy, and Allan Cabelly, *Systematic Management of Human Resources* (Reading, MA: Addison-Wesley, 1979), pp. 135–146.
7. For an example of a computerized system in use at Citibank, see Paul Sheiber, "A Simple Selection System Called 'Job Match,'" *Personnel Journal*, Vol. 58, no. 1 (January 1979), pp. 26–54.
8. For discussions of skill inventories, see, for example, John Lawrie, "Skill Inventories: Pack for the Future," *Personnel Journal* (March 1987), pp. 127–130; John Lawrie, "Skill Inventories: A Developmental Process," *Personnel Journal* (October 1987), pp. 108–110.
9. Alfred Walker, "Management Selection Systems That Meet the Challenge of the 80s," *Personnel Journal*, Vol. 60, no. 10 (October 1981), pp. 775–780.
10. Donald Harris, "A Matter of Privacy: Managing Personnel Data in Computers," *Personnel* (February 1987), pp. 34–39.
11. Amiel Sharon, "Skills Bank Tracks Talent, Not Training," *Personnel Journal* (June 1988), pp. 44–49.
12. This section is based on Harris, "A Matter of Privacy."
13. John Campbell and others, *Managerial Behavior, Performance, and Effectiveness* (New York: McGraw-Hill, 1970), p. 23. See also Allan Halcrow, "Recruitment by Any Other Name Is Turnover," *Personnel Journal*, Vol. 65 (August 1986), pp. 10–15.
14. David Dahl and Patrick Pinto, "Job Posting, an Industry Survey," *Personnel Journal*, Vol. 56, no. 1 (January 1977), pp. 40–41.
15. Jeffrey Daum, "Internal Promotion—Psychological Asset or Debit? A Study of the Effects of Leader Origin," *Organizational Behavior and Human Performance*, Vol. 13 (1975), pp. 404–413.
16. Arthur R. Pell, *Recruiting and Selecting Personnel* (New York: Regents, 1969), pp. 10–12.
17. Ibid., p. 11.
18. This is based on Gary Dessler, *Winning Commitment* (New York: McGraw-Hill Book Company, 1993).
19. Federal Express Employee Handbook, p. 28.
20. Sara Rynes, Robert Breta, Jr., and Barry Gerhart, "The Importance of Recruitment in Job Choice: A Different Way of Looking," *Personnel Psychology*, Vol. 44, no. 3 (Autumn 1991), pp. 487–521.
21. Pell, *Recruiting and Selecting Personnel*, pp. 16–34. See also Barbara Hunger, "How to Choose a Recruitment Advertising Agency," *Personnel Journal*, Vol. 64, no. 12 (December 1985), pp. 60–62. For an excellent review of ads, see Margaret Magnus, *Personnel Journal*, Vols. 64 and 65, no. 8 (August 1985 and 1986), and Bob Martin, "Recruitment Ad Ventures," *Personnel Journal*, Vol. 66 (August 1987), pp. 46–63.
22. John P. Kohl and David B. Stephens, "Wanted: Recruitment Advertising That Doesn't Discriminate," *Personnel* (February 1989), pp. 18–26.
23. Pell, *Recruiting and Selecting Personnel*, pp. 34–42.
24. Stephen Rubenfeld and Michael Crino, "Are Employment Agencies Jeopardizing Your Selection Process?" *Personnel*, Vol. 58 (September–October 1981), pp. 70–77.
25. Ibid.
26. Bureau of National Affairs, "Part-Time and Other Alternative Staffing Practices," *Bulletin to Management*, June 23, 1988, pp. 1–10.
27. This is based on or quoted from Nancy Howe, "Match Temp Services to Your Needs," *Personnel Journal* (March 1989), pp. 45–51.
28. John Wareham, *Secrets of a Corporate Headhunter* (New York: Playboy Press, 1981), pp. 213–225.
29. Pell, *Recruiting and Selecting Personnel*, pp. 56–63; David L. Chicci and Carl Knapp, "College Recruitment from Start to Finish," *Personnel Journal*, Vol. 59, no. 8 (August 1980), pp. 653–657.
30. Allen J. Cox, *Confessions of a Corporate Headhunter* (New York: Trident Press, 1973).
31. Robert Dipboye, Howard Fronkin, and Ken Wiback, "Relative Importance of Applicant Sex, Attractiveness, and Scholastic Standing in Evaluation of Job Applicant Resumes," *Journal of Applied Psychology*, Vol. 61 (1975), pp. 39–48. See also Laura M. Graves, "College Recruitment: Removing the Personal Bias from Selection Decisions," *Personnel* (March 1989), pp. 48–52.
32. Ibid., pp. 39–48.
33. Ibid. See also, "College Recruiting," in *Personnel* (May–June 1980).
34. See, for example, Richard Becker, "Ten Common Mistakes in College Recruiting—or How to Try Without Really Succeeding," *Personnel*, Vol. 52, no. 2 (March–April 1975), pp. 19–28. See also Sara Rynes and John Boudreau, "College Recruiting in Large Organizations: Practice, Evaluation, and Research Implications," *Personnel Psychology*, Vol. 39 (Winter 1986), pp. 729–57.
35. Pell, *Recruiting and Selecting Personnel*, pp. 62–63.
36. Ibid.
37. Ibid., p. 13.
38. The study on employment referrals was published by Bernard Hodes Advertising, Dept. 100, 555 Madison Avenue, New York, N.Y. 10022. See also Allan Halcrow, "Employees Are Your Best Recruiters," *Personnel Journal* (November 1988), pp. 43–49.
39. For further information on this service, you can call CPR at 1-800-368-3093. Their complete address is Career Placement Registry, Inc., 302 Swann Avenue, Alexandria, VA 23301.
40. Harold E. Johnson, "Older Workers Help Meet Employment Needs," *Personnel Journal* (May 1988), pp. 100–105.
41. This is based on Robert W. Goddard, "How to Harness America's Gray Power," *Personnel Journal* (May 1987), pp. 33–40.
42. Glenn McEvoy and Wayne Cascio, "Cumulative Evidence of the Relationship Between Employee Age and Job Performance," *Journal of Applied Psychology*, Vol. 74, no. 1 (February 1989), pp. 11–17.
43. Goddard, "How to Harness America's Gray Power," p. 33.
44. For this and other examples here, see Goddard, "How to Harness America's Gray Power."
45. *B & E Review* (July–September 1990), p. 7.
46. The remainder of this paragraph is based on Robert W. Wendover, "Smart Hiring," *B & E Review* (July–September 1990), pp. 6–15.

47. This is based on Jennifer Laabs, "The Global Talent Search," *Personnel Journal* (August 1991), pp. 38–42.
48. *Recruiting Practices*, Personnel Policy Forum, Survey No. 462 (Washington, DC: Bureau of National Affairs, August 1979), p. 114; reprinted in Stephen P. Robbins, *Personnel: The Management of Human Resources* (Englewood Cliffs, NJ: Prentice Hall, 1982), p. 115. For another view of this see Phillip Swaroff, Alan Bass, and Lizabeth Barclay, "Recruiting Sources: Another Look," *Journal of Applied Psychology*, Vol. 70, no. 4 (1985), pp. 720–728. See also David Caldwell and W. Austin Stivey, "The Relationship Between Recruiting Source and Employee Success: An Analysis by Race," *Personnel Psychology*, Vol. 36, no. 1 (Spring 1983), pp. 67–72.
49. Pell, *Recruiting and Selecting Personnel*, pp. 96–98. See also Wayne Cascio, "Accuracy of Verifiable Biographical Information Blank Responses," *Journal of Applied Psychology*, Vol. 60 (December 1975), for a discussion of accuracy of bio data.
50. Richard Lowell and Jay Deloach, "Equal Employment Opportunity: Are You Overlooking the Application Form?" *Personnel*, Vol. 59 (July–August 1982), pp. 49–55.
51. Wayne Cascio, "Turnover, Biographical Data, and Fair Employment," *Journal of Applied Psychology*, Vol. 61 (October 1976).
52. Richard Rosenbaum, "Predictability of Employee Theft Using Weighted Application Blanks," *Journal of Applied Psychology*, Vol. 61 (1976), pp. 94–98.

CHAPTER 5

EMPLOYEE TESTING AND SELECTION

OVERVIEW

One of your most important management jobs involves recruitment and placement—finding the right person for the right job and hiring him or her. This requires screening candidates, and so we have discussed one important screening technique (application forms). But, as explained in this chapter, most managers also use other selection tools for screening. These include tests, prior work experience, assessment centers, and reference checks. In the following chapter, we then explain a final selection technique, interviewing. Once you select and hire the person you want, your next step will be to orient and train that person. We will discuss these subjects in the following chapters. When you finish studying this chapter, you should be able to discuss basic testing concepts including validity and reliability; explain how to validate a test; describe the pros and cons of work samples, simulations, and management assessment centers; and explain how to conduct a reference check.

THE SELECTION PROCESS

WHY THE SELECTION PROCESS IS IMPORTANT

Employee selection is important for three reasons. First, your own performance will always hinge in part on your subordinates' performance. Employees who haven't the right abilities won't perform effectively, and your performance will therefore suffer.[1] The time to screen out undesirables is thus before they are in the door, not after.

Second, effective screening is important because of what it costs to recruit and hire employees. For example, one expert estimates that the total cost of hiring a manager who earns $60,000 a year is about $47,000, once search fees, interviewing time, reference checking, and travel and moving expenses are taken into consideration.[2] The cost of hiring nonexecutive employees, although not as high proportionally, is still high enough to warrant keeping these costs to a minimum.

Third, good selection is important because of the legal implications of doing it poorly. For one thing, as we explained in Chapter 2, equal employment legislation, guidelines, and court decisions require that you systematically evaluate the effectiveness of your selection procedures to ensure that you are not unfairly discriminating against minorities or women. Second, employers increasingly are being held liable for damages stemming from their "negligent hiring" of workers who subsequently commit criminal acts on the job.[3] Specifically, courts are increasingly finding employers liable for damages when employees with criminal records or other problems took advantage of access to customer homes or other similar opportunities to commit crimes.

Several cases illustrate the problem. In one, *Ponticas* v. *K.M.S. Investments,* an apartment manager with a passkey entered a woman's apartment and assaulted her. Negligence by the owner and the operator of the apartment complex in hiring the apartment manager was found to be the cause of the woman's personal injury. In another case, *Henley* v. *Prince, Georges County,* an employee who turned out to have a criminal background murdered a young boy; management, which knew of the man's prior murder conviction, was held liable.

Two experts argue that the recent increase in negligent hiring cases underscores the need for employees to "read between the lines" and carefully identify what the human requirements are when conducting the job analysis.[4] Specifically, "Negligent hiring litigation points out that ability to do the job is interpreted beyond the type of information typically collected in a job analysis."[5] For example, "'Non-rapist' is unlikely to appear as a required knowledge, skill, or ability in a job analysis of a repair person. Yet, it is that type of job-related requirement that has been the focus of many negligent hiring suits."[6] Employers therefore must navigate the tricky waters of a narrow channel in designing their testing programs. On the one hand, employers should identify the traits required for effective performance. However, "performance" must be  defined not just in terms of the skills to do the job, but also in terms of broader traits such as the trust that is part of many jobs, such as door-to-door salesperson. On the other hand, it could be discriminatory to conclude that candidates with conviction records are automatically not right for certain jobs. Thus, the fear of negligent hiring must be balanced with EEO concerns.

BASIC TESTING CONCEPTS

VALIDITY

A test is basically a sample of a person's behavior. However, with some tests, the behavior being sampled is more clearly recognizable than it is with others. Thus, in some cases the behavior you are sampling is obvious from the test itself. A typing test is an example. Here the test clearly corresponds to some on-the-job behavior, in this case, typing. At the other extreme, there may be no apparent relationship between the items on the test and the behavior. This is the case with projective personality tests, for example. Thus, in the *thematic apperception* test illustrated in Figure 5.1, the person is asked to explain how he or she interprets the blurred picture. That interpretation is then used to draw conclusions about the person's personality and behavior.

In summary, some tests are more clearly representative of the behavior they are supposed to be measuring than others. Because of this, it is much harder to "prove" that some tests are measuring what they are purported to measure—that they're *valid.*

validity
The accuracy with which a test, interview, etc. measures what it purports to measure or fulfills the function it was designed to fill.

A test's **validity** answers the question: "What does this test measure?"[7] With respect to testing for employee selection, the term *validity* often refers to evidence that the test is job related, in other words, that performance on the test is a *valid predictor* of subsequent performance on the job. A selection test must above all be valid since, without proof of its validity, there is no logical or legally permissible reason to continue using it to screen job applicants. In employment testing, there are two main ways to demonstrate a test's validity, *criterion validity* and *content validity.*[8]

Criterion Validity

criterion validity
A type of validity based on showing that scores on the test ("predictors") are related to job performance ("criterion").

Demonstrating **criterion validity** basically involves demonstrating that those who do well on the test also do well on the job, and that those who do poorly on the test do poorly on the job.[9] Thus, the test has validity to the extent that the people with higher test scores perform better on the job. In psychological measurement, a *predictor* is the measurement (in this case, the test score) that you are trying to relate to a *criterion*, like performance on the job. The term *criterion validity* comes from that terminology.

Content Validity

content validity
A test that is "content valid" is one in which the test contains a fair sample of the tasks and skills actually needed for the job in question.

You demonstrate the **content validity** of a test by showing that the test constitutes a fair sample of the content of the job.[10] The basic procedure here is to identify the content of the job in terms of job behaviors that are critical to its performance and then randomly select and include a sample of those tasks and behaviors in the tests. A typing test used to hire a typist is an example. If the typing test is a representative sample of the typist's job, then the test is probably content valid.

Demonstrating content validity sounds easier than it is in practice. Demonstrating that the tasks the person performs on the test are in fact a comprehensive and random sample of the tasks performed on the job and demonstrating

JUST LOOK AT THE PICTURE BRIEFLY (10 TO 15 SECONDS),
TURN THE PAGE, AND WRITE THE STORY IT SUGGESTS.

FIGURE 5.1
Example of a TAT Card

Source: John Atkinson, ed., *Motives in Fantasy, Action, and Society* (New York: Van Nostrand Reinhold, 1958).
Author's note: This test is currently in use.

that the conditions under which the test is taken resemble the work situation are not always easy. For many jobs, other evidence of a test's validity—such as its criterion validity—must therefore be demonstrated as well.

RELIABILITY

A test has two important characteristics, *validity* and *reliability.* Validity is the more important characteristic because if you cannot ascertain what the test is measuring, it is of little use to you.

reliability
The characteristic which refers to the consistency of scores obtained by the same person when retested with the identical or equivalent tests.

Reliability is the second important characteristic of a test and refers to its consistency. It is "the consistency of scores obtained by the same person when retested with the identical tests or with an equivalent form of a test."[11] A test's consistency is very important; if a person scores 90 on an intelligence test on a Monday and 130 when retested on Tuesday, you probably wouldn't have much faith in the test.

There are several ways to estimate a test's stability or reliability. You could administer the same test to the same people at two different points in time, comparing their test scores at time 2 with their scores at time 1: This would be a *retest estimate.* Or you could administer a test and then administer what experts believe to be an equivalent test at a later date: This would be an *equivalent-form* estimate.

A test's *internal consistency* is another measure of its reliability. For example, suppose you have 10 items on a test of vocational interests, all of which are supposed to measure, in one way or another, the person's interest in working out of doors. Here, you could administer the test and then statistically analyze the degree to which responses to these 10 items vary together. This would provide a measure of the internal reliability of the test and is referred to as an *internal comparison* estimate. This is one reason you often find questions that apparently are repetitive on some test questionnaires.

What could cause a test to be unreliable? Imagine for a moment that you are asked to take a test in, say, economics, and then you retake an equivalent test, say, one month later. You find that your score changes dramatically.

There are at least four main *sources of error* that might explain this anomaly. First, the items may do a poor job of *sampling* the material; for example, test 1 focuses more on Chapters 1, 3, 5, and 7, while test 2 focuses more on Chapters 2, 4, 5, and 8. Furthermore, one or more of the questions (items) may not do a good job of even measuring what it is supposed to measure—such as your knowledge of, say, indifference curves. Second, there may be errors due to *chance response tendencies*. For example, the test itself is so boring or hard or inconsequential that you give up and start answering questions at random. (Highly personal questions on a psychological test might elicit the same response.) Third, there might be errors due to changes in the *testing conditions*: For instance, the room next month may be very noisy. And, finally, there could be *changes in the person* taking the test—in this case, you may have studied more, or forgotten more, or your mood may have changed. In any event you can see that many factors can affect a test's stability, its *reliability*. (Reliability and validity are discussed in more detail in the appendix to this chapter.)

HOW TO VALIDATE A TEST

What makes a test like the Graduate Record Examination useful for college admissions directors? What makes a mechanical comprehension test useful for a manager trying to hire a machinist?

The answer to both questions is usually that people's scores on these tests have been shown to be *predictive* of how they perform. Thus, other things being equal, students who score high on the graduate admissions tests also do better in graduate school. Applicants who score higher on the mechanical comprehension test perform better as machinists.

In order for any selection test to be useful, an employer has to be fairly sure that scores on the test are related in a predictable way to performance on the job. In other words, it is imperative that you *validate* the test before using it: The employer has to be sure that test scores are a good *predictor* of some *criterion* like job performance. The *validation process* usually requires the expertise of an industrial psychologist and is coordinated by the human resource department. Line management's contribution comes in clearly describing the job and its requirements. That way the human requirements of the job, and the job's standards of performance, are clear to the psychologist. This *validation process* consists of five steps.

Step 1. Analyze the Job

Your first step is to analyze the job and write job descriptions and job specifications. Here you specify the human traits and skills you believe are required for adequate job performance. For example, must an applicant be aggressive? Is shorthand required? Must the person be able to assemble small, detailed compo-

nents? These requirements become your *predictors*. They are the human traits and skills you believe to be predictive of success on the job. In this first step, you also have to define what you mean by "success on the job," since it is this success for which you want predictors. The standards of success are called *criteria*. You could focus on *production-related criteria* (quantity, quality, etc.), *personnel data* (absenteeism, length of service, etc.), or *judgments* (of persons like supervisors). For an assembler's job, predictors to be tested for might include manual dexterity and patience. Criteria that you would hope to predict with your test might include quantity produced per hour and number of rejects produced per hour.

Some employers make the mistake of carefully choosing predictors (such as manual dexterity) while virtually ignoring the question of which performance criteria are best. Doing so can be a mistake. An illustrative study involved 212 employees of a gas utility company. In this study, the researchers found a significant relationship between the test battery that was used as a predictor and two performance criteria: supervisor ratings of performance and objective productivity indices. However, there was virtually no relationship between the same test battery and an objective quality index or employee self-ratings.[12]

Candidates for the position of data transcriber for the 1990 Census take a standardized test at the facility in Austin, Texas.

Step 2. Choose Your Test

Next choose tests that you think measure the attributes (predictors) that are important to job success. This choice is usually based on experience, previous research, and "best guesses," and you usually won't start off with just one test. Instead, you choose several tests, combining them into a *battery*. This is aimed at measuring a variety of possible predictors, such as aggressiveness, extroversion, and numerical ability. For the assembler's job, a possibility for one test would be the Stromberg Dexterity Test illustrated in Figure 5.4. (See page 165.)

Step 3. Administer Test

Next, administer the selected test to your employees. You have two choices here. First, you can administer the tests to employees presently on the job. You then would compare their test scores with the *current* performance; this is called con*current* validation. Its main advantage is that data on performance are readily available. The disadvantage is that the current employees *may not be representative of new applicants* (who of course are really the ones you are interested in developing a screening test for). For example, current employees have already received on-the-job training and have been screened by your existing selection techniques.[13]

The most dependable way to validate a test is called *predictive validation*. Here the test is administered to *applicants* before they are hired. Then these applicants are hired using only existing selection techniques, not the results of the new tests you are developing. Then, after these people have been on the job for some time, you measure their performance and compare it to their earlier tests. You can then determine if their performance on the test could have been used to predict their subsequent job performance. In the case of our assembler's job, the ideal situation would be to administer the Stromberg Dexterity Test to all applicants. Then ignore the test results and hire assemblers as you usually do. Then, perhaps six months later measure your new assemblers' performance (quantity produced per hour, number of rejects per hour) and compare this performance to their test scores (see step 4).

Step 4. Relate Test Scores and Criteria

The next step is to determine if there is a significant relationship between scores (the predictor) and performance (the criterion). The usual way to do this is to determine the statistical relationship between (1) scores on the test and (2) performance through *correlation analysis*, which shows the degree of statistical relationship.

expectancy chart A graph showing the relationship between test scores and job performance for a large group of people.

If performance on the test and on the job are correlated, you can develop an **expectancy chart**. This presents graphically the relationship between the test and job performance. To do this, split the employees into, say, five groups according to their test scores, with those scoring the highest fifth on the test, the second highest fifth, and so on. Then compute the percentage of high job performance *in each of these five test score groups* and present the data in an expectancy chart like that in Figure 5.2. As illustrated, this shows the likelihood of an employee's being rated a high performer if he or she scores in each of these five test score groups. Thus, a person scoring in the top fifth of the test has a 97% chance of being rated a high performer, while one scoring in the lowest fifth has only a 29% chance of being rated a high performer.[14]

Step 5. Cross-validation and Revalidation

Before putting the test into use, you may want to check it by *cross-validating* it by again performing steps 3 and 4 on a new sample of employees. At a minimum, an expert should revalidate the test periodically.

Note that the procedure you would use to demonstrate *content validity* differs from that used to demonstrate *criterion validity*. Content validity tends to emphasize judgment. Here a careful job analysis is carried out to identify the work behaviors required. Then a sample of those behaviors is combined into a

FIGURE 5.2
Expectancy Chart

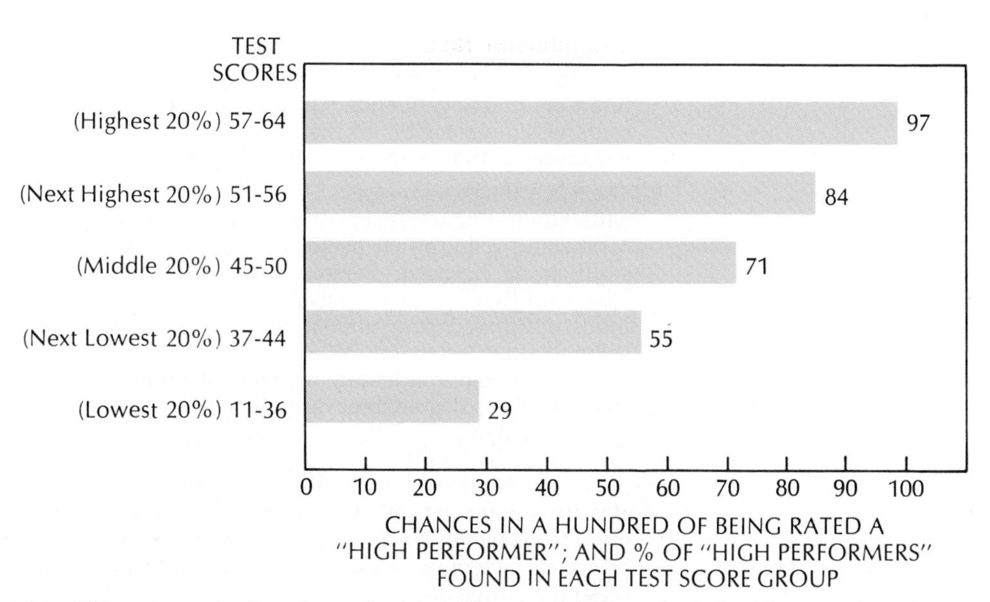

Note: This expectancy chart shows the relation between scores made on the Minnesota Paper Form Board and rated success of junior draftspersons. Example: Those who score between 37 and 44 have a 55% chance of being rated above average; those scoring between 57 and 64 have a 97% chance. Therefore, the higher the score (probably), the higher the person's performance rating on the job. This is because in previous tests 55% of those with scores between 37 and 44 were high performers, while 97% of those with scores between 57 and 64 were high performers.

test that should then be content valid. A typing and shorthand test for a secretary would be an example. *The fact that the test is a comprehensive sample of actual, observable, on-the-job behaviors is what lends the test its content validity.* Criterion validity is determined through the five-step procedure previously described.

TESTING GUIDELINES

Here are some basic guidelines[15] for setting up your testing program:[16]

1. *Use tests as supplements.* Do not use tests as your only selection technique; instead, use them to supplement other techniques like interviews and background checks. There are several reasons for this. First, tests are not infallible. Even in the best of cases the test score usually only accounts for about 25% of the variation in the measure of performance. In addition, tests are often better at telling you which candidates will fail than which will succeed.
2. *Validate the tests in your organization.* Both *legal requirements* and *good testing practice* demand that the test be validated in your own organization. The fact that the same tests have been proven valid in similar organizations is *not* sufficient.
3. *Analyze all your current hiring and promotion standards.* Ask questions such as: "What proportion of minority and nonminority applicants are being rejected at each stage of the hiring process?" and "Why am I using this standard—what does it mean in terms of actual behavior on the job?" Remember that the burden of proof is always on you to prove that the predictor (such as intelligence) is related to success or failure on the job.
4. *Keep accurate records.* It is important that you keep accurate records of why each applicant was rejected. For purposes of the Equal Employment Opportunity Commission, a general note such as "not sufficiently well qualified" would not be enough. State, as objectively as possible, why the candidate was rejected. Remember that your reasons for rejecting the candidate may be subject to validation at a later date.
5. *Begin your validation program now.* If you don't currently use tests, or if you use tests that haven't been validated, begin your validation study now. Preferably make this a predictive validation study: Administer the tests to applicants, hire the applicants without referring to the test scores, and then (at a later date) correlate their test scores with their performance on the job.
6. *Use a certified psychologist.* The development, validation, and use of selection standards (including tests) generally requires the assistance of a qualified psychologist. Most states require that persons who offer psychological services to the public be certified or licensed. Persons engaged in test validation often belong to the *American Psychological Association (APA)* and probably to *Division 14 (Division of Industrial and Organizational Psychology)* as well. Other qualified psychologists belong to the *Society for Industrial and Organizational Psychologists (SIOP)* but not to the APA. Most industrial and organizational psychologists hold a Ph.D. degree (the bachelor's degree is never sufficient). A potential consultant should be able to provide evidence of similar work and experience in the area of test validation. He or she should be familiar with the standards for psychological tests and the manual published by the APA. And the consultant should demonstrate familiarity with existing federal and state laws and regulations applicable to equal rights. The names of previous clients should be provided so you can verify references. Competent professionals generally will not make any claims for extraordinary results or guarantee certain, positive outcomes.
7. *Test conditions are important.* Administer your tests in areas that are reasonably private, quiet, well lighted, and ventilated, and all applicants should take the tests under the same test conditions. Once completed, test results should be held in the strictest confidence and only given to individuals who have a legitimate need for the information and also have the ability to understand and interpret the scores.

▸ Ethical and Legal Questions in Testing

EQUAL EMPLOYMENT OPPORTUNITY IMPLICATIONS FOR TESTING

We've seen that various federal and state laws bar discrimination with respect to race, color, age, religion, sex, disability, and national origin.[17] With respect to testing, these laws boil down to this: (1) You must be able to *prove* that your tests were related to success or failure on the job (validity), and (2) you must *prove* that your tests didn't unfairly discriminate against either minority or non-minority subgroups. The burden of proof rests with you; you are presumed "guilty" until proven innocent and must demonstrate the validity and selection fairness of the allegedly discriminatory item.

Interestingly, even before *Wards Cove* (which, recall from chapter 2, made it easier for a time for employers to avoid equal employment litigation) it appears that a minority of employers were validating their tests. The main reason for noncompliance was apparently not that the guidelines were unfeasible. Instead, compliance can be an expensive inconvenience for the employer. For instance, you have to do a validation study, develop a good performance appraisal method, and do a thorough job analysis.

Yet you can't avoid EEO laws just by phasing out your testing program. EEO guidelines and laws apply to any and all screening or selection devices, including interviews, applications, and references. In other words, the same burden of proving job relatedness falls on interviews and other techniques (including performance appraisals) that falls on tests. In other words, you could be asked to prove the validity and fairness of *any* screening or selection tool that has been shown to have an adverse impact on a protected group.[18] A detailed explanation of test unfairness is presented in the appendix to this chapter.

Your Alternatives

Let's review where we are at this point. Assume that you've used a test and that a rejected minority candidate has demonstrated adverse impact to the satisfaction of a court. How might the person have done this? One way was to show that the selection rate for, say, his racial group was less than four-fifths of that for the group with the highest selection rate. Thus, if 90% of white applicants passed the test but only 60% of blacks, then (since 60% is less than four-fifths of 90%) adverse impact exists.

You would then have three alternatives. One is to choose an alternative selection procedure that does not have an adverse impact. In other words, you could choose a different test or selection procedure, one that does not adversely impact minorities or women.[19]

The second alternative is to produce an explanation of why the test is valid, in other words, why it is a valid predictor of performance on the job. Ideally, you would do this by conducting your own validation study. Under certain circumstances you may also try to show the validity of the test by using information on the test's validity collected elsewhere.[20] In any event, the plaintiff would then have to prove that your explanation for using the test is inadequate.

A third alternative—in this case aimed at avoiding adverse impact, rather than reacting to it—is to monitor the selection device to determine if it has disparate impact. If so, you would then have to determine if the test is valid. In the absence of disparate impact it's generally permissible to use selection devices that may not be valid or otherwise job related—but why would you want to!

Individual Rights of Test Takers and Test Security

Under the American Psychological Association's standard for educational and psychological tests, test takers have certain rights to privacy and information.[21] First, the test taker has the right to the confidentiality of the test results and the right to informed consent regarding the use of these results. Second, the person has the right to expect that only people qualified to interpret the scores will have access to them or that sufficient information will accompany the scores to ensure their appropriate interpretation. Third, he or she has the right to expect that the test is equally fair to all test takers in the sense of being equally familiar.

The tests, in other words, must be *secure*; no person taking the tests should have prior information concerning the questions or answers.[22]

The Issue of Privacy

In addition to the APA's standard, embedded in U.S. law are certain protections regarding an employee's rights to privacy.

At the federal level, there are few restrictions on an employer's right to disseminate information about employees either inside or outside the company. The U.S. Constitution does not expressly provide for the right to privacy, but various U.S. Supreme Court decisions probably protect individuals from intrusive *governmental* action in a variety of contexts.[23] Specifically, if you are a federal employee or (in many jurisdictions) a state or local government employee, there are limits on disclosure of personnel information to other individuals or agencies within or outside the agency.[24] The Federal Privacy Act (although not applicable to employees of private firms) provides an indication of the sorts of informational privacy issues that legislatures are concerned about. The act (1) requires that an agency maintain only such information as is relevant and necessary to accomplish its purpose; (2) requires to the greatest extent practical that the information come directly from the individual; (3) establishes safeguards to ensure the security and confidentiality of records; and (4) gives federal employees the right to inspect personnel files and limits the disclosure of personnel information without an employee's consent.[25]

Beyond this the common law of torts does provide some limited protection as far as disclosing information about employees to people outside the company. The most well-known application here involves defamation (either libel or slander). This basically means that if your employer or former employer discloses information that is false and defamatory and that causes you serious injury, you may be able to sue for defamation of character.[26] In general, though, this is easier said than done. Employers (in providing, say, a recommendation) generally cannot be sued successfully for defamation unless the employee can show "malice" (that is, ill will, culpable recklessness, or disregard of the employee's rights and this is usually hard to prove).[27] An employer may also be sued for interference with business or prospective business relations if it willfully provides information to another for the purpose of harming a former employee. In addition, you should not disclose to another company that a former employee had filed a charge of discrimination or a lawsuit alleging discrimination or other labor law violation since that has been held to constitute unlawful retaliation.

On the other hand, common law as it applies to invasion of privacy has been recognized in various forms in some states. Such cases usually revolve around "public disclosure of private facts." They involve employees suing employers for disclosing to a large number of people true but embarrassing private facts about the employee. For example, your employee personnel file may (and often will) contain information about private facts regarding your health, test results, or job performance you may not want disclosed outside the firm. In invasion-of-privacy suits like these, truth is no defense. One case involved a supervisor in a shouting match with an employee. The supervisor yelled out that the employee's wife had been having sexual relations with certain people. Both the employee and his wife sued the employer for invasion of privacy. The jury found that the employer was liable for invasion of the couple's privacy and awarded damages to both of them. In addition, the jury awarded damages for the couple's additional claim that the supervisor's conduct amounted to an intentional infliction of emotional distress.[28] The point is that in these increasingly litigious times more discretion is required than some employers have shown in the past.

Some guidelines to follow here include

1. **Supervisory training** is very important.[29] Employers should meet with everyone from front-line supervisors up through middle and upper management. Emphasize the importance of confidentiality with regard to information about employees.
2. Next, adopt a policy (particularly in areas like drug testing) that only those who "need to know" will share the information. For example, if an employee has been rehabilitated after a period of drug use and that information is not relevant to the employee's functioning in the workplace, then his or her new supervisor may not "need to know."
3. Third, if you know that for some reason the information to be elicited via testing will *not* be kept confidential, you may limit your liability by disclosing that fact prior to testing. For example, if employees who test positive on a drug test are going to be required to use the company's employee assistance program, that should be explained before the tests are given. Similarly, if supervisors are routinely going to be asked to participate in the rehabilitation phase, then employees should understand that their supervisors will become involved if they test positive.

Types of Tests

We can conveniently classify a test according to whether it measures cognitive (mental) abilities, motor and physical abilities, personality and interests, or achievement.[30]

TESTS OF COGNITIVE ABILITIES

Tests in this group include tests of general reasoning ability (intelligence) and tests of specific mental abilities like memory and inductive reasoning.

Intelligence Tests

Intelligence (IQ) tests are tests of general intellectual abilities. They measure not a single trait, but rather several abilities such as memory, vocabulary, verbal fluency, and numerical ability.

As it was originally used, IQ was literally a quotient. The procedure was to divide a child's mental age (as measured by the intelligence test) by his or her chronological age, and then multiply the results by 100. Thus, if an 8-year-old child answered questions as a 10-year-old might, his or her IQ would be 10 divided by 8, times 100, or 125.

For adults, of course, the notion of mental age divided by chronological age wouldn't make much sense. For example, we wouldn't necessarily expect a 30-year-old individual to be more intelligent than a 25-year-old one. Therefore, an  adult's IQ score is actually a *derived* score. It reflects the extent to which the person is above or below the "average" adult's intelligence score.

Intelligence is often measured with individually administered tests such as the Stanford-Binet Test or the Wechsler Test. Other IQ tests such as the Wonderlic can be administered to groups of people.

Specific Cognitive Abilities

There are also measures of specific mental abilities. These include inductive and deductive reasoning, verbal comprehension, memory, and numerical ability.

Tests in this category are often called *aptitude tests*, since they purport to measure the applicant's aptitudes for the job in question. For example, consider the test of mechanical comprehension illustrated in Figure 5.3. It tests the appli-

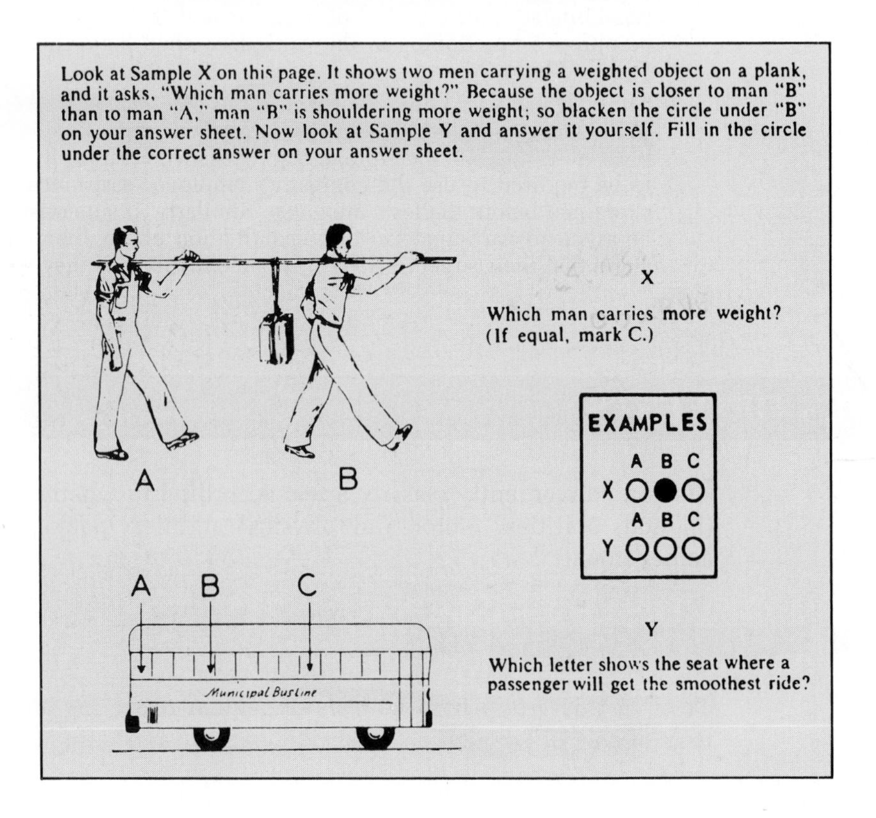

FIGURE 5.3 Two Problems from the Test of Mechanical Comprehension

Source: Reproduced by permission. Copyright 1967, 1969 by The Psychological Corporation, New York, NY. All rights reserved. Author's note: 1969 is latest copyright on this test which is still the main one used for this purpose.

cant's understanding of basic mechanical principles. It therefore, reflects the person's aptitude for jobs—like that of machinist or engineer—that require mechanical comprehension. Other tests of mechanical aptitude include the Mechanical Reasoning Test and the SRA Test of Mechanical Aptitude.

TESTS OF MOTOR AND PHYSICAL ABILITIES

Motor abilities include tests of coordination and dexterity, while *physical abilities* include strength and stamina. There are many motor abilities you might want to measure. These include finger dexterity, manual dexterity, speed of arm movement, and reaction time. The Stromberg Dexterity Test, which is illustrated in Figure 5.4 is an example. It measures the speed and accuracy of simple judgment as well as speed of finger, hand, and arm movements. Other tests include the *Crawford Small Parts Dexterity Test*, the *Minnesota Rate of Manipulation Test*, and the *Purdue Peg Board*.

Tests of *physical abilities* may also be required.[31] Physical abilities include static strength (lifting weights), dynamic strength (like pull-ups), body coordination (as in jumping rope), and stamina.

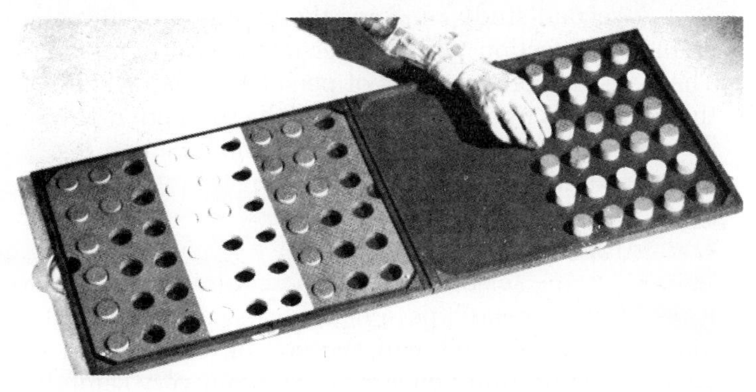

FIGURE 5.4
Minnesota Rate of Manipulation Test (top) and Stromberg Dexterity Test (bottom)

Source: Educational Test Bureau and The Psychological Corporation.

MEASURING PERSONALITY AND INTERESTS

A person's mental and physical abilities are seldom enough to explain the person's job performance. Instead, other factors like the person's motivation and interpersonal skills are important as well. Personality and interests inventories are sometimes used as possible predictors of such intangibles.

Personality tests can measure basic aspects of an applicant's personality, such as introversion, stability, and motivation. Many personality tests are *projective*. Here an ambiguous stimulus like an ink blot or clouded picture is presented to the person taking the test. He or she is then asked to interpret or react to it. Since the pictures are ambiguous, the person's interpretation must come from within—be projected. He or she supposedly *projects* into the picture his or her own emotional attitudes about life. Thus, a security-oriented person might describe the man in Figure 5.1 as "worrying about what he'll do if he's fired from his job." Examples of personality tests (which are more properly called personality *inventories*) include the *Thematic Apperception Test, Guilford-Zimmerman Temperament Survey*, and the *Minnesota Multiphasic Personality Inventory*. The Guilford Zimmerman survey measures personality traits like emotional stability versus moodiness and friendliness versus criticalness. The Minnesota Multiphasic Personality Inventory taps traits like hypochondria and paranoia.

Personality tests—particularly the projective type—are the most difficult tests to evaluate and use. An expert must analyze the test taker's interpretations and reactions and infer from them his or her personality. The usefulness of such tests for selection then assumes you find a relationship between a measurable personality trait (like introversion) and success on the job.[32]

The difficulties notwithstanding, recent studies confirm that personality testing can help companies hire more effective workers. For example, industrial psychologists often talk in terms of the "Big Five" personality dimensions as they apply to personnel testing: extroversion, emotional stability, agreeableness, conscientiousness, and openness to experience.[33] One study focused on the extent to which these five personality dimensions predicted performance (for instance, in terms of job proficiency and training proficiency) for professionals, police officers, managers, sales workers, and skilled/semiskilled workers. Conscientiousness showed consistent relations with all job performance criteria for all the occupations. Extroversion was a valid predictor of performance for the two occupations that involved the most social interaction, namely managers and sales employees. Openness to experience and extroversion predicted training proficiency for all occupations.

A second study confirms the potential usefulness of personality testing in employee selection while underscoring the importance of careful job analysis. These researchers' analysis of personnel testing studies leads them to conclude that under the right circumstances the predictive power of a personality test can be quite high.[34] However, they also conclude that the full potential of using personality traits in personnel selection will be realized only when careful job analysis becomes the "standard practice for determining which traits are relevant to predicting performance on a given job, and when greater attention is directed to the selection of psychometrically sound and valid personality measures."[35] In summary, personality tests can be useful for helping employers predict which candidates will succeed on the job and which will not. However, your validation study must be carried out very carefully.

Interest inventories compare one's interests with those of people in various occupations. Thus, if a person takes the *Strong-Campbell Inventory*, he or she would receive a report comparing his or her interests to those of people already in occupations such as accounting, engineering, management, or medical technology.

Interest inventories have many uses. They are useful in career planning, since a person will likely do better on jobs that involve activities in which he or she is interested. These tests can also be useful as selection tools. Clearly, if you can select people whose interests are roughly the same as those of successful incumbents in the jobs for which you are recruiting, it is more likely that the applicants will be successful on their new jobs.[36]

ACHIEVEMENT TESTS

An achievement test is basically a measure of what a person has learned. Most of the tests you take in school are thus achievement tests. They measure your "job knowledge" in areas like economics, marketing, or personnel.

Achievement tests are also widely used in employment screening. For example, the *Purdue Test for Machinists and Machine Operators* tests the job knowledge of experienced machinists with questions like "what is meant by 'tolerance'?" Other tests are available for electricians, welders, carpenters, and so forth. In addition to job knowledge, other achievement tests measure the applicant's abilities; a typing test is one example.

▸WORK SAMPLES AND SIMULATIONS

work samples
Actual job tasks used in testing applicants' performance.

Work samples and assessment centers can be considered tests. However, they differ from most of the tests discussed previously because they focus on measuring job performance directly.[37] Personality and interests inventories, on the other hand, aim to predict job performance by measuring traits like extroversion or interests.

WORK SAMPLING FOR EMPLOYEE SELECTION

Rationale for Work Sampling

work sampling technique
A testing method based on measuring performance on actual, basic job tasks.

A **work sampling technique** measures how a candidate actually performs some of the job's basic tasks.[38]

There are several advantages to using work sampling. Since you are measuring actual on-the-job tasks, it is harder for the applicant to fake answers. The work sample itself is more clearly relevant to the job you are recruiting for, so in terms of fair employment you may be on safer grounds. The content of the work sample—the actual tasks the person must perform—is not as likely to be unfair to minorities as is a personnel test that inadvertently emphasizes middle-class concepts and values.[39] Work sampling does not delve into the applicant's personality or psyche, so there's almost no chance of it being viewed as an invasion of privacy. Well-designed work samples also exhibit better validity than do tests designed to predict performance.

Basic Work Sampling Procedures

The basic procedure[40] involves choosing several tasks that are crucial to performing the job in question. You then test applicants on each of these tasks. Their performance on each task is monitored by an observer who indicates, on a checklist, how well the applicant performs that task. An example follows.

In developing a work sampling test for maintenance mechanics, experts first listed all the possible tasks (like "install pulleys and belts" and "install and align a motor") that maintenance mechanics would be required to perform. For each task, the experts listed the frequency of performance of the task, and the task's relative importance to the overall job of maintenance mechanic. Thus four crucial tasks here were installing pulleys and belts, disassembling and installing a gear box, installing and aligning a motor, and pressing a bushing into a sprocket.

Next these four tasks were broken down *into the steps needed to complete them*. Each step, of course, could be performed in a slightly different way. Since some approaches were better than others, the experts gave a different weight to different approaches.

This is illustrated in Figure 5.5, which shows one of the steps required for installing pulleys and belts: "checks key before installing." As listed on the checklist, different possible approaches here include checking the key against (1) the shaft, or (2) the pulley, or (3) against neither. Weights reflecting the worth of each of these approaches are shown on the right of the exhibit.

Each applicant was required to perform each of the four tasks, such as installing pulleys and belts. How he or she performed each of the steps was monitored by the test administrator. The latter watched the applicant and indicated on a checklist like that in Figure 5.5 the approach the applicant used. Thus, suppose the applicant checked the key against the pulley before installing it. The test administrator would mark "pulley" for that particular step in the task *installing pulleys and belts*.

Finally, the work sampling test is validated, by determining the relationship between the applicant's scores on the work samples and their actual performance on the job. Then, once it is shown that the work sample is a valid predictor of job success, the employer could begin using it for selection.

MANAGEMENT ASSESSMENT CENTERS

management assessment centers
A situation in which management candidates are asked to make decisions in hypothetical situations and are scored on their performance. It usually also involves testing and the use of management games.

A **management assessment center** is a two- to three-day experience in which about a dozen management candidates perform realistic management tasks (like making presentations) under the watchful eye of expert appraisers; each candidate's potential for management is thereby *assessed* or appraised.[41] The center itself may be just a conference room. However, it is often a special room with a one-way mirror to facilitate the assessors' unobtrusive observations. Examples of the real-life but simulated exercises included in a typical assessment center are as follows:

The in-basket. With this exercise, the candidate is faced with an accumulation of reports, memos, notes of incoming phone calls, letters, and other materials collected in the in-basket of the simulated job he or she is to take over. The candidate is asked to take appropriate action on each of these materials. For example, he or she must write letters, notes, or agendas for meetings. The results of the candidate's actions are then reviewed by the trained evaluators.

Computer Applications in Testing: Computer-Interactive Performance Test

Microprocessors and minicomputers have opened up new possibilities for measuring various types of performance and we should briefly review some of these.[1] One expert classifies the uses of computers in selection into four kinds of applications. The first simply uses the computer as a way to administer a currently available printed test. Using the computer in this way facilitates scoring and the compilation of cumulative norms.

A second way in which computers are used today in selection testing may be called the *adaptive test.* Adaptive tests automatically tailor a sequence of test items to each examinee, contingent on his or her responses to earlier items in the sequence. In tests like these, correct responses generally trigger more difficult items, for instance. The effect is to reduce substantially the number of test items needed, since those that are either too easy or hard for the examinee are not administered.

Third, computers are being used to enhance the administration of tests when dynamics are involved, as in tests of perceptual speed. Here the computer can be used to present signals rapidly and sequentially to test the person's perceptual speed. Similarly, a test of short-term memory, where the stimulus can be removed from the display and recall required later, is another example of an application here.

Fourth, computers are being used to measure human capabilities not measurable (or easily measurable) by printed tests. For example, measuring capabilities like the ability to function under different time pressures, or under different work load conditions, or, for that matter, the ability to concentrate under stress are not human capabilities easily measured by printed tests. Computers are being used in this area, for instance, by measuring the person's ability to concentrate as various stimuli are projected on the screen.

[1]This is based on Edwin A. Fleishman, "Some New Frontiers in Personnel Selection Research," *Personnel Psychology*, Vol. 41, no. 4 (Winter 1988), pp. 679–701.

The leaderless group discussion. A leaderless group is given a discussion question and told to arrive at a group decision. The raters then evaluate each group member's interpersonal skills, acceptance by the group, leadership ability, and individual influence.

Management games. Participants engage in realistic problem solving, usually as members of two or more simulated companies that are competing in the marketplace. Decisions might have to be made about matters like how to advertise and manufacture and how much inventory to keep in stock.

Individual presentations. A participant's communication skills and persuasiveness are evaluated by having the person make an oral presentation of an assigned topic.

FIGURE 5.5
Example of a Work Sampling Question
This is one task in installing pulleys and belts.

CHECKS KEY BEFORE INSTALLING AGAINST:

____	shaft	score	3
____	pulley	score	3
____	neither	score	1

Objective tests. All types of paper-and-pencil tests of personality, mental ability, interests, and achievements might also be a part of an assessment center.

The interview. Most centers also require an interview between at least one of the expert assessors and each participant. Here the latter's current interests, background, past performance, and motivation are assessed.

The agenda for a typical two-day assessment center is presented in Figure 5.6. The figure summarizes the nature of each of the exercises in which the candidates participated.

Effectiveness

Assessment centers are used increasingly as a selection tool.[42] Assessment centers were reportedly first used at the American Telephone & Telegraph Company in the 1950s and are still in use there.

Most studies, including those in the Bell System, suggest that assessment centers are useful for predicting success in management jobs.[43] Studies also indicate that assessment centers, insofar as they sample actual, realistic job behavior, are valid, unbiased selection tools.[44] A study by Hinrichs illustrates the results in this area.[45] In this study, 47 assessment center participants were followed up eight years later to judge how well their assessment center evaluations predicted their future advancement. The overall assessment center rating *was* significantly related to position obtained after eight years for the 30 individuals still with the company.

Yet the same study raises an important question regarding one of the assessment center's main disadvantages, its high cost.[46] The question is whether a center can do its job less expensively than other selection techniques, and here the evidence is not clear. At least one study suggests that the assessment center approach is financially efficient.[47] In his study, however, Hinrichs concluded that a straightforward review of the participants' personnel files did as good a job of predicting which participants would succeed as did their assessment center evaluations.

An Alternative

One alternative has been aptly described as "assessment without a center". It involves assessing job candidates on a series of carefully selected on-the-job activities.[48] The basic approach consists of three steps. First, a *job analysis* is performed to determine the critical tasks and abilities required for each management position. Next, *assessor training* is carried out for the purpose of training selected managers to observe and assess managerial skills like decision making, communication, and technical competence. Next, the program is *implemented.* Here the specially trained assessors assess managerial candidates *on the job*, in terms of their motivation, technical competence, interpersonal skills, and administrative abilities.

THE MINIATURE JOB TRAINING AND EVALUATION APPROACH

In this approach, the job seeker is trained to perform a sample of tasks involved on the job. Immediately following the training his or her ability to perform these tasks is measured. This approach is based on the assumption that a person who

DAY 1

Orientation Meeting

Management Game: "Conglomerate." Forming different types of conglomerates is the goal with four-person teams of participants bartering companies to achieve their planned result. Teams set their own acquisition objectives and must plan and organize to meet them.

Background Interview: A 1½ hour interview conducted by an assessor.

Group Discussion: "Management Problems." Four short cases calling for various forms of management judgment are presented to groups of four participants. In one hour the group, acting as consultants, must resolve the cases and submit its recommendation in writing.

Individual Fact-Finding and Decision-Making Exercise: "The Research Budget." The participant is told that he or she has just taken over as division manager. He or she is given a brief description of an incident in which his or her predecessor has recently turned down a request for funds to continue a research project. The research director is appealing for a reversal of the decision. The participant is given 15 minutes to ask questions to dig out the facts in the case. Following this fact-finding period, he or she must present the decision orally with supporting reasoning and defend it under challenge.

DAY 2

In-Basket Exercise: "Section Manager's In-Basket." The contents of a section manager's in-basket are simulated. The participant is instructed to go through the contents, solving problems, answering questions, delegating, organizing, scheduling and planning, just as he or she might do if he or she were promoted suddenly to the position. An assessor reviews the contents of the completed in-basket and conducts a one-hour interview with the participant to gain further information.

Assigned Role Leaderless Group Discussion: "Compensation Committee." The Compensation Committee is meeting to allocate $8,000 in discretionary salary increases among six supervisory and managerial employees. Each member of the committee (participants) represents a department of the company and is instructed to "do the best he or she can" for the employee from his or her department.

Analysis, Presentation, and Group Discussion: "The Pretzel Factory." This financial analysis problem has the participant role-play a consultant called in to advise Carl Flowers of the C. F. Pretzel Company on two problems: what to do about a division of the company that has continually lost money, and whether the corporation should expand. Participants are given data on the company and are asked to recommend appropriate courses of action. They make their recommendation in a seven-minute presentation after which they are formed into a group to come up with a single set of recommendations.

Final Announcements

DAYS 3 and 4

Assessors meet to share their observations on each participant and to arrive at summary evaluations relative to each dimension sought and overall potential.

FIGURE 5.6
Agenda for a Two–Day Assessment Center

Source: William C. Byham, "The Assessment Center as an Aid in Management Development." Reproduced by special permission from the December 1981 *Training and Development Journal*. Copyright 1981 by the American Society for Training and Development.

can demonstrate the ability to learn and perform a sample of a job will be able to learn and perform the job itself.

The technique has been successful. One study involved a group of navy recruits who had been deemed unacceptable for various naval schools based on their performance on traditional test batteries. The recruits participated in several miniature job training and evaluation situations. One was the "computation and projection miniature training and evaluation situation". Here recruits were taught how to read a simplified plot diagram of the positions of two ships, their headings, and speed and how to extrapolate the new position of each ship and evaluate the danger of collision. Seamen who normally would have been barred from this type of training were found to be competent to pursue computation and projection schooling.

The approach has advantages and disadvantages. Advantages include the fact that it is "content relevant." This means that the recruit is tested with an *actual* sample of the job rather than just with a paper-and-pencil test. This direct approach may also make it more acceptable (and fair) to disadvantaged persons than the usual paper-and-pencil test. On the other hand, with its emphasis on individual instruction during training, this approach is also relatively expensive as a screening device. This higher cost must be weighed against its advantages.[49]

OTHER SELECTION TECHNIQUES

BACKGROUND INVESTIGATIONS AND REFERENCE CHECKS

Use

Most employers try to check and verify the background information and references of job applicants.[50] Estimates of the number of firms checking references range from 93% and up, with about 80% using telephone inquiries. The remainder use other background sources like commercial credit-checking companies and required reference letters.

The actual background investigation/reference check can take many forms. At a minimum, most employers try to verify an applicant's current position and salary with his or her current employer by telephone. Others call the applicant's current and previous supervisors to try to discover more about the person's motivation, technical competence, and ability to work with others. Some employers get background reports from commercial credit-rating companies. The latter can provide information on an applicant's credit standing, indebtedness, reputation, character, and life-style. Some employers ask for written references on their applicants.

Effectiveness

Handled correctly, the background check can be useful. It is an inexpensive and straightforward way of verifying factual information about the applicant, such as current and previous job title, current salary range, dates of employment, and educational background.

However, reference checking can backfire. Laws like the Fair Credit Reporting Act of 1970 increase the likelihood that rejected applicants will successfully demand access to the background information that was compiled and then bring suit against both the source of that information and the recruiting employer. (In one case, a man was awarded $56,000 after being turned down for a job because, among other things, he was called a "character" by a former employer.) From a practical point of view, it is not easy for a reference to prove that the bad appraisal he or she gave an applicant was warranted. The rejected applicant thus has various legal remedies, including suing the reference for defamation of character.[51]

It is not just the fear of legal reprisal that can undermine a reference. Many supervisors don't want to diminish a former employee's chances for a job; others might prefer to give an incompetent employee good reviews if it will get rid of him or her. Even when checking references via the phone, therefore, you have to be careful to ask the right questions and to try to judge if the reference is being evasive in his or her answers and, if so, why.

Human resource managers don't seem to view reference letters as very useful. In one study, 12% replied that reference letters were "highly valuable," 43% call them "somewhat valuable," and 30% viewed them as having "little value," or (6%) "no value." Asked whether they preferred written or telephone references, 72% favored the telephone reference, since it allows a more candid assessment and provides a more interpersonal exchange. Not having a written record is also an appealing feature. In fact, reference letters ranked lowest—seventh out of seven—when rated by these human resource officers as selection tools. Ranked from top to bottom, these tools were, by the way, interview (the top-ranked selection tool), application form, academic record, oral referral, aptitude and achievement tests, psychological tests, and finally, reference letters.[52]

Suggestions

There are several things you can do to make your reference checking more productive.[53] One is to use a structured form as in Figure 5.7. The form helps ensure that you don't overlook important questions. Another suggestion is to use the references suggested by the applicant as merely a source for other references who may know of the applicant's performance. Thus, you might ask each of the applicant's references, "Could you please give me the name of another person who might be familiar with the applicant's performance?" In that way, you begin getting information from references who are assumedly more objective since they weren't referred directly by the applicant.

One suggestion along these lines is to conduct a reference audit rather than just a reference check.[54] The difference between the two is largely a matter of degree.

A thorough reference audit requires contacting at least two superiors, two peers, and two subordinates from each job previously held by the candidate. In doing so, you should find that a reliable picture of the candidate is gradually formed. For example, you will find that the red flags raised by one or two colleagues are in fact problems that can be traced back through several previous jobs and employers. Of course, some employers do have policies that preclude employees (outside the human resources department) from providing reference information. And it is always risky to ask candidates to self-select the references to whom you are to speak. However such audits can and probably will lead to a more accurate picture of your candidate than will the usual poking around that reference checks often involve.

Giving Employment References: Know the Law

You also must be acquainted with what you can and cannot say when *supplying* employment references on former employees. Federal laws that affect references

FIGURE 5.7 Telephone or Personal Interview Form

Source: Adapted by permission of the publisher from *Book of Employment Forms,* American Management Association.

TELEPHONE OR PERSONAL INTERVIEW

☐ FORMER EMPLOYER
☐ CHARACTER REFERENCE

COMPANY ______ ADDRESS ______ PHONE ______

NAME OF PERSON CONTACTED ______ POSITION OR TITLE ______

1. I WISH TO VERIFY SOME FACTS GIVEN BY
(MISS, MRS. MS.)
MR.
WHO IS APPLYING FOR EMPLOYMENT WITH OUR FIRM. WHAT WERE THE DATES OF HIS/HER EMPLOYMENT BY YOUR COMPANY? FROM ______ 19 ___ TO ______ 19 ___

2. WHAT WAS THE NATURE OF HIS/HER JOB? AT START ______
AT LEAVING ______

3. HE/SHE STATES THAT HE/SHE WAS EARNING $ ___ PER ___ WHEN HE/SHE LEFT. IS THAT CORRECT? YES ___ NO ___ $ ______

4. WHAT DID HIS/HER SUPERIORS THINK OF HIM/HER? ______
WHAT DID HIS/HER SUBORDINATES THINK OF HIM/HER? ______

5. DID HE/SHE HAVE SUPERVISORY RESPONSIBILITY? YES ___ NO ___
(IF YES) HOW DID HE/SHE CARRY IT OUT? ______

6. HOW HARD DID HE/SHE WORK? ______

7. HOW DID HE/SHE GET ALONG WITH OTHERS? ______

8. HOW WAS HIS/HER ATTENDANCE RECORD? ______ PUNCTUALITY? ______

9. WHAT WERE HIS/HER REASONS FOR LEAVING? ______

10. WOULD YOU REHIRE HIM/HER? (IF NO) WHY? YES ___ NO ___

11. DID HE/SHE HAVE ANY DOMESTIC, FINANCIAL OR PERSONAL TROUBLE WHICH INTERFERED WITH HIS/HER WORK? YES ___ NO ___

12. DID HE/SHE DRINK OR GAMBLE TO EXCESS? YES ___ NO ___

13. WHAT ARE HIS/HER STRONG POINTS? ______

14. WHAT ARE HIS/HER WEAK POINTS? ______

REMARKS: ______

are the Privacy Act of 1974, the Fair Credit Reporting Act of 1970, the Family Education Rights and Privacy Act of 1974 (and Buckley Amendment of 1974), and the Freedom of Information Act of 1966. These laws give individuals and students the right to know the nature and substance of information in their credit files and files with government agencies and (under the Privacy Act) to review records pertaining to them with any private business that contracts with a federal agency. Therefore, it is quite possible that your comments may eventually be shown to the man or woman you are describing. Also "common law," and in particular the tort of defamation, applies to the information you supply. The communication is defamatory if it is false and tends to harm the reputation of another by lowering him or her in the estimation of the community or by deterring other persons from associating or dealing with him.

Some suggested guidelines for defensible references are summarized in Figure 5.8. As you can see, guidelines include "don't volunteer information," "avoid vague statements," and "do not answer trap questions such as 'would you rehire this person?'" In practice many firms have a policy of not providing any information on former employees except for their dates of employment and position titles.[55]

Being sued for defamation is increasingly a matter of concern for employers. In one case, four employees were terminated for "gross insubordination" after disobeying a supervisor's order to review their expense account reports. In this Minnesota case (*Lewis* v. *Equitable Life Assurance*) the jury found that the employees' expense reports were actually honest. The employees argued for punitive damages under the tort of defamation. They argued that even though the employer did not publicize the defamatory matter to others, it should have known that the employees themselves, in having to defend themselves to future employers, would have to release the (slanderous) reason for their firing. The

FIGURE 5.8 Guidelines for Defensible References

Source: Mary F. Cook, *Human Resources Director's Handbook* (Englewood Cliffs, NJ: Prentice Hall, 1984), p. 93.

1. Don't volunteer information. Respond only to specific company or institutional inquiries and requests. Before responding, telephone the inquirer to check on the validity of the request.
2. Direct all communication only to persons who have a specific interest in that information.
3. State in the message that the information you are providing is confidential and should be treated as such. Use qualifying statements such as "providing information that was requested"; "relating this information only because it was requested"; or "providing information that is to be used for professional purposes only." Sentences such as these imply that information was not presented for the purpose of hurting or damaging a person's reputation.
4. Obtain written consent from the employee or student, if possible.
5. Provide only reference data that relates and pertains to the job and job performance in question.
6. Avoid vague statements such as: "He was an average student"; "She was careless at times"; "He displayed an inability to work with others."
7. Document all released information. Use specific statements such as: "Mr. _____ received a grade of C — an average grade"; "Ms. _____ made an average of two bookkeeping errors each week"; or "This spring, four members of the work team wrote letters asking not to be placed on the shift with Mr. _____."
8. Clearly label all subjective statements based on personal opinions and feelings. Say "I believe . . ." whenever making a statement that is not fact.
9. When providing a negative or potentially negative statement, add the reason or reasons why, or specify the incidents that led you to this opinion.
10. Do not answer trap questions such as "Would you rehire this person?"
11. Avoid answering questions that are asked "off the record."

court agreed and upheld jury awards totaling more than a million dollars to these employees. In other words, the employer may get sued if the employee is terminated for potentially defamatory reasons, even if the employer doesn't publicize the reason for the termination.[56]

PREEMPLOYMENT INFORMATION SERVICES

Computer data bases have made it easier to check background information on candidates than it ever has been before. There was a time not too many years ago when the only source of background information on a candidate was the information he or she provided on the application form and (in some cases) what the employer could obtain through the use of private investigators. Today so-called preemployment information services use data bases to accumulate mounds of information on matters such as worker's compensation histories, credit histories, and conviction records. Employers are increasingly turning to these information services to get the information they need (or think they need) to make the right selection decision. It is then extremely simple when hiring, say, a plant employee to summarily reject any applicants with histories of worker's compensation claims or poor credit on the assumption that such workers "won't work out."

There are two reasons to be very careful in the use of information that relates to an applicant's criminal, credit, and worker's compensation histories.[57] First, as we discussed in Chapter 2, various equal employment laws discourage or prohibit the use of such information in employee screening. For example, under the 1990 Americans with Disabilities Act (ADA), which became effective in July, 1992, employers are prohibited from making preemployment inquiries into the existence, nature, or severity of a disability. As a result, a general request from an employer for information regarding a candidate's previous worker's compensation claims would likely be viewed as unlawful. Instead, the employer would have to ask whether the candidate has the ability to perform a particular function on the job. Similarly (also mentioned in Chapter 2), making employment decisions based on a person's arrest record would likely be viewed as unfairly discriminatory. The reason, again, is that some minorities suffer relatively high arrest rates, although an arrest, of course, does not mean that the person is guilty. On the other hand, use of conviction information for particular jobs (e.g., where security is involved) would be less problematical.

Several EEOC decisions held that employers violated Title VII by denying employment based on a poor credit rating. It held that a poor credit history should not, by itself, preclude a person from getting a job. Instead, the question was whether a good credit history was required as a business necessity.

However, it's not just equal employment laws that suggest prudence in using background data: A great many states specifically ban the use of such information as well. For example, Pennsylvania law provides that felony and misdemeanor convictions "may be considered by the employer only to the extent to which they relate to the applicant's suitability for employment in the position for which he has applied."[58] New York requires employers to notify an applicant before requesting a consumer report. It also requires the employer to obtain the written permission of the applicant before seeking a more extensive investigative report.[59] Under the Federal Fair Credit Reporting Act, employers that take adverse employment action based on a consumer report must follow two rules. First, the employer must advise the employee or candidate of the fact that he or she was turned down based on the consumer report and the name and address of the consumer reporting agency must be supplied. Second, the employer may not obtain a consumer report from a reporting agency under false pretenses.[60]

This being the case, you can see that even the apparently simple process of gathering background information on an applicant has the potential for developing into an explosive situation for an employer. A rejected applicant even somewhat familiar with the law could easily take an employer to court and could win. Some suggestions for collecting background information thus include:

1. Check all applicable state laws.
2. Check beyond applicable state laws, and particularly the impact of equal employment laws.
3. Remember the Federal Fair Credit Reporting Act.
4. Do not obtain information that will not be used.
5. Remember that using arrest information will be highly suspect.
6. Avoid blanket policies (such as "we hire no one with a record of worker's compensation claims").
7. Use information that is specific and job-related.
8. Keep information confidential and up-to-date.
9. Never authorize an unreasonable investigation.[61]

THE POLYGRAPH AND HONESTY TESTING

The polygraph (or "lie detector") machine is a device that measures physiological changes, like increased perspiration. The assumption is that such changes reflect changes in the emotional stress that accompanies lying. The usual procedure is for an applicant (or current employee) to be attached to the machine with painless electronic probes. He or she is then asked a series of obvious, neutral questions by the polygraph expert. These questions might, for instance, confirm that the person's name is John Smith and that he is currently residing in New York.

Under certain conditions, an applicant for the position of security guard with a major defense contractor can be given a polygraph exam as part of the screening process.

Once the person's emotional reactions to giving truthful answers to neutral questions has been ascertained, questions like "have you ever stolen anything without paying for it," "do you use drugs," or "have you ever committed a crime" can be asked. In theory, at least, the expert can then determine with some accuracy whether or not the applicant is lying.

Complaints about offensiveness plus grave doubts about the accuracy of the polygraph culminated in the Employee Polygraph Protection Act being signed into law by President Reagan on June 27, 1988. The law prohibits (with a few exceptions) employers from conducting polygraph examinations of all job applicants and most employees. Also prohibited under this law are other mechanical or electrical devices that attempt to measure honesty or dishonesty, including psychological stress evaluators and voice stress analyzers. Paper-and-pencil tests and chemical testing (as for drugs) are not prohibited under federal laws.[62] Governmental (local, state, or federal) employers can continue to use polygraph exams under the law (but are restricted under a number of state laws). Other employers that can use polygraph tests include industries with national defense or security contracts; certain businesses with nuclear power-related contracts with the Department of Energy; businesses and consultants with access to highly

NOTICE

EMPLOYEE POLYGRAPH PROTECTION ACT

The Employee Polygraph Protection Act prohibits most private employers from using lie detector tests either for pre-employment screening or during the course of employment.

PROHIBITIONS

Employers are generally prohibited from requiring or requesting any employee or job applicant to take a lie detector test, and from discharging, disciplining, or discriminating against an employee or prospective employee for refusing to take a test or for exercising other rights under the Act.

EXEMPTIONS*

Federal, State and local governments are not affected by the law. Also, the law does not apply to tests given by the Federal Government to certain private individuals engaged in national security-related activities.

The Act permits *polygraph* (a kind of lie detector) tests to be administered in the private sector, subject to restrictions, to certain prospective employees of security service firms (armored car, alarm, and guard), and of pharmaceutical manufacturers, distributors and dispensers.

The Act also permits polygraph testing, subject to restrictions, of certain employees of private firms who are reasonably suspected of involvement in a workplace incident (theft, embezzlement, etc.) that resulted in economic loss to the employer.

EXAMINEE RIGHTS

Where polygraph tests are permitted, they are subject to numerous strict standards concerning the conduct and length of the test. Examinees have a number of specific rights, including the right to a written notice before testing, the right to refuse or discontinue a test, and the right not to have test results disclosed to unauthorized persons.

ENFORCEMENT

The Secretary of Labor may bring court actions to restrain violations and assess civil penalties up to $10,000 against violators. Employees or job applicants may also bring their own court actions.

ADDITIONAL INFORMATION

Additional information may be obtained, and complaints of violations may be filed, at local offices of the Wage and Hour Division, which are listed in the telephone directory under U.S. Government, Department of Labor, Employment Standards Administration.

THE LAW REQUIRES EMPLOYERS TO DISPLAY THIS POSTER WHERE EMPLOYEES AND JOB APPLICANTS CAN READILY SEE IT.

**The law does not preempt any provision of any State or local law or any collective bargaining agreement which is more restrictive with respect to lie detector tests.*

U.S. DEPARTMENT OF LABOR

EMPLOYMENT STANDARDS ADMINISTRATION

Wage and Hour Division
Washington, D.C. 20210

*U.S.GPO:1991-0-522-762

WH Publication 1462
September 1988

FIGURE 5.9
Employee Polygraph Notice

classified information, as well as those with counter intelligence-related contracts with the FBI or Department of Justice; and private businesses that are (1) hiring private security personnel, or (2) hiring persons with access to drugs, or (3) doing ongoing investigations involving economic loss or injury to an employer's business, such as a theft. (See Figure 5.9 above.)

Even in the case of ongoing investigations of theft, the employer's right to use polygraphs is quite limited. The first two cases to be decided under the 1988 Employee Polygraph Protection Act were decided in 1992 by a Labor Department administrative law judge.[63] To administer a polygraph test during an ongoing investigation, an employer must meet four standards. First, the employer must show that it suffered an economic loss or injury. Second, it must show that the employee in question had access to the property. Third, asking the employee to take the polygraph must be based on a reasonable suspicion. Finally, the employee who is asked to take the test must be notified of the details of the investigation before the test as well as the questions to be asked on the polygraph test itself.

In these two cases, the administrative law judge decided in favor of one employer, but not in favor of the other. In one case the judge found that the employer had failed to properly notify the 11 employees it tested, thus violating their right under the law to know why they were being investigated. In the second case the administrative law judge ruled that the use of a polygraph test was proper. Here the employer investigated the loss of $135 from a cash register for several months before asking that the employee submit to the test. The employee was given notice of the test 48 hours in advance and the details of the investigation—including the date on which the cash was discovered missing and its amount.[64]

The virtual elimination of the polygraph as a screening device has triggered a burgeoning market for other types of honesty testing devices; there are now a range of these from which to choose. Paper-and-pencil honesty tests are psychological tests designed to predict job applicants' proneness to dishonesty and other forms of counterproductivity.[65] Most of these tests measure attitudes regarding things like tolerance of others who steal, acceptance of rationalizations for theft, and admission of theft-related activities. Tests here include the Phase II profile, the marketing rights to which were recently purchased by Wackenhut Corporation of Coral Gables, Florida (which provides security services to employers). Similar tests are published by London House, Incorporated, and Stanton Corporation.[66]

Several psychologists (including some speaking for the American Psychological Association) have expressed concerns about the proliferation of paper-and-pencil honesty tests.[67] Many of the supportive articles regarding these paper-and-pencil honesty tests have been written by the test publishers themselves, they say. They also argue that additional independent peer review should be conducted before the validity of these devices is accepted.[68]

Given all this, what can an employer do to detect dishonesty? Several things. One expert suggests taking the following steps:

> *Ask blunt questions.*[69] Within the bounds of legality, you can ask very direct questions in the face-to-face interview. For example, says this expert, there is nothing wrong with asking the applicant: "Have you ever stolen anything from an employer?" Other questions to ask include: "Have you recently held jobs other than those listed on your application?" "Have you ever been fired or asked to leave a job?" "What reasons would past supervisors give if they were asked why they let you go?" "Have past employers ever disciplined you or warned you about absences or lateness?" "Is any information on your application misrepresented or falsified?"
>
> *Listen, rather than talk.* Specifically, allow the applicant to do the talking so you can learn as much as possible about the person.

Ask for a credit check. Include a clause in your application form which gives you the right to conduct certain background checks on the applicant including credit checks and motor vehicle reports.

Check all references. Rigorously pursue employment and personal references.

Consider a paper-and-pencil test. Consider utilizing paper-and-pencil honesty tests and psychological tests as a part of your honesty screening program.

Test for drugs. Devise a drug testing program and give each applicant a copy of the policy.

Conduct searches. Establish a search-and-seizure policy. Give each applicant a copy of the policy and require each to return a signed copy. Basically, the policy should state that all lockers, desks, and similar property remain the property of the company and may be inspected routinely.

An Example of an Honesty Screening Program

The Adolf Coors company scrapped its polygraph testing requirement for job applicants. It then substituted a three-step program that all new job applicants have to undergo. The steps include urinalysis, a paper-and-pencil honesty test, and a reference check. The company uses an outside lab to conduct the urinalysis test. Next, applicants take a Stanton Corporation paper-and pencil survey of 83 questions on attitudes toward honesty and theft. The survey company provides Coors with a written report. This report categorizes applicants by levels of risk. For example, low-risk individuals are those who have never been involved in any extensive thefts, while marginal-risk applicants might be tempted to steal if they felt they wouldn't be caught. Finally, applicant references and background checks are performed by a company called Equifax Services. They involve contacting previous employers and educational institutions attended.[70]

A Caution

There are several reasons why great caution should be used in any honesty testing program. First, as noted earlier, considerable doubt has been expressed regarding how valid many (or most) paper-and-pencil honesty testing instruments are. The argument, basically, is that until more widespread evaluations are done, these tests should be used very cautiously, and certainly only as supplements to other techniques like reference checking. Second, on purely humanitarian grounds, one could argue that a rejection (let alone an incorrect rejection) for dishonesty carries with it some more stigma than does being rejected for, say, poor mechanical comprehension or even poor sociability. It's true that others may never know just why you rejected the candidate. However, he or she, having just taken and "failed" what may have been a fairly obvious "honesty test," may leave the premises feeling that his or her treatment was less than proper. Third, questions and tests in this area pose some serious invasion-of-privacy issues, delving as they do into areas such as how you feel about stealing, or whether you have ever stolen anything. There are also more legal constraints that you must watch for. For instance, Massachusetts and Rhode Island both limit the use of paper-and-pencil honesty tests.

GRAPHOLOGY

The use of graphology (handwriting analysis) is based on the assumption that the writer's basic personality traits will express themselves in his or her handwriting.[71] Handwriting analysis thus has some resemblance to projective personality tests.

In graphology, the handwriting analyst studies an applicant's handwriting and signature in order to discover the person's needs, desires, and psychological makeup.[72] According to the graphologist, the writing in Figure 5.10 exemplifies "uneven pressure, poor rhythm, and uneven baselines." The variation of light and dark lines shows a "lack of control" and is "one strong indicator of the writer's inner disturbance."

While many scientists doubt the validity of handwriting analysis, some writers estimate that over 1,000 U.S. companies use handwriting analysis to access applicants for certain strategic positions.[73] And the classified ads of some international newspapers like the *Economist* periodically run advertisements from graphologists offering to aid in an employer's selection process.

FIGURE 5.10 Handwriting Exhibit Used by Graphologist

Source: Reproduced with permission from Kathryn Sackhein, *Handwriting Analysis and the Employee Selection Process* (New York: Quorum Books, 1990) p. 45.

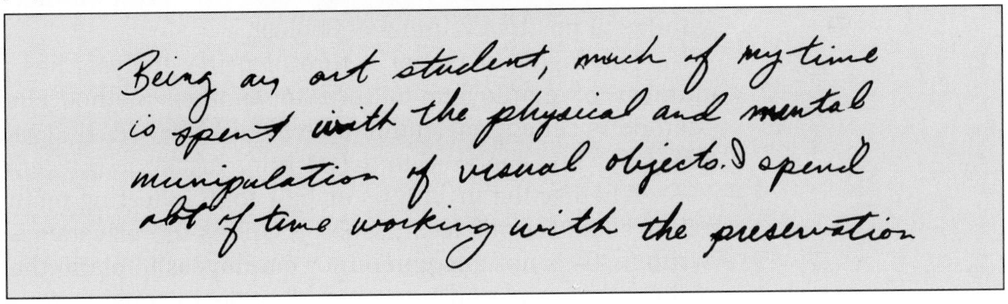

Being an art student, much of my time
is spent with the physical and mental
munipulation of visual objects. I spend
alot of time working with the preservation

PHYSICAL EXAMINATION

A medical examination is usually the next step in the selection process. In some cases the examination takes place after the new employee starts work.[74]

There are five main reasons for requiring preemployment medical exams. The exam can be used to determine that the applicant qualifies for the *physical requirements* of the position and to discover any *medical limitations* that should be taken into account in placing the applicant. The exam will also establish a *record and baseline* of the applicant's health for the purpose of future insurance or compensation claims. The examination can, by identifying health problems, also reduce *absenteeism and accidents* and, of course, detect *communicable diseases* that may be unknown to the applicant. The exam is usually performed by the employer's medical department (in the largest organizations). Smaller employers retain the services of consulting physicians to perform such exams, which are almost always paid for by the employer. In any case remember that under the Americans with Disabilities Act, a person with a disability can't be rejected for the job if he or she is otherwise qualified and if the person could perform the job functions with reasonable accommodation. Under the ADA, a medical exam is permitted during the period between the job offer and commencement of work only if such exams are standard practice for all applications for that job category.[75]

DRUG SCREENING

Drug abuse is a serious problem at work. Counselors at the Cocaine National Help Line polled callers of the 800-Cocaine hot line and found that 75% admitted to occasional cocaine use at work, 69% said that they regularly worked under the influence of a drug, and 25% recorded daily use at work. The U.S. Chamber of Commerce estimates that employee drug and alcohol use costs American employers over $60 billion each year in reduced productivity, accidents, increased sick benefits, and higher worker's compensation claims.[76]

As a result, more employers are conducting drug screening as part of their selection program. The most common practice is to test new applicants just before they are formally hired. Many firms also test current employees when there is reason to believe the person has been using drugs.

Virtually all (96%) of employers that conduct such tests use urine sampling.[77] The preferred initial drug-testing method is the immunoassay test. However, this test cannot differentiate between legal and illegal substances in the same chemical family. For example, popular over-the-counter pain killers like Advil and Nuprin can produce positive results for marijuana. Many firms therefore conduct the more expensive thin-layer chromotography method test to validate a positive immunoassay test.

The highly personal nature of urine analysis has prompted an increasing number of employers to turn to another method, hair follicle testing. The method is called radioimmunoassay of hair (RIAH). It requires a small sample of hair, which is analyzed to detect prior ingestion of illicit drugs.[78]

Whether the urinalysis or hair follicle testing method is used, drug testing raises some serious legal issues.[79] One is the privacy issue. As one attorney has written, "It is not uncommon for employees to claim that drug tests violate their rights to privacy under common law or, in some states, a state statutory or constitutional provision."[80] Since it is less intrusive than urinalysis, hair follicle testing may seem a relatively safe procedure in such cases. Yet hair follicle testing can actually produce even more extensive information of a personal nature than urinalysis. For example, a three-inch hair segment will record six months of drug use. Furthermore, under certain conditions an employer is permitted to reveal private employee information including medical information such as drug test results. However, should drug testing information be promulgated recklessly, or in an unnecessary, unreasonable manner, the employer could be slapped with a suit for defamation.

The Americans with Disabilities Act has implications for drug testing, too. For example, "An individual who has successfully completed or is participating in a supervised drug rehabilitation program and is no longer engaged in the illegal use of drugs is considered to be a qualified individual with a disability."[81] Other laws, including the Federal Rehabilitation Act of 1973 and various state laws, similarly give protection to rehabilitating drug users or to those who have a physical or mental addiction.[82]

What should you do when a job candidate tests positive? Most companies will not hire such candidates, although most will not immediately fire current employees whose tests results are positive.[83] For example, 120 of the 123 companies responding to the question, "If test results are positive, what action do you take?" indicated that applicants checking positive are not hired. Current employees have more legal recourse if dismissed. Current employees therefore must be told the reason for their dismissal if they are dismissed for a positive drug test.[84]

VALIDITY OF VARIOUS SELECTION DEVICES

Table 5.1 summarizes the results of one study of the validity of various selection devices. Tests of actual performance—work samples, peer evaluations, and assessment centers—rate highest. Indirect evaluations, such as psychological tests or academic performance, rate lower.

TABLE 5.1 Validity of Various Selection Devices

PREDICTOR	VALIDITY
Cognitive Ability and Special Aptitude	Moderate
Personality	Low
Interest	Low
Physical Ability	Moderate–High
Biographical Info.	Moderate
Interviews	Low
Work Samples	High
Seniority	Low
Peer Evaluations	High
Reference Checks	Low
Academic Performance	Low
Self Assessments	Moderate
Assessment Centers	High

Source: Neal Schmitt and Raymond Noe, "Personal Selection and Equal Employment Opportunity," in *International Review of Industrial and Organizational Psychology*, ed. Cary L. Cooper and Ivan T. Robertson. Copyright 1986 by John Wiley & Sons, Ltd. Reprinted by permission.

COMPLYING WITH THE IMMIGRATION LAW

Under the Immigration Reform and Control Act of 1986, employees hired in the United States have to prove they are eligible to be employed in the United States. A person does not have to be a U.S. citizen to be employed under this act. However, employers should ask a person who is about to be hired whether he or she is a U.S. citizen or if he or she is an alien lawfully authorized to work in the United States. To comply with this law, the employers should follow the following procedures:[85]

1. Hire only citizens and aliens lawfully authorized to work in the United States.
2. Continue to advise all new job applicants of your policy to such effect.
3. Require all new employees to complete and sign the verification form designated by the Immigration and Naturalization Service (INS) to certify that they are eligible for employment.
4. Examine documentation presented by new employees, record information about the documents on the verification form, and sign the form.
5. Retain the form for three years or for one year past the employment of the individual, whichever is longer.
6. If requested, present the form for inspection by INS or Department of Labor Officers. No reporting is required.

There are two basic ways prospective employees can show their eligibility for employment. One is to show a document such as a U.S. passport or alien registration card with photograph that proves both the person's identity and employment eligibility. However many prospective employees won't have one of these documents. Therefore the other way to verify employment eligibility is to provide a document that proves the person's identity, along with a document showing the person's employment eligibility.

Employers cannot and should not use the so-called I-9 Employment Eligibility Verification form to discriminate in any way based on race or country of national origin. For example, the requirement that you verify employment does not give you any basis to reject an applicant just because he or she is a foreigner, or not a U.S. citizen, or an alien residing in the United States, as long as that person can prove his or her identity and employment eligibility.

SMALL BUSINESS APPLICATIONS

Testing

Just because a company is small doesn't mean it shouldn't engage in personnel testing. Quite the opposite: Hiring one or two mistakes may not be a big problem for a very large firm, but it could cause chaos in a small operation.

There are a number of tests that (while used by big employers too) are so easy to administer they are particularly good for smaller firms. One is the Wonderlic Personnel Test. This deceptively easy-to-use test measures general mental ability. The test, in the form of a four-page booklet, takes under 15 minutes to administer. You first read the instructions and then time the candidate as he or she works through the 50 problems on the two inside sheets. The person's test can then be scored with a scoring key: His or her score is comprised of the number of questions answered correctly. You then compare the person's score to the minimum scores recommended for various occupations (Figure 5.11), determining if the person achieved the minimally acceptable score for the type of job applied for.

A test like this can be useful for helping identify people who are simply not up to the task of doing the job. However, you have to be careful not to misuse it. In the past, for instance, unnecessarily high cutoff scores were required by some employers for some jobs, a tactic which in effect unfairly discriminated against the members of some minority groups. Similarly, it would probably not be either fair or wise to choose between two candidates who both exceeded the minimum score for the job applied for by choosing the one with the higher score. Remember, also, that people of lower ability but higher motivation will often outperform those with higher ability but less motivation. Therefore tests like the Wonderlic are only useful as supplements to a comprehensive screening program. The Wonderlic is available to employers, business owners, and human resource directors with or without previous training in personnel testing.[86]

Another example of a test that is used by large companies but is equally valuable for small ones because of its ease of administration and interpretation is the Predictive Index. The index measures personality traits, drives, and behav-

Position	No. of Questions Answered Correctly in 12 minutes
Administrator	30
Engineer	29
Accountant	28
Programmer	28
Supervisor/Manager	27
Management, Trainee	27
Field Repr. (Sales)	26
Salesman	26
Secretary	25
Accounting Clerk	25
Writer, News, etc.	25
Stenographer	24
Cashier	24
Bookkeeper	24
Foreman	24
Draftsman	23
Receptionist	23
Office, General	23
Lineman, Utility	22
Teller	22
Typist	21
Clerical	21
Key Punch Operator	20
Police, Patrolman	20
Skilled Trades	20
File Clerk	19
Maintenance	18
Telephone Operator	18
General Laborer	17
Factory, General	17
Labor, Skilled	17
Labor, Unskilled	16
Nurses Aide	15
Custodian	8

See the Tables presented in this Manual, "Test Scores by Position Applied For" and "Minimum Occupational Scores for The Wonderlic Personnel Test," for additional data on established scores.

FIGURE 5.11 Minimum Scores on Wonderlic Personnel Test for Various Occupations

Source: Wonderlic Personnel Test Manual (Northfield, IL: E. F. Wonderlic & Associates, Inc., 1983), p. 6.

iors that are work related—in particular, dominance (ranging from submissive to arrogant), extroversion (ranging from withdrawn to gregarious), patience (ranging from volatile to lethargic), and blame avoidance (ranging from sloppy to perfectionist). The Predictive Index test itself is a two-sided sheet in which candidates or current employees check off which words most describe them (such as "helpful" or "persistent"). The test is then easily scored at your office with the use of a scoring template.

The Predictive Index provides valuable information about the candidate. For example, for a job that you know involves painstaking attention to details, you'd want to think twice about a candidate who rates toward the careless end of the range. For an exceedingly boring job, you'd no doubt lean toward the more patient candidates. Each candidate taking the Predictive Index will probably have his or her own unique pattern of responses. However, the Predictive Index program includes 15 standard patterns that are typical of many of the patterns you will see. For example, there is the "social interest" pattern, representing a person who is generally unselfish, congenial, persuasive, patient, and fairly unassuming. This is a person who'd be good with people and a good personnel interviewer, for instance.

Computerized testing programs like those described earlier in this chapter can also be especially useful for small employers. For example, when hiring office help smaller employers typically depend on informal tests of typing, and filing. A much better way to proceed is to use a program like the Minnesota Clerical Assessment Battery published by Assessment Systems Corp. This program runs on a personal computer. It includes a typing test, proofreading test, filing test, business vocabulary test, business math test, and clerical knowledge test. It is therefore useful for evaluating the knowledge and skills of various office positions, including secretary, clerk-typist, bookkeeper, and filing clerk. Because it is computerized, administration and scoring are simplified and each test can be adapted to the particular position being applied for.[87]

▶ Chapter Review

SUMMARY

1. In this chapter we discussed several techniques for screening and selecting job candidates; the first was testing.
2. Test validity answers the question, "What does this test measure?" We discussed criterion validity and content validity.
3. As used by psychologists, the term reliability always means consistency. One way to measure this is to administer the same (or equivalent) test to the same people at two different points in time. Or you could focus on "internal consistency." Here, compare the responses to roughly equivalent items on the same test.
4. There are many types of personnel tests in use, including intelligence tests, tests of physical skills, tests of achievement, aptitude tests, interest inventories, and personality tests.
5. For a selection test to be useful, scores on the test should be related in a predictable way to performance on the job; you must *validate* the test. This involves five steps: (a) analyze the job, (b) choose your tests, (c) administer the test, (d) relate test scores and criteria, and (e) cross-validate and revalidate the test.
6. Under equal rights legislation, an employer may have to be able to prove that his or her tests are predictive of success or failure on the job. This usually involves a predictive validation study, although other means of validation are often acceptable.
7. Some basic testing guidelines include (a) use tests as supplements, (b) validate the tests for appropriate jobs, (c) analyze all current hiring and promotion standards, (d) beware of certain tests, (e) use a certified psychologist, and (f) maintain good test conditions.
8. The work sampling selection technique is based on the assumption that "the best indicator of future performance is past performance." Here you use the applicant's actual performance on the same (or very similar) job to predict his or her future job performance. The steps are (a) analyze applicant's previous work experience, (b) have experts list component tasks for jobs being recruited for, (c) select crucial tasks as work sample measures, (d) break down these tasks into steps, (e) test the applicant, and (f) relate the applicant's work sample score to his or her performance on the job.

9. Management assessment centers are a third screening device and involve exposing applicants to a series of real-life exercises. Performance is observed and assessed by experts, who then check on their assessments by watching the participants when they are back at their jobs. Examples of "real-life" exercises include a simulated business game, an in-basket exercise, and group discussions.
10. Even though most people prefer not to give bad references, most companies still carry out some sort of screening reference check on their candidates. These can be useful in raising red flags, and structured questionnaires can improve the usefulness of the responses you receive.
11. Other selection tools we discussed include the polygraph, honesty tests, graphology, and the physical examination.
12. Employee selection is directly related to employee commitment. Your aim is to select those who have the ability and potential to perform the job successfully. In this chapter we discussed a variety of tools—tests, previous experience, assessment centers—that can help an employer choose the best qualified, most highly committed candidates, those with the potential to do the job. The next step is to hire, orient, and train the new employees, to which we now turn.

KEY TERMS

validity
criterion validity
content validity
reliability
expectancy chart
work samples
work sampling technique
management assessment center

DISCUSSION QUESTIONS

1. Explain what is meant by reliability and validity. What is the difference between them? In what respects are they similar?
2. Explain how you would go about validating a test. How can this information be useful to a manager?
3. Write a short essay discussing some of the ethical and legal considerations in testing.
4. Explain why you think a certified psychologist who is specially trained in test construction should (or should not) always be used by a company developing a personnel test battery.
5. Explain how you would use work sampling for employee selection.

APPLICATION EXERCISES

RUNNING CASE

CARTER CLEANING COMPANY

Honesty Testing

Jennifer and her father have what the latter describes as an easy but hard job when it comes to screening job applicants. It is easy because for two important jobs—the people who actually do the pressing and those who do the cleaning–spotting—the applicants are easily screened with about 20 minutes of on-the-job testing. As with a typist, as Jennifer points out, "a person either knows how to press clothes fast enough or how to use cleaning chemicals and machines, or he or she doesn't, and we find out very quickly by just trying them out on the job."

But, on the other hand, applicant screening for the stores can also be frustratingly *hard* because of the nature of things that Jennifer would like to screen for. Two of the most critical problems facing her company concern employee turnover and employee honesty. As mentioned previously, Jennifer and her father sorely need to implement practices that will reduce the rate of employee turnover. If there is a way to do this through employee testing and screening techniques, Jennifer would like to know about it because of the management time and money that is now being wasted by the never-ending need to recruit and hire new employees.

Of even greater concern to Jennifer and her father is the need to institute new practices to screen out those employees who may be predisposed to steal from the company.

Employee theft is an enormous problem for the Carter Cleaning Centers, and one that is not just limited to employees who handle the cash. For example, the cleaner–spotter and/or the presser often open the store themselves, without a manager (to get the day's work started), and it is not unusual to have one or more of these people steal supplies or "run a route." Running a route means that an employee canvases his or her neighborhood to pick up people's clothes for cleaning and then secretly cleans and presses them in the Carter store, using the company's supplies, gas, and power. It would also not be unusual for an unsupervised person (or his or her supervisor, for that matter) to accept a one-hour rush order for cleaning or laundering, quickly clean and press the item, and return it to the customer for payment without making out a proper ticket for the item or posting the sale. The money, of course, goes into the person's pocket instead of into the cash register.

The more serious problem concerns the store manager and the counter people who actually have to handle the cash. According to Jack Carter, "you would not believe the creativity employees use to get around the management controls we set up to cut down on employee theft." As one extreme example of this felonious creativity, Jack tells the following story: "To cut down on the amount of money my employees were stealing, I had a small sign painted and placed in front of all our cash registers. The sign said: Your entire order *free* if we don't give you a cash register receipt when you pay.—Call 962-0734. It was my intention with this sign to force all our cash–handling employees to place their receipts into the cash register where they would be recorded for my accountants. After all, if all the cash that comes in is recorded in the cash register, then we should have a much better handle on stealing in our stores, right? Well, one of our managers found a diabolical way around this. I came into the store one night and noticed that the cash register that this particular manager was using just didn't look right although the sign was dutifully placed in front of it. It turned out that every afternoon at about 5:00 P.M when the other employees left, this character would pull his own cash register out of a box that he hid underneath all our supplies. Customers coming in would notice the sign and of course the fact that he was meticulous in ringing up every sale. But unbeknownst to them and to us, for about five months the sales that came in for about an hour every day went into his cash register, not mine. It took us that long to figure out where our cash for that store was going."

Questions

1. What would be the advantages and disadvantages to Jennifer's company of routinely administering honesty tests to all its employees?
2. Specifically, what other screening techniques could the company use to screen out theft-prone employees, and how exactly could these be used?
3. How should her company terminate employees caught stealing and what kind of procedure should be set up for handling reference calls about these employees when they go to other companies looking for jobs?

CASE INCIDENT *The Tough Screener*

Everyone who knows Mark Rosen knows he is a very tough owner when it comes to screening applicants for jobs in his firm. His company, located in a large northeastern city, provides financial planning advice to wealthy clients and, related to that, sells insurance and sets up pension plans for individuals and businesses. His firm's clients range from professionals such as doctors and lawyers to business owners, who are fairly sophisticated in financial matters and very busy people. They expect accurate advice provided in a clear and expeditious manner. It is safe to say that Rosen's firm can be no better than its financial advisors.

Mark Rosen has always been described as somewhat autocratic. The need to be very careful about whom he hires has led him to be extraordinarily careful about how he screens his job applicants. Some of his methods are probably beyond reproach. For example, he requires every applicant to provide a list of names and phone numbers for at least five people the applicant worked with at each previous employer to be used as references. The resulting reference check is time consuming but effective.

On the other hand, given recent legislation including the Civil Rights Act of 1991 and the Americans With Disabilities Act, some of his other "tough screening" methods could be problematical. He requires that all applicants take a purported honesty test which he found in the catalog of an office supply store. As another example, he believes it is extremely important to check every viable applicant's credit history and worker's compensation history in order to screen out what he refers to as "potential undesirables." Unbeknownst to his applicants, he runs a credit check on each of them and also retains the services of a firm which checks worker's compensation and driving violation histories.

Questions

1. What specific legal problems do you think Rosen can run into as a result of his firm's current screening methods? What steps would you suggest he take to eliminate these problems?
2. Given what you know about Rosen's business, write a two-page proposal describing an employee testing and selection program that you would recommend for his firm. Say a few words about the sorts of tests, if any, you would recommend and the application blank questions you would ask, as well as other methods including drug screening, and reference checking.

HUMAN RESOURCE MANAGEMENT SIMULATION

Employee selection is covered in the simulation with incident (D). You will be asked to choose one of four finalists for a supervisor's position. This is a hard decision because of the vast differences in education and experience of the candidates and because an element of affirmative action is also involved. Is it better to select the "perfect" candidate in terms of technical expertise, a candidate with better all-around education, or a candidate with more supervisory experience?

APPENDIX 5.1

Special Topics in Testing

▶ RELIABILITY

As discussed in the text, reliability is a characteristic of a test, or of any measurement, that describes its consistency. If the test or measure is free from random errors then it will be consistent and reliable. For example, suppose we have a test that is a measure of mechanical aptitude and it is to be used to assess job applicants as part of a selection procedure. In measurement theory each individual is considered to possess a certain amount of mechanical aptitude and this amount is a conceptual (theoretical) *true score* for that person. The test score for that person will not only include the true score, but include also any other aspects of the testing situation that may cause the obtained score to vary from the true score. These other aspects are considered to be random and they therefore introduce an element of uncertainty as to what the true score is. In other words, we say the obtained score, X, is composed of two parts: (1) a true score, t, (2) a random error score, e, or $X = t + e$. Examples of sources of error that contribute to e include how the examinee felt at the time the test was taken (bad day/good day), variables in the environment such as noise, temperature, ventilation, lighting, and so on, and procedures for administering the test such as unclear instructions, or improper timing of the test. These, and many others, will in general cause the obtained score, X, to vary on repeated measurements of X for the same person even though the true score, t, does not change. From the above it follows that the degree of agreement between X and t is an index of the reduction of random errors that affects the measurement. The correlation coefficient, r_{xt}, which may assume any value 0 to 1.00, is commonly used as a measure of reliability, where 0 means the scores on X are simply random numbers and 1.00 means the scores on X are free from random errors. It can be shown that the reliability coefficient, that is, correlation between t and X, is equal to the percentage of the total variance in test scores that is true score variance, or $r_{xt} = \frac{\sigma_t^2}{\sigma_x^2}$.

Even though the true scores are not directly observable the reliability coefficient can be estimated from the observed X scores by the methods presented on pages 156–157. Essentially each of the methods requires at least two measures from the same person on the same test. The correlation between the two measures yields an estimate of the test's reliability. It is important to note that the method used to estimate the reliability determines what sources of variance are treated as random error. For example, if the test is administered as equivalent forms (p. 156) in a single administration, sources of random error associated with the environment (temperature, noise, and so forth), the persons, and the passage of time such as learning are minimized if not eliminated. On the other hand, a source of error variance is introduced—the difference in the item content or questions between the equivalent forms, for example, are treated as error.

The reliability coefficient, besides showing how consistent or dependable the obtained scores are, has another important application in that it can be used to estimate the amount of error contained in an observed score. A quantity, the standard error of measurement (SEM) can be computed by the following formula: $SEM = S_x = \sqrt{1-r_{xx}}$ where S_x is the standard deviation of test scores in a group of testees and r_{xx} is the computed reliability coefficient (note: r_{xx} is an estimate of r_{xt}). An obtained score plus or minus the SEM or a multiple of it can be used to determine a range of true scores for an individual. For example, if in a group of testees the standard deviation of obtained test scores was 10 and the reliability of the test was .80 the $SEM = 10\sqrt{1-.80} = 4.47$. The true score for an individual who scores 35 is expected to lie between $X \pm 1.96$ SEM or in the range 26 – 44 with 95% confidence. The computation assumes that true scores are normally distributed.

Validity

To express the degree of accuracy for a test the most frequently used method is to compute the validity coefficient of the test for a criterion of interest. The validity coefficient is the correlation between the scores on the test (predictor) and the scores on the criterion for a group of employees. In a predictive validation method, over a period of time, applicants are given the test and hired based on considerations other than the test scores obtained. These might be interviews, information on application blanks, reference checks, and even other tests. At a later time, for those applicants hired, criterion measures are obtained and the correlation between the test scores and the criterion is computed.

The first step in computing the validity coefficient is to display the predictor and criterion measures for each employee in a scatterplot as shown in Figure 5.12. Each point represents the intersection of a predictor score and criterion score for one individual. The circled point shows a person who scored 10 on the predictor at the time of application and 20 on the criterion when job performance was assessed by a supervisor. In this scatterplot it appears that *on average* those who scored higher on the predictor also scored higher on the criterion and vice-versa. Note that for each predictor score there is a range of criterion scores. Compare Figure 5.12 to Figure 5.13 in which there does not appear to be any correspondence between predictor and criterion scores. Based on Figure 5.13 one would say that the *average* criterion score is the same for any predictor score, whether it is high or low.

While inspection of the scatterplot provides an idea of the existence of a relationship between the predictor and criterion scores, the degree of the relationship is more precisely determined by the Pearson Product-moment correlation or the validity coefficient as it is called in the personnel selection context. In this example both predictor and criterion scores are assumed to be measured on interval scales. For other types of measurement in which scales are categorized, for example when the criterion is simply a judgment that the employee meets a standard or does not meet the standard, i.e., a two-point scale, other kinds of validity coefficients such as phi or biserial may be computed.

The validity coefficient provides two kinds of important information. First, it indicates the *direction* of the relationship as positive or negative. A positive relationship, as in Figure 5.12, shows that as the predictor score increases so does the criterion score; a negative relationship exists when an increase in the predictor score is associated with a decrease in criterion score. Second, the size of the validity coefficient indicates the *degree* of relationship between predictor

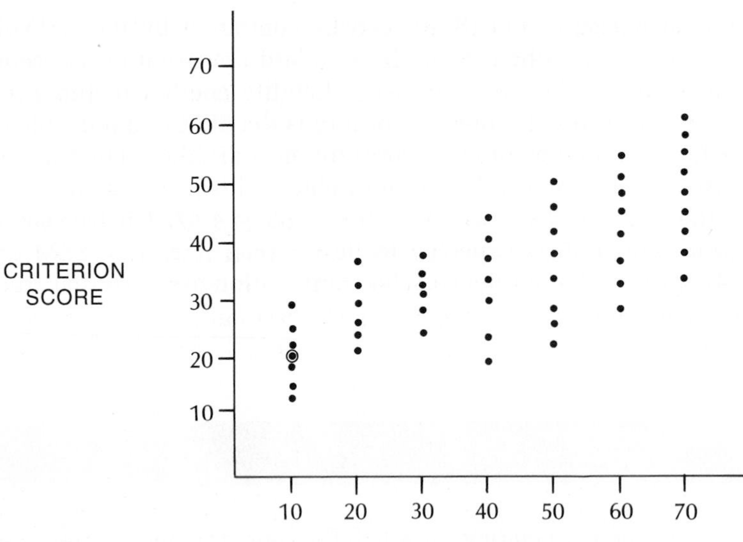

FIGURE 5.12
Predictor Score

and criterion. Because it is a correlation, a validity coefficient may range from −1 through 00 to +1. The closer to +1 or −1 the stronger is the relationship. The validity coefficient is tested for its statistical significance to determine if its value is high enough to be considered different from zero and not just the result of a chance occurrence. If the validity coefficient is not statistically significant, the predictor should not be considered as valid for the criterion. In Figure 5.12 the validity coefficient is .40 for a sample of 50 employees. The statistical test for this correlation is given by the following formula:

$$t = \frac{r\sqrt{n-2}}{\sqrt{1-r^2}}$$

FIGURE 5.13
Criterion Score

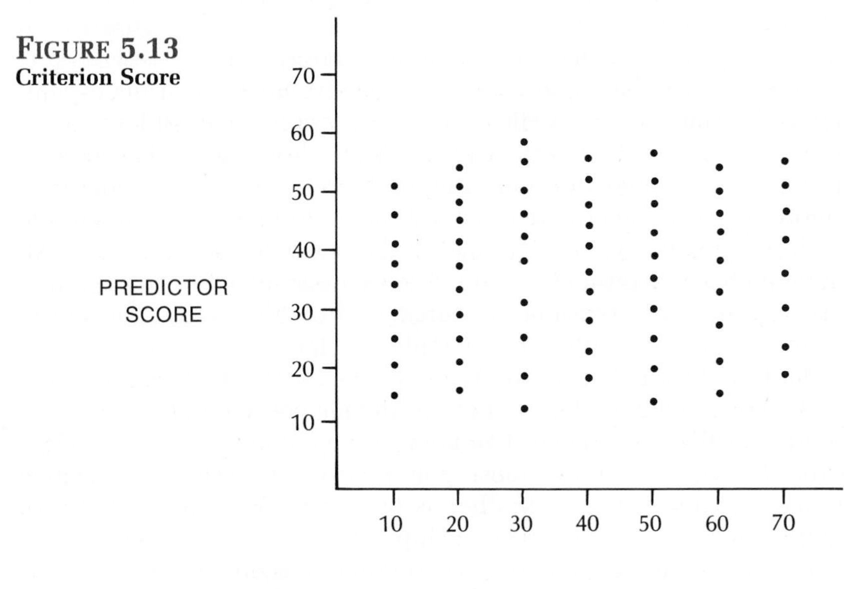

where r is the validity coefficient and n is the sample size from which it was computed. For this example the conclusion is that a correlation of .40 has less than five chances in 100 of occurring by chance and therefore there probably is a true relation between the predictor score and the criterion score.

The validity coefficient may be interpreted as the percentage of improvement in criterion scores from selecting individuals by using the test compared to selecting them based on their criterion score. This means that if *all* applicants were hired and the best 50 were retained after criterion scores were obtained, a test with a validity coefficient of .40 would have selected employees that produced 40% of the criterion performance as the best 50. In other words, the efficiency of a selection instrument is directly and linearly related to its validity.

THE PROBLEM OF TEST UNFAIRNESS

A test might be valid when all applicants are considered, but still discriminate unfairly against *subgroups* of applicants. Thus, suppose a test is administered to 100 applicants, 60 of whom are white and 40 black. You find that for the 100 applicants the test is valid. But on closer examination, it turns out that 80% of the whites are selected, while only 20% of the blacks are selected. The fact that a lower proportion of blacks are selected could put the burden of proof on the employer to prove that the blacks are not being unfairly discriminated against by the test. The employer could be required to validate the test separately for *both* blacks and whites.

Suppose the employer makes separate validation studies and finds the test is in fact valid for both blacks and whites. Then even though the test results in a larger proportion of rejects among blacks than whites, the test is, generally speaking, still legally acceptable. While it *does* "discriminate" between black and white candidates, it probably does not do so *unfairly* since it is valid (it predicts performance) for both groups.

It occasionally happens, however, that while a person's score on the test is a valid predictor of his or her performance on the job, members of one group consistently score better (or worse) than do members of another group and are therefore more likely to be hired. For example, assume an employer decides to hire applicants who will perform on the job in a "good" manner (equivalent to supervisor performance rating of 70–80). Further assume that the selection test is validated separately for whites and nonwhites and found to be valid for both. However, nonwhites who score 60 on the test tend to get "good" on-the-job performance ratings, while whites who score 80 on the test tend to get the "good" ratings.

If the employer decided to use the higher test score (80) as the cutoff score, then mostly whites would be hired, since relatively few nonwhites (for whom 60 was a high score) probably achieved scores as high as 80. (Perhaps nonwhites cannot read as well, for instance, and thus do more poorly, overall, than whites on the test, although once on the job the nonwhite who scores 60 will perform as well as the white who scores 80.)

Such a situation could be *unfairly discriminatory* to the nonwhites. Unfair discrimination exists when persons with equal probabilities of success on the job have unequal probabilities of being hired. In our case, a nonwhite who scores 60 and a white who scores 80 both have equal opportunities for being "good" performers. But since the employer chose to use the higher test score (80) as a cutoff, whites, primarily, were hired, thus unfairly discriminating against those nonwhites (who scored 60) *who had the same probability as the whites who scored 80 of performing in a "good" manner.*

There are two implications. First, employers should, whenever feasible, validate tests separately for both minorities and nonminorities, both to ensure that the test is valid for both and to ascertain whether different cutoff scores for each group might be appropriate.[88] Second, an employer can generally use different cutoff scores for each group (like 80 for whites and 60 for nonwhites) *as long as each cutoff score corresponds to the same level of on-the-job performance* (in our case "good").[89]

On the other hand, your study might show that the test is valid for both blacks and whites. Therefore, although there is adverse impact, the test passes the standards for a business necessity (job relatedness) defense.

This is illustrated in Figure 5.14. Here, note that this test is valid for both groups together and also for the subgroups, since (while most minority candidates are rejected) they are "correctly" identified as probable unsuccessful performers.

Once subgroups are analyzed it can be seen that the test is valid for blacks and whites. Therefore, although there is adverse impact, the test passes the standard for business necessity.

▶ Aspects of the Quest for Validity

Unfortunately, things are not always so simple as they appear, and that is certainly the case when it comes to the matter of validating tests. The five step process laid out earlier is a simple and practical one. However, you should also be aware of and consider certain matters that may complicate your quest to arrive at conclusions regarding the validity of the tests you might want to use.

There is, first, the matter of which criterion to use. In brief, the so-called "criterion problem" revolves around ". . . whether different methods of measuring job performance, such as supervisor ratings, production output, and work samples, result in different validity results for the same test."[90] Basically, the problem here is that there are differences in the correlation coefficient when using different criteria. In other words, the same test could have one correlation coefficient when relating scores on a test to one criterion (perhaps using supervisor ratings), and a quite different coefficient when ration scores on a test to a second or other criteria (perhaps using production output). This obviously demands that care be taken in the choice of criteria. Consideration must also be given to analyzing the correlation between predictor and each criterion with the aim of determining why discrepancies (if any) exist.

The second problem has been described in terms of "disenchantment with the usual validity coefficient." This basically refers to the fact that in many cases basing a test's validity on a single correlation coefficient between predictor and criterion (as is often done) may be flawed for at least two reasons.[91] One is "a

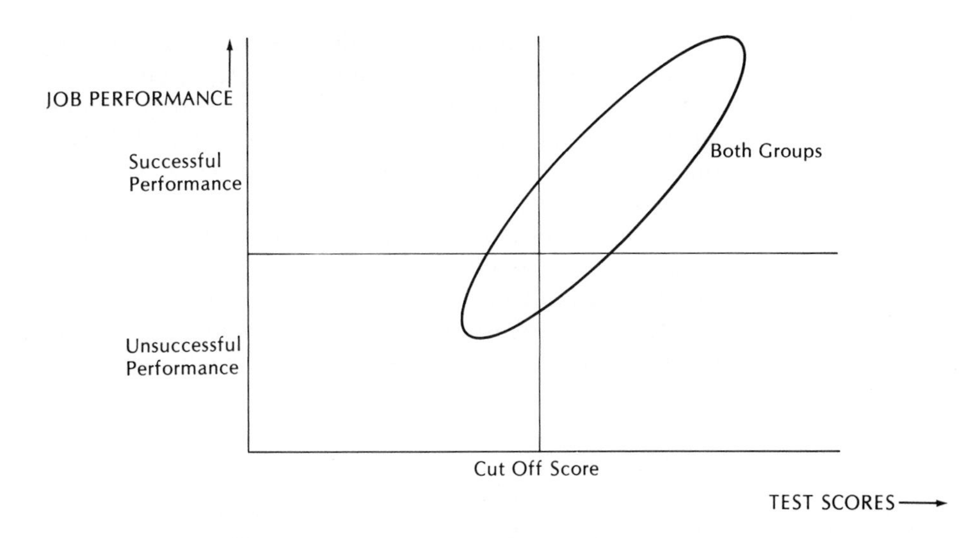

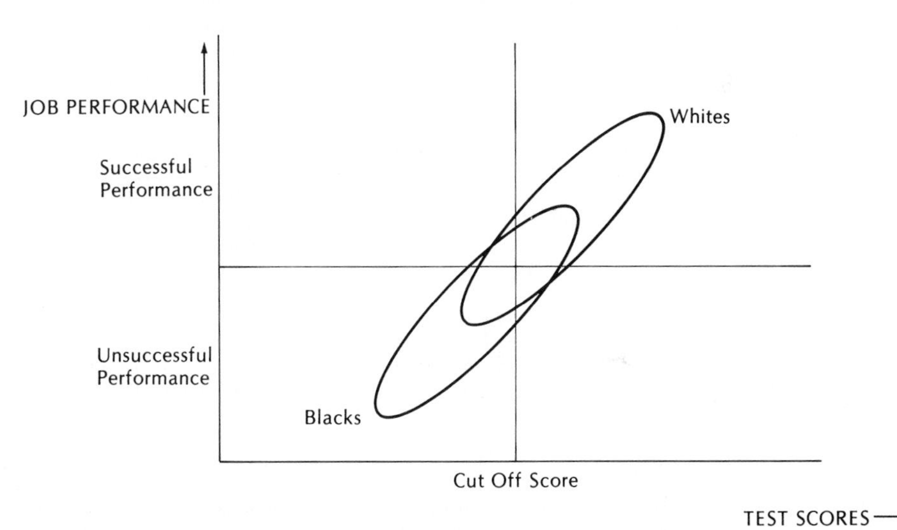

FIGURE 5.14 Validation for Subgroups

Once subgroups are analyzed it can be seen that the test is valid for blacks and whites. Therefore, although there is adverse impact, the test passes the standard for business necessity.

growing awareness that a single bivariate (two-variable) correlation is virtually uninterpretable."[92] For example, you know a correlation coefficient by itself doesn't show cause and effect: Thus (to use an overworked example), a correlation between smoking and cancer (the tobacco industry would contend) doesn't necessarily *prove* that smoking *leads* to cancer; it may simply reflect that fact that other, unmeasured factors (like emotional stress) lead people to both smoke and get cancer. "Thus," (contend some psychologists) "just how much importance can be lent to a single correlation coefficient—in this case, a validity coefficient that correlates test scores (predictor) and performance (criterion)?"

The other reason for the "disenchantment with the usual validity coefficient" is the possible unreliability of the criterion itself. Specifically, a correlation (validity) coefficient may be deemed questionable because of an unreliable criterion (for instance, haphazard performance appraisal) or the fact that other criteria should have been used, or because of other, related problems. (These problems are studied today under the topics of metaanalysis and validity generalization.) For example, the question can be raised as to how valid a validity coefficient is over the entire range of test scores or criterion. Thus a test may do a good job of predicting performance for very high performers and so (unless the researcher is very careful) thereby produce a high-validity coefficient and an apparently valid test. But the point has been made that this apparent validity may not be generalizable to the lower range of test scores. For example, it may turn out that for some reason test scores correlate very highly for a certain range of performance (or for a certain range of test scores), but not nearly as well in other parts of the range.[93] In any event, the bottom line is that someone embarking on a validity study has to take more care than might be immediately apparent.[94]

▶ NOTES

1. Frank Schmidt and others, "Impact of Valid Selection Procedures on Workforce Productivity," *Journal of Applied Psychology*, Vol. 64 (December 1979), pp. 609–626. See also Robert M. Guion, "Changing Views for Personnel Selection Research," *Personnel Psychology*, Vol. 40, no. 2 (Summer 1987), pp. 199–213.
2. Robert E. Sibson, "The High Cost of Hiring," *Nation's Business*, February 1975, p. 85.
3. Bureau of National Affairs, *Bulletin to Management*, September 10, 1987, p. 295.
4. Ann Marie Ryan and Marja Lasek, "Negligent Hiring and Defamation: Areas of Liability Related to Pre–Employment Inquiries," *Personnel Psychology*, Vol. 44, no. 2 (Summer 1991), pp. 293–319.
5. Ibid., p. 302.
6. Ibid.
7. Leona Tyler, *Tests and Measurements* (Englewood Cliffs, NJ: Prentice Hall, 1971), p. 25. More technically, "validity refers to the degree of confidence one can have in inferences drawn from scores, considering the whole process by which the scores are obtained. Stated differently, validity refers to the confidence one has in the meaning attached to scores." (See Guion, "Changing Views for Personnel Selection Research," p. 208.)
8. Strictly speaking, a third way to demonstrate a test's validity is *construct validity.* A construct is a trait such as intelligence. Therefore, to take a simple example, if intelligence is important to the position of engineer, a test that measures intelligence would have construct validity for that position. To prove construct validity, an employer has to prove that the test actually measures the construct *and* that the construct is in turn required for the job. Federal agency guidelines make it difficult to prove construct validity, however, and as a result few employers use this approach as a means of satisfying the federal guidelines. See James Ledvinka, *Federal Regulation of Personnel and Human Resource Management* (Boston: Kent, 1982), p. 113.
9. Bureau of National Affairs, *Primer of Equal Employment Opportunity* (Washington, D.C.: BNA, 1978), p. 18. In practice, proving in court the criterion–related validity of paper–and–pencil tests has been difficult.
10. Ledvinka, *Federal Regulations*, p. 111.
11. Anne Anastasi, *Psychological Patterns* (New York: Macmillan, 1968), reprinted in W. Clay Hamner and Frank Schmidt, *Contemporary Problems in Personnel* (Chicago: St. Claire Press, 1974), pp. 102–109. Discussion of reliability based on Marvin Dunnette, *Personnel Selection and Placement* (Belmont, CA: Wadsworth Publishing Company, Inc., 1966), pp. 29–30.
12. Calvin Hoffman, Bary Nathan, and Lisa Holden, "A Comparison of Validation Criteria: Objective versus Subjective Performance Measures and Self– versus Supervisory Ratings," *Personnel Psychology*, Vol. 44 (1991), pp. 601–619.
13. Based on J. Tiffin and E. J. McCormick, *Industrial Psychology* (Englewood Cliffs, NJ: Prentice Hall, 1965), pp. 104–105; C. H. Lawshe and M. J. Balma, *Principles of Personnel Testing*, 2nd ed. (New York: McGraw–Hill, 1966).
14. Experts sometimes have to develop separate expectancy charts and cutting points for minorities and nonminorities if the validation studies indicate that high performers from either group (minority or nonminority) score lower (or higher) on the test. See our discussion of differential validity in the appendix to this chapter. For a good discussion of how to evaluate a selection test, see Raymond Berger and Donna Tucker, "How to Evaluate a Selection Test," *Personnel Journal*, Vol. 66, no. 6 (February 1987), pp. 88–91.
15. See, for example, Floyd L. Ruch, "The Impact on Employment Procedures of the Supreme Court Decision in the Duke Power Case," *Personnel Journal*, Vol. 50, no. 4 (October 1971), pp. 777–783; Hubert Field, Gerald Bagley, and Susan Bagley, "Employment Test Validation for Minority and Non–minority Production Workers," *Personnel Psychology*, Vol. 30, no. 1 (Spring 1977), pp. 37–46; Ledvinka, *Federal Regulations*, p. 110.
16. See Ruch, "The Impact on Employment Procedures," pp. 777–783, in Hamner and Schmidt, *Contemporary Problems in Personnel*, pp. 117–123; Dale Beach, *Personnel* (New York: Macmillan, 1970); Field, Bagley, and Bagley, "Employing Test Validation for Minority and Nonminority Production Workers," pp. 37–46; M. K. Distefano, Jr., Margaret Pryer, and Stella Craig, "Predictive Validity of General Ability Tests with Black and White Psychiatric Attendants," *Personnel Psychology*, Vol. 29, no. 2 (Summer

1976). Also, see the Winter 1976 issue of *Personnel Psychology*, Vol. 2, no. 4. See also James Norborg, "A Warning Regarding the Simplified Approach to the Evaluation of Test Fairness and Employee Selection Procedures," *Personnel Psychology*, Vol. 37, no. 3 (Autumn 1984), pp. 483–486; Charles Johnson, Lawrence Messe, and William Crano, "Predicting Job Performance of Low Income Workers: The Work Opinion Questionnaire," *Personnel Psychology*, Vol. 37, no. 2 (Summer 1984), pp. 291–299; Frank Schmidt, Benjamin Ocasio, Joseph Hillery, and John Hunter, "Further Within–Setting Empirical Tests of the Situational Specificity Hypothesis in Personnel Selection," *Personnel Psychology*, Vol. 38, no. 3 (Autumn 1985), pp. 509–524.

17. Prentice Hall, "PH/ASPA Survey: Employee Testing Procedures—Where Are They Headed?" *Personnel Management: Policies and Practices*, April 22, 1975, described in James Ledvinka and Lyle Schoenfeldt, "Legal Developments in Employment Testing: Albemarle," *Personnel Psychology*, Vol. 31, no. 1 (Spring 1978), p. 9.
18. Ledvinka and Schoenfeldt, "Legal Developments," p. 9.
19. Ledvinka, *Federal Regulations*, p. 109.
20. Douglas Baker and David Terpstra, "Employee Selection: Must Every Job Test Be Validated?" *Personnel Journal*, Vol. 61 (August 1982), pp. 602–605.
21. This is based on Marilyn Quaintance, "Test Security: Foundations of Public Merit Systems," *Personnel Psychology*, Vol. 33, no. 1 (Spring 1980), pp. 25–32.
22. William Roskind, "DECO Versus NLRB, and the Consequences of Open Testing in Industry," *Personnel Psychology*, Vol. 33, no. 1 (Spring 1980), pp. 3–9; and James Ledvinka, Val Markos, and Robert Ladd, "Long–Range Impact of 'Fair Selection' Standards on Minority Employment," *Journal of Applied Psychology*, Vol. 67, no. 1 (February 1982), pp. 18–36.
23. Susan Mendelsohn and Katheryn Morrison, "The Right to Privacy at the Work Place," Part 1: "Employee Searchers," *Personnel*, July 1988, p. 20.
24. Wayne Outten and Noah A. Kinigstein, *The Rights of Employees* (New York: Bantam Books, 1984), pp. 53–54.
25. Mendelson and Morrisohn, "The Right to Privacy in the Work Place," p. 22.
26. Outten and Kinigstein, *The Rights of Employees*, pp. 54–55.
27. Ibid., p. 55.
28. *Kehr* v. *Consolidated Freightways of Delaware*, Docket No. 86–2126, July 15, 1987, U.S. Seventh Circuit Court of Appeals. Discussed in Commerce Clearing House, *Ideas and Trends*, October 16, 1987, p. 165.
29. For a discussion of these see Commerce Clearing House, *Ideas and Trends*, October 16, 1987, pp. 165–166.
30. Except as noted, this is based largely on Laurence Siegel and Irving Lane, *Personnel and Organizational Psychology* (Homewood, IL: Irwin, 1982), pp. 170–185. See also Tyler, *Tests and Measurements*, pp. 38–79, and Lawshe and Balma, *Principles of Personnel Testing*, pp. 83–160.
31. See, for example, Richard Reilly, Sheldon Zedeck, and Mary Tenopyr, "Validity and Fairness of Physical Ability Tests for Predicting Performance in Craft Jobs," *Journal of Applied Psychology*, Vol. 64, no. 3 (June 1970), pp. 262–274. See also Barten Daniel, "Strength and Endurance Testing," *Personnel Journal*, June 1987, pp. 112–122.
32. If you read note 8, you will see that this approach calls for construct validation which, as was pointed out, is extremely difficult to demonstrate.
33. Murray R. Barrick and Michael K. Mount, "The Big Five Personality Dimensions and Job Performance: A Meta-Analysis," *Personnel Psychology*, Vol. 44, no. 1, Spring 1991, pp. 1–26.
34. Robert Tett, Douglas Jackson, and Mitchell Rothstein, "Personality Measures as Predictors of Job Performance: A Meta-Analystic Review," *Personnel Psychology*, Vol. 44 (1991), p. 732.
35. Ibid.
36. For a study describing how matching (1) task and working condition preferences of applicants with (2) actual job and working conditions can be achieved, see Ronald Ash, Edward Levine, and Steven Edgell, "Study of a Matching Approach: The Impact of Ethnicity," *Journal of Applied Psychology*, Vol. 64, no. 1 (February 1979), pp. 35–41. For a discussion of how a standard clerical test can be used to screen applicants who will have to use video displays, see Edward Silver and Corwin Bennett, "Modification of the Minnesota Clerical Test to Predict Performance on Video Display Terminals," *Journal of Applied Psychology*, Vol. 72, no. 1 (February 1987), pp. 153–155.
37. Emma D. Dunnette and W. D. Borman, "Personnel Selection and Classification Systems," *Annual Review of Psychology*, Vol. 30 (1979), pp. 477–525, quoted in Siegel and Lane, *Personnel and Organizational Psychology*, pp. 182–183.
38. Paul Wernamont and John T. Campbell, "Signs, Samples, and Criteria," *Journal of Applied Psychology*, Vol. 52 (1968), pp. 372–376; James Campion, "Work Sampling for Personnel Selection," *Journal of Applied Psychology*, Vol. 56 (1972), pp. 40–44, reprinted in Hamner and Schmidt, *Contemporary Problems in Personnel*, pp. 168–180; Sidney Gael, Donald Grant, and Richard Ritchie, "Employment Test Validation for Minority and Nonminority Clerks with Work Sample Criteria," *Journal of Applied Psychology*, Vol. 60, no. 4 (August 1974); Frank Schmidt and others, "Job Sample vs. Paper and Pencil Trades and Technical Test: Adverse Impact and Examinee Attitudes," *Personnel Psychology*, Vol. 30, no. 7 (Summer 1977), pp. 187–198.
39. See, for example, George Burgnoli, James Campion, and Jeffrey Bisen, "Racial Bias in the Use of Work Samples for Personnel Selection," *Journal of Applied Psychology*, Vol. 64, no. 2 (April 1979), pp. 119–123.
40. Siegel and Lane, *Personnel and Organizational Psychology*, pp. 182–183.
41. Ann Howard, "An Assessment of Assessment Centers," *Academy of Management Journal*, Vol. 17 (1974), pp. 115–134; see also Louis Olivas, "Using Assessment Centers for Individual and Organizational Development," *Personnel*, Vol. 57 (May–June 1980), pp. 63–67.
42. *Development Dimensions, Inc., 1977–1978 Catalog.* (Pittsburgh: Development Dimensions Press, 1977), discussed in Wayne F. Cascio and Val Silbey, "Utility of the Assessment Center as a Selection Device," *Journal of Applied Psychology*, Vol. 64, no. 4 (April 1979), pp. 107–118.
43. See, for example, Larry Alexander, "An Exploratory Study of the Utilization of Assessment Center Results," *Academy of Management Journal*, Vol. 22, no. 1 (March 1970), pp. 152–157.
44. Steven Norton, "The Empirical and Content Validity of Assessment Centers Versus Traditional Methods of Predicting Management Success," *Academy of Management Review*, Vol. 20 (July 1977), pp. 442–453. Interestingly, a recent review concludes that assessment centers do predict managerial success, but after an extensive review, "we also assert that we do not know why they work." Richard Klimoski and Mary Brickner, "Why Do Assessment Centers Work? The Puzzle of Assessment Center Validity," *Personnel Psychology*, Vol. 40, no. 2 (Summer 1987), pp. 243–260.

45. John Hinrichs, "An Eight Year Follow–up of a Management Assessment Center," *Journal of Applied Psychology*, Vol. 63, no. 5 (October 1978), pp. 596–601.
46. Cascio and Silbey, "Utility of the Assessment Center as a Selection Device." See also Paul R. Sackett, "Assessment Centers and Content Validity: Some Neglected Issues," *Personnel Psychology*, Vol. 40 (Spring 1987), pp. 13–26.
47. David Groce, "A Behavioral Consistency Approach to Decision Making in Employment Selection," *Personnel Psychology*, Vol. 34, no. 1 (Spring 1981), pp. 55–64.
48. Donald Brush and Lyle Schoenfeldt, "Identifying Managerial Potential: An Alternative Assessment Center," *Personnel*, Vol. 57 (May–June 1980), pp. 72–73.
49. Arthur Cosiegel, "The Miniature Job Training and Evaluation Approach: Traditional Findings," *Personnel Psychology*, Vol. 36, no. 1 (Spring 1983), pp. 41–56.
50. See, for example, George Beason and John Belt, "Verifying the Job Applicant's Background," *Personnel Administration*, November–December 1974, pp. 29–32; Bureau of National Affairs, "Selection Procedures and Personnel Records," *Personnel Policies Forum*, No. 114 (September 1976), p. 4. See also Paul Sackett and Michael M. Harris, "Honesty Testing for Personnel Selection: A Review and Critique," *Personnel Psychology*, Vol. 37, no. 2 (Summer 1985), pp. 221–245.
51. For additional information see Lawrence E. Dube, Jr., "Employment References and the Law," *Personnel Journal*, Vol. 65, no. 2 (February 1986), pp. 87–91.
52. Thomas von der Embse and Rodney Wyse, "Those Reference Letters: How Useful Are They?" *Personnel*, Vol. 62, no. 1 (January 1985), pp. 42–46.
53. Tiffin and McCormick, *Industrial Psychology*, pp. 78–79.
54. See Howard M. Fischer, "Select the Right Executive," *Personnel Journal* (April 1989), pp. 110–114.
55. James Bell, James Castagnera, and Jane Patterson Yong, "Employment References: Do you Know the Law?" *Personnel Journal*, Vol. 63, no. 2 (February 1984), pp. 32–36. In order to demonstrate defamation, several elements must be present: (a) the defamatory statement must have been communicated to another party; (b) the statement must be a false statement of fact; (c) injury to reputation must have occurred; and (d) the employer must not be protected under qualified or absolute privilege. For a discussion see Ryan and Lasek, "Negligent Hiring and Defamation," p. 307.
56. This is based on SKRSC Update, May–June 1985, Schachter, Kristoff, Ross, Sprague, and Curialle, California Street, San Francisco, CA.
57. This is based largely on Jeffrey M. Hahn, "Pre-Employment Information Services: Employers Beware?" *Employee Relations Law Journal*, Vol. 17, no. 1 (Summer 1991), pp. 45–69.
58. Ibid., p. 50.
59. Ibid., p. 53.
60. Ibid., p. 51.
61. Based in part on Ibid., pp. 64–66.
62. James Frierson, "New Polygraph Tests Limits," *Personnel Journal* (December 1988), pp. 84–89.
63. See Bureau of National Affairs, "Polygraph Law Parameters Outlined," *Bulletin to Management*, July 30, 1992, p. 234.
64. For additional detail on the legal aspects of polygraph testing, see Robert Faley, "Legal Issues Concerning Polygraph Testing in the Public Sector," *Public Personnel Management*, Vol. 19, no. 4, (Winter 1990) pp. 365–379.
65. John Jones and William Terris, "Post–Polygraph Selection Techniques," *Recruitment Today* (May–June 1989), pp. 25–31.
66. Norma Fritz, "In Focus: Honest Answers–Post Polygraph," *Personnel* (April 1989), p. 8.
67. Bureau of National Affairs, *Bulletin to Management*, September 10, 1987, p. 296.
68. See, for example, Kevin Murphy, "Detecting Infrequent Deception," *Journal of Applied Psychology*, Vol. 72, no. 4 (November 1987), pp. 611–614, for a discussion of the difficulty of using such tests to provide convincing evidence of deception.
69. These are based on Commerce Clearing House, *Ideas and Trends*, December 29, 1988, pp. 222–223. See also Bureau of National Affairs, "Divining Integrity Through Interview," *Bulletin to Management*, June 4, 1987, p. 184.
70. This example is based on Bureau of National Affairs, *Bulletin to Management*, February 26, 1987, p. 65.
71. See, for example, "Corporate Lie Detectors Under Fire," *Business Week*, January 13, 1973. For a discussion of how to improve the validity of the polygraph test, see Robert Forman and Clark McCauley, "Validity of a Positive Control Polygraph Test Using the Field to Practice Model," *Journal of Applied Psychology*, Vol. 71, no. 4 (November 1986), pp. 691–698.
72. Ulrich Sonnemann, *Handwriting Analysis as a Psychodiagnostic Tool* (New York: Grune & Stratton, 1950), pp. 144–145.
73. Jitendra Sharma and Harsh Vardham, "Graphology: What Handwriting Can Tell You about an Applicant," *Personnel*, Vol. 52, no. 2 (March–April 1975), pp. 57–63. Note that one recent empirical study resulted in the conclusion that "we find ourselves compelled to conclude that it is graphology, rather than just our small sample of graphologists, that is invalid." These researchers conclude that when graphology does seem to "work," it does so because the graphologist is reading a spontaneously written autobiography of the candidate and is thereby obtaining biographical information about the candidate from that essay. See Gershon Ben–Shakhar, Maya Bar–Hillel, Yoram Bilu, Edor Ben–Abba, and Anat Flug, "Can Graphology Predict Occupational Success? Two Empirical Studies and Some Methodological Ruminations," *Journal of Applied Psychology*, Vol. 71, no. 4 (November 1986), pp. 645–653.
74. Joseph Famularo, *Handbook of Modern Personnel Administration* (New York: McGraw–Hill, 1972), pp. 12–17, 18.
75. Mick Haus, "Pre-Employment Physicals and the ADA," *Safety and Health*, February 1992, pp. 64–65.
76. Ian Miners, Nick Nykodym, and Diane Samerdyke–Traband, "Put Drug Detection to the Test," *Personnel Journal*, Vol. 66, no. 8 (August 1987), pp. 191–197.
77. Eric Rolfe Greenberg, "Workplace Testing: Who's Testing Whom?" *Personnel*, May 1989, pp. 39–45.
78. Chris Berka and Courtney Poignand, "Hair Follicle Testing—An Alternative to Urinalysis for Drug Abuse Screening," *Employee Relations Today*, Winter 1991–1992, pp. 405–409.
79. This is based on Ann M. O'Neill, "Legal Issues Presented by Hair Follicle Testing," *Employee Relations Today*, Winter 1991–1992, pp. 411–415.
80. Ibid., p. 411.
81. Ibid., p. 413.
82. For an additional perspective on drug testing as it applies to public agencies and unions see, for example, Nancy C. O'Neill, "Drug Testing in Public Agencies: Are Personnel Directors Doing Things Right?," *Public Personnel Management*, Vol. 19, no. 4 (Winter 1990), pp. 391–397; Michael H. LeRoy, "The Presence of Drug Testing in the Workplace and Union Member Attitudes," *Labor Studies Journal*, Fall 1991, pp. 33–42.

83. Eric Rolfe Greenberg, "Workplace Testing: Results of a New AMA Survey," *Personnel* (April 1988), p. 40.
84. Michael A. McDaniel, "Does Pre–Employment Drug Use Predict on the Job Suitability?" *Personnel Psychology*, Vol. 41, no. 4 (Winter 1988), pp. 717–729.
85. These are quoted from Commerce Clearing House, *Ideas and Trends*, May 1, 1987, pp. 70–71.
86. For information about ordering the Wonderlic, contact E. F. Wonderlic and Associates, Inc., 820 Frontage Rd., Northfield, IL 60093. Their phone number is 312/446–8900.
87. Reach Assessment Systems Corporation at 2233 University Ave., Suite 440, St. Paul, MN 55114, 612/647–9220.
88. David Robertson, "Update on Testing and Equal Opportunity," *Personnel Journal*, Vol. 56, no. 3 (March 1977), reprinted in Craig Schneier and Richard Beatty, *Personnel Administration Today* (Reading, Mass.: Addison–Wesley, 1978), p. 300.
89. Virginia R. Boehm, "Negro–White Differences in Validity of Employment and Training Selection Procedures: Summary of Research Evidence," *Journal of Applied Psychology*, Vol. 56 (1972), pp. 33–39, in Hamner and Schmidt, *Contemporary Problems in Personnel*, pp. 126–134. See also John Hunter and Frank Schmidt, "Differential and Single Group Validity of Employment Tests by Race: A Critical Analysis of Three Recent Studies," *Journal of Applied Psychology*, Vol. 63, no. 1 (1978), pp. 1–11. Note that the need for differential test scores is a separate problem from that of *differential validity*. Differential validity exists when the validity coefficients for two groups are significantly different in a statistical sense. Differential validity thus refers to the predictive capability of the test for each group. When a test is validated separately for two groups—say, white and nonwhite—it could thus turn out that (1) the test is *differentially valid*, in that the validity coefficients (the correlation between test score and job performance) are different for the two groups, and/or (2) different cutting scores are needed for each group, since using the same cutting score might be unfairly discriminatory to one group. In practice, *differential validity* is generally not a serious problem. Finally, also note that while the need for different cutting scores is an important source of test unfairness, there are other ways to use a test unfairly. One could, for instance (to use an extreme example), give nonminority candidates the test answers ahead of time.
90. Barry R. Nathan and Ralph A. Alexander, "A Comparison of Criteria for Test Validation: A Meta–analytic Investigation," *Personnel Psychology*, Vol. 41, no. 3 (Autumn 1988), pp. 517–535.
91. Guion, "Changing Views for Personnel Selection Research," pp. 207–208.
92. Ibid., p. 207.
93. For a discussion, see David A. Waldman and Bruce J. Avolio, "Homogeneity of Test Validity," *Journal of Applied Psychology*, Vol. 74, no. 2 (April 1989), pp. 371–374.
94. For a discussion of how to evaluate psychological tests, see, for example, Robin Inwald, "How to Evaluate Psychological/Honesty Tests," *Personnel Journal*, May 1988, pp. 40–46. Dr. Inwald suggests a number of pointers, including beware of tests for which little or no validation research exists; beware of studies that are not based on the prediction model of validation; beware of studies that do not tell you how many people were incorrectly predicted to have job problems; beware of studies (or tests) that claim to successfully predict dangerous, violent, or nonviolent behavior or tendencies because violent behavior "cannot be predicted"; beware of studies that report significant correlations as their evidence of validity (since unusually high correlations would be questionable); beware of studies that use small numbers of participants to predict important job performance outcomes; beware of studies that have not been cross–validated; beware of claims that tests are valid for use with occupational groups for whom validation studies have not yet been conducted; beware of studies based on individuals filling out questionnaires or tests anonymously; beware of studies that have not used real job candidates as subjects for their validation efforts; and beware of tests whose validation studies have been designed, conducted, and published only by the test developer or publishing company without replication by other independent psychological agencies.

CHAPTER 6

INTERVIEWING CANDIDATES AND BUILDING A TOTAL SELECTION PROGRAM

OVERVIEW

We first discuss the types of interviews, as well as the pros and cons of interviewing. We next turn to some of the factors that affect the usefulness of interviews. We then present some specific guidelines for improving your "batting average" as an interviewer—and as an interviewee. When you finish studying this chapter, you should be able to discuss each of the current interviewing mistakes; and explain how to conduct an effective interview.

▶ INTRODUCTION

The screening tool that's used most often (and sometimes exclusively) is the *selection interview*. Interviews give you a chance to size up the candidate personally, and to pursue questioning in a way that tests cannot. They give you an opportunity to make judgments on the candidate's enthusiasm and intelligence. And they give you an opportunity to assess subjective aspects of the candidate—facial expressions, appearance, nervousness, and so forth. Interviews can therefore be a *very* potent screening tool.

Yet all too often interviews are not used to their best advantage. The interviewer himself or herself may be nervous, and pertinent questions aren't asked, for instance. The result is that the findings on the reliability and validity of interviews could lead one to believe that interviews are worthless, when it's not the interview but the ineptness of the interviewer that creates the problem.

How useful *is* the interview? The evidence shows that an interview's usefulness depends on how it is carried out. Much of the earlier research gave selection interviews low marks in terms of reliability and validity.[1] However, more recent studies show that an interview properly administered *is* a useful screening device.[2] The key to an interview's usefulness is the manner in which it is administered.[3] In this chapter we therefore focus on the problems that can undermine interviews, and how to avoid them. First, though, we review the basic types of interviews.

TYPES OF INTERVIEWS

There are several basic types of interviews.

Nondirective

nondirective interview An unstructured conversational-style interview. The interviewer pursues points of interest as they come up in response to questions.

In a **nondirective interview**, you ask questions as they come to mind. There is no special format to follow, and the conversation can wander off in various directions. As an interviewer you may have a job specification as a guide and you may or may not ask the same or similar questions of each applicant. Often, each interview starts off about the same, but the unstructured nature of the interview lets you wander far afield, asking questions based on the candidate's last statements. This allows you to pursue points of interest as they develop.

Directive Interview

directive interview An interview following a set sequence of questions.

In a **directive** (or structured) **interview** you follow a predetermined sequence of questions, perhaps using a structured interview form as in Figure 6.1. If you'll review that figure for a moment, you'll notice that a form like this is only meant to be a general guide and that, as it says, "All of the items may not apply in every instance." The main advantages of using a form like this is that it's very comprehensive. There is thus less likelihood of forgetting to ask a particular question of applicant. With a form like this, in other words, all the applicants tend to be asked all of the necessary questions by all the interviewers.

Again, though, you'll notice that a form like this isn't meant to lock you into a particular set of questions, with no variability on your part. The form does mention, again, that you may skip some items. Furthermore, space is provided

FIGURE 6.1
Structured Interview Guide

APPLICANT INTERVIEW GUIDE

To the interviewer: This Applicant Interview Guide is intended to assist in employee selection and placement. If it is used for all applicants for a position, it will help you to compare them, and it will provide more objective information than you will obtain from unstructured intereviews.

Because this is a general guide, all of the items may not apply in every instance. Skip those which are not applicable and add questions appropriate to the specific position. Space for additional questions will be found at the end of the form.

Federal law prohibits discrimination in employment on the basis of sex, race, color, national origin, religion, disability, and, in most instances, age. The laws of most states also ban some or all of the above types of discrimination in employment as well as discrimination based on marital status or ancestry. Interviewers should take care to avoid any questions which suggest that an employment decision will be made on the basis of any such factors.

Job Interest

Name_______________ Position applied for_______________

What do you think the job (position) involves?_______________

Why do you want the job (position)?_______________

Why are you qualified for it?_______________

What would your salary requirements be?_______________

What do you know about our company?_______________

Why do you want to work for us?_______________

Current Work Status

Are you now employed? _____ Yes_____ No. If not, how long have you been unemployed?_______________

Why are you unemployed?_______________

If you are working, why are you applying for this position?_______________

When would you be available to start work with us?_______________

Work Experience

(Start with the applicant's current or last position and work back. All periods of time should be accounted for. Go back at least 12 years, depending upon the applicant's age. Military service should be treated as a job.)

Current or last employer_______________ Addresss_______________

Dates of employment: from_______________ to_______________

Current or last job title_______________

What are (were) your duties?_______________

Have you held the same job throughout your employment with that company? _____ Yes _____ No. If not, describe the various jobs you have had with that employer, how long you held each of them, and the main duties of each._______________

____

What was your starting salary?_______________ What are you earning now?_______________ Comments_______________

____

Name of your last or current supervisor_______________

What did you like most about that job?_______________

What did you like least about it?_______________

Why are you thinking of leaving?_______________

Why are you leaving right now?_______________

Interviewer's comments or observations_______________

____

FIGURE 6.1 (continued)

What did you do before you took your last job? ______________________

Where were you employed? ______________________

Location ______________ Job title ______________

Duties ______________________

Did you hold the same job throughout your employment with that company? _______Yes _______ No. If not, describe the jobs you held, when you held them and the duties of each. ______________________

____

What was your starting salary? ____________What was your final salary?____________

Name of your last supervsor______________________

May we contact that company? _______Yes _______No.

What did you like most about that job?______________________

What did you like least about that job?______________________

Why did you leave that job?______________________

Would you consider working there again? ______________________

Interviewer: If there is any gap between the various periods of employment, the applicant should be asked about them. ______________________

Interviewer's comments or observations ______________________

____

What did you do prior to the job with that company?______________________

What other jobs or experience have you had? Describe them briefly and explain the general duties of each.

____

Have you been unemployed at any time in the last five years? _______Yes _______No. What efforts did you make to find work? ______________________

What other experience or training do you have which would help qualify you for the job you applied for? Explain how and where you obtained this experience or training.______________________

____

Educational Background

What education or training do you have that would help you in the job for which you have applied?________

____

Describe any formal education you have had. (Interviewer may substitute technical training, if relevant.) _____

____

Off-Job Activities

What do you do in your off-hours? ____Part-time job ____Athletics____ Spectator sports_____Clubs ____Other

Please explain. ______________________

Interviewer's Specific Questions

Interviewer: Add any questions to the particular job for which you are interviewing, leaving space for brief answers. (Be careful to avoid questions which may be viewed as discriminatory.)

____

____

____

Personal

Would you be willing to relocate? _______Yes _______No

Are you willing to travel? ______Yes _______No

(continued)

FIGURE 6.1 (continued)

What is the maximum amount of time you would consider traveling? ____________

____

Are you able to work overtime? ____________

What about working on weekends? ____________

Self-Assessment

What do you feel are your strong points? ____________

____

What do you feel are your weak points? ____________

____

Interviewer: Compare the applicant's responses with the information furnished on the application for employment. Clear up any discrepancies. ____________

____

Before the applicant leaves, the interviewer should provide basic information about the organization and the job opening, if this has not already been done. The applicant should be given informaiton on the work location, work hours, the wage or salary, type of remuneration (salary or salary plus bonuses, etc.), and other factors that may affect the applicant's interest in the job.

Interviewer's Impressions

Rate each characteristic from 1 to 4, with 1 being the highest rating and 4 being the lowest.

Personal Characteristics	1	2	3	4	Comments
Personal appearance					
Poise, manner					
Speech					
Cooperation with interviewer					
Job-related Characteristics					
Experience for this job					
Knowledge of job					
Interpersonal relationships					
Effectiveness					

Overall rating for job

1	2	3	4	5
___ Superior	___ Above Average (well qualified)	___ Average (qualified)	___ Marginal (barely qualified)	___ Unsatisfactory

Comments or remarks ____________

____

____

Interviewer ____________ Date ____________

for additional questions that you may want to add to customize the form for the particular job for which you are recruiting. Not all interviewers are comfortable or competent at formulating questions or at the give and take of the typical interview. In such instances, a structured form like the one shown in Figure 6.1 can be particularly useful, since it presents the interviewer with all the questions laid out in a simple and easy to use format.[4]

Situational Interview

situational interview A series of job-related questions with "preferred" answers that are asked of all job applicants.

A **situational interview**[5] is really a series of job-related questions with predetermined "preferred" answers that are consistently asked of all interviewees for a particular job. It is similar to the directive interview in that you ask a predetermined, structured set of questions. But with the situational interview you can also ask job-related questions, questions that have been developed through job analysis. Acceptable answers are then chosen by a panel of supervisors who can then rate each applicant's answers to the job-related questions that are asked. The situational interview helps you to (1) *identify acceptable answers* ahead of time and (2) *get consensus among interviewers* regarding the acceptability of these answers. It thus results in more reliable interviews. This technique is described more fully later in this chapter.

Serialized or Sequential Interview

Most employers require that applicants be interviewed by several persons before reaching a decision. Each interviewer looks at the applicant from his or her own point of view, asks different questions, and forms an independent opinion of the candidate.

serialized interview An interview in which the applicant is interviewed sequentially by several supervisors and each rates the applicant on a standard form.

In a **serialized interview**[6] each interviewer rates the candidate on a standard evaluation form, and the ratings are compared before the hiring decision is made. Assuming the form focuses on skills and traits that are required for satisfactory job performance, the serialized interview should result in more reliable and valid interviews than would a nondirective approach.

Panel Interview

panel interview An interview in which a group of interviewers questions the applicant, a method similar to a press conference.

The **panel interview** involves having the candidate interviewed by a group (or panel) of interviewers.

This approach has several advantages. A regular interview often involves having candidates cover basically the same ground over and over again with each interviewer. The panel interview, on the other hand, lets each interviewer pick up on the candidate's answers, much as reporters do in press conferences. This approach can thus elicit deeper and more meaningful responses than are normally produced by a series of one-on-one interviews. However, this type of interview can also place extra stress on the candidate. It may thus inhibit responses that would be elicited in a one-on-one interview. One variant is the *mass interview* in which several candidates are interviewed at once by a panel. Here the panel poses a problem to be solved and then sits back and watches which of the candidates takes the lead in formulating an answer.

Stress Interview

stress interview An interview in which the applicant is made uncomfortable by a series of often rude questions. This technique helps identify hypersensitive applicants and those with low or high stress tolerance.

The objective of the **stress interview** is to determine how an applicant will react to stress on the job. To use this approach, you should be skilled in its use and should be sure that stress is, in fact, an important characteristic of the job.

In the typical stress interview, the applicant is made uncomfortable by being put on the defensive by a series of frank (and often discourteous) questions from the interviewer. The interviewer usually probes for weaknesses in the applicant's background. Having identified these, the interviewer can then focus on them, hoping to get the candidate to lose his or her composure. Thus, a candidate for customer relations manager who obligingly mentions that she's had

Computer Application in Interviewing: The Computer-Aided Interview

Computer–aided interviews are built on the principles of patterned and structured interviews. The basic idea is to present the applicant with a series of questions regarding his or her background, experience, education, skills, knowledge, and work attitudes, questions that relate to a specific job for which the person has applied.[1] The questions are presented in a multiple choice format, one at a time, and the applicant is expected to respond to the questions on the computer screen by pressing a key corresponding to desired responses. Here are some sample interview questions for a person applying for a job in a retail store:[2]

Are you applying to work part time or full time?

A. Part time (less than 40 hours per week).
B. Full time (40 hours per week).
C. Whatever is available.

The position for which you are applying may require you to lift boxes that weigh 25 to 30 pounds. Will this be a problem for you?

A. It will definitely be a problem.
B. It might be a problem.
C. It will not be a problem.

Have you ever had a job where you worked directly with customers?

A. Yes.
B. No.
C. If yes. . . .

How would your supervisor rate your customer service skills?

A. Outstanding.
B. Above average.
C. Average.
D. Below average.
E. Poor.

Note that the last question would be asked only if the applicant answered yes to the previous question.

Computer-aided interviews usually precede and supplement the face-to-face interview. At the end of the computer-aided interview a printed report is produced that lists all interview questions, applicants' responses, and follow-up comments and questions to be asked such as "give me some examples of why your supervisor would rate your customer service skills as outstanding" for the interviewer to ask. The typical computer-aided interview involves about 100 questions and is completed in under 20 minutes.

Computer-aided interviews can have some enormous benefits. Their ability to branch to follow-up questions allows topics to be pursued as they might be in a face-to-face interview; a lot of information can thus be obtained quickly without the interviewers' services. Several of the interpersonal interview problems we'll discuss later in this chapter (such as making a snap judgment about the interviewee based on his or her appearance) are also obviously avoided with this nonpersonal approach to interviewing. Particularly for larger companies with the resources to develop job-specific computer-aided interviews the savings in interviewer time and in avoiding hiring mistakes can be considerable.[3]

[1]This is based on Douglas D. Rodgers, "Computer-Aided Interviewing Overcomes First Impressions," *Personnel Journal*, April 1987, pp. 148–152.
[2]These are based on, and quoted from Ibid.
[3]For additional information on computer-aided interviewing's benefits, see, for example, Christopher Martin and Denise Nagao, "Some Effects of Computerized Interviewing on Job Applicant Responses," *Journal of Applied Psychology*, Vol. 74, no. 1 (February 1989), pp. 72–80.

four jobs in the past two years might be told that frequent job changes reflect irresponsible and immature behavior. If the applicant then responds with a reasonable explanation of why the job changes were necessary, another topic might be pursued. On the other hand, if the person reacts with anger and disbelief, this might be taken as a symptom of low tolerance for stress.

This approach has its advantages and disadvantages. On the one hand, it can be a good way for identifying applicants who are hypersensitive and who might be expected to overreact to mild criticism with anger and abuse. On the other hand, the interviewer who uses this approach should be sure that a thick skin and an ability to handle stress are really required for the job, and will also need the skills to keep the interview (and hysterical interviewee) under control.

Appraisal Interview

appraisal interview A discussion following a performance appraisal in which supervisor and employee discuss the employee's rating and possible remedial actions.

In this chapter we emphasize the selection interview. However, there are other circumstances that require interviews, most notably the interview that usually follows the performance appraisal. After the appraisal, the supervisor and subordinate will usually meet to discuss the latter's rating and the remedial action (if any) that's required. Many of the concepts and techniques explained in the present chapter are applicable to the **appraisal interview**. However, a complete explanation of the appraisal interview will be postponed until Chapter 10.

INTERVIEWING AND THE LAW: EMPLOYMENT DISCRIMINATION "TESTERS"

Interviewers who are trained in the nature of equal employment law will avoid asking the sorts of questions that make firms run afoul of the law, questions concerning, for instance, candidates' marital status, child care arrangements, ethnic background, and worker's compensation history. Over the past few years the increasing use of employment discrimination testers has made such training even more important for the process of interviewing.[7] Testers will be indistinguishable from legitimate applicants, both minority and nonminority, male and female. But they won't be ordinary applicants. As defined by the EEOC, testers are "individuals who apply for employment which they do not intend to accept, for the sole purpose of uncovering unlawful discriminatory hiring practices."[8] Their role, in other words, is to unearth discriminatory practices at your firm. Your firm's interviewers—perhaps you—are thus the first line of defense when a tester comes to call.

Although they're not really seeking employment, testers have legal standing, both with the courts and with the EEOC. As described in its "Policy Guidance on the Use of Testers in the Employment Selection Process," the EEOC takes the position that testers can file charges under Title VII and may be useful in unearthing employment discrimination.[9] Courts have also recognized the use of testers even though their primary motive is not to seek jobs but to test for discrimination.[10] A case filed in 1991 illustrates the usual tester approach. A private, nonprofit civil rights advocacy group sent four university students—two white, two black—to an employment agency, supposedly in pursuit of a job. Although the testers were given backgrounds and training to make them appear almost indistinguishable from each other in terms of qualifications, the white applicants and black applicants were allegedly treated quite differently. For example, both

white applicants were given interviews and offered jobs, while the two black testers got neither interviews nor job offers.[11] A study by the Urban Institute suggests that such unequal treatment is "entrenched and widespread."[12]

An employer's best strategy, of course, is to be actively nondiscriminatory. However, a prudent employer will also take steps in planning the interview process and conducting the actual interviews to ensure that its interviewers avoid tester claims. We can summarize these steps as follows:[13]

1. Caution interviewers that testers may be posing as applicants.
2. Train interviewers to make careful notes during and after the interview to substantiate the differences among applicants and to record responses to questions and other items of interest not on the applicant's resume or application.
3. Try to avoid differences in the interviews themselves, perhaps through the use of an interview checklist.

4. If an applicant appears disinterested in the position, note specific signs of such "disinterest."
5. Consider using a point system for interviews. Assign applicants a certain number of points for relevant education, employment stability, work experience, and other criteria related to success on the job.
6. Have applicants execute a statement acknowledging that they are applying for the job out of a sincere interest in the job and for no other purpose. Signing that and later returning with a claim as a "tester" could show evidence of deceit if there is a lawsuit.
7. Remember that these testers often enter the employment process with phony resumes and fabricated qualifications, thus emphasizing the importance of carefully checking references.
8. Consider establishing an internal dispute resolution procedure that applicants and employees can turn to if they have an employment-related complaint against the firm. This can result in less expensive resolution than taking the matter to court.

In general, this matter of testers underscores the importance of having well-trained interviewers and a well-thought-out interview process. More specifically, it underscores the need to standardize and structure the interview process, using the sorts of techniques described later in the chapter.

▶ Common Interviewing Mistakes

INTRODUCTION

Earlier we said the usefulness of interviews depends mostly on how they're carried out. Since there are several common interviewing mistakes that undermine the interview's usefulness, we should explain these first, since knowledge of the mistakes is the first step in avoiding them.

SNAP JUDGMENTS

Interviewers usually make up their minds about candidates during the first few minutes of the interview. Prolonging the interview past this point usually adds little to change the decisions. One researcher even found that in 85% of the cases the interviewer had already made up his or her mind about the candidate *before* the interview even began, on the basis of the applicant's application form and personal appearance!

The problem is especially bad when you get negative feedback about the candidate before the interview. In one study, the researchers found that interviewers who received unfavorable reference letters about applicants were likely to give the applicant less credit for past successes and to hold the person more personally responsible for past failures. Furthermore, the final decision to accept or reject an applicant was always tied to what the interviewer *expected* of the person, based on the reference.[14]

NEGATIVE EMPHASIS

Interviewers are also influenced more by unfavorable than favorable information about the candidate. Similarly, interviewers' impressions are much more likely to change from favorable to unfavorable than unfavorable to favorable. In fact, the interview itself is often mostly a search for negative information.

When you combine this negative emphasis with the fact that interviewers tend to make snap judgments, you can see why most interviews are loaded against the applicant. An applicant who is initially highly rated could easily end up with a low rating, given the fact that unfavorable information tends to carry more weight in the interview. And an interviewee who begins with a poor rating will find it difficult to overcome that first bad impression during the interview.[15]

NOT KNOWING THE JOB

Interviewers who don't know precisely what the job entails and what sort of candidate is best suited for it usually develop incorrect stereotypes about what a good applicant is. They then erroneously match interviewees with their incorrect stereotypes. On the other hand, interviewers who have a clear understanding of what the job entails hold interviews that are more useful.

Take this example. In one study, 30 professional interviewers were used.[16] Half of them were just given a brief description of the jobs for which they were recruiting. Specifically, they were told "the eight applicants here represented by their application blanks are applying for the position of secretary." In contrast, the other 15 interviewers were given much more explicit job information:

> The eight applicants . . . are applying for the position of executive secretary. The requirements are typing speed of 60 words per minute, stenography speed of 100 words per minute, dictaphone use and bilingual ability in either French, German, or Spanish. . . .

The results were clear. The 15 interviewers who had more job information generally agreed among themselves about each candidate's potential, while those without complete job information did not. Interviewers who did not have full job information also did not discriminate very well among the applicants and tended to give all applicants high ratings.

PRESSURE TO HIRE

You may also do a worse job of interviewing when under pressure to hire more candidates. Here's an example. In one study a group of managers was told to assume that they were behind in their recruiting quota. A second group was told that they were already ahead of their quota. Those who were told they were behind evaluated the same recruits much more highly than did the other group of managers.[17]

CANDIDATE-ORDER ERROR

candidate-order error An error of judgment on the part of the interviewer due to interviewing one or more very good or very bad candidates just before the interview in question.

Candidate-order error means that the order in which you see applicants can affect how you rate them.

In one study, managers were asked to evaluate a candidate who was "just average" after first evaluating several "unfavorable" candidates. The average candidate was evaluated much more favorably than he might otherwise have been, since in contrast to the unfavorable candidates the average one looked better than he actually was.

This can be a major problem. In some studies, only a small part of the applicant's rating was based on his or her actual potential. Most of the applicant's rating was based on the effect of having followed very favorable or unfavorable candidates.[18]

NONVERBAL BEHAVIOR

As an interviewer you may also be unconsciously influenced by the applicant's nonverbal behavior. For example, several studies have shown that applicants who demonstrate greater amounts of eye contact, head moving, smiling, and other similar nonverbal behaviors are rated higher. In fact, these nonverbal behaviors often account for more than 80% of the applicant's rating.[19] In one study, 52 human resource specialists reviewed videotaped job interviews in which what the applicants said—their verbal content—was identical. However, the interviewees' nonverbal behavior differed markedly. The interviewees in one group had been instructed to exhibit minimal eye contact, a low energy level, and low voice modulation. The interviewees in a second group demonstrated the opposite behavior. Of the 26 personnel specialists who saw the high–eye contact, high–energy-level candidate, 23 would have invited him or her for a second interview. All 26 of the personnel people who saw the low–eye-contact, low–energy-level candidate would not have recommended that person for a second interview.[20] One implication is that an otherwise inferior candidate who is trained to "act right" in an interview will often be appraised more highly than will a more competent applicant without the right nonverbal interviewing skills.

Another facet of this problem is the role played by the applicant's attractiveness, and whether the person is male or female.[21] In one study, researchers found that whether attractiveness was a help or a hindrance to job applicants depended on the sex of the applicant and the nature of the job. Attractiveness was consistently an advantage for male applicants seeking white-collar jobs. Yet attractiveness was advantageous for female interviewees only when the job was *nonmanagerial.* When the position the woman was being interviewed for was *managerial*, there was a tendency for the person's attractiveness to work against her—in terms of recommendation for hiring and suggested starting salary. One explanation may be that interviewers tend to equate attractiveness with femininity. Thus attractive ("more feminine") women are seen as less fit for "masculine-type" jobs like that of manager, quite aside from the women's actual qualifications or the talents actually needed for the job.

It will also not come as a surprise to many women that how they dress will also affect the interviewer's selection decisions. In one study, 77 human resource administrators attending a conference evaluated videotapes of women interviewing for management positions. The women were dressed in one of four styles ranging from a light beige dress in a soft fabric (style 1) to a bright aqua suit with a short belted jacket (style 2) to a beige tailored suit with a blazer jacket (style 3) to "the most masculine" outfit, a dark navy, tailored suit and a white blouse with an angular collar (style 4). A comparison of the hiring recommendations associated with each style suggests that, up to a point, the more masculine the style, the more favorable the hiring recommendations were. Specifically, applicants received more favorable hiring recommendations as style masculinity increased from style 1 to style 3. However, they then turned down for those applicants wearing style 4 (the most masculine style), which, one must surmise, was considered "too masculine" for the interviewers. The findings may not apply to every individual. However, they suggest that it would be better for women to risk dressing "too masculine" rather than "too feminine" when applying for a management position.[22]

In summary, seven common interviewing mistakes are: snap judgments; negative emphasis; not knowing the job; pressure to hire; candidate order; the effect of nonverbal factors, and emphasis on physical factors that are not job related. Understanding these common mistakes is the first step toward avoiding them.

▶ THE EFFECTIVE INTERVIEW

STEPS IN THE INTERVIEW

Your interview should ideally contain five steps: plan, establish rapport, question, close, and review.[23]

Planning the Interview

First, you should plan the interview in advance. Specifically, review the candidate's application and resume, and note any areas that are vague or that may indicate strengths or weaknesses. You should review the job specification so that you'll go into the interview with a clear picture of the traits of an ideal candidate.

Also plan the location in which the interview will take place. Ideally, it should be a private room. Telephone calls should not be put through, and other interruptions should be minimized.

Establishing Rapport

Next, greet the candidate and take steps to put the person at ease. The interviewing room itself should be conducive to reducing tensions and establishing rapport. It should be private, quiet, and lacking in distractions. You might want to start the interview by asking noncontroversial questions—perhaps about the weather or the traffic conditions that day. A few minutes spent on questions like these can go far toward reducing the applicant's tension. This should enable the person to respond more completely and intelligently to your questions.

In addition to reducing tensions, *establishing rapport* has another aim. It can help you make a friend of the applicant, whether the person is eventually offered a job or not. As a rule, all applicants—even unsolicited drop-ins—should get friendly, courteous treatment, not only on humanitarian grounds but because your reputation is on the line.

The panel interview provides an effective way of allowing interviewers to follow-up on each other's questions.

Ask Questions

The interview next moves to the *asking questions* stage. As explained previously there are several approaches you can use here: nondirective, for instance, or structured. Similarly, the questioning can be carried out on a one-to-one basis, by a panel, or by a series of interviewers.

In any event, there are several things to keep in mind when asking questions. First, avoid questions that can be answered "Yes" or "No." Instead, ask questions that require more elaborate answers. Don't put words in the applicant's mouth (for instance by asking, "You *have* called on discount stores, haven't you?"), and don't telegraph the desired answer, for instance by nodding or smiling when the right answer is given. Don't interrogate the applicant as if the person is a prisoner, and don't be patronizing, sarcastic, or inattentive. Don't monopolize the interview by rambling. Similarly, don't let the applicant dominate the interview so you can't ask all your questions. Instead, *do* ask open-ended questions, and *listen* to the candidate's answer to encourage him or her to express himself or herself fully.

Close the Interview

Toward the close of the interview, there should be time to answer any questions the candidate may have, and (if appropriate) to advocate your firm to the candidate.

Try to end all interviews on a positive note. The applicant should be told if there is an interest in his or her background and, if so, what the next step will be. Similarly, rejections should be made diplomatically, for instance with a statement like, "Although your background is impressive, there are some other candidates whose experience is closer to our requirements." If the applicant is still being considered, but a decision can't be reached at once, the person should be told this. If your policy is instead to inform candidates of their status in writing, this should be done within a few days of the interview.

Review the Interview

After the candidate leaves, you should review your notes of the interview, fill in the structured interview guide (if this was not done during the interview), and review the interview while it's still fresh in your mind. Remember that snap judgments and a negative emphasis are two common interviewing mistakes.

Carefully reviewing the interview after the candidate has left can help you minimize these two problems.

SUMMARY OF INTERVIEWING GUIDELINES

1. *Use a structured form.* Interviews based on structured guides like those in Figures 6.1 and 6.2 usually result in the better interviews.[24] By forcing you to adhere to a standard sequence of interview items, they help reduce your tendency to let unfavorable information bias your opinions. They also help you more accurately recall the information produced in the interview and help ensure that all interviewers ask all candidates the same questions. At a minimum, you should write out your questions before the interview.

2. *Delay your decision.* Interviewers often make their decisions before they ever see the candidate—on the basis of his or her application form, for instance—or during the first few minutes of the interview. Another principle of good interviewing is thus to delay your decision as long as possible. Try to keep a record of the interview, and review this record after the interview. Make your decision then.[25] We also know that the quality of the applicant will influence how long it takes you to make a decision, with the quickest decisions being made on the worst candidates—those that get off to the worst start, in terms of their answers to the interviewers' questions.[26] The time allotted for the interview is another important factor. Allotting more time for an interview will thus make you less likely to make a premature decision.[27, 28]

3. *Focus on traits that are more accurately assessed in the interview.* Some traits are more accurately assessed during interviews than others. These include the candidate's intelligence, ability to get along with others, and motivation to work. As two researchers conclude,

> the results rather consistently indicate two areas which both contribute heavily to interview decisions and show greatest evidence of validity . . . personal relations, and motivation to work. In other words, perhaps the interviewer should seek information on two questions: "What is the applicant's motivation to work?" and "Would he or she adjust to the social context of the job?" Such an approach would leave the assessment of abilities, aptitudes, and biographical data to other, and in all likelihood, more reliable and valid sources.[29]

4. *Get the interviewee to talk.* The main reason for the interview is to find out about the applicant. To do this, you must get the person to talk. Make the applicant feel at ease early in the interview, perhaps with some general comment about the organization and the job. Avoid asking too many direct questions. Also, draw out an applicant's opinions and feelings by repeating the person's last comment as a question (such as "You didn't like your last job?"). Some sample questions (such as "Why do you feel qualified for this job?" and "What attracted you to us?") are presented in Figure 6.3.

5. *Comply with equal employment requirements.* Remember that your employer may be called on to explain the selection procedures and questions used in the interview. You should therefore be alert to bias. Also, make periodic checks of the number of minorities hired or recommended, along with the jobs they are recommended for. Using a structured interview form is also advisable, since it can be standardized and validated as a selection tool for EEOC purposes.[30]

CANDIDATE RECORD NAP 100 (10/77)

CANDIDATE NUMBER I U 921 (1-7) | NAME (LAST NAME FIRST) (8-27) | COLLEGE NAME | COLLEGE CODE (28-30)

INTERVIEWER NUMBER 0 (33-40)
INTERVIEWER NAME

SOURCE(41) Campus C Walk-in W Intern I Agency A

RACE (42) White W Black B Asian A Hispanic H Native Am. NA

SEX (43) Male M Female F

Init. Cont. Date (46-51)

DEGREE (53) Bachelors B Masters M Law L Major:

AVERAGE (A = 4.0) Overall (54-55) Acctg (56-57)

CLASS STANDING (58-59) Top 10% 10 Top 25% 25 Top Half 50 Bottom Half 75

CAMPUS INTERVIEW EVALUATIONS

ATTITUDE – MOTIVATION – GOALS

POOR ☐ AVERAGE ☐ GOOD ☐ OUTSTANDING ☐
(POSITIVE, COOPERATIVE, ENERGETIC, MOTIVATED, SUCCESSFUL, GOAL-ORIENTED)
COMMENTS:

COMMUNICATIONS SKILLS-PERSONALITY-SALES ABILITY

POOR ☐ AVERAGE ☐ GOOD ☐ OUTSTANDING ☐
(ARTICULATE, LISTENS, ENTHUSIASTIC, LIKEABLE, POISED, TACTFUL, ACCEPTED, CONVINCING)
COMMENTS:

EXECUTIVE PRESENCE – DEAL WITH TOP PEOPLE

POOR ☐ AVERAGE ☐ GOOD ☐ OUTSTANDING ☐
(IMPRESSIVE, STANDS OUT, A WINNER, REMEMBERED, LEVELHEADED, AT EASE, AWARE)
COMMENTS:

INTELLECTUAL ABILITIES

POOR ☐ AVERAGE ☐ GOOD ☐ OUTSTANDING ☐
(INSIGHTFUL, CREATIVE, CURIOUS, IMAGINATIVE, UNDERSTANDS, REASONS, INTELLIGENT, SCHOLARLY)
COMMENTS:

JUDGMENT – DECISION MAKING ABILITY

POOR ☐ AVERAGE ☐ GOOD ☐ OUTSTANDING ☐
(MATURE, SEASONED, INDEPENDENT, COMMON SENSE, CERTAIN, DETERMINED, LOGICAL)
COMMENTS:

LEADERSHIP

POOR ☐ AVERAGE ☐ GOOD ☐ OUTSTANDING ☐
(SELF-CONFIDENT, TAKES CHARGE, EFFECTIVE, RESPECTED, MANAGEMENT MINDED, GRASPS AUTHORITY)
COMMENTS:

CAMPUS INTERVIEW SUMMARY

INVITE (Circle)	AREA OF INTEREST (Circle)	SEMESTER HRS.	OFFICES PREFERRED:	SUMMARY COMMENTS:
YES NO	AUDIT TAX	Acct'g.	No. 1	
DATE AVAILABLE	MCS ABC	Audit	No. 2	
	Other	Tax	No. 3	

FIGURE 6.2 **Structured Interview Form for College Applicants**

As explained in Chapter 2, *federal* equal employment laws generally do not prohibit interviewers from asking most questions, but the EEOC does look with suspicion on certain inquiries. As we explained, dubious questions include those concerning marital status, child care, availability for Saturday or Sunday work, arrest record, or any other questions that could have an adverse impact on women or minorities.[31]

FIGURE 6.3
Interview questions to expect

Source: H. Lee Rust, *Job Search, The Complete Manual for Job Seekers* (New York, AMACOM, 1991), pp. 232–233.

1. Did you bring a résumé?
2. What salary do you expect to receive?
3. What was your salary in your last job?
4. Why do you want to change jobs or why did you leave your last job?
5. What do you identify as your most significant accomplishment in your last job?
6. How many hours do you normally work per week?
7. What did you like and dislike about your last job?
8. How did you get along with your superiors and subordinates?
9. Can you be demanding of your subordinates?
10. How would you evaluate the company you were with last?
11. What were its competitive strengths and weaknesses?
12. What best qualifies you for the available position?
13. How long will it take you to start making a significant contribution?
14. How do you feel about our company—its size, industry, and competitive position?
15. What interests you most about the available position?
16. How would you structure this job or organize your department?
17. What control or financial data would you want and why?
18. How would you establish your primary inside and outside lines of communication?
19. What would you like to tell me about yourself?
20. Were you a good student?
21. Have you kept up in your field? How?
22. What do you do in your spare time?
23. What are your career goals for the next five years?
24. What are your greatest strengths and weaknesses?
25. What is your job potential?
26. What steps are you taking to help achieve your goals?
27. Do you want to own your own business?
28. How long will you stay with us?
29. What did your father do? Your mother?
30. What do your brothers and sisters do?
31. Have you ever worked on a group project and, if so, what role did you play?
32. Do you participate in civic affairs?
33. What professional associations do you belong to?
34. What is your credit standing?
35. What are your personal likes and dislikes?
36. How do you spend a typical day?
37. Would you describe your family as a close one?
38. How aggressive are you?
39. What motivates you to work?
40. Is money a strong incentive for you?
41. Do you prefer line or staff work?
42. Would you rather work alone or in a team?
43. What do you look for when hiring people?
44. Have you ever fired anyone?
45. Can you get along with union members and their leaders?
46. What do you think of the current economic and political situation?
47. How will government policy affect our industry or your job?
48. Will you sign a noncompete agreement or employment contract?
49. Why should we hire you?
50. Do you want the job?

THE STRUCTURED INTERVIEW

The *structured* or *situational* interview is defined as *a series of job-related questions with predetermined answers that are consistently asked of all applicants for a particular job.*[32] The procedure involves having a committee of persons who are familiar with the job develop job-related interview questions, questions that are based on the actual duties of the job. These people then meet and reach consensus regarding what are and are not acceptable answers to these questions. The procedure consists of five steps as follows.

Step 1. Job Analysis

First, write a description of the job in terms of job duties, required knowledge, skills, abilities, and other worker qualifications.

Step 2. Evaluate the Job Duty Information

The job analysis results in a list of job duties. Next, rate each job duty on its importance to job success and on the amount of time required to perform it compared to other tasks. The aim here is to identify the main duties on the job.

Step 3. Develop Interview Questions

The employees who helped develop and evaluate the job duties are then asked to develop the actual interview questions. The interview questions are based on the listing of job duties, with more interview questions devoted to the more important job duties.

A situational interview contains several types of questions. *Situational questions* pose a hypothetical job situation, such as "What would you do if the machine suddenly began heating up?" *Job knowledge questions* assess job knowledge that is both essential to job performance and must be known prior to entering the job. These often deal with technical aspects of a job (such as "What is a ratchet wrench?"). *Worker requirements questions* usually take the form of "willingness questions." They include questions on the applicant's willingness and motivation to work, to do repetitive physical work, to travel, to relocate, and so forth.

The employees who develop the questions will also choose, for each question, *critical incidents* that reflect especially good or poor performance. For example, a critical incident-based situational question that could be asked of a supervisor is as follows:

> Your spouse and two teenage children are sick in bed with a cold. There are no relatives or friends available to look in on them. Your shift starts in three hours. What would you do in this situation?

Step 4. Develop Benchmark Answers to Interview Questions

Next, a five-point answer rating scale is constructed for each critical incident question, with specific answers developed for a good answer (a 5 rating), a marginal answer (a 3 rating), and a poor answer (a 1 rating).

For example, take the situational question earlier ("your spouse and two teenage children are sick in bed . . ."). Each member of the team that was developing the questions and answers was asked to write good, marginal, and poor answers based on "things you have actually heard said in an interview by people who subsequently were considered good, marginal, or poor as the case may be on the job." Each person then reads his or her answers to the other group members. After a group discussion, consensus is reached on the answers to use as 5, 3, and 1 benchmarks. The three benchmarks for the example question were "I'd stay home—my spouse and family come first" (1), "I'd phone my supervisor and explain my situation" (3), and "since they only have colds, I'd come to work" (5). Similarly, a set of questions and corresponding answers is written for each of the other important job duties.

Step 5. Appoint Interview Committee and Implement

The interview committee should consist of three to six members, preferably the same employees who participated in the job analysis and the writing of the interviews and answers. Members of the committee may also come from supervisors above the job to be filled or include the job incumbent, peers, and human resource representatives. The same interview members should be used throughout the interviewing for the job.[33]

Before the interview, the job duties and questions and benchmark interview answers are distributed to the committee members and reviewed. Next, the interview itself is conducted by committee members, usually in a quiet, comfortable, nonstressful atmosphere. Ideally, one member of the panel is designated to introduce the applicant to the panel and to ask all questions of all applicants in this and succeeding interviews, to ensure consistency. However, all panel members record and rate the applicant's answers on the rating scale sheet, by indicating where the candidate's answer to each question falls relative to the ideal 1, 3, or 5 answers. At the end of the interview, each applicant is directed to someone who explains the follow-up procedures and answers any questions the applicant has.[34]

Small Business Applications

Many of the points discussed in this chapter can be combined in a practical interview procedure for a small business. Such a procedure is especially useful when time and resources are scarce and when a quick way of assessing the job duties and the questions to ask is required. The procedure consists of four steps as follows:[35]

1. Develop behavioral specifications for the job.
2. Determine what basic factors to probe for.
3. Use an interview plan.
4. Match the candidate to the job.

DEVELOP BEHAVIORAL SPECIFICATIONS

First, specify the behaviors you will look for in candidates. Here, it is convenient to classify these behaviors into four basic types: *intellectual capacity, motivation, personality strengths and limitations,* and *knowledge and experience.*

Intellectual capacity refers to the person's intelligence and problem-solving capacity, and to specific intellectual aptitudes such as for mathematics or understanding mechanical activities. In assessing your candidate's intellectual capacity you'll be interested in both the person's intellectual capacity or potential, and the person's desire to apply that intellectual capacity. For example, some very smart people may be superficial. Intellectual capacity is most accurately assessed through paper-and-pencil tests. However, there are some areas you can probe in the interview to assess the person's capacities.

Motivation refers to the person's interests, aspirations, and energy level. *Personality strengths and limitations* refers to the candidate's psychological adjustment and to the nature and quality of the interpersonal relationships he or she has had. Here, you should be especially wary of self defeating patterns of behavior, such as extreme impatience or a desire to speak one's mind to the point of being abrasive. Finally, with *knowledge and experience* you might want to focus on short verbal tests that probe what the candidate knows (or does not know) as it relates to the job.

Developing Behavioral Specifications for the Job: What to Look for in the Candidate

Even a one-person business can develop a set of criteria regarding the kind of person that would be best for the job. A quick and efficient way of formulating such specifications is to ask the following questions:

Knowledge-Experience Factor: What must the candidate know about to perform the job? What experience is absolutely necessary to perform the job?

Motivation Factor: What should the person like doing to enjoy this job? Is there anything the person should not dislike? Are there any essential goals or aspirations the person should have? Are there any unusual energy demands on the job? How critical is the person's drive and motivation?

Intellectual Factor: Are there any specific intellectual aptitudes required (mathematics, mechanical, etc.)? How complex are the problems to be solved? What must a person be able to demonstrate he or she can do intellectually? How should the person problem solve (cautiously, deductively, etc.)?

Personality Factor: What are the critical personality qualities needed for success on the job (ability to withstand boredom, decisiveness, stability, etc.)? How must the job incumbent handle stress, pressure, and criticism? What kind of interpersonal behavior is required in the job up the line, at peer level, down the line, and outside the firm with customers?

SPECIFIC FACTORS TO PROBE IN THE INTERVIEW

Next, use a combination of open-ended questions like those in Figure 6.3 to probe the candidate's suitableness for the job as follows:

Intellectual Factor: Here probe such things as complexity of tasks the person has performed, grades in school, test results (including scholastic aptitude tests, etc.), and how the person organizes his or her thoughts and communicates.

Motivation Factor: Probe such areas as the person's likes and dislikes (for each thing done, what he or she liked or disliked about it), the person's aspirations (including the validity of each goal in terms of why he or she chose that goal), and the person's energy level, perhaps by asking them what they do on, say, a "typical Tuesday."

Personality Factor: Probe by looking for self-defeating patterns of behavior (aggressiveness, compulsive fidgeting, etc.) and by probing the person's past interpersonal relations. Here, ask probing questions about the person's past interactions (working in a group at school, working with sorority sisters, leading the work team on the last job, etc.). Also try to judge the person's behavior in the interview itself—is the person personable? shy? outgoing?

USING AN INTERVIEW PLAN

You should also devise and use an interview plan to guide the interview. John Drake[36] says that significant stages to cover include

- High school
- College
- Work experiences—summer, part time
- Work experience—full time (one by one)
- Goals and ambitions
- Reactions to the job you are interviewing for
- Self-assessments (by the candidate of his or her strengths and weaknesses)
- Military experiences
- Present outside activities

Your basic approach is to follow your plan, perhaps starting with an open-ended question for each topic, such as "Could you tell me about what you did when you were in high school?" Keep in mind that you are trying to elicit information on four main traits—intelligence, motivation, personality, and knowledge and experience. You can then accumulate information on each of those four traits as the person talks. Particular areas that you want to follow up on can usually be pursued by asking such questions as "Could you elaborate on that please?," or by probing such things as the complexity of tasks performed, test grades, what they like and dislike, and what their actual interactions were like.

MATCH CANDIDATE TO THE JOB

If you followed your interview plan and probed for the four factors, you should now be able to summarize the candidate's general strengths and limitations. You should also be able to draw some solid conclusions about the person's intellectual capacity, knowledge/experience, motivation, and personality. Your next step should be to compare your conclusions to both the job description and to the list of behavioral specifications developed as explained earlier. You should then have a rational basis for matching the candidate to the job, one based on an analysis of the traits and aptitudes actually required.

Building Employee Commitment

A Total Selection Program

Companies today need employees who are committed to their firms—employees who identify with the firm's values and goals and treat their firms like their own. However, the time to start building such commitment is before—not after—employees are hired.[37] Increasingly, therefore, progressive companies like Saturn, Delta, and Federal Express use what we might term value-based hiring practices. They don't just look at applicants' job-related skills. They try to get a sense of the person and his or her destiny and personal qualities and values. They identify common experiences and values that may flag the applicant's future fit and success with the firm. They give their applicants realistic previews of what to expect. And, perhaps most important, they put enormous effort into combining interviews and other screening procedures into total selection programs in order to find the best people. As Fujio Cho, president of Toyota Motor Manufacturing USA, put it:

> You might be surprised, but our selection and hiring process is an exhaustive, painstaking system designed not to fill positions quickly, but to find the right people for those positions. What are we looking for? First, these people must be able to think for themselves . . . be problem solvers . . . and second, work in a team atmosphere. Simply put, we need strong minds, not strong backs. . . . We consider the selection of a team member as a long-term investment decision. Why go to the trouble of hiring a questionable employee only to have to fire him later?[38]

As summarized in Figure 6.4 Toyota's hiring process involves about 20 hours and six phases, spread over five or six days. The Kentucky Department of Employment Services conducts Phase I. Here applicants fill out application forms summarizing their work experience and skills and view a video describing Toyota's work environment and selection system. This takes about an hour and gives applicants a realistic preview of work at Toyota and of the hiring process's extensiveness. Many applicants simply drop out at this stage.

Phase II is aimed at assessing the applicant's technical knowledge and potential and in Toyota's case is also conducted by the Kentucky Department of Employment Services. Here applicants take the U.S. Employment Services' General Aptitude Test Battery (GATB), which helps identify problem-solving skills and learning potential, as well as occupational preferences. Skilled trades applicants (experienced mechanics and so forth) also take a six-hour tool and die or general maintenance test. Kentucky Employment Services scores all tests and submits the files to Toyota. (Many state employment offices will arrange similar prescreening services for firms doing heavy recruiting in their areas, and many will also administer GATB tests for most firms in their areas.)

Toyota takes over the screening process in Phase III. The aim here is to assess applicants' interpersonal and decision-making skills. All applicants participate in four hours of group and individual problem-solving and discussion activities in the firm's assessment center. This is a separate location where applicants engage in exercises under the observation of Toyota screening experts.

THE PROCESS			
Phase I	Orientation/Application Fill out an application and view a video of the Toyota work environment and selection system process (1 hour)		
	Objective:		To explain the job and collect information about work experiences and skills
	Conducted:		Kentucky Department of Employment Services
Phase II	Technical Skills Assessment Pencil/Paper tests		
		General knowledge test (2 hours) Tool & die or general maintenance test (6 hours)[1]	
	Objective:		To assess technical knowledge and potential
	Conducted:		Kentucky Department of Employment Services
Phase III	Interpersonal Skills Assessment		
		Group and individual problem-solving activities (4 hours) Production assembly simulation (5 hours)[2]	
	Objective:		To assess interpersonal and decision-making skills
	Conducted:		Toyota Motor Manufacturing
Phase IV	Toyota Assessment Group interview and evaluation (1 hour)		
	Objective:		To discuss achievements and accomplishments
	Conducted:		Toyota Motor Manufacturing
Phase V	Health Assessment Physical exam and drug/alcohol tests (2½ hours)		
	Objective:		To determine physical fitness
	Conducted:		Scott County General Hospital and University of Kentucky Medical Center
Phase VI	On-the-Job Observation Observation and coaching on the job after being hired (6 months)		
	Objective:		To assess job performance and develop skills
	Conducted:		Toyota Motor Manufacturing

[1] Skilled trades only
[2] Production only

FIGURE 6.4 Summary of Toyota Hiring Process
Based on Toyota Motor Manufacturing, USA Inc. documents.

The group discussion exercises help show how individual applicants interact with others in their group. In a typical exercise participants playing roles as company employees constitute a team responsible for choosing new features for next year's car. Team members first individually rank 12 features based upon market appeal and then suggest one feature not included on the list. They must then come to a consensus on the best rank ordering.

The problem-solving exercises are usually administered individually and are aimed at assessing each applicant's problem-solving ability, in terms of facets such as insight, flexibility, and creativity. In one typical exercise, for example, an applicant is given a brief description of a production problem and is asked to formulate questions that will help him or her better understand the causes of the problem. He or she then gets a chance to ask questions of a resource person, one with considerable information about the problem's cause. At the end of this question-and-answer period, the candidate fills out a form, listing the problem's causes, recommended solutions, and the reasons for suggesting these solutions.

Also, in Phase III, production line assembly candidates participate in a five-hour production assembly simulation. In one of these, candidates play the roles of the management and work force of a firm that makes electrical circuits. During a series of planning and manufacturing periods, the team must decide which circuits should be manufactured and how to effectively assign people, materials, and money to produce them.

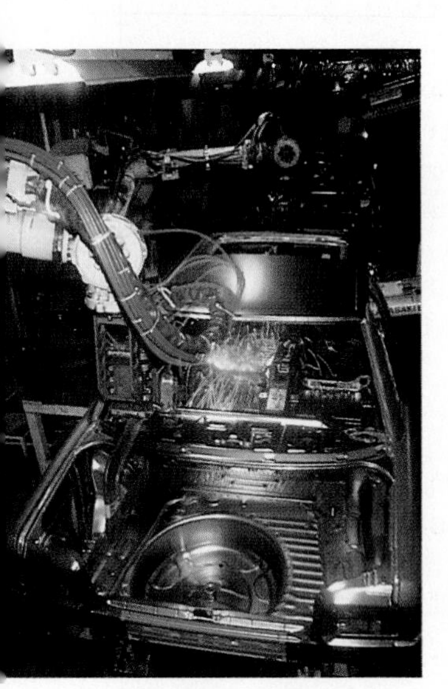

The commitment of Toyota's U.S.A. team-member employees is a major part of the reason why the Camry (being assembled here at the plant in Georgetown, Kentucky) consistently wins quality awards.

A one-hour group interview constitutes Phase IV. Here groups of candidates discuss their accomplishments with Toyota interviewers. This phase helps give the Toyota assessors a more complete picture of what drives each candidate, in terms of those things each is proudest of and most interested in. Phase IV also gives Toyota another opportunity to watch its candidates interact with each other in groups. Those who successfully complete Phase IV (and are tentatively tapped as Toyota employees) then undergo two-and-a-half hours of physical and drug/alcohol tests at area hospitals (Phase V). Finally, Phase VI involves closely monitoring, observing, and coaching the new employees on the job, to assess their job performance and to develop their skills during their first six months at work.

The firm's personnel chief has said that the first thing you have to do in designing a hiring process such as Toyota's is "to know what you want." At Toyota they are looking, first, he said, for interpersonal skills, due to the firm's emphasis on team interaction.

Similarly, the whole thrust of Toyota's "kaizen" production process is to improve work processes through worker commitment, and so reasoning and problem-solving skills are crucial human requirements too. This emphasis on kaizen—on having the workers themselves improve the system—helps explain Toyota's emphasis on hiring an intelligent, educated work force. The GATB and problem-solving simulations have in fact helped produce such a work force. "Those who did the best in their education did the best in the simulations," said one personnel officer. One hundred percent of Toyota workers have at least a high school degree or equivalent, and many plant employees (including assemblers) are college educated.

Quality is one of Toyota's central values, and so the firm also seeks a history of quality commitment in the people it hires. This is one reason for the group interview, the one that focuses on accomplishments. By asking candidates about the things they are proudest of, Toyota gets a better insight into the person's values regarding quality and doing things right. This is very important in a firm devoted to having employees build quality into its cars each step of the way.

Toyota is also looking for employees "who have an eagerness to learn, and a willingness to try it not only their way, but our way and the group's way." After all, Toyota's production system is based on consensus decision making, job rotation, and flexible career paths, and these require open-minded, flexible team players, not dogmatists. The firm's group decision-making and problem-solving exercises help identify such people.

In summary, high-commitment firms like Toyota use total value-based hiring programs to select employees whose values are compatible with those of the firm. While firms go about this in various ways, five common themes are apparent at Toyota. First, value-based hiring requires that you've clarified your firm's own values. Whether it's excellence, kaizen/continuous improvement, integrity, or some other, value-based hiring begins with clarifying what those values are.

Second, high-commitment firms such as Toyota commit the time and effort for an exhaustive screening process. Eight to 10 hours of interviewing even for entry-level employees is not unusual, and firms like Toyota will spend 20 hours or more with someone before deciding to hire. Many are rejected.

Third, the screening process does not just identify knowledge and technical skills. Instead, the candidates' values and skills are matched with the needs of the firm. Teamwork, kaizen, and flexibility are central values at Toyota; therefore, problem-solving skills, interpersonal skills, and commitment to quality are crucial human requirements.

Fourth, value-based hiring always includes realistic job previews. High-commitment firms are certainly interested in "selling" good candidates. But it's more important to make sure that the candidates know what working in the firms is going to be like and, even more important, what sorts of values the companies cherish.

Finally, self-selection is an important screening practice at most of these firms. In some firms this just means realistic previews. At others, practices such as long "probationary" periods in entry-level jobs help screen out those who do not fit. And, in firms like these, the screening process itself demands a sacrifice of employees: the time and effort is always extensive.

Guidelines for Interviewees

Before you get into a position where you have to do interviewing, you will probably have to navigate some interviews yourself. Here are some hints for excelling in your interview.

When being interviewed, the first thing to understand is that interviews are used primarily to help employers determine what you are like as a person.[39] In other words, information regarding how you get along with other people and your desire to work is of prime importance in the interview; your skills and technical expertise are usually best assessed through tests and a study of your educational and work history. Interviewers will look first for crisp, articulate answers. Specifically, whether you respond concisely, cooperate fully in answering questions, state personal opinions when relevant, and keep to the subject at hand are by far the most important elements in influencing the interviewer's decision.

There are seven things to do to get that extra edge in the interview.

First, *preparation is essential.* Before the interview, learn all you can about the employer, the job, and the people doing the recruiting. At the library, look through business periodicals to find out what is happening in the employer's field. Who is the competition? How are they doing? Try to unearth the employer's problems. Be ready to explain why you think you would be able to solve such problems, citing some of your *specific accomplishments* to make your case.

Second, *uncover the interviewer's real needs.* Spend as little time as possible answering your interviewer's first questions and as much time as possible getting him or her to describe his or her needs. Determine what the person is looking to get accomplished, and the type of person he or she feels is needed. Use open-ended questions here such as: "Could you tell me more about that?"

Third, *relate yourself to the interviewer's needs.* Once you know the type of person your interviewer is looking for and the sorts of problems he or she wants solved, you are in a good position to describe your own accomplishments *in terms of the interviewer's needs.* Start by saying something like "one of the problem areas you've said is important to you is similar to a problem I once faced." Then, state the problem, describe your solution, and reveal the results.[40]

Fourth, *think before answering.*[41] Answering a question should be a three-step process: Pause—Think—Speak. *Pause* to make sure you understand what the interviewer is driving at, *think* about how to structure your answer, and then *speak.* In your answer, try to emphasize how hiring you will help the interviewer solve his or her problem.

Fifth, *appearance and enthusiasm are important.* Appropriate clothing, good grooming, a firm handshake, and the appearance of controlled energy are important.

Sixth, *make a good first impression.* Remember that studies show that in most cases interviewers make up their minds about the applicant during the first minutes of the interview. A good first impression may turn to bad during the interview, but it is unlikely. Bad first impressions are almost impossible to overcome. One expert suggests paying attention to the following "key interviewing considerations":

1. Appropriate clothing
2. Good grooming
3. A firm handshake
4. The appearance of controlled energy
5. Pertinent humor and readiness to smile
6. A genuine interest in the employer's operation and alert attention when the interviewer speaks
7. Pride in past performance
8. An understanding of the employer's needs and a desire to serve them
9. The display of sound ideas
10. Ability to take control when employers fall down on the interviewing job

Sample questions you can ask are presented in Figure 6.5. They include "Would you mind describing the job for me?" and "Could you tell me about the people who would be reporting to me?"

Seventh, remember that your *nonverbal behavior* may broadcast more about you than the verbal content of what you say. Here, maintaining *eye contact* is very important. In addition, speak with enthusiasm, nod agreement, and remember to take a moment to frame your answer (pause, think, speak) so that you sound articulate and fluent.

FIGURE 6.5
Interview questions to ask

Source: H. Lee Rust, *Job Search, The Complete Manual for Job Seekers*, (New York, AMACOM, 1991), pp. 234–235.

1 What is the first problem that needs attention of the person you hire?
2. What other problems need attention now?
3. What has been done about any of these to date?
4. How has this job been performed in the past?
5. Why is it now vacant?
6. Do you have a written job description for this position?
7. What are its major responsibilities?
8. What authority would I have? How would you define its scope?
9. What are the company's five-year sales and profit projections?
10. What needs to be done to reach these projections?
11. What are the company's major strengths and weaknesses?
12. What are its strengths and weaknesses in production?
13. What are its strengths and weaknesses in its products or its competitive position?
14. Whom do you identify as your major competitors?
15. What are their strengths and weaknesses?
16. How do you view the future for your industry?
17. Do you have any plans for new products or acquisitions?
18. Might this company be sold or acquired?
19. What is the company's current financial strength?
20. What can you tell me about the individual to whom I would report?
21. What can you tell me about other persons in key positions?
22. What can you tell me about the subordinates I would have?
23. How would you define your management philosophy?
24. Are employees afforded an opportunity for continuing education?
25. What are you looking for in the person who will fill this job?

▸ CHAPTER REVIEW

SUMMARY

1. There are several basic types of interviews, including situational, nondirective, structured, sequential, panel, stress, and appraisal interviews.
2. We discussed several factors and problems that can undermine the usefulness of an interview. These are making premature decisions, the fact that unfavorable information predominates, the extent to which the interviewer knows the requirements of the job, being under pressure to hire, the candidate-order effect, visual cues, and traits such as enthusiasm.
3. The five steps in the interview include: plan, establish rapport, question the candidate, close the interview, and review the data.
4. Guidelines for interviewers include: use a structured guide, know the requirements of the job, focus on traits you can more accurately evaluate (like motivation), let the interviewee do most of the talking, delay your decision, and remember the EEOC requirements.
5. The steps in a structured or situational interview include: job analysis, evaluate the job duty information, develop interview questions with critical incidents, develop benchmark answers, appoint interview committee, and implement.

6. As an interviewee, keep in mind that interviewers tend to make premature decisions and let unfavorable information predominate; your appearance and enthusiasm are important; you should get the interviewer to talk; it is important to prepare before walking in—get to know the job and the problems the interviewer wants solved; and you should stress your enthusiasm and motivation to work, and how your accomplishments match your interviewer's need.
7. A quick procedure for conducting an interview involves developing behavioral specifications; determining the basic intellectual, motivation, personality, and experience factors to probe for; using an interview plan; and then matching the individual to the job.
8. Value-based hiring can contribute directly to increasing the commitment in your organization. It helps you select the best qualified candidates—ones who have the values and potential to do the job. However, it assumes that management has clarified the values it cherishes (such as quality at Toyota).

KEY TERMS

nondirective interview
situational interview
structured interview
serialized interview
panel interview
stress interview
appraisal interview
candidate-order error

DISCUSSION QUESTIONS

1. Do interviews have to be a waste of time? Why? Why not?
2. Explain at least six factors that affect the usefulness of interviews.
3. Discuss our guidelines for being a more effective interviewer.
4. Write a short presentation entitled "How to Be Effective as an Interviewee."

APPLICATION EXERCISES

RUNNING CASE

CARTER CLEANING COMPANY

The Better Interview

Like virtually all the other personnel management–related activities at Carter Cleaning Centers, the company currently has no organized approach to interviewing job candidates. Store managers, who do almost all the hiring, have a few of their own favorite questions that they ask. But in the absence of any guidance from top management, they all admit their interview performance leaves something to be desired. Similarly, Jack Carter himself is admittedly most comfortable dealing with what he calls the "nuts and bolts" machinery aspect of his business and has never felt particularly comfortable having to interview management or other job interviewees. Jennifer is sure that lack of formal interviewing practices, procedures, and training account for some of the employee turnover and theft problems. She therefore wants to do something to improve her company's batting average in this important area.

Questions

1. In general, what can Jennifer do to improve her employee interviewing practices? Should she develop interview forms that list questions for management and nonmanagement jobs, and if so what form should these take and what questions should be included?

2. Should she implement a training program for her managers, and if so, what, specifically, should the content of such an interview training program be? In other words, if she did decide to start training her management people to be better interviewers, what should she tell them and how should she tell it to them?

CASE INCIDENT *The Out-of-Control Interview*

Maria Fernandez is a bright, popular, and well-informed mechanical engineer who graduated with an engineering degree from State University in June 1992. During the spring preceding her graduation she went out on many job interviews, most of which she thought were courteous and reasonably useful in giving both her and the prospective employer a good impression of where each of them stood on matters of importance to both of them. It was, therefore, with great anticipation that she looked forward to an interview with the one firm in which she most wanted to work, Apex Environmental. She had always had a strong interest in cleaning up the environment and firmly believed that the best use of her training and skills lay in working for a firm like Apex, where she thought she could have a successful career while making the world a better place.

The interview, however, was a disaster. She walked into a room in which five men, including the president of the company, two vice presidents, the marketing director, and another engineer began throwing questions at her that she felt were aimed primarily at tripping her up rather than finding out what she could offer by way of engineering skills. The questions ranged from unnecessarily discourteous ("Why would you take a job as a waitress in college if you're such an intelligent person?") to irrelevant and sexist ("Are you planning on settling down and starting a family any time soon?"). Then, after the interview, she met with two of the gentlemen individually (including the president) and the discussions focused almost exclusively on her technical expertise. She thought that these later discussions went fairly well. However, given the apparent aimlessness and even mean-spiritedness of the panel interview, she was astonished when several days later she got a job offer from the firm.

The offer put her in the position of having to consider several matters. From her point of view the job itself was perfect—she liked what she would be doing, the industry, and the location of the firm. And, in fact, the president had been quite courteous in subsequent discussions, as had been the other members of the management team. She was left wondering whether the panel interview had been intentionally tense to see how she'd stand up under pressure, and, if so, why they would do such a thing.

Questions

1. How would you explain the nature of the panel interview which Maria had to endure? Specifically, do you think it reflected a well-thought-out interviewing strategy on the part of the firm or carelessness on the part of the firm's management? If it was carelessness, what would you do to improve the interview process at Apex Environmental?
2. Would you take the job offer if you were Maria? If you're not sure, is there any additional information that would help you make your decision, and if so, what is it?
3. The job of applications engineer for which Maria was applying requires: (1) excellent technical skills with respect to mechanical engineering; (2) a commitment to working in the area of pollution control; (3) the ability to deal well and confidently with customers who have engineering problems; (4) a willingness to travel worldwide; and (5) a very intelligent and well-balanced person. What questions would you ask when interviewing applicants for the job?

Human Resource Management Simulation

You will notice in incident D that the candidates describe themselves very differently. How much weight should be placed on an interview? What if the candidate had a bad day before the interview? Also, incident B involves job design. To what extent should the candidate be made aware of the detailed specifications of a job? Could such detail "turn off" a job candidate?

Notes

1. Neal Schmitt, "Social and Situational Determinants of Interview Decisions: Implications for the Employment Interview," *Personnel Psychology*, Vol. 29 (Spring 1976), pp. 79–101; Lynn Ulrich and Don Trumbo, "The Selection Interview Since 1949," *Psychological Bulletin*, Vol. 63 (1965), pp. 100–116. See, however, Frank Landy, "The Validity of the Interview in Police Officer Selection," *Journal of Applied Psychology*, Vol. 61 (1976), pp. 193–198. See also Vincent Loretto, "Effective Interviewing Is Based on More than Intuition," *Personnel Journal*, Vol. 65 (December 1986), pp. 101–107; George Dreher et al., "The Role of the Traditional Research Design in Underestimating the Validity of the Employment Interview," *Personnel Psychology*, Vol. 41, no. 2 (Summer 1988), pp. 315–318; and M. M. Harris, "Reconsidering the Employment Interview: A Review of Recent Literature and Suggestions for Future Research," *Personnel Psychology*, Vol. 42, 1989, pp. 691–726.
2. Richard Arvey and James Campion, "The Employment Interview: A Summary and Review of Recent Research," *Personnel Psychology*, Vol. 35 (Summer 1982), pp. 281–322. See also Richard Arvey, Howard Miller, Richard Gould, and Philip Burch, "Interview Validity for Selecting Sales Clerks," *Personnel Psychology*, Vol. 40 (Spring 1987), pp. 1–12; and Amanda Phillips and Robert Dipboye, "Correctional Tests of Predictions from a Process Model of the Interview," *Journal of Applied Psychology*, Vol. 74, no. 1 (February 1989), pp. 41–52.
3. Frank Landy and Don Trumbo, *Psychology of Work Behavior* (Homewood, IL: Dorsey Press, 1976), p. 185. See also Arvey et al., "Interview Validity for Selecting Sales Clerks," pp. 1–12.
4. A similar, but more structured interview form, is called the patterned interview. It is aimed at obtaining facts about the applicant's technical competence, as well as uncovering personality patterns, attitudes, and motivation. See, for example, Arthur Pell, *Recruiting and Selecting Personnel* (New York: Regents, 1969), pp. 120–121.
5. See G. Latham et al, "The Situational Interview," *Journal of Applied Psychology*, Vol. 65 (1980), pp. 422–427; Elliott Pursell, Michael Campion, and Sara Gaylord, "Structured Interviewing: Avoiding Selection Problems," *Personnel Journal*, Vol. 59 (November 1980), pp. 907–912. See also Jeff Weekley and Joseph Gier, "Reliability and Validity of the Situational Interview for a Sales Position," *Journal of Applied Psychology*, Vol. 72, no. 3 (August 1987), pp. 484–487. See also Michael A. Campion, Elliott Pursell, and Barbara Brown, "Structured Interviewing: Raising the Psychometric Properties of the Employment Interview," *Personnel Psychology*, Vol. 41, no. 1 (Spring 1988), pp. 25–42; and Steven Maurer and Charles Fay, "Effect of Situational Interviews, Conventional Structured Interviews, and Training on Interview Rating Agreement: An Experimental Analysis," *Personnel Psychology*, Vol. 41, no. 2 (Summer 1988), pp. 329–344.
6. Arthur Pell, *Recruiting and Selecting Personnel* (New York: Regents, 1969), p. 119.
7. This is based on John F. Wymer III and Deborah A. Sudbury, "Employment Discrimination 'Testers'—Will Your Hiring Practices 'Pass'?" *Employee Relations Law Journal*, Vol. 17, no. 4 (Spring 1992), pp. 623–633.
8. Ibid., pp. 624–625.
9. Bureau of National Affairs, *Daily Labor Report*, December 5, 1990 at D-1.
10. See for example *Lea* v. *Cone Mills Corp.*, 438 F2d 86 (1971).
11. Wymer and Sudbury, "Employment Discrimination 'Testers,'" p. 629.
12. Urban Institute, *Opportunities Denied, Opportunities Diminished: Discrimination in Hiring.*

13. Adapted from Wymer and Sudbury, "Employment Discrimination 'Testers,'" pp. 631–632.

14. S. W. Constantin, "An Investigation of Information Favorability in the Employment Interview," *Journal of Applied Psychology*, Vol. 61 (1976), pp. 743–749. It should be noted that a number of the studies discussed in this chapter involve having interviewers evaluate interviews based on written transcripts (rather than face to face) and that a study suggests that this procedure may not be equivalent to having interviewers interview applicants directly. See Charles Gorman, William Grover, and Michael Doherty, "Can We Learn Anything About Interviewing Real People from Interviews' of Paper People? A Study of the External Validity Paradigm," *Organizational Behavior and Human Performance*, Vol. 22, no. 2 (October 1978), pp. 165–192. See also John Binning et al., "Effects of Pre-interview Impressions on Questioning Strategies in Same and Opposite Sex Employment Interviews," *Journal of Applied Psychology*, Vol. 73, no. 1 (February 1988), pp. 30–37; and Sebastiano Fisicaro, "A Reexamination of the Relation Between Halo Error and Accuracy," *Journal of Applied Psychology*, Vol. 73, no. 2 (May 1988), pp. 239–246.

15. David Tucker and Patricia Rowe, "Relationship Between Expectancy, Casual Attribution, and Final Hiring Decisions in the Employment Interview," *Journal of Applied Psychology*, Vol. 64, no. 1 (February 1979), pp. 27–34. See also Robert Dipboye, Gail Fontenelle, and Kathleen Garner, "Effect of Previewing the Application on Interview Process and Outcomes," *Journal of Applied Psychology*, Vol. 69, no. 1 (February 1984), pp. 118–128.

16. Don Langdale and Joseph Weitz, "Estimating the Influence of Job Information on Interviewer Agreement," *Journal of Applied Psychology*, Vol. 57 (1973), pp. 23–27; for a review of how to determine the human requirements of a job, see Anthony W. Simmons, "Selection Interviewing," *Employment Relations Today*, Winter 1991, pp. 305–309.

17. R. E. Carlson, "Selection Interview Decisions: The Effects of Interviewer Experience, Relative Quota Situation, and Applicant Sample on Interview Decisions," *Personnel Psychology*, Vol. 20 (1967), pp. 259–280.

18. R. E. Carlson, "Effects of Applicant Sample on Ratings of Valid Information in an Employment Setting," *Journal of Applied Psychology*, Vol. 54 (1970), pp. 217–222.

19. See Arvey and Campion, "The Employment Interview," p. 305.

20. T. V. McGovern and H. E. Tinsley, "Interviewer Evaluations of Interviewees' Nonverbal Behavior," *Journal of Vocational Behavior*, Vol. 13 (1978), pp. 163–171. See also Keith Rasmussen, Jr., "Nonverbal Behavior, Verbal Behavior, Resume Credentials, and Selection Interview Outcomes," *Journal of Applied Psychology*, Vol. 60, no. 4 (1984), pp. 551–556; Robert Gifford, Cheuk Fan Ng, and Margaret Wilkinson, "Nonverbal Cues in the Employment Interview: Links Between Applicant Qualities and Interviewer Judgments," *Journal of Applied Psychology*, Vol. 70, no. 4 (1985), pp. 729–736; Scott T. Fleischmann, "The Messages of Body Language in Job Interviews," *Employee Relations*, Vol. 18, no. 2 (Summer 1991), pp. 161–166.

21. Madelaine Heilmann and Lewis Saruwatari, "When Beauty Is Beastly: The Effects of Appearance and Sex on Evaluation of Job Applicants for Managerial and Nonmanagerial Jobs," *Organizational Behavior and Human Performance*, Vol. 23 (June 1979), pp. 360–372. See also Tracy McDonald and Milton Hakel, "Effects of Applicant Race, Sex, Suitability, and Answers on Interviewers' Questioning Strategy and Ratings," *Personnel Psychology*, Vol. 38, no. 2 (Summer 1985), pp. 321–334. See also M. S. Singer and Christine Sewell, "Applicant Age and Selection Interview Decisions: Effect of Information Exposure on Age Discrimination in Personnel Selection," *Personnel Psychology*, Vol. 42, no. 1 (Spring 1989), pp. 135–154.

22. Sandra Forsythe, Mary Frances Drake, and Charles Cox, "Influence of Applicants' Dress on Interviewers' Selection Decisions," *Journal of Applied Psychology*, Vol. 70, no. 2 (1985), pp. 374–378.

23. Pell, *Recruiting and Selecting Personnel*, pp. 103–115.

24. Carlson, "Selection Interview Decisions," pp. 259–280.

25. William Tullar, Terry Mullins, and Sharon Caldwell, "Effects of Interview Length and Applicant Quality on Interview Decision Time," *Journal of Applied Psychology*, Vol. 64 (December 1979), pp. 669–674. See also McDonald and Hakel, "Effects of Applicants' Race, Sex, Suitability, and Answers," pp. 321–334.

26. Tullar et al., "Effects of Interview Length."

27. Ibid., p. 674.

28. See David Tucker and Patricia Rowe, "Consulting the Application Form Prior to the Interview: An Essential Step in the Selection Process," *Journal of Applied Psychology*, Vol. 63, no. 3 (1977), pp. 283–287.

29. Landy and Trumbo, *Psychology of Work Behavior*.

30. Robert Dipboye, Richard Arvey, and David Terpstra, "Equal Employment and the Interview," *Personnel Journal*, Vol. 55 (October 1976).

31. Frederic M. Jablin, "Use of Discrimination Questions in Screening Interviews," *Personnel Administrator*, Vol. 27, no. 3 (March 1982), pp. 41–44; also see Clifford M. Koen, Jr., "The Pre-employment Inquiry Guide," *Personnel Journal*, Vol. 59, no. 10 (October 1980), pp. 825–829.

32. This section based on Pursell, Campion, and Gaylord, "Structured Interviewing," and Latham et al., "The Situational Interview." See also Michael A. Campion, Elliott Pursell, and Barbara Brown, "Structured Interviewing," pp. 25–42, and Weekley and Gier, "Reliability and Validity of the Situational Interview," pp. 484–487.

33. Pursell et al., "Structured Interviewing," p. 910.

34. From a speech by industrial psychologist Paul Green and contained in Bureau of National Affairs, *Bulletin to Management*, June 20, 1985, pp. 2–3.

35. This is based on John Drake, *Interviewing for Managers: A Complete Guide to Employment Interviewing* (New York: AMACOM, 1982).

36. Ibid.

37. Based on Gary Dessler, *Winning Commitment* (New York: McGraw-Hill Book Company, 1993).

38. Speech to the City Club, November 15, 1991, Cleveland, Ohio.

39. James Hollandsworth, Jr., and others, "Relative Contributions of Verbal, Articulative, and Nonverbal Communication to Employment Decisions in the Job Interview Setting," *Personnel Psychology*, Vol. 32 (Summer 1979), pp. 359–367. See also Sara Rynes and Howard Miller, "Recruiter and Job Influences on Candidates for Employment," *Journal of Applied Psychology*, Vol. 68, no. 1 (1983), pp. 147–154.

40. Richard Payne, *How to Get a Better Job Quickly* (New York: New American Library, 1979).

41. J. G. Hollandsworth, R. C. Ladinski, and J. H. Russel, "Use of Social Skills Training in the Treatment of Extreme Anxiety of Deficient Verbal Skills," *Journal of Applied Psychology*, Vol. 11 (1979), pp. 259–269.

VIDEO CASE 1
—Conclusion—

WOMEN IN THE WORK FORCE

In the Introduction to Video Case 1 on page 75, we asked several important questions that you should now reconsider.

As the video vividly illustrates, setting up an antidiscrimination policy and passing stringent antidiscrimination laws is no guarantee that discrimination will not continue. As Ellen Galinsky of the Families and Work Institute says, "What we're really talking about is changing a culture, and that isn't going to be quick and easy."

The video also shows that being a plaintiff in a discrimination case can be an exasperating and time-consuming process; the average length of an investigation by the EEOC is 248 days. In many cases, the company will muster all the evidence it can to protect itself, and "without hard evidence, it's the company's word against the employee and in some cases it's a gray area." Clearly, reducing discrimination requires a "culture" change on the part of the employer, one that usually comes about only with the active and obvious commitment of the firm's top management.

A comprehensive testing and selection process should include several specific testing and selection techniques. Among these are application forms, tests (including, for example, tests of intelligence, specific cognitive abilities, motor and physical abilities, personality and interests, and achievements), work sampling, management assessment centers, and background investigations and interviews. Regardless of the technique, personnel managers should always consider several guidelines in developing the testing and selection process. First, they should ensure that an application blank, test, or interview item is *valid*—in other words, that performance on the item is a valid predictor of subsequent job performance. The technique should also be *reliable,* so that the test scores obtained by one person are consistent when that person is retested with an identical test or with an equivalent form of the test. Equal employment opportunity issues as well as ethical and privacy-rights issues should also be considered.

Once you have recruited, selected, and placed an employee on the job, the next task is to orient and train him or her. We turn to these topics next, in Part 2.

PART 2

Training and Development

VIDEO CASE 2
—Introduction—

ASSEMBLY LINE TEAMS ARE BETTER TRAINED AND MORE EFFICIENT

from ABC News, "World News Tonight," February 24, 1993

In Part 1 of this book, we covered the important topics of recruitment and placement—in particular, job analysis, personnel planning and recruiting, employee testing and selection, and interviewing job candidates. We saw that in recruitment and placement we are concerned with identifying the human requirements of the job, choosing feasible job candidates, and then testing and selecting those who will best fulfill the job's demands.

But as we'll now see in Part 2, hiring the right people doesn't guarantee their success. They must also be trained to do their jobs and their performance appraised to make sure they are doing their jobs satisfactorily. Therefore in this second part of the book—Training and Development—we'll turn to the following topics:

Chapter 7: Orientation and Training
Chapter 8: Developing Managers
Chapter 9: Managing Quality and Productivity
Chapter 10: Appraising Performance
Chapter 11: Managing Careers

Actually, as we'll see in this Part, training employees doesn't just mean teaching them how to do their jobs. Training and development fosters employee commitment by helping employees to use their skills fully and by involving them in their work. As you consider the video case and read the next five chapters, keep the following questions in mind. Video Case 2 illustrates how companies today are using training and team-building techniques to help win their employees' commitment.

- Why do you think companies such as Square D give their employees so much training?
- In what way do you think *training* is a big part of career *development*?
- How do you think you can use training, development, and team-building practices to boost quality so that eventually you might eliminate the need for separate quality inspectors?

CHAPTER 7

ORIENTATION AND TRAINING

OVERVIEW

Once you've successfully recruited and selected employees, your next step is to orient and train them. This is the time you provide them with the information and skills they need to be successful on their new jobs. In this chapter, we first explain orientation, which (with training) is used to assimilate the new employee into the organization. We then describe training, which involves determining what skills must be taught and then teaching them. When you finish studying this chapter, you should be able to discuss how to set up an orientation program; explain how to identify training needs; discuss the nature of the basic training techniques used in industry; and discuss several training techniques used for special purposes, such as AIDS education.

▸ ORIENTATION AND SOCIALIZATION

ORIENTATION

employee orientation A procedure for providing new employees with basic background information about the firm.

Employee orientation means providing new employees with basic background information about the employer, information that they need to perform their jobs satisfactorily. This basic information includes such facts as how to get on the payroll, how to obtain identification cards, what the working hours are, and who the new employee will be working with. Orientation is actually one component of the employer's new-employee socialization process, an ongoing process that involves instilling in all employees the prevailing attitudes, standards, values, and patterns of behavior that are expected by the organization and its departments. The employee's initial orientation, if handled correctly, can help reduce the new employee's first-day jitters as well as the reality shock the person might otherwise experience. **Reality shock** refers to the discrepancy between what the new employee expected from his or her new job, and the realities of it.

reality shock That state which results from the discrepancy between what the new employee expected from his or her new job, and the realities of it.

Orientation programs range from brief introductions to lengthy, formal programs. In the latter, the new employee is usually given a handbook or printed materials that cover matters like working hours, performance reviews, getting on the payroll, and vacations, as well as a tour of the facilities. As illustrated in Figure 7.1,[1] other information typically includes employee benefits, personnel policies, the employee's daily routine, company organization and operations, and safety measures and regulations.

There is the real possibility that courts will find that your employee handbook's contents represent a contract with the employee. Therefore disclaimers should be included that make it clear that statements of company policies, benefits, and regulations do not constitute the terms and conditions of an employment contract either express or implied. Think twice before including statements in your handbook such as "no employee will be fired without just cause" or statements that imply or state that employees have tenure; they could be viewed as legal and binding commitments.

In this class for nurses' aides the supervisor continues orientation by explaining the exact nature of the job, introducing new colleagues, and familiarizing the new employees with the workplace.

In most firms, the first part of the orientation is performed by the human resource specialist, who explains such matters as working hours and vacation. The employee is then introduced to his or her new supervisor. The latter continues the orientation by explaining the exact nature of the job, introducing the person to his or her new colleagues, and familiarizing the person with the workplace.

Some companies also provide special new employee anxiety-reduction seminars. For example, when the Texas Instruments Company found out how high the anxiety level of its new employees was, it initiated special full-day seminars. These focused on information about the company and the job and allowed many opportunities for questions and answers. The new employees were told what to expect in terms of rumors and hazing from old employees. They were also told that it was very likely they would succeed on their jobs. These special seminars proved to be very useful. By the end of the first month, the new employees who had participated in the seminar were performing much better than were those who had not.[2] Orientation is one activity that contributes to the new employee's successful socialization into the firm; some other socialization activities are discussed next.

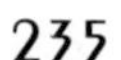

FIGURE 7.1 Contents of Orientation

Source: *Handbook of Modern Personnel Administration* by Joseph Famularo. Copyright 1985, McGraw-Hill Book Company. Used with permission of McGraw-Hill, Inc.

Orientation Checklist
(Small southern manufacturing company)

HOURLY & SALARIED EMPLOYEE ORIENTATION GUIDE CHECKLIST

NOTE: ALL APPROPRIATE INFORMATION MUST BE DISCUSSED WITH EACH NEW EMPLOYEE

SUPERVISOR: This form is to be used as a guide for the orientation of new employees in your department.

In order to avoid duplication of instruction the information indicated below has been given to the employee by the Personnel Department.

PERSONNEL DEPARTMENT

EEO BOOKLET		ABSENCES - TARDINESS	
INSURANCE PROGRAM BOOKLET		VETERANS' RE-EMPLOYMENT RIGHTS & RESERVE STATUS	
SALARY CONTINUANCE INSURANCE BOOKLET		UNITED FUND	
SAFETY BOOKLET		VACATIONS	
PENSION PLAN BOOKLET		JURY DUTY	
EMPLOYEE HANDBOOK/LABOR AGREEMENT/RULES BOOKLET		SICK BENEFITS — A & S — LIMITATIONS, ETC.	
MATCHING GIFTS		LEAVE OF ABSENCE - MATERNITY - MEDICAL, ETC.	
EDUCATIONAL ASSISTANCE PROGRAM		SERVICE AWARDS	
PATENT AGREEMENT		VISITORS	
I.D. CARD		HOLIDAYS	
CREDIT UNION		FOOD SERVICES	
STOCK PURCHASE PLAN		FIRST AID & REQUIREMENTS OF REPORTING INJURY	
SAVINGS BOND PLAN		DIFFICULTIES, COMPLAINTS, DISCRIMINATION & GRIEVANCE PROCED.	
PROBATIONARY PERIOD		MILL TOUR	
PAY, SALARY, PROMOTIONS AND TRANSFERS		TERMINATION NOTICE AND PAY ESP. VACATION ALLOWANCE (VOLUNTARY RESIGNATION)	
TRANSPORTATION			
TIME SHEET		INTRODUCTION TO GUARDS	
PERSONAL RECORDS		(OTHERS)	
BULLETIN BOARDS			
PERSONAL MAIL			
PARKING FACILITIES			

SIGNATURE OF EMPLOYEE:	WITNESS:	DATE

SUPERVISOR: The following is a check list of information necessary to orient the new employee to the job in your department. Please check off each point as you discuss it with the employee and return to the Personnel Department within three days following employee placement on the job:

INTRODUCTION TO FELLOW EMPLOYEES		HOURS OF WORK - OVERTIME - CALL IN PROCEDURES	
TOUR OF DEPARTMENT		REST, LUNCH PERIODS	
EXPLANATION OF NEW EMPLOYEE'S JOB, RESPONSIBILITIES AND PERFORMANCE EVALUATIONS		SUPPLY PROCEDURE	
		LINE OF AUTHORITY	
LAVATORY			
PHONE CALLS - PERSONAL/COMPANY			

SIGNATURE OF SUPERVISOR:	DATE

I have received a copy of the appropriate materials listed above and have had explained to me the information outlined. I understand this information concerning my employment with (Company name). Also, in case of voluntary separation (resignation) I understand the Company's policy, that in order to be eligible for any due vacation allowance, I must give my supervisor at least two weeks' notice in writing prior to my last day of work.

SIGNATURE OF EMPLOYEE:	WITNESS:	DATE

BUILDING EMPLOYEE COMMITMENT

Orientation and Socialization

In many firms today "orientation" goes well beyond providing basic information about such things as hours of work. More and more companies, as previously mentioned, are finding that the orientation period can be used for other purposes, including familiarizing the new employee with the company's cherished goals and values. Orientation thus begins the process of synthesizing the employee's and the company's goals, a process that's one step toward winning the employee's commitment to the firm and its values and goals.

The orientation (it is called an "assimilation") program at Toyota Motor Manufacturing USA is a case in point. While it covers traditional topics such as company benefits, it's mostly intended to convert Toyota's new employees to the firm's ideology of quality, teamwork, personal development, open communication, and mutual respect. It lasts four days and can be summarized as:

DAY ONE. Day one begins at 6:30 A.M. with an overview of the program, a welcome to the company, and a discussion of the firm's organization structure and human resource department by the firm's vice-president for human resources. It devotes about an hour and a half to discussing Toyota history and culture, and about two hours to employee benefits. Another two hours are then spent discussing Toyota's policies about the importance of quality and teamwork.

DAY TWO. The second day starts with about two hours devoted to "communication training—TMM way of listening." Here the importance of mutual respect, teamwork, and open communication is emphasized. The rest of the day is then devoted to general orientation issues. These include safety, environmental affairs, the Toyota production system, and the firm's library.

DAY THREE. Again, this day begins with two-and-a-half to three hours devoted to communication training, in this case the "TMM way of making requests and giving feedback." The rest of the day is spent covering matters such as Toyota's problem-solving methods, quality assurance hazard communications, and safety.

DAY FOUR. Teamwork is stressed in the morning session. Topics include teamwork training, Toyota's suggestion system, and the Toyota Team Member Activities Association. Day four also covers basic team-member skills such as what work teams are responsible for, and how to work together as a team. The afternoon specifically covers fire prevention and fire extinguishers training.

Employees thus complete the four-day orientation/assimilation/socialization process having been steeped in—and it is hoped converted to—Toyota's ideology, in particular its mission of quality and its values of teamwork, kaizen/continuous improvement, and problem solving. That is a big step toward winning new employees' commitment to Toyota and its goals and values.

INTRODUCTION TO TRAINING

training
The process of teaching new employees the basic skills they need to perform their jobs.

Training involves giving new or present employees the skills they need to perform their jobs. Training might thus involve showing a machinist how to operate his new machine, a new salesperson how to sell her firm's product, or a new supervisor how to interview and appraise employees. Whereas technical training is aimed at providing employees with the skills they need to perform their current jobs, *management development* (explained in Chapter 8) is training of a more long-term nature. Its aim is to develop current or future management employees for some future jobs with the organization or to solve some organizational problem concerning, for instance, poor interdepartmental communication. The techniques used in both training and development are often the same, however. Therefore, distinguishing between the two is always somewhat arbitrary.

Whether called training or development, training today is big business. For example, one survey concluded that *Personnel Journal* subscriber companies spent over $5.3 billion on training and development in a recent year, a 38% jump from two years earlier.[3]

As suggested by the Toyota training example previously discussed, the purposes served by training are much broader today than they have been in the past. Training used to be a fairly narrow and routine affair in most firms. The aim was usually to impart the technical skills needed to do one's job. This might involve training assemblers to solder wires, salespeople to close a deal, or teachers to devise a lesson plan.

Training is used by more and more firms today to achieve two additional aims. First, as at Toyota, other, broader skills are being taught to the firm's employees: These include, as you'll recall, such things as problem-solving skills, communication skills, and team-building skills. Second, more firms are taking advantage of the fact that training can enhance employee commitment. Few things illustrate a firm's commitment to its people more than providing continuing opportunities to better one's self. Therefore, training opportunities can help mold employee commitment. This is one of the reasons why firms like Toyota and Saturn provide about two weeks of training per year for all employees.

The expansion of training's role reflects the fact that "the game of economic competition has new rules," as one expert says.[4] In particular, it's no longer enough to just be very efficient. Surviving and thriving today requires speed and flexibility on the part of the firm. And they require responding to customers' needs with respect to quality, variety, customization, convenience, and timeliness. Meeting these new standards requires a work force that is more than just technically trained. It requires people who are capable of analyzing and solving job-related problems, working productively on teams, and "switching gears" and shifting from job to job as well.

Unfortunately, a "training gap" exists and may even be widening. While some companies—IBM, Xerox, Texas Instruments, and Motorola, for instance—devote 5 to 10% of their payroll dollars to training activities, the average training investment by U.S. firms (while large in dollar terms) is less than 2 percent of payroll.[5] Experts estimate that between 42 and 90 percent of American workers need further training to get them up to speed.[6] In any case, training is moving to center stage as a means of improving employers' competitiveness.

THE BASIC TRAINING PROCESS

Any training program ideally consists of four steps, which are summarized in Figure 7.2. The purpose of the *assessment* step is to determine training needs. Then, if one or more needs that can be eliminated through training are identified, *training objectives* should be set; here you specify in observable, measurable terms the performance you expect to obtain from the employees who are to be trained. In the *training* step the actual training techniques are chosen and the training takes place. Finally, there should be an *evaluation* step. Here the trainees' pre- and post-training performances are compared, and the effectiveness of the training program is thus evaluated.

FIGURE 7.2 The Four Basic Steps in Training

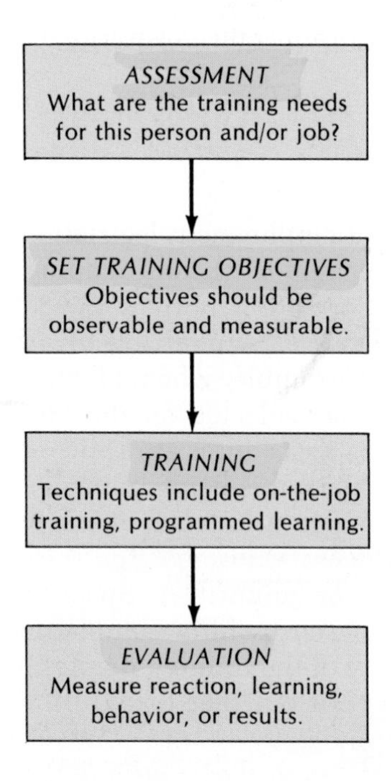

ASSESSMENT
What are the training needs for this person and/or job?
SET TRAINING OBJECTIVES
Objectives should be observable and measurable.
TRAINING
Techniques include on-the-job training, programmed learning.
EVALUATION
Measure reaction, learning, behavior, or results.

TRAINING AND LEARNING

Training is essentially a learning process. To train employees, it is therefore useful to know something about how people learn. Some suggestions follow:

Make the material meaningful: It is easier for trainees to understand and remember material that is meaningful. To accomplish this:[7]

1. At the start of training, provide the trainees with a bird's-eye view of the material to be presented. Knowing the overall picture facilitates learning.
2. Use a variety of familiar examples when presenting material.
3. Organize the material so that it is presented in a logical manner and in meaningful units.
4. Try to use terms and concepts that are already familiar to trainees.
5. Use as many visual aids as possible.

Provide for transfer to learning: Make sure to facilitate the transfer of learning from the training site to the job site. To do this:[8]

1. Maximize the similarity between the training situation and the work situation.
2. Provide adequate training practice.
3. Label or identify each feature of the machine and/or step in the process.

Motivate the trainee: As all students know, learning is easiest when someone is motivated to learn. To facilitate motivation:[9]

1. People learn best by doing. Try to provide as much realistic practice as possible.
2. Trainees learn best when correct responses on their part are immediately reinforced, perhaps with a quick "well done."
3. Trainees learn best when they learn at their own pace. If possible, let trainees pace themselves.

LEGAL ASPECTS OF TRAINING

As explained in Chapter 2, equal employment legislation makes it illegal to discriminate unfairly against applicants or current employees on the basis of the person's age, race, sex, religion, or national origin. Several aspects of your training program must therefore be assessed with an eye toward the program's impact on women and minorities.[10] For example, when adverse impact exists and relatively few women or minorities are selected for the training program, you may have to show that the admissions procedures are valid—that they predict performance on the job for which the person is being trained.

Similarly, suppose you plan to use "completion of training" as a job criterion. You should then attempt to show that the training program itself has no adverse impact on women or minorities. Specifically, these individuals should have as much chance of successfully completing the training as white males. If they do not, the validity of the training requirements should be demonstrated. For example, it could turn out that the reading level of your training manuals is too high for many minority trainees, and that they are thus doing poorly in the program *quite aside from their aptitude for the jobs for which they are being trained.* In such a case, your training program may be found to be unfairly discriminatory.

▶ ASSESSING TRAINING NEEDS

INTRODUCTION

The first step in training is to determine what training, if any, is required. Assessing the training needs of employees who are new to their jobs is a fairly straightforward matter. Your main task is to determine what the job entails and to break it down into subtasks, each of which is then taught to the new employee. But assessing the training needs of *present* employees can be more complex. Here the need for training is usually prompted by problems (like excess scrap). You therefore have the added task of deciding whether or not training is the solution. Often, for instance, performance is down because the standards aren't clear or because the person is just not motivated.

task analysis A detailed study of a job to identify the skills required, so that an appropriate training program may be instituted.

performance analysis Careful study of performance to identify a deficiency and then correct it with new equipment, a new employee, a training program, or some other adjustment.

The two main techniques for determining training requirements are *task analysis* and *performance analysis.* About 19% of employers reporting in one survey said they used **task analysis**—an analysis of the job's requirements—to determine the training required.[11] Task analysis is especially appropriate for determining the training needs of employees who are *new* to their jobs. **Performance analysis** involves appraising the performance of *current* employees to determine if training could reduce performance problems like excess scrap or low output. Other techniques reportedly used to identify training needs include supervisor's reports, personnel records, management requests, observations, tests of job knowledge, and questionnaire surveys.[12]

Training will also reflect your firm's overall human resource plans and the goals of the enterprise. Thus, suppose a department store chain plans to double their stores in the South. This means that plans must be made for staffing these new stores. These plans will in turn require that employees be selected and trained for the projected store openings.

TASK ANALYSIS: ASSESSING THE TRAINING NEEDS OF NEW EMPLOYEES

Task analysis is used for determining the training needs of employees who are new to their jobs. Particularly with lower-echelon workers, it is common to hire inexperienced personnel and train them.[13] Here your aim is to develop the skills and knowledge required for effective performance, and so the training is usually based on task analysis—*a detailed study of the job to determine what specific skill*—like soldering (in the case of an assembly worker) or interviewing (in the case of a supervisor)—*are required.*

The *job description* and job specification are helpful here. These list the specific duties and skills required on the job and become the basic reference point in determining the training required for performing the job.

Task Analysis Record Form

Some employers also use a *task analysis record form.* This consolidates information regarding the job's tasks and required skills in a form that's especially helpful for determining training requirements. As illustrated in Table 7.1, a task analysis record form contains six types of information:

Column 1. Here the job's main tasks and subtasks are listed. For example, if one major task is "Operate paper cutter," subtasks 1.1 through 1.5 might include "Start motor," "Set cutting distance," "Place paper on cutting table," "Push paper up to cutter," and "Grasp safety release with left hand."

Column 2. Here you indicate the *frequency* with which the task and subtasks are performed. For example, is it performed only once at the beginning of the shift, or many times, hour after hour?

Column 3. Here indicate the *standards of performance* for each task and subtask. These show the level to be attained by the trainee and should be as specific as

TABLE 7.1 Tasks Analysis Record Form

TASK LIST	WHEN AND HOW OFTEN PERFORMED	QUANTITY AND QUALITY OF PERFORMANCE	CONDITIONS UNDER WHICH PERFORMED	SKILLS OR KNOWLEDGE REQUIRED	WHERE BEST LEARNED
1. Operate paper cutter	4 times per day		Noisy press room: distractions		
1.1 Start motor					
1.2 Set cutting distance		±tolerance of 0.007 in.		Read gauge	On the job
1.3 Place paper on cutting table		Must be completely even to prevent uneven cut		Lift paper correctly	"
1.4 Push paper up to cutter				Must be even	"
1.5 Grasp safety release with left hand		100% of time, for safety		Essential for safety	On the job but practice first with no distractions
1.6 Grasp cutter release with right hand				Must keep both hands on releases	"
1.7 Simultaneously pull safety release with left hand and cutter release with right hand				"	"
1.8 Wait for cutter to retract		100% of time, for safety		"	"
1.9 Retract paper				Wait till cutter retracts	"
1.10 Shut off		100% of time, for safety			"
2. Operate printing press					
2.1 Start motor					
. . .					

Note: Task analysis record form showing some of tasks and subtasks performed by printing pressman.

possible. They should be expressed in measurable terms like "± tolerance of 0.007 in.," "Twelve units per hour," or "Within two days of receiving the order," for instance.

COLUMN 4. Here indicate the *conditions* under which the tasks and subtasks are to be performed. This is especially important if the conditions are crucial to the training—for example, where (as in the case of an air traffic controller) the person normally has to work under conditions of turmoil and stress.

Column 5. This is the heart of the task analysis form; here you list the *skills* or *knowledge* required for each of the tasks and subtasks. Here you specify exactly what knowledge or skills you must teach the trainee. Thus, for the subtask "Set cutting distance" the person must be taught how to read the gauge.

Column 6. Here you indicate whether the task is learned best *on* or *off the job.* Your decision is based on several considerations. Safety is one: For example, prospective jet pilots must learn something about the plane off the job, in a simulator, before actually getting behind the controls.

PERFORMANCE ANALYSIS: DETERMINING THE TRAINING NEEDS OF CURRENT EMPLOYEES

Performance analysis means verifying that there is a significant performance deficiency and determining if that deficiency should be rectified through training or by some other means (such as changing the machinery or transferring the employee).

The first step is to appraise your employee's performance. In other words, to improve your employee's performance, you must first determine what the person's performance is now and what you would like it to be. Examples of specific performance deficiencies follow:

> I expect each salesperson to make ten new contracts per week, but John averages only six.
>
> Other plants our size average no more than two serious accidents per month; we're averaging five.

The heart of performance analysis is to distinguish between *can't do* and *won't do* problems. First, determine if it's a can't do problem and, if so, its specific causes: Employees who don't know what to do or what your standards are; obstacles in the system such as lack of tools or supplies; the need for job aids, such as color-coded wires that show assemblers which wire goes where; poor selection that results in hiring people who haven't the skills to do the job; or inadequate training. On the other hand, it might be a won't do problem. Here employees could do a good job if they wanted to. If so, the reward system might have to be changed, perhaps installing an incentive system.

SETTING TRAINING OBJECTIVES

Setting concrete, measurable training objectives is the bottom line that should result from determining training needs. For example:

> Given a tool kit and a service manual, the technical representative will be able to adjust the registration (black line along paper edges) on this Xerox duplicator within 20 minutes according to the specifications stated in the manual.[14]

Objectives specify what the trainee will be able to accomplish after successfully completing the training program.[15] They thus provide a focus for the efforts of both the trainee and the trainer and a benchmark for evaluating the success of the training program.

▸ TRAINING AND TRAINING TECHNIQUES

After determining your employees' training needs and setting training objectives, the actual training can take place. The advantages and disadvantages of the most popular training techniques follow.

ON-THE-JOB TRAINING

on-the-job training (OJT)
Training a person to learn a job while working at it.

On-the-job training (OJT) involves having a person learn a job by actually performing it on the job. Virtually every employee, from mailroom clerk to company president, gets some on-the-job training when he or she joins a firm. In many companies, OJT is the *only* type of training available to employees. It usually involves assigning new employees to experienced workers or supervisors who then do the actual training.[16]

In a Textron assembly plant a newly hired employee receives on-the-job, in-depth training.

There are several types of on-the-job training. The most familiar is the *coaching or understudy method.* Here the employee is trained on the job by an experienced worker or the trainee's supervisor. At lower levels the coaching may just involve having trainees acquire the skills for running the machine by observing the supervisor. But this technique is also widely used at top-management levels. The position of *assistant to* is often used to train and develop the company's future top managers, for instance. *Job rotation* in which the employee (usually a management trainee) moves from job to job at planned intervals is another OJT technique. *Special assignments* similarly give lower-level executives firsthand experience in working on actual problems.

OJT has several advantages. It is relatively *inexpensive*; trainees learn while producing, and there is no need for expensive off-job facilities like classrooms or programmed learning devices. The method also *facilitates learning* since trainees learn by actually doing the job and get quick feedback about the correctness of their performance.

However, there are several trainer-related factors to keep in mind when designing OJT programs.[17] The trainers themselves should be carefully trained and given the necessary training materials. (Often, instead, an experienced worker is simply told to "go train John.") Experienced workers who are chosen as trainers should be thoroughly trained in the proper methods of instruction—in particular the principles of learning, explained previously, and perhaps the job instruction technique that we address next. A useful step-by-step job instruction approach for giving a new employee on-the-job training is as follows:

STEP 1: PREPARATION OF THE LEARNER

1. Put the learner at ease—relieve the tension.
2. Explain why he or she is being taught.
3. Create interest, encourage questions, find out what the learner already knows about his or her job or other jobs.
4. Explain the why of the whole job and relate it to some job the worker already knows.
5. Place the learner as close to the normal working position as possible.
6. Familiarize the worker with the equipment, materials, tools, and trade terms.

STEP 2: PRESENTATION OF THE OPERATION

1. Explain quantity and quality requirements.

2. Go through the job at the normal work pace.
3. Go through the job at a slow pace several times, explaining each step. Between operations, explain the difficult parts, or those in which errors are likely to be made.
4. Again go through the job at a slow pace several times; explain the key points.
5. Have the learner explain the steps as you go through the job at a slow pace.

STEP 3: PERFORMANCE TRYOUT

1. Have the learner go through the job several times, slowly, explaining to you each step. Correct mistakes, and if necessary, do some of the complicated steps the first few times.
2. You, the trainer, run the job at the normal pace.
3. Have the learner do the job, gradually building up skill and speed.
4. As soon as the learner demonstrates ability to do the job, let the work begin, but don't abandon him or her.

STEP 4: FOLLOW-UP

1. Designate to whom the learner should go for help if he or she needs it.
2. Gradually decrease supervision, checking work from time to time against quality and quantity standards.
3. Correct faulty work patterns that begin to creep into the work, and do it before they become a habit. Show why the learned method is superior.
4. Compliment good work; encourage the worker until able to meet the quality/quantity standards.

JOB INSTRUCTION TRAINING

job instruction training (JIT)
Listing of each of a job's basic tasks, along with a "key point" for each, in order to provide step-by-step training for employees.

Many jobs consist of a logical sequence of steps and are best taught step by step. This step-by-step process is called **job instruction training (JIT)**. It involves listing all necessary steps in the job, each in its proper sequence. Alongside each step you also list a corresponding "key point" (if any). The steps show *what* is to be done, while the key points show *how* it's to be done—and *why*. Here is an example of a job instruction training sheet for teaching a trainee how to operate a large motorized paper cutter.

STEPS	KEY POINTS
1. Start motor	None
2. Set cutting distance	Carefully read scale—to prevent wrong-sized cut
3. Place paper on cutting table	Make sure paper is even—to prevent uneven cut
4. Push paper up to cutter	Make sure paper is tight—to prevent uneven cut
5. Grasp safety release with left hand	Do not release left hand—to prevent hand from being caught in cutter
6. Grasp cutter release with right hand	Do not release right hand—to prevent hand from being caught in cutter
7. Simultaneously pull cutter and safety releases	Keep both hands on corresponding releases—to avoid hands being on cutting table
8. Wait for cutter to retract	Keep both hands on releases—to avoid having hands on cutting table
9. Retract paper	Make sure cutter is retracted; keep both hands away from releases
10. Shut off motor	None

LECTURES

Lecturing has several advantages. It is a quick and simple way of providing knowledge to large groups of trainees, as when the sales force must be taught the special features of some new product. While written material like books and manuals could be used instead, they may involve considerable printing expense, and don't permit the give and take of questioning that lectures do.

Some useful guidelines for presenting your lecture can be summarized as follows:[18]

Give your listeners signals to help them follow your ideas. For instance, if you have a list of items, start by saying something like "There are four reasons why the sales reports are necessary. . . . The first . . . the second . . . "

Don't start out on the wrong foot. For instance, don't start with any irrelevant joke or story or by saying something like "I really don't know why I was asked to speak here today."

Keep your conclusions short. Just summarize your main point or points in one or two succinct sentences.

Be alert to your audience. Watch body language for "closed" signals like fidgeting and arms crossed.

Maintain eye contact with the trainees in the program. At a minimum you should look at each section of trainees during your presentation.

Make sure that everyone in the room can hear. Talk loudly enough so that you can be heard by people in the last row and if necessary repeat questions that you get from trainees from the front of the room.

Control your hands. Get in the habit of leaving your hands hanging naturally at your sides rather than drifting to your face, and then your pockets, then your back, and so on.

Avoid putting your hands near your face. This can block your voice projection and also give the impression that you lack confidence in what you are saying.

Talk from notes rather than from a script. Write out clear, legible notes on large index cards and then use these as an outline, rather than memorizing the whole presentation.

Eliminate bad habits. Beware of distracting bad habits like jiggling coins in your pocket or pulling on an earlobe.

Practice. If you have the time, make sure to rehearse under conditions similar to those under which you will actually give your presentation.

AUDIOVISUAL TECHNIQUES

Using audiovisual techniques like films, closed-circuit TV, audiotapes, or videotapes can be very effective, and this technique is widely used.[19] At Weyerhaeuser Company, for instance, portions of films like *Bridge on the River Kwai* have been used as a basis for discussing interpersonal relationships in the company's management school. The Ford Motor Company uses films in its dealer training sessions to simulate problems and reactions to handling various customer complaints.

Audiovisuals are more expensive than are conventional lectures but offer some advantages. Consider using them in the following situations: first, *when there is a need to illustrate how a certain sequence should be followed over time,* such as when teaching wire soldering or telephone repair, the stop action, instant reply, or fast- or slow-motion capabilities of audiovisuals can be useful; second, when there is *a need to expose trainees to events not easily demonstrable in live lectures,* such as a visual tour of a factory or open-heart surgery; third, when *the training is going to be used organizationwide* and it is too costly to move the trainers from place to place.

There are three options when it comes to obtaining your company's video: You can buy an existing videotape or film; you can make your own; or you can have a production company produce the video for you. Dozens of businesses issue catalogs listing audiovisual programs on topics ranging from applicant interviewing to zoo management.

Teletraining

Companies today are also experimenting with *teletraining*, through which a trainer in a central location can train groups of employees at remote locations via television hookups.[20] For example, AMP, Incorporated, uses satellites to train its engineers and technicians at 165 sites in the United States and 27 other countries. (The firm makes electrical and electronic connection devices.) To reduce costs for one training program, AMP supplied the program content. PBS affiliate WITF, Channel 33 of Harrisburg, Pennsylvania, supplied the equipment and expertise needed to broadcast the training program to five AMP facilities in North America.[21]

PROGRAMMED LEARNING

programmed learning
A systematic method for teaching job skills involving presenting questions or facts, allowing the person to respond, and giving the learner immediate feedback on the accuracy of his or her answers.

Whether the programmed instruction devise is a textbook or computer, **programmed learning** consists of three functions:

1. Presenting questions, facts, or problems to the learner.
2. Allowing the person to respond.
3. Providing feedback on the accuracy of his or her answers.

A page from a programmed instruction book for learning calculus is presented in Figure 7.3. Note how facts and questions are presented. The learner can then respond, and the book then gives feedback on the accuracy of his or her answers.

The main advantage of programmed learning is that it reduces training time by about one-third.[22] In terms of the principles of learning listed earlier, programmed instruction can also facilitate learning since it lets trainees learn at their own pace, provides immediate feedback, and reduces the risk of error. On the other hand, trainees do *not* learn much more with programmed learning than they would with a textbook. Therefore, the cost of developing the manuals and software for programmed instruction has to be weighed against the accelerated but not improved learning that should occur.

VESTIBULE OR SIMULATED TRAINING

vestibule or **simulated training**
Training employees on special off-the-job equipment, as in airplane pilot training, whereby training costs and hazards can be reduced.

Vestibule or **simulated training** is a technique in which trainees learn on the actual or simulated equipment they will use on the job, but are actually trained off the job. *Vestibule training* therefore aims to obtain the advantages of on-the-job training without actually putting the trainee on the job. Vestibule training is virtually a necessity on jobs where it is too costly or dangerous to train employees on the job. It is therefore useful for training new assembly-line workers where putting them right to work could slow production. Similarly when safety is a concern—as with pilots—it may be the only practical alternative.

Vestibule training may just involve placing in a separate room the equipment the trainees will actually be using on the job. However, it often involves the use of equipment simulators. In pilot training, for instance, the main advantages of flight simulators are as follows:[23]

Safety. Crews can practice hazardous flight maneuvers in a safe, controlled environment.

Learning efficiency. The absence of conflicting air traffic and radio chatter that exists in real flight situations enables total concentration on the business of learning how to fly the craft.

Money. The cost of flying a flight simulator is only a fraction of the cost of flying an aircraft. This includes savings on maintenance costs, pilot trainer cost, fuel cost, and the cost of not having the aircraft in regular service.

FIGURE 7.3 A Page from a Programmed Textbook
Source: Daniel Kleppner and Norman Ramsey, *Quick Calculus.* Copyright © 1985 by John Wiley & Sons, Inc. Reprinted by permission.

Sec. 2 Graphs

---

17 The most direct way to plot the graph of a function $y = f(x)$ is to make a table of reasonably spaced values of x and of the corresponding values of $y = f(x)$. Then each pair of values (x,y) can be represented by a point as in the previous frame. A graph of the function is obtained by connecting the points with a smooth curve. Of course, the points on the curve may be only approximate. If we want an accurate plot we just have to be very careful and use many points. (On the other hand, crude plots are pretty good for most purposes.)

Go to 18.

---

18 As an example, here is a plot of the function $y = 3x^2$. A table of values of x and y is shown and these points are indicated on the graph.

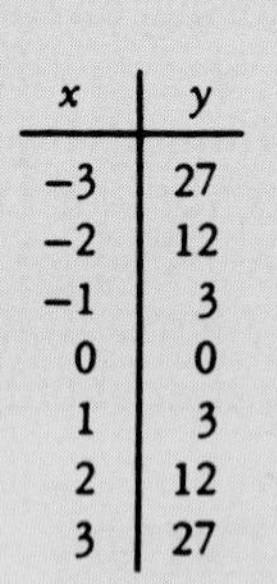

x	y
−3	27
−2	12
−1	3
0	0
1	3
2	12
3	27

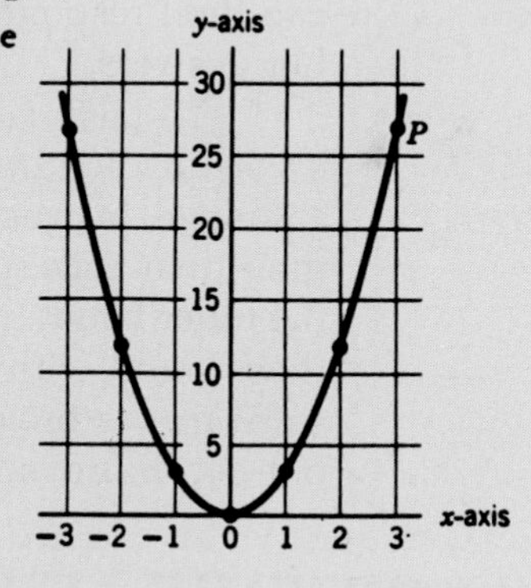

To test yourself, encircle below the pair of coordinates that corresponds to the point P indicated in the figure.

[(3,27) | (27,3) | none of these]

Check your answer. If correct, go on to 19. If incorrect study frame 16 once again and then go to 19.

Computer Application in Training: Computer-Assisted Instruction

Many firms are now using computers to facilitate the training process. Computer-assisted instruction (CAI) systems like Control Data's Plato have several advantages. They provide *self-paced* individualized instruction that is one on one and easy to use, and trainees get *immediate feedback* to their input. CAI also provides *accountability* in that tests are taken on the computer so that management can monitor each trainee's progress and needs. A CAI training program can also be *easily modified* to reflect technological innovations in the equipment for which the employee is being trained. This training also tends to be more *flexible* in that trainees can usually use the computer almost any time they want, and thus get their training when they prefer. Computer-assisted instruction systems like Plato can also provide *simulation* capabilities. Specifically, the system can be designed to simulate complex or difficult tasks and to challenge trainees with "what if" questions like, "If wind velocity on the ground is 80 knots, then what will happen if you decrease your aircraft velocity below its stall speed?"

Some examples of how systems like Plato are being used can help to illustrate the usefulness of CAIs. In some schools, security analyst trainees are able to learn and manipulate various stock valuation models, by programming in various assumptions about economic growth rates and risks; they can thus assess how changes in these factors will influence the price of these stocks.

Plato is also being used to train airline pilots. Part of a pilot's training includes time in a cockpit trainer, in a flight simulator, and in an actual airplane—all expensive pieces of equipment. The Plato system minimizes the amount of time spent in the simulator and thus reduces training costs. By using this computerized system, pilots familiarize themselves with the complicated instrument panel before working with the actual equipment in a simulator or airplane. This is illustrated in the accompanying figure.[1] While a textbook, film, or lecture could present photos of the same instruments, none could provide the almost realistic reactions and problems supplied by the CAI system.[2]

[1] *Plato: A New Way to Solve Training Problems.* Control Data Corporation sales brochure.

[2] *Ibid.* See also Nancy Madlin, "Computer-Based Training Comes of Age," *Personnel*, Vol. 64 no. 11 (November 1987), pp. 64–65; Marilyn Gist, et al., "The Influence of Training Method and Trainees Age on the Acquisition of Computer Skills," *Personnel Psychology*, Vol. 41 no. 2 (Summer 1988), pp. 255–266; Ralph E. Ganger, "Computer-Based Training," *Personnel Journal*, Vol. 68, no. 6 (June 1989), pp. 116–123; John Spirig, "CBT—Computer Based Training—Holds Benefits for a Changing User Community," *Employment Relations Today*, Winter 1990–1991, pp. 325–328; and Ralph Ganger, "HRIS Logs on to Strategic Training," *Personnel Journal*, August 1991, pp. 50–55.

Pilot Training with Plato

Note: The Plato System (right) is used to train pilots in the use of complicated instrument panels.

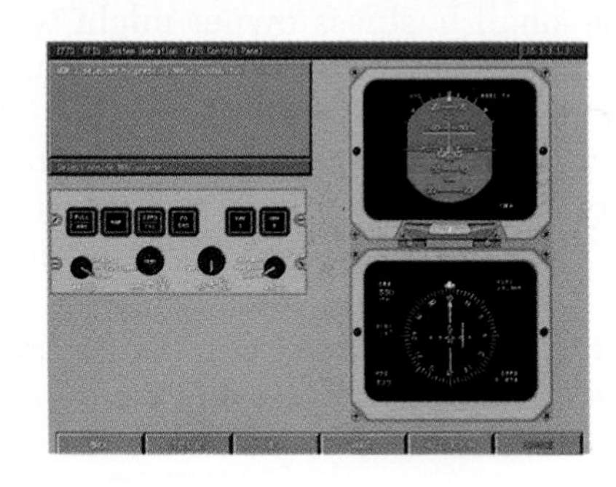

SMALL BUSINESS APPLICATIONS

Training

It does not pay to spend a lot of time hiring the best employees if the employees you hire aren't properly trained. In the book *Made in America*, a group of MIT researchers concluded, for instance, that superior training is one reason Japanese firms have often pulled ahead of American firms within the same industries. Japanese firms will spend weeks in meticulous training programs developing their workers' expertise, while comparable American firms often all but ignore the training process.

Again because so much is riding on such a relatively few employees, it is important that smaller firms, too, carefully train their employees. The concepts and techniques explained in this chapter should enable you to do so. In addition, here is a practical procedure you can use. It contains five steps.

Step 1. Set Training Objectives

First, write down your training objectives. For example, if your objective is to reduce an existing problem (such as too much scrap), or get new assemblers up to speed within two weeks, these objectives should be stated.

Step 2. Write a Detailed Job Description

As explained in Chapter 3, a detailed job description is the heart of any training program. A job description should list the daily and periodic tasks of each job, along with a summary of the steps in each task. Thus, for the job of printer presented in Table 7.1, a main task is "operate paper cutter." Below this, perhaps in paragraph form, the press operator's job description should then explain how the paper cutter should be operated, including steps such as start motor, set cutting distance, and place paper on cutting table. In other words, the job description should list *what* is to be done as well as *how* to do it.

Step 3. Task Analysis Record Form

Next, develop a task analysis record form as summarized in Table 7.1. However, for practical purposes, the small business owner might want to use an abbreviated task analysis record form containing only four columns. In the first, list *tasks* (including what is to be performed in terms of each of the main tasks, and the steps involved in each task). In column B, list *performance standards* (in terms of quantity, quality, accuracy, etc.). In column C, list *trainable skills required*. Here list things the employee must know or do to perform the task. This column provides you with specific skills (such as "Keep both hands on releases") that you'll want to make sure to stress in your training program. In the fourth column, list *aptitudes required*. These are the human aptitudes (such as mechanical comprehension, tolerance for boredom, and so on) that the employee should have to be trainable for the task and for which the employee can be screened ahead of time.

Step 4. Develop Job Instruction Sheet

Next, develop a job instruction sheet for the job. As explained, the job instruction training sheet should list the steps in each task (as listed on the job description, and task analysis record form), as well as key points for each.

Step 5. Prepare Training Program for the Job

Finally, you should now be ready to prepare all the final training documents and media for the job. Build the training manual for the job around the training sequence, listing steps in each job task, and key points.

At a minimum, your training program should thus include the job description, task analysis record form, job instruction sheet, and trainer's manual. The latter contains a summary of the objectives of the training program, the three forms mentioned earlier, and a listing of the trainable skills required. For the trainee, the "training manual" might simply then consist of an introduction to the job and explanation of where the job fits in with the other jobs in the plant or office as well as a job description and job instruction sheet.

You also have to make a decision regarding what media to use in your training program. A simple but effective on-the-job training program using current employees or supervisors as trainers requires only the materials we just described. However, it could turn out that the nature of the job or the number of trainees requires producing or purchasing special audio or visual tapes or films, a slide presentation, or more extensive printed materials.

Training For Special Purposes

Increasingly today training employees involves more than just training them to perform their jobs effectively. Instead, training for special purposes—how to deal with AIDS and adjusting to diversity, for instance—is required too. A sampling of such special purpose training programs follows.

LITERACY TRAINING TECHNIQUES

Functional illiteracy is a serious problem for many employers. By some estimates there are 25 million American adults 17 years old and older who are "functional illiterates" either because they can't read at all or can only read up to a third- or fourth-grade level.[24] Yet as the U.S. economy shifts from goods to services, there is a corresponding need for workers who are more skilled, more literate, and able to perform at least basic arithmetic skills.

Employers are responding to this problem in two main ways. First, companies are testing prospective employees' *basic skills*. Of the 1,005 companies that responded to an American Management Association (AMA) survey on workplace testing, for instance, 345 companies (34.3%) indicated that they conduct basic skills testing.[25] In 89% of the responding companies job applicants who are deficient in basic skills are refused employment. At about 3% of the other companies current employees and candidates for promotion are tested (and often rejected) based on their literacy scores.

The second response is to institute basic skills and literacy programs. Based on the AMA survey, the areas in which remedial training are needed tend to be fairly evenly split among mathematics, reading, and writing.

One simple approach is to have supervisors focus on basic skills by giving employees writing and speaking exercises. After the exercise is completed, the supervisor can then provide personal feedback.[26] One way to do this is to convert materials used in the employees' jobs into instructional tools. For example, if an employee needs to use a manual to find out how to replace a certain machine part, he or she should be taught how to use an index to locate the relevant section.[27] Another approach is to bring in outside professionals like teachers from a local high school or community college to institute, say, a remedial reading or writing program. Having employees attend adult education or high school evening classes is another option.

Another approach is to use an interactive video disk (IVD). This technique combines the drama of video with the power of microcomputers.[28] An example is Principles of Alphabet Literacy (PALS). It uses animated video and a computer-stored voice to enable nonreaders to associate sounds with letters and letters with words, and to use the words to create sentences.[29] A second IVD program is call SKILLPAC. This program, subtitled English for Industry, was designed mostly for nonnative English speakers. It combines video, audio, and computer technologies to teach language skills in the context of the specific workplace situation in which those skills will be used.[30]

AIDS EDUCATION

Many of the estimated one million Americans infected with the AIDS virus are in the work force, and this creates anxiety for many non-infected employees and a dilemma for many employers. On the one hand, infected individuals must be allowed to remain on their jobs, both for moral and legal reasons. On the other hand, the infected person's co-workers often require some type of training in order to reduce anxieties and maximize the chances that the employees will be able to work together effectively as a team.

Many firms therefore institute AIDS education programs. The program instituted in the Wellesley, Massachusetts office of Sun Life of Canada, a life insurance company, is typical.[31] Groups of 20 to 30 employees attended 90-minute seminars. In addition to providing detailed information on AIDS, the seminars provided a forum for discussion and questions. Management employees attended three-hour seminars of 10 to 12 people each. These covered additional AIDS-related issues, including the need for confidentiality, the potential impact of discrimination laws, and the company's AIDS policy.

There was reportedly little resistance to holding or attending these seminars, in part because the existence of the seminars and the reasons for them were widely communicated in the company's newsletters. Some management employees initially expressed skepticism about devoting so many hours to AIDS education but after their sessions most reportedly felt differently. Based on pre- and post-seminar questionnaires, the company believes that the seminars were useful in getting employees to learn the facts about AIDS, cleared up misconceptions, and helped to put personal concerns of many employees to rest.

GLOBAL HRM

Training

As firms expand operations abroad it becomes more important to train foreign nationals. For example, recall Gillette International's program that brought local foreign talent to the Boston headquarters for training in the techniques, policies, and values of the firm before they assumed new jobs in their home country.

Training employees abroad involves more than translating existing programs into other languages. Cultural differences influence both the applicability of training material and the reactions of trainees to the programs. Here are some suggestions for conducting training programs abroad.[33]

1. Understand the taboos and turn-ons of the participants' culture. For example, in Japan, risk taking is by and large taboo. You may therefore find that you get no volunteers to participate in a training role-play exercise because doing so is taking a risk. Similarly, in the Middle East, role-plays are games that are for children, not for adults.
2. Critiquing other people in public is taboo in some Far Eastern cultures. Therefore, even something so simple as getting a volunteer to be an "observer" in a training discussion or role-play could be difficult with trainees here because the role of the observer is often to critique the other participants' behavior.
3. Saving face and not putting people in embarrassing situations is important not just in the Far East. In Middle Eastern countries, and in East and West Africa and some European cultures including Spain and Italy, criticizing trainees or making them look foolish is not advisable. In fact, putting them in any activity in which their behavior will be discussed, debriefed, and/or criticized can create problems.
4. In some cultures you'll find it difficult to get feedback on your effectiveness as a trainer. Even if you violate a taboo, the trainees may be reluctant to tell you so, because to do so would be to criticize you and cause you to lose face.
5. Make sure to understand how the job you are training your trainees to do is viewed in their native culture. In the U.S. for instance, it's appropriate to tell the sales people to write introductory letters to high-level executives to gain entry to their organizations. In Japan doing so would be highly unusual. Instead, repeated personal visits to drop off business cards is often required to gain entry.
6. Consider the effects of jet lag and diet changes. For example, while it may be 4:00 P.M.. in Boston where you're doing your training, your French participants' body clocks may be set to a more tired 9:00 P.M. Similarly, Japanese participants may expect a rice meal, and all participants fresh from overseas would probably do better with mineral water than soda.

VALUES TRAINING

Many training programs today are aimed at educating employees about the firm's most cherished values and (it is hoped) convincing employees that these should be their values as well.

The training programs at Saturn Corporation illustrate this. For example, their new-employee orientation/training program is similar in this regard to Toyota's. At Saturn, the first two days are devoted to discussions of benefits, safety and security, and the company's production process—just-in-time delivery, materials management, and so forth.[34] However, in days three and four the focus shifts to Saturn's values. Here the firm's top managers spend about an hour and a half discussing Saturn's values. Then, all new employees get their copy of Saturn's "mission card." This allows the trainees and trainer to go through each of the Saturn values listed on the card—teamwork, trust and respect for the individual, and quality, for example—to illustrate its meaning. Short exercises are also used here. Thus the new employees might be asked "If you saw a team member do this . . . what would you do?" Or, "If you saw a team member 'living' this value, what would you see?"

For their part, Saturn's supervisors get "converted" to Saturn's values in part through a special two-day leadership seminar called "Values and Beliefs." The program's basic aim is to familiarize supervisors with Saturn's core values and illustrate how to translate them from words into actions. Part one, for instance, explains how values influence behavior and cautions managers to beware of any disparities between stated and operative values: "It's what you do, not what you say that sends the real signal to workers about what your department's operative values are," say the trainers. Thus talking "trust" while insisting on time clocks may be contradictions because the time clocks seem to say "We don't trust you." (There are no time clocks at Saturn.)

Succeeding sessions use lectures and exercises to explain and illustrate each of Saturn's basic values. Illustrations of core Saturn values such as "respect for people," "make our employees full partners," "build customer satisfaction through teamwork;" and "put quality in all we do" are presented here. The aim is to make believers of Saturn leaders through the use of illustrative examples of what these values mean (i.e., what does "respect for people" mean, and how does it manifest itself?).

DIVERSITY TRAINING

With a work force that is becoming increasingly diverse, many more firms find they have to implement diversity training programs. As a personnel officer for one firm put it, "We're trying to create a better sensitivity among our supervisors about the issues and challenges women and minorities face in pursuing their careers."[35] Therefore, diversity training often involves creating better sensitivity among non-supervisors as well, with the aim of creating more harmonious working relationships among a firm's employees.

A supervisory training program at Kinney Shoe Corp. provides an example.[36] The firm conducts eight-hour seminars for Kinney Shoe executives and store managers. The program is called "Valuing Diversity." In part, the seminars are aimed at showing participants how their own upbringing affects the assumptions they make and their behavior. For example, the firm's studies indicated that managers responsible for hiring might make an assumption about an applicant's intelligence based on the person's accent and poor English-speaking skills. The manager might assume, in other words, that the person hasn't the skills to sell shoes, although he or she certainly could sell effectively.

The Kinney "Valuing Diversity" program also shows how people from different cultures react differently to situations in the workplace. It does this by presenting a number of situations. For example, one situation illustrates the fact that a Native American worker might be embarrassed by public praise from his or her supervisor.

CUSTOMER-SERVICE TRAINING

Today almost two-thirds of Americans are in customer-service (rather than manufacturing) jobs and, furthermore, more and more companies are finding it necessary to compete based on the quality of their service. It's no longer enough, for instance, to have a clean room at a decent price when you check into a Hilton. To stay competitive employers like Hilton find they have to provide total customer service, from courteous bellhops to easy parking to speedy check-outs.

Many companies are therefore setting up customer-service training programs. The basic aim here is to train all employees to treat the company's customers in a courteous and hospitable manner. The saying "The customer is always right" may be an old one, but it's one that's been rediscovered and is being emphasized by countless service companies today. However, putting the customer first requires employee customer-service training.

The customer-service training at Alamo Rent-a-Car is an example.[37] They call it the "Best Friends" program. Carried out in the early 1990s, it involved spending millions of dollars for introducing new customer-service policies and indoctrinating and retraining Alamo employees in the practices of excellent customer-service.

"Best Friends" consisted of a five-day orientation/customer-service training program. First, employees are familiarized with Alamo's history, its growth and expansion, and the company's expectations regarding customer service and the firm's work ethics. The program then shifts to customer-service training. This includes segments on the importance of exceptional customer service, how to define it, illustrative examples of exceptional customer service, and the specific employee skills needed to deliver such fine service.

In addition to these general sessions, Alamo employees also received customer-service training related specifically to their jobs. For example, service agents got training on the firm's extensive car preparation test which aims to assure that customers get cars that are clean and running properly.

Early results suggest the training program has been successful. While other factors may have contributed to the improvements, sales complaints were down 15% from the year before training commenced. Similarly, rudeness complaints were down 50% from pre-training levels. The firm's business transactions jumped by 30% in one year.

TRAINING FOR TEAMWORK AND EMPOWERMENT

worker involvement programs
Programs that aim to boost organizational effectiveness by getting employees to participate in the planning, organizing, and managing of their jobs.

An increasing number of firms today use work teams and empowerment to improve their effectiveness. They adapt "teamwork" as a value and then organize the work to be done around close-knit work teams. They then empower these teams to get their jobs done, which means giving them the authorization and the ability to do their jobs. Both the team approach and worker empowerment are components of what many firms call worker involvement programs. **Worker involvement programs** aim to boost organizational effectiveness by getting employees to participate in the planning, organizing, and general managing of their jobs.

However, many firms find that "teamwork" doesn't just happen: Instead, employees must be trained to be good team members. That is why (as discussed earlier in this chapter) firms like Toyota and Saturn spend considerable sums training new employees to be good team members. You may recall, for instance, that Toyota devotes hours to training new employees to listen to each other and to cooperate. And, throughout the training process, Toyota's dedication to teamwork is stressed. Short exercises are used to illustrate examples of good and bad teamwork and to mold new employees' attitudes regarding what good teamwork is.

Some firms use outdoor training such as Outward Bound programs to build teamwork.[38] Outdoor training usually involves taking a firm's management team out into rugged, mountainous terrain. There they learn team spirit and cooperation and the need to trust and rely on each other by overcoming physical obstacles. As one participant put it, "Every time I climbed over a rock, I needed someone's help."[39] An example of one activity is the "trust fall." Here an employee has to slowly lean back and fall backwards from a height of, say, 10 feet into the waiting arms of 5 or 10 team members. The idea is to build trust, and particularly trust in one's colleagues.

On an assembly line such as the one above, workers, as part of a team, can improve their effectiveness if they are empowered through training to make decisions.

Not all employees are eager to participate in such activities. Firms such as Outward Bound have potential participants fill out extensive medical evaluations to make sure participants can safely engage in risky outdoor activities. Others feel that the outdoor activities are too contrived to be applicable back at work. However, they do illustrate the lengths to which employers will go to build teamwork.

Empowering employees (either individually or as teams) also almost always requires a lot of training. It is rarely enough to just tell the members of a group that they're "empowered" to do all the buying and selling and planning involved in producing, say, the auto component they are responsible for. Instead, extensive training is required to ensure they have the skills to do the job.

Many companies today use work teams or special "quality circles" to analyze job-related problems and to come up with solutions. (A quality circle is a group of five to ten employees, often a work team, who meet for an hour or two each week during work hours to analyze a problem on their job and to develop solutions to it.) As a result, much of the approximately 320 hours of training a new Saturn employee receives is devoted to developing the sorts of problem-solving and analysis skills he or she will need to help the work team be empowered—in this case, to analyze and solve problems. Training in the use of basic statistical analysis tools and basic accounting is an example.

Evaluating the Training Effort

After trainees have completed their training programs (or perhaps at planned intervals during the training), the program should be evaluated to see how well its objectives have been met. Thus, if assemblers should be able to solder a junction in 30 seconds, or a Xerox technician repair a machine in 30 minutes, then the program's effectiveness should be measured based on whether these goals are met. It is unfortunate (but true) that most managers do not spend much time appraising the effects of their training programs. For example, are your trainees learning *as much* as they can? Are they learning *as fast* as they can? Is there a *better method* for training them? These are some of the questions you can answer by properly evaluating your training efforts.

There are two basic issues to address when evaluating a training program. The first is the design of the evaluation study and, in particular, whether *controlled experimentation* will be used. The second is *what training effect to measure.*

CONTROLLED EXPERIMENTATION

experimentation Formal methods for testing the effectiveness of a training program, preferably with before and after tests and a control group.

Ideally, the best method to use in evaluating a training program involves controlled **experimentation**. In a controlled experiment, both a training group and a control (no training) group are used. Data (for instance, on quantity of production or quality of soldered junctions) should be obtained both before and after the training effort in the group exposed to training and before and after a corresponding work period in the control group. In this way, it is possible to determine to what extent any change in performance in the training group resulted from the training itself, rather than from some organizationwide change like a raise in pay; the latter, one assumes, would have affected employees in both the training and control groups. In terms of current practices, however, one survey found that something less than half the companies responding attempted to obtain before and after measures from trainees; the number of organizations using control groups was negligible.[40] One expert suggests at least using an evaluation form like the one shown in Figure 7.4 to evaluate the development program.[41]

WHAT TRAINING EFFECTS TO MEASURE

There are four basic categories of training outcomes or effects that can be measured:

1. *Reaction.* First, evaluate trainees' reactions to the program. Did they like the program? Did they think it worthwhile?
2. *Learning.* Second, you can test the trainees to determine if they learned the principles, skills, and facts they were to learn.
3. *Behavior.* Next ask whether the trainees' behavior on the job changed because of the training program. For example, are employees in the store's complaint department more courteous toward disgruntled customers than previously?
4. *Results.* Last, but probably most importantly, ask: "What final results were achieved in terms of the training objectives previously set? Did the number of customer com-

EVALUATION OF OUTSIDE MANAGEMENT DEVELOPMENT PROGRAMS

Name__________ Title__________ Date__________

Program Attended:

Name of program__________ Dates__________

Location__________ Fee__________

Organization presenting program__________

1. How accurately did the program announcement describe what was covered at the program?
   ________Very accurately ________Fairly accurately ________Inaccurately
2. To what extent did the subject content meet your needs and interests?
   ________Very well ________To some extent ________Very little
3. How effective were the speakers and conference leaders?
   ________Excellent ________Very good ________Good ________Fair ________Poor
4. How were the facilities, meals, etc?
   ________Excellent ________Very good ________Good ________Fair ________Poor
5. What benefits do you feel you gained?
   ________Knowledge of what other companies were doing.
   ________New theory and principles that are pertinent.
   ________Ideas and techniques that can be applied on the job.
   ________Other (please explain).
6. How would you rate the entire program in relation to time and cost?
   ________Excellent ________Very good ________Good ________Fair ________Poor
7. Would you like to attend a future program presented by the same organization?
   ________Definitely ________Possibly ________No
8. Would you recommend that others from your company attend programs presented by the same organization?
   ________Yes ________No ________Not sure
   If yes, who should attend?__________
9. Other comments__________

FIGURE 7.4
A Sample Outside-Training Evaluation Form
Source: Reprinted, by permission of the publisher, from "Effective Supervisory Training and Development, Part 3: Outside Programs," *Personnel* (February 1985), p. 42 © 1985, American Management Association, New York. All rights reserved.

plaints about employees drop? Did the reject rate improve? Did scrappage cost decrease? Was turnover reduced? Are production quotas now being met?" and so forth. Improved results are, of course, especially important. The training program may succeed in terms of the reactions from trainees, increased learning, and even changes in behavior. But if the results are not achieved, then in the final analysis, the training has not achieved its goals. If so, the problem may lie in the training program. Remember, though, that the results may be inadequate because the problem was not amenable to training in the first place.

CHAPTER REVIEW

SUMMARY

1. In this chapter we focused on technical skills training for new employees and for present employees whose performance is deficient. For either, uncovering training requirements involves analyzing the cause of the problem and determining what (if any) training is needed. Remember to ask, "Is it a training problem?" Make sure the "problem" is not being caused by some more deep-rooted problem like poor selection or low wages.
2. We discussed some principles of learning that should be understood by all trainers. The guidelines include: make the material meaningful (by providing a bird's-eye view, familiar examples, organizing the material, splitting it into meaningful chunks, and using familiar terms and visual aids); make provision for transfer of training; and try to motivate your trainee.
3. We discussed several training techniques. *Job instruction training* is useful for training on jobs that consist of a logical sequence of steps. *Vestibule* training combines the advantages of on- and off-the-job training.

4. On-the-job training is a third technical training technique. It might involve the understudy method, job rotation, or special assignments and committees. In any case, it should involve four steps: preparing the learner, presenting the operation (or nature of the job), performance tryouts, and a follow-up. Other training methods include audiovisual techniques, lectures, and computer-assisted instruction.
5. Most managers don't spend time evaluating the effects of their training program although they should. In measuring the effectiveness of a training program there are four categories of outcomes you can measure: reaction, learning, behavior and results. In some cases where training seems to have failed, it may be because training was not the appropriate solution.

KEY TERMS

employee orientation
reality shock
training
task analysis
performance analysis
on-the-job training (OJT)
job instruction training (JIT)
programmed learning
vestibule or simulated
training
worker involvement programs
experimentation

Discussion Questions

1. "A well-thought-out orientation program is especially important for employees (like recent graduates) who have had little or no work experience." Explain why you agree or disagree with this statement.
2. You're the supervisor of a group of employees whose task it is to assemble tuning devices that go into radios. You find that quality is not what it should be and that many of your group's tuning devices have to be brought back and reworked; your own boss says that "You'd better start doing a better job of training your workers."
   a. What are some of the "staffing" factors that could be contributing to this problem?
   b. Explain how you would go about assessing whether it is in fact a training problem.
3. Explain how you would apply our "principles of learning" in developing a lecture, say, on "orientation and training."
4. Pick out some task with which you are familiar — mowing the lawn, tuning a car — and develop a job instruction training sheet for it.

Application Exercises

RUNNING CASE

Carter Cleaning Company

The New Training Program

At the present time the Carter Cleaning Centers have no formal orientation or training policies or procedures, and Jennifer believes this is one reason why the standards that she and her father would like employees to adhere to are generally not followed.

Several examples can illustrate this. In dealing with the customers at the front counters the Carters would prefer that certain practices and procedures be used. For example, all customers should be greeted with what Jack refers to as a "big hello." And any garments they drop off should immediately be inspected for any damage or unusual stains so these can be brought to the customer's attention, lest the customer later return to pick up the garment and erroneously blame the store for the damage or the unusual stain. The garments are then supposed to be immediately placed together in a nylon sack to separate them from other customers' garments. The ticket also has to be carefully written up with the customer's name, telephone number, and the date precisely and clearly noted on all copies. The counterperson is also supposed to take the opportunity to try to sell the customer some additional services, such as waterproofing, if a raincoat has been dropped off, or simply notifying the customer that "you know now that people are doing their spring cleaning, we're having a special on drapery cleaning all this month." Finally, as the customer leaves, the counterperson is supposed to make some courteous comment like "Have a nice day" or "Drive safely." Each of the other jobs in the stores—pressing, cleaning and spotting, periodically maintaining the coin laundry equipment, and so forth—similarly contain certain steps, procedures, and most important, standards which the Carters would prefer to see adhered to.

The company has also had other problems, Jennifer feels, because of a lack of adequate employee training and orientation. For example, two new employees became very upset last month when they discovered that they were not paid at the end of the week, on Friday, but instead were paid (as are all Carter employees) on the following Tuesday. The Carters use the extra two days in part to give them time to obtain everyone's hours and compute their pay. The other reason they do it, according to Jack, is that "frankly, when we stay a few days behind in paying employees it helps to ensure that they at least give us a few days notice before quitting on us. While we are certainly obligated to pay them anything they earn, we find that psychologically they seem to be less likely to just walk out on us Friday evening and not show up Monday morning if they still haven't gotten their pay from the previous week. This way they at least give us a few days' notice so we can find a replacement."

Other matters that could be covered during an orientation, says Jennifer, include company policy regarding paid holidays, lateness and absences, health and hospitalization benefits (there are none, other than worker's compensation) and general matters like maintaining a clean and safe work area, personal appearance and cleanliness, filling in time sheets, personal telephone calls and mail, company policies regarding matters like substance abuse, and eating or smoking on the job.

Jennifer believes that implementing orientation and training programs would help to ensure that employees know how to do their jobs the right way. And she and her father further believe that it is only when employees understand the right way to do their jobs that there is any hope that their jobs will in fact be accomplished the way the Carters want them to be accomplished.

Questions

1. Specifically what should the Carters cover in their new employee orientation program and how should they cover this information?
2. In the personnel management course Jennifer took the book suggested using a task analysis record form to identify tasks performed by an employee. "Should we use a form like this for the counterperson's job and if so what, roughly speaking, would the completed, filled-in form look like?"
3. Which specific training techniques should she use to train her pressers, her cleaner-spotters, her managers, and her counterpeople, and why?

CASE INCIDENT: *Boeing's New Computer System*

In 1990 the Boeing Commercial Airline Group in Seattle was about to install in its commercial spare parts department the largest computing system it had ever developed. The department sells spare parts to commercial airlines. The purpose of the new computer system was to automate many of the department's tasks, including inventory updates, customer inquiry responses, and pricing.

Boeing managers knew that installation of the new computer system would require extensive retraining of its employees. It would impact almost all of the 700 people in the spare parts department, and not just in terms of the technical aspects of using the new computer system. For one thing, the department's offices would become virtually paperless. And perhaps even more scary to the employees was the fact that they would have to spend much more of their day working at their computer terminals. In addition, interpersonal relationships would become more interdependent because each employee would be more reliant on information that others entered accurately onto the computer. Employees had to understand that suddenly they had many more "customers" relying on them—customers who, in fact, were other spare parts department employees.

As the training coordinator put it, "We realized that providing technical training alone wouldn't be enough to insure a successful implementation." The new system's users would need tools to handle the changes they would experience when the system came online. The training group wanted to make sure that it minimized the stress and confusion that implementation could potentially create. More to the point though, it wanted to make sure that all the employees using the new system became "customer-oriented" in terms of providing the information their colleagues/customers in the spare parts department required.

Given the functional diversity of the group, Boeing knew a challenge lay ahead. Half of the group worked in a warehouse and was responsible for shipping, receiving, and storing parts. The other half worked in an office thirty miles away. Furthermore, it was a diverse group in terms of educational attainment.

In deciding the nature of the training program, Boeing had a variety of options to choose from. Because there already was an entire in-house training department, one option was to have *it* do the training. On the other hand, preparing 700 people in a very short time might require the services of a consulting, training, and development firm geared to getting a program like this up and running. The training department also had to consider the specific types of training to be used, such as seminars, video instruction, lectures, or books. One San Francisco-based firm under consideration was well known for being able to quickly develop large scale training programs that were generally based around seminars which utilized written and visual material, participative exercises, examples, and lectures.

However, before deciding whether the training program would be managed internally or by a consulting firm, Boeing knew that it had to be more clear about the actual training objectives. For instance, in addition to the purely technical aspects of the training, there was the need to make the employees who used the system more customer-oriented. Possibly, employee communication and assertiveness skills had to be developed so that they could make their needs known if there was particular information they wanted from the system that was not being provided by the employees who would now input that data.

Questions

1. What sort of training do you think the spare parts department employees require?
2. How would you go about determining what the specific training objectives should be?
3. Do you think it's advisable for Boeing to go to an outside consulting firm to put together this program, or would you recommend handling it internally?
4. Whether done internally or through the consulting firm, explain how you would go about designing the necessary training program.

Source: This case incident is based on Steve Thieme, "Customer-Service Training Supports Work Systems," *Personnel Journal,* Vol. 72, No. 4, pp. 63–65.

Human Resource Management Simulation

You will have an opportunity in the simulation to budget an orientation program. Do you think it is worth the cost? To what extent does an effective orientation program help retain employees?

Training is also a key element in the simulation. You will need to decide whether you train those employees you promote. Although training costs for internal promotions and open-market hiring costs are relatively equal, the organization believes that supervisors and managers will be better prepared by the training program to assume managerial positions in the organization. Your team will need to wrestle with the decision of promoting (and training) from within or hiring qualified people from outside the organization. In addition, you will need to budget for technical and nontechnical types of training.

Incident F involves a budgetary decision concerning several training requests. As you make this decision, remember that almost all decisions involve setting precedent. Whatever you decide to do, you may be asked to do it again in the future.

Notes

1. Joseph Famularo, *Handbook of Modern Personnel Administration* (New York: McGraw-Hill, 1972), pp. 23.7–23.8. See also Ronald Smith, "Employee Orientation: Ten Steps to Success," *Personnel Journal*, Vol. 63, no. 12 (December 1984), pp. 46–49.
2. See also Walter St. John, "The Complete Employee Orientation Program," *Personnel Journal*, Vol. 59 (May 1980), pp. 373–378.
3. Morton E. Grossman, "The $5.3 Billion Bill for Training," *Personnel Journal* (July 1986), p. 54.
4. This is based on Anthony F. Carnevale, "America and the New Economy," *Training and Development Journal*, Vol. 44, no. 11 (November 1990), pp. 31ff.
5. Ibid.
6. Ibid.; "The Training Gap," *Training and Development Journal*, March 1991, p. 9.
7. Carnevale, based on Kenneth Wexley and Gary Yukl, *Organizational Behavior and Personnel Psychology* (Homewood, IL: Richard D. Irwin, 1977), pp. 289–295; E. J. McCormick and J. Tiffin, *Industrial Psychology* (Englewood Cliffs, NJ: Prentice-Hall, 1974), pp. 232–340.
8. Wexley and Yukl, *Organizational Behavior*, pp. 289–295.
9. R. E. Silverman, *Learning Theory Applied to Training* (Reading, MA: Addison Wesley, 1970), Chapter 8; McCormick and Tiffin, *Industrial Psychology*, pp. 239–240.
10. This is based on Kenneth Wexley and Gary Latham, *Developing and Training Human Resources in Organizations* (Glenview, IL: Scott, Foresman, 1981), pp. 22–27. Note that these legal aspects apply equally to technical training and management development. See also Ron Zemke, "What is Technical Training, Anyway?" *Training*, Vol. 23, no. 7 (July 1986), pp. 18–22. See also Bureau of National Affairs, "Sexual Harassment: Training Tips," *Fair Employment Practices*, June 25, 1987, p. 84.
11. Bureau of National Affairs, *Training Employees*, Personnel Policies Forum, Survey 88 (Washington, DC: November 1965), p. 5. For further discussion of conducting a needs analysis, see Kenneth Nowack, "A True Training Needs Analysis," *Training & Development Journal*, April 1991, pp. 69–73.
12. B. M. Bass and J. A. Vaughan, "Assessing Training Needs," in Craig Schneier and Richard Beatty, *Personnel Administration Today* (Reading, MA: Addison-Wesley, 1978), p. 311. See also Ronald Ash and Edward Leving, "Job Applicant Training and Work Experience Evaluation: An Empirical Comparison of Four Methods," *Journal of Applied Psychology*, Vol. 70, no. 3 (1985), pp. 572–576, and John Lawrie, "Break the Training Ritual," *Personnel Journal*, Vol. 67, no. 4 (April 1988), pp. 95–97.
13. McCormick and Tiffin, *Industrial Psychology*, p. 245. See also James C. Georges, "The Hard Realities of Soft Skills Training," *Personnel Journal*, Vol. 68, no. 4 (April 1989), pp. 40–45; Robert H. Buckham, "Applying Role Analysis in the Workplace," *Personnel*, Vol. 64, no. 2 (February 1987), pp. 63–65; and J. Kevin Ford and Raymond Noe, "Self-Assessed Training Needs: The Effects of Attitudes Towards Training, Management Level, and Function," *Personnel Psychology*, Vol. 40, no. 1 (Spring 1987), pp. 39–54.
14. J.P. Cicero, "Behavioral Objectives for Technical Training Systems," *Training and Development Journal*, Vol. 28 (1973), pp. 14–17. See also Larry D. Hales, "Training: A Product of Business Planning," *Training and Development Journal*, Vol. 40, no. 7 (July 1986), pp. 87–92, and Arnold H. Wensky and Robert Legendre, "Training Incentives," *Personnel Journal*, Vol. 68, no. 4 (April 1989), pp. 102–108.
15. I.L. Goldstein, *Training: Program Development and*

Evaluation (Monterey, CA: Wadsworth, 1974). See also Stephen B. Wehrenberg, "Learning Contracts," *Personnel Journal*, Vol. 67, no. 9 (September 1988), pp. 100–103, and Murray B. Heibert and Norman Smallwood, "Now for a Completely Different Look at Needs Analysis," *Training and Development Journal*, Vol. 41, no. 5 (May 1987), pp. 75–79.
16. Wexley and Latham, *Developing and Training*, p. 107.
17. Ibid., pp. 107–112. Four steps in on-the-job training based on William Berliner and William McLarney, *Management Practice and Training* (Homewood, IL: Irwin, 1974), pp. 442–443. See also Robert Sullivan and Donald Miklas, "On-the-Job Training That Works," *Training and Development Journal*, Vol. 39, no. 5 (May 1985), pp. 118–120, and Stephen B. Wehrenberg, "Supervisors as Trainers: The Long-Term Gains of OJT," *Personnel Journel*, Vol. 66, no. 4 (April 1987), pp. 48–51.
18. Donald F. Michalak and Edwin G. Yager, *Making the Training Process Work* (New York, Harper & Row, 1979), pp. 108–111. See also Richard Wiegand, "Can *All* Your Trainees Hear You?" *Training and Development Journal*, Vol. 41, no. 8 (August 1987), pp. 38–43.
19. Wexley and Latham, *Developing and Training*, pp. 131–133. See also Teri O. Grady and Mike Matthews, "Video . . . Through the Eyes of the Trainee," *Training*, Vol. 24, no. 7 (July 1987), pp. 57–62.
20. Mary Boone and Susan Schulman, "Teletraining: A High-Tech Alternative," *Personnel*, Vol. 62, no. 5 (May 1985), pp. 4–9. See also Ron Zemke, "The Rediscovery of Video Teleconferencing," *Training*, Vol. 23, no. 9 (September 1986), pp. 28–36; and Carol Haig, "Clinics Fill Training Niche," *Personnel Journal*, Vol. 66, no. 9 (September 1987), pp. 134–140.
21. Joseph Giusti, David Baker, and Peter Braybash, "Satellites Dish Out Global Training," *Personnel Journal*, June 1991, pp. 80–84.
22. G.N. Nash, J.P. Muczyk, and F.L. Vettori, "The Role and Practical Effectiveness of Programmmed Instruction," *Personnel Psychology*, Vol. 24 (1971), pp. 397–418.
23. Wexley and Latham, *Developing and Training*, p. 141. See also Raymond Wlozkowski, "Simulation," *Training and Development Journal*, Vol. 39, no. 6 (June 1985), pp. 38–43.
24. Harold W. McGraw, Jr., "Adult Functional Illiteracy: What to Do About It," *Personnel*, October 1987, p. 38; Catherine Petrini, "Literacy Programs Make the News," *Training and Development Journal*, February 1991, pp. 30–36.
25. This is based on Ellen Sherman, "Back to Basics to Improve Skills," *Personnel*, July 1989, pp. 22–26.
26. Ibid., p. 24.
27. Bureau of National Affairs, *Bulletin to Management*, December 17, 1987, p. 408.
28. Nancy Lynn Bernardon, "Let's Erase Illiteracy from the Workplace," *Personnel* (January 1989), pp. 29–32.
29. Ibid. The PALS course was developed by educator Dr. John Henry Martin.
30. Ibid., p. 32. SKILLPAC was created by the Center for Applied Linguistics and Dr. Arnold Packer, senior research fellow at the Hudson Institute in Indianapolis, Indiana.
31. Jeffrey Mello, "AIDS Education in the Work Place," *Training and Development Journal*, December 1990, pp. 65–70.
32. Jennifer Laabs, "The Global Talent Search," *Personnel Journal*, August 1991, pp. 38–42.
33. Pat McCarthy, "The Art of Training Abroad," *Training and Development Journal*, November 1990, pp. 13–18.
34. This is adapted from Gary Dessler, *Winning Commitment* (New York: McGraw-Hill, 1993), Chapter 7.
35. See Joyce Santora, "Kinney Shoes Steps Into Diversity," *Personnel Journal*, September 1991, p. 74.
36. This is based on Ibid., pp. 72–77.
37. Joyce Santora, "Alamo's Drive for Customer Service," *Personnel Journal*, April 1991, pp. 42–44.
38. This is based on Jennifer Laabs, "Team Training Goes Outdoors," *Personnel Journal*, June 1991, pp. 56–63.
39. Ibid., p. 56.
40. R.E. Catalano and D.L. Kirkpatrick, "Evaluating Training Programs—The State of the Art," *Training and Development Journal*, Vol. 22, no. 5 (May 1968), pp. 2–9. See also J. Kevin Ford and Steven Wroten, "Introducing New Methods for Conducting Training Evaluation and for Linking Training Evaluation to Program Redesign," *Personnel Psychology*, Vol. 37, no. 4 (Winter 1984), pp. 651–666. See also Basil Paquet et al., "The Bottom Line," *Training and Development Journal*, Vol. 41, no. 5 (May 1987), pp. 27–33.; Harold E. Fisher and Ronald Weinberg, "Make Training Accountable: Assess Its Impact," *Personnel Journal*, Vol. 67, no. 1 (January 1988), pp. 73–75; and Timothy Baldwin and J. Kevin Ford, "Transfer of Training: A Review and Directions for Future Research," *Personnel Psychology*, Vo. 41, no. 1 (Spring 1988), pp. 63–105.
41. Donald Kirkpatrick, "Effective Supervisory Training and Development," Part 3: "Outside Programs," *Personnel*, Vol. 62, no. 2 (February 1985), pp. 39–42. See also James Bell and Deborah Kerr, "Measuring Training Results: Key to Managerial Commitment," *Training and Development Journal*, Vol. 41, no. 1 (January 1987), pp. 70–73. Among the reasons training might not pay off on the job are a mismatching of courses and trainee's needs, supervisory slip-ups (with supervisors signing up trainees and then forgetting to have them attend the sessions when the training session is actually given), and no help applying skills back on the job. For a discussion, see Ruth Colvin Clark, "Nine Ways to Make Training Pay Off on the Job," *Training*, Vol. 23, no. 11 (November 1986), pp. 83–87. See also Herman Birnbrauer, "Troubleshooting Your Training Program," *Training and Development Journal*, Vol. 41, no 9 (September 1987), pp. 18–20.

CHAPTER 8

DEVELOPING MANAGERS

OVERVIEW

Management development is similar to training since it is aimed at providing managers with the leadership skills they need to do their jobs. In this chapter we explain the main management development methods, including job rotation, leadership training, role playing, and management games. When you finish studying this chapter, you should be able to discuss basic on-the-job and off-the-job development techniques such as job rotation, and management games, and describe special-purpose development techniques such as organizational development.

▸ NATURE & PURPOSE OF MANAGEMENT DEVELOPMENT

management development
Any attempt to improve current or future management performance by imparting knowledge, changing attitudes, or increasing skills.

Management development is any attempt to improve current or future managerial performance by imparting knowledge, changing attitudes, or increasing skills. It thus includes in-house programs like courses, coaching, and rotational assignments, professional programs like American Management Association Seminars, and university programs like executive MBA programs.[1]

An ultimate aim of such development programs is, of course, to enhance the future performance of the organization itself. As a result, the management development *process* seeks to (1) assess and satisfy the company's needs (for instance, to fill future executive openings, or to make the firm more responsive) by (2) appraising the manager's performance and needs and then (3) developing the managers themselves.

Management development is a very big business. It is estimated that over 1 million American managers participate in management development programs yearly,[2] for a cost to American industry alone of several billion dollars a year.[3]

Management development is important for several reasons. The main reason is that promotion from within is a major source of management talent. One survey of 84 employers reported that about 90% of supervisors, 73% of middle-level managers, and 51% of executives were promoted from within; virtually all these managers, in turn, required some development to prepare them for their new or prospective jobs. Similarly, management development facilitates organizational continuity by preparing employees and current managers to smoothly assume higher-level positions. It also helps to socialize management trainees by developing in them the right values and attitudes for working in the firm.[4]

THE MANAGEMENT DEVELOPMENT PROCESS

Given its aim (of balancing the company's needs with the developmental needs of its managers), the management development process consists of two basic sets of tasks: (1) personnel (managerial) planning and forecasting, and (2) manager needs—analysis and development. As explained in Chapter 4 ("Personnel Planning and Recruiting"), the personnel planning process involves projecting personnel (in this case management) positions to be filled, and then comparing the projected openings with the inside and outside candidates who are available. Companywide and individualized management development programs are then laid out to ensure that properly trained and developed managers are available when they are needed.

A management development program may be companywide, and basically open to all or most new or potential management recruits. Thus, the new college graduate may join Enormous Corp. and become part of (with two dozen colleagues) the companywide management development program. Here, she may be rotated through a preprogrammed series of departmental assignments and educational experiences, all aimed at identifying (for both her and the company) her management potential, and at providing the breadth of experience (in, say, production and finance) that will make her more valuable in her first "real" assignment as group product leader. Here, superior candidates may be slotted onto a "fast track," a development program that prepares them more quickly to assume senior-level commands.

On the other hand, the management development program may be even more individualized, in that it is aimed at filling a specific position, such as CEO, perhaps with one of two potential candidates. When it is an executive position to be filled, the process is usually called **succession planning**. Succession planning refers to a process of (1) personal planning and forecasting and (2) management needs analysis and development through which senior-level openings are planned for and eventually filled.

succession planning A process through which senior-level openings are planned for and eventually filled.

Career interests and aspirations, as well as performance appraisal, play crucial roles in management development. People do best on jobs that they like and for which they are suited. Therefore the development program should give the person a chance to assess his or her interests, as well as include some more formal career interests testing. Performance appraisal, meanwhile, serves to monitor the person's progress and potential, and to highlight what sorts of development activities might be needed to correct or compensate for deficiencies.

A typical management development program involves several steps. First, an *organization projection* is made; here you project your department's management needs based on factors like planned expansion or contraction. Next the personnel department reviews its *management skills inventory* to determine the management talent now employed. These inventories, you may recall, contain data on things like educational and work experience, career preferences, and performance appraisals. Next management *replacement charts* are drawn. These summarize potential candidates for each of your management slots, as well as each person's development needs. As shown in Figure 8.1, the development needs for a future division vice-president might include *job rotation* (to obtain more experience in the firm's finance and production divisions), *executive development programs* (to provide training in strategic planning), and assignment for two weeks to the employer's *in-house management development center.*

FIGURE 8.1 Management Replacement Chart Showing Development Needs of Future Divisional Vice-President

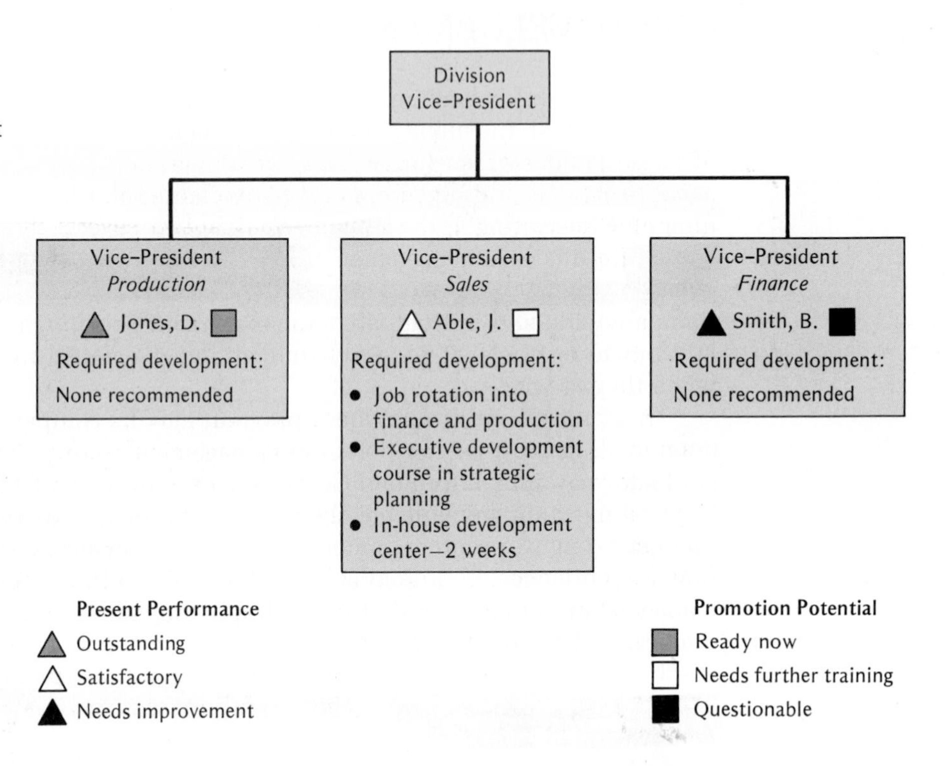

POPULARITY OF VARIOUS DEVELOPMENT TECHNIQUES

On-the-job experiences (supplemented by coaching, rotational assignments, and other in-house training) are, by far, the most popular form of management development. This is illustrated by the following table, which shows the percentages for techniques reported by personnel managers as being the "most important means of development" in their firms.[5]

MEANS OF DEVELOPMENT	PERCENTAGE REPORTING MOST IMPORTANT (%)
On-the-job experience	68.2
Coaching by superiors	20.9
In-house classroom	4.7
Rotational assignment	2.4
University programs	2.3
Consultant programs	1.1
Other	1.1

▶ MANAGERIAL ON-THE-JOB TRAINING

On-the-job training is one of the most popular development methods. Important techniques here include job rotation, coaching/understudy approach, junior boards, and action learning.

JOB ROTATION

job rotation
A management training technique that involves moving a trainee from department to department to broaden his or her experience and identify strong and weak points.

With **job rotation** you move management trainees from department to department to broaden their understanding of all phases of the business.[6] The trainee—often a recent college graduate—may spend several months in each department; this not only helps broaden his or her experience, but also helps the person discover the jobs he or she prefers. The person may just be an observer in each department but more commonly gets fully involved in its operations. He or she thus learns the department's business by actually doing it, whether it involves sales, production, finance, or some other function.

Job rotation has several other advantages.[7] In addition to providing a well-rounded training experience for each person, it helps avoid stagnation through the constant introduction of new points of view in each department. It also tests the trainee and helps identify the person's strong and weak points. Periodic job changing can also improve interdepartmental cooperation; managers become more understanding of each other's problems, while rotation also widens the trainee's acquaintances among management.

Rotation does have disadvantages. It encourages "generalization" and tends to be more appropriate for developing general line managers than functional staff experts. You also have to be careful not to forget inadvertently a trainee at some deserted outpost.

There are several things you can do to improve a rotation program's success.[8] The program should be tailored to the needs and capabilities of the individual trainee, and not be a standard sequence of steps that all trainees take. The trainee's interests, aptitudes, and career preferences should be considered, along with the employer's needs; the length of time the trainee stays in a job should then be determined by how fast he or she is learning. Furthermore, the managers to whom these people are assigned should themselves be specially trained to provide feedback and to monitor performance in an interested and competent way.

The Goodyear Tire and Rubber Company's training program for college graduates is a good example of job rotation.[9] Each trainee's program is tailored to match his or her experience, education, and vocational preference. Programs vary from 6 to 15 months, beginning with 3 weeks in an orientation program becoming thoroughly acquainted with Goodyear. (Here they study the organization's structure, company objectives, and basic manufacturing processes and participate in informal meetings with top company officials.) After an additional month of factory orientation, trainees discuss their career interests with top-level managers and select up to six assignments in special departments, each of which will last about one month. (For example, a chemical engineering graduate might rotate through departments for fabric development, chemical materials development research, central process engineering, process development, and chemical production.) Trainees then select specific job assignments as the starting point of their careers.

GLOBAL HRM

Global Job Rotation and Management

As firms expand multinationally, the phrase *job rotation* is taking on a new meaning. At firms like Shell and British Petroleum (BP), rotating managers globally is a primary means through which the firms maintain their flexibility and responsiveness even as they grow to an enormous size.

The rationale for extensive global job rotation was summarized as follows by a Shell senior executive:

> The word summarizing today's business outlook is uncertainty, and the response must be flexibility. For a complex, international, multifunctional organization like the Shell group, the prerequisite for flexibility is a highly skilled, mobile, international body of staff.[10]

The advantage of global job rotation (rotating managers from, say, positions in Sweden to those in New York, and from New York to Japan) is that it builds a network of informal ties—an informal information network—that assures superior cross-border communication and mutual understanding as well as tight control.

The improved communication and understanding stem from the personal relationships that are forged as the managers spend time in the firm's various locations. But these activities can also enhance organizational control. When employees from a firm's global locations are rotated, or brought together at, say, the Harvard Business School or Europe's INSEAD for a management training program, the aim is more than just teaching basic skills. The aim is also to build a stronger identification with the company's culture and values. The point is that job rotation and other developmental activities do more than just develop management and executive skills. By creating shared values and a consistent view of the firm and its goals, management development activities like these can facilitate communication and assure that through a sense of shared values and purpose the firm's policies are followed, even with a minimum reliance on more traditional forms of control.[11]

COACHING/UNDERSTUDY APPROACH

In the coaching/understudy approach, the trainee works directly with the person he or she is to replace; the latter is in turn responsible for the trainee's coaching. Normally, the understudy relieves the executive of certain responsibilities, thereby giving the trainee a chance to learn the job.[12] This helps ensure that the employer will have trained managers to assume key positions when they're vacated due to retirement, promotions, transfers, or terminations. It also helps guarantee the long-run development of company-bred top managers.

To be effective, the executive has to be a good coach and mentor. Furthermore, this person's motivation to train the replacement will depend on the quality of the relationship between them. Some executives are also better at delegating responsibility, providing reinforcement, and communicating than are others; this, too, will affect the results.

JUNIOR BOARDS

junior board
A method of providing middle-management trainees with experience in analyzing company problems by inviting them to sit on a junior board of directors and make recommendations on overall company policies.

Unlike job rotation (which aims to familiarize the trainees with the problems of each department), **junior boards** aim to give promising middle managers experience in analyzing overall company problems. The idea of a junior board (also sometimes called *multiple management*) is to give trainees top-level analysis and policymaking experience by having 10 to 12 of them sit on a "junior" board of directors. The members of such committees come from various departments. They make recommendations regarding top-level issues like organization structure, executive compensation, and interdepartmental conflict to the official board of directors. This technique provides middle-management trainees with on-the-job training and experience in dealing with organization-wide problems.

ACTION LEARNING

action learning
A training technique by which management trainees are allowed to work full time analyzing and solving problems in other departments or government agencies.

Action learning[13] involves giving middle-management trainees released time to work full time on projects, analyzing and solving problems in departments other than their own. The trainees meet periodically with a four- or five-person project group, where their findings and progress are discussed and debated.

Action learning was first used in England, but it is similar to (and grounded in) other, earlier development techniques. It is similar to the *junior boards* previously discussed except that trainees generally work full time on their projects, rather than analyzing a problem as a committee as they would on junior boards.

It is also similar to just giving a management trainee a special assignment or project. However, with action learning several trainees meet once a week as a project group to compare notes and discuss each other's projects. Action learning often involves cooperation among several employers. For example, an employee from General Electric might be assigned to a government agency for his research project, while the agency might assign one of its managers to GE for hers.

The idea of developing managers this way has pros and cons. It gives trainees real experience with actual problems, and to that extent it can develop skills like problem analysis and planning. Furthermore, the trainees (working with the others in the group) can and do find solutions to major problems. The main drawback is that in releasing trainees to work on outside projects, the employer loses, in a sense, the full-time services of a competent manager.

▶ BASIC OFF-THE-JOB DEVELOPMENT TECHNIQUES

There are many techniques you can use to develop managers off the job, perhaps in a conference room at headquarters or off the premises entirely at a university or special seminar. These techniques are addressed next.

THE CASE STUDY METHOD

case study method A development method in which the manager is presented with a written description of an organizational problem to diagnose and solve.

The **case study method** involves presenting a trainee with a written description of an organizational problem. The person then analyzes the case in private, diagnoses the problem, and presents his or her findings and solutions in a discussion with other trainees.[14] The case method approach is aimed at giving trainees realistic experience in identifying and analyzing complex problems in an environment in which their progress can be subtly guided by a trained discussion leader. Through the class discussion of the case, the trainee learns that there are usually many ways to approach and solve complex organizational problems. He or she also learns that his or her own solution is often influenced by his or her needs and values.

The case method has five main features:[15] (1) the use of actual organizational problems; (2) the maximum possible involvement of participants in stating their views, inquiring into other's views, confronting different views, and making decisions; resulting in (3) a minimal degree of dependence on the faculty members who, in turn (4) hold the position that there are rarely any right or wrong answers, that cases are incomplete and so is reality, and (5) who still strive to make the case method as engaging as possible through creation of appropriate levels of drama. As you can see, the instructor plays (or should play) a crucial role.[16] The person should be not a lecturer or expounder of principles lifted from textbooks, but rather a catalyst and coach. The instructor should also be a helpful source of information, while asking probing questions to elicit lively debate among trainees.

Problems to Avoid

Unfortunately, the case approach (as used in practice) often falls far short of this mark.[17] In practice, faculty often dominate classroom discussions by asking students questions that they then themselves proceed to answer, by answering specific questions asked by students, and by presenting statements of the facts about the case. Faculty also use "mystery to achieve mastery" by intentionally withholding information (for instance regarding what the company actually did and what its competitors were doing at the time when the case was written) with the aim of maintaining control of the classroom discussion. In one study of the case method, Argyris found that there were inconsistencies between the approach that the faculty espoused and what they actually did. For example, (1) faculty say there are no right or wrong answers, yet some faculty members do take positions and give answers; (2) faculty say there are many different points of view possible; yet they seem to select viewpoints and organize them in a way to suggest that they have a preferred route. Finally, few attempts were made by the faculty to relate the trainee's behavior in the classroom to their behavior back home.

There are several things you can do to make the case approach more effective. If possible, the cases should be actual cases from the trainee's own firm. This will help ensure that trainees understand the background of the case, as well as make it easier for trainees to transfer what is learned to their own jobs and situations. Argyris also contends that instructors have to guard against dominating the case analysis and make sure that they remain no more than a catalyst or coach. Finally, they must carefully prepare the case discussion and let the students discuss the case in small groups before class.[18]

MANAGEMENT GAMES

management game A development technique in which teams of managers compete with one another by making computerized decisions regarding realistic but simulated companies.

In a computerized **management game**, trainees are divided into five- or six-person companies, each of which has to compete with the other in a simulated marketplace. Each company sets a goal (such as "maximize sales") and is told it can make several decisions. For example, the group may be allowed to decide (1) how much to spend on advertising, (2) how much to produce, (3) how much inventory to maintain, and (4) how many of which product to produce. Usually the game itself compresses a two- or three-year period into days, weeks, or months. As in the real world, each company usually cannot see what decisions the other firms have made, although these decisions do affect their own sales. For example, if a competitor decides to increase its advertising expenditures, that firm may end up increasing its sales at the expense of yours.

Management games can be good development tools. People learn best by getting actively involved in the activity itself, and the games can be useful for gaining such involvement. Games are almost always interesting and exciting for the trainees because of their realism and competitiveness. They help trainees develop their problem-solving skills, as well as focus their attention on the need for planning, rather than on just putting out fires. The companies also usually elect their own officers and develop their own divisions of work; the games can thus be useful for developing leadership skills and for fostering cooperation and teamwork.

Management games also have their drawbacks. One problem is that the game can be expensive to develop and implement, particularly when (as is usually the case) it's computerized. Games also usually force the decision makers to choose alternatives from a closed list (for instance, they might have choices of only three levels of production); in real life managers are more often rewarded for creating new, innovative alternatives. On the whole, though, trainees almost always react favorably to a well-run game, and it is a good technique for developing problem-solving and leadership skills.

OUTSIDE SEMINARS

Many organizations put on special seminars and conferences aimed at providing skill-building training for managers. The American Management Associations (AMA), for instance, provide thousands of courses in areas such as the following:

General management
Human resources
Sales and marketing
International management
Finance
Information systems and technology
Manufacturing and operations management
Purchasing, transportation, and physical distribution
Packaging
Research and technology management
General and administrative services
Insurance and employee benefits

The courses themselves range from "how to sharpen your business writing skills" to "strategic planning" and "assertiveness training for managers."[19] The outline of a typical course is presented in Fig. 8.2; it is for a course in "advanced management techniques for experienced supervisors." As you can see, it is a two-and-a-half day advanced course for first-line manufacturing supervisors with three to five years experience who want to enhance their management skills. Topics covered include review of management and organization concepts, developing effective interpersonal skills, communication, motivation, and developing leadership skills. Many of the AMA courses can also be presented on site at the employer's place of business if ten or more employees are enrolled. Other organizations offering management development services include AMR International, Inc., the Conference Board, and Xerox Educational Systems.

Many of these programs offer *continuing education units (CEUs)* for course completion. Earning CEUs for course completion provides, says the AMA, a recognized measure of educational accomplishment, one that is today used by more than 1,000 colleges to record successful program completions. CEUs generally can't be used to obtain degree-granting credit at most colleges or universities, but they do provide a record of the fact that the trainee participated in and completed a special conference or seminar.

UNIVERSITY-RELATED PROGRAMS

Colleges and universities provide three types of management development activities. First, many schools provide *continuing education programs* in leadership, supervision, and the like. As with the AMA, these range from one- to four-day programs to executive development programs lasting one to four months.

4208Q/Advanced Management Techniques for Experienced Supervisors: How to Work Effectively With People and Within the Organization

Who Should Attend:
An advanced course for First-Line Manufacturing Supervisors with 3-5 years' experience who want to enhance their management skills. Especially useful for supervisors who have completed course #4271—The Management Course For New Manufacturing Supervisors, or course #4202—Productivity Improvement Methods and Techniques.

Key Topics:

- Review of management and organization concepts and how they relate to today's employees: planning, organizing, coordinating, controlling; authority, responsibility, accountability, reportability; dollar relationship to human resources utilization and lost time
- How to develop effective interpersonal skills: understanding behavior and personality; relating to people as individuals; self-awareness and opportunities to develop; how to positively affect attitudes and working relationships; team development; how to develop a warmer, more relaxed climate in dealing with people; how to come across firmly but fairly.
- The communication workshop for supervisors: develop increased listening skills; writing and speaking clearly, concisely, and with more organization; how to use communication to reduce stress and fear; assertiveness in communication; how to sell your ideas to management
- The motivation workshop for supervisors: analyzing management style and its role in motivation; creating an environment where employees will work effectively; behavioral foundation for self-motivation; relating program content to actual problem situations.
- Developing your leadership skills: how you are perceived by others; habits that reduce your leadership potential; applying course content to leadership development

Special Feature:
Examination of the supervisor's role—defining responsibilities, duties, authority, and the restriction of authority. **Discussions** on worker psychology—how the supervisor can effectively motivate, and the importance of communications. **Discussion** of various discipline techniques—when and where to use them and their effects on performance and morale. **Presentation** on reviewing employee performance with emphasis on improving their production and morale.

FIGURE 8.2 Content for a Typical Middle-Management American Management Association Training Program
Source: American Management Association

The Advanced Management Program of the Graduate School of Business Administration at Harvard University is an example of one of these longer programs. As can be seen in Figure 8.3, each class in this program consists of a group of experienced managers from all regions of the world. The program uses cases and lectures to provide an employer's top-level management talent with the latest management skills, as well as with practice in analyzing complex organizational problems. Similar programs include the Executive Program of the Graduate School of Business Administration at the University of California at Berkeley, the Management Development Seminar at the University of Chicago, and the Executive in Business Administration Program of the Graduate School of Business at Columbia University. Most of these programs take the executives away from their jobs, putting them in university-run learning environments for their entire stay. The Columbia University program, for instance, is offered at Arden House in the Ramapo Mountains of New York.

Second, many colleges and universities also offer *individualized courses* in areas like business, management, and health care administration. Managers can take these as matriculated or nonmatriculated students to fill gaps in their

What's innovative, time-tested, diverse, intense, global, and develops leaders?

FIGURE 8.3 Ad for Harvard Executive Training Program

backgrounds. Thus, a prospective division manager with a gap in her experience with accounting controls might sign up for a two-course sequence in managerial accounting.

Finally, many schools, of course, also offer *degree programs* such as the MBA or Executive MBA. The latter is a Master of Business Administration degree program geared especially to middle managers and above, who generally take their courses on weekends and proceed through the program with the same group of colleagues.

Executive Development programs such as this one at Stanford University, help prepare talented mid-level managers to move into executive roles.

The Employer's Contribution

The employer usually plays a role in university-related programs.[20] First, many employers offer *tuition refunds* as an incentive for employees to develop job-related skills. Thus, engineers may be encouraged to enroll in technical courses aimed at keeping them abreast of changes in their field. Supervisors may be encouraged to enroll in programs to develop them for higher-level management jobs.

Employers are also increasingly granting technical and professional employees extended *sabbaticals*—periods of time off—for attending a college or university to pursue a higher degree or to upgrade skills. For example, Bell Laboratories has a program that includes a tuition refund and released time for up to one year of on-campus study. In addition, the company has a doctoral support program that permits tuition refund and released time for studies one day a week (and, for some, a full year's study on campus to meet residence requirements).

Some companies have experimented with offering selected employees in-house degree programs in cooperation with colleges and universities. Many also offer a variety of in-house lectures and seminars by university staff.

For example, Technicon, a high-tech medical instruments company, asked Pace University to offer an executive education program for its key middle managers. The theme of the 14-month program was successful management of high-tech businesses. The coursework covered topics ranging from finance to executive communication.[21]

Universities and corporations are also experimenting with video-linked classroom education. For example, the School of Business and Public Administration at California State University, Sacramento, and a Hewlett-Packard facility in Roseville, California, are video-linked. A video-link allows for classroom learning on campuses with simultaneous broadcasting to other locations via telephone communication lines.

ROLE PLAYING

role playing
A training technique in which trainees act out the parts of people in a realistic management situation.

The aim of **role playing** is to create a realistic situation and then have the trainees assume the parts (or roles) of specific persons in that situation.[22]

One such role—that of Walt Marshal, supervisor—from a famous role-playing exercise called the New Truck Dilemma is presented in Figure 8.4. Roles like these for each of the participants (when combined with the general instructions for the role-playing exercise) can lead to a spirited discussion among the role players, particularly when each throws himself or herself into the role, rather than merely acting. The idea of the exercise is to solve the problem at hand and thereby develop trainees' skills in areas like leadership and delegating.

Walt Marshall — Supervisor of Repair Crew

You are the head of a crew of telephone maintenance workers, each of whom drives a small service truck to and from the various jobs. Every so often you get a new truck to exchange for an old one, and you have the problem of deciding to which of your crew members you should give the new truck. Often there are hard feelings, since each seems to feel entitled to the new truck, so you have a tough time being fair. As a matter of fact, it usually turns out that whatever you decide is considered wrong by most of the crew. You now have to face the issue again because a new truck, a Chevrolet, has just been allocated to you for assignment.

In order to handle this problem you have decided to put the decision up to the crew. You will tell them about the new truck and will put the problem in terms of what would be the fairest way to assign the truck. Do not take a position yourself, because you want to do what they think is most fair.

FIGURE 8.4
Typical Role in a Role-Playing Exercise

Source: Norman R. F. Maier and Gertrude Casselman Verser, *Psychology in Industrial Organizations*, 5th ed., p. 190. Copyright 1982 by Houghton Mifflin Company. Used by permission of the publishers.

Role playing can be an enjoyable and inexpensive way to develop many new skills. With the New Truck Dilemma exercise, for instance, participants learn the importance of fairness in bringing about acceptance of resource allocation decisions. The role players can also give up their inhibitions and experiment with new ways of acting. For example, a supervisor could experiment with both a considerate and autocratic leadership style, whereas in the real world the person might not have this harmless way of experimenting. According to Maier, role playing also trains a person to be aware of and sensitive to the feelings of others.[23]

Role playing has some drawbacks. An exercise can take an hour or more to complete, only to be deemed a waste of time by participants if the instructor doesn't prepare a wrap-up explanation of what the participants were to learn. Some trainees also feel that role playing is childish, while others, having had a bad experience with the technique, are reluctant to participate at all.

BEHAVIOR MODELING

behavior modeling A training technique in which trainees are first shown good management techniques (in a film), are then asked to play roles in a simulated situation, and are then given feedback and praise by their supervisor.

Behavior modeling involves (1) showing trainees the right (or "model") way of doing something, (2) letting each person practice the right way to do it, and then (3) providing feedback regarding his or her performance.[24] It has been used, for example, to:

1. Train first-line supervisors to handle common supervisor-employee interactions better. This includes giving recognition, disciplining, introducing changes, and improving poor performance.
2. Train middle managers to better handle interpersonal situations involving, for example, giving directions, discussing performance problems, and discussing undesirable work habits.

3. Train employees (and their supervisors) to take and give criticism, ask and give help, and establish mutual trust and respect.

The basic behavior modeling procedure can be outlined as follows:

1. *Modeling.* First, trainees watch films or videotapes that show model persons behaving effectively in a problem situation. In other words, trainees are shown the right way to behave in a simulated but realistic situation. The film might thus show a supervisor effectively disciplining a subordinate, if teaching how to discipline is the aim of the training program.
2. *Role playing.* Next the trainees are given roles to play in a simulated situation; here they practice and rehearse the effective behaviors demonstrated by the models.
3. *Social reinforcement.* The trainer provides reinforcement in the form of praise and constructive feedback based on how the trainee performs in the role-playing situation.
4. *Transfer of training.* Finally, trainees are encouraged to apply their new skills when they are back on their jobs.

Example

An example can help illustrate the basic behavior modeling technique.[25] The training group (which consisted of first-line supervisors) was divided into 2 groups of 10, with each group meeting for 2 hours each week for 9 weeks. The sessions focused on management skills like orienting new employees, giving recognition, motivating poor performers, and correcting poor work habits.

Each training session followed the same format. First, the topic (such as handling a complaining employee) was introduced by two trainers. Next a film was presented that depicted a supervisor "model." He or she effectively handled a complaining employee by following several guidelines that were shown in a film immediately before and after the "model film" was presented. (In the case of handling a complaining employee, these guidelines included: avoid responding with hostility or defensiveness; ask for and listen openly to the employee's complaint; restate the complaint for thorough understanding; and recognize and acknowledge his or her viewpoint.) Next there was a group discussion of the model supervisor's effectiveness in demonstrating the desired behaviors, such as: "Did the person avoid responding with hostility or defensiveness?" Next the trainees practiced (via role playing) the desired behaviors in front of the class and got feedback from the class on their effectiveness in demonstrating the desired behaviors.[26]

IN-HOUSE DEVELOPMENT CENTERS

in-house development centers
A company-based method for exposing prospective managers to realistic exercises to develop improved management skills.

Some employers have established **in-house development centers**. These centers usually combine classroom learning (lectures and seminars, for instance) with other techniques like assessment centers, in-basket exercises, and role playing to help develop managers.

For example, the CBS School for Management, as it is called, is set in country club surroundings in Old Westbury, New York.[27] Its basic aim is to give young managers firsthand experience at decision making.

To accomplish this, both their general management program (for upper-level managers) and professional management programs (for entry-level managers) stress the solution of concrete business problems through working with

Computer Applications in Management Development: A Computerized Managerial Assessment and Development Program

There are a number of Computerized Management Assessment and Development programs that can facilitate an employer's development process. One particularly useful example of such a management development tool is called ACUMEN[1]

ACUMEN is a sophisticated managerial assessment and development program. The Education Version of ACUMEN consists of three elements: instructions, a self-assessment, and an assessment report. After spending approximately 20 minutes interacting with ACUMEN's IBM-compatible program, you will receive a visual display or hard-output "management profile" that focuses on 12 basic management traits:

1. *Humanistic-helpful.* Measures your inclination to see the best in others, to encourage their growth and development, to be supportive.
2. *Affiliation.* Measures the degree of friendliness, sociability, and outgoing tendencies you are likely to exhibit.
3. *Approval.* Measures your need to seek others' approval and support in order to feel secure and worthwhile as a person.
4. *Conventional.* Measures your need to conform, follow the rules, and meet the expectations of those in authority.
5. *Dependence.* Measures your tendency to be compliant, passive, and dependent on others.
6. *Apprehension.* Measures your tendency to experience anxiety and self-blame.
7. *Oppositional.* Measures your tendency to take a critical, questioning, and somewhat cynical attitude.
8. *Power.* Measures your tendency to be authoritarian and controlling.
9. *Competition.* Measures your need to be seen as the best and, to some extent, to maintain a self-centered attitude.
10. *Perfectionism.* Measures your need to seek perfection, and your tendency to base your self-worth on your own performance.
11. *Achievement.* Measures your need to achieve and have an impact on things.
12. *Self-actualization.* Measures your level of self-esteem, interest in self-development, and general drive to learn about and experience life to the fullest extent.

When you complete the self-assessment, ACUMEN analyzes your responses and generates scores on the twelve scales. Each scale represents a particular attitude, or thinking style. The way you think (your thinking style) affects:

- What you strive to achieve (your *goals*).
- Your effectiveness as a *leader.*
- How you relate to and *communicate* with other people.
- Whether you view *change* as positive or negative.
- How you respond to crises and *stress.*

The major aim of ACUMEN is to help you develop a fuller understanding and appreciation of how your own thinking styles and personal dispositions play a role in your productivity and management effectiveness. ACUMEN's analysis of your assessment responses, presented in graphic or textual form, provides this information.

When you view a graphic profile display, you will notice that each scale's extension is of varying length. On the circular graph, some scales extend a long away from the center of the circle while other segments are relatively short. Similarly, scales on the bar graph will vary in length. The longer extensions indicate styles that are more prominent in your profile. By comparing the extensions, you will be able to find the thinking styles that have the most impact on your own behavior.

The text printout on each scale provides you with detailed assessment and development information for each scale. For example, you might find you have a high score on the Humanistic Helpful Scale. You're told here that you are likely to enjoy developing, helping and teaching others, like to motivate others, and attempt to see the best in others. So far so good. However on the Oppositional Scale your low score indicates a fairly accepting, agreeable type of person. Up to a point, these may be laudable traits for managers. But in terms of development, you should (the printout says) "beware of being too reticent about making critical comments" (which you will have to do as a manager). In summary, a computerized management tool like ACUMEN can be very valuable, both for assessing management aptitudes (say, for future promotability) and for providing detailed development advice for the trainee.

[1]ACUMEN is a Trademark of Human Factors Advanced Technology Group. This box from "What ACUMEN Is and How It Works," by HFATG.

At programs such as the CBS School for Management, teaching methods include the use of videotape and computer simulation.

people. The programs use various teaching methods but stress computerized case exercises. In one exercise, for instance, each student acts as a regional sales manager and has to make decisions regarding how to deal with a star saleswoman who wants to leave. As trainees make decisions (like whether or not to boost the saleswoman's salary to entice her to stay), the computer indicates the implications of the decision; thus, if she is paid more, others may also want that increase in pay. At the end of each day students get printouts evaluating their decisions with respect to setting goals, organizing work, managing time, and supervising subordinates.

Fortune magazine calls Crotonville, General Electric's Management Development Institute, the Harvard of corporate America. Run by a former Harvard Business School professor, the firm's 160-page catalog offers a wide array of management development courses. These range from entry-level programs in manufacturing and sales to a course for English majors called "Everything You Always Wanted to Know About Finance," as well as advanced management training.[28] Many of the firm's programs emphasize what GE calls action learning. This development method goes beyond the usual case approach used by many business schools. As one participant summed up, "It wasn't a game. Six groups of us—total strangers—were assigned real company issues to tackle. We went to the businesses, interviewed the key players, developed real solutions, presented them to company officers and got their honest feedback . . . and along the way, our groups became teams."[29]

Special Management Development Techniques

There are also various **special management development techniques** that are aimed at developing leadership ability, increasing the manager's sensitivity to others, and reducing interdepartmental conflict.

LEADER MATCH TRAINING

leader match training A program that identifies types of leaders and teaches them how to fit their leadership style to their situation.

Leader match training is aimed at teaching managers how to fit their leadership style to the situation and is based on several assumptions. First, it assumes that whether a people-oriented or production-oriented style is appropriate depends on the degree of situational control the leader can exercise. This is summarized in Figure 8.5. Fred Fiedler, who developed this technique, contends that production-oriented leaders do best in situations where they can exercise either very high control or in situations where they have very little control. People-oriented leaders, on the other hand, do best in middle-of-the-road situations where they can exercise moderate amounts of control.

Fiedler explains his findings as follows: He says that in very-high control situations—where the leader's word is "law" and the job is very routine—the group is ready to be directed and the subordinates expect to be told what to do. On the other hand, in the very-low-control situation—where the leader can't hire or fire, and the job to be done is nonroutine—the group will fall apart without the leader's active intervention and control. Thus, in both high- and low-control situations, a more no-nonsense, production- or task-oriented leadership style is called for. In the middle range, says Fiedler, the situation is not so clear cut, and the biggest problem is often that disagreements may break out and undermine the group's performance. Here the leader must be supportive and people oriented, because it is important that he or she coax the subordinates to work together and with the leader.

The leader match program is in the form of a manual that contains questionnaires that enable the leader to assess his or her natural leadership style, as well as the degree of control inherent in his or her situation.[30] Fiedler contends that the problem for leaders consists of getting into and remaining in situations where they can perform well. He also argues that it is usually easier to change your situation (or to at least choose the right situation) than it is to change your leadership style. He therefore presents several prescriptions aimed at enabling you to fit your style to the situation: For example, a task-oriented leader who finds herself misplaced in a situation of moderate control should take actions that give her more control of the situation, perhaps by having her boss give her the authority to hire and fire subordinates unilaterally.[31]

VROOM-YETTON LEADERSHIP TRAINING

Vroom-Yetton leadership training A development program for management trainees that focuses on decision making with varying degrees of input from subordinates.

Vroom-Yetton leadership training focuses on developing your ability to determine the degree to which your subordinates should be allowed to participate in the decisions that must be made. First, Vroom and Yetton say there are several degrees of participation (as summarized in Figure 8.6), ranging from *no* participation to *minimum* participation, *more* participation, *still more* participation, and finally *consensus* management, or total participation. Next, Vroom and Yetton say that the right degree of participation depends on seven attributes of the situation, including the importance of the quality of the decision, the extent to which you possess sufficient information to make a high-quality decision by yourself, and the extent to which the problem is routine and structured or ambiguous and complicated. (These seven attributes are summarized in Table 8.1.) Finally, Vroom and Yetton present a chart for determining the appropriate-

Leader Type	CONTROL ALLOWED BY SITUATION: High Control (Leader's Word Is "Law")	Moderate Control	Low Control (Situation Itself Gives Leader Little Control)
People-oriented	*Performance:* Poor	*Performance:* Good	*Performance:* Poor
Task-oriented	*Performance:* Good.	*Performance:* Poor.	*Performance:* Relatively good.

FIGURE 8.5 Effects of People-Oriented and Task-Oriented Leaders in Various Situations

ness of employee participation in the form of a decision tree, as shown in Figure 8.7. To use this figure, trainees are taught to work from left to right. First, determine whether the *quality of decision* is important; then determine if you have *sufficient information to make a high-quality decision*, and so forth. By answering each question "yes" or "no", the trainee can work his or her way across the decision tree and thereby determine the degree of participation that is best.

In the development program based on this model, trainees are first taught the rudiments of the approach, such as the differences between the management styles, and the questions that must be asked to identify the nature of the problem (such as "How important is the quality of the decision?"). Next they are given case incident problems that briefly summarize the situation facing the trainees. For example, "Suppose you are the captain of a submarine that is being shelled by enemy torpedo boats. You must decide whether to sink to the bottom and wait for them to pass, or to surface and make a run for it in open waters. Which management style would you choose?" Trainees then use the decision tree to determine the best style, starting with the first column on the left. (This particular example is presented as a discussion question at the end of this chapter.) The results of training managers in the use of the Vroom-Yetton model indicate that the training is effective.[32]

DEVELOPING O.K. MANAGERS: TRANSACTIONAL ANALYSIS

transactional analysis (TA) A method for helping two people communicate and behave on the job in an adult manner by understanding each other's motives.

Transactional analysis (TA) is aimed at analyzing the interpersonal "transactions" or communications between yourself and your subordinates. It can supposedly enable you to better analyze any interpersonal situation you find yourself in by helping answer such questions as: "Why am I saying what I am saying to this subordinate?" and "Why is she saying what she is saying to me?"

To use transactional analysis, a person has to be able to analyze the particular *ego state* that he or she is in, and also that of the person being spoken to. There are three such ego states: *parent, adult,* and *child.*

When a person is in a particular ego state, he or she *behaves in characteristic ways.* Characteristics of a person acting in the *parent* state include being overprotective, distant, dogmatic, indispensible, and upright. A person in this state tends to argue not on the basis of logical facts, but on the basis of rules, or ways that were successful in the past. The person thus argues and explains much like his or her parent might have, all the while wagging a finger to show displeasure. A person operating in this mode is usually not an O.K. manager.

FIGURE 8.6 Five Degrees of Participative Leadership

Source: R. H. George Field, "A Test of Vroom-Yetton Normative Model of Leadership," *Journal of Applied Psychology*, vol. 67, no. 5 (October 1982), pp. 523–532. Copyright 1982 by the American Psychological Association. Reprinted by permission.

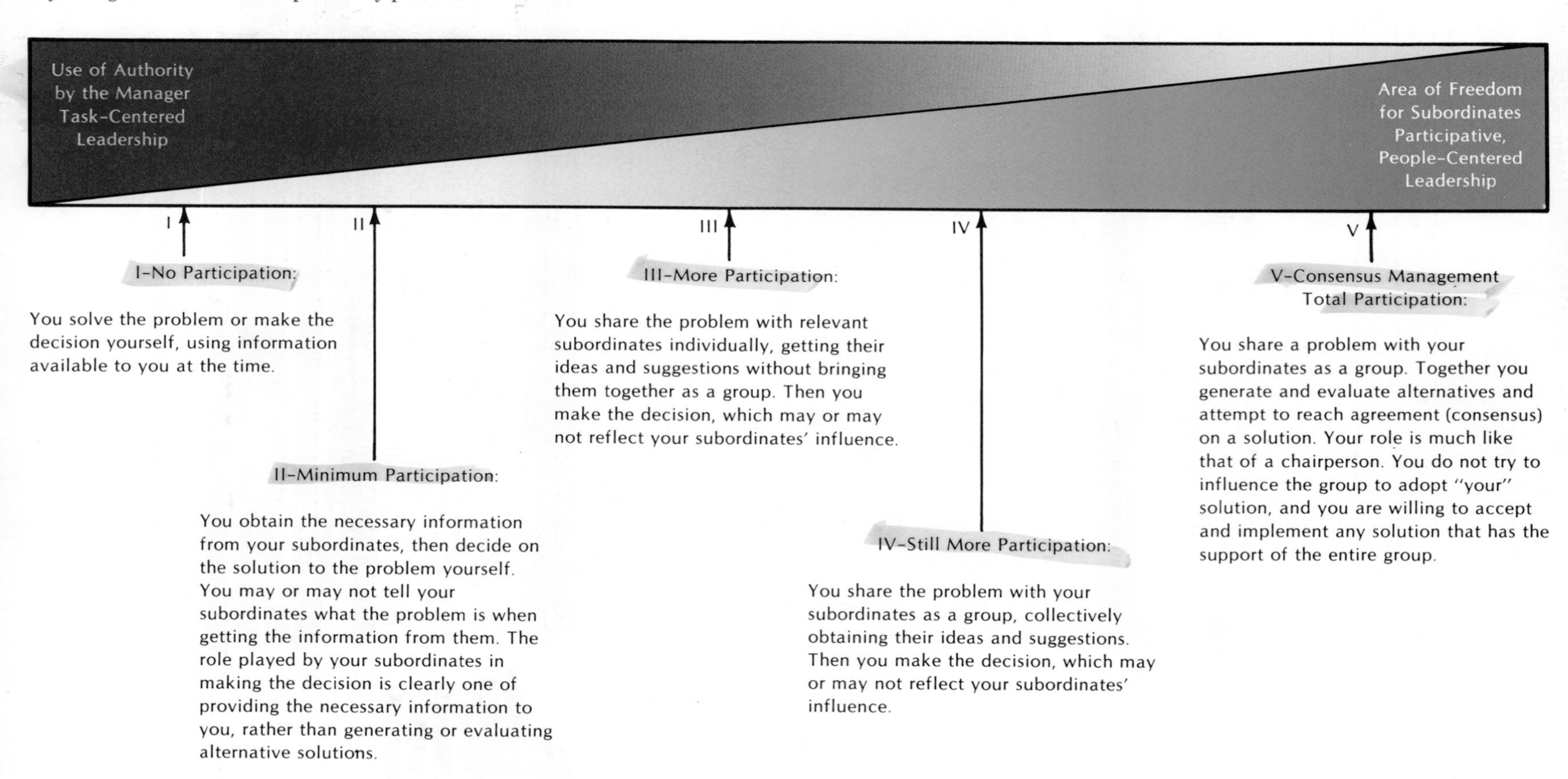

Use of Authority
by the Manager
Task-Centered
Leadership
Area of Freedom
for Subordinates
Participative,
People-Centered
Leadership
I
II
III
IV
V
I-No Participation:
You solve the problem or make the decision yourself, using information available to you at the time.
II-Minimum Participation:
You obtain the necessary information from your subordinates, then decide on the solution to the problem yourself. You may or may not tell your subordinates what the problem is when getting the information from them. The role played by your subordinates in making the decision is clearly one of providing the necessary information to you, rather than generating or evaluating alternative solutions.
III-More Participation:
You share the problem with relevant subordinates individually, getting their ideas and suggestions without bringing them together as a group. Then you make the decision, which may or may not reflect your subordinates' influence.
IV-Still More Participation:
You share the problem with your subordinates as a group, collectively obtaining their ideas and suggestions. Then you make the decision, which may or may not reflect your subordinates' influence.
V-Consensus Management
Total Participation:
You share a problem with your subordinates as a group. Together you generate and evaluate alternatives and attempt to reach agreement (consensus) on a solution. Your role is much like that of a chairperson. You do not try to influence the group to adopt "your" solution, and you are willing to accept and implement any solution that has the support of the entire group.

TABLE 8.1 Diagnostic Questions Used in the Vroom-Yetton Model

PROBLEM ATTRIBUTES	DIAGNOSTIC QUESTIONS
(These determine the degree of participation that is appropriate.)	(These enable you to diagnose the presence or absence of each attribute.)
A. The importance of the quality of the decision	Is there a quality requirement such that one solution is likely to be more rational than another?
B. The extent to which the leader possesses sufficient information/expertise to make a high-quality decision by him- or herself	Do I have sufficient information to make a high-quality decision?
C. The extent to which the problem is structured	Is the problem structured?
D. The extent to which acceptance or commitment on the part of subordinates is critical to the effective implementation of the decision	Is acceptance of decision by subordinates critical to effective implementation?
E. The prior probability that the leader's autocratic decision will receive acceptance by subordinates	If you were to make the decision by yourself, is it reasonably certain that it would be accepted by your subordinates?
F. The extent to which the subordinates are motivated to attain the organizational goals as represented in the objectives explicit in the statement of the problem	Do subordinates share the organizational goals to be obtained in solving this problem?
G. The extent to which subordinates are likely to be in conflict over preferred solutions	Is conflict among subordinates likely in preferred solutions?

A person in the *child* ego state reflects all those behaviors that we normally attribute to childishness. For example, this person tends to take illogical, precipitous actions that provide him or her with immediate satisfaction. In an argument or discussion, this person's actions may include temper tantrums, silent compliance, coyness, and giggling.

A person in the *adult* state takes a rational, logical approach. He or she processes new data, carefully seeks out new information, thoughtfully considers these data, and then bases the argument on the facts. An adult manager is usually an O.K. manager: He or she is not out to "get" his or her subordinates, or to maneuver them into embarrassing positions. Instead, an adult manager is interested in confronting and solving problems in a straightforward, sensible manner by considering all points of view and arriving at a solution.

ORGANIZATIONAL DEVELOPMENT

Perhaps your organization suddenly has to adapt to a competitor's new and unique product. Or perhaps you're faced with emerging conflict between several

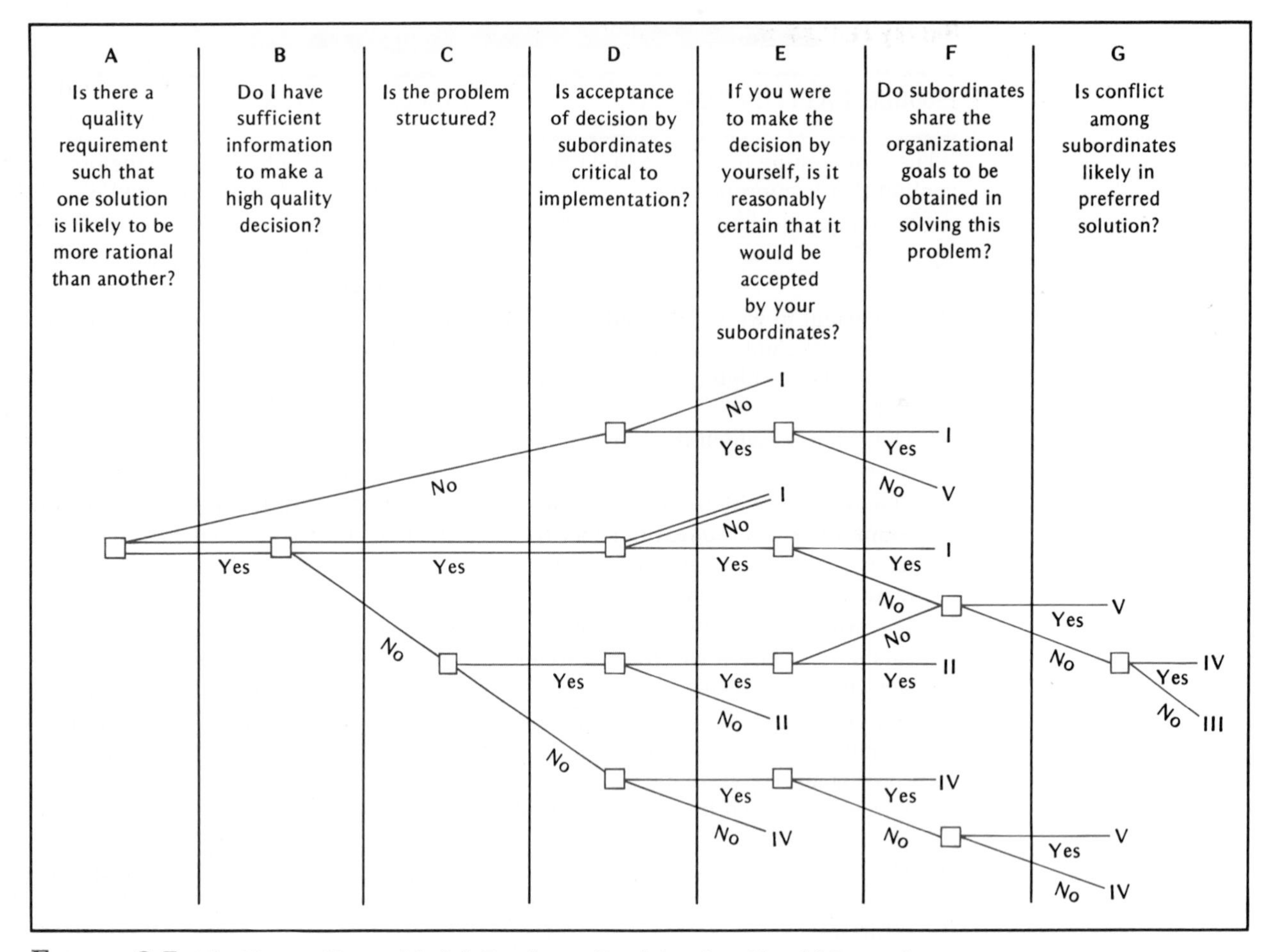
A
Is there a quality requirement such that one solution is likely to be more rational than another?
B
Do I have sufficient information to make a high quality decision?
C
Is the problem structured?
D
Is acceptance of decision by subordinates critical to implementation?
E
If you were to make the decision by yourself, is it reasonably certain that it would be accepted by your subordinates?
F
Do subordinates share the organizational goals to be obtained in solving this problem?
G
Is conflict among subordinates likely in preferred solution?
Yes
No
I
II
III
IV
V

FIGURE 8.7 The Vroom-Yetton Model: Employee Participation Should Depend on the Decision

organizational development (OD) A program aimed at changing the attitudes, values, and beliefs of employees so that employees can improve the organization.

of your department heads—conflict that is undermining the unit's creativity and flexibility. These are the kinds of situations that lead managers to turn to **organizational development (OD)**. OD is defined as a program that is aimed at changing the attitudes, values, and beliefs of employees so that *the employees themselves* can identify and implement the sorts of technical changes (reorganizations, redesigned facilities, and the like) that are required, usually with the aid of an outside "change agent" or consultant.

The common denominator underlying most OD interventions is called *action research.* This involves (1) *gathering data about the organization* and its operations and attitudes, with an eye toward solving some particular problem (e.g., conflict between the sales and production departments); (2) *feeding back* these data to the parties (employees) involved; and then (3) having these parties *team-plan solutions* to the problems. In OD, the participants always get involved in gathering data about themselves and their organization, analyzing it, and planning solutions based on it.[33] Popular OD efforts include survey feedback, sensitivity training, and team building.

Survey Feedback

survey feedback
A method which involves surveying employees' attitudes and providing feedback to department managers so that problems can be solved by the managers and employees.

Survey feedback is a method which involves surveying employees' attitudes and providing feedback to department managers so that problems can be solved by the managers and employees. Using attitude surveys such as the one in Figure 8.8 can be a useful OD technique. They can be used to dramatically underscore the existence of some problem like low morale and as a basis for discussion among employees for developing alternative solutions. Finally, they can also be used to follow up on any change to see if it has been successful in terms of changing the participant's attitudes.

Scott Meyers has proposed an *involvement approach* to using attitude surveys.[34] At Texas Instruments, where this approach was developed, a questionnaire like that in Figure 8.8 is administered to a 10 to 20% sample of employees throughout the company. Profiles like the one in Figure 8.9 are then prepared from the results and delivered to each of the approximately 160 department managers. The heavy solid line shows the *company* average for this year and is the same on every department's profile. The thin solid line is this year's *department* results, while the dashed line is last year's results. As you can see, each department manager can thus compare his or her department's results for each item to both the total company results and to his or her last year's profile.

This feedback provides a useful basis upon which managers and employees can identify problems and discuss and solve them. To avoid making departmental managers defensive, the process usually involves having survey results fed directly back to them rather than to top management. Then the department head presents and discusses these results in general terms in a group meeting of his or her department, before handing them to a committee of employees. These five or six people meet as often as necessary to analyze the results and make recommendations to the department manager. The latter, in turn, analyzes these recommendations with his or her boss, and the final recommendations are transmitted back to departmental employees. Problems and recommendations might include, for instance, "new employees are sometimes hired for good jobs that old employees could fill," so "post job openings on bulletin boards and explain procedure for bidding for these jobs."

Sensitivity Training

sensitivity training
A method for increasing employees' insights into their own behavior by candid discussions in groups led by special trainers.

Sensitivity training aims to increase a participant's insights into his or her behavior and the behavior of others *by encouraging an open expression of feelings in the trainer-guided T-Group "laboratory."*[35] (The "T" is for training.) The assumption is that newly sensitized employees will then find it easier to work together amicably as a team. Sensitivity training seeks to accomplish its aim (of increased interpersonal sensitivity) by requiring frank, candid discussions in the T-Group, discussions of participant's personal feelings, attitudes, and behavior. Participants in such a group are encouraged to inform each other truthfully of how their behavior is being seen and to interpret the kind of feelings it produces.[36] As a result, it is a controversial method surrounded by heated debate and is used much less today than in the past.[37]

team building
Improving the effectiveness of teams such as corporate officers and division directors through use of consultants, interviews, and team-building meetings.

Team Building

Team building refers to a group of OD techniques aimed at improving the effectiveness of teams at work. And, in fact, the characteristic OD stress on action

This questionnaire is designed to help you give us your opinions quickly and easily. There are no "right" or "wrong" answers—it is your own, honest opinion that we want. Please do not sign your name.

DIRECTIONS:
Check ( ) one box for each statement to indicate whether you agree or disagree with it. If you cannot decide, mark the middle box.

EXAMPLE:
I would rather work in a large city than in a small town — Agree ? Disagree 2☐ 1☐ 0☐

1. The hours of work here are O.K. — Agree ? Disagree 2☐ 1☐ 0☐
2. I understand how my job relates to other jobs in my group — Agree ? Disagree 2☐ 1☐ 0☐
3. Working conditions in TI are better than in other companies — Agree ? Disagree 2☐ 1☐ 0☐
4. In my opinion, the pay here is lower than in other companies — Agree ? Disagree 2☐ 1☐ 0☐
5. I think TI is spending too much money in providing recreational programs — Agree ? Disagree 2☐ 1☐ 0☐
6. I understand what benefits are provided for TIers — Agree ? Disagree 2☐ 1☐ 0☐
7. The people I work with help each other when someone falls behind, or gets in a tight spot — Agree ? Disagree 2☐ 1☐ 0☐
8. My supervisor is too interested in her/his own success to care about the needs of other TIers — Agree ? Disagree 2☐ 1☐ 0☐
9. My supervisor is always breathing down our necks; he watches us too closely — Agree ? Disagree 2☐ 1☐ 0☐
10. My supervisor gives us credit and praise for work well done — Agree ? Disagree 2☐ 1☐ 0☐
11. I think badges should reflect rank as well as length of service — Agree ? Disagree 2☐ 1☐ 0☐
12. If I have a complaint to make, I feel free to talk to someone up-the-line — Agree ? Disagree 2☐ 1☐ 0☐
13. My supervisor sees that we are properly trained for our jobs — Agree ? Disagree 2☐ 1☐ 0☐
14. My supervisor sees that we have the things we need to do our jobs — Agree ? Disagree 2☐ 1☐ 0☐
15. Management is really trying to build the organization and make it successful — Agree ? Disagree 2☐ 1☐ 0☐
16. There is cooperation between my department and other departments we work with — Agree ? Disagree 2☐ 1☐ 0☐
17. I usually read most of Texins News — Agree ? Disagree 2☐ 1☐ 0☐
18. They encourage us to make suggestions for improvements here — Agree ? Disagree 2☐ 1☐ 0☐
19. I am often bothered by sudden speed-ups or unexpected slack periods in my work — Agree ? Disagree 2☐ 1☐ 0☐
20. Qualified TIers are usually overlooked when filling job openings — Agree ? Disagree 2☐ 1☐ 0☐
21. Compared with other TIers, we get very little attention from management — Agree ? Disagree 2☐ 1☐ 0☐
22. Sometimes I feel that my job counts for very little in TI — Agree ? Disagree 2☐ 1☐ 0☐
23. The longer you work for TI the more you feel you belong — Agree ? Disagree 2☐ 1☐ 0☐
24. I have a great deal of interest in TI and its future — Agree ? Disagree 2☐ 1☐ 0☐
25. I have little opportunity to use my abilities in TI — Agree ? Disagree 2☐ 1☐ 0☐
26. There are plenty of good jobs in TI for those who want to get ahead — Agree ? Disagree 2☐ 1☐ 0☐
27. I often feel worn out and tired on my job — Agree ? Disagree 2☐ 1☐ 0☐
28. They expect too much work from us around here — Agree ? Disagree 2☐ 1☐ 0☐
29. The company should provide more opportunities for employees to know each other — Agree ? Disagree 2☐ 1☐ 0☐
30. For my kind of job, working conditions are O.K. — Agree ? Disagree 2☐ 1☐ 0☐
31. I'm paid fairly compared with other TIers — Agree ? Disagree 2☐ 1☐ 0☐
32. Compared with other companies, TI benefits are good — Agree ? Disagree 2☐ 1☐ 0☐
33. A few people I work with think they run the place — Agree ? Disagree 2☐ 1☐ 0☐
34. The people I work with get along well together — Agree ? Disagree 2☐ 1☐ 0☐
35. My supervisor has always been fair in his/her dealings with me — Agree ? Disagree 2☐ 1☐ 0☐
36. My supervisor gets employees to work together as a team — Agree ? Disagree 2☐ 1☐ 0☐
37. I have confidence in the fairness and honesty of management — Agree ? Disagree 2☐ 1☐ 0☐
38. Management here is really interested in the welfare of TIers — Agree ? Disagree 2☐ 1☐ 0☐
39. Most of the higher-ups are friendly toward us — Agree ? Disagree 2☐ 1☐ 0☐
40. I work in a friendly environment — Agree ? Disagree 2☐ 1☐ 0☐
41. My supervisor lets us know what is expected of us — Agree ? Disagree 2☐ 1☐ 0☐
42. We don't receive enough information from top management — Agree ? Disagree 2☐ 1☐ 0☐
43. I know how my job fits in with other work in this organization — Agree ? Disagree 2☐ 1☐ 0☐
44. TI does a poor job of keeping us posted on the things we want to know about TI — Agree ? Disagree 2☐ 1☐ 0☐
45. I think TI informality is carried too far — Agree ? Disagree 2☐ 1☐ 0☐
46. You can get fired around here without much cause — Agree ? Disagree 2☐ 1☐ 0☐
47. I can be sure of my job as long as I do good work — Agree ? Disagree 2☐ 1☐ 0☐
48. I have plenty of freedom on the job to use my own judgment — Agree ? Disagree 2☐ 1☐ 0☐
49. My supervisor allows me reasonable leeway in making mistakes — Agree ? Disagree 2☐ 1☐ 0☐
50. I really feel part of this organization — Agree ? Disagree 2☐ 1☐ 0☐
51. The people who get promotions in TI usually deserve them — Agree ? Disagree 2☐ 1☐ 0☐
52. I can learn a great deal on my present job — Agree ? Disagree 2☐ 1☐ 0☐

(PLEASE CONTINUE ON REVERSE SIDE)

FIGURE 8.8
Attitude Questionnaire of Texas Instruments, Inc.

learning—on letting the trainees solve the problem—is perhaps most evident when the OD program is aimed at improving a team's effectiveness. Data concerning the team's performance are collected and then fed back to the members of the group. The participants then examine, explain, and analyze the data and develop specific action plans or solutions for solving the team's problems.

The typical team-building program begins with the consultant's interviewing each of the group members and the leader prior to the group meeting—ask-

Item	Agree 2	? 1	Disagree 0
53. My job is often dull and monotonous	☐	☐	☐
54. There is too much pressure on my job	☐	☐	☐
55. I am required to spend too much time on the job	☐	☐	☐
56. I have the right equipment to do my work	☐	☐	☐
57. My pay is enough to live on comfortably	☐	☐	☐
58. I'm satisfied with the way employee benefits are handled here	☐	☐	☐
59. I wish I had more opportunity to socialize with my associates	☐	☐	☐
60. The people I work with are very friendly	☐	☐	☐
61. My supervisor welcomes our ideas even when they differ from her/his own	☐	☐	☐
62. My supervisor ought to be friendlier toward us	☐	☐	☐
63. My supervisor lives up to his promises	☐	☐	☐
64. We are kept well informed about TI's business prospects and standing with competitors	☐	☐	☐
65. Management ignores our suggestions and complaints	☐	☐	☐
66. My supervisor is not qualified for his/her job well	☐	☐	☐
67. My supervisor has the work well organized	☐	☐	☐
68. I have ample opportunity to see the end results of my work	☐	☐	☐
69. My supervisor has enough authority and backing to perform his job well	☐	☐	☐
70. I do not get enough instruction about how to do a job	☐	☐	☐
71. You can say what you think around here	☐	☐	☐
72. I know where I stand with my supervisor	☐	☐	☐
73. When terminations are necessary, they are handled fairly	☐	☐	☐
74. I am very much underpaid for the work I do	☐	☐	☐
75. I'm really doing something worthwhile in my job	☐	☐	☐
76. I'm proud to work for TI	☐	☐	☐
77. Many TIers I know would like to see the union get in	☐	☐	☐
78. I received fair treatment in my last performance review	☐	☐	☐
79. During the past six months I have seriously considered getting a job elsewhere	☐	☐	☐
80. TI's problem-solving procedure is adequate for handling our problems and complaints	☐	☐	☐
81. I would recommend employment at TI to my friends	☐	☐	☐
82. My supervisor did a good job in discussing my last performance review with me	☐	☐	☐
83. My pay is the most important source of satisfaction from my job	☐	☐	☐
84. Favoritism is a problem in my area	☐	☐	☐
85. I have very few complaints about our lunch facilities	☐	☐	☐
86. Most people I know in this community have a good opinion of TI	☐	☐	☐
87. I usually read most of my division newspaper	☐	☐	☐
88. I can usually get hold of my supervisor when I need her/him	☐	☐	☐
89. Most TIers are placed in jobs that make good use of their abilities	☐	☐	☐
90. I receive adequate training for my needs	☐	☐	☐
91. I've gone as far as I can in TI			
92. My job seems to be leading to the kind of future I want	☐	☐	☐
93. There is too much personal friction among people at my level in the company	☐	☐	☐
94. The amount of effort a person puts into his/her job is appreciated at TI	☐	☐	☐
95. Filling in this questionnaire is a good way to let management know what employees think	☐	☐	☐
96. I think some good will come out of filling in a questionnaire like this one	☐	☐	☐

97 Please check on term which most nearly describes the kind of work you do: 1 ☐ Clerical or office 2 ☐ Production 3 ☐ Technical 4 ☐ Maintenance 5 ☐ Manufacturing 6 ☐ R & D 7 ☐ Engineering 8 ☐ Other

98 1 ☐ Hourly 2 ☐ Salaried | 99 1 ☐ Male 2 ☐ Female | 100 Do you supervise 3 or more TIers? 1 ☐ Yes 2 ☐ No

Name of your department:

Please write any comments or suggestions you care to make in the space below.

FIGURE 8.8 (continued)

ing them what their problems are, how they think the group functions, and what obstacles are in the way of the group's performing better.[38] (Or the consultant may interview the entire group at once, using open-ended questions such as: "What things do you see getting in the way of this group's being the better one? Sometimes, an attitude survey is used to gather the basic background data for the meetings.) The consultant usually then categorizes the interview data into themes and presents themes to the group at the beginning of the meeting.

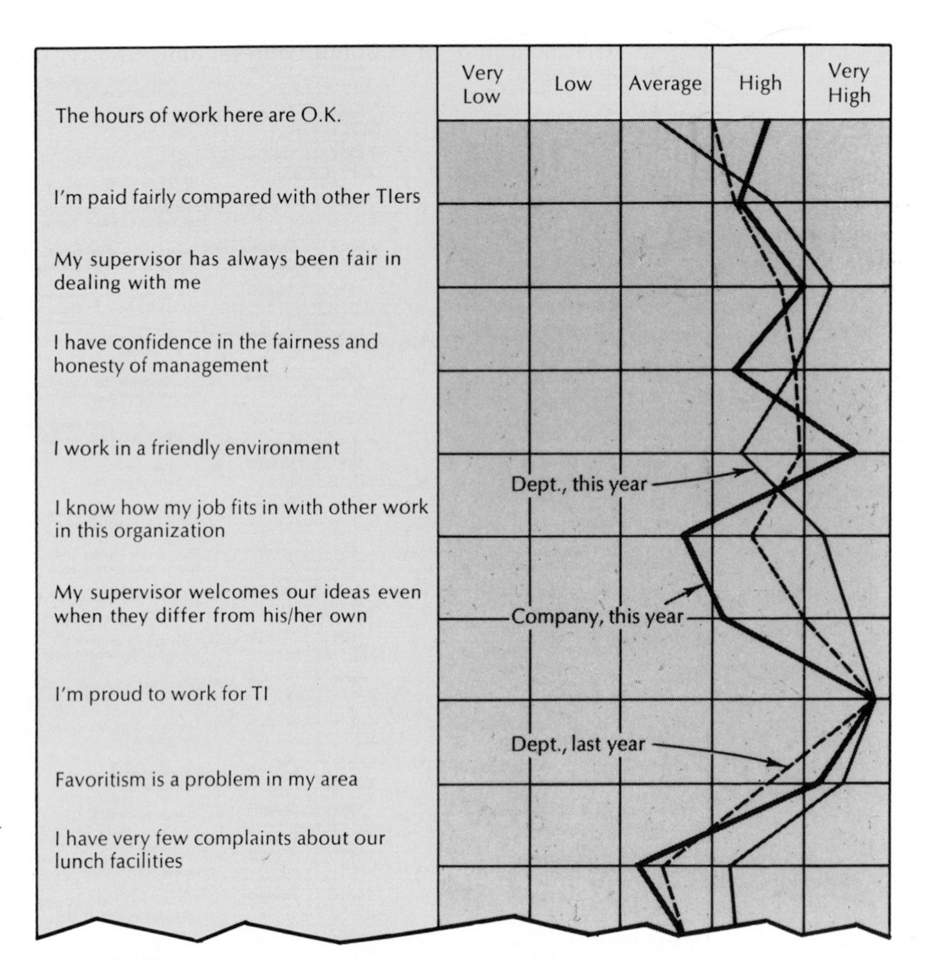
Very Low
Low
Average
High
Very High
The hours of work here are O.K.
I'm paid fairly compared with other TIers
My supervisor has always been fair in dealing with me
I have confidence in the fairness and honesty of management
I work in a friendly environment
I know how my job fits in with other work in this organization
My supervisor welcomes our ideas even when they differ from his/her own
I'm proud to work for TI
Favoritism is a problem in my area
I have very few complaints about our lunch facilities
Dept., this year
Company, this year
Dept., last year

FIGURE 8.9
Attitude Survey Profile

Note: Attitude survey results are usually summarized and a profile prepared showing departments' results on each item this year, compared with (1) department last year, and (2) total company results this year.

Themes might include, for example, "Not enough time to get my job done," or "I can't get any cooperation around here." The themes are then ranked by the group in terms of their importance. The most important ones then form the agenda for the meeting. The group then examines and discusses the issues, examines the underlying causes of the problem, and begins work on some solution to the problems.

During one of these sessions it is likely that certain nonagenda items will emerge as a result of the participant's interaction. In discussing the theme "I can't get any cooperation around here," for instance, the group's discussion might uncover the fact that the group's manager is not providing enough direction. She might be allowing vacuums to develop that are leading to conflict and a breakdown of cooperation. These new items or problems, as well as the agenda items (or themes), are generally pursued under the guidance of the consultant. Next, some steps are formulated to bring about the changes deemed desirable. Then a follow-up meeting is often scheduled. Here it is determined whether the steps have been implemented successfully.

Notice how the typical team-building intervention relies on the *participants* themselves doing the research: Information about the group's problems is obtained from the group; members of the group then analyze and discuss the data in an atmosphere of cooperativeness; and, finally, the participants develop solutions or action steps for solving the problems that *they themselves* have identified.

managerial grid
A matrix that represents different possible leadership styles.

"9,9" managers
A manager with this rating is highly concerned with people *and* with production.

Grid training is a formal approach to team building designed by Blake and Mouton.[39] As summarized in Table 8.2 Grid training is based on a device called the **managerial grid**. This represents different possible leadership styles (specifically whether the leader is more concerned with people or production).

The Grid program is aimed, first, at developing **"9,9" managers**—managers who are interested in getting results by being high on both their concern for production and for people; they want to get results through committed, cooperative subordinates, say Blake and Mouton. The Grid program assumes that possessing such a style makes it easier for you to work with your subordinates, superiors, and peers in analyzing group, intergroup, and organizational problems and developing action steps to solve these problems.

EXECUTIVE DEVELOPMENT: KEY FACTORS FOR SUCCESS

The idea that there are several key factors for an executive development program's success is illustrated by the results of a survey of executive development practices in 12 leading corporations.[40] This study found a surprisingly high degree of consensus among the 12 firms regarding the characteristics of ineffective and effective executive development processes. In particular, five major success criteria were listed by over 75% of the survey participants.

FIVE KEY FACTORS FOR SUCCESS

These five key factors were as follows:

1. Extensive and visible involvement by the chief executive (CEO) is critical.

In all but one of the companies, extensive and visible involvement by the CEO was described as "essential" and "the single most important determinant" of success for the executive development program. This extensive involvement helped guarantee that the company's executive development process was consistent with the direction in which the CEO wanted to see the company go. It also lent the process a credibility unachievable in any other way.

TABLE 8.2 Summary of Managerial Grid Leadership Styles

TYPE OF LEADER AS RANKED ON GRID	CONCERN FOR PEOPLE	CONCERN FOR PRODUCTION
(1-1)	Low	Low
(1-9)	High	Low
(9-1)	Low	High
(9-9)	High	High

2. Corporations with a successful executive development process have a clearly articulated and understood executive development policy and philosophy.

In other words, the executive development process should ideally be built around a clearly articulated philosophy and purpose. For example, 10 of the 12 companies surveyed listed four common objectives of their executive development processes: ensuring that qualified executives would be available to fill current and future assignments; serving as a major vehicle to perpetuate the organization's heritage and shape its culture by communicating its mission, beliefs, values, and management practices; preparing executives to respond to the complex business issues of the changing environment by providing managers with the experience, knowledge, and skills they need in future assignments; and developing a cadre of individuals prepared to assume senior-level general management responsibilities.

3. Successful executive development policies and strategies are directly linked to the corporation's business strategies, objectives, and challenges.

Nine of the 12 companies emphasized that their executive development policies and strategies were consciously linked to the company's business plans and objectives. For example, plans to expand overseas, diversify into new product lines, or consolidate manufacturing operations have implications for management/executive development activities. In the successful programs the development process was molded around the company's plans.

4. Successful executive development processes include three main elements: an annual succession planning process; planned on-the-job developmental assignments; and customized, internal, executive education programs supplemented by the selected use of university programs.

All the companies surveyed were emphatic in insisting that a development program could not be successful without all three ingredients. And they all emphasized that all three ingredients together—succession planning, development assignments, and customized programs—added up to a total executive development process.

With respect to succession planning (planning which individuals would be available to fill which slots as they opened), all the companies engaged in several specific activities. In all 12 companies *replacement plans* were in place and were actively managed for key positions and individuals. Second, *development needs* are continually identified (based on these replacement plans), and plans are developed and implemented to address these development needs. Third, a formal, annual planning and review phase is in place to assess each *candidate's progress* and to review the company's replacement plans.

With respect to on-the-job development (the second ingredient), "all the study participants agreed that it was the single most effective developmental tool available to organizations." The four types of on-the-job experience used most often were: assignment of people to membership on task forces assembled to address specific issues, job rotation experiences lasting from one to two years, overseas assignments, and temporary assignments of relatively short duration.

With respect to the third ingredient, executive education, all the companies offered a mix of external university-type programs and customized internal programs. Some of the companies expressed concern about the prohibitive costs of the external programs although virtually all sent selected employees to them.

5. Executive development is the responsibility of line management rather than of the human resources function.

In all but one of the companies in this survey, the role of the human resource department was seen as crucial but advisory. Specifically, members of the personnel department or training staff served as facilitators of the executive development process and as a resource for line management regarding what development programs and activities to use and how to use them. However, the actual responsibility for achieving the goals of the executive development program—to fill future positions, or to eliminate current managerial shortcomings, for instance—is the responsibility of line management.

Global HRM

Selecting and developing executives to run the employer's overseas operations present management with a dilemma. There is what one expert calls "an alarmingly high failure rate when executives are relocated overseas." This failure rate is usually caused by poor and inappropriate selection and preplacement development.[41] However, in an increasingly globalized economy, employers will have to develop managers for overseas assignments despite these difficulties.

A number of companies, including Dow, Colgate-Palmolive, and Ciba-Geigy, have developed and implemented international executive relocation programs that are working successfully. In addition to the general requirements for successful executive development programs previously listed, preparing and training executives for overseas assignments should include the following considerations as well:

1. Choose international assignment candidates whose educational backgrounds and experiences are appropriate for overseas assignments. As in most other endeavors, the best predictor of future performance is often a person's past performance. In this case the person who has already accumulated a track record of successfully adapting to foreign cultures (perhaps through college studies and overseas summer internships) will more likely succeed as an international transferee.
2. Choose those whose personalities and family situations can withstand the cultural changes they will encounter in their new environments. When many of these executives fail, it is not because they themselves couldn't adapt, but because their spouses or children were unhappy in their new foreign setting. Thus the person's family situation probably should have more influence on the assignment than it would in a domestic assignment.
3. Brief candidates fully and clearly on all relocation policies. Here, it is important that transferees be given a realistic preview of what the assignment will entail, including the company's policies regarding matters such as moving expenses, salary differentials, and benefits (such as paid schooling for the employees' children). Given the expense of such a move—for both the employer and employee—surprises are best held to a minimum.
4. Give executives and their families comprehensive training in their new company's culture and language. At Dow Chemical, for instance, orientation begins with a

briefing session, during which the transfer policy is explained in detail to the relocating executive. He or she is also given a briefing package compiled by the receiving area containing important information on local matters (such as shopping and housing). In addition, an advisor—often the spouse of a recently returned expatriate—will visit the transferee and his or her spouse to explain what sort of emotional issues they are likely to face in the early stages of the move—such as feeling remote from relatives, for instance. The option of attending a two-week language and cultural orientation program offered by a school like Berlitz is also extended. At Colgate-Palmolive a two-year orientation program prepares trainees for assignment in an international subsidiary.

5. Provide all relocating executives with a mentor to monitor their overseas careers and help them secure appropriate jobs with the company when they repatriate. At Dow, for instance, each expatriate is assigned a "mentor." This person is usually a high-level supervisor in the expatriate's particular function. The overseas assignee keeps his or her mentor up-to-date on his or her activities. For his or her part, the mentor keeps track of the expatriate's career while he or she is overseas. Specifically, all job changes and compensation actions involving the expatriate must be reviewed with and supported by the mentor. This helps to avoid the problem of having expatriates feel "lost" overseas, particularly in terms of career progress.
6. Establish a repatriation program that helps returning executives and their families readjust to their professional and personal lives in their home country. At Dow, for instance, the head of the overseas assignee's department or division gives the transferee a letter stating that the foreign subsidiary guarantees that he or she will be able to return to a job at least at the same level as the one he is leaving. As much as a year in advance of the expatriate's scheduled return to headquarters, his or her new job is arranged by the person's mentor.[42]

SMALL BUSINESS APPLICATIONS

The president of a smaller enterprise faces both unique advantages and disadvantages when it comes to developing employees for higher-level executive roles. On the negative side, this president does not have the resources or time to develop full-blown executive succession programs or to fund many outside programs like sending potential executives away to the Harvard Business school. Yet at the same time the president of a smaller firm has the advantage of working closer with and knowing more about each of his or her employees than does the CEO of a bigger, less personal firm.

A relative lack of resources notwithstanding, the smaller firm's president has few needs more important than that of developing senior managers. For most small firms with successful products, it is not a lack of financing that holds them back, but a lack of management talent. This is because all growing firms inevitably reach the point where the entrepreneur/owner can no longer solely make all the decisions. For the Dows and Mercks of the world, the question of succession planning and executive development is mostly a question of selecting the best of the lot and then developing them: There is usually an adequate supply of talent given these companies' enormous influx of new recruits. For the smaller company, the problem usually is not one of selecting the best of the lot. Instead, it's making sure that key positions are filled and that the president will have the foresight to know when to surrender one set of reins over a part of the company's operations.

There are thus four main steps in the smaller company's executive development process:

Step 1. Problem Assessment

Particularly here the executive development process must begin with an assessment of the company's current problems and the owner's plans for the company's future. Obviously, if the owner/entrepreneur is satisfied with the current size of the firm and has no plans to retire in the near future, no additional management talent may be required.

On the other hand, if plans call for expansion, or current problems seem to be growing out of control, management development/succession planning might be the key. It often happens, for instance, that as the small company evolves from a mom and pop operation to a larger firm the management system that adequately served the owner in the past is no longer effective. Problems arise as manufacturing orders that were previously profitable now incur overtime costs and excessive waste, and the informal order-writing process can no longer keep up with the volume of orders.

At this point the president must assess the problems in his or her firm. Begin with an analysis of the company's financial statements. For example, what is the trend of key financial ratios, such as the ratio of manufacturing costs to sales, or of sales overhead to sales? Are your profit margins level, or heading up or down? Are fixed costs remaining about the same, or heading up as a percentage of sales? Next, analyze the organization function by function. In sales, is the backlog of orders growing? In manufacturing, are there inventory problems that require attention? In accounting, are you getting the accounting reports that you need and are the monthly and end-of-year reports produced in a timely fashion? Does the company have a personnel system in place such that as many personnel matters as possible—recruitment, testing, selection, training and so forth—are routinized and carried out in an effective manner? The point is that the owner must continually assess the problems in his or her firm with an eye toward determining when and if new management talent is required.

Step 2. Management Audit

One reason management selection and development is so important in small firms is that the "problems" assessed in step 1 are often just symptoms of inadequate management talent in smaller firms. It's simply not possible for the owner/entrepreneur to run a $5 million company the way he or she did when the company was one-tenth the size. Therefore the lack of adequate management is a depressingly familiar cause for many of the problems in the small growing firm.

Therefore, use the problems found in step 1 as a starting point in conducting a management audit of the people you now have helping you manage your firm. One simple and effective way to do this is by evaluating them on the traditional management functions of planning, organizing, staffing, leading, and controlling. For example, within their own areas of responsibility have they instituted plans, policies, and procedures that enable their activities to be carried out efficiently? Have they organized their activities in such a way that their subordinates have job descriptions and understand what their responsibilities are? In terms of staffing, have they selected competent employees, are their people adequately oriented and trained, and are the pay rates within their group viewed as fair and equitable? In terms of leadership, is the morale in their department satisfactory, and do their people seem to enjoy what they are doing? Is the person's interpersonal relations with other members of your team satisfactory? And in terms of control, has the person recommended and/or instituted a set of reports that provide him and you with the information you need to assess adequately how that department is doing?

Step 3. Analysis of Development Needs

Your next step is to determine whether any inadequacies uncovered in step 2 can be remedied via some type of development program. At one extreme, the person may not have the potential to grow beyond what he or she is now, and here development may serve no purpose. At the other extreme, the problems uncovered may just reflect a lack of knowledge. For example, sending your bookkeeper/accountant back to school for a course or two in management accounting could alleviate the problem. Another question to answer here is whether you (the owner/entrepreneur) may be responsible for some of the problems yourself, and whether you should direct yourself to some management development program (or out of the firm altogether).

Step 4. Identify Replacement Needs

Your assessment may lead to the need to recruit and select new management talent. Here, as explained in Chapter 3, you should determine ahead of time the intellectual, personality, interpersonal, and experience criteria to be used. You should also map out an on-the-job development program that gives the person the breadth of experience he or she needs to perform the job.

▶ CHAPTER REVIEW

SUMMARY

1. Management development is aimed at preparing employees for some future jobs with the organization, or at solving organization-wide problems concerning, for instance, inadequate interdepartmental communication.
2. On-the-job experience is by far the most popular form of management development. However, the preferred techniques differ by organizational level, with in-house programs being preferred for first-line supervisors and external conferences and seminars more widely used for top executives.
3. Managerial on-the-job training includes job rotation, coaching, junior boards, and action learning. Basic off-the-job techniques include case studies, management games, outside seminars, university-related programs, role playing, behavior modeling, and in-house development centers. We also explained several special management development techniques, including leader match, Vroom-Yetton training, TA, and organizational development.
4. Organizational development (OD) is an approach to instituting change in which employees themselves play a major role in the change process by providing data, by obtaining feedback on problems, and by team planning solutions. We described several OD methods including sensitivity training, Grid development, and survey feedback.
5. Grid programs (and other intergroup team-building efforts) aim at developing better problem solving and more cooperativeness at work through the "action research" process. Each work group analyzes work team problems and generates action plans for solving them. Then this same approach is used by special intergroup teams so that companywide problems are solved.

6. Successful development programs require CEO involvement; a clear development policy; linkage to plans; succession planning and development; and line responsibility.

KEY TERMS

- management development
- succession planning
- job rotation
- junior board
- action learning
- case study method
- management game
- role playing
- behavior modeling
- in-house development centers
- special management development techniques
- leader match training
- Vroom-Yetton leadership training
- transactional analysis (TA)
- organizational development (OD)
- survey feedback
- sensitivity training
- team building
- grid training
- managerial grid
- "9,9" managers

DISCUSSION QUESTIONS

1. How does the involvement approach to attitude surveys differ from simply administering surveys and returning the results to top management?
2. Compare and contrast three organizational development techniques.
3. Review the "submarine captain" example from page 281 of the Vroom-Yetton method discussion, and use their chart and technique to determine what approach the captain should use.
4. Describe the pros and cons of five management development methods.
5. Discuss the key considerations in a typical small business management development program.

APPLICATION EXERCISES

RUNNING CASE

Carter Cleaning Company

Developing Managers

"Management development? Did you say management development? Jennifer, you're my daughter and I love you but I can't believe that with all the problems we're facing here—strong competition, softening economy, 400% turnover, employee theft, and supply and waste management cartage costs that are going through the roof—you actually want me to consider setting up some kind of a program that will turn that bunch of deadbeats that we have as managers into nice guys. I love you, Jenny, but please let's focus on the problems that we have to get solved today."

Actually, Jennifer was not altogether surprised with her father's reaction, but she did believe that her dad was being more than a little shortsighted. For example, she knew that some successful organizations, like Club Med, had a policy of rotating managers annually to help avoid their getting "stale," and she wondered whether such a program would make sense at Carter's. She also felt that some type of simulations might help managers do a better job of dealing with their customers and subordinates, and she further believed that periodic off-site meetings between her, her father, and the store managers might help to identify and solve problems with the stores. Outside seminars in areas like modern cleaning techniques might also help to boost the current store managers' interest and performance and, of course, there is also the possibility of scheduling potential managers (like a few of the current cleaner-spotters) for management development as well. The company really didn't have much money to spend on matters like this though, and Jennifer knew that to sell the idea to her father she would need a very concrete, tight set of recommendations.

Questions

1. Given a budget of $750, what type of management development program can Jennifer formulate for her current store managers? The proposal must include the specific activities (like job rotation) in which her managers should engage over the next four months.
2. Would it be worthwhile for the company to administer an attitude survey of all their employees? Jennifer knows she doesn't have a big company, but she is curious as to whether employees would anonymously express their concerns and their likes and dislikes and perhaps even help identify problems like employee theft that they are encountering on their job. If they do go ahead with the survey, what questions should they ask?

CASE INCIDENT: *What We Need Around Here Is Better Human Relations*

Hank called his three highest-ranking managers together for a surprise luncheon meeting. "Have lunch on United Mutual," said Hank, "I have an important topic I want to bring to your attention."

After Madeline, Raymond, and Allen ordered lunch, Hank launched into the agenda:

"As office manager, I think we have to move into a rigorous human relations training and development program for our front-line supervisors. It's no longer a question of whether we should have a program, it's now a question of what kind and when."

Allen spoke out, "Okay, Hank, don't keep us in suspense any longer. What makes you think we need a human relations program?"

"Look at the problems we are facing. Twenty-five percent turnover among the clerical and secretarial staffs; productivity lower than the casualty insurance industry national standards. What better reasons could anybody have for properly training our supervisory staff?"

Madeline commented, "Hold on Hank. Training many not be the answer. I think our high turnover and low productivity are caused by reasons beyond the control of supervision. Our wages are low and we expect our people to work in cramped, rather dismal office space."

Hank retorted, "Nonsense. A good supervisor can get workers to accept almost any working conditions. Training will fix that."

"Hank, I see another problem," said Allen. "Our supervisors are so overworked already that they will balk at training. If you hold the training on company time, they will say that they are falling behind in their work. If the training takes place after hours or on weekends, our supervisors will say that they are being taken advantage of."

"Nonsense," replied Hank. "Every supervisor realizes the importance of good human relations. Besides that, they will see it as a form of job enrichment."

"So long as we're having an open meeting, let me have my input," volunteered Raymond. "We are starting from the wrong end by having our first-line supervisors go through human relations training. It's our top management who needs the training the most. Unless they practice better human relations, you can't expect such behavior from our supervisors. How can you have a top management that is insensitive to people and a bottom management that is sensitive? The system just won't work."

"What you say makes some sense," said Hank, "but I wouldn't go so far as to say top management is insensitive to people. Maybe we can talk some more about the human relations program after lunch."

Questions

1. What do you think Hank means by "human relations training"?
2. Should Hank go ahead with his plans for the human relations training and development program? Why or why not?
3. What do you think of Raymond's comment that top management should participate in human relations training first?
4. What is your opinion of Hank's statement that good leadership can compensate for poor working conditions?
5. If you were in Hank's situation, would you try to get top management to participate in a human relations training program?
6. What type of training and development activities would you recommend for first-line supervisors at United Mutual? How would you analyze the need for such a program?
7. What other factors could be causing the problems Hank refers to?

Source: Andrew J. Dubrin, *Human Relations: A Job Oriented Approach*, pp. 343–44. © 1988. Reprinted by permission of Prentice Hall, Englewood Cliffs, NJ.

HUMAN RESOURCE MANAGEMENT SIMULATION

The training budget in the simulation includes training for promotions from within, as well as other types of managerial and supervisory training. In the simulation, sufficient training will reduce costs, increase productivity, lower turnover, decrease accidents, and increase moral. Clearly, training *is* important!

NOTES

1. Lester A. Digman, "Management Development: Needs and Practices," *Personnel*, Vol. 57 (July–August 1980), pp. 45–57. See also James Cureton, Alfred Newton, and Dennis Tesolowski, "Finding Out What Managers Need," *Training and Development Journal*, Vol. 40, no. 5 (May 1986), pp. 106–107.
2. William Kearney, "Management Development Programs Can Pay Off," *Business Horizons*, Vol. 18 (April 1975), pp. 81–88.
3. According to a survey by Digman, the median percentage of executives receiving training during a typical year was 23%; middle managers, 38%; and first-line supervisors, 20%.
4. "Trends in Corporate Education and Training," Report no. 870 (1986), The Conference Board, 845 Third Avenue, New York, NY 10022.
5. Lise Saari et al., "A Survey of Management Training and Education Practices in U.S. Companies," *Personnel Psychology* (Winter 1988), pp. 731–743.
6. Dale Yoder et al., *Handbook of Personnel Management and Labor Relations* (New York: McGraw-Hill, 1958), pp. 10–27; for a recent review see William Rothwell, H. C. Kazanas, and Darla Haines, "Issues and Practices in Management Job Rotation Programs as Perceived by HRD Professionals," *Performance Improvement Quarterly*, Vol. 5, no. 1 (1992), pp. 49–69.
7. Ibid. See also Jack Phillips, "Training Supervisors Outside the Classroom," *Training and Development Journal*, Vol. 40, no. 2 (February 1986), pp. 46–49.
8. Kenneth Wexley and Gary Latham, *Developing and Training Resources in Organizations*, (Glenview, IL: Scott, Foresman, 1981), p. 118.
9. Ibid, pp. 118–119.
10. Quoted in Paul Evans, Yves Doz, and Andre Laurent, *Human Resource Management in International Firms* (New York: St. Martin's Press, 1990), p. 123.
11. Ibid.
12. Wexley and Latham, *Developing and Training*, p. 207.
13. This is based on Nancy Fox, "Action Learning Comes to Industry," *Harvard Business Review*, Vol. 56 (September–October, 1977), pp. 158–168.
14. Wexley and Latham, *Developing and Training*, p. 193.
15. Chris Argyris, "Some Limitations of the Case Method: Experiences in a Management Development Program," *Academy of Management Review*, Vol. 5, no. 2 (1980), pp. 291–298. For a discussion of the advantages of case studies over traditional methods, see, for example, Eugene Andrews and James Noel, "Adding Life to the Case Study," *Training and Development Journal*, Vol. 40, no. 2 (February 1986), pp. 28–33.
16. David Rogers, *Business Policy and Planning* (Englewood Cliffs, NJ: Prentice Hall, 1977), pp. 532–533.

17. Argyris, "Some Limitations of the Case Method," pp. 292–295.
18. Rogers, *Business Policy and Planning*, p. 533.
19. Mona Pintkowski, "Evaluating the Seminar Marketplace," *Training and Development Journal*, Vol. 40, no. 1 (January 1986), pp. 74–77.
20. Joseph Famularo, *Handbook of Modern Personnel Administration* (New York: McGraw-Hill, 1972), pp. 21.7–21.8. For an interesting discussion of how to design a management game that is both educational and stimulating, see Beverly Loy Taylor, "Around the World in 80 Questions," *Training and Development Journal*, Vol. 40, no. 3 (March 1986), pp. 67–70.
21. Lawrence G. Bridwell and Alvin B. Marcus, "Back to School—A High Tech Company Sent Its Managers to Business School—to Learn "People" Skills," *Personnel Administrator*, Vol. 32, no. 3 (March 1987), pp. 86–91.
22. John Hinrichs, "Personnel Testing," in Marvin Dunnette, ed., *Handbook of Industrial and Organizational Psychology* (Chicago: Rand McNally, 1976), p. 855.
23. Norman Maier, Allen Solem, and Ayesha Maier, *The Role Play Technique* (San Diego, CA: University Associates, 1975), pp. 2–3.
24. This section based on Allen Kraut, "Developing Managerial Skill via Modeling Techniques: Some Positive Research Findings—A Symposium," *Personnel Psychology*, Vol. 29, no. 3 (Autumn 1976), pp. 325–361.
25. Gary Latham and Lise Saari, "Application of Social-Learning Theory to Training Supervisors Through Behavior Modeling," *Journal of Applied Psychology*, Vol. 64, no. 3 (June 1979), pp. 239–246. Note that in one study in which managers were substituted for professional trainers, the researchers concluded that while behavior modeling resulted in favorable reactions and an increase in learning, it did not produce behavior change on the job or improved performance results. The researchers here conclude that behavior modeling could be improved by such techniques as persuading supervisors that the new behaviors that they are asked to learn are more effective than their current behaviors. See also James Russell, Kenneth Wexley, and John Hunter, "Questioning the Effectiveness of Behavior-Modeling Training in an Industrial Setting," *Personnel Psychology*, Vol. 37, no. 3 (Autumn 1984), pp. 465–481.
26. Herbert Meyer and Michael Raich, "An Objective Evaluation of Behavior-Modeling Training Program," *Personnel Psychology*, Vol. 36, no. 4 (Winter 1983), pp. 755–761.
27. "A Surprise CBS Morale Booster," *Business Week*, October 20, 1980, pp. 125–126.
28. Thomas Stewart, "How GE Keeps Those Ideas Coming," *Fortune*, August 12, 1991, p. 43.
29. J. L. Noel and R. Charan, "Leadership Development at GE's Crotonville," *Human Resource Management* (April 1988), p. 434, quoted in Marshall Whitmire and Philip Nienstedt, "Lead Leaders into the 90s," *Personnel Journal* (May 1991), p. 80.
30. Fred Fiedler, Martin Chambers, and Linda Mahar, *Improving Leadership Effectiveness: The Leader Match Concept* (New York: John Wiley, 1977).
31. Fred Fiedler and Linda Mahar, "The Effectiveness of Contingency Model Training: A Review of the Validation of Leader Match," *Personnel Psychology*, Vol. 32 (Spring 1979), pp. 45–62; Lewis Csoka and Paul Bons, "Manipulating the Situation to Fit the Leader Style: Two Validation Studies to Leader Match," *Journal of Applied Psychology*, Vol. 53 (June 1978), pp. 295–300; Boris Kabanoff, "A Critique of Leader Match and Its Implications for Leadership Research," *Personnel Psychology*, Vol. 34 (Winter 1981), pp. 749–764; Samuel Shiflett, "Is There a Problem with the LPC Score in Leader Match?" *Personnel Psychology*, Vol. 34 (Winter 1981), pp. 765–769; Arthur Jago and James Ragan, "The Trouble with Leader Match Is That It Doesn't Match Fiedler's Contingency Model," *Journal of Applied Psychology*, Vol. 71, no. 4 (November 1986), pp. 555–559; Martin Chemers and Fred E. Fiedler, "The Trouble with Assumptions: A Reply to Jago and Ragan," *Journal of Applied Psychology*, Vol. 71, no. 4 (November 1986), pp. 560–563.
32. See, for example, R. H. George Field, "A Test of the Vroom-Yetton Normative Model of Leadership," *Journal of Applied Psychology*, Vol. 67, no. 5 (October 1982), pp. 523–532.
33. Mark Frohman, Marshall Sashkin, and Michael Kavanagh, "Action Research as Applied to Organization Development," *Organization and Administrative Science*, Vol. 7 (Spring–Summer 1976), pp. 129–142; Paul Sheibar, "The Seven Deadly Sins of Employee Attitude Surveys," *Personnel*, Vol. 66, no. 6 (June 1989), pp. 66–71. See also George Gallup, "A Surge in Surveys," *Personnel Journal*, Vol. 67, no. 8 (August 1988), pp. 42–43.
34. M. Scott Meyers, "How Attitude Surveys Help You Manage," *Training and Development Journal*, Vol. 21 (October 1967), pp. 34–41. For a good explanation of how to conduct attitude surveys, see, for example, David York, "Attitude Surveying," *Personnel Journal*, Vol. 64, no. 5 (May 1985), pp. 70–73.
35. Based on J. P. Campbell and M. D. Dunnette, "Effectiveness of T-Group Experiences in Managerial Training and Development," *Psychological Bulletin*, Vol. 7 (1968), pp. 73–104.
36. Robert J. House, "T-Group Training: Good or Bad?" *Business Horizons*, Vol. 22 (December 1979), pp. 69–77.
37. John Kimberly and Warren Nielson, "Organization Development and Change in Organizational Performance," *Administrative Science Quarterly*, Vol. 20, no. 2 (June 1975); Peter Smith, "Controlled Studies of the Outcome of Sensitivity Training," *Psychological Bulletin*, Vol. 82 (1976), pp. 597–622. See also Rosemary Caffarella, "Managing Conflict: An Analytical Tool," *Training and Development Journal*, Vol. 38, no. 2 (February 1984), pp. 34–38.
38. Wendell French and Cecil Bell, Jr., *Organization Development* (Englewood Cliffs, NJ: Prentice-Hall, 1978). See also David M. Zakeski, "Reliable Assessments of Organizations," *Personnel Journal*, Vol. 67, no. 12 (December 1988), pp. 42–44.
39. Robert Blake and Jane Mouton, *The Managerial Grid* (Houston: Gulf, 1964). For an interesting description of the effectiveness of team building in solving a management problem, see, for example, Barry Miller and Ronald Phillips, "Team Building on a Deadline," *Training and Development Journal*, Vol. 40, no. 3 (March 1986), pp. 54–58.
40. Julie A. Fenwick-MacGrath, "Executive Development: Key Factors for Success," *Personnel* (July 1988), pp. 68–72.
41. Paul Blocklyn, "Developing the International Executive," *Personnel* (March 1989), pp. 44–47.
42, This section based on Ibid.

CHAPTER 9

MANAGING QUALITY AND PRODUCTIVITY

OVERVIEW

In this chapter we focus on four important programs—alternative work arrangements, quality circle programs, total quality management programs, and self-directed teams, all of which can boost quality and productivity. Each of these programs also contributes to employee commitment by providing employees with more opportunities for flexibility, creativity, and responsibility than they might otherwise have. When you finish studying this chapter, you should be able to discuss the pros and cons of alternative work arrangements; explain how to make quality circles more effective; describe how to implement total quality management programs; and explain how to create self-managing work teams.

INTRODUCTION

Many changes are occurring in the environment of human resource management. Information technology (PCs, etc.) increasingly demands a more sophisticated, better-trained work force. Of the 16 million or so jobs to be added by the U.S. economy in the 1990s, virtually all will be in service jobs. These are jobs (like consultants, salespeople, food service workers, and nurses) that don't readily lend themselves to highly restrictive work rules or supervisory practices. At the same time the supply of available labor is growing more slowly than in the past, and the average age of that work force is rising—two more factors putting a premium on using new methods for getting the best out of your work force. And superimposed over all this is the change in work itself (and in how modern businesses are managed), changes that reflect the increasing globalization and need for responsiveness that corporate success today requires.

These changes are influencing the personnel management methods employers use, and nowhere is this more apparent than in their worker reward and involvement systems. In particular, employers are increasingly utilizing techniques like quality improvement programs and flexible work arrangements. Programs like these aim at eliciting the best that workers can offer, by treating them responsibly, by giving them more discretion over their jobs, and by giving them the opportunity to use their problem-solving skills at work. Some of the most important of these methods are discussed in this chapter and include such closely related programs as

ALTERNATIVE WORK ARRANGEMENTS. These generally involve allowing employees to design relatively flexible workdays and/or workweeks for themselves so as to better accommodate the employees' personal needs and preferences.

QUALITY CIRCLE PROGRAMS. These include the establishment of specially trained work teams that meet periodically (usually weekly) to analyze and solve problems in their work areas.

COMPANYWIDE QUALITY IMPROVEMENT (QI) PROGRAMS. These programs are instituted to improve the quality of the employer's product or services; the basic approach involves a coordinated, companywide effort built around monitoring customer satisfaction and using employee teams and involvement to continually improve quality.

SELF DIRECTED TEAMS. These are created by techniques aimed at enabling work teams to self-direct their work activities.

ALTERNATIVE WORK ARRANGEMENTS

FLEXTIME

flextime
A plan whereby employees build their workday around a core of midday hours.

Flextime is a plan whereby employees' flexible workdays are built around a core of midday hours, such as 11 to 2. It is called flextime because workers determine their own starting and stopping hours. For example, they may opt to work from 7 to 3 or 11 to 7. Well over 15% of the U.S. work force is on a flextime schedule, not counting professionals, managers, and self-employed persons who customarily set their own work hours anyway.[1]

Flextime in Practice

In practice, most employers who use flextime allow employees only limited freedom regarding the hours they work. This is summarized in Table 9.1, which shows the earliest starting time, latest starting time, and core periods that are most popular. As you can see, employers still try to hold fairly close to the traditional 9 to 5 day. For example, in 67% of the companies employees can't start work before 7 A.M., and in almost all firms employees must not clock in before 6 A.M.. Similarly, in about half the firms, employees can't start work later than 9

TABLE 9.1 Typical Flextime Schedules

FLEXTIME STARTING TIMES			
Earliest Starting Time	Percent of Respondents	Latest Starting Time	Percent of Respondents
Before 6 A.M.	10	8–9 A.M.	55
6–7 A.M.	21	9–10 A.M.	31
7–8 A.M.	67	10–11 A.M.	9
8–9 A.M.	2	11–12 Noon	0
After 9 A.M.	0	After 12 Noon	5

FLEXTIME CORE HOURS		WORK WEEK SCHEDULING	
Time	Percent of Respondents	Scheduling Plan	Percent of Respondents
8 A.M.–3 P.M.	5	5 days, 40 hours	64
8 A.M.–4 P.M.	19	5 days, 37½ hours	18
8 A.M.–5 P.M.	10	5 days, 35 hours	8
9 A.M.–3 P.M.	15	5 days, 38¾ hours	3
9 A.M.–4 P.M.	28	5 days, 36¼ hours	2
9 A.M.–5 P.M.	6	4 days, 40 hours	1
10 A.M.–2 P.M.	4	All others	4
10 A.M.–3 P.M.	3		
10 A.M.–4 P.M.	5		
11 A.M.–3 P.M.	3		
Noon–6 P.M.	1		

Note: Types of industries represented are business and human services (including government agencies, medical institutions, educational institutions, nonprofit organizations, employment agencies, consulting firms, and publishing firms), 39%; banking/financial/insurance, 28%; manufacturing/processing, 21%; retail/wholesale sales and distribution, 7%. Number of employees in represented companies: very small companies (1–100), 24%; small companies (101–1,000), 37%; medium-sized companies (1,000–10,000), 24%; large companies (over 10,000), 10%.

Source: *1986 AMS Flexible Work Survey* (Willow Grove, PA: Administrative Management Society, 1986), pp. 3, 4, 9.

A.M., and employees in about 40% of the firms must be in by 10 A.M.. Therefore, the effect of flextime for most employees is to give them about 1 hour leeway in terms of starting before 9 or leaving after 5. Similarly, about 15% of the employers made 9 A.M.–3 P.M. their core period, while another 28% made their core period 9 A.M.–4 P.M.

The Pros and Cons of Flextime

Some flextime programs have been quite successful.[2] Because less time is lost due to tardiness, the ratio of worker-hours worked to worker-hours paid (a measure of productivity) increases. It has also been shown to reduce absenteeism and to cut down on "sick" leave being used for personal matters. The hours actually worked seem to be more productive, and there is less slowing down toward the end of the workday. Workers tend to leave early when work is slack and work later when it is heavy. The use of flextime also seems to be related to an increased receptiveness on the part of employees to changes in other procedures.

Flextime is also advantageous for the workers. It may reduce the tedium associated with the timing of their work and democratize their work. It also tends to reduce the distinction between managers and workers and requires more delegation of authority by supervisors.

There are also disadvantages. Flextime is complicated to administer and may be impossible to implement where large groups of workers must work interdependently.[3] It also requires the use of time clocks or other time records, and this can be disadvantageous from the point of view of workers.

Surveys covering some 445 employees (including drug companies, banks, electronics firms, and government agencies) indicate that the percentage of employees reporting productivity increases as a result of flextime programs ranges from a low of 5% or 10% in some firms to about 95% in one airline. On the whole, about 45% of employees involved in flextime programs report that the program has resulted in improved productivity.[4] The failure rate of flextime is also remarkably low, reportedly 8%, according to one study.[5]

Conditions for Success

There are several things you can do to make your flextime program more successful.[6] *Management resistance*—particularly at the supervisory level and particularly before the program is actually tried—has torpedoed several programs before they became operational, so supervisory indoctrination programs are important prerequisites to success. Second, flextime is usually more successful with clerical, professional, and managerial jobs, and less so with factory jobs (the nature of which tend to demand interdependence among workers). Third, experience indicates that the greater the flexibility of a flextime program, the greater the benefits the program can produce (although the disadvantages, of course, multiply as well). Fourth, how the program is installed is important; a flextime project director to oversee all aspects of the program should be appointed, and frequent meetings should take place between supervisors and employees to allay their fears and clear up misunderstanding. A pilot study, say, in one department, is advisable.[7]

Also, flextime may be especially valuable for the employer when the group must share limited resources. For example, computer programmers often spend as much as two-thirds of their time waiting to make computer runs. In situations like these, flextime may be especially beneficial. As one researcher concludes,

"because flextime expands the amount of time that the computer is available to the programmer, this allows its usage to be spread over more hours, and the time in queues to make runs and get output back is reduced."[8]

THREE- AND FOUR-DAY WORKWEEKS

four-day workweek An arrangement that allows employees to work four ten-hour days instead of the more usual five eight-hour days.

A number of employers have also switched to a **four-day workweek**. Here employees work four 10-hour days instead of the more usual five 8-hour days.

Advantages

Compressed workweek plans have been fairly successful since they have several advantages (see Table 9.2). Productivity seems to increase since there are fewer start-ups and shutdowns. Workers are more willing to work some evenings and Saturdays as part of these plans. According to one study 80% of the firms on such plans reported that the plan "improves business results"; three-fifths said that production was up and almost two-fifths said that costs were down. Half the

TABLE 9.2 Advantages and Disadvantages of Flextime (in rank order)

RANK ORDER	ADVANTAGES
1	Improves employee attitude and morale
2	Accommodates working parents
3	Results in fewer traffic problems—workers can avoid congested streets and highways
4	Increases production
5	Decreases tardiness
6	Accommodates those who wish to arrive at work before interruptions begin
7	Facilitates employee scheduling of medical, dental, and other types of appointments
8	Decreases absenteeism
9	Accommodates the leisure-time activities of employees
10	Decreases turnover
	DISADVANTAGES
1	Lack of supervision during all hours of work
2	Finding key people unavailable at certain times
3	Causes understaffing at times
4	Accommodating employees whose output is the input for other employees is a problem
5	Inability to schedule meetings at convenient times
6	Employee abuse of flextime program
7	Keeping track of hours worked or accumulated is a problem
8	Planning work schedules is difficult
9	Inability to coordinate projects

Source: *1986 AMS Flexible Work Survey* (Willow Grove, PA: Administrative Management Society, 1986), p. 4.

firms also reported higher profits. Even the four-day firms *not* reporting positive results reported that cost and profit factors at least remained the same. One study suggests that the four-day workweek is generally effective (in terms of reducing paid overtime, reducing absenteeism, and improving efficiency). Furthermore, workers also gain; there is a 20% reduction in commuter trips and an additional day off per week. Additional savings (for example, in child care expenses) may also occur.[9]

However, there has not been a lot of experience with shortened workweeks, and it is possible that the improvements are short-lived. In one study, for instance, 4-day weeks resulted in greater employee satisfaction and productivity and less absenteeism when evaluated after 13 months, but these improvements were not found after 25 months.[10] A recent review of 3-day, 38-hour workweeks concluded that compressed workweek schedules have significant positive and long-lasting effects on the organization if handled properly. Regardless of individual differences, those employees who had experienced the 3/38 schedule reacted favorably to it, particularly if they had participated in the decision to implement the new program and if their jobs had been enriched by the schedule change. Fatigue did not appear to be a problem in this survey.[11]

Disadvantages

There are also some disadvantages, some of them potentially quite severe (see Table 9.2). Tardiness, for example, may become a problem. Of more concern is the fact that fatigue was cited by a number of firms as a principal drawback of the four-day workweek (note that fatigue was a main reason for adopting 8-hour days in the first place).

OTHER FLEXIBLE WORK ARRANGEMENTS

job sharing
A concept that allows two or more people to share a single full-time job.

work sharing
A temporary reduction in work hours by a group of employees during economic difficulties to prevent layoffs.

flexiplace
A flexible work arrangement in which employees are allowed or encouraged to work at home or in a satellite office closer to home.

Employers are also taking other steps to accommodate their employees' needs. **Job sharing** is a concept that allows two or more people to share a single full-time job. For example, two people may share a 40-hour-per-week job, with one working mornings and the other working afternoons. About 10% of the firms questioned in one survey indicated that they allow for job sharing.[12] **Work sharing** refers to a temporary reduction in work hours by a group of employees during economic hard times as a way of preventing layoffs; thus 400 employees may all agree to work (and get paid for) only 35 hours per week in order to avoid having the firm lay off 30 workers. **Flexiplace**, in which employees are allowed or encouraged to work at home or in a satellite office closer to home, is another example of a flexible work arrangement that is becoming more popular today.

Telecommuting is another option. Here employees work at home, usually with video displays, and use telephone lines to transmit letters, data, and completed work back to the home office. For example, Best Western Hotels in Phoenix is using the residents of the Arizona Center for Women, a minimum-security prison, as an office staff. It is estimated that some 7 million Americans are telecommuting today, in various jobs from lawyer to clerk to computer expert.[13]

Still other employers, especially in Europe, are switching to a plan they call *flexyears*. Under this plan, employees can choose (at six-month intervals) the number of hours they want to work each month over the next year. A full-timer, for instance, might be able to work up to 173 hours a month. In a typical flexyear arrangement, an employee who wants to average 110 hours a month might work 150 hours in January (when the children are at school and when the company needs extra help to cope with the January sales). In February, she may work only 70 hours because she wants to, say, go skiing.[14]

USING QUALITY CIRCLE PROGRAMS

quality circle
A group of five to ten specially trained employees who meet on a regular basis to identify and solve problems in their work area.

A **quality circle** is a group of five to ten specially trained employees who meet for an hour once a week for the purpose of spotting and solving problems in their work area.[15] The circle is usually composed of a work group, people who work together to produce a specific component or service.

STEPS IN ESTABLISHING A QUALITY CIRCLE

The four steps in establishing and leading a quality circle include *planning, training, initiation*, and *operating*.

Planning the Circle

The planning phase usually takes about one month and typically begins with a top-level executive making the decision to implement the quality circle (QC) technique. This usually leads to identifying and selecting a consultant who will assist top management in implementing the quality circles in the firm. However, in some cases an in-house *facilitator* will be identified and sent out for special circle methods training. The facilitator then returns to the firm and handles the tasks the consultant would otherwise have been responsible for.

One of the most important steps in this first phase involves selecting the quality circle *steering committee.* The steering committee becomes the group that directs quality circle activities in the organization. The committee is usually multidisciplinary in that it draws on employees from functions such as production, human resources, quality control, training, marketing, engineering, finance, and the union. The success of the quality circle concept often hinges on how committed to the technique workers feel top management is. Therefore, the steering committee almost always has at least one or two top managers as members.

The steering committee has several responsibilities. Perhaps most important, it should establish circle objectives in terms of the kinds of *bottom-line improvements* they would like to see. Yardsticks include reduced errors and enhanced quality, more effective teamwork, and an increased attitude of problem prevention. At the same time, the steering committee determines actions that are considered outside the charter of the circles—for instance, benefits and salaries, employment practices, policies on discharging employees, personalities, and grievances. The steering committee also chooses the in-house facilitator, the person who will be responsible for daily coordination of the firm's quality circle activities. In most cases the facilitator devotes full time to the quality circle tasks and is responsible for such specific quality circle duties as

coordinating the activities of the circles, training leaders for each circle, attending circle meetings and providing expert advice and backup coordination, and maintaining records to reflect circle achievements.

Initial Training

In the second phase, the facilitator and pilot project circle leaders meet (usually with the consultant) to be trained in basic QC philosophy, implementation, and operation. This training course typically takes four days and includes various activities. On the first day, the consultant meets with the leaders to discuss the nature and objectives of quality circles. On the remaining days, trainees use case studies to learn quality circle leadership techniques.

Initiating the Circles

This quality circle is examining a production problem involving an automated soup manufacturing process.

Initiating the pilot program's circles begins with department managers conducting quality circle familiarization meetings with employees, with the facilitator, circle leaders, and (ideally) an executive participating as speakers. Employees are told they will be contacted later regarding whether or not they want to join a circle. Then, circle leaders contact each employee to determine circle membership, and the circles are constituted. The facilitator distributes manuals for circle leaders at this point; they contain an overview of the QC idea, as well as an explanation of data collection and problem-solving techniques.

The Circle in Operation

Next, each circle can turn to problem solving and analysis. In practice, this involves five steps: problem identification, problem selection, problem analysis, solution recommendations, and solution review by management. Each step is explained next.

Problem Identification. The problems identified by circle members are usually mundane and may not be especially interesting to anyone outside the circle's work area. These problems might include how to keep the area cleaner, how to improve the work group's product quality, or how to speed up the packing of the work group's crates.

Problem Selection. Next, members select the number one problem they wish to focus on. Circle members usually know better than anyone else what impediments are making it difficult for them to do their jobs. They are thus in the best position to prioritize problems.

Problem Analysis. In this next step, circle members collect and collate data relating to the problem and analyze them using data collection, analysis, and problem-solving techniques for which they are especially trained.

It is important to stress that it is the group members, rather than outside experts or the group leader/supervisor, who solve the problem. A big benefit—perhaps the biggest benefit—derived from quality circles is the sense of satisfaction that members get from being involved in the actual problem analysis process. If they are prohibited from analyzing the problem by an inept leader, they will not only miss this sense of satisfaction but may actually resent (rather than be committed to) implementing the solution. Quality circles are as much a people-building opportunity as a quality-improving one. To derive all the benefits from a circle the members themselves must thus be involved in the problem selection, analysis, and implementation.

Solution Recommendations. The group's solution is then presented to management by group members, with the aid of charts and graphs they prepare themselves. The presentation is usually oral rather than written and more often than not is voluntarily prepared by employees on their own time at break, lunch, and after work.

Solution Review and Decision by Management. Quality circles usually operate through the management chain of command. The presentation is made to the individual to whom the supervisor (frequently the circle leader) reports, not to the steering committee or to somebody on the executive level. Top managers may be present as observers.

According to one source, from 85% to 100% of circle suggestions are approved by the manager, often in the presentation meeting itself. Occasionally the manager will need some verification of studies done and may even ask a staff person to assist in the verification. In those unusual instances when a manager must decline a recommendation, he or she is trained to explain why it was turned down, so as not to dampen the enthusiasm of the circle members.

There are several predictable problems that quality circles encounter which you should plan to avoid. One is skepticism on the part of employees that this is "just another program," one that will probably evaporate once the initial excitement wears off. Gaining top management's commitment to quality circles is thus crucial for such a program's success. Some employees will complain that the circles are doomed because "management never pays attention to us anyway." Here again, the best solution is to underscore top management's commitment to the quality circle program. Selecting problems outside the circle's areas of expertise is another familiar problem, as when a production group decides to work on a shipping problem. Circle leaders therefore should be trained to keep their members on track and to caution them to focus on problems within their own areas—where they are the experts. Other area's problems can be handed over to those areas' circles or handed up the line where interdisciplinary teams can try to tackle them. Finally, some of the greatest resistance to the circles will come not from the employees but from the supervisors themselves, perhaps because they fear that the circles may undermine their traditional authority. This is another reason why top management's commitment is essential—to let supervisors know that the firm takes this program very seriously.

MAKING QUALITY CIRCLES MORE EFFECTIVE

By the mid-1980s, the original wave of employer enthusiasm and support for quality circle programs had begun to wane for several reasons. Perhaps the main reason was that many QCs failed to produce measurable cost savings for the sponsoring employers, in part because their bottom-line aims were too vague. And in many other firms, the participative QCs simply proved incompatible with the management styles and cultures existing in those firms.

Studies of quality circle effectiveness generally confirm the often spotty records achieved by quality circle programs.[16] Many of the so-called studies of QC effectiveness are actually anecdotal case studies. Here the researcher simply reports his or her observations regarding the effectiveness of quality circle programs based on perceived results and estimated dollar savings. In one such study, a company steering committee reported annualized savings of over

$400,000 in one year, reflecting a three-to-one return on investment. Such results are impressive. However, since it is a case study, it's not possible to conclude that it was the quality circle program itself that created the savings rather than, say, some parallel changes such as improvements in the firm's financial incentive plan.

Results of more careful experimental studies of quality circles generally indicate that the majority of such programs are successful but that many still are not. One, for instance, showed an initial improvement in attitudes, behaviors, and effectiveness but then a decline in each to the initial levels.[17] Results of one recent quality circle study are probably typical. As the researcher concluded: "The fact that two of the four circles had actual cost savings ($9,600 and $11,280), none had noticeable quality improvements, all worked on job improvement issues, and that three of the four were evaluated as successful by facilitators seem indicative of general quality circle performance."[18] Such spotty results, plus the cost of implementing their circles, prompted many firms to phase out their QC programs.

Rather than throw out the baby with the bath water, though, many firms today are taking steps to make their QCs more effective. Some firms are turning to what are in essence second-generation QCs, ones that are geared more specifically to preventing problems through a companywide quality management approach. To distinguish them from traditional quality circles, these new work groups are often referred to by other names such as employee participation teams (EPTs) or quality improvement program teams.

Some of the differences between traditional quality circles and these "second generation" employee participation teams can be illustrated by the new programs now in place at Northrop Corporation and at Honeywell Corporation. At Northrop the groups are no longer voluntary and now involve all workers on the shop floor. The groups are responsible for setting improvement targets and keeping reports on their progress, and they compete with other groups to achieve goals. At Honeywell Corporation (one of the pioneer users of QCs), the company has replaced about 700 of its traditional quality circles with about 1,000 work groups. As is characteristic of the second generation of quality circles, these Honeywell groups are generally not voluntary and involve instead most shop-floor employees. And, in contrast to the bottom-up approach of quality circles, problems are often assigned to work groups by management.

Beyond tightening up the running of the teams themselves, other firms have found that instituting quality circles without corresponding changes in management styles and company culture is futile.

One major banking company ran into problems with their quality circle program: Their experience is illustrative of these problems, and how they were solved by one service company.[19] The bank instituted quality circle teams to improve efficiency, communications, and team spirit. However, when asked how they liked their quality circle program, participants reportedly used words such as "nuisance," "a joke," and "very unproductive" to describe circle meetings. Participants claimed there were no ideas generated during the sessions, that the sessions themselves were dull and boring, and that most felt a lack of emotional involvement. Most also claimed they really didn't understand what they were to do or accomplish with the quality circles. An investigation led to the conclusion that it was widespread apprehension among employees that was undermining the program: The underlying culture at the bank was just not conducive to a participative quality circle program.

Several changes were implemented to change this culture. In a program like this, the bottom-up participation that management wants to encourage must be fostered by a fundamental change in philosophy from top management on down. In other words, managers must make it clear to everyone that they will listen to and act on employees' input, they must create trust and confidence by example, and they must take other steps to show in concrete terms that they mean what they say about wanting employee input. This firm began by changing some policies that contradicted this sort of approach. For example, the annual polygraph examinations (which were legal at the time) and the time clock were eliminated. An interdepartmental employee quality circle committee was instituted. This committee in turn established a two-way dialogue between management and workers through regularly scheduled meetings. The basic theme of these meetings was company profitability for survival; it was explained repeatedly that such profitability was the surest route to job security.

As a result of their experience, the consultants to this project suggest the following guidelines for introducing a QC program:

1. Level with the chief executive officer about the organization's current state of management and employee thinking.
2. The CEO and senior officials must be models for change in implementing constructive ideas.
3. Make the program voluntary.
4. In the beginning, provide group members with solvable problems. Be prepared to change structures, policies, and procedures. Keep objectives simple.
5. Emphasize that these are not complaint sessions.
6. Communicate and educate every person in the organization about the program. Emphasize that group members need support.
7. Establish a climate of care and feedback.
8. Involve line managers and make them leaders of the groups whenever possible.
9. Provide additional training to complement quality circle training. Introduce the circles as an ongoing process of good supervision to the supervisors themselves.[20]

▸ Total Quality Management Programs

INTRODUCTION

As the experience of the banking company suggests, there is a lot more to implementing successful quality circle programs than organizing several groups and telling them to "go at it." At the bank, for instance, management philosophies and styles had to be changed, and a new company culture (complete with no more polygraphs, and so on) had to be molded.

In fact, we now know that the most successful QC programs aren't run in vacuums, but are often part of comprehensive companywide quality improvement programs: The teams' quality improvement projects are conducted within companywide plans and quality targets and goals; efforts are made to ensure the full support of middle managers; extensive training opportunities are provided; and the culture and reward systems are geared to encouraging employee involvement. Comprehensive quality improvement programs like this go by many names

Computer Applications in Incentives: Attitude Surveys

According to a Louis Harris survey reported by *Industry Week*,[1] in 1989 fewer employees were satisfied with their jobs than in 1988. The reasons given were based on a dissonance between expectations and experiences in ethical management behavior, concern for employees, and communication. Mergers and acquisitions have only exacerbated the feelings of mistrust of management. Companies that value their workers apparently get input from them on company policies, perceptions of management, work or company restructuring, benefit packages (current and proposed changes), or reasons for turnover.

The use of employee attitude surveys has grown since 1944 when the National Industrial Conference Board "had difficulty finding fifty companies that had conducted opinion surveys."[2] Today most companies are aware of the need for employee anonymity, the impact of both the design of the questions and also their sequence, and the importance of effective communication, including the purpose of the survey before it's taken and feedback to the employees after it's completed. Computerization of surveys can provide anonymity, if there is no audit trail to the user, especially for short answers that are entered rather than written or typed on a distinguishable machine.

Survey software packages are available that generate questions in a number of standard topics and can be customized by modifying existing questions or by adding questions. If the survey is computerized, then reports can be generated with ease to provide snapshots of a given period of time, trend analysis, and breakdowns according to various demographics. You may be interested in responses by age, sex, job categories, departments, divisions, functions or geography.

The survey may be conducted by placing microcomputers in several locations convenient for employee use. Employees are advised where the computers will be, for how long, and when the data will be collected (e.g., daily at 5 p.m. for 3 weeks). The screen should not be viewable by supervisors or passersby. While there may be some risk that employees will take the survey more than once, there are comparable risks with other methods. (For example, who completes the survey mailed to the employee's home?)

In addition to the survey topics previously listed, managers may be interested in knowing how they are perceived by their peers and subordinates. Packages that may be customized are available which allow the manager to complete a self-assessment tool used to compare self-perceptions to the opinions of others. This comparison may assist in the development of a more effective manager. The same protection for anonymous participation is required as is the necessity for communicating the purpose of the assessment and feedback to participants.

Employees who are leaving the company are often asked their opinions during a formal or informal exit interview. Concerned about future references, employees often state innocuous reasons for leaving, reasons known to be acceptable to the company. However, if the exiting employees could respond to computer questions (such as, If you could change some aspect of supervision, what would it be? If you could change some aspect of our benefits, what would it be?) and be assured that answers would not be looked at until several people had responded, more helpful information might be learned.

[1]Stanley J. Modica, "Whatever It Is, It's Not Working," *Industry Week*, Vol. 238, no. 14 (July 17, 1989), p. 27.

[2]Martin Wright, "Helping Employees Speak Out About Their Jobs and the Workplace," *Personnel*, Vol. 63 (September 1986), p. 56.

including total quality management (TQM), quality improvement process (QIP), and total quality control (TQC).[21] Regardless of labels, TQM is always a total corporate focus on meeting and often exceeding customers' expectations and significantly reducing the cost resulting from poor quality by shaping a new management system and corporate culture.[22]

Also regardless of the labels, most total quality management programs follow common guidelines. One TQM expert summarizes these as follows:[23]

1. Realize the need for improvement and find a compelling reason for adopting a TQM process.
2. Design an organization structure for managing the quality "journey."
3. Explicitly state your firm's quality policy and show everyone in the firm that you are committed to it.
4. Devise ways to continually seek customer feedback.
5. Measure employee attitudes particularly with respect to TQM, identify quality "gaps," and devise means to close the gap.
6. Use quality improvement teams to identify and solve quality problems.
7. Make quality improvement part of your overall planning process such that quality improvement priorities can then permeate the quality improvement work of all employees and teams.
8. Turn the organization chart upside down: In other words, make it clear that each manager is really there to provide the support and assistance that his or her subordinates need to improve quality and satisfy the company's customers.
9. Have all teams use the *plan, do, check, act cycle: Plan* the quality improvement process for each unit by identifying the goals to be achieved, the tasks to be accomplished, and the customers' needs to be met; *do* implement the plan by having the teams actually do the work; *check* the results continuously by monitoring customers; and *act* on the feedback to improve the system.
10. TQM requires extensive training and retraining of all employees. For example, they need training in statistical problem-solving techniques and in interpersonal communications.
11. Continually involve managers in the quality improvement process to ensure you have their commitment.
12. Celebrate your successes and recognize your heroes.
13. Get the commitment of your vendors to the total quality management process.

The Malcolm Baldrige National Quality Award is an honor bestowed on selected companies such as Federal Express.

Two major awards recognize companies that institute highly effective quality improvement programs. As explained later, the Deming Prize (named after Dr. W. Edwards Deming and awarded by the Union of Japanese Scientists and Engineers) was the first such award. In 1987 Congress established the Malcolm Baldrige National Quality Award to promote quality awareness, recognize quality achievements of U.S. companies, and publicize successful quality strategies.[24] The award is considered by many in the United States to be the "Nobel Prize" for quality. Each year up to two companies can be chosen from three business categories—manufacturing, service, and small business—to receive the award. The 150 judges pore over information regarding such things as each applicant firm's leadership, human resources, quality assurance programs, and customer satisfaction. Firms winning the Baldrige have included Cadillac Motor Car Division, Federal Express Corp., and Motorola, Inc.

Miami-based Florida Power & Light Company (FPL), Florida's largest utility, was the first company outside Japan to win the Deming Prize. Awarded annually (and since 1986 outside Japan) by the Union of Japanese Scientists and Engineers, the prize recognizes outstanding achievement in quality control management. The steps taken by the company to achieve this difficult task help to illustrate the activities involved in implementing comprehensive company-wide total quality management programs, and the role of HR management in doing so.

THREE BASIC FEATURES OF THE PROGRAM

FPL's quality improvement program contains three basic components or phases: policy deployment, quality in daily work, and quality improvement teams. Policy deployment "is the process through which company management works together to focus resources on achieving customer satisfaction"; quality in daily work means "that each employee applies quality improvement practices to all his or her activities to improve the quality of products and services"; and quality improvement teams mean that employees working in teams engage in solving quality problems.

Policy Deployment

One problem traditional quality circle programs run into is a lack of direction of the circles themselves. In many applications, in other words, the circles themselves identify problems to study without any coherent direction from top management regarding what the high-priority problems should be.

Policy deployment provides such direction. At FPL the policy deployment process begins by finding out what FPL customers actually want and then compiling these needs in a customer needs table. In other words, annual surveys are made of customer needs and these are then summarized and prioritized into five or six main categories of needs. These needs then drive the "corporate agenda"—the plans regarding where the company and the team should focus their efforts.

The point of the policy deployment process, according to the company, is to concentrate company resources on a few priority issues. Recently, for instance, the objectives emerging from the customer needs assessment included:

- Improve public confidence in safety programs.
- Reduce the number of complaints to the Florida Public Service Commission.
- Improve the reliability of electric service.
- Continue to emphasize safe, reliable, and efficient operation of nuclear plants.
- Strengthen fossil unit reliability, and availability.

These objectives are then translated into more measurable terms, such as "increase fossil plant availability to about 95% of total time by 1994." Measurable objectives like these, which FPL refers to as *policies*, are then distributed to all FPL employees via what they call their *Annual Guide to Corporate Excellence*. This publication folds out into a wall chart and, as the company puts it, "Hung in offices throughout FPL, it reminds one and all to check whether their QI teams and daily work are contributing to the corporate vision."[25] It is thus through this process that the measurable quality objectives (or "policies") of FPL are deployed throughout the company, thus giving this process its name.

In summary, the entire thrust of quality improvement at FPL is to identify customer needs and then satisfy them. Company plans, objectives, and measurable policies are formulated based on the annual survey of customer needs. These policies (and top management's corresponding plans for FPL) then become the guidelines within which the quality improvement teams do their work.

Quality Improvement Teams

FPL uses four kinds of quality improvement teams or circles: functional teams, cross-functional teams, task teams, and lead teams. (In total, about 1,700 quality improvement teams operate at FPL.) *Functional teams* are comprised of volunteers who typically work together as natural work units on a daily basis. These teams generally choose their own problems and meet one hour each week. The basic aim here is to involve first-line employees in improving their daily work activities so as to enhance the quality of their work life and to develop their skills. *Cross-functional teams* are ongoing teams that are formed to address problems that cut across organizational boundaries. *Task teams* are comprised of members who are appointed from one or more departments to work on specific problems. Task teams spend various amounts of time in meetings, depending upon the urgency of the problem. They are usually constituted specifically to support policy deployment or locally identified high priority issues. When the problem of a task team is solved, the team is disbanded.

Finally, *lead teams* are headed by a vice-president or other manager and serve as steering committees for the activities of the teams that operate in their areas. It is the lead team, for instance, that determines how and which team members are selected to serve on which teams, and establishes guidelines regarding frequency and duration of team meetings.

The basic customer-oriented policies (such as "improve reliability of service") emerging from the policy deployment process forms the framework within which quality improvement teams focus their efforts. While the teams then generally select their own problem topics (called "themes"), certain topics are off limits. These include the company's union agreement, absenteeism, pay, salaries, promotions, the apprenticeship program, and in general safety rules produced by a joint safety committee.

Four Main Features of FPL QI Teams

It is informative to review four main features of FPL's quality improvement teams: training, facilitators, computerization, and "quality improvement stories."

Team members undergo extensive training and this is one area in which the company's human resource management system has a major impact on its quality circle and quality improvement programs. One training program is called "Team member training." This is open to all employees who are in the process of becoming team members. In this two-day program employees receive training in special techniques such as statistical quality control and in group decision-making techniques such as brainstorming. Workbooks, case studies, and video presentations are used.

Other training programs include the "team member training course," for "team members who are ready to move on to more advanced statistical quality control," the "team leader training course" (in which individuals about to assume team leadership learn about such things as how to identify, prioritize, analyze, and solve quality-related problems), and the "project team training course" for individuals forming project teams.

Three other features of FPL quality improvement teams are pertinent. *Facilitators*—employees who have completed team leader training and want to move on to provide assistance to other teams—coach team leaders and help coordinate quality improvement efforts between teams and functional units. The company also uses a *management information system* called "Information Central." This keeps the files on team membership and on the projects each team is working on. Finally, teams present their proposals regarding problems and solutions to management via *quality improvement stories*. This is basically a seven-step structured set of instructions as follows:

> *Step 1.* The team must provide an overall reason for solving the targeted problem, based on FPL's stated high-priority needs.
>
> *Step 2.* Here, they must describe the current situation. To do this, tools such as histograms, Pareto diagrams, control charts, graphs, and check sheets are used to collect data on all aspects of the theme or problem area and to study the theme from various viewpoints.
>
> *Step 3.* In this third *analysis step*, the cause of the problem is identified using techniques such as cause-and-effect diagrams and Pareto diagrams.
>
> *Step 4. Countermeasures* are presented based on tools and techniques such as cost-benefit analysis and an analysis of countermeasure barriers and potential aids. In this step, the structured instructions for the FPL story format call for the team to develop and evaluate potential countermeasures, develop an action plan, and obtain cooperation and approvals for their proposed plan.
>
> *Step 5. Results* are reported to confirm that the problem and its root causes have been decreased and that the target for improvement has been met. Here (as is stressed throughout the company's quality improvement program) results are reported in concrete terms, for instance using histograms and Pareto diagrams.
>
> *Step 6.* Next, the team must explain how it has *standardized* the countermeasures it presented. They must explain how the work process has been changed, how employees have been trained on the revised process and countermeasures, and how the team suggests replicating the countermeasures in other company departments.
>
> *Step 7.* Finally, *future plans* are summarized, usually with respect to moving the team on to its next problem or theme.

With about a thousand stories presented per year there is no shortage of examples of quality improvement team efforts. One team discovered that it was bird droppings, not inclement weather, that caused some of FPL's high-voltage lines to short out fairly often. As another example, FPL put many of its teams to work analyzing the company's trucks, equipment, and processes, with the aim of improving safety. One quality improvement team decided to focus on a safety problem faced by meter readers (who are the company's most injured employees): frequent dog bites. A team decided that if they could find a way to warn the meter readers that a dog was normally around the house, the employee would be better prepared. Furthermore, if necessary, a call could be made to the home just prior to the meter reader's visit, so that the dog could be locked up. Their recommendation was that a postcard should be placed into bills periodically asking if the homeowner has a dog. They got 20,000 cards back. Meter reading at FPL is done with an electronic reading machine. This electronic reader is now programmed to beep when a meter reader gets to a home where there is a dog. Calls are also made to the homes of dog owners on the morning of the visit. This has resulted in a huge increase in safety companywide.

Quality in Daily Work

In addition to using quality improvement teams, FPL uses "quality in daily work" (QIDW) to spread the gospel of satisfying customer needs throughout the company. Here, individual employees are urged to identify their "customers" and their needs, keeping in mind that the customer may be external or internal (i.e., within the company). It is also stressed that employees should understand their job responsibilities and the quality standards to be met. The basic thrust of QIDW is to encourage individual employees to take a quality improvement–perspective approach to their work, on an individual basis.

HUMAN RESOURCE MANAGEMENT AND THE QUALITY IMPROVEMENT EFFORT

FPL managers and employees learned a lot about how to build an effective QI program over the years. For example, FPL's initial approach to quality improvement was to institute just a quality circle program. These circles were generally not operating within the context of quality improvement objectives and policies like those now produced by the company's policy deployment process. Furthermore, the original circle program was erroneously designed around a separate, parallel "organization within an organization." Each of these original teams had facilitators appointed to them and the regular departmental supervisors were told in no uncertain terms "don't mess with them." Based on FPL's experience, there are many personnel-related steps to take that can help to ensure a more effective quality improvement program. Some HR guidelines based on FPL's experience are as follows:

- Recognize that instituting quality improvement teams and a quality improvement program means doing so *within the context of a policy deployment–type process* so that the program has direction.
- *Do not institute quality circles as separate, parallel organization structures.* Instead, institute the teams in layers from top to bottom using the natural organization structure to form the teams. Simply trying to superimpose quality circles outside of the normal chain of command elicited resistance from the supervisors, many of whom made comments like "I don't know what these people are doing—they're not helping me do my job."[26] The teams should, to the greatest extent possible, be composed of natural work units. Employ existing reporting systems and remain compatible with existing organization structure as much as possible.
- *Do not treat the quality improvement program as if it has an end.* It is important to emphasize that a quality improvement program that is successful is really a systematic way of doing business, one that has no end.
- *Training is essential.* In Japan (and in a successful program like that at FPL) quality improvement is successful largely because training continually upgrades the problem analysis and statistics skills of even first-line employees. This training is crucial both to provide the required analytical skills and also to emphasize the firm's commitment to the program.
- Whether or not the company achieves its quality goals is, although very important, almost secondary. The important thing is creating an organization of *self-directed quality seekers* within the framework of customer-oriented quality objectives and policies. Give employees the skills they need to analyze and solve problems; then get them to analyze and solve the problem, and follow up on their suggestions. The new culture that emerges is at the heart of the program.

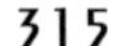

- FPL found that a *management by objectives program is not enough* to accomplish these sorts of aims, by the way. MBO did not provide for the kind of analysis and follow-up demanded by a quality improvement program.
- Do not focus exclusively on "boosting productivity," or assume that emphasizing quality means that productivity will necessarily fall. In fact (and this is very important) FPL and other companies instituting these kinds of programs find that *as quality increases so does productivity*—and costs will actually go down. However, some quality improvements will be more cost effective than others, so it is still important to keep quality improvements cost effective.
- As previously explained, assessing customer needs as a first step in policy deployment should result in a corporate agenda of prioritized needs to be met. It is important here to *work on only a few needs* at once: Do not dilute your resources.
- *Employee recognition and employee satisfaction are essential.* Personal satisfaction and intrinsic rewards come from the responsibility of seeing that "quality begins with me." It also comes from encouraging employees to identify and devise countermeasures against problems, and from giving them the tools and leeway necessary to get this job done. This attitude, FPL found, develops over time from confidence that "my ideas count, they will be given an audience, and they can affect change." In fact, when FPL asked their employees early in the program what they wanted most they didn't say "more money." They said they wanted their suggestions implemented and wanted recognition from their supervisors; these are two important things that the quality improvement teams provided for.
- Also reward *individual and team efforts in a more concrete manner*, not generally with money but with rewards like merchandise or pins. These, the company found, "stay with the employee-suggester for years, and serve as continual recognition/reinforcers of a job well done." Furthermore, it is essential that individual and team suggestions be implemented.
- Quality circle programs are generally best implemented within the context of more comprehensive quality improvement programs. Related to this, remember that a quality improvement program is more than the sum of its parts: it is not just an incentive program, or a quality circle program or a training program, for instance. Most important, *quality improvement requires instituting a new culture in the firm*, one that values (and focuses all employees' thoughts on) the central issue of continually seeking out and instituting incremental quality improvements to meet customer needs. Individually (through QIDW) and collectively (through quality improvement teams), employees thus must be given the skills to identify, analyze, and solve quality problems, as well as the motivation to do so. Producing a new company culture that encourages this kind of behavior may be the biggest challenge that a quality-seeking company (and its HR unit) has to face; the task of molding a company like this can take years. In any case the first steps need to be taken by top management: "From the board of directors to every supervisor, management must adopt the principles and language of quality, follow the processes, set examples and guide others. A substantial commitment is necessary for employee education, and for awareness and recognition programs. These programs require reallocation of budgets and personnel, and will take time to produce results but will be worth it."[27]
- In carrying out changes like these, one of the most remarkable aspects of the quality improvement program effort is that *both the company and the employee gain.* Satisfying customer needs is the *raison d'être* of any company: An effective quality improvement program will help to ensure that customer needs are met, and that the company is successful. But at the same time (as this is occurring), comprehensive companywide quality improvement programs like FPL's also help ensure that in many ways employees' most important personal needs—not just for money, but to achieve difficult goals and to grow and to self-actualize—are met. In doing so, QI programs boost (or should boost) the quality of work life in the firm, and to that extent the employees' personal growth, satisfaction, and sense of accomplishment.

CREATING SELF-DIRECTED TEAMS

THE NATURE OF SELF-DIRECTED TEAMS

Individuals in this team of construction workers have a high level of commitment to the group and its work goals, due, in part, to their shared experiences.

In the 1950s psychologist Rensis Likert formulated what, for later generations of organizational experts, would become the classic explanation of cohesive work teams.[28] He said, first, that the leadership and other processes of the organization must be such as to ensure that each employee will view the experience as to ensure that each employee will view the experience as one that builds and maintains his or her sense of personal worth and importance.[29] Furthermore, said Likert,

> The most important source of satisfaction for this desire is the response we get from the people we are close to, in whom we are interested, and whose approval and support we are eager to have. The face-to-face groups with whom we spend the bulk of our time are, consequently, the most important to us. [Therefore,] management will make full use of the potential capacities of its human resources only when each person in an organization is a member of one or more effectively functioning work groups that have a high degree of group loyalty.[30]

From a practical point of view, Likert might have added, employees probably tend to develop their first and perhaps most intense commitment to the people in their work groups and to their group's norms and ideals. To many people at work the company itself—what it is, where it's going, what its values are—is often little more than an abstraction. But the people with whom they work everyday—the door trim team at Saturn, the menswear group at the Penney's store, the securities group at Goldman Sachs—are real and worthy of their commitment. You can't let your teammates down.

For many firms the ideal situation, as Likert saw, is to organize work around small close-knit teams whose goals are high and whose aims are the same as the firm's. And this is what more and more firms today are doing, firms such as Saturn, Toyota, Corning, and Texas Instruments. Specifically, they and others like them are increasingly organizing the work around small self-contained teams, teams that are variously labeled self-managed teams, high-performance teams, autonomous work groups or, simply, superteams.[31] Whatever they're called, all such **self-directed teams** have certain things in common. Each team generally performs natural sets of interdependent tasks, such as all the steps needed to assemble a Saturn door. They all use consensus decision making to choose their own team members, solve job-related problems, design their own jobs, and schedule their own break time. And their jobs are always enriched in that they carry out many of the jobs formerly accomplished by the management staff, such as dealing with vendors and overseeing quality. Finally, self-directed teams are also highly trained to solve problems, to design jobs, to interview candidates, and to understand financial reports.

self-directed teams Highly trained work groups that use consensus decision making and broad authority to "self-direct" their activities.

SELF-DIRECTED TEAMS IN ACTION

Several examples of such companies can illustrate the basic approach. When it opened its Blacksburg, Virginia, plant in 1989, Corning, Inc., "decided to use multiskilled, team-based production in tandem with automation as a means of 'challenging people instead of forcing them to do dumb, stupid jobs.'" As a result, "The firm sorted through 8,000 job applicants and hired 150 with the best problem-solving ability and the willingness to work in a team setting. The majority had finished at least one year of college."[32] The relative expense of these kinds of practices has apparently paid off. A Blacksburg team, comprised of workers with interchangeable skills, can retool a line to produce a different type of filter in only ten minutes, for instance, six times faster than workers in traditional filter plants. Corning is now converting its 27 other factories to team-based production, as well.

The practices used at Toyota Motor Manufacturing, USA, also illustrate the basic approach. Team building here begins with the firm's commitment to the teamwork principle. For example, their "Team Member Handbook" states their commitment "To work as a team with mutual respect and equal opportunities for all: our abilities are maximized when we work together in a cooperative manner toward common goals. Mutual trust and respect for each other are the basis on which team spirit is developed."[33]

At most Japanese auto firms, including Toyota and Honda, employees wear uniforms in an effort to emphasize that everyone belongs to a team.

All factory work is then organized around work teams. For example, there are teams of about five to ten people in charge of door installations, assembly trim, power train conveyance, stamping tool and die, and body weld. There are no individuals on the plant floor; every Toyota employee belongs to a work team.

Toyota then uses several practices to assure smoothly functioning work teams. Once hired, employees are steeped in the terminology and techniques of teamwork.[34] As mentioned, there are no employees in the plant, only team members. There is no employee handbook; there is a team member handbook. There is no employee activities association; there is a team member activities association, and so on. "Teamwork training" begins during initial orientation, as new team members meet their teams and are trained in the interpersonal techniques that make for good teamwork. The closeness is enhanced by letting work teams recruit and select their own new members.

The monthly *Toyota Topics* magazine then continuously publicizes the accomplishments of team work heroes. An article in the June 1990 *Toyota Topics* describes the accomplishments of a body weld maintenance group this way:

> Because production goes on around the clock, each maintenance shift plays an important role in making sure everything on the line is running smoothly when the next shift takes over. One example of how this group pulls together in a difficult situation was evident when a wiring harness inside a robot went bad one night in late April. Several team members removed the bad harness while several others removed the good wiring harness from a robot not in use and reinstalled it in the other robot. "The problem occurred at about 3:30 a.m.," Dennis Waltz explained. "By the time the first shift came on at 6:30 we had the countermeasure in place." That took a lot of teamwork and hard work.

The article goes on to explain that Dennis and the group were especially grateful to an earlier shift group leader in body weld, who had often stayed after his shift to assist in technical training and problem solving.[35]

The feeling that they're all there to share the group's work comes across when you speak with team members themselves. For example, one body shop team member said that one of the things he liked about Toyota was the "Toyota teamwork—on every other job I've had people wouldn't contribute or help each other out, but it's the complete opposite here. Here everyone depends on someone else."[36]

Building Employee Commitment

Empowering Work Teams

Employees tend to be committed to employers who let them "actualize" at work—in other words, develop and use their skills and gifts to the maximum degree. Empowering their work teams and enriching their jobs thus helps employers like Saturn win their employees' commitment.[37]

Ideally, job enrichment and worker empowerment should always go hand-in-hand.[38] Enrichment means building challenge and achievement into workers' jobs by changing their jobs' content—letting them order and inspect their own goods, schedule their own day, and so forth. Empowerment, as the term is increasingly used, means authorizing *and enabling* workers to do their jobs.

Enriching jobs should thus give employees more challenging jobs to do, while empowering them should give them the skills, authority, and discretion they need to actually do them. "Enrich and empower" at work thus means doing three things: (1) Enriching employees' jobs by changing the content of these jobs —letting employees plan their own work, control their own scrap, and obtain their own supplies, for instance; (2) giving them the training, tools, and support they need to enable them to do their new jobs; and (3) insisting that all managers follow through by actually letting the workers use their new, broader authority to do their jobs. The total effect, as we'll see, can be exhilarating for all concerned.

Saturn provides a good example of the three "enrich and empower" components in action. At Saturn, all production work is accomplished by work teams, and the work assignments of all work teams are highly enriched. This is evident from the 30 "work unit functions" for which all teams are responsible.

A sampling of the 30 functions is presented in Figure 9.1. As you can see, all teams are responsible for a broad range of functions, including to "resolve their own conflicts; plan their own work; make their own job assignments; make selection decisions of new members; perform to their own budget; and obtain their own supplies." Saturn's documenting of the 30 functions clarifies the responsibilities of each team and helps legitimate the broad-based authority the teams are to exercise.

Second, the teams and their members get the skills and tools to do their jobs, since "empowerment" without "ability" is just a sham. For example, you can't expect workers to use consensus decision making and make their own job assignments without giving them the training and decision-making tools that will help them do so.

Saturn thus provides both the tools and the training. RASI cards are examples of the tools. As shown in Figure 9.2, RASI stands for Responsibility, Approval, Support, and Inform. Teams are trained to use the RASI process to specify the level of each person's involvement as they use consensus decision making to solve team problems and determine courses of action. Suppose a door installation team decides to look for new suppliers for some item. Individual roles and responsibilities will be assigned according to the RASI process: Mike and Tina might be responsible for initiating the action and ensuring it is carried out; Lynn and Karl must approve or veto the recommended action; and so on.

But training in the RASI process is just a fraction of the empowerment-producing training these people receive. New Saturn team members get at least

Each Saturn team will

1. Use consensus decision making: No formal leader (will be) apparent in the process. . . . All members of the work unit who reach consensus must be at least 70% comfortable with the decision, and 100% committed to its implementation.
3. Make their own job assignments: A work unit . . . ensures safe, effective, efficient, and equal distribution of the work unit tasks to all its members.
5. Plan their own work: The work unit assigns timely resources for the accomplishment of its purpose to its customers while meeting the needs of the people within the work unit.
6. Design their own jobs: This should provide the optimum balance between people and technology and include the effective use of manpower, ergonomics, machine utilization, quality, cost, job task analysis, and continuous improvement.
8. Control their own material and inventory: Work directly in a coordinated manner with suppliers, partners, customers, and indirect/product material resource team members to develop and maintain necessary work unit inventory.
9. Perform their own equipment maintenance: Perform those tasks that can be defined as safe, and those they have the expertise, ability, and knowledge to perform effectively.
13. Make selection decisions of new members into the work unit: A work unit operating in a steady state has responsibility for determining total manpower requirements, and selection and movement of qualified new members from a candidate pool will be in accordance with the established Saturn selection process.
14. Constantly seek improvement in quality, cost, and the work environment: The work unit is responsible for involving all work unit members in improving quality, cost, and the work environment in concert with Saturn's quality system.
18. Determine their own methods: The work unit is responsible for designing the jobs of its team members consistent with the requirements of the Saturn production system and comprehending the necessary resources and work breakdown required.
21. Provide their own absentee replacements: The work unit is responsible for the attendance of its members. . . . The work unit will be required to plan for and provide its own absentee coverage.
22. Perform their own repairs: The work unit will have the ultimate responsibility for producing a world-class product that meets the needs and requirements of the customer. In the event a job leaves the work unit with a known or unknown nonconformance to specification, the originating work unit will be accountable for corrective action and repair.

FIGURE 9.1
Sampling of the 30 Saturn Work Team Functions

320 hours of training in their first year and then receive at least 92 hours per year thereafter. And, remember that at Saturn "training" doesn't just mean how to screw in bolts or position doors. Instead, the emphasis is on broadening the employee and developing new skills, with the aim of making each person "all he or she can be." The emphasis is on learning new things and on broadening the person's horizons, for instance with problem-solving training.

Third, high-commitment firms follow through with supervisory action. In other words they make sure their managers actually let their people do their jobs as assigned. Team members thus made comments like these:

> "You don't have anyone who is supervisor—you don't experience supervision—we are supervised very loosely, if at all."

FIGURE 9.2 Saturn RASI Card

RASI— Clarifies level of involvement; agree who owns the task, assign that person the "R". All other group members would assume A, S, or I positions depending on their role in relation to the task. Only one "R" can be assigned per task.

	Individual Roles and Responsibilities
R Responsibility	• Owns task (accountable and responsible) • Initiates action • Ensures the action is carried out • Performs tasks or delegates to appropriate others • Involves other team members appropriately
A Approval	• Approves or vetos the recommended action • Assures members are properly involved • Ensures resources are available for implementation • Sets parameters
S Support	• Provides support and resources • Shares knowledge and expertise • Questions and challenges • Offers options and input
I Inform	• Listens to assure understanding • Uses information • Keeps feedback loops open • Questions and expresses opinions

(FRONT)

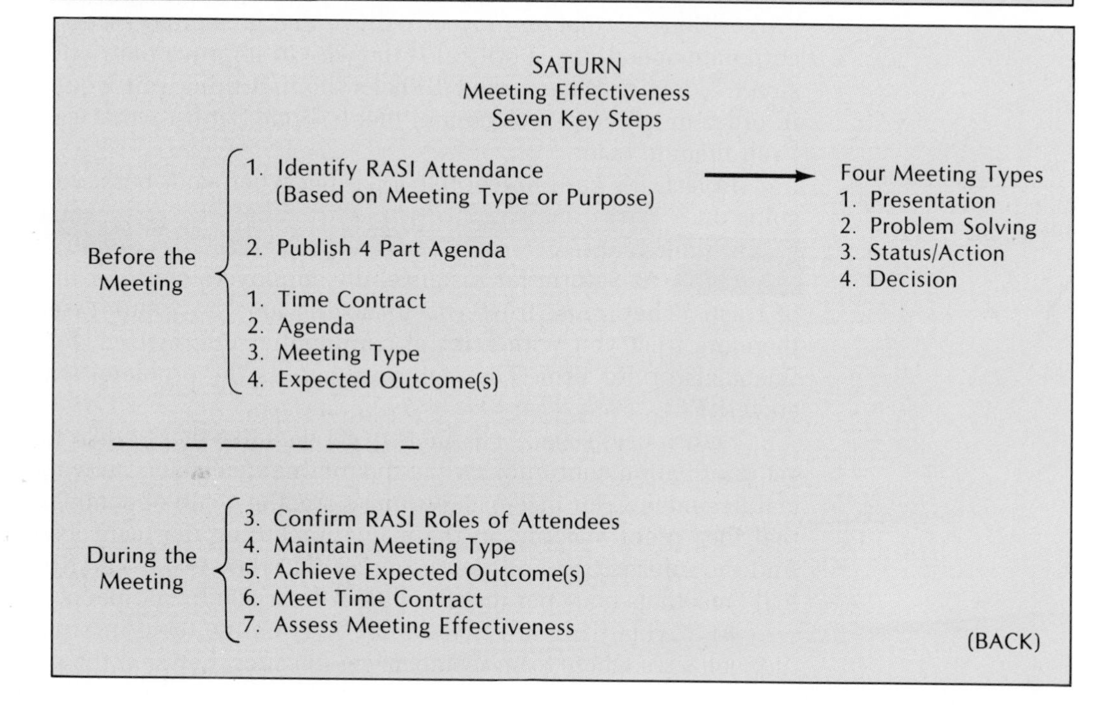

SATURN
Meeting Effectiveness
Seven Key Steps

Before the Meeting

1. Identify RASI Attendance (Based on Meeting Type or Purpose) → Four Meeting Types
   1. Presentation
   2. Problem Solving
   3. Status/Action
   4. Decision
2. Publish 4 Part Agenda
   1. Time Contract
   2. Agenda
   3. Meeting Type
   4. Expected Outcome(s)

During the Meeting

3. Confirm RASI Roles of Attendees
4. Maintain Meeting Type
5. Achieve Expected Outcome(s)
6. Meet Time Contract
7. Assess Meeting Effectiveness

(BACK)

"We become responsible to the people (the team members) we work with everyday. What I do affects my coworkers; in other firms you're treated like children—here we're treated like adults."

"In terms of budgeting, such as buying tools, we go through our own suppliers and choose the best and we know that in that way we'll affect the quality of the car."

"If an issue comes up the work team handles it—all on our team must be agreeable or we don't leave the room until we're 100% committed, 70% comfortable."

"We are responsible to make our jobs more cost effective, . . . etc."

MAKING SELF-DIRECTED TEAMS MORE EFFECTIVE

As you can see from our discussion to this point, several factors contribute to the success of any effort aimed at organizing work around self-directed teams. These include a commitment to the teamwork principle, steeping employees in the terminology and techniques of teamwork, and continuously publicizing the accomplishments of teamwork heroes.

Two teamwork success ingredients should be further emphasized. First, as summarized in Table 9.3, *insufficient training* is consistently listed as the single biggest barrier to effective self-directed teams. We've seen that at firms such as Toyota, team-member training is extensive. As also summarized in Table 9.3, team training usually emphasizes problem solving and communication skills. For example, 83% of responding companies with team training teach team members problem-solving skills. There is also an emphasis on training team members to communicate more effectively and to hold more effective meetings.[39]

Second, *communications* between top management and the teams should be open and freely flowing if the teams are to do their jobs. As one study of team-based employee programs recently concluded, "These results support the proposition . . . that employees believe that greater access to information about corporate operations is critical if they are to improve their effectiveness in decision making."[40] When asked "What's the first thing you would tell a boss to do in order to get employee commitment?," one Saturn work team said in unison, "Tell them to listen."[41]

In fact, it's hard to feel like a partner when your boss won't tell you what's going on.[42] Firms that want to win their employees' commitment therefore tend to give their people extensive data on the performance of and prospects for their operations. At Saturn, for instance, the employees consider this mostly a matter of trust. "They must trust you to do the job," says one assembler, "and they therefore trust you with a lot of confidential information, for instance, on the financials of our firm. They tell you 'here is the problem, what would you do about it?' "[43]

Saturn uses several channels to get data like these down to the troops. They get information continuously via the internal television network and from financial documents, for instance. Furthermore, the chain of command is fairly flat so that the "point" people on the teams, including the team leaders, can quickly find the information and the resources that they need. The firm also has "town hall" meetings once per month, with at least 500 to 700 people attending.

At Toyota there are twice-a-day five-minute team information meetings at their job sites where team members get the latest news on the plant. There is also

TABLE 9.3 Developing Self-directed Teams

BARRIERS TO SELF-DIRECTED TEAMS	
Barriers	Percentage of respondents that mentioned each
Insufficient training	54
Supervisor resistance	47
Incompatible systems	47
Lack of planning (implementation was too fast)	40
Lack of management support	31
Lack of union support	24

The results are from a 1990 survey by DDI, AQP, and *Industry Week*.

TYPES OF TEAM TRAINING	
Type of training	Percentage of responding companies that offer each
Problem solving	83
Meeting skills	65
Communication skills	62
Handling conflict	61
SDT (self-directed teams) roles and responsibilities	58
Quality tools and concepts	56
Evaluating team performance	39
Work flow and process analysis	36
Selecting team members	35
Presentation skills	35
Influencing others	29
Budgeting	14

The results are from a 1990 survey by DDI, AQP, and *Industry Week*.

Source: Richard Wellins and Jill George, "The Key to Self-directed Teams," *Training & Development Journal*, April 1991, p. 29.

a TV in each work site break area. The TV runs continuously, presenting plantwide information from the in-house Toyota broadcasting center. There are also quarterly "round table" discussions between two management and selected nonsupervisory staff. They also have an in-house newsletter.

Federal Express uses daily Fed Ex TV broadcasts—seen by about 70% of Fed Ex employees each day—to disseminate company information almost instantaneously.

The point is, companies like these work very hard to keep the lines of communication wide, wide open. This in turn contributes to the sense of trust that's crucial if the self-directed teams are to be relied upon, for instance, to schedule their own break times and to deal with their vendors. In turn, this commitment to open communication and fostering trust reflects the values of these firms' top managers, in particular the value of putting their people first and building their firms around highly committed employees.

▶ CHAPTER REVIEW

SUMMARY

1. *Flextime* is a plan whereby employees' flexible work days are built around a core of midday hours, such as 11 to 2. It seems to improve employee attitudes and morale, increases production, and decreases tardiness; however, unavailability of key people at certain times and, generally, scheduling activities like meetings can be problems. Flextime and other flexible work arrangements are aimed in part at tapping employees' needs to be treated as responsible human beings, and to that extent they boost quality of work life.
2. A *quality circle* is a group of five to ten specially trained employees who meet for an hour once a week for the purpose of spotting and solving problems in their work area.
3. Steps in establishing a *quality circle* program include planning, training, initiating, and operating. Problems to be aware of include: attitudes such as, "This is just another program," and "Management pays no attention to our ideas"; selecting problems outside the circle's expertise; problems that are too difficult to handle; scheduling problems; and fear of interference from the union.
4. Comprehensive companywide quality improvement programs like that at FPL basically aim at improving the customer-orientation of a firm by appealing to employees' higher-order needs. A framework of objectives or policies is first laid out based on satisfying customers' needs. Then a comprehensive program of training, incentives, quality circles, and (in general) culture-modification is carried out to appeal to employees' sense of responsibility. As at FPL, it's not just the specific techniques (like selection, or training, or incentives) that ensure high performance; the culture of the firm—its basic shared values and attitudes—is important, too.
5. Self-directed teams carry out interdependent tasks, and use consensus decision-making to choose the other team members, solve job-related problems, design their own jobs, schedule their own break times, and do much of their own work planning and review. At firms such as Saturn, such teams contribute to building commitment, by enriching and empowering employees' jobs.

KEY TERMS

flextime	work sharing	quality circle
four-day workweek	flexiplace	self directed teams
job sharing		

DISCUSSION QUESTIONS

1. What steps would you take to institute self-directed work teams?
2. Explain the steps involved in operating a circle (including problem identification and problem selection).
3. Explain how you would set up a companywide quality improvement program.
4. Explain the pros and cons of flextime and the four-day workweek.

▶ APPLICATION EXERCISES

RUNNING CASE

CARTER CLEANING COMPANY

The Quality Circle Program

As a recent graduate and a person who keeps up with the business press, Jennifer is not unfamiliar with the benefits of nonfinancial motivation such as quality circle programs.

Jack has actually installed a total quality program of sorts at Carter, and it has been in place for about five years. He holds employee meetings periodically but particularly when there is a serious problem in a store—such as very poor quality work or too many breakdowns—he schedules a meeting with all the employees in that store and meets with them as soon as the store closes. Hourly employees get extra pay for these meetings, and they actually have been fairly useful in helping Jack to identify several problems. Jennifer is now curious as to whether these employee meetings should be formalized and perhaps a formal quality circle program initiated.

Questions

1. Would you recommend a quality circle program to Jennifer? Why? Why not?
2. Given what you know about the supervision of these stores, would you recommend a management by objectives program for store managers? Why or why not?
3. Are new work arrangements such as flextime or four-day workweeks practical at Carter? Why?

CASE INCIDENT: *Is the Honeymoon Over at Flat Rock?*

It began in 1986 with such great promise: Mazda Motor Corp. was going to build an assembly plant in Flat Rock, Michigan—just outside Detroit—that would eventually provide thousands of high-paying and secure jobs. By 1990, however, conditions had seriously deteriorated and Mazda's honeymoon with Flat Rock seemed to have come to an end. Four top U.S. managers had quit the company since 1988, and now Japanese executives had taken the senior posts that Americans once held. The company was on its fourth director of labor relations since hiring began in 1986. Unionized workers were boycotting Mazda's suggestion box, a cornerstone of Japanese-style management. Workers complained of job stress and increased injuries and absenteeism was running approximately ten percent, which was higher than other Japanese plants in the U.S. But let's start at the beginning, when Mazda began the task of staffing its new plant.

All job candidates applying at Flat Rock for assembly jobs went through a five-step screening process that was specifically designed to assess interpersonal skills, aptitude for teamwork, planning skills, and flexibility. This screening process encompassed a lot more than taking a paper-and-pencil test, enduring a few interviews, and providing some references. At Mazda, applicants also had to perform tasks that simulated jobs that they might do on the actual factory floor. For example, applicants might bolt fenders onto a car or attach hoses in a simulated engine compartment. This helped Mazda's management to match workers' abilities with specific job requirements, and it also provided applicants with a realistic preview of what they were getting into.

For the initial work force, 10,000 out of 100,000 candidates passed the five-step screening process. Of these, only 1,300 were hired. The cost of screening each one of these new employees was about $13,000 per worker.

But new hirees didn't just report to the factory floor and join a work team. First, they had to undergo detailed training. That started with a three-week hodgepodge of sessions in which they learned about interpersonal relations, charting quality, stimulating creativity, and the like. This was followed by three days devoted to learning Mazda's philosophy of increasing efficiency through continual improvement. After this basic training came job-specific training. Line workers, for example, spent five to seven more weeks picking up specific technical skills, then spent another three or four weeks being supervised on the assembly line.

Why did Mazda go to all this expense and effort? The company wanted literate, versatile employees who would accept the company's emphasis on teamwork, loyalty, efficiency, and quality. Moreover, it wanted to weed out any troublemakers. What Mazda got was a work force more educated and nearly a generation younger than the old line auto workers at most Big Three plants. Mazda also wanted smooth relations with its workers. So it invited the United Auto Workers to organize the plant's employees before operations began. What went wrong? How could all this preparatory work have resulted in a disgruntled work force? The following highlights a few of the causes.

The high turnover among U.S. managers created instability. U.S. managers complained about being left out of the information network. Major decisions were controlled by Mazda executives in Japan or local Japanese superiors. Each morning, for instance, U.S. managers get a "laundry list" from their Japanese "adviser" telling them just what they were supposed to do that day.

Workers' complaints were numerous. They said that the Japanese managers didn't listen to them. They criticized the company's policy for continuous improvement, claiming that this translates into a never-ending push to cut the number of worker-hours spent building each car. To support their argument, they pointed out that American plants use fifteen to twenty percent more workers to produce a similar number of cars. Workers said that even Mazda's team system, which is supposed to give employees more authority and flexibility, is a gimmick. Power is gradually taken away from team leaders; flexibility is a one-way street that management uses to control workers; and the team system encouraged workers to pressure each other to keep up the rapid pace.

Japanese executives at Flat Rock responsed by publicly lambasting workers for lacking dedication. As to the high turnover in the management ranks, Japanese executives admit that Mazda's practice of making decisions by consensus often gives the appearance of keeping authority away from its U.S. executives. But Japanese executives can also claim that the American workers just have not adapted to Mazda's way of doing business. In spite of worker complaints, management can proudly point to the fact that independent experts give Flat Rock's cars high marks for quality; every bit, in fact, as good as those built in Japan.

Questions

1. Contrast Mazda's selection and training process with those more typically used for manufacturing workers.
2. "Mazda's management doesn't understand the American worker." Do you agree or disagree with this statement? Discuss.
3. What suggestions, if any, would you make to Flat Rock's top management regarding its employee practices that might reduce absenteeism, turnover, and improve employee job satisfaction?

Source: Stephen Robbins, *Organizational Behavior* (Englewood Cliffs, NJ: Prentice Hall, 1993), pp. 593–5. Based on W. J. Hampton, "How Does Japan Inc. Pick Its American Workers?," *Business Week,* October 3, 1988, pp. 84–88; G. A. Patterson, "Mazda-UAW's Michigan Honeymoon Is Over," *The Wall Street Journal,* April 17, 1990, p. B1; and J. J. Fucini and S. Fucini, *Working For the Japanese* (New York: Free Press, 1990).

HUMAN RESOURCE MANAGEMENT SIMULATION

Incident B addresses some of the topics involved in alternative work arrangements. Incident H involves the creation of self-directed teams. Does your team feel the organization is ready for some of these techniques, or should you wait until you have all your other problems ironed out?

Quality issues may be addressed through the quality-budget expenditure that you will be making each decision period. The quality of the goods produced (or services rendered) by your firm is listed on the report each period. An index has been established with a range from 100 (high quality) down to 0 (extremely low quality). Currently, the organization has a quality index of 50. This represents "average" quality. Although quality control is not normally the responsibilty of a Human Resources Director, it is incorporated in the simulation because it is closely related to such HR areas as grievances, training, and turnover. Currently, quality is checked at the end of the process (post-process control). Various programs are provided in the simulation manual to address the quality issue in your organization.

Your team will also be given the opportunity to support an employee-participation program. Programs range from voluntary problem-solving groups to formal quality-circle programs. To simplify the decision-making process, you must decide whether to budget $10,000 each quarter for a participation program. The budget includes funds for establishing and supervising these new programs as well as paying the time of employees when they are attending meetings and not doing their regular job.

▶ NOTES

1. Donald Peterson, "Flexitime in the United States: The Lessons of Experience," *Personnel*, Vol. 57 (January–February 1980), pp. 21–37; *1987 AMS Flexible Work Survey* (Willow Grove, PA: Administrative Management Society, 1987); Commerce Clearing House, "ASPA/CCH Survey on Alternative Work Schedules," June 26, 1987; Bureau of National Affairs, "Flexible Work Schedules," *Bulletin to Management*, September 3, 1992, pp. 276–277.
2. Peterson, "Flexitime in the United States," p. 22.
3. Stanley Nollen, "Does Flexitime Improve Productivity?" *Harvard Business Review*, Vol. 56 (September–October 1977), pp. 12–22.
4. Ibid.
5. Stanley Nollen and Virginia Martin, *Alternative Work Schedules Part One: Flextime* (New York: AMACOM, 1978), p. 44.
6. Peterson, "Flexitime in the United States," pp. 29–31.
7. Another problem is that some employers let workers "bank" extra hours by working, say, 45 hours one week so they need work only 35 hours the next week. The problem is that in the 45-hour week the employees should, strictly speaking, be paid an overtime rate for the extra 5 hours worked. Some employers handle this problem by letting hours worked vary from day to day but requiring each week to be a 40-hour week. Others are experimenting with letting workers accumulate hours and be paid overtime if necessary. See J. C. Swart, "Flexitime's Debit and Credit Option," *Personnel Journal*, Vol. 58 (January–February 1979), pp. 10–12.
8. David Ralston, David Gustafson, and William Anthony, "Employees May Love Flextime, but What Does It Do to the Organization's Productivity?" *Journal of Applied Psychology*, Vol. 70, no. 2 (1985), pp. 272–279.
9. Herbert Northrup, "The Twelve Hour Shift in the North American Mini-steel Industry," *Journal of Labor Research*, Vol. 12, no. 3 (Summer 1991), pp. 261–278; Charlene Marner Solomon, "24-hour Employees," *Personnel Journal*, Vol. 70, no. 8 (August 1991), pp. 56ff.
10. Ibid. See also John Ivancevich and Herbert Lyon, "The Shortened Work Week: A Field Experiment," *Journal of Applied Psychology*, Vol. 62, no. 1 (1977), pp. 34–37.
11. Janina Latack and Lawrence Foster, "Implementation of Compressed Work Schedules: Participation and Job Redesign as Critical Factors for Employee Acceptance," *Personnel Psychology*, Vol. 38, no. 1 (Spring 1985), pp. 75–92. Interestingly, one way to determine how your employees will react to a 4/40 or flextime work schedule apparently is to ask them ahead of time. One study suggests that these will be the reactions that emerge three to six months after commencement of the program. See Randall B. Dunham, Jon L. Pierce, and Maria B. Castaneda, "Alternative Work Schedules: Two Field Quasi-Experiments," *Personnel Psychology*, Vol. 40, no. 2 (Summer 1987), pp. 215–242.
12. Commerce Clearing House, *Ideas and Trends*, February 26, 1982, p. 61.
13. "These Top Executives Work Where They Play," *Business Week*, October 27, 1986, p. 132.
14. "After Flexible Hours, Now It's Flexiyear," *International Management* (March 1982), pp. 31–32.
15. This section based on Donald Dewar, *The Quality Circle Guide to Participation Management* (Englewood Cliffs, NJ: Prentice-Hall, 1980). See also James Thacker and Mitchel Fields, "Union Involvement in Quality-of-Work Life Efforts: A Longitudinal Investigation," *Personnel Psychology*, Vol. 40, no. 1 (Spring 1987), pp. 97–112. They conclude that unions' fears of QCs may be misplaced and that after quality-of-work-life involvement, "A majority of the rank and file members who perceived QWL—quality of work life—as successful gave equal credit for the success to both union and management. The rank and file members who perceived QWL as unsuccessful tended to blame management for the lack of success." See also Anat Rafaeli, "Quality Circles and Employee Attitudes," *Personnel Psychology*, Vol. 38 (Fall 1985), pp. 603–615; Mitchell Lee Marks, Edward Hackett, Philip Mirvis, and James Grady, Jr., "Employee Participation in a Quality Circle Program: Impact on Quality of Work Life, Productivity, and Absenteeism," *Journal of Applied Psychology*, Vol. 71, no. 1 (February 1986), pp. 61–69, and "Quality Circles: A New Generation," *BNA Bulletin to Management*, Vol. 38, no. 2 (January 1987), pp. 10–15. See also Preston C. Bottger and Philip Yetton, "Improving Group Performance by Training in Individual Problem Solving," *Journal of Applied Psychology*, Vol. 72, no. 4 (November 1987), pp. 651–657, and Murray R. Barrick and Ralph Alexander, "A Review of Quality Circle Efficacy and the Existence of Positive-Finding Bias," *Personnel Psychology*, Vol. 40, no. 3 (Autumn 1987), pp. 579–592.
16. This is based on Everett Adam, Jr., "Quality Circle Performance," *Journal of Management*, Vol. 17, no. 1 (1991), pp. 25–39.
17. R. W. Griffin, "Consequences of Quality Circles in an Industrial Setting: A Longitudinal Assessment," *Academy of Management Journal*, Vol. 31, no. 2 (1988), pp. 338–358; reported in Adam, "Quality Circle Performance," p. 27.
18. Adam, "Quality Circle Performance," p. 38.
19. Gopal Pati, Robert Salitore, and Saundra Brady, "What Went Wrong with Quality Circles?" *Personnel Journal* (December 1987), pp. 83–89.
20. Ibid., p. 86.
21. Thomas Berry, *Managing the Total Quality Transformation* (New York: McGraw-Hill, 1991), p. 1.
22. Ibid., p. xv.
23. These are adapted from ibid., pp. 53–54.
24. This is based on Shari Caudron, "How Xerox Won the Baldrige," *Personnel Journal* (April 1991), p. 100.
25. "Building a Quality Improvement Program at Florida Power & Light," *Target* (Fall 1988), p. 6.
26. Private conversation with Wayne Brunetti, Executive Vice-President, Florida Power & Light Company.
27. "Building a Quality Improvement Program at Florida Power & Light," *Target* (Fall 1988), p. 8.
28. The following is adapted from Gary Dessler, *Winning Commitment* (New York: McGraw-Hill, 1993), Chapter 5.
29. Rensis Likert, *New Patterns of Management* (New York: McGraw-Hill, 1961), p. 103.
30. Ibid., p. 104.
31. See for example Brian Dumaine, "Who Needs a Boss?" *Fortune* May 7, 1990, p. 52; David Hames, "Productivity-Enhancing Work Innovations: Remedies for What Ails Hospitals?" *Hospital & Health Services Administration*, Vol. 36, no. 4 (Winter 1991), pp. 551–552.
32. John Hoerr, "Sharpening Minds for a Competitive Edge," *Business Week*, December 17, 1990, p. 72.
33. Toyota Motor Manufacturing, USA, Inc., Team Member Handbook, February 1988, p. 11.

34. This is based on internal company documents and is adapted from Dessler, *Winning Commitment*, Chapter 5.
35. *Toyota Topics*, June 1990, p. 8.
36. Dessler, *Winning Commitment*, Chapter 5, personal interview.
37. For a discussion see ibid., Chapters 2, 5, and 10.
38. This is based on ibid., Chapter 10.
39. See Richard Wellins and Jill George, "The Key to Self-Directed Teams," *Training & Development Journal* (April 1991), pp. 26–31.
40. Richard Majuka and Timothy Baldwin, "Team-Based Employee Involvement Programs: Effects of Design and Administration," *Personnel Psychology*, Vol. 44 (1991), p. 806.
41. Dessler, *Winning Commitment*, Chapter 4.
42. This is based on ibid.
43. Personal interview.

CHAPTER 10

APPRAISING PERFORMANCE

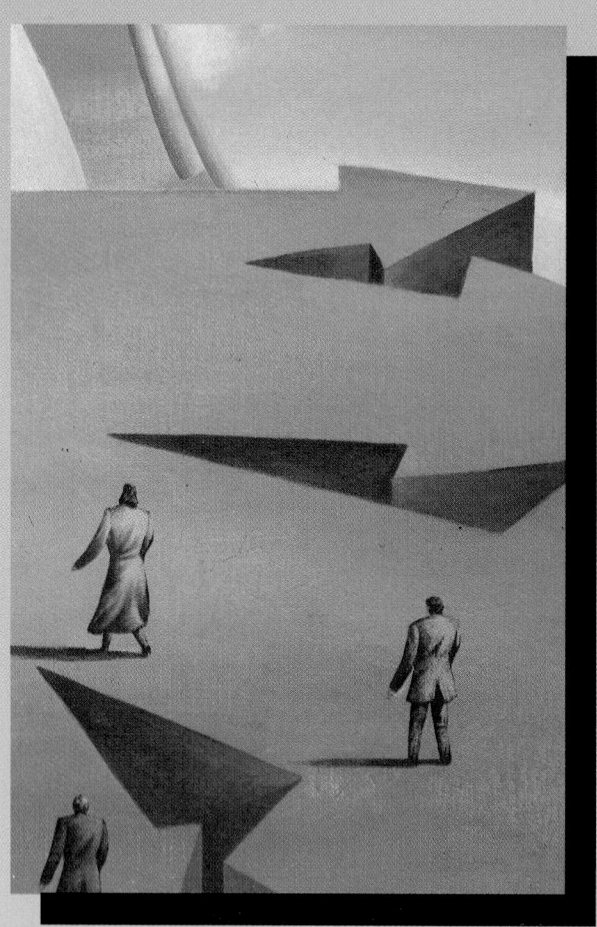

OVERVIEW

In this chapter, we explain how to use several appraisal techniques and how to avoid common performance appraisal problems. Next, we explain how to review the appraisal with your subordinate. When you finish studying this chapter, you should be able to administer at least four performance appraisal tools; list and discuss the pros and cons of several appraisal tools; explain the problems to be avoided in appraising performance; and discuss the pros and cons of using different potential raters to appraise a person's performance.

You have probably already had some experience with performance appraisal scales. For example, some colleges ask students to rank instructors on scales such as the one in Table 10.1. Do you think this is an effective scale? Do you see any ways to improve it? These are two of the questions you should be in a better position to answer by the end of this chapter.

▶ Why Should You Appraise Performance?

There are several reasons to appraise performance.[1] Appraisals provide information upon which *promotion* and *salary* decisions can be made. Second, they provide an opportunity for you and your subordinate to sit down and *review* the subordinate's work-related behavior. This in turn allows both of you to develop a plan for correcting any deficiencies the appraisal might have unearthed and lets you reinforce the things the subordinate does right. Finally, the appraisal can and should be central to your firm's career planning process because it provides a good opportunity to review the person's career plans in light of his or her exhibited strengths and weaknesses.

Evaluating Faculty for Promotion and Tenure

Classroom Teaching Appraisal by Students

Teacher ____________ Course ____________
Term ____________ Academic Year ____________

Thoughtful student appraisal can help improve teaching effectiveness. This questionnaire is designed for that purpose, and your assistance is appreciated. Please do not sign your name.

Use the back of this form for any further comments you might want to express; use numbers 10, 11, and 12 for any additional questions that you might like to add.

Directions: Rate your teacher on each item, giving the highest scores for exceptional performances and the lowest scores for very poor performances. Place in the blank space before each statement the rating that most closely expresses your view:

Exceptional			Moderately Good			Very Poor	Don't Know
7	6	5	4	3	2	1	X

____ 1. How do you rate the agreement between course objectives and lesson assignments?
____ 2. How do you rate the planning, organization, and use of class periods?
____ 3. Are the teaching methods and techniques employed by the teacher appropriate and effective?
____ 4. How do you rate the competence of the instructor in the subject?
____ 5. How do you rate the interest of the teacher in the subject?
____ 6. Does the teacher stimulate and challenge you to think and to question?
____ 7. Does he or she welcome differing points of view?
____ 8. Does the teacher have a personal interest in helping you in and out of class?
____ 9. How would you rate the fairness and effectiveness of the grading policies and procedures of the teacher?
____ 10. ____________

Faculty Evaluation Rating Forms

____ 11. ____________
____ 12. ____________
____ 13. Considering all the above items, what is your overall rating of this teacher?
____ 14. How would you rate this teacher in comparison with all others you have had in the college or university?

Table 10.1
Classroom Teaching Appraisal by Students

Source: Richard I. Miller, *Evaluating Faculty for Promotion and Tenure* (San Francisco: Jossey-Bass Publishers, 1987), pp. 164–165.

THE SUPERVISOR'S ROLE IN APPRAISAL

The supervisor usually does the actual appraising and must be familiar with the appraisal techniques, understand (and avoid) problems that can cripple an appraisal, and conduct the appraisal fairly.

The human resource department serves a policy-making and advisory role. In one survey, for example, about 80% of the firms responding said the human resource department provides *advice and assistance* regarding which appraisal tool to use but leaves final decisions on appraisal procedures to operating division heads; in the rest of the firms the personnel office prepares detailed forms and procedures and insists that all departments use them.[2] Personnel is also responsible for training supervisors to improve their appraisal skills. Finally, personnel is responsible for monitoring the use of the appraisal system, particularly in regard to ensuring that the format and criteria being measured comply with EEO laws and don't become outdated. In one survey, for example, half the employers were in the process of revising their appraisal programs, while others were conducting reviews to see how well their programs were working.[3]

STEPS IN APPRAISING PERFORMANCE

Performance appraisal involves three steps: define the job, appraise performance, and provide feedback. *Defining the job* means making sure that you and your subordinate agree on his or her duties and job standards. *Appraising performance* means comparing your subordinate's actual performance to the standards set in step one; this usually involves some type of rating form. Third, performance appraisal usually requires one or more *feedback sessions* during which the subordinate's performance and progress are discussed and during which plans are made for any development that is required.

PERFORMANCE APPRAISAL PROBLEMS

Some appraisals fail because subordinates are not told ahead of time exactly what is expected of them in terms of good performance. Other appraisals fail because of problems in the forms or procedures used to actually appraise the performance; a lenient supervisor might rate all subordinates "high," for instance, although many are actually unsatisfactory. Still other problems arise during the interview–feedback session, problems that include arguing and poor communications. These and other problems are summarized in Figure 10.1.

▶ HOW TO DEFINE THE JOB

CLARIFY WHAT PERFORMANCE YOU EXPECT

The job description often isn't sufficient to clarify what you want your subordinate to do. This is because most are written not for specific jobs but for groups of jobs. All sales managers in the firm might have the same job description, for

Problems can occur at any stage in the evaluation process. Some of the pitfalls to avoid in performance appraisals are:

1. *Lack of standards.* Without standards, there can be no objective evaluation of results, only a subjective guess or feeling about performance.

2. *Irrelevant or subjective standards.* Standards should be established by analyzing the job output to ensure that standards are job related.

3. *Unrealistic standards.* Standards are goals with motivating potential. Those that are reasonable but challenging have the most potential to motivate.

4. *Poor measures of performance.* Objectivity and comparison require that progress toward standards or accomplishment of standards be measurable. Examples of measurable standards include quantifiable measures such as 10 rejects per 1,000 units or 10 sales per 100 calls, as well as qualitative measures, such as projects completed or not completed.

5. *Rater errors.* Rater errors include rater bias or prejudice, halo effect, constant error, central tendency, and fear of confrontation.

6. *Poor feedback to employee.* Standards and/or ratings must be communicated to the employee in order for the performance evaluation to be effective.

7. *Negative communications.* The evaluation process is hindered by communication of negative attitudes, such as inflexibility, defensiveness, and a nondevelopmental approach.

8. *Failure to apply evaluation data.* Failure to use evaluations in personnel decision making and personnel development negates the primary purpose of performance evaluations. The use and weighting of multiple criteria as well as the frequency of evaluation also present problems.

FIGURE 10.1 Common Performance Evaluation Problems

Source: John E. Oliver, "Performance Appraisals That Fit," *Personnel Journal,* Vol. 64, no. 6 (June 1985), p. 69.

instance, although as the boss of a sales manager you may have specific ideas regarding what you expect *your* sales manager to do. For example, the job description may list duties such as "supervise sales force" and "is responsible for all phases of marketing the division's products." However, you may expect your sales manager to personally sell at least $600,000 worth of products per year by handling the division's two largest accounts; keep the sales force happy; and keep customers away from the executives (including you).[4]

To operationalize this it is helpful to set measurable standards for each of these activities. The "personal selling" activity can be measured in terms of how many dollars of sales he or she generates personally. "Keeping the sales force happy" might be measured in terms of turnover (on the assumption that less than 10% of the sales force will quit in any given year if morale is high). "Keeping customers away from executives" can be measured in terms of "customer complaints reaching top management," with a standard of "no more than ten customer complaints per year" being the sales manager's target.

▶ The Appraisal Itself: Appraisal Methods

GRAPHIC RATING SCALE TECHNIQUE

graphic rating scale A scale that lists a number of traits and a range of performance for each. The employee is then rated by identifying the score that best describes his or her level of performance for each trait.

The **graphic rating scale** is the simplest and most popular technique for appraising performance. Figure 10.2 shows a typical rating scale. It lists traits (such as quality and quantity) and a range of performance (from unsatisfactory to outstanding) for each. Each subordinate is rated by circling or checking the score that best describes his or her performance for each trait. The assigned values for the traits are then totaled.

Instead of appraising generic traits or factors (such as quality and quantity), many firms specify the duties to be appraised. For example, review Figure 10.3.[5] It shows an appraisal form for the position of administrative secretary. In this case the job's five main sets of duties have been taken from the job description and prioritized. Importance ratings are thus indicated as percentages at the top of each of the five categories (typing and stenography, reception, and so on). There is also a place on the form for comments, and for evaluation of "general performance" attributes like reporting for work on time and observing work rules.

ALTERNATION RANKING METHOD

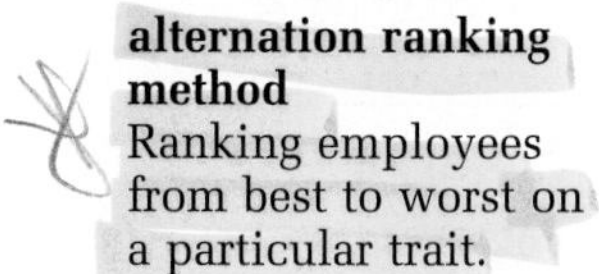

alternation ranking method Ranking employees from best to worst on a particular trait.

Another method for evaluating employees is to rank them from best to worst on some trait. Since it is usually easier to distinguish between the worst and best employees than to just rank them, an **alternation ranking method** is most popular. First, list all subordinates to be rated, and then cross out the names of any not known well enough to rank. Then, on a form such as that in Figure 10.4, indicate the employee who is the highest on the characteristic being measured and also the one who is the lowest. Then choose the next highest and the next lowest, *alternating* between highest and lowest until all the employees to be rated have been ranked.

PAIRED COMPARISON METHOD

paired comparison method Ranking employees by making a chart of all possible pairs of the employees for each trait and indicating which is the better employee of the pair.

The **paired comparison method** helps make the ranking method more effective. For every trait (quantity of work, quality of work, and so on), every subordinate is compared to every other subordinate in pairs.

Suppose there are five employees to be rated. In the paired comparison method you make a chart, as in Figure 10.5, of all possible pairs of employees *for each trait*. Then for each trait indicate (with a + or –) who is the better employee of the pair. Next, the number of times an employee is rated better is added up. In Figure 10.5, employee Maria ranked highest for quality of work, while Art was ranked highest for creativity.

FIGURE 10.2 **One Page of a Two-Page Graphic Rating Scale with Space for Comments**

Performance Appraisal

Employee Name______________________________ Title______________________

Department ______________________________ Employee Payroll Number ______________

Reason for Review: ☐ Annual ☐ Promotion ☐ Unsatisfactory Performance

☐ Merit ☐ End Probation Period ☐ Other ____________

Date employee began present position _____/_____/_____

Date of last appraisal _____/_____/_____ Scheduled appraisal date _____/_____/_____

Instructions: Carefully evaluate employee's work performance in relation to current job requirements. Check rating box to indicate the employee's performance. Indicate N/A if not applicable. Assign points for each rating within the scale and indicate in the corresponding points box. Points will be totaled and averaged for an overall performance score.

RATING IDENTIFICATION

O – Outstanding – Performance is exceptional in all areas and is recognizable as being far superior to others.

V – Very Good – Results clearly exceed most position requirements. Performance is of high quality and is achieved on a consistent basis.

G – Good – Competent and dependable level of performance. Meets performance standards of the job.

I – Improvement Needed – Performance is deficient in certain areas. Improvement is necessary.

U – Unsatisfactory – Results are generally unacceptable and require immediate improvement. No merit increase should be granted to individuals with this rating.

N – Not Rated – Not applicable or too soon to rate.

GENERAL FACTORS	RATING	SCALE	SUPPORTIVE DETAILS OR COMMENTS
1. **Quality –** The accuracy, thoroughness and acceptability of work performed.	O ☐ V ☐ G ☐ I ☐ U ☐	100-90 90-80 80-70 70-60 below 60	Points
2. **Productivity –** The quantity and efficiency of work produced in a specified period of time.	O ☐ V ☐ G ☐ I ☐ U ☐	100-90 90-80 80-70 70-60 below 60	Points
3. **Job Knowledge –** The practical/technical skills and information used on the job	O ☐ V ☐ G ☐ I ☐ U ☐	100-90 90-80 80-70 70-60 below 60	Points
4. **Reliability –** The extent to which an employee can be relied upon regarding task completion and follow up.	O ☐ V ☐ G ☐ I ☐ U ☐	100-90 90-80 80-70 70-60 below 60	Points
5. **Availability –** The extent to which an employee is punctual, observes prescribed work break/ meal periods and the overall attendance record.	O ☐ V ☐ G ☐ I ☐ U ☐	100-90 90-80 80-70 70-60 below 60	Points
6. **Independence –** The extent of work performed with little or no supervision.	O ☐ V ☐ G ☐ I ☐ U ☐	100-90 90-80 80-70 70-60 below 60	Points

FIGURE 10.3 Sample Performance Appraisal Form Source: James Buford, Jr., Bettye Burkhalter, and Grover Jacobs, "Link Job Descriptions to Performance Appraisals," *Personnel Journal* (June 1988), pp. 135–136.

Name ____________________
Position ____________________
Rating period from ____________ to ____________
Rater name ____________________
Rater title ____________________
Department ____________________

Rating Scale Key

1 Fails to meet job requirements
2 Essentially meets job requirements
3 Fully meets job requirements
4 Meets job requirements with distinction
5 Exceeds job requirements

Figure 1

PART II Rating Scales for Task Areas

Position: Administrative Secretary
Duties and Responsibilities

A. Typing and stenography PCT. (30%)	RATING: 1 ☐ 2 ☐ 3 ☐ 4 ☐ 5 ☐
Producing accurate typewritten documents in the proper format at 60wpm from a variety of sources, including oral dictation: From oral dictation, dictating machine, shorthand notes or standard formats, transcribes correspondence for general manager; transcribes minutes of meetings; types notices, agendas, schedules, and other internal material; types surveys for trade associations; compiles and types operating reports and other reports, including text and tables; types copy for trade magazines and newspapers; composes and types letters, memoranda, copy and other documents as needed or on request.	Comments
B. Reception PCT. (25%)	RATING: 1 ☐ 2 ☐ 3 ☐ 4 ☐ 5 ☐
Receiving and recording initial contacts in person or on the telephone and courteously assisting callers or visitors: Answers incoming telephone calls, takes message, provides information or routes call to appropriate individual; greets visitors, provides information or directs to appropriate office or individual; acts as hostess and provides incidental services to visitors in waiting status; operates automatic answering service; maintains log of callers and visitors to cooperative.	Comments
C. Scheduling PCT. (20%)	RATING: 1 ☐ 2 ☐ 3 ☐ 4 ☐ 5 ☐
Managing calendar efficiently including arranging appointments, meetings, travel and similar activities; maintains calendar and makes appointments for general manager, board members and other staff; prepares requests for reimbursement for official travel; assists with arrangements of annual meeting; makes arrangements for in-service training meetings, including rooms, coffee breaks and food service when necessary; schedules use of organizational facilities; arranges lodging, travel and fees for outside speakers and consultants.	Comments
D. Filing and records management PCT. (15%)	RATING: 1 ☐ 2 ☐ 3 ☐ 4 ☐ 5 ☐
Creating and maintaining appropriate filing systems and promptly locating and retrieving needed material upon request: Develops space allocation plan and filing system for correspondence, minutes, reports, regulations and related material; places material into proper location in file; searches for and retrieves material from files; culls, files and removes material to central location or destroys as needed; maintains and preserves vital records; organizes data from file search into usable format.	Comments
E. General office service PCT. (10%)	RATING: 1 ☐ 2 ☐ 3 ☐ 4 ☐ 5 ☐
Performing related office duties in accordance with acceptable practice and prescribed procedures; processes mail through postage meter, records readings and posts; opens and distributes incoming mail; makes copies of documents; maintains petty cash fund; clips articles from papers and magazines related to the organization; maintains bulletin board; performs other job duties as assigned.	Comments

FIGURE 10.3

PART III: Performance Appraisal Form

Does the employee report for and remain at work as required? ☐ yes ☐ no   If no, please explain.

Does the employee follow instructions and observe work rules? ☐ yes ☐ no   If no, please explain.

Does the employee get along and cooperate with co-workers on the job? ☐ yes ☐ no   If no, please explain.

Does the employee have the knowleges, skills, abilities and other qualifications needed for successful job performance? ☐ yes ☐ no   If no, please explain.

Describe any specific actions employee needs to take to improve job performance.

Summarize this employee's overall job performance as determined in your joint discussion.

PART IV: Signatures

This report is based on my observation and knowledge of both the employee and the job.

My signature indicates that I have reviewed this appraisal. It does not mean that I agree with the results.

Supervisor   Date

Reviewer   Date

Employee   Date

ALTERNATION RANKING SCALE

For the Trait: ____________________

For the trait you are measuring, list all the employees you want to rank. Put the highest-ranking employee's name on line 1. Put the lowest-ranking employee's name on line 20. Then list the next highest ranking on line 2, the next lowest-ranking on line 19, and so on. Continue until all names are on the scale.

Most-highest ranking employee

1. ____________	11. ____________
2. ____________	12. ____________
3. ____________	13. ____________
4. ____________	14. ____________
5. ____________	15. ____________
6. ____________	16. ____________
7. ____________	17. ____________
8. ____________	18. ____________
9. ____________	19. ____________
10. ____________	20. ____________

Least-lowest ranking employee

FIGURE 10.4
Alternation Ranking Scale

FORCED DISTRIBUTION METHOD

forced distribution method
Similar to grading on a curve; predetermined percentages of ratees are placed in various performance categories.

The **forced distribution method** is similar to "grading on a curve." With this method, predetermined percentages of ratees are placed in performance categories. For example, you may decide to distribute employees as follows:

15% high performers
20% high-average performers
30% average performers
20% low-average performers
15% low performers

One practical way to do this is to write each employee's name on a separate index card. Then, for each trait being appraised (quality of work, creativity, and so on), place the employee's card in one of the appropriate performance categories.

An Example

Merck and Company, with about 31,000 employees, has used a forced distribution appraisal method with some success. It is used for all exempt employees who receive merit pay increases based on their performance ratings.

Merck's reason for instituting a forced distribution system is informative.[6] It was instituted when they found that 80% of their exempt employees were

FOR THE TRAIT "QUALITY OF WORK"					
	Employee Rated:				
As Compared to:	A Art	B Maria	C Chuck	D Diane	E José
A Art		+	+	−	−
B Maria	−		−	−	−
C Chuck	−	+		+	−
D Diane	+	+	−		+
E José	+	+	+	−	
		↑ Maria Ranks Highest Here			

FOR THE TRAIT "CREATIVITY"					
	Employee Rated:				
As Compared to:	A Art	B Maria	C Chuck	D Diane	E José
A Art		−	−	−	−
B Maria	+		−	+	+
C Chuck	+	+		−	+
D Diane	+	−	+		−
E José	+	−	−	+	
	↑ Art Ranks Highest Here				

FIGURE 10.5
Ranking Employees by the Paired Comparison Method
Note: + means "better than," − means "worse than." For each chart, add up the number of +'s in each column to get the highest-ranked employee.

receiving ratings of 4 and above on their 5-point scale. In other words, employees who had significant accomplishments were getting only slightly higher ratings than were those who did a good but not extraordinary job. As a result, neither the performance appraisal system nor the merit pay plan had the effects on motivation that Merck wanted. Its main purpose was to provide for greater differentiation among employees, so outstanding employees could be identified.

At Merck, all exempt employees now receive an annual performance appraisal in December. They meet with their supervisors to review their accomplishments for the year (compared with previously established goals) and receive one of five ratings: EX (exceptional), WD (with distinction), HS (high Merck standard), RI (room for improvement), and NA (not acceptable).

However, only limited percentages of a manager's subordinates can fall in each of the five categories. For example, 5% of the department's employees can receive EX ratings, 15% can receive WD ratings, and the vast majority—70%—should fall in the "high Merck standard" middle level of the range. In other words, this system forces the supervisor to identify no more than 20% of his or her exempt employees as above average, when compared with their Merck peers.

The program is working well, since the company has worked hard to overcome forced distribution's inherent problems. For example, it's not realistic to force a manager with only four or five employees to distribute them into five classes. They therefore use a "roll-up" system. Here several departments in the same division are reviewed together for the purpose of meeting the percentage distribution requirements of the rating system. (At each "roll-up" meeting, the supervisor can argue for two out of five employees receiving an EX rating.) The big problem, though, was getting employees who viewed themselves as high achievers to understand that getting an HS (high Merck standard) does not equate to getting a C on a report card.

Still, at Merck (or when rating college students, for that matter), there is always the question of whether the person's absolute or relative performance should be appraised. On balance, however, the Merck program has been successful, particularly in helping Merck identify high achievers and reward them.

CRITICAL INCIDENT METHOD

critical incident method
Keeping a record of uncommonly good or undesirable examples of an employee's work-related behavior and reviewing it with the employee at predetermined times.

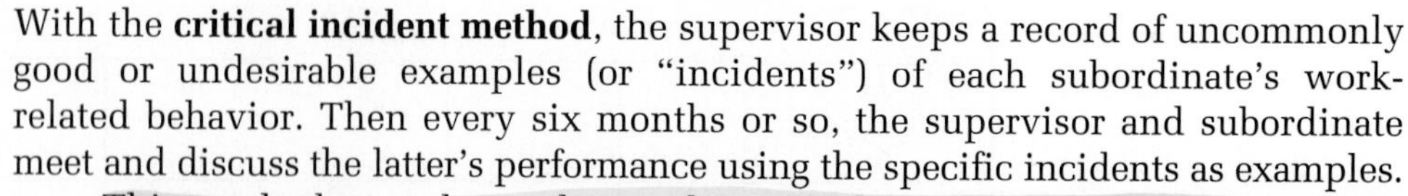

With the **critical incident method**, the supervisor keeps a record of uncommonly good or undesirable examples (or "incidents") of each subordinate's work-related behavior. Then every six months or so, the supervisor and subordinate meet and discuss the latter's performance using the specific incidents as examples.

This method can always be used to supplement another appraisal technique, and as such it has several advantages. For one thing, it provides you with some specific hard facts for explaining the appraisal. It ensures that you think about the subordinate's appraisal all during the year (because the incidents must be accumulated); the rating therefore does not just reflect the employee's most recent performance. Keeping a running list of critical incidents should also provide some concrete examples of what specifically your subordinate can do to eliminate any performance deficiencies.

You can gear the critical incident method directly to the specific job expectations laid out for the subordinate at the beginning of the year. Thus, in the example presented in Table 10.2, one of the assistant plant manager's continuing duties was to supervise procurement and to minimize inventory costs. The critical incident shows that he let inventory storage costs rise 15%; this provides a specific example of what performance he must improve in the future.

The critical incident method is often used to supplement a ranking technique. It is useful for identifying specific examples of good and poor performance and planning how deficiencies can be corrected. It is not as useful, by itself, for comparing employees or, relatedly, for making salary decisions.

NARRATIVE FORMS

Some firms use narrative forms to evaluate personnel. For example, the form used in Figure 10.6 presents the "Performance Improvement Plan" used by one

TABLE 10.2 Examples of Critical Incidents for an Assistant Plant Manager

CONTINUING DUTIES	TARGETS	CRITICAL INCIDENTS
Schedule production for plant	Full utilization of personnel and machinery in plant; orders delivered on time	Instituted new production scheduling system; decreased late orders by 10% last month; increased machine utilization in plant by 20% last month
Supervise procurement of raw materials and inventory control	Minimize inventory costs while keeping adequate supplies on hand	Let inventory storage costs rise 15% last month; overordered parts "A" and "B" by 20%; underordered part "C" by 30%
Supervise machinery maintenance	No shutdowns due to faulty machinery	Instituted new preventive maintenance system for plant; prevented a machine breakdown by discovering faulty part

FIGURE 10.6 Performance Improvement Plan

Source: Joseph J. Famularo, *Handbook of Personnel Forms, Records, and Reports* (New York: McGraw-Hill, 1982), pp. 216–219.

PERFORMANCE IMPROVEMENT PLAN

Name ______________________ Date ______________

Position Title ______________________ Dept./Div. ______________

I. **PURPOSE AND OBJECTIVE**
This form and process is designed to assist the supervisor in analyzing *how* an employee is performing his or her work, that is, the individual skills and knowledge they use in performing their job responsibilities. The primary objective for you in completing this Performance Analysis and subsequent discussions with the employee is to help the person improve.

II. **STEPS IN THE PROCESS**

A. **Performance Factors and Skills** — The individual skills and performance factors represent the major abilities that are required of most employees to perform their jobs. After reading the description of each factor, assign a rating of the employee's skill proficiency using the following guide:

S — Strength
SA — Satisfactory
N — Needs improvement
NA — Not Applicable

Space is provided at the end of this form to write out performance factors/skills which you may consider to be important and are not found on this form. We suggest, however, that you avoid adding personality traits that do not influence performance.

B. **Performance Analysis and Examples** — This section is provided for you to support your judgment with specific *performance related* examples of observed behavior. These examples should be stated in terms of what the employee did or said (in completing a task or project) as it relates to the performance factor.

C. **Improvement Plan** — Specific actions should be listed in this section that will be taken to assist the employee in those areas that require performance improvement. It is suggested that supervisor and subordinate develop this plan jointly in a discussion session. These actions should focus on activities, tasks, training, expanded job duties, etc., that will afford the employee an opportunity to develop the needed skill. The written Improvement Plan should also state *who* is responsible for completing each step, a *timetable* for completion and a *feedback/followup* process that will monitor the progress.

D. **Discussion with the Employee** — The performance rating and analysis of each factor or skill must be discussed with the employee. The principal focus of this meeting should be on problem solving, i.e., to stimulate the employee to think about the probable causes of the skill or knowledge deficiency and to generate ideas on how to bring about performance improvement in these areas. Working together, supervisor and employee should examine the cause of each deficiency and then jointly develop and agree upon a logical course of action for improvement. The Improvement Plan should be realistic, written down, and followed up in future sessions.

multinational Company to evaluate the progress and the development of its exempt employees. As you can see, the person's supervisor is asked (1) to rate the employee's performance in terms of standard and (2) to present critical examples and an improvement plan designed to aid the employee in meeting or exceeding these position standards. A summary performance appraisal discussion then focuses on problem solving.[7]

FIGURE 10.6 (continued)

Performance Factors/Skills	Performance Analysis & Examples	Improvement Plan
PLANNING — Forecasting, setting objectives, establishing strategies and courses of action, budgeting, scheduling, programming, and outlining procedures.		
ORGANIZING — Grouping of activities to achieve results, delegating, staffing, and using available resources.		
DIRECTING — Ability to guide and supervise. Stresses the processes of motivating, communicating, and leading.		
CONTROLLING — Developing performance standards, measuring results, and taking corrective action.		
DEVELOPING PEOPLE — Evaluating performance and potential, providing training and development, coaching and counseling and resolving personnel problems.		

BEHAVIORALLY ANCHORED RATING SCALES

behaviorally anchored rating scale (BARS) An appraisal method that aims at combining the benefits of narrative critical incidents and quantified ratings by anchoring a quantified scale with specific narrative examples of good or poor performance.

A **behaviorally anchored rating scale (BARS)** aims at combining the benefits of narrative critical incidents and quantified ratings by anchoring a quantified scale with specific narrative examples of good or poor performance, as in Figure 10.7. Its proponents claim that it provides better, more equitable appraisals than do the other tools we discussed.[8]

Developing a BARS typically requires five steps:[9]

1. *Generate critical incidents.* Persons who know the job being appraised (job holders and/or supervisors) are asked to describe specific illustrations (critical incidents) of effective and ineffective performance.
2. *Develop performance dimensions.* These people then cluster these incidents into a smaller set (say, five or ten) of performance dimensions. Each cluster (dimension) is then defined.

FIGURE 10.6 (continued)

PROBLEM ANALYSIS — Determining pertinent data, differentiating significant from less significant facts, defining interrelationships, and arriving at sound practical solutions.		
DECISION-MAKING — Evaluating and selecting among alternative courses of action quickly and accurately.		
INTERPERSONAL RELATIONS — Effectiveness in relating to others at all organizational levels. Sensitive to the needs of others.		
COMMUNICATION — Ability to get ideas across in a clear and persuasive manner. Skilled in listening to and seeking clarification of other's point of view.		
EQUAL OPPORTUNITY — Supports and implements goals of affirmative action plan for minorities and females.		

3. *Reallocate incidents.* Another group of people who also know the job then reallocate the original critical incidents. They are given the clusters' definitions and the critical incidents and asked to reassign each incident to the cluster they think fits best. Typically, a critical incident is retained if some percentage (usually 50% to 80%) of this second group assigns it to the same cluster as did the group in step 2.
4. *Scale the incidents.* This second group is generally asked to rate (7- or 9-point scales are typical) the behavior described in the incident as to how effectively or ineffectively it represents performance on the appropriate cluster's dimension.
5. *Develop final instrument.* A subset of the incidents (usually six or seven per cluster) are used as "behavioral anchors" for each dimension.

Example

Three researchers developed a BARS for grocery checkout clerks who were working in a large western grocery chain.[10] They collected a number of critical incidents and then clustered them into eight performance dimensions:

FIGURE 10.6 (continued)

Performance Factors/Skills	Performance Analysis & Examples	Improvement Plan
JOB KNOWLEDGE — An understanding of the functional components of own job as well as an awareness of work relationships with other areas. Knowledge of one's specialized and technical field of work.		
SAFETY AND HEALTH — Actively promotes and upholds the Corporation's Safety & Health principles. Initiates and works for realistic goals.		

KNOWLEDGE AND JUDGMENT
CONSCIENTIOUSNESS
SKILL IN HUMAN RELATIONS
SKILL IN OPERATION OF REGISTER
SKILL IN BAGGING
ORGANIZATIONAL ABILITY OF CHECKSTAND WORK
SKILL IN MONETARY TRANSACTIONS
OBSERVATIONAL ABILITY

They then developed a behaviorally anchored rating scale for one of these dimensions, "knowledge and judgment." Similar to Figure 10.7, it contained a scale (ranging from 1 to 9) for rating performance from "extremely poor" to "extremely good." Notice also that the typical BARS is *behaviorally anchored* with specific critical incidents. Thus, in the supermarket example, there was a specific critical incident ("by knowing the price of items, this checker would be expected to look for mismarked and unmarked items"); this helped anchor or

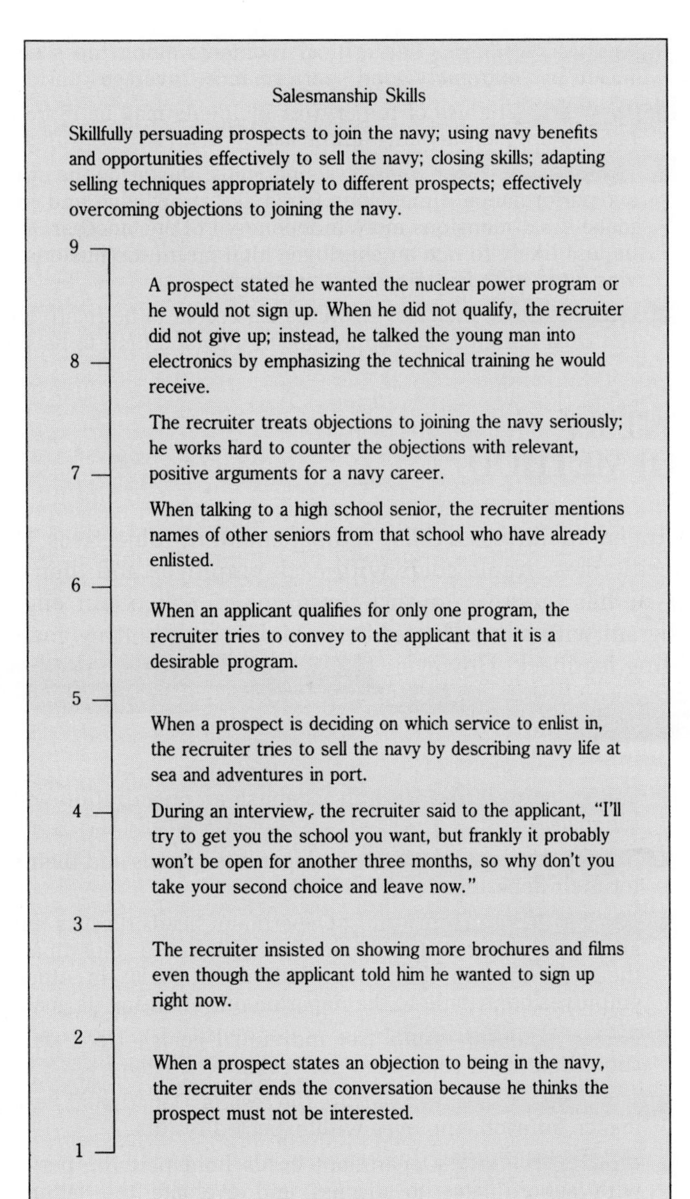

Salesmanship Skills
Skillfully persuading prospects to join the navy; using navy benefits and opportunities effectively to sell the navy; closing skills; adapting selling techniques appropriately to different prospects; effectively overcoming objections to joining the navy.
9
A prospect stated he wanted the nuclear power program or he would not sign up. When he did not qualify, the recruiter did not give up; instead, he talked the young man into electronics by emphasizing the technical training he would receive.
8
The recruiter treats objections to joining the navy seriously; he works hard to counter the objections with relevant, positive arguments for a navy career.
7
When talking to a high school senior, the recruiter mentions names of other seniors from that school who have already enlisted.
6
When an applicant qualifies for only one program, the recruiter tries to convey to the applicant that it is a desirable program.
5
When a prospect is deciding on which service to enlist in, the recruiter tries to sell the navy by describing navy life at sea and adventures in port.
4
During an interview, the recruiter said to the applicant, "I'll try to get you the school you want, but frankly it probably won't be open for another three months, so why don't you take your second choice and leave now."
3
The recruiter insisted on showing more brochures and films even though the applicant told him he wanted to sign up right now.
2
When a prospect states an objection to being in the navy, the recruiter ends the conversation because he thinks the prospect must not be interested.
1

FIGURE 10.7
Behaviorally Anchored Performance Category

Source: Walter C. Borman, *Behavior Based Rating Scales* in Ronnald A. Berk (Ed.) *Performance Assessment: Methods & Applications* (Baltimore: The Johns Hopkins University Press, 1986), p. 103.

specify what was meant by "extremely good" performance. Similarly, there are other critical incident anchors along the scale.

Advantages

Developing a BARS can be more time-consuming than developing other appraisal tools, such as graphic rating scales. But BARS are also said to have important advantages.[11]

1. *A more accurate gauge.* People who know the job and its requirements better than anyone else develop BARS. The resulting BARS should therefore be a good gauge of performance on that job.

2. *Clearer standards.* The critical incidents along the scale help to clarify what is meant by "extremely good" performance, "average" performance, and so forth.
3. *Feedback.* The use of the critical incidents may be more useful in providing feedback to the people being appraised.
4. *Independent dimensions.* Systematically clustering the critical incidents into five or six performance dimensions (such as "knowledge and judgment") should help to make the dimensions more independent of one another. For example, a rater should be less likely to rate an employee high on *all* dimensions simply because he or she was rated high in "conscientiousness."
5. *Consistency.*[12] BARS evaluations also seem to be relatively consistent and reliable, in that different raters' appraisals of a person tend to be similar.

THE MANAGEMENT BY OBJECTIVES (MBO) METHOD

management by objectives (MBO) Involves setting specific measurable goals with each employee and then periodically reviewing the progress made.

Stripped to its essentials, **management by objectives (MBO)** involves setting specific measurable goals with each employee and then periodically discussing his or her progress toward these goals. You could engage in a modest MBO program with subordinates by participatively setting goals and periodically providing feedback. However, the term MBO almost always refers to a comprehensive *organization-wide goal-setting and appraisal program* that consists of six main steps:

1. *Set the organization's goals.* Establish an organization-wide plan for next year and set goals.
2. *Set departmental goals.* Here, department heads and their superiors jointly set goals for their departments.
3. *Discuss departmental goals.* Department heads discuss the department's goals with all subordinates in the department (often at a department-wide meeting) and ask them to develop their own individual goals; in other words, how can each employee contribute to the department's attaining its goals?
4. *Define expected results* (set individual goals). Here, department heads and their subordinates set short-term performance targets.
5. *Performance reviews: measure the results.* Department heads compare actual performance for each employee with expected results.
6. *Provide feedback.* Department heads hold periodic performance review meetings with subordinates to discuss and evaluate the latters' progress in achieving expected results.

One of the foundations of a good Management By Objectives program is open communication which fosters employee commitment to goals.

Problems to Avoid

There are three problems in using MBO. Setting *unclear, unmeasurable objectives* is the main problem. Setting an objective such as "will do a better job of training" is useless. On the other hand, "will have four subordinates promoted during the year" is a measurable objective.

Second, MBO is *time-consuming.* Taking the time to set objectives, to measure progress, and to provide feedback can take several hours per employee per year over and above the time you already spend doing each person's appraisal.

Third, setting objectives with the subordinate sometimes turns into a *tug of war,* with you pushing for higher quotas and the subordinate pushing for lower ones. Knowing the job and the person's ability is thus important. To motivate performance the objectives must be fair and attainable. The more you know about the job and this person's ability, the more confident you can be about the standards you set.

MIXING THE METHODS

In practice, most firms combine several appraisal tools. An example is presented in Figure 10.8. This presents a form used to appraise the performance of managers in a large airline. Notice that it is basically a graphic rating scale, with descriptive phrases included to define the traits being measured. But there is also a "comments" section below each trait. This lets the rater jot down several critical incidents. The quantifiable ranking method permits comparisons of employees and is therefore useful for making salary, transfer, and promotion decisions. The critical incidents provide specific examples of good or poor performance.[13]

▶ APPRAISING PERFORMANCE: PROBLEMS AND ISSUES

DEALING WITH THE FIVE MAIN RATING SCALE APPRAISAL PROBLEMS

There are five main problems that can undermine appraisal tools such as graphic rating scales: unclear standards, halo effect, central tendency, leniency or strictness, and bias.

Unclear Standards

unclear performance standards
An appraisal scale that is too open to interpretation; instead, include descriptive phrases that define each trait and what is meant by standards like "good" or "unsatisfactory."

Unclear performance standards are one problem. For example, look at the graphic rating scale in Table 10.3. Although the chart seems objective enough, it would probably result in unfair appraisals. This is because the traits and degrees of merit are open to interpretation. For example, different supervisors would probably define "good" performance, "fair" performance, and so on differently. The same is true of traits such as "quality of work" or "creativity."

There are several ways to rectify this problem. The best way is to develop and include descriptive phrases that define each trait, as in Figure 10.2. There, the form specified what was meant by "outstanding," "superior," and "good" quality of work. This results in appraisals that are more consistent and more easily explained.

Halo Effect

halo effect
In performance appraisal, the problem that occurs when a supervisor's rating of a subordinate on one trait biases the rating of that person on other traits.

The **halo effect** means that your rating of a subordinate on one trait (such as "gets along with others") biases how you rate that person on other traits (such as "quantity of work"). This problem often occurs with employees who are especially friendly (or unfriendly) toward the supervisor. For example, an unfriendly employee will often be rated unsatisfactory for all traits rather

MAJOR PERFORMANCE STRENGTHS/WEAKNESSES

Read the definitions of each management factor below and choose the ranking which most accurately describes the employee. If, after reading the definition, it is determined that the skill area was not demonstrated because of the nature of the employee's position, indicate as Non-Applicable (N/A). Your evaluation on each of the management factors below should relate directly to the employee's actual performance on the job.

PLANNING SKILL – Degree to which incumbent:	Ranking Code	(CHECK ONE)	
– Assessed and established priorities of result area. – Designed realistic short and long range plans. – Formulated feasible timetables. – Anticipated possible problems and obstacles toward reaching required results.	1	Far exceeds requirements	
	4	Usually meets requirements	
	3	Fully meets requirements	
	2	Usually exceeds requirements	
	5	Fails to meet requirements	

Comments:

ORGANIZING SKILL – Degree to which incumbent:	Ranking Code	(CHECK ONE)	
– Grouped activities for optimal use of personnel and material resources in order to achieve goals. – Clearly defined responsibilities and authority limits of subordinates. – Minimized confusion and inefficiencies in work operations.	3	Fully meets requirements	
	2	Usually exceeds requirements	
	5	Fails to meet requirements	
	1	Far exceeds requirements	
	4	Usually meets requirements	

Comments:

CONTROLLING SKILL – Degree to which incumbent:	Ranking Code	(CHECK ONE)	
– Established appropriate procedures to be kept informed of subordinate's work progress. – Identified deviations in work goal progress. – Adjusted to deviations in work to ensure that established goals were met.	5	Fails to meet requirements	
	4	Usually meets requirements	
	3	Fully meets requirements	
	2	Usually exceeds requirements	
	1	Far exceeds requirements	

Comments:

Note: This is one page from a multipage form used to appraise managers.

FIGURE 10.8 One Page from a Typical Management Appraisal Form

than just for the trait "gets along well with others." Being aware of this problem is a major step toward avoiding it. Supervisory training can also alleviate the problem.[14]

Central Tendency

central tendency
A tendency to rate all employees the same way, such as rating them all average.

Many supervisors have a **central tendency** when filling in rating scales. For example, if the rating scale ranges from 1 to 7, they tend to avoid the highs (6 and 7) and lows (1 and 2) and rate most of their people between 3 and 5. If you use a graphic rating scale, this central tendency could mean that all employees are simply rated "average." Such a restriction can distort the evaluations making them less useful for promotion, salary, or counseling purposes. *Ranking* employees (instead of using a graphic rating scale) can avoid this central tendency problem because all employees must be ranked and thus can't all be rated average. Recall that this is a main advantage of the ranking approach.

Leniency or Strictness

strictness/leniency
The problem that occurs when a supervisor has a tendency to rate all subordinates either high or low.

Some supervisors tend to rate all their subordinates consistently high (or low), just as some instructors are notoriously high graders and others are not. This **strictness/leniency** problem is especially serious with graphic rating scales because the supervisor can conceivably rate *all* subordinates either high or low. When you must *rank* subordinates, you are forced to distinguish between high and low performers. Strictness/leniency is thus not a problem with the ranking or forced distribution approach.

In fact, if you must use a graphic rating scale, it may be a good idea to *assume* a distribution of performances—that, say, only about 10% of your people should be rated "excellent," 20% "good," and so forth. In other words, try to get a spread (unless, of course, you are sure all your people really do fall into just one or two categories).

Bias

bias
The tendency to allow individual differences such as age, race, and sex affect the appraisal rates these employees receive.

Individual differences among ratees (in terms of characteristics like age, race, and sex) can affect the ratings they get, often quite apart from each ratee's actual performance.[15] In one study, for instance, researchers found a systematic tendency to evaluate older ratees (over 60 years of age) lower on "performance capacity" and "potential for development" than younger employees.[16] The ratee's race and sex can also affect the person's rating. However, here the **bias** is not necessarily consistently against minorities or women, as it seems to be in the case of older workers. In one study, high-performing females were often rated significantly higher than were high-performing males. Similarly, low-performing blacks were often rated significantly higher than were low-performing whites.[17]

An interesting picture of how age can distort evaluations emerges from a study of registered nurses. When the nurses were 30–39 years old, they and their

TABLE 10.3 A Graphic Rating Scale with Unclear Standards

	EXCELLENT	GOOD	FAIR	POOR
Quality of work				
Quantity of work				
Creativity				
Integrity				

Note: For example, what exactly is meant by "good," "quantity of work," and so forth?

supervisors each rated the nurses' performance virtually the same. In the 21–29 category, supervisors actually rated nurses higher than they rated themselves. However, for the 40–61 nurse age category, the supervisors rated nurses' performance lower than the nurses rated their own performance. The conclusion here may be that supervisors are tougher in appraising older subordinates. Specifically, they don't give them as much credit for their success, while attributing any low performance to their lack of ability.[18]

The employee's previous performance can also affect the evaluation of his or her current performance.[19] The actual error can take several forms. Sometimes the rater may systematically overestimate improvement on the part of a poor worker or decline on the part of a good worker, for instance. In some situations—especially when the change in behavior is more gradual—the rater may simply be insensitive to changes in the ratee's behavior. In any case, it is important when rating performance to do so objectively. Try to block out the influence of things such as previous performance, age, or race.

HOW TO AVOID APPRAISAL PROBLEMS

There are at least three things you can do to minimize the impact of appraisal problems such as bias and central tendency. First, be sure to be familiar with the problems as just discussed. Understanding the problem can help you avoid it.

Second, choose the right appraisal tool. Each tool, such as the graphic rating scale or critical incident method, has its own advantages and disadvantages. For example, the ranking method avoids central tendency but can cause ill feelings when employees' performances are in fact all actually "high" (Table 10.4).

TABLE 10.4 Important Advantages and Disadvantages of Appraisal Tools

	ADVANTAGES	DISADVANTAGES
Graphic rating scales	Simple to use; provides a quantitative rating for each employee.	Standards may be unclear; halo effect, central tendency, leniency, bias can also be problems.
Alternation ranking	Simple to use (but not as simple as graphic rating scales). Avoids central tendency and other problems of rating scales.	Can cause disagreements among employees and may be unfair if all employees *are*, in fact, excellent.
Forced distribution method	End up with a predetermined number of people in each group.	Appraisal results depend on the adequacy of your original choice of cutoff points.
Critical incident method	Helps specify what is "right" and "wrong" about the employee's performance; forces supervisor to evaluate subordinates on an ongoing basis.	Difficult to rate or rank employees relative to one another.
Behaviorally anchored rating scale	Provides behavioral "anchors." BARS is very accurate.	Difficult to develop.
MBO	Tied to jointly agreed upon performance objectives.	Time-consuming.

Third, training supervisors to eliminate rating errors such as halo, leniency, and central tendency can help them avoid these problems.[20] In a typical training program, raters are shown a videotape of jobs being performed and are asked to rate the worker. Ratings made by each participant are then placed on a flip chart and the various errors (such as leniency and halo) are explained. For example, if a trainee rated all criteria (such as quality, quantity, etc.) about the same, the trainer might explain that halo error had occurred. Typically, the trainer gives the correct rating and then illustrates the rating errors the participants made.[21] According to one study, computer-assisted appraisal training improved managers' ability to conduct performance appraisal discussions with their subordinates.[22]

Rater training is also no panacea for reducing rating errors or improving the accuracy of appraisals. From a practical point of view, several factors, including the extent to which pay is tied to performance ratings, union pressure, employee turnover, time constraints, and the need to justify ratings may be more important than training. This means that improving an appraisal's accuracy involves not only training but also reducing outside factors such as union pressure and time constraints.[23]

EQUAL EMPLOYMENT AND PERFORMANCE APPRAISAL

Since the passage of Title VII courts have addressed various issues (including promotion, layoff, and compensation decisions) in which performance appraisals played a significant role.[24] As summarized in Table 10.5, they have often found that the inadequacies of the employer's appraisal system lay at the root of some illegal discriminatory action.[25]

One case involved layoff decisions. Here the court held that the firm had violated Title VII when on the basis of poor performance ratings it laid off several Spanish-surnamed employees.[26] The court concluded that the practice was illegal because:

1. The appraisals were based on subjective supervisory observations.
2. The appraisals were not administered and scored in a standardized fashion.
3. Two of the three supervisory evaluators did not have daily contact with the employees being evaluated.

An important aspect of this case was that the court in effect accepted performance appraisals as tests. In other words, they concluded that the performance appraisal procedure used by the company had to comply with EEOC employee selection guidelines and that in this case it did not. While the appraisals *were* based on the "best judgments and opinions" of the appraisers, they were *not* based on any objective criteria that were supported by some kind of record of validity.

Based on this, some experts have contended that the performance appraisal development process should comply with the strict guidelines for developing any test; however today most assume this is not required.[27] For example, two writers concluded that insisting on such validation can be "potentially damaging as it could eventually place the profession in a position it cannot satisfactorily defend."[28]

TABLE 10.5 Appraisal: A Summary of Court Cases and Significant Rulings

CASE	YEAR	COURT	PREVAILING PARTY	SIGNIFICANT RULING(S)
Griggs v. *Duke Power Company*	1971	Supreme	Employee	EEOC guidelines first endorsed. Adverse impact requires demonstration of job relatedness. Employer intent to discriminate irrelevant.
Marquez v. *Omaha District Sales Office, Ford Division of the Ford Motor Company*	1971	Appeals, 8th Circuit	Employee	Documentation necessary. Misuse of legal appraisal system may violate Title VII.
Rowe v. *General Motors*	1972	Appeals, 5th Circuit	Employee	Lack of appraiser training condemned. Subjective performance standards condemned. Communication of performance standards required.
Brito v. *Zia Company*	1973	Appeals, 10th Circuit	Employee	Performance appraisals are "employment tests." Adverse impact requires demonstration of validity of appraisal system. Objective performance standards should supplement subjective standards. Standardized administration and scoring of appraisals required.
Wade v. *Mississippi Cooperative Extension Service*	1974	District	Employee	Job analysis required. Appraisal on general traits condemned.
Albemarle Paper Company v. *Moody*	1975	Supreme	Employee	Appraisals as criteria must be job related. Endorsement of EEOC guidelines regarding criterion development.
Patterson v. *American Tobacco Company*	1978	Appeals, 4th Circuit	Employee	Job analysis necessary. Objective performance standards required.
Ramirez v. *Hofheinz*	1980	Appeals, 5th Circuit	Organization	Subjective performance standards supported. Past record of employer important.
Carpenter v. *Stephen F. Austin State University*	1983	Appeals, 5th Circuit	Employee	Updated analysis. Performance standards required to be demonstrably job related. Appraiser training required.
Chamberlain v. *Bissel, Inc.*	1982	District	Employee	Failure to warn of declining performance in evaluations
Grant v. *C&P Telephone Co.*	1984	District Court of DC	Organization	The plaintiff's work records were not only reviewed by upper level personnel, he was warned repeatedly that termination was imminent if his work did not improve.
Nord v. *U.S. Steel*	1985	11th Circuit	Employee	The plaintiff successfully demonstrated that she had good performance appraisals before requesting a promotion. After request, her appraisals became negative, leading to her eventual termination.
John F. Winslow v. *Federal Energy Regulatory Commission*	1987	District	Employee	Employers lack of documentation undermined employer's credibility.
Romei v. *Shell Oil Co.*	1991	New York Superior Court	Employee	Raises possibility that employer can be sued for libel for what is put in performance appraisal.

Sources: Based on Sami M. Abbasi, Kenneth W. Hollman, and Joe H. Murrey, Jr., "Employment at Will: An Eroding Concept in Employment Relationships," *Labor Law Journal*, Vol. 38, no. 1 (January 1987), pp. 26-27; Gerald Barrett and Mary Kernan, "Performance Appraisal and Terminations: A Review of Court Decisions Since *Brito* v. *Zia* with Implications for Personnel Practices," *Personnel Psychology*, Vol. 40, no. 3 (Autumn 1987), pp. 489-501; David Martin and Kathryn Bartol, "The Legal Ramifications of Performance Appraisal: An Update," *Employee Relations Law Journal*, Vol. 17, no. 2 (Autumn 1991), pp. 257–286.

This being the case, a checklist for developing a defensible appraisal process includes the following:[29]

1. Conduct a job analysis to ascertain characteristics (such as "timely project completion") required for successful job performance. Graphically:

   Job Analysis ⟶ Performance Standards ⟶ Performance Appraisal

2. Incorporate these characteristics into a rating instrument. (Note that while the professional literature recommends rating instruments that are tied to specific job behaviors, i.e., BARS, the courts routinely accept less sophisticated approaches such as graphic rating scales.)
3. Make sure that definitive performance standards are provided to all raters and ratees.
4. Use clearly defined individual dimensions of job performance (like quantity or quality) rather than undefined, global measures of job performance (like "overall performance").
5. When using graphic rating scales, avoid abstract trait names (for example, loyalty, honesty) unless they can be defined in terms of observable behaviors.
6. Employ subjective supervisory ratings (in terms of essays, for instance) only as one component of the overall appraisal process.
7. Train supervisors to use the rating instrument properly. This includes instructions on how to apply performance appraisal standards ("outstanding," etc.) when making judgments. In six of ten cases decided against the employer, the plaintiffs were able to show that subjective standards had been applied unevenly to minority and majority employees.[30]
8. Allow appraisers substantial daily contact with the employee being evaluated.
9. Whenever possible, have more than one appraiser conduct the appraisal and conduct all such appraisals independently. This process can help to "cancel out" individual errors and biases on the part of individual appraisers.
10. Utilize formal appeal mechanisms and a review of ratings by upper-level personnel.
11. Document evaluations and reasons for the termination decision (if any).
12. Where appropriate, provide corrective guidance to assist poor performers in improving their performance. Courts look favorably on this practice.

WHO SHOULD DO THE APPRAISING?

Who should actually rate an employee's performance? Several options exist.

Appraisal by the Immediate Supervisor

Supervisors' ratings are the heart of most appraisal systems. This is because getting a supervisor's appraisal is relatively easy and also makes a great deal of sense. The supervisor should be—and usually is—in the best position to observe and evaluate his or her subordinate's performance.

Using Peer Appraisals

The appraisal of an employee by his or her peers can be effective in predicting future management success. From a study of military officers, for example, we know that peer ratings were quite accurate in predicting which officers would be promoted and which would not.[31] In another study that involved more than 200 industrial managers, peer ratings were similarly useful in predicting who would be promoted.[32] One potential problem is "logrolling." Here all the peers simply get together to rate each other high.

With more firms using self-managing teams, peer or "team" appraisals are becoming more popular. At Digital Equipment Corporation, for example, an employee due for an appraisal chooses an appraisal "chairperson" each year. This person then selects one supervisor and three other peers to evaluate the employee's work.[33]

Using Rating Committees

Many employers use rating committees to evaluate employees. These committees are usually composed of the employee's immediate supervisor and three or four other supervisors.

There are several advantages to using multiple raters. While there may be a discrepancy in the ratings made by the different supervisors, the composite ratings tend to be more reliable, fair, and valid than those of individual raters.[34] Several raters can help cancel out problems like bias and halo effect on the part of individual raters. Furthermore, when there *are* differences in raters' ratings, they usually stem from the fact that raters at different levels often observe different facets of an employee's performance; the appraisal ought to reflect these differences.[35] Even when a committee is not used, it is common to have the appraisal reviewed by the manager immediately above the one who makes the appraisal. This was found to be standard practice in 16 of 18 companies surveyed in one study.[36]

This food service supervisor is conducting a feedback session about his performance during today's major banquet not only to gain information on his performance, but also to keep communications open and build employee commitment.

Self-ratings

Some employers use employees' self-ratings of performance (usually in conjunction with supervisors' ratings). The basic problem is that most studies show that employees consistently rate themselves higher than they are rated by supervisors or peers.[37] In one study, for example, it was found that when asked to rate their own job performances, 40% of the employees in jobs of all types placed themselves in the top 10% ("one of the best"), while virtually all remaining employees rated themselves either in the top 25% ("well above average"), or at least in the top 50% ("above average"). Usually, no more than 1% or 2% will place themselves in a below-average category, and then those are almost invariably in the top below-average category.

Self-appraisals should thus be used carefully. Supervisors requesting self-appraisals should know that their appraisals and the self-appraisals may accentuate differences and rigidify positions.[38] Furthermore, even if self-appraisals are not formally requested, each employee will enter the performance-review meeting with his or her own self-appraisal in mind, and this will usually be higher than the supervisor's rating.

Appraisal by Subordinates

More firms today let subordinates anonymously evaluate their supervisors' performance, a process many call *upward feedback*.[39] When conducted throughout the firm the process helps top managers diagnose management styles, identify potential "people" problems, and take corrective action with individual managers, as required. Such subordinate ratings are especially valuable when used for developmental rather than evaluative purposes.[40]

The Federal Express program is typical and is called Survey Feedback Action (SFA). SFA involves three phases. First, the survey itself is a standard, anonymous form given each year to every employee. The items on it are designed to gather information about those things that help and hinder employees in their work environment. Sample items include: Can tell my manager what I think; My manager tells me what is expected; My manager listens to my concerns; My manager keeps me informed; Upper management listens to ideas from my level; Fed Ex does a good job for our customers; In my environment we use safe work practices; and Paid fairly for this kind of work. Results of the survey for a work group are then compiled and returned to the manager. To ensure anonymity the smaller units do *not* receive their own results. Instead, their results are folded in with those of several other similar work units until a department of 20 or 25 people obtains the overall group's results.

The second phase involves a feedback session between the manager and his or her work group. The session's goal is to identify specific concerns or problems, examine specific causes for these problems, and devise action plans to correct the problems. As a result, managers are trained to ask probing questions. For example, suppose a low-scoring survey item was "I feel free to tell my manager what I think." Managers are trained to ask their groups questions such as "What restrains you?" (timing, specific behaviors); and "What do I do that makes you feel that I'm not interested?"

The feedback meeting should result in a third, "action plan" phase. The plan itself is a list of actions that the manager will take to address employees' concerns and hopefully boost results. Managers thus get an action planning worksheet containing four columns: What is the concern?, What's your analysis?, What's the cause?, and What should be done?

THE APPRAISAL INTERVIEW

MAIN TYPES OF INTERVIEWS

There are basically three types of **appraisal interviews**, each with its own objectives. They are summarized next.[41]

PERFORMANCE APPRAISAL INTERVIEW TYPE	APPRAISAL INTERVIEW OBJECTIVE
(1) Satisfactory—Promotable	(1) Make development plans
(2) Satisfactory—Not promotable	(2) Maintain performance
(3) Unsatisfactory—Correctable	(3) Plan correction
Unsatisfactory—Uncorrectable	Fire or tolerate (no interview needed)

In the last situation (unsatisfactory—uncorrectable), there is usually no need for any appraisal interview because the person's performance is not correctable anyway.

Satisfactory—Promotable

In this interview the person's performance is satisfactory and there is a promotion ahead. This is the easiest of the three appraisal interviews. Your objective is to discuss the person's career plans and to develop a specific action plan for the educational and professional development the person needs to move to the next job.

Satisfactory—Not Promotable

This interview is for employees whose performance is satisfactory but for whom promotion is not possible. Perhaps the person has reached his or her level of competence or perhaps there is no more room in the company. Some employees are also happy where they are and don't want a promotion.[42] Your objective here is not to improve or develop the person but to maintain satisfactory performance.

This is not easy. You will have to find incentives that are important to the person and are enough to maintain satisfactory performance. These might include extra time off, a small bonus, some extra authority to handle a somewhat enlarged job, and reinforcement, perhaps in the form of an occasional "well done!"

Unsatisfactory—Correctable

When the person's performance is unsatisfactory but correctable, the interview objective is to lay out an action plan (as explained later) for correcting the unsatisfactory performance.

HOW TO PREPARE FOR THE APPRAISAL INTERVIEW

There are three things to do.[43] First, *assemble the data*. Study the person's job description, compare the employee's performance to the standards, and review the files of the employee's previous appraisals. Next, *prepare the employee*. Give your employees at least a week's notice to review their work, read over their job descriptions, analyze problems, and gather their questions and comments. Finally, *choose the time and place*. Find a mutually agreeable time for the interview and allow enough time for the entire interview. Interviews with lower-level personnel like clerical workers and maintenance staff should take no more than an hour. Appraising management employees often takes two or three hours. Be sure the interview is done in a private place where you won't be bothered by phone calls or visitors.

HOW TO CONDUCT THE INTERVIEW

There are four things to keep in mind here:[44]

1. *Be direct and specific*. Talk in terms of objective work data. Use examples such as absences, tardiness, quality records, inspection reports, scrap or waste, orders processed, productivity records, material used or consumed, timeliness of tasks or projects, control or reduction of costs, numbers of errors, costs compared to budgets, customer correspondence, product returns, order processing time, inventory level and accuracy, accident reports, and so on.
2. *Don't get personal*. Don't say "*You're* too slow in producing those reports." Instead, *try* to compare the person's performance to a *standard* ("These reports should normally be done within 10 days"). Similarly, don't compare the person's performance to that of other people ("He's quicker than you are").
3. *Encourage the person to talk*. *Stop* and *listen* to what the person is saying; ask open-ended questions such as "What do you think we can do to improve the situation?"

Use a command such as "go on" or "tell me more." Restate the person's last point as a question, such as, "You don't think you can get the job done?"

4. *Don't tiptoe around.* Don't get personal, but do make sure the person leaves knowing specifically what he or she is doing right *and doing wrong*. Give specific examples; make sure the person understands, and get agreement before he or she leaves on how things will be improved, and by when. Develop an action plan such as this:

ACTION PLAN

Date: May 18

For: John, Assistant Plant Manager
Problem: Parts inventory too high
Objective: Reduce plant parts inventory by 10% in June

Action Steps	*When*	*Expected Results*
Determine average monthly parts inventory	6/2	Establish a base from which to measure progress
Review ordering quantities and parts usage	6/15	Identify overstock items
Ship excess parts to regional warehouse and scrap obsolete parts	6/20	Clear stock space
Set new ordering quantities for all parts	6/25	Avoid future overstocking
Check records to measure where we are now	7/1	See how close we are to objective

How to Handle a Defensive Subordinate

Defenses are a very important and familiar aspect of our lives. When a person is accused of poor performance, the first reaction will often be *denial*. By denying the fault, the person avoids having to question his or her competence. Others react to criticism with *anger and aggression*. This helps them let off steam and postpones confronting the immediate problem until they are able to cope with it. Still others react to criticism by *retreating* into a shell.

In any event, understanding and dealing with defensiveness is an important appraisal skill. Psychologist Mortimer Feinberg suggests the following:

1. *Recognize that defensive behavior is normal.*
2. *Never attack a person's defenses.* Don't try to "explain someone to themselves" by saying things like "you know the real reason you're using that excuse is because you can't bear to be blamed for anything." Instead, try to concentrate on the act itself ("sales are down") rather than on the person ("you're not selling enough").
3. *Postpone action.* Sometimes the best thing to do is to do nothing at all. People frequently react to sudden threats by instinctively hiding behind their "masks." But, given sufficient time, a more rational reaction takes over.

4. *Recognize your own limitations.* Don't expect to be able to solve every problem that comes up, especially the human ones. More important, remember that a supervisor should not try to be a psychologist. Offering your people understanding is one thing; trying to deal with deep psychological problems is another matter entirely.

Argumentative behavior on the part of the manager during a performance appraisal meeting undermines the usefulness of the evaluation process.

How to Criticize a Subordinate

When some criticism is required, it should be done in a manner that helps the person maintain his or her dignity and sense of worth. Specifically, criticism should be done in private and should be done constructively. Provide examples of critical incidents and specific suggestions of what could be done and why. Avoid once-a-year "critical broadsides" by giving feedback on a daily basis, so that at the formal review there are no surprises. Never say the person is "always" wrong (since no one is ever "always" wrong or right). Finally, criticism should be objective and free from any personal biases on your part.

How to Ensure That the Appraisal Interview Leads to Improved Performance

You should clear up job-related problems and set improvement goals and a schedule for achieving them. In one study the researchers found that whether or not subordinates expressed *satisfaction* with their appraisal interview depended mostly on three things: not feeling threatened during the interview; having an opportunity to present their ideas and feelings and to influence the course of the interview; and having a helpful and constructive supervisor conduct the interview.[45]

However, you don't just want subordinates to be satisfied with their appraisal interviews. Your main aim is to get them to improve their subsequent performance. Here researchers found that *clearing up job-related problems with the appraisee* and *setting measurable performance targets and a schedule for achieving them*—an action plan—were the actions that consistently led to improved performance.

How to Handle a Formal Written Warning

There will be times when your employee's performance is so poor that a formal written warning is required. Such written warnings serve two purposes: (1) They may serve to shake your employee out of his or her bad habits, and (2) they can help you defend your decision both to your own boss and (if needed) to the courts. Written warnings should thus identify the standards under which the employee is judged, make it clear that the employee was aware of the standard, specify any violation of the standard, and show the employee had an opportunity to correct his or her behavior.

▸ PERFORMANCE APPRAISAL IN PRACTICE

How do employers actually go about appraising performance? What tools do they use? A survey of current practice suggests the following:[46]

Computer Application in Performance Appraisal: Performance Analysis

One measure of the performance of HRM interviewers is how long the people they place stay with the company. This retention measure can be quantified, which makes it suitable for computerization. Personnel/HRM professionals often begin their careers interviewing applicants, sometimes without adequate training in interviewing techniques. And one purpose of an effective performance appraisal system is to pinpoint areas in which an employee needs further training.

If company research shows a high turnover rate of employees within the first six months of employment, for example, this implies mismatches between the employee and the position. The problem may be an inadequate job analysis (or its outcome, a poor job description), inaccurate job specifications, or a poorly trained interviewer. The first step is to establish what the retention rates are, both for interviewer and for the supervisor. (The supervisors are recorded because of their significant impact on retention, regardless of the input of HRM in the hiring process.)

Retention rates can be calculated by capturing the names, race, sex, position code of job applied for, department code where referred, and supervisor's code (a unique number or letters assigned to each supervisor who has hiring responsibilities). By linking this spreadsheet to one that lists new hires and one that lists terminations, retention rates can be calculated regularly. A macro (which combines several keystrokes into one set of directions taking two keystrokes) can link the spreadsheets, complete the calculations, and print the report.

A table can be constructed in which supervisors who have hired someone in the specified time frame are identified by a unique number or a two- or three-letter abbreviation. Each time a new employee is hired, one column of data would include the supervisor's identification. Through a data base count or extraction, you can total the number of employees hired by each supervisor in that time period. You can count only those supervisors to whom a given interviewer referred applicants by adjusting the formula to perform that discrimination of data. This is particularly helpful if the interviewer feels that one supervisor significantly impacted the retention rate negatively. This is an example of "What if. . .?" which allows managers to see how a change in facts affects the outcome—and possibly the manager's decision.

While retention rates should not be used as the sole measure of the effectiveness of an interviewer, it offers one objective performance measure on which to base decisions about future goals and/or training.

Almost all companies responding do have formal appraisal programs. About 93% of smaller organizations (those with fewer than 500 employees) have such programs. About 97% of large organizations have them.

Rating scales are by far the most widely used appraisal technique. About 62% of small organizations use rating scales, 20% use essays, and about 19% use MBO. Among large organizations, 51% use rating scales, just over 23% use essays, and about 17% use MBO.

However, those using ratings as the main appraisal technique typically also require narrative comments to justify ratings and to describe employee strengths and weaknesses and document development plans.[47] Those using essays as the main appraisal technique usually require an overall quantitative performance rating to facilitate employee comparisons for compensation decisions.

Ninety-two percent of appraisals are made by the employee's immediate supervisor. These appraisals are in turn reviewed by the appraiser's supervisor in 74% of the responding organizations.

Only about 7% of the organizations use self-appraisal in any part of the overall appraisal process.

Virtually all (99%) of employees are informed of the results of their appraisals. Overall, about 77% are given a chance to respond with written comments on their appraisals.

In 69% of companies, appraisals are done annually.

Instructions are important: 82% of employers provide written instructions for appraisers, and 60% provide training.

CHAPTER REVIEW

SUMMARY

1. Appraising performance plays a crucial role in improving motivation at work. People want and need feedback regarding how they are doing, and appraisal provides an opportunity for you to give them that feedback. And if performance is not up to par, the appraisal conference provides an opportunity to review your subordinate's progress and map out a plan for rectifying any performance deficiencies that might be identified.
2. Before the appraisal, make sure to clarify what performance you expect so that the employee knows what he or she should be shooting for. Ask, in other words, "What do I really expect this person to do?"
3. We described several performance appraisal tools, including the graphic rating scale, alternation ranking method, forced distribution method, BARS, MBO, and critical incident method.
4. Each of these techniques has its own advantages and disadvantages. Appraisal problems to beware of include unclear standards, the halo effect, the central tendency, the leniency or strictness problem, and bias.
5. Most subordinates probably want some specific explanation or examples regarding why they were appraised high or low and, for this, compiling *critical incidents* can be useful. Here, a running record of uncommonly good or undesirable examples of each person's work-related behavior should be maintained. This approach can be useful for identifying specific examples of good and poor performance in terms of the specific activities you expect your subordinates to perform. Even if your firm requires that you summarize the appraisal in a form like a graphic rating scale, maintaining a list of critical incidents can be useful when the time comes to discuss the appraisal with your subordinate.
6. It is important that your subordinate view the appraisal as a fair one, and in this regard there are four things you can do: Evaluate his or her performance frequently; make sure you are familiar with the person's performance; make sure there is an agreement between you and your subordinate concerning his or her job duties; and finally, solicit the person's help when you formulate plans for eliminating performance weaknesses.
7. There are three types of appraisal interviews, each with its own objectives. One is for performance that is unsatisfactory but correctable. Here, the objective of the interview is to lay out an action plan for correcting the unsatisfactory performance. The second type of interview is for employees whose performance is satisfactory but for whom promotion is not possible. Your objective here is not to improve or

develop the person but to maintain satisfactory performance. Finally, there is the satisfactory—promotable interview in which the main objective is to discuss the person's career plans and to develop a specific action plan for the educational and professional development the person needs to move on to the next job.

8. To prepare for the appraisal interview there are three things to do: Assemble the data, prepare the employee, and choose the time and place.
9. In actually conducting the interview, the main things to keep in mind are to set the tone at the start of the interview, be as positive as you can, summarize your own and your employee's views, and then develop an action plan like the one presented in this chapter.
10. To bring about some constructive change in your subordinate's behavior it is important to get the person to talk in the interview. Do's for encouraging the person to talk include: Try silence, use open-ended questions, state questions in terms of a problem, use a command question, use choice questions to try to understand the *feelings* underlying what the person is saying, and restate the person's last point as a question. On the other hand, *don't* do all the talking, use restrictive questions, be judgmental, give free advice, get involved with name calling, ridicule, digress, or use sarcasm.
11. The best way to handle a defensive subordinate is to proceed very carefully. Specifically, recognize that defensive behavior is normal, never attack a person's defenses, postpone actions, and recognize your own limitations.
12. If you are genuinely interested in using the appraisal interview to improve your subordinate's subsequent performance, the most important thing you should aim to accomplish is to clear up job-related problems and set improvement goals and a schedule for achieving them.

KEY TERMS

graphic rating scale
alternation ranking method
paired comparison method
forced distribution method
critical incident method
behaviorally anchored rating scale (BARS)
management by objectives (MBO)
unclear performance standards
halo effect
central tendency
strictness/leniency
bias
appraisal interviews

DISCUSSION QUESTIONS

1. Discuss the pros and cons of at least four performance appraisal tools.
2. Develop a graphic rating scale for the following jobs: secretary, engineer, directory assistance operator.
3. Evaluate the rating scale in table 10.1. Discuss ways to improve it.
4. Explain how you would use the alternation ranking method, the paired comparison method, and the forced distribution method.
5. Over the period of a week, develop a set of critical incidents covering the classroom performance of one of your instructors.
6. Explain in your own words how you would go about developing a behaviorally anchored rating scale.
7. Explain the problems to be avoided in appraising performance.
8. Discuss the pros and cons of using different potential raters to appraise a person's performance.
9. Explain the four types of appraisal interview objectives and how they affect how you manage the interview.
10. Explain how to conduct an appraisal interview.
11. Answer the question: "How would you get the interviewee to talk during an appraisal interview?"

APPLICATION EXERCISES

RUNNING CASE

CARTER CLEANING COMPANY

The Performance Appraisal

After spending several weeks on the job, Jennifer was surprised to discover that her father had not formally evaluated any employee's performance for all the years that he had owned the business. Jack's position was that he had "a hundred higher priority things to attend to," such as boosting sales and lowering costs, and, in any case, many employees didn't stick around long enough to be appraisable anyway. Furthermore, contended Jack, manual workers such as those doing the pressing and the cleaning did periodically get positive feedback in terms of praise from Jack for a job well done or criticism, also from Jack, if things did not look right during one of his swings through the stores. Similarly, Jack was never shy about telling his managers about store problems so that they, too, got some feedback on where they stood.

This informal feedback notwithstanding, Jennifer believes that a more formal appraisal approach is needed. She believes that there are criteria such as quality, quantity, attendance, and punctuality that should be evaluated periodically even if a worker is paid on piece rate. Furthermore, she feels quite strongly that the managers need to have a list of quality standards for matters such as store cleanliness, efficiency, safety, and adherence to budget on which they know they are to be formally evaluated.

Questions

1. Is Jennifer right about the need to evaluate the workers *formally*? The managers? Why or why not?
2. Develop a performance appraisal method for the workers and managers in each store.

CASE INCIDENT: *Appraising the Secretaries at Sweetwater U*

Rob Winchester, newly appointed vice-president for administrative affairs at Sweetwater State University, faced a tough problem shortly after his university career began. Three weeks after he came on board in September Sweetwater's president, Rob's boss, told him that one of his first problems would involve ways to improve the appraisal system used to evaluate secretarial and clerical performance at Sweetwater U. Apparently, the main difficulty was that the performance appraisal was traditionally tied directly to salary increases given at the end of the year. So most administrators were less than accurate when they used the graphic rating forms that were the basis of the clerical staff evaluation. In fact, what usually happened was that each administrator simply rated his or her clerk or secretary as "excellent." This cleared the way for all support staff to receive a maximum pay increase every year.

But the current university budget simply did not have enough money to fund another "maximum" annual increase for every staffer. Furthermore, Sweetwater's president felt that the custom of providing invalid feedback to each secretary on his or her year's performance was not a healthy situation, so he had asked the new vice-president to revise the system. In October, the vice-president sent a memo to all administrators telling them that in the future no more than half of the secretaries reporting to any particular administrator could be appraised as "excellent." This move, in effect, forced each supervisor to begin ranking his or her secretaries for quality of performance. The vice-president's memo met widespread resistance immediately—from administrators, who were afraid that many of their secretaries would begin leaving for more lucrative jobs in private industry, and from secretaries, who felt that the new system was unfair and reduced each secretary's chance of receiving a maximum salary. A handful of secretaries began quietly picketing outside the president's home on the university campus. The picketing, caustic remarks by disgruntled administrators, and rumors of an impending "slowdown" by the secretaries (there were about 250 on the campus) made Rob Winchester wonder whether he had made the right decision by setting up forced ranking. He knew, however, that there were a few performance appraisal experts in the School of Business, so he decided to set up an appointment with them to discuss the matter.

He met with them the next morning. He explained the situation as he had found it: The present appraisal system had been set up when the university first opened ten years earlier, and the appraisal form had been developed primarily by a committee of secretaries. Under that system, Sweetwater's administrators fill out forms similar to the one shown in Table 10.3. This once-a-year appraisal (in March) had run into problems almost immediately since it was apparent from the start that administrators vary widely in their interpretations of job standards, as well as in how conscientiously they filled out the forms and supervised their secretaries. Moreover, the defects of this procedure had become conspicuous at the end of the first year when it became obvious to everyone that each secretary's salary increase was tied directly to the March appraisal. For example, those rated "excellent" received the maximum increases, those rated "good" received smaller increases, and those given neither rating received only the standard across-the-board cost-of-living increase. Since universities in general—and Sweetwater U in particular—have paid secretaries somewhat lower salaries than those prevailing in private industry, some secretaries left in a huff that first year. From that time on most administrators simply rated all secretaries as excellent in order to save themselves staff turnover, thus ensuring each a maximum increase. In the process, they also avoided the hard feelings aroused by the significant performance differences otherwise highlighted by administrators.

Two of the Sweetwater experts agreed to consider the problem, and in two weeks they came back to the vice-president with the following recommendations. First, the form used to rate the secretaries was grossly insufficient. As written, it was unclear what "excellent" or "quality of work" meant, for example. As a result, most of the administrators they had spoken to were unclear as to the meaning of each item in the rating. They recommended instead a form like that in Figure 10.2. In addition, they recommended that the vice-president rescind his earlier memo and no longer attempt to force university administrators arbitrarily to rate at least half their secretaries as something less than excellent. The two consultants pointed out that this was, in fact, an unfair procedure since it was quite possible that any particular administrator might have staffers who were all or virtually all excellent—or conceivably, although less likely, all below standard. The experts said that the way to get all the administrators to take the appraisal process more seriously was to stop tying it to salary increases. In other words, they recommended that every administrator fill out a form like that in Figure 10.2 for each of his or her secretaries at least once a year and then use this form for the basis of a counseling session. Salary increases, however, would have to be made on some basis other than the performance appraisal so that administrators would no longer hesitate to fill out the rating forms honestly.

The vice-president thanked the two experts and went back to his office to ponder their recommendations. Some of the recommendations (such as substituting the new rating form for the old) seemed to make sense. Nevertheless, he still had serious doubts as to the efficacy of any graphic rating form, particularly if he were to decide in favor of his original forced-ranking approach. The experts' second recommendation—to stop tying the appraisals to automatic salary increases—made sense but raised at least one very practical problem: If salary increases were not to be based on performance appraisals, on what were they to be based? He began wondering whether the experts' recommendations weren't simply based on ivory tower theorizing.

Questions

1. Do you think that the experts' recommendations will be sufficient to get most of the administrators to fill out the rating forms properly? Why? Why not? What additional actions (if any) do you think will be necessary?
2. Do you think that Vice-President Winchester would be better off dropping the use of graphic rating forms, substituting instead one of the other techniques we discussed in this chapter, such as a ranking method?
3. What performance appraisal system would you develop for the secretaries if you were Rob Winchester? Defend your answer.

HUMAN RESOURCE MANAGEMENT SIMULATION

Your firm does not currently have a formal performance appraisal system. Some employees complain that the supervisors and managers give raises and perks to those they like and not necessarily to those who are most productive. Decreased turnover, increased morale, and higher productivity should result from a formal performance appraisal system.

In addition, incident E will provide several options for creating your own performance appraisal program. An important aspect of your selection will be to answer the question "Who should do the appraising?" Your team should discuss the consequences of each alternative. You will also be required to select the type of rating scale you are going to use. Because your firm has never had a formal appraisal system, should you select something straightforward and simple, or a more complex scale that will do the job in the longer run?

▶ NOTES

1. Kenneth Teel, "Performance Appraisal: Current Trends, Persistent Progress," *Personnel Journal* (April 1980), pp. 296–301. See also Christina Banks and Kevin Murphy, "Toward Narrowing the Research-Practice Gap in Performance Appraisals," *Personnel Psychology*, Vol. 38, no. 2 (Summer 1985), pp. 335–346. For a description of how to implement an improved performance appraisal system, see, for example, Ted Cocheu, "Performance Appraisal: A Case in Point," *Personnel Journal*, Vol. 65, no. 9 (September 1986), pp. 48–53; William H. Wagel, "Performance Appraisal with a Difference," *Personnel*, Vol. 64, no. 2 (February 1987), pp. 4–6; and Jeanette Cleveland et al., "Multiple Uses of Performance Appraisal: Prevalence and Correlates," *Journal of Applied Psychology*, Vol. 74, no. 1 (February 1989), pp. 130–135; Ian Carlton and Martyn Sloman, "Performance Appraisal in Practice," *Human Resource Management Journal*, Vol. 2, no. 3 (Spring 1992), pp. 80–94.
2. Teel, "Performance Appraisal," p. 301.
3. Ibid. See also Martin Friedman, "Ten Steps to Objective

Appraisals," *Personnel Journal*, Vol. 65, no. 6 (June 1986).
4. For a recent discussion see Gary English, "Tuning Up for Performance Management," *Training and Development Journal* (April 1991), pp. 56–60.
5. This is based on James Buford, Jr., Bettye Burkhalter, and Grover Jacobs, "Link Job Descriptions to Performance Appraisals," *Personnel Journal* (June 1988), pp. 132–140.
6. This is based on Commerce Clearing House, "Merck's New Performance Appraisal/Merit Pay System Is Based on Bell-Shaped Distribution," *Ideas and Trends*, May 17, 1989, pp. 88–90.
7. Commerce Clearing House Editorial Staff, "Performance Appraisal: What Three Companies Are Doing," Chicago, 1985. See also Richard Girard, "Are Performance Appraisals Passe?" *Personnel Journal*, Vol. 67, no. 8 (August 1988), pp. 89–90, which explains how companies can appraise performance using incidents instead of formal performance appraisals.
8. See, for example, Timothy Keaveny and Anthony McGann, "A Comparison of Behavioral Expectation Scales and Graphic Rating Scales," *Journal of Applied Psychology*, Vol. 60 (1975), pp. 695–703. See also John Ivancevich, "A Longitudinal Study of Behavioral Expectation Scales: Attitudes and Performance," *Journal of Applied Psychology* (April 1980), pp. 139–146.
9. Based on Donald Schwab, Herbert Heneman III, and Thomas DeCotiis, "Behaviorally Anchored Scales: A Review of the Literature," *Personnel Psychology*, Vol. 28 (1975), pp. 549–562. For a discussion, see also Uco Wiersma and Gary Latham, "The Practicality of Behavioral Observation Scales, Behavioral Expectations Scales, and Trait Scales," *Personnel Psychology*, Vol. 30, no. 3 (Autumn 1986), pp. 619–628.
10. Lawrence Fogli, Charles Hulin, and Milton Blood, "Development of First Level Behavioral Job Criteria," *Journal of Applied Psychology*, Vol. 55 (1971), pp. 3–8. See also Terry Dickenson and Peter Fellinger, "A Comparison of the Behaviorally Anchored Rating and Fixed Standard Scale Formats," *Journal of Applied Psychology* (April 1980), pp. 147–154.
11. Keaveny and McGann, "A Comparison of Behavioral Expectation Scales," pp. 695–703; Schwab, Heneman, and DeCotiis, "Behaviorally Anchored Rating Scales"; and James Goodale and Ronald Burke, "Behaviorally Based Rating Scales Need Not Be Job Specific," *Journal of Applied Psychology*, Vol. 60 (June 1975).
12. Wayne Cascio and Enzo Valenzi, "Behaviorally Anchored Rating Scales: Effects of Education and Job Experience of Raters and Ratees," *Journal of Applied Psychology*, Vol. 62, no. 3 (1977), pp. 278–282. See also Gary P. Latham and Kenneth N. Wexley, "Behavioral Observation Scales for Performance Appraisal Purposes," *Personnel Psychology*, Vol. 30, no. 2 (Summer 1977), pp. 255–268; H. John Bernardin, Kenneth M. Alvares, and C. J. Cranny, "A Recomparison of Behavioral Expectation Scales to Summated Scales," *Journal of Applied Psychology*, Vol. 61, no. 5 (October 1976), p. 564; Frank E. Saal and Frank J. Landy, "The Mixed Standard Rating Scale: An Evaluation," *Organizational Behavior and Human Performance*, Vol. 18, no. 1 (February 1977), pp. 19–35; Frank J. Landy et al., "Behaviorally Anchored Scales for Rating the Performance of Police Officers," *Journal of Applied Psychology*, Vol. 61, no. 6 (December 1976), pp. 750–758; and Kevin R. Murphy and Joseph Constans, "Behavioral Anchors as a Source of Bias in Rating," *Journal of Applied Psychology*, Vol. 72, no. 4 (November 1987), pp. 573–577.
13. See Martin Levy, "Almost-Perfect Performance Appraisals," *Personnel Journal*, Vol. 68, no. 4 (April 1989), pp. 76–83, for a good example of how one company fine tuned its form for individual performance.
14. Teel, "Performance Appraisal," pp. 297–298.
15. For a discussion of this see, for example, Wayne Cascio, *Applied Psychology in Personnel Management* (Reston, VA: Reston, 1978), pp. 337–341.
16. B. Rosen and T. H. Gerdee, "The Nature of Job Related Age Stereotypes," *Journal of Applied Psychology*, Vol. 61 (1976), pp. 180–183.
17. William J. Bigoness, "Effect of Applicant's Sex, Race and Performance on Employer's Performance Ratings: Some Additional Findings," *Journal of Applied Psychology*, Vol. 61 (February 1976). See also Duane Thompson and Toni Thompson, "Task-Based Performance Appraisal for Blue Collar Jobs: Evaluation of Race and Sex Effects," *Journal of Applied Psychology*, Vol. 70, no. 4 (1985), pp. 747–753.
18. Gerald Ferris, Valerie Yates, David Gilmore, and Kendrith Rowland, "The Influence of Subordinate Age on Performance Ratings and Casual Attributions," *Personnel Psychology*, Vol. 38, no. 3 (Autumn 1985), pp. 545–557. As another example, see Gregory Dobbins and Jeanne Russell, "The Biasing Effects of Subordinate Likeableness on Leader's Responses to Poor Performers: A Laboratory and Field Study," *Personnel Psychology*, Vol. 39, no. 4 (Winter 1986), pp. 759–778. See also Michael E. Benedict and Edward Levine, "Delay and Distortion: Passive Influences on Performance Appraisal Effectiveness," *Journal of Applied Psychology*, Vol. 73, no. 3 (August 1988), pp. 507–514, and James Smither et al., "Effect of Prior Performance Information on Ratings of Present Performance: Contrast Versus Assimilation Revisited," *Journal of Applied Psychology*, Vol. 73, no. 3 (August 1988), pp. 487–496.
19. Kevin Murphy, William Balzer, Maura Lockhart, and Elaine Eisenman, "Effects of Previous Performance on Evaluations of Present Performance," *Journal of Applied Psychology*, Vol. 70, no. 1 (1985), pp. 72–84. See also Kevin Williams, Angelo DeNisi, Bruce Meglino, and Thomas Cafferty, "Initial Decisions and Subsequent Performance Ratings," *Journal of Applied Psychology*, Vol. 71, no. 2 (May 1986), pp. 189–195.
20. W. C. Borman, "Effects of Instruction to Avoid Halo Error in Reliability and Validity of Performance Evaluation Ratings," *Journal of Applied Psychology*, Vol. 65 (1975), pp. 556–560; Borman points out that since no control group (a group of managers who did not undergo training) was available, it is possible that the observed effects were not due to the short five-minute training experience. G. P. Latham, K. N. Wexley, and E. D. Pursell, "Training Mangers to Minimize Rating Errors in the Observation of Behavior," *Journal of Applied Psychology*, Vol. 60 (1975), pp. 550–555; John Ivancevich, "Longitudinal Study of the Effects of Rater Training on Psychometric Error in Ratings," *Journal of Applied Psychology*, Vol. 64 (1979), pp. 502–508. For a related discussion, see, for example, Bryan Davis and Michael Mount, "Effectiveness of Performance Appraisal Training Using Computer Assistance Instruction and Behavior Modeling," *Personnel Psychology*, Vol. 37 (Fall 1984), pp. 439–452.
21. Walter Borman, "Format and Training Effects on Rating Accuracy and Rater Errors," *Journal of Applied Psychology*, Vol. 64 (August 1979), pp. 410–412, and Jerry Hedge and Michael Cavanagh, "Improving the Accuracy of Performance Evaluations: Comparison of Three Methods of Performance Appraiser Training," *Journal of Applied Psychology*, Vol. 73, no. 1 (February 1988), pp. 68–73.
22. Davis and Mount, "The Effectiveness of Performance Appraisal Training," *Personnel Psychology*, Vol. 37, pp. 439–452.

23. Dennis Warnke and Robert Billings, "Comparison of Training Methods for Improving the Psychometric Quality of Experimental and Administrative Performance Ratings," *Journal of Applied Psychology*, Vol. 64 (April 1979), pp. 124–131. See also Timothy Athey and Robert McIntyre, "Effect of Rater Training on Rater Accuracy: Levels of Processing Theory and Social Facilitation Theory Perspectives," *Journal of Applied Psychology*, Vol. 72, no. 4 (November 1987), pp. 567–572.
24. This is based primarily on Gary Lubben, Duane Tompason, and Charles Klasson, "Performance Appraisal: The Legal Implications of Title VII," *Personnel* (May–June 1980), pp. 11–21.
25. Shelley Burchett and Kenneth DeMeuse, "Performance Appraisal and the Law," *Personnel*, Vol. 62, no. 7 (July 1985), pp. 34–35.
26. See also Ian Carlson and Martyn Sloman, "Performance Appraisal in Practice," *Human Resource Management*, Vol. 2, No. 3, Spring 1992, pp. 80–94.
27. See for example Caryn Beck-Dudley and Glenn McEvoy, "Performance Appraisals and Discrimination Suits: Do Courts Pay Attention To Validity?", *Employee Responsibilities and Rights*, Vol. 4, No. 2, June 1991, pp. 149–163.
28. Gerarld Barrett and Mary Kernan, "Performance Appraisal and Terminations: A Review of Court Decisions Since *Brito* v. *Zia* with Implications for Personnel Practices," *Personnel Psychology*, Vol. 40, no. 3 (Autumn 1987), p. 499.
29. Wayne Cascio and H. John Bernardin, "Implications of Performance Appraisal Litigation for Personnel Decisions," *Personnel Psychology* (Summer 1981), pp. 211–212, and Barrett and Kernan, "Performance Appraisal and Terminations," pp. 489–504.
30. Barrett and Kernan, "Performance Appraisal and Terminations," p. 501.
31. R. G. Downey, F. F. Medland, and L. G. Yates, "Evaluation of a Peer Rating System for Predicting Subsequent Promotion of Senior Military Officers," *Journal of Applied Psychology*, Vol. 61 (April 1976), and Glenn McEvoy and Paul Buller, "User Acceptance of Peer Appraisals in an Industrial Setting," *Personnel Psychology*, Vol. 40, no. 4 (Winter 1987), pp. 785–798.
32. Allan Kraut, "Prediction of Managerial Success by Peer and Training Staff Ratings," *Journal of Applied Psychology*, Vol. 60 (February 1975). See also Michael Mount, "Psychometric Properties of Subordinate Ratings of Managerial Performance," *Personnel Psychology*, Vol. 37, no. 4 (Winter 1984), pp. 687–702.
33. Carol Norman and Robert Zawacki, "Team Appraisals—Team Approach," *Personnel Journal* (September 1991), pp. 101–103.
34. Robert Libby and Robert Blashfield, "Performance of a Composite as a Function of the Number of Judges," *Organizational Behavior and Human Performance*, Vol. 21 (April 1978), pp. 121–129; Walter Borman, "Exploring Upper Limits of Reliability and Validity in Job Performance Ratings," *Journal of Applied Psychology*, Vol. 63 (April 1978), pp. 135–144; M. M. Harris and J. Schaubroeck, "A Meta-Analysis of Self-Supervisor, Self-Peer, and Peer-Supervisor Ratings," *Personnel Psychology*, Vol. 41 (1988), pp. 43–62.
35. Walter C. Borman, "The Rating of Individuals in Organizations: An Alternate Approach," *Organizational Behavior and Human Performance*, Vol. 12 (1974), pp. 105–124.
36. Teel, "Performance Appraisal," p. 301.
37. George Thornton III, "Psychometric Properties of Self-appraisal of Job Performance," *Personnel Psychology*, Vol. 33 (Summer 1980), p. 265; Cathy Anderson, Jack Warner, and Cassie Spencer, "Inflation Bias in Self-assessment Evaluations: Implications for Valid Employee Selection," *Journal of Applied Psychology*, Vol. 69, no. 4 (November 1984), pp. 574–580. See also Shaul Fox and Yossi Dinur, "Validity of Self-assessment: A Field Evaluation," *Personnel Psychology*, Vol. 41, no. 3 (Autumn 1988), pp. 581–592; and John W. Lawrie, "Your Performance: Appraise It Yourself!" *Personnel*, Vol. 66, no. 1 (January 1989), pp. 21–33, a good explanation of how self-appraisals can be used at work.
38. Herbert Myer, "Self-appraisal of Job Performance," *Personnel Psychology*, Vol. 33 (Summer 1980), pp. 291–293; Robert Holzbach, "Rater Bias in Performance Ratings: Superior, Self, and Peer Ratings," *Journal of Applied Psychology*, Vol. 63, no. 5 (October 1978), pp. 579–588. Herbert G. Heneman III, "Comparison of Self and Superior Ratings of Managerial Performance," *Journal of Applied Psychology*, Vol. 59 (1974), pp. 638–642; Richard J. Klimoski and Manuel London, "Role of the Rater in Performance Appraisal," *Journal of Applied Psychology*, Vol. 59 (1974), pp. 445–451; Hubert S. Field and William H. Holley, "Subordinates' Characteristics, Supervisors' Ratings, and Decisions to Discuss Appraisal Results," *Academy of Management Journal*, Vol. 20, no. 2 (1977), pp. 215–221. See also Robert Steel and Nestor Ovalle II, "Self-appraisal Based Upon Supervisory Feedback," *Personnel Psychology*, Vol. 37, no. 4 (Winter 1984), pp. 667–685. See also Gloria Shapiro and Gary Dessler, "Are Self-appraisals More Realistic Among Professionals or Nonprofessionals in Health Care?" *Public Personnel Management*, Vol. 14 (Fall 1985), pp. 285–291; James Russell and Dorothy Goode, "An Analysis of Managers' Reactions to Their Own Performance Appraisal Feedback," *Journal of Applied Psychology*, Vol. 73, no. 1 (February 1988), pp. 63–67; and Harris and Shaubroeck, "A Meta-Analysis of Self-Supervisor, Self-Peer, and Peer-Supervisor Ratings," pp. 43–62.
39. Manuel London and Arthur Wohlers, "Agreement Between Subordinate and Self-Ratings in Upward Feedback," *Personnel Psychology*, Vol. 44 (1991), pp. 375–390.
40. Ibid., p. 376.
41. See also Jerald Greenberg "Using Explanations to Manage Impressions of Performance Appraisal Fairness," *Employee Responsibilities and Rights*, Vol. 4, No. 1, March 1991, pp. 51–60.
42. Johnson, *The Appraisal Interview Guide*, Chapter 9.
43. Judy Block, *Performance Appraisal on the Job: Making It Work* (New York: Executive Enterprises Publications, 1981), pp. 58–62. See also Terry Lowe, "Eight Ways to Ruin a Performance Review," *Personnel Journal*, Vol. 65, no. 1 (January 1986).
44. Block, *Performance Appraisal on the Job*.
45. Ronald Burke, William Weitzel, and Tamara Weis, "Characteristics of Effective Employee Performance Review and Development Interviews: Replication and Extension," *Personnel Psychology*, Vol. 31 (Winter 1978), pp. 903–919. See also Joane Pearce and Lyman Porter, "Employee Response to Formal Performance Appraisal Feedback," *Journal of Applied Psychology*, Vol. 71, no. 2 (May 1986), pp. 211–218.
46. Allan Locher and Kenneth Teel, "Appraisal Trends," *Personnel Journal* (September 1988), pp. 139–145. This paper describes a survey sent to 1,459 organizations belonging to the Personnel and Industrial Relations Association of Southern California; 324 companies responded.
47. Ibid., p. 140.

CHAPTER 11

MANAGING CAREERS

OVERVIEW

In many cases, the key to a firm's winning commitment from their employees is offering them a chance to have a successful and fulfilling career. In this chapter we discuss the factors (such as interests) that affect career choices. Next, we describe some guidelines for making an employee's first assignment more effective. We then explain important promotion-related decisions that firms have to make (such as whether seniority or competence will be the criterion). Finally, we describe "career management in practice" and explain how firms actually use practices such as career-oriented appraisals to develop employees and help win their commitment. When you finish studying this chapter you should be able to discuss factors that influence career decisions; explain how you'd go about making effective first-job assignments; and describe practices firms use to help their employees have more successful careers.

▶ Introduction: HR Career Management

Personnel activities like screening, training, and appraising serve two basic roles in organizations. First, their traditional role has been to staff the organization—to fill its positions with employees who have the requisite interests, abilities, and skills. Increasingly, however, these activities are taking on a second role—that of ensuring that the long-run interests of the employees are protected by the organization and that, in particular, the employee is encouraged to grow and realize his or her full potential. Referring to *staffing* or *personnel management* as *human resource management* reflects this second role. A basic assumption underlying the focus on human resource management is that the organization has an obligation to utilize its employees' abilities to the fullest and to give each employee a chance to grow and to realize his or her full potential, and to develop a successful career.[1] One way this trend is manifesting itself is in the increased emphasis many firms are placing on **career planning and development**, an emphasis, in other words, on giving employees the assistance and opportunities that will enable them to form realistic career goals and realize them.

career planning and development
Giving employees the assistance to form realistic career goals and the opportunities to realize them.

Activities like personnel planning, screening, and training play a big role in the career development process. Personnel planning, for example, can be used not just to forecast open jobs but to identify potential internal candidates and the training they would need to fill these jobs. Similarly, an organization can use its periodic employee appraisals not just for salary decisions but for identifying the development needs of individual employees and of ensuring that these needs are met. All the staffing activities, in other words, can be used to satisfy the needs of both the organization and the individual in such a way that they both gain: the organization from improved performance from a more committed work force and the employee from a richer, more challenging career.[2]

▶ Factors That Affect Career Choices

The first step in planning a career (your own or someone else's) is to learn as much as you can about the person's interests, aptitudes, and skills.

IDENTIFY THE PERSON'S CAREER STAGE

career cycle
The stages through which a person's career evolves.

Each person's career goes through stages, and it is important that you understand the nature of this **career cycle**. It is important because the stage you are in will influence your knowledge of and preference for various occupations. The main stages one's career goes through can be summarized as follows:[3]

growth stage
Period from birth to age 14 during which the person develops a self-concept by identifying with and interacting with other people such as family, friends, and teachers.

Growth Stage

The **growth stage** lasts roughly from birth to age 14 and is a period during which the person develops a self-concept by identifying with and interacting with other people such as family, friends, and teachers. Toward the beginning of this period, role playing is important, and children experiment with different ways of acting; this helps them to form impressions of how other people react to different behaviors and contributes to their developing a unique self-concept, or identity. Toward the end of this stage, the adolescent (who by this time has developed some preliminary ideas of what his or her interests and abilities are) begins some realistic thinking about alternative occupations.

Exploration Stage

exploration stage The period from around ages 15 to 24 during which a person seriously explores various occupational alternatives, attempting to match these alternatives with his or her interests and abilities.

The **exploration stage** is the period, roughly from ages 15 to 24, during which a person seriously explores various occupational alternatives. The person attempts to match these alternatives with what he or she has learned about them, and about his or her own interests and abilities from school, leisure activities, and part-time work. Some tentative broad occupational choices are usually made during the beginning of this period. This choice is refined as the person learns more about the choice and about him- or herself. Then, toward the end of this period, a seemingly appropriate choice is made and the person tries out for a beginning job.

Probably the most important task the person has in this and the preceding stage is that of developing a realistic understanding of his or her abilities and talents. Similarly, the person must make sound educational decisions based on reliable sources of information about occupational alternatives.

Establishment Stage

establishment stage The period, roughly from ages 24 to 44, that is the heart of most people's work lives.

trial substage The period from about age 25 to 30 during which the person determines whether or not the chosen field is suitable and if it is not, attempts to change it.

stabilization substage The period, roughly from age 30 to 40, during which firm occupational goals are set and more explicit career planning is made to determine the sequence for accomplishing these goals.

midcareer crisis substage The period occurring between the mid-thirties and mid-forties during which people often make a major reassessment of their progress relative to their original career ambitions and goals.

The **establishment stage** spans roughly ages 24 to 44 and is the heart of most people's work lives. Sometime during this period (toward the beginning, it is hoped), a suitable occupation is found and the person engages in those activities that help him or her earn a permanent place in it. Often (and particularly in the professions) the person locks on to a chosen occupation early. But in most cases, this is a period during which the person is continually testing his or her capabilities and ambitions against those of the initial occupational choice.

The establishment stage is itself comprised of three substages. The **trial substage** lasts from about ages 25 to 30: During this period the person determines whether or not the chosen field is suitable; if it is not, several changes might be attempted. (Jane Smith might have her heart set on a career in retailing, for example, but after several months of constant travel as a newly hired assistant buyer for a department store, she might decide that a less travel-oriented career such as that in market research is more in tune with her needs.) Roughly between the ages of 30 and 40, the person goes through a **stabilization substage**. Here firm occupational goals are set and the person does more explicit career planning to determine the sequence of promotions, job changes, and/or any educational activities that seem necessary for accomplishing these goals. Finally, somewhere between the mid-thirties and midforties, the person may enter the **midcareer crisis substage**. During this period people often make a major reassessment of their progress relative to original ambitions and goals. They may find that they are not going to realize their dreams (such as being company president) or that, having accomplished what they set out to do, their dreams are not all they were cut out to be. Also during this period, people have to decide how important work and career are to be in their total life. It is often during this midcareer substage that the person is, for the first time, faced with the difficult decisions of what he or she really wants, what really can be accomplished, and how much must be sacrificed to achieve it.

maintenance stage The period from about ages 45 to 65 during which the person secures his or her place in the world of work.

Maintenance Stage

Between the ages of 45 to 65, many people simply slide from the stabilization substage into the **maintenance stage**. During this latter period the person has typically created for him- or herself a place in the world of work and most efforts are now directed to securing that place.

decline stage The period during which many people are faced with the prospect of having to accept reduced levels of power and responsibility.

Decline Stage

As retirement age approaches, there is often a deceleration period. Here many people face the prospect of having to accept reduced levels of power and responsibility and learn to accept and develop new roles as mentor and confidante for those who are younger. There is then the more or less inevitable retirement, after which the person is faced with the prospect of finding alternative use for the time and effort formerly expended on his or her occupation.

IDENTIFY OCCUPATIONAL ORIENTATION

John Holland The career-counseling expert who carried out research with his *Vocational Preference Test.*

Career-counseling expert **John Holland** says that a person's personality (including values, motives, and needs) is another important determinant of career choices. Specifically, he says there are six basic "personal orientations" that determine the sorts of careers to which people are drawn. For example, a person with a strong *social orientation* might be attracted to careers that entail interpersonal rather than intellectual or physical activities and to occupations such as social work. Based on research with his *Vocational Preference Test (VPT),* Holland found six basic personality types or orientations.[4]

1. *Realistic orientation.* These people are attracted to occupations that involve physical activities requiring skill, strength, and coordination. Some examples include forestry, farming, and agriculture.
2. *Investigative orientation.* These people are attracted to careers that involve cognitive (thinking, organizing, understanding) rather than affective (feeling, acting, or interpersonal and emotional) activities. Examples include biologist, chemist, and college professor.
3. *Social orientation.* These people are attracted to careers that involve interpersonal rather than intellectual or physical activities. Examples include clinical psychology, foreign service, and social work.
4. *Conventional orientation.* These people prefer careers that involve structured, rule-regulated activities, as well as careers in which it is expected that the employee subordinate his or her personal needs to those of the organization. Examples include accountants and bankers.
5. *Enterprising orientation.* These people are attracted to careers that involve verbal activities aimed at influencing others. Examples include managers, lawyers, and public relations executives.
6. *Artistic orientation.* People here are attracted to careers that involve self-expression, artistic creation, expression of emotions, and individualistic activities. Examples include artists, advertising executives, and musicians.

Most people have more than one orientation (they might be social, realistic and investigative, for example), and Holland believes that the more similar or compatible these orientations are, the less internal conflict or indecision a person will face in making a career choice. To help illustrate this, Holland suggests placing each orientation in one corner of a hexagon, as in Figure 11.1. As you can see, the model has six corners, each of which represents one personal orientation (for example, enterprising). According to Holland's research, the closer two orientations are in this figure, the more compatible they are. Holland believes that if your number one and number two orientations fall side by side, you will have an easier time choosing a career. However, if your orientations turn out to be opposite (such as realistic and social), you may experience more indecision in making a career choice because your interests are driving you toward very different types of careers.

occupational orientation
The theory developed by John Holland that says there are six basic personal orientations that determine the sorts of careers to which people are drawn.

In Table 11.1, we have summarized some of the occupations that have been found to be the best match for each of these six personal **occupational orientations**. For example, people with realistic orientations often gravitate toward occupations such as carpentry, engineering, farming, forestry, highway patrol, and machinist. Those with investigative orientations gravitate toward astronomy, biology, and chemistry.

IDENTIFY SKILLS

Successful performance depends not just on motivation but on ability as well. You may (for example) have a Conventional orientation, but whether you have the *skills* to be an accountant, banker, or credit manager will largely determine *which specific occupation* you choose in the end. Therefore, you have to identify your skills—or those of your employees.

occupational skills
The skills needed to be successful in a particular occupation. According to the *Dictionary of Occupational Titles,* occupational skills break down into three groups depending on whether they emphasize data, people, or things.

An Exercise

One useful exercise for identifying **occupational skills** is as follows: Take a blank piece of paper and write in the heading "The Most Enjoyable Occupational Tasks I Have Had." Then write a short essay that describes the tasks. Make sure to go into as much detail as you can about your duties and responsibilities and what it was about each task that you found enjoyable. (In writing your essay, by the way, notice that it's not necessarily the most enjoyable *job* you've had but the most enjoyable *task* you've had to perform; you may have

FIGURE 11.1
Choosing an Occupational Orientation

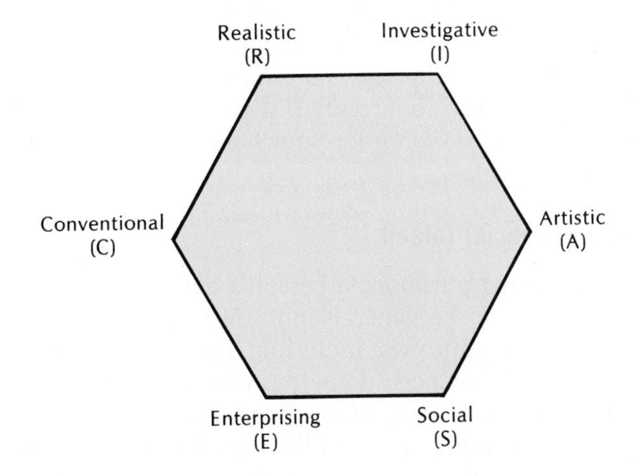

TABLE 11.1 Occupations Scoring High on Each Occupational Orientation Theme

REALISTIC	INVESTIGATIVE	ARTISTIC	SOCIAL	ENTERPRISING	CONVENTIONAL
Consider these occupations if you score *high* here:					
Agribusiness managers	Biologists	Advertising executives	Auto sales dealers	Agribusiness managers	Accountants
Carpenters	Chemists	Art teachers	Guidance counselors	Auto sales dealers	Auto sales dealers
Electricians	Engineers	Artists	Home economics teachers	Business education teachers	Bankers
Engineers	Geologists	Broadcasters	Mental health workers	Buyers	Bookkeepers
Farmers	Mathematicians	English teachers	Ministers	Chamber of Commerce executives	Business education teachers
Foresters	Medical technologists	Interior decorators	Physical education teachers	Funeral directors	Credit managers
Highway patrol officers	Physicians	Medical illustrators	Recreation leaders	Life insurance agents	Executive housekeepers
Horticultural workers	Physicists	Ministers	School administrators	Purchasing agents	Food service managers
Industrial arts teachers	Psychologists	Musicians	Social science teachers	Realtors	IRS agents
Military enlisted personnel	Research and development managers	Photographers	Social workers	Restaurant managers	Mathematics teachers
Military officers	Science teachers	Public relations directors	Special education teachers	Retail clerks	Military enlisted personnel
Vocational agricultural teachers	Sociologists	Reporters	YMCA/YWCA directors	Store managers	Secretaries

Note: for example, if you score high on "realistic," consider a career as a carpenter, engineer, farmer, and so on.

Source: Reproduced by special permission of the publisher, Consulting Psychologists Press, Inc., Palo Alto, CA 94306, from *Manual for the SVIV-SCII,* Fourth Edition, by Jo-Ida C. Hansen and David P. Campbell. © 1985 by the Board of Trustees of Leland Stanford Junior University.

had jobs that you really didn't like except for one of the specific duties or tasks in the job, which you really enjoyed.) Next, on other sheets of paper, do the same thing for two other tasks you have had. Now, go through your three essays and *underline the skills that you mentioned the most often.* For example, did you enjoy putting together and *coordinating* the school play when you worked in the principal's office one year? Did you especially enjoy the hours you spent in the library *doing research* for your boss when you worked one summer as an office clerk?[5]

aptitudes
These include intelligence, numerical aptitude, mechanical comprehension, and manual dexterity, as well as talents such as artistic, theatrical, or musical ability that play an important role in career decisions.

Aptitudes and Special Talents

For career planning purposes, a person's aptitudes are usually measured with a test battery such as the general aptitude test battery (GATB). This instrument measures various aptitudes including intelligence and mathematical ability. Considerable work has been done to relate aptitudes, such as those measured by the GATB, to specific occupations. For example, the U.S. Department of Labor's *Dictionary of Occupational Titles* lists the nature and titles of hundreds of occupations, along with the aptitudes required for success in these occupations.[6]

IDENTIFYING CAREER ANCHORS

Edgar Schein
Based on his research at the Massachusetts Institute of Technology, he identified five career anchors: creativity, managerial, security, technical, autonomy/independence.

career anchors
A concern or value that you will not give up if a choice has to be made.

Edgar Schein says that career planning is a continuing process of discovery—one in which a person slowly develops a clearer occupational self-concept in terms of what his or her talents, abilities, motives, needs, attitudes, and values are. Schein also says that as you learn more about yourself, it becomes apparent that you have a dominant **career anchor**, a *concern or value that you will not give up if a choice has to be made.* Career anchors, as their name implies, are the pivots around which a person's career swings; a person becomes conscious of them as a result of learning about his or her talents and abilities, motives and needs, and attitudes and values. Based on his research at the Massachusetts Institute of Technology, Schein believes that career anchors are difficult to predict ahead of time because they are evolutionary and a product of a process of discovery. Some people may never find out what their career anchors are until they have to make a major choice—such as whether to take the promotion to the headquarters staff or strike out on their own by starting a business. It is at this point that all the person's past work experiences, interests, aptitudes, and orientations converge into a meaningful pattern (or career anchor) that helps show what is personally the most important. Based on his study of MIT graduates, Schein identified five career anchors.[7]

Bill Gates, CEO of Microsoft, has built his career and company around the managerial-competence and creativity-career anchors.

Technical/Functional Career Anchor

People who have a strong technical/functional career anchor tend to avoid decisions that would drive them toward general management. Instead, they make decisions that will enable them to remain and grow in their chosen technical or functional fields.

Managerial Competence as a Career Anchor

Other people showed a strong motivation to become managers, "and their career experience enables them to believe that they have the skills and values necessary to rise to such general management positions." A management position of high responsibility is these peoples' ultimate goal. When pressed to explain why they believed they had the skills necessary to gain such positions, many answered that they were qualified for these jobs because of what they saw as their *competencies* in a combination of three areas: (1) analytical competence (ability to identify, analyze, and solve problems under conditions of incomplete information and uncertainty); (2) interpersonal competence (ability to influence, supervise, lead, manipulate, and control people at all levels); and (3) emotional competence (the capacity to be stimulated by emotional and interpersonal crises rather than exhausted or debilitated by them, and the capacity to bear high levels of responsibility without becoming paralyzed).

Creativity as a Career Anchor

Some of the graduates had gone on to become successful entrepreneurs. To Schein these people seemed to have a need "to build or create something that was entirely their own product—a product or process that bears their name, a company of their own, or a personal fortune that reflects their accomplishments." For example, one graduate had become a successful purchaser, restorer, and renter of townhouses in a large city; another had built a successful consulting firm.

Autonomy and Independence as Career Anchors

Some seemed driven by the need to be on their own, free from the dependence that can arise when a person elects to work in a large organization where promotions, transfers, and salary decisions make them dependent on others. Many of these graduates also had a strong technical/functional orientation. However, instead of pursuing this orientation in an organization, they had decided instead to become consultants, working either alone or as part of a relatively small firm. Others had become professors of business, free-lance writers, and proprietors of a small retail business.

Security as a Career Anchor

A few of the graduates were mostly concerned with long-run career stability and job security. They seemed willing to do what was required to maintain job security, a decent income, and a stable future in the form of a good retirement program and benefits.

For those interested in *geographic security,* maintaining a stable, secure career in familiar surroundings was generally more important than was pursuing superior career choices, if choosing the latter meant injecting instability or insecurity into their lives—by forcing them to pull up roots and move to another city. For others, security meant *organizational security.* They might today opt for government jobs, where tenure still tends to be a way of life. They were much more willing to let their employers decide what their careers should be.

Assessing Career Anchors

To help you identify career anchors, take a few sheets of blank paper and write out your answers to the following questions:[8]

1. What was your major area of concentration (if any) in high school? Why did you choose that area? How did you feel about it?
2. What is (or was) your major area of concentration in college? Why did you choose that area? How did you feel about it?
3. What was your first job after school (include military if relevant)? What were you looking for in your first job?
4. What were your ambitions or long-range goals when you started your career? Have they changed? When? Why?
5. What was your first major change of job or company? What were you looking for in your next job?
6. What was your next major change of job, company, or career? Why did you initiate or accept it? What were you looking for? (Do this for each of your major changes of job, company, or career.)
7. As you look back over your career, identify some times you have especially enjoyed. What was it about those times that you enjoyed?
8. As you look back, identify some times you have not especially enjoyed. What was it about those times you did not enjoy?
9. Have you ever refused a job move or promotion? Why?
10. Now review all your answers carefully, as well as the descriptions for the five career anchors (managerial competence, technical/functional, security, creativity, autonomy). Based on your answers to the questions, rate each of the anchors from 1 to 5; 1 equals low importance, 5 equals high importance.
    Managerial competence ____
    Technical/functional competence ____
    Security ____ Creativity ____ Autonomy ____

WHAT DO YOU WANT TO DO?

We have explained occupational orientations, skills, and career anchors and the role these play in choosing a career. But there is (at least) one more exercise you should try that can prove enlightening. That is to answer the question, "If you could have any kind of job, what would it be?" Invent your own job if need be, and don't worry about what you *can* do—just what you *want to do.*[9]

IDENTIFYING HIGH-POTENTIAL OCCUPATIONS

Learning about yourself is only half the job of picking an occupation. You also have to identify those occupations that are right (given your occupational orientations, skills, career anchors, and occupational preferences) as well as those which will be in high demand in the years to come.

Finding Out About Occupations and Careers

Investigating occupations can take hours (or perhaps days or weeks) of library research. The *Dictionary of Occupational Titles* is the bible of the vocational field and lists detailed job descriptions for more than 20,000 occupations. The *Dictionary of Occupational Titles* provides, for each title, a listing of the responsibilities, duties, and procedures for each job in the manual. Also listed for each job are the physical demands of the job, as well as individual working conditions, and (based on the judgment of experts) the interests, aptitudes, educational requirements, and vocational preparation required of those seeking each job. The *Occupational Outlook Handbook* gives an outline for about 700 occupations, including the prospects for the occupation and the major work, required training, earnings, and working conditions. There is also an *Occupational Outlook Handbook for College Graduates,* and the U.S. Employment Service publishes *Occupations in Demand,* a comprehensive listing of jobs most frequently requested of 2,500 job service offices around the country. *Occupations in Demand* provides information on local areas having large numbers of openings, industries requesting workers, pay ranges, and average number of openings available. It also lists jobs not requiring previous work experience.

Occupational Outlook Quarterly is published every three months and provides information on (among other things) occupations that are most in demand. Another source is the *Encyclopedia of Careers and Vocational Guidance,* which provides descriptions of over 650 occupations. For information on federal jobs and filling out applications, try the U.S. Office of Personnel Management's *Handbook X118,* which gives detailed job descriptions for hundreds of government positions. The U.S. Office of Education, in conjunction with Harvard University, has developed a computerized career information system called the *Guidance Information System* (GIS). Using this computerized system, you provide input on your occupational preferences and skills. The system then suggests one or more feasible matching occupations.

There are two basic things you or your employee can and should do to improve the career decisions you make.[10] First, you have to *take charge* of your own career by understanding that there are major decisions to be made and that making them requires considerable personal planning and effort. In other words, you cannot leave your choices in the hands of others but must decide where you want to go in terms of a career and what job moves and education are required to get there. Related to this, you have to become an effective *diagnostician.* You have to determine (through career counseling, testing, self-diagnostic books, and so on) what your talents or values are and how these fit with the sorts of careers you are considering.[11] In other words, the key to career planning is self-insight—into what you want out of a career, into your talents and limitations, and into your values and how they will fit in with the alternatives being considered. As Schein points out: "Too many people never ask, much less attempt to answer, these kinds of questions. It was shocking to me when I conducted the interviews for the MIT panel study and discovered how many respondents said they had never in 10 years of their careers asked themselves the kinds of questions which I was asking just to fill in the details of their job history."[12]

Career Management and the First Assignment

CAREER-MANAGEMENT GUIDELINES

Understanding your employee's occupational interests, anchors, and skills and then placing him or her onto a career track that's most fitting is one way to use "personnel" to help optimize personal growth and development. Factors to keep in mind about the important first assignment include:

Avoid Reality Shock

Perhaps at no other stage in the person's career is it more important for the employer to take career development into account than at the initial entry stage during which the person is recruited, hired, and given a first assignment and boss. For the employee this is a period during which he or she has to develop a sense of confidence, learn to get along with the first boss and with coworkers, learn how to accept responsibility, and, most important, gain an insight into his or her talents, needs, and values as they relate to initial career goals. For the new employee, in other words this is (or should be) a period of *reality testing* during which his or her initial hopes and goals first confront the reality of organizational life and of the person's talents and needs.

For many first-time workers, this turns out to be a disastrous period, one in which their often naive expectations first confront the realities of organizational life. The young MBA or CPA, for example, might come to the first job seeking a challenging, exciting assignment in which to apply the new techniques learned in school and to prove his or her abilities and gain a promotion. In reality, however, the trainee is often turned off by being relegated to an unimportant low-risk job where he or she "can't cause any trouble while being tried out;" or by the harsh realities of interdepartmental conflict and politicking; or by a boss who is neither rewarded for nor trained in the unique mentoring tasks needed to properly supervise new employees.[13] **Reality shock** refers to the results of a period that may occur at the initial career entry when the new employee's high job expectations confront the reality of a boring, unchallenging job.

reality shock
Results of a period that may occur at the initial career entry when the new employee's high job expectations confront the reality of a boring, unchallenging job.

Provide Challenging Initial Jobs

Most experts therefore agree that one of the most important things you can do is provide new employees with challenging first jobs. In one study of young managers at AT&T, for example, the researchers found that the more challenging a person's job was in his or her first year with the company, the more effective and successful the person was even five or six years later.[14] Based on his own research, Hall contends that challenging initial jobs provide "one of the most powerful yet uncomplicated means of aiding the career development of new employees."[15] In most organizations, however, providing such jobs seems more the exception than the rule. In one survey of research and development organizations, for example, only 1 out of 22 companies had a formal policy of giving challenging first assignments.[16] And this, as one expert has pointed out, is an example of "glaring mismanagement" when one considers the effort and money invested in recruiting, hiring, and training new employees.[17]

Other firms are generally different—they "front-load" the job challenge by giving new employees considerable responsibility. At Saturn and Toyota even assembly workers are assigned at once to self-managing teams of highly skilled and motivated colleagues where they must quickly learn to be productive team members. At Goldman Sachs young professionals are expected to contribute at once and immediately find themselves on teams involved in challenging projects. As one manager there said:[18]

> Even with fairly new employees, the partner in charge will usually not be the first one to speak when a project team meets with a client—often the newest member will; you take the responsibility and you're supported by the team. That's what attracts people to Goldman Sachs, the ability to make decisions early.

Making a major presentation to an important client is one way to front-load entry level jobs with challenge and to foster employee commitment.

The merchandising manager trainee position at JC Penney's (their entry-level management position) is another good example. A trainee almost straight out of college might be assigned the job of supervising the jeans section in the menswear department. Fresh from college, in other words, he or she would be responsible (under the guidance of his or her manager) for the section's display, inventory management, customer service, and staffing. As one Penney's manager put it, "From my first day as a merchandising manager trainee—straight out of college—I was running the 'store within a store.' JC Penney gives you guidance as you go along but won't hold your hand. You're kind of 'bracketed' in what you can do but you're basically running your own little shop."[19]

The new merchandise manager trainees remain as trainees for about 12 months. During this time they are responsible for training themselves. To facilitate this process, they receive various training manuals, including "The Role of a First Level Supervisor." This describes the trainee's responsibilities for activities including customer service, sales, gross profit, merchandising, visual merchandising, sales promotion, staffing, and time management. Each new trainee is also assigned a mentor—usually a merchandising manager or senior merchandising manager. The mentor provides guidance and weekly appraisals. The training program, however, is self-administered: The trainee is responsible for teaching him- or herself the merchandising job's details.

Trainees are appraised weekly by their mentors according to a schedule. At the end of week two, for instance, their personal selling skills are appraised. In week three their visual merchandising skills are appraised, and in week four their sales leadership, and so on.

At the end of eight weeks the trainee gets an extensive appraisal. At this point he or she meets with three people—the store manager, merchandising manager, and senior merchandising manager—and has what one manager referred to as a "very frank, outgoing discussion." A typical comment might be, "You're going to have to be much more outgoing if you want a successful career here." They "lay it on the table" as one executive said, telling the trainee where he or she stands, what progress is being made, and what development is required.

After six months trainees usually move into new assignments, where they assume more responsibility, usually running larger departments. At the end of a year they're generally ready for promotion to merchandising manager.

Provide Realistic Job Previews in Recruiting

Providing recruits with realistic previews of what to expect once they begin working in the organization can be an effective way of minimizing reality shock and improving their long-term performance. Schein points out that one of the biggest problems recruits (and employers) encounter during the crucial entry stage is getting accurate information in a "climate of mutual selling."[20] The recruiter (anxious to hook good candidates) and the candidate (anxious to present as favorable an impression as possible) often give and receive unrealistic information during the interview. The result is that the interviewer may not form a realistic picture of the candidate's career goals, while at the same time the candidate forms an unrealistically favorable image of the organization.[21]

Realistic job previews can significantly improve the survival rate among employees who are being hired for relatively complex jobs like those of management trainee, salesperson, or life insurance agent.[22] They are also used very successfully by firms such as Toyota and Saturn to show assembler recruits what their jobs will be like and how demanding the environments will be at these firms.

Be Demanding

There is often a "Pygmalion effect"[23] in the relationship between a new employee and his or her boss.[24] In other words, the more you expect and the more confident and supportive you are of your new employees, the better they will perform. Therefore, as two experts put it, "Don't assign a new employee to a 'dead wood,' undemanding, or unsupportive supervisor."[25] Instead, choose specially trained, high-performing, supportive supervisors who can set high standards for new employees during their critical exploratory first year.

Provide Periodic Job Rotation and Job Pathing

The best way new employees can test themselves and crystallize their career anchors is by trying out a variety of challenging jobs. By rotating the person to jobs in various specializations—from financial analysis to production to human resource, for example—the employee gets an opportunity to assess his or her aptitudes and preferences. At the same time, the organization gets a manger with a broader multifunctional view of the organization.[26] One extension of this is called *job pathing,*[27] which involves carefully sequenced job assignments.

Career-Oriented Performance Appraisals

Edgar Schein says that supervisors must understand that valid performance appraisal information is in the long run more important than protecting the

COMPUTER APPLICATION IN CAREER COUNSELING

One of the thorniest problems a job-hunter faces is the relative dearth of qualified advisors out there to help in the job search. As explained elsewhere, some employers have a policy of retaining outplacement specialists for the purpose of providing career counseling and job search help to the employees they lay off. However, such qualified outplacement specialists generally (though not always) deal exclusively with employer-paid assignments: You can't just walk into one and have them help you, in other words. Beyond this, the field of job search help runs the gamut from the generally qualified college career counseling centers (which can help you with your career choice) to (at the other extreme) the sometimes less-than-reputable "job search experts" who may charge an up-front fee of $2,000 or more and give you very little in return.

Some personnel managers, realizing the shortage of qualified help but not being able to commit to the substantial fees that outplacement specialists often charge, provide computer-assisted programs to help discharged employees with their career and job search decisions. These computerized programs are generally also available to anyone who asks. They cost from $100 to $300.

One good example of such a computerized program is Career Navigator, published by outplacement specialist Drake Bean Morin, Inc., 100 Park Avenue, New York, New York 10017. The program contains both a comprehensive manual and a set of computer disks. It covers all the steps a job searcher would normally go through, from identifying career interests through sending thank you letters after a job is obtained.

For example, section 2 ("Know Yourself") takes you step by step through a program in which you identify your interests, define your values, identify your accomplishments, and identify your skills. Here, you'll not only be able to zero in on several ideal job preferences; you will also generate a list of accomplishment statements that will be useful for building your resume and conducting interviews later in your job search.

Succeeding sections of the program take you step by step through the job search itself. By interacting with the computer you will learn how to use the telephone effectively, to write effective letters (the program will actually print these out for you, in the proper format), and how to interview effectively. The computerized program will help you create your resume and will print it out for you (again in the proper format). And, it will help you organize a job research campaign plan and give you a computerized printout of weekly action plans. It will even assess your weekly progress. It then gives you help in negotiating your offers, evaluating them, and even in assessing the first three months on the new job.

short-term interests of one's immediate subordinates.[28] Therefore, he says, supervisors need concrete information regarding the appraisee's potential career path—information, in other words, about the nature of the future work for which he or she is appraising the subordinate, or which the subordinate desires.[29]

Encourage Career-Planning Activities

Employers also have to take steps to increase employees' involvement in their own career planning and development. For example, some employers are experimenting with activities designed specifically to make employees aware of the need for career planning and of improving career decisions. Here, for example, employees might learn about the rudiments of career planning and the stages in one's career and engage in various activities aimed at crystallizing career anchors and formulating more realistic career goals.[30] Similarly, employers are increasingly engaging in career-counseling meetings (perhaps as part of the performance appraisal meeting) during which the employee and his or her supervisor (or perhaps a human resource director) assess the employee's progress in light of his or her career goals and identify development needs.[31]

▶ MANAGING PROMOTIONS AND TRANSFERS

MAKING PROMOTION DECISIONS

There are three main promotion-related decisions employers must make, and how these decisions are made will affect your employees' motivation, performance, and commitment.

Decision 1: Seniority or Competence?

Probably the most important decision concerns whether promotion will be based on seniority or competence, or some combinations of the two. From the point of view of motivation, promotion based on competence is best. However, your ability to use competence as a sole criterion depends on several things, most notably whether or not your firm is unionized or governed by civil service requirements. Union agreements often contain a clause that emphasizes seniority in promotions, such as: "In the advancement of employees to higher paid jobs when ability, merit, and capacity are equal, employees with the highest seniority will be given preference."[32] Although this might seem to leave the door open for giving a person with less seniority (but slightly better ability) the inside track for a job, labor arbitrators have generally held that when clauses such as these are binding only *substantial differences in abilities can be taken into account.* In one case, for example, the arbitrator ruled that seniority should be disregarded only when an employee with less seniority stood "head and shoulders" above the employees with greater seniority.[33] Similarly, many organizations in the public sector are governed by civil service regulations that emphasize seniority rather than competence as the basis for promotion.[34]

Decision 2: How Is Competence Measured?

When promotion *is* to be based on competence, you'll have to decide how competence will be defined and measured. Defining and measuring *past* performance is a fairly straightforward matter: The job is defined, standards are set, and one or more appraisal tools are used to record the employee's performance. But promotion also requires predicting the person's *potential*; thus, you must have some valid procedure for predicting a candidate's future performance.

Many employers simply use prior performance as a guide and extrapolate, or assume, that (based on the person's prior performance) he or she will perform well on the new job. This is the simplest procedure to use.

On the other hand, some employers uses tests to evaluate promotable employees[35] and to identify those employees with executive potential.[36] Others use assessment centers to assess management potential.

Decision 3: Formal or Informal?

Next (particularly if you decide to promote based on competence), you have to decide if the process will be a formal or informal one. Many employers still depend on an informal system. Here, the availability and requirements of open positions are kept secret. Promotion decisions are then made by key managers from among employees they know personally and also from among those who, for one reason or another, have impressed them.[37] The problem is that when you don't make employees aware of what jobs are available, what the criteria are for promotion, and how promotion decisions are made, the link between performance and promotion is cut. The effectiveness of promotion as a reward is thereby diminished.

Many employers therefore do establish formal, published promotion policies and procedures. Here, employees are generally provided with a formal promotion policy statement that describes the criteria by which promotions are awarded. Formal systems often include a job-posting policy. This states that open positions and their requirements will be posted and circulated to all employees. As explained in Chapter 4, many employers also compile detailed information on the qualifications of employees, while others use work force replacement charts. Computerized information systems can be especially useful for maintaining qualifications inventories on hundred or thousands of employees. The net effect of such actions is twofold: (1) an employer ensures that all qualified employees are considered for openings; and (2) promotion becomes more closely linked with performance in the minds of employees.

HANDLING TRANSFERS

Reasons for Transfers

A transfer involves a movement from one job to another, usually with no change in salary or grade. There are several reasons why such changes take place. *Employees* may seek transfers for personal enrichment, for more interesting jobs, for greater convenience—better hours, location of work, and so on—or for jobs offering greater possibilities for advancement.[38] *Employers* may transfer a worker from a position where he or she is no longer needed to one where he or she is needed, or to retain a senior employee (bumping where necessary a less senior person in another department), or (more generally) to find a better fit for the employee within the firm. Finally, many firms today are endeavoring to boost productivity by eliminating management layers. Transfers are thus increasingly a way to give employees who might have nowhere else to move in their firms opportunities for some diversity of job assignment and, therefore, personal growth.

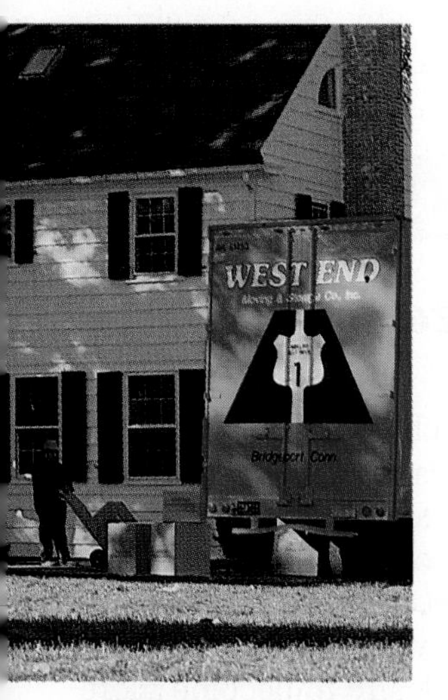

Changing jobs for career advancement may mean uprooting the family on a regular basis.

Effect on Family Life

Many firms have had policies of routinely transferring employees from locale to locale, either to give their employees more exposure to a wide range of jobs or to fill open positions with trained employees. Such easy-transfer policies have fallen into disfavor, though. This is partly because of the cost of relocating employees (paying moving expenses, buying back the employee's current home, and perhaps financing his or her next home, for instance) and partly because it was assumed that frequent transfers had a bad effect on an employee's family life.

One study suggests that the latter argument, at least, is without merit.[39] The study compared the experiences of "mobile" families who had moved on the average of once every two years with "stable" families who had lived in their communities for more than eight years.

In general, the stable families were no more satisfied with their marriages and family life or children's well-being than were the mobile families. In fact, mobile men and women believed their lives to be more interesting and their capabilities greater than did stable men and women. Likewise, they were more satisfied with their family lives and marriage than were stable men and women.

However, mobility *was* associated with dissatisfaction with social relationships among men and women (for instance, in terms of "opportunities to make friends at work and in the community"). Developing new social relationships was cited as a problem for children of mobile parents, with "missing old friends and making new friends" a bigger problem for teenagers than for young children.

The major finding, though, was that for these people there were few differences between mobile and stable families. Few families in the mobile group believed moving was easy. However, these families were as satisfied with all aspects of their lives (except social relationships) as were stable families. Yet—this study notwithstanding—there is no doubt that employees do resist geographical transfers more today than they did even a few years ago. In one study, for instance, "the proportion of top executives who were 'eager' or 'willing' to make a geographic move has dropped ten percentage points to 51.5% since 1979, while 45% described themselves as reluctant."[40]

BUILDING EMPLOYEE COMMITMENT

Helping Employees to Self-Actualize

You will come to a point when you will ask if you've achieved all you could have achieved, given your skills, your gifts, and your dreams for yourself, and woe to the firm that prevented you from doing so.[41] Few needs are as strong as the need to fulfill your dreams, to become all you are capable of becoming. Firms that don't cater to this need lose their best employees, or drift along with increasingly bitter, unhappy, and uncommitted ones. It was the psychologist Abraham Maslow who said that the ultimate need is "the desire to become more and more what one is, to become anything that one is capable of becoming." Self-actualization, to Maslow, meant that "what man *can* be, he *must* be. . . . It refers to the desire for self-fulfillment, namely, to the tendency for him to become actualized in what he is potentially."[42] An important key to winning your employees' commitment is thus to help them self-actualize—to become all they can be.[43]

Ironically, many companies not only do not commit to fulfilling this need, they actively thwart it. As a healthy person matures and approaches adulthood, said Chris Argyris, he or she moves to a state of increased activity, independence, and stronger interests.[44] The person also becomes capable of behaving in a greater variety of ways and tends to have a much longer time perspective. And as he or she matures from the subordinate role of a child to an equal or superordinate role as an adult, the person also develops more awareness of and control over his or her actions. Often, said Argyris, the typical company with its short-cycle jobs, autocratic supervision, and relative dearth of growth opportunities thwarts these normal maturation changes by forcing employees into dependent, passive, and subordinate roles.

Not surprisingly, progressive firms such as Delta, Saturn, and Federal Express do things differently. They all engage in practices that aim to ensure that all employees have every opportunity to actualize—to use all their skills and gifts at work, and become all they can be. Of course, "actualizing" doesn't have to mean just promotions or career success. Certainly, these are very important. But the crucial question is whether employees have the opportunity to develop and use all their skills and become—as Maslow would say—all they can be. Training employees to expand their skills and solve problems at work (as described in Chapters 7 and 8), enriching their jobs and empowering them to plan and inspect their own work (Chapter 9), and helping them continue their educations and grow (Chapters 7 and 8) are some other ways to achieve this.

EXAMPLES OF CAREER MANAGEMENT/ PROMOTION FROM WITHIN PROGRAMS

Yet, for many employees "becoming all you can be" does boil down to career progress. Many firms today therefore have comprehensive career management/promotion from within programs.

The distinction between promotion from within *programs* and *policies* is important. Many firms already have promotion from within *policies.* At JC Penney, "We believe in promotion from within whenever a unit's requirements and an associate's qualifications provide a suitable match. Promotions are based primarily on such factors as performance (including productivity), dependability, initiative, and availability."[45] At Federal Express "open positions are filled, whenever possible, by qualified candidates from within the existing workforce."[46] At IBM "promotion is from within—and also based on merit."[47] At Delta Airlines "Delta hires at entry-level, then trains and develops personnel to promote them to higher levels of responsibility."[48] At Toyota, where the team leader and group leader positions are stepping stones to all management positions in the plant, "it is TMM's philosophy to consider its current workforce when attempting to fill team leader and group leader job openings. [Furthermore] TMM is committed to filling open positions in the office classifications by promotions from within whenever possible. New hires are considered only after efforts to promote from within have been exhausted."[49]

However, there is more to a successful promotion from within program than a strong statement of policy. Thus promotion from within at the more progressive firms such as Federal Express generally means a five-part program, consisting of a promotion from within policy (previously discussed); value-based hiring; developmental activities; career-oriented appraisals; and a coordinated system of career records and job postings.

Promotion from Within and Value-Based Hiring

Promotion from within is aided first by value-based hiring, which we explained in Chapter 6. As one Delta manager said: "First of all, we hire for the future. . . . The employment process favors applicants who have the potential for promotion for a good reason. Delta subscribes almost entirely to a promotion from within policy. Except for a handful of people with specialized skills, everyone is hired in at entry-level."[50] The story is much the same at other progressive firms. You can't really commit to promotion from within when the people you hire haven't the potential to develop to the point at which they're promotable. Hiring people who have promotion potential and values that are synchronous with those of the firm is thus a requisite step in any promotion from within program.

Developmental Activities

Next, these firms provide the educational and training resources needed to help employees identify and develop their promotion potential. At Ben & Jerry's, promotional development is encouraged with programs of career planning, company internships, and tuition assistance. Ben & Jerry's employees are encouraged to attend a sequence of eight four-hour career planning seminars, the aim of which is to help employees think about and plan their careers. Employees who have completed the seminars and want to learn about other jobs within the firm can then spend two or three days interning at another company job, on paid time. The firm offers up to 90% funding for tuition reimbursement for up to three courses per year. It also provides many classes, seminars, counseling and tutoring, both on company premises and off. These include community and college courses; business writing, taught by the community college of Vermont and including one-on-one tutoring; computer classes, in which employees can earn a certificate from Ben & Jerry's information services group; adult basic education tutoring and high school diploma program; management development counseling one-on-one, by invitation and request; professional development classes and seminars; and financial planning seminars and individual counseling.

At Ben & Jerry's corporate headquarters employees' development is an integral part of career management.

Other firms also spend lavishly on developing employees' potential. For example, IBM—even with their recent cutbacks—still has one of the most extensive training and education programs in industry. In its advanced education program IBM sponsors part-time or full-time advanced education programs at outside colleges and universities. "Consistent with IBM's goal to encourage individual career development," employees may also receive educational leaves of absence without pay after two years of satisfactory full-time employment, as part of IBM's educational leave of absence program.[51]

IBM's extensive employee development program is available to all employees on a voluntary basis. IBM emphasizes here that it is each employee's responsibility to make the decisions regarding the development that's appropriate given his/her work interests and future goals. Managers are then charged with determining their employees' interest in participating in these programs and understanding the development needs of their employees. IBMers usually pursue their desired development activities with their own personal commitment of time and energy. But in doing so they're encouraged by the firm: "While participation in employee development planning is not, in itself, a guarantee of promotion, transfer or change in job, it can be helpful to you in setting your work goals and enhancing your capabilities."[52] The company's tuition refund plan also fully reimburses employees for the cost of tuition and other eligible education fees for approved courses and programs given by any accredited college, university, high school, business, or technical school.

Saturn Corp. also has a career development program. A career growth workshop uses vocational guidance tools (including a skills assessment disk and other "career gap analysis tools") to help employees identify career-related skills and the development needs they require. This career growth workshop, according to one employee, "helps you assess yourself, and takes four to six hours. You use it for developing your own career potential. The career disk identifies your weaknesses and strengths: you assess yourself, and then your team assesses you."[53] Tuition reimbursement and other development aids are then available to help employees develop the skills they need to get ahead.

No career-assessment, training, or education programs can guarantee an employee will be promoted, of course. Particularly in this era of consolidations, many employees will plateau, rising no higher at their firms. However, these firms' educational assistance and development programs do help guarantee that all employees have the opportunity to formulate realistic pictures of their career abilities, interests, and occupational options. And, they help ensure that all employees have an equal opportunity to make themselves promotable at their firms. These programs also make it easier for employees to choose and make lateral moves, ones that will let them broaden and challenge themselves. And, they provide a continuing opportunity for each employee to grow, by learning new subjects and meeting new academic challenges. Here is how one Saturn assembler summed it up:

> I'm an assembler now, and was a team leader for two-and-a-half years. My goal is to move into our people-systems [personnel] unit. I know things are tight now, but I know that the philosophy here is that the firm will look out for me—they want people to be all they can be. I know here I'll go as far as I can go; that's one reason I'm so committed to Saturn."[54]

Career-Oriented Appraisals

Next, career-oriented firms stress career-oriented appraisals. They don't just assess past performance, in other words. Instead, the supervisor and the appraisee are charged with linking the latter's past performance, career preferences, and developmental needs in a formal career plan.

JC Penney is a good example here. As illustrated in Figure 11.2, their Management Appraisal form requires both a "promotability recommendation" and "projections for associate development."

Here is how it works. Prior to the annual appraisal the associate and his or her manager review Penney's Management Career Grid (Figure 11.3). The grid itemizes all supervisory positions at JC Penney (grouped by operations jobs, merchandise jobs, personnel jobs, and general management jobs) and includes specific job titles such as "regional catalog sales manager," "cosmetic market coordinator," "regional training coordinator," and "project manager, public affairs." The firm also provides a "work activities scan sheet." This basically contains thumbnail job descriptions for all the grid's jobs.

Date & Initials Midyear Follow Up
9/10/90 GPT / PPS

Management Characteristics and Strategic Directions: Fill in letter for each using ratings below. See reverse for definitions.
Ratings: O = Outstanding G = Good S = Satisfactory ND = Needs Development TN = Too New to Rate or Not Applicable

I. Leadership G II. Awareness ND III. Sense of Urgency ND IV. Judgement G V. Planning & Organizing G VI. Team Process Participation G VII. Fashion Credibility G VIII. EEO Management G

Additional Comments, Strengths and Opportunities Lee achieved very solid results in Men's -- nice sales, good team development and depth of lines. Shoes is a real opportunity for Lee. Many decisions must be made more quickly by Lee, using merchandise systems better.

OVERALL PERFORMANCE RATING 3
(See reverse for instructions)

Manager Signature	Date of Appraisal	Reviewer Signature	Date of Review	Associate Signature	Date of Appraisal	Is this associate willing to move residence? (Check One)
Garry D. Turner	4-15-91	Phil Adams	4-1-91	Lee Smith	4/15/91	[X] Yes [ ] Not Now

See Associate Career Grid for Instructions

Promotability Recommendation: Enter letter here → B

A This Year B Second or third year C Fourth or fifth year
D Can grow with job E Recommend lateral transfer F Is at responsibility level
G Recommend less responsibility H Promotable this store I Too New To Rate

High Potential: Check if this associate has exceptional growth potential, top 5% in drive and ability [ ]

Projections for Associate Development	Year 1992 Position Title	Year 1992 Position Code/Volume	Year 19__ Position Title	Year 19__ Position Code/Volume
First Choice Projection	Sr.Merch.Mgr.	4300		
Alternate Projection				

DP. 2036 (Rev. 2/90) T.O.C. # 008-7427-1000

FIGURE 11.2 Portion of JC Penney's Appraisal Form
Note: Career orientation of appraisal.

The Management Career Grid also identifies typical promotional routes. As the instructions indicate: "When projecting the next assignment for a management associate, you should consider not only merchandise positions but also operations and personnel positions as well as general management positions."

Promotional projections can cross the four groups, as well as up one or two job levels. Thus, a senior merchandising manager might be projected for promotion to either assistant buyer or general merchandise manager. ("Assistant buyer" is classified as a general management job at Penney's since buying is done centrally. The potential general merchandise manager job is a merchandise group job, two levels above the person's current senior merchandising manager position.)

Career Records/Jobs Posting Systems

Finally, most of these firms have a career records/jobs posting system. The basic purpose of such systems is to ensure that the career goals and skills of inside candidates are matched openly, fairly, and effectively with promotional opportunities.

Goldman Sach's Internal Placement Center (IPC) is one example.[55] Its aim is to offer

> Goldman Sachs employees interested in pursuing career opportunities in different areas of the firm the resources to locate and apply for job openings. The IPC also makes it simpler for managers to consider qualified internal candidates when filling open positions, and furnishes managers with information about openings that could provide career development opportunities for their employees.[56]

There are five steps in the IPC process. For each open position, the hiring manager can first choose to conduct an internal, external, or combined (internal and external) search, but "an internal or combined search is strongly encouraged."[57] Next, the manager and recruiter fill out a job description form for the open position. The form includes job title, department and manager, a descrip-

Instructions and Use of Grid for Making Associate Projections of Development

1) **Promotability - Enter the appropriate Promotability letter in the box provided. If the answer to Promotability is D, F, or I, leave the "High Potential" and "Projections for Associate Development" sections blank.**

2) **High Potential - The High Potential box should be checked if this associate has exceptional growth potential — is within the top 5% in drive and ability. Please keep in mind that appraisal ratings and high potential ratings while related reflect two distinct judgments — performance in current assignment versus exceptional potential for growth. A "1" rated associate, is not necessarily high potential or vice versa.**

		FIELD MANAGEMENT	
OPERATIONS		**MERCHANDISE**	
Position Title/Volume	Code	Position Title/Volume	Code
Regional Operations Manager	1002	Manager of Geographic Markets	1017
		Manager of Business Planning	1025
		District Manager	1121
		Store Manager 30+ D.S.	0109
		Entity Store Manager	0110
		Store Manager 22 - 30 D.S.	0108
		Store Manager 15 - 22 D.S.	0107
		Regional Business Planning Manager	1026
		Store Manager 10 - 15 D.S.	0106
		Store Manager Under 10 D.S.	0105
Regional Catalog Sales Center Manager	1150	Regional Merchandiser/Geographic Markets	1146
Regional Programs Manager	1100		
Regional Systems Manager	1027		
		Store Manager 5 - 10 S.L.	0104
Regional Catalog Sales Manager	1139	Business Planning Manager	**40( )0
District Operations Manager	2290	District Special Events & Publicity Manager	2800
District Operations/Personnel Manager	2310	Store Merchandise & Marketing Manager	4260
Regional Loss Prevention Manager	4804		
Operations Manager 30+ D.S.	1329	Store Manager 3 - 5 S.L.	0103
District Merchandise Systems Coordinator	2330	General Merchandising Manager 30+ D.S.	4299
D.L.D.C. Manager	3750	General Merchandising Manager 22 - 30 D.S.	4298
Operations Manager 25 - 30 D.S.	1328	Store Manager 1 - 3 S.L.	0102
		Regional Visual Merchandising Mgr - Geo. Mkts.	1085
		Regional Visual Merchandising Mgr - Metro Mkts.	1092
Regional Loss Prevention Representative	4805		
Regional Styling Salon Sales Manager	1109	General Merchandising Manager 15 - 22 D.S.	4297
Regional Maintenance Manager	1165	General Merchandising Manager 10 - 15 D.S.	4296
Regional Telecommunications Manager	1028	General Merchandising Manager under 10 D.S.	4295
District Loss Prevention Manager	5620	Store Manager under 1 S.L.	0101
		Multiple Unit D.L.D.C. Merchandiser	4450
Operations/Personnel Manager 10 - 25 D.S.	5356	D.L.D.C. Merchandiser	3760
D.L.D.C. Operations Manager	4930	District Merchandise Publicity Coordinator	5580
Systems Implementation & Training Manager	1130	Special Lines Market Coordinator	2340
Catalog Sales Center Manager	1010	District Visual Merchandising Manager	5630
Sales Support Manager	3210	Cosmetic Market Coordinator	0700
		Visual Merchandising Manager	4650
		Senior Merchandising Manager	4300
		Department Sales Manager	3460
		Shoe Department Manager	5590
		Cosmetic Manager	0710
(Functional Title) Manager	4980	Merchandising Manager	4310
		Fine Jewelry Manager	3360
		Multi Store Fine Jewelry Manager	4470
		Fine Jewelry Merchandiser	3370
		Shoe Department Merchandiser	5600
		Cosmetic Merchandiser	0720
		Merchandising Manager Trainee	4330

FIGURE 11.3 Portion of JC Penney's Management Career Grid

tion of the position's responsibilities and duties, and a summary of qualifications required for the position. Third, listings of current job opportunities are posted in the Internal Placement Center and in the reception area on each floor. Fourth, any employee interested in applying for an open position submits an IPC application and current resume to the Internal Placement Center.

Finally, the process of reviewing an employee's application begins with the IPC coordinator and the recruiter assessing each applicant's qualifications. Within two weeks after submitting his or her application, the employee is informed by the IPC coordinator at his or her home address about the status of the application. (This is the case whether or not the employee is selected to be interviewed for a position.) Those chosen as candidates then start their interviews.

Federal Express has its own job postings/career coordination system called JCATS, for Job Change Applicant Tracking System. Announcements of new job openings via this electronic system usually take place every Friday. All employees posting for the position get numerical scores based on job performance and length of service and are then advised as to whether or not they were chosen as candidates.

Retirement counseling on issues like Social Security and financial planning is becoming more important as conditions facing older workers become more complex.

At JC Penney, regional managers (who oversee several stores) and regional personnel managers get lists of promotable people from store managers. The regions and districts also keep their own career-related files on supervisory personnel, and there are an additional 4,000 files or so at the JC Penney corporate office. The four functional divisions (merchandising, operations, personnel, and general management) also have files.

The question of who gets what files is largely determined by each associate's chosen career path (as determined by the yearly appraisal). Thus someone who aims to move from merchandising manager to assistant buyer would have a file set up in the general management offices.

JC Penney also has an employee data base on over 18,000 managers—where they're located, their appraisal codes, their chosen career routes, and so on. A senior executive reviews all recommendations for interregional or interdepartmental transfers. And the chief operating officer evaluates all the appraisals and career plans for all employees down through the director level. The result, says one of the firm's top personnel officers, is an ongoing dialogue between mangers and subordinates regarding their careers. They are always discussing—at least annually, usually a lot more often—what this person will be doing in the next 12 months, and what his or her career options are. And in turn the store manager is discussing the same thing regarding the individual with his or her own district manager. The emphasis is always on how to help this subordinate grow.[58]

RETIREMENT

Retirement for most employees is a bittersweet experience. For some it is the culmination of their careers, a time when they can relax and enjoy the fruits of their labor without worrying about the problems of work. For others, it is the retirement itself that is the trauma, as the once busy employee tries to cope with being suddenly "nonproductive" and with the strange (and not entirely pleasant) experience of being home every day with nothing to do. For many retirees, in fact, maintaining a sense of identity and selfworth without a full-time job is the single most important task they'll face. And it's one that employers are increasingly trying to help their retirees cope with, as a logical last step in the career management process.[59]

Preretirement Counseling

About 30% of the employers in one recent survey said they had formal preretirement programs aimed at easing the passage of their employees into retirement.[60] The most common preretirement practices were:

Explanation of Social Security benefits (reported by 97% of those with preretirement education programs)

Leisure-time counseling (86%)

Financial and investment counseling (84%)

Health counseling (82%)

Living arrangements (59%)

Psychological counseling (35%)

Counseling for second careers outside the company (31%)

Counseling for second careers inside the company (4%)

Among employers that did *not* have preretirement education programs, 64% believed that such programs were needed, and most of these said their firms had plans to develop them within two or three years.

Another important trend here is that of granting part-time employment to employees as an alternative to outright retirement. Several recent surveys of blue- and white-collar employees showed that about half of all employees over age 55 would like to continue working part-time after they retire, and employers can probably be expected to build such alternatives into their career-management processes.

▶ CHAPTER REVIEW

SUMMARY

1. The key to managing your career is insight into what you want out of a career, into your talents and limitations, and into your values and how they fit with the alternatives you are considering.
2. The main stages in a person's career include: growth stage (roughly birth to age 14), exploration stage (roughly 15 to 24), establishment stage (roughly ages 24 to 44, the heart of most people's work lives), maintenance stage (45 to 65), and decline stage (preretirement). The establishment stage itself may consist of a trial substage, a stabilization substage, and a midcareer crisis substage.
3. The first step in planning your career is to learn as much as you can about your own interest, aptitudes, and skills. Start by identifying your occupational orientation: realistic, investigative, social, conventional, enterprising, and artistic. Next, identify your skills and rank them from high to low.
4. Next, identify your career anchors: technical/functional, managerial, creativity, autonomy, and security. Then ask yourself what you want to do.
5. There are many sources you can turn to for learning about occupations and careers. These include the *Dictionary of Occupational Titles,* the *Occupational Outlook Handbook, Occupational Outlook Quarterly,* the *Encyclopedia of Careers and Vocational Guidance,* and the Office of Personnel Management's *Handbook X118.*
6. The supervisor plays an important role in the career management process. Some important guidelines include: avoid reality shock, be demanding, provide realistic job previews, conduct career-oriented performance appraisals, and encourage job rotation.
7. In making promotion decisions, you have to decide between *seniority and competence,* a *formal or informal system,* and how to *measure competence.*
8. More firms today engage in practices aimed at helping employees "be all they can be," in other words, self-actualize. Training, job enrichment, and educational opportunities are examples. However for many employees self-actualizing boils down to promotions and career progress. Many firms thus institute comprehensive career management/promotion from within programs.

9. Value-based hiring and developmental activities are two important components of such programs. Value-based hiring is important because promotion from within assumes you have employees who are promotable in the first place. Career developmental activities (including career assessment and planning) help employees identify their career interests and more intelligently plan career moves.
10. Career-oriented appraisals play a crucial role in managing careers. Here the supervisor and appraisee link the latter's past performance, career preferences, and developmental needs to develop an appropriate career plan for the employee.
11. Career records/job posting systems are also important. Maintaining career-related data on employees and then openly posting all jobs ensures that the career goals and skills of inside candidates are matched openly and fairly with promotional opportunities.

KEY TERMS

career planning and development
career cycle
growth stage
exploration stage
establishment stage
trial substage
stabilization substage
midcareer crisis substage
maintenance stage
decline stage
John Holland
occupational orientation
occupational skills
aptitudes
Edgar Schein
career anchors
reality shock

DISCUSSION QUESTIONS

1. Briefly describe each of the stages in a typical career.
2. What is a career anchor? What are the main types of career anchors discussed in this chapter?
3. What are the main types of occupational orientations discussed in this chapter?
4. Describe some important sources of information you could use to learn about careers of interest to you.
5. Develop a resume for yourself, using the guidelines presented in this chapter. (See the appendix.)
6. Write a one-page essay stating "Where I would like to be career-wise ten years from today."
7. Explain career-related factors to keep in mind when making the employee's first assignments.

APPLICATION EXERCISES

RUNNING CASE

CARTER CLEANING COMPANY

The Career Planning Program

Career planning has always been a pretty low priority item for Carter Cleaning, since "just getting workers to come to work and then keeping them honest is enough of a problem," as Jack likes to say. Yet, Jennifer thought it might not be a bad idea to give some thought to what a career planning program might involve for Carter. A lot of their employees had been with them for years in dead-end jobs, and she frankly felt a little bad for them: "Perhaps we could help them gain a better perspective on what they want to do," she thought. And she definitely believed that the store management group needed some better career direction if Carter Cleaning was to develop and grow.

Questions

1. What would be the advantages to Carter Cleaning of setting up such a career planning program?
2. Who should participate in the program? All employees? Selected employees?
3. Describe the program you would propose for injecting a career planning and development perspective into the Carter Cleaning Centers.

CASE INCIDENT 2 *Reality Shock*

Maria Blanco didn't know what to do. After graduating from Columbia University in 1992, she'd taken a job with a major New York talent agency, thinking she could pursue her first love, entertainment. The agency had a reputation for being like "family" but it turned out that it was like no family she'd ever known. The personnel director seemed to go out of his way to diminish the employee's importance by making comments like "If you want to leave, go ahead. I've got another 1000 applicants just like you."

She spent her first year working in the mailroom and was now trying to figure out whether to leave for another big agency like CAA, or a small one, or change careers altogether. "This is not what I got an economics degree for," she thought. Now, in the summer of 1993, she was facing a very tight job market and hadn't been able to save a penny all year. All she knew was that she was miserable.

Questions

1. What would you do now if you were Maria? Why?
2. What could the talent agency have done to avoid problems like this?

HUMAN RESOURCE MANAGEMENT SIMULATION

Managing promotions is one of the principal decisions in the simulation. Do you promote from within or hire qualified people from outside the organization? While promoting from within increases morale, organizations also need "new blood" to bring new ideas and methods into the organization.

Incident N will give you some idea as to how hard some promotion decisions are. The basic question raised is: "To what extent should a person's outside activities effect his or her ability to be promoted?"

APPENDIX 11.1

Finding the Right Job

▶ HELPING YOU GET THE RIGHT JOB

You have identified your occupational orientation, skills, and career anchors and have picked out the occupation you want and laid plans for a career. And (if necessary) you have embarked on the required training. Your next step is to find a job that you want in the company and locale you want to work in. The following are some techniques for doing so.

JOB SEARCH TECHNIQUES

Do Your Own Research

Perhaps the most direct way of unearthing the job you want where you want it is to pick out the geographic area in which you want to work and find out all you can about the companies in that area that appeal to you and the people you have to contact in those companies to get the job you want. Most public libraries have local directories. For example, the reference librarian in one Fairfax County, Virginia, library made the following suggestions for patrons seeking information on local businesses:

Industrial Directory of Virginia
Industrial Directory of Fairfax County
Principal Employers of the Washington Metro Area
The Business Review of Washington

Some other general reference material you can use includes *Who's Who in Commerce and Industry, Who's Who is America, Who's Who in the East,* and *Poor's Register.* Using these guides, you can find the person in each organization who is ultimately responsible for hiring people in the position you seek.

Personal Contacts

According to one survey, the most popular way to seek job interviews, especially for jobs paying $30,000 or more, is to rely on personal contacts such as friends and relatives.[61] For example, one Department of Labor study indicates that about 19% of managers get their jobs through friends and about 6% got them through relatives. The way to proceed is to let as many *responsible* people as you can know that you are in the market for a job and, specifically, what kind of job you want. (Beware, though, if you are currently employed and don't want your job search getting back to your current boss; if that is the case, better just pick out two or three *very* close friends and tell them that it is absolutely essential that they be discreet in poking around and looking for a job for you.)

No matter how close your friends or relatives are to you, by the way, you don't want to impose too much on them by shifting the burden of your job search to them. Therefore, it is sometimes best to ask them just for the name of someone they think you should talk to in the kind of firm in which you'd like to work, and then do the digging yourself.

Answering Advertisements

Most experts agree that this is a low-probability way to get a job, and it becomes increasingly less likely that you will get a job this way as the level of a job increases. Answering ads, in other words, is fine for jobs that pay under $20,000 per year, but its highly unlikely that as you move up in management you are going to get your job by simply answering classified ads. Low probability though it be, good sources of classified ads for professionals and managers include *the New York Times,* the *Wall Street Journal,* and a separate *Wall Street Journal* listing of job openings.

Be very careful in replying to blind ads, however. Some executive search firms and companies will run ads even when no position exists just to gauge the market, and there is always the chance that you can be trapped into responding to your own firm. In responding to these ads, also be sure to create the right impression with the materials you submit; check the typing, style, grammar, neatness, and so forth, and check your resume to make sure it is geared to the job for which you are applying. In your cover letter, be sure to have a paragraph or so in which you specifically address why your background and accomplishments are appropriate to the job being advertised; you must respond clearly to the company's identified needs.

Employment Agencies

Agencies are especially good at placing people in jobs up to about $30,000 but can be useful for higher paying jobs as well. Their fees for professional and management jobs are usually paid by the employer. Assuming you know the job you want, review eight or so back issues of the Sunday classified ads (in your library) to identify the agencies that consistently handle the positions you want. Approach three or four initially, preferably in response to specific ads, and avoid signing any contract that gives an agency exclusive right to place you.

Executive Recruiters

These firms are retained by employers to seek out top talent for their clients, and their fees are always paid by the employer. They fill positions in the $40,000 and up category, although $50,000 is often the lower limit. They do not do career counseling, but if you know the job you want, it pays to contact a few. Send your resume and a cover letter summarizing your job objective in precise terms (including job title and size company you want), work-related accomplishments, current salary, and salary requirements. They are listed in the Yellow Pages under "Executive Search Consultants," but beware, since some *non*search firms now also use the "Executive Search" label. Remember that with a search firm you never pay a fee. A list of executive recruiters is also available for $3.00 from the Management Information Service of the American Management Association, 135 West 50th Street, New York, NY 11020.

Career Counselors

These people will not help you find a job per se; rather, they specialize in aptitude testing and career counseling. They are listed in the Yellow Pages under "Career Counseling" or "Vocational Guidance." Their services usually cost $200 or $300 and include psychological testing and interviews with an experienced career counselor. Check the firm's services, prices, and history as well as the credentials of the person you will be dealing with.

Executive Marketing Consultants

These firms manage your job-hunting campaign. They are generally not recruiters and *do not have jobs to fill.* Depending on the services you choose, your cost will range from $300 to $4,000 or more. The process may involve months of weekly meetings. Services include resume and letter writing, interview skill building, and developing a full job-hunting campaign. Before approaching one, though, you should *definitely* do some in-depth self-appraisal (as explained in this chapter) and read books like Richard Bolles's *The Quick Job Hunting Map* and *What Color Is Your Parachute?*

Then check out three or four of these firms (they are listed in the Yellow Pages under "Executive Search Consultants") by visiting each and asking: What exactly is your program? How much does each service cost? Are there any extra costs, such as charges for printing and mailing resumes? What does the contract say? After what point will you get no rebate if you're unhappy with the services? Then, review your notes, check the Better Business Bureau, and decide which of these firms (if any) is for you.

WRITING YOUR RESUME

Your resume is probably your most important selling document, one that can determine if you "make the cut" and get offered a job interview. Here are some resume pointers, as offered by employment counselor Richard Payne and other experts.[62] An example of a good resume is presented in Figure 11.4.

Introductory Information

Start your resume with your name, address, and telephone number. Using your office phone number, by the way, can indicate either that (1) your employer knows you are leaving or (2) that you don't care if he or she finds out. You're usually better off using your home phone number.

Job Objective

State your job objective next. This should summarize in one sentence the specific position you want, where you want to do it (type and size of company), and a special reason an employer might have for wanting you to fill the job. For example, "Production manager in a medium-size manufacturing company in a situation in which strong production scheduling and control experience would be valuable." Always try to put down the most senior title you know you can expect to secure, keeping in mind the specific job for which you are applying.

CONRAD D. STAPLETON
77 Pleasantapple Way
Coltsville, NY 10176
(914) 747-1012

CONFIDENTIAL

JOB OBJECTIVE:	*Senior Product Manager* in a situation requiring extensive advertising and promotion experience.
PRESENT POSITION	VALUE-PLUS DIVISION, INTERCONTINENTAL CORPORATION
1986-Present	*Product Manager,* NEW PRODUCTS, LAUNDRYON SOAP and CARBOLENE CLEANER, reporting to Group Product Manager.
	Recommended and obtained test market authorization, then managed all phases of development of THREE test brands, scheduled for introduction during Fall/Winter 1986. Combined first year national volume projects to $20 million, with advertising budget of $6 million. Concurrently developing several new products for 1987 test marketing.
	Also responsible for two established brands: LAUNDRYON SOAP, a $7 million brand, and CARBOLENE CLEANER, a $4 million regional brand. Currently work with three advertising agencies on test and established brands.
1983-1985	*Product Manager,* WEEKENDER PAINTS, a $6 million brand.
	Developed and implemented a repositioning of this brand (including new copy and new package graphics) to counter a 10-year sales downtrend averaging 10% a year. Repositioning increased test market volume 16%, and national volume 8% the following year.
	Later initiated development of new, more competitive copy than advertising used during repositioning. Test area sales increased 35%. National airing is scheduled for Fall 1986.
	Developed plastic packaging that increased test market volume 10%.
	Also developed and implemented profit improvement projects which increased net profit 33%.
1982	*Product Manager,* SHINEZY CAR WASH, a $4 million brand.
	Initiated and test marketed an improved aerosol formula and a liquid refill. Both were subsequently expanded nationally and increased brand volume 26%.
	RICHARDS-DONALDS COMPANY
1981-1982	*Assistant Product Manager,* reporting to Product Manager.
	Concurrent responsibility on PAR and SHIPSHAPE detergents. Developed locally tailored annual promotion plans. These resulted in 30% sales increase on PAR and stabilization of SHIPSHAPE volume.
1980-1981	*Product Merchandising Assistant*
	Developed and implemented SUNSHINE SUDS annual promotion plan.

(continued)

FIGURE 11.4 Example of a Good Resume

Source: Richard Payne, *How to Get a Better Job Quicker* (New York: Signet, 1988), pp. 80–81.

Job Scope

Indicate the scope of your responsibility in each of your previous jobs, starting with your most recent position. For each of your previous jobs, write a para-

CONRAD D. STAPLETON . . . page 2

1979-1980	Academic Leave of Absence to obtain MBA. See EDUCATION.
1977-1979	*Account Manager*, Field Sales.
	Account Manager for Shopper's Pal, the most difficult chain in Metropolitan Westchester. Achieved sales increase of 10% and distribution of all Lever products, introduced while I was on territory. Based on this performance was awarded Food'N Things Cooperatives, the second most difficult account, and achieved similar results.
EDUCATION	READING SCHOOL, University of Maryland
	MBA in Marketing Management. Average grade 3.5 out of 4.0 Thesis: "The Distribution of Pet Supplies through Supermarkets," graded 4.0 out of 4.0. Courses included quantitative methods, finance, accounting and international business.
	ELTON COLLEGE, Kansas City, Missouri
	BA in Liberal Arts. Was one of 33, out of freshman class of 110, who completed four years of this academically rigorous program. Theses required each year. Judge in Student Court during senior year.
PERSONAL	Single, U.S. Citizen.

FIGURE 11.4
(continued)

graph that shows job title, who you reported to directly and indirectly, who reported to you, how many people reported to you, the operational and human resource budgets you controlled, and what (in one sentence) your job entailed.

Your Accomplishments

Next (and this is *very important*) indicate your "worth" in each of the positions you held. This is the heart of your resume. It shows, for each of your previous jobs, (1) the concrete action you took and why you took it and (2) the specific result of your action—the "payoff." For example, "As production supervisor, I introduced a new process to replace costly hand soldering of component parts. The new process reduced assembly time per unit from 30 to 10 minutes and reduced labor costs by over 60 percent." Use several of these worth statements for each job.

Length

Keep you resume to two pages or less and list education, military service (if any), and personal background (hobbies, interests, associations) on the last page.

Personal Data

Do not put personal data regarding age, marital status, or dependents on top of page one. If you must include it, do so at the end of the resume, where it will be read after the employer has already formed an opinion of you.

Finally, two last points. First, do not produce a slipshod resume: Avoid overcrowded pages, difficult-to-read copies, typographical errors, and other problems of this sort. Second, do not use a make-do resume—one from ten years ago. Produce a new resume for each job you are applying for, gearing your job objective and worth statements to the job you want.

HANDLING THE INTERVIEW

You have done all your homework and now the big day is almost here; you have an interview next week with the person who is responsible for hiring for the job you want. What do you have to do to excel in the interview? Here are some suggestions. (Also review interviewing in Chapter 6 at this point.)

Prepare, Prepare, Prepare

First, remember that preparation is essential. Before the interview, learn all you can about the employer, the job, and the people doing the recruiting. At the library, look through business periodicals to find out what is happening in the employer's field. Who is the competition? How are they doing?

Uncover the Interviewer's Needs

Spend as little time as possible answering your interviewer's first questions and as much time as possible getting the person to describe the needs: What the person is looking to get accomplished and the type of person needed. Use open-ended questions, such as "Could you tell me more about that?"

Relate Yourself to the Person's Needs

Once you have a handle on the type of person your interviewer is looking for and the sorts of problems he or she wants solved, you are in a good position to describe your own accomplishments *in terms of the interviewer's needs.* Start by saying something like, "One of the problem areas you've indicated is important to you is similar to a problem I once faced." Then, state the problem, describe your solution, and reveal the results.

Think Before Answering

Recall (from Chapter 6) that answering a question should be a three-step process: pause, think, speak. Pause to make sure you understand what the interviewer is driving at, think about how to structure your answer, and then speak. In your answer, try to emphasize how hiring you will help the interviewer solve his or her problem.

Appearance and Enthusiasm Are Important

Appropriate clothing, good grooming, a firm handshake, and the appearance of controlled energy are important.

First Impressions Count

Studies of interviews show that in almost 80% of the cases, interviewers make up their minds about the applicant during the first few minutes of the interview. A good first impression may turn to bad during the interview, but it is unlikely. Bad first impressions are almost impossible to overcome.

▶ Notes

1. J. Richard Hackman and J. Lloyd Suttle, *Improving Life at Work* (Santa Monica, CA: Goodyear, 1977); see also David Bowen and Edward Lawler, "Total Quality-Oriented Human Resources Management," *Organizational Dynamics*, Vol. 20, No. 4, Spring 1992, pp. 29–41.
2. Hackman and Suttle, *Improving Life at Work,* p. 4.
3. Donald Super and others, *Vocational Development: A Framework for Research* (New York: Teachers College Press, 1957), and Edgar Schein, *Career Dynamics: Matching Individual and Organizational Needs* (Reading, MA: Addison-Wesley, 1978).
4. John Holland, *Making Vocational Choices: A Theory of Careers* (Englewood Cliffs, NJ: Prentice-Hall, 1973).
5. Richard Bolles, *The Quick Job Hunting Map* (Berkeley, CA: Ten Speed Press, 1979), pp. 5–6
6. Ibid., p. 5.
7. Schein, *Career Dynamics,* pp. 128–129.
8. Ibid., pp. 257–262.
9. This example is based on Richard Bolles, *The Three Boxes of Life* (Berkeley, CA: Ten Speed Press, 1976).
10. Schein, *Career Dynamics,* pp. 252–253.
11. For self-diagnosis books, see, for example, G. A. Ford and G. L. Lippitt, *A Life Planning Workbook* (Fairfax, VA: NTL Learning Resources, 1972).
12. Schein, *Career Dynamics,* p. 253.
13. Richard Bolles, *What Color Is Your Parachute?* (Berkeley, CA: Ten Speed Press, 1976), p. 86.
14. *The Guidance Information System,* Time Share Corporation, 630 Oakwood Avenue, West Hartford, CT 06110, described in Andrew Dubrin, *Human Relations: A Job-Oriented Approach* (Reston, VA: Reston, 1982), p. 358.
15. Gail Martin, "The Job Hunters Guide to the Library," *Occupational Outlook Quarterly* (Fall 1980), p. 10.
16. Robert Jameson, *The Professional Job Changing System* (Verona, NJ: Performance Dynamics, 1975).
17. Richard Payne, *How to Get a Better Job Quicker* (New York: New American Library, 1987).
18. Personal interview March, 1992.
19. Personal interview March, 1992.
20. Ibid.
21. Richard Reilly, Mary Tenopyr, and Steven Sperling, "The Effects of Job Previews on Job Acceptance and Survival Rates of Telephone Operator Candidates," *Journal of Applied Psychology,* Vol. 64 (1979).
22. Schein, *Career Dynamics,* p. 19.
23. J. Sterling Livingston, "Pygmalion in Management," *Harvard Business Review,* Vol. 48 (July–August 1969), pp. 81–9.
24. Joel Ross, *Managing Productivity* (Reston, VA: Reston, 1979).
25. Douglas Hall and Francine Hall, "What's New in Career Management?" *Organizational Dynamics,* Vol. 4 (Summer 1976).
26. H. G. Kaufman, *Obsolescence and Professional Career Development* (New York: AMACOM, 1974).
27. Hall & Hall, "What's New in Career Management?" p. 350.
28. See, for example, Terri Scandurg, "Mentorship and Career Mobility: An Empirical Investigation," *Journal of Organizational Behavior,* Vol. 13, Nr. 2, March 1992, pp. 169–174.
29. Schein, *Career Dynamics,* p. 19.
30. See, for example, D. B. Miller, *Personal Vitality* (Reading, MA: Addison-Wesley, 1977), and *Personal Vitality Workbook* (Reading, MA: Addison-Wesley, 1977).
31. Albert Griffith, "Career Development: What Organizations Are Doing About It," *Personnel,* Vol. 57 (1980), pp. 63–69; see also Kenneth Brousseau, "Career Dynamics in The Baby Boom and Baby Bus Era," *Journal of Organizational Change Management,* Vol. 3, No. 3, 1990, pp. 46–58.
32. See for example, Daniel Quinn Mills, *Labor-Management Relations* (New York: McGraw-Hill, 1986), pp. 387–396.
33. James Healy, "The Factor of Ability in Labor Relations," in *Arbitration Today,* Proceedings of the Eighth Annual Meeting of the National Academy of Arbitrators, 1955, pp. 45–54, quoted in Pigors and Meyers, *Personnel Administration,* p. 283.
34. Charles Halaby, "Bureaucratic Promotion Criteria," *Administrative Science Quarterly,* Vol. 23 (September 1978), pp. 466–484.
35. Gary Dessler, *Winning Commitment* (NY: McGraw-Hill, 1993), pp. 144–9.
36. Ibid.
37. See Joseph Famularo, *Handbook of Modern Personnel Administration* (New York: McGraw-Hill, 1972), p. 17.
38. See, for example, Richard Chanick, "Career Growth for Baby Boomers," *Personnel Journal*, January 1992, Vol. 71, No. 1, pp. 40–46.
39. Ibid.
40. Commerce Clearing House, "Top Executives Are Growing Reluctant to Relocate," *Ideas and Trends,* December 10, 1982, p. 218.
41. This is based on Gary Dessler, *Winning Commitment* (New York: McGraw-Hill, 1993), Chapter 10.
42. Abraham Maslow, "A Theory of Human Motivation," *Psychological Review,* Vol. 50 (1943), pp. 370–396, reprinted in Michael Matteson and John Ivancevich, *Management Classics* (Santa Monica: Goodyear Publishing Co., 1977), p. 336.
43. Abraham Maslow, Ibid.
44. Chris Argyris, *Integrating the Individual and the Organization* (New York: John Wiley & Sons, 1964).
45. JC Penney Associate Handbook, p. 3.
46. Federal Express Employee Handbook, p. 28.
47. About Your Company, IBM Handbook, p. 17.
48. Delta Policies and Procedures Manual.
49. Toyota Team Member Handbook, p. 82.
50. Paulette O'Donnell speech, pp. 4-5.
51. About Your Company, IBM Handbook, p. 188.
52. Ibid., p. 188.
53. Personal interview March, 1992.
54. Personal interview March, 1992.
55. Goldman Sachs, "Internal Placement Center: Guidelines for Managers."
56. Ibid., p. 1.
57. Ibid.
58. Personal interview March, 1992.
59. Remember certain highly paid executives and employees receiving pensions of at least $25,000 a year at retirement can be forced to retire at 65, under federal law.
60. "Preretirement Education Programs," *Personnel,* Vol. 59 (May–June 1982), p. 47. Also see Daniel Halloran, "The Retirement Identity Crisis—and How to Beat It," *Personnel Journal,* Vol. 64 (May 1985), pp. 38–40 and Silvia Odenwald, "Pre-Retirement Training Gathers Steam," *Training and Development Journal,* Vol. 40, no. 2 (February 1986), pp. 62–63.
61. Jameson, *The Professional Job Changing System.* See also Kenneth McRae, "Career-Management Planning: A Boon to Managers and Employees," *Personnel,* Vol. 62, no. 5 (May 1985), pp. 56–60.
62. Payne, *How to Get a Better Job Quicker.*

VIDEO CASE 2

—Conclusion—

ASSEMBLY LINE TEAMS ARE BETTER TRAINED AND MORE EFFICIENT

When we introduced Video Case 2 on page 233, we asked some questions that you should now review.

Companies such as Square D and Saturn do spend enormous sums of money on employee training and development. However, as Chapters 7 through 11 and the video make clear, these companies don't do so simply to give employees the basic skills they need to do their jobs satisfactorily. Certainly, techniques such as on-the-job training, job instruction training, lectures, and audio visual tools are invaluable for building job-related skills. But, beyond that, training and development can play a crucial role in employees' career development. In the video, plant manager Tom Palmer says, "I've had people look me in the eye and say, 'You know, at one time I was told by management, you're not paid to think. Just do your job.' And when you think about it, that's tragic."

We've seen in Part 2 that many firms, recognizing this no-think attitude, are instituting worker empowerment and team-building programs aimed at enabling workers to think on the job. Training is necessarily part of any such program. Like all of us (and, indeed, most of us will end up as employees), employees are motivated to become all that they can be; training and development is a vehicle through which they can attain that goal.

We've also seen in these chapters, and in the video, that fostering employee commitment (through techniques such as empowerment, training, and team buliding) can pay off when it comes to quality-consciousness. Whether it's the self-managing teams discussed in Chapter 9 or the work teams in the accompanying video, it's apparent that committed employees are most firms' best guarantee of high-quality work. As with "Team 440" in the video (which "finished it's 57th day without a rejection for errors or defects"), the time to stop errors is not at the final inspection point but during the production process. This, however, requires committed employees.

Once your employees are trained and appraised, they must be compensated. We now turn to this topic.

PART 3

Compensation

VIDEO CASE 3

—Introduction—

ABC NEWS

EMPLOYEE PENSION FUNDS

from ABC News, "Business World," July 7, 1991

Part 1 focused on recruiting and selecting employees; Part 2 dealt with the issues of training and development and the techniques companies use to train, develop, and appraise their employees. In Part 2 we also discussed techniques such as team building and total-quality management programs, as well as the overall impact that programs such as these have on developing employees' careers.

Now, in Part 3 we turn to the subject of employee compensation and particularly to:

Chapter 12: Establishing Pay Plans

Chapter 13: Pay-For-Performance and Financial Incentives

Chapter 14: Benefits and Services

Video Case 3 describes one increasingly important component of most firms' compensation plan, employee pensions. The video makes the point that most people don't think about retirement until they're in their 50s, and that most people—especially those under 40—"probably know almost nothing about their retirement funds, such as how they're invested." But it's a pretty safe bet that you will eventually retire from your career; so if you haven't thought about pensions until now, this may be as good a time as any to start. As you read Chapters 12, 13, and 14 and watch the video, consider the following questions.

1. What are the factors you'd want to consider before deciding what to pay various people in your department?
2. What are some of the main types of financial incentives you could use to boost performance?
3. With all the "downsizing" and forced (not to mention voluntary) mobility of employees these days, how do you think companies' pension plans are going to be affected?

CHAPTER 12

ESTABLISHING PAY PLANS

OVERVIEW

Developing a pay plan involves evaluating the relative worth of jobs (through the technique of job evaluation), and then pricing each job using wage curves and pay grades. In this chapter four evaluation methods (ranking, classification, point, and factor comparison) are explained as is the process for developing wage curves and pay grades. When you finish studying this chapter, you should be able to describe the job evaluation process; discuss the legal considerations in compensation; explain what is meant by compensable factors; and perform a job evaluation using the ranking method.

▸ BASIC ASPECTS OF COMPENSATION

COMPENSATION AT WORK

employee compensation All forms of pay or rewards going to employees and arising from their employment.

Employee compensation refers to all forms of pay or rewards going to employees and arising from their employment.[1] Employee compensation has two components. It includes *direct financial payments* in the form of wages, salaries, incentives, commissions, and bonuses; and *indirect payments* in the form of financial benefits like employer-paid insurance and vacations. In this chapter we explain how to formulate a plan for paying employees a fixed wage or salary; succeeding chapters cover financial incentives and bonuses and employee benefits.

THE ROLES OF MONEY IN WORK MOTIVATION

Psychologists know that people have many needs, only some of which can be satisfied directly with money. Other needs—for achievement, affiliation, power, or self-actualization, for instance—also motivate behavior but can only be satisfied indirectly (if at all) by money.

Yet even with all our more modern motivation techniques (like job enrichment), there's no doubt that money is still the most important motivator. As two researchers put it:

> Pay in one form or another is certainly one of the mainsprings of motivation in our society. . . . The most evangelical human relationist insists it is important, while protesting that other things are too (and are, perhaps in his view, nobler). It would be unnecessary to belabor the point if it were not for a tendency for money drives to slip out of focus in a miasma of other values and other practices. As it is, it must be repeated: Pay is the most important single motivator used in our organized society.[2]

BASES FOR DETERMINING PAY

Time clocks may become a relic of the past as more organizations trust their employees to track their own time.

There are essentially two bases on which to pay employees: increments of time and volume of production.

Compensation Based on Time

Most employees are paid on the basis of the time they put in on the job. For example, blue-collar workers are usually paid hourly or daily *wages*; this is often called *day work*. Some employees—managerial, professional, and usually secretarial and clerical—are *salaried*. They are compensated on the basis of a set period of time (like a week, month, or year), rather than hourly or daily.

Piecework

The second basis on which employees are paid is called *piecework*. Piecework ties compensation directly to the amount of production (or number of "pieces") the worker produces. It is therefore most popular as an incentive pay system. In one simple version, a worker's hourly wage is divided by the standard number of units he or she is expected to produce in one hour. Then for each unit produced over and above this standard, the worker is paid an incentive rate (per piece). Salespeople's commissions are another example of compensation tied to "production" (in this case, sales).

▶ BASIC CONSIDERATIONS IN DETERMINING PAY RATES

There are four basic factors you should consider before deciding how much to pay your employees: specifically, legal, union, policy, and equity factors should be considered.

LEGAL CONSIDERATIONS IN COMPENSATION

There are, first, laws that affect the compensation you pay in terms of minimum wages, overtime rates, and benefits. The most important of these laws follows.[3]

Davis-Bacon Act
A law passed in 1931 that sets wage rates for laborers employed by contractors working for the federal government.

1931 Davis-Bacon Act

This act provides for the secretary of labor to set wage rates for laborers and mechanics employed by contractors working for the federal government. Amendments to the act provide for employee benefits and require contractors or subcontractors to make necessary payment for these benefits.

Walsh-Healey Public Contract Act
A law from 1936 that requires minimum wage and working conditions for employees working on any government contract amounting to more than $10,000.

1936 Walsh-Healey Public Contract Act

This act sets basic labor standards for employees working on any government contract that amounts to more than $10,000. The law contains minimum wages, maximum hours, and safety and health provisions. It requires that time and a half be paid for work over 8 hours a day and 40 hours a week.

Fair Labor Standards Act
Congress passed this act in 1936 to provide for minimum wages, maximum hours, overtime pay, and child labor protection. The law has been amended many times and covers most employees.

1938 Fair Labor Standards Act

This act, originally passed in 1938 and since amended many times, contains minimum wage, maximum hours, overtime pay, equal pay, recordkeeping, and child labor provisions covering the majority of American workers—virtually all those engaged in the production and/or sales of goods for interstate and foreign commerce. In addition, agricultural workers and those employed by certain larger retail and service companies are included.

One important provision of the Fair Labor Standards Act governs overtime pay. It states that overtime must be paid at a rate of at least one and a half times normal pay for any hours worked over 40 in a workweek. Thus, if a worker covered by the act works 44 hours one week, he or she must be paid for 4 of those hours at a rate equal to one and a half times the hourly or weekly base rate the person would have earned for 40 hours. For example, if the person earns $5 an hour (or $200 for a 40-hour week), he or she would be paid at the rate of $7.50 per hour (5 times 1.5) for each of the 4 overtime hours worked, or a total of $30 extra. If the employee instead receives time off for the overtime hours, the number of hours granted off must also be computed at the one and a half time rate so that, for example, a person working 4 hours overtime would be granted 6 hours off, in lieu of overtime pay.

The act also established a minimum wage for those covered by the act. This minimum wage not only sets a floor or base wage for employees covered by the act, but also serves as an index that usually leads to increased wages for practically all workers whenever the minimum wage is raised. (The minimum wage in 1993 was $4.25 for the majority of those covered by the act.) The act also contains Child Labor Provisions. These prohibit employing minors between 16 and 18 years of age in hazardous occupations such as mining and carefully restricts employment of those under 16.

Certain categories of employees are exempt from the act or certain provisions of the act, and particularly from the act's overtime provisions. An employee's exemption depends on the responsibilities, duties, and salary of the job. However, bona fide executives, administrative, and professional employees (like architects) are generally exempt from the minimum wage and overtime requirements of the act.[4]

Equal Pay Act of 1963 An amendment to the Fair Labor Standards Act designed to require equal pay for women doing the same work as men.

1963 Equal Pay Act

This act is an amendment to the Fair Labor Standards Act. It states that employees of one sex may not be paid wages at a rate lower than that paid to employees of the opposite sex for doing roughly equivalent work. Specifically, if the work requires equal skills, effort, and responsibility and is performed under similar working conditions, employees of both sexes must receive equal pay unless the differences in pay are based on a seniority system, a merit system, the quantity or quality of production, or "any factor other than sex." The act, in other words, takes into consideration that differences in pay may exist for men and women performing essentially the same jobs if those differences are based on such considerations as merit or the quality or quantity of the person's work. Unfortunately, even today, though, the average woman who works can still only expect to earn about 70 cents for each $1 earned by the average man who is working in the same occupation.[5]

Civil Rights Act This law makes it illegal to discriminate in employment because of race, color, religion, sex, or national origin.

1964 Civil Rights Act

Title VII of this act is known as the Equal Employment Opportunity Act of 1964. It established the Equal Opportunity Employment Commission (EEOC). Title VII makes it an unlawful employment practice for an employer to discriminate against any individual with respect to hiring, compensation, terms, conditions, or privileges of employment because of *race, color, religion, sex,* or *national origin.*

Employee Retirement Income Security Act (ERISA) The law that provides government protection of pensions for all employees with company pension plans. It also regulates vesting rights (employees who leave before retirement may claim compensation from the pension plan).

1974 Employee Retirement Income Security Act (ERISA)

This act, in effect, renegotiated every pension contract in the country. It provides for the creation of government-run employer-financed corporations to protect employees against a failing pension plan. In addition, it set regulations regarding vesting rights. (Vesting refers to the equity the employees build up in their pension plan should their employment be terminated before retirement.) It also covers portability rights (the transfer of an employee's vested rights from one organization to another) and contains fiduciary standards to prevent dishonesty in the funding of pension plans.

The Tax Reform Act of 1986

The Tax Reform Act of 1986 represents the most extensive overhaul of the tax code in over 40 years.[6] It affected employee compensation in two ways. The most familiar feature of the law is the reduction of the individual tax rates to just two brackets of 15% and 28%, which means employees take home more of their wages and salaries. In brief, the 15% tax bracket applies to taxable income up to $17,850 for singles, $25,288 for heads of households, and $29,750 for married couples filing joint returns. The 28% tax rate applies to income over those figures.

The second feature that affects compensation is its treatment of employee benefits. The basic intent of this feature of the act was to increase benefits coverage for rank-and-file employees while reducing tax-favored benefits that can be provided to highly paid employees. The new deficit-reduction bill being considered by Congress may dramatically alter tax rates in the 1990s.

Other Legislation Affecting Compensation

Various other laws directly or indirectly impact your compensation decisions.[7] The *Age Discrimination in Employment Act of 1967* (ADEA) originally prohibited discrimination in hiring individuals between 40 and 65 years old and applied to employers with 25 or more employees (and labor organizations with 25 or more members). ADEA protected workers with respect to compensation, terms, conditions, or privileges of employment. ADEA was amended in 1986 (effective January 1, 1987) to prohibit employers from requiring retirement at any age. The new law covers private employers with 20 or more employees, state and local governments, employment agencies that serve covered employers, and labor unions with 25 or more members. State and local governments have seven years before mandatory retirement is eliminated for police officers, prison guards, and firefighters. The seven-year exclusion also includes tenured university professors.[8]

Each of the 50 states has its own worker's compensation laws, which today cover over 85 million workers. Among other things, the aim of these laws is to provide a prompt, sure, and reasonable income to victims of work-related accidents. The *Social Security Act of 1935* has been amended several times. It is aimed at protecting American workers from total economic destitution in the event of termination of employment beyond their control. Employers and employees contribute equally to the benefits provided by this act. *This act also provided for unemployment compensation*—jobless benefits—for workers unemployed through no fault of their own for up to 26 weeks in duration. ("Social Security" payments—payments to those who are disabled or retired, for instance—are discussed in Chapter 14.) The *federal wage garnishment law* limits the amount of an employee's earnings that can be garnished in any one week and protects the worker from discharge due to garnishment.

UNION INFLUENCES ON COMPENSATION DECISIONS

Labor relations laws and court decisions also impact compensation decisions. The National Labor Relations Act of 1935 (or Wagner Act) and associated legislation and court decisions legitimatized the labor movement. It gave it legal protection and gave employees the right to self-organization, to bargain collectively, and to engage in concerted activities for the purpose of collective bargaining or other mutual aid or protection. Historically, the wage rate has been the main issue in collective bargaining. However, other issues including time off with pay, income security (for those in industries with periodic layoffs), cost-of-living adjustment, and various benefits—like health care—are also important.[9]

In addition, the National Labor Relations Board (NLRB)—the group created by the National Labor Relations Act to oversee employer practices and to ensure that employees receive their rights—has made a series of rulings that underscore the need to involve union officials in developing the compensation package. For example, the employee's union must be provided with a written explanation of an employer's "wage curves"—the graph that relates jobs to pay rate. It is also entitled to know the salary of each employee in the bargaining unit.[10]

Union Attitudes Toward Compensation Decisions

Several studies shed some light on union attitudes toward compensation plans and underscore a number of commonly held union fears.[11] Many union leaders fear than any system (like a time and motion study) used to evaluate the worth of a job can become a tool for management malpractice. They tend to feel that no one can judge the relative value of jobs better than the workers themselves. And, they feel that management's usual method of using several *compensable factors* (like "degree of responsibility") to evaluate and rank the worth of jobs can be a manipulative device for restricting or lowering the pay of workers. One implication seems to be that the best way to gain the cooperation of union members in evaluating the worth of jobs is to request and use their active involvement in the process of evaluating the relative worth of jobs and in assigning fair rates of pay to these jobs. On the other hand, management has to ensure that its prerogatives—such as to use the appropriate "job evaluation" technique to assess the relative worth of jobs—are not surrendered.

COMPENSATION POLICIES

Your *compensation policies* will also influence the wages and benefits you pay, since these policies provide the basic compensation guidelines in several important areas. One is whether you want to be a leader or a follower regarding pay. For example, one hospital might have a policy of starting nurses at a wage at least 20% above the prevailing market wage. Other important topics usually covered by policies include the basis for salary increases, promotion and demotion policies, overtime pay policy, and policies regarding probationary pay and leaves for military service, jury duty, and holidays. Compensation policies are usually written by the human resource or compensation director in conjunction with top management.[12]

EQUITY AND ITS IMPACT ON PAY RATES

The *need for equity* is perhaps the most important factor in determining pay rates, and there are two types of equity to address: external equity and internal equity. Externally, pay must compare favorably with wages in other organizations or you'll find it hard to attract and retain qualified employees. Pay rates must also be equitable internally: Each employee should view his or her pay as equitable given other employees' pay rates in the organization. Some firms administer employee attitude surveys to obtain information from employees regarding their perceptions and feelings regarding the firm's compensation system. Questions typically addressed by such employee compensation surveys include "How satisfied are you with your pay?," "What criteria were used for your recent pay increase?," and "What factors do you believe are used when your pay is determined?"[13]

In practice, the process of establishing pay rates while assuring external and internal equity involves five steps:

1. Conduct a *salary survey* of what other employers are paying for comparable jobs (to help ensure *external equity*).
2. Determine the worth of each job in your organization through *job evaluation* (to ensure *internal equity*).
3. Group similar jobs into *pay grades*.
4. Price each pay grade by using *wage curves*.
5. Fine tune pay rates.

Each of these steps is explained in the next section of this chapter.

▶ ESTABLISHING PAY RATES

STEP 1. CONDUCT THE SALARY SURVEY

Introduction

salary survey
A survey aimed at determining prevailing wage rates. A good salary survey provides specific wage rates for specific jobs. Formal written questionnaire surveys are the most comprehensive, but telephone surveys and newspaper ads are also sources of information.

benchmark job
A job that is used to anchor the employer's pay scale and around which other jobs are arranged in order of relative worth.

Compensation or **salary surveys** play a central role in the pricing of jobs. Virtually every employer (regardless of size) therefore conducts such surveys for pricing one or more jobs.[14]

You'll use salary surveys in three ways. First, 20% or more of any employers' positions are usually *priced directly* in the marketplace, based on a formal or informal survey of what comparable firms are paying for comparable jobs. Second, survey data are used to price **benchmark jobs**, jobs that are used to anchor the employer's pay scale and around which other jobs are then slotted based on their relative worth to the firm. (*Job evaluation*, explained next, is the technique used to determine the relative worth of each job.) Finally, surveys also collect data on *benefits* like insurance, sick leave, and vacation time and so provide a basis on which to make decisions regarding employee benefits.

There are many ways you can conduct a salary survey. According to one British study, about 71% of the employers questioned rely to some extent on informal communication with other employers as a way of obtaining comparative salary information.[15] And 55% regularly review newspaper ads as a means of collecting comparative salary information, while 33% survey employment agencies to determine the wages for at least some of their jobs. About two-thirds of the firms also used commercial or professional surveys—surveys conducted by organizations like the American Management Association (or, in this case, their British counterparts). Finally, 22% of the firms also conducted formal questionnaire-type surveys with other employers.

Formal and Informal Surveys by the Employer

Most employers rely heavily on formal or informal surveys of what other employers are doing.[16] Informal telephone surveys are good for collecting data on a relatively small number of easily identified and quickly recognized jobs, such as when a bank's human resource director wants to determine the salary at which a newly open cashier's job should be advertised. This informal phone technique is also good for checking discrepancies, such as when the human resource director wants to confirm if some area banks are really paying tellers 10% more than his or her bank. Informal discussions among human resource specialists at professional conferences (like local meetings of the Society for Human Resource Management) are other occasions for informal salary surveys.

Perhaps 20% to 25% of employers use formal questionnaire surveys to collect compensation information from other employers. One page from such a survey is presented in Figure 12.1. It is part of a questionnaire that inquires about things like number of employees, overtime policies, starting salaries, and paid vacations.

For a salary survey to be useful, it must be sufficiently specific: 60% of the respondents in one study claimed that job categories were too broad or imprecise, for instance. Therefore, make sure you construct your survey with enough detail to make it useful.[17]

Commercial, Professional, and Government Salary Surveys

Many employers also rely on surveys published by various commercial firms, professional associations, or government agencies.

For example, the *Bureau of Labor Statistics (BLS)* annually conducts three types of surveys: (1) area wage surveys, (2) industry wage surveys, and (3) professional, administrative, technical, and clerical (PATC) surveys.

The BLS annually performs about 200 *area wage surveys*. These focus on clerical and manual occupations and provide pay data for jobs. This is illustrated in Table 12.1. As with this table, an employer could use this information as an input in pricing various jobs. Area wage surveys also provide data on weekly work schedules, paid holidays and vacation practices, and health insurance pension plans, as well as on shift operations and differentials.

Industry wage surveys provide data similar to that in the area wage surveys, but by industry, rather than geographic area. They thus provide national pay data for workers in selected jobs for industries like building, trucking, and printing.

PATC surveys provide pay data on 80 occupational levels in the fields of accounting, legal services, personnel management, engineering, chemistry, buying, clerical supervisory, drafting, and clerical. They provide information on straight-time earnings as well as production bonuses, commissions, and cost-of-living increases.

The American Management Association of New York (AMA) conducts and furnishes executive, managerial, and professional compensation data as one of its services. For example, its *executive compensation service* provides about a dozen compensation reports on domestic executive positions as well as several foreign reports. The top-management report includes information from almost 4,000 firms covering about 31,000 executives in 75 top positions in 53 industries.[18] The information covers both salaries and bonuses earned by these executives. The AMA also publishes a middle-management report providing similar

FIGURE 12.1
Compensation Survey

Source: David Belcher and Thomas Atchison, *Compensation Administration* (Englewood Cliffs, NJ: Prentice Hall, 1987), pp. 112–113.

Name of organization participating in the survey: ____________________
Address: ____________________ Industry: ____________________
Code No.: ____________________ Date this form was completed: ____________________
Data furnished by: Name ____________________ Title ____________________

1. Briefly describe major products (or services) of your reporting unit: ____________________

2. Employment:
   Total number of employees in company, division, or plant for which survey data is reported:
   Hourly ____
   Nonexempt salaried ____
   Exempt salaried ____
   Total ____
3. General increase and structure adjustments:
   a. During the past twelve months, has your firm granted a general increase to employees in the following classifications?
      Hourly ____ No ____ Yes Amount or %____ Date ____
      Nonexempt salaried ____ No ____ Yes Amount or %____ Date ____
      Exempt salaried ____ No ____ Yes Amount or %____ Date ____
   b. During the same period, did you have a structure adjustment?
      Hourly ____ No ____ Yes Amount or %____ Date ____
      Nonexempt salaried ____ No ____ Yes Amount or %____ Date ____
      Exempt salaried ____ No ____ Yes Amount or %____ Date ____
4. Merit increases:
   a. Does your firm maintain a merit increase budget for granting pay increases during a time period?
      Hourly ____ No ____ Yes
      Nonexempt salaried ____ No ____ Yes
      Exempt salaried ____ No ____ Yes
   b. If no, what was the approximate salary increase for the last period?
      Hourly $____
      Nonexempt salaried $____
      Exempt salaried $____
   c. If yes (if you have a merit increase budget), it is:

	Merit	*Promotion*	*Total*
Hourly	____:____%	____:____%	____:____%
Nonexempt salaried	____:____%	____:____%	____:____%
Exempt salaried	____:____%	____:____%	____:____%

   d. What are the dates of your current budget year?
      From ____________ to ____________, inclusive.
5. Union? ____ Yes ____ No
   If yes, list by name: ____________________

6. Cost of Living:
   Do you grant a cost-of-living allowance? ____ No ____ Yes
   If yes, what is the current amount and group involved? ____________________

7. Are any employee groups on automatic progression? ____ No ____ Yes
   If yes, groups, frequency, and amount: ____________________

8. Does your firm grant pay increases on an anniversary date or fixed calendar date(s)?

	Anniversary Date	Fixed Calendar	Date(s)
Hourly	____	____	____
Nonexempt	____	____	____
Exempt	____	____	____

9. What is the frequency of your salary increases?

	Times per Year 1	2	3	Other
Hourly	____	____	____	____
Nonexempt	____	____	____	____
Exempt	____	____	____	____

10. Any additional information that might help us interpret your pay data: ____________________

data on about 15,000 executives in 73 key jobs in about 650 firms. Its report on administrative and technical positions covers employee positions beneath middle management in about 600 companies. Its supervisory management compensation report surveys about 700 companies and 55 categories of first-line managers and staff supervisors.

The Administrative Management Society (AMS) conducts an annual survey of 13 clerical jobs, 7 data processing jobs, and various middle-management jobs in about 130 cities in the United States, Canada, and the West Indies (including many not covered by the BLS area wage surveys). The AMS surveys report data on salaries, length of workweeks, overtime, paid holidays, and the extent of union membership among survey participants for over 600,000 employees. They can provide a useful reference for employers making compensation decisions in the cities surveyed by the AMS. Private consulting and/or executive recruiting companies like Hay Associates, Heidrick and Struggles, and Hewitt Associates annually publish data covering the compensation of top and middle management and members of boards of directors. Professional organizations like the Society for Human Resource Management and the Financial Executives Institute publish surveys of compensation practices covering members of their associations.

For many firms, jobs are priced directly, based on formal or informal salary surveys. In most cases, though, surveys are used to price benchmark jobs around which other jobs are then slotted based on their relative worth. Determining the relative worth of a job is the purpose of *job evaluation*, to which we now turn.

STEP 2. DETERMINE THE WORTH OF EACH JOB: JOB EVALUATION

Purpose of Job Evaluation

job evaluation
A systematic comparison done in order to determine the worth of one job relative to another.

Job evaluation is aimed at determining a job's relative worth. It involves a formal and systematic comparison of jobs in order to determine the worth of one job relative to another and eventually results in a wage or salary hierarchy. The basic procedure of job evaluation is to compare the *content of jobs* in relation to one another, for example, in terms of their effort, responsibility, and skills. Suppose you know (based on your salary survey and compensation policies) how to price key benchmark jobs and can use job evaluation to determine the relative worth of all the other jobs in your firm relative to these key jobs. Then you are well on your way to being able to equitably price all the jobs in your organization.

Compensable Factors

compensable factor
A fundamental, compensable element of a job, such as skill, effort, responsibility, or working conditions.

Job evaluation involves comparing jobs to one another based on their content; it is the job's **compensable factors** that constitute what we mean by content.

There are two basic approaches you could use for comparing several jobs. First, you could take a more intuitive approach. You might decide that one job is "more important" than another, and not dig any deeper into why—in terms of specific job-related factors.

As a second alternative, you could compare your jobs to one another by focusing on certain basic factors each of the jobs have in common. In compensation management, these basic factors are called *compensable factors*. They are

TABLE 12.1 Average Straight-Time Weekly Earnings for Selected Office Occupations in 5 Areas, June–September 1986[1]

OCCUPATION AND LEVEL[2]	ALBANY–SCHENECTADY–TROY, NY	ANAHEIM–SANTA ANA–GARDEN GROVE, CA	BALTIMORE, MD	BILLINGS, MT	BOSTON, MA
	September	September	August	July	August
Secretaries	$385.50	$414.50	$377.50	$335.00	$385.00
Secretaries I	287.50	354.50	297.50	275.50	297.00
Secretaries II	310.50	347.00	336.50	—	350.50
Secretaries III	381.50	424.50	389.00	348.00	374.00
Secretaries IV	420.50	475.00	453.50	—	452.50
Secretaries V	450.50	558.50	519.50	—	498.00
Stenographers	—	—	451.00	—	352.50
Stenographers I	327.00	—	454.50	—	331.00
Stenographers II	369.00	—	—	—	—
Transcribing-machine typists	—	—	—	—	—
Typists	285.50	254.00	294.50	—	259.50
Typists I	234.00	242.00	238.00	—	239.00
Typists II	370.00	—	358.00	—	305.50
Word processors	—	354.50	309.50	278.50	330.00
Word processors I	—	318.50	291.50	268.50	288.00
Word processors II	—	390.00	337.50	—	366.00
File clerks	201.00	228.50	252.50	194.50	223.50
File clerks I	197.00	224.50	278.50	—	216.00
File clerks II	—	—	232.50	—	236.50
File clerks III	—	—	—	—	288.00
Messengers	—	271.50	247.50	—	221.50
Receptionists	—	246.00	240.50	—	296.00
Switchboard operators	296.50	265.00	272.00	240.00	277.50
Switchboard operator–receptionists	254.50	275.50	241.00	231.00	272.50
Order clerks	250.50	323.00	241.00	—	283.00
Order clerks I	—	281.50	233.00	—	256.50
Order clerks II	—	372.00	—	—	352.50
Accounting clerks	312.00	326.50	300.00	271.00	301.50
Accounting clerks I	—	275.00	235.00	253.50	221.00
Accounting clerks II	264.00	311.00	260.50	263.00	287.00
Accounting clerks III	322.00	367.50	308.50	306.00	325.00
Accounting clerks IV	398.00	417.00	481.00	—	394.50
Payroll clerks	377.50	329.50	331.50	297.50	334.00
Key entry operators	295.00	310.50	285.00	267.50	284.50
Key entry operators I	253.50	293.50	267.50	240.00	273.50
Key entry operators II	345.00	341.50	324.00	—	328.50

[1]Hourly earnings excluding premium pay for overtime and work on weekends, holidays, and late shifts.

[2]Percent increases have been adjusted to reflect a 12-month period even though the time span between annual surveys may have been other than 12 months.

Source: U.S. Department of Labor, Bureau of Labor Statistics, *Occupational Earnings and Wages, Trends in Metropolitan Areas, 1986 Summary 86–10.*

the factors that determine your definition of job content. They are the basic factors that determine how the jobs compare to each other. And, they are the basic factors that help determine the compensation paid for each job.

Some employers develop their own compensable factors. However, most use factors that have been popularized by packaged job evaluation systems or by federal legislation. For example, the Equal Pay Act focuses on four compensable factors—*skills, effort, responsibility,* and *working conditions*—holding that women in jobs that are about the same as men's (in terms of these factors) should be paid the same. As another example, the job evaluation method popularized by the Hay consulting firm focuses on three compensable factors: *know-how, problem solving,* and *accountability.*

The compensable factors you focus on depend on the nature of the job and the method of job evaluation that is to be used. For example, you might choose to focus on the compensable factor *decision making* (among others) for a manager's job, while that factor might be inappropriate for the job of assembler.

Identifying compensable factors plays a pivotal role in job evaluation. In job evaluation each job is usually compared with all comparable jobs *using the same compensable factors.* You thus evaluate the same elemental components for each job and are then better able to compare jobs to each other—for example, in terms of the degree of skills, effort, responsibility, and working conditions present in each job.[19]

Planning and Preparation for the Job Evaluation

Job evaluation is mostly a judgmental process, one that demands close cooperation between supervisors, personnel specialists, and the employees and their union representatives. The main steps involved include identifying the need for the program, getting cooperation, and then choosing an evaluation committee; the latter then carries out the actual job evaluation.[20]

Identifying the need for job evaluation should not be difficult. For example, dissatisfaction reflected in high turnover, work stoppages, or arguments may result from the inequities of paying employees different rates for similar jobs.[21] Similarly, managers may express uneasiness with the current, informal way of assigning pay rates to jobs, accurately sensing that a more systematic means of assigning pay rates would be more equitable.

Next, since employees may fear that a systematic evaluation of their jobs may actually reduce their wage rates, *getting employee cooperation* (for the evaluation) is a second important step. You can tell employees that, as a result of the impending job evaluation program, wage rate decisions will no longer be made just by management whim; that job evaluation will provide a mechanism for considering the complaints they have been expressing, and that no present employee's rate will be adversely affected as a result of the job evaluation.[22]

Next, you have to *choose a job evaluation committee,* and there are two reasons for doing so. First, the committee should bring to bear the points of view of several people who are familiar with the jobs in question, each of whom may have a different perspective regarding the nature of the jobs. Second (assuming the committee is composed at least partly of employees), the committee approach can help ensure greater acceptance by employees of the job evaluation results.

The committee itself usually consists of about five members, most of whom are employees. While management has the right to serve on such committees,

their presence can be viewed with suspicion by employees and "it is probably best not to have managerial representatives involved in committee evaluation of nonmanagerial jobs. . . ."[23] However, a personnel specialist can usually be justified on the grounds that he or she has a more impartial image than line managers and can provide expert assistance in the job evaluation. One method is to have this person serve in a nonvoting capacity. Union representation is possible. In most cases, though, the union's position is that it is only accepting job evaluation as an initial decision technique and is reserving the right to appeal the actual job pricing decisions through grievance or bargaining channels.[24] Once constituted, each committee member then receives a manual explaining the job evaluation process and special instructions and training that explain how to conduct a job evaluation.

The evaluation committee serves three main functions. First, it usually identifies 10 or 15 key benchmark jobs. These will be the first jobs to be evaluated and will serve as the anchors or benchmarks against which the relative importance or value of all other jobs can be compared and slotted into a hierarchy of jobs. Next, the committee may select compensable factors (although the human resource department will usually choose these as part of the process of determining the specific job evaluation technique to be used). Finally, the committee turns to its most important function, actually evaluating the worth of each job. For this, the committee will probably use one of the following job evaluation methods: the ranking method, the job classification method, the point method, or the factor comparison method.

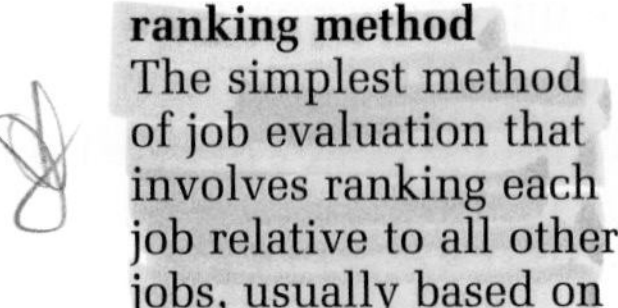

ranking method
The simplest method of job evaluation that involves ranking each job relative to all other jobs, usually based on overall difficulty.

Ranking Method of Job Evaluation

The simplest job evaluation method involves ranking each job relative to all other jobs, usually based on some overall factor like "job difficulty." There are several steps involved in ranking jobs.

1. *Obtain job information*. The first step is job analysis. Job descriptions for each job are prepared and these are (usually) the basis on which the rankings are made. (Sometimes job specifications also are prepared, but the job ranking method usually ranks jobs according to "the whole job" rather than a number of compensable factors. Therefore, job specifications—which provide an indication of the demands of the job in terms of problem solving, decision making, and skills, for instance—are not quite as necessary with this method as they are for other job evaluation methods.)
2. *Select raters and jobs to be rated*. It is often not practical to make a single ranking of all jobs in an organization. The more usual procedure involves ranking jobs by department or in "clusters" (i.e., factory workers, clerical workers). This eliminates the need for having to compare directly, say, factory jobs and clerical jobs.
3. *Select compensable factors*. In the ranking method, it is common to use just one factor (such as job difficulty) and to rank jobs on the basis of "the whole job." Regardless of the number of factors you choose, it's advisable to explain the definition of the factor(s) to the evaluators carefully so that they evaluate the jobs consistently.
4. *Rank jobs*. Next, the jobs are ranked. The simplest way to do this involves giving each rater a set of index cards, each of which contains a brief description of a job. These cards are then ranked from lowest to highest. Some managers use an "alternation ranking method" for making the procedure more accurate. Here you take the cards, first choosing the highest, and then the lowest, then the next highest and next lowest and so forth until all the cards have been ranked. Since it is usually easier to choose extremes, this approach facilitates the ranking procedure. A job ranking is

illustrated in Table 12.2. Jobs in this small health facility are ranked from maid up to office manager. The corresponding pay scales are shown on the right.

5. *Combine ratings.* It's usual to have several raters rank the jobs independently. Then, once this is accomplished, the rating committee (or you) can simply average the rankings.

PROS AND CONS. This is the simplest job evaluation method, as well as the easiest to explain. And it usually takes less time to accomplish than other methods.

Some of its drawbacks derive more from how it's used than the method itself. For example, there's a tendency to rely too heavily on "guesstimates." Similarly, ranking provides no yardstick for measuring the value of one job relative to another. For example, job No. 4 may in fact be five times "more valuable" than job No. 5, but with the ranking system all you know is that one job ranks higher than the other. Ranking is usually more appropriate for small organizations that can't afford the time or expense of developing a more elaborate system.

classification (or grading) method
A method for categorizing jobs into groups.

classes
Dividing jobs into classes based on a set of rules for each class, such as amount of independent judgment, skill, physical effort, and so forth, required for each class of jobs. Classes usually contain similar jobs—such as all secretaries.

grades
A job classification system synonymous with class. Grade descriptions are written based on compensable factors listed in classification systems, such as the federal classification system. Grades often contain dissimilar jobs, such as secretaries, mechanics, and firefighters.

Job Classification (or Grading) Evaluation Method

This is a simple, widely used method in which jobs are categorized into groups. The groups are called **classes** if they contain similar jobs (like all "fiscal assistant IVs"), or **grades** if they contain jobs that are similar in difficulty but are otherwise different. Thus, in the federal government's pay grade system, a "press secretary" and a "fire chief" might both be graded "GS–10" (GS stands for General Schedule).

There are several ways to categorize jobs. One is to draw up "class descriptions" (the analogs of job descriptions) and place jobs into classes based on their correspondence to these descriptions. Another is to draw up a set of classifying rules for each class (e.g., How much independent judgment, skill, physical effort, and so on, does the class of jobs require?). You then categorize the jobs according to these rules.

The usual procedure is to choose compensable factors and then develop class or grade descriptions that describe each class in terms of amount or level of compensable factor(s) in jobs. The federal classification system in the United States, for example, employs the following compensable factors: (1) difficulty

TABLE 12.2 Job Ranking by Olympia Health Care

RANKING ORDER	ANNUAL PAY SCALE
1. Office manager	$28,000
2. Chief nurse	27,500
3. Bookkeeper	19,000
4. Nurse	17,500
5. Cook	16,000
6. Nurse's aide	13,500
7. Maid	10,500

After ranking, it becomes possible to slot additional jobs between those already ranked and to assign an appropriate wage rate.

and variety of work, (2) supervision received and exercised, (3) judgment exercised, (4) originality required, (5) nature and purpose of interpersonal work relationships, (6) responsibility, (7) experience, and (8) knowledge required. Based on these compensable factors, a **grade description** like that in Figure 12.2 is written. Then the evaluation committee reviews all job descriptions and slots each job into its appropriate class or grade; in the federal government system, for instance, the positions of automotive mechanic, welder, electrician, and machinist are classified as being in grade GS–10.

grade description Written descriptions of the level of, say, responsibility and knowledge required by jobs in each grade. Similar jobs can then be combined into grades or classes.

The job classification method has several advantages. The main one is that most employers usually end up classifying jobs anyway, regardless of the job

FIGURE 12.2 Examples of Grade-Level Definitions in the Federal Government

Source: Douglass Bartley, *Job Evaluation* (Reading, MA: Addison-Wesley Publishing Company, Inc., 1981), p. 36.

GRADE	DEFINITION
GS-1	Includes those classes of positions the duties of which are to perform, under immediate supervision, with little or no latitude for the exercise of independent judgment— (A) the simplest routine work in office, business, or fiscal operations; or (B) elementary work of a subordinate technical character in a professional, scientific, or technical field.
GS-2	Includes those classes of positions the duties of which are— (A) to perform, under immediate supervision, with limited latitude for the exercise of independent judgment, routine work in office, business, or fiscal operations, or comparable subordinate technical work of limited scope in a professional, scientific, or technical field, requiring some training or experience; or (B) to perform other work of equal importance, difficulty, and responsibility, and requiring comparable qualifications.
GS-3	Includes those classes of positions the duties of which are— (A) to perform, under immediate or general supervision, somewhat difficult and responsible work in office, business or fiscal operations, or comparable subordinate technical work of limited scope in a professional, scientific, or technical field, requiring in either case— (i) some training or experience; (ii) working knowledge of a special subject matter; or (iii) to some extent the exercise of independent judgment in accordance with well-established policies, procedures, and techniques; or (B) top perform other work of equal importance, difficulty, and responsibility, and requiring comparable qualifications.
GS-4	Includes those classes of positions the duties of which are— (A) to perform, under immediate or general supervision, moderately difficult and responsible work in office, business, or fiscal operations, or comparable subordinate technical work in a professional, scientific, or technical field, requiring in either case— (i) a moderate amount of training and minor supervisory or other experience;

evaluation method that they use. They do this to avoid having to work with and price an unmanageable number of jobs; with the job classification method all your jobs, of course, are already grouped into several classes. The disadvantages are that it is difficult to write the class or grade descriptions, and considerable judgment is required in applying them. Yet many employers (including the U.S. government) use this method with success, and the government, in fact, has concluded that using a more quantitative method (like the two explained next) would cost much more than the additional accuracy warrants.[25]

Point Method of Job Evaluation

point method
The job evaluation method in which a number of compensable factors are identified and then the degree to which each of these factors is present on the job is determined.

The **point method** is a more quantitative job evaluation technique. It involves identifying (1) several compensable factors, *each having several degrees*, as well as (2) the degree to which each of these factors is present in the job. Thus, assume that there are five degrees of *responsibility* your jobs could contain. And assume a different number of *points* is assigned to each degree of each factor. Then, *once your evaluation committee determines the degree to which each compensable factor (like "responsibility") is present in the job*, you can add up the corresponding points for each factor and arrive at a total point value for the job. The result is thus a quantitative point rating for each job. The point method is apparently the most widely used job evaluation method and is explained in detail in the appendix to this chapter.

Factor Comparison Job Evaluation Method

factor comparison method
A widely used method of ranking jobs according to a variety of skill and difficulty factors, then adding up these rankings to arrive at an overall numerical rating for each given job.

The **factor comparison method** is also a quantitative technique and entails deciding which jobs have more of the chosen compensable factors than others. The method is actually a refinement of the ranking method. With the ranking method, you generally look at each job as an entity and rank the jobs on some overall factor like job difficulty. With the factor comparison method, you rank each job *several times—once for each compensable factor you choose*. For example, jobs might be ranked first in terms of the compensable factor "skill." Then they are ranked according to their "mental requirements," and so forth. Then these rankings are combined for each job into an overall numerical rating for the job. This is also a widely used method and is also explained in more detail in the appendix to this chapter.

STEP 3. GROUP SIMILAR JOBS INTO PAY GRADES

pay grade
A pay grade is comprised of jobs of approximately equal difficulty.

Once a job evaluation method has been used to determine the relative worth of each job, the committee can turn to the task of assigning pay rates to each job, but it will usually want to first group jobs into **pay grades**. If the committee used the ranking, point method, or factor comparison method it *could* assign pay rates to *each* individual job.[26] But for a larger employer such a pay plan would be difficult to administer, since there might be different pay rates for hundreds or even thousands of jobs. And even in smaller organizations there is a tendency to try to simplify wage and salary structures as much as possible. Therefore, the committee will probably want to group similar jobs (similar in terms of their ranking or number of points, for instance) into grades for pay purposes. Then, instead of having to deal with hundreds of pay rates, it might only have to focus on, say, 10 or 12 pay grades.[27]

A pay grade is comprised of jobs of approximately equal difficulty or importance as determined by job evaluation. If the point method was used, the pay grade consists of jobs falling within a range of points. If the ranking plan was used, the grade consists of all jobs that fall within two or three ranks. If the classification system was used, then the jobs are already categorized into classes or grades. (If the factor comparison method is used, the grade will consist of a specified range of pay rates, as explained in the appendix to this chapter.) Ten to 16 grades per "job cluster" (factory jobs, clerical jobs, etc.) is common.

STEP 4. PRICE EACH PAY GRADE—WAGE CURVES

wage curve
Shows the relationship between the value of the job and the average wage paid for this job.

The next step is to assign pay rates to each of your pay grades. (Of course, if you chose *not* to slot jobs into pay grades, pay rates would instead have to be assigned to each individual job.) Assigning pay rates to each pay grade (or to each job) is usually accomplished with a **wage curve**.

The wage curve depicts graphically the pay rates *currently* being paid for jobs in each pay grade relative to the points or rankings assigned to each job or grade, as determined by the job evaluation. An example of a wage curve is presented in Figure 12.3. Note that pay rates are shown on the vertical axis, while the pay grades (in terms of points) are shown along the horizontal axis. The purpose of the wage curve is to show the relationship between (1) the value of the job as determined by one of the job evaluation methods and (2) the current average pay rates for your grades.

The pay rates on the graph are traditionally those now paid by the organization. If there is reason to believe that the present pay rates are substantially out of step with the prevailing market pay rates for these jobs, benchmark jobs within each pay grade are chosen and priced via a compensation survey. These new market-based pay rates are then the wage rates plotted on the wage curve.

There are several steps in pricing jobs with a wage curve. First, *find the average pay for each pay grade*, since each of the pay grades consists of several jobs. Next, plot the pay rates for each pay grade as was done in Figure 12.3. Then fit a line (called a *wage line*) through the points just plotted. This can either be done freehand or by using a statistical method. Finally, *price jobs*. Wages along the wage line are the target wages or salary rates for the jobs in each pay grade. If the current rates being paid for any of your jobs or grades fall well above or below the wage line, that rate may be "out of line"; raises or a pay freeze for that job may be in order. Your next step, then, is to *fine tune* your pay rates.

STEP 5. FINE TUNE PAY RATES

Finally, the pay rates for each pay grade are fine tuned. This will involve correcting out-of-line rates and (usually) developing rate ranges.

Developing Rate Ranges

rate ranges
A series of steps or levels within a pay grade, usually based upon years of service.

Most employers do not just pay one rate for all jobs in a particular pay grade. Instead, they develop **rate ranges** for each grade so that there might, for instance, be 10 levels or "steps" and 10 corresponding pay rates within each pay grade. This approach is illustrated in Table 12.3, which shows the pay rates and steps for some of the federal government pay grades. As of the time of this pay

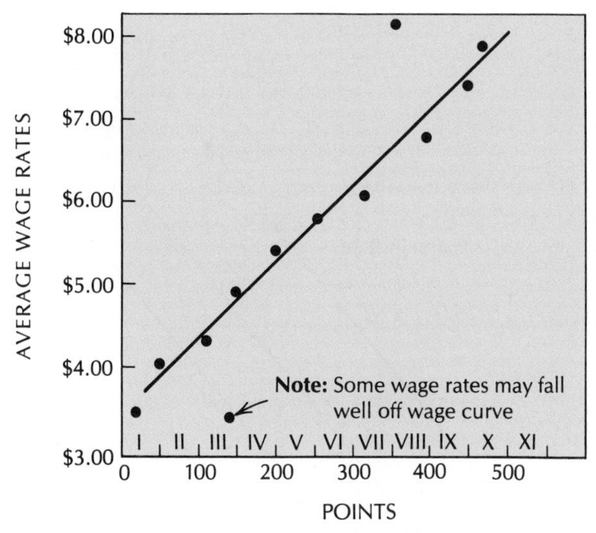

FIGURE 12.3
Plotting a Wage Curve

Note: The average pay rate for jobs in each grade (Grade I, Grade II, Grade III, etc.) are plotted, and the wage curve fitted to the resulting points.

schedule, for instance, employees in positions that were classified in grade GS–10 could be paid annual salaries of between $24,011 and $31,211, depending on the level or step at which they were hired into the grade, the amount of time they were in the grade, and their merit increases (if any). Another way to depict the rate ranges for each grade is with a *wage structure*, as in Figure 12.4. The wage structure *graphically* depicts the range of pay rates (in this case, per hour) to be paid for each pay grade.

There are several benefits in using rate ranges for each pay grade. First, the employer can take a more flexible stance with respect to the labor market. For example, it makes it easier to attract experienced, higher-paid employees into a pay grade where the starting salary for the lowest step may be too low to attract such experienced personnel. Rate ranges also allow you to provide for performance differences between employees within the same grade or between those with differing seniorities. As in Figure 12.4, most employers structure their rate ranges to overlap a bit so that an employee with more experience or seniority may earn more than an entry-level person in the next higher pay grade.

The rate range is usually built around the wage line or curve. One alternative is to arbitrarily decide on a maximum and minimum rate for each grade,

TABLE 12.3 Federal Government Pay Schedule: Grades GS 8–GS 10

	RATES AND STEPS WITHIN GRADE									
GRADE	1	2	3	4	5	6	7	8	9	10
GS–8	19,740	20,398	21,056	21,714	22,372	23,030	23,688	24,346	25,004	25,662
GS–9	21,804	22,531	23,258	23,985	24,712	25,439	26,166	26,893	27,620	28,347
GS–10	24,011	24,811	25,611	26,411	27,211	28,011	28,811	29,611	30,411	31,211

Note: Federal grades range from GS–1 to top grade of GS–18 (annual rate of $84,157).
Source: The U.S. Office of Personnel Management.

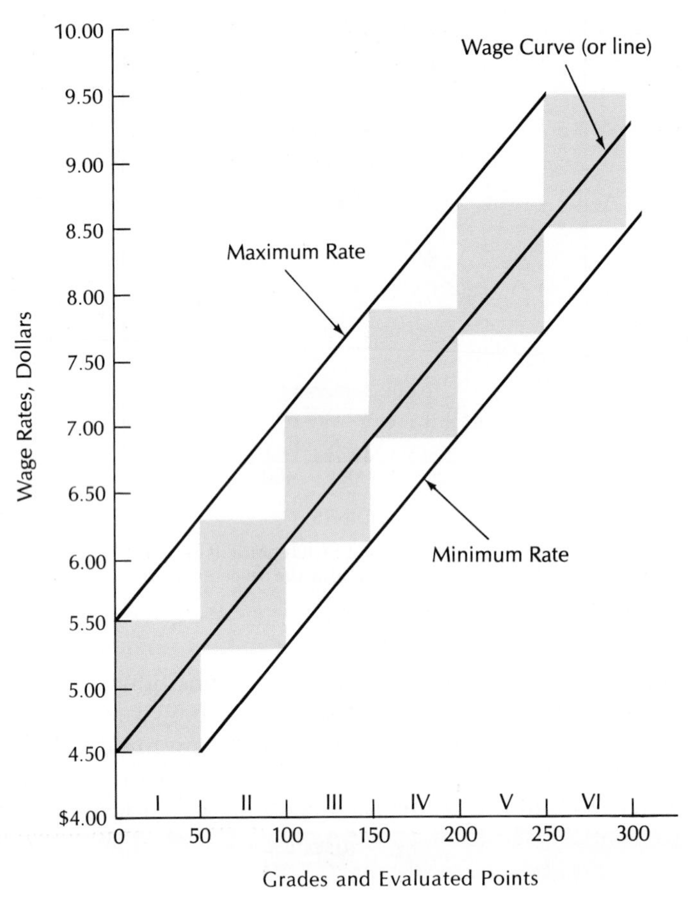

FIGURE 12.4
Wage Structure

Note: This shows overlapping wage classes and maximum–minimum wage ranges.

such as 15% above and below the wage line. As an alternative, some employers allow the rate range for each grade to become wider for the higher pay ranges, reflecting the greater demands and performance variability inherent in these more complex jobs.

Correcting Out-of-Line Rates

It is possible (as shown in Figure 12.3) that the wage rate for a job may fall well off the wage line (or well outside the rate range for its grade). *This means that the average pay for that job is currently too high or too low*, relative to other jobs in the firm. If a point falls well below the line, a pay raise for the job may be required. If the plot falls well above the wage line, pay cuts or a pay freeze may be required.

For underpaid employees, the problem is easy to solve. Underpaid employees should have their wages raised to the minimum of the rate range for their pay grade, assuming you want to retain the employees and have the funds. This can be done either immediately or in one or two steps.

Rates being paid to overpaid employees are often called red circle, flagged, or overrates, and there are several ways to cope with this problem. One is to freeze the rate paid to employees in this grade until general salary increases bring the other jobs into line with it. A second alternative is to transfer or promote some or all of the employees involved to jobs for which they can legitimately be paid their current pay rates. The third alternative is to freeze the rate for six months, during which time you try to transfer or promote the employees involved. If you cannot, then the rate at which these employees are paid is cut to the maximum in the pay range for their pay grade.

▶ CURRENT TRENDS IN COMPENSATION

IS JOB EVALUATION A "BARRIER TO EXCELLENCE"?

An increasing number of firms, such as Toyota Motor Manufacturing, USA, don't use job evaluation systems like Hay's to compute point values for jobs or to classify jobs by pay grade. They argue, basically, that to do so hinders adaptability because "with a point system, you can't move people as easily from job to job."[28] Their argument is that in, say, a typical General Motors plant, workers' jobs are narrowly defined and assigned a number of points. Therefore, moving employees from job to job as needs change becomes problematical. At Toyota, and a growing number of firms, therefore, there are only three plant job classifications: Division I includes all production team members; Division II includes all general maintenance team members; and Division III includes all tool and die members. Employees' pay is then tied to the skills they accumulate, rather than the specific jobs they do. As a result, it's easier to move them from job to job as needs change.

In fact, one expert argues that quantitative plans such as Hay's actually reward unadaptability.[29] She says that in some of these quantitative plans, compensable factors such as "know-how" range from "highly routine" to "highly independent" and that if you identify a job as being "highly routine" in terms of know-how, it's unlikely you'll be encouraging the job incumbents to think independently or be flexible.[30] Instead, they'll be inclined to keep doing the specific, routine jobs to which they are assigned.

ALTERNATIVES TO JOB EVALUATION

There are two popular alternatives to traditional job evaluation: pay for skill/knowledge and market pricing.

Skill-Based Pay

With skill-based pay, you are paid for the range, depth, and types of skills and knowledge you are capable of using, rather than for the job you currently hold.[31] According to one expert, there are several key differences between skill-based pay (SBP) and evaluation-driven job-based pay (JBP):[32]

1. *Competence testing.* With JBP, you receive the pay attached to your job regardless of whether or not you develop the competence needed to perform the job effectively. With SBP, your base pay is not tied to the job, but to your skills. You have to be certified as competent in the skills required by the job to get a pay increase.

2. *Effect of job change*. With JBP, your pay usually changes automatically when you switch jobs. With SBP that's not necessarily so. Before getting a pay raise, you must first demonstrate proficiency at the skills required by the new job.
3. *Seniority and other factors*. Pay in JBP systems is often tied to "time in grade" or seniority: In other words, the longer you're in the job, the more you get paid, regardless of how well you perform. SBP systems are based on skills, not seniority.
4. *Advancement opportunities*. Typically (but not always) there tend to be more opportunities for advancement with SBP plans than with JBP plans because of the companywide focus on skill building. A corollary to this is that SBP enhances organizational flexibility by making it easier for workers to move from job to job because their skills (and thus their pay) are more portable.

A skill-based pay plan was implemented at a General Mills manufacturing facility.[33] In this case, General Mills sought to boost the commitment and flexibility of its plant work force by implementing what it referred to as a high-involvement/high-performance work system, of which skill-based pay was one element. (Other elements included egalitarian management practices such as no reserved parking spaces for management and hiring practices that ensured a special effort was made to recruit employees who represented a strong fit with the flexible, team-based organizational culture in the plant.)

In this plant, the workers were paid based on their attained skill levels. There were basically four classifications (or "blocks") of jobs, corresponding to the four production areas: mixing, filling, packaging, and materials. Within each of these blocks workers could attain three levels of skill. Level 1 indicates limited ability, such as knowledge of basic facts and ability to perform simple tasks without direction.[34] Level 2 means the employee attained partial proficiency and could, for instance, apply technical principles on the job. Attaining Level 3 means the employee is fully competent in the area and could, for example, analyze and solve production problems. Each block or production area had a different average wage rate. There were therefore 12 pay levels (four blocks with three pay levels each) in the plant.

A new employee could start in any block, but always at Level 1. If after several weeks the employee was able to complete certification at the next higher skill level, his or her salary was correspondingly raised. Furthermore, employees were continually rotated from production area (or block) to production area. To be rotatable into a block, however, the employee had to achieve Level 2 performance within that skill block.

The system encouraged the learning of new skills. It also fostered flexibility by encouraging workers to learn multiple skills and willingly switch from block to block. The actual pricing of the 12 skill levels was accomplished in part by making the lowest of the 12 plant skill levels' wage rate equal to the average entry level wage rate for similar jobs in the community. (Notice, therefore, that even with skill-based pay you still can't entirely escape from evaluating jobs, market pricing them, and ranking them relative to one another in some fashion.)

Market Pricing

The second basic alternative to job evaluation is to value jobs directly, in the market. This basically involves preparing concise, lucid job descriptions and then comparing the prices paid for similar jobs in the market.[35] To some extent, of course, all job evaluation plans are at some point "market based." However, with most job evaluation plans only a relatively few benchmark jobs are market priced. Non–benchmark jobs are then slotted around these based on their values.

WHY JOB EVALUATION PLANS ARE STILL WIDELY USED

It's estimated that quantitative job evaluation systems such as the point and factor comparison plans are still used by 60 to 70% of all U.S. firms.[36] There are several reasons for this. Proponents of the point plan argue that individual differences in skill attainment certainly *can* be taken into consideration even when point-type plans are used, since most firms have salary ranges for groups of similar jobs. These salary ranges often reflect differences in the skills attained by, say, different people who may be working on the very same job.[37] Job evaluation advocates also argue that a job description is not necessarily a job restriction since it's naive to "believe that employees automatically limit their behavior to what is written on a piece of paper."[38] Furthermore, they say, there's no reason why job evaluation needs to be limited to specific jobs. Instead, one could theoretically evaluate the "job" of doing a whole project and from there ascertain the problem solving, accountability, and knowledge that a worker would need to successfully accomplish all the jobs involved in that specific project.

The fact that (as we've seen) neither skill-based pay nor market-based pay entirely eliminates the need for evaluating the worth of one job relative to others in the firm is another argument in favor of job evaluation. But in the final analysis the relative ease and security of having a quantitative system for valuing jobs probably is the major reason for the continued widespread use of quantitative plans. Use of these quantitative plans has also recently been facilitated by the development of computerized plans, as explained in the accompanying computer applications box.

BUILDING EMPLOYEE COMMITMENT

Compensation Management

The pay plans at well-known and progressive firms such as Saturn Corporation can help illustrate the current trends in job evaluation and compensation management. As at the General Mills plant previously mentioned, the compensation plans at firms like Saturn are elements in more comprehensive programs aimed at fostering employee commitment. These elements, as we've seen, include value-based hiring, career-oriented appraisals, and extensive employee involvement programs. Their compensation plans therefore tend to reflect the trust with which these firms treat their employees, and the fact that employees are and should be treated as partners in the business.

The compensation policies at Saturn Corp. are typical.[39] Saturn's pay plan is built on four principles—salary, trust, few classifications, and pay-for-performance. All Saturn employees are salaried, and there are no time clocks in the facility. To report your hours you go to a keyboard and punch in the number of hours you worked. While there are some checks and balances, the process is basically an honor system. "What it comes down to," said one operating technician, "is a matter of trust."[40]

There are also (as at Toyota) relatively few job classifications. Virtually all

Computer Applications In Compensation: Computerized Job Evaluations

As explained more fully in the appendix to this chapter, using a quantitative job evaluation plan such as the point plan can be a fairly time-consuming matter. This is because accumulating the information on "how much" of each compensable factor the job contains has traditionally been done through an often tedious process in which evaluation committees debate the level of each compensable factor in a job. They then write down their consensus judgments and manually compute each job's point values.

According to one expert, CAJE—computer-aided job evaluation—can dramatically streamline this whole process.[1] Computer-aided job evaluation, she says, can simplify job analysis, help keep job descriptions up-to-date, increase evaluation objectivity, reduce the time spent in committee meetings, and ease the burden of system maintenance. CAJE "features electronic data entry, computerized checking of questionnaire responses and automated output—not only of job evaluations, but also of a variety of compensation reports."[2] Most CAJE systems have two main components. There is a structured questionnaire. This contains items such as "enter total number of employees who report functionally to this position." Second, all CAJE systems are built around statistical models. These statistical models allow the computer program to price jobs more or less automatically, based upon inputted information on such things as prices of benchmark jobs, current pay, and current pay grade midpoints.

Another expert points out that CAJE does not replace but enhances traditional evaluation systems.[3] He says that you still need a traditional job evaluation system to provide "the initial solid analysis of benchmark jobs"—in other words, to identify the relative worth of these benchmark jobs. Then CAJE "streamlines and speeds the job evaluation process for 'non-benchmark' jobs."[4]

1. Sondra O'Neal, "CAJE: Computer-Aided Job Evaluation for the 1990s," *Compensation and Benefits Review* (November–December 1990), pp. 14–19.
2. Ibid.
3. Lauren & Dufetel, Job Evaluation: Still at the Frontier," *Compensation and Benefits Review* (July–August 1991), p. 64.
4. Ibid.

the assembly employees are classified as "operating technicians" as are all nonskilled trades members such as machinists. In addition, there are four additional classifications for skilled trades members.

Pay-for-performance is important, too. Under the reward system originally envisioned in the memorandum of agreement between Saturn and the UAW, about 20% of each employee's pay was to be "at risk." Specifically, each employee's base compensation was to equal 80% of straight time wages (base plus COLA) of the average of competitive rates in the U.S. automobile manufacturing industry. Over and above that a reward system was to be developed that would be based on factors such as achievement of specific objective productivity targets; performance in terms of individual and work unit performance; quality bonuses; and, eventually, a "Saturn sharing formula" through which profits were to be shared above a specified level of return to Saturn. At a minimum, therefore, 20% of each person's pay was to be at risk and to be earned back if the individual and the company met its productivity goals. Over and above that, a profit-sharing formula was to kick in. At the present time, a slower than expected start up at Saturn has forced the firm to reduce the at-risk component and thus boost the "guaranteed" component of the pay. For now, there is thus only 5 percent at risk. Taking a modified skill-based approach, employees can earn that 5 percent back by meeting specified training goals (by attending training sessions, improving their skills, and so on). In summary, the trend in firms like these is to

1. Offer packages of above average pay combined with incentives and extensive benefits
2. Build a compensation package that puts a significant portion of pay at risk
3. Emphasize self-reporting of hours worked, rather than devices like time clocks
4. Build a pay plan that encourages employees to think of themselves as partners. This means that they should have a healthy share of the profits in good years and share in the downturn during bad times.
5. Provide a package of benefits that makes it clear that they view their employees as long-term investments.

A GLIMPSE INTO THE FUTURE

The evolving practices in firms like Saturn provide us with a glimpse into the future of compensation management, and that future is here now, as far as many firms are concerned. Here's what several compensation experts say we can expect.

First, with an increasing emphasis on flexibility and on empowering employees, "In the U.S. companies in the year 2000, most traditional job descriptions and hourly employee job classifications will be fed unceremoniously into the paper shredder."[41] Replacing them will be greater latitude for employees to evolve their responsibilities to meet customer needs as they see fit and an increasing emphasis on paying employees for their competencies rather than just for the responsibilities and activities in a job description. Measurement systems and rewards will continue to focus on paying for improved results.

Construction workers of today are often compensated for their work through the method of skill-based pay which originated with the guilds of the Middle Ages.

One aspect of this—skill-based pay—(see previous discussion) will actually be a return to the compensation methods of the far distant past. Under the apprentice systems that started with the guilds of the Middle Ages, apprentices had to demonstrate competence at their trade before being promoted to journeymen, and then to masters. So when firms like General Mills or Saturn or Motorola condense dozens or hundreds of job classifications into a few broad bands and then base pay differentials on skill levels we're really returning, to some extent, to the past. In summary, competency or skill-based pay will become increasingly prevalent.[42]

One expert also suggests that as firms like IBM break themselves into small, decentralized pieces the whole concept of centrally determined compensation plans may become obsolete.[43] He says that at some point managers of decentralized units should simply get salary budgets and then "set pay levels for new hires, determine pay increases, decide when to give raises, and make all other decisions concerning cash compensation for the employees reporting to them."[44]

There will also be a growing emphasis on pay for improved results and on nontraditional pay (also called "alternative rewards"). This is summarized in Figure 12.5. Traditional pay plans based on job descriptions, job evaluations, and salary structures tend to focus, says this expert, on creating order, reinforcing the hierarchy, and directing behavior.[45] In the future (and for many firms the future is now), the emphasis will shift from paying for the job to paying for the employee's contribution. Thus, the focus will shift from creating order and directing behavior to encouraging involvement and commitment, and to rewarding positive results. Nontraditional or alternative pay plans for doing this include competency or skill-based pay and the sorts of spot awards, team incentives, and gainsharing discussed in Chapter 13.

PRICING MANAGERIAL AND PROFESSIONAL JOBS

Developing a compensation plan to pay executive, managerial, and professional personnel is similar in many respects to developing a plan for any employees.[46] The basic aims of the plan are the same in that your goal is to attract good employees and maintain their commitment. Furthermore, the basic methods of job evaluation—classifying jobs, ranking them, or assigning points to them, for instance—are about as applicable to managerial and professional jobs as to production and clerical ones.

Yet for managerial and professional jobs, job evaluation only provides a partial answer to the question of how to pay these employees, because these jobs differ from production and clerical jobs in several respects. For one thing, managerial and professional jobs tend to emphasize nonquantifiable factors like judgment and problem solving more than do production and clerical jobs. Second, there is a tendency to pay managers and professionals based on ability—based on their performance or on what they can do—rather than on the basis of "static" job demands like working conditions. Developing compensation plans for managers and professionals therefore tends to be a relatively complex matter, one in which job evaluation, while still important, usually plays a secondary role to nonsalary issues like bonuses, incentives, and benefits.

FIGURE 12.5
Examples of Traditional and Nontraditional Pay

Source: Sibson & Company, Inc. Reproduced in Charles Cumming, "Will Traditional Salary Administration Survive the Stampede to Alternative Rewards?" *Compensation and Benefits Review* (November–December 1992), p. 45.

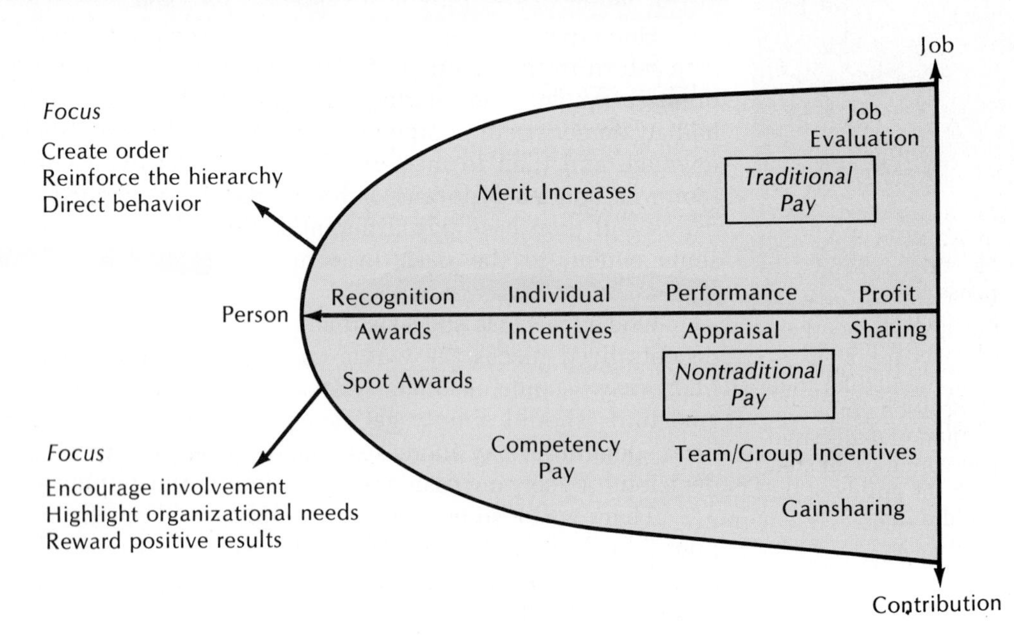

COMPENSATING MANAGERS

Basic Compensation Elements

There are five elements in a manager's compensation package: salary, benefits, short-term incentives, long-term incentives, and perquisites.[47]

The amount of salary managers are paid is usually a function of the value of the person's work to the organization and how well the person is discharging these responsibilities. As with other jobs, the value of the person's work is usually determined through job analysis and salary surveys and the resulting fine tuning of salary levels. Salary is the cornerstone of executive compensation, since it is on this element that the other four are layered, with benefits, incentives, and perquisites normally awarded in some proportion to the manager's base pay.

The other four elements include benefits, short- and long-term incentives, and perquisites. *Benefits* (including time off with pay, health care, employee services, survivors protection, and retirement coverage) are discussed in Chapter 14. *Short-term incentives* are designed to reward managers for attaining short-term (normally yearly) goals. *Long-term incentives* are aimed at rewarding the person for long-term performance (in terms of increased market share and the like). Incentives are discussed in Chapter 13. *Perquisites* (perks for short) begin where benefits leave off and are usually given to only a select few executives based on organizational level and (possibly) past performance. Perks include use of company cars, yachts, and executive dining rooms. These benefits are also covered in Chapter 14.

Executive compensation tends to emphasize performance incentives more than do other employees' pay plans, since organizational results are more likely to directly reflect the contributions of executives than those of lower-echelon employees. The heavy incentive component of executives' compensation can be illustrated with some examples of the highest paid U.S. executives.[48] Recently, for instance, the president of United Technologies earned a salary of $545,000 and a bonus of $480,000 and exercised his long-term incentive stock option to earn an additional $1,946,000; for the chairman of Rockwell International, his salary component was $460,000, the bonus was $655,000, and the long-term income was $1,055,000, for total compensation of $2,170,000. The president of Levi Strauss earned a salary of $276,000, a bonus of $125,000, and long-term income of $1,256,000. In general, bonuses today equal 25% or more of a typical executive's base salary in many countries, including the United States, the United Kingdom, France, and Germany.[49]

Michael Eisner, CEO of Walt Disney Co., had official 1992 compensation of almost $7,500,000 which didn't include his exercise and sale of stock options worth much more.

Determinants of Executive Pay

Compensation levels like these have prompted some writers to ask whether top managers are not overpaid. One even contends that the stockholders and public resent

> the prospect that key executives are becoming a privileged class, receiving special contracts or bonuses along with their extensive perquisites and often spectacular salaries—regardless of the performance of their companies. The rewards should not be, as a judge once said "a misuse or waste of corporate funds, or a gift to a favored few." Executive compensation practices that undermine public trust must be changed, or capitalists themselves will become a major force undermining capitalism.[50]

In point of fact, there *is* considerable disagreement regarding what determines executive pay and therefore whether top executives are worth what they are paid. At the lower levels of management (like first-line supervisor), there is no debate; supervisors' pay grades are usually set so that their median salaries are 10% to 25% above those of the highest paid workers supervised. And many employers even pay supervisors for scheduled overtime, although the Fair Labor Standards Act does not require them to do so.[51]

It is at the topmost management levels that questions regarding pay abound. The traditional wisdom is that a top manager's salary is closely tied to the size of the firm.[52] Yet two experts who tested this idea by studying the relationship between pay and responsibility for the 148 highest-paid executives in the United States concluded that "the level of executive responsibility (as measured by total assets, total sales, total number of shares in the company, total value of the shares, and total corporate profits) is not an important variable in determining executive compensation."[53] Instead, say these experts, an executive's pay is mostly determined by the industry in which he or she works, and the "corporate power structure," since executives who also serve on their firms' boards of directors "are, to a large degree, dictators of their own destiny."

Yet there is conflicting evidence. In one study, for instance, the researcher found that a statistical analysis of the total cash compensation of the chief executive officers of 129 companies showed that they *were* paid for both responsibility and performance. This researcher found that four compensable factors—company size, profitability, number of employees, and experience—accounted for 83% of the differences in pay. Therefore, says this writer, it appears "that there are rational, acceptable, and abiding principles that govern the total cash compensation of top executives in manufacturing firms."[54]

In any case, shareholder activism is combining with congressional reform and other changes to tighten up the restrictions on what firms pay their top executives.[55] For example, the Securities and Exchange Commission voted in 1992 to approve final rules regarding executive compensation communications. The chief executive officer's pay is always to be disclosed as well as other officers' pay if their compensation (salary and bonus) exceeds $100,000. And for bankers, the Federal Deposit Insurance Act of 1991 contains a prohibition on excessive compensation. One result is that boards of directors must act responsibly in reviewing and setting executive pay. That includes, says one expert, determining the key performance requirements of the executive's job; assessing strategic and compensation appropriateness of the firm's current practices; conducting a pay-for-performance survey; and testing shareholder acceptance of the board's pay proposals.[56]

Managerial Job Evaluation

Despite questions regarding the rationality of executive pay levels, job evaluation still plays an important role in pricing executive and managerial jobs, at least in most firms. According to one expert, "the basic approach used by most large companies to ensure some degree of equity among various divisions and departments is to classify all executive and management positions into a series of grades, to which a series of salary ranges is attached."[57]

As with nonmanagerial jobs, one alternative is to rank the executive and management positions in relation to each other, grouping those of equal value. However, the job classification and point evaluation methods are also used, with compensable factors like scope of the position, complexity, difficulty, and creative demands.

COMPENSATING PROFESSIONAL EMPLOYEES

Compensating nonsupervisory professional employees like engineers and scientists presents some unique problems.[58] Investigative work like this puts a heavy premium on creativity and problem solving, compensable factors that are not easily compared or measured. Furthermore, the professional's economic impact on the firm is often related only indirectly to the person's actual effort; for example, the success of an engineer's invention depends on many factors, like how well it is produced and marketed.

The job evaluation methods we explained previously can be used for evaluating professional jobs.[59] The compensable factors here tend to focus on problem solving, creativity, job scope, and technical knowledge and expertise. Both the point method and factor comparison methods have been used, although the job classification method seems most popular. Here a series of grade descriptions are written, and then a position is slotted into the grade having the most appropriate definition.

Yet, in practice, traditional methods of job evaluation are rarely used for professional jobs since "it is simply not possible to identify factors and degrees of factors which meaningfully differentiate among the values of professional work."[60] "Knowledge and the skill of applying it," as one expert notes, "are extremely difficult to quantify and measure."[61]

As a result, most employers use a market-pricing approach in evaluating professional jobs. They price professional jobs in the marketplace to the best of their ability to establish the values for benchmark jobs. These benchmark jobs and the employer's other professional jobs are then slotted into a salary structure. Specifically, each professional discipline (like mechanical engineering or electrical engineering) usually ends up having four to six grade levels, each of which requires a fairly broad salary range. This approach helps ensure that the employer remains competitive when bidding for professionals whose attainments vary widely and whose potential employers are literally found worldwide.

▶ CURRENT ISSUES IN COMPENSATION MANAGEMENT

THE ISSUE OF COMPARABLE WORTH

The Issue

Should women who are performing jobs *equal* to men or just *comparable* to men be paid the same as men? This is the basic issue in **comparable worth**.

comparable worth The concept by which women (who are usually paid less than men) can claim that men in *comparable* (rather than strictly equal) jobs are paid more.

Equal pay legislation in the United States and other industrialized countries has a history of debate over whether "equal" or "comparable" should be the standard for comparison when comparing men's and women's jobs.[62] For years, "equal" was the standard in the United States, though "comparable" was and is used in Canada and many European countries.[63] In the United States, for instance, the 1963 Equal Pay Act prohibits sex-based pay discrimination, in that an "employer is prohibited from discriminating between employees on the basis of sex by paying wages to employees . . . at a rate less than the rate at which wages are paid to employees of the opposite sex . . . for equal work on jobs the performance of which requires equal skill, effort and responsibility, and which are performed under similar working conditions." For years, courts interpreted this to mean that an employee had to prove not only a disparity of wages between males and females, but also that the disparity exists in *substantially equal jobs* in order to show a case of sex discrimination exists against the employer.[64] As a result of court rulings, though, some experts now believe that *comparable worth* may become the standard in the United States.[65]

The issue of comparable worth refers to the requirement to pay equal wages for jobs of comparable (rather than strictly equal) value to the employer. In a limited sense, this means jobs that (while not equal) *are at least quite similar*, jobs such as assemblers on one line versus assemblers on a different assembly line. In its broadest sense, though, *comparable worth includes comparing quite dissimilar jobs*, such as nurses to fire truck mechanics, nurses to public works mechanics, secretaries to parking lot attendants, nurses to tree trimmers, or secretaries to electricians.[66]

The Gunther Supreme Court Case

A pivotal case here was *Gunther* v. *County of Washington*. It involved Washington County, Oregon, prison matrons who claimed sex discrimination because male prison guards, whose jobs were somewhat different, received substantially higher pay.[67] In this case, the county had evaluated the men's jobs as having 5% more "job content" (based on a point evaluation system) than the female jobs and paid the males 35% more.

While the Supreme Court's decision for the female employee specifically stated that this was not a comparable worth case, many experts believed that the effect of the decision would make comparable worth the main consideration in future equal pay lawsuits. Prior to the *Gunther* case, wage discrimination claims based on sex had to be argued under the 1963 Equal Pay Act, so that the aggrieved employee had to show that the pay disparity existed in substantially equal jobs. In the *Gunther* case, however, the Supreme Court held that a sex-based pay discrimination case could be argued under Title VII of the 1964 Civil Rights Act. It was relatively difficult to prove pay discrimination under the Equal Pay Act, since the man and woman involved had to have the same or equal jobs. Under Title VII of the 1964 Civil Rights Act, it appears that it will be easier to compare men's and women's wages in comparable, rather than just equal, jobs.

However, the concept of comparable worth was subsequently dealt a severe blow by the Ninth Circuit Court of Appeals, which ruled on the appeal of a State of Washington case that also first helped put comparable worth in the spotlight. The appeals court overturned a U.S. district court's ruling, rejecting the idea that the payment of wages based on the prevailing rates in the market can be in and of itself evidence of intentional discrimination. The court, in *AFSCME* v. *State of Washington*, also ruled that there was nothing in Title VII that was intended to "abrogate fundamental economic principles such as the laws of supply and demand or to prevent employers from competing in the labor market." However, as one law firm puts it, "until the U.S. Supreme Court rules on this issue, employers should continue to be cautious in initiating job evaluation studies and in perpetuating known wage disparities between male dominated and female dominated jobs, where the jobs are arguably of 'comparable value.'"[68] An agreement was subsequently announced whereby the state of Washington agreed to pay 35,000 employees in female-dominated jobs almost $500 million in pay raises over seven years, in settlement of this suit.

Comparable Worth and Job Evaluation

The issue of *comparable worth* has important implications for an employer's job evaluation procedures. In virtually every comparable worth case that reached a court, the claim revolved around the use of the point method of job evaluation. Here each job is evaluated in terms of several factors (like effort, skill, and responsibility) and then assigned points based on the degree of each factor present in the job. As a result, point plans actually encourage assigning "comparable worth" ratings to different jobs. There are two sides to the problem. In the more familiar case, two positions such as Clerk-Typist IV and Junior Engineer might be evaluated as having the same number of points (and therefore comparable worth). This would seem to imply that both jobs should be paid the same, although in practice market wage rates may be much higher for the (male-dominated) junior engineers than for the (female-dominated) clerk-typist.[69] Sometimes, in other words, jobs that are evaluated as having comparable worth to a firm might each have very different values out in the market; to pay them both the same could then be viewed as questionable.

The other side of the problem concerns the possibility of bias in the job evaluation plan itself. In particular, some traditional job evaluation point plans "tend to result in higher point totals for jobs traditionally held by males than for those traditionally held by females."[70] For example, the factor "supervisory responsibility" might heavily weight chain of command factors such as number of employees supervised and downplay the importance of functional authority or gaining the voluntary cooperation of other employees. The solution, says one expert, is to rewrite the factor rules in job evaluation plans so as to give more weight to the sorts of activities that female-dominated positions frequently emphasize.[71]

Implications

The comparable worth issue has several implications for compensation management. Some argue that quantitative job evaluation methods like the point method need not be discarded, just used more wisely. For example, one approach is to stress prevailing market rates in pricing jobs, and then only use an evaluation method (like the point method) to slot in those jobs for which a market price is not readily available.[72] Another practical solution (says one writer) is to allow employers to price their jobs as they see fit, but to ensure that women have equal access to all jobs, as do men; the idea here is to eliminate the wage discrimination issue by eliminating sex-segregated jobs.[73] To avoid "comparable worth" problems some questions to ask include the following:

> Are your job duties and responsibilities clearly documented either by a job analysis questionnaire or a job description? Are they reviewed and updated annually?
>
> When was your pay system last reviewed? If more than three years have passed, serious inequities could exist.
>
> Do you have any circumstances where your system indicates that jobs are comparable, even in the marketplace, but you are paying those jobs occupied by females or minorities less than predominantly male and/or white jobs?
>
> When was the last time you statistically checked the effect of your pay system on females and minorities? Could it be that you have discrimination in fact, though not in intent?
>
> Is your pay system clearly documented in a salary administration manual? If not, the credibility and defensibility of your pay practices are ripe for challenge.[74]

THE ISSUE OF PAY SECRECY

There are basically two opposing points of view with respect to the question "Should employees know what other employees in the organization are being paid?" The basic argument *for* "open pay" is that it improves employee motivation, and the basic thinking here is as follows: If employees believe that greater effort does not result in greater rewards then, generally speaking, greater effort (and therefore motivation) will not be forthcoming. On the other hand, if employees *do* believe that there is a direct relationship between effort and rewards then greater effort would result. Proponents of "open pay" contend that workers who do *not* know each other's pay cannot easily assess how effort and rewards are related, or whether they are equitably paid, and as a result of this motivation tends to suffer. (They cannot, for example, say "Smith doesn't work hard, so is paid less than Jones, who works hard.") The opposing argument is that in practice there *are* usually real inequities in the pay scale, perhaps because of the need to hire someone "in a hurry," or because of the superior sales ability of a particular applicant. And even if the employee in a similar job who is being paid more actually deserves the higher salary because of his or her effort, skill, or experience, it's possible that lower paid colleagues, viewing the world through their own point of view, may still convince themselves that they are underpaid relative to him or her.

The research findings to this point are sketchy. In one study a researcher found that managers' satisfaction with their pay increased following their firms' implementation of an open pay policy.[75] A survey conducted by the Bureau of National Affairs found that less than half the firms responding gave employees access to salary schedules. Those not providing such information indicated, among other things, that "secrecy prevents much quibbling . . . ," "salary is a delicate matter . . . ," open pay "could well lead to unnecessary strain and dissatisfaction among managers . . . ," and "open systems too often create misunderstandings and petty complaints." The author of this study notes that "whether the inequities result from a growth situation or some other factor, it is clear that some inequities and openness are incompatible."[76] The implication for compensation management seems to be that a policy of open pay can, under the best of conditions, improve employees' satisfaction with their pay and (possibly) their effort as well. On the other hand, if conditions are not right—and especially if there are any lingering inequities in the employer's pay structure—moving to an open pay policy is not advisable.

THE ISSUE OF INFLATION AND COMPENSATION MANAGEMENT

Inflation and how to cope with it has been another important issue in compensation management. According to one estimate, a family of four earning $21,000 in 1975 would have to have earned just over $48,000 by 1990 to maintain the same purchasing power because of inflation, and because the family would move to higher income tax brackets as their income increased.[77]

A related problem—*salary compression*—was ranked as a major problem by 15% of the respondents in one study. Salary compression is a result of inflation. Its symptoms include (1) higher starting salaries, thereby compressing current employees' salaries; (2) unionized hourly pay increases that overtake supervisory and nonunion hourly rates; and (3) the recruitment of new college graduates at salaries above those of current job holders.[78]

Dealing with salary compression is a tricky problem.[79] On the one hand, you do not want your long-termers to be treated unfairly or to become inordinately dissatisfied and possibly leave with their accumulated knowledge and expertise. On the other hand, the fact remains that mediocre performance or lack of assertiveness may in many cases explain the low salaries rather than salary compression.

In any case, there are several solutions to the pay compression problem.[80] As distasteful as it is to many employers to pay employees simply for seniority, you can institute a program of providing raises based on longevity. These raises could be distributed in flat dollar amounts, or as a percentage of base pay, or as a combination of the two. Second (as explained more fully in Chapter 13), a much more aggressive merit pay program can be installed. This may at least help reduce the morale problems associated with pay compression, since employees know they have the potential for earning higher raises. Third, supervisors can be authorized to recommend "equity" adjustments for selected incumbents who are both highly valued by the organization and also viewed as unfairly victimized by pay compression.

Inflation has also put some employers' pension plans in peril.[81] An executive who retired at the beginning of 1982 had lost about 45% of the purchasing power of a fixed-dollar company pension by 1990, for instance, a frightening state of affairs for retirees whose pensions are not indexed to inflation. While the rate of increase of consumer prices has recently slowed, some fear that inflation is only dormant and that rapid price increases will again occur.

In the 1970s and early 1980s, employers tried to cope with inflation's impact in many ways. More employers granted across-the-board salary increases either in lieu of or in addition to performance-based merit increases. Others changed their pension plans to index them to inflation so that the value of the pension payments increased along with the rise in the price of goods.[82] Others changed the compensation mix to decrease the emphasis on taxable income like wages and salary and to substitute nontaxable benefits like flexible work hours, dental plans, day care centers, and group legal and auto insurance plans.[83]

The cost-of-living adjustment (or COLA) clause is another way employers tried to cope with inflation.[84] The COLA or escalator clause is designed to maintain the purchasing power of the wage rate and operates as follows. Specified increases in the Consumer Price Index trigger increases in the wage rate, with the magnitude of the increase depending on the negotiated COLA formula.[85] The most common formula provides a 1 cent per hour wage adjustment for each 0.3% or 0.4% change in consumer prices.[86] Nonunion employees often then receive a similar adjustment. Periodically, the employer takes a portion of the dollar COLA adjustment and builds it into the employee's base salary, a procedure known as "baking in."[87] Again, though, COLAs have become less of a concern to unions as inflation has moderated. The COLA clause was first adopted by the United Auto Workers and the General Motors Corporation in 1950; a study by the Bureau of Labor Statistics indicates that about 40% of the major union contracts negotiated recently (covering 6.5 million workers) contained COLA provisions, down from 58% and 9.3 million workers in 1980.[88]

In fact, General Motors Corporation is eliminating COLAs for its 125,000 salaried employees. GM had previously instituted a pay-for-performance system and, pleased with the results, decided to expand it to all salaried workers. This move may signal the end of COLAs in the next UAW contract.[89]

THE ISSUE OF COST-OF-LIVING DIFFERENTIALS

Cost-of-living differences between localities have escalated from occasional inconveniences into serious compensation problems. For example, a family of four might live in Atlanta for just over $39,000 per year while the same family's annual expenditures in Chicago or Los Angeles would be over $46,000. Deciding whether and how to have differential pay rates for employees living in different locales and how to handle employees' moving from one area to another is thus an important compensation issue today.

Employers are using several methods to handle cost-of-living differentials. The main approach is to give the transferred person a nonrecurring payment, usually in a lump sum, or perhaps spread over one to three years.[90] Other employers pay a differential for ongoing costs in addition to a one-time allocation. For example, one employer pays a differential of $6,000 per year to people earning $35,000 to $45,000 who are transferred from Atlanta to Minneapolis. The first $6,000 is a lump sum at the time of the move, and in the second year the employee gets another $6,000 in four quarterly increments. Employees already living in Minneapolis (or any other high-cost area) are not given any adjustment.[91] Other companies simply increase the employee's base salary rate. They give the person an automatic raise equal to the amount that living costs in the new locale exceed those in the old, in addition to any other promotion-based raise the employee may get.

GLOBAL HRM

The Issue of Compensating Overseas Employees

The question of cost-of-living differentials has particular relevance to multinational firms. The annual cost of sending a U.S. expatriate manager from the United States to Europe varies widely according to the country. For example, it's estimated that the annual cost of keeping a U.S. expatriate in France might average $193,000, while in neighboring Germany the cost would be $246,000.[92]

Such wide discrepancies of course raise the issue of how multinational firms should compensate overseas employees. The issue is particularly important today, in part because of the growing need to staff overseas operations, and in part because of the increasing frequency with which managers and professionals are moved from country to country.

Two basic international compensation policies seem to be most popular today: home-based versus host-based.[93]

Under a home-based salary policy, an international transferee's base salary reflects his or her home country's salary structure. Additional allowances are then tacked on for cost-of-living differences and housing and schooling costs, for instance. This is a reasonable approach for short-term assignments and avoids the problem of having to change the employee's base salary every time that he or she moves. However, it can result in some difficulty at the host office if, say, employees from several different countries at the same office are all being paid different base salaries for essentially performing the same tasks.

In the host-based plan the base salary for the international transferee is tied to the host country's salary structure. In other words, the manager from New York who is sent to France would have his or her base salary changed to the prevailing base salary for that position in France, rather than keep his or her New York base salary. Of course, cost-of-living, housing, schooling, and other allowances are tacked on here as well. This approach can cause some consternation to our New York manager who might, for instance, see his or her base salary plummet with a transfer to Bangladesh. Conversely, he or she may face the problem of frequent salary fluctuations if he or she moves from country to country fairly often.

There's no definitive best way to deal with the international compensation problem. One compensation expert suggests a compromise, namely basing the person's new base salary on a percentage of home country salary, plus the higher of a percentage of (1) host country salary or (2) the amount required in host country currency to maintain a home country standard of living in the host location.[94]

Small Business Applications

Developing a pay plan that is internally and externally equitable is no less important in a small firm than in a large one. Paying wage rates that are too high for the area may be unnecessarily expensive, and paying less may guarantee poor-quality help and rapid turnover. Similarly, wage rates that are internally inequitable will reduce morale and cause the president to be badgered mercilessly by employees demanding raises "The same as Joe down the hall." The president who wants to concentrate on major issues like sales would thus do well to institute a rational pay plan as soon as possible.

DEVELOPING A WORKABLE PAY PLAN

Your first step should be to conduct a wage survey. The basic methods for doing so were described earlier in this chapter, but in the smaller business you'll generally depend on less formal methods for collecting this information.

Three sources here can be especially useful. A careful perusal of the Sunday classified newspaper ads should yield useful information on wages offered for jobs similar to those you are trying to price. Second, your local Job Service office can be a wealth of information, compiling as it does extensive information on pay ranges and averages for many of the jobs listed in the *Dictionary of Occupational Titles.* (This is another reason for using job titles that are consistent with those in the DOT.) The Job Service office can provide information on wages within the local area served by that office, as well as on the geographic region served by the group of Job Service offices of which your office is one member. Finally, local employment agencies, always anxious to establish ties that could grow into business relationships, should be able to provide fairly good data regarding pay rates for different jobs.

Next, if you employ more than 20 employees or so, conduct at least a rudimentary job evaluation. For this, you will first require job descriptions, since these will be the source of data regarding the nature and worth of each job.

You will usually find it easier to split employees into three groups—managerial/professional, office/clerical, and plant personnel. For each of the three groups, determine the compensable factors to be evaluated and then rank or assign points to each job based on the job evaluation.

For each job or class of jobs (i.e., assemblers), you will want to create a pay range. The procedure for doing so was described earlier. However, in general, you should choose as the midpoint of your range the target salary as required by your job evaluation and then produce a range of about 30% around this average, broken into a total of five steps.

While it doesn't always work, you may find it useful to experiment with using the *Dictionary of Occupational Titles* data–people–things scores as a simple job evaluation method. As explained earlier (on page 90) the experts at the Department of Labor have gone to considerable trouble to produce data–people–things scores for each job in the *Dictionary of Occupational Titles*.

There are many situations in which these scores can be used for job evaluation purposes although they are not designed to be so used. Assigning job evaluation ratings to jobs based on the data–people–things scores seems to work best when you're dealing with jobs that are fairly similar in many respects. It often works well in evaluating all manufacturing jobs in a company's plant, for instance. Here you may have a range of jobs such as textile loom fixer, production supervisor, weaver, production crew member, and fabricator. Strictly speaking, the data–people–things scores for each job reflect the degree to which each of these three factors is present in each job (for instance, the degree to which the job requires manipulating data, dealing with people, or dealing with things). These scores are listed in the *Dictionary* for each job title. Therefore it is simple for you to, say, add up the D + P + T numerical score for each job to see if it produces for you what appears to be a logical hierarchy of jobs (in terms of their value to the company). Again, this approach is not for everyone, but it is so simple that it is worth a try. Of course, a weighting scheme could be included if you believed that one factor should be weighted more heavily than the others.

COMPENSATION POLICIES

You must also have policies on compensation-related matters. For example, you have to have a policy on when and how raises are computed. Many small-business owners make the mistake of appraising employees on their anniversary date, a year after they are hired. The problem here is that the raise for one employee then becomes the standard for the next, and so on, for each of your employees. This produces a never-ending cycle of appraisals and posturing for ever higher raises.

The better alternative is to have a policy of once-a-year raises during a standard appraisal period, preferably about four weeks before the budget for next year must be produced. In this way, the administrative headache of conducting these appraisals and awarding raises is dealt with during a one- or two-week period. Furthermore, the total required raise money (which of course has to be outlined in advance by the company president) is then known more precisely when next year's budget is compiled. Other compensation policies include amount of holiday and vacation pay (as explained in the next chapter), overtime pay policy, method of pay (i.e., weekly, biweekly, monthly), garnishments, and time card or sign-on sheet procedures.

LEGAL ISSUES

There are, as mentioned earlier in this chapter, a number of federal, state, and local laws to which small (and large) employers must adhere. Local and state laws will often cover companies not covered by the Fair Labor Standards Act, but the latter is actually quite comprehensive. It covers most employees of enterprises engaged in activities affecting interstate or foreign commerce. Retail and service companies are covered if their annual gross volume of business is not less than $362,500 a year and any other type of business is covered if its volume is not less than $250,000 a year.[95]

Misclassification of exempt employees is probably the biggest mistake made by smaller firms. As noted earlier, some employees are exempt from the overtime and/or minimum wage requirements of the FLSA. A common small-business mistake is to assume that putting employees on a yearly salary exempts them from the overtime provisions of the act. You cannot make those workers exempt simply by paying them a yearly salary, nor can you make them exempt by claiming they are "managers" because they spend some of their time supervising other employees. Strictly speaking, employees have to spend at least 50% of their time actually supervising other employees to be classified as executive, managerial, or supervisory employees. It is not enough that they spend 80% of their time doing the same work as the people they supervise, and only 20% of their time actually supervising.[96]

There are other common wage-hour traps to avoid.[97] With respect to meal and break periods, an employee must generally be paid for meal periods unless the period is at least 20 minutes long, the employee is completely relieved of duties, and the employee can leave his or her work post. Also beware of how you handle compensatory time off. Many smaller employers believe they can have an employee work, say, 45 hours in one week, pay the person for 40 hours and give them compensatory time off of 5 hours in the following week. Under the law, this is not legal, for two reasons. First, if there is to be compensatory time off, the employer must provide 1½ hours off for each overtime hour worked. Thus, if someone works 42 hours in one week, he or she should receive 3 hours of compensable time. Furthermore, you cannot manipulate the pay period, for instance, by generally paying for a pay period that ranges from Monday morning through Sunday night but then temporarily changing the pay period to Saturday morning through Friday night in order to accommodate the need to work extra hours on a weekend because of a rush job.[98] Great care also must be taken when it comes to paying for time recorded. For example, suppose employees are required to clock in. They consistently clock in 15 minutes early or get into the habit of not clocking out for lunch. Here, it is possible that an inspector from the wage and hour division may conclude that the employees were underpaid, since there is no record that they were clocked out for the period for which they were docked.

Also beware of how you use so-called independent contractors. Many small businesses hire management consultants or, say, part-time bookkeepers to keep their books and then classify these people as independent contractors. Independent contractors are, as their name implies, not employed by the firm and are thus not eligible for benefits, unemployment compensation, worker's compensation, or all other benefits accruing to the firm's employees. At first glance, this seems like a cost-effective way to run a firm, and to some extent it can be. However, care must be taken not to try to call people who are legitimately employees "independent contractors" just to get around paying them benefits. There are many factors that determine whether a person is in fact an independent contractor. For example, a worker who is required to comply with another person's instructions about when, where, and how he or she is to work is ordinarily considered an employee, not an independent contractor.[99]

▸ Chapter Review

SUMMARY

1. There are two bases on which to pay employees compensation: increments of time and volume of production. The former includes hourly or daily wages and salaries. Basing pay on volume of production ties compensation directly to the amount of production (or number of "pieces" the worker produces).
2. Establishing pay rates involves five steps, each of which is explained in this chapter: conduct salary survey, evaluate jobs, develop pay grades, use wage curves, and fine tune pay rates.
3. Job evaluation is aimed at determining the relative worth of a job. It involves comparing jobs to one another based on their content, which is usually defined in terms of compensable factors like skills, effort, responsibility, and working conditions.
4. The ranking method of job evaluation involves five steps: (a) obtain job information, (b) select clusters of jobs to be rated, (c) select compensable factors, (d) rank jobs, and (e) combine ratings (of several raters). This is a simple method to use, but there is a tendency to rely too heavily on guesstimates. The classification (or grading) method is a second qualitative approach that involves categorizing jobs based on a "class description" or "classification rules" for each class.
5. The point method of job evaluation requires identifying a number of compensable factors and then determining the degree to which each of these factors is present in the job. As explained in the appendix, it involves nine steps: (a) determine types of jobs to be evaluated, (b) collect job information, (c) select compensable factors, (d) define compensable factors, (e) define factor degree, (f) determine relative weights of factors, (g) assign point values to factors and degrees, (h) develop a job evaluation manual, and (i) rate the jobs. This is a quantitative technique, and many packaged plans are readily available.
6. The factor comparison method (as explained in the appendix) is a quantitative job evaluation technique that entails deciding which jobs have more of certain compensable factors than others. It is one of the most widely used job evaluation methods and entails eight steps: (a) obtain job information, (b) select key jobs, (c) rank key jobs by factors, (d) distribute wage rates by factors for each job, (e) rank jobs by wage rates, (f) compare the two sets of ranking to screen out unusable key jobs, (g) construct the job comparison scale, and (h) use the job comparison scale. This is a systematic, quantifiable method. However, it is also a difficult method to implement. Steps (e) and (f) can be skipped if you prefer.
7. Most managers group similar jobs into wage or pay grades for pay purposes. These are comprised of jobs of approximately equal difficulty or importance as determined by job evaluation.
8. The wage curve (or line) shows the average target wage for each pay grade (or job). It can help show you what the average wage for each grade *should be*, and whether any present wages (or salaries) are out of line. Developing a wage curve involves four steps: (a) find the average pay for each pay grade, (b) plot these wage rates for

each pay grade, (c) draw the wage line, and (d) price jobs, after plotting present wage rates.

9. Developing a compensation plan for executive, managerial, and professional personnel is complicated by the fact that factors like performance and creativity must take precedence over "static" factors like working conditions. Market rates, performance, and incentives and benefits thus play a much greater role than does job evaluation for these employees.
10. Four main compensation issues we discussed were comparable worth, pay secrecy, inflation, and cost-of-living differentials.

KEY TERMS

employee compensation
Davis-Bacon Act
Walsh-Healey Public Contract Act
Fair Labor Standards Act
Equal Pay Act
Civil Rights Act
Employee Retirement Income Security Act (ERISA)
salary surveys
benchmark job
job evaluation
compensable factor
ranking method
classification (or grading) method
classes
grades
grade description
point method
factor comparison method
pay grade
wage curve
rate ranges
comparable worth

DISCUSSION QUESTIONS

1. What is the difference between exempt and nonexempt jobs?
2. Should the job evaluation depend on an appraisal of the job holder's performance? Why? Why not?
3. What is the relationship between compensable factors and job specifications?
4. What are the pros and cons of the following methods of job evaluation: ranking, classification, factor comparison, point method?
5. In what respect is the factor comparison method similar to the ranking method? How do they differ?

APPLICATION EXERCISES

RUNNING CASE

Carter Cleaning Company

The New Pay Plan

Carter Cleaning Centers does not have a formal wage structure nor does it have rate ranges or use compensable factors. Wage rates are based almost exclusively on those prevailing in the surrounding community and are tempered with an attempt on the part of Jack Carter to maintain some semblance of equity between what workers with different responsibilities in the stores are paid.

Needless to say, Carter does not make any formal surveys when determining what his company should pay. He peruses the want ads almost every day and conducts informal surveys among his friends in the local chapter of the laundry and cleaners trade association. While Jack has taken a "seat-of-the-pants" approach to paying employees, his salary schedule has been guided by several basic pay policies. While many of his colleagues adhere to a policy of paying absolutely minimum rates, Jack has always followed a policy of paying his employees about 10% above what he feels are the prevailing rates, a policy that he believes reduces turnover while fostering employee loyalty. Of somewhat more concern to Jennifer is her father's policy of paying men about 20% more than women for the same job. Her father's explanation is "They're stronger and can work harder for longer hours, and besides they all have families to support."

Questions

1. Is the company at the point where it should be setting up a formal salary structure complete with a job evaluation? Why?
2. Is Jack Carter's policy of paying 10% more than the prevailing rates a sound one, and how could that be determined?
3. Similarly, is Carter's male–female differential wise and if not, why not?

CASE STUDY *Job Evaluation for Bank Managers*

The chairman of the board of directors of the Second National Bank has proposed that all managerial positions be included in the bank's job evaluation plan. He has talked with executives in several large business organizations in which such a practice has been found entirely possible and helpful. He proposed this action to the board at its latest meeting. The president asked that no action be taken until he could discuss it with those who would be affected.

Most of the middle-management group appear to be opposed to such a procedure. The president, while trying to remain neutral, has expressed a fear that if salaries are fitted to job evaluation, he will lose his best people. Many department heads and assistants insist that their jobs simply can't be rated on the scale used for subordinate positions. Others argue that no individual or small group can possibly know what their jobs involve. It is also argued that the qualities for which managers are paid are so varied and intangible that no systematic comparison of jobs makes sense.

The personnel manager and her staff are united in favoring the idea. The chairman of the board, through the president, has asked the human resource department to prepare a statement in favor of the development, explaining what it would do and how it would be done.

Question

You have been assigned the responsibility for a first draft of this statement, to be directed to the rest of the personnel staff for discussion. What would your statement say?

Source: Dale Yoder and Paul D. Standohar, *Personnel Management & Industrial Relations* (Englewood Cliffs, NJ: Prentice Hall, 1982), p. 361.

HUMAN RESOURCE MANAGEMENT SIMULATION

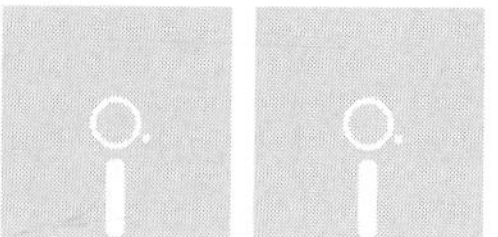

The simulation requires your team to make decisions concerning the amount of compensation for five levels of employees. Currently your firm is paying less than local comparable jobs and this is affecting your turnover and morale. However, budget constraints require that you plan ahead for any wage increases carefully. One key consideration is whether to give employees at all levels a small increase in a given decision period or to give a larger increase to one level at a time.

APPENDIX 12.1

Quantitative Job Evaluation Methods

THE FACTOR COMPARISON JOB EVALUATION METHOD

The factor comparison technique is a *quantitative* job evaluation method. It has many variations and appears to be one of the most widely used, the most accurate, and most complex job evaluation method.

It entails deciding which jobs have more of certain compensable factors than others and is actually a refinement of the ranking method. With the ranking method you generally look at each job as an entity and rank the jobs. With the factor comparison method you rank each job *several times—once for each compensable factor you choose.* For example, jobs might be ranked first in terms of the factor "skill." Then they are ranked according to their "mental requirements." Next, they are ranked according to their "responsibility," and so forth. Then these rankings are combined for each job into an overall numerical rating for the job. Here are the required steps:

Step 1. Obtain Job Information

This method requires a careful, complete job analysis. First, job descriptions are written. Then job specifications are developed, preferably in terms of the compensable factors the committee had decided to use. *For the factor comparison method, these compensable factors are usually* (1) *mental requirements,* (2) *physical requirements,* (3) *skill requirements,* (4) *responsibility* and (5) *working conditions.* Typical definitions of each of these five factors are presented in Figure 12.6.

Step 2. Select Key "Benchmark" Jobs

Next, 15 to 25 key jobs are selected by the job evaluation committee. These jobs will have to be representative of the range of jobs under study. Thus, they have to select "benchmark jobs" that are acceptable reference points, ones that represent the full range of jobs to be evaluated.

Step 3. Rank Key Jobs by Factors

Here evaluators are asked to rank the key jobs on each of the five factors (mental requirements, physical requirements, skill requirements, responsibility, and working conditions). This ranking procedure is based on job descriptions and job specifications. Each committee member usually makes this ranking individually, and then a meeting is held to develop a consensus (among raters) on each job. The result of this process is a table, as in Table 12.4. This shows how each key job ranks on *each* of the five compensable factors.

Step 4. Distribute Wage Rates by Factors

This is where the factor comparison method gets a bit more complicated. In this step the committee members have to divide up the present wage now being paid

TABLE 12.4 Ranking[1] Key Jobs by Factors

	MENTAL REQUIREMENTS	PHYSICAL REQUIREMENTS	SKILL REQUIREMENTS	RESPONSIBILITY	WORKING CONDITIONS
Welder	1	4	1	1	2
Crane operator	3	1	3	4	4
Punch press operator	2	3	2	2	3
Security guard	4	2	4	3	1

[1] 1 is high, 4 is low.

for *each key job*, distributing it among the five compensable factors. They do this in accordance with their judgments about the importance to the job of each factor. For example, if the present wage for the job of common laborer is $4.26, our evaluators might distribute this wage as follows:

Mental requirements	$0.36
Physical requirements	2.20
Skill requirements	0.42
Responsibility	0.28
Working conditions	1.00
Total	$4.26

You make such a distribution for all key jobs.

Step 5. Rank Key Jobs According to Wages Assigned to Each Factor

Here you again rank each job, factor by factor. But here the ranking is based on the wages assigned to each factor. For example (see Table 12.5) for the "mental requirements" factor, the welder job ranks first, while the security guard job ranks last.

Each member of the committee first makes this distribution working independently. Then the committee meets and arrives at a consensus concerning the money to be assigned to each factor for each key job.

Step 6. Compare the Two Sets of Rankings to Screen Out Unusable Key Jobs

You now have two sets of rankings for each key job. One was your original ranking (from step 3). This shows how each job ranks on each of the five compensable factors. The second ranking reflects, for each job, the wages assigned to each factor. You can now draw up a table like the one in Table 12.6.

For each factor, this shows *both* rankings for each key job. On the left is the ranking from step 3. On the right is the ranking based on wages paid. For each factor, the ranking based on the amount of the factor (from step 3) should be

1. Mental Requirements

Either the possession of and/or the active application of the following:

A. (inherent) Mental traits, such an intelligence, memory, reasoning, facility in verbal expression, ability to get along with people and imagination.

B. (acquired) General education, such as grammar and arithmetic; or general information as to sports, world events, etc.

C. (acquired) Specialized knowledge such as chemistry, engineering, accounting, advertising, etc.

2. Skill

A. (acquired) Facility in muscular coordination, as in operating machines, repetitive movements, careful coordinations, dexterity, assembling, sorting, etc.

B. (acquired) Specific job knowledge necessary to the muscular coordination only; acquired by performance of the work and not to be confused with general education or specialized knowledge. It is very largely training in the interpretation of sensory impressions.

Examples

(1) In operating an adding machine, the knowledge of *which key* to depress for a sub-total would be skill.

(2) In automobile repair, the ability to determine the significance of a certain knock in the motor would be skill.

(3) In hand-firing a boiler, the ability to determine from the appearance of the firebed how coal should be shoveled over the surface would be skill.

3. Physical Requirements

A. Physical effort, as sitting, standing, walking, climbing, pulling, lifting, etc.; both the amount exercised and the degree of the continuity should be taken into account.

B. Physical status, as age, height, weight, sex, strength and eyesight.

4. Responsibilities

A. For raw materials, processed materials, tools, equipment and property.

B. For money or negotiable securities.

C. For profits or loss, savings or methods' improvement.

D. For public contact.

E. For records.

F. For supervision.

(1) Primarily the complexity of supervision *given* to subordinates; the number of subordinates is a secondary feature. Planning, direction, coordination, instruction, control and approval characterize this kind of supervision.

(2) Also, the degree of supervision *received*. If Jobs A and B gave no supervision to subordinates, but A received much closer immediate supervision than B, then B would be entitled to a higher rating than A in the supervision factor.

To summarize the four degrees of supervision:

Highest degree – gives much – gets little
High degree – gives much – gets much
Low degree – gives none – gets little
Lowest degree – gives none – gets much

5. Working Conditions

A. Environmental influences such as atmosphere, ventilation, illumination, noise, congestion, fellow workers, etc.

B. Hazards—from the work or its surroundings.

C. Hours.

FIGURE 12.6 Sample Definitions of Five Factors Typically Used in Factor Comparison Method Source: Jay L. Otis and Richard H. Leukart, *Job Evaluation: A Basis for Sound Wage Administration*, p. 181. ©1954, renewed 1983. Reprinted by permission of Prentice Hall, Englewood Cliffs, NJ.

about the same as the ranking based on the wages assigned to the job (step 5). If there's much of a discrepancy, it suggests that the key job might be a "fluke," and from this point on, such jobs are no longer used as key jobs. (Many managers don't bother to screen out "unusable" key jobs. To simplify things, they skip our steps 5 and 6, going instead from step 4 to step 7; this is an acceptable alternative.)

TABLE 12.5 Ranking[1] Key Jobs by Wage Rates

	HOURLY WAGE	MENTAL REQUIRE-MENTS	PHYSICAL REQUIRE-MENTS	SKILL REQUIRE-MENTS	RESPONSIBILITY	WORKING CONDITIONS
Welder	$9.80	4.00(1)	0.40(4)	3.00(1)	2.00(1)	0.40(2)
Crane operator	5.60	1.40(3)	2.00(1)	1.80(3)	0.20(4)	0.20(4)
Punch press operator	6.00	1.60(2)	1.30(3)	2.00(2)	0.80(2)	0.30(3)
Security guard	4.00	1.20(4)	1.40(2)	0.40(4)	0.40(3)	0.60(1)

[1] 1 is high, 4 is low.

Step 7. Construct the Job-Comparison Scale

Once you've identified the usable, "true" key jobs, the next step is to set up the job-comparison scale (Table 12.7). (Note that there's a separate column for each of the five comparable factors.) To develop it, you'll need the assigned wage table from step 4.

For each of the factors (for all key jobs), you write the job next to the appropriate wage rate. Thus in the assigned wage table (Table 12.5), the welder job has $4.00 assigned to the factor "mental requirement." Therefore, on the job comparison scale (Table 12.7) write "welder" in the "mental requirements" factor column, next to the "$4.00" row. Do the same for all factors for all key jobs.

Step 8. Use the Job-Comparison Scale

Now, all the other jobs to be evaluated can be slotted, factor by factor, into the job-comparison scale. For example, suppose you have a job of plater that you want to slot in. You decide where the "mental requirements" of the plater job would fit as compared with the mental requirements of all the other jobs listed. It might, for example, fit between punch press operator and inspector. Similarly, you would ask where the "physical requirements" of the plater's job fit as compared with the other jobs listed. Here you might find that it fits just

TABLE 12.6 Comparison of Factor and Wage Rankings

	MENTAL REQUIRE-MENTS		PHYSICAL REQUIRE-MENTS		SKILL REQUIRE-MENTS		RESPONSIBILITY		WORKING CONDITIONS	
	A[1]	$[2]	A[1]	$[2]	A[1]	$[2]	A[1]	$[2]	A[1]	$[2]
Welder	1	1	4	4	1	1	1	1	2	2
Crane operator	3	3	1	1	3	3	4	4	4	4
Punch press operator	2	2	3	3	2	2	2	2	3	3
Security guard	4	4	2	2	4	4	3	3	1	1

[1] Amount of each factor based on step 3.

[2] Ratings based on distribution of wages to each factor from step 4.

TABLE 12.7 Job (Factor) Comparison Scale

	MENTAL REQUIREMENTS	PHYSICAL REQUIREMENTS	SKILL REQUIREMENTS	RESPONSIBILITY	WORKING CONDITIONS
.20	....	....	....	Crane Operator	Crane Operator
.30	....	....	....	....	Punch Press Operator
.40	....	Welder	Sec. Guard......	Sec. Guard......	Welder
.50					
.60	....	....	....	....	Sec. Guard
.70					
.80				Punch Press Operator	
.90					
1.00					
1.10				(Plater)	
1.20	Sec. Guard				
1.30	....	Punch Press Operator			
1.40	Crane Operator..	Sec. Guard	(Inspector)......	(Plater)	
1.50	....	(Inspector)......	....	....	(Inspector)
1.60	Punch Press Operator				
1.70	(Plater)				
1.80	....	....	Crane Operator	(Inspector)	
1.90					
2.00	....	Crane Operator..	Punch Press .... Operator	Welder	
2.20	....	(Plater)			
2.40	(Inspector)......	....	....	....	(Plater)
2.60					
2.80					
3.00	....	....	Welder		
3.20					
3.40					
3.60					
3.80					
4.00	Welder				
4.20					
4.40					
4.60					
4.80					

below crane operator. You would do the same for each of the remaining three factors.

An Example

Let us work through an example to clarify the factor comparison method. We'll just use four key jobs to simplify the presentation—you'd usually start with 15 to 25 key jobs.

Step 1. First, we do a job analysis.

Step 2. Here we select our four key jobs: welder, crane operator, punch press operator, and security guard.

Step 3. Here (based on the job descriptions and specifications) we rank key jobs by factor, as in Table 12.4.

Step 4. Here we distribute wage rates by factor, as in Table 12.5.

Step 5. Then we rank our key jobs according to wage rates assigned to each key factor. These rankings are shown in parentheses in Table 12.5.

Step 6. Next, compare your two sets of rankings. In each left-hand column (marked A) is the job's ranking from step 3 based on the *amount* of the compensable factor. In each right-hand column (marked $) is the job's ranking from step 5, based on the wage assigned to that factor, as in Table 12.6.

In this case, there are no differences between any of the pairs of A (amount) and $ (wage) rankings, so *all* our key jobs are usable. If there had been any differences (for example, between the A and $ rankings for the welder job's mental requirement factor) we would have dropped that job as a key job.

Step 7. Now we construct our job comparison scale as in Table 12.7. For this, we use the wage distributions from step 4. For example, let us say that in steps 4 and 5 we assigned $4.00 to the mental requirement factor of the welder's job. Therefore, we now write "welder" on the $4.00 row under the "mental requirements" column as in Table 12.7.

Step 8. Now all our other jobs can be slotted, factor by factor, into our job-comparison scale. We do *not* distribute wages to each of the factors for our other jobs to do this. *We just decide where, factor by factor, each of our other jobs should be slotted.* We've done this for two other jobs in the factor comparison scale: They're shown in parentheses. Now we also know what the wages for these two jobs should be, and we can also do the same for *all* our jobs.

A Variation

There are several variations to this basic factor comparison method. One involves converting the dollar values on the factor comparison chart (Table 12.7) to points. (You can do this by multiplying each of the dollar values by 100, for example.) The main advantage in making this change is that your system would no longer be "locked in" to your present wage rates. Instead, each of your jobs would be compared with one another, factor by factor, in terms of a more "constant" point system.

Pros and Cons

We've presented the factor comparison method at some length because it is (in one form or another) a very widely used job evaluation method. Its wide use derives from several advantages: First, it is an accurate, systematic, quantifiable method for which detailed step-by-step instructions are available. Second, jobs are compared to other jobs to determine a *relative* value. Thus, in the job comparison scale you not only see that the welder requires *more* mental ability than a plater; you can also determine about *how much more* mental ability is required—apparently about twice as much ($4.00 versus $1.70). (This type of calibration is not possible with the ranking or classification methods.) Third, this is also a fairly easy job evaluation system to explain to employees.

Probably the most serious *disadvantage* of the factor comparison method is its complexity. While it is fairly easy to explain the factor comparison scale and its rationale to employees, it is difficult to show them how to *build* one. In addition, the use of the five factors is an outgrowth of the technique developed by its originators. Yet, using the same five factors for all organizations and for all jobs in an organization may not always be appropriate.

THE POINT METHOD OF JOB EVALUATION

The point method is widely used. Basically, it requires identifying several compensable factors (like skills and responsibility), each with several degrees, and also the *degree* to which each of these factors is present in the job. A different number of points is usually assigned for each degree of each factor. So once you determine the degree to which each factor is present in the job, you need only add up the corresponding number of points for each factor and arrive at an overall point value for the job.[100] Here are the steps:

Step 1. Determine Clusters of Jobs to be Evaluated

Because jobs vary widely by department, you usually will not use one point rating plan for all jobs in the organization. Therefore, the first step is usually to *cluster* jobs, for example into shop jobs, clerical jobs, sales jobs, and so forth. Then the committee will generally develop a point plan for one group (or cluster) at a time.

Step 2. Collect Job Information

This involves job analysis and writing job descriptions and job specifications.

Step 3. Select Compensable Factors

Here select compensable factors, like education, physical requirements, or skills. (Often each cluster of jobs may require its own compensable factors.)

Step 4. Define Compensable Factors

Next, carefully define each compensable factor. This is to ensure that the evaluation committee members will each apply the factors with consistency. Some examples of definitions are presented in Figure 12.7. The definitions are often drawn up or obtained by the human resource specialist.

Step 5. Define Factor Degrees

Next, define each of several degrees for each factor so that raters may judge the amount or "degree" of a factor existing in a job. Thus, for the factor "complexity" you might choose to have six degrees, ranging from "job is repetitive" through "requires initiative" (definitions for each degree are shown in Figure 12.7). The number of degrees usually does not exceed five or six, and the actual number depends mostly on judgment. Thus if all employees either work in a quiet, air conditioned office, or in a noisy, hot factory, then two degrees would probably suffice for the factor "working conditions." One need not have the same number of degrees for each factor, and should limit degrees to the number necessary to distinguish among jobs.

Step 6. Determine Relative Values of Factors

The next step is to decide how much weight (or how many total points) to assign to each factor. This is important because for each cluster of jobs some factors are

Example of One Factor in a Point Factor System (Complexity/Problem Solving)

The mental capacity required to perform the given job as expressed in resourcefulness in dealing with unfamiliar problems, interpretation of data, initiation of new ideas, complex data analysis, creative or developmental work.

Level	Point Value	Description of Characteristics and Measures
0	0	Seldom confronts problems not covered by job routine or organizational policy; analysis of data is negligible. *Benchmark:* General secretary, switchboard/receptionist.
1	40	Follows clearly prescribed standard practice and demonstrates straightforward application of readily understood rules and procedures. Analyzes noncomplicated data by established routine. *Benchmark:* Statistical clerk, billing clerk.
2	80	Frequently confronts problems not covered by job routine. Independent judgment exercised in making minor decisions where alternatives are limited and standard policies established. Analysis of standardized data for information of or use by others. *Benchmark:* Social worker, executive secretary.
3	120	Exercises independent judgment in making decisions involving nonroutine problems with general guidance only from higher supervision. Analyzes and evaluates data pertaining to nonroutine problems for solution in conjunction with others. *Benchmark:* Nurse, accountant, team leader.
4	160	Uses independent judgment in making decisions that are subject to review in the final stages only. Analyzes and solves nonroutine problems involving evaluation of a wide variety of data as a regular part of job duties. Makes decisions involving procedures. *Benchmark:* Associate director, business manager, park services director.
5	200	Uses independent judgment in making decisions that are not subject to review. Regularly exercises developmental or creative abilities in policy development. *Benchmark:* Executive director.

FIGURE 12.7
Example of One Factor in a Point Factor System

Source: Richard W. Beatty and James R. Beatty, "Job Evaluation," Ronald A. Berk (Ed.) *Performance Assessment: Methods and Applications* (Baltimore: Johns Hopkins University Press, 1986), p. 322.

bound to be more important than others. Thus, for executives the "mental requirements" factor would carry far more weight than would "physical requirements." The opposite might be true of factory jobs.

So, the next step is to determine the relative values or "weights" that should be assigned to each of the factors. Assigning factor weights is generally done by the evaluation committee. The committee members carefully study factor and degree definitions, and then determine the relative value of the factors for the cluster of jobs under consideration. Here is one method for doing this:

First, assign a value of 100% to the highest-ranking factor. Then assign a value to the next highest factor *as a percentage of its importance to the first factor*, and so forth. For example,

Decision making	100%
Problem solving	85%
Knowledge	60%

Next, sum up the total percentage (in this case 100% + 85% + 60% = 245%). Then convert this 245% to a 100% system as follows:

Decision making:	100 ÷ 245 = 40.82 =	40.8%
Problem solving:	85 ÷ 245 = 34.69 =	34.7%
Knowledge:	60 ÷ 245 = 24.49 =	24.5%
Totals		100.0%

Step 7. Assign Point Values to Factors and Degrees

In step 6 total weights were developed for each factor, in percentage terms. Now assign points to each factor as in Table 12.8. For example, suppose it is decided to use a total number of 500 points in the point plan. Then since the factor "decision making" had a weight of 40.8%, it would be assigned a total of 40.8% × 500 = 204 points.

Thus it was decided to assign 204 points to the "decision-making" factor. *This automatically means that the highest degree for the decision-making factor would also carry 204 points.* Then assign points to the other degrees for this factor, usually in equal amounts from the lowest to the highest degree. For example, divide 204 by the number of degrees (say, 5); this equals 40.8. Then the lowest degree here would carry about 41 points. The second degree would carry 41 plus 41, or 82 points.. The third degree would carry 123 points. The fourth degree would carry 164 points. Finally, the fifth and highest degree would carry 204 points. Do this for each factor (as in Table 12.8).

Step 8. Write the Job Evaluation Manual

Developing a point plan like this usually culminates in a "point manual" or "job evaluation manual." This simply consolidates the factor and degree definitions and point values into one convenient manual.

Step 9. Rate the Jobs

Once the manual is complete, the actual evaluations can begin. Raters (usually the committee) use the manual to evaluate jobs. Each job, based on its job

TABLE 12.8 Evaluation Points Assigned to Factors and Degrees.

	1ST DEGREE POINTS	2ND DEGREE POINTS	3RD DEGREE POINTS	4TH DEGREE POINTS	5TH DEGREE POINTS
Decision making	41	82	123	164	204
Problem solving	35	70	105	140	174
Knowledge	24	48	72	96	123

description and job specification, is evaluated factor by factor to determine the number of points that should be assigned to it. First, committee members determine the *degree* (1st degree, 2nd degree, etc.) to which each factor (like decision making) is present in the job. Then they note the corresponding *points* (see Table 12.8) that were previously assigned to each of these degrees (in step 7). Finally, they add up the points for all factors, arriving at a *total point value* for the job. Raters generally start with rating key jobs, obtaining consensus on these. Then they rate the rest of the jobs in the cluster.

"Packaged" Point Plans

Developing a point plan of one's own can obviously be a time-consuming process. For this reason a number of groups (such as the National Electrical Manufacturer's Association and the National Trade Association) have developed standardized point plans. These have been used or adapted by thousands of organizations. They contain ready-made factor and degree definitions and point assignments for a wide range of jobs, and can often be used with little or no modification. One survey of U.S. companies found that 93% of those using a ready-made plan rated it successful.

Pros and Cons

Point systems have their advantages, as their wide use suggests. This is a quantitative technique that is easily explained to and used by employees. On the other hand, it can be difficult to develop a point plan, and this is one reason many organizations have opted for ready-made plans. In fact, the availability of a number of ready-made plans probably accounts in part for the wide use of point plans in job evaluation.

▸ Notes

1. Thomas Patten, Jr., *Pay: Employee Compensation and Incentive Plans* (New York: Free Press, 1977), p. 1. See also Jerry McAdams, "Why Reward Systems Fail," *Personnel Journal*, Vol. 67, no. 6 (June 1988), pp. 103–113; James Whitney, "Pay Concepts for the 1990s," Part I, *Compensation and Benefits Review*, Vol. 20, no. 2 (March–April 1988), pp. 33–44; and James Whitney, "Pay Concepts for the 1990s," Part II, *Compensation and Benefits Review*, Vol. 20, no. 3 (May–June 1988), pp. 45–50.
2. Orlando Behling and Chester Schriesheim, *Organizational Behavior* (Boston: Allyn & Bacon, 1976), p. 233.
3. Based partly on Richard Henderson, *Compensation Management* (Reston, VA: Reston, 1980).
4. A complete description of exemption requirements as found in U.S. Department of Labor, *Executive, Administrative, Professional & Outside Salesmen Exempted from the Fair Labor Standards Act* (Washington, DC: U.S. Government Printing Office, 1973).
5. Earl Mellor, "Weekly Earnings in 1985: A Look at More than 200 Occupations," *Monthly Labor Review*, Vol. 109, no. 9 (September 1986), pp. 27–34; Bureau of National Affairs, *Fair Employment Practices*, 1988, p. 27. See also John R. Hellenbeck et al., "Sex Differences in Occupational Choice, Pay, and Worth: A Supply-Side Approach to Understanding the Male-Female Wage Gap," *Personnel Psychology*, Vol. 40, no. 4 (Winter 1987), pp. 715–744.
6. Commerce Clearing House, *Ideas and Trends in Personnel*, October 31, 1986, pp. 169–171.
7. Henderson, *Compensation Management*, pp. 88–99.
8. Michael R. Carrell and Frank E. Kuzmits, "Amended ADEA's Effects on Human Resources Strategies Remain Dubious," *Personnel Journal*, Vol. 66, no. 5 (May 1987).
9. Henderson, *Compensation Management*, pp. 101–127.
10. Ibid., p. 115.
11. Edward Hay, "The Attitude of the American Federation of Labor on Job Evaluation," *Personnel Journal*, Vol. 26 (November 1947), pp. 163–169; Howard James, "Issues in Job Evaluation: The Union's View," *Personnel Journal*, Vol. 51 (September 1972), pp. 675–679; Henderson, *Compensation Management*, pp. 117–118; Harold Jones, "Union Views on Job Evaluations: 1971 vs. 1978," *Personnel Journal*, Vol. 58 (February 1979), pp. 80–85.
12. Joseph Famularo, *Handbook of Modern Personnel Administration* (New York: McGraw-Hill, 1972), pp. 27–29. See also Bruce Ellig, "Strategic Pay Planning," *Compensation and Benefits Review*, Vol. 19, no. 4 (July–August 1987),

pp. 28–43; Thomas Robertson, "Fundamental Strategies for Wage and Salary Administration," *Personnel Journal*, Vol. 65, no. 11 (November 1986), pp. 120–132. One expert cautions against conducting salary surveys based on job title alone. He recommends job-content salary surveys that examine the content of jobs according to the size of each job so that, for instance, the work of the president of IBM and that of a small clone manufacturer would not be inadvertently compared. See Robert Sahl, "Job Content Salary Surveys: Survey Design and Selection Features," *Compensation and Benefits Review* (May–June 1991), pp. 14–21.

13. Vicki Kaman and Jodie Barr, "Employee Attitude Surveys for Strategic Compensation Management," *Compensation and Benefits Review* (January–February 1991), pp. 52–65.
14. "Use of Wage Surveys," *BNA Policy and Practice Series* (Washington, DC: Bureau of National Affairs, 1976), pp. 313–314. In a recent survey of compensation professionals, uses of salary survey data were reported. The surveys were used most often to adjust the salary structure and ranges. Other uses included determining the merit budget, adjusting individual job rates, and maintaining pay leadership. D. W. Belcher, N. Bruce Ferris, and John O'Neill, "How Wage Surveys Are Being Used," *Compensation and Benefits Review* (September–October 1985), pp. 34–51. For further discussion, see, for example, Kent Romanoff, Ken Boehm, and Edward Benson, "Pay Equity: Internal and External Considerations," *Compensation and Benefits Review*, Vol. 18, no. 3 (May–June 1986), pp. 17–25.
15. Helen Murlis, "Making Sense of Salary Surveys," *Personnel Management*, Vol. 17 (January 1981), pp. 30–33. For an explanation of how market analysis can be used to ensure fair and competitive pay for all jobs in the organization, see, for example, Peter Olney, Jr., "Meeting the Challenge of Comparable Worth," Part 2, *Compensation and Benefits Review*, Vol. 19, no. 3 (May–June 1987), pp. 45–53.
16. Henderson, *Compensation Management*, pp. 260–269.
17. Joan O'Brien and Robert Zawacki, "Salary Surveys: Are They Worth the Effort?" *Personnel*, Vol. 62, no. 10 (October 1985), pp. 70–74.
18. Patten, *Pay*, p. 177.
19. You may have noticed that job analysis as discussed in Chapter 3 can be a useful source of information on compensable factors, as well as on job descriptions and job specifications. For example, a quantitative job analysis technique like the position analysis questionnaire generates quantitative information on the degree to which the following five basic factors are present in each job: having decision-making/communication/social responsibilities, performing skilled activities, being physically active, operating vehicles or equipment, and processing information. As a result, a job analysis technique like the PAQ is actually as (or some say, more) appropriate as a job evaluation technique in that jobs can be quantitatively compared to one another on those five dimensions and their relative worth thus ascertained. Another point worth noting is that you may find that a single set of compensable factors is not adequate for describing all your jobs. Many managers, therefore, divide their jobs into job clusters. For example, you might have a separate job cluster for factory workers, for clerical workers, and for managerial personnel. Similarly, you would then probably have a somewhat different set of compensable factors for each job cluster.
20. A. N. Nash and F. J. Carroll, Jr., "Installation of a Job Evaluation Program," from *Management of Compensation* (Monterey, CA: Brooks/Cole, 1975), reprinted in Craig Schneier and Richard Beatty, *Personnel Administration Today: Readings and Commentary* (Reading, MA: Addison-Wesley, 1978), pp. 417–425; and Henderson, *Compensation Management*, pp. 231–239. According to one survey, about equal percentages of employers use individual interviews, employee questionnaires, or observations by personnel representatives to obtain the actual job evaluation information. See Mary Ellen Lo Bosco, "Job Analysis, Job Evaluation, and Job Classification," *Personnel*, Vol. 62, no. 5 (May 1985), pp. 70–75. See also Howard Risher, "Job Evaluation: Validity and Reliability," *Compensation and Benefits Review*, Vol. 21, no. 1 (January–February 1989), pp. 22–36; and David Hahn and Robert Dipboye, "Effects of Training and Information on the Accuracy and Reliability of Job Evaluations," *Journal of Applied Psychology*, Vol. 73, no. 2 (May 1988), pp. 146–153.
21. See, for example, Donald Petri, "Talking Pay Policy Pays Off," *Supervisory Management* (May 1979), pp. 2–13.
22. As explained later, the practice of *red circling* is used to delay downward adjustments in pay rates that are presently too high given the newly evaluated jobs. See also E. James Brennan, "Everything You Need to Know About Salary Ranges," *Personnel Journal*, Vol. 63, no. 3 (March 1984), pp. 10–17.
23. Nash and Carroll, "Installation of a Job Evaluation," p. 419.
24. Ibid.
25. C. F. Lutz, "Quantitative Job Evaluation in Local Government in the United States," *International Labor Review* (June 1969), pp. 607–619.
26. If you used the job classification method, then of course the jobs are already classified.
27. David Belcher, *Compensation Administration* (Englewood Cliffs, NJ: Prentice Hall, 1973), pp. 257–276.
28. Personal interview with Toyota Motor Manufacturing, USA, Inc., personnel officer.
29. For example see Edward Lawler, *Compensation and Benefits Review* (March–April 1986); and Edward E. Lawler, "Paying the Person: A Better Approach to Management?" *Human Resource Management Review*, Vol. 1, no. 2 (Summer 1991), pp. 145–154.
30. See Sondra M. Emerson, "Job Evaluation: A Barrier to Excellence?" *Compensation and Benefits Review* (January–February 1991), pp. 39–51; see also Nina Gupta and G. Douglas Jenkins, "Job Evaluation: An Overview," *Human Resource Management Review*, Vol. 1, no. 2 (Summer 1991), pp. 91–95; Thomas Mahoney, "Job Evaluation: Endangered Species or Anachronism?" *Human Resource Management Review*, Vol. 1, no. 2 (Summer 1991), pp. 155–162; Nan J. Weiner, "Job Evaluation Systems: A Critique," *Human Resource Management Review*, Vol. 1, no. 2 (Summer 1991), pp. 119–132.
31. Gerald Ledford, Jr., "Three Case Studies on Skill-Based Pay: An Overview," *Compensation and Benefits Review* (March–April 1991), pp. 11–23.
32. Ibid., p. 12.
33. Gerald Ledford, Jr., and Gary Bergel, "Skill-Based Pay Case Number 1: General Mills," *Compensation and Benefits Review*, (March–April 1991), pp. 24–38; see also Gerald Barrett, "Comparison of Skill-Based Pay with Traditional Job Evaluation Techniques," *Human Resource Management Review*, Vol. 1, no. 2 (Summer 1991), pp. 97–105.
34. This is based on Ledford and Bergel, "Skill-Based Pay Case Number 1," pp. 28–29.
35. Jay Schuster, Patricia Zingheim, and Marvin Dertien, "The Case for Computer Assisted Market-Based Job Evaluation," *Compensation and Benefits Review* (May–June 1990), pp. 44–54.
36. Emerson, "Job Evaluation," p. 39.

37. This is based on Laurent Dufetel, "Job Evaluation: Still at the Frontier," *Compensation and Benefits Review*, (July–August 1991), pp. 53–67.
38. Ibid. p. 54.
39. This is based on Gary Dessler, *Winning Commitment* (New York: McGraw-Hill, 1993), Chapter 9.
40. Personal interview.
41. Jude Rich, "Meeting the Global Challenge: A Measurement and Reward Program for the Future," *Compensation and Benefits Review* (July–August 1992), p. 27.
42. Ibid., p. 28.
43. A. W. Smith, Jr., "Structuralist Salary Management: A Modest Proposal," *Compensation and Benefits Review* (July–August 1992), pp. 22–25.
44. Ibid., p. 23.
45. Charles Cumming, "Will Traditional Salary Administration Survive the Stampede to Alternative Rewards?" *Compensation and Benefits Review* (November–December 1992), pp. 42–47.
46. Dale Yoder, *Personnel Management and Industrial Relations* (Englewood Cliffs, NJ: Prentice Hall, 1970), pp. 643–645; Famularo, *Handbook of Modern Personnel Administration*, pp. 32.1–32.6 and 30.1–30.8.
47. Bruce Ellig, *Executive Compensation—A Total Pay Perspective* (New York: McGraw-Hill, 1982), pp. 9–10. See also Bryan J. Brooks, "Trends in International Executive Compensation," *Personnel*, Vol. 64, no. 5 (May 1987), pp. 67–71.
48. "No Sign of Recession in Pay at the Top," *Business Week*, May 10, 1982, pp. 76–80. See also Peter D. Sherer, Donald Schwab, and Herbert Henneman, "Managerial Salary-Raise Decisions: A Policy-Capturing Approach," *Personnel Psychology*, Vol. 40, no. 1 (Spring 1987), pp. 27–38.
49. Towers, Perrin, Forster & Crosby, *News Release*, June 1987, p. 3.
50. John Baker, "Are Corporate Executives Overpaid?" *Harvard Business Review*, Vol. 56 (July–August 1977), p. 52.
51. Ernest C. Miller, "Setting Supervisors' Pay at Pay Differentials," *Compensation Review*, Vol. 10 (Third Quarter 1978), pp. 13–16.
52. Nardash Agarwal, "Determinants of Executive Compensation," *Industrial Relations*, Vol. 20, no. 1 (Winter 1981), pp. 36–45. See also John A. Fossum and Mary Fitch, "The Effects of Individual and Contextual Attributes on the Sizes of Recommended Salary Increases," *Personnel Psychology*, Vol. 38, no. 3 (Autumn 1985), pp. 587–602.
53. Kenneth Foster, "Does Executive Pay Make Sense?" *Business Horizons* (September–October 1981), pp. 47–51.
54. Foster, "Does Executive Pay Make Sense?" p. 50.
55. This is based on William White, "Managing the Board Review of Executive Pay," *Compensation and Benefits Review* (November–December 1992), pp. 35–41.
56. Ibid., pp. 38–40; see also H. Anthony Hampson, "Tying CEO Pay to Performance: Compensation Committees Must Do Better," *The Business Quarterly*, Vol. 55, no. 4 (Spring 1991), pp. 18–22.
57. Famularo, *Handbook of Modern Personnel Administration*, pp. 32.1–32.6. See also Peter Sherer, et al., "Managerial Salary-Raise Decisions," pp. 27–38.
58. Famularo, *Handbook of Modern Personnel Administration*, pp. 30.1–30.15.
59. Ibid., pp. 30.1–30.5. See also Patric Moran, "Equitable Salary Administration in High-Tech Companies," *Compensation and Benefits Review*, Vol. 18, no. 5 (September–October 1986), pp. 31–40.
60. Robert Sibson, *Compensation* (New York: AMACOM, 1981), p. 194.
61. Ibid.
62. Helen Remick, "The Comparable Worth Controversy," *Public Personnel Management Journal* (Winter 1981), pp. 371–383.
63. Ibid., p. 377.
64. James Brinks, "The Comparable Worth Issue: A Salary Administration Bomb Shell," *Personnel Administrator*, Vol. 26 (November 1981), pp. 37–40. See also Sarah L. Rynes et al., "Effects of Market Survey Rates, Job Evaluation, and Job Gender on Job Pay," *Journal of Applied Psychology*, Vol. 74, no. 1 (February 1989), pp. 114–123.
65. Ibid.
66. Ibid., p. 38; U.S. Department of Labor, *Perspectives on Working Women: A Data Book*, October 1980.
67. *County of Washington* v. *Gunther;* U.S. Supreme Court, No. 80–429 (June 8, 1981).
68. SKRSC Update, Schachter, Kristoff, Ross, Sprague, and Curiale, California Street, San Francisco, CA., September–October 1985. For further information on comparable worth, see U.S. Commission of Civil Rights, *Comparable Worth: Issue for the 80's*, Vols. 1 and 2, June 6–7, 1984. See also Walter Fogel, "Intentional Sex-Based Pay Discrimination: Can It Be Proven?" *Labor Law Journal*, Vol. 27, no. 5 (May 1986), pp. 291–299.
69. See also David Thomsen, "Compensation and Benefits—More on Comparable Worth," *Personnel Journal*, Vol. 60 (May 1981), pp. 348–349. See also Marvin Levine, "Comparable Worth in the 1980s: Will Collective Bargaining Supplant Legislative and Judicial Interpretations?" *Labor Law Journal*, Vol. 38, no. 6 (June 1987), pp. 323–335; and Peter Olney, Jr., "Meeting the Challenge of Comparable Worth," Part II, *Compensation and Benefits Review*, Vol. 19, no. 3 (May–June 1987), pp. 45–53.
70. Mary Gray, "Pay Equity Through Job Evaluation: A Case Study," *Compensation and Benefits Review* (July–August 1992), p. 46.
71. Ibid., pp. 46–51.
72. Brinks, "The Comparable Worth Issue," p. 40.
73. Michael Carter, "Comparable Worth: An Idea Whose Time Has Come?" *Personnel Journal*, Vol. 60 (October 1981), p. 794; and Peter Olney, Jr., "Meeting the Challenge of Comparable Worth," Part I, *Compensation and Benefits Review*, Vol. 19, no. 2 (March–April 1987), pp. 34–44.
74. Brinks, "The Comparable Worth Issue," p. 40.
75. Charles M. Futrell, "Effects of Pay Disclosure on Satisfaction for Sales Managers: A Longitudinal Study," *Academy of Management Journal*, Vol. 21, no. 1 (March 1978), pp. 140–144.
76. Mary G. Miner, "Pay Policies: Secret or Open? and Why?" *Personnel Journal*, Vol. 53 (February 1974), reprinted in Richard Peterson, Lane Tracy, and Alan Cabelly, *Readings in Systematic Management in Human Resources* (Reading, MA: Addison–Wesley, 1979), pp. 233–239.
77. Margaret Yao, "Inflation Outruns Pay of Middle Managers, Increasing Frustration," *Wall Street Journal*, June 9, 1981, p. 1. See also, "The Impact of Inflation on Wage and Salary Administration," *Personnel*, Vol. 58 (November–December 1981), p. 55.
78. This section based on or quoted from "The Impact of Inflation on Wage and Salary Administration," p. 55.
79. Wendell C. Lawther, "Ways to Monitor (and Solve) the Pay Compression Problem," *Personnel* (March 1989), pp. 84–87.
80. Ibid., p. 87.
81. Robert Dockson and Jack Vance, "Retirement in Peril: Inflation and the Executive Compensation Program," *California Management Review*, Vol. 24 (Summer 1981), pp. 87–94.

82. Ibid.
83. Joan Lindroth, "Inflation, Taxes, and Perks: How Compensation Is Changing," *Personnel Journal,* Vol. 60 (December 1981), pp. 934–940.
84. Clarence Deitch and David Dilts, "The COLA Clause: An Employer Bargaining Weapon?" *Personnel Journal,* Vol. 61 (March 1982), pp. 220–223.
85. Patten, *Pay,* p. 181.
86. Deitch and Dilts, "The COLA Clause," p. 221.
87. Patten, *Pay,* p. 182.
88. "Collective Bargaining in 1987," *Monthly Labor Review* (January 1987), p. 34.
89. "Dun's Business Monthly," Vol. 129, no. 1 (January 1987), p. 18. See also, "End of an Era: COLA's on the Way Out," *Compensation and Benefits Review,* Vol. 18, no. 2 (March–April 1986), p. 4.
90. Rugus Runzheimer, Jr., "How Corporations Are Handling Cost of Living Differentials," *Business Horizons,* Vol. 23 (August 1980), p. 39.
91. Ibid., p. 39.
92. Jack Anderson, "Compensating Your Overseas Executives, Part II: Europe in 1992," *Compensation and Benefits Review* (July–August 1990), p. 28.
93. This is based on ibid., pp. 29–31.
94. Ibid., p. 31.
95. Wayne Outten and Noah Kinigstein, *The Rights of Employees* (New York: Bantam Books, 1983), pp. 201–202.
96. Commerce Clearing House, "How to Avoid the Ten Most Common Wage-Hour Traps," *Ideas and Trends,* March 10, 1989, p. 43.
97. Ibid.
98. With more companies establishing all-salaried work forces, firms are seeking to erase, to as great an extent as possible, the distinction between exempt and nonexempt employees. As a result, there are some exceptions that permit fluctuating workweeks. See Christopher Martin and Jerry Newman, "The FLSA Overtime Provision: A New Controversy?" *Compensation and Benefits Review* (July–August 1991), pp. 60–63.
99. For a full discussion see Peter Gold and Michael Esposito, "The Right to Control: Are Your Workers Independent Contractors or Employees?" *Compensation and Benefits Review* (July–August 1992), pp. 30–37.
100. For a discussion, see, for example, Roger Plachy, "The Point Factor Job Evaluation System: A Step-by-Step Guide, Part I," *Compensation and Benefits Review,* Vol. 19, no. 4 (July–August 1987), pp. 12–27; Roger Plachy, "The Case for Effective Point-Factor Job Evaluation, Viewpoint I," *Compensation and Benefits Review,* Vol. 19, no. 2 (March–April 1987), pp. 45–48; Roger Plachy, "The Point-Factor Job Evaluation System: A Step-by-Step Guide, Part II," *Compensation and Benefits Review,* Vol. 19, no. 5 (September–October 1987), pp. 9–24; and Alfred Candrilli and Ronald Armagast, "The Case for Effective Point-Factor Job Evaluation, Viewpoint II," *Compensation and Benefits Review,* Vol. 19, no. 2 (March–April 1987), pp. 49–54. See also Robert J. Sahl, "How to Install a Point-Factor Job Evaluation System," *Personnel,* Vol. 66, no. 3 (March 1989), pp. 38–42.

CHAPTER 13

PAY-FOR-PERFORMANCE AND FINANCIAL INCENTIVES

OVERVIEW

In this chapter we explain how to use financial incentive plans—plans that tie pay to performance—to motivate employees. Several types of incentive plans, including piecework, the standard hour plan, commissions, and stock options are explained. Next we discuss why incentive plans fail, and when to use them. When you finish studying this chapter, you should be able to compare and contrast at least six types of incentive plans; explain at least five reasons why incentive plans fail; discuss when to use—and when not to use—incentive plans; and establish and administer an effective incentive plan.

▸ MONEY AND MOTIVATION: BACKGROUND

Frederick Taylor
Father of the scientific management movement, according to which a fair day's work should depend on a careful, formal process of inspection and observation.

fair day's work
Frederick Taylor's observation that haphazard setting of piecework requirements and wages by supervisors was not sufficient, and that careful study was needed to define acceptable production quotas for each job.

scientific management
Implies careful, "scientific" study of all the factors that go into work and includes workers' motivation and job satisfaction, as well as optimum production.

The use of financial incentives—financial rewards paid to workers whose production exceeds some predetermined standard—was popularized by **Frederick Taylor** in the late 1800s. As a supervisory employee of the Midvale Steel Company, he had become concerned with what he called "systematic soldiering"—the tendency of employees to work at the slowest pace possible and produce at the minimum acceptable level. What especially intrigued him was the fact that some of these same workers still had the energy to run home and work on their cabins, even after a hard 12-hour day. Taylor knew that if he could find some way to harness this energy during the workday, huge productivity gains would be achieved.

At this time, primitive piecework systems were already in use, but they were generally ineffective. Workers were paid a piece rate based on informally arrived at quotas for each piece they produced. However, rate cutting on the part of employers was flagrant, and the workers knew that if their earnings became excessive, their pay per piece would be cut. As a result, most workers produced just enough to earn a decent wage, but little enough so that their rate per piece would not be cut. One of Taylor's great insights was in seeing the need for a standardized, acceptable view of a **fair day's work**. As he saw it, this fair day's work should depend not on the vague estimates of supervisors but on a careful, formal, scientific process of inspection and observation. It was this need to evaluate each job *scientifically* that led to what became known as the **scientific management** movement. In turn, scientific management gave way in the Depression-plagued 1930s to the human relations movement and its focus on satisfying workers' social needs. The strong interest today in quality improvement programs and employee commitment is a continuation of that theme.

Increasingly, though, this growing emphasis on quality improvement and commitment-building programs is creating a renaissance for financial incentive or pay-for-performance plans. One expert estimates, for instance, that pay-for-performance—pay that puts some part of base salary at risk or that pays individuals or teams based on the achievement of quality or quantity goals—will rise to 15–20% of compensation for all U.S. employees over the next few years.[1] Today one expert estimates that such variable pay constitutes less than 5% of U.S. workers' compensation.[2] That is why (as in Figure 12.5 page 426), traditional job-oriented pay plans are quickly giving way to contribution-based plans, and the sorts of spot awards, team incentives, and gainsharing discussed later in the chapter.

As always, there are competitive reasons for the growing emphasis on this form of compensation. For one thing, today's new interest in cutting costs, restructuring, and boosting performance leads one logically to look toward linking pay and performance as did compensation managers of Taylor's day.

But the growing emphasis on pay-for-performance today is also rooted in the trend toward quality improvement and employee commitment programs. The entire thrust of programs like these is to treat workers more like partners and to encourage them to think of the business and its goals as their own. To the extent that the employer does treat employees like partners and fosters commitment, it is reasonable to pay them more like partners, too, by linking pay more directly to performance.

TYPES OF INCENTIVE PLANS

There are many incentive plans in use and a number of ways to categorize them. For simplicity we will classify the plans as follows: incentives for production employees; incentives for managers and executives; incentives for salespeople; merit pay as an incentive (primarily for white-collar and professional employees); and organization-wide incentives.

▸ INCENTIVES FOR PRODUCTION EMPLOYEES

PIECEWORK PLANS

piecework
A system of pay based on the number of items processed by each individual worker in a unit of time, such as items per hour or items per day.

Piecework is the oldest type of incentive plan, as well as the most commonly used. Earnings are tied directly to what the worker produces by paying the person a "piece rate" for each unit he or she produces. Thus, if Tom Smith gets 40 cents apiece for stamping out door jambs, then he would make $40 for stamping out 100 a day and $80 for stamping out 200.

Developing a workable piece-rate plan requires both job evaluation and (usually) industrial engineering. Job evaluation enables you to assign an hourly wage rate to the job in question. But the crucial issue in piece-rate planning is the production standard, and these standards are usually developed by industrial engineers. The standards are usually stated in terms of a standard number of minutes per unit or a standard number of units per hour. In Tom Smith's case, the job evaluation indicated that his door-jamb stamping job was worth $8 an hour. The industrial engineer determined that 20 jambs per hour was the standard production rate. Therefore, the piece rate (for each door jamb) was $8.00 divided by 20 = $0.40 per door jamb.

straight piecework plan
Under this pay system each worker receives a set payment for each piece produced or processed in a factory or shop.

guaranteed piecework plan
The minimum hourly wage plus an incentive for each piece produced above a set number of pieces per hour.

With a **straight piecework plan**, Tom Smith would simply be paid on the basis of the number of door jambs he produced; there would be no guaranteed minimum wage. However, after passage of the Fair Labor Standards Act it became necessary for most employers to guarantee their workers a minimum wage. With a **guaranteed piecework plan**, Tom Smith would be paid $4.25 per hour (the minimum wage) whether or not he stamped out 10.6 door jambs per hour (at $0.40 each). But as an incentive he would also be paid at the piece rate of $0.40 for each unit he produced over 10.6.

Piecework (to most people) implies *straight piecework*, a strict proportionality between results and rewards regardless of the level of output. Thus, in Smith's case, he continues to get 40 cents apiece for stamping out door jambs, even if he stamps out many more than planned, say, 500 per day. On the other hand, certain types of piecework incentive plans call for a sharing of productivity gains between worker and employer such that the worker does not receive full credit for all production above normal.[3]

Advantages and Disadvantages

Piecework incentive plans have several advantages. They are simple to calculate and easily understood by employees. Piece-rate plans appear equitable in principle, and their incentive value can be powerful since rewards are directly tied to performance.

Piecework also has some disadvantages. A main disadvantage is its somewhat unsavory reputation among many employees, a reputation based on some employers' habit of arbitrarily raising production standards whenever they found their workers earning "excessive" wages. In addition, piece rates are stated in monetary terms (like 40 cents per piece). Thus, when a new job evaluation results in a new hourly wage rate the piece rate must also be revised; this can be a big clerical chore. Another disadvantage is more subtle; since the piece rate is quoted on a per piece basis, in workers' minds production standards become tied inseparably to the amount of money earned. When an attempt is then made to revise production standards, it meets considerable worker resistance, even if the revision is fully justified.[4]

In fact, the industrial engineered specificity of piecework plans represents the seeds of piecework's biggest disadvantage these days. Piecework plans tend to be tailor made for relatively specialized jobs in which employees do basically the same narrow tasks over and over again many times a day. This in turn fosters a certain rigidity: Employees become preoccupied with producing the number of units needed. They become less willing to concern themselves with meeting quality standards or switching from job to job (since doing so could reduce the person's productivity).[5] They tend to be trained to perform only a limited number of tasks. Similarly, attempts to introduce new technology or innovative processes may be more likely to fail insofar as they require major adjustments to engineered standards and negotiations with employees. Equipment tends not to be as well maintained (since employees are focusing on maximizing each machine's output).

Problems such as these have led a number of firms to drop their piecework plans (as well as their standard hour plans, discussed later) and to substitute team-based incentive plans or programs such as gainsharing, which we will also discuss. Plans such as gainsharing have the advantage of being more comprehensive than piecework plans. In particular, there are built-in mechanisms such as suggestion plans for creating team spirit and encouraging quality and productivity improvement.

STANDARD HOUR PLAN

standard hour plan A plan by which a worker is paid a basic hourly rate but is paid an extra percentage of his or her base rate for production exceeding the standard per hour or per day. Similar to piecework payment but based on a percent premium.

The **standard hour plan** is very similar to the piece-rate plan, with one major difference. With a piece-rate plan the worker is paid a particular *rate per piece* that he or she produces. With the standard hour plan the worker is rewarded by a *percent premium that equals the percent by which his or her performance is above standard.* The plan assumes that the worker has a guaranteed base rate.

As an example, suppose the base rate for Smith's job is $8 per hour. (The base rate may, but need not, equal the hourly rate determined by the job evaluation.) And again assume that the production standard for Smith's job is 20 units per hour, or 3 minutes per unit. Suppose that in one day (8 hours) Smith produces 200 door jambs. According to the production standard, this *should have taken Smith 10 hours* (200 divided by 20 per hour); instead it took him 8 hours. He produced at a rate that is 25% (40 divided by 160) higher than the standard rate. The standard rate would be 8 hours times 20 (units per hour) = 160: Smith *actually* produced 40 more, or 200. He will therefore be paid at a rate that is 25% above his base rate for the day. His base rate was $8 per hour times 8 hours equals $64. So he'll be paid 1.25 times 64 or $80.00 for the day.

The standard hour plan has most of the advantages of the piecework plan and is fairly simple to compute and easy to understand. But the incentive is expressed in units of time instead of in monetary terms (as it is with the piece-rate system). Therefore, there is less tendency on the part of workers to link their production standard with their pay. Furthermore, the clerical job of recomputing piece rates whenever hourly wage rates are reevaluated is avoided.[6]

TEAM OR GROUP INCENTIVE PLANS

team or group incentive plan
A plan in which a production standard is set for a specific work group, and its members are paid incentives if the group exceeds the production standard.

Some employers use **team or group incentive plans**, and there are several ways to do this.[7] One approach is to set work standards for each member of the group and maintain a count of the output of each member. Members are then paid based on one of three formulas: (1) All members receive the pay earned by the highest producer, (2) all members receive the pay earned by the lowest producer, or (3) all members receive payment equal to the average pay earned by the group. The second approach is to set a production standard based on the final output of the group as a whole; all members then receive the same pay, based on the piece rate that exists for the group's job. The group incentive can be based on either the piece rate or standard hour plan, but the latter is somewhat more prevalent.

A third option is to simply choose a measurable definition of group performance or productivity that the group can control. You could, for instance, use broad criteria such as total labor hours per final product. In other words, the carefully engineered standards of piecework or standard hour plans are not necessarily required here.

There are several reasons to use a team incentive plan. Sometimes several jobs are interrelated, as they are on project teams. Here one worker's performance reflects not only his or her own effort but that of coworkers as well; here team incentives make sense. Team plans also reinforce group planning and problem solving and help ensure collaboration.[8]

One writer points out that in Japan "the first rule is never reward only one individual." Instead, employees are rewarded as a group in order to reduce jealousy, make group members indebted to one another (as they would be to the group), and encourage a sense of cooperation.[9] There tends to be less bickering among group members over who has "tight" production standards and who has loose ones. Group incentive plans also facilitate on-the-job training, since each member of the group has an interest in getting new members trained as quickly as possible.[10]

The chief disadvantage of group plans is that each worker's rewards are no longer based just on his or her own efforts. To the extent that the person does not see his or her effort leading to the desired reward, a group plan may be less effective than an individual plan. In one study, however (in which the researchers arranged to pay the group based on the performance of its best member), the group incentive plan proved as effective as an individual incentive plan in improving performance.[11]

▶ INCENTIVES FOR MANAGERS AND EXECUTIVES

Because of the role managers play in determining divisional and corporate profitability, most employers pay their managers and executives some type of bonus or incentive.[12] One survey found, for instance, that about 90% of large companies pay managers and executives annual ("short-term") bonuses,[13] while another found that about 70% of small firms have such plans.[14] Similarly, long-term incentive plans (like stock options), which are intended to motivate and reward management for the corporation's long-term growth and prosperity, are used by over 50% of U.S. firms.[15] The widespread use of these bonuses may reflect the fact that they can and do pay for themselves by improving management and thus organizational performance.[16] We can conveniently distinguish between short-term and long-term management incentives.

SHORT-TERM INCENTIVES: THE ANNUAL BONUS

annual bonus
Plans that are designed to motivate short-term performance of managers and are tied to company profitability.

Most firms have **annual bonus** plans aimed at motivating the short-term performance of their managers and executives. Unlike salaries (which are rarely reduced to reflect a falloff in performance), short-term incentive bonuses can easily result in plus or minus adjustments of 25% or more in total pay.

There are three basic issues to be considered when awarding short-term incentives: eligibility, fund-size determination, and individual awards. *Eligibility* is usually decided in one of three ways. The first criterion is *key position*. Here a job-by-job review is conducted to identify the key jobs (typically only line jobs) that have measurable impact on profitability. The second approach to determining eligibilty involves setting a *salary level* cutoff point; here all employees earning over a threshold amount are automatically eligible for consideration for short-term incentives. Finally, eligibility can be determined by *salary grade*. This is a refinement of the salary cutoff approach and assumes that all employees at a certain grade or above should be eligible for the short-term incentive program.[17] The simplest approach is just to use *salary level* as a cutoff.[18] As a rule, bonus eligibility begins somewhere around $40,000 to $50,000.[19]

In general, the size of the bonus is usually greater for top-level executives. Thus, an executive with a $150,000 salary may be able to earn another 80% of his or her salary as a bonus, while a manger in the same firm earning $80,000 can earn only another 30%. Similarly, a supervisor might be able to earn up to 15% of his or her base salary in bonuses. Average bonuses range from a low of 10% to a high of 80% or more: A typical company might establish a plan whereby executives could earn 45% of base salary, managers 25%, and supervisory personnel 12%.

How Much to Pay Out (Fund Size)

Next, a determination must be made regarding *fund determination*—the amount of bonus money that will be available—and there are several formulas used to do this. For example, some companies use a *nondeductible formula*. Here a straight percentage (usually of the company's net income) is used to create the short-term incentive fund. Others use a *deductible formula* on the assumption that the short-term incentive fund should begin to accumulate only after the firm has met a specified level of earnings threshold.

In practice, what proportion of profits is usually paid out as bonuses? There are no hard and fast rules, and some firms do not even have a formula for developing the bonus fund.[20] One alternative is to reserve a minimum amount of the profits, say, 10% for safeguarding stockholders' investment, and then to establish a fund for bonuses equal to, say, 20% of the corporate operating profit before taxes in excess of this base amount. Thus, if the operating profits were $100,000, then the management bonus fund might be 20% of $90,000 or $18,000.[21] Some other illustrative formulas used for determining the executive bonus fund are as follows:

> Ten percent of net income after deducting 5% of average capital invested in business.
>
> Twelve and one-half percent of the amount by which net income exceeds 6% of stockholders' equity.
>
> Twelve percent of net earnings after deducting 6% of net capital.[22]

Deciding Individual Awards

The third issue is deciding the *individual awards* to be paid. Typically a target bonus is set for each eligible position and adjustments are then made for greater or less than targeted performance. A maximum amount, perhaps double the target bonus, may be set. Performance ratings are obtained for each manager and preliminary bonus estimates are computed. Estimates for the total amount of money to be spent on short-term incentives are thereby made and compared with the bonus fund available. If necessary, the individual estimates are then adjusted.

A related question concerns whether managers will receive bonuses based on individual performance, corporate performance, or both. The thing to keep in mind here is that there is a difference between a profit-sharing plan and a true, individual incentive bonus. In a profit-sharing plan, each person gets a bonus based on the company's results, regardless of the person's actual effort. With a true individual incentive, it is the manager's individual effort and performance that is rewarded with a bonus.

Here, again, there are no hard and fast rules. Top-level executive bonuses are generally tied to overall corporate results (or divisional results if the executive is, say, the vice-president of a major division). The assumption here is that corporate results reflect the person's individual performance. But as one moves further down the chain of command, corporate profits become a less accurate gauge of a manager's contribution. Here (say with supervisory personnel or with the heads of functional departments) the person's individual performance is a more logical determinant of his or her bonus.

Many experts argue that in most organizations managerial and executive-level bonuses should be tied to *both* organizational and individual performance, and there are several ways to do this.[23] Perhaps the simplest is the *split award method*, which breaks the bonus into two parts. Here the manager actually gets two separate bonuses, one based on his or her individual effort and one based on the organization's overall performance. Thus a manager might be *eligible* for an "individual performance" bonus of *up to* $10,000 but receive an individual performance bonus of only $8,000 at the end of the year, based on his or her individual performance evaluation. In addition, though, the person might also receive a second bonus of $8,000 based on the *company's* profits for the year.

Thus, even if there are no company profits, the high-performing manager would still get an individual-performance bonus.

One drawback to this approach is that it pays too much to the marginal performer, even if his or her own performance is mediocre, since he or she at least gets that second, company-based bonus. One way to get around this is by using the *multiplier method*. For example, a manager whose individual performance was "poor" might not even receive a company-performance-based bonus, on the assumption that the bonus should be a *product* of individual and corporate performance. When either is very poor, the product is zero.

Whichever approach is used, the basic point to keep in mind is that truly outstanding performers should never be paid less than their normal reward, regardless of organizational performance, and should get substantially larger awards than do other managers. They are people the company cannot afford to lose, and their performance should always be adequately rewarded by the organization's incentive system—marginal or below average performers should never receive awards that are normal or average, and poor performers should be awarded nothing. The money saved on those people should be given to above average performers.[24]

LONG-TERM INCENTIVES

Long-term incentives are intended to motivate and reward management for the corporation's long-term growth and prosperity and to inject a long-term perspective into the executive's decisions. If only short-term criteria were used, a manager could, for instance, increase profitability by reducing plant maintenance, a tactic that might, of course, catch up with the company over two or three years. Another purpose of these plans is to encourage executives to stay with the company by providing them with the opportunity to accumulate capital (like company stock) based on the firm's long-term success. Long-term incentives or **capital accumulation programs** are most often reserved for senior executives.[25] There are six popular long-term incentive (for capital accumulation) plans: stock options, stock appreciation rights, performance achievement plans, restricted stock plans, phantom stock plans, and book value plans.[26] The popularity of these plans changes over time due to economic conditions and trends, internal company financial pressures, changing attitudes toward long-term incentives and changes in tax law as well as other factors. A recent example was the impact of the 1986 Tax Reform Act, which lowered rates and established a new set of rules on benefit plans.[27] A basic purpose of long-term incentives like incentive stock options was to reduce the after-tax bite of taxes on the executive's incentive pay. The reduction in maximum tax rates and the elimination of favorable treatment for capital gains of the 1986 act thus increased the value of cash as a substitute for such incentives.[28] Tax changes in 1993 should reverse these effects.

capital accumulation programs
Long-term incentives most often reserved for senior executives. Six popular plans include stock options, stock appreciation rights, performance achievement plans, restricted stock plans, phantom stock plans, and book value plans.

stock option
The right to purchase a stated number of shares of a company stock at a stated price during a stated period of time. An executive is given the right to purchase shares in the future at today's price. If the company grows, share prices may rise and the executive may benefit, assuming the economy is stable.

Stock Options

A **stock option** is the right to purchase a specific number of shares of company stock at a specific price during a period of time; the executive thus hopes to profit by exercising his or her option in the future, *but at today's price.* The assumption is that the price of the stock will go up, rather than down or stay the same. Unfortunately, this depends partly on considerations outside the executives control, such as general economic conditions. Stock price *is*, of course, affected by the firm's profitability and growth, and to the extent the executive can affect these factors the stock option can be an incentive. However, in one survey it was found that over half the executives saw little or no relation between their performance and the value of their stock options.[29]

One alternative to stock options is a *book value plan*. Here managers are permitted to purchase stock at current book value, a value anchored in the value of the company's assets. Executives here can earn dividends on the stock they own, and as the company grows the book value of their shares may grow too. When these employees leave the company, they can then sell the shares back to the company at the new higher book value.[30] The book value approach avoids the uncertainties of the stock market, emphasizing instead reasonable growth.

Other Plans

There are several other types of popular long-term incentive plans. *Stock appreciation rights* (SARs) are usually combined with stock options; they permit the recipient to either exercise the option (by buying the stock) or instead to take any appreciation in the stock price in cash, stock, or some combination of these. A *performance achievement plan* awards shares of stock that are earned for the achievement of predetermined financial targets, such as profit or growth in earnings per share. With *restricted stock plans*, shares are usually awarded without cost to the executive but with certain restrictions that are specified in the Internal Revenue Code. For example, there is risk of forfeiture if an executive leaves the company before the specified time limit elapses. Finally, under *phantom stock plans* executives receive not shares but "units" that are similar to shares of company stock. Then at some future time they receive value (usually in cash) equal to the appreciation of the "phantom" stock that they own.[31]

Whichever long-term plan is used, a growing concern today is achieving a "better balance between the personal motives and financial incentives of executives and their fiduciary responsibility to shareholders.[32] The problem is that traditional executive incentives often don't build in any real risk for the executive, and so the executives' and the shareholders' interests could diverge. Often, for instance, options can be exercised with little or no cash outlay by the executive who then turns around and quickly sells his or her stock. There is therefore a growing emphasis on long-term executive incentives that build more executive risk into the formula.[33]

Performance Plans

The need to tie executive's pay more clearly to the firm's performance while building in more risk has led many more firms to institute *performance plans*. Performance plans "are plans whose payment or value is contingent on financial performance measured against objectives set at the start of a multi-year period."[34] For example, the executive may be granted so-called performance units. These grants are similar to annual bonuses but the measurement period is longer than a year. Thus the executive might be able to achieve, say, a $100,000 grant in units, valued at $50 per unit in proportion to his or her success in meeting the assigned financial goals.

Implementing Long-Term Incentives

The results of one study by consultants McKinsey and Company, Inc., indicate that the simple expedient of giving managers stock options may be the simplest and wisest route as far as providing long-term incentives for top executives. In the McKinsey study about one-half the companies surveyed had stock options only and about one-half had performance-based plans in which managers were given cash bonuses for long-term performance.

The results indicated that in most cases the return to shareholders of companies with long-term cash performance incentives did not differ significantly from those companies that had only stock-based incentive plans (like stock options). This was so even though companies that paid cash bonuses had spent more to fund their incentive plans. Their most serious problem in awarding cash bonuses lay in identifying the proper performance measures. The survey concludes that successful long-term incentive plans should (1) use measures of performance that correlate with shareholder wealth creation (that is, return on equity and growth), not earnings per share growth; (2) establish valid target levels and communicate them clearly to participants; and (3) provide for target adjustment under certain well-defined circumstances (in other words, the performance standards can be modified if market conditions warrant it).[35]

Long-Term Incentives for Overseas Executives

Developing effective long-term incentives for a firm's overseas operations presents some tricky problems, particularly with regard to taxation. For example, extending a U.S. stock option plan to local nationals in a firm's overseas operations could subject them to immediate taxation on the stocks, even though the shares could not be sold because of requirements built in to the U.S.-based plan.[36]

The problem extends to U.S. executives stationed overseas as well. For example, it's not unusual for an executive to be taxed $40,000 on $140,000 of stock option income if he or she is based in the United States. However, if that same person receives the same $140,000 stock option income while stationed overseas, he or she may be subject to both the $40,000 U.S. tax, plus a foreign income tax (depending on the country) of perhaps $94,000. Therefore, not taking into consideration the overseas country's tax burden has the effect of either virtually eliminating the incentive value of the stock from the executive's point of view or dramatically boosting the cost of the stock to the company (assuming the company pays the foreign income tax). In any case, firms can't assume that they can simply export their executives' incentive programs. Instead, various factors including tax treatment, the regulatory environment, and foreign exchange controls must be considered as well.[37]

▶ Incentives for Salespeople

Compensation plans for salespeople have typically relied heavily on incentives in the form of sales commissions, although this varies by industry. In the tobacco industry, for instance, salespeople are usually paid entirely via commissions, while in the transportation equipment industry salespeople tend to be paid by salary. However, the most prevalent approach is to use a combination of salary and commissions to compensate salespeople.[38]

The widespread use of incentives for salespeople is due to three things: tradition, the unsupervised nature of most sales work, and the assumption that incentives are needed to motivate salespeople. The pros and cons of salary, commission, and combination plans are as follows:

SALARY PLAN

In a salary plan salespeople are paid a fixed salary, although there may be occasional incentives in the form of bonuses, sales contest prizes, and the like.[39]

There are several reasons to use straight salary. The plan works well when your main objective is prospecting work (in terms of finding new clients) or where the salesperson is mostly involved in account servicing, such as developing and executing sales and product training programs for a distributor's sales force, or participating in national and local trades shows.[40] Jobs like these are often found in industries that sell technical products. This is one reason why the aerospace and transportation equipment industries have a relatively heavy emphasis on salary plans for their salespeople.

There are advantages to paying salespeople on a straight salary basis. Salespeople know in advance what their income will be, and the employer also has fixed, predictable sales force expenses. It makes it simple to switch territories or quotas or to reassign salespeople, and it can develop a high degree of loyalty among the sales staff. Commissions tend to shift the salesperson's emphasis to "making the sale" rather than prospecting and cultivating long-term customers. Such a long-term perspective *is encouraged* by straight salary compensation.

However, the salary plan has disadvantages. The main one is that it does not depend on results.[41] In fact, salaries are often tied to seniority (rather than to performance), and this can be demotivating to potentially high-performing salespeople, who see seniority—not performance—being rewarded.

COMMISSION PLAN

Commission plans pay salespeople in direct proportion to their sales—for results, and only for results.

The commission plan has several advantages. Salespeople have the greatest possible incentive, and there is a tendency to attract high-performing salespeople who see that effort will clearly lead to rewards. Sales costs are proportional to sales (rather than fixed), and the company's selling investment is reduced. The commission basis is also easy to understand and compute.

But the commission plan also has drawbacks. Salespeople focus on making a sale and on high-volume items; cultivating dedicated customers and working to push hard-to-sell items may be neglected. Wide variances in income between salespeople may occur; this can lead to a feeling that the plan is inequitable. More serious is the fact that salespeople are encouraged to neglect nonselling duties like servicing small accounts. In addition, pay is often excessive in boom times and very low in recessions.

COMBINATION PLAN

Most companies pay their salespeople a combination of salary and commissions, and there is a sizable salary component in most such plans. The most frequent percentage split reported in one study was 80% base salary and 20% incentives.

A close second was a 70/30 split, with a 60/40 split being the third most frequent reported arrangement.[42]

Combination plans provide not only some of the advantages of both straight salary and straight commission plans, but also some of the disadvantages of each. Salespeople have a floor to their earnings so their families' security is ensured. Furthermore, the company can direct its salespeople's activities by detailing what services the salary component is being paid for, while the commission component provides a built-in incentive for superior performance.

Awards for special performance on the job take many forms; recognition of the employee is the key factor.

However, the salary component is not tied to performance, and the employer is therefore trading away some of the incentive value of what the person is paid. Combination plans also tend to become complicated, and misunderstandings can result. This might not be a problem with a simple "salary plus commission" plan, but most plans are not so simple. For example, there is a "commission plus drawing account" plan, where a salesperson is paid basically on commissions but can *draw on future earnings* to get through low sales periods. Similarly, in the "commission plus bonus" plan, salespeople are again paid primarily on the basis of commissions. However, they are also given a small bonus for directed activities like selling slow-moving items.

An example can help illustrate complexities of the typical combination plan. In one company, for instance, the following three-step formula is applied:

Step 1: Sales volume up to $18,000 a month. Base salary plus 7% of gross profits plus 1/2% of gross sales.

Step 2: Sales volume from $18,000 to $25,000 a month. Base salary plus 9% of gross profits plus 1/2% of gross sales.

Step 3: Over $25,000 a month. Base salary plus 10% of gross profits plus ½% of gross sales.

In all cases, base salary is paid every two weeks, while the earned percentage of gross profits and gross sales is paid monthly.[43]

special awards Individual bonuses, such as TVs, paid on the basis of performance ratings.

The sales force also may get various **special awards.**[44] At Oakite Company, for instance, several recognition-type awards are used to boost sales. For example, there are a President's Cup for the Top Division Manager and a VIP Club for the top 10% of the sales force in total dollars sales. The VIP Club is well publicized within the firm and has a lot of prestige attached to it. Other firms such as Airwick Industries award televisions and Lenox china as special sales awards.

▶ INCENTIVES FOR OTHER PROFESSIONALS

MERIT PAY AS AN INCENTIVE

merit pay Any salary increase awarded to an employee based on his or her individual performance.

merit raise Merit raise is another term for merit pay.

Merit pay or **merit raise** is any salary increase that is awarded to an employee based on his or her individual performance. It is different from a bonus in that it represents a continuing increment, whereas the bonus represents a one-time payment. Although the term *merit pay* can apply to the incentive raises given to any employees—exempt or nonexempt, office or factory, management or nonmanagement—the term is more often used with respect to white-collar employees and particularly professional, office, and clerical employees.

Merit pay has both advocates and detractors and is the subject of much debate.[45] Advocates argue that only pay (or other rewards) tied directly to performance can motivate improved performance. They contend that the effect of awarding pay raises across the board (without regard to individual performance) may actually detract from performance by showing employees they'll be rewarded the same regardless of how they perform.

On the other hand, merit pay detractors present some good reasons why merit pay plans can backfire. One is that the usefulness of the merit pay plan depends on the validity of the performance appraisal system, and if performance appraisals are viewed as unfair, so, too, will the merit pay that is based on them.[46] Similarly, supervisors often tend to minimize differences in employee performance when computing merit raises. They instead give most employees about the same raise, either because of a reluctance to alienate some employees or because of a desire to give everyone a raise that will at least help them stay even with the cost of living. A third problem is that almost every employee thinks he or she is an above-average performer; being paid a below-average merit increase can thus be demoralizing.[47] However, while problems like these can undermine a merit pay plan, there seems little doubt that merit pay can and does improve performance. But you must make sure that the performance appraisals are carried out effectively.[48]

Merit Pay: Two New Options

Traditional merit pay plans have two basic characteristics: (1) merit increases are usually granted to employees at a designated time of the year in the form of a higher base salary (or "raise"), and (2) the merit raise is usually based exclusively on individual performance (although the overall level of company profits may affect the total sum available for merit raises).[49] Two adaptations of merit pay plans are becoming more popular today. One awards merit raises in one lump sum once a year. The other ties awards to both individual and organizational performance.

Lump-sum merit raises are attractive for several reasons. Traditional merit increases are cumulative, while some lump-sum merit raises are not. Since the employee's merit raise (of, say 5% of his or her base salary) is awarded in one lump sum, the rise in payroll expenses can be significantly slowed. (Traditionally, someone with a salary of $20,000 per year might get a 5% increase. This moves her to a new base salary of $21,000. If she gets another 5% increase next year then the new merit increase of 5% is tacked on not just to the $20,000 base salary but to the extra $1,000 she received last year.) Another advantage is that lump-sum merit raises can help contain benefit costs, since the level of benefit coverage is often tied to a person's current base pay. Lump-sum merit increases can also be more dramatic motivators than traditional merit pay raises. For example, a 5% lump-sum merit increase to our $20,000 employee is $1,000, as opposed to a traditional weekly increment of $19.25 for 52 weeks. Knowing that base salary levels are not being permanently impacted by merit pay decisions can also give management more flexibility (say, in a particularly good year) to award somewhat higher lump-sum merit raises.

Moving to a lump-sum merit pay plan like this requires considering several points. Perhaps most important, if you are going to surrender the merit pay tool often used for raising base salaries, any substantial base salary inequities should first be eliminated. That way, weaker performers' salaries are not permanently frozen in above higher performers' salaries. The timing of the merit increases may also become more important, since you must now consider the impact of the lump-sum payments on our company's cash flow.

Another merit pay option is to award lump-sum merit pay based on both individual and organizational performance. A sample matrix for doing so is presented in Table 13.1. In this example the company's performance might be measured by rate of return or sales divided by payroll costs. Company performance is then weighted equally with the employee's performance as measured by his or her performance appraisal. Thus, an outstanding performer would still receive a lump-sum award even if the organization's performance was marginal. However employees with unacceptable performance would receive no lump-sum awards even for a year in which the organization's performance was outstanding. The advantage of this approach is that it forces employees to focus on organizational goals like profitability and improved productivity. The drawback is that it can reduce the motivational value of the reward by reducing the impact of the employee's own performance on the reward.[50]

INCENTIVES FOR PROFESSIONAL EMPLOYEES

Professional employees are those whose work involves the *application of learned knowledge to the solution of the employer's problems.* They include lawyers, doctors, economists, and engineers. Professionals almost always reach their positions through prolonged periods of formal study.[51]

TABLE 13.1 Lump-Sum Award Determination Matrix (an example)

	THE ORGANIZATION'S PERFORMANCE (WEIGHT = 0.50)				
THE EMPLOYEE'S PERFORMANCE (WEIGHT = .50)	Outstanding (1.00)	Excellent (0.80)	Commendable (0.60)	Marginal or Acceptable (0.40)	Unacceptable (0)
Outstanding (1.00)	1.00	0.90	0.80	0.70	0.50
Excellent (0.80)	0.90	0.80	0.70	0.60	0.40
Commendable (0.60)	0.80	0.70	0.60	0.50	0.30
Acceptable (0.00)	—	—	—	—	—
Unacceptable (0.00)	—	—	—	—	—

Source: John F. Sullivan, "The Future of Merit Pay Programs," *Compensation and Benefits Review* (May–June 1989), p. 29.

Instructions. To determine the dollar value of each employee's incentive award, (1) multiply the employee's annual, straight time wage or salary as of June 30 times his or her maximum incentive award and (2) multiply the resultant product times the appropriate percentage figure from this table. For example, if an employee had an annual salary of $20,000 on June 30 and a maximum incentive award of 7% and if her performance and the organization's performance were both "excellent," the employee's award would be $1,120: ($20,000 × 0.07 × 0.80 = $1,120).

Pay decisions regarding professional employees involve unique problems. One is that for most professionals money has historically been less important as an incentive than it has been for other employees. This is partly because professionals tend to be paid well anyway, and partly because they tend to already be driven—by the desire to produce high-caliber work, and to receive recognition from colleagues.

However, that's not to say that professionals don't want financial incentives. For example, studies in industries like pharmaceuticals and aerospace consistently show that firms with the most productive research and development groups have incentive pay plans for their professionals, usually in the form of bonuses. There is usually a conservative relationship between bonus and salary, in other words, smaller portions of total pay in the form of bonuses. The time cycle of the professionals' incentive plans also tends to be longer than a year, reflecting long development time often involved in designing, developing, and marketing a new product.

While not strictly incentives, there *are* many nonsalary items professionals must have to do their best work. These range from better equipment and facilities and a supportive management style to support for professional journal publications.

REWARDING KEY CONTRIBUTORS

How do organizations typically reward their key contributors? According to a *Hay Executive and Key Contributor Compensation Survey* of high-technology firms about 76% of the participants reported having some type of formal or informal key contributor plan. As you can see in Figure 13.1, 83% of the firms with key contributor programs used cash in a lump-sum payment to pay key contributors. About half of these firms used some type of stock payment plan (stock options or stock grants) to reward key contributors. With respect to cash payments, maximum opportunities for individuals ranged from $5,000 to $30,000 (typically $5,000) for key personnel. Other rewards used included nonmonetary rewards like automobiles, trips, and research funding, as well as sabbaticals, public recognition, freedom-to-choose projects, and "general work-life improvements."[52]

FIGURE 13.1
Vehicles Used to Reward Key Contributors

Source: Michael F. Spratt and Bernadette Steele, "Rewarding Key Contributors," *Compensation and Benefits Review* (July–August 1985), p. 30.

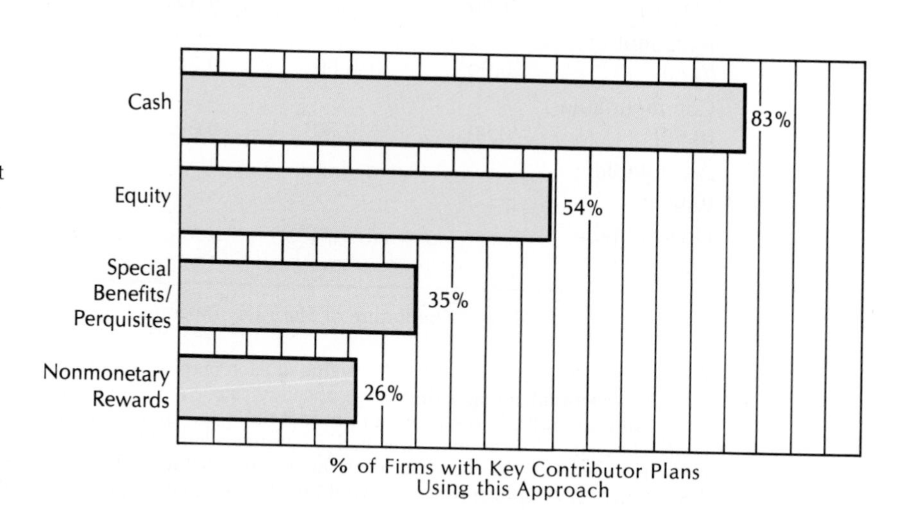

CUSTOMER SERVICE INCENTIVE PLANS

Firms are also developing merit pay–type plans to reward employees for their contributions to the firm's customer service standards. One such program was instituted at the Aetna Life & Casualty Company.[53]

This plan had two components. The base pay program compensated employees based on their sustained overall performance. However, the customer service–based Star Performance Plan used one-time bonuses to reward employees for superior contributions, particularly in the area of customer service.[54] First, customer service standards were set. These included: The employee exhibits knowledge of the customer and his or her needs; the employee exhibits concern for others and their opinions; and the employee is accessible to customers. Annual bonuses were then distributed to star performers from a fund that represented 2% of the firm's annual base salaries.

▶ ORGANIZATION-WIDE INCENTIVE PLANS

Many employers have incentive plans in which virtually all employees can participate, namely, profit sharing, employee stock ownership, and Scanlon plans.

PROFIT-SHARING PLANS

profit-sharing plan
A plan whereby most employees share in the company's profits.

In a **profit-sharing plan**, most employees receive a share of the company's profits. Research on the effectiveness of such plans is sketchy. In one survey, about half the companies believed their profit-sharing plans had been beneficial,[55] but these benefits are not necessarily in terms of increased performance and motivation. Instead, the benefits are probably more subtle. For example, these plans may increase each worker's sense of commitment, participation, and partnership. They may also reduce turnover and encourage employee thrift.

There are several types of profit-sharing plans. The most popular are cash plans. Here a percentage of profits (usually 15% to 20%) is distributed as profit shares at regular intervals. One example of this is the *Lincoln Incentive System*, which was first instituted at the Lincoln Electric Company of Ohio. In one version employees work on a guaranteed piecework basis, and total annual profits (less taxes, 6% dividends to stockholders, and a reserve for investment) are distributed each year among employees based on their merit rating.[56] The Lincoln plan also includes a suggestion system that pays individual workers rewards for savings resulting from suggestions. The Lincoln plan has been quite successful.

Profit sharing has perhaps reached its logical conclusion in Japan. Many employees receive a semiannual bonus that reflects the performance of the enterprise. The amount of this bonus is usually the equivalent of 5 to 6 months' salary for each employee.[57]

There are also *deferred profit-sharing plans*. Here a predetermined portion of profits is placed in each employee's account under the supervision of a trustee. There is a tax advantage to such plans, since income taxes are deferred, often until the employee retires and he or she is thus taxed at a lower tax rate.

EMPLOYEE STOCK OWNERSHIP PLAN (ESOP)

Employee Stock Ownership Plan (ESOP)
This plan usually involves having a corporation contribute shares of its own stock to a trust in which additional contributions are made annually. The trust distributes the stock to employees on retirement or separation from service.

Under the most basic form of ESOP, a corporation contributes shares of its own stock—or cash to be used to purchase such stock—to a trust, one established to purchase shares of the firm's stock for employees.[58] These contributions are generally made annually in proportion to total employee compensation, with a limit of 15% of compensation. The trust holds the stock in individual employee accounts and distributes the stock to employees upon retirement or other separation from service (assuming the employee has worked long enough to earn ownership of the stock).

An employee stock ownership plan has several advantages. The corporation receives a tax deduction when it makes its contribution. The deduction is equal to the fair market value of the shares that are transferred to the trustee. Corporations can claim an income tax deduction for dividends paid on ESOP-owned stock.[59] Employees are not taxed until they receive a distribution from the trust, usually at retirement when their tax rate is reduced. The Employee Retirement Income Security Act (ERISA) allows a firm to borrow against employee stock held in trust and then repay the loan in pretax rather than after-tax dollars, another tax incentive for using such plans.[60] The Deficit Reduction Act of 1984 and the Tax Reform Act of 1986 both included substantial tax advantages for ESOP formation, and ESOPs thereafter became a common vehicle for financing acquisitions. The Revenue Reconciliation Act of 1989 reduced several of the tax benefits associated with ESOPs but the programs remain popular nevertheless.

Research suggests that ESOPs do encourage employees to develop a sense of ownership in and commitment to the firm.[61] They do so in part because they provide opportunities for increased financial incentives, create a new sense of ownership, and help to build teamwork.[62]

SCANLON PLAN

Scanlon plan
An incentive plan developed in 1937 by Joseph Scanlon and designed to encourage cooperation, involvement, and sharing of benefits. Plan involves attitudes, suggestions by workers, and benefits formulas.

Few would argue with the fact that the most powerful way of ensuring commitment is to synchronize the organization's goals with those of its employees: to ensure in other words, that the two sets of goals overlap, and that by pursuing his or her goals, the worker pursues the employer's goals as well. Many techniques have been proposed for obtaining this idyllic state, but few have been implemented as widely or successfully as the **Scanlon plan**, an incentive plan developed in 1937 by Joseph Scanlon, a United Steel Worker's Union official.[63]

The Scanlon plan is actually remarkably progressive considering that it was developed almost 60 years ago. It actually contains many of the elements that we today associate with commitment-building programs and quality improvement plans. The Scanlon plan itself has been refined over the years by organizations such as Scanlon Plan Associates, a nonprofit support group for organizations that have Scanlon plans. As currently implemented Scanlon plans have the following basic features:[64] The first is the *philosophy of cooperation* on which it is based. It assumes that managers and workers have to rid themselves of the "us" and "them" attitudes that normally inhibit employees from developing a sense of ownership in the company. It substitutes instead a climate in which everyone cooperates because he or she understands that economic rewards are contingent on honest cooperation. A pervasive philosophy of cooperation must therefore exist in the firm for the plan to succeed.[65]

A second feature of the plan is what its practitioners refer to as *identity.* This means that to focus employee involvement, the company's mission or purpose must be clearly articulated and employees must fundamentally understand how the business operates in terms of customers, prices, and costs, for instance. *Competence* is a third basic feature. The program today, say three experts, "explicitly recognizes that a Scanlon Plan demands a high level of competence from employees at all levels."[66] Successfully implementing the plan therefore assumes that hourly employees can competently perform their jobs as well as identify and implement improvements, and that supervisors have the leadership skills for the participative management that is crucial to a Scanlon plan.

The Weirton, West Virginia Steel plant is a successful ESOP in a highly competitive industry. (See page 470 for a discussion of ESOP).

The fourth feature of the plan is the *involvement system.*[67] This takes the form of two levels of committees—the departmental level and the executive level. Productivity-improving suggestions are presented by employees to the appropriate departmental-level committees, which then selectively transmit valuable suggestions to the executive-level committee. The latter then decides whether to implement the suggestion.

The fifth element of the plan is the *sharing of benefits formula.* Basically, the Scanlon plan assumes that employees should share directly in any extra profits resulting from their cost-cutting suggestions. If a suggestion is implemented and successful, all employees usually share in 75% of the savings. For example, assume that the normal monthly ratio of payroll costs to sales is 50%. (Thus, if sales are $600,000, payroll costs should be $300,000.) Assume suggestions are implemented and result in payroll costs of $250,000 in a month when sales were $550,000, and payroll costs *should have been* $275,000 (50% of sales). The saving attributable to these suggestions is $25,000 ($275,000 minus $250,000). Workers would typically share in 75% of this ($18,750) while $6,250 would go to the firm. In practice, a portion, usually one-quarter of the $18,750, is set aside for the months in which labor costs exceed the standard.

The Scanlon plan has been quite successful at reducing costs and fostering a sense of sharing and cooperation among employees. In one study, labor costs were cut by 10%, and grievances were cut in half after implementation of such a plan.[68]

Yet Scanlon plans do fail, and there are several conditions required for their success. They are usually more effective when there is a relatively small number of participants, generally less than 1,000. They are more successful when there are stable product lines and costs, since it is important that the labor costs/sales ratio remains fairly stable. Good supervision and healthy labor relations seem essential. And, of course, it is crucial that there be strong commitment to the plan on the part of management, particularly during the confusing phase-in period.[69]

GAINSHARING PLANS

gainsharing
An incentive plan that engages employees in a common effort to achieve productivity objectives and share the gains.

The Scanlon plan is actually an early version of what today is known as a **gainsharing plan**, an incentive plan that engages many or all employees in a common effort to achieve a company's productivity objectives; resulting incremental cost savings gains are shared among employees and the company.[70] In addition to the Scanlon plan, other popular types of gainsharing plans include the Rucker and Improshare plans.

The basic difference in these plans is in the formula used to determine employee bonuses.[71] The Scanlon formula divides payroll expenses by total sales. The Rucker plan uses sales value minus materials and supplies all divided into payroll expenses as the formula's ratio. The Improshare plan is different, in that it creates production standards for each department. The Scanlon and Rucker plans include participative management systems using committees. Improshare does not include a participative management component but instead considers participation an outcome of the bonus plan. In a survey of 223 companies with gainsharing plans, 95 of the responding firms had custom-designed plans, while the rest used standardized plans like Scanlon, Rucker, or Improshare.[72]

Steps in Gainsharing Plan

The employer wishing to implement its own gainsharing plan should address eight basic steps.[73] First, establish general plan objectives. These might include the company's need to improve productivity, or reinforce teamwork, for instance.

Second, define specific performance measures. These usually include productivity measures such as labor or hours or cost per unit produced, loans processed per hour, or total cost per full-time employee. Possible financial measures usable here include profits before interest and taxes, and return on net assets. The third step is the funding formula, such as "payroll expenses divided by total sales." This creates the pot of dollars that is shared among participants. (In one study, by the way, an average of 46.7% of incremental gains were provided to employees with the remainder staying with the company.)[74] Fourth, determine a method for dividing and distributing the employees' share of the gains among the employees themselves. Typical methods here include equal percentage of pay or equal shares, although some plans also try to modify awards to a limited degree based on individual performance. Fifth, the size of the payment must be meaningful enough to get participants' attention and motivate their behavior. One expert suggests a potential of 4–5% of pay and a 70–80% chance of achieving such an objective as an effective combination. The sixth component is the payment form, which is usually in cash but occasionally in common stock or deferred cash. Seventh, you must decide how frequently bonuses are to be paid. This in turn depends on the performance measures used: Most financial performance measures tend to be computed annually, while labor productivity measures tend to be computed quarterly or monthly.

Finally, the eighth component is the support or participative system to be used to involve the employees. Here the systems most commonly used include steering committees, update meetings, suggestion systems, coordinators, problem-solving teams, department committees, training programs, newsletters, inside auditors, and outside auditors.

Making the Plan Work

The gainsharing approach to incentives is simple in concept, but several issues must be addressed to ensure that your plan works in practice.[75] First, in most gainsharing plans, employee involvement is the single most crucial factor to its success. Obviously if your employees mistrust your motives for installing the plan, or do not believe their suggestions will be listened to, or believe that for some reason the plan will backfire, the plan will not likely succeed. In general, therefore, top management and supervisory personnel have to support participatory management actively and willingly to make these plans work. Furthermore, they generally work better with a work force that is technically knowledgeable, motivated by higher compensation and more involvement, and interested in learning more about the financial ramifications of their work. Employee opinion surveys are often used to gather information to predict how a work force will react to a gainsharing plan. Topics to touch on in such a survey include employee satisfaction, degree of confidence and trust in supervisor, perceived supervisory competence, level of interdepartmental cooperation, willingness to make suggestions, current level of job performance, and willingness to participate in job-related decision making.[76]

AT-RISK PAY PLANS

A growing number of firms including Saturn Corp., Toyota Motor Manufacturing, and DuPont are implementing new organization-wide incentive plans. These are sometimes called variable pay plans but are essentially plans that put some portion of the employee's pay at risk, subject to the firm meeting its financial goals.

The basic characteristic of all these at-risk pay plans is that some portion of the employee's base salary is at risk. In the DuPont plan, for instance, the employee's at-risk pay is a maximum of 6%. This means each employee's base pay will be 94% of his or her counterpart's salary in other (non-at-risk) DuPont departments.[77] At Saturn, the at-risk component was initially designed to be about 20% but was recently cut back to 5% as discussed earlier. The "at-risk" approach is aimed in part at paying employees more like they are partners. It is actually similar to much more extensive programs in Japan in which the "at-risk" portion might be 50–60% of a person's yearly pay. To the extent that at-risk pay is part of a more comprehensive program aimed at turning employees into committee partners—programs stressing values of trust and respect, extensive communications, and participation and opportunities for advancement, for instance—at-risk programs should be successful.

▶ DEVELOPING EFFECTIVE INCENTIVE PLANS

INCENTIVE PLAN PROBLEMS

There are a number of reasons why incentive plans fail, most of which can be explained in terms of what we know about human motivation. For motivation to take place, the worker must believe that effort on his or her part will lead to rewards, *and* he or she must want that reward. In most cases where incentive plans fail, it is because one or both of these conditions are not met.[78] *Unfair standards*—standards that are too high or unattainable—are thus one cause for incentive plan failure. A second is the real or imagined fear that *rates will be cut or standards raised* if performance exceeds the standard for too long a time. Rate cuts have long been the nemesis of incentive plans, and the problem persists to this day, for instance, among manufacturers who reduce a salesperson's territory as soon as his or her commissions become "excessive." *Group restrictions* and peer pressure can work both for and against the plan. If a group views the plan as fair, it can keep loafers in line and maintain high production. But if for any reason the group views the plan as unfair it will—through education, ostracism, or punishment—see that the production levels of group members are held down. Other plans fail because employees *do not understand them* either because the plan is too complex or because it is not communicated to employees in an understandable way.

So far we have discussed some of the causes of such failures. Now let us turn to some specific guidelines for developing effective incentive plans.[79]

1. *Ensure that effort and rewards are directly related.* Your incentive plan should reward employees in *direct proportion* to their increased productivity. Employees must also perceive that they can *actually do the tasks* required. Thus, the standard has to be attainable, and you have to provide the necessary tools, equipment, and training.[80]

Computer Application in Financial Incentives: Appraisal Statistics

Remember that effective merit pay plans are always built on a foundation of fair and accurate appraisals. Some supervisors "grade" more stringently than others; some truly have mostly stars; and others are subject to the traditional rating errors. Comparing the results of various departments or divisions may flag certain problems for closer examination.

After accumulating appraisal data from various departments and/or supervisors, extract the particular area(s) you would like to review. You may extract more than one area at a time by sorting the data first by department (in ascending alphabetical order) and then by supervisor's last name (again in ascending alphabetical order).

Then, examine statistical averages and variances. Too little variance indicates a central tendency—a supervisor who does not want to distinguish between employees, so all are rated average. Looking at the minimum and maximum scores actually awarded will tell whether or not there is a restricted range—in other words, another indication of little differentiation between employees. Of course, the range may be restricted on the high side (an "easy grader") or the low side. If there is very little difference in ratings, then superior performers are not getting reinforcement and poor performers are not being given clear expectations of what they must do to improve. Penley and Penley point out that small variance indicates ". . . undifferentiated feedback to the employees."[1]

You may also wish to examine the timeliness of appraisals. If your company policy is to appraise the employee on or before the anniversary of hiring date, then that month and day are entered. In another column, enter the date the appraisal was actually done. By subtracting the appraisal date from the hire date, you are able to quickly view the timeliness of appraisals. This is possible because packages such as Lotus 1–2–3 store Gregorian dates based on the number of days since December 31, 1899.[2]

By analyzing the results of the appraisal process, it is possible to see problem areas that demand further training. Cleaning up these problems may well be a prerequisite to installing an effective incentive plan.

[1] Larry E. Penley and Yolanda E. Penley, *Human Resources Simulation: Using Lotus 1–2–3* (Carrollton, TX: South-Western Publishing Co., 1988), p. 121.

[2] Gregory T. LeBlond and Douglas Ford Cobb, *Using Lotus 1–2–3* (Indianapolis: Que Corporation, 1983), p. 169.

2. *The plan must be understandable and easily calculable by the employees.* Employees should be able to calculate easily the rewards they will receive for various levels of effort.
3. *Set effective standards.* This requires several things. The standards should be viewed as *fair* by your subordinates. They should be set high, but *reasonable*—there should be about a 50:50 chance of success. And the goal should be *specific*—this is much more effective than telling someone to "do your best."
4. *Guarantee your standards.* View the standard as a *contract* with your employees. Once the plan is operational, use great caution before decreasing the size of the incentive in any way.[81]
5. *Guarantee an hourly base rate.* Particularly for plant personnel it's usually advisable to guarantee employees' base rate.[82] They'll therefore know that no matter what happens they can at least earn a minimum guaranteed base rate.

IN SUMMARY: WHEN TO USE INCENTIVE PLANS

There are two bases on which you can compensate employees: time and output. Straight salary or wages involve compensating employees based on increments of time (such as hourly, daily, or weekly). Incentive plans (calling for piecework or commissions) involve compensating employees based on their output.[83] Under what conditions should you pay employees on a time basis? On an output (incentive) basis? Here are some guidelines (as summarized in Table 13.2).

When To Pay On A Time Basis

1. *When units of output are difficult to distinguish and measure.* Straight salary or wages (or perhaps a group incentive plan) is more appropriate here.
2. *When employees are unable to control quantity of output.* When employees have little control over the quantity of output (such as on machine-paced assembly lines) pay based on time is more appropriate.
3. *When delays in the work are frequent and beyond employees' control.* It is impractical to tie workers' pay to their output if production delays are beyond their control.

TABLE 13.2 **When to Base Pay on Incentives Instead of Time**

	BASE PAY ON INCENTIVES	BASE PAY ON TIME
Units of output	Easy to measure	Hard to measure
Employee's control of output	They can control it	They can't
Work delays	Under employee's control	Beyond employee's control
Quality	Not too important	Paramount
Good supervision and agreement on what is a "fair day's work"	No	Yes
Must know precise labor costs to stay competitive	Yes	No

4. *When quality considerations are especially important.* Virtually all incentive plans tie pay to the quantity, rather than the quality of output. When quality is a primary consideration pay based on time is more appropriate.
5. *When precise advance knowledge of unit labor costs is not required by competitive conditions.* Installing an incentive plan often requires an investment in industrial engineering, methods analysis, and computation of unit labor costs. If such precise cost control is not required by competitive conditions, it is probably not worthwhile to develop them just to install an incentive plan.

When Payment Should Be Based On Output (Incentive Plans)

Similarly, pay based on *output* would be preferable if:

1. Units of output can be measured.
2. There is a clear relationship between employee effort and quantity of output.
3. The job is standardized, the work flow is regular, and delays are few or consistent.
4. Quality is less important than quantity or, if quality is important, it is easily measured and controlled.
5. Competitive conditions require that unit table costs be known and precise.[84]

BUILDING EMPLOYEE COMMITMENT

Example of a Total Compensation Program

Progressive firms today are increasingly using at-risk pay, financial incentives, and various alternative rewards (such as spot awards). The aim is to boost quality and productivity by using innovative compensation tools as part of their commitment-building programs. Federal Express provides a good example.[85]

At Federal Express, quarterly pay reviews and periodic national and local salary surveys are used to maintain salary ranges and pay schedules that are competitive. Internal equity is maintained through the use of the Hay system of job evaluation. Under the Hay system, all salaried Federal Express positions are evaluated on three factors: know-how, problem solving, and accountability. For each job, points are assigned for each of the three factors, and the total number of points then equates to a corresponding grade level. (Each grade level has a range of job evaluation points.) Federal Express jobs are slotted into these grades based on the number of points as derived by the Hay system.

The result of all this job evaluation is a set of salary ranges such that salaries for each Federal Express position tend to be equitable relative to other Federal Express jobs. At the same time (thanks to the salary surveys), the base salaries are highly competitive as compared with similar jobs in the market. Federal Express defines market as "where we recruit" each pay group. The primary market for the pilot and maintenance groups is the airline/air freight industry, for instance. The pay rates of their direct competitors in the air freight industry are compared for the field and hub hourly pay group. The exempt salaried market consists of major national companies, since these jobs are recruited nationally. Nonexempt salaried employees generally are hired locally. Therefore, the local market is surveyed for this pay group to determine Federal Express's market position.

For virtually all Federal Express positions base salary alone would probably make pay competitive with market rates. However, there is also a heavy emphasis on pay-for-performance. As one manager put it, "We are convinced people want to see a relationship between performance and reward. . . . I think people want to know that when they knock themselves out to reach their part of our 100% customer satisfaction goal, their efforts will not go unnoticed."[86] Federal Express therefore has as number of pay-for-performance programs.

Merit Program. All salaried employees receive merit salary increases based on their individual performance. Many hourly employees also now receive merit increases rather than automatic step progression increases to recognize individual performance. The performance appraisal process at Federal Express provides the vehicle for rating employees' performance and for "sharing that information for the individual's development and making pay increase recommendations based on sustained performance. It is [therefore] essential that performance appraisals are fair and accurately measure performance to ensure the integrity of the pay-for-performance principle."[87]

Pro Pay. Many hourly Federal Express employees can receive lump-sum merit bonuses once they reach the top of their pay range. Pro Pay is paid only if the employee has been at the top of his or her pay range for a specified period of time (normally six months) and it's only paid if he or she has had an above-average performance review.

Star/Superstar Program. Salaried employees with a specified performance rating may be nominated for a Star or Superstar bonus. Employees who are designated a Star or Superstar receive a lump-sum bonus. Stars represent up to the top 10% of performers in each division, while Superstars represent up to the top 1% of performers in each division.

Profit Sharing. Federal Express's profit-sharing plan distributes profits based on the overall profit levels of the corporation. The board of directors annually sets the amount paid, based on pretax profits. Payments to the plan can be in the form of stock, cash, or both and are usually made semiannually in June and December. The plan is designed to integrate with the firm's pension and savings plans to provide a comprehensive retirement program.

MBO/MIC and PBO/PIC Programs. These are individual incentive plans for managers and professionals. They were developed to provide management and many exempt employees the opportunity to receive financial rewards for helping attain corporate, departmental, and divisional objectives. The MIC and PIC programs (management incentive compensation and professional incentive compensation) components generally reward achievement of divisional and corporate profit goals.[88] The MBO (or PBO) bonuses are tied to individual attainment of people, service, or profit-related goals. Thus for a regional sales manager, a "people" goal could be an improvement in the person's leadership index score on the firm's annual survey feedback action survey.[89]

Bravo Zulu Voucher Program. The Bravo Zulu Voucher Program was established to give managers the ability to provide immediate rewards to employees for outstanding performance above and beyond the normal requirements of the job. Bravo Zulu vouchers may be in the form of a check or may include some other form of reward (such as dinner vouchers or theater tickets). (Bravo Zulu is a title borrowed from the U.S. Navy's semaphore signal for "well done.") It's estimated that more than 150,000 times a year a Federal Express manager presents an employee with one of these awards which averages about $50.[90]

Golden Falcon Award. The Golden Falcon Award is given to permanent employees who demonstrate service to customers that is above and beyond the call of duty. Candidates are usually nominated based on unsolicited internal or external customer letters citing the candidate's outstanding performance. Nominated candidates are reviewed by the Golden Falcon committee and the final selection is made by the chief operating officer. Winners are announced monthly through company publications and/or video programs. They receive a Golden Falcon lapel pin and shares of Federal Express common stock.

With the exception of the merit program, all of these pay-for-performance programs are forms of **variable compensation**. In other words, Pro Pay, Star/Superstar, profit sharing, MBO/MIC, PBO/PIC, Bravo Zulu, and Golden Falcon awards are paid as one-time lump-sum awards, separate from base pay. They all let the company reward outstanding performance without permanently increasing its fixed payroll costs. The variability also reflects changes in business conditions and allows Federal Express to react to adverse economic conditions while maintaining its full employment policy.

variable compensation Financial rewards paid as one-time awards that do not permanently increase fixed payroll costs.

Like other progressive firms, Federal Express also offers a feast of worker benefits. We will discuss such benefits in Chapter 14.

Small Business Applications

In addition to the incentives-implementation methods discussed to this point, there are several other hints that will improve incentive-planned effectiveness.

ADAPT INCENTIVES FOR NONEXEMPTS TO THE FAIR LABOR STANDARDS ACT

Particularly for smaller companies that may not be familiar with this problem, it is important to keep in mind that under the FLSA, only certain kinds of bonuses are excludable from overtime pay calculations.[91] The basic problem is that overtime rates must be paid to nonexempt employees based on their previous week's earnings, and unless the incentive bonuses are structured properly the amount of the bonuses themselves becomes part of the week's wages. They must then be included in base pay when computing any overtime that week.

Certain bonuses are excludable from overtime pay calculations. For example, Christmas and gift bonuses that are not based on employees' hours worked, or paid pursuant to a contract, or so substantial that employees consider them a part of their wages do not have to be included in overtime pay calculations. Similarly, purely discretionary bonuses in which the employer retains discretion over whether the bonus will be paid and the amount of the bonus are also excludable.

The problem is that many other types of incentive pay definitely must be included in your calculations. Under the FLSA, bonuses to be included in overtime pay computations include those promised to newly hired employees; those provided in union contracts or other agreements; and those announced to induce employees to work more productively, steadily, rapidly, or efficiently or to induce them to remain with the company. Such bonuses would include individual and group production bonuses, bonuses for quality and accuracy of work, efficiency bonuses, attendance bonuses, length-of-service bonuses, and sales commissions.[92]

To see how incentive bonuses can impact overtime pay, consider the following example. Alison works 45 hours in a particular week at a straight time rate of $5.00 an hour. In that week she also earns a production bonus of $18.00. Her new regular rate for that week becomes 45 × $5.00 = $225.00 + $18.00 = $243.00, and $243.00 divided by 45 equals $5.40 per hour. Her new hourly rate is therefore $5.40 per hour for that week. Additional half-time pay is due her for the 5 hours overtime she worked. Her total weekly pay for that week is therefore $243.00 + 5 (½ times $5.40) = $256.50.

The problem can be even more complicated with gainsharing and other productivity-related bonuses since these are usually paid over intervals longer than a single pay period. Here, determining the new regular rate for overtime pay calculations can be deferred until after the bonus is determined. However, at that point the bonus must be apportioned over the workweeks in which it was earned. This actually requires employers to go back and recalculate overtime rates for all of those weeks, retroactively. This can be very time-consuming, as you can imagine.

According to one expert, an expeditious way of getting around this problem is to design your incentive bonuses as a percentage-of-wage bonus.[93] Basing the bonus awarded on a percentage of each employee's total pay—straight time and overtime for the period involved—protects the company from liability for any additional overtime pay under the FLSA. One way to do it is to design the incentive plan so that it generates a percentage that is applied to all wages. For example, each employee is paid a bonus equal to a predetermined percentage of his or her salary. This percentage can be based on the number of weeks he or she is in the plan, or the person's level of participation, or some other criteria.

CONSIDER THE CURRENT BUSINESS STAGE OF THE COMPANY

In designing your incentive plan, you should also consider your firm's life-cycle stage.[94] For example, small companies experiencing rapid growth usually prefer a broader based profit-sharing plan to the more complicated individual incentive- or gainsharing-type plans. For one thing, profit-sharing plans tend to be simpler and less expensive to implement and require much less planning and administrative paperwork. Furthermore, small firms' employees tend to feel a more direct tie to the company's profitability than do those embedded in much larger firms. Similarly, companies in a survival or turnaround situation or ones threatened by takeover may also opt for less complicated profit-sharing plans.

That way top and middle managers can focus all their energies on the crisis rather than on the administrative effort required to implement gainsharing or individualized incentive plans.

STRESS PRODUCTIVITY AND QUALITY MEASURES IF POSSIBLE

Remember that profitability is not always the same as productivity and that it is usually productivity and quality for which employees should be held accountable, not profitability. The reason is that productivity and quality are controllable, whereas profitability may be influenced by factors like competition and government regulations. As a result, unless it is a more simple overall profit-sharing plan that you are opting for, be careful to formulate your productivity and/or quality standards carefully, focusing on measures that employees can actually control.

GET EMPLOYEE INPUT IN SYSTEM DESIGN

It is usually a mistake to implement an incentive plan without input from your employees. Therefore, many employers use a program design team composed of selected employees and supervisors. They work with the compensation specialist in the development of the plan, perhaps by explaining idiosyncrasies that need to be taken into consideration or by helping them understand the culture and attitudes in the plant.

▶ CHAPTER REVIEW

SUMMARY

1. The scientific use of financial incentives can be traced back to Frederick Taylor. While such incentives became somewhat less popular during the human relations era, most writers today agree that they can be quite effective.
2. Piecework is the oldest type of incentive plan. Here a worker is paid a piece rate for each unit he or she produces. With a *straight* piecework plan, workers are paid on the basis of the number of units produced. With a *guaranteed* piecework plan each worker receives his or her base rate (such as the minimum wage) regardless of how many units he or she produces.
3. Other useful incentive plans for plant personnel include the standard hour plan and group incentive plans. The former rewards workers by a percent premium that equals the percent by which their performance is above standard. Group incentive plans are useful where the workers' jobs are highly interrelated.
4. Several incentive plans for white-collar personnel were discussed. Most sales personnel are paid on some type of salary plus commission (incentive) basis. The trouble with straight commission is that there is a tendency to focus on "big-ticket" or "quick-sell" items and to disregard long-term customer building. Management employees are often paid according to some bonus formula that ties the bonus to, for example, increased sales. Stock options are one of the most popular executive incentive plans.

5. Profit sharing and the Scanlon plan are examples of organization-wide incentive plans. The problem with such plans is that the link between a person's efforts and rewards is sometimes unclear. On the other hand, such plans may contribute to developing a sense of commitment among employees. Gainsharing and merit plans are two other popular plans.
6. When incentive plans fail it is usually because (a) the worker does not believe that effort on his or her part will lead to obtaining the reward, or (b) the reward is not important to the person. Specific incentive plan problems therefore include unfair standards, fear of a rate cut, group restrictions, lack of understanding, and lack of required tools or training.
7. We suggest using incentive plans when units of output are easily measured, employees can control output, the effort–reward relationship is clear, work delays are under employee's control, quality is not paramount, and the organization must know precise labor costs anyway (to stay competitive).

KEY TERMS

Frederick Taylor
fair day's work
scientific management
piecework
straight piecework
guaranteed piecework plan
standard hour plan
team or group incentive plan
attendance incentive plan
annual bonus
capital accumulation programs
stock option
special awards
merit pay
merit raise
profit-sharing plan
Employee Stock Ownership Plan (ESOP)
Scanlon plan
gainsharing
variable compensation

DISCUSSION QUESTIONS

1. Compare and contrast six types of incentive plans.
2. Explain five reasons why incentive plans fail.
3. Describe the nature of some important management incentives.
4. When and why would you pay a salesperson a salary? A commission? Salary and commission combined?

APPLICATION EXERCISES

RUNNING CASE

CARTER CLEANING COMPANY

The Incentive Plan

The question of whether to pay Carter Cleaning Center employees an hourly wage or an incentive of some kind has always intrigued Jack Carter.

His basic policy has been to pay employees an hourly wage, except that his managers do receive an end-of-year bonus depending, as Jack puts it, "on whether their stores do well or not that year."

He has, however, experimented in one store with incentive plans, with mixed results. Jack knows that a presser should press about 25 "tops" (jackets, dresses, blouses) per hour. Most of his pressers do not attain this ideal standard, though. In one instance, a presser named Walt was paid $6 per hour, and Jack noticed that regardless of the amount of work he had to do, Walt always ended up making about $180 at the end of the week. If it was a holiday week, for instance, and there were a lot of clothes to press he might average 22 to 23 tops per hour (someone else did pants) and so he'd earn perhaps $190 to 200 and still finish up each day in time to leave by 3:00 P.M. so he could pick up his children at school. But when things were very slow in the store his productivity would drop to perhaps 12 to 15 pieces an hour, so that at the end of the week he'd still end up earning close to $180, and in fact not go home much earlier than he did when it was busy.

Jack spoke with Walt several times and while Walt always promised to try to do better, it gradually became apparent to Jack that Walt was simply going to earn his $180 per week no matter what. While Walt never told him so directly it dawned on Jack that Walt had a family to support and was not about to earn less than his "target" wage regardless of how busy or slow the store was. The problem was the longer Walt kept pressing each day the longer the steam boilers and compressors had to be kept on to power his machines and the fuel charges alone ran close to $5 per hour. Jack clearly needed some way short of firing Walt to solve the problem, since the fuel bills were eating up his profits.

His solution was to tell Walt that instead of an hourly $6 wage he would henceforth pay him 25 cents per item pressed. That way, said Jack to himself, if he presses 25 items per hour at 25 cents he will in effect get a small raise and will get more items pressed per hour and will therefore be able to shut the machines down earlier.

On the whole, the experiment worked well. Walt generally presses 25 to 35 pieces per hour now. He gets to leave earlier, and with the small increase in pay he generally earns his target wage. Two problems have arisen though. The quality of Walt's work dipped a bit, and his manager has to spend a minute or two each hour counting the number of pieces Walt pressed that hour. Otherwise Jack is fairly pleased with the results of his incentive plan and he's wondering whether to extend it to other employees and other stores.

Questions

1. Should this plan in its present form be extended to pressers in the other stores?
2. Should other employees be put on a similar plan? Why? Why not?
3. Is there another incentive plan you think would work better for the pressers?
4. A store manager's basic job is to keep total wages to no more than 30% of sales and to maintain both the fuel bill and the supply bill at about 9% of sales. Managers can also directly affect sales by ensuring courteous customer service and by ensuring that the work is done properly. What suggestions would you make to Jennifer and her father for an incentive plan for store managers?

CASE INCIDENT *Sales Quotas*

The Superior Floor Covering Company has an incentive program for its salespeople. Incentive earnings are based on the amount of sales in relation to an assigned quota.

The quota is computed each year by management, taking into account the number and type of customers in each salesperson's territory and the previous year's sales records for the company and for its competitors. In the administration of this incentive program, the following problems have arisen. Suggest the solutions you would consider in elimination these difficulties. Note also the parallels between the problems here and those involving blue-collar, manufacturing incentive plans.

Questions

1. Some of the best salespeople now have too many accounts in the area assigned to them. From the company's point of view, it would be advantageous to reduce the size of the districts covered by each of these representatives and to add several new salespeople who could give more thorough coverage. The outstanding salespeople resent this proposal, however, claiming that it would penalize them for their success.

2. The top-earning salespeople also complain that their base quotas increase each year, reflecting their previous success. This, too, they feel is discrimination against success.
3. Management believes that the company is not acquiring as many new accounts as it should. So-called missionary work, trying to induce a store that has not previously purchased Superior products to become a customer, takes more time and energy than selling old customers. Also, the results of this missionary work may not show up for several years. The present incentive plan gives no credit for this type of work.
4. When business is booming within a salesperson's territory, he or she may receive high bonus earnings even without great effort. When there is a great deal of unemployment in the territory or when competition decides to lower prices to penetrate this new market, his or her bonus earnings may decline even though sales efforts are at a maximum.

Source: George Strauss and Leonard R. Sayles, *Personnel: The Human Problems of Management*, 4th ed. (Englewood Cliffs, NJ: Prentice Hall, 1980), p. 636. Reprinted by permission.

HUMAN RESOURCE MANAGEMENT SIMULATION

Incident G gives your team an opportunity to select a compensation plan for the firm. In making your selection, you may want to consider your organization's short-term needs with the idea that you can develop a longer-range plan at a later date.

NOTES

1. Jude Rich, "Meeting the Global Challenge: A Measurement and Reward Program for the Future," *Compensation and Benefits Review* (July–August 1992), p. 27.
2. Ibid., p. 28.
3. Richard Henderson, *Compensation Management* (Reston, VA: Reston, 1979), p. 363. For a discussion of the increasing use of incentives for blue-collar employees, see, for example, Richard Henderson, "Contract Concessions: Is the Past Prologue?" *Compensation and Benefits Review*, Vol. 18, no. 5 (September–October 1986), pp. 17–30.
4. David Belcher, *Compensation Administration* (Englewood Cliffs, NJ: Prentice Hall, 1973), p. 314.
5. For a discussion of these, see Thomas Wilson, "Is It Time to Eliminate the Piece Rate Incentive System?" *Compensation and Benefits Review* (March–April 1992), pp. 43–49.
6. *Measured day work* is a third type of individual incentive plan for production workers. See, for example, Mitchell Fein, "Let's Return to MDW for Incentives," *Industrial Engineering* (January 1979), pp. 34–37.
7. Henderson, *Compensation Management*, pp. 367–368. See also David Swinehart, "A Guide for More Productive Team Incentive Programs," *Personnel Journal*, Vol. 65, no. 7 (July 1986).
8. James Nickel and Sandra O'Neal, "Small Group Incentives: Gainsharing in the Microcosm," *Compensation and Benefits Review* (March–April 1990), p. 24.
9. Jon P. Alston, "Awarding Bonuses the Japanese Way," *Business Horizons*, Vol. 25 (September–October 1982), pp. 6–8.
10. See, for example, Peter Daly, "Selecting and Assigning a Group Incentive Plan," *Management Review* (December 1975), pp. 33–45. For an explanation of how to develop a successful group incentive program, see K. Dow Scott and Timothy Cotter, "The Team That Works Together Earns Together," *Personnel Journal*, Vol. 63 (March 1984), pp. 59–67.
11. Manuel London and Greg Oldham, "A Comparison of Group and Individual Incentive Plans," *Academy of Management Journal,"* Vol. 20, no. 1 (1977), pp. 34–41. Note that the study was carried out under controlled conditions in a laboratory setting. See also Thomas Rollins, "Productivity-Based Group Incentive Plans: Powerful, But Use with Caution," *Compensation and Benefits Review,* Vol. 21, no. 3 (May–June 1989), pp. 39–50; discusses several popular group incentive plans, including gainsharing, and lists dos and don'ts for using them.
12. W. E. Reum and Sherry Reum, "Employee Stock Ownership Plans: Pluses and Minuses," *Harvard Business Review,* Vol. 55 (July–August 1976), pp. 133–143; Ralph Bavier, "Managerial Bonuses," *Industrial Management* (March–April 1978), pp. 1–5. See also James Thompson, L. Murphy Smith, and Alicia Murray, "Management Performance Incentives: Three Critical Issues," *Compensation and Benefits Review*, Vol. 18, no. 5 (September–October

1986), pp. 41–47.
13. Bureau of National Affairs, *Bulletin to Management*, January 6, 1983, p. 1.
14. James Brinks, "Executive Compensation: Crossroads of the 80s," *Personnel Administrator*, Vol. 26 (December 1981), p. 24.
15. "Long-Term Incentives: Trends and Approaches," *Personnel*, Vol. 57 (July–August 1982), pp. 60–61.
16. S. B. Prasod, "Top Management Compensation and Corporate Performance," *Academy of Management Journal* (September 1974), pp. 554–558; John Bouike, "Performance Bonus Plans: Boom for Managers and Stockholders," *Management Review* (November 1975), pp. 13, 18; "How Pay and Save Grows and Grows," *Forbes*, April 16, 1979, p. 113.
17. Bruce R. Ellig, "Incentive Plans: Short-Term Design Issues," *Compensation Review*, Vol. 16, no. 3 (Third Quarter 1984), pp. 26–36.
18. Bruce Ellig, *Executive Compensation—A Total Pay Perspective* (New York: McGraw–Hill, 1982), p. 187.
19. Ibid., p. 187.
20. Ibid., p. 188.
21. See, for example, Bavier, "Managerial Bonuses," pp. 1–5. See also Charles Tharp, "Linking Annual Incentive Awards to Individual Performance," *Compensation and Benefits Review*, Vol. 17 (November–December 1985), pp. 38–43.
22. Ellig, *Executive Compensation*, p. 189.
23. F. Dean Hildebrand, Jr., "Individual Performance Incentives," *Compensation Review*, Vol. 10 (Third Quarter 1978), p. 32.
24. Ibid., pp. 28–33.
25. Edward Redling, "The 1981 Tax Act: Boom to Managerial Compensation," *Personnel*, Vol. 57 (March–April 1982), pp. 26–35.
26. The following based on ibid.
27. See both William M. Mercer–Meidinger, Inc., "How Will Reform Tax Your Benefits?" *Personnel Journal*, Vol. 65, no. 12 (December 1986), pp. 49–63, and Jack H. Schechter, "The Tax Reform Act of 1986: Its Impact on Compensation and Benefits," *Compensation and Benefits Review*, Vol. 18, no. 6 (November–December 1986), pp. 11–24.
28. See also Paul Bradley, "Justify Executive Bonuses to the Board," *Personnel Journal* (September 1988), pp. 116–125, and his "Long Term Incentives: International Executives Need Them Too," *Personnel* (August 1988), pp. 40–42.
29. Belcher, *Compensation Administration*, p. 548; Schechter, "The Tax Reform Act of 1986," p. 23. See also Rein Linney and Charles Marshall, "ISOs vs. NQSOs: The Choice Still Exists," *Compensation and Benefits Review*, Vol. 19, no. 1 (January–February 1987), pp. 13–25.
30. Basically, book value per share equals the firm's assets minus its prior (basically debt) liabilities, divided by the number of shares. See, for example, John Annas, "Facing Today's Compensation Uncertainties," *Personnel*, Vol. 33, no. 1 (January–February 1976).
31. Ray Stata and Modesto Maidique, "Bonus System for Balanced Strategy," *Harvard Business Review*, Vol. 59 (November–December 1980), pp. 156–163; Alfred Rappaport, "Executive Incentives Versus Corporate Growth," *Harvard Business Review*, Vol. 57 (July–August 1978), pp. 81–88. See also Crystal Graef, "Rendering Long-Term Incentives Less Risky for Executives," *Personnel*, Vol. 65, no. 9 (September 1988), pp. 80–84.
32. Ira Kay, "Beyond Stock Options: Emerging Practices in Executive Incentive Programs," *Compensation and Benefits Review* (November–December 1991), p. 19.
33. For a discussion see ibid., pp. 18–29.
34. Jeffrey Kanter and Matthew Ward, "Long-Term Incentives for Management, Part 4: Performance Plans," *Compensation and Benefits Review* (January–February 1990), p. 36.
35. Jude Rich and John Larson, "Why Some Long-Term Incentives Fail," *Compensation Review*, Vol. 16 (First Quarter 1984), pp. 26–37. See also Eric Marquardt, "Stock Option Grants: Is Timing Everything?" *Compensation and Benefits Review*, Vol. 20, no. 5 (September–October 1988), pp. 18–22.
36. Robert Klein, "Compensating Your Overseas Executives, Part 3: Exporting U.S. Stock Option Plans to Expatriates," *Compensation and Benefits Review* (January–February 1991), pp. 27–38.
37. For a discussion see ibid.
38. This section based primarily on John Steinbrink, "How to Pay Your Sales Force," *Harvard Business Review*, Vol. 57 (July–August 1978), pp. 111–122.
39. Straight salary by itself is not, of course, an incentive compensation plan as we use the term in this chapter.
40. Steinbrink, "How to Pay," p. 112.
41. T. H. Patten, "Trends in Pay Practices for Salesmen," *Personnel*, Vol. 43 (January–February 1968), pp. 54–63.
42. Steinbrink, "How to Pay," p. 115.
43. In the salary plus bonus plan, salespeople are paid a basic salary and are then paid a bonus for carrying out specified activities. For a discussion of how to develop a customer-focused sales compensation plan, see, for example, Mark Blessington, "Designing a Sales Strategy with the Customer in Mind," *Compensation and Benefits Review* (March–April 1992), pp. 30–41.
44. This is based on "Sales Incentives Get the Job Done," *Sales and Marketing Management*, September 14, 1981, pp. 67–120.
45. See, for example, Herbert Meyer, "The Pay for Performance Dilemma," *Organizational Dynamics* (Winter 1975), pp. 39–50; Thomas Patten, Jr., "Pay for Performance or Placation?" *Personnel Administrator*, Vol. 24 (September 1977), pp. 26–29; William Kearney, "Pay for Performance? Not Always," *MSU Business Topics* (Spring 1979), pp. 5–16. See also Hoyt Doyel and Janet Johnson, "Pay Increase Guidelines with Merit," *Personnel Journal*, Vol. 64 (June 1985), pp. 46–50.
46. Nathan Winstanley, "Are Merit Increases Really Effective?" *Personnel Administrator*, Vol. 27 (April 1982), pp. 37–41. See also William Seithel and Jeff Emans, "Calculating Merit Increases: A Structured Approach," *Personnel*, Vol. 60, no. 5 (June 1985), pp. 56–68.
47. James T. Brinks, "Is There Merit in Merit Increases?" *Personnel Administrator*, Vol. 25 (May 1980), p. 60.
48. *Merit Pay: Fitting the Pieces Together* (Chicago: Commerce Clearing House, 1982).
49. Suzanne Minken, "Does Lump Sum Pay Merit Attention?" *Personnel Journal* (June 1988), pp. 77–83. Two experts suggest using neither straight merit pay nor lump sum merit pay but rather tying the merit payment to the duration of the impact of the employee's work so that, for instance, the merit raise might last for two or three years. See Jerry Newman and Daniel Fisher, "Strategic Impact Merit Pay," *Compensation and Benefits Review* (July–August 1992), pp. 38–45.
50. John F. Sullivan, "The Future of Merit Pay Programs," *Compensation and Benefits Review* (May–June 1988), pp. 22–30.
51. This section based primarily on Robert Sibson, *Compensation* (New York: AMACOM, 1981), pp. 189–207.
52. Michael Sprat and Bernadette Steele, "Rewarding Key Contributors," *Compensation and Benefits Review*, Vol. 17 (July–August 1985), pp. 24–37.

53. Kyle Burns, "A Bonus Plan That Promotes Customer Service," *Compensation and Benefits Review* (September–October 1992), pp. 15–20.
54. See ibid., pp. 16–17.
55. Bert Metzger and Jerome Colletti, "Does Profit Sharing Pay?" (Evanston, IL: Profit Sharing Research Foundation, 1971), quoted in Belcher, *Compensation Administration*, p. 353. See also D. Keith Denton, "An Employee Ownership Program That Rebuilt Success," *Personnel Journal*, Vol. 66, no. 3 (March 1987), pp. 114–118.
56. Belcher, *Compensation Administration*, p. 351.
57. Mary O'Connor, "Employee Profit Sharing in Japan," *Personnel Journal*, Vol. 60 (August 1981), p. 614.
58. Based on Randy Swad, "Stock Ownership Plans: A New Employee Benefit," *Personnel Journal*, Vol. 60 (June 1981), pp. 453–455.
59. See James Brockardt and Robert Reilly, "Employee Stock Ownership Plans After the 1989 Tax Law: Valuation Issues," *Compensation and Benefits Review* (September–October 1990), pp. 29–36.
60. Donald Sullivan, "ESOPs," *California Management Review*, Vol. 20, no. 1 (Fall 1977), pp. 55–56. For a discussion of the effects of employee stock ownership on employee attitudes, see Katherine Klein, "Employee-Stock Ownership and Employee Attitudes: A Test of Three Models," *Journal of Applied Psychology*, Vol. 72, no. 2 (May 1987), pp. 319–331.
61. Everett Allen, Jr., Joseph Melone, and Jerry Rosenbloom, *Pension Planning* (Homewood, IL: Irwin, 1981), p. 316. Note that the Tax Reduction Act of 1975 has also led to the creation of the so-called TRAFOP. This is basically a regular employee stock ownership plan, except that a portion of the investment tax credit that employers receive for investing in capital equipment can be invested in the employee stock ownership plan.
62. William Smith, Harold Lazarus, and Harold Murray Kalkstein, "Employee Stock Ownership Plans: Motivation and Morale Issues," *Compensation and Benefits Review* (September–October 1990), pp. 37–46.
63. Brian Moore and Timothy Ross, *The Scanlon Way to Improved Productivity: A Practical Guide* (New York: Wiley, 1978), p. 2.
64. These are based in part on Steven Markham, K. Dow Scott, and Walter Cox, Jr., "The Evolutionary Development of a Scanlon Plan," *Compensation and Benefits Review* (March–April 1992), pp. 50–56.
65. J. Kenneth White, "The Scanlon Plan: Causes and Correlates of Success," *Academy of Management Journal*, Vol. 22 (June 1979), pp. 292–312.
66. Markham et al., "The Evolutionary Development of a Scanlon Plan," p. 51.
67. Moore and Ross, *The Scanlon Way*, pp. 1–2.
68. George Sherman, "The Scanlon Plan: Its Capabilities for Productive Improvement," *Personnel Administrator* (July 1976).
69. White, "The Scanlon Plan," pp. 292–312. For a discussion of the Improshare plan see Roger Kaufman, "The Effects of Improshare on Productivity," *Industrial and Labor Relations Review*, Vol. 45, no. 2, 1991, pp. 311–322.
70. Barry W. Thomas and Madeline Hess Olson, "Gainsharing: The Design Guarantees Success," *Personnel Journal* (May 1988), pp. 73–79.
71. See Theresa A. Welbourne and Louis Gomez–Mejia, "Gainsharing Revisited," *Compensation and Benefits Review* (July–August 1988), pp. 19–28.
72. Carla O'Dell and Jerry McAdams, *People, Performance, and Pay* (American Productivity Center and Carla O'Dell, 1987), p. 34.
73. Thomas and Olson, "Gainsharing," pp. 75–76.
74. O'Dell & McAdams, *People, Performance, and Pay*, p. 42.
75. Jeffrey Ewing, "Gainsharing Plans: Two Key Factors," *Compensation and Benefits Review* (January–February 1989), pp. 49–53.
76. See, for example, Moore and Ross, *The Scanlon Way to Improved Productivity*, pp. 157–164; Ewing, "Gainsharing Plans," pp. 51–52. For a description of the implementation of a gainsharing plan in health care institutions see Steven Markham et al., "Gainsharing Experiments in Health Care," *Compensation and Benefits Review* (March–April 1992), pp. 57–64.
77. Robert McNutt, "Sharing Across the Board: DuPont's Achievement Sharing Program," *Compensation and Benefits Review* (July–August 1990), pp. 17–24.
78. See Ronald Goettinger, "Why Isn't Your Incentive Compensation Working?" *Personnel Journal*, Vol. 60 (November 1981), pp. 840–841.
79. Robert Opsahl and Marvin Dunnette, "The Role of Financial Compensation in Industrial Motivation," *Psychological Bulletin*, Vol. 66 (1966), pp. 94–118.
80. See for example James Gutherie and Edward Cunningham, "Pay for Performance: The Quaker Oats Alternative," *Compensation and Benefits Review*, Vol. 24, no. 2, March–April, 1992, pp. 18–23.
81. Gary Yukl and Gary Latham, "Consequences of Reinforcement Schedules and Incentives Magnitudes fcr Employee Performance: Problems Encountered in an Industrial Setting," *Journal of Applied Psychology*, Vol. 60 (June 1975).
82. Louden and Deagan, *Wage Incentives*, p. 26.
83. Based on Belcher, *Compensation Administration*, pp. 309–311. See also Edward Lawler III, "Reward Systems," in J. R. Hackman and J. L. Suttle, *Improving Life at Work* (Santa Monica, CA: Goodyear, 1977), pp. 191–219. See also Kent E. Romanoff, "The Ten Commandments of Performance Management," *Personnel*, Vol. 66, no. 1 (January 1989), pp. 24–28.
84. Belcher, *Compensation Administration*, pp. 309–310.
85. The following is based on Gary Dessler, *Winning Commitment* (New York: McGraw–Hill Book Company, 1993), Chapter 9.
86. Blueprints for Service Quality: The Federal Express Approach (New York: AMA Membership Publication Division, 1991), pp. 31–32.
87. "Compensation at Federal Express," company document, P. 8.
88. Unless otherwise indicated the section on pay-for-performance is based on "Compensation at Federal Express," pp. 8–9.
89. Blueprints for Service Quality, p. 32.
90. Blueprints for Service Quality, pp. 34–35.
91. This is based on William E. Buhl, "Keeping Incentives Simple for Nonexempt Employees," *Compensation and Benefits Review* (March–April 1989), pp. 14–19.
92. Ibid., pp. 15–16.
93. Ibid., pp. 17–18.
94. The following are based on Michael J. Cissell, "Designing Effective Reward Systems," *Compensation and Benefits Review* (November–December 1987), pp. 49–56.

CHAPTER 14

BENEFITS AND SERVICES

OVERVIEW

In this chapter we discuss four types of employee benefits plans: supplemental pay benefits (such as unemployment insurance), insurance benefits (such as worker's compensation), retirement benefits (such as pensions), and employee services (such as dining facilities). We explain that employees' preferences for various benefit plans differ, and it is therefore useful to individualize an organization's benefits package. When you finish studying this chapter, you should be able to explain the main features of at least 10 employee benefit plans; cite the policy areas that must be considered in regard to vacations and holidays; cite the four key policy areas involved in pension plans; and discuss how employees' ages affect their choice of benefits.

▶ Introduction

benefits
Any supplements to wages given to employees. They may include health and life insurance, vacation, pension, education plans, and discounts on company products, for instance.

Financial incentives are paid to *specific* employees whose work is above standard. Employee **benefits,** on the other hand, are available to all employees and include such things as health and life insurance, vacations, and child care facilities.

Administering benefits today represents an increasingly specialized and expensive task. It demands specialized expertise because workers are becoming more sophisticated in financial matters and are therefore demanding new types of benefits, and because federal legislation—concerning pregnancy benefits, for instance—requires that benefit plans comply with new laws. Furthermore, benefit plans became increasingly expensive to administer during the 1980s. Benefit costs as a percentage of payroll rose from 25.5% in 1961 to about 38% today. That translated to about $6.00 per payroll hour, or $12,402 per year per employee in 1992 according to the U.S. Chamber of Commerce.[1] In terms of the costs of specific benefits, payments for time not worked (vacations, sick days, and so on) represent just over 10% of the average employer's payroll. Medical and related benefits account for about 10% of payroll; legally required benefits (Social Security, for instance) represent almost 9%; and other benefits including retirement and savings plans and life insurance account for the remaining 8.5% of payroll taken up by benefits.[2]

Unfortunately, employees often don't know the market value and high cost (to the employer) of their benefits. The results of one study indicate that this problem can be overcome with what the researchers call an information-enhancement approach. This involves, for instance, indicating the benefits' true cost on each employee's pay stub.

There are many benefit plans, and to simplify our discussion, they are classified as (1) pay supplements (for time not worked), (2) insurance benefits, (3) retirement benefits, (4) services.

▶ Supplemental Pay Benefits

supplemental pay benefits
Benefits for time not worked such as unemployment insurance, vacation and holiday pay, and sick pay.

All firms provide **supplemental pay benefits**—benefits, in other words, for time not worked. These include unemployment insurance (if the person is laid off), vacation and holiday pay, sick pay, severance pay (if the person is terminated), and supplemental unemployment benefits (which guarantee income if the plant is closed down for a period). We'll discuss each benefit in turn.

UNEMPLOYMENT INSURANCE

unemployment insurance
Provides weekly benefits if a person is unable to work through some fault other than his or her own.

All states have **unemployment insurance** or compensation acts. These provide for weekly benefits if a person is unable to work through some fault other than his or her own. The benefits derive from an *unemployment tax* on employers that can range from 0.1% to 5% of taxable payroll in most states. States (to repeat) each have their own unemployment laws; however, these all follow federal guidelines. Your organization's unemployment tax reflects its experience with personnel terminations.

Unemployment benefits are meant for workers who are terminated through no fault of their own. Thus (strictly speaking), a worker who is fired for chronic lateness does not have a legitimate claim to benefits. But in practice many managers take a lackadaisical attitude toward protecting their employers against unwarranted claims. Employers therefore end up spending thousands of dollars more per year on unemployment taxes than would be necessary if they protected themselves against such claims.

One way to protect your employer is by carefully reviewing the personnel procedures itemized in Table 14.1. Determine whether you could answer yes to questions such as "Do you tell employees whom to call when they're late?" or "Do you have a rule that three days absence without calling in is reason for automatic discharge?" By establishing policies and rules in these areas you will be

TABLE 14.1 An Unemployment Insurance Cost Control Survey

CAUSE—DO YOU . . .	YES	NO	SOMETIMES
Lateness			
1. Tell employees whom to call when late	____	____	____
2. Keep documented history of lateness and warning notices	____	____	____
3. Suspend chronically late employees before discharging them	____	____	____
Absenteeism			
1. Tell employees whom to call when absent	____	____	____
2. Rule that three days' absence without calling in is reason for automatic discharge	____	____	____
3. Keep documented history of absence and warning notices	____	____	____
4. Request doctor's note on return to work	____	____	____
Illness			
1. Keep job open, if possible	____	____	____
2. Offer leave of absence	____	____	____
3. Request doctor's note on return to work	____	____	____
Pregnancy			
1. Follow EEOC ruling, "no discharge"	____	____	____
2. Request doctor's note indicating how long employee may work	____	____	____
3. Change jobs within company when practical			
4. Offer maternity leave	____	____	____
Leave of Absence			
1. Make written approval mandatory	____	____	____
2. Stipulate date for return to work	____	____	____
3. Offer position at end of leave	____	____	____
Leave Job Voluntarily			
1. Conduct exit interview	____	____	____
2. Obtain a signed resignation statement	____	____	____
3. Mail job abandonment letter	____	____	____
4. Mail job review questionnaire three to six months after separation	____	____	____
Layoff			
1. Hire employees with established "benefit year" if you anticipate layoffs	____	____	____
2. Keep employees on when the cost to replace them would more than offset paying their salary	____	____	____
3. Transfer employees to different departments	____	____	____
4. Have a flexible workweek that reflects high and low periods of productivity	____	____	____

TABLE 14.1 (continued)

CAUSE—DO YOU . . .	YES	NO	SOME-TIMES
5. Temporarily lay off employees for one week during slack periods			
6. Attempt to find temporary or part-time jobs for laid-off employees			
Job Refusal			
1. Issue a formal notice to employees collecting benefits to return to work			
2. Require new employees to stipulate in writing their availability to work overtime, night shifts, etc.			
Not Qualified			
1. Set probationary periods to evaluate new employees			
2. Conduct follow-up interviews one to two months after hire			
Deliberate Unsatisfactory Performance			
1. Document all instances, recording when and how employees did not meet job requirements			
2. Require supervisors to document the steps taken to remedy the situation			
3. Require supervisors to document employee's refusal of advice and direction			
Violation of Company Rule			
1. Make sure all policies and rules of conduct are understood by all employees			
2. Require all employees to sign a statement acknowledging acceptance of these rules			
3. Meet with employee and fill out documented warning notice			
4. Discharge at the time violation occurs, or suspend			

CAUSE—DO YOU	YES	NO	SOME-TIMES
Wrong Benefit Charges			
1. Check state charge statement for			
(a) correct employee			
(b) correct benefit amount			
(c) correct period of liability			
Claim Handling			
1. Assign a claims supervisor or central office to process all separation information			
2. Respond to state claim forms on time			
3. Use proper terminology on claim form and attach documented evidence regarding separation			
4. Attend hearings and appeal unwarranted claims			
5. Conduct availability checks and rehire employees collecting benefits			
Administration			
1. Have a staff member who knows unemployment insurance laws and who			
(a) works with the personnel department to establish proper use of policies and procedures			
(b) anticipates and reports costly turnover trends			
(c) successfully protests unwarranted claims and charges for unemployment benefits			
(d) recommends appropriate tax remedies:			
1. Verify the contribution rate assigned by the state			
2. Test for Rate Modification			
3. Test for Voluntary Contribution and advisability of a joint account			

continued

TABLE 14.1 (continued)

CAUSE—DO YOU . . .	YES	NO	SOME-TIMES
4. Determine advantage of transfer of experience resulting from mergers, acquisition, or other corporate charges	____	____	____
Communication			
1. Hold periodic workshops with key personnel to review procedures and support effort to reduce turnover costs	____	____	____
2. Immediately investigate who or what is responsible for costly errors and why	____	____	____
Management Reports			
1. Point to turnover problems as they occur by			
(a) location	____	____	____
(b) department	____	____	____
(c) classification of employee	____	____	____
(d) job position			
2. Evaluate the effectiveness of current policies and procedures used to			
(a) recruit	____	____	____
(b) select	____	____	____
(c) train	____	____	____
(d) supervise	____	____	____
(e) separate	____	____	____
3. Help create policies and procedures for			
(a) less costly layoffs	____	____	____
(b) increased survival rate	____	____	____
(c) retention of employees	____	____	____

Explanation: Each "no" or "sometimes" answer represents an area where you lack control; each "yes" is a strong point that acts to save you money.

Source: Reprinted from the January 1976 issue of *Personnel Administrator*. Copyright 1976, the American Society for Personnel Administration.

able to show that an employee's termination was a result of the person's inadequate performance (rather than lack of work or some other cause beyond his or her control). Some additional guidelines for cutting unemployment insurance costs include:

The first step in filing an unemployment compensation claim is filling out the paperwork.

Understand the unemployment insurance code. Many states publish an updated employer's guide annually with names such as "Twenty-seven Ways to Avoid Losing Your Unemployment Appeal." You or someone on your staff should become an expert in understanding the unemployment insurance code in your state and how the system works.

Train managers and supervisors. Train your managers and supervisors to use a checklist such as the one in Table 14.1. Don't let otherwise ineligible, dismissed employees successfully apply for unemployment compensation.

Conduct exit interviews. If you conduct exit interviews with everyone who leaves your organization, you can use the information in protesting unemployment claims.

Verify unemployment claims. Remember to check every unemployment claim against the individual's personnel file. Make sure to double-check the reasons the employee gives for why he or she left your employ.

File on a timely basis. Make sure to file your protest (against a former employee's claim) on a timely basis. In most states you have 10 days in which to protest a claim.

Know your local unemployment insurance official. Most unemployment officers appreciate cooperative employers and are historically understaffed and overworked. Taking a hostile, adversarial position may undermine your ability to get the benefit of their doubt on a claim you might otherwise have won.

Audit the annual benefit charges statement. Once a year you will receive a benefit charges statement regarding the status of your unemployment compensation account. Thoroughly audit this since errors (such as inaccurate charges against your account) may be included in it.[3]

In summary, persons in most states are eligible for unemployment benefits if they were terminated through no fault of their own. If they quit without good cause or if they refuse a suitable position or if they are discharged through misconduct of some type, they are *not* eligible. Your unemployment tax is based on the number of former employees who are eligible for (and receive) unemployment benefits. It is therefore to the employer's advantage to set clear policies and procedures concerning matters such as lateness, absenteeism, and job refusal.

VACATIONS AND HOLIDAYS

Specific policies concerning holidays and vacations vary from employer to employer. Paid vacations may vary from 1 week per year to 4 weeks or more. Paid holidays may range from a minimum of 4 or 5 to as many as 13 or more. But regardless of the organization, there are certain key personnel policy areas that must be addressed.[4]

Eligibility requirements. Your plan should specify the length of service required in order to earn vacations and the length of vacation time. Some plans call for the employee gradually to accumulate vacation time, for example, one hour of vacation time for each week of service.

Vacation pay. Some plans give the employee his or her regular base rate of pay while on vacation; others provide for vacation pay based on average earnings.

Earned right. Some organizations provide for accrued vacation time that is paid if an employee leaves before taking his or her vacation.

With respect to *holidays*, key personnel policy areas include:

Number of paid holidays. This varies from a minimum of about 5 to 13 or more. Some common holidays are

New Year's Day	Thanksgiving Day
Memorial Day	Martin Luther King's Birthday
Independence Day	President's Day
Labor Day	Christmas Day
Veterans' Day	

Provision for holidays on a Saturday or Sunday. Employees are often given the following Monday off when the holiday falls on a Sunday and Friday off when a holiday falls on a Saturday.

Premium pay for work on a regular holiday. Most organizations provide for some premium—such as time-and-a-half—to employees who work on a holiday.

SICK LEAVE

sick leave
Provides pay to an employee when he or she is out of work because of illness.

Sick leave provides pay to an employee when he or she is out of work because of illness. Most sick leave policies grant full pay for a specified number of "permissible" sick days—usually up to about 12 per year. The so-called sick days are usually accumulated at the rate of, say, one day per month of service.

In the past, most organizations haven't rewarded employees who didn't take their sick days. (Thus, if the worker wasn't "out sick" for his or her permissible seven or eight days per year, he or she simply lost the time off.) Since this acted as a somewhat illogical negative incentive system, there's been a tendency for organizations to buy back unused sick leave time. They do this by paying their employees a daily equivalent pay for each sick leave day not used. One drawback to this is that it can encourage sick employees to come to work regardless of their illness.[5]

SEVERANCE PAY

severance pay
A one-time payment some employers provide when terminating an employee.

Some employers provide **severance pay**—a one-time payment—when terminating an employee. The payment may range from three or four days' wages to as much as one year's salary. Others today provide "bridge" severance pay by keeping employees (especially managers) on the payroll for several months till they've found a new job.

Such payments make sense on several grounds. It is a humanitarian gesture as well as good public relations. In addition, most managers expect employees to give them at least one or two weeks' notice if they plan to quit; it therefore seems appropriate to provide at least one or two weeks' severance pay if an employee is being terminated.

Plant closings around the country have put thousands of employees out of work, often with little or no notice and no severance pay. Many states have been attempting to fight such closings, and a recent Supreme Court ruling (*Fort Halifax Packing Co.* v. *Coyne*, 1987) paves the way for states to cushion the economic impact of such closings. The Court has ruled that states may force employers to provide severance pay to workers who lose their jobs because of plant closings. In the *Fort Halifax* case, laid-off packing company workers will be paid amounts ranging from $490 to $8,680.[6] The Worker Adjustment and Retraining Notification ("plant closing") Act of 1989 requires covered employers to give employees 60 days' written notice of plant closures or mass layoffs.

SUPPLEMENTAL UNEMPLOYMENT BENEFITS

supplemental unemployment benefits
Provide for a "guaranteed annual income" in certain industries where employers must shut down to change machinery or due to reduced work. These benefits are paid by the company and supplement unemployment benefits.

These benefits provide, in effect, for a "guaranteed annual income." In some industries (such as auto making), shutdowns to reduce inventories or change machinery are common, and in the past employees were laid off or furloughed and had to depend on unemployment insurance. **Supplemental unemployment benefits** are paid by the company and *supplement* unemployment benefits, thus enabling the workers to better maintain their standards of living. Supplemental benefits are becoming more prevalent in collective bargaining agreements. They provide supplemental unemployment benefits (over and above state employment compensation) for three contingencies: layoffs, reduced workweeks, and relocation. These plans are normally found in heavy manufacturing operations such as in the auto and steel industries. Here, weekly or monthly plant shutdowns are typical, and some plan for guaranteeing minimum annual income is more appropriate.

▶ INSURANCE BENEFITS

WORKER'S COMPENSATION

insurance benefits Include worker's compensation benefits, life insurance plans, and hospitalization, medical, and disability insurance.

worker's compensation Provides employer-funded income and medical benefits to work-related accident victims or their dependents, regardless of fault.

Worker's compensation laws[7] are aimed at providing sure, prompt income and medical benefits to work-related accident victims or their dependents, regardless of fault.[8] Every state has its own worker's compensation law. However, there has been continuing congressional interest in the past few years in establishing minimum national standards for state compensation laws, and this has provided an impetus for improving employer's job-related accident and illness benefits. Improvements have included expanded medical coverage, increased weekly benefits, and rehabilitation provisions.[9] Some states have their own insurance programs. However, most require employers to carry worker's compensation insurance with private state-approved insurance companies.

Worker's compensation benefits can be either monetary or medical. In the event of a worker's death or disablement, the person's dependents are paid a cash benefit based on prior earnings—usually one-half to two-thirds of the worker's average weekly wage, per week of employment. In most states there is a set time limit—such as 500 weeks—for which benefits can be paid. If the injury causes a specific loss (such as an arm), the employee may receive additional benefits based on a statutory list of losses, even though he or she may return to work. In addition to these cash benefits, employers must furnish medical, surgical, and hospital services needed by the employee.

For an injury or illness to be covered by worker's compensation, it is only necessary to provide that it arose while the employee was on the job. It does not matter that the employee may have been at fault; if he or she was on the job when the injury occurred, he or she is entitled to worker's compensation. For example, suppose all employees are instructed to wear safety goggles when working at their machines. One worker does not and is injured while on the job. The company must still provide worker's compensation benefits. The fact that he was at fault in no way waives his claim to benefits.

Worker's compensation is usually handled by state administrative commissions. However, neither the state nor the federal government contributes any funds for worker's compensation. *Employers* are responsible for insuring themselves or for arranging for the appropriate coverage through an insurance company.

The employment provisions of the Americans with Disabilities Act will influence how most employers handle worker's compensation cases. For one thing (as mentioned in Chapter 2) ADA provisions generally prohibit employers from inquiring about an applicant's worker's compensation history, a practice that was widespread prior to the passage of the ADA. Furthermore, the ADA will make it more important that injured employees get back to work more quickly or are accommodated if their injury has led to a disability. Failing to let an employee who is on worker's compensation because of an injury return to work, or failing to accommodate him or her, could lead to litigation under ADA.[10]

Controlling Workers' Compensation Costs

Minimizing the number of worker's compensation claims is an important goal for all employers. While the claims themselves will generally be paid by the employer's insurance company, the costs of the premiums are a function of the number and amounts of claims that are paid. Minimizing such claims is thus important.

In practice, there are three main ways you can reduce such claims. First (as explained in more detail in Chapter 18, Employee Safety and Health), you can screen out accident-prone workers and also reduce accident-causing conditions in your facilities. Second, you can reduce the accidents and health problems that trigger these claims, for instance, by instituting effective safety and health programs and by complying with government standards on these matters.

Finally, you can institute rehabilitation programs for injured employees, since worker's compensation costs increase the longer an employee is unable to return to work. The object here is to institute corrective physical therapy programs (including exercise equipment, career counseling to guide injured employees into new, less strenuous jobs, and nursing assistance, for instance) so as to reintegrate recipients back into your work force.[11]

LIFE INSURANCE

group life insurance Provides for lower rates for the employer or employee and includes all employees, including new employees, regardless of health or physical condition.

Most employers provide **group life insurance** plans for their employees. Because it is a group plan, it contains several important advantages for employers and employees. As a group, employees can obtain lower rates than if they bought such insurance as individuals. And group plans usually contain a provision for including all employees—including new ones—regardless of health or physical condition.

In most cases the employer pays 100% of the base premium, which usually provides life insurance equal to about two years' salary. Additional life insurance coverage is then paid for by the employee. In some cases the cost of even the base premium is split 50:50 or 80:20 between the employer and employee, respectively. In general, there are three key personnel policy areas to be addressed: the benefits-paid schedule (benefits are usually tied to the annual earnings of the employee); supplemental benefits (continued life insurance coverage after retirement, double indemnity, and so on); and financing (the amount and percent that the employee contributes).[12]

HOSPITALIZATION, MEDICAL, AND DISABILITY INSURANCE

Most employers—about 92% of medium and large firms and 69% of small firms—make available to their employees some type of hospitalization, medical, and disability insurance; along with life insurance, these benefits form the cornerstone of almost all benefit programs.[13] Hospitalization, health, and disability insurance is aimed at providing protection against hospitalization costs and loss of income arising from accidents or illness occurring from off-the-job-causes. Most employers purchase such insurance from life insurance companies, casualty insurance companies, or Blue Cross (for hospital expenses) and Blue Shield (for physician expenses) organizations.

Most health insurance plans provide, at a minimum, *basic hospitalization, surgical*, and *medical insurance* for all eligible employees as a group. As with life insurance, group rates are usually lower than individual rates and are generally available to all employees—including new ones—regardless of health or physical condition. Most basic plans pay for hospital room and board, surgery charges, and medical expenses (such as doctors' visits to the hospital). Some group plans also provide *major medical* coverage to meet high medical expenses that result from long-term or serious illnesses; with hospitalization costs rapidly rising this is an increasingly popular option.

Many employers are also sponsoring health-related insurance plans covering things like eye care and dental services. In fact, dental insurance plans have been one of the fastest-growing items over the past few years, with the number of persons in the United States with dental coverage growing to over 100 million today.[14] In most employer-sponsored dental plans, participants must pay a specified amount of deductible dental expenses (typically $25 or $50 each year) before the plan kicks in with benefits. In a majority of the cases the participants in such plans have premiums paid for entirely by their employers, though.[15]

Accidental death and dismemberment coverage is another option. It provides a fixed lump-sum benefit in addition to life insurance benefits when death is accidental. It also provides a range of benefits in case of accidental loss of limbs or sight. Other options provide payments for diagnostic visits to the doctor's office, vision care, hearing aid plans, payment for prescription drugs, and dental care plans. Employers must provide the same health care benefits to employees over the age of 65 that are provided to younger workers, even though the older workers are eligible for the federally funded *Medicare* health insurance plan.[16]

Disability insurance is aimed at providing income protection or compensation for loss of salary due to illness or accident. The disability payments usually begin when normal sick leave is used up and may continue to provide income to age 65 or beyond.[17] The disability benefits usually range from 50 to 75% of the employee's base pay if he or she is disabled.

health maintenance organization (HMO) A prepaid health care system that generally provides routine round-the-clock medical services as well as preventive medicine in a clinic-type arrangement for employees, who pay a nominal fee in addition to the fixed annual fee the employer pays.

The **Health Maintenance Organization (HMO)** Act of 1973 was aimed at stimulating a nationwide prepaid health care system, *requiring* employers to offer an HMO as an alternative to conventional group health plans. Many employers therefore offer membership in an HMO as a hospital/medical option. The HMO itself is a medical organization consisting of several specialists (surgeons, psychiatrists, and so on). The HMO generally provides routine round-the-clock medical services at a specific site and usually stresses preventive medicine in a clinic-type arrangement to employees who pay a nominal fee. The HMO also receives a fixed annual fee per employee from the employer (or employer and employee), regardless of whether any service actually is provided.[18]

Reducing Health Benefits' Costs

The average cost per employee of health benefits has risen from about $300 in 1980 to over $3,600 today in some firms; giant firms like General Motors spend hundreds of millions of dollars per year just on health care benefits.[19] Caught between rising benefits costs and the belt tightening occurring in firms today, managing and reducing health care costs now therefore tops many manager's to-do lists. As a result, beginning in the early 1980s, many employers have been changing their medical plans to do the following.

1. Move away from "first-dollar" medical benefits. In 1982, only about 30% of the surveyed companies required employees to pay a front-end deductible on hospital expenses. By 1990, the percentage had more than doubled, with 70% using a deductible.

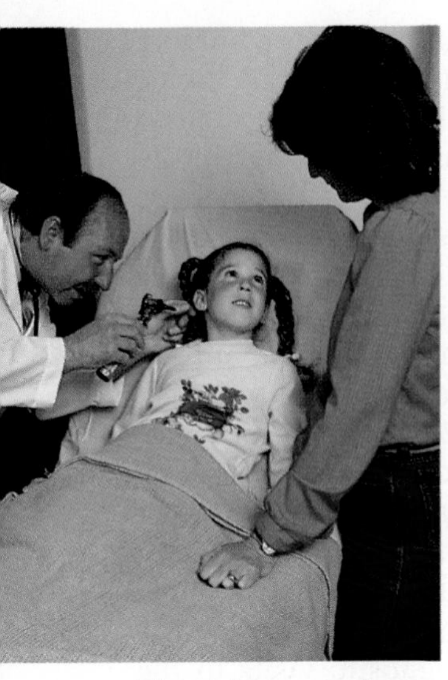
The rising cost of health care coverage has become a primary concern of the 1990s.

2. Increase annual deductibles. In 1982, the average deductible was $100. Today, almost 40% use a deductible of $150 or more.
3. Reimburse less than 100% of hospital costs. In 1982, 67% of companies provided full reimbursement for hospital costs versus only 42% of companies in 1990.
4. Limit the annual out-of-pocket medical expenses an employee pays. Interestingly, the number of plans with a "stop-loss" amount, which limits the out-of-pocket expense an employee would have to pay during a year, has increased from 80% to 89% recently. In other words, while employers are asking employees to pay higher deductibles, the companies are giving employees more protection against catastrophic medical expenses.
5. Require medical contributions. Whereas only 31% of employers required employee contributions to their medical premiums in 1982, about 46% of plans required them by 1990.[20]
6. More firms are moving to *managed care* programs. Managed care refers to the practice by which health maintenance organizations and the somewhat similar preferred provider organizations (PPOs) channel patients to the most cost-efficient providers of care, including physicians and hospitals.[21] Such a case management procedure—in which, for instance, a general practitioner serves as a gatekeeper and channels the patient to the appropriate specialist and/or hospital, as needed—was cited as "very effective" by 69% of the employers in one survey that use it.[22]
7. More and more firms are also focusing on health promotion and preventive health care as a way of reducing their health care program costs. For example, according to one survey, 56% of the firms were sponsoring drug and alcohol abuse programs; 31% were offering stop-smoking sessions; 45% were providing physical fitness classes; and 18% have exercise facilities on company premises. Most employers—70%—were training employees in first aid and CPR. Most of the employers were also increasing their communication efforts: 69% explain the problem of rising health care costs to employees and 54% offer tips about how to use company health benefits wisely.[23]
8. More firms today are cutting their health insurance bills by reducing retirees' benefits. At some firms, such as Primerica, retirees argue that paid health insurance was part of the retirement benefits that they were promised, and that such cuts are thus unethical and possibly illegal.

Managing Health Care Costs: AIDS

By now, the fatal nature of AIDS—Acquired Immune Deficiency Syndrome—is unfortunately well known to everyone.[24] However, in addition to the human suffering caused by AIDS, its potential impact on insurance companies and employers' insurance plans must be considered. Estimates of the anticipated costs of treating an AIDS patient exceed $150,000 per claimant, but as of 1991 the actual cost to insurers was considerably less. According to one survey, AIDS-related claims represented less than 1% of 1991 medical insurance claims costs for seven out of ten health insurers. The average estimated claims payout per AIDS case was about $68,000 in that year, still a very considerable sum.[25]

The problem is that reining in these costs is hampered by several unique aspects of the AIDS disease. While the disease at the present time is always terminal, intensive medical intervention is usually necessary for only short periods of time. For most of the time, the need is more custodial than anything else, and can often be as well administered at home or in nonhospital facilities as inside hospitals themselves. Yet while reduced costs are therefore possible with alternative treatment facilities, most employers' medical plans don't cover such alternative treatment facilities. Such plans are thus self-defeating in requiring more expensive care where such care is not needed. There is also a constellation of psychological barriers that inhibit early diagnosis and more cost-effective treatment. Many AIDS sufferers are reluctant to discuss their illness with their employers for fear of losing their job and/or their insurance benefits. At the same time, the reactions of fearful coworkers to AIDS sufferers often further impedes open discussions of the problem. The very nature of the disease also makes traditional cost-containment efforts virtually useless: obtaining second surgical opinions, outpatient surgery, or mandating psychiatric restrictions have little or no bearing in the treatment of AIDS, for instance.

Several insurance companies have concluded that the best way to control the cost of AIDS is to rethink the benefits plans themselves, with an eye toward providing required care in the least costly way. This often means treating the AIDS sufferer in his or her home and allowing this cost to be paid under the benefits plan (as is usually not allowed now). The emphasis increasingly will thus be on *individual case management (ICM)*. Here a special ICM nurse will be assigned to the patient and an alternative treatment plan will be designed. The plan itself will be individualized, taking into consideration the patient's ability to care for himself or herself, the availability of others who are able to help in the person's treatment, and the age and condition of the patient. A case history can illustrate this:

> When the patient was admitted to the hospital, the insurance carrier's precertification office questioned him at length and determined that he was suffering from a late stage of mylobacterium intracellular, an opportunistic disease most commonly found among AIDS patients. After six weeks in the hospital, the patient was discharged to an intensive home care routine costing $390 per day. If he had remained in the hospital, the cost would have been $1,100 per day. The attempt at home care lasted only 12 days, at which time the patient's condition degenerated to a point where permanent hospitalization was necessary. Even this modest success with home care resulted in a savings to the plan of $8,520.[26]

In summary, several steps recommended by one expert to help contain the health care benefits costs associated with AIDS are as follows:

> Medical plans should be expanded to provide coverage for outpatient services and alternate treatment facilities.
>
> Individual care management should be used to find the most appropriate type of care for each individual.
>
> Employers should not penalize or stigmatize those employees who admit they have AIDS.[27]

Mental Health Benefits

The mental health component of their health plans is the fastest-rising benefits cost for many employers. It's estimated that employers spend just over 8% of their health plan dollars on mental health treatment.[28] These costs are rising quickly, because of widespread drug and alcohol problems in society; an increase in the number of states (to 29 today) that require employers to offer a minimum package of mental health benefits; other health care claims being higher for employees with high mental health claims.

For the employer, the bottom line is that the cost of mental health care benefits is substantial. In one financial services firm in New York City, the company found that its mental health benefits jumped 61% in one year, for instance.

The first step in slowing rising mental health benefits is for employers to identify whether and to what extent a problem exists. Thus, this financial services firm rejected the idea of placing across-the-board limits on mental health coverage. Instead, it redesigned the mental health portion of its health benefits plan. The new plan emphasizes a utilization review to certify treatment; increased outpatient benefits; and a selected network of cost-efficient providers along with the provision of customized treatment plans in a negotiated provider network. The new program cut mental health benefit plans significantly while still providing needed benefits for company employees.[29]

The Pregnancy Discrimination Act

Pregnancy Discrimination Act (PDA)
An amendment to Title VII of the Civil Rights Act that prohibits sex discrimination based on "pregnancy, childbirth, or related medical conditions." It requires employers to provide benefits—including sick leave and disability benefits and health and medical insurance—the same as for any employee not able to work because of disability.

The **Pregnancy Discrimination Act (PDA)**, technically an amendment to Title VII of the Civil Rights Act, became law in 1978. It aimed at prohibiting sex discrimination based on "pregnancy, childbirth, or related medical conditions."[30] Before enactment of this law, temporary disability benefits for pregnancies were generally paid in the form of either sick leave or disability insurance, if at all. However, while most employers provide temporary disability income to their employees for up to 26 weeks for most illnesses, those that provided benefits for pregnancy usually limited benefits to only 6 weeks for normal pregnancies. Many believed that the shorter duration of pregnancy benefits constituted discrimination based on sex, and it was this issue that the Pregnancy Discrimination Act was aimed at settling.

Specifically, the act requires employers to treat women affected by pregnancy, childbirth, or related medical conditions the same as any employees not able to work, with respect to all benefits, including sick leave and disability benefits, and health and medical insurance. Thus, it is now illegal for most employers to discriminate against women by providing benefits of lower amount or duration for pregnancy, childbirth, or related medical conditions. For example, if an employer provides up to 26 weeks of temporary disability income to employees for all illnesses, it is now required to provide up to 26 weeks for pregnancy and childbirth also, rather than the more typical 6 weeks that prevailed before the act.

Interestingly, even some feminist groups have come out against granting special pregnancy benefits to women. They say it mediates against equality in the workplace by seeking special treatment with regard to selected issues. Furthermore, they argue that special benefits for pregnancy make women of childbearing age potentially more expensive employees and thus increase the likelihood they will be discriminated against, for instance, in hiring. It remains to be seen what the final disposition of this matter will be.

In the meantime, though, states and companies are moving ahead on their own. For example, about 15 states, as well as Dade County, Florida, have passed parental leave laws. And many firms, including Campbell Soup and American Express, have policies allowing up to three months' unpaid leaves for all employees—male and female—with a newborn at home. We'll return to a discussion of parental leave shortly.

COBRA Requirements

The ominously titled COBRA—The Comprehensive Omnibus Budget Reconciliation Act—requires most private employers to make available to terminated or retired employees and their families continued health benefits for a period of time, generally 18 months. The former employee must pay for this coverage, as well as a small fee for administrative costs.

You need to take care in administering COBRA, especially when it comes to informing employees of their COBRA rights. For one thing, you don't want a terminated or retired employee to get injured and then come back and claim that he or she didn't know that his or her insurance coverage could have been continued. Also, you want to comply with the law. Therefore, when a new employee first becomes eligible for your company's insurance plan, an explanation of COBRA rights should be received and acknowledged. More important, any employees who are separated from the company for any reason should have to sign a form acknowledging that they have received and understand their COBRA rights.

▸ RETIREMENT BENEFITS

SOCIAL SECURITY

Social Security
Provides three types of benefits: retirement income at the age of 62 and thereafter; survivor's or death benefits payable to the employee's dependents, regardless of age at time of death; and disability benefits payable to disabled employees and their dependents. These benefits are payable only if the employee is insured under the Social Security Act.

Many people assume that **Social Security** is something they collect only when they are old, but it actually provides three types of benefits. First are the familiar **retirement benefits**. These provide you with an income if you retire at age 62 or thereafter *and* are insured under the Social Security Act. Second, there are *survivor's* or death benefits. These provide monthly payments to your dependents regardless of your age at death, again assuming you were insured under the Social Security Act. Finally, there are *disability payments*. These provide monthly payments to you and your dependents if you become totally disabled for work and meet certain specified work requirements.[31] The Medicare program (which provides a wide range of health services to people 65 or over) is also administered through the Social Security system.

Social Security (technically, federal old age and survivor's insurance) is paid for by a tax on the employee's wages; employees and their employer share equally in this tax. If you are self-employed, you pay the entire sum, less 2% of your self-employment income.

PENSION PLANS

pension plans
Plans that provide a fixed sum when employees reach a predetermined retirement age or when they can no longer work due to disability.

group pension plan
A plan in which the employer and/or employee makes a set contribution to a pension fund.

There are three basic types of **pension plans**.[32] In the **group pension plan**, the employer (and possibly the employee) makes a set contribution to a pension fund. A second type of pension plan is actually a **deferred profit-sharing plan**. Here, a certain amount of profits is credited to each employee's account. These benefits are then distributed to the employee (or his or her dependents) upon retirement or death. Finally, under **savings plans** employees set aside a fixed percentage of their weekly wages for their retirement; the company usually matches from 50% to 100% of the employee's contribution.[33]

The basic types of pension plans can be further subdivided. For example, we can distinguish between defined benefit pension plans and defined contribution benefit plans.[34] A **defined benefit** pension plan contains a formula for determining retirement benefits so that the actual benefits to be received are defined ahead of time. For example, the plan might include a formula that designates a dollar amount or a percentage of annual salary for predicting the individual's eventual pension. On the other hand, a **defined contribution** plan specifies what contribution the employer will make to a retirement or savings fund set up for the employee. The defined contribution plan does not define the eventual bene-

deferred profit-sharing plan
A plan in which a certain amount of profits is credited to each employee's account, payable at retirement, termination, or death.

savings plan
A plan in which employees contribute for their retirement a fixed percentage of their weekly wage, usually matched by a certain percentage by the employer.

defined benefit
A plan that contains a formula for determining retirement benefits.

defined contribution
A plan in which the employer's contribution to employees' retirement or savings funds are specified.

fit amount, only the periodic contribution to the plan. In a defined benefit plan, the employee knows ahead of time what his or her retirement benefits will be upon retirement. With a defined contribution plan, the employee cannot be sure of his or her retirement benefits. Those benefits depend on both the amounts contributed to the fund plus the retirement fund's investment earnings.

There is also the so-called 401(k) Plan, based on Section 401(k) of the Internal Revenue Code. Under 401(k) employees can have a portion of their compensation that would otherwise be paid in cash put into a company profit-sharing or stock bonus plan by the employer. This results in a pretax reduction in salary, so the employee isn't taxed on those dollars until after he or she retires (or removes the money from the pension fund). Some employers also match a portion of what the employee contributes to the 401(k) plan. One attraction of 401(k) is that employees often have a range of investment options for the 401(k) funds including mutual stock funds and bond funds.

There are two major types of defined contribution plans.[35] In *savings and thrift plans*, employees contribute a portion of their earnings to a fund; this contribution is usually matched in whole or in part by the employer. In *deferred profit-sharing plans* employers typically contribute a portion of their profits to the pension fund, regardless of the level of employee contribution.

The entire area of pension planning is an extremely complicated one, partly because of the many federal laws governing pensions. For example, companies want to ensure that their pension contributions are tax deductible and it's therefore necessary to adhere to the pertinent income tax codes. We've also seen (in Chapter 12) that the Employee Retirement Income Security Act of 1974 (ERISA) restricts what companies can, cannot, and must do in regard to pension plans (more on this in a moment). In unionized companies, the union must be allowed to participate in the administration of the pension plan (under the Taft-Hartley Act).

While an employer usually must develop a pension plan to meet its own unique needs, there are several key policy issues to consider.[36]

Membership requirements. For example, what is the minimum age or minimum service at which employees become eligible for a pension?

Benefit formula. This usually ties the pension to the employee's final earnings, or an average of his or her last three or four years' earnings.

Retirement requirements. Although 65 is often considered a "standard" retirement age, federal law prohibits forced retirement of any competent employee. Yet most people opt for early retirement.[37] In companies such as General Motors, for example, only a small proportion of production and office workers retire as late as 65.[38] Partly due to union pressure and partly because early retirement helps open up jobs for younger employees, many employers now encourage early retirement. For example, some plans call for "30 and out." This permits an employee to retire after 30 years of continuous service, regardless of the person's age. In some cases—such as in the U.S. Army and among New York City employees—employees can retire with reduced pensions after 20 years of continuous service, regardless of the employee's age.[39]

Funding. The question of how the plan is to be funded is another key issue. One aspect is whether the plan will be contributory or noncontributory. In the former, contributions to the pension funds are made by both employees and the employer. In a noncontributory fund—the prevailing type, by the way—only the employer contributes. Another aspect of this is that many pension plans are underfunded. Although under the Employee Retirement Income Security Act most pension plans are now "guaranteed" (as explained following), the fact of the matter is that an alarming number of employers' pension funds do not have adequate funds to cover expected pension benefits.[40]

These workers have come together to discuss pension and retirement options under their employer's retirement system.

vesting
Provision that money placed in a pension fund cannot be forfeited for any reason.

Vesting. **Vesting** is another critical issue in pension planning. It refers to the money that the employer and employee have placed in the latter's pension fund *that cannot be forfeited for any reason.* The employees' contributions are always theirs and cannot be forfeited. However, until the passage of ERISA—the Employee Retirement Income Security Act—in 1974, the employer's contribution was not necessarily vested. Thus, suppose a person worked for a company for 30 years and the company then went out of business one year before he or she was to retire at age 65. Unless that employee's rights to the company's pension contributions were *vested*—due to a union agreement or company policy, for instance—he or she might well not have a pension.[41]

ERISA AND THE TAX REFORM ACT OF 1986

Employee Retirement Income Security Act (ERISA)
Signed into law by President Ford in 1974 to require that pension rights be vested, and protected by a government agency, the PBGC.

As a reaction to problems such as these, the **Employee Retirement Income Security Act (ERISA)** was signed into law in 1974.[42]

Debate regarding regulation of pension funds had actually begun in 1965, at which time private retirement plans covered some 25 million workers. At that time plans were paying nearly $2.75 billion annually in benefits to almost 2.5 million beneficiaries and had accumulated reserves in excess of $75 billion. By the end of 1974 (when ERISA was enacted), the assets of all private pension plans were close to $200 billion. Today more than 35 million workers are covered by employer pension plans. ERISA was aimed at protecting the interests of such workers and in stimulating the growth of pension plans.

Before enactment of ERISA, pension plans often failed to deliver expected benefits to employees. For example, when the Studebaker Auto Company went out of business in 1964, it terminated its pension plan; this left nearly 8,500 participants with either sharply reduced benefits or none at all. Any number of reasons—business failure, inadequate funding—could result in employees' losing their expected pensions.

Under ERISA, pension rights had to be vested under one of three formulas.[43]

100% vesting after 10 years of service (often referred to as *cliff vesting*).

25% vesting after 5 years, increasing 5% a year to 50% vesting after 10 years, and by 10% a year to 100% vesting after 15 years.

50% vesting after 5 years of service if the employee's age and years of service total 45 (or after 10 years of service if less), and increasing by 10% a year thereafter.

However, the Tax Reform Act of 1986 further tightened up these vesting rules and is now the law of the land. As of today, participants in a pension plan must have a nonforfeitable right to 100% of their accrued benefits after five years of service. Or, as an alternative, the employer may choose to phase in vesting over a period of from three to seven years. Under the Tax Reform Act of 1986 an employer can require that an employee complete a period of no more than two years' service to the company before becoming eligible to participate in the plan. However, if you require more than one year of service the plan must grant employees full and immediate vesting rights at the end of their required service.[44]

Pension Benefits Guarantee Corporation (PBGC)
Established under ERISA to assure that pensions meet vesting obligations; also insures pensions should a plan terminate without sufficient funds to meet its vested obligations.

Among other things, the **Pension Benefits Guarantee Corporation (PBGC)** was established under ERISA to assure that pensions meet vesting obligations; the PBGC also insures pensions should a plan terminate without sufficient funds to meet its vested obligations.[45]

Several factors are making some experts uncomfortable about the security of employees' pensions, despite the existence of the Pension Benefit Guarantee Corp.[46]

First, PBGC guarantees only defined benefit plans, not defined contribution plans. Furthermore, PBGC payments are not unlimited. It will pay an individual a pension of up to roughly $27,000 per year, for instance. This may seem like a lot, but it might not be to, say, an airline pilot who retired expecting a pension of $70,000 per year. Furthermore, according the PBGC, more and more employers are terminating their defined benefit plans and replacing them with (uninsured) defined contribution plans. (Legislation is being considered to deal with this problem.)

Finally, many companies have been eliminating their defined benefit plans and replacing them with annuities purchased from insurance companies. Most of the defined benefit plans were covered by the PBGC, but the annuities are not. The problem is that an increasing number of insurance firms are going bankrupt. This can leave the employees with worthless annuities, and therefore no pensions.

FASB 87 AND THE OMNIBUS BUDGET RECONCILIATION ACT OF 1987

The problem of underfunded or unfunded pension plans also helped prompt the Financial Accounting Standards Board to introduce "Employers Accounting for Pensions," commonly known as FASB 87. This rule (which is one of a multitude of rules to which certified public accountants in the United States must adhere) mandates that:[47]

1. For both reported earnings and balance sheet calculations, accounting for defined benefits plans (those in which participating employees receive previously agreed upon *defined* benefits when they retire) must estimate the size of the liability the employer is accumulating by using market interest rates. Since the cost of funding specific, defined benefits (of, say, $1,000 per month) 20 years from now will rise with a rise in market interest rates, this means that the reported liability to the employer will reflect more closely the plan's actual cost than it did previously.
2. The corporate balance sheet must include the unfunded liability of an underfunded pension plan.
3. If changes in the surplus of the plan (should the plan have a surplus) exceed 10% of its assets or liabilities, such changes must be reflected in the earnings statement in the form of operating earnings.

Note that Statement No. 87 does not apply to defined *contribution* plans. Unlike defined benefits plans, defined contribution plans do not guarantee how much money an employee will receive on retirement, but only what each party's contribution to the plan will be. The Omnibus Budget Reconciliation Act of 1987 lays out further rules regarding the funding of pension liabilities.[48]

WORKING WOMEN AND RETIREMENT BENEFITS

The number of women in the work force almost doubled in the 1970s and 1980s, and women will account for 64% of the growth of the work force in the 1990s. This increase has created pressure on the part of women and many women's groups to change three particular aspects of pension laws that they believe are discriminatory on the basis of sex:

The traditional rules regarding the accumulation of pension credits

The limited right of a homemaker to her spouse's workplace pension

The gender-based actuarial tables used to calculate the rate at which accrued pensions are paid

As a result of this pressure, changes have already been made. The Retirement Equity Act seeks to increase women's share of private sector retirement benefits by changing some of ERISA's rules. For example, prior to the Retirement Equity Act, a woman who left her job to have a child before she was vested and remained at home until the child reached school age was likely to lose what credits she had previously amassed; she would have to start over again when she returned to work. Now, a nonvested employee who leaves the employer's service and then comes back within five years can get credit for that earlier service, and employees who are absent from work because of pregnancy, childbirth, adoption, or infant care are protected against break-in-service penalties for a year. The act also lowers the maximum age from 25 to 21 that a private pension plan can require an employee to attain before he or she can participate in the plan. It also allows women on maternity leave for up to five years to retain certain pension benefits and to require a spouse's written permission before a pension plan participant can waive survivor benefits. In a divorce settlement, the act also authorizes the court to award a person the right to part of the former spouse's pension as part of the benefit.[49]

Furthermore, on July 16, 1983, the U.S. Supreme Court decided that sex-based longevity tables which distinguish between men and women can no longer be used and that if employees contribute toward their benefits, men and women must be charged the same and paid the same. Previously, separate tables were used to account for the fact that women have a longer life expectancy than men and therefore are likely to receive their pension payments for a longer period of time.

INDIVIDUAL RETIREMENT ACCOUNTS

individual retirement accounts (IRA) Pension plans qualified under tax laws to receive favorable tax treatment; established individually by employees

An **individual retirement account,** or **IRA** pension plan, has the following basic features. Under the Economic Recovery Tax Act of 1981 (ERTA), anyone who earned an income—even if he or she was already enrolled in a company pension plan—could invest in an IRA.[50] The person could make a tax-deductible investment of up to $2,000 in his or her IRA. If the person also contributed to a separate IRA for his or her nonworking spouse, they could make an overall contribution of $2,250. Those who wanted to establish such plans found a multitude of financial institutions that had established IRA-investment vehicles. For example, money could be invested through savings banks, insurance companies, brokerage houses, and mutual funds. In addition to the fact that the annual investments were tax deductible, the income earned on the investment (the financial institution might invest the funds in stocks or bonds, for instance) was *tax deferred.* That means you don't pay taxes on the income until you cash in your accounts.[51] This usually occurs after you retire, when your tax bracket is probably lower than it is while you're working.

The 1986 Tax Reform Act has had a major effect on IRAs, changing many of the previous provisions. The law states that no deductible IRA contribution can be made by active participants in an employer-sponsored retirement plan, or their spouses, if their income is above $50,000 (adjusted gross income) on joint returns, or $35,000 on single returns. If income falls between $40,000 and $50,000 on joint returns or $25,000-$35,000 on single returns, the amount that can be deducted is reduced.[52]

RECENT TRENDS

golden offerings Offers to current employees aimed at encouraging them to retire early—perhaps even with the same pensions they would expect if they retired at, say, age 65.

Retirement benefits are getting a new twist with the so-called **golden offerings**—early retirement windows and other voluntary separation arrangements. These so-called golden offerings appear to correlate with the state of the economy and are aimed at avoiding mandatory layoffs by offering special retirement packages to long-term employees. According to one survey of a cross section of industries and locations across the United States, about one-third of companies offered such voluntary separation plans in the past few years, while another 9% were considering an offering.

Early Retirement Windows

early retirement window A type of "golden offering" by which employees are encouraged to retire early, the incentive being liberal pension benefits plus, perhaps, a cash payment.

Most of the plans take the form of **early retirement window** arrangements. Here, only older employees (often age 50+) are eligible to participate. The "window" represents the fact that the company opens up (for a limited time only) the chance for an employee to retire earlier than usual. The financial incentive is usually a combination of improved or liberalized pension benefits plus a cash payment. One expert concludes that early retirement has become the method of choice for reducing midmanagement and white-collar work forces, with about 13% of 362 employers surveyed providing such early retirement windows in one recent year.[53]

Other voluntary separation plans operate more like "bonuses" for leaving and may apply even to recent hires. The offerings are usually made regardless of age. The financial incentive is typically a cash payment which varies substantially by company but often is in the range of one week's pay per year of service. About one-third of those employees eligible to walk through the early retirement windows typically accept the offer, while about one-fourth of those offered other separation plans do likewise.[54]

Early retirement windows like these must be used with caution if you are to avoid charges of age discrimination. The problem is that age discrimination is the fastest-growing type of discrimination claim today, and unless structured properly, early retirement programs can be challenged as de facto programs for forcing the discharge of older employees against their will.[55] While it is generally legal to use incentives like early retirement benefits to encourage individuals to choose early retirement, the employee's decision must be voluntary. In fact, in several cases individuals who were eligible for and elected early retirement later challenged their early retirement by claiming that their decision was not voluntary. In one case, for instance (*Paolillo* v. *Dresser Industries, Inc.*), employees were told on October 12 that they were eligible to retire under a "totally voluntary" early retirement program and that they must inform the company by October 18 to take advantage of this benefit. However, they were not informed of the details of the program (such as the amount of medical insurance and pension benefits for each individual employee) until October 15. This did not leave them much time, so that employees who had at first elected early retirement were able to subsequently sue, claiming coercion. The U.S. Court of Appeals for the Second Circuit (New York) agreed with their claim, arguing that an employee's decision to retire must be voluntary and without undue strain.[56]

As an employer you must therefore exercise great caution in encouraging employees to take early retirement. The decision must be voluntary and "without undue strain," and the waivers that they sign should meet certain EEOC guidelines. In particular, in agreeing to accept early retirement and waive future Age Discrimination in Employment Act claims, the waiver itself must be knowing and voluntary, not provide for the release of prospective rights or claims, and not be an exchange for consideration that included benefits to which the employee was already entitled. It should give the employee ample opportunity to think over the agreement and seek advice from legal counsel.[57]

Employee Services Benefits

While an employer's insurance and retirement benefits account for the main part of its benefits costs, most also provide a range of services including personal services (such as counseling), job-related services (such as child care facilities), and executive perquisites (such as company cars and plans for its executives).

PERSONAL SERVICES BENEFITS

First, many companies provide service benefits in the form of personal services that most employees need at one time or another. These include credit unions, legal services, counseling, and social and recreational opportunities.

Credit Unions

Credit unions are usually separate businesses that are established with the assistance of the employer. Employees usually become members of a credit union by purchasing a share of the credit union's stock for $5 or $10. Members can then deposit savings that accrue interest at a rate determined by the credit union's board of directors. Perhaps more important to most employees, loan eligibility and the rate of interest paid on the loan are usually more favorable than those found in banks and finance companies.

Counseling Services

Employers are also providing a wider range of counseling services to employees. These include financial counseling (for example, in terms of how to overcome existing indebtedness problems); family counseling (covering marital problems, and so on); career counseling (in terms of analyzing one's aptitudes and deciding on a career); job placement counseling (for helping terminated or disenchanted employees find new jobs); and preretirement counseling (aimed at preparing retiring employees for what many find is the trauma of retiring). Many employers also make available to employees a full range of legal counseling through legal insurance plans.[58] In the *open panel* legal plan, employees can choose their own attorney and then be reimbursed according to the fee schedule in the policy. In the *closed panel* legal plan, employees are required to use one of a number of specified attorneys, who are paid directly by the insurance plan.

Employee Assistance Programs (EAPs)

Employee Assistance Program (EAP)
A formal employer program for providing employees with counseling and/or treatment programs for problems such as alcoholism, gambling, or stress.

An employee assistance plan (EAP) is a formal employer program for providing employees with counseling and/or treatment programs for problems such as alcoholism, gambling, or stress. It is estimated that 50–75% of all employers with 3,000 or more employees now offer EAPs,[59] and there are four basic models in use today.[60] In the *in-house model* the entire assistance staff is employed by the company. In the *out-of-house model* the company contracts a vendor to provide employee assistance staff and services either in its own offices, the company's offices, or a combination of both. In the *consortium model* several companies pool their resources to develop a collaborative EAP program. Finally, in the *affiliate model*, a vendor already under contract to the employer subcontracts to a local professional rather than use its own salaried staff. This is usually to service employees in a client company location in which the EAP vendors do not have an office. Key ingredients for ensuring a successful EAP program include:[61]

Specify goals and philosophy. The short- and long-term goals expected to be achieved for both the employee and employer should be specified.

Develop a policy statement. Next, a comprehensive EAP policy statement should be prepared. This should define the purpose of the program, employee eligibility, the roles and responsibility of various personnel in the organization, and procedures for taking advantage of the plan.

Ensure professional staffing. Give careful consideration to the professional and state licensing requirements as they apply to the people staffing these facilities. If necessary, retain the services of an experienced person to consult with you in drawing up job specifications for the required staff.

Maintain confidential record-keeping systems. Everyone involved with the EAP—including secretaries and support staff—must understand the importance of confidentiality. Furthermore, make sure files are locked, access is limited and monitored, and identifying information (which might otherwise find itself in an employee's computerized records) is kept to a minimum.

Provide supervisory training. While this needn't involve extensive training, supervisors should certainly understand the program's policies, procedures, and services as well as the company's policies regarding confidentiality. And perhaps more important, all supervisors should get some training regarding the outward symptoms of problems like alcoholism as well as how to encourage employees to use the services of the EAP.

Be aware of legal issues. For example, in most states counselors must disclose suspicions of child abuse to an appropriate state agency: Your in-house counselors thus put your company in the legal position of having to comply in such an instance. Three ways to safeguard your interests here include retaining legal advice on establishing your EAP, carefully screening the credentials of the staff you hire, and obtaining professional liability insurance for the EAP.

Other Personal Services

Finally, some employers also provide a wide range of social and recreational opportunities for their employees, including company-sponsored athletic events, dance clubs, annual summer picnics, craft activities, and parties.[62] In practice, the benefits you can offer are limited only by your creativity in thinking up new benefits. One study of innovative benefits, for instance, found Canadian companies offering the following benefits, among others:

Lakefront vacations—the company owns lakeshore property and rents cottages and campsites to employees at low rates.

Weight loss program—several companies subsidize costs of weight loss workshops.

Adoption benefit—companies pay amounts of $500 to $1,500 per child for adoption costs.

Company country club—the company maintains a golf course, tennis courts, and football and baseball fields.

Cultural subsidy—the company will pay 33% of the cost of tickets to cultural activities such as theater, ballet, museum, and so on up to $100 per year per employee.

Lunch-and-learn program—interested employees can attend lunchtime talks on a variety of subjects, including stress management, weight control, computer literacy, fashion, and travel.

Home assistance—employees may use up to $1,500 of their annual profit-sharing award to save for a down payment on a house or to reduce their down payment, up to a maximum of $15,000.[63]

JOB-RELATED SERVICES BENEFITS

Job-related services (that are aimed directly at helping employees perform their jobs) such as assistance in moving and day care centers constitute a second group of services.

Parental Leave and The Family and Medical Leave Act of 1993

Parental leave is increasingly a benefit whose time has come. It's estimated that about half of workers today are women and that 80% of them are expected to become pregnant at some time during their work lives.[64] Partly as a response to this, the Family and Medical Leave Act of 1993 was signed into law by President Clinton February 5, 1993. Among its provisions, the law stipulates that:

1. Private employers of 50 or more employees must provide eligible employees up to 12 weeks of unpaid leave for their own serious illness, the birth or adoption of a child, or the care of a seriously ill child, spouse, or parent.
2. Employers may require employees to take any paid sick leave or annual leave as part of the 12-week leave provided in the law.
3. Employees taking leave are entitled to receive health benefits while they are on unpaid leave under the same terms and conditions as when they were on the job.
4. Employers must guarantee employees the right to return to their previous or an equivalent position with no loss of benefits at the end of the leave; however, the law provides a limited exception from this provision to certain highly paid employees.

Many employers were already voluntarily instituting such plans. For example, in a survey of 384 of the nation's largest 1,500 companies, it was found that 95% of employers provided disability leave to pregnant women under their health insurance benefit plans. Fifty-two percent of employers provided job-protected, unpaid leave to women (for one to three months), and 37% provided a similar job-protected, unpaid leave to men when a child was born. Many other employers are reevaluating their parental leave policies. The range of possibilities might include:[65]

Disability leave with full or partial salary reimbursement

Additional unpaid leave of one to three months

A transition period of part-time work for one month to one year

Reinstatement to the same or a comparable job at all stages of the leave.

Employers interested in implementing some type of child care leave have to be careful to avoid running afoul of the equal employment laws, and particularly Title VII. For example, the Equal Employment Opportunity Commission recently warned that child care leave offered only to female employees may violate Title VII by discriminating against male employees. In other words, employers must provide (or refuse to provide) child care leave to males if they do so to female employees.[66] If the allowable leave only covered pregnancy disability it would probably *not* apply to men since men are not subject to pregnancy. It's therefore essential that employers wishing to formulate child leave policies clearly distinguish between leave allowed for pregnancy disability and leave allowed for child care. If your intention is to give only female employees pregnancy disability leave, don't describe your pregnancy leave as a "child care leave" policy. Instead, be very specific about the purpose of the leave policy and the allowable duration of the leave—such as "from the eighth month of pregnancy, until one year after the female employee gives birth."[67]

Subsidized Child Care

Today, over 50% of all American women with children under 6 years old are in the work force, up from 32% of 1970, and 19% in 1960.[68] One increasingly popular benefit stemming directly from that trend is *subsidized day care.*[69] Many employers simply investigate the day care facilities in their communities and recommend certain ones to interested employees. But more employers are setting up company-sponsored day care facilities themselves, both to attract young mothers to the payroll and to reduce absenteeism. Often (as at the Wang Laboratories day care facility in Lowell, Massachusetts), the center is a private tax-exempt venture run separately from but subsidized by the firm. Employees are charged $30 a week for a child's care, and about 75 children from 2 to 4 years old are now enrolled. Where successful, the day care facility is usually close to the workplace (often in the same building), and the employer provides 50% to 75% of the operating costs. To date, however, the publicity these programs have received exceeds their actual use, with most surveys showing fewer than 5% of employers providing subsidized day care.

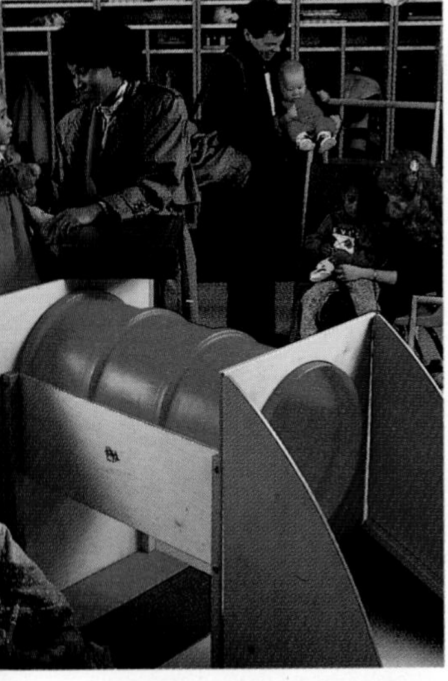

Subsidizing day care facilities for children of employees has many benefits for the employer including less employee absenteeism.

A survey found that employers can gain considerably by instituting subsidized day care centers; increased ability to attract employees, lower absenteeism, improved morale, favorable publicity, and lower turnover are some of the benefits attributed to day care programs.[70] To make sure the program is worthwhile and that its costs do not get out of hand, however, good planning is needed. This often starts with a questionnaire to survey employees in order to answer such questions as: "What would you be willing to pay for care for one child in a child care center near work?" and "Have you missed work during the past six months because you needed to find new care arrangements?" To date the evidence regarding the actual effects of employer-sponsored child care on employee absenteeism, turnover, productivity, recruitment, or job satisfaction is positive, particularly with respect to reducing obstacles to coming to work and improving workers' attitudes.[71]

Elder Care

With the average age of the U.S. population rising, elder care is increasingly a concern for many employers and individuals. Similar in some respects to child care, elder care is designed to help employees who must help elderly parents or relatives who are not fully able to care for themselves.[72]

From the point of view of the employer, elder care benefits are important for much the same reason as are child care benefits: The responsibility for caring for an aging relative can and will impact the employee's performance at work. A number of employers are therefore instituting elder care benefits, including flexible hours, long-term care insurance coverage, and company-sponsored elder care centers.

The elder care program instituted by Aerospace Company helps to illustrate what a typical program involves. Utilizing a program kit made available by the American Association of Retired Persons, the company program involved:

1. A lunchtime elder care fair. Here 31 community organizations involved with providing services to older people came to explain to employees the services that were available.
2. Next, there were 10 lunchtime information sessions for employees aimed at explaining various aspects of elder care, such as independent versus dependent living and housing, the aging process, and legal concerns of elder care.
3. Finally, the company also distributed AARP's publication entitled "Care Management Guide." This lists potential problems associated with elder care in a question-and-answer format.

Stride Rite Corp., the shoe manufacturer, recently opened an on-site elder care facility at its Cambridge, Massachusetts, headquarters. Several start-up obstacles had to be overcome before the facility was opened. For one thing, Massachusetts requires one counselor for every eight elders. The question of what to charge also had to be answered. Stride Rite decided to offer the elder care services at a discounted flat rate.[73] Employees have been slow to use the program.

Subsidized Employee Transportation

As gasoline prices rise, some employers are providing subsidized employee transportation.[74]

Such transportation can take several forms. In one large program the Seattle First National Bank negotiated separate contracts with a transit system to provide free year-round transportation to more than 3,000 of the bank's employees. At the other extreme, some employers just facilitate employee car pooling, perhaps by acting as the central clearing house to identify employees from the same geographic areas who work the same hours.

Food Services

Food services are provided in some form by most employers; they let employees purchase meals, snacks, or coffee, usually at relatively low prices. Most food operations are nonprofit, and, in fact, some firms provide food services below cost. The advantages to the employee are clear, and for the employer it can mean ensuring that employees do not drift away for long lunch hours. Even employers that do not provide full dining facilities generally make available food services such as coffee wagons or vending machines for the convenience of employees.

Educational Subsidies

Educational subsidies such as tuition refunds have long been a popular benefit for employees seeking to continue or complete their educations. Educational subsidies range from total payment of all tuition and expenses to some percentage of expenses to a flat fee per year of, say, $250 to $300. Some employers have experimented with providing in-house college programs such as Master of Business Administration programs, in which college faculty teach courses on the employer's premises. Other in-house educational programs include remedial work in basic literacy and training for improved supervisory skills. As far as tuition reimbursement programs are concerned, one survey found that nearly all companies (of 619 companies surveyed) pay for courses directly related to an employee's present job. Most companies also reimburse non–job-related courses (such as a secretary taking an accounting class) that pertain to the company business (79%) and those that are part of a degree program (66%). Furthermore, about 14% of the employers pay for self-improvement classes such as a foreign language, even though they are unrelated to company business or the employee's job.[75]

EXECUTIVE PERQUISITES

Perquisites (perks, for short) are usually given to only a select few executives, usually based on organizational level.

Perks can range from the substantial to the (almost) insignificant. In addition to his $200,000 annual salary, for instance, the president of the United States has an expense account of $50,000 for household expenses and entertainment, $100,000 for travel, and pays no rent for using the White House or Camp David (not to mention a fleet of limousines, *Air Force One*, and various helicopters!)[76] At the other extreme, perks may entail little more than the right to use the executive washroom.

In between these extremes are a multitude of popular perks. These include: *management loans* (which typically enable senior officers to exercise their stock options); *salary guarantees* (also known as "golden parachutes"), to protect executives even if their firms are the targets of acquisitions or mergers; *financial counseling* (to handle top executive's investment programs); and *relocation benefits*, often including subsidizing mortgages, buying back the executive's current house, and paying for the actual move.[77] A potpourri of other executive perks would include time off with pay (including work at home, sabbaticals, and severance pay), outplacement assistance, company cars, chauffeured limousines, security systems, company planes and yachts, executive dining rooms, physical fitness programs, legal services, tax assistance, liberal expense accounts, club membership, season tickets, credit cards, and children's education. As you can see, employers have many ways of making their hard-working executives' lives as pleasant as possible!

▶ FLEXIBLE BENEFITS PROGRAM

flexible benefits program Individualized plans allowed by employers to accommodate employee preferences for benefits.

"Variety is the spice of life," the saying goes. This applies very well to company benefits, since the benefits that one worker finds attractive may be unattractive to another. As a result, there is a trend toward **flexible benefits programs** today.

EMPLOYEE'S PREFERENCES FOR VARIOUS BENEFITS

Two researchers carried out a study that provides some insight into employee's preferences for various benefits.[78] They mailed questionnaires covering seven possible benefit options to 400 employees of a Midwest public utility company. Properly completed questionnaires were received from 149 employees (about 38% of those surveyed). The seven benefit options were as follows:

1. A five-day work week with shorter working days of 7 hours and 35 minutes.
2. A four-day work week consisting of 9 hours and 30 minutes each day.
3. Ten Fridays off each year with full pay. This includes 10 three-day weekends per year, in addition to any three-day weekends previously scheduled.
4. Early retirement through accumulating 10 days per year until retirement age. The retirement age will be 65 minus the number of accumulated days. Full pay will continue until age 65 is reached.
5. Additional vacation of two weeks per year with full pay. The additional vacation will be added to the present vacation.
6. A pension increase of $75 per month.
7. Family dental insurance. The company will pay the entire cost of family dental insurance.

Finally, employees were also asked to show their relative preference for a *pay increase of 5%*, in addition to any general wage increase negotiated.

Results

Two extra weeks of vacation was clearly the most preferred benefit, while the pay increase was second in preference. Overall, the shorter workday was by far the least preferred benefit option.

But this is not the full story; the employee's age, marital status, and sex influenced his or her choice of benefits. For example, younger employees significantly favored the *family dental plan* over older employees. Younger employees also showed a greater preference for the *four-day work week*. As might be expected, preference for the *pension* option increased significantly with employee age. Married workers showed more preference for the *pension* increase and for the family dental plan than did single workers. The preference for the family dental plan increased sharply as the number of dependents increased. In addition, the survey did not include health care benefits (which are a major concern to all employees today) as a benefit option.

Because employees do have different preferences for benefits, some employers let employees individualize their benefits plans.[79]

THE "CAFETERIA" APPROACH

The *cafeteria benefit plan* enables employees to pick and choose from available options and literally, develop their own benefit plan.

The basic idea is to allow the employee to put together his or her own benefit plan, subject to two constraints. First, the employer has to set total cost limits carefully. (This limits what it will spend for each total benefits package.) Second, each benefit plan must include certain *non*optional items. These include, for example, Social Security, worker's compensation, and unemployment insurance.

Subject to these two constraints, employees can pick and choose from the available options. Thus, a young married employee might opt for the company's life and dental insurance plans, while an older employee opts for an approved pension plan. The list of possible options would probably include many of the benefits discussed in this chapter: vacations, insurance benefits, pension plans, educational services, and so on.

An example of a flexible compensation plan was instituted at IDS Financial Services, a Minneapolis-based American Express subsidiary. The 2,500 IDS employees covered by the plan automatically got core benefits that included a minimal level of life insurance, a number of vacation days based upon years of service, short-term disability that pays 100% of salary and gradually drops to 70% over time, long-term disability that begins after a 150-day absence, and an attendance bonus that is earned when no health-related time off is taken during the year. However, the company also contributed 5% of salary that the employee can use toward any one or a combination of three options: One choice is to put all or part of the 5% in a tax-deferred savings plan. (For the first 3% the employee puts in, the company will add another 2½%). A second option is to take all or part of the 5% as cash. Option 3 is to put a portion of the entire credit toward extra benefits including medical coverage, life insurance, long-term disability, and vacation (employees can buy up to 5 days).[80]

Building this type of individual choice into a benefit plan can obviously be advantageous, but there are also disadvantages. The main problem is that the implementation of a cafeteria plan can involve substantial clerical and administrative costs. Each employee's benefits have to be carefully priced out and updated periodically, and even a medium-sized company would undoubtedly have to use a computer to administer such a plan.[81] Although most employees favor flexible benefits, many don't like to spend the time involved in choosing among available benefit options. Various consulting firms have therefore developed computerized games such as one called "FlexSelect." This is a user-friendly interactive program for personal computers that helps employees make choices under a flexible benefits program.[82]

Cafeteria-type, flexible benefits plans are spreading fast, with many new employers adding these plans every year. It is estimated that well over 1,400 companies are now on-line with some form of choice making among employee benefits.[83]

COMPUTERS AND BENEFITS ADMINISTRATION

Whether it is a flexible benefits plan or some other, computers play an important role in benefits administration. For even a smaller company with 40 to 50 employees, the administrative problems of keeping track of the benefits status of each employee can be a time-consuming task as employees are hired and separated, and as they utilize or want to change their benefits. Even a fairly straightforward problem like keeping track of who is eligible for vacations, and when, becomes a chore when a lot of employees are involved. As a result, most companies at least make use of some sort of benefits spreadsheet (see the accompanying box) to facilitate tracking benefits. Others use packaged software to update things like vacation eligibility and to trigger, say, a memo to a supervisor when one of his or her subordinates is overdue for some time off.

Keeping Employees Informed

Computers are also being used to inform employees about their benefits and to answer routine questions that might otherwise go unasked or take a human resource manager's time.[84] Such questions include: "In which option of the medical plan am I enrolled?" "Who are my designated beneficiaries for the life insurance plan?" "If I retire in two years, what will be my monthly retirement income?" and "What is my current balance in the company savings plan?"

At General Foods Corporation, for instance, employees use a computer system called "Benefits Window." Benefits Window gives employees the capability of easily looking up information about their benefits at centrally located interactive Kiosks situated around the facilities. As illustrated in Figure 14.1, employ-

Computer Applications in Benefits: Benefits Spreadsheet

In the 1990s, companies will continue to be concerned about controlling benefits costs. One prerequisite to this is to be fully aware of how much the benefits offered are actually costing the company, on an ongoing basis. A benefits spreadsheet will provide this information.

The spreadsheet should list the following: each employee (by name or number), the job code (so you can compare benefits by job category in response to ERISA requirements); pay rate (annual, monthly, or hourly, since subsequent spreadsheet formulas will than calculate the appropriate rate for the benefit being considered); department (if you wish to compare departments or divisions); and each benefit listed, all in separate columns. In order to accurately track your current liabilities for benefits accrued but not used, list separate columns for liability and use of these benefits.

For example, suppose you want a report on accrued vacations. In the liability column, calculate the accumulation minus use, times current hourly rate of pay. It is this column that will highlight how costly it is to allow employees to accumulate vacation or sick leave from year to year. If an employee accrues at a $10 an hour rate now but does not use the vacation time until retirement, the cost of those hours could easily double or treble, as his or her pay rises.

EMPLOYEE BENEFITS

- Your Current Status in GF Plans
- Your Beneficiaries
- Value of Your TIP Account
- Before-tax TIP Loans
- Value of Your Contributory Retirement Account
- Your Reimbursement Account Status
- Value of Your ESOP Account (Coming Soon)
- Retirement Income Projection (Coming Soon)

EXIT

Note: With "Benefits Window" employees use an interactive computer display to look up information about their benefits.

FIGURE 14.1
Employee Benefits Menu

Source: Anthony J. Barra, "Employees Keep Informed with Interactive KIOSKs," *Personnel Journal* (October 1988), p.46. Reprinted with permission.

ees can punch in their Social Security numbers and then identify such basic plan items as their beneficiaries, the value of their Thrift Investment Plan (TIP) accounts, the value of their contributory retirement accounts, and the value of their ESOP accounts.

SMALL BUSINESS APPLICATIONS

Benefits and Employee Leasing

As explained in Chapter 4 (Personnel Planning and Recruiting), some employers use employee leasing firms to reduce or eliminate the need to recruit and screen employees with their own in-house staff. Leasing firms usually arrange to have all the employer's employees transferred to the employee leasing firm. The employee leasing firm thus becomes the legal employer and handles all employee-related paperwork. This usually includes recruiting, hiring, paying tax liabilities (Social Security payments, unemployment insurance, and so on), as well as, often, day-to-day details like performance appraisals (with the assistance of the on-site supervisor).

The idea of having a leasing company take over the time-consuming job of managing personnel can be attractive. However, it is with respect to benefits management that employee leasing is often most advantageous. For many smaller employers the most serious personnel problem they face is getting insurance. Even group rates for things like life or health insurance can still be quite high when only 20 or 30 employees are involved.

This is when employee leasing comes in. Remember that the leasing firm is the legal employer of your employees. Therefore, your employees are absorbed into a much larger insurable group, along with other employers' former employees. The bottom line is that the employee leasing company can thus often provide benefits that much smaller companies cannot obtain or cannot obtain at anywhere near as favorable a cost. As a small-business owner, you may thereby be able to get insurance for your people that you couldn't otherwise obtain. Furthermore, there will be some instances in which an employee leasing arrangement actually costs an employer virtually nothing, even with the leasing firm's fee. This is because the fee may be more than outweighed by the reduced benefits cost to the employer, plus the in-house labor costs savings gained by letting the leasing company handle HRM.[85]

Employee leasing may sound too good to be true, and it often is. Many employers are understandably uncomfortable letting a third party become the legal employer of their employees (who literally have to be terminated by the employer and rehired by the leasing firm). There is also the matter of the somewhat erratic history of some employee leasing firms, a number of which have gone out of business after apparently growing successfully for several years. Such a business failure leaves the original employer with the need to hire back all its employees, and with the problem of finding new insurance carriers to take on the job of insuring these "new" employees. The original insurance plan may have prevented the original insurer from cutting off services to the employer's employees. But if the health history of your employees has taken a turn for the worse, it may be hard to repurchase insurance at any price. Furthermore, Congress is continually tinkering with the tax code in such a way as to reduce employee leasing's insurance benefits' attractiveness.

If you decide to go with a leasing firm there are several common sense guidelines to use. Of course, check the prospective leasing firm with your local Better Business Bureau. Get a full list of local clients so you can completely check the leasing firm's references. Furthermore:[86]

> Employee leasing is a relatively specialized field given the legal and tax code ramifications of what they do. Therefore, work with a leasing firm that specializes in leasing rather than one that offers leasing as only part of its services.
>
> Choose a financially stable and well-managed leasing firm. You should try to check the firm's capitalization and credit ratings. Also look at the number of years it has been in business.
>
> Look for a firm that provides benefits that are at least as good or better than those you now offer.
>
> Make sure the firm pays its bills. If the leasing firm does not pay its insurance premiums on time, it could be a catastrophe for your firm. The leasing firm may be the legal entity responsible for the payments. However, from a practical point of view, it is your employees who will be left without insurance, and this will turn into a problem for your firm.
>
> Finally, review their policies. Remember that most leasing firms will not just administer your own firm's personnel policies. Instead, they will institute their own personnel policies (regarding, for instance, performance appraisals, periodic review for raises, and so on). It is therefore important to ensure their personnel policies are consistent with yours and that any inconsistencies are worked out before the transition.

▶ BENEFITS TODAY AND TOMORROW

THE BENEFITS PICTURE TODAY

A majority of companies in the United States today do offer at least some fringe benefits to their employees.[87] For example, as noted earlier, about 92% of medium and larger firms and 69% of smaller firms provide health insurance. Of these, about 60% provide an HMO option, 25% provide a PPO option, and 90% provide some type of group dental plan benefits. The use of supplemental health benefits is extensive too: Between 25% and 45% of responding companies (depending on size) provide vision care plan benefits; about 50% have a prescription drug plan; about 55% have some type of employee assistance programs; and about 40% of the responding companies provide health education/promotion/wellness programs.

Most respondents even provide retirement/pension benefits. For example, 88% of large companies (those with 5,000 or more employees), 78% of medium-sized companies (500–4,999), and 73% of smaller companies (fewer than 500 employees) provide defined contribution plans,while about 67% of all the firms have defined benefit plans.

In addition, most employers also offer death and disability benefits. For example, about 76% of all companies regardless of size provide group life insurance benefits, about 85% provide accidental death and disability insurance, and 85% provide long-term disability insurance.

THE BENEFITS SCENE TOMORROW

Benefits directors from 100 major U.S. industrial companies offered their predictions regarding employee benefits in the 1990s in a survey conducted by Hewitt Associates, a large consulting and actuarial firm.[88] Against a backdrop of changing demographics—in particular an increase in the average age of employees and the proportion of women in their work force—it is not surprising that about half the respondents expect the average benefit cost to increase.

However, benefit costs are not projected to increase across the board. For example, these experts expect little change in the areas of life insurance, disability, and time off. But with regard to retirement benefits, almost half predict that costs will rise. On the other hand, the trend toward early retirement appears to have bottomed out. As a result, many of the experts expect less use in the future of special early retirement windows.

From a list of possible emerging benefits practices, the respondents chose several as being the most likely to become more popular. Eighty percent said there will be more use of flexible benefits plans as a way to maintain benefits during the period of cost squeeze. Furthermore, 82% expect an increase in long-term care coverage such as that provided by nursing homes (not currently covered adequately under Medicare or most private plans). Between 70 and 80% of the respondents also expect more use of flextime and an increase in elder care benefits. Most also expect much wider use of employer-sponsored day care. Almost all the respondents (92%) expected computerization to be used widely to facilitate benefits administration and particularly the administration of flexible benefits plans.

Use of wellness incentives and other cost containment strategies is likely to increase. So will portability, which refers to the ability of the employee to take his or her benefits from employer to employer (for instance, an employee could credit 8 years of accumulated pension benefits to a new employer's 20-year pension plan).[89]

BUILDING EMPLOYEE COMMITMENT

Example of a Benefits Program

The extensive benefits plan at Federal Express explains, in part, the employee commitment that many associate with that firm's workers. It's therefore useful to briefly summarize that firm's overall benefits program at this point.[90]

The firm's retirement benefits are exceptional. Retirement benefits at Federal Express actually consist of several plans to help the employee prepare for his or her retirement. The pension plan, profit-sharing plan, and employee stock ownership plan (as well as company-sponsored savings plans) combine to provide employees with a good income at retirement. The firm's pension plan alone provides employees with a fixed percentage of their salary. The normal retirement benefit payable at age 60 is 2% of the employee's final average pay times the employee's years of credited service (up to 25 years). That means that an employee's pension benefit at age 60 with 25 years of service with the company will be 50% of the person's final average pay. Final average pay is the average of the total compensation received during the highest paid five consecutive years of the employee's last 15 years before retirement or disability. And that, according to the firm's head of personnel, means highest average total pay, including overtime and incentives.

All full-time permanent or part-time employees who have completed at least three consecutive months of employment with Federal Express can also participate in the firm's employee stock purchase plan. This lets them purchase Federal Express stock without commission through payroll deductions in an amount varying from 1% to a maximum of 10% of their total salary. These deductions accumulate for a designated period, at the end of which time Federal Express purchases the shares of stock for all participants.

There's more. The firm's tuition refund program lets any permanent employee with one year of continuous service receive financial reimbursement up to a maximum annual amount for his or her continuing education. Employees earn two weeks of vacation after one year with the firm, three weeks after five years, four weeks after ten years, and five weeks of vacation after twenty years with Federal Express.

But for some employees the best is last. Federal Express participates with other airlines that offer interline benefits in a discount travel program. Employees who have completed a minimum of six months of continuous service in a permanent status are eligible to participate. And (in a benefit that most employers would find hard to match) permanent employees are eligible to use Federal Express aircraft jump seats for travel. Permanent employees may travel for personal or business purposes and make their arrangements through the jump seat reservations office in Memphis—which takes the request by phone and confirms it. There is also a computerized system called "Free Bird" which lets employees make the reservations themselves. Then they just have to be at the airport at least two hours prior to the flight, and away they go.

▸ CHAPTER REVIEW

SUMMARY

1. The financial *incentives* we discussed are usually paid to specific employees whose work is above standard. Employee *benefits*, on the other hand, are available to *all* employees based on their membership in the organization. We discussed four types of benefit plans: pay supplements, insurance, retirement benefits, and services.
2. Supplemental pay benefits provide pay for time not worked. They include unemployment insurance, vacation and holiday pay, severance pay, and supplemental unemployment benefits.
3. Insurance benefits are another type of employee benefit. Worker's compensation, for example, is aimed at ensuring prompt income and medical benefits to work accident victims or their dependents regardless of fault. Most employers also provide group life insurance and group hospitalization, accident, and disability insurance.
4. Two types of retirement benefits were discussed: Social Security and pensions. Social Security does not just cover retirement benefits but survivors and disability benefits as well. There are three basic types of pension plans: group, deferred profit sharing, and savings plans. One of the critical issues in pension planning involves *vesting*—the month that employer and employee have placed in the latter's pension fund, which cannot be forfeited for any reason. ERISA basically ensures that pension rights become vested and protected after a reasonable amount of time.
5. Most employers also provide benefits in the form of employee services. These include food services, recreational opportunities, legal advice, credit unions, and counseling.
6. Surveys suggest two conclusions regarding employee's preferences for benefits. First, *overall*, time off (such as two extra weeks' vacation) seems to be the most preferred benefit. Second, the employee's age, marital status, and sex clearly influence his or her choice of benefits. (For example, younger employees were significantly more in favor of the family dental plan than were older employees.) This suggests the need for individualizing the organization's benefit plans.
7. The *cafeteria approach* allows the employee to put together his or her own benefit plan, subject to total cost limits and the inclusion of certain nonoptional items. Several firms have installed cafeteria plans; they require considerable planning and computer assistance.

KEY TERMS

benefits
supplemental pay benefits
unemployment insurance
sick leave
severance pay
supplemental unemployment benefits
insurance benefits
worker's compensation
group life insurance
health maintenance organization (HMO
Pregnancy Discrimination Act
Social Security
retirement benefits
pension plans
group pension plan
deferred profit-sharing plan
savings plan

defined benefit
defined contribution
vesting
Employee Retirement Income Security Act (ERISA)
Pension Benefits Guarantee Corporation (PBGC)
individual retirement account (IRA)
golden offerings
early retirement window
employee services benefits
flexible benefits programs

DISCUSSION QUESTIONS

1. You are applying for a job as a manager and are at the point of negotiating salary and benefits. What questions would you ask your prospective employer concerning benefits? Describe the benefits package you would try to negotiate for yourself.
2. Explain how you would go about minimizing your organization's unemployment insurance tax.
3. Explain how ERISA protects employees' pension rights.
4. In this chapter we presented findings concerning the preferences by age, marital status, and sex for various benefits. Basically, what were these findings and how would you make use of them if you were a human resource manager?

APPLICATION EXERCISES

RUNNING CASE

Carter Cleaning Company

The New Benefit Plan

Carter Cleaning Centers has traditionally provided only legislatively required benefits for its employees. These include participation in their state's unemployment compensation program, Social Security, and worker's compensation (which is provided through the same insurance carrier that insures the stores for such hazards as theft and fire). The principals of the firm—Jack, Jennifer, and their families—have individual family-supplied health and life insurance.

At the present time, Jennifer can see several things wrong with the company's policies regarding benefits and services. First, she wants to do a study to determine whether similar companies' experiences with providing health and life insurance benefits suggest they enable these firms to reduce employee turnover and perhaps pay lower wages. Jennifer is also concerned with the fact that at the present time the company has no formal policy regarding vacations or paid days off or sick leave. Informally, at least, it is understood that employees get one week vacation after one year's work, but in the past the policy regarding paid vacations for days such as New Year's and Thanksgiving has been very inconsistent: Sometimes employees who have been on the job only two or three weeks are paid fully for one of these holidays while at other times employees who have been with the firm for six months or more have been paid for only half a day. Jennifer knows that this policy must be made more consistent.

She also wonders whether it would be advisable to establish some type of day care center for the employees' children. She knows that for many of the employees, including Walt, the children either have no place to go during the day (they are preschoolers) or have no place to go after school, and she wonders if a benefit such as day care would be in the best interests of the company.

Questions

1. Draw up a policy statement regarding vacations, sick leave, and paid days off for Carter Cleaning Centers.
2. What are the advantages and disadvantages to Carter Cleaning Centers of providing its employees with health, hospitalization, and life insurance programs?
3. How should Jennifer go about determining whether a day care center would be advisable for the company?

CASE INCIDENT *Sick Leave in Spring Valley*

Slashes in federal aid programs to cities, a decline in revenue from a 2 percent sales tax, and higher costs in everything from cleaning supplies to wages had brought hard times to the elected officials of Spring Valley. The combination of these factors made it seem impossible for Robert Donizetti—the city manager—and the budget committee of the city council to provide a balanced budget for the city.

Situated in a northwestern state, Spring Valley had a population of 12,000, a declining one that matched its declining revenue. In casting about for means to finance the small city's operations, Donizetti saw few opportunities for increasing the revenue. In the past year one of its chief employers, the Acme Manufacturing Company, had been forced to close its local factory, and all parts of the local economy had been affected by the national business recession. Hence, Donizetti went carefully over departmental budgets seeking ways to cut costs and eliminate waste.

One area in which Donizetti decided savings could be effected was through changes in policy concerning sick leave. The city's work force consisted of only about 150 full-time employees, and figures in Donizetti's office showed that sick leave in the past six years averaged 7.34 days per year per employee. This was not only costly in dollars in terms of Spring Valley's budget but it meant a loss of labor efficiency and productivity. His statistics showed that female and older employees used more sick leave than males and younger workers. Donizetti prepared the following tables of sick leave averages by age and sex for the budget committee:

SICK LEAVE IN SPRING VALLEY BY SEX, 1988–1993

Year	Male	Female
1988	6.1	7.9
1989	5.9	7.7
1990	6.4	8.4
1991	6.3	8.7
1992	6.5	8.5
1993	6.8	8.9

SICK LEAVE IN SPRING VALLEY BY AGE, 1988–1993

Year	Under 30	Over 30
1988	5.1	6.8
1989	5.3	8.4
1990	5.7	8.1
1991	5.5	7.7
1992	5.8	8.3
1993	5.6	8.6

Spring Valley had not had many labor conflicts. Employee relations were handled through the human resource director, William Danforth, and the City Employees' Association, whose president was Jessica Blum. In respect to sick leave, the city had in recent years agreed to include in it family care, doctor appointments, and emergency time off for such events as funerals.

After study of the problem, Donizetti recommended that the City Employees' Association and the human resource department together devise a sick leave incentive program. It would serve as an incentive to save sick leave, as a deterrent to sick-leave abuse, and as an equitable plan for the different uses of sick leave.

On June 6 the human resource department presented its proposal. Under its plan, employees would be reimbursed on February 1 of each year for 20 percent of the sick leave credits accumulated during the past year. An employee would have to have built up 45 sick leave days in order to draw cash payments, a move intended to reduce turnover in employment in the city.

The City Employees' Association made a counterproposal that included a choice by the employee to consider sick leave as vacation time or else to triple it and add it to retirement service. Unused credits diverted to retirement were to be made at a rate of 100 percent.

The main point of contention at this stage concerned the percentage of sick leave credit for which an employee might be reimbursed. The city offered no alternative to minimum yearly reimbursement while the employees demanded that some sort of retirement-related incentive be adopted. After several fruitless negotiations, the two parties agreed to present the problem to a fact finder. His or her findings and suggestions for resolution of the issues would be used as a basis for further negotiations. The fact finder chosen, Alison Cartaret, conducted private hearings with both parties and submitted his report on July 15.

Questions

1. Assume that you are the fact finder in the case. Analyze the sick leave problem in Spring Valley and propose a plan equitable to both parties.
2. If you were the city manager, entrusted with pursuing the best interests of the city, which provisions in the proposal would you accept and which would you attempt to change?
3. Assume that you are the union negotiator. Which provisions would you accept and which would you attempt to change?

HUMAN RESOURCE MANAGEMENT SIMULATION

Your organization offers very meager fringe benefits to its employees. These benefits are currently 11% of wages and include social security tax (FICA); unemployment insurance; a low-benefit, high-deductible health care plan; and worker's compensation insurance. Your team will need to assess your firm's fringe benefits and decide what new benefits are needed. Although your budget constraints will make large improvements impossible, do not let this keep you from making progress toward a better benefit program for your employees. A "cafeteria" plan is also available.

▶ NOTES

1. Employee Benefit Costs," *BNA Bulletin to Management*, January 16, 1992, pp. 12–13.
2. Ibid. p. 12.
3. This is based on Bonnie De Clark, "Cutting Unemployment Insurance Costs," *Personnel Journal*, Vol. 62 (November 1983), pp. 868–870.
4. Robert E. Sibson, *Wages and Salaries: A Handbook for Line Managers* (New York: American Management Association, 1967), pp. 236–237. See also Richard L. Bunning, "A Prescription for Sick Leave," *Personnel Journal*, Vol. 67, no. 8 (August 1988), pp. 44–49; explains how one company set up an effective sick leave policy based on positive reinforcement rather than discipline.
5. Miriam Rothman, "Can Alternatives to Sick Pay Plans Reduce Absenteeism?" *Personnel Journal*, Vol. 60 (October 1981), pp. 788–791.
6. *San Francisco Chronicle*, June 2, 1987, p. 10.
7. Joseph Famularo, *Handbook of Modern Personnel Administration* (New York: McGraw-Hill, 1972), pp. 51–62.
8. Richard Henderson, *Compensation Management* (Reston, VA: Reston, 1979), p. 250. For an explanation of how to reduce worker's compensation costs, see Betty Strigel Bialk, "Cutting Worker's Compensation Costs," *Personnel Journal*, Vol. 66, no. 7 (July 1987), pp. 95–97.
9. Henderson, *Compensation Management*, p. 90. Also see Bureau of National Affairs, Worker's Compensation Total Disability Benefits by State," 1989, pp. 172–173, for a list showing worker's compensation by state.
10. "Worker's Compensation and ADA," *BNA Bulletin to Management*, August 6, 1992, p. 248.
11. See, for example, Bialk, "Cutting Workers' Compensation Costs," pp. 95–97.
12. Sibson, *Wages and Salaries*, p. 235.
13. "Employee Benefits in Small Firms," Bureau of National Affairs *Bulletin to Management*, June 27, 1991, pp. 196–197.
14. Rita Jain, "Employer-Sponsored Dental Insurance Eases the Pain," *Monthly Labor Review* (October 1988), p. 18. "Employee Benefits," Commerce Clearing House *Ideas and Trends in Personnel*, January 23, 1991, pp. 9–11.
15. Ibid., p. 23.
16. Bureau of National Affairs, *Bulletin to Management*, December 23, 1982, p. 1; "TEFRA—The Tax Equity and Fiscal Responsibility Act of 1982," *Personnel*, Vol. 59 (November–December 1982), p. 43.
17. A.N. Nash and S.J. Carroll, Jr., "Supplemental Compensation," in *Perspectives on Personnel: Human Resource Management*, in Herbert Heneman III and Donald Schwab, eds. (Homewood, IL: Irwin, 1978), p. 223.
18. Thomas Snodeker and Michael Kuhns, "HMO's: Regulations, Problems, and Outlook," *Personnel Journal*, Vol. 60 (August 1981), pp. 629–631.
19. "Health Care Costs Continue to Climb," *BNA Bulletin to Management*, February 6, 1992, p. 33.
20. Hewitt Associates, "Health Care Costs Becoming Shared Responsibility," *News and Information*, June 21, 1984. See also, *Health Care Cost Containment* (New York: William Mercer-Meidinger, 1984), as discussed in *Compensation Review* (Fourth Quarter 1984), pp. 8–9; and Thomas Paine, "Outlook for Compensation and Benefits: 1986 and Beyond," Hewitt Associates, October 30, 1985. See also John Parkington, "The Trade-off Approach to Benefits Cost Containment: A Strategy to Increase Employee Satisfaction," *Compensation and Benefits Review*, Vol. 19, no. 1 (January–February 1987), pp. 26–35; Hewitt Associates, "Employer-Sponsored Medical Plans Designed to Make Employees Better Health Care Consumers, Study Says, *News and Information*, July 28, 1989 (100 Half Day Road, Lincolnshire, IL 60015); Janet Norwood, "Measuring the Cost and Incidence of Employee Benefits," *Monthly Labor Review*, Vol. 111, no. 8 (August 1988), pp. 3–8; Robert C. Penzkover, "Health Incentives at Quaker Oats," *Personnel Journal*, Vol. 68, no. 3 (March 1989), pp. 114–118; and Anne Skagen, "Managing Health Care Costs," Part III, "Focus on Case Management," *Compensation and Benefits Review*, Vol. 20, no. 6 (November–December 1988), pp. 56–63; Hewitt Associates, *News and Information*, February 6, 1990.
21. Robert Jenkins, "The Strengths and Scope of Managed Health Care Today," *Employment Relations Today*, (Spring 1992), pp. 43–50.
22. "Managing Health Care Costs," *BNA Bulletin to Management*, August 27, 1992, p. 272.
23. Hewitt Associates, "Employers Trim Future Health Care Costs by Keeping Employees 'Well,'" *News and Information*, June 7, 1984; and Morton Grossman and Margaret Magnus, "The Boom in Benefits," *Personnel Journal*, (November, 1988), pp. 51–55. See also "Could Wellness Programs Thrive?" *Personnel*, Vol. 65, no. 3 (March 1988), pp. 6–7; lists specific examples of wellness programs now in place. See also Marjorie Blanchard, "Wellness Programs," *Personnel Journal*, Vol. 68, no. 5 (May 1989), pp. 30–31, for examples of wellness program benefits, and BNA, "Benefit Cost Containment Trend Continues," 1989, p. 2, for examples of how companies are proceeding.
24. The following is based on Michael Gomez, "Managing Health Care Costs," Part I, "The Dilemma of AIDS," *Compensation and Benefits Review* (September–October 1988), pp. 23–31, and Nancy Breuer, "AIDS Issues Haven't Gone Away," *Personnel Journal*, January 1992, Vol. 71, no. 1, pp. 47–49.
25. AIDS Insurance Costs Examined," *BNA Bulletin to Management*, July 23, 1992, p. 226.
26. Quoted from Gomez, "Managing Health Care Costs," p. 28.
27. Ibid., p. 31.
28. This is based on Thomas C. Billet, "Managing Health Care Cots," Part II, "Coping with Mental Health," *Compensation and Benefits Review* (September–October 1988), pp. 32–36.
29. Ibid., pp. 35–36.
30. This is based on Paul Greenlaw and Diana Foderaro, "Some Practical Implications of the Pregnancy Discrimination Act," *Personnel Journal*, Vol. 58 (October 1979), pp. 677–681. See also Commerce Clearing House "Supreme Court Says Giving Women Pregnancy Leave Is Lawful Even in the Case Where Men Receive No Disability Leave Whatever," *Ideas and Trends in Personnel*, January 23, 1987, pp. 9–10.
31. Jerome B. Cohen and Arthur Hanson, *Personnel Finance* (Homewood, IL: Irwin, 1964), pp. 312–320. See also BNA, January 14, 1988, pp. 12–13. This article explains changes in the Social Security law and presents an exhibit showing how to estimate your Social Security benefits.
32. See Henderson, *Compensation Management*, pp. 289–290; Famularo, *Handbook*, pp. 37.1–37.9; Edward Katz, "The Unsung Benefits of Employee Savings Plans," *Personnel Journal*, Vol. 58 (January 1979), pp. 30–31; Edward Redling, "Voluntary Deferred Compensation—Off Again, On Again, *Personnel*, Vol. 56 (1979), pp. 64–67.

33. See Evert Allen, Jr., Joseph Melone, and Jerry Rosenbloom, *Pension Planning* (Homewood, IL: Irwin, 1981).
34. Avy Graham, "How Has Vesting Changed Since Passage of Employee Retirement Income Security Act?" *Monthly Labor Review* (August 1988), pp. 20–25.
35. Ibid., p. 20.
36. Sibson, *Wages and Salaries*, p. 234.
37. For a discussion of demographic trends with specific reference to average age of employees, see, for example, D. Quinn Mills, "Human Resources in the 1980's," *Harvard Business Review*, Vol. 58 (July–August 1979), pp. 154–163.
38. *The Economist*, August 5, 1978, p. 57.
39. For a discussion of the pros and cons of early retirement, see, for example, Jeffrey Sonnenfelt, "Dealing with the Aging Workforce," *Harvard Business Review*, Vol. 57 (November–December 1978), pp. 81–92.
40. A.F. Ehrbar, "Those Pension Plans Are Even Weaker Than You Think," *Fortune*, Vol. 94 no. 5 (November 1977), pp. 104–107, discussed in H. Chruden and A. Sherman, Jr. *Personnel Management* (Cincinnati: South-Western 1980), pp. 500–501. See also Carroll Roarty, "How Merabank Lowered Pension Costs Without Lowering Morale," *Personnel Journal*, Vol. 66, no. 11 (November 1987), pp. 64–71, which relates how this bank changed its profit sharing and pension plans and saved money without sacrificing morale.
41. See Irwin Tepper, "Risk vs. Return in Pension Fund Investment," *Harvard Business Review*, Vol. 56 (March–April 1977), pp. 100–107, and William Rupert, "ERISA: Compliance May Be Easier Than You Expect and Pay Unexpected Dividends," *Personnel Journal*, Vol. 55 (April 1976).
42. Robert Paul, "The Impact of Pension Reform on American Business," *Sloan Management Review*, Vol. 18 (Fall 1976), pp. 59–71. See also John M. Walbridge, Jr., "The Next Hurdle for Benefits Manager: Section 89," *Compensation and Benefits Review*, Vol. 20, no. 6 (November–December 1988), pp. 22–35.
43. Henderson, *Compensation Management*, p. 292.
44. Bureau of National Affairs, "Tax Reform Act: Major Changes in Store for Compensation Programs," *Bulletin to Management*, October 9, 1986, p. 1.
45. In fact, unfunded pension liabilities of American firms have continued to grow. "Pension Survey: Unfunded Liabilities Continue to Grow," *Business Week*, August 25, 1980, pp. 94–97. See also James Benson and Barbara Suzaki, "After Tax Reform," Part III, "Planning Executive Benefits," *Compensation and Benefits Review*, Vol. 20, no 2 (March–April 1988), pp. 45–57; and BNA, February 23, 1989, p. 57. "Post-Retirement Benefits Impact of FASB New Accounting Rule."
46. For a discussion see Milton Zall, "Understanding the Risks to Pension Benefits," *Personnel Journal*, (January 1992), pp. 62–69.
47. Robert Arnott and Peter Bernstein, "The Right Way to Manage Your Pension Fund," *Harvard Business Review* (January–February 1988), pp. 95–102. See also 401(k): *Cash or Deferred Arrangements,* Coopers & Lybrand (USA), 1991.
48. A task force of consultants from William A. Mercer Meidinger Hansen, Inc. "The Omnibus Budget Reconciliation Act of 1987: What It Means to Pensions and Employee Benefits," *Compensation and Benefits Review* (March–April 1988), pp. 14–32.
49. Judith Mazo, "Another Compliance Challenge for Employers: The Retirement Equity Act," *Personnel*, Vol. 62, no. 2 (February 1985), pp. 43–49. See also Deborah Nikkel, "HIRS Implementation: A Systematic Approach," *Personnel*, Vol. 62, no. 2 (February 1985), pp. 66–69. See also Jack Schechter, "The Impact of Tax Reform on Employee Benefits: A Half Time Report," *Personnel,* Vol. 65, no. 1 (January 1988), pp. 46–51.
50. Randy Cepuch, "Should You Put IRA on the Payroll?" *Personnel Journal*, Vol. 61 (November 1982), p. 812.
51. Allen et al., *Pension Planning*, pp. 406–410. Note that self-employed individuals can establish Keogh (for H.R. 10) pension plans. Basically, 15% of earned income (or up to $7.500) can be invested in such a plan; if the person is not only self-employed but also the owner of the business, then all his or her full-time employees must also be covered by the plan.
52. Willam M. Mercer-Meidinger, Inc., "How Will Reform Tax Your Benefits?" *Personnel Journal*, Vol. 65, no. 12 (1986), pp. 52–53. See also Steven Baderian and Ivy Stempel, "Coping with COBRA," *Compensation and Benefits Review*, Vol. 19, no. 3 (May–June 1987), pp 28–36.
53. "Trends," *BNA Bulletin to Management*, May 7, 1992, p. 143.
54. "Plan Design and Experience in Early Retirement Windows and in Other Voluntary Separation Plans," prepared by the staff of Hewitt Associates, 1986. See also Eugene Seibert and Jo Anne Seibert, "Retirement Windows," *Personnel Journal*, Vol. 68, no. 5 (May 1989) pp. 30–31, examples of wellness program benefits.
55. Marco Colosi, Philip Rosen, and Sara Herrin, "Is Your Early Retirement Package Courting Disaster?" *Personnel Journal*, (August 1988) pp. 59–67.
56. *Paolillo* v. *Dresser Industries*, 821F.2d81 (2d cir. 1987).
57. See also Eugene Seibert and Jo Anne Seibert, "Look into Window Alternatives," *Personnel Journal* (May 1989), pp. 80–87.
58. See Henderson, *Compensation Management*, pp. 336–339. See also Lewis Burger, "Group Legal Service Plans: A Benefit Whose Time Has Come," *Compensation and Benefits Review*, Vol. 18, no. 4 (July–August 1986), pp. 28–34.
59. Richard T. Hellan, "Employee Assistance: An EAP Update: A Perspective for the '80s," *Personnel Journal*, Vol. 65, no. 6 (1986), p. 51.
60. See Dale Masi and Seymour Friedland, "EAP Actions & Options," *Personnel Journal* (June 1988), pp. 61–67.
61. These are based on ibid.
62. "Employee Benefit Costs," Bureau of National Affairs. *Bulletin to Management*, January 16, 1992, pp. 12–14.
63. The Research Staff of Hewitt Associates, *Innovative Benefits*, Hewitt Associates, 160 Bloor Street East, Toronto, Ontario.
64. This is based on Margaret Meiers, "Parental Leave and the Bottom Line," *Personnel Journal* (September 1988), pp. 108–115.
65. Ibid., pp. 110–112.
66. L. Lynne Pulliman, "Pregnancy Disability and Child Care Leave: What Does Title VII Require?" *Employee Relations Law Journal*, Vol. 17, no. 3 (Winter 1991–1992), pp. 511–518.
67. For a discussion see ibid., pp. 516–517.
68. Jennifer S. MacLeod, "Meeting the Needs of Today's Working Parents," *Employment Relations Today*, Vol. 13, no. 2 (Summer 1986), p. 127. See also Susan Velleman, "A Benefit to Meet Changing Needs: Child-Care Assistance," *Compensation and Benefits Review*, Vol. 19, no. 3 (May–June 1987), pp. 54–58, and June O'Neill, "A Flexible Work Force: Opportunities for Women," *Journal of Labor Relations,* Vol. 13, no. 1, Winter 1992, pp. 67–72.
69. *Dun's Review* (July 1981), p. 49. See also Velleman, "A Benefit to Meet Changing Needs," pp. 54–62; Bureau of National Affairs, "Child Care Benefits Offered by Employers," *Bulletin to Management* March 17, 1988, pp. 84–85.

For a discussion of other employer child care options and the costs and problems of implementing them, see Caroline Eichman and Barbara Reisman, "How Small Employers Are Benefitting from Offering Child Care Assistance," *Employment Relations Today* (Spring 1992), pp. 51–62.

70. "Employers and Child Care: Establishing Services Through the Workplace," Women's Bureau, U.S. Department of Labor, Washington, D.C., 1982. See also BNA, "Special Survey on Child Care Assistance Programs," *Bulletin to Management*, March 26, 1987. Donald J. Peterson and Douglas Massengill, "Child Care Programs Benefit Employers, Too," *Personnel*, Vol. 65, no. 5 (May 1988), pp. 58–62, and Toni A. Campbell and David E. Campbell, "Employers and Child Care," *Personnel Journal*, Vol. 67, no. 4 (April 1988), pp. 84–87.
71. Lorri Johnson, "Effectiveness of An Employee-Sponsored Child Care Center," *Applied H.R.M. Research*, Vol. 2, no. 1, Summer 1991, pp. 38–67.
72. Commerce Clearing House, "As the Population Ages, There Is Growing Interest in Adding Elder Care to the Benefits Package," *Ideas and Trends*, August 21, 1987, pp. 129–131.
73. "Elder Care: A Maturing Benefit," *BNA Bulletin to Management*, February 20, 1992, pp. 50, 55.
74. Mary Zippo, "Subsidized Employee Transportation: A Three Way Benefit," *Personnel*, Vol. 57 (May–June 1980), pp. 40–41.
75. Hewitt Associates, Survey of Educational Reimbursement Programs, 1984.
76. Bruce Ellig, *Executive Compensation—A Total Pay Perspective* (New York: McGraw-Hill, 1982), p. 141.
77. Lindroth, "Inflation Taxes, and Perks," p. 939.
78. J. Brad Chapman and Robert Ottermann, "Employee Preference for Various Compensation and Fringe Benefit Options" (Berea, OH: ASPA Foundation, 1975). See also, William White and James Becker, "Increasing the Motivational Impact of Employee Benefits, *Personnel* (January–February 1980), pp. 32–37, and Barney Olmsted and Suzanne Smith, "Flex for Success!" *Personnel*, Vol. 66, no. 6 (June 1989), pp. 50–55.
79. Ibid.; Albert Cole, "Flexible Benefits Are a Key to Better Employee Relations," *Personnel Journal* (January 1983) pp. 49–53. See also, Lance Tane, "Guidelines to Successful Flex Plans: Four Companies' Experiences," *Compensation and Benefits Review*, Vol. 17 (July–August, 1985), pp. 38–45; Peter Stonebraker, A Three-Tier Plan for Cafeteria Benefits," *Personnel Journal*, Vol. 63, no. 12 (December 1984), pp. 50–53; and Commerce Clearing House, "Flexible Benefits: Will They Work for You?" Chicago, 1983; and George F. Dreher, Ronald A. Ash, and Robert D. Bretz, "Benefit Coverage and Employee Cost: Critical Factors in Explaining Compensation Satisfaction," *Personnel Psychology*, Vol. 41, no. 2 (Summer 1988), pp. 237–254.
80. Barbara Anne Soloman, "The Change to 'Flexible': No Easy Task," *Personnel*, Vol. 62, no. 5 (May 1985), pp. 10–12.
81. Henderson, *Compensation Management*, p. 312; "Flexible Benefits Are Spreading Fast," *Dun's Business Month*, September 1981, pp. 82–84. See Caroline A. Baker, "Flex Your Benefits," *Personnel Journal*, Vol. 67, no. 5 (May 1988) pp. 54–58, for discussion of the pros and cons of three basic approaches to flexible benefits.
82. For information about this program, contact Towers, Perrin, Forster, and Crosby, 245 Park Avenue, New York, NY 10167. Hewitt Associates similarly has a program called FlexSystem (Hewitt Associates, New York, NY). See also John Parkington, "The 'Trade-Off' Approach to Benefits Cost Containment: A Strategy to Increase Employee Satisfaction," *Compensation and Benefits Review*, Vol. 19, no. 1 (January–February 1987), pp. 35–36, which explains a simple way of determining what your employees prefer in benefits.
83. "Benefits Policies," *BNA Bulletin to Management*, March 5, 1992, p.71.
84. This is based on Anthony Barra, "Employees Keep Informed with Interactive KIOSKs," *Personnel Journal* (October 1988), pp. 43–51.
85. For a discussion see, for example, Marvin Selter, "On the Plus Side of Employee Leasing," *Personnel Journal* (April 1986), pp. 87–91; David Altaner, "Employees for Lease," *Weekly Business News/Sun Sentinel*, November 9, 1987, pp. 8–9.
86. John Naisbitt, "Employee Leasing Takes Off," *Success!* (April 1986), p. 12.
87. Morton Grossman and Margaret Magnus, "The Boom in Benefits," *Personnel Journal* (November 1988), pp. 51–59; "Employee Benefits in Smaller Firms," Bureau of National Affairs, *Bulletin to Management*, June 27, 1991, pp. 196–197.
88. Thomas Paine, "Benefits in the 1990s," *Personnel Journal*, (March 1988) pp. 82–92.
89. "Compensation in the Year 2000," *BNA Bulletin to Management*, February 27, 1992, p. 64.
90. This is based on Gary Dessler, *Winning Employee Commitment* (New York: McGraw-Hill Book Company, 1993), Chapter 9.

VIDEO CASE 3

—Conclusion—

EMPLOYEE PENSION FUNDS

In the Introduction to Video Case 3 on page 401, we asked several important questions that you should now refer to.

In Part 3 we focused on employee compensation and saw that there are many factors employers have to take into account in formulating compenation plans. Certainly, federal and state laws are one—including, for example, the Fair Labor Standards Act. Other, perhaps more practical factors include the questions of external and internal equity: Salaries have to be in line with what other employers are paying, or your firm may not be able to attract qualified candidates. And salaries must be internally equitable as well, since employees doing similar jobs do not like to find out that they are being paid at different rates. Employee commitment is another factor to be considered. Behavioral techniques such as worker empowerment aren't enough to make employees feel committed. Instead, firms usually build their commitment practices on a strong foundation of equitable financial rewards.

Firms today are using a wide array of financial incentives—often under the banner of "pay for performance." In addition to traditional incentives, such as piecework plans and merit pay, companies are instituting gain-sharing plans, for example, as well as yearly bonus awards and various spot award plans such as those at Federal Express.

There's little doubt that, along with widespread efforts to build commitment, organizational downsizing continues, as does employee mobility. This in turn has implications for how companies structure their pension plans. For one thing (as the video points out), because employees are so mobile, more and more of them want pensions—or so-called lump-sum distributions—that they can walk away with in mid-career. (In other words, employees leave the firm before retirement and take a "lump sum" with them when they go.) Similarly, we are seeing a switch away from traditional, defined benefits plans that specify what pension benefits employees get when they retire to defined contribution plans in which there is a defined contribution (but not necessarily a set retirement benefit).

In Part 4 we turn to the topics of collective bargaining, and union-management relations.

PART 4

Labor Relations

VIDEO CASE 4
—Introduction—

WILL UNIONS HAVE TO CONTINUE STRUGGLING TO GET NEW MEMBERS?

from ABC News, "Business World," September 6, 1992

In Part 3 we discussed employee compensation, including establishing pay plans, financial incentives, and benefits and services.

Now, in Part 3 we turn to the important topic of labor relations, and in particular:

Chapter 15: Basics of Labor Relations
Chapter 16: Collective Bargaining

Just a few years ago many people were predicting the eventual demise of the American labor movement. As we'll see in the next two chapters, a variety of social and technological trends seems to be reducing the need for unions. Indeed, union membership in the United States has dropped dramatically throughout most of the 1970s and 1980s. It's interesting, therefore, that in June 1993 news reports described how the new president of General Motors was closing down assembly operations in several Mexican plants in order to bring production back to plants in Texas and Michigan. This would help to provide more job security for GM's unionized United States work force and thereby reduce the traditional hostility that existed between GM and its unions.

The video describes tensions existing between GM and its unions toward the end of 1992, as well as the problems the United Auto Workers is having organizing the new Japanese and German auto plants that are coming to the United States. As you read Chapters 15 and 16, consider these questions:

1. How will the growing emphasis on quality improvement programs and worker involvement affect unionization efforts?
2. What are the elements of an effective grievance procedure?

CHAPTER 15

BASICS OF LABOR RELATIONS

OVERVIEW

After briefly discussing the history of the American labor movement we describe some basics of labor legislation, including the subject of unfair labor practices. We also describe the union actions you can expect during the union drive and election. When you finish studying this chapter, you should be able to deal more effectively with a unionization drive and a bargaining session; discuss "five sure ways" to lose a National Labor Relations Board (NLRB) election; discuss the main features of at least three major pieces of labor legislation; and present examples of what to expect during the union drive and election.

▶ INTRODUCTION: THE LABOR MOVEMENT

Today over 16 million American workers belong to unions—a number that amounts to around 16% of the total number of men and women working in America today. In some industries—mining, construction, transportation—it is almost impossible to get a job without joining a union. And unions do not just appeal to private sector blue-collar workers. More and more white-collar workers and public employees are turning to unions as well.

Why are unions important? How did they get that way? What do unions want of their members? Why do workers join unions? These are some of the questions addressed in this chapter.[1]

A BRIEF HISTORY OF THE AMERICAN UNION MOVEMENT

To understand what unions are and what they want, it is useful to understand "where they've been." The first thing to understand is that unions have been around for quite some time. As early as 1790, for example, skilled craftsmen (shoemakers, tailors, printers, and so on) organized themselves into trade unions. They posted their "minimum wage" demands and had "tramping committees" go from shop to shop to ensure that no member accepted a lesser wage.

Samuel Gompers formed the AFL in 1886.

From these earliest unions to the present time, the history of the union movement has been one of alternate expansion and contraction. Union membership grew until a major depression around 1837 resulted in a decline in membership. Membership then began increasing as America entered its Industrial Revolution. In 1869 a group of tailors met and formed the Knights of Labor; the "Knights" were interested in political reform and agitation and often sought political changes. By 1885 it had 100,000 members and (as a result of winning a major strike against a railroad) exploded to 700,000 members the following year. Partly because of their focus on social reform (and partly due to a series of unsuccessful strikes), the Knights' membership dwindled rapidly thereafter. By 1893 (when they were dissolved) they had virtually no members.

In 1886 Samuel Gompers formed the American Federation of Labor. It consisted mostly of skilled workers and (unlike the Knights) eschewed social reform for practical "bread and butter" gains for its members. The Knights of Labor had engaged in a "class struggle" to alter the form of society and *thereby* get a bigger chunk of benefits for its members. Gompers, on the other hand, aimed at raising day-to-day wages and improving the working conditions of his constituents. The AFL grew rapidly until after World War I, at which point its membership exceeded 5½ million people.

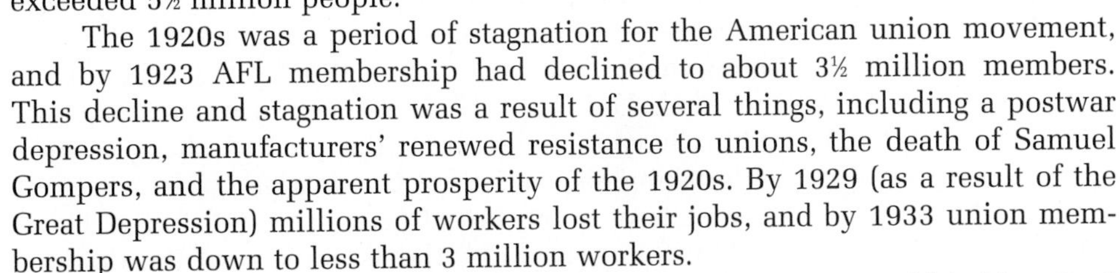

The 1920s was a period of stagnation for the American union movement, and by 1923 AFL membership had declined to about 3½ million members. This decline and stagnation was a result of several things, including a postwar depression, manufacturers' renewed resistance to unions, the death of Samuel Gompers, and the apparent prosperity of the 1920s. By 1929 (as a result of the Great Depression) millions of workers lost their jobs, and by 1933 union membership was down to less than 3 million workers.

Membership began to increase in the mid-1930s. As part of his New Deal programs, President Roosevelt passed the National Industrial Recovery Act which, among other things, made it easier for labor to organize. Other federal laws (as well as prosperity and World War II) also contributed to the rapid increase in membership, which topped out at about 21 million workers in the 1970s. Then membership again began to decline, to about 16.6 million wage and salary workers in 1991.[2]

Today, the labor movement is undergoing dramatic changes, as it has been for more than ten years. At the present time, organized labor's share of the work force in the United States is down to 16% and is still dropping; if this trend persists, by the year 2000 unions will represent only 13% of all nonfarm workers, down from a peak of about 34% in 1955. The union membership proportion is dropping rapidly because the number of union members is falling while total employment is rising.[3]

RECENT TRENDS IN UNIONIZATION

Several things have contributed to this decline. Traditionally, unions have appealed mostly to blue-collar workers, and the proportion of blue-collar jobs has been decreasing as service sector and white-collar service jobs have increased. Furthermore, several economic factors, including intense international competition, outdated equipment and factories, mismanagement, new technology, and government regulation, have hit those industries (like mining and manufacturing) that have traditionally been unionized. Other changes, including the deregulation of trucking, airlines, and communications, have helped to erode union membership as well.[4] The effect of all this has been the permanent layoff of hundreds of thousands of union members, the permanent closing of company plants, the relocation of companies to nonunion settings (either in the United States or overseas), and mergers and acquisitions that have eliminated union jobs and impacted collective bargaining agreements.

Furthermore, there now exists what *Business Week* refers to as a "growing web of laws and court rulings" that provides the sorts of protection that up to a few years ago only unions could provide. Foremost on the list are those court decisions (discussed elsewhere in this book) that erode the employment-at-will doctrine and make it more difficult for employers in many states to fire employees without just cause. On this and many other fronts, employee rights regarding job security, privacy, occupational safety, equal employment opportunities, pension vesting, and pay policies are now provided by law. To that extent, the role formerly played by unions has been reduced.[5]

Unions Reassert Themselves

Of course, unions are aware of these trends and are acting to reassert their dominance as employees' representatives. The AFL-CIO has released a study by its Committee on the Evolution of Work titled "The Changing Situation of Workers and Their Unions." The main conclusion of this study was that the country's unions have "fallen behind the pace of change." As a result, the AFL-CIO is undertaking new activities. One is a program to train 1,000 unionists in the fundamentals of how to react (and not react) to the TV camera and how to better explain themselves and the aspirations of the union movement to the general public. Another is a new organizing drive for service workers beginning with the health care industry and firms such as Blue Cross/Blue Shield.[6]

In fact, during the last ten years or so, the major union effort has been aimed at organizing white-collar workers. Service-oriented industries—insurance, banking, retail trade, government—are now being organized by unions, for example. More than 10% of white-collar workers have already become unionized. The number is increasing rapidly, particularly among professionals (many of whom work in the public sector).[7]

In summary, unions are becoming more activist today, for instance in terms of advertising for workers and aggressively pursuing white-collar workers. Beyond that (as we'll see in this and Chapter 16), they are taking other activist steps, including sophisticated "corporate campaigns" aimed at winning over reluctant corporate boards of directors, and using their pension plan clout to win control of firms.[8] Whether this is enough to arrest union membership declines remains to be seen.

WHY DO WORKERS ORGANIZE?

Much time and money has been spent trying to analyze "why workers unionize," and many theories have been proposed. Yet there is no simple answer to the question, partly because each worker probably joins for his or her own unique reasons.

Yet it does seem clear that workers do not unionize just to get more pay or better working conditions. These are important factors and, in fact (for whatever reason), the weekly earnings of union members are about $120 higher than are those of nonunion employees.[9] Yet the urge to unionize more often seems to boil down to the belief on the part of workers that it is only through unity that they can get their fair share of the "pie" and also protect themselves from the arbitrary whims of management. In practice, this usually means that low morale and poor communication tend to lead to unionization, as does fear of job loss. Yet in reality unions have not always been able to protect job security, as evidenced by the huge loss of union jobs in manufacturing industries and airlines over the past few years.[10]

In 1937 these union teachers were dismissed and protested by sitting down outside the administration's offices.

Research Findings

Generally, it is often dissatisfaction with basic bread-and-butter issues that leads to pro union voting, rather than noneconomic issues such as opportunities for achievement on the job (although noneconomic issues are often important as well). This is illustrated in Table 15.1, which summarizes the correlation between *job satisfaction* and *voting for union representation* in one study. Notice that dissatisfaction with basic issues such as job security and wages was most strongly correlated with a vote for the union, while the employees' satisfaction with things such as supervisor and type of work was less so.[11] The author of this study contends, by the way, that dissatisfaction alone will not automatically lead to unionization. First, she says, *dissatisfied employees must first believe they are without the ability to influence a change in the conditions causing the dissatisfaction.* Then, she adds, a large enough group of employees would have to believe it could improve things through collective action. Dissatisfied employees who believe the union will be instrumental in achieving their goals thus present a potent combination.[12]

The bottom line (to repeat) is that the urge to unionize often boils down to the belief on the workers' part that it is only through unity that they can get their

TABLE 15.1 Correlation Between Job Satisfaction and Voting for Union Representation

ISSUE	CORRELATION WITH VOTE FOR UNION
Are you satisfied with the job security at this company?	–.42
Are you satisfied with your wages?	–.40
Taking everything into consideration, are you satisfied with this company as a place to work?	–.36
Do supervisors in this company treat all employees alike?	–.34
Are you satisfied with your fringe benefits?	–.31
Do your supervisors show appreciation when you do a good job?	–.30
Do you think there is a good chance for you to get promoted in this company?	–.30
Are you satisfied with the type of work you are doing?	–.14

Source: Adapted from Jeanne M. Brett, "Why Employees Want Unions," *Organizational Dynamics*, Spring 1980, p. 51. © 1980 by AMACOM, a division of American Management Associations.

fair share of the pie and also protect themselves from the arbitrary whims of management. Here is how one writer describes the reasons behind the early unionization of automobile workers:

> In the years to come, economic issues would make the headlines when union and management met in negotiations. But in the early years the rate of pay was not the major complaint of the autoworkers. . . . Specifically, the principal grievances of the autoworkers were the speed-up of production and the lack of any kind of job security. As production tapered off, the order in which workers were laid off was determined largely by the whim of foremen and other supervisors. The system encouraged workers to curry favor by doing personal chores for supervisory employees—by bringing them gifts or outright bribes. The same applied to recalls as production was resumed. The worker had no way of knowing when he would be laid off, and had no assurance when, or whether, he would be recalled. . . . Generally, what the workers revolted against was the lack of human dignity and individuality, and a working relationship that was massively impersonal, cold, and nonhuman. They wanted to be treated like human beings—not like faceless clockcard numbers.[13] [See Figure 15.1 for a picture of early auto plant working conditions.][14]

WHAT DO UNIONS WANT? WHAT ARE THEIR AIMS?

union security
Unions' desire to establish security for themselves by gaining the right to represent a firm's workers.

We can generalize by saying that unions have two sets of aims, one for *union security* and one for *improved wages, hours, working conditions,* and *benefits* for their members.

Union Security

First (and probably foremost), unions seek to establish **security** for themselves. They fight hard for the right to represent a firm's workers and to be the *exclusive*

FIGURE 15.1
Early Auto Plant Working Conditions

Source: Warner Pflug, *The UAW in Pictures* (Detroit: Wayne State University Press, 1971), p. 14.

Note: In addition to the back-breaking work required in the early auto plants, health hazards were an ever-present danger. Lighting was often poor, dust filled the air, and unguarded moving belts led to many injuries.

bargaining agent for all employees in the unit. (Here, they negotiate contracts for all employees *including* those not members of the union.) Five types of union security are possible.

closed shop
A form of union security in which the company can hire only union members. This was outlawed in 1947 but still exists in some industries (such as printing).

union shop
A form of union security in which the company can hire nonunion people but they must join the union after a prescribed period of time and pay dues. (If they do not, they can be fired.)

agency shop
A form of union security in which employees who do not belong to the union must still pay union dues (on the assumption that union efforts benefit all workers).

open shop
Perhaps the least attractive type of union security from the union's point of view, the workers decide whether or not to join the union; and those who do not do not pay dues.

maintenance of membership arrangement
A form of union security in which employees do not have to belong to the union; however, union members employed by the firm must maintain membership in the union for the contract period.

1. **Closed Shop.**[15] The company can hire only union members. This was outlawed in 1947 but still exists in some industries (such as printing).
2. **Union Shop.** The company *can* hire nonunion people but they must join the union after a prescribed period of time and pay dues. (If not, they can be fired.)
3. **Agency Shop.** Employees who do not belong to the union still must pay union dues (on the assumption that the union's efforts benefit *all* the workers).
4. **Open Shop.** It is up to the workers whether or not they join the union—those who do not do not pay dues.
5. **Maintenance of Membership Arrangement.** Employees do not have to belong to the union. However, *union members* employed by the firm *must* "maintain membership" in the union for the contract period.

Improved Wages, Hours, and Benefits for Members

Once their security is assured, unions fight to better the lot of their members—to improve their wages, hours, and working conditions, for example. The typical labor agreement also gives the union a role in personnel management activities, including recruiting, selecting, compensating, promoting, training, and discharging employees.

THE AFL-CIO

What It Is

The **American Federation of Labor and Congress of Industrial Organizations (AFL-CIO)** is a voluntary federation of about 100 national and international labor unions in the United States. It was formed by the merger of the AFL and CIO in 1955, with the AFL's George Meany as its first president. For many people, it has become synonymous with the word "union" in America.

There are about 2½ million workers who belong to unions that are not affiliated with the AFL-CIO. Of these workers, about one-half belong to the largest "independent" union, the United Auto Workers (about 1 million members).[16] The formerly independent Teamsters union, with about 2 million members, rejoined the AFL-CIO in October 1987.

The Structure of the AFL-CIO

There are three layers in the structure of the AFL-CIO (and other American unions). First, there is the *local* union. This is the union the worker joins and to which he or she pays dues. It is also usually the local union that signs the collective bargaining agreement determining the wages and working conditions. The local is in turn a single chapter in the *national* union. For example, if you were a typesetter in Detroit, you would belong to the local union there, but the local union is one of hundreds of local chapters of the International Typographical Union, with headquarters in Colorado Springs.

The third layer in the structure is the *national federation*, in this case, the AFL-CIO. This federation is comprised of about 100 national (and international) unions, which in turn comprise more than 60,000 local unions.

Most people tend to think of the AFL-CIO as the most important part of the labor movement, but it is not. The AFL-CIO itself really has little power, except what it is allowed to exercise by its constituent national unions. Thus, the president of the teachers' union wields more power in that capacity than in his capacity as a vice-president of the AFL-CIO. Yet as a practical matter the AFL-CIO does act as a spokesperson for labor, and its president, Lane Kirkland, has accumulated political clout far in excess of some "figurehead" president.

▶ UNIONS AND THE LAW

BACKGROUND

Until about 1930 there were no special labor laws. Employers were not required to engage in collective bargaining with employees and were virtually unrestrained in their behavior toward unions: The use of spies, blacklists, and the firing of "agitators" was widespread. "Yellow dog" contracts (whereby management could require *non*union membership as a condition for employment) were widely enforced. Most union weapons—even strikes—were held illegal.

This one-sided situation lasted in America from the Revolution to the Great Depression (around 1930). Since then (in response to changing public attitudes, values, and economic conditions) labor law has gone through three clear changes: from "strong encouragement" of unions, to "modified encouragement coupled with regulation," and finally to "detailed regulation of internal union affairs."[17]

PERIOD OF STRONG ENCOURAGEMENT: THE NORRIS-LAGUARDIA ACT (1932) AND THE NATIONAL LABOR RELATIONS OR WAGNER ACT (1935)

The Norris-LaGuardia and National Labor Relations (Wagner) acts marked a shift in labor law from repression to strong encouragement of union activity.[18] The first of these acts was passed during the Depression. During this time unemployment was rampant, and many policymakers felt that only through bargaining collectively could employees improve their work situations.

Norris-LaGuardia Act This law marked the beginning of the era of strong encouragement of unions and guaranteed to each employee the right to bargain collectively "free from interference, restraint, or coercion."

The **Norris-LaGuardia Act** set the stage for a new era in which union activity was *encouraged*. It guaranteed to each employee the right to bargain collectively "free from interference, restraint, or coercion." It declared yellow dog contracts unenforceable. And it limited the courts' abilities to issue injunctions for activities such as peaceful picketing and payment of strike benefits.

Yet this act did little to restrain employers from fighting labor organizations by whatever means they could muster. Therefore, in 1935 the National Labor Relations (or Wagner) Act was passed to add "teeth" to the Norris-LaGuardia Act. It did this by (1) banning certain *unfair labor practices*; (2) providing for secret ballot elections and majority rule (for determining whether a firm's employees were to unionize); and (3) creating the **National Labor Relations Board (NLRB)** for enforcing these two provisions.

National Labor Relations Board (NLRB)
The agency created by the Wagner Act to investigate unfair labor practice charges and to provide for secret ballot elections and majority rule in determining whether or not a firm's employees want a union.

National Labor Relations (or Wagner) Act
This law banned certain types of unfair labor practices and provided for secret ballot elections and majority rule for determining whether or not a firm's employees want to unionize.

unfair labor practices
Under the Wagner Act, it is unfair for management to "interfere with, restrain, or coerce employees" in exercising their legally sanctioned right of self-organization.

Employer Unfair Labor Practices

The **Wagner Act** deemed "statutory wrongs" (but not crimes) five employer **unfair labor practices:**

1. It is unfair for employers to "interfere with, restrain, or coerce employees" in exercising their legally sanctioned right of self-organization.
2. It is an unfair practice for company representatives to dominate or interfere with either the formation or administration of labor unions. Among other management actions found to be unfair under practices 1 and 2 are bribery of employees, company spy systems, moving a business to avoid unionization, and blacklisting union sympathizers.
3. Companies are prohibited from discriminating in any way against employees for their legal union activities.
4. Employers are forbidden from discharging or discriminating against employees simply because the latter had filed "unfair practice" charges against the company.
5. Finally, it made it an unfair labor practice for employers to refuse to bargain collectively with their employees' duly chosen representatives.

An unfair labor practice charge is filed (see Figure 15.2) with the National Labor Relations Board. The board then investigates the charge and determines if formal action should be taken. Possible actions (as summarized in Figure 15.3) include dismissal of the complaint, request for an injunction against the employer, or an order that the employer cease and desist.

From 1935 to 1947

Union membership increased quickly after passage of the Wagner Act in 1935. Other factors (such as an improving economy and aggressive union leadership) contributed to this as well. But by the mid-1940s the tide had begun to turn. Largely because of a series of massive postwar strikes, public policy began to shift against what many viewed as the union excesses of the times. The stage was set for passage of the Taft-Hartley Act of 1947.

PERIOD OF MODIFIED ENCOURAGEMENT COUPLED WITH REGULATION: THE TAFT-HARTLEY ACT (1947)

Taft-Hartley Act
Also known as the Labor–Management Relations Act, this law prohibited union unfair labor practices and enumerated the rights of employees as union members. It also enumerated the rights of employers.

The **Taft-Hartley** (or Labor–Management Relations) **Act** reflected the public's less enthusiastic attitudes toward unions. It amended the National Labor Relations (Wagner) Act. Its provisions were aimed at limiting unions in four ways: (1) by prohibiting *union* unfair labor practices, (2) by enumerating the rights of employees as union members, (3) by enumerating the rights of employers, and (4) by allowing the president of the United States to temporarily bar *national emergency* strikes.

Union Unfair Labor Practices

The Taft-Hartley Act enumerated several labor practices that unions were prohibited from engaging in:

FORM EXEMPT UNDER 44 U.S.C. 3512

FORM NLRB 501 (2-81)

UNITED STATES OF AMERICA
NATIONAL LABOR RELATIONS BOARD
CHARGE AGAINST EMPLOYER

INSTRUCTIONS: File an original and 4 copies of this charge with NLRB Regional Director for the region in which the alleged unfair labor practice occurred or is occurring.

DO NOT WRITE IN THIS SPACE	
CASE NO.	DATE FILED

1. EMPLOYER AGAINST WHOM CHARGE IS BROUGHT

a. NAME OF EMPLOYER

b. NUMBER OF WORKERS EMPLOYED

c. ADDRESS OF ESTABLISHMENT *(street and number, city, State, and ZIP code)*

d. EMPLOYER REPRESENTATIVE TO CONTACT

e. PHONE NO.

f. TYPE OF ESTABLISHMENT *(factory, mine, wholesaler, etc.)*

g. IDENTIFY PRINCIPAL PRODUCT OR SERVICE

h. THE ABOVE-NAMED EMPLOYER HAS ENGAGED IN AND IS ENGAGING IN UNFAIR LABOR PRACTICES WITHIN THE MEANING OF SECTION 8(a), SUBSECTIONS (1) AND ______ *(list subsections)* OF THE NATIONAL LABOR RELATIONS ACT, AND THESE UNFAIR LABOR PRACTICES ARE UNFAIR LABOR PRACTICES AFFECTING COMMERCE WITHIN THE MEANING OF THE ACT.

2. BASIS OF THE CHARGE *(be specific as to facts, names, addresses, plants involved, dates, places, etc.)*

BY THE ABOVE AND OTHER ACTS, THE ABOVE-NAMED EMPLOYER HAS INTERFERED WITH, RESTRAINED, AND COERCED EMPLOYEES IN THE EXERCISE OF THE RIGHTS GUARANTEED IN SECTION 7 OF THE ACT.

3. FULL NAME OF PARTY FILING CHARGE *(if labor organization, give full name, including local name and number)*

4a. ADDRESS *(street and number, city, State, and ZIP code)*

4b. TELEPHONE NO.

5. FULL NAME OF NATIONAL OR INTERNATIONAL LABOR ORGANIZATION OF WHICH IT IS AN AFFILIATE OR CONSTITUENT UNIT *(to be filled in when charge is filed by a labor organization)*

6. DECLARATION

I declare that I have read the above charge and that the statements therein are true to the best of my knowledge and belief.

By ______ (signature of representative or person filing charge) ______ (title, if any)

Address ______ ______ (telephone number) ______ (date)

WILLFULLY FALSE STATEMENTS ON THIS CHARGE CAN BE PUNISHED BY FINE AND IMPRISONMENT
(U.S. CODE, TITLE 18, SECTION 1001)

FIGURE 15.2 NLRB Form 501: Filing an Unfair Labor Practice Charge

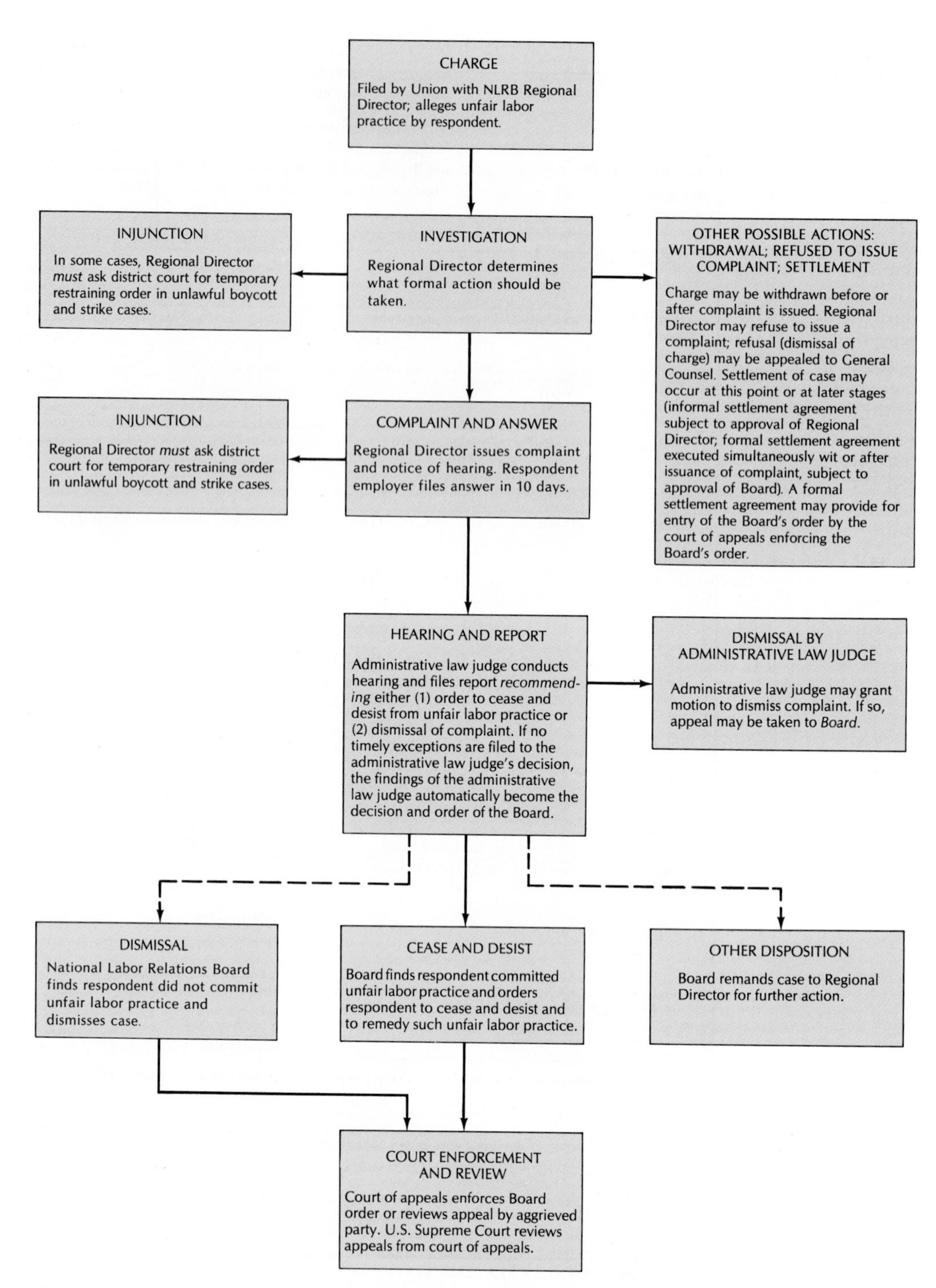

FIGURE 15.3 Possible Actions NLRB Can Take When It Receives Unfair Labor Practice Charge

Source: Adapted from Bruce Feldacker, *Labor Guide to Labor Law* 3/e (Reston, VA: Reston, 1990), p. 15.

union unfair labor practices
The Taft-Hartley Act banned unions from restraining or coercing employees from exercising their guaranteed bargaining rights; prohibited unions from causing an employer to discriminate in any way against an employee in order to encourage or discourage membership in a union; prohibited a union from refusing to bargain "in good faith" with the employer about wages, hours, and other employment conditions; and prohibited a union from engaging in "featherbedding."

right-to-work laws
Legislation that outlawed labor contracts that made union membership a condition for retaining employment.

1. First, unions were banned from restraining or coercing employees from exercising their guaranteed bargaining rights. For example, some specific union actions the courts have held illegal under this provision include stating to an antiunion employee that he or she will lose his or her job once the union gains recognition; issuing patently false statements during union organizing campaigns; making threats of reprisal against employees subpoenaed to testify against the union at NLRB hearings.
2. It is also an unfair labor practice for a union to cause an employer to discriminate in any way against an employee in order to encourage or discourage his or her membership in a union. In other words, the union cannot try to force an employer to fire a worker because he or she doesn't attend union meetings, opposes union policies, or refuses to join a union. There is one exception to this. Where a closed or union shop prevails (and union membership is therefore a prerequisite to employment), the union may demand discharge for a worker who fails to pay his or her initiation fees and dues.
3. It is an unfair labor practice for a union to refuse to bargain "in good faith" with the employer about wages, hours, and other employment conditions. Certain strikes and boycotts are also considered unfair union labor practices.
4. It is also an unfair labor practice for a union to engage in "featherbedding." (Here an employer is required to pay an employee for services not performed.)

Rights of Employees

The Taft-Hartley Act also protected the rights of *employees* against their unions. For example, many people felt that compulsory unionism violated the basic American right of freedom of association. New **right-to-work laws** sprang up in 19 states (mainly in the South and Southwest). These outlawed labor contracts that made union membership a condition for keeping one's job. In New York, for example, many printing firms have union shops. There, you can't work as a press operator unless you belong to a printers' union. In Florida such union shops—except those covered by the Railway Labor Act—are illegal. There, printing shops typically employ both union and nonunion press operators. This provision also allowed an employee to present grievances directly to the employer (without going through the union) and required the employee's authorization before union dues could be subtracted from his or her paycheck.

Rights of Employers

The Taft-Hartley Act also explicitly gave *employers* certain rights. First, it gave them full freedom to express their views concerning union organization. For example, you can as a manager tell your employees that in your opinion unions are worthless, dangerous to the economy, and immoral. You can even, generally speaking, hint that unionization (and subsequent high-wage demands) might result in the permanent closing of the plant (but not its relocation). Employers can set forth the union's record in regard to violence and corruption (if appropriate) and can play upon the racial prejudices of workers (by describing the union's philosophy toward integration). In fact, your only major restraint is that you must avoid threats, promises, coercion, and direct interference with workers who are trying to reach a decision. There can be no threat of reprisal or force or promise of benefit.[19]

The employer (1) cannot meet with employees on company time within 24 hours of an election or (2) suggest to employees that they vote against the union *while they are at home or in the employer office*, although he or she *can* while in their work area or where they normally gather.

National Emergency Strikes

national emergency strikes
Strikes that might "imperil the national health and safety."

The Taft-Hartley Act also allows the U.S. president to intervene in **national emergency strikes.** These are strikes (for example, on the part of steel firm employees) that might "imperil the national health and safety." The president may appoint a board of inquiry and, based on its report, apply for an injunction restraining the strike for 60 days. If no settlement is reached during that time, the injunction can be extended for another 20 days. During this last period, employees are polled (in a secret ballot) to ascertain their willingness to accept the employer's last offer.

PERIOD OF DETAILED REGULATION OF INTERNAL UNION AFFAIRS: THE LANDRUM-GRIFFIN ACT (1959)

Landrum-Griffin Act
The law aimed at protecting union members from possible wrongdoing on the part of their unions.

In the 1950s, Senate investigations revealed unsavory practices on the part of some unions, and the result was the **Landrum-Griffin Act** (officially, the Labor–Management Reporting and Disclosure Act). An overriding aim of this act was to protect union members from possible wrongdoing on the part of their unions. It also was an amendment to the National Labor Relations (Wagner) Act.

Bill of Rights

First, this law contains a "bill of rights" for union members. Among other things, this provides for certain rights in the nomination of candidates for union office. It also affirms a member's right to sue his or her union and ensures that no member can be fined or suspended without due process—which includes a list of specific charges, time to prepare defense, and a fair hearing. It also requires that officers provide copies of the collective bargaining agreement to all union members.

Union Elections

This act also laid out ground rules regarding union elections. For example, national (and international) unions must elect officers at least once every five years, using some type of secret ballot mechanism. Also, local unions must elect officers at least every three years, again by secret ballot. The elections must adhere to the union's constitution and bylaws, and every member in good standing is entitled to one vote.

Union Officers

The act also regulates the kind of person who can serve as a union officer. For example, persons convicted of felonies (bribery, murder, and so on) are barred from holding union officer positions for a period of five years after conviction.

Employer Wrongdoing

The Senate investigating team also discovered some flagrant examples of employer wrongdoing. Union agents had been bribed, and so-called "labor relations consultants" had been used to buy off union officers, for example.

Such bribery had been a federal crime starting with the passage of the Taft-Hartley Act. But the Landrum-Griffin Act greatly expanded the list of unlawful employer actions. For example, companies can no longer pay their own employees to entice them into not joining the union. It also requires reports from unions and employers, covering things such as use of labor relations consultants.

LABOR LAW TODAY

The Labor Law Reform Bill was debated by the U.S. Senate, and although it did not pass (and is not law), its proposals help illustrate some of the ways the union movement hopes to bolster its sagging numbers.[20]

One of organized labor's aims with this bill was to make it harder for "antiunion" companies to resist being organized. For example, some companies—such as J. P. Stevens, a textile firm headquartered in the Southeast—had a long history of engaging in protracted litigation in order to resist union organizing efforts. The purpose of this bill, then, was to close some of the loopholes of previous labor laws and make it more difficult for confrontation-oriented employers to maneuver around existing laws.

Recent NLRB and Court Decisions

Against the backdrop of such efforts, the question of whether the courts and the NLRB are contributing to a more encouraging or discouraging climate for unions today is not entirely clear cut. On the one hand, some NLRB decisions favor unions. In one case (known as the *Jean Country* case), a union and a shopping center took their case to the NLRB. The basic question was whether the union could picket a store (Jean Country) on private property in a shopping mall. Under the old rule (which dated back to 1986), the NLRB would balance the union's right to engage in labor activity with the property owner's right to decide how the property should be used. It would then decide whose rights prevailed in that instance. Technicalities aside, in this case the NLRB basically modified its rule, thus making it easier for unions to show why their rights should prevail.[21]

On the other hand, many important recent NLRB and court decisions have gone against unions, and this could have the effect of weakening workers' union rights. For example, in one decision[22] the NLRB in effect made it harder for workers adversely affected by outrageous violations to take legal action. It required that they seek administrative redress instead. In another decision,[23] the NLRB held it would no longer evaluate the impact of misleading employer campaign statements upon worker free choice in a representation election.[24]

The Supreme Court's decision in *TWA* v. *Independent Federation of Flight Attendants* is another instance of the court's strengthening management's hand. For the first time, the Supreme Court held that management can announce it will continue to operate during a strike, "and that employees *in the bargaining unit* who wish to work during the strike will be considered the new permanent holders of any jobs they fill, assuming they want to stay in those jobs."[25] Strikers who want to return to work must wait for an opening to occur, said the Court. This may prove discouraging to union members considering a walkout, given the employer's right to also bring in outside replacements. In a 1992 case reminiscent of the *Jean Country* case previously discussed, the Supreme Court held that union organizers do not have the right to trespass on private property to get their message to employees. As long as the employees are not inaccessible—as they would be if they lived on company property, for instance—the court said non-employee union organizers would have to stay off the employer's property.[26]

This means, said one NLRB member, that in the future unions will have to show "extreme difficulty" in reaching employees in order to gain access to private property.[27] The pendulum today seems to have swung a bit more toward discouragement of union activities. Clinton Administration actions may change this.

▶ The Union Drive and Election

It is through the union drive and election that a union tries to be recognized to represent employees.[28] This process involves five basic steps: (1) initial contact, (2) authorization cards, (3) hearing, (4) campaign, and (5) the election.

STEP 1. INITIAL CONTACT

During the *initial contact* stage, the union determines the employees' interest in organizing, and an organizing committee is established.

The initiative for the first contact between the employees and the union may come from the employees, from a union already representing other employees of the firm, or from a union representing workers elsewhere. Sometimes a union effort starts with a disgruntled employee contacting the local union to learn how to organize his or her place of work. Sometimes, though, the campaign starts when a union decides it wants to expand to representing other employees in the firm or when the company looks like an easy target. In any case, there is an initial contact between a union representative and a few employees.

Once an employer becomes a target, a union official usually assigns a representative to assess employee interest. The representative visits the firm to find out if enough employees are interested to make a union campaign worthwhile. He or she also identifies employees who would make good leaders in the organizing campaign and calls them together to create an **organizing committee.** The objective here is to "educate the committee about the benefits of forming a union, the law and procedures involved in forming a local union, and the issues management is likely to raise during a campaign."[29]

organizing committee Employees of a firm, identified by union officials as good prospects, who are established as a committee to be educated about the benefits of forming a union.

The union must follow certain guidelines when it starts contacting employees. The law allows union organizers to solicit employees for membership as long as it doesn't endanger the performance or safety of the employees. Therefore, much of the contact often takes place off the job, for example, at home or at eating places near work. Organizers can also safely contact employees on company grounds during off hours (such as lunch or break time). Under some conditions, union representatives may solicit employees at their work stations, but this is rare. Yet, in practice, there will be much informal organizing going on at the workplace as employees debate the merits of organizing. In any case, this *initial contact* stage may be deceptively quiet. In some instances the first inkling management has of a union campaign is the distribution or posting of a handbill soliciting union membership.

Labor Relations Consultants

Labor relations consultants are increasingly having an impact on the bargaining process, with both management and unions now being supplemented by trained

COMPUTER APPLICATIONS IN LABOR RELATIONS: COMPUTERS ASSIST BOTH LABOR AND MANAGEMENT

Both sides of labor–management relations may benefit from the use of computers. Management may track grievances to see where and on what subjects training is needed. Labor may find that computers provide new ways to assist members.

Management is able to track trends in grievances within any given time period for the whole company, a division or department, or a particular supervisor or group of supervisors. For example, the researcher might hypothesize that supervisors with less than one year of experience in their positions might generate more grievances than experienced supervisors. If this proves to be true, then either new supervisors should be trained before starting in the position or should be offered frequent training sessions during their first year. However, research might prove that in some departments, this hypothesis is not true. Thus, if there are a number of grievances from a large department, an investigation might reveal the need for (1) managerial training, probably defined by the subject of the grievances, (2) better communication on a topic (such as the importance of following safety rules), or (3) the development of a process that allows more input from employees before instituting new policies. Grievance topics may be coded for easy computer tracking. Grievances may incorporate more than one code.

Labor, too, can benefit from computerization. With the demographic changes in the workplace, labor is searching for new ways to meet the needs of its members and potential members. One area of concern that has continued for many years is for job security due to mergers and acquisitions that have cost many employees their jobs. Another is the trend toward service industries and away from manufacturing that has led to a need for knowledgeable workers who are more highly educated. A third is the many low-paying jobs that have been generated by the service industry. When closed shops were legal, the union hall was the place to find a job. This function has now generally been replaced by temporary employment agencies. However, unions could still fulfill this function for the benefit of their members. Not only are there many craft and skill workers who need the kind of expertise offered by unions to adequately find placement, there are many technical and knowledge-based workers who need to keep up to date on skills, equipment, and procedures through both information sharing and hands-on training. Computer-based networks nationwide would help to adjust the unemployment caused by having skills in one location and jobs in another. As Hallett suggests, unions could become "the single best source of information, training, standards, and individuals [with] specific skills and talents."[1] With the support of international unions, locals could be linked effectively and relatively inexpensively (using telephone lines) to provide this source of information, thus assuring their members a degree of job security.

[1]Geffrey J. Hallet, "Unions in Our Future?" *Personnel Administration*, Vol. 31, no. 4 (April 1986), pp. 40–94.

outside advisors. These advisors may be law firms, researchers, psychologists, labor relations specialists, or public relations firms. In any case, their role is to provide advice and related services to both management and unions, not only when a vote is anticipated (although this is when most of them are used) but at other times as well. For the employer, the consultant's services may range from ensuring that the firm properly fills out routine forms, to managing the whole

An important element in organizing union drives is handing out literature to employees at the plant gate.

union campaign. Unions, on the other hand, may use public relations firms to improve their image or specialists to manage "corporate campaigns" aimed at pressuring the firm's shareholders and creditors into influencing management to agree to the union's demands.

The use by management of consultants (who are often referred to disparagingly by unions as "union busters") has apparently grown tremendously over the past 25 years. A study by the AFL-CIO's Department of Organization and Field Services concluded, for example, that management consultants were involved in 85% of the elections they surveyed and that the consultant "ran the show" for the employers 72% of the time.[30] The widespread use of such consultants—only some of whom are actually lawyers—has raised the question of whether these consultants have advised their clients to engage in activities that are illegal or questionable under various labor laws. One tactic, for instance, is to delay the union vote with lengthy hearings at the NLRB. The longer the delay in the vote, it is argued, the more time the employer has to drill antiunion propaganda into the employees. During these delays employees who are not antiunion can be eliminated and the bargaining unit can be packed with promanagement employees.[31] Other consultants are accused of advising employers to lie to the NLRB, for example, by backdating memoranda in order to convince the board that the wage increase being offered was decided months before the campaign ever began.[32]

The ethics of the matter aside, any employers using such consultants are required to report their use. For example, under the Labor–Management Reporting and Disclosure Act of 1959, employers must report "any agreement or arrangement with a labor relations consultant or other independent contractor or organization pursuant to which such person undertakes activities where an object thereof, directly or indirectly, is to persuade employees to exercise or not to exercise, or persuade employees as to the manner of exercising, the right to organize and bargain collectively. . . .[33] Unions, for their part, may be expected to file complaints such as that presented in Figure 15.4 informing the Labor Department of unreported consultant activities.

STEP 2. OBTAINING AUTHORIZATION CARDS

authorization cards In order to petition for a union election, the union must show that at least 30% of employees may be interested in being unionized. Employees indicate this interest by signing authorization cards.

In order to petition the NLRB for the right to hold an election, the union must show that a sizable number of employees *may* be interested in being organized. The next step is thus for union organizers to try to get the employees to sign **authorization cards.** Thirty percent of the eligible employees in an appropriate bargaining unit must sign before an election can be petitioned.

During this stage, both union and management typically use various forms of propaganda. The union claims it can improve working conditions, raise wages, increase benefits, and generally get the workers better deals. Management need not be silent; it can attack the union on ethical and moral grounds and could cite the cost of union membership, for example. Management can also explain its track record, express facts and opinions, and explain the law applicable to organizing campaigns and the meaning of the duty to bargain in good faith (if the union should win the election) to its employees. However, neither side can threaten, bribe, or coerce employees, and an employer may not make promises of benefit to employees or make unilateral changes in terms and conditions of employment that were not planned to be implemented prior to the onset of union organizing activity.

FIGURE 15.4
Labor Relations Consultant Complaint Form

Source: Reproduced in *Labor Relations Consultants: Issues, Trends, and Controversies—A BNA Special Report*, Bureau of National Affairs, 1985, pp. 68–69.

COMPLAINT OF EMPLOYER NON-COMPLIANCE WITH THE REPORTING REQUIREMENTS OF THE LABOR-MANAGEMENT REPORTING AND DISCLOSURE ACT OF 1959*

(See accompanying instructions)

TO: The Honorable Secretary of Labor of the United States:

The undersigned wishes to advise you of the existence of facts indicating that the employer named below has engaged in reportable conduct under Section 203(a) of the Labor Management Reporting and Disclosure Act of 1959 (LMRDA). Accordingly, this will request that you advise the undersigned promptly of whether the named employer has filed the appropriate reports with the United States Department of Labor concerning such activity. If so, please provide a copy of such report(s) to the undersigned with an appropriate billing, if any.**

If no report has been filed by the named employer, the undersigned hereby requests that you conduct an investigation in accordance with your authority under Section 601 of the LMRDA If you determine that a violation exists, or that reporting by the employer will be required in the future, the undersigned requests that you obtain compliance from the employer now or at the appropriate time and that you advise the undersigned accordingly.

A. Employer concerning whom Complaint is being filed:
   1. Name: ____________________
   2. Street Address: ____________________
   3. City, State and Zip Code: ____________________
   4. Type of establishment (factory, hospital, retail store, office, etc.): ____________________
   5. Principal product or service: ____________________

B. Consultant, if any, which the employer has engaged to perform reportable conduct:
   1. Name: ____________________
   2. Street Address: ____________________
   3. City, State and Zip Code: ____________________
   4. Type of consultant (individual, attorney, consulting firm, trade association, psychologist, public official, etc.): ____________________

C. 1. The named employer is required to report under Section 203(a) of the Act because: [Place an "X" in those boxes which apply]
   a. It made an agreement or arrangement with, or a payment to, a "labor relations consultant" or other person or organization for that party to undertake any activity intended to persuade employees about whether or how to exercise their rights to join, form or assist a union and/or to bargain collectively. Specifically, the employer:
      ☐ Hired a labor relations consultant to handle his labor relations, which included activities intended to persuade employees either directly or indirectly about how to exercise their organizing or bargaining rights.

(CONTINUED ON OTHER SIDE)

**I understand that the first 9 reports are free and that the charge thereafter is 10 cents per page. I also understand that most reports do not exceed two or three pages.

What Management Can Do

There are also several steps management can take with respect to the authorization cards themselves. For example, the NLRB has ruled that "an employer may lawfully inform employees of their right to revoke their authorization cards, even when employees have not solicited such information." The employer can also distribute pamphlets such as the one in Figure 15.5, which explains just *how* employees can revoke their cards.[34] However, management can go no

☐ Paid a consultant to make a speech or write an advertisement or other material to convince employees not to unionize or to seek decertification.
☐ Paid a consultant to organize anti-union activities or committees among employees.
☐ Other (describe below).

b. It made an agreement or arrangement with, or a payment to, any such party to supply the employer with information about the activities of employees or a union in connection with a labor relations matter involving the employer (other than information for use solely in connection with a legal proceeding, such as an arbitration case, administrative hearing, or court proceeding). Specifically, the employer:

☐ Hired a labor relations consultant to research the union's history or organizational structure and activities for use as propaganda during a union election campaign.
☐ Paid a consultant to obtain copies of other contracts the union has with other companies in order to prepare for collective bargaining.
☐ Other (describe below).

c. It made any expenditure to obtain the type of information referred to in (b) above. Specifically, the employer:

☐ Paid for copies of reports filed with the government by a union which is trying to organize the employer's employees.
☐ Other (described below).

d. It made a payment to an employee (including a supervisor) to persuade other employees about how to exercise their legal rights to organize and bargain collectively without informing all employees about the payments beforehand or at the time they were made. Specifically, the employer:

☐ Secretly paid an employee to convince other employees not to unionize.
☐ Paid a supervisor to convince employees that the union they were joining would do them more harm than good.
☐ Other (describe below).

e. It made an expenditure in connection with the commission of an unfair labor practice. Specifically, the employer:

☐ Paid a supervisor to threaten employees with punishment for their attempts to join a union.
☐ Hired a lawyer or consultant to engage in "surface bargaining," that is, going through the motions of bargaining without really trying to come to an agreement.
☐ Paid for the printing and distribution of any letter or other written matter which makes promises of benefit or threats of reprisal regarding union activities or sympathies.
☐ Other (describe below):

2. Set forth the activities, arrangements and/or expenditures you have marked above. Be specific as to names, dates and places (use additional sheets if needed):

D. Individual or organization submitting complaint:
1. Name:__________
2. Street Address:__________
3. City, State and Zip Code:__________
4. Telephone Number:__________
5. If organization, individual to contact:__________

____
SIGNATURE **DATE**

3

FIGURE 15.4
(continued)

further than explaining to employees the procedure for card revocation and furnishing resignation language such as that in Figure 15.5. Any type of *material* assistance—postage and stationery, for instance, is prohibited. The employer also cannot check to determine which employees have actually revoked their authorization cards.

What can you do about educating employees who have not yet decided whether to sign their cards? Above all, it is an unfair labor practice to tell employees that they cannot sign a card or to give them the impression that it is against their best interests to do so. What you *can* do, though, is explain the legal and practical consequences of signing or not signing. For example, management *can* prepare its supervisors to be able to explain what the card authorizes the union to do. This is important, because most cards don't just authorize the union to petition an election. For example, the authorization card in Figure 15.6 actually does three things: It lets the union seek a representation election (it can be used as evidence that 30% of your employees have an interest in organizing); it designates the union as a bargaining representative in all employment matters; and it means the employee has applied for membership in the union and that he or she will be subject to union rules and bylaws. The latter is especially important; the union, for instance, may force the employee to picket and fine any member who does not comply with union instructions. Explaining the serious legal and practical implications of signing the card can thus be an effective management weapon. Finally, do not look through signed authorization cards if confronted with them by union representatives. Doing so could be construed as an unfair labor practice by the NLRB, which could view it as spying on those who signed. It could also later form the basis of a charge alleging discrimination due to union activity if someone who signed a card is subsequently disciplined. Examining signed cards could also give rise to a claim that the union should be recognized as the employees' bargaining representative without an election: The union could claim the employer no longer has a good faith doubt that a majority of the employees signed cards authorizing the union to represent them, since it saw the cards.

FIGURE 15.5
Sample Language Approved by the NLRB for Explaining How to Revoke Authorization Card

Source: Reproduced with permission from *Human Resources Management Ideas and Trends Newsletter*, August 20, 1982, published and copyrighted by Commerce Clearing House, Inc., Chicago, IL 60646.

In its *White* decision, the NLRB found the following question and answer, included in a pamphlet distributed to employees, to be unobjectionable –

Question: How do I go about getting my union card back from the union?

Answer: Some unions will not return signed authorization cards once they have them. I don't know what Local [name] would do. If an employee wants the card back, a certified letter can be sent to the union and a copy to the NLRB. Whether or not an employee chooses to try to get an authorization card returned is solely that employee's decision. Here are the addresses [of the union and the NLRB] for your information.

In another decision, the Board found no objection to a sample letter management distributed to its employees –

To: Local 294, Hotel, Motel & Restaurant Workers
[address]

I hereby request a withdrawal from [the union]. If this request is not granted, I am terminating my union membership, effective immediately.

Name ______________________ Membership No. ______________

Date ______________________

Morco, Inc. dba Towne Plaza Hotel, 1981, 258 NLRB No. 16, 1981-82 CCH NLRB ¶ 18, 47B

Note: Sample of acceptable information an employer can give employees to facilitate the latter withdrawing their authorization cards.

FIGURE 15.6
Sample Authorization Card

Source: Reproduced with permission from *Human Resources Management Ideas and Trends Newsletter*, August 20, 1982, published and copyrighted by Commerce Clearing House, Inc., Chicago, IL 60646.

UNITED GLASS AND CERAMIC WORKERS
OF NORTH AMERICA, AFL-CIO, CLC

OFFICIAL MEMBERSHIP APPLICATION AND AUTHORIZATION

I, hereby apply for membership in the United Glass and Ceramic Workers of North America, AFL-CIO, CLC. I hereby designate and authorize the United Glass and Ceramic Workers of North America, AFL-CIO, CLC, as my collective bargaining representative in all matters pertaining to wages, rates of pay and other conditions of employment. I also authorize the United Glass and Ceramic Workers of North America, AFL-CIO, CLC, to request recognition from my employer as my bargaining agent.

SIGNATURE OF APPLICANT ____________________

EMPLOYED BY ____________________

APPLICATION RECEIVED BY ____________________

DATE ____________________

During this stage, unions can picket the company, subject to three constraints: (1) They must file a petition for an election within 30 days after the start of picketing; (2) the firm cannot already be lawfully recognizing another union; and (3) there cannot already have been a valid NLRB election during the past 12 months.

STEP 3. HOLD A HEARING

Once the authorization cards are collected, one of two things can occur. If the employer chooses *not* to contest union recognition, no hearing is needed and a "consent election" is held immediately. If the employer chooses not to contest the union's right to an election and/or the scope of the bargaining unit and/or which employees are eligible to vote in the election, no hearing is needed and the parties can stipulate an election. If an employer *does* wish to contest the union's right, it can insist on a hearing to determine those issues. An employer's decision about whether to insist on a hearing is a strategic one based upon the facts of each case and whether it feels it needs additional time to develop a campaign to try to persuade a majority of its employees not to elect a union to represent them.

Most companies do contest the union's right to represent their employees, and decline to voluntarily recognize the union, claiming that a significant number of their employees do not really want the union. It is at this point that the U.S. Labor Department's National Labor Relations Board gets involved. The NLRB is usually contacted by the union, which submits NLRB Form 502 (Figure 15.7). Based on this, the regional director of the NLRB sends a hearing officer to investigate. The examiner sends both management and union a notice of representation hearing (NLRB Form 852, Figure 15.8). This states the time and place of the hearing.

There are usually two main issues to be investigated in this hearing. First, does the record indicate that there is enough evidence to hold an election? (For example, did 30% or more of the employees in an appropriate bargaining unit sign the authorization cards?) Second, the examiner also must decide what the bargaining unit will be. The latter is an especially crucial matter for the union,

FIGURE 15.7 NLRB Form 502: Request from Union for Holding an NLRB Hearing

FORM NLRB-502
(5-85)

FORM EXEMPT UNDER 44 U.S.C. 3512

UNITED STATES GOVERNMENT
NATIONAL LABOR RELATIONS BOARD
PETITION

DO NOT WRITE IN THIS SPACE	
Case No.	Date Filed

INSTRUCTIONS: Submit an original and 4 copies of this Petition to the NLRB Regional Office in the Region in which the employer concerned is located. If more space is required for any one item, attach additional sheets, numbering item accordingly.

The Petitioner alleges that the following circumstances exist and requests that the National Labor Relations Board proceed under its proper authority pursuant to Section 9 of the National Labor Relations Act.

1. PURPOSE OF THIS PETITION *(If box RC, RM, or RD is checked and a charge under Section 8(b)(7) of the Act has been filed involving the Employer named herein, the statement following the description of the type of petition shall not be deemed made.)* **(Check One)**

☐ **RC-CERTIFICATION OF REPRESENTATIVE -** A substantial number of employees wish to be represented for purposes of collective bargaining by Petitioner and Petitioner desires to be certified as representative of the employees.

☐ **RM-REPRESENTATION (EMPLOYER PETITION) -** One or more individuals or labor organizations have presented a claim to Petitioner to be recognized as the representative of employees of Petitioner.

☐ **RD-DECERTIFICATION -** A substantial number of employees assert that the certified or currently recognized bargaining representative is no longer their representative.

☐ **UD-WITHDRAWAL OF UNION SHOP AUTHORITY -** Thirty percent (30%) or more of employees in a bargaining unit covered by an agreement between their employer and a labor organization desire that such authority be rescinded.

☐ **UC-UNIT CLARIFICATION -** A labor organization is currently recognized by Employer, but Petitioner seeks clarification of placement of certain employees: *(Check one)* ☐ In unit not previously certified. ☐ In unit previously certified in Case No. ______________.

☐ **AC-AMENDMENT OF CERTIFICATION -** Petitioner seeks amendment of certification issued in Case No. ______________
Attach statement describing the specific amendment sought.

2. Name of Employer	Employer Representative to contact	Telephone Number

3. Address(*es*) of Establishment(*s*) involved *(Street and number, city, State, ZIP code)*

4a. Type of Establishment *(Factory, mine, wholesaler, etc.)*	4b. Identify principal product or service

5. Unit Involved *(In UC petition, describe* **present** *bargaining unit and attach description of proposed clarification.)*	6a. Number of Employees in Unit:
Included	Present
	Proposed *(By UC/AC)*
Excluded	6b. Is this petition supported by 30% or more of the employees in the unit? * ____ Yes ____No *Not applicable in RM, UC, and AC

(If you have checked box RC in 1 above, check and complete EITHER item 7a or 7b, whichever is applicable)

7a.☐ Request for recognition as Bargaining Representative was made on *(Date)* ______________ and Employer declined recognition on or about *(Date)*______________ *(If no reply received, so state).*

7b.☐ Petitioner is currently recognized as Bargaining Representative and desires certification under the Act.

8. Name of Recognized or Certified Bargaining Agent *(If none, so state)*	Affiliation
Address and Telephone Number	Date of Recognition or Certification

9. Expiration Date of Current Contract, If any *(Month, Day, Year)*	10. If you have checked box UD in 1 above, show here the date of execution of agreement granting union shop *(Month, Day, and Year)*

11a. Is there now a strike or picketing at the Employer's establishment(*s*) Involved? Yes ________ No ________	11b. If so, approximately how many employees are participating?

11c. The Employer has been picketed by or on behalf of *(Insert Name)* ______________, a labor organization, of *(Insert Address)* ______________ Since *(Month, Day, Year)* ______________

12. Organizations or individuals other than Petitioner *(and other than those named in items 8 and 11c)*, which have claimed recognition as representatives and other organizations and individuals known to have a representative interest in any employees in unit described in item 5 above. *(If none, so state)*

Name	Affilation	Address	Date of Claim *(Required only if Petition is filed by Employer)*

I declare that I have read the above petition and that the statements are true to the best of my knowledge and belief.

____
(Name of Petitioner and Affilation, if any)

By ______________________________ ______________
(Signature of Representative or person filing petition) *(Title, if any)*

Address ______________________________ ______________
(Street and number, city, State, and ZIP Code *(Telephone Number)*

WILLFUL FALSE STATEMENTS ON THIS PETITION CAN BE PUNISHED BY FINE AND IMPRISONMENT (U. S. CODE, TITLE 18, SECTION 1001)

bargaining unit The group of employees the union will be authorized to represent.

for employees, and for the employer. The **bargaining unit** is the group of employees that the union will be authorized to represent and bargain collectively for. If the entire organization is viewed as a bargaining unit, the union will represent all employees. (For example, it might end up representing all profes-

FIGURE 15.8 NLRB Form 852: Notice of Representation Hearing

FORM NLRB-852
(6-61)

UNITED STATES OF AMERICA

BEFORE THE NATIONAL LABOR RELATIONS BOARD

Case No.

NOTICE OF REPRESENTATION HEARING

The Petitioner, above named, having heretofore filed a Petition pursuant to Section 9 (c) of the National Labor Relations Act, as amended, 29 U.S.C. Sec 151 et seq., copy of which Petition is hereto attached, and it appearing that a question affecting commerce has arisen concerning the representation of employees described by such Petition,

YOU ARE HEREBY NOTIFIED that, pursuant to Section 3(b) and 9(c) of the Act, on the day of , 19 , at

a hearing will be conducted before a hearing officer of the National Labor Relations Board upon the question of representation affecting commerce which has arisen, at which time and place the parties will have the right to appear in person or otherwise, and give testimony.

Signed at on the day of , 19

Regional Director, Region
National Labor Relations Board

sional white-collar and blue-collar employees, although the union is oriented mostly toward blue-collar workers.) However, only nonsupervisory, nonmanagerial, and nonconfidential employees may be represented by a union; professional and nonprofessional employees may be included in the same bargaining unit only if the professionals agree to it. If your firm disagrees with the examiner's decision regarding the bargaining unit, you can challenge the decision. This will require a separate step and NLRB ruling.

There are also other questions to be addressed in the NLRB hearing. These include: "Does the employer qualify for coverage by the NLRB?" "Is the union a labor organization within the meaning of the National Labor Relations Act?" "Do any existing collective bargaining agreements or prior elections bar the union from holding a representation election?"

Finally, if the results of the hearing are favorable for the union, the NLRB will direct that an election be held. It will issue a Decision and Direction of Election notice to that effect, and NLRB Form 666 (Figure 15.9) will be sent to the employer to post.

STEP 4. THE CAMPAIGN

During the campaign that precedes the election, both the union and the employer make appeals to employees for their votes; the most prevalent union and management campaign issues are summarized in Tables 15.2 and 15.3. The union emphasizes that it will prevent unfairness, set up a grievance/seniority system, and improve unsatisfactory wages. Union strength, they'll say, will give employees a voice in determining wages and working conditions. For its part, management will emphasize that improvements such as those the union promises don't require unionization, and that wages are equal to or better than they would be with a union contract. Management will also emphasize the financial cost of union dues; the fact that the union is an "outsider"; and that if the union wins, a strike may follow.[35] It can even attack the union on ethical and moral grounds, while insisting that employees will not be as well off and may lose freedom. But neither side can threaten, bribe, or coerce employees.

STEP 5. THE ELECTION

Finally the election can be held within 30 to 60 days after the NLRB issues its Decision and Direction of Election. The election is by secret ballot and the NLRB provides the ballots (see Figure 15.10), voting booth, and ballot box and counts the votes and certifies the results of the election.

The union becomes the employees' representative if it wins the election, and winning means getting a majority of the votes *cast, not* a majority of the workers in the bargaining unit. (It is also important to keep in mind that when an employer commits an unfair labor practice, a "no union" election may be reversed. As representatives of their employer, supervisors must therefore be very careful not to commit such "unfair" practices.)

FIGURE 15.9 NLRB Form 666: Notice to Employees

Form NLRB 666
(7–72)

★ NOTICE TO EMPLOYEES

FROM THE

National Labor Relations Board

A PETITION has been filed with this Federal agency seeking an election to determine whether certain employees want to be represented by a union.

The case is being investigated and NO DETERMINATION HAS BEEN MADE AT THIS TIME by the National Labor Relations Board. IF an election is held Notices of Election will be posted giving complete details for voting.

It was suggested that your employer post this notice so the National Labor Relations Board could inform you of your basic rights under the National Labor Relations Act.

YOU HAVE THE RIGHT under Federal Law

- **To self-organization**
- **To form, join, or assist labor organizations**
- **To bargain collectively through representatives of your own choosing**
- **To act together for the purposes of collective bargaining or other mutual aid or protection**
- **To refuse to do any or all of these things unless the union and employer, in a state where such agreements are permitted, enter into a lawful union security clause requiring employees to join the union.**

It is possible that some of you will be voting in an employee representation election as a result of the request for an election having been filed. While NO DETERMINATION HAS BEEN MADE AT THIS TIME, in the event an election is held, the NATIONAL LABOR RELATIONS BOARD wants all eligible voters to be familiar with their rights under the law IF it holds an election.

The Board applies rules which are intended to keep its elections fair and honest and which result in a free choice. If agents of either Unions or Employers act in such a way as to interfere with your right to a free election, the election can be set aside by the Board. Where appropriate the Board provides other remedies, such as reinstatement for employees fired for exercising their rights, including backpay from the party responsible for their discharge.

NOTE:

The following are examples of conduct which interfere with the rights of employees and may result in the setting aside of the election.

- **Threatening loss of jobs or benefits by an Employer or a Union**
- **Misstating important facts by a Union or an Employer where the other party does not have a fair chance to reply**
- **Promising or granting promotions, pay raises, or other benefits, to influence an employee's vote by a party capable of carrying out such promises**
- **An Employer firing employees to discourage or encourage union activity or a Union causing them to be fired to encourage union activity**
- **Making campaign speeches to assembled groups of employees on company time within the 24-hour period before the election**
- **Incitement by either an Employer or a Union of racial or religious prejudice by inflammatory appeals**
- **Threatening physical force or violence to employees by a Union or an Employer to influence their votes**

Please be assured that IF AN ELECTION IS HELD every effort will be made to protect your right to a free choice under the law. Improper conduct will not be permitted. All parties are expected to cooperate fully with this agency in maintaining basic principles of a fair election as required by law. The National Labor Relations Board as an agency of the United States Government does not endorse any choice in the election.

NATIONAL LABOR RELATIONS BOARD
an agency of the
UNITED STATES GOVERNMENT

THIS IS AN OFFICIAL GOVERNMENT NOTICE AND MUST NOT BE DEFACED BY ANYONE

FIGURE **15.9** **(continued)**

HOW TO LOSE AN NLRB ELECTION

Of the 3,600 or so collective bargaining elections held recently, about half were lost by companies.[36] Yet according to a study by the University Research Center many of these elections should probably *not* have been lost. According to expert Matthew Goodfellow, there is no sure way an employer can win an election. However, there are five sure ways an employer could *lose* one.

Reason 1. Asleep at the Switch

In 68% of the companies studied (of those that lost to the union) executives were caught unaware, having not paid attention to symptoms of low employee morale. In these companies turnover and absenteeism had increased, productivity was erratic, and safety was poor. Grievance procedures were rarely used. When the first reports of authorization cards being distributed began trickling

TABLE 15.2 Prevalent Union Campaign Issues

ISSUE	PERCENT OF CAMPAIGNS
Union will prevent unfairness, set up grievance procedures/ seniority system	82%
Union will improve unsatisfactory wages	79
Union strength will provide employees with voice in wages, working conditions	79
Union, not outsider, bargains for what employees want	73
Union has obtained gains elsewhere	70
Union will improve unsatisfactory sick leave/insurance	64
Dues/initiation fees are reasonable	64
Union will improve unsatisfactory vacations/holidays	61
Union will improve unsatisfactory pensions	61
Employer promises/good treatment may not continue without union	61
Employees choose union leaders	55
Employer will seek to persuade/frighten employees to vote against union	55
No strike without vote	55
Union will improve unsatisfactory working conditions	52
Employees have legal right to engage in union activity	52

Source: Adapted from *Union Representation Elections: Law and Reality*, by Julius G. Getman, Stephen B. Goldberg, and Jeanne B. Herman. Copyright 1976 by Russell Sage Foundation. Reprinted by permission of Basic Books, Inc., Publishers.

TABLE 15.3 Prevalent Management Campaign Issues

ISSUE	PERCENT OF CAMPAIGNS
Improvements not dependent on unionization	85%
Wages good/equal to/better than under union contract	82
Financial costs of union dues outweigh gains	79
Union is outsider	79
Get facts before deciding; employer will provide facts and accept employee decision	76
If union wins, strike may follow	70
Loss of benefits may follow union win	67
Strikers will lose wages; lose more than gain	67
Unions not concerned with employee welfare	67
Strike may lead to loss of jobs	64
Employer has treated employees fairly/well	60
Employees should be certain to vote	54

Source: Adapted from *Union Representation Elections: Law and Reality*, by Julius G. Getman, Stephen B. Goldberg, and Jeanne B. Herman. Copyright 1976 by Russell Sage Foundation. Reprinted by permission of Basic Books, Inc., Publishers.

UNITED STATES OF AMERICA
National Labor Relations Board
OFFICIAL SECRET BALLOT
FOR CERTAIN EMPLOYEES OF

Do you wish to be represented for purposes of collective bargaining by –

MARK AN "S" IN THE SQUARE OF YOUR CHOICE

YES ☐ NO ☐

DO NOT SIGN THIS BALLOT. Fold and drop in ballot box.
If you spoil this ballot return it to the Board Agent for a new one.

FIGURE 15.10
Sample NLRB Ballot

back to top managers, they usually responded with a knee-jerk reflex action. A barrage of one-way communications ensued in which top management bombarded workers with letters describing how the company was "one big family" and calling for a "team effort."

It is interesting that even once union efforts had begun, management often made no serious effort to ascertain *from the employees themselves* what it was that troubled them enough to force them into the arms of the union. As the researcher points out, "what must be done—even at the last minute—is to uncover the issues that vex employees." Keep in mind, though, that this can be a ticklish business. Knowing *what* questions to ask and *how* (without committing unfair labor practices) and knowing how to work within NLRB rules that inhibit "corrective actions" (such as giving everyone a raise) in the preelection period usually require specialized training.[37]

Yet the best strategy is to not be caught asleep in the first place:

> Overall, prudence dictates that management spend time and effort even when the atmosphere is calm testing the temperature of employee sentiments and finding ways to remove irritants. Doing that cuts down on the possibility that an election will ever take place. . . .

In practice, nonunionized employers often have human resource policies that reduce the sort of dissatisfaction that often precedes a unionization effort. At Diamond Shamrock Corporation, for instance, job security, competitive wages, and a corporate benefits plan that is the same for both white-collar and blue-collar workers have helped make this a large nonunionized firm.[38]

Reason 2. Appointing a Committee

Of the losing companies 36% formed a committee to manage the campaign. According to the expert, there are three fallacies in this:

1. *Promptness* is the essence of the election situation, and committees are notorious for deliberation.
2. Most of the members of such a committee are *neophytes* so far as an NLRB situation is concerned. Their views therefore are mostly reflections of wishful thinking rather than experience.
3. A committee's decision is usually a homogenized decision, with everyone seeking to compromise differences. The result is often close to the most conservative opinion—but not necessarily the most knowledgeable or most effective one.

This expert suggests, instead, giving full responsibility to a single decisive executive. This person should in turn be assisted by a human resource director and a consultant/advisor with broad experience in labor relations.

Reason 3. Concentrating on Money and Benefits

In 54% of the elections studied the company lost the election because top management concentrated on the "wrong" issues: money and benefits. As this expert puts it:

> Employees may want more money, but quite often if they feel the company treats them fairly, decently, and honestly, they are satisfied with reasonable, competitive rates and benefits. It is only when they feel ignored, uncared for, and disregarded that money becomes a major issue to express their dissatisfaction.

Reason 4. Industry Blind Spots

The researcher found that in some industries employees felt more ignored and disregarded than in others. For example, in industries that are highly automated (such as paper manufacturing and automotive), there was some tendency for executives to regard hourly employees as "just cogs in the machinery," although this is changing today as firms such as Chrysler implement more quality improvement programs. Here (as in reason 3) the solution is to begin paying more serious attention to the needs and attitudes of employees.

Reason 5. Delegating Too Much to Divisions or Branches

For companies with plants scattered around the country, unionization of one or more plants tends to lead to unionization of others. Organizing several of the plants gives the union a "wedge" in the form of a contract that can be used to tempt other plants' workers.

Part of the solution here is to keep our first four "reasons" in mind and thereby keep those first few plants from being organized. Beyond that, firms with multiplant operations should not blindly relegate all decisions concerning personnel and industrial relations to plant managers. Effectively dealing with unionization—taking the "pulse" of the workers' attitudes, knowing what is bothering them, reacting appropriately when the union first appears, and so on—generally requires strong centralized guidance from the head office and its human resource staff.

THE SUPERVISOR'S ROLE

The extent to which you as a supervisor can help or hinder your employer's attempts to limit union organizing activity depends on your knowledge of union organizing rules. When you are not thoroughly familiar with what you can and cannot do to legally hamper organizing activities, your effect may be to commit an unfair labor practice. You could thereby (1) cause a new election to be held after your company has won a previous election, or (2) cause your employer to have to forfeit the second election and go directly to contract negotiation. In one case, for example, a plant superintendent reacted to a union's initial organizing attempt by prohibiting distribution of union literature in the plant's lunchroom. Since solicitation of off-duty workers in nonwork areas is generally legal, the company subsequently allowed the union to post union literature on the company's bulletin board and to distribute union literature in nonworking areas inside the plant. However, the NLRB still ruled that the initial act of prohibiting distribution of the literature in the lunchroom was an unfair labor practice, one that was not "made right" by the company's subsequent efforts. In this case, the NLRB used the action of the plant superintendent as one reason for invalidating an election that the company had won.[39] To avoid such problems, employers should do two things: First, they should develop clear rules governing distribution of literature and solicitation of workers. Second, they should train supervisors in how to administer these rules.[40]

RULES REGARDING LITERATURE AND SOLICITATION

There are a number of steps an employer can take to legally restrict union organizing activity.[41]

> *Non*employees can always be barred from soliciting employees during their work time—that is, when the employee is on duty and not on a break. Thus, if the company cafeteria is open to whoever is on the premises, union organizers *can* solicit off-duty employees who are in the cafeteria but not the cafeteria workers (such as cooks) who are not on a break.
>
> Employers can usually stop employees from soliciting other employees for any purpose if one or both employees are on paid-duty time and not on a break.
>
> Most employers (not including retail stores, shopping centers, and certain other employers) can bar nonemployees from the building's interiors and work areas as a right of private property owners. In certain cases, nonemployees can also be barred from exterior private property areas such as parking lots—if there is a business reason (such as safety) and the reason is not just to interfere with union organizers.
>
> *Employees* can be denied access to interior or exterior areas only if the employer can show that the rule is required for reasons of production, safety, or discipline.
>
> In general, off-duty employees cannot be considered to have the same status as nonemployees. They therefore cannot be prohibited from remaining on the premises or returning to the premises unless this prohibition is also required for reasons of production, safety, or discipline.

Finally, note that these restrictions are only valid provided they are not imposed in a discriminatory manner. For example, if employees are permitted to collect money for wedding, shower, and baby gifts; or sell Avon products or Tupperware; or engage in other solicitation during their working time, the employer will not be able to lawfully prohibit them from union soliciting during work time; to do so would discriminate on the basis of union activity, which is an unfair labor practice. Two examples of specific rules aimed at limiting union organizing activity are thus as follows:

> Solicitation of employees on company property during working time interferes with the efficient operation of our business. Nonemployees are not permitted to solicit employees on company property for any purpose. Except in break areas where both employees are on break or off the clock, no employee may solicit another employee during working time for any purpose.
>
> Distribution of literature on company property not only creates a litter problem but also distracts us from our work. Nonemployees are not allowed to distribute literature on company property. Except in the performance of his or her job, an employee may not distribute literature unless both the distributor and the recipient are off the clock or on authorized break in a break area or off company premises. Special exceptions to these rules may be made by the company for especially worthwhile causes such as United Way, but written permission must first be obtained and the solicitation will be permitted only during break periods.[42]

The Need for Training

In addition to instituting rules, supervisors should be trained in their use. There are several things to keep in mind here. First, the overall aim of the program should be to familiarize supervisors with the rules governing organizing activity (as discussed); if possible, there should be an emphasis on what supervisors *can* do, rather than on what they can't do. (Typically in these training sessions, the don'ts far outnumber the do's, and the effect is to inhibit supervisory action.) Training should also be given in advance of a union organizing attempt; once the union has begun its efforts, training is often too late, since some supervisors have already inadvertently committed unfair labor practices. The training should also provide a practice session in which supervisors can apply the do's and don'ts. For example, they should be exposed to simulations of the kinds of situations they may encounter and be given an opportunity to apply what they have learned; case studies can be useful here.[43]

Other Unfair Labor Practices

You also have to keep in mind that there are a lot more ways to commit unfair labor practices than simply keeping union organizers off your private property. For example, one company recently decided to have a cookout and paid day off two days before a union representation election. The National Labor Relations Board held that this was too much of a coincidence, and that it represented coercive conduct. The union had lost the first vote, but won the second vote as a result.[44]

GUIDELINES FOR EMPLOYERS WISHING TO STAY UNION FREE

In addition to establishing rules and providing training, several additional guidelines for preserving a union-free workplace include:

1. *Practice preventive employee relations.* Fair discipline policies; open worker–management communications; and fair salaries, wages, and benefits can contribute to preserving a union-free workplace.
2. Recognize the importance of location. Unions have traditionally been weaker in the South and Southwest than in the North, Northeast, or Far West, for instance.

3. *Seek early detection.* Detect union-organizing activity as early as possible, and remember that your best source here is probably your first-line supervisors. These people should be trained to look for changes in employee behavior. In addition, you and your people should also look for direct signs of union activity such as posters, buttons, and authorization cards.
4. *Do not volunteer.* Obviously, never voluntarily recognize a union without a secret election supervised by the NLRB.
5. *Beware the authorization cards.* As previously explained, authorization cards must be handled correctly. When confronted by the union submitting authorization cards get another manager in as a witness and do not touch (or, worse, count or examine in any way) the cards. When the organizer leaves, call your lawyer.
6. *Present your case.* Again, present your case to your employees forcefully and relentlessly. Executives' speeches to employees during working hours, informal meetings in the dining areas, and informational letters are all good tools.
7. *Postpone the election.* There may be an advantage in postponing the election as much as possible. This will give you more time to prepare and communicate your case and could wear down the union's resolve and majority.
8. *Pick your time carefully.* Within the guidelines set by the NLRB you should carefully choose the time and date of the election. For example, you may find that employees are in a better frame of mind on Friday than on Monday and that payday affords you an opportunity to get in the final word by stuffing some information in their pay envelopes.[45]
9. *Consider your options.* Finally, consider the option of *not* staying union free. While we have emphasized staying union free, some employers do opt to let the union in. Union membership may make health benefits available at group rates that many employers could not afford; and industry- or association-wide wage agreements can remove the burden of having to negotiate salaries and raises with each of your employees. Some unions may be easier to get along with than others, if you have a choice. Therefore, consider your options.

DECERTIFICATION ELECTIONS: WHEN EMPLOYEES WANT TO OUST THEIR UNION

Winning an election and signing an agreement do not necessarily mean that the union is in the company to stay—quite the opposite. The same law that grants employees the right to unionize also provides a way for them to legally terminate their union's right to represent them. The process is known as *decertification*, and it has been exercised increasingly in recent years. In 75% of these elections, the employees voted for decertification.[46] (Unions have won on average 48% of the total representation elections held over the past few years.[47])

Decertification campaigns don't differ much from certification campaigns (those leading up to the initial election).[48] For its part, the union organizes membership meetings, house-to-house visits, mails literature into the homes, and uses phone calls, NLRB appeals, and, sometimes, threats and harassment to win the election.[49] For its part, managers use meetings—including one-on-one meetings, small-group meetings, and meeting with entire units—as well as legal or expert assistance, letters, improved working conditions and (sometimes) subtle and not-so-subtle threats in its attempts to win a decertification vote.

Employers are also increasingly turning to consultants. These consultants (who claim they act as "marriage brokers" between workers and management)[50] provide, among other things, managers and supervisors with detailed advice concerning how to behave during the preelection period.[51] According to at least one account, some of these consultants may even explain how to pay an illegal pay raise in the middle of a union organizing campaign on the assumption that "the probability is that you will never get caught. If you do get caught the worst that can happen is a second election and the union loses 96% of these elections."[52]

On the whole, however, these consultants' strategies seem to be to assist management in improving their communications with the shop floor and in identifying and eliminating the basic pressures that led to the pro-union vote in the first place. Ideally, therefore, this is usually not a last-minute effort. Instead, a promanagement vote on either a certification or decertification election tends to be the result of long-term sensible actions on the part of management, actions which have as their goal winning the trust and confidence of employees:

> Decertification cannot be accomplished just at election time. You must earn the confidence of employees over at least a year's period of time, through effective performance evaluation programs, personnel development programs, and overall good communication between employees and management during the contract.[53]

▶ CHAPTER REVIEW

SUMMARY

1. Union membership has been alternately growing and shrinking since as early as 1790. A major milestone was the creation, in 1886, of the American Federation of Labor by Samuel Gompers. Most recently the trend in unionization has been toward organizing white-collar workers, particularly since the proportion of blue-collar workers has been declining. In any case, we saw that while wages and benefits are important factors in unionization, workers are also seeking fair, humane, and equitable treatment.
2. In addition to improved wages and working conditions, unions seek security when organizing. We discussed five possible arrangements, including the closed shop, the union shop, the agency shop, the open shop, and maintenance of membership.
3. The AFL-CIO is a national federation comprised of 109 national (and international) unions. It can exercise only that power it is allowed to exercise by its constituent national unions.
4. During the period of strong encouragement of unions, the Norris-LaGuardia and Wagner acts were passed; these marked a shift in labor law from repression to strong encouragement of union activity. They did this by banning certain types of unfair labor practices, by providing for secret ballot elections, and by creating the National Labor Relations Board.
5. The Taft-Hartley Act reflected the period of modified encouragement coupled with regulation. It enumerated the rights of employees with respect to their unions, enumerated the rights of employers, and allowed the president to temporarily bar national emergency strikes. Among other things, it also enumerated certain union unfair labor practices. For example, it banned unions from restraining or coercing employees from exercising their guaranteed bargaining rights. And employers were explicitly given the right to express their views concerning union organization.
6. The Landrum-Griffin Act reflected the period of detailed regulation of internal union affairs. It grew out of discoveries of wrongdoing on the part of both management and union leadership and contained a "bill of rights" for union members. (For example, it affirms a member's right to sue his or her union.)
7. There are four steps in a union drive and election: the initial contact, obtaining authorization cards, holding a hearing with the NLRB, and the election itself. Remember that the union need only win a majority of the votes *cast, not* a majority of the workers in the bargaining unit.

8. There are five surefire ways to lose an NLRB election: Be caught sleeping at the switch, form a committee, emphasize money and benefits, have an industry blind spot, and delegate too much to divisions. Supervisors should be trained regarding how to administer the employer's union literature and solicitation rules.

KEY TERMS

union security
closed shop
union shop
agency shop
open shop
maintenance of membership arrangement
American Federation of Labor and Congress of Industrial Organizations (AFL-CIO)
Norris-LaGuardia Act
National Labor Relations Board (NLRB)
Wagner Act
unfair labor practices
Taft-Hartley Act
union unfair labor practices
right-to-work laws
national emergency strikes
Landrum-Griffin Act
organizing committee
authorization cards
bargaining unit

DISCUSSION QUESTIONS

1. Explain the structure and purpose of the AFL-CIO.
2. Discuss five sure ways to lose an NLRB election.
3. Describe some important tactics you would expect the union to use during the union drive and election.
4. Briefly explain why "labor law has gone through a cycle of repression and encouragement."
5. Explain in detail each step in a union drive and election.

APPLICATION EXERCISES

RUNNING CASE

CARTER CLEANING COMPANY

The Union Arrives

Last week something happened at one of the Carter stores that upset Jack and Jennifer. As is often the case, one of the workers involved with cleaning and spotting had to be fired because of poor-quality work. The nature of the business is such that employees are continually quitting, being fired, and being rehired somewhere else, and the fact is it is not unusual for a worker in the industry to have worked in all or most of the stores in a geographic area during the period of five or so years. Because job switching is so much a part of the industry, Jack and Jennifer were therefore taken aback when Bob, the man who was fired, reacted almost violently. He threw a bottle of chemicals to the floor, began shouting that Jack was "incompetent, unfair, and unfit to be an employer," and proceeded to warn that he was forthwith driving to the local headquarters of the textile workers union to get them to begin organizing the Carter's firm. Subsequently, several of Carter's store managers reported that employees were talking among themselves much more animatedly during lunch than they usually do and that a man who one manager believes is a local union representative has been meeting with the employees after work as well.

Questions

1. Is it possible that the firm is in the first stages of an organizing campaign? How could Jack and Jennifer find out for sure?
2. What steps should they take now to determine if such organizing activity is going on?
3. If this firm is being organized, what steps should they take next?

CASE INCIDENT *France Rivet Company*

The France Rivet Company has no union. Many efforts have been made to organize employees, but no union has asked for recognition as bargaining agent. Whether any or a large proportion of employees may be union members is not known by the employer.

During the past two days, however, pickets representing an international industrial union have appeared before the plant. They carry banners describing the employer as "unfair." The industrial relations director has talked to a half-dozen employees. He asked them if they belonged to a union or if they knew why the plant is being picketed. All answers were negative.

Up to this time, the pickets have been rather ineffective. Few, if any, employees have been prevented from working. Trucks have continued deliveries. Some feeling of tension, however, is apparent; employees obviously dislike crossing the picket line. Customers may also object, although none is known to have avoided the plant on that account.

The industrial relations director, however, is under pressure to get rid of the pickets. Plant officials and managers are afraid they may shut out customers or interfere with both receiving and shipping of materials. Several managers have suggested that the whole procedure is a shakedown—that some union official is getting set to ask for a payoff. Other members of the managerial group think legal action should be taken; they want the industrial relations director to get an injunction. The firm's business is nationwide.

Questions

1. What, in your opinion, should the industrial relations director say or do?
2. Has he handled the matter properly to this point?
3. Prepare a memorandum he might hand to his firm's top managers in which he predicts what are likely to be the significant developments and suggests what action, if any, will be appropriate.

Source: Dale Yoder, *Personnel Management and Industrial Relations*, 6th ed., pp. 480–481. © 1970. Reprinted by permission of Prentice Hall, Englewood Cliffs, NJ.

HUMAN RESOURCE MANAGEMENT SIMULATION

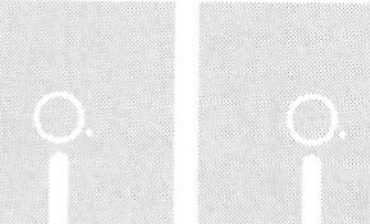

There is always a possibility that your firm will become organized by a labor union. Danger signals include low morale, lower than average wages and/or benefits, and a high accident rate. You will have an opportunity to discuss unionization and several approaches to it in incident L.

▸ NOTES

1. Parts of this section are based on Paul A. Samuelson, *Economics* (New York: McGraw-Hill, 1967), Chapter 7; Dale Yoder, *Personnel Management and Industrial Relations* (Englewood Cliffs, NJ: Prentice Hall, 1970), Chapter 16; Arthur Sloane and Fred Witney, *Labor Relations* (Englewood Cliffs, NJ: Prentice Hall, 1977); Leonard Sayles and George Strauss, *Managing Human Resources* (Englewood Cliffs, NJ: Prentice Hall, 1977), Chapter 7; Edwin Beal,

Edward Wickersham, and Philip Kienast, *The Practice of Collective Bargaining* (Homewood, IL: Irwin, 1976), Chapter 2; Gordon Bloom and Herbert Northrup, *Economics of Labor Relations* (Homewood, IL: Irwin, 1977), Chapter 2; and Dennis Chamot, "Professional Employees Turn to Unions," *Harvard Business Review*, Vol. 54, no. 3 (May–June 1976). Also see Bernard Bass and Charles Mitchell, "Influences on the Felt Need for Collective Bargaining in Business and Science Professionals," *Journal of Applied Psychology*, Vol. 61, no. 6 (December 1976), pp. 770–772; Harold W. Davey, *Contemporary Collective Bargaining* (Englewood Cliffs, NJ: Prentice Hall, 1972), pp. 342–360.

2. "Union Membership in 1991," *BNA Bulletin to Management*, March 5, 1992, pp. 68–69.
3. "Beyond Unions: A Revolution in Employee Rights Is in the Making," *Business Week*, July 8, 1985, p. 72; Bureau of National Affairs, "Union Membership in 1988," *Bulletin to Management*, April 13, 1989.
4. "AFL-CIO Launching New Strategy to Win Over Nonunion Workers," *Compensation and Benefit Review*, Vol. 18, no. 5 (September–October 1986), p. 8; Shane R. Premeaux, R. Wayne Moody, and Art Bethke, "Decertification: Fulfilling Unions' 'Destiny'?" *Personnel Journal*, Vol. 66, no. 6 (June 1987), p. 144; and Peter A. Susser, "The Labor Impact of Deregulation," *Employment Relations Today*, Vol. 13, no. 2 (Summer 1986), pp. 117–123.
5. "Beyond Unions," pp. 72–77.
6. Commerce Clearing House, *Ideas and Trends*, January 10, 1986, p. 7.
7. Sar Levitan and Frank Gallo, "Collective Bargaining and Private Sector Employment," *Monthly Labor Review* (September 1989), pp. 24–33.
8. Dennis Chamot, "Unions Need to Confront the Results of New Technology," *Monthly Labor Review* (August 1987), p. 45. Closely related to unions, *employee associations* of government employees have grown steadily over the past few years. For a discussion, see Sar Levitan and Frank Gallo, "Can Employee Associations Negotiate New Growth?" *Monthly Labor Review* (July 1989), pp. 5–13.
9. From the Bureau of Labor Statistics; discussed in "Union Wages," *BNA Bulletin to Management*, April 2, 1992, pp. 100–101.
10. W. Clay Hamner and Frank Schmidt, "Work Attitude as Predictors of Unionization Activity," *Journal of Applied Psychology*, Vol. 63, no. 4 (1978), pp. 415–421. See also Amos Okafor, "White Collar Unionization: Why and What to Do," *Personnel*, Vol. 62, no. 8 (August 1985), pp. 17–20.
11. Jeanne Brett, "Why Employees Want Unions," *Organizational Dynamics* (Spring 1980), and John Fossum, *Labor Relations* (Dallas, TX: Business Publications, 1982), p. 4.
12. Clive Fullager and Julian Barling, "A Longitudinal Test of a Model of the Antecedents and Consequences of Union Loyalty," *Journal of Applied Psychology*, Vol. 74, no. 2 (April 1989), pp. 213–227. Adrienne Eaton, Michael Gordon and Jeffrey Keefe, "The Impact of Quality of Work Life Programs and Grievance Systems Effectiveness on Union Commitment," *Individual and Labor Relations Review*, Vol. 45, no. 3, April 1992, pp. 591–604.
13. Warner Pflug, *The UAW in Pictures* (Detroit: Wayne State University Press, 1971), pp. 11–12.
14. See also M. Gordon and others, "Commitment to the Union: Development of a Measure and an Examination of Its Correlates," *Journal of Applied Psychology* (August 1980), pp. 474–499. For an interesting discussion of this see Bert Klandermans, "Perceived Cost and Benefits of Participation in Union Action," *Personnel Psychology*, Vol. 39, no. 2 (Summer 1986), pp. 379–398.
15. These are based on Richard Hodgetts, *Introduction to Business* (Reading, MA: Addison-Wesley, 1977), pp. 213–214.
16. "Boardroom Reports," The Conference Board, New York, December 15, 1976, p. 6. See also "Perspectives on Employment," *Research Bulletin #194*, 1986, The Conference Board, 845 Third Avenue, New York, N.Y. 10020.
17. The following material is based on Sloane and Witney, *Labor Relations*, p. 137.
18. Ibid., p. 106.
19. Ibid., p. 121.
20. Quoted from D. Quinn Mills, "Flawed Victory in Labor Law Reform," *Harvard Business Review*, Vol. 57 (May–June 1979), pp. 92–102. The law also proposed to increase the size of the NLRB from five to seven members and to permit the board to speed its process of review of decisions by administrative law judges. See also "Labor's Long Winter May Be Coming to an End," *Business Week*, February 23, 1987, p. 140.
21. Commerce Clearing House. This is based on "NLRB Announces New Rule on When Unions Can Picket Stores in Malls," *Ideas and Trends*, November 2, 1988, pp. 181–184. Jean Country and Brook Shopping Centers, Inc., as nominee for Dollar Land Syndicate (Retail and Wholesale Employees Union, Local 305, AFL-CIO), 291 NLRB No. 4, Sept. 27, 1988. It should be noted that the NLRB held that in balancing the interests involved, it was essential to consider whether those seeking to exercise the right to organize on private property had reasonable alternative means of doing so without trespassing on the owner's property. Previously, the NLRB had held it must sometimes refrain from considering that issue in determining whether such organizational rights could be exercised under a balancing test. In a 1992 case, *Lechmere, Inc.* v. *NLRB*, "the court has been asked to decide whether an operator of a chain of New England retail stores committed an unfair labor practice when it prevented non-employee union organizers from distributing union literature on a company property." The issue again raises the question—first raised by the Supreme Court 35 years ago in *NLRB* v. *Babcok & Wilcox* as to whether union organizers can be banned from company premises when they can easily contact employees "through the usual channels" of communication. On January 27, 1992, the Supreme Court decided in favor of the employer in this case. For a discussion of this see Craig Hukill, "Labor and the Supreme Court: Significant Issues of 1991–92," *Monthly Labor Review* (January 1992), p. 35.
22. Clear Pine Moldings.
23. Midland National Life Insurance Company.
24. This is based on "Taft Act Losing Teeth," a summary of a speech by Professor Charles Craver of the George Washington University. National Law Center, in Bureau of National Affairs, *Bulletin to Management*, March 16, 1989, p. 88.
25. Commerce Clearing House, "Supreme Court Ruling Gives Management Greater Power to Fill Jobs During a Strike," *Ideas and Trends*, March 23, 1989, p. 46.
26. *Lechmere Inc.* v. *National Labor Relations Board*, U.S. S. Ct., No. 90-970, 1/27/92.
27. "Difficulties Foreseen for Union Organizing Efforts," *BNA Bulletin to Management*, February 13, 1992, p. 42.
28. See William J. Glueck, "Labor Relations and the Supervisor," in M. Jean Newport, *Supervisory Management: Tools and Techniques* (St. Paul, MN: West, 1976), pp. 207–234. See also "Big Labor Tries the Soft Sell," *Business Week*, October 13, 1986, p. 126.
29. William Fulmer, "Step by Step Through a Union Election," *Harvard Business Review*, Vol. 60 (July–August 1981), pp. 94–102.
30. *Labor Relations Consultants: Issues, Trends, Controversies* (Rockville, MD: Bureau of National Affairs, 1985), p. 7.

31. Ibid., p. 71.
32. Ibid., p. 72.
33. Ibid., p. 62.
34. Commerce Clearing House, "More on Management's Preelection Campaign Strategy," *Ideas and Trends in Personnel*, August 20, 1982, pp. 158–159.
35. Fulmer, "Step by Step," p. 94. See also "An Employer May Rebut Union Misrepresentations," Bureau of National Affairs, *Bulletin to Management*, January 16, 1986, p. 17.
36. Based on Matthew Goodfellow, "How to Lose an NLRB Election," *Personnel Administrator*, Vol. 23 (September 1976), pp. 40–44. Union win–loss ratio based on "Union Win–Loss Ratio Stable in '88," Bureau of National Affairs, *Bulletin to Management*, April 20, 1989, p. 121.
37. This is one reason why the use of consultants in this area is increasing. See, for example, "American Union Busting," *The Economist*, November 17, 1979, pp. 39–50.
38. Stuart Dien and Kenneth Rose, "Formal Policies and Procedures Can Forestall Unionization," *Personnel Journal*, Vol. 61 (April 1982), pp. 275–277.
39. Frederick Sullivan, "Limiting Union Organizing Activity Through Supervisors," *Personnel*, Vol. 55 (July–August 1978), pp. 55–65. Richard Peterson, Thomas Lee, and Barbara Finnegan, "Strategies and Tactics in Union Organizing Campaigns," *Industrial Relations*, Vol. 31, no. 2, Spring 1992, pp. 370–381.
40. Ibid., p. 60.
41. Ibid., pp. 62–65.
42. Ibid., pp. 64–65. The appropriateness of these sample rules may be affected by factors unique to an employer's operation, and they should therefore be reviewed by the employer's attorney before implementation.
43. For a discussion, see James Rand, "Preventive-Maintenance Techniques for Staying Union-Free," *Personnel Journal*, Vol. 59 (June 1980), pp. 497–508. See also John Teeter, "Inadvisable Advice: Writs on Employers' Counseling of Employees with Regard to Unfair Labor Practice Proceedings," *Industrial Relations Law* Journal, Vol. 12, No. 2, 1990, pp. 292–339.
44. B&D Plastics Inc. 302 NLRB No. 33, 1991, 137 LRRM 1039; discussed in "No Such Things as a Quote Free Lunch," *BNA Bulletin to Management*, May 23, 1991, pp. 153–154.
45. Charles Wentz, Jr., "Preserving a Union-Free Workplace," *Personnel* (October 1987), pp. 68–72.
46. Francis T. Coleman, "Once a Union, Not Always a Union," *Personnel Journal*, Vol. 64, no. 3 (March 1985), p. 42. See total article, pp. 42–45, for an excellent discussion of the benefits of decertification for both employers and workers. See also "Decertification: Fulfilling Unions' Destiny?" *Personnel Journal*, Vol. 66 (June 1987), pp. 144–148.
47. "Union Win Rate in 1991," *BNA Bulletin to Management*, March 26, 1992, pp. 92–93.
48. William Fulmer, "When Employees Want to Oust Their Union," *Harvard Business Review*, Vol. 56 (March–April 1978), pp. 163–170; Coleman, "Once a Union, Not Always a Union," pp. 42–45. See also "Decertification: Fulfilling Unions' Destiny?" pp. 144–148.
49. Fulmer, "When Employees Want to Oust Their Union," p. 167.
50. *The Economist*, November 17, 1979, p. 50.
51. See also William Fulmer and Tamara Gilman, "Why Do Workers Vote for Union Decertification?" *Personnel*, Vol. 58 (March–April 1981), pp. 28–35, and Shane Premeaux et al., "Managing Tomorrow's Unionized Workers," *Personnel* (July 1989), pp. 61–64, for a discussion of some important differences (in preferred management styles) between unionized and nonunionized employees.
52. Ibid.
53. Fulmer, "When Employees Want," p. 168. See also "Decertification: Fulfilling Unions' Destiny?" p. 148; and James Thacker et al., "The Factor Structure of Union Commitment: An Application of Confirmatory Factor Analysis," *Journal of Applied Psychology*, Vol. 74, no. 2 (April 1989), pp. 228–232.

COLLECTIVE BARGAINING

CHAPTER 16

OVERVIEW

The union drive and election are just the first phase of the union's interaction with your firm. Collective bargaining and contract administration come next. The other phases—also discussed in this chapter—include preparing for negotiations and actually bargaining. When you finish studying this chapter, you should be able to explain how to prepare for union contract negotiations; list at least 10 hints on collective bargaining; and define impasse, mediation, and strike.

▸ INTRODUCTION: WHAT IS COLLECTIVE BARGAINING?

When (and if) the union is recognized as your employees' representative, a day is set for meeting at the bargaining table. Here representatives of management and the union meet to negotiate a labor agreement. This will contain agreements on specific provisions covering wages, hours, and working conditions.

collective bargaining The process through which representatives of management and the union meet to negotiate a labor agreement.

What exactly is **collective bargaining?** According to the National Labor Relations Act:

> For the purpose of (this act) to *bargain collectively* is the performance of the mutual obligation of the employer and the representative of the employees to meet at reasonable times and confer in good faith with respect to wages, hours, and terms and conditions of employment, or the negotiation of an agreement, or any question arising thereunder, and the execution of a written contract incorporating any agreement reached if requested by either party, but such obligation does not compel either party to agree to a proposal or require the making of a concession.

In plain language, this means that both management and labor are required, under law, to negotiate wages, hours, and terms and conditions of employment "in good faith." In a moment we will see that the *specific* terms that are negotiable (since "wages," "hours," and "conditions of employment" are too broad to be useful in practice) have been clarified by a series of court decisions.

WHAT IS "GOOD FAITH"?

good faith bargaining A term that means both parties are communicating and negotiating. Also, that proposals are being matched with counterproposals and that both parties are making every reasonable effort to arrive at agreements. It does not mean that either party is compelled to agree to a proposal.

Bargaining in **good faith** is the cornerstone of effective labor–management relations. It means that both parties communicate and negotiate. It means that proposals are matched with counterproposals and that both parties make every reasonable effort to arrive at an agreement.[1] It does *not* mean that either party is compelled to agree to a proposal. Nor does it *require* that either party make any specific concessions (although as a practical matter, some may be necessary).

When Is Bargaining Not "in Good Faith"?

As interpreted by the NLRB and the courts, a violation of the requirement for good faith bargaining may include the following:

1. *Surface bargaining.* This involves merely going through the motions of bargaining, without any real intention of completing a formal agreement.
2. *Concession.* Although not required to make a concession, the courts' and Board's definitions of good faith suggest that a willingness to compromise is an essential ingredient in good faith bargaining.
3. *Proposals and demands.* The NLRB considers the advancement of proposals as a factor in determining overall good faith.
4. *Dilatory tactics.* The law requires that the parties meet and "confer at reasonable times and intervals." Obviously, refusal to meet at all with the union does not satisfy the positive duty imposed on the employer.
5. *Imposing conditions.* Attempts to impose conditions that are so onerous or unreasonable as to indicate bad faith will be scrutinized by the Board.
6. *Unilateral changes in conditions.* This is viewed as a strong indication that the employer is not bargaining with the required intent of reaching an agreement.

7. *Bypassing the representative.* An employer violates its duty to bargain when it refuses to negotiate with the union representative. The duty of management to bargain in good faith involves, at a minimum, recognition that this *statutory representative* is the one with whom the employer must deal in conducting bargaining negotiations.
8. *Commission of unfair labor practices during negotiations.* Doing so may reflect upon the good faith of the guilty party.
9. *Providing information.* Information must be supplied to the union, upon request, to enable it to understand and intelligently discuss the issues raised in bargaining.
10. *Bargaining items.* Refusal to bargain on a "mandatory" item (one *must* bargain over these) or insistence on a "permissive" item (one *may* bargain over these) is usually viewed as bad faith bargaining.[2] (We will present these items in the following discussion.)

THE NEGOTIATING TEAM

Both union and management send a negotiating team to the bargaining table. The management team is usually smaller, consisting of perhaps three or four persons. If the employer is large enough to have a vice-president or director of industrial relations, that person would undoubtedly be on the team. In addition, there might be a line manager and perhaps one or two attorneys from a law firm that specializes in labor law. On the union side will be the local's business agent, as well as several of its officers. Your shop's union steward (local union representative) might attend, as well as a representative of the national union. The latter might be the chief spokesperson for the union. More typically, though, he or she provides expert advice and helps maintain consistency among the local agreements that are reached across the country.

Preparations

Both teams usually go into the bargaining sessions having "done their homework." Union representatives have sounded out union members on their desires and conferred with union representatives of related unions. In large industrial unions (such as the Auto Workers), negotiation objectives are usually set by top national officers.

Management uses a number of techniques and procedures to prepare for bargaining. First, it prepares the data on which to build its bargaining position.[3] Pay and benefit data are compiled and include comparisons to local pay rates and rates paid for similar jobs within the industry. Data on the distribution of your work force (in terms of age, sex, and seniority, for instance) are also important, since these factors determine what you will actually pay out in benefits. Internal economic data regarding cost of benefits, overall earnings levels, and the amount and cost of overtime are important as well. Management will also "cost" the current labor contract and determine the increased cost—total, per employee, and per hour—of the union's demands. Another important step here is to *identify probable union demands.* Here you will use information from grievances and feedback from supervisors to determine ahead of time what the union's demands might be (and thus prepare counteroffers and arguments ahead of time).[4] Attitude surveys (to test the reactions of employees to various sections of the contract that management may feel require change) and informal conferences with local union leaders (to discuss the operational effectiveness of the contract and to send up trial balloons on management ideas for change) are other popular tactics.

THE ACTUAL BARGAINING SESSIONS

BARGAINING ITEMS

Labor law sets out categories of items that are subject to bargaining: These are *mandatory, voluntary,* and *illegal* items.

voluntary bargaining items
Items in collective bargaining, over which bargaining is neither illegal nor mandatory—neither party can be compelled against its wishes to negotiate over those items.

Voluntary (or permissible) **bargaining items** are neither mandatory nor illegal; they become a part of negotiations only through the joint agreement of both management and union. Neither party can be compelled against its wishes to negotiate over voluntary items. You cannot hold up signing your contract because the other party refuses to bargain on a voluntary item.

illegal bargaining items
Items in collective bargaining that are forbidden by law; for example, the clause agreeing to hire "union members exclusively" would be illegal in a right-to-work state.

Illegal bargaining items are, of course, forbidden by law. The clause agreeing to hire "union members exclusively" would be illegal in a right-to-work state, for example.

mandatory bargaining items
Items in collective bargaining that a party must bargain over if they are introduced by the other party—for example, pay.

There are about 70 basic items over which bargaining is **mandatory** under the law, and some are presented in Figure 16.1. They include wages, hours, rest periods, layoffs, transfers, benefits, and severance pay. Others are added as the law evolves. For instance, drug testing evolved into a mandatory item as a result of court decisions in the 1980s.[5]

MANDATORY	PERMISSIVE	ILLEGAL
Rates of pay	Indemnity bonds	Closed shop
Wages	Management rights as to union affairs	Separation of employees based on race
Hours of Employment	Pension benefits of retired employees	Discriminatory treatment
Overtime pay	Scope of the bargaining unit	
Shift differentials	Including supervisors in the contract	
Holidays	Additional parties to the contract such as the international union	
Vacations	Use of union label	
Severance pay	Settlement of unfair labor changes	
Pensions	Prices in cafeteria	
Insurance benefits	Continuance of past contract	
Profit sharing plans	Membership of bargaining team	
Christmas bonuses	Employment of strike breakers	
Company housing, meals, and discounts		
Employee security		
Job performance		
Union security		
Management-union relationship		
Drug testing of employees		

FIGURE 16.1
Bargaining Items

Source: Michael R. Carrell and Christina Heavrin, *Collective Bargaining and Labor Relations: Cases, Practice, and Law,* (New York: Macmillan Publishing Company, 1991), pp. 127.

BARGAINING STAGES[6]

Bargaining typically follows several stages of development.[7] *First*, each side presents its demands. (At this stage both parties are usually quite far apart on some issues.) *Second*, there is a reduction of demands. (At this stage each side trades off some of its demands to gain others.) *Third* comes the subcommittee studies: The parties form joint subcommittees to try to work out reasonable alternatives. *Fourth*, an informal settlement is reached and each group goes back to its sponsor: Union representatives check informally with their superiors and the union members; management representatives check with top management. *Finally*, once everything is in order, a formal agreement is fine-tuned and signed.

Some Hints on Bargaining

Reed Richardson has the following advice for bargainers:[8]

1. Be sure you have set clear objectives for every bargaining item and you understand on what grounds the objectives are established.
2. *Do not hurry.*
3. When in doubt, *caucus* with your associates.
4. Be *well prepared* with firm data supporting your position.
5. Always strive to keep some *flexibility* in your position. Don't get yourself out on a limb.
6. Don't just concern yourself with what the other party says and does; *find out why*. Remember that economic motivation is not the only explanation for the other party's conduct and actions.
7. Respect the importance of *face saving* for the other party.
8. Constantly be alert to the *real intentions* of the other party with respect not only to goals but also priorities.
9. Be a good *listener*.
10. Build a reputation for being *fair but firm*.
11. Learn to *control your emotions*; don't panic. Use emotions as a tool, not an obstacle.
12. Be sure as you make each bargaining move that you know its *relationship* to all other moves.
13. Measure each move against your *objectives*.
14. Pay close attention to the *wording* of every clause negotiated; words and phrases are often a source of grievances.
15. Remember that collective bargaining negotiations are, by their nature, part of a *compromise* process. There is no such thing as having all the pie.
16. Learn to *understand* people and their personalities.
17. Consider the impact of present negotiations on those in *future years*.

IMPASSES, MEDIATION, AND STRIKES[9]

impasse
A situation in which the parties cannot reach settlement, usually because one party is demanding more than the other will offer.

Impasse Defined

In collective bargaining, an **impasse** occurs when the parties are not able to move further toward settlement. An impasse usually occurs because one party is demanding more than the other will offer. Sometimes an impasse can be resolved through a "third party," a disinterested person such as a mediator or arbitrator. If the impasse is not resolved in this way, a work stoppage, or *strike*, may be called by the union to bring pressure to bear on management.[10]

Third-Party Involvement

third-party involvement Interventions by a third party used to overcome an impasse, such as mediation, fact-finding, and arbitration.

mediation Intervention in which a neutral third party tries to assist the principals toward reaching agreement.

fact-finder A neutral party who studies the issues in a dispute and makes a public recommendation for settlement.

arbitration The most definitive type of third-party intervention, in which the arbitrator usually has the power to determine and dictate the settlement terms.

Three types of third-party interventions are used to overcome an impasse: mediation, fact-finding, and arbitration. With **mediation** a neutral third party tries to assist the principals toward reaching agreement. The mediator usually holds meetings with each party to determine where each stands regarding their position, and then this information is used to find some common ground for further bargaining. The mediator is always a go-between. As such, he or she communicates assessments of the likelihood of a strike, the possible settlement packages available, and the like. The mediator does not have the authority to fix a position or make a concession.

In certain situations (as in a national emergency dispute where the president of the United States determines that it would be a national emergency for a strike to occur), a *fact-finder* may be appointed. A **fact-finder** is a neutral party who studies the issues in a dispute and makes a public recommendation of what a reasonable settlement ought to be.[11] For example, presidential emergency fact-finding boards have successfully resolved impasses in certain critical transportation disputes.

Arbitration is the most definitive type of third-party intervention, since the arbitrator often has the power to determine and dictate the settlement terms. Unlike mediation and fact-finding, arbitration can thus guarantee a solution to an impasse. With binding arbitration, both parties are committed to accepting the arbitrator's award. With nonbinding arbitration, they are not. Arbitration may also be voluntary or compulsory (in other words, imposed by a government agency). In the United States, voluntary binding arbitration is the most prevalent.

Strikes

strike Refusal by employees to work until their demands are met by the employer.

economic strike A strike that results from a failure to agree on the terms of a contract.

unfair labor practice strike A strike aimed at protesting illegal conduct by the employer.

wildcat strike An unauthorized strike occurring during the term of a contract.

sympathy strike A strike that takes place when one union strikes in support of the strike of another.

There are four main types of **strikes.** An **economic strike** results from a failure to agree on the terms of a contract—from an impasse, in other words. **Unfair labor practice strikes,** on the other hand, are aimed at protesting illegal conduct by the employer. A **wildcat strike** is an unauthorized strike occurring during the term of a contract. A **sympathy strike** occurs when one union strikes in support of the strike of another.[12] Picketing is one of the first activities occurring during a strike. The purpose of picketing is to inform the public about the existence of the labor dispute and (often) to encourage others to refrain from doing business with the struck employer.

Employers can make several responses when they become the object of a strike. One is to *shut down* the affected area and thus halt their operations until the strike is over. A second alternative is to *contract out* work during the duration of the strike in order to blunt the effects of the strike on the employer. A third alternative is for the employer to *continue operations*, perhaps using supervisors and other nonstriking workers to fill in for the striking workers. A fourth alternative is the hiring of replacements for the strikers. In an economic strike, such replacements can be deemed "permanent" and would not have to be let go to make room for strikers who decided to return to work. If the strike was an unfair labor practice strike, the strikers would be entitled to return to their jobs upon making an unconditional offer to do so. Major work stoppages (those involving a thousand or more workers) have dropped significantly over the past 10 years or so, from about 140 in 1981 to about 40 in 1991.[13]

Preparing for the Strike

When a strike is imminent, you'll have to make plans to deal with it. For example, two experts say that when a strike is imminent or already under way, following these guidelines can minimize confusion.[14]

Failure of contract talks in 1990 caused these employees of the *New York Daily News* to picket as part of an economic strike.

- Pay all striking employees what they are owed on the first day of the strike.
- Secure the facility. Supervisors should be on the alert for strangers on the property and access should be controlled. The company should consider hiring guards to protect replacements coming to and from work, and to watch and control the picketers, if necessary.
- Notify all customers. You may decide not to notify customers but to respond to inquiries only. A standard official response to all customers should be prepared and should be merely informative.
- Contact all suppliers and other persons with whom you do business who will have to cross the picket line. Establish alternative methods of obtaining supplies.
- Make arrangements for overnight stays in the facility and for delivered meals, in case the occasion warrants such action.
- Notify the local unemployment office of your need for replacement workers.
- Photograph the facility before, during, and after picketing. If necessary, install videotape equipment and a long-distance microphone to monitor picket line misconduct.
- Record any and all facts concerning strikers' demeanor and activities and such incidents as violence, threats, mass pickets, property damage, or problems. Record police responses to request for assistance.
- Gather the following evidence: number of pickets and their names; time, date, and location of picketing; wording on every sign carried by pickets; and descriptions of picket cars and license numbers.

Other Alternatives

boycott
The combined refusal by employees and other interested parties to buy or use the employer's products.

lockout
A refusal by the employer to provide opportunities to work.

Management and labor each have one other weapon in their arsenal to try to break an impasse and achieve their aims. Unions sometimes try to organize **boycotts,** with the aim of pressuring the employer into making concessions. In fact, some unions are now hiring "boycott consultants" to organize the "corporate campaigns" that put pressure on related firms—such as banks that hold the employer's main loans. In this way the union hopes to pressure the employer and its owners into agreeing to its terms.

For its part, employers can try to break an impasse with the use of a *lockout.* A **lockout** is a refusal by the employer to provide opportunities to work. Here, the employees are (sometimes literally) locked out and prohibited from doing their jobs (and thus getting paid).

A lockout is not generally viewed as an unfair labor practice by the NLRB. For example, if your product is a perishable one (such as vegetables), then a lockout may be a legitimate tactic to neutralize or decrease union power. A lockout is only viewed as an unfair labor practice by the NLRB when the employer acts for a prohibited purpose. It is not a prohibited purpose to try to bring about a settlement of negotiations on favorable terms to the employer. Lockouts today are not widely used, though; employers are usually reluctant to cease operations when employees are willing to continue working (even though there may be an impasse at the bargaining table).[15] However, in 1989, baseball players went on strike, and the owners threatened a lockout; the players then returned to work.

THE AGREEMENT ITSELF

The actual agreement may be 20 or 30 pages, or more than 100. It may contain just general declarations of policy or a detailed specification of rules and procedures. The tendency today is toward the longer, more detailed contract. This is largely a result of the increased number of items the agreements have been covering.

The main sections of a typical contract cover subjects such as these:

1. Management rights
2. Union security and dues checkoff
3. Grievance procedures
4. Arbitration of grievances
5. Disciplinary procedures
6. Compensation rates
7. Hours of work and overtime
8. Benefits: vacations, holidays, insurance, pensions
9. Health and safety provisions
10. Employee security–seniority provisions
11. Contract expiration date

But this list just shows the main categories of subjects. The Bureau of National Affairs in Washington has published a "contract clause finder" which you can use as a checklist to guide your discussions during bargaining.

CHANGES TO EXPECT AFTER BEING UNIONIZED

It goes without saying that unionization of your employees will have profound effects on you and your organization. Professor Dale Beach says there are five basic areas in which the union's impact will be felt:[16] It will restrict management's freedom of action; it will result in union pressure for uniformity of treatment of all employees; it will require improved human resources policies and practices; it will require one spokesperson to be used for the employees; and it will lead to centralization of labor relations decision making.

Perhaps the most obvious impact of unionization is that it restricts management's freedom of action. Decisions such as who gets laid off when business is slow, who gets to work overtime, and who gets a raise will now be subject to challenge by the union, for example.

Partly because of the prospect of such challenges (and partly because the union contract contains written provisions regarding pay, benefits, promotion, and the like), unionization also leads to a systematizing, centralizing, and sophistication of the employer's human resources policies, procedures, and rules. With unionization, for instance, your employer might take steps to (1) advise all plant managers that union-related questions should be referred to the headquarters' labor relations specialist; (2) formulate a compensation plan and particularly a system of wage classes; and (3) develop an improved, more objective procedure for appraising employee performance, so that union challenges are more easily defended against.

CONTRACT ADMINISTRATION: GRIEVANCES

THE IMPORTANT ROLE OF CONTRACT ADMINISTRATION

grievance
Any factor involving wages, hours, or conditions of employment that is used as a complaint against the employer.

grievance procedure
An orderly system whereby employer and union determine whether or not the contract has been violated.

day-to-day collective bargaining
The process of grievance resolution through which the collective bargaining agreement's clauses are interpreted (but *not* renegotiated).

Hammering out a labor agreement is not the last step in collective bargaining; in some respects, it is just the beginning. No labor contract can ever be so complete that it covers all contingencies and answers all questions. For example, suppose the contract says you can only discharge an employee for "just cause." You subsequently discharge someone for speaking back to you in harsh terms. Was it within your rights to discharge this person? Was speaking back to you harshly "just cause"?

Problems like this are usually handled and settled through the **grievance procedure** of the labor contract. This procedure provides an orderly system whereby employer and union determine whether or not the contract has been violated.[17] It is the vehicle for administering the contract on a day-to-day basis. Through this grievance process various clauses are interpreted and given meaning and the contract is transformed into a "living organism." (Remember, though, that this **day-to-day collective bargaining** involves *interpretation* only; it usually does *not* involve negotiating new terms or altering existing ones.)[18]

WHAT ARE THE SOURCES OF GRIEVANCES?

From a practical point of view it is probably easier to list those items that *don't* precipitate grievances than to list the ones that do. Just about any factor involving wages, hours, or conditions of employment has and will be used as the basis of a grievance.

However, some grievances are more serious than others since they are usually more difficult to settle. Discipline cases and seniority problems (including promotions, transfers, and layoffs) would top this list. Others would include grievances growing out of job evaluations and work assignments, overtime, vacations, incentive plans, and holidays.[19] Here are five actual examples of grievances as presented by Reed Richardson:[20]

> *Absenteeism.* An employer fired an employee for excessive absences. The employee filed a grievance stating that there had been no previous warnings or discipline related to excessive absences.
>
> *Insubordination.* An employee on two occasions refused to obey a supervisor's order to meet with him unless a union representative was present at the meeting. As a result, the employee was discharged and subsequently filed a grievance protesting discharge.
>
> *Overtime.* Sunday overtime work was discontinued after a department was split. Employees affected filed a grievance protesting loss of the overtime work.
>
> *Plant rules.* The plant had a posted rule barring employees from eating or drinking during unscheduled breaks. The employees filed a grievance claiming the rule was arbitrary.
>
> *Seniority.* A junior employee was hired to fill the position of a laid-off senior employee. The senior employee filed a grievance protesting the action.

Always Ask: What Is the Real Problem?

Remember that a grievance is often just a symptom of an underlying problem. For example, an employee's concern for his or her security may prompt a grievance over a transfer, work assignment, or promotion. Sometimes bad relations between supervisors and subordinates are to blame: This is often the cause of grievances over "fair treatment," for example. Organizational factors such as automated jobs or ambiguous job descriptions that frustrate or aggravate employees also cause grievances. Union activism is another cause; for example, the union may solicit grievances from workers to underscore ineffective supervision. Problem employees are yet another cause of grievances. These are individuals, who, by their nature, are negative, dissatisfied, and grievance prone.[21] *Disciplinary measures*—a major source of grievances—and *dismissal*—a frequent result of disciplinary measures—are explained in Chapter 17.

THE GRIEVANCE PROCEDURE

Most collective bargaining contracts contain a carefully worded grievance procedure. This specifies the various steps in the procedure, time limits associated with each step, and specific rules such as "all charges of contract violation must be reduced to writing."

Grievance procedures differ from firm to firm. Some contain simple two-step procedures. Here the grievant, union representative, and company representative first meet to discuss the grievance. If a satisfactory solution is not found, the grievance is brought before an independent "third-person" arbitrator, who hears the case, writes it up, and makes a decision.

At the other extreme, the grievance procedure may contain six or more steps. The first step might be for the grievant and shop steward to meet informally with the grievant's supervisor to try to find a solution. If one is not found, a formal grievance is filed and a meeting scheduled among the employee, shop steward, and the supervisor's boss. The next steps involve meetings between higher and higher echelon managers. Finally, if top management and the union cannot reach agreement, the grievance may go to arbitration.

An Example of What to Expect

Professors Arthur Sloane and Fred Witney say that the best way to demonstrate the working of a grievance procedure is through an example. They present the following as an actual situation that typifies the grievance process in industry.[22]

Background

Tom Swift, a member of Local 1000, was employed by the Apex Manufacturing Company for a period of five years. His production record was excellent, he caused management no trouble, and during his fourth year of employment he received a promotion. One day Swift began preparations to leave the plant 20 minutes before quitting time. He put away his tools, washed up, got out of his overalls, and put on his street clothes. Jackson, an assistant supervisor in his department, observed Swift's actions. He immediately informed Swift that he was going to the "front office" to recommend his discharge. The next morning Swift reported for work, but Jackson handed Swift a pay envelope. In addition to wages, it included a discharge notice. The notice declared that the company discharged Swift because he had made ready to leave the plant 20 minutes before quitting time. Swift immediately contacted his union steward, Sue Thomas. Swift told Thomas the circumstances, and the steward believed that the discharge constituted a violation of the collective bargaining contract. A clause in the agreement provided that an employee could be discharged only for "just cause." Disagreeing with the assistant supervisor and the "front office," shop steward Thomas felt that the discharge was *not* for just cause.

Step 1: The steps in processing the complaint through the grievance procedure were clearly outlined in the collective bargaining agreement. First, it was necessary to present the grievance to the supervisor of the department in which Swift worked. Both Thomas and Swift approached the supervisor, and the written grievance was presented to him. The supervisor was required to give his answer on the grievance within 48 hours after receiving it. He complied with the time requirements, but his answer did not please Swift or Thomas. The supervisor supported the action of the assistant supervisor and refused to recommend the reinstatement of Swift.

Step 2: Not satisfied with the action of the supervisor, the labor union (through Thomas the steward) initiated the second step of the grievance procedure. This step required the appeal of the complaint to the superintendent of the department in which Swift worked. The superintendent supported the decisions of his supervisor and assistant supervisor. Despite the efforts of the steward (who vigorously argued the merits of Swift's case), the department superintendent refused to reinstate the worker. Hence the second step of the grievance procedure was exhausted, and the union and the employee were still not satisfied with the results. (Keep in mind that the vast majority of grievances *are* usually settled in these first two steps of the grievance procedure.)

Step 3: Accordingly, the union went to the third step of the grievance procedure. Grievance personnel for the third step included the general manager and her representative from the company; the labor union was represented by the organization's plantwide grievance committee. The results of the negotiation at this third step proved satisfactory to Swift, the union, and the company. After 45 minutes of spirited discussion, the management group agreed with the union that discharge was not warranted in this particular case. (Management's committee, by the way, was persuaded by the following set of circumstances. Everyone conceded that Swift had an outstanding record before the dismissal occurred. In addition, the discussion revealed that Swift had asked the department supervisor whether there was any more work to be done before he left his bench to prepare to leave for home. The supervisor had replied in the negative. Finally, it was brought out that Swift had had a pressing problem at home which he claimed was the motivating factor in his desire to prepare to leave early.) It was concluded that Swift would be reinstated in his job but would be penalized by a three-day suspension without pay.

Step 4: What would have occurred if the company and the labor union had *not* reached a satisfactory agreement at the third step of the grievance procedure? In this particular contract, the grievance procedure provided for a fourth step. Grievance procedure personnel at the fourth step included (for the company) the vice-president in charge of industrial relations or her representative and (for the union) an officer of the international union or his representative.[23] In most agreements, a final step would require taking the grievance outside the company to arbitration. (The arbitrator's decision generally cannot be appealed to the courts except in discrimination cases.)

GRIEVANCE HANDLING IN NONUNION ORGANIZATIONS

Virtually every labor agreement signed today contains a grievance procedure clause, but the fact is that *non*unionized employers need such procedures as well. We'll discuss those procedures in the following chapter.

GUIDELINES FOR HANDLING GRIEVANCES

Developing the Proper Environment

The best way to "handle" a grievance is to develop a work environment in which grievances don't occur in the first place.[24] Because of this, *constructive grievance handling* depends first on your ability to recognize, diagnose, and correct the causes of potential employee dissatisfaction (causes such as unfair appraisals, inequitable wages, or poor communications) *before* they become formal grievances.

Some Guidelines: Do's and Don'ts [25]

As a manager, your behavior in handling grievances is very important. You are on the "firing line" and must therefore steer a course between fair treatment of employees and maintaining the rights and prerogatives of management. Walter Baer has developed a list of do's and don'ts that you will find useful guides in handling grievances.[26] Some of the most critical ones are presented next:

DO

Investigate and handle each and every case as though it may eventually result in an arbitration hearing.

Talk with the employee about his or her grievance; give the person a good and full hearing.

Require the union to identify specific contractual provisions allegedly violated.

Comply with the contractual time limits of the company for handling the grievance.

Visit the work area of the grievance.

Determine if there were any witnesses.

Examine the grievant's personnel record.

Fully examine prior grievance records.

Treat the union representative as your equal.

Hold your grievance discussions privately.

Fully inform your own supervisor of grievance matters.

DON'T

Discuss the case with the union steward alone—the grievant should definitely be there.

Make arrangements with individual employees that are inconsistent with the labor agreement.

Hold back the remedy if the company is wrong.

Admit to the binding effect of a past practice.

Relinquish your rights as a manager to the union.

Settle grievances on the basis of what is "fair." Instead, stick to the labor agreement, which should be your only standard.

Computer Application In Collective Bargaining: Estimating Offers Costs With Computers

Management students, whether they ultimately work for management or labor, are usually introduced to gaming—computer simulations that answer "what if . . ." questions. Sometimes the simulations are complex strategies; sometimes they are as basic as looking at cash-flow projections. These same concepts may be applied to labor–management negotiations. When labor suggests a 5% wage increase the first year, followed by 3% each of the next two years, management counters with 3, 3, 5, understanding that their proposal will cost less over the course of the three years. However, costing out other benefits may not be as easily understood. Therefore, programs which rapidly calculate the dollar cost of benefits (both direct and indirect costs) offer the opportunity for more knowledgeable bargaining.[1]

To quickly calculate the costs of offers or counteroffers, a simple table based on the percent of (1) each step in salary ranges, or (2) each employee's annual pay, or (3) a particular benefit can be created. For example, if each wage step is 4% higher than the one below, and the first step of each grade equals the middle step of the previous grade, simply changing the first grade's first step in the table of the wage plan will update it. Then, by linking this table to the rate each employee is paid (keyed to that table), the new total cost is available. If an employee is paid at the rate of step 4, grade 3, a cell address next to that employee's name tells the company what is budgeted for that employee. If that employee has worked an average of 100 hours overtime each of the last three years, a formula would be placed next to the employee's name which includes the cell address plus the hourly rate (if the wage plan is not in hourly figures) times 100 (to represent the 100 hours).

If one side suggests that the benefits package should be raised by 7% to include so many dollars for child care, the negotiator should have available the number of employees who have expressed an interest in this benefit and how many children are involved as well as a range of possible costs of child care in the area. By combining this information with the current percentage of payroll assigned to benefit costs, it will be clear whether or not the 7% is a realistic figure of probable costs. The negotiator might be willing to give 5% and, with data of probable use and cost figured in, be able to negotiate a wording of the benefit that will better control costs, keeping them within the intended range.

Computers, then, help to prepare the negotiator for the bargaining sessions and could possibly shorten the time spent bargaining. If bargaining is done off-site, portable or laptop computers with 30 or 40 megabyte memories provide support.

[1]M. Steven Potash, "A Scientific Approach to Bargaining," ABA Journal (January, 1986), p. 58.

Bargain over items not covered by the contract.

Treat as arbitrable claims demanding the discipline or discharge of managers.

Give long written grievance answers.

Trade a grievance settlement for a grievance withdrawal (or try to make up for a bad decision in one grievance by bending over backward in another).

Deny grievances on the premise that "your hands have been tied by management."

Agree to informal amendments in the contract.

▸ The Future Of Unionism

UNIONS FALL ON HARD TIMES

The 1970s and 1980s were hard times for unions, and during those years their roles dropped steeply. About 22% of the nonfarm U.S. work force belonged to unions in 1975. By 1992 that figure had dropped to about 16%. This slide actually began in the early 1950s. By then, recall, most easily organized workers in industries like mining, transportation, and manufacturing had already unionized.

By the 1970s and 1980s, other changes were occurring. Most of the new jobs being created in our economy were in the service sector, and today roughly two-thirds of the work force is employed in service firms. These workers have never been highly unionized. Many work part-time, and the typical firm is small. This makes it harder and more costly for unions to organize them, in part because it requires dealing with many more employers.[27]

The last 10 years have also been an era of restructuring for American industry. Faced with intense global competition, outdated equipment, and corporate raiders, hundreds of thousands of union members have been laid off as firms tried to consolidate and boost their profits.

In a major test for unions, workers at Nissan Motor Manufacturing Corp., U.S.A., in Smyrna, Tennessee, rejected the United Auto Workers in the first union vote at a U.S. auto plant wholly-owned by a Japanese firm.[28] After a bitter, 18-month union organizing campaign, workers voted more than two to one against UAW representation in 1989, apparently because pay, job security, and management practices were already so favorable at the plant.

Double-breasting is another way that companies are putting unions under more pressure. It refers to a tactic whereby employers avoid their obligations under union contracts by establishing and running nonunion companies to which they may transfer union work. The NLRB permits this under certain circumstances. It is, for instance, a common practice in the construction industry.

Also, as explained in Chapter 15, the labor laws and court rulings for which unions fought so long are now in place. Ironically, they—along with more progressive human resource management practices in many firms—provide just the sorts of protection (of occupational health or plant closing warnings, for instance) that up to a few years ago only unions could provide.[29]

Beyond this, technology will influence unionization. Computer systems and other modern technologies may reduce labor demand, for instance. Electronic work (as in processing credit card claims) is also highly portable compared with factory work. Modern office work—and its workers—can thus be shifted almost literally at the touch of a button from a facility in one state to another, and even overseas.[30]

WHAT'S NEXT FOR UNIONS?

Does this all mean that we no longer need unions? Probably not. But what it does mean is a change in the way that unions operate and in how they see their role.

This seems to mean several changes in the way that unions do business. First, unions are increasingly going after a "piece of the pie" in terms of ownership and control of corporations. As a United Steelworkers Union president put it, "We are not going to sit around and allow management to louse things up like they did in the past."[31] Today, for one thing, over 8 million workers have a piece of their employers through employee stock ownership plans. Recall that these ESOPs are basically pension plans through which a company's employees accumulate shares of their company's stock. As a result, nonmanagement employees now sit on boards of directors at more than 300 firms in their role as representatives of the firm's employee stock ownership plans.

Second, unions are becoming both more aggressive and more sophisticated in the way that they present themselves to the public. The AFL-CIO has a program to train a thousand unionists in the fundamentals of how to come across well on television, for instance. At the same time unions are making a major effort to organize white-collar workers, with more than 10% of white-collar workers already unionized. Unions are also, as we'll see, entering into more cooperative pacts with employers, for instance working with them in developing team-based employee participation programs.

In the early days of President Clinton's new Democratic administration a more optimistic union movement was already beginning to map out a new strategy. Among other changes being planned was an effort aimed at eliminating some of the previous administrations' executive owners, some of which had the effect of impeding unions' organizing efforts. More changes will undoubtedly take place as well.

Building Employee Commitment

The sorts of quality circles and total quality management programs discussed in Chapter 9 are a two-edged sword as far as unions are concerned. On the one hand they can be the basis for building better communications and for boosting union–management harmony. On the other hand they may undercut union security by building relationships between labor and management that make unions obsolete. Unions are therefore a bit indecisive when it comes to the subject of commitment-building participation programs.

Based on the research, at least, worker participation programs don't seem to be the threat union leaders fear they may be. One study, for instance, found few differences between how quality programs' participants and nonparticipants viewed the performance of their unions.[32] Another researcher found that quality program participants were actually more involved in and satisfied with the union than were nonparticipants.[33]

Perhaps the critical issue is whether or not the union is involved in helping develop and implement the total quality program. For example, one study concluded that union officers were much less likely to view the quality program negatively when they were involved in designing and implementing it.[34] Similarly, in another study, the researchers found that "union members who participated in [such] programs were less likely than nonparticipants to view [them] as a threat to the union, and also remained more loyal to the union."[35] The idea that involving the union in the participation program can be useful seems to have occurred in programs like that at Saturn Corp., which we'll turn to in a moment. First, though, let's consider what can happen when unions resist. One way they do this is by filing unfair labor practices against the employer.

Are Employee Participation Programs Unfair Labor Practices?

The proliferation of employee participation programs—quality circles, quality improvement programs, quality of work life teams, and so on—has added urgency to a question that's been debated in labor relations circles for over 50 years: Are employee participation programs like these "sham unions" and therefore illegal under the National Labor Relations Act? At the present time they are "subject to serious legal challenge under the National Labor Relations Act (NLRA)."[36]

To understand the problem, it's useful to know that a principal goal of the National Labor Relations (or Wagner) Act was to outlaw so-called sham unions. Two years before passage of the NLRA the National Recovery Act of 1933 tried to give employees the right to organize and bargain collectively. This in turn triggered an enormous increase in "sham unions," unions that were actually company-supported organizations aimed at keeping legitimate unions out. As Senator Robert Wagner explained then, "at the present time genuine collective bargaining is being thwarted immeasurably by the proliferation of company unions."[37] These sham unions were one of the principal factors motivating Senator Wagner to sponsor the 1935 National Labor Relations Act.

The problem is that because of the way the NLRA is written and frequently interpreted, participative programs such as quality circles and quality improvement teams could be viewed as sham unions. In part, this is because the NLRA defines a "labor organization" as

> Any organization of any kind, or any agency or employee representation committee or plan, in which employees participate and which exists for the purpose, in whole or in part, of dealing with employers concerning grievances, labor disputes, wages, rates of pay, hours of employment, or conditions of work.[38]

The matter of whether various types of worker participation plans are sham unions has thus been a matter of contention for many years. Senator Wagner specifically said that his bill did not "prevent employers from forming or assisting associations which exist to promote the health and general welfare of workers or to provide group insurance or for similar purposes."[39] In some cases—such as *NLRB* v. *Ampex Corporation*—the courts and the NLRB have held that a firm's participation committees *were* labor organizations and were therefore prohibited by the NLRA. In others, such as *Sears, Roebuck and Company*,[40] the decision has been that committees—in this case, an employee communications committee comprised of one employee from each of 10 departments that met with management to discuss such matters as uniforms, tools, and equipment—did *not* fit the definition of labor organization and was therefore permissible under the NLRA.[41]

It seems that whether or not an employer's participation program will be viewed as an impermissible labor organization revolves around at least two things. One is the question of "dominance." Thus, if the employer formulates the idea for the organization (committees); creates them; controls the development of their constitution or governing rules; maintains control over the committees' functions; controls the internal management of the program; controls or participates in the program's meetings; or allows the organization—in this case committees—to meet on its premises and use its supplies while paying employees for time spent in committee meetings, the organizations *could* be considered impermissibly dominated by the employer. The NLRB has frequently taken the approach that even potential domination is impermissible. Courts, though, have often taken the position that *actual* domination had to be shown before a violation is established: in other words, that the employees' freedom of choice was actually dominated by the employer.[42]

The actual role of the participation committees is the second consideration. Thus if the committees focus exclusively on issues such as quality and productivity improvement, they may be more likely to be viewed by the courts as outside the purview of the National Labor Relations Act. On the other hand, if the committees become involved in union-type matters such as wages, working conditions, and hours of work, they may be more likely to be viewed as basically unions. Thus in the Electromation Corp. case decided in 1992 by the NLRB, the firm set up "action committees" to advise management regarding matters such as absenteeism/infractions, pay progression, and the attendance bonus plan. When a teamsters local lost a certification election at this firm, they filed an unfair labor practice act with the NLRB. They claimed, in part, that the action committees were unlawfully dominated labor organizations. The NLRB decided in favor of the union but did not really clarify when and under what conditions participation programs might be acceptable. The matter will probably move slowly through the courts.

For now, two experts urge employers to take prudent steps to avoid having their employee participation programs viewed as sham unions. The steps to take are as follows:[43]

1. If you want to establish participation programs, involve employees in the formation of these programs to the greatest practical extent.
2. Continually emphasize to employees that the committees exist for the *exclusive purpose* of addressing such issues as quality and productivity. Stress that they are not intended to be vehicles for "dealing with" management on items that are generally viewed as "mandatory" bargaining items between unions and management, such as pay and working conditions.
3. Of course, make sure you don't try to set up such committees at the same time union-organizing activities are beginning in your facility.
4. Comprise committees of volunteers, rather than elected employee representatives. Also rotate membership frequently to ensure broad employee participation.
5. The employer and its managers and supervisors should participate in the day-to-day activities of the committees as little as possible. Employers want to avoid even the suspicion of unlawful interference in these committees, or, worse, the perception of domination.

Employee Participation Programs at Saturn Corp.

Union–management relations have a long history of harmony at Saturn Corp. GM involved the United Auto Workers (UAW) in the firm's earliest planning stages, and joint GM/UAW study groups hammered out agreement on virtually every aspect of the new company and plant. What came out of this may be the prototype of unionized companies of the future. There are no hourly employees at Saturn Corp. All are on salary, and there is (as we mentioned) a heavy emphasis on performance-based pay. Every supervisory employee at Saturn—from front-line supervisors up through the president of the firm—is "paired" with a union partner and virtually all work-related decisions are made together.

Progressive relationships with the UAW union help companies such as Saturn Corporation grow and avoid the fate of this closed GM plant in California.

The union–management cooperation that characterizes Saturn stems, it should be stressed, from the deep commitment to employees and to cooperation that both the union and the company share. For example, as the UAW's partner to Saturn Corporation's head of personnel puts it:

> Our philosophy is, we care about people . . . and it shows. We involve people in decisions that affect them. I came here from the Mesina, New York, GM foundry and managers there, like a lot of the other managers you'll come across, take the position that "I'll tell you what to do, and that's what you'll do." In fact, some of those managers from the foundry are here now. But on the whole those who are here now are different, and the basic difference is wrapped up in the question, "Do you really believe in people?" Saturn's commitment really comes down to how you feel about people—your attitudes—more than anything, because all the other Saturn programs—the work teams, the extensive training, the way people are paid—all flow from these people's attitudes.[44]

As if to underscore this, the firm's union contract stresses much the same point:

> We believe that all people want to be involved in decisions that affect them, care about their job, take pride in themselves and in their contributions, and want to share in the success of their efforts. By creating an atmosphere of mutual trust and respect, recognizing and utilizing individual expertise and knowledge in innovative ways, providing the technologies and education for each individual, we will enjoy a successful relationship and a sense of belonging to an integrated business system capable of achieving our common goals which ensures security for our people and success for our business and communities.

Such attitudes and such an agreement provide a glimpse, one would hope, of the union–management relationships of the future.

Indeed, this approach—merging the employers and the union's interests through the vehicle of participative management—is spreading. For example, at Corning, the firm is converting all of its 28 U.S. factories to team-based production and they are doing it in partnership with the American Flint Glass Workers Union (AFGW).[45]

At Corning (whose participative, team-based programs were discussed in Chapter 9), the union plays a major role in the team-based production program's success. As at Saturn, union and management signed a joint philosophical statement which in this case was called "A partnership in the workplace." It articulates six "essential values" including "recognition of the rights of workers to participate in decisions that affect their working lives."[46] As part of its new role, the union has a hand in the content and administration of all the firm's training programs, and work redesign committees (which include shop floor workers) work on restructuring their jobs. What we may be moving toward, proposes this expert, is an era in which union–management relations are more similar to what they've traditionally been in countries like Germany and Japan, where both the workers and their unions traditionally have considerable input in how their firms are run.[47]

modern operating agreements
A type of labor contract designed to give workers a greater say in how their jobs are performed through inclusion of work teams, fewer job classifications, and pay-for-knowledge systems.

Increasingly, new types of labor contracts called **modern operating agreements (MOA)** are being signed to memorialize these new, more cooperative union–management arrangements. Unlike traditional union agreements, MOAs "are designed to give hourly workers a greater say in how their jobs are performed. The agreements establish work teams, decentralize decision making, include union representatives on key plant operating committees, reduce the number of job classifications, and use a pay-for-knowledge system that links employees' wage rates to the number of different operations they can perform."[48] Increasingly, in other words, the labor agreements of tomorrow will probably reflect employers' growing awareness of the need to win their employees' commitment.

Chapter Review

SUMMARY

1. Bargaining collectively "in good faith" is the next step if and when the union wins the election. Good faith means that both parties communicate and negotiate, and that proposals are matched with counterproposals. We discussed the structure of the negotiating teams and their preparations. We also discussed the actual bargaining sessions and the distinction between mandatory, voluntary, and illegal bargaining items. We also listed some hints on bargaining, including do not hurry, be prepared, find out why, and be a good listener.
2. An impasse occurs when the parties aren't able to move further toward settlement. *Third-party involvement*—namely, arbitration, fact-finding, or mediation—is one alternative. Sometimes, though, a *strike* occurs. Preparing for the strike involves such steps as securing the facility, notifying all customers, and photographing the facility. Boycotts and lockouts are two other "anti-impasse" weapons sometimes used by labor and management.
3. Grievance handling has been called "day-to-day collective bargaining." It involves the continuing interpretation of the collective-bargaining agreement (but usually not its renegotiation).
4. Just about any management action might lead to a grievance, but the most serious actions involve discipline cases, seniority problems, actions growing out of a job evaluation and work assignments, and overtime and benefits. But remember that a grievance is often just a symptom; always try to find the underlying problem.
5. Most agreements contain a carefully worded grievance procedure. It may be a two-step procedure or (at the other extreme) involve six or more steps. In any case, the steps usually involve meetings between higher and higher echelon managers until (if agreement isn't reached) the grievance goes to arbitration. Grievance handling is as important in nonunion organizations as in those that are unionized.
6. Disciplinary actions are one big source of grievances. Discipline should be based on rules, adhere to a system of progressive penalties, and permit an appeals process. Other "fairness" guidelines include the fact that the discipline should be in line with the way management usually responds to similar incidents. Other important guidelines include emphasize rules, remember that the burden of proof is on you, and don't fail to get the facts.

KEY TERMS

collective bargaining
good faith bargaining
voluntary bargaining items
illegal bargaining items
mandatory bargaining items
impasse
third-party involvement
mediation
fact-finder
arbitration
strikes
economic strike
unfair labor practice strike
wildcat strike
sympathy strike
boycott
lockout
grievance
grievance procedure
day-to-day collective bargaining

DISCUSSION QUESTIONS

1. Discuss what you, as a supervisor, should keep in mind about how to prepare for union contract negotiations.
2. What is meant by good faith bargaining? When is bargaining not in good faith?
3. You are the president of a small (30 employees) firm. While you are not unionized, you would like to have an appeals process that would serve a purpose similar to that of a grievance procedure. Discuss what this appeals process might entail.
4. Define *impasse, mediation,* and *strike,* and explain the techniques that are used to overcome an impasse.

APPLICATION EXERCISES

RUNNING CASE

CARTER CLEANING COMPANY

The Grievance

On visiting one of Carter Cleaning Company's stores Jennifer was surprised to be taken aside by a long-term Carter employee, who met her as she was parking her car. "Murray (the store manager) told me I was suspended for two days without pay because I came in late last Thursday," said George. "I'm really upset, but around here the store manager's word seems to be law, and it sometimes seems like the only way anyone can file a grievance around here is by meeting you or your father like this in the parking lot." Jennifer was very disturbed by this revelation, and promised the employee she would look into it and discuss the situation with her dad. In the car heading back to headquarters she began mulling over what Carter Cleaning Company's alternatives might be.

Questions

1. Do you think it is important for Carter Cleaning Company to have a formal grievance process? Why or why not?
2. Based on what you know about the Carter Cleaning Company, outline the steps in what you think the ideal grievance process would be for this company.
3. In addition to the grievance process, can you think of anything else that Carter Cleaning Company might do to make sure that grievances and gripes like this one get expressed, and also get heard by top management?

CASE INCIDENT *Botched Batch*

"All right, I admit I made an error in preparing those data processing disks, but I told the operations manager about it right away, and he could have stopped the computer run," protested Bonnie Flint. "Seeing as how I've always been one of your best workers, how can you justify suspending me and rescinding my promotion, and not doing anything to him?"

"The simple fact is that if you hadn't been negligent, we wouldn't have had to deal with a whole string of problems that cost us several thousand dollars to correct," replied human resources manager Judy Martin. "Since you were primarily responsible for the foul-up, you deserve the discipline."

Was the disciplinary decision proper?

Facts

A computer department employee made an entry error that botched up an entire run of computer reports. Efforts to rectify the situation produced a second set of improperly run reports. As a result of the series of errors, the employer incurred extra costs of $2,400, plus a weekend of overtime work by other computer department staffers. Management suspended the employee for three days for negligence, and also revoked a promotion for which she previously had been approved.

Protesting the discipline, the employee stressed that she had attempted to correct her error in the early stages of the run by notifying the manager of computer operations of her mistake. Maintaining that the resulting string of errors could have been avoided if the manager had followed up on her report and stopped the initial run, the employee argued that she had been treated unfairly because the manager had not been disciplined even though he compounded the problem, while she was severely punished. Moreover, citing her "impeccable" work record and management's acknowledgement that she had always been a "model employee," the worker insisted that the denial of her previously approved promotion was "unconscionable."

Questions

1. Do you believe the disciplinary decision was proper?
2. What changes, if any, would you make in this firm's disciplinary process?

Award

(Please do *not* read beyond here until after you have completed answering the questions, above.) The arbitrator upholds the three-day suspension but decides that the promotion should be restored.

Discussion

"There is no question," the arbiter notes, that the employee's negligent act "set in motion the train of events which resulted in running two complete sets of disks reflecting improper information." Stressing that the employer incurred substantial cost because of the error, the arbiter cites "unchallenged" testimony that management had commonly issued three-day suspensions for similar infractions in the past. Thus, the arbiter decides, the employer acted with just cause in meting out an "even-handed" punishment for the negligence.

Turning to the denial of the already approved promotion, the arbitrator says that this action should be viewed "in the same light as a demotion for disciplinary reasons." In such cases, the arbiter notes, management's decision normally is based on a pattern of unsatisfactory behavior, an employee's inability to perform, or similar grounds. Observing that management had never before reversed a promotion as part of a disciplinary action, the arbiter says that by tacking on the denial of the promotion in this case, the employer substantially varied its disciplinary policy from its past practice. Since this action on management's part was not "even handed," the arbiter rules, the promotion should be restored.

Pointers

Arbiters tend to frown on management decisions to demote an employee for temporary performance problems on the grounds that such a penalty constitutes a "permanent punishment." For example, in one case, an arbitrator emphasized that "permanent demotion is not a proper form of discipline where an employee's capabilities are conceded and his performance generally is satisfactory, but where his attitudes of the moment are improper." Stressing that undesirable behavior, such as occasional carelessness or a failure to obey instructions, usually can be corrected by suspending the employee for a reasonable period, the arbiter noted that such discipline does not "offend the basic seniority rights of the employee and does not inflict upon the employee an indeterminate sentence."

Source: Bureau of National Affairs, *Bulletin to Managers*, September 13, 1985, p. 3.

Human Resource Management Simulation

One item of particular importance that a union always provides to employees is a formal method of handling grievances. The simulation offers an option for your firm to establish a formal grievance program—something it currently does not have. The grievance panel consists of an even number of employees and supervisors. Such programs increase morale by helping employees feel they have a "court of last resort." As with any program in the simulation, your team will need to do a qualitative cost-benefit analysis before undertaking such a program.

NOTES

1. Dale Yoder, *Personnel Management* (Englewood Cliffs, NJ: Prentice Hall, 1972), p. 486. See also Michael Ballot, *Labor-Management Relations in a Changing Environment* (New York: John Wiley and Sons, 1992), pp. 169–425.
2. Quoted in Reed Richardson, *Collective Bargaining by Objectives* (Englewood Cliffs, NJ: Prentice Hall, 1977), p. 150; adapted from Charles Morris, ed., *The Developing Labor Law* (Washington, DC: Bureau of National Affairs, 1971), pp. 271–310.
3. John Fossum, *Labor Relations* (Dallas, TX: Business Publications, 1982), pp. 246–250.
4. *Boulwareism* is the name given to a strategy, now generally held in disfavor, by which the company, based on an exhaustive study of what it thought its employees wanted, made but one offer at the bargaining table and then refused to bargain any further unless convinced by the union on the basis of new facts that its original position was wrong. The NLRB subsequently found that the practice of offering the same settlement to all units, insisting that certain parts of the package could not differ among agreements and communicating to the employees about how negotiations were going, amounted to an illegal pattern. Fossum, *Labor Relations*, p. 267.
5. Commerce Clearing House, "Drug Testing/Court Rulings," *Ideas and Trends*, January 25, 1988, p. 16.
6. Bargaining items based on Richardson, *Collective Bargaining*, pp. 113–115; bargaining stages based on William Glueck, "Labor Relations and the Supervisor," in M. Gene Newport, *Supervisory Management* (St. Paul, MN: West, 1976), pp. 207–234.
7. See also Yoder, *Personnel Management*, pp. 517–518.
8. Richardson, *Collective Bargaining*, p. 150.
9. Fossum, *Labor Relations*, pp. 298–322.
10. Although considerable research has been done on the subject, it's not clear what sorts of situations precipitate impasses. At times, however, it seems that the prospect of having the impasse taken to an arbitrator actually "chills" the negotiation process. Specifically, if neither the union nor the management negotiators want to make the tough political decision to make the tough choices, they might consciously or unconsciously opt to declare an impasse knowing that the arbitrator will then have to take the heat. See Linda Babcock and Craig Olson, "The Causes of Impasses in Labor Disputes," *Industrial Relations*, Vol. 31, no. 2 (Spring 1992), pp. 348–360.
11. Fossum, *Labor Relations*, p. 312. See also Thomas Watkins, "Assessing Arbitrator Competence," *Arbitration Journal*, Vol. 47, No. 2, June 1992, pp. 43–48.
12. Ibid., p. 317.
13. "Work Stoppages," *BNA Bulletin to Management*, March 19, 1992, pp. 84–85.
14. Stephen Cabot and Gerald Cureton, "Labor Disputes and Strikes: Be Prepared," *Personnel Journal*, Vol. 60 (February 1981), pp. 121–126.
15. For a discussion of the cost of a strike see Woodruff Imberman, "Strikes Cost More than You Think," *Harvard Business Review*, Vol. 57 (May–June 1979), pp. 133–138. The NLRB held in 1986 in *Harter Equipment, Inc.*, 280 NLRB No. 71, that an employer could lawfully hire temporary replacements during the course of a lockout, in the absence of proof of specific antiunion motivation, in order to bring economic pressure to bear upon a union to support a legitimate bargaining position.
16. Dale Beach, *Personnel* (New York: Macmillan, 1975), pp. 117–119.
17. Arthur A. Sloane and Fred Witney, *Labor Relations*, 5th ed. (Englewood Cliffs, NJ: Prentice Hall, 1977), pp. 229–231.
18. Richardson, *Collective Bargaining*, p. 184.
19. Lester Bittel, *What Every Supervisor Should Know* (New York: McGraw-Hill, 1974), p. 308, based on a study of 1,000 grievances made by the American Arbitration Association.
20. Richardson, *Collective Bargaining*.
21. J. Brad Chapman, "Constructive Grievance Handling," in M. Gene Newport, *Supervisory Management* (St. Paul: West Publishing Co., 1976), pp. 253–274.
22. Quoted from Sloane and Witney, *Labor Relations*, pp. 219–221. Copyright 1985. Reprinted by permission of Prentice Hall, Englewood Cliffs, NJ.
23. Ibid., p. 221.
24. See, for example, Clyde Summers, "Protecting All Employees Against Unjust Dismissal," *Harvard Business Review*, Vol. 58 (January–February 1980), pp. 132–139; and George Bohlander and Harold White, "Building Bridges: Non-Union Employee Grievance Systems," *Personnel* (July 1988), pp. 62–66.
25. Newport, *Supervisory Management*, p. 273, for an excellent checklist.
26. For a full discussion of these and others, see Walter Baer, *Grievance Handling: 101 Guides for Supervisors* (New York: American Management Association, 1970). For an interesting discussion of major league baseball's grievance arbitration system, see Glenn Wong, "Major League Baseball's Grievance Arbitration System: A Comparison with Nonsport Industry," *Labor Law Journal* , Vol. 38, no. 2 (February 1987), pp. 84–99.
27. "Perspectives on Employment," *Research Bulletin #194* (1986), The Conference Board, 845 Third Avenue, New York, N.Y. 10020.
28. Bureau of National Affairs, "Union 'No' at Nissan," *Bulletin to Management*, August 10, 1989, pp. 249–250.
29. "Beyond Unions: A Revolution in Employee Rights Is in the Making," *Business Week*, July 8, 1985, pp. 72–77.
30. Dennis Chamot, "Unions Need to Confront the Results of New Technology," *Monthly Labor Review* (August 1987), p. 45.
31. "The Battle for Corporate Control," *Business Week*, May 18, 1987, p. 107.
32. Thomas Kochan, Harry Katz, and Nancy Mower, *Worker Participation and American Unions: Threat or Opportunity* (Kalamazoo, MI: W. E. Upjohn, 1984).
33. Nil Verma, "Employee Involvement Programs: Do They Alter Worker Affinity Towards Unions?" *Proceedings of the 39th Annual Meetings* (New Orleans, December 1986) (Madison, WI: Industrial Relations Research Association, 1987), pp. 306–312.
34. Adrienne Eaton, "The Extent and Determinants of Local Union Control of Participative Programs," *Industrial and Labor Relations Review*, Vol. 43, no. 5 (1990), pp. 604–620.
35. Adrienne Eaton, Michael Gordon, and Jeffrey Keefe, "The Impact of Quality of Work Life Programs and Grievance System Effectiveness on Union Commitment," *Industrial and Labor Relations Review*, Vol. 45, no. 3 (April 1992), p. 591.

36. This is based on Kenneth Jenero and Christopher Lyons, "Employee Participation Programs: Prudent or Prohibited?" *Employee Relations Law Journal*, Vol. 17, no. 4 (Spring 1992), pp. 535–566.
37. 78 Congressional Records 4229, 4230 (1934).
38. Jenero and Lyons, "Employee Participation Programs," p. 539.
39. Ibid., p. 540.
40. *Sears, Roebuck and Company*, 274 NLRB 230 (1985).
41. For a discussion see Jenero and Lyons, "Employee Participation Programs," pp. 546–547.
42. See ibid., p. 551, for instance.
43. These are based on ibid., pp. 564–565.
44. Personal interview.
45. For a discussion of this see John Hoerr, "What Should Unions Do?" *Harvard Business Review* (May–June 1991), pp. 30–45. See also Roy Marshall, "The Future Role of Government in Industrial Relations," *Industrial Relations*, Vol. 31, No. 1, Winter 1992, pp. 31–49.
46. Ibid., p. 39.
47. Ibid., pp. 42–43; for an additional view on this topic see David Blanchflower and Richard Freeman, "Unionism in the United States and Other Advanced OECD Countries," *Industrial Relations*, Vol. 31, no. 1 (Winter 1992), pp. 56–79.
48. "New Agreements Improve Labor Relations," *Bulletin to Management*, September 5, 1991, p. 279 and Joseph D. Reid, "Future Unions," *Industrial Relations*, Vol. 31, No. 1, Winter 1992, pp. 122–136.

VIDEO CASE 4

—Conclusion—

WILL UNIONS HAVE TO CONTINUE STRUGGLING TO GET NEW MEMBERS?

In the Introduction to Video Case 4 on page 527, we asked several important questions that you should now refer to.

Up to this point the United Auto Workers has had mixed results in organizing Japanese auto facilities in the United States. As Mr. Fraser in the video mentions, three plants—the Toyota/GM plant in Freemont, California, the Mitsubishi plant in Normal, Illinois, and the Mazda plant in Michigan were organized by the UAW. On the other hand, several major plants including the Nissan plant in Smyrna, Tennessee, and the Toyota Motor Manufacturing plant in Georgetown, Kentucky, have not been organized; and at the present time it appears that the new BMW plant in South Carolina also will not be organized by the UAW (although that could change).

It's hard to pinpoint the reasons that some of these attempts at organizing have failed while others have succeeded, although several factors seem to stand out: Nonorganized plants are in geographic areas that have historically not been strongholds of unionization; as a result, many of Toyota's and Nissan's employees in these plants have never been unionized. On the other hand, there is a strong tradition of unionization in areas such as Michigan and Illinois. Beyond that, Toyota and Nissan took great pains to pay very competitive salaries to their employees (as Mr. Fraser mentions, in the video). But, in addition, these employers have also endeavored to create a work environment that fosters employee commitment—a work environment characterized by team building, worker involvement, empowerment, and healthy two-way communications. Therefore, although the jury is still out on this issue, one could reasonably argue that the growing emphasis on team-building and involvement programs may undermine the unions' abilities to organize their workers. (At the same time, recent decisions, such as the one in the Electromation case discussed in Chapter 15, may yet impede the forward progress of such worker-involvement programs.)

Nevertheless, there's no doubt that grievance procedures (such as those in place in virtually all unionized firms and in many nonunionized firms, as well) can be instrumental in fostering better labor–management relations. As we've seen in the last two chapters, employees need and deserve a vehicle through which they can express dissatisfaction regarding treatment by their supervisors or the firm; and grievance procedures should provide just such a vehicle. With that, let's turn to the last part of this book—and particularly to Chapter 17 on guaranteed fair treatment.

PART 5

Employee Security and Safety

VIDEO CASE 5

—Introduction—

ABCNEWS

DRINKING AND FLYING

from ABC News, "Prime Time Live," February 2, 1991

In this final part of the book we turn to the issues of employee security and safety and in particular to:

Chapter 17: Guaranteed Fair Treatment

Chapter 18: Employee Safety and Health

Chapter 19: Strategic Issues in Human Resource Management

According to the National Institute of Alcohol Abuse and Alcoholism, 10% of all Americans have alcohol problems. As a result, when it comes to employee security and safety, alcoholism and other forms of drug abuse are a very serious problem. The video describes a situation in which a Northwest Airlines captain and two other members of his crew were arrested in Minneapolis for flying "under the influence" with 58 passengers aboard. Witnesses and the bar tab showed that, prior to the flight, the crew drank six pitchers of beer and the captain drank 19 rum and cokes. Not all incidents of drug abuse on the job are going to have the potentially serious consequences that such abuse has for airline pilots. However, the fact that such highly trained and responsible people as airline pilots would fly inebriated makes one wonder how widespread the problem of drug and alcohol abuse must be among the general population of employees.

The video describes some of the problems surrounding the identification and treatment of employee drug abusers. As you read Chapters 17, 18, and 19 consider these questions:

1. What are some of the steps you would take to reduce accidents at work?
2. How do top management's values influence employee security and safety?
3. What is the role of human resource management in implementing the organization's strategic plan?

CHAPTER 17

GUARANTEED FAIR TREATMENT

OVERVIEW

We begin by describing three techniques employers use to build healthy two-way communications—"Speak Up!," "What's Your Opinion?," and "top-down" programs. We then describe the central role played by "guaranteed fair treatment" programs in giving employees a vehicle through which to express concerns and to appeal disciplinary actions. We then turn to discussions of how to effectively manage dismissals and other separations such as layoffs and retirements. When you finish studying this chapter you should be able to explain the role of communication and guaranteed fair treatment processes in fostering employee commitment; explain how to discipline a subordinate; and describe the steps in managing a layoff.

BUILDING EMPLOYEE COMMITMENT

Building Two-Way Communications

Guaranteeing fair treatment to employees begins with listening to them, but most firms don't seem to be listening. Hay Research did a survey of 750,000 middle managers and compared data from 1985–1987 with those from 1988–1990. The percentage of middle managers who expressed a favorable attitude on "information given to employees" fell from 85% in 1985-87 to 69% in the later survey. "Top management listening to their problems and complaints" elicited favorable attitudes from 42% in the early survey, and 35% in 1988-1990.[1] Louis Harris & Associates polled office workers and their managers on behalf of the Steelcase Office Furniture Company; they concluded that what top management thinks their workers want is much different from what those workers say they want. For example, workers ranked "more honest communications between employees and senior management" higher than management's choice, "job security." Opinion Research Corporation surveyed 100,000 middle managers; supervisors; professionals; salespeople; and technical, clerical and hourly workers of Fortune 500 companies a few years ago. Except for the sales group all employees believed top management now was less willing to listen to their problems than five years earlier.[2]

This is generally not the case in firms with more progressive HRM practices. Managers of these firms know that commitment is built on trust, and that trust requires floods of two-way communications. These firms thus do more than express a willingness to hear and be heard. They also set up programs that guarantee such a flood of two-way talk. There are basically four types of programs: *speak up* programs for voicing concerns and making inquiries; periodic survey-type programs for expressing *opinions*; various *top-down* programs for keeping employees informed; and *guaranteed fair treatment* programs for filing grievances and complaints.

"SPEAK UP!" PROGRAMS

Grievance matters like those discussed in Chapter 16 are the tip of the iceberg when it comes to the sorts of concerns that employees have. These run the gamut from malfunctioning vending machines to unlit parking lots to a manager's spending too much of the department's money on travel.

About 30 years ago an IBM facility in San Jose, California, launched a program called "What's On Your Mind?" Several years later the program's name was changed to **"Speak up!"** and the program went worldwide.[3] Since then the program has been used more than 450,000 times by employees in more than 40 countries. Its basic aim is to give employees a confidential channel for speaking their minds.

speak up! programs Communications programs that allow employees to register questions, concerns, and complaints about work-related matters.

What makes the program unique is its anonymity. Employees may ask questions or make comments and receive a reply without revealing their identity to anyone except the Speak Up! administrator.

The program works to protect the employee's identity as soon as a Speak Up! form is filed. The form itself is a combination letter-envelope, is easily available to all employees, and is self-addressed to the Speak Up! administrator. On the top is a detachable stub. Here employees print their name, home address, and IBM location and indicate if they prefer to discuss the matter with a qualified person (usually by phone). There is also a space for the hand-written concerns, along with a note that "Your Speak Up! will be typed so that your handwriting cannot be identified." The form is completed, folded, and mailed.

When it's received, a Speak Up! administrator removes the name stub from the form and assigns the form a file number. The stub itself is then secured in a locked box and no one—except the Speak Up! administrator—ever sees the writer's name. All information that could possibly identify the writer or a third party is deleted from the Speak Up! comments. The Speak Up! is then typed and assigned to an investigator for an answer.

The investigator is usually the highest level manager who knows about the Speak Up! concern. Answers are usually provided within 10 working days unless the Speak Up! requires more extensive investigation.

All nonanonymous Speak Up! inquiries get written replies. Responses are individual letters signed by the manager who investigated the matter. The Speak Up! administrator first checks all responses for accuracy and completeness. He or she then personally addresses an envelope and mails the answer to the employee's home. The letters are mailed through U.S. mail—never along with internal company mail—to further assure anonymity. The program is managed by IBM's communication organization through 80 Speak Up! administrators around the world.

Employees are encouraged to write Speak Up! requests at any time but are told that they might first consider talking to their own manager, reviewing the employee handbook, or calling the department involved to get a direct answer. Similarly, the IBM Suggestion Program is generally used to propose ideas that could save the company time or money. What the Speak Up! program does is let employees jump the normal chain of command. It lets them express their comments, concerns, or suggestions directly to someone who is responsible for the activity in question.

Toyota Motor Manufacturing similarly tells its employees "Don't spend time worrying about something . . . speak up!" At Toyota, the main Speak Up! communication channel is called the "hotline."[4] Its purpose is to provide Toyota team members with an additional method of bringing questions or problems to the attention of the company.

Here's how it works. The hotline is available 24 hours a day. Employees are instructed to pick up any phone, dial the hotline extension (the number is posted on the plant bulletin boards), and deliver their message to the recorder.

All inquiries received on the hotline are guaranteed to be reviewed by the general manager of human resources and to be thoroughly investigated by the firm. If it's decided that a particular question would be of interest to other Toyota team members, then the inquiry, along with the company's response, is typed up and posted on plant bulletin boards within seven days of the date the call was received. If a personal response is desired, employees have to leave their name when they call; otherwise the calls are anonymous. In general, though, employees are told that their identity remains confidential, and that there will be no attempt to identify a particular hotline caller. Toyota is not the only firm with a hotline, by the way. Publix has a 24-hour 800-number "WOW" line for employees' suggestions, complaints, and ideas.

"Speak Up" programs like IBM's and Toyota's produce several benefits. They let management continuously monitor employee feelings and concerns;

they make it clear that employees have several channels through which to communicate concerns and get responses; and the net effect is that there's less chance that small problems will grow into big ones.

WHAT'S YOUR OPINION?

opinion surveys Communication devices that use questionnaires to regularly ask employees their opinions about the company, management, and work life.

Most of these firms also administer periodic anonymous **opinion surveys**. At IBM the opinion survey regularly asks employees their opinions about the company, management, and work life. The stated purpose of the IBM opinion survey "is to aid management at all levels in identifying and solving problems."[5] The standard practice with most of these firms' surveys is to have department heads conduct feedback sessions after the survey results are compiled, in order to share the results and work on solutions.

The Federal Express program is typical and is called Survey Feedback Action (SFA). SFA is primarily a method for measuring and then improving the "people" aspect of the business. It is an anonymous survey that allows employees to express feelings about the company and their managers, and to some extent about service, pay, and benefits. Each manager then has an opportunity to use the results to help design a blueprint for improving work group commitment.

SFA involves three phases. First, the survey itself is a standard, anonymous questionnaire given each year to every employee. The questions are designed to gather information about what helps and hinders employees in their work environment. Sample items include:

Can tell my manager what I think.
My manager tells me what is expected.
My manager listens to my concerns.
My manager keeps me informed.
Upper management listens to ideas from my level.
Fed Ex does a good job for our customers.
In my environment we use safe work practices.
I am paid fairly for this kind of work.

Results of the survey for a work group are then compiled and returned to the manager. To ensure anonymity the smaller units do *not* receive their own results. Instead, their results are folded in with those of several other similar work units until a department of 20 or 25 people obtains the overall group's results.

The second phase involves a feedback session between the manager and his or her work group. The session's goal is to identify specific concerns or problems, examine specific causes for these problems, and devise action plans to correct the problems. As a result, managers are trained to ask probing questions. For example, suppose the low-scoring survey item was "I feel free to tell my manager what I think." Managers are trained to ask their groups questions such as "What restrains you? (timing, specific behaviors) and "What do I do that makes you feel that I'm not interested?"

The feedback meeting should result in a third, "action plan" phase. The plan itself is a list of actions that the manager will take to address employees' concerns and boost results. Managers thus get an action planning worksheet containing four columns: What is the concern? What's your analysis? What's the cause? and What should be done?

TOP-DOWN PROGRAMS

It's hard to develop commitment when your boss won't tell you what's going on. Firms like Saturn and Federal Express therefore give their people extensive data on the performance of and prospects for their operations.

At Saturn the employees consider this mostly a matter of trust. "They must trust you to do the job," says one, "and they therefore trust you with a lot of confidential information, for instance on the financials of our firm. They tell you 'here is the problem, what would you do about it?'"

top-down programs
Communications activities including in-house TV centers, frequent roundtable discussions, and in-house newsletters that provide continuing opportunities for the firm to let all employees be updated on important matters regarding the firm.

The firm uses several **top-down programs** to get data to all employees. "The communication is excellent," says one assembler. "We get information continuously via the internal television network, and from financial documents." "And the hierarchy is pretty flat here," says another, "so the point people on the teams, including the team leaders, can quickly find the information and the resources that you need." One union leader says, "We have 'town hall' meetings once per month, and usually have at least 500 to 700 people attending. That plus the broadcasts usually make sure that everyone's knowledge base is up—you better know the facts if you want to work here."

Toyota stresses that the old saying about knowledge being power doesn't apply at its plant: Management works hard to share all it knows with every team member. There are twice-a-day five-minute team information meetings at job sites where employees get the latest news about the plant. There's also a TV in each work-site break area. The TV runs continuously, presenting plant-wide information from the in-house Toyota broadcasting center. There are quarterly "roundtable" discussions between top management and selected nonsupervisory staff, as well as the in-house newsletter. The hotline described earlier in this chapter is another channel of top-down information, in that it gives management a chance to answer, publicly, any anonymous (or nonanonymous) questions team members might have. The plant's general manager points out that Mr. Cho, the firm's president, is often in the plant, fielding questions, providing performance information, and ensuring that his general managers, managers, and team members—in fact all in the company—are "aware of Toyota's goals and where we are heading."

▶ GUARANTEED FAIR TREATMENT & EMPLOYEE DISCIPLINE

GUARANTEED FAIR TREATMENT AT WORK

guaranteed fair treatment
Employer programs that are aimed at ensuring that all employees are treated fairly, generally by providing formalized, well-documented and highly publicized vehicles through which employees can appeal any eligible issues.

We saw in Chapter 16 that the potential for grievances and discontent is always present in any firm. Just about any factor involving wages, hours, or conditions of employment has and will be used as the basis of a grievance in most firms. Discipline cases and seniority problems (including promotions, transfers, and layoffs) would probably top the list. Others would include grievances growing out of job evaluations and work assignments, overtime, vacations, incentive plans, and holidays.

Whatever the source of grievances, most firms today (and virtually all unionized ones) give their people channels through which to air grievances. A grievance procedure helps to ensure that every employee's grievance is heard and treated fairly, and unionized firms do not hold a monopoly on such fair treatment. So even in nonunionized firms, formal grievance procedures can help ensure that labor-management peace prevails.

Programs such as Federal Express's Guaranteed Fair Treatment go far beyond most grievance procedures for several reasons: (1) Special, easily available forms make filing the grievance easy; (2) employees are encouraged to use the system; and (3) the highest levels of top management are routinely involved in reviewing complaints. As their employee handbook says:

> Perhaps the cornerstone of Federal Express' 'people' philosophy is the guaranteed fair treatment procedure (GFTP). This policy affirms your right to appeal any eligible issue through this process of systematic review by progressively higher levels of management. Although the outcome is not assured to be in your favor, your right to participate within the guidelines of the procedure is guaranteed. At Federal Express, where we have a 'people-first' philosophy, you have a right to discuss your complaints with management without fear of retaliation.[6]

Employee commitment at Federal Express has been fostered by CEO Fred Smith's people-first values.

The net effect is twofold: Complaints don't get a chance to accumulate; and it helps to ensure that all managers think twice before doing anything unfair, since their actions will likely be brought to their bosses' attention. In fact, each Tuesday morning, a group of five Federal Express executives gathers to review and rule on employee complaints and grievances filed through the program. They include CEO Fred Smith, Chief Operating Officer James Barksdale, the firm's chief personnel officer, and two other senior vice-presidents.[7]

Eligible Concerns. GFTP is available to all permanent Fed Ex employees. It covers all concerns regarding matters such as job promotion and the application of compensation policies or discipline affecting the individual complainant. Basically, as the firm's handbook points out, "If for any reason you are a recipient of discipline, you will have access to the GFTP."[8]

Steps. The Fed Ex guaranteed fair treatment procedure contains three steps. In step one, *management review*, the complainant submits a written complaint to a member of management (manager, senior manager, or managing director) within seven calendar days of the occurrence of the eligible issue. Then the manager, senior manager, and managing director of the employee's group review all relevant information; hold a telephone conference and/or meeting with the complainant; make a decision to either uphold, modify, or overturn management's action; and communicate their decision in writing to the complainant and the department's personnel representative. All of this occurs within 10 calendar days of receipt of the complaint.

In step two, *officer complaint*, the complainant submits a written complaint to an officer (vice-president or senior vice-president) of the division within seven calendar days of the step one decision. The vice-president and senior vice-president then review all relevant information; conduct an additional investigation, when necessary; make a decision to either uphold, overturn, or modify management's action, or initiate a board of review; and communicate their decision in writing to the complainant with copies to the department's personnel representative and the complainant's management. As in step one, the step two review generally occurs within 10 calendar days of receipt of the complaint.

Finally, in step three, *executive appeals review*, the complainant submits a written complaint within seven calendar days of the step two decision to the employee relations department. This department then investigates and prepares a GFTP case file for the appeals board executive review. The appeals board—CEO Smith, COO Barksdale, the chief personnel officer, and three senior vice-presidents—then reviews all relevant information; makes a decision to either uphold, overturn, or initiate a board of review or to take other appropriate action; and generally does this within 14 calendar days of receipt of the complaint. Barring the formation of a separate board of review, the appeals board's decision is final.

A board of review is used when there is a question of fact regarding the complaint. It's actually a five-member jury of Federal Express employees.[9] Two are chosen by the complaining employee from a list of names submitted by the board chair. Three are selected by the board chair from a list of names submitted by the employee. Board chairpersons are chosen from the ranks of management at the director level or above and receive special training for this responsibility.

Documentation. Packets of forms in folders entitled "Guaranteed Fair Treatment Procedure" are used to file GFTP-registered complaints and are available from the personnel department. They include a fact sheet listing the complainant's name and work history; a GFTP tracking sheet to keep track of the complaint at each step; and instructions and space for management's rationale (for instance, in terms of applicable policies and procedures), a write-up from the personnel department, and places for key documents (termination letters, and so on). There is also space for back-up material including witness statements, medical statements, and training records. These packets are widely available and easily accessible.

open-door program
IBM's fair-treatment program, which gives every IBM employee the right to appeal the actions of his or her supervisor by taking the concern to successively higher levels of management.

IBM's fair-treatment program is called **open-door.** It gives every employee the right to appeal the actions of his or her supervisors.

Employees are told to first discuss the problem with their immediate manager, their manager's manager, their personnel manager, or their branch or site manager. If that doesn't solve the problem, they are instructed to go to the senior management in their business unit.

skip-level interview
Also known as the executive interview, this is an IBM program in which employees are periodically invited to speak to a manager one or more levels above that of their manager for the purpose of ensuring more fair, open communications throughout the firm.

There are two other avenues available at IBM for openly expressing concerns about fairness. First, if employees don't get satisfactory answers via the normal process, they may discuss the matter with IBM's chairperson by mail, or personally if the chairperson finds it appropriate. The **skip-level interview** is the second. This is sometimes also referred to as the *executive interview, cross-talk,* or *second-level* interview. Here, employees are periodically invited to speak to a manager one or more levels above that of their manager. Participation is voluntary, but employees may also request to have such an interview. Programs like those at IBM and Toyota haven't the structure and formality of Fed Ex's guaranteed fair treatment program. However, they do help ensure healthy communication regarding disciplinary matters and that employees' voices are heard.

FAIRNESS IN DISCIPLINING

discipline
A procedure that corrects or punishes a subordinate because a rule or procedure has been violated.

The purpose of **discipline** is to encourage employees to behave sensibly at work, where "sensible" behavior is defined as adhering to rules and regulations. In an organization, rules and regulations serve about the same purpose that laws do in society, and discipline is called for when one of these rules or regulations is violated.[10] A fair and just discipline process is based on three prerequisites: *rules and regulations*; *a systems of progressive penalties*; and *an appeals process*. Programs like Fed Ex's Guaranteed Fair Treatment and IBM's open-door help ensure their employees a real appeals process. Let's turn now to the other prerequisites of a fair discipline process: rules and regulations and a system of progressive penalties.

Prerequisites to Disciplining

The first prerequisite is a set of clear *rules and regulations*. These rules address things like theft, destruction of company property, drinking on the job, and insubordination.[11] Examples of rules include:

> Poor performance is not acceptable. Each employee is expected to perform his or her work properly and efficiently and to meet established standards of quality.
>
> Liquor and drugs do not mix with work. The use of either during working hours or reporting for work under the influence of either is strictly prohibited.
>
> The vending of anything in the plant without authorization is not allowed, nor is gambling in any form permitted.

The purpose of these rules is to inform employees ahead of time as to what is and is not acceptable behavior. Employees have to be told, preferably in writing, what is not permitted. This is usually done during the employee's orientation. The rules and regulations are usually listed in the employee orientation handbook.

A system of progressive penalties is a second prerequisite to effective disciplining. Penalties may range from oral warnings to written warnings to suspension from the job to discharge. The severity of the penalty is usually a function of the type of offense and the number of times the offense has occurred. For example, most companies issue warnings for the first unexcused lateness. However, for a fourth offense, discharge is the more usual disciplinary action.

Finally, you should have an *appeals process* as part of your disciplinary process; this helps to ensure that discipline is meted out fairly and equitably. Programs like Guaranteed Fair Treatment illustrate how to do this.

DISCIPLINE GUIDELINES

It is important to ensure that your disciplinary actions will be viewed as fair and thus worthy of being upheld by an impartial arbitrator. Based on past disciplinary cases, here are important guidelines that arbitrators may look for when deciding whether there was "just cause" for your disciplinary action:

> *The discipline should be in line with the way management usually responds to similar incidents.* In one case the employer's rule stated that "leaving the plant without permission during working hours" made the worker subject to immediate discharge. A worker did leave the plant and was thus discharged. The arbitrator later found that employees frequently left the plant while they were clocked in and went openly into town for personal matters. Since the rule was not consistently applied in the past, the arbitrator ruled that the worker was wrongfully discharged.[12]
>
> *The employee should be adequately warned of the consequences of his or her alleged misconduct.* The person should be told of any undesirable behavior that is noted and the consequences that may result if the employee chooses not to change that behavior.

The rule that allegedly was violated should be "reasonably related" to the efficient and safe operation of the particular work environment. Employees, in other words, are usually allowed by arbitrators to question the reason behind any rule or order.

Management must adequately investigate the matter before administering discipline. Furthermore, the investigation must be fair and objective.

The investigation should produce substantial evidence of misconduct.

Applicable rules, orders, or penalties should be applied evenhandedly and without discrimination.

The penalty should be reasonably related to the misconduct and to the employee's past history. In other words, each employee should be judged on the basis of his or her personal record; only then should the appropriate discipline be imposed.[13]

Other important disciplining guidelines include the following:

Right to counsel. All union employees have the right to bring help when they are called in for an interview that they reasonably believe might result in disciplinary action. Typically, unionized employees may bring a union representative and nonunion employees—who hopefully will be told of their rights—may bring a coworker. Note that this is a legal right that employees have according to the National Labor Relations Board.[14]

Don't rob your subordinate of his or her dignity.[15] Discipline your subordinate in private (unless he or she requests counsel) and avoid entrapment. Don't deliberately rig a situation that causes the employee to require disciplining.

Remember that the burden of proof is on you. In our society, a person is always considered innocent until proven guilty.

Get the facts. Don't base your decision on hearsay evidence. Don't base it just on your "general impression." Instead, get the facts.

Don't act while angry. Very few people can be objective and sensible when they are angry.

DISCIPLINE WITHOUT PUNISHMENT

Discipline traditionally has two major potential shortcomings. First (though fairness guidelines like those previously mentioned can take the edge off this) no one ever feels good about being punished. Yet that is exactly what discipline is: an employee does something wrong, and he or she is punished. There may therefore be a residual of bad feelings among all involved. A second shortcoming is that, as the saying goes, "a person convinced against his or her will is of the same opinion still." In other words, forcing your rules on employees may gain short-term compliance, but not their active cooperation when you are not on hand to enforce the rules.

"Discipline without punishment" (or "nonpunitive discipline") is aimed at avoiding these disciplinary problems. This is accomplished by gaining the employees' acceptance of your rules and by reducing the punitive nature of the discipline itself.

Here is an example. Assume there has been a breach of discipline (such as disregarding safety rules) or unsatisfactory work performance (such as carelessness in handling materials). In such a case, the following steps would constitute a typical nonpunitive approach to discipline.[16]

Step 1: First, issue an "oral reminder." As a supervisor, your goal here is to get the employee to agree to solve the problem. You will meet privately with the employee and (instead of warning him or her of possible disciplinary sanctions) remind the person of (1) the reason for the rule and (2) the fact that he or she has a responsibility to meet performance standards. Keep a written record of the incident in a separate working file in your desk rather than in the employee's personnel file.

Step 2: Should another incident arise within six weeks, issue the employee a formal "written reminder," a copy of which is placed in the personnel file. In addition, a second discussion is held privately with the employee, again without any threats. As in step 1, the aim is to discuss the need for the rule and to obtain the employee's acceptance of the need to act responsibly at work. Make sure the person understands the rule and your explanation for why improvement is required, and express your confidence in the person's ability to act responsibly at work. Should another such incident occur in the next six weeks, a follow-up meeting *might* be held. Here reiterate the need to act responsibly, and investigate the possibility that the person is ill-suited to or bored with the job. Usually, though, the next step (after the written reminder, step 2) would be step 3, a paid one-day leave.

Step 3: A paid one-day "decision-making leave" is the next step. If another incident occurs in the next six weeks or so, the employee is told to take a one-day leave with pay to stay home and consider whether or not the job is right for him or her and whether or not the person wants to abide by the company's rules. The fact that the person is paid for the day is a final expression of the company's hope that the employee can and will act responsibly with respect to following the rules. When the employee returns to work, he or she meets with you, and gives you a decision regarding whether or not the rules will be followed. At that point (assuming a positive response), you again explain your confidence in the employee, and if necessary, work out a brief action plan to help the person change his or her behavior.

Step 4: If no further incidents occur in the next year or so, the one-day suspension would be purged from the person's file. If the behavior repeats itself, dismissal (see later discussion) would be required.

The process must of course be changed to take care of exceptional circumstances. Criminal behavior or in-plant fighting might be grounds for immediate dismissal, for instance. And if several incidents occurred at very close intervals, step 2—the written warning—might be skipped.

Does the nonpunitive approach to discipline work? Preliminary evidence suggests that it does. Employees seem to welcome the less punitive aspects, and don't seem to abuse the system by misbehaving to get a free day off with pay. Grievances, sick leave usage, and disciplinary incidents all seem to drop in firms using these new procedures. However, there will still be times when dismissals—discussed next—will be required.

▶ MANAGING DISMISSALS

dismissal
Involuntary termination of an employee's employment with the firm.

Dismissal is the most drastic disciplinary step you can take toward an employee[17] and is thus one that must be taken with deliberate care. Specifically, the dismissal should be *just,* in that *sufficient cause* exists for the dismissal. Furthermore, the dismissal should occur only after *all reasonable steps* taken to rehabilitate or salvage the employee have failed. However, there are undoubtedly times when dismissal is required, and in these instances it should be carried out forthrightly.[18]

GROUNDS FOR DISMISSAL

Reasons for dismissal can be classified as either unsatisfactory performance, misconduct, lack of qualifications for the job, or changed requirements of the job. *Unsatisfactory performance* may be defined as a persistent failure to perform assigned duties or to meet prescribed standards on the job.[19] Specific reasons here include excessive absenteeism, tardiness, a persistent failure to meet normal job requirements, or an adverse attitude toward the company, supervisor, or fellow employees. *Misconduct* may be defined as deliberate and willful violation of the employer's rules and may include stealing, rowdyism, and insubordination. *Lack of qualifications for the job* is defined as an employee's incapability of doing the assigned work although the person is diligent. Since the employee in this case may be trying to do the job, it is especially important that every effort be made to salvage him or her. *Changed requirements of the job* may be defined as an employee's incapability of doing the work assigned after the nature of the job has been changed. Similarly, an employee may have to be dismissed when his or her job is eliminated. Here again, the employee may be industrious, so every effort should be made to retrain or transfer this person, if possible.

insubordination Willful disregard or disobedience of the boss's authority or legitimate orders; criticizing the boss in public.

Insubordination is sometimes the grounds for dismissal although it may be harder to prove than are other grounds for dismissal. Stealing, chronic tardiness, and poor quality work are fairly concrete grounds for dismissal, while insubordination is sometimes harder to translate into words. To that end it may be useful to remember that some acts are or should be considered insubordinate whenever and wherever they occur. These include:

1. Direct disregard of the boss's authority. At sea, this is called mutiny.
2. Flat out disobedience of, or refusal to obey, the boss's orders—particularly in front of others.
3. Deliberate defiance of clearly stated company policies, rules, regulations, and procedures.
4. Criticizing the boss in public. Contradicting or arguing with him or her is also negative and inappropriate.
5. Blatantly ignoring the boss's reasonable instructions.
6. Contemptuous display of disrespect; making insolent comments, for example; and, more important, portraying these feelings in the attitude shown while on the job.
7. Showing disregard for the chain of command by going around the immediate supervisor or manager with a complaint, suggestion, or political maneuver. Although the employee may be right, that may not be enough to save him or her from the charges of insubordination.
8. Leading or participating in an effort to undermine and remove the boss from power. If the effort doesn't work (and it seldom does), those involved will be "dead in the water."[20]

Of course, as in most other human endeavors, it is dangerous to take the position that any of these acts should "always" lead to dismissal. Even at sea (as the movie *The Caine Mutiny* illustrates), there may be extenuating circumstances for the apparent insubordination. Cases like these should therefore be reviewed by the supervisor's boss.

TERMINATION AT WILL

termination at will The idea, based in law, that the employment relationship can be terminated "at will" by either the employer or the employee for any reason.

For more than 100 years the prevailing rule in the United States has been that without an employment contract, the employment relationship can be terminated "at will" by either the employer or the employee. In other words, the employee could resign for any reason, at will, and the employer could similarly dismiss an employee for any reason, at will. Today, however, dismissed employees are increasingly taking their cases to court, and, in many states, employers are finding that they no longer have a blanket right to fire. Instead, federal laws and various state court rulings increasingly limit management's right to dismiss employees at will.

Consider an example. You're fired for no apparent reason and given two weeks' pay and two hours to leave the firm. You've worked for this company for almost three years with consistently good reviews. Your job, you know, was not dissolved. Instead, you were replaced by someone with less seniority and experience—and at lower pay. You ask your supervisor why you were fired, and he says he just can't tell you. What legal recourse do you have?

George Steinbrenner, principal owner of the New York Yankees baseball team, has had a lot of practice in dismissing employees—including the late Billy Martin, whom he fired as manager—a number of times.

Increasingly, today, the answer to this question depends on the state where you work.[21] The United States today is one of the few remaining industrialized countries without federal legislation addressing management's right to dismiss employees at will. And in only three states—Michigan, Pennsylvania, and Wisconsin—has legislation been introduced that would erode the "at-will" rule. Yet, today, despite this dearth of laws, discharged employees are turning to their state courts for relief—and winning their cases.

In 20 states—California, Connecticut, Idaho, Illinois, Indiana, Kansas, Maryland, Massachusetts, Michigan, Missouri, Montana, New Hampshire, New Jersey, New York, Oregon, Pennsylvania, Texas, Virginia, Washington, and West Virginia—courts have ruled that there are "public policy exceptions" to the common law doctrine that employees may be discharged for any reason an employer chooses. They have held, for instance, that it is against "public policy" for an employer to fire an employee because the person refused to give false testimony in court to protect the employer, or refused to sell a drug that the employee knew was tainted.

In 13 states—California, Connecticut, Idaho, Louisiana, Maine, Massachusetts, Michigan, Montana, Nebraska, New Hampshire, North Carolina, Oklahoma, and Washington—courts have taken the position that company manuals or handbooks (or even employment interviews) may constitute "implied contracts" to which an employer is legally bound to adhere. In Idaho, for instance, the state Supreme Court ruled in *Jackson* v. *Minidoka Irrigation* that the employee handbook was an enforceable employment contract with respect to discharge hearing, retirement benefits, and vacation pay.

Courts in 7 states—Florida, Illinois, Minnesota, Missouri, North Dakota, South Carolina, and Washington—have granted limited exceptions to the at-will doctrine for other reasons. In Florida, for instance (where the employment at-will rule is still strictly adhered to) a court in *Chatelier* v. *Robertson* found for the employee, who had transferred his business to his employer in exchange for lifetime employment but was subsequently fired.

Finally, remember that employees may also be protected by existing federal laws. The Civil Rights Act (and state fair employment laws) prohibit employers from discharging employees because of their age, race, sex, religion, or national origin. Under federal law, for instance, if the employee is over 40 and is replaced by someone younger—even if that person is also over 40—the dismissed employee may have a basis for an age discrimination charge. As another example, employees who report safety violations at their place of work are generally protected from discharge by the Occupational Safety and Health Act.

AVOIDING WRONGFUL DISCHARGE SUITS

wrongful discharge
An employee dismissal that does not comply with the law or does not comply with the contractual arrangement stated or implied by the firm via its employment application forms, employee manuals, or other promises.

With the increased likelihood that terminated employees can and will sue for **wrongful discharge,** it behooves you as an employer to protect yourself against wrongful discharge suits. The time to do that is now, rather than after mistakes have been made and suits have been filed. Here is what one expert recommends to avoid wrongful discharge suits.

- Have applicants sign the *employment application* and make sure it contains a clearly worded statement that employment is for no fixed term and that the employer can terminate at any time. In addition, the statement should include a written statement informing the job candidate that "nothing on this application can be changed."
- You should also review your *employee manual* to look for and delete statements that could prejudice your defense in a wrongful discharge case. For example, delete any reference to the fact that "employees can be terminated only for just cause" (unless you really mean that). Also consider *not* outlining progressive discipline procedures in the manual since you may be obligated to stick with the rules and follow the steps exactly or be sued for failing to do so. Similarly, references to probationary periods or permanent employment may be unwise since they imply a permanence you may not really mean to imply.
- Make sure that no one in a position of authority makes *promises* you do not intend to keep, such as by saying that "if you do your job here, you can't get fired."
- You should have clear written rules listing infractions that may require *discipline* and *discharge*, and then make sure to adhere to the rules. Generally, employees must be given an opportunity to correct unacceptable behavior, and you should deal with your worst offenders first and be careful not to single out any one person.
- If a rule is broken, you should get the worker's side of the story in front of witnesses, preferably in writing. Then make sure to *check out* the story, getting both sides of the issue.
- Before taking any irreversible steps, *review* the person's personnel file. For example, long-seniority employees may merit more opportunities to correct their actions than newly hired workers.
- Finally, consider *"buying out"* a wrongful discharge claim with settlement pay. Do not stand in the way of a terminated employee's future employment since a person with a new job is less likely to bring a lawsuit against the former employer than someone who remains unemployed.[22]
- Other mistakes to avoid include:

  Don't discharge anyone who is about to vest in employee benefits.

  Don't discharge a female employee just before maternity leave.

  Don't "constructively discharge" employees by placing them in a lower paying job in hopes of a resignation.

  Don't try to induce employees to waive existing rights in exchange for gaining other rights.

  Don't deviate from internal complaint resolution guidelines and procedures.

  Don't oversell promises of job security in handbooks or oral discussions.[23]

DISMISSAL PROCEDURES

In the event of a dismissal, these additional steps should be followed in developing your dismissal procedures:

Hold warning discussions before any final action. An employee must be made aware that he or she is not performing satisfactorily.

Make sure you have written confirmation of the final warning.

Prepare a checklist of all property that should be accounted for, including computer disks and manuals.

Change security codes and locks previously used by discharged individuals.

If the dismissal involves large numbers of employees (say, 25 or more), prepare and secure approval for a news release.

Always prepare for the possibility that the discharged individual may act irrationally or even violently either immediately or in weeks to come.

Decide beforehand how you are going to handle telling other employees about this person's dismissal. An informal departmental meeting of those directly involved with this person is usually sufficient.

THE TERMINATION INTERVIEW

termination interview The interview in which an employee is informed of the fact that he or she has been dismissed.

Dismissing an employee is one of the most difficult tasks you'll face at work.[24] The dismissed employee—even though warned many times in the past—will often still react with total disbelief or even violence. Guidelines for the **termination interview** itself are as follows:

STEP 1. Plan the interview carefully. According to experts at Hay Associates, this means:

Schedule the meeting on a day early in the week.

Make sure the employee keeps the appointment time.

Never inform an employee over the phone.

Ten minutes should be sufficient for notification.

Avoid Fridays, preholidays, and vacation times when possible.

Use a neutral site, never your own office.

Have employee agreements, human resources file, release announcement (internal and external) prepared in advance.

Be available at a time after notification.

Have phone numbers ready for medical or security emergencies.

STEP 2. Get to the point. Do not beat around the bush by talking about the weather or by making other small talk. As soon as the employee enters your office, give the person a moment to get comfortable, and then inform the person of your decision.

STEP 3. Describe the situation. Briefly, in three or four sentences, explain why the person is being let go. For instance, "Production in your area is down four percent, and we are continuing to have quality problems. We have talked about these problems several times in the past three months and the solutions are not being followed through. We have to make a change."[25] Remember to describe the situation, rather than attacking the employee personally by saying things like "your production is just not up to par." Also emphasize that the decision is final and irrevocable; other in-house positions were explored, management at all levels concurs, and all relevant factors—performance, workload, and so on—were considered. Don't take more than 10–15 minutes for the interview.

STEP 4. Listen. It is important to continue the interview until the person appears to be talking freely and reasonably calmly about the reasons for his or her termination and the support package (including severance pay) he or she is to receive. Do not get into arguments; instead, *actively listen* and get the person to talk by using open-ended questions, restating his or her last comment, and using silence and a nod of your head. Use the Behavioral Reaction Chart (Figure 17.1) to gauge the person's reaction and to decide how best to proceed.

STEP 5. Discuss the severance package. Next, carefully review all elements of the severance package. Describe severance payments, benefits, access to office support people, and how recommendations will be handled. However, under no conditions should any promises or benefits beyond those already in the support package be implied. Do not promise to "look into" something and get back to the subordinate at a later date. This will simply complicate the termination process. The termination should be complete when the person leaves your office.

FIGURE 17.1
Behavioral Reaction to Termination and Suggested Response
Source: Hay Associates, Philadelphia, Pa. 19103

Hostile and angry	Defensive and bargaining	Formal and procedural (lawsuit?)	Stoic	Crying/ sobbing
Hurt Anger Disappointment Relief	Guilt Fear Uncertainty Disbelief	Vengeful Suppressed Controlled	Shock Disbelief Numbness	Sadness Grief Worry
•Summarize what you have heard in a tentative style: "It sounds as if you are pretty angry about this." •Avoid confronting the anger or becoming defensive. •Remain objective; stick to the facts and give the employee helpful information.	•Let the employee know you realize this is a difficult time for him or her as well as for yourself. •Don't get involved in any bargaining discussions. •Offer reassurance about the future and connect this to the counseling process.	•Allow the employee freedom to ask any questions as long as they pertain to his or her own case. •Try to avoid side issues and discussion of "political" motivations. •Keep the tone formal. This is a good way to lead into the role the career counselor will play.	•Communicate to the employee that you recognize his or her shock and say the details can be handled later if the employee prefers. •Ask if there are any specific questions for the moment. If not, tell the employee about the career counselor and make the introduction.	•Allow the person an opportunity to cry if that occurs. Just offer some tissues. •Avoid inane comments such as "What are you crying about, it's not that important." •When the person regains composure, press on with the facts and explain the counseling process.

STEP 6. Identify the next step. The terminated employee may be disoriented and unsure of what to do next. You should explain where the employee should go upon leaving your office. Remind the person who to contact at the company regarding questions about the support package or references.

MANAGING SEPARATIONS: LAYOFF AND RETIREMENT

INTRODUCTION

Non-disciplinary separations are a fact of life in organizations and can be initiated by either employer or employee. For the employer, reduced sales or profits may require *layoffs,* for instance, while employees may terminate their employment so as to *retire* or to seek better jobs.

The "Plant Closing" Law

plant closing law The Worker Adjustment and Retraining Notification Act, which requires notifying employees in the event an employer decides to close its facility.

Until recently there were no federal laws requiring notification of employees in the event an employer decided to close its facility. However, on February 4, 1989, the Worker Adjustment and Retraining Notification Act (popularly known as the **"Plant Closing" law**) became effective. Basically, the law requires employers of 100 or more employees to give 60 days notice before closing a facility or starting a layoff *of 50 people or more.* The law does not prevent the employer from closing down, nor does it require the saving of jobs. The Worker Adjustment and Retraining Notification Act simply seeks to give employees time to seek other work or retraining by giving them advance notice of the close down.

As more U.S. firms relocate their manufacturing plants to foreign countries in order to minimize costs, workers in San Antonio, Texas protest the signing of any free trade agreements which, they think, encourage such action.

Not all plant closings and layoffs are covered by the law, although many are. As an employer you are responsible for giving notice to employees who will or reasonably may be expected to experience a covered "employment loss." Employment losses include terminations (other than discharges for cause, voluntary departures, or retirement), layoffs exceeding six months, or reductions of more than 50% in employees' work hours during each month of any six-month period. Generally speaking, workers who are reassigned or transferred to certain employer-sponsored programs or who are given an opportunity to transfer or relocate to another employer location within a reasonable commuting distance need not be notified. While there are exceptions to the law, the penalty for failing to give notice is fairly severe: one day's pay and benefits to each employee for each day notice that should have been given, up to 60 days.

The law is not entirely clear about how the notice to employees must be worded. However, if you write a letter to individual employees to be laid off, a paragraph toward the end of the letter that might suit the purpose would be as follows:

> Please consider this letter to be your official notice, as required by the federal Plant Closing law, that your current position with the company will end 60 days from today because of a (layoff or closing) that is now projected to take place (on October 9). After that day your employment with the company will be terminated, and you will no longer be carried on our payroll records or be covered by any company benefit programs. Any questions concerning the plant closing law or this notice will be answered in the personnel office.[26]

MANAGING LAYOFFS

Layoff Defined

layoff
A situation in which there is a temporary shortage of work so that employees are told there is no work for them but that management intends to recall the employee when work is again available.

Layoff refers to a situation in which three conditions are present: (1) There is no work available for the employee who is being sent home; (2) management expects the no-work situation to be temporary and probably short term; and (3) management intends to recall the employee when work is again available.[27] A layoff is therefore not a *termination*, which is a permanent severing of the employment relationship, although some employers do use "layoff" as a euphemism for discharge or termination.

Bumping/Layoff Procedures

bumping/layoff procedures Detailed procedures that determine who will be laid off if no work is available; generally allow employees to use their seniority to remain on the job.

Employers who encounter frequent business slowdowns and layoffs usually draw up detailed procedures that allow employees to use their seniority to remain on the job. Most layoff procedures have these features in common:[28]

1. For the most part, seniority is the ultimate determiner of who will work.
2. Seniority can give way to merit or ability but usually only when none of the senior employees is qualified for a particular job.
3. Seniority is usually based on the date the employee joined the organization, not the date he or she took a particular job.
4. Because seniority is usually companywide, an employee in one job is usually allowed to bump or displace an employee in another job provided the more senior employee is able to do the job in question without further training.

Alternatives to Layoffs

Many employers today recognize the enormous investments they made in recruiting, screening, and training their employees and in developing their commitment and loyalty. As a result, many employers are more hesitant to lay off employees at the first signs of business decline. Instead, they are using new approaches to either blunt the effects of the layoff or eliminate the layoffs entirely.

voluntary reduction in pay plan
An alternative to layoffs in which all employees agree to reductions in pay to keep everyone working.

voluntary time off
An alternative to layoffs in which some employees agree to take time off to reduce the employer's payroll and avoid the need for a layoff.

rings of defense
An alternative layoff plan in which temporary supplemental employees are hired with the understanding that they may be laid off at any time.

There are several alternatives to layoff. With the **voluntary reduction in pay plan** all employees agree to reductions in pay in order to keep everyone working. Other employers arrange to have all or most of their employees accumulate their *vacation time* and to concentrate their vacations during slow periods. Temporary help thus does not have to be hired for vacationing employees during peak periods, and employment automatically falls off when business declines. Other employees agree to take **voluntary time off,** which again has the effect of reducing the employer's payroll and avoiding the need for a layoff. Control Data Corporation avoids layoff with what they call their **rings of defense** approach. In their plan, temporary supplemental employees are hired with the understanding that their work is of a temporary nature and they may be laid off at any time or fired. Then when layoffs come, the first "ring of defense" is the cadre of supplemental workers.[29]

Outplacement Counseling[30]

Outplacement counseling is a systematic process by which a terminated person is trained and counseled in the techniques of (1) self-appraisal and (2) securing a new job that is appropriate to his or her needs and talents.[31] As the term is generally used, outplacement does not mean the employer takes responsibility

outplacement counseling
A systematic process by which a terminated person is trained and counseled in the techniques of self-appraisal and securing a new position.

for placing the terminated person in a new job. Instead, it is a counseling service whose purpose is to provide the person with advice, instructions, and a sounding board to help formulate career goals and successfully execute a job search. Outplacement counseling thus might more accurately (but more ponderously) be called "career counseling and job search skills for terminated employees." The counseling itself is done either by the employer's in house specialist or by outside consultants. The outplacement counseling is considered part of the terminated employee's support or severance package.

Outplacement counseling is usually conducted by special firms set up for this purpose, firms such as Drake Bean Morim Inc., and Right Associates Inc. Middle- and upper-level managers who are let go will typically have office space and secretarial services they can use at local offices of such firms.

Exit Interviews

exit interview
Interviews, usually conducted by the human resource department, with any and all employees who are leaving the firm for any reason and which are aimed at eliciting information about the job or related matters that might give the employer a better insight into what is right or what is wrong about the company.

Many employers conduct final **exit interviews** with employees who are leaving the firm. They are usually conducted by the human resource department and are aimed at eliciting information about the job or related matters that might give the employer a better insight into what is right—or what is wrong—about the company. The assumption, of course, is that since the employee is leaving, he or she will be candid.

That the person will be candid is questionable. The person might have his own ax to grind, for instance, and could use the exit interview to try to retaliate against former foes. Or the person might simply not want to cause trouble that might come back to haunt her when she needs references for a new job.

In fact, based on the results of one survey, the kind of information you can expect to obtain from exit interviews is questionable. The researchers found that at the time of separation, 38% of those leaving blamed "salary and benefits," while only 4% blamed "supervision." Followed up 18 months later, though, 24% blamed supervision and only 12% blamed salary and benefits. Getting to the real problem during the exit interview may thus require some heavy digging.[32]

ADJUSTING TO DOWNSIZINGS AND MERGERS

downsizings
Refers to the process of reducing, usually dramatically, the number of people employed by the firm.

When a **downsizing** or merger requires a reduction in force, attention must also be given to the employees not dismissed. Certainly those dismissed should be treated fairly. But it is often those "left behind" that you'll need to build your business around.

Dealing with the Survivors Immediately After the Downsizing

In terms of your survivors, you will face one of two situations immediately following the downsizing.[33] First, you may anticipate no further reductions, and here you can assure your people of that. However, remember not to promise that no further reductions will occur unless that is really what you mean.

The second situation is more difficult because here you know that future reductions will probably take place. The best you can do is to be honest with those remaining, explaining that while future downsizings will probably occur they will be informed of these reductions as soon as possible. Here you may well experience a transitory drop in productivity and an increased attrition, but the alternative is being dishonest with all the people involved.

Specific Steps to Take

A postdownsizing program instituted at Duracell, Inc., illustrates the steps involved in a well-conceived program. After several months of planning, the program began with a series of *announcement activities.*[34] These included a full staff meeting at the facility, followed by a program in which every employee was informed individually of his or her status with the firm. In addition, each survivor received a description of the support services and assistance being made available to those leaving Duracell. This helped reduce the survivors' concern about their friends and former colleagues.

Next, there was an *immediate follow-up* phase during the first few days after the announcement. Here survivors were split into groups that included the senior management of the facility. At these sessions, employees were encouraged to discuss how they felt about the layoffs and to express their concerns and feelings about their future with the company and the future of the facility as a team.

A mechanism for providing *long-term support* was also built into the program. Here, key management was encouraged to meet with the remaining staff frequently and informally in order to provide ongoing support to these people in an "open-door" atmosphere. Finally, there was a follow-up meeting with the survivors about two months after the downsizing to make sure all concerns had been aired and addressed.[35]

Handling the Merger/Acquisition

In terms of dismissals and downsizings, mergers or acquisitions are usually one sided: In many mergers, in other words, one company essentially acquires the other, and it is often the employees of the latter that find themselves out looking for new jobs.

In such a situation the employees in the acquired firm will be hypersensitive to mistreatment of their colleagues. It thus behooves you to take care that those let go are treated with courtesy. Seeing your former colleagues fired is bad enough for morale. Seeing them fired under conditions which look like bullying rubs salt in the wound and poisons the relationship for years to come. As a rule, therefore,[36]

- Avoid the appearance of power and domination.
- Avoid win/lose behavior.
- Remain businesslike and professional in all dealings.
- Maintain as positive a feeling about the acquired company as possible.
- Remember that the degree to which your organization treats the acquired group with care and dignity will impact the confidence, productivity, and commitment of those remaining.

LIFETIME EMPLOYMENT WITHOUT GUARANTEES

Job security and employee commitment go hand-in-hand. For one thing, the cost involved in value-based hiring and in extensively training, empowering, and actualizing employees presumes the firm is committed to keeping them around. That is why Toyota USA's president has said that "At Toyota we hire people who we hope will stick around for 30 or 40 years or the remainder of their working years. So we always try to remember that hiring a 30-year employee who will earn $30,000 to $40,000 a year is really a million dollar plus decision for us."[37] Furthermore, commitment is a two-way street: Employees are committed to companies that are committed to them and few things express an employer's commitment like the goal of lifetime employment. It is an ultimate manifestation of the fact that the firm's destiny is inextricably intertwined with that of its staff. That's why firms like Toyota, Saturn, and Federal Express follow a policy that one could call **lifetime employment without guarantees.**

lifetime employment without guarantees
Refers to a commitment on the part of firms like Toyota and Saturn to do all that is reasonably possible to avoid layoffs and non-performance-based dismissals while recognizing that ultimately the employment relationship must be "at-will."

Take Toyota. On the one hand, the firm's documents and managers' comments continually refer to lifetime employment. The team member handbook for instance, states it this way:

> Lifetime employment is our goal—the ultimate result of you and the company working together to ensure TMM's success. We believe that job security is fundamental to the development of motivated employees. We also know that career employees have a significant stake in the company's success. If TMM is profitable, your job will be secure and you will receive a fair salary over the course of your career. We feel we have hired the best to make up our Toyota team. Job security demands that you must do everything possible to maximize the efficiency of the company in order to maintain its competitive edge in the marketplace. We count on you to help us search for a better way . . . to obtain success . . . job security at TMM.[38]

But in reality, there are not guarantees. For example, the team member handbook also prominently displays the usual "employment-at-will" disclaimer found in virtually all company handbooks these days:

> All employment relationships at TMM will be 'employment-at-will' arrangements. This means that either the team member or TMM may terminate the employment relationships at any time and for any reason. No contract, implied or otherwise, will be considered to exist between TMM and any TMM team member.[39]

Fujio Cho, CEO of the Toyota U.S.A. subsidiary, stands with cars produced at the Georgetown, Kentucky plant—a testing ground for joining Japan's lifetime employment concept with the realities of the U.S. automobile industry.

Yet Toyota employees are convinced—probably for good reason—that their jobs are secure as long as they do them. As one body shop team member said, "They always say they'd never lay someone off. In lean times, we'd be kept on to make the process more efficient."[40]

That kind of confidence is probably not misplaced. While the plant hasn't been in operation long enough to test the "no layoff" policy, Toyota USA's president publicly takes the position that the firm would in fact redeploy, not dismiss, its people if times got tough:

> At TMM we have not yet reached the point of making adjustments in production. However, should adjustments become necessary, TMM would use it as an opportunity for further training of our team members, as we call our employees. Team members would use this time to work on their kaizen ideas [continual improvement], which they have been too busy to pursue when production is in full swing.[41]

As previously mentioned, firms like Toyota take several steps to help ensure that employment is indeed "for keeps": temporary, part-time employees provide the slack that helps these firms downsize without laying off permanent employees; as much as 10–20% of compensation is "at risk" and drops when sales or profits plummet; and, perhaps most important, these firms' high commitment usually lets them stay "lean and mean" and thus more efficient and flexible than their competitors.

RETIREMENT

retirement
The point at which a person gives up one's work, usually around the age of 60–65, but increasingly earlier today due to firms' early-retirement incentive plans.

Retirement for most employees is a bittersweet experience. For some it is the culmination of their careers, a time when they can relax and enjoy the fruits of their labor without worrying about the problems of work. For others, it is the retirement itself that is the trauma, as the once busy employee tries to cope with being suddenly "nonproductive" and with the strange (and not entirely pleasant) experience of being home every day with nothing to do. For many retirees, in fact, maintaining a sense of identity and self-worth without a full-time job is the single most important task they'll face. And it's one that employers are increasingly trying to help their retirees cope with, as a logical last step in the career management process.[42]

Preretirement Counseling

pre-retirement counseling
Counseling provided to employees who are about to retire, and which covers matters such as benefits advice, second careers, and so on.

About 30% of the employers in one survey said they had formal preretirement programs aimed at easing the passage of their employees into retirement.[43] The most common preretirement practices were

Explanation of Social Security benefits (reported by 97% of those with preretirement education programs)
Leisure-time counseling (86%)
Financial and investment counseling (84%)
Health counseling (82%)
Living arrangements (59%)
Psychological counseling (35%)
Counseling for second careers outside the company (31%)
Counseling for second careers inside the company (4%)

Among employers that did *not* have preretirement education programs, 64% believed that such programs were needed, and most of these said their firms had plans to develop them within two or three years.

Another important trend here is that of granting part-time employment to employees as an alternative to outright retirement. Several recent surveys of blue- and white-collar employees showed that about half of all employees over age 55 would like to continue working part-time after they retire.

▶ CHAPTER REVIEW

SUMMARY

1. Managers of more progressive firms know that commitment is built on trust, and that trust requires floods of two-way communications. Firms like this therefore set up programs such as Guaranteed Fair Treatment, Speak Up!, opinion surveying, and Top-Down for keeping employees informed.
2. Firms give employees vehicles through which to "speak their minds." For example, IBM's Speak Up! and Toyota's hot line provide employees with anonymous channels through which they can express concerns to top management.
3. Firms such as IBM and Federal Express also engage in periodic anonymous opinion surveys. These provide standardized channels thorough which management can take the pulse of employee attitudes. Top-down programs—including roundtable discussions, in-house TV broadcasts, and top managers continuously mingling with the rank-and-file—are some techniques firms use to ensure healthy top-down communications.

4. Guaranteed Fair Treatment programs, such as the one at Federal Express, help to ensure that grievances are handled fairly and openly. Steps include management review, officer complaint, and executive appeals review. Packets of forms are used to facilitate the filing of Guaranteed Fair Treatment program complaints.
5. A fair and just discipline process is based on three prerequisites: rules and regulations, a system of progressive penalties, and an appeals process. We listed a number of discipline guidelines, including discipline should be in line with the way management usually responds to similar incidents; management must adequately investigate the matter before administering discipline; and don't rob your subordinate of his or her dignity.
6. We discussed a new approach to discipline called discipline without punishment. The basic aim here is to gain acceptance to rules by reducing the punitive nature of the discipline itself. In particular, employees are given a paid day off to consider their infraction before more punitive disciplinary steps are taken.
7. Managing dismissals is an important part of any supervisor's job. Among the reasons for dismissal are unsatisfactory performance, misconduct, lack of qualifications, changed job requirements, and insubordination. In dismissing one or more employees, however, remember that "termination at will" as a policy has been weakened by exceptions in many states. Furthermore, great care should be taken to avoid wrongful discharge suits. For example, delete statements from your employee manual that could prejudice your defense, have clear written rules regarding discipline and discharge, and don't "constructively discharge" employees by placing them in a lower paying job in hopes of a resignation.
8. Dismissing an employee is always difficult and the termination interview should be handled properly. Specifically, plan the interview carefully (for instance, early in the week), get to the point, describe the situation, and then listen until the person has expressed his or her feelings. Then discuss the severance package and identify the next step.
9. Nondisciplinary separations such as layoffs and retirements occur all the time. The "Plant Closing" law (the Worker Adjustment and Retraining Notification Act) sets down requirements to be followed with regard to official notice before operations with 50 or more people are to be closed down.
10. Many firms today seek alternatives to layoffs. These include voluntary reduction in pay plans, voluntary time off, and the "rings of defense" approach which involves using temporary, part-time employees who are let go in adverse times.
11. Job security and employee commitment go hand in hand. That's why firms like Toyota, Saturn, and Federal Express emphasize what might be called "lifetime employment without guarantees." On the one hand, these firms do all they can to ensure job security and in return they expect their employees to commit themselves to the firm and its goals. Yet even in these firms "employment at will" is the rule. This means that either the employee or the firm may terminate the employment relationship at any time and for any reason.

KEY TERMS

Speak Up!
opinion survey
top-down programs
guaranteed fair treatment
open-door
skip-level interview
discipline
dismissal
insubordination
termination at will
wrongful discharge
termination interviews
"Plant Closing" law
layoff
bumping/layoff procedures
voluntary reduction in pay plan
voluntary time off
rings of defense
outplacement counseling
exit interviews
downsizings
lifetime employment without guarantees
retirement
preretirement counseling

DISCUSSION QUESTIONS

1. Explain the role of communications and guaranteed fair treatment in fostering employee commitment.
2. Describe some of the specific techniques you would use to foster top-down communication in an organization.
3. Describe the similarities and differences between a program such as Federal Express's guaranteed fair treatment program and a typical union grievance procedure.
4. Explain how you would ensure fairness in disciplining, discussing particularly the prerequisites to disciplining, disciplining guidelines, and the new "discipline without punishment" approach.
5. Why is it important in what some consider our highly litigious society to manage dismissals properly?
6. What are the techniques you would use as alternatives to layoffs? What do such alternatives have to do with what we refer to as "lifetime employment without guarantees"? Why do you think alternatives like these are important, given industry's need today for highly committed employees?

APPLICATION EXERCISES

RUNNING CASE

CARTER CLEANING COMPANY

Guaranteeing Fair Treatment

Being in the laundry and cleaning business, the Carters have always felt strongly about not allowing employees to smoke, eat, or drink in their stores. Jennifer was therefore surprised to walk into a store and find two employees eating lunch at the front counter. There was a large pizza in its box, and the two of them were sipping colas and eating slices of pizza and submarine sandwiches off paper plates. Not only did it look messy, but there were also grease and soda spills on the counter and the store smelled from onions and pepperoni, even with the four-foot wide exhaust fan pulling air out through the roof. In addition to being a turnoff to customers, the mess on the counter increased the possibility that a customer's order might actually become soiled in the store.

While this was a serious matter, neither Jennifer nor her father felt that what the counter people were doing was grounds for immediate dismissal, partly because the store manager had apparently condoned their actions. The problem was they didn't know what to do. It seemed to them that the matter called for more than just a warning, but less than dismissal.

Questions

1. Should a disciplinary system be established at Carter's Cleaning Centers?
2. If so, what should it cover, and how would you suggest they deal with the errant counter people?

CASE INCIDENT *Job Insecurity at IBM*

For over fifty years IBM was known for its policy of job security. Throughout all those years it had never laid off any employees, even as the company was going through wrenching changes. For example, in the late 1970s and 1980s, IBM had to close down its punch card manufacturing plants and division but the thousands of employees who worked in those plants were simply given an opportunity to move to comparable jobs in other IBM divisions.

Unfortunately, IBM's full-employment policy is evaporating, and fast. As IBM's computer industry market share dropped throughout the 1980s both its sales revenue and profits began to erode. By 1991 it had become apparent that a drastic restructuring was needed. The firm therefore accelerated its downsizing efforts, instituting various early retirement and incentive plans aimed at getting employees voluntarily to leave IBM. Various imaginative schemes were introduced, including spinning off certain operations to groups of employees who then quit IBM while becoming independent consultants, doing tasks very similar to those they used to do while employees of IBM. By 1992, however, at least 40,000 more employees still had to be trimmed and by 1993 it had become apparent that IBM's cherished full employment policy had to be discarded. For the first time, IBM began laying off employees, beginning with about 300 employees of the firm's Armonk, New York headquarters.

Questions

1. What do you think accounts for the fact that a company like IBM can have high commitment but still lose market share, sales, and profitability? In other words, why do you think employee commitment did not translate into corporate success as well as it might have at IBM?
2. What sorts of steps do you think IBM could have taken in order to continue to avoid layoffs? If you don't think any such steps were feasible, explain why.
3. Given IBM's experience with its full employment policy, what do you think are the implications for other companies thinking of instituting full employment policies of their own?

HUMAN RESOURCE MANAGEMENT SIMULATION

Two incidents in the simulation pertain to this chapter. Incident K requires your team to make a decision concerning which, if any, outplacement services you offer to an employee that you are discharging. Remember that whatever you do, you are setting a precedent for future cases. Further, keep in mind that you are making a strong statement to your employees about fairness when you make decisions about outplacement.

Incident M concerns the actions you will take in disciplining an employee. There are two ways to look at this incident—one from the viewpoint of the company (the bottom line and precedent), and the other from the viewpoint of the employee. You may want to role-play each side to reach your decision.

NOTES

1. Anne B. Fisher, "Morale Crisis," *Fortune*, November 18, 1991, p. 70.
2. This is based on Allan Farnham, "The Trust Gap," *Fortune*, December 4, 1989, p. 57.
3. *Think Magazine*, Vol. 55, no. 6 (1989).
4. Toyota Motor Manufacturing, U.S.A., Inc., *Team Member Handbook* (February 1988), pp. 52–53.
5. All about Your Company, IBM Employee Handbook, p. 184. The section on building employee commitment and the material quoted in it is based on Gary Dessler, *Winning*

Commitment (New York: McGraw-Hill, 1993), pp. 37–51.
6. The Federal Express Employee Handbook, August 7, 1989, p. 89.
7. *Blueprints for Service Quality: The Federal Express Approach*, AMA Management Briefing (New York: AMA Membership Publications Division, 1991), p. 42.
8. Ibid. p. 89.
9. Ibid. p. 45.
10. Lester Bittel, *What Every Supervisor Should Know* (New York: McGraw-Hill, 1974), p. 308; based on a study by the American Arbitration Association of 1,000 grievances.
11. Commerce Clearing House, *Personnel Practices/Communications* (Chicago: CCH, 1982), pp. 2351–2352.
12. Commerce Clearing House, *Ideas and Trends in Personnel*, April 8, 1982, p. 88.
13. Commerce Clearing House, "One Thing Unions Offer Is "Fair Discipline—But Management Can Offer That Too," *Ideas and Trends in Personnel*, September 3, 1982, p. 168.
14. Commerce Clearing House, "Non-union Employees, NLRB Rules, Have the Right to Help During Questioning by Management," *Ideas and Trends in Personnel*, August 6, 1982, p. 151.,
15. These are based on George Odiorne, *How Managers Make Things Happen* (Englewood Cliffs, NJ: Prentice Hall, 1961), pp. 132–143; see also Bittel, *What Every Supervisor Should Know*, pp. 285–298.
16. Nonpunitive discipline discussions based on David Campbell et al., "Discipline Without Punishment—At Last," *Harvard Business Review* (July–August 1985), pp. 162–178; and Gene Milbourn, Jr., "The Case Against Employee Punishment," *Management Solutions* (November 1986), pp. 40–45. Mark Sherman and Al Lucia, "Positive Discipline and Labor Arbitration," *Arbitration Journal*, Vol. 47, No. 2, June 1992, pp. 56–58.
17. Joseph Famularo, *Handbook of Modern Personnel Administration* (New York, McGraw-Hill, 1972), pp. 65.3–65.5.
18. Ibid.
19. Ibid., pp. 65.4–65.5.
20. From a press release dated August 6, 1987. The Goodrich & Sherwood Company, 521 Fifth Avenue, New York, NY 10017. Reprinted in Commerce Clearing House, *Ideas and Trends*, October 2, 1987, p. 157.
21. Bureau of National Affairs, *The Employment-at-Will Issue* (Washington, DC: BNA, 1982). See also Emily Joiner, "Erosion of the Employment at Will Doctrine, *Personnel*, Vol. 61, no. 5 (September–October 1984), pp. 12–18; Harvey Steinberg, "Where Law and Personnel Practice Collide: The At Will Employment Crossroad," *Personnel*, Vol. 62, no 6 (June 1985), pp. 37–43.
22. Based on a speech by Peter Panken and presented in BNA, *Bulletin to Management*, June 20, 1985, pp. 11–12.
23. Based on comments by attorney Richard Curiale in BNA, *Bulletin to Management*, November 17, 1983, p. 8. See also BNA, *Bulletin to Management*, May 18, 1989, p. 154; averting wrongful discharge litigation, specific guidelines. Also see Commerce Clearing House, "How to Discharge: Some Guidelines," *Ideas and Trends in Personnel*, January 11, 1988, p. 4. Except as noted, this section was based on Miriam Rothman, "Employee Termination, I: A Four-Step Procedure," *Personnel* (February 1989), pp. 31–35; and Steven Jesseph, "Employee Termination, II: Some Do's and Don'ts," *Personnel* (February 1989), pp. 36–38.
24. William J. Morin and Lyle York, *Outplacement Techniques* (New York: AMACOM, 1982) pp. 101–131, and F. Leigh Branham, "How to Evaluate Executive Outplacement Services," *Personnel Journal*, Vol. 62 (April 1983), pp. 323–326.
25. Morin and York, *Outplacement Techniques*, p. 117.
26. Quoted from Commerce Clearing House, *Ideas and Trends*, August 9, 1988, p. 133; see also Bureau of National Affairs, "Plant Closing Notification Rules: A Compliance Guide," *Bulletin to Management*, May 18, 1989. See also Nancy Ryan, "Complying with the Worker Adjustment and Retraining Notification Act (WARNACT)," *Employee Relations Law Journal*, Vol. 18, No. 1, Summer 1993, pp. 169–176.
27. Commerce Clearing House, *Personnel Practices/Communications*, p. 1402.
28. Ibid., p. 1410.
29. Commerce Clearing House, *Ideas and Trends in Personnel*, July 9, 1982, p. 131; Robert Tomasko, "Downsizing: Layoffs and Alternatives to Layoffs," *Compensation and Benefits Review*, Vol. 23, no. 4 (July–August 1991), pp. 19–32.
30. Commerce Clearing House, *Ideas and Trends in Personnel*, July 9, 1982, pp. 132–146.
31. Ibid., p. 132.
32. Joseph Zarandona and Michael Camuso, "A Study of Exit Interviews: Does the Last Word Count?" *Personnel*, Vol. 62, no. 3 (March 1985), pp. 47–48.
33. This is based on Steven Jesseph, "Employee Termination, II: Some Do's and Don'ts," *Personnel* (February 1989), pp. 36–38.
34. Les Feldman, "Duracell's First Aid for Downsizing Survivors," *Personnel Journal* (August, 1989), p. 94.
35. Ibid.
36. These are based on Dan Kleinman, "Witness to a Merger," *Personnel Journal* (November 1988), pp. 64–67.
37. Alex Warren, speech to the City Club, Cleveland, Ohio, November 15, 1991, p. 7.
38. Team Member Handbook, Toyota Motor Manufacturing, U.S.A., February 1988, p. 102.
39. Ibid., p. 103.
40. Personal interview, March, 1992.
41. Fujio Cho, "Employee Motivation by Applying The Toyota Promotion System," speech to the Asian Business Club of Harvard Business School, March 4, 1991, p. 2.
42. Remember that certain highly paid executives and employees who will receive pensions of at least $25,000 a year at retirement can be forced to retire at 65, under federal law.
43. "Preretirement Education Programs," *Personnel*, Vol. 59 (May–June 1982), p. 47. For a discussion of why it is important for retiring employees to promote aspects of their lives aside from their careers, see Daniel Halloran, "The Retirement Identity Crisis—and How to Beat It," *Personnel Journal*, Vol. 64 (May 1985), pp. 38–40. For an example of a program aimed at training preretirees to prepare for the financial aspects of their retirement, see, for example, Silvia Odenwald, "Pre-Retirement Training Gathers Steam," *Training and Development Journal*, Vol. 40, no. 2 (February 1986), pp. 62–63; "Pay Policies," Bureau of National Affairs *Bulletin to Management*, March 29, 1990, p. 103.

CHAPTER 18

EMPLOYEE SAFETY AND HEALTH

OVERVIEW

Every manager needs a working knowledge of OSHA—the Occupational Safety and Health Act—and so we discuss its purpose, standards, and inspection procedures, as well as the rights and responsibilities of employees and employers under OSHA. We also stress the importance of the supervisor in safety and the importance of obtaining top management's commitment to safety. There are three basic causes of accidents—chance occurrences, unsafe conditions, and unsafe acts—and we explain how to deal with them. We discuss techniques for preventing accidents, as well as four employee health problems: alcoholism, drug addiction. emotional illness, and stress. When you finish studying this chapter, you should be able to explain the basic facts about OSHA—its purpose, standards, inspection, and rights and responsibilities; explain the supervisor's role in safety; explain what causes unsafe acts; and describe five techniques for reducing accidents.

WHY EMPLOYEE SAFETY AND HEALTH ARE IMPORTANT

The subject of safety and accident prevention is of tremendous concern to managers for several reasons. For one thing, the figures concerning work-related accidents are staggering. The National Safety Council reports, for example, that for a recent year there were more than 11,000 deaths and almost 6 million injuries resulting from accidents at work—that's over eight cases per 100 full-time workers in 1991. And many safety experts feel that such figures seriously underestimate the actual number of injuries.[1]

But figures like these don't tell the full story. They don't reflect the human suffering incurred by the injured workers and their families. They don't reflect the economic costs incurred by these people's employers—costs that averaged over $23,000 per serious accident in the early 1990s.[2] Nor do they reflect the legal implications. For example, the owners of a Hamlet, North Carolina, food processing plant were sued and imprisoned because exit doors were bolted when a tragic fire occurred in 1992; in 1991 a federal jury found a construction contractor guilty on federal criminal charges for violating three OSHA regulations after three of his employees were killed in a sewage tunnel explosion;[3] in 1992 a company president charged with making false statements to OSHA got a sentence of 8 to 14 months in jail.[4]

BASIC FACTS ABOUT OCCUPATIONAL SAFETY LAW

PURPOSE

Occupational Safety and Health Act
The law passed by Congress in 1970 "to assure so far as possible every working man and woman in the nation safe and healthful working conditions and to preserve our human resources."

Occupational Safety and Health Administration (OSHA)
The agency created within the Department of Labor to set safety

The **Occupational Safety and Health Act**[5] was passed by Congress in 1970; its purpose, as stated by Congress, was "to assure so far as possible every working man and woman in the nation safe and healthful working conditions and to preserve our human resources." The only employers not covered under the act are self-employed persons, farms in which only immediate members of the farm employer's family are employed, and certain workplaces that are already protected by other federal agencies or under other statutes. Federal agencies are covered by the act, although provisions of the act usually don't apply to state and local governments in their role as employers.

Under the provisions of the act, the **Occupational Safety and Health Administration (OSHA)** was created within the Department of Labor. The basic purpose of OSHA is to set safety and health standards, standards that apply to almost all workers in the United States. The standards are enforced through the Department of Labor, and to ensure compliance, OSHA has inspectors working out of branch offices throughout the country.

OSHA STANDARDS

OSHA operates under the "general" standard that each employer:

shall furnish to each of his employees employment and a place of employment which are free from recognized hazards that are causing or are likely to cause death or serious physical harm to his employees.

In carrying out this basic mission, OSHA is responsible for promulgating legally enforceable standards. The standards themselves are contained in five volumes, covering general industry standards, maritime standards, construction standards, other regulations and procedures, and a field operations manual.

The standards are very complete and seem to cover just about any hazard one could think of, in great detail. For example, a small part of the standard governing scaffolds is presented in Figure 18.1. Note also that OSHA regulations don't just enumerate recommended standards (like the one describing what guard rails should look like, in Figure 18.1). For example, provisions of OSHA's Hazard Communication Standard require employers to establish hazard communication programs to inform employees about chemical hazards. Hazards have to be communicated through training programs, container labels, and particularly materials safety data sheets (known as MSDS), which list the nature of a treatment for hazardous substances.

OSHA RECORDKEEPING PROCEDURES

Under OSHA, employers with 11 or more employees must maintain records of occupational injuries and illnesses as they occur. (Employers having 10 or fewer employees are exempt from recordkeeping unless they are selected to participate in the annual statistical survey carried out by the Bureau of Labor Statistics.)

Both occupational injuries and occupational illnesses must be reported. An occupational illness is any abnormal condition or disorder caused by exposure to environmental factors associated with employment. Included here are acute and chronic illnesses that may be caused by inhalation, absorption, ingestion, or direct contact with toxic substances or harmful agents. As summarized in Figure 18.2, *all* occupational illnesses must be reported.[6] Similarly, *most* occupational injuries also must be reported. Specifically, occupational injuries must be recorded if they result in medical treatment (other than first aid), loss of consciousness, restriction of work (one or more lost workdays), restriction of motion, or transfer to another job.[7] If an on-the-job accident occurs that results in the death of an employee or in the hospitalization of five or more employees, all employers, regardless of size, must report the accident, in detail, to the nearest OSHA office. A form used to report occupational injuries or illness is shown in Figure 18.3.

FIGURE 18.1 OSHA Standards Example

Source: *General Industry Standards and Interpretations,* U.S. Department of Labor, OSHA (Volume 1: Revised 1989, Section 1910.28(b) (15)), p. 67.

Guardrails not less than 2″ × 4″ or the equivalent and not less than 36″ or more than 42″ high, with a midrail, when required, of a 1″ × 4″ lumber or equivalent, and toeboards, shall be installed at all open sides on all scaffolds more than 10 feet above the ground or floor. Toeboards shall be a minimum of 4″ in height. Wire mesh shall be installed in accordance with paragraph (a) (17) of this section.

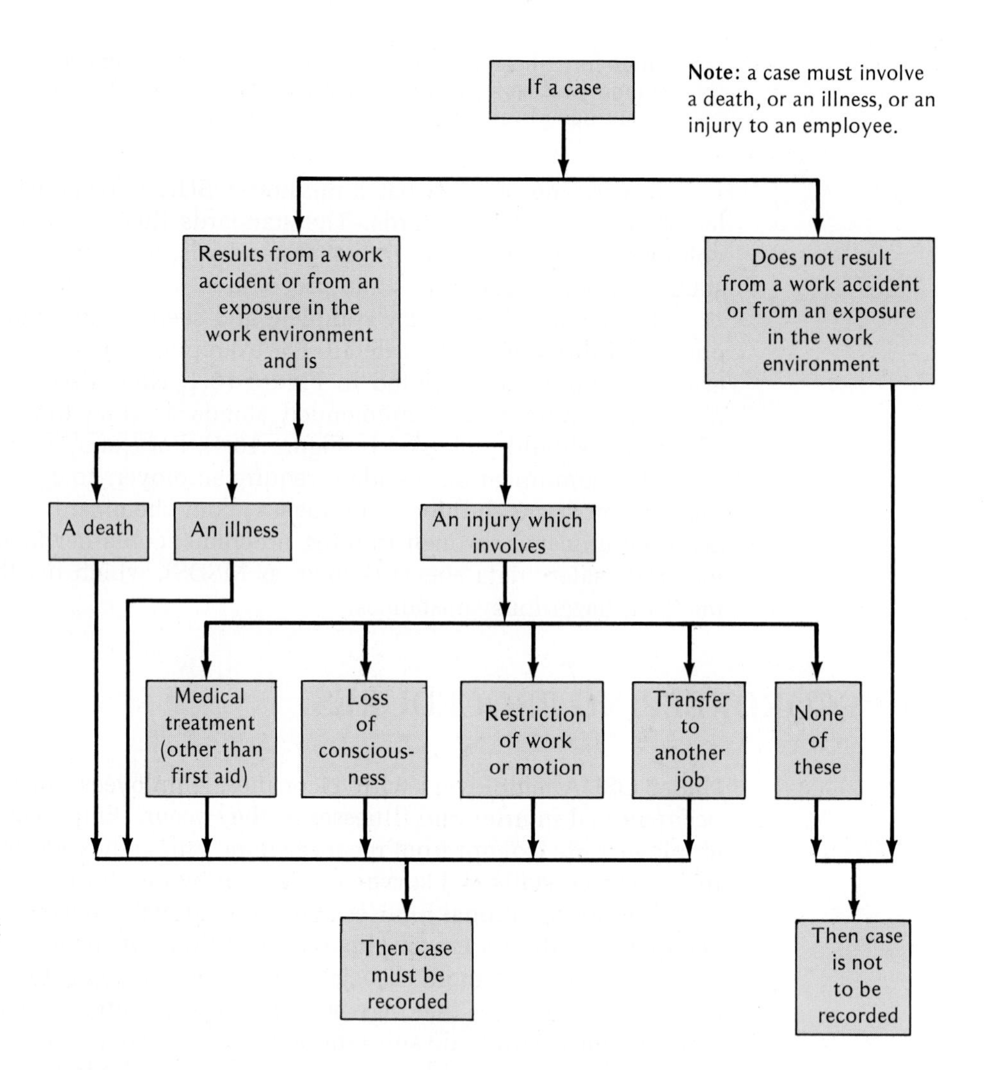

FIGURE 18.2
What Accidents Must Be Reported Under the Occupational Safety and Health Act (OSHA)

INSPECTIONS AND CITATIONS

OSHA standards are enforced through inspections and (if necessary) citations. Originally every employer covered by the act was subject to inspection by OSHA compliance officers who were authorized to "enter without delay and at reasonable times any factory, plant, establishment . . . where work was performed . . . ," and to "inspect and investigate during regular working hours, and at other reasonable times, . . . any such place of employment and all pertinent conditions, structures, machines, . . . and to question privately any such employer, owner, operator, agent or employee."[8] However, OSHA may not conduct warrantless inspections without an employer's consent. It may, however, inspect after acquiring a judicially authorized search warrant or its equivalent.[9]

Inspection Priorities

OSHA has a list of inspection priorities. Imminent danger situations get top priority. This is a condition where it is likely a danger exists that can cause death or serious physical harm immediately. Second priority is given to investigation

FIGURE 18.3
Form Used to Record Occupational Injuries and Illnesses

OSHA No. 101
Case or File No. ____________

Form approved
OMB No. 44R 1453

Supplementary Record of Occupational Injuries and Illnesses

EMPLOYER

1. Name ____________
2. Mail address ____________
(No. and street) (City or town) (State)
3. Location, if different from mail address ____________

INJURED OR ILL EMPLOYEE

4. Name ____________ Social Security No. ____________
(First name) (Middle name) (Last name)
5. Home address ____________
(No. and street) (City or town) (State)
6. Age ____________ 7. Sex: Male ____________ Female ____________ (Check one)
8. Occupation ____________
(Enter regular job title, *not* the specific activity he/she was performing at time of injury.)
9. Department ____________
(Enter name of department or division in which the injured person is regularly employed, even though he/she may have been temporarily working in another department at the time of injury.)

THE ACCIDENT OR EXPOSURE TO OCCUPATIONAL ILLNESS

10. Place of accident or exposure ____________
(No. and street) (City or town) (State)
If accident or exposure occurred on employer's premises, give address of plant or establishment in which it occurred. Do not indicate department or division within the plant or establishment. If accident occurred outside employer's premises at an identifiable address, give that address. If it occurred on a public highway or at any other place which cannot be identified by number and street, please provide place references locating the place of injury as accurately as possible.
11. Was place of accident or exposure on employer's premises? ____________ (Yes or No)
12. What was the employee doing when injured? ____________
(Be specific. If he/she was using tools or equipment or handling material, name them and tell what he/she was doing with them.)
13. How did the accident occur? ____________
(Describe fully the events which resulted in the injury or occupational illness. Tell what happend and how it happened. Name any objects or substances involved and tell how they were involved. Give full details on all factors which led or contributed to the accident. Use separate sheet for additional space.)

OCCUPATIONAL INJURY OR OCCUPATIONAL ILLNESS

14. Describe the injury or illness in detail and indicate the part of body affected. ____________
(e.g.: amputation of right index finger at second joint; fracture of ribs; lead poisoning; dermatitis of left hand, etc.)
15. Name the object or substance which directly injured the employee. (For example, the machine or thing he/she struck against or which struck him/her; the vapor or poison inhaled or swallowed; the chemical or radiation which irritated the skin; or in cases of strains, hernias, etc., the thing he/she was lifting, pulling, etc.)
16. Date of injury or initial diagnosis of occupational illness ____________
(Date)
17. Did employee die? ____________ (Yes or No)

OTHER

18. Name and address of physician ____________
19. If hospitalized, name and address of hospital ____________

Date of report ____________ Prepared by ____________
Official position ____________

of catastrophes, fatalities, and accidents that have already occurred. (Such situations must be reported to OSHA within 48 hours.) Third priority is given to valid employee complaints of alleged violation of standards. Next in priority are periodic special emphasis inspections, aimed at high-hazard industries, occupations, or substances. Finally, random inspections (and reinspections) generally have last priority.

An OSHA safety inspector visits the plant to check on reported violations of federal safety and health regulations.

OSHA no longer follows up on *every* employee complaint with an inspection. The thrust now is to focus on priority problems.[10] Under its priority system, OSHA conducts an inspection within 24 hours when a complaint indicates an immediate danger, and within 3 working days when a serious hazard exists. For a "nonserious" complaint filed in writing by a worker or a union, OSHA will respond within 20 working days. Otherwise, "nonserious" complaints are handled by writing to the employer and requesting corrective action.

Of the 71,303 OSHA inspections made recently, more than 72% were concentrated on high-hazard worksites. The agency cited 119,706 alleged violations and assessed penalties totaling $9,190,039.[11] Lockheed Aeronautical was hit with nearly $1.5 million in proposed penalties, for instance.

The Inspection Itself

Before an inspection, the OSHA inspector becomes familiar with as many relevant facts as possible about the worksite.[12] The inspection itself begins when the OSHA officer arrives at the place of work. He or she displays official credentials and asks to meet an employer representative. (You should always insist on seeing the officer's credentials, which include photograph and serial number.) The officer explains the purpose of the visit, the scope of the inspection, and the standards that apply. An authorized *employee* representative is also given an opportunity to accompany the officer during the inspection. Other employees will also be consulted during the inspection and the inspector can stop and question workers (in private if necessary) about safety and health conditions. Each employee is protected under the act from discrimination for exercising his or her disclosure rights.

Finally (after checking the premises and employer's records), a closing conference is held between the inspector and the employer representative. Here the inspector discusses what has been found in terms of apparent violations for which a citation may be issued or recommended. The inspector does *not* indicate any proposed penalties. Only the OSHA area director has that authority. At this point the employer can produce records to show compliance efforts.

Citations and Penalties

citations
Summons informing employers and employees of the regulations and standards that have been violated in the workplace.

After the inspection report is submitted to the OSHA office, the area director determines what citations, if any, will be issued. The **citations** inform the employer and employees of the regulations and standards that have been violated and of the time set for rectifying the problem. These citations must be posted at or near the place the violation occurred. Under some circumstances the inspector can post a citation immediately (to ensure that employees receive protection in the shortest possible time).

OSHA can also impose penalties. With changes mandated by the Omnibus Budget Reconciliation Act of 1990, these now range up to $7,000 for serious violations and from $5,000 to $70,000 for willful or repeat violations. There is also a maximum of $7,000 a day in penalties for a failure to rectify a violation.

In general, OSHA calculates penalties based on the gravity of a particular violation and usually takes into consideration such factors as the size of the business, the firm's compliance history, and the employer's good faith. In practice, OSHA must have a final order from the independent Occupational Safety and Health Review Commission (OSHRC) in order to enforce a penalty. While that appeals process has been sped up of late, an employer who files a notice of contest can still drag out an appeal for years, according to OSHRC's current head.[13]

THE RESPONSIBILITIES AND RIGHTS OF EMPLOYERS AND EMPLOYEES

As summarized in Figure 18.4, both employers and employees have responsibilities and rights under the Occupational Safety and Health Act. Employers, for example, are responsible for meeting their duty to provide "a workplace free from recognized hazards," for being familiar with mandatory OSHA standards and for examining workplace conditions to make sure they conform to applicable standards. Employers have the right to seek advice and off-site consultation from OSHA, to request and to receive proper identification of the OSHA compliance officer before inspection, and to be advised by the compliance officer of the reason for an inspection.

Employees also have rights and responsibilities, but they *cannot* be cited for violations of their responsibilities. They are responsible, for example, for complying with all applicable OSHA standards, for following all employer safety and health rules and regulations, and for reporting hazardous conditions to the supervisor. Employees have a right to demand safety and health on the job without fear of punishment. Employers are forbidden to punish or discriminate against workers who complain to OSHA about job safety and health hazards.

Dealing with Employee Resistance

While employees have a responsibility to comply with OSHA standards, the fact is they often resist complying, and in most such cases the *employer* remains liable for any penalties.[14] The problem of employee resistance is typified by the refusal of longshoremen to wear hard hats as mandated by the OSHA requirements. Employers have attempted to defend themselves against penalties for such noncompliance by citing worker intransigence and fear of wildcat strikes and walkouts. Yet in most cases courts have held that employers were liable for safety violations at the workplace regardless of the fact that the violations were due to employee resistance.[15] The result is that an employer is often in a difficult position: On the one hand, the courts and OSHA claim that employers must vigorously seek employee compliance; on the other hand, doing so is often all but impossible.

There are several tactics you can use to overcome this problem.[16] First, the courts have held that an employer can bargain in good faith with its union for the right to discharge or discipline any employee who disobeys an OSHA standard. Yet most unions have thus far refused to bargain over hard hats (and many other OSHA issues) because they oppose having penalties assessed against their members. As a second alternative, one expert suggests greater use of arbitration in safety disputes. Arbitration is already widely used to resolve employee grievances. The use of a formal arbitration process by aggrieved employers could pro-

FIGURE 18.4 Employer/Employee Rights and Responsibilities Under OSHA

Source: U.S. Department of Labor, *All About OSHA* (Washington, DC: U.S. Government Printing Office, 1992).

Employer Responsibilities and Rights

Employers have certain responsibilities and rights under the Occupational Safety and Health Act of 1970.

The checklists that follow provide a review of many of these. Employer responsibilities and rights in states with their own occupational safety and health programs are generally the same as in federal OSHA states.

Responsibilities

As an employer, you must:

- Meet your general duty responsibility to provide a workplace free from recognized hazards that are causing or are likely to cause death or serious physical harm to employees, and comply with standards, rules and regulations issued under the Act.
- Be familiar with mandatory OSHA standards and make copies available to employees for review upon request.
- Inform all employees about OSHA.
- Examine workplace conditions to make sure they conform to applicable standards.
- Minimize or reduce hazards.
- Make sure employees have and use safe tools and equipment (including appropriate personal protective equipment), and that such equipment is properly maintained.
- Use color codes, posters, labels, or signs when needed to warn employees of potential hazards.
- Establish or update operating procedures and communicate them so that employees follow safety and health requirements.
- Provide medical examinations when required by OSHA standards.
- Provide training required by OSHA standards (e.g., hazard communication, lead, etc).[1]
- Report to the nearest OSHA office within 48 hours any fatal accident or one that results in the hospitalization of five or more employees.
- Keep OSHA-required records of work-related injuries and illnesses, and post a copy of the totals from the last page of OSHA No. 200 during the entire month of February each year. (This applies to employers with 11 or more employees.)
- Post, at a prominent location within the workplace, the OSHA poster (OSHA 2203) informing employees of their rights and responsibilities. (In states operating OSHA-approved job safety and health programs, the state's equivalent poster and/or OSHA 2203 may be required.)
- Provide employees, former employees and their representatives access to the Log and Summary of Occupational Injuries and Illnesses (OSHA No. 200) at a reasonable time and in a reasonable manner.
- Provide access to employee medical records and exposure records to employees or their authorized representatives.
- Cooperate with the OSHA compliance officer by furnishing names of authorized employee representatives who may be asked to accompany the compliance officer during an inspection. (If none, the compliance officer will consult with a reasonable number of employees concerning safety and health in the workplace.)
- Not discriminate against employees who properly exercise their rights under the Act.
- Post OSHA citations at or near the worksite involved. Each citation, or copy thereof, must remain posted until the violation has been abated, or for three working days, whichever is longer.
- Abate cited violations within the prescribed period.

Rights

As an employer, you have the right to:

- Seek advice and off-site consultation as needed by writing, calling or visiting the nearest OSHA office. (OSHA will not inspect merely because an employer requests assistance.)
- Be active in your industry association's involvement in job safety and health.
- Request and receive proper identification of the OSHA compliance officer prior to inspection.
- Be advised by the compliance officer of the reason for an inspection.
- Have an opening and closing conference with the compliance officer.
- Accompany the compliance officer on the inspection.
- File a Notice of Contest with the OSHA area director within 15 working days of receipt of a notice of citation and proposed penalty.
- **Apply to OSHA for a temporary variance from a standard if unable to comply because of the unavailability of materials, equipment or personnel needed to make necessary changes within the required time.**
- **Apply to OSHA for a permanent variance from a standard if you can furnish proof that your facilities or method of operation provide employee protection at least as effective as that required by the standard.**
- **Take an active role in developing safety and health standards through participation in OSHA Standards Advisory Committees, through nationally recognized standards-setting organizations, and through evidence and views presented in writing or at hearings.**
- **Be assured of the confidentiality of any trade secrets observed by an OSHA compliance officer during an inspection.**
- **Submit a written request to NIOSH for information on whether any substance in your workplace has potentially toxic effects in the concentrations being used.**

vide a relatively quick and inexpensive method for resolving an OSHA-related complaint. Other employers have turned to positive reinforcement and training for the purpose of gaining employee compliance; more on this shortly.

FIGURE 18.4 (continued)

Employee Responsibilities and Rights

Although OSHA does not cite employees for violations of their responsibilities, each employee "shall comply with all occupational safety and health standards and all rules, regulations, and orders Issued under the Act" that are applicable.

Employee responsibilities and rights in states with their own occupational safety and health programs are generally the same as for workers in federal OSHA states.

Responsibilities

As an employee, you should:

- Read the OSHA poster at the jobsite.
- Comply with all applicable OSHA standards.
- Follow all employer safety and health rules and regulations, and wear or use prescribed protective equipment while engaged in work.
- Report hazardous conditions to the supervisor.
- Report any job-related injury or illness to the employer, and seek treatment promptly.
- Cooperate with the OSHA compliance officer conducting an inspection if he or she inquires about safety and health conditions in your workplace.
- Exercise your rights under the Act in a responsible manner.

11(c) Rights: Protection for Using Rights

Employees have a right to seek safety and health on the job without fear of punishment. That right is spelled out in Section 11(c) of the Act.

The law says employers shall not punish or discriminate against workers for exercising rights such as:

- Complaining to an employer, union, OSHA or any other government agency about job safety and health hazards;
- Filing safety or health grievances;
- Participating on a workplace safety and health committee or in union activities concerning job safety and health; and,
- Participating in OSHA inspections, conferences, hearings, or other OSHA-related activities.

If an employee is exercising these or other OSHA rights, the employer is not allowed to discriminate against that worker in any way, such as through firing, demotion, taking away seniority or other earned benefits, transferring the worker to an undesirable job or shift, or threatening or harassing the worker.

If the employer has knowingly allowed the employee to do something in the past (such as leaving work early), he or she may be violating the law by punishing the worker for doing the same thing following a protest of hazardous conditions. If the employer knows that a number of workers are doing the same thing wrong, he or she cannot legally single out for punishment the worker who has taken part in safety and health activities.

Workers believing they have been punished for exercising safety and health rights must contact the nearest OSHA office within 30 days of the time they learn of the alleged discrimination. A union representative can file the 11(c) complaint for the worker.

The worker does not have to complete any forms. An OSHA staff member will complete the forms, asking what happened and who was involved.

Following a complaint, OSHA investigates. If an employee has been illegally punished for exercising safety and health rights, OSHA asks the employer to restore that worker's job earning and benefits. If necessary, and if it can prove discrimination, OSHA takes the employer to court. In such cases the worker does not pay any legal fees.

If a state agency has an OSHA-approved state program, employees may file their complaint with either federal OSHA or the state agency under its laws.

Other Rights

As an employee, you have the right to:

- Review copies of appropriate OSHA standards, rules, regulations and requirements that the employer should have available at the workplace.
- Request information from your employer on safety and health hazards in the area, on precautions that may be taken, and on procedures to be followed if an employee is involved in an accident or is exposed to toxic substances.
- Receive adequate training and information on workplace safety and health hazards.
- Request the OSHA area director to investigate if you believe hazardous conditions or violations of standards exist in your workplace.
- Have your name withheld from your employer, upon request to OSHA, if you file a written and signed complaint.
- Be advised of OSHA actions regarding your complaint and have an informal review, if requested, of any decision not to inspect or to issue a citation.
- Have your authorized employee representative accompany the OSHA compliance officer during the inspection tour.
- Respond to questions from the OSHA compliance officer, particularly if there is no authorized employee representative accompanying the compliance officer.
- Observe any monitoring or measuring of hazardous materials and have the right to see these records, and your medical records, as specified under the Act.
- Have your authorized representative, or yourself, review the Log and Summary of Occupational Injuries (OSHA No. 200) at a reasonable time and in a reasonable manner.
- Request a closing discussion with the compliance officer following an inspection.
- Submit a written request to NIOSH for information on whether any substance in your workplace has potentially toxic effects in the concentration being used and have your name withheld from your employer if you so request.
- Object to the abatement period set in the citation issued to your employer by writing to the OSHA area director within 15 working days of the issuance of the citation.
- Participate in hearings conducted by the Occupational Safety and Health Review Commission.
- Be notified by your employer if he or she applies for a variance from an OSHA standard, and testify at a variance hearing and appeal the final decision.
- Submit information or comment to OSHA on the issuance, modification, or revocation of OSHA standards and request a public hearing.

THE CHANGING NATURE OF OSHA

The Occupational Safety and Health Act and Administration both have been criticized on many grounds, and it is not unusual for the U.S. Congress to have more than 100 OSHA reform bills on its agenda.[17] Critics have argued, for example, that too many OSHA rules are nit-picking, and that OSHA has had an overly adverse effect on small businesses.

In response, OSHA made several changes in its policies and procedures. Small businesses with 10 or fewer employees no longer have to file accident reports or undergo routine inspections, and the accident report itself has been simplified and condensed.[18] As mentioned, OSHA inspectors must also now obtain warrants before entering an employer's premises.

In 1981, the funding of OSHA was severely reduced by the Republican administration. In addition, the Reagan administration issued an executive order requiring no regulatory action be "undertaken unless potential benefits to society from the regulation outweigh the potential costs to society." This action did much to stop the initiation of further OSHA health and safety standards.[19]

On August 1, 1991, the Comprehensive Occupational Safety and Health Reform Act was introduced into both houses of Congress. While the act did not become law, it remains a high priority for the AFL-CIO and many members of Congress and provides an insight into the OSHA changes we might expect over the next few years with a Democratic administration.[20] As one expert said, "The Bill is sweeping in its scope and, if enacted as proposed, will significantly increase the adversarial nature of safety and health enforcement."[21]

The proposed act has five main components:

1. *Safety and Health Programs.* Section 101 of the act would have required employers to produce and maintain safety and health programs that provide worker training and education aimed at reducing or eliminating hazards and preventing injuries and illnesses to employees.
2. *Safety and Health Committees and Employee Representatives.* Section 201 of the act would have required employers to establish joint labor–management safety and health committees to inspect the workplace, review injury and illness records, and make safety recommendations to the employer.
3. *OSHA Standards.* This act would have expedited the adoption of new OSHA standards, for instance, by setting tight deadlines for issuing proposed and final rules.
4. *Enforcement.* The act would have compelled more aggressive enforcement by OSHA and strengthened OSHA's authority, for instance by mandating "special emphasis inspections" of high-risk workplaces and by dramatically increasing the penalties for noncompliance.
5. *Expansion of Coverage.* Another section of the bill would have amended the act's definition of "employer" to include the United States and any state or political subdivision of a state.

THE SUPERVISOR'S ROLE IN SAFETY

As a safety-minded manager, your basic aim must be *to instill in your workers the desire to work safely.* Minimizing hazards (by ensuring that spills are wiped up, machine guards are adequate, and so forth) is important, but no matter how safe the workplace is, there will be accidents unless workers *want* to act safely and do. Of course, you could try closely watching each subordinate, but most managers know this won't work. In the final analysis, your best (and perhaps only) alternative is to instill in workers the desire to work safely. Then, when needed, enforce your safety rules.[22]

TOP MANAGEMENT COMMITMENT

Most safety experts agree that safety commitment must begin with top management. Historically, for example, DuPont's accident rate has been much lower than that of the chemical industry as a whole. (In its U.S. plants, DuPont had an annual rate of 0.12 accidents per 100 workers, which was one twenty-third of the National Safety Council's average rate for all manufacturers in that year. If DuPont's record had been average, it would have spent more than $26 million in additional compensation and other costs, or 3.6 percent of its profits. To recover the difference, DuPont would have had to boost sales by about $500 million, given the company's 5.5% net return on sales at that time.[23] And this good safety record is probably partly due to an organizational commitment to safety, a commitment evident in the following description:[24]

> One of the best examples I know of in setting the highest possible priority for safety takes place at a DuPont Plant in Germany. Each morning at the DuPont Polyester and Nylon Plant the director and his assistants meet at 8:45 to review the past 24 hours. The first matter they discuss is not production, but safety. Only after they have examined reports of accidents and near misses and satisfied themselves that corrective action has been taken do they move on to look at output, quality, and cost matters.

In summary, without the full commitment of all levels of management, any attempts to reduce unsafe acts by workers will meet with little success. And the first-line supervisor is a critical link in the chain of management. As one safety expert states: "If the supervisor does not take safety seriously, those under him or her will not either. . . ."

WHAT CAUSES ACCIDENTS

THE THREE BASIC CAUSES OF ACCIDENTS

There are three basic causes of accidents in organizations: chance occurrences, unsafe conditions, and unsafe acts on the part of employees. Chance occurrences (such as walking past a plate-glass window just as someone hits a ball through it) contribute to accidents but are more or less beyond management's control: we will therefore focus on *unsafe conditions* and *unsafe acts.*

UNSAFE CONDITIONS (WORK-RELATED ACCIDENT-CAUSING FACTORS)

unsafe conditions
The mechanical and physical conditions that cause accidents.

Unsafe Conditions (of one sort or another) are one main cause of accidents. They include such things as:

Improperly guarded equipment
Defective equipment
Hazardous procedure in, on, or around machines or equipment
Unsafe storage: congestion, overloading
Improper illumination—glare, insufficient light
Improper ventilation—insufficient air change, impure air source[25]

The basic remedy here is to eliminate or minimize unsafe conditions. For example, OSHA standards address the mechanical and physical conditions that cause accidents. Furthermore, a checklist of "unsafe conditions" can be useful for spotting problems. One such checklist is presented in Figure 18.5; another can be found in the appendix to this chapter.

While accidents can happen anywhere, there are some "high danger" zones. About one-third of industrial accidents occur around forklift trucks, wheelbarrows, and other handling and lifting areas, for example. The most serious accidents usually occur near metal and woodworking machines and saws or around transmission machinery like gears, pulleys, and flywheels. Falls on stairs, ladders, walkways, and scaffolds are the third most common cause of industrial accidents. Hand tools (like chisels and screwdrivers) and electrical equipment (extension cords, electric drop lights, and so on) are other big accident causers.[26]

Three Other Work-Related Accident Factors

In addition to the unsafe conditions we just discussed, three more work-related factors contribute to accidents: *the job itself, the work schedule,* and the *psychological climate* of the workplace.

For example, some *jobs* are inherently more dangerous than others. According to one study, for example, the job of crane operator results in about three times more accident-related hospital visits than does the job of supervisor. Similarly, some departments' work is inherently safer than others'. For example, the bookkeeping department will usually have fewer accidents than the shipping department.

Work schedules and *fatigue* also affect accident rates. Accident rates usually don't increase too noticeably during the first five or six hours of the workday. But beyond that, the accident rate increases faster than the increase in the number of hours worked. This is due partly to fatigue and partly to the fact that accidents occur more often during night shifts.

Finally, many experts believe that the *psychological climate* of the workplace affects the accident rate. For example, accidents occur more frequently in plants with a high seasonal layoff rate and where there is hostility among employees, many garnisheed wages, and blighted living conditions. Temporary stress factors such as high workplace temperature, poor illumination, and a congested workplace are also related to accident rates. One writer says these find-

I. GENERAL HOUSEKEEPING

- Adequate and wide aisles–no materials protruding into aisles.
- Parts and tools stored safely after use–not left in hazardous positions that could cause them to fall
- Even and solid flooring–no defective floors or ramps that could cause falling or tripping accidents
- Waste cans and sand pails–safely located and properly used
- Material piled in safe manner–not too high or too close to sprinkler heads
- Floors–clean and dry
- Firefighting equipment–unobstructed
- Work benches orderly
- Stockcarts and skids safely located, not left in aisles or passageways
- Aisles kept clear and properly marked no air lines or electric cords across aisles

II. MATERIAL HANDLING EQUIPMENT AND CONVEYANCES

On all conveyances, electric or hand, check to see that the following items are all in sound working conditions:

- Brakes–properly adjusted
- Not too much play in steering wheel
- Warning device–in place and working
- Wheels–securely in place; properly inflated
- Fuel and oil–enough and right kind
- No loose parts
- Cables, hooks or chains—not worn or otherwise defective
- Suspended chains or hooks conspicuous
- Safely loaded
- Properly stored

III. LADDERS, SCAFFOLD, BENCHES, STAIRWAYS, ETC.

The following items of major interest to be checked:

- Safety feet on straight ladders
- Guard rails or hand rails
- Treads, not slippery
- No splintered, cracked, or rickety
- Properly stored
- Extension ladder ropes in good condition
- Toeboards

IV. POWER TOOLS (STATIONARY)

- Point of operation guarded
- Guards in proper adjustment
- Gears, belts, shafting, counterweights guarded
- Foot pedals guarded
- Brushes provided for cleaning machines
- Adequate lighting
- Properly grounded
- Tool or material rests properly adjusted
- Adequate work space around machines
- Control switch easily accessible
- Safety glasses worn
- Gloves worn by persons handling rough or sharp materials
- No gloves or loose clothing worn by persons operating machines

V. HAND TOOLS AND MISCELLANEOUS

- In good condition–not cracked, worn, or otherwise defective
- Properly stored
- Correct for job
- Goggles, respirators, and other personal protective equipment worn where necessary

VI. WELDING

- Arc shielded
- Fire hazards controlled
- Operator using suitable protective equipment
- Adequate ventilation
- Cylinder secured
- Valves closed when not in use

VII. SPRAY PAINTING

- Explosion-proof electrical equipment
- Proper storage of paints and thinners in approved metal cabinets
- Fire extinguishers adequate and suitable; readily accessible
- Minimum storage in work area

VIII. FIRE EXTINGUISHERS

- Properly serviced and tagged
- Readily accessible
- Adequate and suitable for operations involved

FIGURE 18.5 Checklist of Mechanical or Physical Accident-Causing Conditions

Source: Courtesy of the American Insurance Association. From "A Safety Committee Man's Guide," 1–64.

ings mean that workers who work under stress, or who feel their jobs are threatened or insecure, have more accidents than those who do not.[27]

WHAT CAUSES UNSAFE ACTS (A SECOND BASIC CAUSE OF ACCIDENTS)

unsafe acts Behavior tendencies and undesirable attitudes that cause accidents.

There is little doubt that **unsafe acts** (not unsafe conditions) are the main cause of accidents, and that *people* cause these unsafe acts.

Most safety experts and managers long ago discovered that it is impossible to eliminate accidents just by reducing unsafe conditions. This is because *people* cause accidents, and no one has found a sure-fire way to make employees work safely. The result is a number of unsafe acts such as:

Failing to use safe attire or personal protective equipment
Throwing materials
Operating or working at unsafe speeds—either too fast or too slow
Making safety devices inoperative by removing, adjusting, disconnecting them
Using unsafe equipment or using equipment unsafely
Using unsafe procedures in loading, placing, mixing, combining
Taking unsafe positions under suspended loads
Lifting improperly
Distracting, teasing, abusing, startling, quarreling, horseplay

Unsafe acts such as these can undermine even the best attempts on your part to minimize unsafe conditions. We should therefore discuss the causes of unsafe acts.[28]

Personal Characteristics and Accidents

Ernest McCormick and Joseph Tiffin have developed a model that summarizes how personal characteristics (such as personality) are linked to accidents; it is presented in Figure 18.6. They say that personal characteristics (personality, motivation, and so on) serve as the basis for certain "behavior tendencies"—such as the tendency to take risks—and undesirable attitudes. These behavior tendencies in turn result in unsafe acts—such as failure to follow procedures and inattention. In turn, such unsafe acts increase the probability of a person's having an accident.

Are There "Accident-Prone" People?

You have probably come across people whom you would consider "accident prone." (Perhaps it is the person who is always dropping things or bumping into doors or falling, for instance.) But to a psychologist, the phrase "accident prone" means something quite specific. It implies the possession of those *qualities* or *traits* that have been found from research to lead to an undue number of accidents.[29] Thus, to most psychologists, accident proneness is a *personality type*, and a person who is accident prone can be identified by a number of specific and measurable personality traits.

Most experts doubt that accident proneness is universal—that there are some people who will have many accidents no matter what situation they are put in. Instead, the consensus seems to be that the person who is accident prone on one job may not be on a different job—that accident proneness is "situational." We will discuss some of the relevant findings.

What Traits Characterize Accident-Prone People?

For years psychologists have tried to determine what package of traits distinguishes those who are accident prone from those who are not. The original interest in this was based on the discovery that a small percentage of workers (say, 20%) were responsible for a large percentage (say, 70%) of the accidents. Researchers assumed that the workers having more accidents were accident prone and set about trying to find a bundle of traits that made them so.

Today, it is generally recognized that these original findings were somewhat inaccurate and misleading; they were more a result of the statistical analysis than the accident proneness of the workers. (One problem was the small number of accidents per worker the researchers had to deal with. For example, suppose you flip a coin many, many times. Over the long run you would expect to get one-half heads and one-half tails. But suppose you just flipped the coin three or four times. Here you might well get three tails in a row or four heads. In that case you obviously would not consider yourself "head prone" or "tail prone," yet that is about what early researchers concluded from the accident-proneness experiments.)

In any case, years of research failed to unearth any set of traits that accident repeaters seemed to have in common. Today, we believe that the personal traits that contribute to accidents probably differ from situation to situation. For example, *personality traits* (such as emotional stability) may distinguish accident-prone workers on jobs involving risk; and *motor skills* may distinguish accident-prone workers on jobs involving coordination. In fact, many human traits *have* been found to be related in accident repetition *in specific situations.*[30]

Vision

Vision is related to accident frequency for many jobs. For example, passenger car drivers, intercity bus drivers, and machine operators who have high visual skills have fewer injuries than those who do not.[31]

Age and Length of Service

We also know that accidents are generally most frequent between the ages of 17 and 28, declining thereafter to reach a low in the late fifties and sixties.[32] While

FIGURE 18.6
How Personal Factors May Influence Employee Accident Behavior

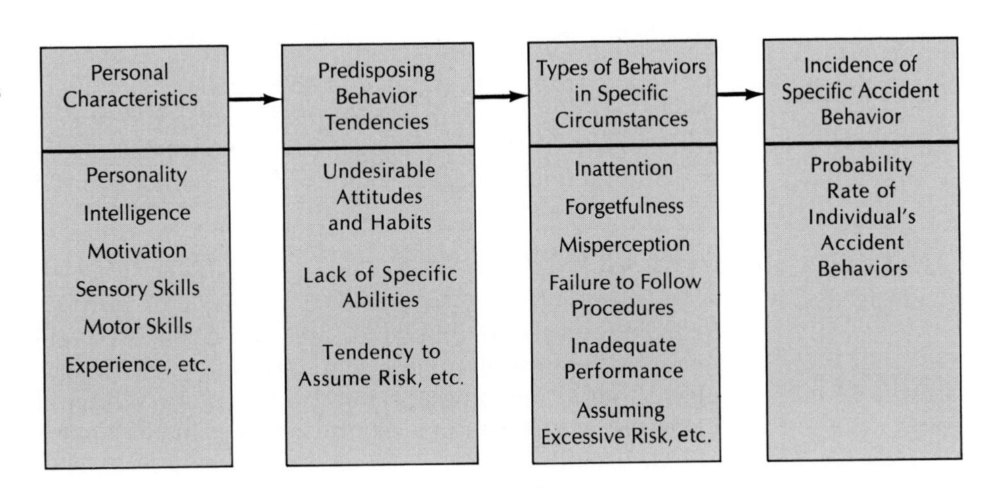

different patterns might be found with different jobs, this age factor seems to be a fairly general one.

Perceptual Versus Motor Skills

One researcher concludes that "where [a worker's] perceptual skill is equal to, or higher than, his motor skill, the employee is a relatively safe worker. But where the perception level is *lower* than the motor level, the employee is accident prone and his accident proneness becomes greater as this difference increases."[33] This theory seems to be a twist on the "look before you leap" theme; a worker who reacts quicker than he or she can perceive is more likely to have accidents.

Vocational Interests

In the Strong-Campbell Vocational Interest Inventory (discussed in Chapter 5), there are scales for, among other things, aviator and banker. One researcher equated "adventuresomeness" with the aviator scale and "cautiousness" with the banker scale. He then developed an "accident-proneness" index by subtracting the second from the first. Then, in a study of both hazardous and nonhazardous jobs in a food-processing plant, he found that employees with high accident-proneness scores had higher accident rates on *both* the hazardous and nonhazardous jobs.

In summary, these findings do not provide a complete list of the personal traits that have been found to be related to higher accident rates. Some researchers, for example, believe that accident proneness is a type of deviant behavior that is characterized by impulsiveness and is found in *all* accident-prone people.[34] What they *do* suggest is that *for specific jobs* it seems to be possible to identify accident-prone individuals and to screen them out.

▶ How to Prevent Accidents

BASIC APPROACHES TO PREVENTING ACCIDENTS

The National Safety Council says that accident prevention depends on the three E's—engineering, education, and enforcement: The job should be *engineered* for safety, employees should be *educated* in safe procedures; and safety rules should be *enforced*.[35] But, in practice, accident prevention boils down to two basic activities: reducing unsafe conditions and reducing unsafe acts.

REDUCING UNSAFE CONDITIONS

Reducing unsafe conditions is, first, a job for safety engineers: Their job is to remove or reduce physical hazards. However, all supervisors and managers can play a role in reducing unsafe conditions. Use a brief checklist like the one in Figure 18.5. The Self-inspection Checklist in the appendix to this chapter can also be useful.

REDUCING UNSAFE ACTS THROUGH SELECTION AND PLACEMENT

Company safety rules, posted in a highly visible form, play a useful role in plant accident prevention programs.

One way to reduce accidents is to screen out accident-prone persons before they are hired. Accidents are similar to other types of poor performance. You should therefore be interested in screening out these people, just as you might want to screen out applicants who are potentially "short tenure," "theft prone," or "low performers." We discussed the techniques for doing so in Chapters 4 to 6.

Remember that the Americans with Disabilities Act (which went into effect in 1992 for employers of 25 or more) has particular relevance for safety-related screening decisions. For example, many employers used to routinely inquire about applicants' worker's compensation history prior to hiring, in part to avoid habitual worker's compensation recipients and (perhaps) in part to avoid hiring accident-prone individuals. Today, under the ADA, it is unlawful to inquire about an applicant's prior worker's compensation injuries and claims in order to screen out prior claimants. Similarly, you cannot ask applicants whether they have a disability nor can you require applicants to take tests that tend to screen out those with disabilities. However, you can ask whether an applicant has the ability to perform a job and even ask "Do you know of any reason why you would not be able to perform the various functions of the job you are seeking?"[36]

Given that caveat, psychologists have still had some success in screening out individuals who might be accident prone for some specific job. The basic technique involves identifying the human trait (such as visual skill) that might be related to accidents on the job. Then determine whether scores (on this trait) are indeed related to accidents on the job.[37] For example:

> *Emotional stability and personality tests.* Psychological tests—especially tests of emotional stability—have been used to screen out accident-prone taxicab drivers. Here the test was especially effective when administered under disturbing and distracting conditions. In this case, researchers found that taxi drivers who made five or more errors on such tests averaged three accidents, while those who made fewer than five averaged only 1.3 accidents.[38]
>
> *Measures of muscular coordination.* We also know that *coordination* is a predictor of safety for certain jobs. In one study, more than 600 employees were divided into two groups according to test scores on coordination tests. Here it was found that the poorest quarter had 51% more accidents than those in the better three quarters.[39]
>
> *Tests of visual skills.* Good vision plays a part in preventing accidents in many occupations, including driving and operating machines. In a study (in a paper mill) 52 accident-free employees were compared with 52 accident-prone employees. Here the researcher found that 63% of the no-accident group passed a vision test, while only 33% of the accident group passed it.[40]

In summary, Professor Norman Maier concludes that:

> Of great practical importance is the fact that there is a definite relationship between these accident-proneness tests and proficiency on the job. By selecting employees who do well—that is, score low—on accident-proneness tests, managers can reduce accidents and improve the caliber of the employees at the same time.[41]

Genetic Screening for Employment Purposes

Some have proposed using genetic screening for reducing injuries and disease at work. This approach, which uses genetic tests, is based on the belief that individual differences in susceptibility to toxic exposure exists—that, in other words, some people are just genetically more susceptible to, say, chemical pollutants than are others. Genetic tests would provide information that is predictive of an individual's health status on the job.

However, genetic screening on the job will be slow to evolve for two reasons. First, there is strong evidence that genetic differences are distributed unequally across different ethnic populations, so genetic screening would elicit charges of employment discrimination. Second, genetic testing may run afoul of other legal roadblocks. For example, genetic monitoring of employees for changes in genetic material as a result of repeated work exposure may jeopardize an employer's defense by showing a consistent, incremental pattern of genetic impairment over years of exposure to a toxic agent. In summary, as one expert concludes, "the foreseeable future promises far-reaching scientific advances that will permit the employment applications of G.S. practices." However, whether such applications will ever become widespread remains a matter of conjecture.[42]

REDUCING UNSAFE ACTS THROUGH PROPAGANDA

Many organizations use propaganda of one sort or another—such as safety posters—as part (or all) of their safety programs. Such posters (and other propaganda) can be useful. In one study, for example, their use apparently increased safe behavior by more than 20%.[43]

On the other hand, you can't substitute posters for a comprehensive safety program; instead, they should be used in conjunction with other attempts to reduce unsafe conditions and acts. For example, key posters to your own safety program. Thus, if you are emphasizing protective gloves this month, the "poster of the month" should underscore this emphasis. It is also important to change posters frequently.[44]

REDUCING UNSAFE ACTS THROUGH TRAINING

We also know that experience reduces accidents. Since training can provide a substitute for experience, it follows that safety training can also reduce accidents. Such training is especially appropriate with new employees. You should instruct them in safe practices and procedures, warn them of potential hazards, and work on developing their predisposition toward safety. OSHA has published two booklets, "Training Requirements Under OSHA" and "Teaching Safety and Health in the Workplace," that are useful here.

REDUCING UNSAFE ACTS THROUGH POSITIVE REINFORCEMENT

Introduction

Safety programs based on positive reinforcement have improved safety at work.[45] One program was instituted in a wholesale bakery that bakes, wraps and transports pastry products to retail outlets nationwide.[46] An analysis of the safety-related conditions existing in the plant before the study suggested a number of areas that needed improvement. For example, new hires received no formal safety training and safety was rarely mentioned on a day-to-day basis. Commercial safety posters were placed at the entrance to the work area and on a bulletin board in the dining room but were often not updated for six months. No single person was responsible for safety. Similarly, employees received little or no positive reinforcement for performing safely. Managers said little or nothing to employees who took the time to act safely. Although the accident rate had been climbing, many employees had yet to experience an injury because of performing unsafely, so this "punishment" was also missing.

The Safety Program

The safety program stressed positive reinforcement and training. A reasonable goal (in terms of observed incidents performed safely) was set and communicated to workers to ensure that they knew what was expected of them in terms of good performance. Next came a training phase. Here employees were presented with safety information during a 30-minute training session. Employees were shown pairs of slides (35mm transparencies) which depicted scenes that were staged in the plant. In one transparency, for example, the wrapping supervisor was shown climbing over a conveyor; the parallel slide illustrated the supervisor walking around the conveyor. After viewing an unsafe act, employees were asked to describe verbally what was wrong ("what's unsafe here?"). Then, once the problem had been aired, the same incident was again shown performed in a safe manner and the safe-conduct rule was explicitly stated ("go around, not over or under conveyors").

At the conclusion of the training phase the employees were shown a graph with their pretraining safety record (in terms of observed incidents performed safely) plotted. They were encouraged to consider increasing their performance to the new safety goal for the following reasons: for their own protection; to decrease costs for the company; and, last, to help the plant get out of last place in the safety ranking of the parent company. Then the graph and a list of safety rules (do's and don'ts) were posted in a conspicuous place in the work area.

Reinforcement and Safety

The graph then played an important role in the final, "positive reinforcement" phase of the study. Whenever observers walked through the plant collecting safety data, they posted on the graph the percentage of incidents they had seen performed safely by the group as a whole, thus providing the workers with feedback on their safety performance. Workers could then compare their current safety performance with both their previous performance and with their assigned goal. In addition, supervisors praised workers when they performed selected incidents safely. Safety in the plaint subsequently improved markedly.[47]

REDUCING UNSAFE ACTS THROUGH TOP MANAGEMENT COMMITMENT

According to one researcher, "one of the most consistent findings in the literature is that in factories having successful safety programs, there was a strong management commitment to safety."[48] In practice, this commitment manifests itself in top management's being personally involved in safety activities on a routine basis; giving safety matters high priority in company meetings and production scheduling; giving the company safety officer high rank and status; and including safety training in new workers' training.

SUMMARY: HOW TO REDUCE ACCIDENTS

1. Check for and if possible *remove unsafe conditions*; use a checklist like the one presented in the appendix to the chapter. If the hazard cannot be removed, guard against it (for instance, with guardrails) or if necessary use personal protective equipment such as goggles or safety shoes.
2. Through *selection*, try to screen out employees who might be accident prone for the job in question (but remember the requirements of the Americans with Disabilities Act).
3. Establish a *safety policy* emphasizing that the firm will do everything practical to eliminate or reduce accidents and injuries and emphasizing the importance of accident and injury prevention at your firm.
4. Set specific *loss control goals*. Analyze the number of accidents and safety incidents and then set specific safety goals to be achieved, for instance in terms of frequency of lost-time injuries per number of full-time employees.[49]
5. Encourage and *train your employees* to be safety conscious; show them that top management and all supervisors are serious about safety.
6. Enforce *safety rules*.
7. Conduct *safety and health inspections* regularly. Also investigate all accidents and "near misses" and have a system in place for letting employees notify management about hazardous conditions.[50]

CONTROLLING WORKER'S COMPENSATION COSTS

According to one report, worker's compensation costs soared over the 1980s, with the average claim costing $34,000 in 1990, twice the average cost of a claim in 1980.[51] While these costs are generally paid by the employer's insurance carrier, the insurance premiums themselves are proportional to the firm's worker's compensation experience rate. Thus, the more worker's compensation claims a firm has, the more the firm will pay in insurance premiums.

There are several aspects to reducing worker's compensation claims:

Before the accident. The appropriate time to begin "controlling" worker's compensation claims is before the accident happens, not after. This involves taking all the steps previously summarized. For example, remove unsafe conditions, screen out employees who might be accident prone for the job in question (remembering the ADA, however), and establish a safety policy and loss control goals.

After the accident. The occupational injury or illness can obviously be a traumatic event for the employee, and how the employer handles it can influence the injured worker's reaction to it. From the employee's point of view, he or she is going to have specific needs and specific questions, such as where to go for medical help, and whether or not he or she will be paid for any time off. It is usually at this point that the employee decides whether or not to retain a worker's compensation attorney to plead his or her case. Employers are therefore admonished to provide first aid and make sure the worker gets quick medical attention; make it clear that you are interested in the injured worker and his or her fears and questions; document the accident; file any required accident reports; and encourage a speedy return to work.[52]

Facilitate the employee's return to work. According to one discussion of managing worker's compensation costs:

> Perhaps the most important and effective thing an employer can do to reduce costs is to develop an aggressive return-to-work program, including making light-duty work available. Surely the best solution to the current workers' compensation crisis, for both the employer and the employee, is for the worker to become a productive member of the company again instead of a helpless victim living on benefits.[53]

EMPLOYEE HEALTH: PROBLEMS AND REMEDIES[54]

ALCOHOLISM AND SUBSTANCE ABUSE

Among the most frustrating health problems today are the problems of worker alcoholism, drug addiction, and substance abuse—all of which seem to be increasing.[55]

Alcoholism is a serious and widespread disease, one not confined to "skid row" individuals. In fact, 50% of alcoholics are women, 25% are white-collar workers, 45% are professional/managerial personnel, 37% are high school graduates, and 50% have completed or attended college. Most are members of households. Some experts estimate that as many as 50% of all "problem employees" in industry are actually alcoholics. In one auto assembly plant, 48.6% of the grievances filed over the course of one year were alcohol-related.[56] In the United States alone substance abusers cost employers about $30 billion in lost production alone and account for 40% of all industrial fatalities.

The use of drugs, especially in the workplace, is a growing concern for U.S. companies, and has led to increased numbers of alcohol and drug abuse counseling programs.

The effects of alcoholism on the worker and the work are severe.[57] Both the quality and quantity of the work decline sharply. A form of "on-the-job absenteeism" occurs as efficiency declines. The alcoholic's on-the-job accidents do *not* appear to increase significantly, apparently because he or she becomes much more cautious (but his or her effectiveness suffers as well). However, the *off*-the-job accident rate is three to four times higher than for nonalcoholics. Contrary to popular opinion, turnover among alcoholics is not unusually high. The morale of other workers is affected as they have to do the work of their alcoholic peer.

Recognizing the alcoholic on the job is also a major problem. The early symptoms are often similar to those of other problems and are thus hard to classify. The supervisor is not a psychiatrist, and without specialized training, identifying—and dealing with—the alcoholic is a difficult task.

A chart showing observable behavior patterns that indicate alcohol-related problems is presented in Table 18.1. As you can see, alcohol-related problems range from tardiness (in the earliest stages of alcohol abuse) to prolonged unpredictable absences in its later stages.[58]

Traditional Techniques Used to Deal with These Problems

Disciplining, discharge, in-house counseling, and referral to an outside agency are the four traditional techniques for dealing with these problems. (Discipline short of discharge is used more often with alcoholics than for dealing with drug problems or emotional illness. Discharge is frequently used to deal with alcoholism and drug problems; it is almost never used in the case of serious emotional illness.)[59]

In-house counseling, one example of an *employee assistance program*, is used often in dealing with alcoholics and those with emotional disorders. In most

TABLE 18.1 Observable Behavior Patterns

STAGE	ABSENTEEISM	GENERAL BEHAVIOR	JOB PERFORMANCE
I Early	Tardiness Quits early Absence from work situations ("I drink to relieve tension")	Complaints from fellow employees for not doing his or her share Overreaction Complaints of not "feeling well" Makes untrue statements	Misses deadlines Commits errors (frequently) Lower job efficiency Criticism from the boss
II Middle	Frequent days off for vague or implausible reasons ("I feel guilty about sneaking drinks"; "I have tremors")	Marked changes Undependable statements Avoids fellow employees Borrows money from fellow employees Exaggerates work accomplishments Frequent hospitalization Minor injuries on the job (repeatedly)	General deterioration Cannot concentrate Occasional lapse of memory Warning from boss
III Late Middle	Frequent days off; several days at a time Does not return from lunch ("I don't feel like eating"; "I don't want to talk about it"; "I like to drink alone")	Aggressive and belligerent behavior Domestic problems interfere with work Financial difficulties (garnishments, and so on) More frequent hospitalization Resignation: does not want to discuss problems Problems with the laws in the community	Far below expectation Punitive disciplinary action

TABLE 18.1 (continued)

IV Approaching Terminal Stage	Prolonged unpre–dictable absences ("My job interferes with my drinking")	Drinking on the job (probably) Completely undependable Repeated hospitalization Serious financial problems Serious family problems: divorce	Uneven Generally incompetent Faces termination or hospitalization

Note: Based on content analysis of files of recovered alcoholics in five organizations. From *Managing and Employing the Handicapped: The Untapped Potential,* by Gopal C. Pati and John I. Adkins, Jr., with Glenn Morrison (Lake Forest, IL: Brace-Park, Human Resource Press, 1981).

Source: Gopal C. Pati and John I. Adkins, Jr., The Employer's Role in Alcoholism Assistance," Vol. 62, no. 7 (July 1983), p. 570.

cases the counseling is offered by the personnel department or the company's medical staff. Immediate supervisors who have received special training also provide counseling in many instances.

Many companies use outside agencies such as Alcoholics Anonymous, psychiatrists, and clinics to deal with the problems of alcoholism and emotional illness. Outside agencies are used less often in the case of drug problems.

Trice[60] suggests a number of specific actions managers can take to deal with employee alcoholism—actions which all involve supervisory training or company policy. He says supervisors should be trained to identify the alcoholic and the problem he or she creates. Employers should also establish a company policy that recognizes alcoholism as a health problem and places it within the firm's health plan.

The Drug-Free Workplace Act

Today, because of the seriousness of the problem and the passage of a new federal law, most employers are taking additional steps to deal with alcohol and substance abuse on the job. The federal Drug-Free Workplace Act of 1988 became effective on March 18, 1989. It requires employers with federal government contracts or grants to ensure a drug-free workplace by taking (and certifying that they have taken) a number of steps. Specifically, to be eligible for contract awards or grants, employers must agree to:

Publish a policy prohibiting the unlawful manufacture, distribution, dispensing, possession, or use of controlled substances in the workplace.

Establish a drug-free awareness program that informs employees about the dangers of workplace drug abuse.

Inform employees that they are required, as a condition of employment, not only to abide by the employer's policy, but also to report any criminal convictions for drug-related activities in the workplace.

Notify the federal contracting or granting agency of any criminal convictions of employees for illegal drug activity in the workplace.

Take appropriate personnel action against any employee convicted of a criminal drug offense.

Make a "good faith" effort to maintain a drug-free workplace by complying with the law's requirements.[61]

GUIDELINES FOR DEALING WITH SUBSTANCE ABUSE

Beyond this, there are a number of guidelines to follow. First, develop a *formal written policy* on substance abuse on the job. This should clearly state management's philosophy and position on drug abuse and on the use and possession of illegal drugs on company premises and set standards for appropriate conduct both on and off the job. The policy should also list the methods (such as urinalysis) that might be used to determine the causes of poor performance and state the company's views on rehabilitation, including workplace counseling. Specific penalties for policy violations should be noted. This policy should then be communicated to all employees.

Supervisors, says one expert, should be the company's first line of defense in combating drug abuse in the workplace but should not try to become company detectives or medical diagnosticians. Guidelines supervisors should follow include:

If an employee appears to be under the influence of drugs or alcohol, ask how the employee feels and look for signs of impairment such as slurred speech. An employee judged to be unfit for duty may be sent home, but not fired on the spot.

Make a written record of your observations and follow up each incident. In addition to issuing a written reprimand, managers should inform workers of the number of warnings the company will tolerate before requiring termination.

Troubled employees should be referred to the company's employee assistance program.

Additional steps the employer can take to combat substance abuse on the job include *administering urine tests, conducting workplace inspections* (searching employees for illegal substances), and *using undercover agents* (which should be used only as a last resort, according to one expert).[62]

Legal Considerations

Guidelines such as those just listed may entail legal risks: Employees have sued successfully for invasion of privacy, wrongful discharge, defamation, and illegal searches. Therefore, before implementing any drug control program:

Ask: *How would you inform workers about your substance abuse policy*? Providing employees with adequate notice of rules and procedures for handling drug-related problems is "critical to avoiding wrongful discharge allegations." Use employee handbooks, bulletin board postings, pay inserts, and the like to publicize your substance abuse plans.

Ask: *What testing, such as urinalysis, will be required of prospective and current employees*? If you decide to implement drug-screening programs, you have to be careful to choose appropriate tests that include reliable procedures for analysis, verification, and retesting. The conditions under which testing may occur and the procedures for handling employees who refuse to be tested should be explained.

Ask: *What accommodations would you make for employees who voluntarily seek treatment for drug or alcohol problems?* Since substance abuse is considered a physical handicap under federal and some state laws, you may be required to make "reasonable accommodations" for employees who enter alcohol or drug treatment programs.

Ask: *Is supervisory training provided?* Since managers are often the first to observe signs of trouble on the job, they should be taught how to recognize and document possible substance-abuse–related problems.

Other factors must be considered. For example, searches on company property even without prior notice may be legal so long as they are conducted in a reasonable manner and avoid violating employees' privacy expectations. Similarly, conducting internal undercover investigations may be legal and even advised if there are repeated reports of employees using or selling drugs on the job. However, any such activities may trigger employee lawsuits and should be conducted only after a thorough review of their legal implications.[63]

THE PROBLEMS OF JOB STRESS AND BURNOUT

Sometimes, problems such as alcoholism and drug abuse are a consequence of stress, especially *job stress.* Here job-related factors such as overwork, relocation, and problems with customers eventually put the person under so much stress that some pathological reaction such as drug abuse results.

There are two main sources of job stress: environmental and personal.[64] First, a variety of external, *environmental factors* can lead to job stress. These include your work schedule, pace of work, job security, route to and from work, and the number and nature of customers or clients. However, no two people will react to the same job in the very same way, since *personal factors* also influence stress. For example, type A personalities—people who are workaholics and who feel driven to always be on time and meet deadlines—normally place themselves under greater stress than do others. Similarly, your tolerance for ambiguity, patience, self-esteem, health and exercise, work, and sleep patterns can also affect how you react to stress. Add to job stress the stress caused by nonjob problems like divorce, and, as you might imagine, many workers are "accidents waiting to happen."

Regardless of its source, job stress has serious consequences for both the employee and the organization. The human consequences of job stress include anxiety, depression, anger, and various physical consequences, such as cardiovascular disease, headaches, and accidents. In some cases it can lead to other human consequences, including drug abuse, over and under eating, and poor interpersonal relations. Stress also has serious consequences for the organization, including reductions in the quantity and quality of job performance, increased absenteeism and turnover, and increased grievances.

Yet stress is not necessarily dysfunctional. Some people, for example, only work well under a little stress and find they are more productive as a deadline approaches. Others find that stress may result in a search that leads to a better job or to a career that makes more sense, given the person's aptitudes. A modest level of stress may even lead to more creativity if a competitive situation results in new ideas being generated.[65] As a rule, however, employers don't worry about the sorts of modest stress that lead to such positive consequences. Instead, and for obvious reasons, they focus on dysfunctional stress and its negative consequences.

There are a number of things you can do to alleviate stress, ranging from commonsense remedies such as getting more sleep and eating better to more exotic remedies such as biofeedback and meditation. Finding a more suitable job, getting counseling, and planning and organizing each day's activities are other sensible responses.[66] In his book *Stress and the Manager*, Dr. Karl Albrecht suggests the following to reduce stress on the job.[67]

> Building rewarding, pleasant, cooperative relationships with as many of your colleagues and employees as you can.
>
> Don't bite off more than you can chew.
>
> Build an especially effective and supportive relationship with your boss.
>
> Understand his or her problems and help the boss to understand yours.
>
> Negotiate realistic deadlines on important projects with your boss. Be prepared to propose deadlines yourself, instead of having them imposed on you.
>
> Study the future. Learn as much as you can about likely coming events and get as much lead time as you can to prepare for them.
>
> Find time every day for detachment and relaxation.
>
> Take a walk now and then to keep your body refreshed and alert.
>
> Make a noise survey of your office area and find ways to reduce unnecessary noise.
>
> Get away from your office from time to time for a change of scene and a change of mind.
>
> Reduce the amount of trivia to which you give your attention. Delegate routine paperwork to others whenever possible.
>
> Limit interruptions. Try to schedule certain periods of "uninterruptibility" each day and conserve other periods for your own purposes.
>
> Don't put off dealing with distasteful problems.
>
> Make a constructive "worry list." Write down the problems that concern you and beside each write down what you're going to do about it, so that none of the problems will be hovering around the edges of your consciousness.

The organization and its human resources specialists and supervisors also play a big role in identifying and remedying job stress. For the supervisor, this typically involves monitoring each subordinate's performance to identify symptoms of stress, and then informing the person of the organizational remedies that may be available, such as job transfers or counseling. The personnel specialist's role includes using attitude surveys to identify organizational sources of stress; refining selection and placement procedures to ensure effective person–job match; and providing career planning aimed at ensuring that the employee moves toward a job that makes sense in terms of his or her aptitudes.

BURNOUT

burnout
The total depletion of physical and mental resources caused by excessive striving to reach some unrealistic work-related goal.

Dr. Herbert Freudenberger, an expert on the overachiever, says that today many people may be falling victim to **burnout**—the total depletion of physical and mental resources caused by excessive striving to reach some unrealistic work-related goal. Burnout, he contends, is often the end result of too much job stress, especially when that stress is combined with the fact that you become preoccupied with attaining unattainable work-related goals. In his book, *Burnout: How to Beat the High Cost of Success*, Freudenberger lists some of these other signs of possible impending burnout:[68]

You are unable to relax.

You identify so closely with your activities that when they fall apart you do too.

The positions you worked so hard to attain often seem meaningless now.

You are working more now but enjoying it less.

Your need for a particular crutch such as smoking, liquor, or tranquilizers is increasing.

You are constantly irritable, and family and friends are often commenting that you don't look well.

You would describe yourself as a workaholic and constantly strive to obtain your work-related goals to the exclusion of almost all outside interest.

Who Suffers from Burnout?

Burnout, Freudenberger says, is mostly limited to dynamic goal-oriented individuals who are overdedicated to whatever they undertake. The potential burnout victim thrives on intensity, often setting up his or her life to lurch from crisis to crisis, deadline to deadline. Burnout victims usually don't lead well-balanced lives, in that virtually all their energies are focused on achieving their work-related goals. The burnout victim is usually a workaholic from whom the constant stress of seeking an unattainable goal to the exclusion of other activities can lead to physical and perhaps mental collapse.

What, then, can a candidate for burnout do? Here are some suggestions:

Break your patterns. First, survey how you spend your time. For example, are you doing a variety of things or the same one over and over? The more well rounded your life is, the more protected you are against burnout. If you've stopped trying new activities, start them again—for instance, travel or new hobbies.

Get away from it all periodically. Schedule occasional periods of introspection into your life, during which you can get away from your usual routine, perhaps alone, to get a perspective on where you are and where you are going.

Reassess your goals in terms of their intrinsic worth. Are the goals you've set for yourself attainable? Are they really worth the sacrifices you'll have to make?

Think about your work. Could you do as good a job without being so intense or by also pursuing some outside interests?

Reduce stress. Organize your time more effectively, build a better relationship with your boss, negotiate realistic deadlines, find time during the day for detachment and relaxation, reduce unnecessary noise around your office, and limit interruptions.

Avoiding Stress-Related Disability Claims

In addition to the obvious humanitarian reasons for reducing work stress, there are good economic and legal reasons for doing so, too. It has been estimated that stress-related disability claims account for 11% of all occupational disease claims and, in addition, courts are increasingly giving stress-related claims a sympathetic ear. As of now, only Florida, Georgia, and Kansas do not compensate employees disabled by stress.[69] Most other states do compensate workers for stress-related claims as long as the source of the stress is at least unusual (such as inconsistent supervision). But in some states "unusual circumstances" are not even required: In one case the employee received worker's compensation for suffering a mental breakdown after assuming new duties.[70] Other jurisdictions around the country have awarded worker's compensation for stress resulting from inconsistent job performance evaluations, criticism of job performance by supervisors, and lack of adequate communication. Minimizing such claims usually begins with good supervision and includes, at a minimum, the following steps:

Adequately train supervisors. Make them aware of the possible disability implications of creating stressful situations. Train them in interpersonal skills, performance evaluation, communication, discipline and discharge, and other matters like conflict management.

Adequate communications. Let employees know that channels of communication are open and that if they have a problem it can be brought to top management's attention.

Use attitude surveys. Use a survey to monitor attitudes and in particular supervisor-caused stress.

Good hiring. Make sure you do your best to hire the right people for the right job and to make sure they have realistic previews of what the job entails. Check references carefully, and watch how your applicant acts in the interview, since the interview itself is a stressful situation.

ASBESTOS EXPOSURE AT WORK

There are four major occupational respiratory diseases caused by asbestos, silica, lead, and carbon dioxide. Of these, asbestos has become a major concern, in part because of publicity surrounding asbestos in buildings such as schools constructed before the mid-1970s. Major efforts are now underway to rid these buildings of the cancer-causing asbestos.

As with other respiratory diseases at work, the problem with asbestos derives from its presence in the workplace air. The heaviest exposures were to the tens of thousands of workers engaged in general building renovation. Other at-risk workers include those involved with automatic brake and clutch repair and those in the tire industry, which uses talc, a product with asbestos-like minerals.

Sensing a serious problem, the U.S. Labor Department issued new rules to sharply lower worker exposure to asbestos. They dropped the allowable level of asbestos in the workplace air from 2 fibers a cubic centimeter to 0.2 fibers, averaged over an eight-hour day. The new standard is expected to reduce the risk of worker cancer from 64 per 1000 workers to about 6.7 per 1000; the risk of asbestosis is expected to fall from 50 per 1000 workers to 5 per 1000. Unions are pushing for further reductions to 0.1 fibers per cubic centimeter.

OSHA standards require several actions with respect to preventing asbestos-related disease. They require that companies monitor the air whenever an employer expects the level of asbestos to rise to one-half the allowable limit. (You would therefore have to monitor if you expected asbestos levels of 0.1 fibers per cubic centimeters in this case.) Second, engineering controls—walls, special filters, and so forth—are required to maintain an asbestos level that complies with OSHA standards. Respirators can only be used if additional efforts are still required to achieve compliance.

Unlike obvious workplace hazards such as broken guardrails, the effects of respiratory hazards like asbestos are insidious. In the case of asbestosis or asbestos-related cancer, the effects may not show up for years, if ever. The insidious nature of these health hazards is thus one reason to reduce their occurrence in your firm; the practical need to comply with OSHA standards is another. A major lawsuit—the National Tire Workers Litigation Project—aimed at suing on behalf of tire workers with asbestosis provides another incentive for reducing this occupational health hazard.

VIDEO DISPLAY HEALTH PROBLEMS AND HOW TO AVOID THEM

Many workers today—from stockbrokers and editors to accountants and clerks—must spend hours each day working with video display terminals (VDTs); this is creating a new set of health problems at work. According to a study by the National Institute for Occupational Safety and Health, short-term eye problems like burning, itching, and tearing as well as eye strain and eye soreness are common complaints of video display operators. Surveys have found that 47% to 76% of operators complain of such problems, and while no permanent vision problems have surfaced yet, long-term studies are under way. The institute's studies have also addressed the possible radiation, muscular, and stress problems of working at a video display. With respect to radiation, researchers conclude that "the VDT does not present a radiation hazard to the employees working at or near a terminal."[71] (However, that point today remains a matter of heated debate). A new NIOSH study calmed some VDT-related fears when it concluded that pregnant women who use computer monitors do not run any greater risk of having miscarriages than do women who are not exposed to VDTs.[72]

But backaches and neckaches *are* widespread among display users. This is often because employees try to compensate for display problems like glare and immovable keyboards by maneuvering into awkward body positions. Researchers also found that employees who used VDTs and had heavy work loads were prone to psychological distress like anxiety, irritability, and fatigue.

The institute has therefore provided general recommendations regarding the use of VDTs. These can be summarized as follows:

1. Give employees rest breaks. The institute recommends a 15-minute rest break after 2 hours of continuous VDT work for operators under moderate work loads and 15-minute breaks every hour for those with heavy work loads.
2. Design the maximum flexibility into the work station so that it can be adapted to the individual operator. For example, use movable keyboards, adjustable chairs with midback supports, and a video display in which screen height and position are independently adjustable.
3. Reduce glare with things such as shades over windows, proper positioning of terminal screen hoods, antiglare VDT screen filters, and recessed or indirect lighting.
4. VDT workers should have a complete preplacement vision exam to ensure properly corrected vision for reduced visual strain.

Many VDT vision problems can be reduced by using the right equipment and a little common sense. Some simple techniques are summarized in Figure 18.7. As you can see, the basic worker-task relationship is fairly straightforward when paperwork tasks are involved, since the light just bounces from the ceiling to the paper and then to the worker's eyes. But once a VDT is added, your employee may find himself or herself dealing with direct glare as well as reflected glare in addition to the visual demands of watching the small screen. Therefore, as Figure 18.7 illustrates, adjustable stands, partitions, venetian blind-

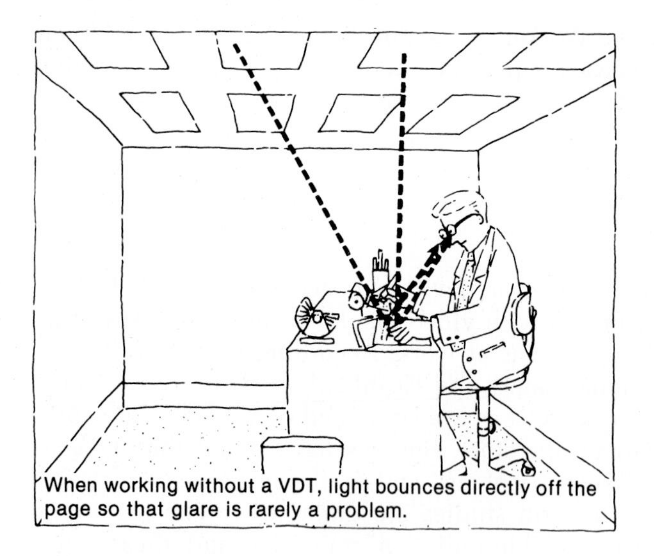

When working without a VDT, light bounces directly off the page so that glare is rarely a problem.

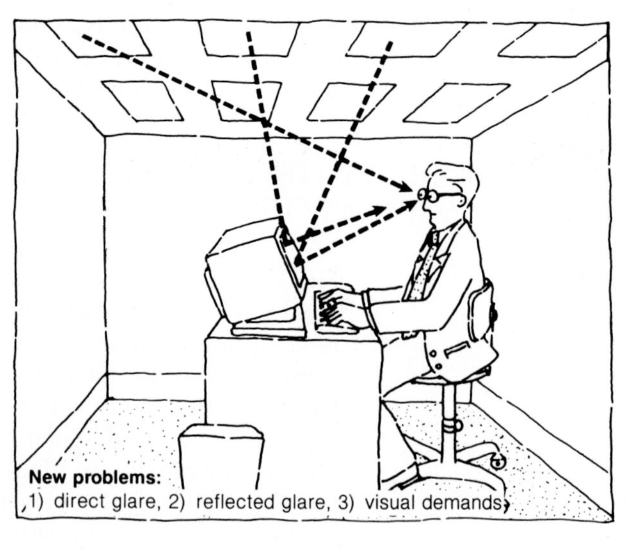

New problems:
1) direct glare, 2) reflected glare, 3) visual demands

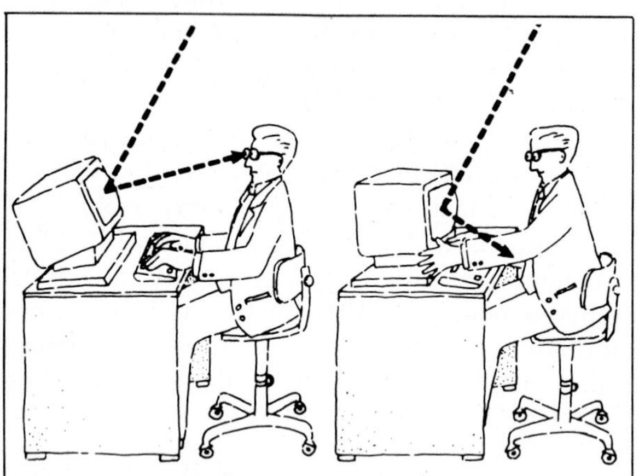

The fixed position of the VDT on the left causes light from an overhead light source to reflect off the task surface and into the operator's eyes. By installing an adjustable stand, as shown on the right, the VDT can be repositioned so reflected light misses the operator's eyes.

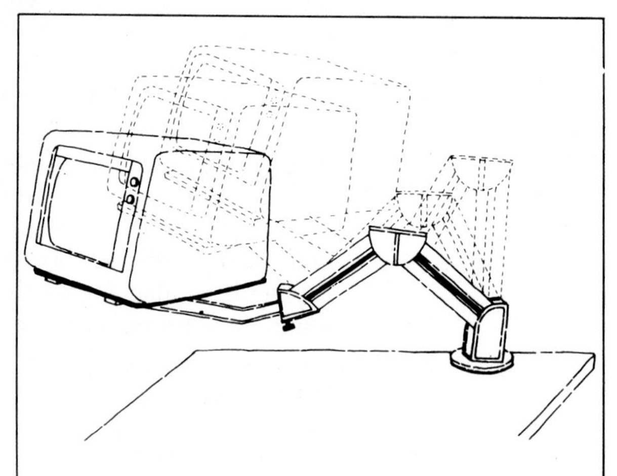

The most effective VDT stands permit almost unlimited adjustment of task position.

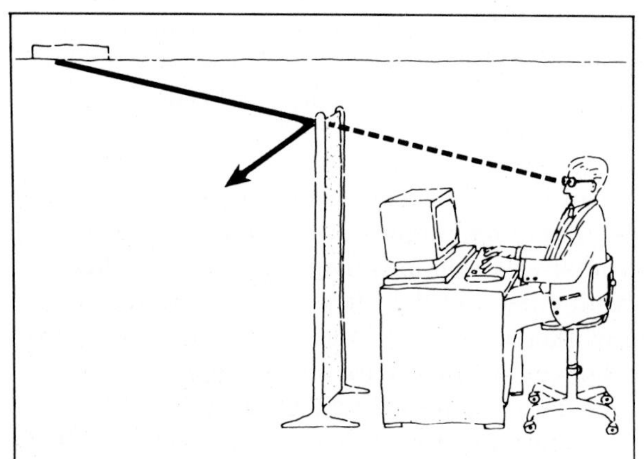

Floor-mounted partitions can be used to block light from light sources, but other corrective measures usually produce more effective results.

FIGURE 18.7
Simple Techniques for Reducing VDT Vision Problems

Source: Bureau of National Affairs, "Solutions to VDT Viewing Problems," *Datagraph*, November 5, 1987, pp. 356, 357.

type window controls, screen filters, and fully adjustable VDT stands can help minimize VDT-caused visual problems.[73]

AIDS AND THE WORKPLACE

As everyone knows by now, AIDS—Acquired Immune Deficiency Syndrome—is a disease that undermines the body's immune system, leaving the person susceptible to a wide range of serious and usually fatal diseases.

Some of the most crucial AIDS-related questions employers must deal with concern their legal responsibilities in dealing with AIDS sufferers. While case law is only now evolving on this issue, several tentative conclusions are warranted. First, an employer cannot single out an employee to be tested for AIDS because to do so would be to subject the person to discriminatory treatment. Similarly, you can probably require a physical exam that includes an AIDS test as a condition of employment but refusing to hire the person because of positive test results could put you at risk of a handicap discrimination suit. Mandatory leave cannot be required of a person with AIDS unless work performance has deteriorated, and preemployment inquiries about AIDS (such as inquiries about any other illnesses or disabilities) would not be advisable given the prohibitions of the Americans with Disabilities Act. Providing sympathy and support and making reasonable accommodations to persons with AIDS, and using education and counseling to deal with the fears of the person's coworkers seem to be the only concrete prescriptions for dealing with the concerns this disease will elicit at work.[74]

Developing an AIDS Policy

From a practical point of view your procedure for dealing with AIDS will usually begin with a statement of your firm's AIDS policy.

The purpose of the AIDS policy is twofold: to reassure employees regarding the impossibility of spreading AIDS through casual contact, and to lay out the legal rights of employees who are diagnosed with an AIDS-related condition. The policy therefore usually contains a medical overview of what we know about AIDS and lists a number of supervisors' responsibilities such as maintaining confidentiality of all medical conditions and records.[75]

WORKPLACE SMOKING

The Nature of the Problem

Smoking is a serious problem for employees and employers. The congressional Office of Technology Assessment estimates that each employee-smoker costs an employer between $2,000 and $5,000 yearly, for instance.[76] These costs derive from higher health and fire insurance, as well as increased absenteeism and reduced productivity (which occurs when, for instance, a smoker takes a ten-minute break to finish a cigarette down the hall). Studies even show that for some reason smokers have a significantly greater risk of occupational accidents than do nonsmokers, as well as much higher absenteeism rates. In a study of

COMPUTER APPLICATIONS IN OCCUPATIONAL SAFETY: USING COMPUTERS TO MONITOR SAFETY

Companies that must comply with state and federal laws (OSHA,[1] RCRA,[2] OSHA Hazard Communication Law,[3] and SARA[4]) are obligated to file federal reports, monitor employee exposure to various hazards to note trends, and provide employees with information on hazards in their workplaces. Computers can assist in all three areas.

Reporting

Most federal forms can be formatted and formulated on a company's computer so that only the raw data need to be entered. The computer will perform the instructed calculations and print out the results in an acceptable format. If a piece of information has been input in error, only the figure needs to be changed. Recalculations are automatic. With some forms, the typing of results takes several hours. This task is completed in minutes with a computer. One of several programs available for providing the correct information in proper sequence is PRO–AM, by Safety, Inc.

Monitoring

Computers can track personal exposure level (PEL) for noise, particulates, vapors, or other contaminates for a given location, giving timely warnings of trigger points. A dosimeter sensor can be plugged into a personal computer to translate readings on an hourly basis. Not only does this protect, say, the hearing of workers, it can also spot equipment that needs servicing if, for example, a given decibel level indicates increased friction. Trends of various hazards can also be plotted for work redesign to make the workplace safer.

Communicating

The effectiveness of training in any area depends in part on the Hawthorne Effect: the degree to which the student feels that the training is important and accurate. In communicating the hazards of a workplace, employees might not listen because they feel that *they* will not be exposed to those particular hazards, or that they are already careful, or that their work situation does not support those safeguards. If the supervisors push for results to the point of ignoring torn gloves, holes in respirators, inadequate ventilation, or workers who are not wearing safety glasses, then employees will ignore the training. Also, employees may not understand key parts of the training.

Interactive computers can help with some of these problems. If an employee is assigned to work with a hazardous substance that was discussed with her a few weeks before, the knowledge may have become hazy. Access to a personal computer can allow the employee to refresh her memory on how to handle the substance and what to avoid doing. If there are words within the explanation that are not clear, an interactive program will allow the employee to question that word (and any words in the subsequent definition) until she is ready to return to the original explanation. How recently an employee has reviewed the information correlates with the degree of retention, and computer-assisted instruction provides training any time the employee needs help.

[1]Occupational Safety and Health Act, 1970.
[2]Resource Conservation and Recovery Act, 1980.
[3]1986.
[4]Superfund Amendments Reauthorization Act, 1986, which requires Material Safety Data Sheets.

Boston postal workers, this was so even controlling for other factors such as drug use, age, exercise habits, and race.[77] Employers today are also being hit with lawsuits brought by nonsmoking employees who are (perhaps rightfully) concerned with inhaling secondhand smoke. And for the smokers, of course, smoking is associated with numerous health problems. Smoking at work is therefore a serious problem.

What You Can and Cannot Do

Suppose you want to institute a smoking ban, or a policy against hiring any smokers in the future: What are your legal rights? The answer depends on several things, including the state in which you are located, whether or not your firm is unionized, and the details of the situation. Fourteen states regulate smoking in the private sector workplace, and here your position would be stronger if you decided to impose a smoking ban. (States restricting private worksite smoking are Arkansas, Connecticut, Florida, Missouri, Minnesota, Montana, Nebraska, Nevada, New Jersey, New York, Utah, Vermont, Washington, and West Virginia.)[78] There are no hard and fast rules, though. For example, in states in which the termination-at-will doctrine has been modified by the courts, firing an employee who refuses to quit smoking could present legal problems. And a union contract generally means that instituting a smoking ban for unionized employees who formerly were allowed to smoke means altering "conditions of work." It is therefore subject to collective bargaining.

In general, though, you do not have to hire smokers. Specifically, you can deny a job to a smoker as long as you do not use "smoking" as a surrogate for some other kind of discrimination. The EEOC, in other words, says that a policy of not hiring smokers is legal as long as the rules apply to all applicants and employees.[79] You therefore can institute a policy now against hiring people who smoke.

The problem arises, of course, when you try to implement smoking restrictions in a facility where you already have smokers. Here the best advice seems to be to proceed with aid of counsel or one step at a time, starting with restrictions that are not too confining.

Smoking Policies

This notwithstanding, employer smoking bans are on the rise, either because of health concerns, economic concerns, or the fear that nonsmoking employees will themselves sue for a workplace free of secondhand smoke. In one survey of 283 employers, for instance, one-quarter of the organizations polled prohibited smoking anywhere on company premises—up from 14% the previous year. (More than four out of five insurance companies and utilities banned smoking in the workplace.) Beyond that, the number of companies with some type of smoking policies has also shot up, from 16% in 1980 to 60% in 1988.[80]

From a practical point of view most employers probably should be considering some smoking restrictions. As summarized in Figure 18.8, policies can range from total prohibitions down to "smokers and nonsmokers should courteously work out a compromise among themselves."

Policy A

It is the policy of the company to hire nonsmokers only. Smoking is prohibited off the job, and smoking is prohibited on the job.

Policy B

Smoking is prohibited in all areas on company premises.

Policy C

Smoking is prohibited in all areas in company buildings.

Policy D

Smoking is prohibited in all areas in company buildings, with few exceptions. Smoking is permitted in the smoking section of the cafeteria (or room with a similar function in your company, if there is no cafeteria); in specially designated smoking rooms (smoking lounges); and in private offices, which may be designated "smoking permitted" or "no smoking" by the occupant.

Policy E

Smoking is prohibited in all common areas except those designated "smoking permitted." Smoking is permitted in specially designated smoking rooms (smoking lounges).
In open offices and in shared workspace areas where smokers and nonsmokers work together, where smokers' and nonsmokers' preferences are in conflict, employees and management will endeavor to find a satisfactory compromise. On failure to find a compromise, the preferences of the nonsmoker will prevail.
Private offices may be designated "smoking permitted" or "no smoking" by the occupant.

Policy F

It is the policy of the company to respect the preferences of both smokers and nonsmokers in company buildings. Where smokers' and nonsmokers' preferences are in conflict, employees and management will endeavor to find a satisfactory compromise. On failure to reach a compromise, the preferences of the nonsmoker will prevail.

Policy G

The company places no restrictions on employee smoking (the company does not have a smoking policy).

"Smoking Permitted" is synonymous with "Designated Smoking Area." The latter term is increasing in usage.

A basic assumption is that all companies have policies prohibiting smoking in areas where there are safety and fire hazards and where sensitive equipment may be damaged. In reference to the scale above, the term "smoking policy" refers to a written statement or statements that place restrictions on smoking and intend to accommodate health concerns.

FIGURE 18.8
Degrees of Restrictions on Employee Smoking—A Scale

Source: J. Carroll Swart, "Corporate Smoking Policies: Today and Tomorrow," *Personnel* (August 1988), p. 62.

▸ CHAPTER REVIEW

SUMMARY

1. The area of safety and accident prevention is of concern to managers at least partly because of the staggering number of deaths and accidents occurring at work. We said there are three reasons for safety programs: moral, legal, and economic.

2. The purpose of OSHA is to ensure every working person a safe and healthful workplace. OSHA standards are very complete and detailed, and are enforced through a system of inspections in which inspectors, following a list of inspection priorities, visit workplaces. These inspectors can issue citations and recommend penalties to their area directors.
3. Supervisors play a key role in safety to monitor workers. Workers have a responsibility to act safely. A commitment to safety on the part of top management that is filtered down through the management ranks is an important aspect of any safety program.
4. There are three basic causes of accidents: chance occurrences, unsafe conditions, and unsafe acts on the part of employees. Unsafe *conditions* (such as defective equipment) are one big cause of accidents. In addition, three other work-related factors (the job itself, the work schedule, and the psychological climate) also contribute to accidents.
5. Unsafe *acts* on the part of employees are a second basic cause of accidents. Such acts are to some extent the result of certain behavior tendencies on the part of employees, and these tendencies are possibly the result of certain personal characteristics.
6. Most experts doubt that there are accident-prone people who have accidents regardless of the job. Instead, the consensus seems to be that the person who is accident prone in one job may not be on a different job. For example, vision is related to accident frequency for drivers and machine operators but might not be for other jobs, such as accountants.
7. There are several approaches you could use to prevent accidents. One is to reduce unsafe *conditions* (although this is somewhat more in the domain of safety engineers). The other approach is to reduce unsafe *acts*—for example, through selection and placement, training, positive reinforcement, propaganda, and top management commitment.
8. Alcoholism, drug addiction, stress, and emotional illness are four important and growing health problems among employees. Alcoholism is a particularly serious problem and one that can drastically lower the effectiveness of your organization. Techniques including disciplining, discharge, in-house counseling, and referrals to an outside agency are used to deal with these problems.
9. Stress and burnout are other potential health problems at work. Reducing job stress involves such things as getting away from work for a while each day, delegating, and developing a "worry list."
10. Asbestosis, video display health problems, AIDS, and workplace smoking are other employee health problems discussed in this chapter.

KEY TERMS

Occupational Safety and Health Act

Occupational Safety and Health Administration (OSHA)

citations

unsafe conditions

unsafe acts

burnout

DISCUSSION QUESTIONS

1. How would you go about providing a safer environment for your employees to work in?
2. Discuss how you would go about minimizing the occurrence of unsafe acts on the part of your employees.
3. Discuss the basic facts about OSHA—its purpose, standards, inspection, and rights and responsibilities.

4. Explain the supervisor's role in safety.
5. Explain what causes unsafe acts.
6. Answer the question, "Is there such a thing as an accident-prone person?"
7. Describe at least five techniques for reducing accidents.
8. Analyze the legal and safety issues concerning AIDS.
9. Explain how you would reduce stress at work.

Application Exercises

RUNNING CASE

Carter Cleaning Company

The New Safety Program

Employees' safety and health are very important matters in the laundry and cleaning business. Each facility is a small production plant in which machines, powered by high-pressure steam and compressed air, work at high temperatures washing, cleaning, and pressing garments often under very hot, slippery conditions. Chemical vapors are continually produced, and caustic chemicals are used in the cleaning process. High temperature stills are almost continually "cooking down" cleaning solvents in order to remove impurities so that the solvents can be reused. If a mistake is made in this process—like injecting too much steam into the still—a "boilover" occurs, in which boiling chemical solvent erupts out of the still and over the floor and anyone who happens to be standing in its way.

As a result of these hazards and the fact that chemically hazardous waste is continually produced in these stores, several government agencies (including OSHA and the EPA) have instituted strict guidelines regarding the management of these plants. For example, posters have to be placed in each store notifying employees of their right to be told what hazardous chemicals they are dealing with and what the proper method for handling each chemical is. Special waste-management firms must be used to pick up and properly dispose of the hazardous waste.

A chronic problem the Carters (and most other laundry owners) have is the unwillingness on the part of the cleaning–spotting workers to wear safety goggles. Not all the chemicals they use require safety goggles, but some—like the hydrofluorous acid used to remove rust stains from garments—are very dangerous. The latter is kept in special plastic containers, since it dissolves glass. The problem is that wearing safety goggles can be troublesome. They are somewhat uncomfortable. They also become smudged easily and thus cut down on visibility. As a result, Jack has always found it almost impossible to get these employees to wear their goggles.

Questions

1. How should the firm go about identifying hazardous conditions that should be rectified?
2. Would it be advisable for the firm to set up a procedure for screening out accident-prone individuals?
3. How would you suggest the Carters get all employees to behave more safely at work? Also, how would you advise them to get those who should be wearing goggles to wear the goggles?

CASE INCIDENT *Hartley Corporation*

The Hartley Corporation is composed of ten autonomous divisions and corporate headquarters. The case focuses on the Bien Works. Its organization is given in Figure 18.9.

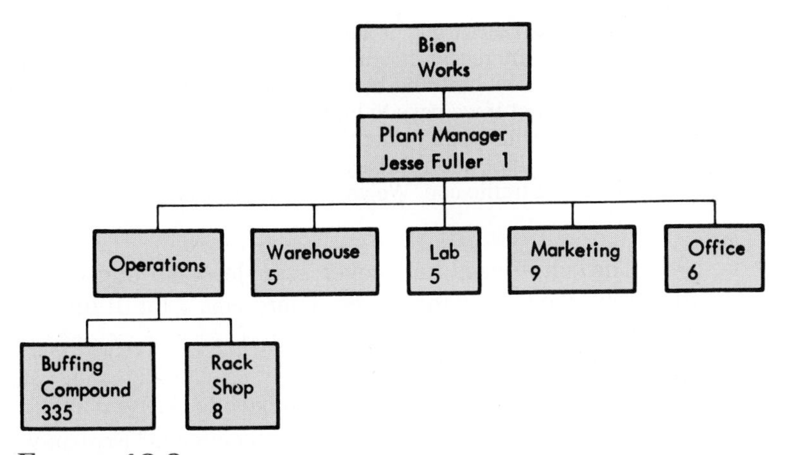

FIGURE 18.9
Organization Chart: Bien Works

Bien Works is housed in a building erected in 1904. The building is five stories high. The top two are not used, since the floors are too dangerous. The second and third floors have holes and rotted places in them.

The third floor holds the rack shop, lab, and marketing departments. The second floor contains the office, some warehousing, and some buffing compound production lines. The first floor contains the warehousing for heavier materials and the rest of the manufacturing lines. The main operation is manufacturing. The rack shop is a support unit to make racks for drying chemicals. The work is nonunion.

Jesse Fuller has been with Hartley for 20 years, all of it in conjunction with the Bien Works. He holds a B.S. in chemistry from City University of New York. He worked his way through college. He's done almost everything at Bien. He started as a supervisor in the manufacturing unit. He's run the rack shop, supervised the warehouse for two years, sold the compounds. The office and lab are white-collar or technical jobs, so he's not worked there. His employees like him, although they are a bit afraid of him, too. He has a terrible temper, which he loses about once a month. When this happens, everyone tries to get out of his way.

Jesse is now 53 years old. He's happy with the Bien Works. He likes the town and wouldn't move. Bien is like his own firm, since he's isolated geographically from Hartley.

Since Bien makes more money for Hartley than his budget calls for, it lets Jesse alone. He has lower turnover than expected. Absenteeism is also low. His safety record is about average. All in all, Hartley and Jesse are happy with the Bien Works.

Except for OSHA. For some reason, the OSHA inspector came around Bien often. The local inspector was James Munsey. In April, he came to Bien when Jesse was at a meeting at Hartley. He determined that the buffing manufacturing was producing unsafe gases. As is his right, he shut the plant down that day. Jesse flew back and modified the gas filters. James passed the filters, and Bien started production again.

In May, James came back and shut the plant again when Jesse was at a Rotary meeting. Again, the filters were cleaned and modified. This time Jesse was really angry. After the plant was reopened and James gone, Jesse held a meeting of all employees. At the meeting, he said:

> Look, this OSHA guy is killing us. This is an old works. We can't afford to be shut down. At my recent meeting at corporate headquarters, I tried to make the case that we needed a new building here. The sharp pencil boys pointed out that we are profitable now but not if we have to build a new plant. The industry is overcrowded, and Hartley will close this plant rather than spend money on it. If we get shut down or have to buy a lot of antipollution garbage, they could shut us down. That OSHA guy is the enemy—just like a traffic cop. We've got to pull together, or we could all sink together.

The employees had never seen Jesse so angry before, and they feared for their jobs now more than ever. There was a lot of unemployment in the area.

Questions

1. What do you think of Jesse's approach to safety?
2. What changes, if any, would you recommend? Explain why.

Source: William F. Glueck and George Stevens, *Cases and Exercises in Personnel/Human Resources Management*, 3d ed. (Plano, Tx.: Business Publications, 1983), pp. 145–146. Copyright 1983, Business Publications, Inc. Reprinted by permission.

HUMAN RESOURCE MANAGEMENT SIMULATION

One of the problems facing the HR Director of your firm is an accident rate higher than it should be. Some of the causes of this are a higher-than-average turnover rate, a less-than-satisfactory morale level, and a lack of any type of accident prevention or safety program. The accident rate for the organization (as measured by employee-days lost per 1 million employee-hours) is 494. The simulation allows you to start and maintain a safety program for your firm. Your accident rate will be printed on your quarterly status report and you can monitor your progress.

Incident J also allows your team to emphasize safety if you want to budget for it. Incident I gives your team an opportunity to consider various health, assistance, and wellness issues.

APPENDIX 18–1

Self-inspection Checklists

General

Develop Your Own Checklist.

These Are Only Sample Questions.

	OK	ACTION NEEDED
1. Is the required OSHA workplace poster displayed in your place of business as required where all employees are likely to see it?	☐	☐
2. Are you aware of the requirement to report all workplace fatalities and any serious accidents (where 5 or more are hospitalized) to a federal or state OSHA office within 48 hours?	☐	☐
3. Are workplace injury and illness records being kept as required by OSHA?	☐	☐
4. Are you aware that the OSHA annual summary of workplace injuries and illnesses must be posted by February 1 and must remain posted until March 1?	☐	☐
5. Are you aware that employers with 10 or fewer employees are exempt from the OSHA recordkeeping requirements, unless they are part of an official BLS or state survey and have received specific instructions to keep records?	☐	☐
6. Have you demonstrated an active interest in safety and health matters by defining a policy for your business and communicating it to all employees?	☐	☐
7. Do you have a safety committee or group that allows participation of employees in safety and health activities?	☐	☐
8. Does the safety committee or group meet regularly and report, in writing, its activities?	☐	☐
9. Do you provide safety and health training for all employees requiring such training, and is it documented?	☐	☐
10. Is one person clearly in charge of safety and health activities?	☐	☐

Source: OSHA Handbook for Small Business.

	OK	ACTION NEEDED
11. Do all employees know what to do in emergencies?	☐	☐
12. Are emergency telephone numbers posted?	☐	☐
13. Do you have a procedure for handling employee complaints regarding safety and health?	☐	☐

Develop Your Own Checklist.

These Are Only Sample Questions.

Workplace

ELECTRICAL WIRING, FIXTURES AND CONTROLS

	OK	ACTION NEEDED
1. Are your workplace electricians familiar with the requirements of the National Electrical Code (NEC)?	☐	☐
2. Do you specify compliance with the NEC for all contract electrical work?	☐	☐
3. If you have electrical installations in hazardous dust or vapor areas, do they meet the NEC for hazardous locations?	☐	☐
4. Are all electrical cords strung so they do not hang on pipes, nails, hooks, etc?	☐	☐
5. Is all conduit, BX cable, etc., properly attached to all supports and tightly connected to junction and outlet boxes?	☐	☐
6. Is there no evidence of fraying on any electrical cords?	☐	☐
7. Are rubber cords kept free of grease, oil and chemicals?	☐	☐
8. Are metallic cable and conduit systems properly grounded?	☐	☐
9. Are portable electric tools and appliances grounded or double insulated?	☐	☐
10. Are all ground connections clean and tight?	☐	☐
11. Are fuses and circuit breakers the right type and size for the load on each circuit?	☐	☐
12. Are all fuses free of "jumping" with pennies or metal strips?	☐	☐
13. Do switches show evidence of overheating?	☐	☐
14. Are switches mounted in clean, tightly closed metal boxes?	☐	☐

	OK	ACTION NEEDED
15. Are all electrical switches marked to show their purpose?	☐	☐
16. Are motors clean and kept free of excessive grease and oil?	☐	☐
17. Are motors properly maintained and provided with adequate overcurrent protection?	☐	☐
18. Are bearings in good condition?	☐	☐
19. Are portable lights equipped with proper guards?	☐	☐
20. Are all lamps kept free of combustible material?	☐	☐
21. Is your electrical system checked periodically by someone competent in the NEC?	☐	☐

EXITS AND ACCESS

	OK	ACTION NEEDED
1. Are all exits visible and unobstructed?	☐	☐
2. Are all exits marked with a readily visible sign that is properly illuminated?	☐	☐
3. Are there sufficient exits to ensure prompt escape in case of emergency?	☐	☐
4. Are areas with limited occupancy posted and is access/egress controlled to persons specifically authorized to be in those areas?	☐	☐
5. Do you take special precautions to protect employees during construction and repair operations?	☐	☐

Develop Your Own Checklist.

These Are Only Sample Questions.

FIRE PROTECTION

	OK	ACTION NEEDED
1. Are portable fire extinguishers provided in adequate number and type?	☐	☐
2. Are fire extinguishers inspected monthly for general condition and operability and noted on the inspection tag?	☐	☐
3. Are fire extinguishers recharged regularly and properly noted on the inspection tag?	☐	☐
4. Are fire extinguishers mounted in readily accessible locations?	☐	☐

Develop Your Own Checklist.

These Are Only Sample Questions.

	OK	ACTION NEEDED
5. If you have interior standpipes and valves, are these inspected regularly?	☐	☐
6. If you have a fire alarm system, is it tested at least annually?	☐	☐
7. Are plant employees periodically instructed in the use of extinguishers and fire protection procedures?	☐	☐
8. If you have outside private fire hydrants, were they flushed within the last year and placed on a regular maintenance schedule?	☐	☐
9. Are fire doors and shutters in good operating condition?	☐	☐
Are they unobstructed and protected against obstruction?	☐	☐
10. Are fusible links in place?	☐	☐
11. Is your local fire department well acquainted with your plant, location and specific hazards?	☐	☐
12. Automatic Sprinklers:		
Are water control valves, air and water pressures checked weekly?	☐	☐
Are control valves locked open?	☐	☐
Is maintenance of the system assigned to responsible persons or a sprinkler contractor?	☐	☐
Are sprinkler heads protected by metal guards where exposed to mechanical damage?	☐	☐
Is proper minimum clearance maintained around sprinkler heads?	☐	☐

HOUSEKEEPING AND GENERAL WORK ENVIRONMENT

	OK	ACTION NEEDED
1. Is smoking permitted in designated "safe areas" only?	☐	☐
2. Are NO SMOKING signs prominently posted in areas containing combustibles and flammables?	☐	☐
3. Are covered metal waste cans used for oily and paint soaked waste?	☐	☐
Are they emptied at least daily?	☐	☐
4. Are paint spray booths, dip tanks, etc., and their exhaust ducts cleaned regularly?	☐	☐

	OK	ACTION NEEDED
5. Are stand mats, platforms or similar protection provided to protect employees from wet floors in wet processes?	☐	☐
6. Are waste receptacles provided, and are they emptied regularly?	☐	☐
7. Do your toilet facilities meet the requirements of applicable sanitary codes?	☐	☐
8. Are washing facilities provided?	☐	☐
9. Are all areas of your business adequately illuminated?	☐	☐
10. Are floor load capacities posted in second floors, lofts, storage areas, etc.?	☐	☐
11. Are floor openings provided with toe boards and railings or a floor hole cover?	☐	☐
12. Are stairways in good condition with standard railings provided for every flight having four or more risers?	☐	☐
13. Are portable wood ladders and metal ladders adequate for their purpose, in good condition and provided with secure footing?	☐	☐
14. If you have fixed ladders, are they adequate, and are they in good condition and equipped with side rails or cages or special safety climbing devices, if required?	☐	☐
15. For Loading Docks:		
Are dockplates kept in serviceable condition and secured to prevent slipping?	☐	☐
Do you have means to prevent car or truck movement when dockplates are in place?	☐	☐

MACHINES AND EQUIPMENT

	OK	ACTION NEEDED
1. Are all machines or operations that expose operators or other employees to rotating parts, pinch points, flying chips, particles or sparks adequately guarded?	☐	☐
2. Are mechanical power transmission belts and pinch points guarded?	☐	☐
3. Is exposed power shafting less than 7 feet from the floor guarded?	☐	☐
4. Are hand tools and other equipment regularly inspected for safe condition?	☐	☐

Develop Your Own Checklist.

These Are Only Sample Questions.

	OK	ACTION NEEDED
5. Is compressed air used for cleaning reduced to less than 30 psi?	☐	☐
6. Are power saws and similar equipment provided with safety guards?	☐	☐
7. Are grinding wheel tool rests set to within 1/8 inch or less of the wheel?	☐	☐
8. Is there any system for inspecting small hand tools for burred ends, cracked handles, etc.?	☐	☐
9. Are compressed gas cylinders examined regularly for obvious signs of defects, deep rusting or leakage?	☐	☐
10. Is care used in handling and storing cylinders and valves to prevent damage?	☐	☐
11. Are all air receivers periodically examined, including the safety valves?	☐	☐
12. Are safety valves tested regularly and frequently?	☐	☐
13. Is there sufficient clearance from stoves, furnaces, etc., for stock, woodwork, or other combustible materials?	☐	☐
14. Is there clearance of at least 4 feet in front of heating equipment involving open flames, such as gas radiant heaters, and fronts of firing doors of stoves, furnaces, etc.?	☐	☐
15. Are all oil and gas fired devices equipped with flame failure controls that will prevent flow of fuel if pilots or main burners are not working?	☐	☐
16. Is there at least a 2-inch clearance between chimney brickwork and all woodwork or other combustible materials?	☐	☐
17. For Welding or Flame Cutting Operations: Are only authorized, trained personnel permitted to use such equipment?	☐	☐
Have operators been given a copy of operating instructions and asked to follow them?	☐	☐
Are welding gas cylinders stored so they are not subjected to damage?	☐	☐
Are valve protection caps in place on all cylinders not connected for use?	☐	☐
Are all combustible materials near the operator covered with protective shields or otherwise protected?	☐	☐
Is a fire extinguisher provided at the welding site?	☐	☐
Do operators have the proper protective clothing and equipment?	☐	☐

Develop Your Own Checklist.

These Are Only Sample Questions.

Materials

		OK	ACTION NEEDED
1.	Are approved safety cans or other acceptable containers used for handling and dispensing flammable liquids?	☐	☐
2.	Are all flammable liquids that are kept inside buildings stored in proper storage containers or cabinets?	☐	☐
3.	Do you meet OSHA standards for all spray painting or dip tank operations using combustible liquids?	☐	☐
4.	Are oxidizing chemicals stored in areas separate from all organic material except shipping bags?	☐	☐
5.	Do you have an enforced NO SMOKING rule in areas for storage and use of hazardous materials?	☐	☐
6.	Are NO SMOKING signs posted where needed?	☐	☐
7.	Is ventilation equipment provided for removal of air contaminants from operations such as production grinding, buffing, spray painting and/or vapor degreasing, and is it operating properly?	☐	☐
8.	Are protective measures in effect for operations involved with X-rays or other radiation?	☐	☐
9.	For Lift Truck Operations: Are only trained personnel allowed to operate forklift trucks?	☐	☐
	Is overhead protection provided on high lift rider trucks?	☐	☐
10.	For Toxic Materials: Are all materials used in your plant checked for toxic qualities?	☐	☐
	Have appropriate control procedures such as ventilation systems, enclosed operations, safe handling practices, proper personal protective equipment (e.g., respirators, glasses or goggles, gloves, etc.) been instituted for toxic materials.	☐	☐

Develop Your Own Checklist.

These Are Only Sample Questions.

Employee Protection

Develop Your Own Checklist. These Are Only Sample Questions.

	OK	ACTION NEEDED
1. Is there a hospital, clinic or infirmary for medical care near your business?	☐	☐
2. If medical and first-aid facilities are not nearby, do you have one or more employees trained in first aid?	☐	☐
3. Are your first-aid supplies adequate for the type of potential injuries in your workplace?	☐	☐
4. Are there quick water flush facilities available where employees are exposed to corrosive materials?	☐	☐
5. Are hard hats provided and worn where any danger of falling objects exists?	☐	☐
6. Are protective goggles or glasses provided and worn where there is any danger of flying particles or splashing of corrosive materials?	☐	☐
7. Are protective gloves, aprons, shields or other means provided for protection from sharp, hot or corrosive materials?	☐	☐
8. Are approved respirators provided for regular or emergency use where needed?	☐	☐
9. Is all protective equipment maintained in a sanitary condition and readily available for use?	☐	☐
10. Where special equipment is needed for electrical workers, is it available?	☐	☐
11. When lunches are eaten on the premises, are they eaten in areas where there is no exposure to toxic materials, and not in toilet facility areas?	☐	☐
12. Is protection against the effects of occupational noise exposure provided when the sound levels exceed those shown in Table G-16 of the OSHA noise standard?	☐	☐

▶ NOTES

1. Bureau of National Affairs, "Occupational Injuries and Illnesses," *Bulletin to Management*, January 16, 1986, pp. 20–21; Bureau of National Affairs, "Occupational Injuries and Illnesses," *Bulletin to Management*, December 17, 1992, pp. 396–397.
2. *Workers' Compensation Manual for Managers and Supervisors* (Chicago: Commerce Clearing House, Inc., 1992), p. 12.
3. *U.S.* v. *S.A. Healy Company*, DC E Wis, No. 90-CR-123, 2/20/91.
4. *U.S.* v. *Mickey*, DC N Ohio, 1-92-CR-0380, 12/4/92.
5. Much of this is based on "All About OSHA" (revised), U.S. Department of Labor, Occupational Safety and Health Administration (Washington, DC, 1980).
6. Bureau of National Affairs, "OSHA Hazard Communication Standard Enforcement," *Bulletin to Management*, February 23, 1989, p. 13.
7. "What Every Employer Needs to Know About OSHA Record Keeping," U.S. Department of Labor, Bureau of Labor Statistics (Washington, DC, 1978), report 412–3, p. 3.
8. "All About OSHA," p. 18.
9. "Supreme Court Says OSHA Inspectors Need Warrants," *Engineering News Record*, June 1, 1978, pp 9–10. W. Scott Railton, "OSHA Gets Tough on Business," *Management Review*, Vol. 80, No. 12, December 1991, pp. 28–29.
10. Michael Verespej, "OSHA Revamps Its Inspection Policies," *Industry Week*, September 17, 1979, pp. 19–20. See also Horace E. Johns, "OSHA's Impact," *Personnel Journal*, Vol. 67, no. 11 (November 1988), pp. 102–107.
11. Bureau of National Affairs, *Bulletin to Management*, January 16, 1986, p. 23; see also Bureau of National Affairs, *Bulletin to Management*, March 30, 1989, p. 103.
12. This section is based on "All About OSHA," pp. 23–25.
13. Bureau of National Affairs, "OSHA Instruction on Penalties," *Bulletin to Management*, February 7, 1991, p. 33; Commerce Clearing House, "OSHA Will Begin Higher Fines March 1st," *Ideas and Trends in Personnel*, January 23, 1991, p. 14; John Bruening, "OSHRC on the Comeback Trail," *Occupational Hazards* (January 1991), pp. 33–36.
14. Roger Jacobs, "Employee Resistance to OSHA Standards: Toward a More Reasonable Approach," *Labor Law Journal* (April 1979), pp. 219–230.
15. Ibid., p. 220.
16. These are based on ibid., pp. 227–230.
17. Michael Verespej, "Has OSHA Improved?" *Industry Week*, August 4, 1980, p. 50.
18. "What Every Employer Needs to Know About OSHA Record Keeping."
19. Willie Hammer, *Occupational Safety Management and Engineering*, 3rd ed. Englewood Cliffs, N.J.: Prentice Hall, 1985, pp. 62–63.
20. See Stephen Yohay, "Comprehensive OSHA Reform a Serious Prospect," *Employee Relations Law Journal*, Vol. 17, no. 4 (Spring 1992), pp. 661–672.
21. Ibid., p. 662.
22. Lester Bittel, *What Every Supervisor Should Know*, (New York: McGraw-Hill, 1974), p.25. For an example of an effective safety training program, see, for example, Michael Pennacchia, "Interactive Training Sets the Pace," *Safety and Health*, Vol. 135, no. 1 (January 1987), pp. 24–27, and Philip Poynter and David Stevens, "How to Secure an Effective Health and Safety Program at Work," *Professional Safety*, Vol. 32, no. 1 (January 1987), pp. 32–41.
23. David S. Thelan, Donna Ledgerwood, and Charles F. Walters, "Health and Safety in the Workplace: A New Challenge for Business Schools," *Personnel Administrator*, Vol. 30, no. 10 (October 1985), p. 44.
24. Hammer, *Occupational Safety Management and Engineering*.
25. "A Safety Committee Man's Guide," Aetna Life and Casualty Insurance Company, Catalog 872684.
26. Ibid., pp. 17–21. OSHA has identified ten major causes of accidents: inadequate training, inability to do the job, lack of job understanding, improper tools and equipment, poor quality materials, poor maintenance, poor work environment, incorrect shop routing, tight work schedules, and overly tight schedules. See Myron Peskin and Frances McGrath, "Industrial Safety: Who is Responsible and Who Benefits," *Business Horizons,* Vol. 35, No. 3, May–June 1992, pp. 66–70.
27. Willard Kerr, "Complementary Theories of Safety Psychology," in Edwin Fleishman and Alan Bass, *Industrial Psychology* (Homewood, IL: Dorsey Press, 1974), pp. 493–500.
28. List of unsafe acts from "A Safety Committee Man's Guide," Aetna Life and Casualty Insurance Company.
29. A.G. Arbous and J.E. Kerrich, "The Phenomenon of Accident Proneness," *Industrial Medicine and Surgery*, Vol. 22 (1953), pp. 141–148, reprinted in Fleishman and Bass, *Industrial Psychology*, p. 485.
30. Ernest McCormick and Joseph Tiffin, *Industrial Psychology* (Englewood Cliffs, NJ: Prentice Hall, 1974), pp. 522–523; Norman Maier, *Psychology and Industrial Organization* (Boston: Houghton-Mifflin, 1965), pp. 458–462; Milton Blum and James Nayler, *Industrial Psychology* (New York: Harper & Row, 1968), pp. 519–531. For example, David DeJoy, "Attributional Processes and Hazard Control Management in Industry," *Journal of Safety Research*, Vol. 16 (Summer 1985), pp. 61–71.
31. McCormick and Tiffin, *Industrial Psychology*, p. 523.
32. John Miner and J. Frank Brewer, "Management of Ineffective Performance," in Marvin Dunnette, ed., *Handbook of Industrial and Organizational Psychology* (Chicago: Rand McNally, 1976), pp. 995–1031; McCormick and Tiffin, *Industrial Psychology*, pp. 524–525. Younger employees probably have more accidents also, at least in part because they fail to perceive specific situations as being as risky as do older employees. See, for example, Peter Finn and Barry Bragg, "Perceptions of the Risk of an Accident by Young and Older Drivers," *Accident Analysis and Prevention*, Vol. 18, no. 4 (August 1986). See also Olivia Mitchell, "The Relation of Age to Workplace Injuries," *Monthly Labor Review*, Vol. 111, no. 7 (July 1988), pp, 8–13.
33. Blum and Nayler, *Industrial Psychology*, p. 522.
34. Miner and Brewer, "Management of Ineffective Performance," in Dunnette, ed., *Handbook of Industrial and Organizational Psychology*, pp. 1004–1005.
35. Bittel, *What Every Supervisor Should Know*, p. 249.
36. *Workers' Compensation Manual for Managers and Supervisors*, pp. 22–23.
37. Maier, *Psychology and Industrial Organization*, pp. 463–467; McCormick and Tiffin, *Industrial Psychology*, pp. 533–536; and Blum and Nayler, *Industrial Psychology*, pp. 525–527.
38. D. Wechsler, "Test for Taxicab Drivers," *Journal of Personnel Research*, Vol. 5 (1926), pp. 24–30, quoted in Maier, *Psychology and Industrial Organization*, p. 64. See also Leo DeBobes, "Psychological Factors in Accident Prevention," *Personnel Journal*, Vol. 65 (January 1986). See

also Curtiss Hansen, "A Causal Model of the Relationship Among Accidents, Biodata Personality, and Cognitive Factors," *Journal of Applied Psychology*, Vol 74, no. 1 (February 1989), pp. 81–90.
39. Maier, *Psychology and Industrial Organization*, p. 463.
40. S.E. Wirt and H.E. Leedkee, "Skillful Eyes Prevent Accidents," Annual Newsletter, National Safety Council, Industrial Nursing Section, November 1945, pp. 10–12, quoted in Maier, *Psychology and Industrial Organization*, p. 466.
41. Maier, *Psychology and Industrial Organization*, p. 464.
42. Judy D. Olian, "Genetic Screening for Employment Purposes," *Personnel Psychology*, Vol. 37, no. 3 (Autumn 1984), pp. 423–438.
43. S. Laner and R. J. Sell, "An Experiment on the Effect of Specially Designed Safety Posters," *Occupational Psychology*, Vol. 34 (1960), pp. 153–169, in McCormick and Tiffin, *Industrial Psychology*, p. 536.
44. McCormick and Tiffin, *Industrial Psychology*, p. 537. A group of international experts met in Belgium in 1986 and concluded that a successful safety poster must be simple and specific and reinforce safe behavior rather than negative behavior. See "What Makes an Effective Safety Poster," *National Safety and Health News*, Vol. 134, no. 6 (December 1986), pp. 32–34.
45. OSHA has published two useful training manuals: *Training Requirements of OSHA Standards* (February 1976) and *Teaching Safety and Health in the Work Place*, U.S. Department of Labor, Occupational Safety and Health Administration (1976); J. Surry, "Industrial Accident Research: Human Engineering Approach" (Toronto: University of Toronto, Department of Industrial Engineering, June 1968), Chapter 4, quoted in McCormick and Tiffin, *Industrial Psychology*, p. 534. For an example of a very successful incentive program aimed at boosting safety at Campbell Soup Company, see Frederick Wahl, Jr., "Soups on for Safety," *National Safety and Health News*, Vol. 134, no. 6 (December 1986), pp. 49–53.
46. Judi Komaki, Kenneth Barwick, and Lawrence Scott, "A Behavioral Approach to Occupational Safety: Pinpointing and Reinforcing Safe Performance in a Food Manufacturing Plant," *Journal of Applied Psychology*, Vol. 63 (August 1978), pp. 434–445.
47. Judi Komaki, Arlene Heinzmann, and Lorealie Lawson, "Effect of Training and Feedback: Component Analysis of a Behavioral Safety Program," *Journal of Applied Psychology*, Vol. 65 (June 1980), pp. 261–270.
48. Dove Zohar, "Safety Climate in Industrial Organization: Theoretical and Implied Implications," *Journal of Applied Psychology*, Vol. 65 (February 1980), p. 97. For a discussion of the importance of getting employees involved in managing their own safety program, see John Lutness, "Self–managed Safety Program Gets Workers Involved," *Safety and Health*, Vol. 135, no. 4 (April 1987), pp. 42–45.
49. *Workers' Compensation Manual for Managers and Supervisors*, p. 24. James Frierson, "An Analysis of ADA Provisions on Denying Employment Because of a Risk of Future Injury," *Employee Relations Law Journal*, Vol. 17, No. 4, Spring 1992, pp. 603–622.
50. Bureau of National Affairs, "Workplace Safety: Improving Management Practices," *Bulletin to Management*, February 9, 1989, pp. 42 and 47; see also Marlene Morgenstern, "Workers' Compensation: Managing Costs," *Compensation and Benefits Review* (September–October 1992), pp. 30–38.
51. *Workers' Compensation Manual for Managers and Supervisors*, p. 10.
52. See, for example, ibid., pp. 36–39.
53. Ibid., p. 51.
54. This section based largely on Miner and Brewer, "Management of Ineffective Performance," pp. 1005–1023.
55. James Schreir, "Survey Supports Perceptions: Work-Site Drug Use Is on the Rise," *Personnel Journal* (October 1987), pp. 114–118. Pallassana Balgopal, "Combating Alcoholism in Industries: Implications for Occupational Social Work," *Management and Labor Studies*, Vol. 17, No. 1, January 1992, pp. 33–42.
56. Gopal Pati and John Adkins, Jr., "The Employer's Role in Alcoholism Assistance," *Personnel Journal*, Vol. 62, no. 7 (July 1983), pp. 568–572. For a discussion of how the work environment can encourage drug dealing, see Richard Lyles, "Should the Next Drug Bust Be in Your Company?" *Personnel Journal*, Vol. 63 (October 1984), pp. 46–49.
57. Harrison Trice, "Alcoholism and the Work World," *Sloan Management Review*, no. 2 (Fall 1970), pp. 67–75, reprinted in W. Clay Hamner and Frank Schmidt, *Contemporary Problems in Personnel*, rev. ed., (Chicago, St. Clair Press, 1977), pp. 496–502. Note also that dependence on ordinary substances can be as devastating as hard drug problems. See, for example, Peter Minetos, "Are You Addicted to Legal Drugs?" *Safety and Health*, Vol. 136, no. 2 (August 1987), pp. 46–49.
58. Pati and Adkins, "Employer's Role in Alcoholism Assistance." See also, Commerce Clearing House, "How Should Employers Respond to Indications an Employee May Have an Alcohol or Drug Problem?" *Ideas and Trends*, April 6, 1989, pp. 53–57.
59. Based on Miner and Brewer, "Management of Ineffective Performance." The survey was conducted jointly by the American Society for Personnel Administration and the Bureau of National Affairs. The results were based on an analysis of the questionnaire data made by Professors Miner and Brewer, who acknowledge the assistance of John B. Schappi, associate editor of the Bureau of National Affairs, and Mary Green Miner, director of BNA Surveys, in making this information available.
60. Trice, "Alcoholism and the Work World." See also Larry A. Pace and Stanley J. Smits, "Substance Abuse: A Proactive Approach," *Personnel Journal*, Vol. 68, no. 4 (April 1989), pp. 84–90, and Commerce Clearing House, "Typical Behavior Changes in an Employee with a Drinking Problem," *Ideas and Trends*, April 6, 1989, p. 56.
61. This is quoted from Bureau of National Affairs, "Drug-Free Workplace: New Federal Requirements," *Bulletin to Management*, February 9, 1989, pp. 1–4. Note that the Drug-Free Workplace Act does not mandate or mention testing employees for illegal drug use.
62. From Henry Balevic, "Drug Abuse in the Workplace" (Personnel Services, Inc., 2303 W. Meadowview Road, Greensboro, NC 27407), reprinted in Bureau of National Affairs, *Bulletin to Management*, August 29, 1985, p. 72. Stanley Smits and Larry Pace, "Workplace Substance Abuse: Establish Policies," *Personnel Journal* (May 1989), pp. 88–93.
63. Bureau of National Affairs, *Bulletin to Management*, December 19, 1985, p. 200. Based on a speech by San Francisco attorneys Victor Schacter and Robert Kristoff. See also Alfred Klein, "Employees Under the Influence—Outside the Law?" *Personnel Journal*, Vol. 65, no. 9 (September 1986), pp. 56–58; Martin Aron, "Drug Testing: The Employer's Dilemma," *Labor Law Journal*, Vol. 38, no. 3 (March 1987), pp. 157–165; Bureau of National Affairs, "Drug Testing 'To Do' List: *Bulletin to Management*, August 10, 1989, p. 250.
64. This is based on Terry Beehr and John Newman, "Organizational Stress, Employer Health, and Organizational Effectiveness: A Factor Analysis, Model, and Literature Review," *Personnel Psychology*, Vol. 31 (Winter 1978),

pp. 665–699. See also Stephan Motowizlo, John Packard, and Michael Manning, "Occupational Stress: Its Causes and Consequences for Job Performance," *Journal of Applied Psychology*, Vol. 71, no. 4 (November 1986), pp. 618–629.

65. Andre DuBrin, *Human Relations: A Job Oriented Approach* (Reston, VA: Reston, 1978), pp. 66–67.
66. John Newman and Terry Beehr, "Personal and Organizational Strategies for Handling Job Stress: A Review of Research and Opinion," *Personnel Psychology* (Spring 1979), pp. 1–43. See also Bureau of National Affairs, "Work Place Stress: How to Curb Claims," *Bulletin to Management*, April 14, 1988, p. 120.
67. Karl Albrecht, *Stress and the Manager* (Englewood Cliffs, NJ: Spectrum, 1979).
68. Herbert Freudenberger, *Burn-Out* (Toronto: Bantam Books, 1980). See also Susan Jackson, Richard Schwab, and Randall Schuler, "Toward an Understanding of the Burnout Phenomenon," *Journal of Applied Psychology*, Vol. 71, no. 4 (November 1986), pp. 630–640, and James R. Redeker and Jonathan Seagal, "Profits Low? Your Employee's May Be High!" *Personnel*, Vol. 66, no. 6 (June 1989), pp. 72–76. See also Cary Cherniss, "Long Term Consequences of Burnout: An Exploratory Study," *Journal of Organizational Behavior,* Vol. 13, No. 1, January 1992, pp. 1–11.
69. This is based on Philip Voluck and Herbert Abramson, "How to Avoid Stress-Related Disability Claims," *Personnel Journal* (May 1987), pp. 95–98.
70. For a discussion, see ibid., p. 96.
71. See, for example, Michael Smith and others, "An Investigation of Health Complaints and Job Stress in Video Display Operations," *Human Factors* (August 1981), pp. 387–400; see also Bureau of National Affairs, "How to Protect Workers from Reproductive Hazards," *Fair Employment Practices*, July 23, 1987, pp. 89–90. See also Commerce Clearing House, "Suffolk County New York Passes Law Covering Employers with Twenty Terminals or More Regarding VDT Regulation," *Ideas and Trends*, 1988, p. 48.
72. Bureau of National Affairs, "No Link Found Between VDTs and Miscarriages," *Bulletin to Management*, March 21, 1991, p. 81.
73. Bureau of National Affairs, "Solutions to VDT Viewing Problems," *Bulletin to Management*, November 5, 1987, pp. 356–357.
74. Bureau of National Affairs, "AIDS and the Workplace: Issues, Advice, and Answers," *Bulletin to Management*, November, 14, 1985, pp. 1–6. See also David Ritter and Ronald Turner, "AIDS: Employer Concerns and Options," *Labor Law Journal*, Vol. 38, no. 2 (February 1987), pp. 67–83, and Bureau of National Affairs, "How Employers Are Responding to AIDS in the Workplace," *Fair Employment Practices*, February 18, 1988, pp. 21–22. For a complete guide to services and information regarding "The Work Place and AIDS," see *Personnel Journal*, Vol. 66, no. 10 (October 1987), pp. 65–80. See also William H. Wager, "AIDS: Setting Policy, Educating Employees at Bank of America," *Personnel*, Vol. 65, no. 8 (August 1988), pp. 4–10. See also Margaret Magnus, "AIDS: Fear and Ignorance," *Personnel Journal*, Vol. 67, no. 2 (February 1988), pp. 28–32, for poll regarding major workplace comments associated with AIDS.
75. Commerce Clearing House, "The Wells Fargo AIDS Policy," *Ideas and Trends*, April 5, 1988, pp. 52–53.
76. Marco Colossi, "Do Employees Have the Right to Smoke?" *Personnel Journal* (April 1988), pp. 72–79.
77. Bureau of National Affairs, "Where There's Smoke There's Risk," *Bulletin to Management*, January 30, 1992, pp. 26 and 31.
78. Commerce Clearing House, "State Laws Regulating Smoking," *Ideas and Trends*, January 9, 1987, pp. 4–5.
79. Jim Collison, "Workplace Smoking Policies: Sixteen Questions and Answers," *Personnel Journal* (April 1988), p. 81.
80. Bureau of National Affairs, "Smoking Bans on the Rise," *Bulletin to Management*, March 16, 1989, p. 82.

CHAPTER 19

STRATEGIC ISSUES IN HUMAN RESOURCE MANAGEMENT

OVERVIEW

In this chapter we explain how various trends such as demographic changes influence human resource management and its evolving role—in terms of dealing with an aging work force, for instance. We'll see that personnel's role is changing in many ways today, and in particular in the degree to which the human resource manager must be involved with strategic planning. At the end of this chapter we tie together what we have said to this point. This should help you to develop a unifying philosophy of personnel management and to reemphasize how HRM can help win your employees' commitment. When you finish studying this chapter, you should be able to discuss the trends influencing the nature of work and the work force in the 1990s; explain the impact these trends will have on the personnel management (HRM) function; discuss HRM's role in strategic planning; and better understand what your philosophy of personnel management is or might be.

▶ THE EVOLVING ROLE OF HRM

THE EVOLUTION OF PERSONNEL MANAGEMENT

Personnel management has evolved in three main stages.[1] In the early 1900s personnel people first took over hiring and firing from supervisors, ran the payroll department, and administered benefit plans. It was a job consisting largely of ensuring that procedures were followed. As technology in such areas as testing and interviewing began to emerge, personnel began to play an expanded role in employee selection, training, and promotion.

The emergence of a strong union movement in the 1930s drove the second expansion of personnel's role. Companies now needed the personnel department to counter the union's efforts to organize the company or (failing that) to deal effectively with the union.

The third change was triggered by the discrimination legislation of the 1960s and 1970s. Because of the large penalties that lawsuits could bring to a company, effective personnel practices became more important. In this phase (as in phase 2), personnel continued to provide expertise in areas like recruitment, screening, and training, albeit in a more expanded role. Notice, though, that whether dealing with unions (phase 2) or equal employment (phase 3), personnel gained status as much for what it could do to protect the organization from problems as for the positive contribution it made to the firm's effectiveness.

Today, "personnel" is speeding through phase 4, and its role is shifting and must continue to shift from protector and screener to planner and change agent. The metamorphosis of personnel into human resource management reflects this, and in fact today's and tomorrow's human resources department will be very different than in the past.

SPECIFIC CHANGES

There are, first, some specific ways in which the human resources function will change.[2]

Employee Benefits

Changing demographics and a changing work force will demand changes in employee benefits. For instance, elder care—direct or indirect care provided to aging relatives—will become more popular as employees and their relatives get older.

Furthermore, the tendency toward earlier retirement seems to have bottomed out. The expectation for the next decade is for a very gradual increase in the retirement age: For example, the average retirement age is expected to increase for salaried employees in 40% of the companies recently surveyed and for union employees in about one-third of them. Less than 20% of the respondents expect a decrease in this average age.[3] The United States has already adopted a gradual increase in the normal retirement age for Social Security purposes.

Consistent with the gradually rising retirement age, about one-third of the organizations surveyed expected early retirement windows to be used less frequently than in the past. In turn, the firm's gradually aging work force will trigger other personnel management changes, as employers have to cope with elder care, motivating plateaued workers, upgrading employees' skills, and instituting more flexible work hours.

Designing New Organizations

Peter Drucker contends that automation will require changes in job design, in the flow of work, and in organizational relationships.[4] Automation on the factory floor requires, for instance, that first-line supervisors change into genuine managers. The traditional functions of first-line supervision are being eroded by automation and either transferred to the work force or built into the process. And, of course, implementing "people" changes like these is traditionally the responsibility of the human resource management function.

Adjusting to Knowledge Workers

Even in the smokestack industries the manual labor component of the work force now accounts for no more than 25%. In most other industries, it is down to one-sixth or less. Productivity of white-collar workers and especially of the rapidly growing groups of knowledge workers—systems analysts, consultants, accountants, and so on—is thus the big productivity challenge in developed countries. And the critical factors in knowledge work productivity are things like attitudes, work flow, job relationships, and the designs of jobs and teams. And, again, says Drucker, these are all jobs for the human resources manager.

Restructuring Career Ladders and Compensation

The continued movement of women into management positions has implications for both career development and recruiting programs.

The shift to knowledge work and knowledge workers also creates a need to rethink and to restructure career ladders, compensation, and recognition.[5] The traditional career ladder in most businesses has only managerial rungs. But for most knowledge workers, a promotion to a management job is a wrong reward, says Drucker. The good ones often prefer to keep on doing professional or technical work. This, says Drucker, is not a new problem. Thirty years ago General Electric Company established "parallel ladders" of advancement and rewards for "individual professional contributors." The shift to knowledge work will also force us to rethink the traditional organizational structure. The existing structure—derived from the nineteenth-century military—sees the manager as the boss, with everybody else as the subordinate. In the knowledge-based organization, knowledge workers are the "bosses," and the "manager" is in a supporting role as their planner and coordinator. But this means that jobs—their responsibilities, relationships, and rewards—have to be thought through and redesigned, again, probably, by the human resource management group.

Recruitment

As discussed, the number of new workers available to the labor force is expected to grow much more slowly over the next 10 years than it has in the past. This will make recruitment more difficult. As one expert puts it: "In a scarce labor market, the human resource department needs to differentiate itself and the company from the competition so that they can attract the desirable, highly qualified job seekers who are in demand.[6] Recruiting top-notch candidates during the next 10 years will therefore be a very challenging task.

Training

The training function will take on added importance in the next 10 years as increasingly complex knowledge jobs must be filled in part by a work force that is often ill prepared educationally to meet the new challenges.[7] Increasingly, human resource management will be called upon to implement a growing range of training programs, from basic skills and literacy training up through computer skills training and training interpersonal communications and leadership. Thus in this area, too, the role of personnel will have to expand in the next few years.

THE CHANGING ROLE OF PERSONNEL/HUMAN RESOURCE MANAGEMENT

The role of personnel will change in three other major ways. There will be an expansion of its consultative role, a new emphasis on its line function, and an increase in its role in developing and implementing corporate strategy.

First, personnel's traditional role as consultant to the company should increase in the years ahead; in fact, top HRM jobs are increasingly demanding a proven track record in providing top-notch consulting services on previous jobs. As firms must cope with shorter product life cycles, increased competition, and a more sophisticated work force, HRM's expert advice in areas like redesigning organizations, monitoring attitudes, instituting quality improvement teams, and molding company culture will be in high demand.

Paradoxically, while personnel's consultative/staff role will expand, its line role will expand as well. Drucker points out, in fact, that there are already quite a few precedents for "personnel" being a line function. He notes that it has always been so in the largest Japanese firms and in the military, where "personnel" might make, say, staffing decisions more or less unilaterally. And the Vatican's "personnel department," which picks and appoints the bishops of the Catholic church, is strictly a "line department." Today, even the most prestigious and influential American human resources department generally only advises and assists line managers. To make the jump to a more line-oriented role, the way these departments are staffed will probably change, too. For example, the vice-president for human resource management may increasingly have a top-level operating background and come up through the ranks before assuming the personnel role.

But perhaps the most striking change in personnel will be its growing role in developing and implementing corporate strategy. Traditionally corporate strategy—the company's plan for how it will balance its internal strengths and weaknesses with external opportunities and threats in order to maintain a competitive advantage—was a job primarily for the company's operating (line) managers. Thus Company X's president might decide to enter new markets, drop product lines, or embark on a five-year cost-cutting plan. He or she would then more or less leave the personnel implications of that plan (hiring or firing new workers, hiring outplacement firms for those fired, and so on) to be carried out by personnel. Today things are different. Strategies increasingly involve merging employees from different firms, and companies face demographic and work force changes described earlier in this book. It is now increasingly necessary to involve personnel in the earliest stages of developing the firm's strategic plan. Human resource management will move from "reactor" to "developer and implementer" of strategy.

▶ STRATEGIC PLANNING AND HRM

STRATEGIC PLANNING DEFINED

To understand the human resources manager's role in strategic planning, we should begin by reviewing what "strategic planning" means.

strategic plan
Course of action the firm plans to pursue in becoming the sort of enterprise it wants to be, given the firm's external opportunities and threats and its internal strengths and weaknesses.

A company's **strategic plan** outlines the course of action the firm plans to pursue in becoming the sort of enterprise that it wants to be, given the firm's external opportunities and threats and its internal strengths and weaknesses. Deciding whether Mom and Pop's Supermarket will compete with Enormous Markets head to head by building similar superstores or deciding what sorts of competitive advantage Burger King should use to compete with McDonald's both involve strategic planning.

An organization's strategic plan always seeks to balance two sets of forces: the company's external opportunities and threats, on the one hand, and its internal strengths and weaknesses, on the other. Companies that successfully balance these external and internal forces succeed, as McDonald's has by diversifying its product line beyond Big Macs, by extending store hours, and by expanding overseas. Those that don't, fail, as happened to the original Braniff Airlines several years ago. Its plan to pursue external opportunities and expand worldwide was inconsistent with its limited "internal" financial and managerial resources.

To illustrate more clearly what strategic planning is all about and how such plans fail, consider several more examples. Starting in the early 1900s, W. T. Grant's grew to a nationwide chain, competing with Woolworth's and Kresge's in the "5&10" category. Around 1970 Grant's management decided to change strategy and to convert the stores to "Grant's City" stores. They were to be large, K-mart–type stores, selling a wide range of clothing, home furnishings, and appliances at discount prices—a great strategy for the external market, perhaps, but the wrong one for Grant's. Grant's was unprepared internally to execute the new strategy effectively—its people couldn't properly handle big-ticket credit sales, for instance—and the firm was out of business within three years.

Delta Airlines' strategy is another good example. Delta's strategy has always been based on several basic components. It organized its flights around a hub-and-spoke system with flights from, say, Miami connecting with flights to New York in the Atlanta hub. It kept its fleet new by cycling out older planes early, before maintenance costs grew too high. And it maintained a nonunion high-committed work force with intelligent and progressive human resource management. This helped to ensure that customers got superior service. It also ensured that employees would willingly shift from job to job as the need arose with, say, a reservations clerk filling in for a baggage handler when the going got rough. As a result, while Delta workers are individually very well paid, Delta's total labor bill is proportionately less than many of its competitors, since the staff is used more efficiently.

In practice, strategies like Delta's succeed or fail for one of two reasons (and this is where the human resource manager comes in, by the way). A strategy may fail because it is simply a *poor strategy*, in that it doesn't fit the market or the company's strengths and weaknesses—that's a big part of why Braniff didn't make it, for example. Second, a firm's strategy can fail because of poor *execution*. In part, that's probably why Grant's went down in failure following a strategy essentially the same as that of K-mart. On the other hand, Delta Airlines' strategy (and that of companies like McDonald's and Domino's Pizza, to name a few) generally succeeded because (1) they were good strategies (balancing the firms' external threats and opportunities, and internal strengths and weaknesses) which were also (2) perfectly executed. Today, the HR manager must increasingly play a pivotal role in strategic planning to ensure the plan is a good one that succeeds.

HRM'S ROLE IN STRATEGIC PLANNING

There are three ways the human resource department helps top management formulate and execute the company's strategic plans: first, by helping supply intelligence regarding the company's external opportunities and threats; second, by supplying intelligence about the company's internal strengths and weaknesses; and third, by helping execute the plan, for instance, by eliminating a weakness that could be an impediment to the plan.

External Opportunities and Threats

Let's look at a few examples. The HR manager can, first, help the CEO formulate the strategic plan by supplying intelligence about the company's external opportunities and threats. For example, labor power projections regarding labor availability must be crucial to firms like Burger King (and others) that depend so heavily on entry-level labor. For a company like Burger King, the strategic implications of a diminishing entry-level labor pool include the need for increased automation of facilities and just possibly the need to reduce the growing dependence on company-owned stores and thus shift the recruiting burden to local franchises. Installing smaller, less labor-intensive drivethrough locations is another strategic possibility that could emerge from such strategic input.

HRM is in a unique position to supply other data on external opportunities and threats as well. Details regarding advanced incentive plans being used by competitors, opinion survey data from employees that elicit suggestions about customer complaints, and information about pending legislation like labor laws or mandatory health insurance are some other examples.

Internal Strengths and Weaknesses

Second, personnel can also help top management formulate strategy by supplying information regarding the company's internal strengths and weaknesses.

For example, many plans fail because they are not compatible with the company's current human resources. At W. T. Grant's, the lack of trained personnel to manage the firm's new credit system helped cripple the company's plan. Twenty-five years ago or so the downfall of Ford's Edsel car was in part preordained by the unavailability at Ford of enough accountants and other middle managers to implement Ford's new Edsel Division.

The whole area of mergers and acquisitions is ripe for HRM's input. While financial and business considerations will usually prevail here, it is usually useful (and often essential) for the CEO to also know about matters like morale problems in the acquired firm, incompatibility of corporate cultures, and potential problems in merging compensation, seniority, and benefit plans. For example, just two months after it officially acquired Crocker National Corporation,

Wells Fargo surveyed 1,500 Crocker employees to make sure that if there was a problem, they knew about it as quickly as possible.

HRM, therefore, should be a source of strategic input regarding the company's strengths and weaknesses. This certainly applies to obvious areas like management talent and competitiveness of the firm's compensation plan. But increasingly it must include less obvious matters such as the attractiveness of a merger candidate in human resource terms, the potential people problems likely to occur as a result of introducing a new technology, and the human resource benefits and drawbacks of pursuing one strategic plan or another.

Successful Execution

Finally, HRM should be heavily involved in the successful *execution* of the company's strategic plan, for instance, by helping to eliminate weaknesses that could inhibit the plan. Today personnel is already heavily involved in the execution of most firms' downsizing and restructuring strategies, in terms of outplacing employees, instituting pay for performance plans, reducing health care costs, and retraining employees. However, these activities are probably just the tip of the iceberg, considering the trends evolving today. Intensifying domestic and international competition, the changing nature of the work force, jobs that are increasingly complex and based on information technology, and continuing merger and divestiture activities mean that management will have to base strategic decisions more than ever on personnel considerations. Creating the right company culture, keeping key personnel after a merger, matching training needs and people with jobs, and solving the human problems (stress and low morale, for example) that can arise when employees' jobs are put in jeopardy are a few examples of the sorts of activities the human resource manager will play in helping execute the strategic plan.[8] But perhaps more to the point is this: In an increasingly service and high-tech economy, *committed employees* (not just "manufacturing efficiency" or "low overall costs" or some other factor) will increasingly be the competitive advantage of choice. And this, as we've seen, will thrust HRM into the role of implementing the practices needed to help win that sort of commitment.

STRATEGIC HUMAN RESOURCE MANAGEMENT: EXAMPLES

The programs carried out by the human resource department at Colgate-Palmolive provide an example of HRM's role in strategy development and implementation.

Colgate-Palmolive Company is a global manufacturing company with sales of over $5 billion that recently received new "marching orders." After assuming the presidency several years ago, the new CEO developed and communicated a new strategic direction for the company based on what he called his "corporate initiatives."[9] Among other things, the new strategy emphasized concentrating on new products, being the low-cost producer, simplifying businesses and structures, pushing decision making down, promoting entrepreneurial action, and improving morale and motivation. The new strategy was aimed at making Colgate a leaner, more responsive competitor in its global markets and in focusing the company more clearly on health-related products.

Consistent with this new strategy, several major steps were made almost at once. Four major businesses were divested, including two sports and recreation companies. A major reorganization took place that eliminated one level of senior management. Additional resources were diverted to new product development and research and development. And the human resource programs at Colgate-Palmolive got a new mandate to help Colgate achieve its new goals.

The programs laid out for Colgate HRM provide a glimpse of how HRM today is being pressed to get involved in strategic management. At Colgate-Palmolive, HRM was directed by the president to develop and execute programs designed to create a company culture that would achieve the following:

> Encourage a spirit of teamwork and cooperation within and among business units in working toward common objectives, with an emphasis on identifying, acknowledging, and rewarding personal and unit excellence.
>
> Foster entrepreneurial attitudes among the managers and innovative thinking among all employees.
>
> Emphasize the commonality of interest between the employees and shareholders.[10]

To that end, numerous HRM programs had to be designed. For example, the company's executive incentive compensation plan was redesigned to place more emphasis on individual performance and achieving operating targets. Employee benefits were redesigned to make them more flexible and responsive to employees' needs. At the same time, cost controls and employee variable pay costs were instituted, two changes that were accomplished by effectively communicating both the changes and the reasons for them. The bottom line was that by implementing a number of programs (including those aimed at redesigning compensation and benefits), HRM was able to contribute to a refocusing of Colgate employees' efforts in a manner that contributed to the execution of Colgate's strategic plan.

PERSONNEL POLICIES AND STRATEGIC IMPLEMENTATION

policies
Guides to action that assure consistency under a particular set of circumstances and within the framework of the company's plan.

As at Colgate, the implementation of a strategic plan generally involves formulating more specific departmental **policies**, "guides to action that assure consistency under a particular set of circumstances and within the framework of the company's plan."[11] These in turn guide the activities of the departments in question. Thus suppose your strategy is to maximize unit sales while reducing costs. This leads to a *production* policy to stress mass-produced items (rather than hand-built ones) and to a *distribution* policy to stress franchised sales (since this might create more sales quicker than would slowly building a company-owned set of dealers).

Much the same applies to *personnel* policies. Personnel policies regarding such matters as how much to pay, how to screen candidates, how disciplinary matters are dealt with, how incentives are earned, or how aggressively affirmative action will be pursued don't (or shouldn't) just emerge spontaneously. Instead, *personnel policies should follow from and be consistent with the company's basic mission and plan.* And, as in Colgate's case, they should enable the company and its managers to better implement that plan.

Some examples help illustrate how.[12] At Vulcan Materials Company in Birmingham, Alabama, maintaining its number one position in construction products means being a low-cost leader. This means personnel policies that stress encouraging productivity, absenteeism control, and high worker safety. Burlington Industries is embarked on a different strategic plan. Facing highly competitive pressures in the textile industry, it had to sell off some businesses, reduce the number of employees, and work hard to consolidate plants and decentralize. Here personnel policies had to help the company get more responsive to customers' needs, since these needs (for different textiles) change so rapidly. Here, therefore, training policies emphasize how to improve employee decision making and team effort as well as understanding the customer's needs, developing customer linkages, and improving delegation and decision making (to help make the firm more responsive).

Tandy Corporation is another example of how personnel policies are formulated to support company strategy. In the case of this electronics/computer firm, success depends largely on the profitability of its retail sales. In turn, these sales are based on the sales ability of retail sales employees, most of whom are selling items (like computers and electronic instruments) that require solid product knowledge and an intelligent sales effort.

At Tandy, therefore, personnel policies (regarding selection and compensation, for instance) are aimed at attracting, hiring, and motivating the kinds of people required for Tandy's success. For example, Tandy's selection policy must emphasize identifying candidates who will be successful selling Tandy's products, since 80% of the company's employees are in direct sales. To this end, Tandy developed a computerized program to administer a skill assessment profile. This is aimed at determining a candidate's aptitude for activities like qualifying customers, making sales presentations, closing sales, and providing after-sales customer service. Similarly, its training policies emphasize effective sales training, and its compensation policy puts a heavy premium on sales performance: In fact, 75% of the management compensation plans at Tandy, including that of the vice-president of human resources, are tied to the company's profits.[13]

AUDITING THE HRM FUNCTION

While the firm's personnel policies and focus should be consistent with the company's strategic plan, the bottom line should always be: "To what extent is HRM effectively carrying out its function?" In other words designing a set of policies and an HRM philosophy that is consistent with where the company wants to go is only part of the job. Effectively carrying out those functions is another.

Several suggestions have been made for how to assess how a firm's HR department is actually doing. One approach is to use accounting and statistical techniques to calculate the cost of human resources, for instance the dollar investment in human assets that good training provides. In this way the bottom-line contribution of HRM can be concretely assessed.[14] For an employer with the wherewithal to conduct such a program, it may well be worth considering. A second, less rigorous, but still effective approach follows.

The HR Review

At a minimum, an "HR review" should be conducted, one aimed at tapping top managers' opinions regarding how effective HRM has been. Former New York

Computer Application in Strategic HRM: Expert Systems in HRM

An Expert System is a program that attempts to simulate how human experts solve problems. This is done by entering knowledge from one or more "expert" sources into what is known as a "knowledge base." This knowledge base includes the rules for solving a specific type of problem. When a user queries the expert system, the rules are evaluated, and the user is presented with an "expert" answer.[1]

Users of electronic spreadsheets (like Lotus 1-2-3 and VP Planner Plus) are already building knowledge systems to handle complex problems. Current uses include producing sales reports quickly when products, data, or rules change frequently. One-time reports using relatively small data bases can be combined with macros to use the time of the manager or professional more efficiently. This type of system is called a *performance aid.* The user sets the rules (*if* this is the situation, *do* that, *otherwise* do this), which can be combined (AND) or contrasted (OR) with other rules.

In HRM, knowledge systems are useful in several areas. For example, as cafeteria benefit plans proliferate, the interaction of decisions made by employees may violate a rule that requires that at least 60% of the employees must choose term life insurance in order for that benefit to be offered at a group rate. The computerized HRM aid could signal management of that fact, as well as allow employees to ask "what-if" questions to see the impact of various decisions on outcomes such as income tax rate, total retirement income, early retirement, or net pay after deferring income.

Knowledge systems are also valuable in reviewing the impact of changes in career ladders, in the weighting of elements in job analysis, and in the effect of recruitment on such outcomes as total wage and benefits costs, EEO categories, and promotional opportunities. Risk managers can more accurately assess the cost of various combinations of benefit packages and differing experience ratings of health plans. Supervisors can more clearly evaluate the impact of merit pay with computer systems that establish percentage increases based on performance ratings. The company can also judge the bottom line impact of various percentage raises for various levels of demonstrated accomplishment based on performance appraisal. While small knowledge systems are useful in contract negotiations, large expert systems will give more accurate estimates of strategic decisions on HRM without bias or emotion and without overlooking significant details.

With the demographic shifts in the United States and the increasing rate of change in the external environment, HR managers must be able to offer ways for companies to remain competitive domestically and internationally. Knowledge-based expert systems will become a part of the arsenal.

[1]Mary Lynn Manns, unpublished manuscript, February 19, 1990.

Mayor Ed Koch used to ask New Yorkers "How am I doing?" While an "HR review" is more comprehensive than that, its value lies in its simplicity. Such a review should contain two parts: what should be and what is.[15]

The question "what should be" refers to the broad aims of the HRM department and involves two things. It should start, first, with a very broad philosophy or *vision statement.* This might envision HRM as being "recognized as an excellent resource rather than a bureaucratic entity, a business-oriented function, and the conscience of the company," for example. This vision might also enumerate the characteristics of the HRM staff, for instance, as "experts in their areas of responsibility, demonstrating a commitment to excellence, and being creative, analytical problem solvers." The vision statement should thus set the tone for HRM.

Second, this broad vision gets more focus with an HRM *mission statement.* This describes what the mission of the department should be, for instance "to contribute to the achievement of the company's business objectives by assisting the organization in making effective and efficient use of employee resources and, at the same time, assisting employees at all levels in creating for themselves satisfying and rewarding work lives.[16]

Next, the HR review's focus shifts to an evaluation of "what is." This part of the evaluation consists of six steps and involves input from the corporate HRM staff, division heads, divisional HRM heads, and those other experts (like the benefits administrator) that report directly to the head of corporate HRM. The issues to be addressed are as follows:

1. *What are the HRM functions?* Here those providing input (division heads and so forth) give their opinions about what they think HRM's functions should be. The list can be extensive, ranging from EEO enforcement and managing health benefits, to employee relations management, recruitment and selection, training, and even community relations management. The important point here is to crystallize what HRM and its main "clients" believe are HRM's functions.
2. *How important are these functions?* The participants then rate each of these functions on a 10-point scale of importance, ranging from low (1–3) to medium (4–7) to high (8–10). This provides an estimate of how important each of the 15 or 20 identified HRM functions are in the views of HRM executives and of their clients (like division managers).
3. *How well is each of the functions performed?* Next, have the same participants evaluate how well each of these HRM functions is actually being performed. Here, for example, you may find that four functions—say, employee benefits, compensation, employee relations, and recruiting—receive "high" ratings from more than half of the raters. Other functions may get "medium" or "low" ratings.
4. *What needs improvement?* The next step is to determine which of the functions rated most important rate as high, or medium, or low in terms of "how well is each of the functions performed?" Functions (like "labor relations") that are assessed as highly important but evaluated as low in terms of performance will require the quickest attention. To formalize the comparison of importance and performance ratings, have the participants compare the median importance and performance ratings for each of the 15 to 20 functions identified in step 1.

   More important, the discussions at this stage will help identify the HRM functions in which the department has to improve its performance. The discussions arising at this point should help to pinpoint specific problems that contributed to the "low performance" ratings and help provide recommendations for improving HRM's performance on low-rated functions (say, selection, or training).
5. *How effectively does the corporate HR function use resources?* This next step consists of checks to determine if the HRM budget is being allocated and spent in a way that's consistent with the functions HRM should be stressing. First, make an estimate of where the HRM dollars are being spent—for instance, on recruiting, EEO compliance, compensation management, and so on. Also try to distinguish between ongoing work and new programs (such as a quality improvement program that may be installed two years hence). Questions to ask here are: "Is expense allocation consistent with the perceived importance and performance of each of the HRM functions?" and "Should any dollars be diverted to low-performing functions to improve their effectiveness?"

6. *How can HR become optimally effective?* This final step is aimed at allowing you one last, broader view of the areas that need improvement and how they should be improved. For example, at this step it may be apparent that a large divisionally organized company needs to strengthen divisional and on-site HRM staffs so that responsibilities for certain HRM functions can be moved closer to the user.

▶ TOWARD A PHILOSOPHY OF HR MANAGEMENT

THE NEED FOR A PHILOSOPHY

In Chapter 1 we said that people's actions are always based in part on the assumptions they make and that this was especially true in regard to human resource management. The basic assumptions you make about people—Can they be trusted? Do they dislike work? Can they be creative? Why do they act as they do?—comprise your philosophy of personnel management. And the people you hire, the training you provide, your leadership style all reflect (for better or worse) this basic philosophy.

Yet throughout this book we have emphasized the "nuts and bolts" of personnel/HR management by focusing on the concepts and techniques all managers need to carry out their personnel-related tasks. It is therefore easy to lose sight of the fact that these techniques, while important, cannot be administered effectively without some unifying philosophy. For, to repeat, it is this philosophy or *vision* that helps guide you in deciding *what people to hire, what training to provide,* and *how to motivate employees.*

For more and more employers, the essence of the difference between "personnel management" and "human resource management" is indeed a philosophical one; it revolves around the latter's emphasis on improving the firm's quality of work life which means that employees are able to satisfy their important personal needs by working in the organization. In practice, this means providing employees with fair, equitable treatment; an opportunity for each employee to use his or her skills to the utmost and to self-actualize; open, trusting communications; an opportunity to take an active role in making important job-related decisions; adequate and fair compensation; and a safe and healthy work environment. However this emphasis on boosting the quality of work life—on satisfying employees' important personal needs at work, and thereby winning their commitment—goes beyond mere techniques. This is because the commitment in your firm will reflect not just techniques but your basic values and assumptions about people. Thus a Theory Y leader who believes the best about his or her subordinates will probably treat them in a way that enhances their quality of work life. In an organization with the opposite assumptions, you can be sure that a lower quality of work life will prevail as the manager tries to closely monitor and control each worker's actions.

Related to this, every personnel decision you make affects your employees' quality of work life in some way. Thus *selection* should emphasize placing the right person on the right job, where the person can have a more satisfying, actualizing experience. Similarly, an equitable grievance procedure will help protect employee rights and dignity and therefore contribute to the quality of work life of your employees. Every personnel action you take, in other words, affects your employees' quality of work life, and your actions will in turn reflect your basic assumptions about people. It is when your personnel actions are geared not just to satisfying your organization's staffing needs but also to satisfying your employees' needs to grow and to self-actualize that your *personnel management system* can be properly referred to as a *human resource management system.*

BUILDING EMPLOYEE COMMITMENT

A Recap

Many employers translate such an HRM philosophy into practices that win their employees' commitment. Commitment-building HRM practices that we described in this book include the following:

Establish people-first values. As explained earlier in the book, "You start the process of boosting employee commitment by making sure you know how you and your top managers really feel about people." In other words, you must be willing to commit to the idea that your employees are your most important assets and that they can be trusted, treated with respect, involved in making on-the-job decisions, and encouraged to grow and reach their full potential. Then put those values in writing, hire and promote into management people who have people-first values from the start, and translate your people-first values into actions every day.

Guaranteed fair treatment. Establish a "super" grievance procedure that guarantees fair treatment of all employees in all grievance and disciplinary matters. Boost upward and downward communications with Speak Up! programs. Institute multiple, formal, easy-to-use channels that employees can use to express concerns and gripes and to get answers to matters that concern them. Also use periodic opinion surveys such as survey-feedback-action, and use every opportunity to tell employees "what's going on" in your organization.

Value-Based hiring. The time to start building commitment is before—not after—employees are hired. High-commitment firms are thus very careful about whom they hire. Start by clarifying your firm's own values and ideology so that its elements can be part of your firm's screening process. Then make your screening process exhaustive, for instance by designing screening tools like structured interviews to help select applicants based, in part, on their values. Recruit actively so that those who are hired see that many were rejected and that they are therefore part of an elite. Go on to provide candid, realistic previews of what working at your firm will be like. Remember that self-selection is important—for instance, use long probationary periods or a long, exhaustive screening process that deserves some "sacrifice" on the part of employees.

Employee Security. Practice "lifetime employment without guarantees." While specifying that all employment relationships will be "employment-at-will" arrangements, emphasize your commitment to lifetime employment without guarantees with statements such as: "Stable employment and continual improvement of the well-being of our team members are essential and can be obtained through the smooth, steady growth of our company." Company practices that facilitate employee security include a compensation plan that places much of each employee's salary at risk, using large numbers of temporary or part-time employees, and cross-training employees to wear "several hats."

The rewards package. Build a pay plan that encourages employees to think of themselves as partners. This means employees should have a healthy share of the profits in good years and share in the downturn during bad times. Therefore, put a significant portion of pay at risk. Institute stock ownership plans that encourage employees to see they have a significant investment in your firm. Emphasize self-reporting of hours worked, rather than devices like time clocks.

Actualize employees. We saw that few needs are as strong as the need to fulfill our dreams, to become all we are capable of becoming. High-commitment firms therefore engage in actualizing practices, practices that aim to ensure that all employees have every opportunity to actualize—to use all their skills and gifts at work, and become all they can be. To do this, commit to actualizing, front-load new employees' jobs with challenge, enrich and empower workers' jobs, and institute comprehensive promotion-from-within/career progress programs.

Practices like these serve a dual role in organizations. They create a work environment that helps to ensure that employees can use their aptitudes and skills to the fullest and satisfy their important personal needs by working in the organization. At the same time they can help an employer to win the commitment of its employees by creating a situation in which the employees' and employer's goals become one. Employees then (it is hoped) do their jobs not just because they have to do these jobs, but because they want to do them—they do their jobs as if they own the company. And in an era that requires levels of worker flexibility, creativity, quality, and initiative such as the world has never known, *committed employees* are a firm's best competitive edge.[17]

▶ CHAPTER REVIEW

SUMMARY

1. Demographic, social, economic, and technological trends are forcing changes on organizations and on personnel. These trends include, for instance, a dramatic slowdown in the growth of the labor force and an increasing emphasis on knowledge-based work.
2. In the face of trends like these, the role of human resource management is evolving. Specific ways in which the personnel function will change include changes in employee benefits, new organization structures, restructuring career ladders, dealing with an aging work force, experimenting with new recruitment methods, and doing more training of workers to help them cope with the new knowledge-based jobs.
3. Perhaps the most striking change in personnel will be its evolving role in developing and implementing corporate strategy. A company's strategic plan outlines the course of action the firm plans to pursue in becoming the sort of enterprise that it wants to be given its external opportunities and threats and its internal strengths and weaknesses. To this end, personnel helps top management to formulate and execute the company's strategic plan by helping to supply intelligence regarding the company's external opportunities and threats, by supplying intelligence about the company's internal strengths and weaknesses, and by helping execute the plan, for instance, by eliminating a weakness that could be an impediment to the plan.
4. A policy is a guide to action that ensures consistency under a particular set of circumstances and within the framework of the company's strategic plan.
5. Commitment-building HRM practices include: Establish people-first values; Guarantee Fair Treatment; use value-based hiring; provide employee security; emphasize rewards package; actualize employees (front-load challenge, enrich and empower, stress promotion from within programs).

KEY TERMS

strategic plan policies

DISCUSSION QUESTIONS

1. Write an essay titled "My Philosophy of Personnel Management."
2. Explain how each chapter in this book affects motivation and the quality of work life.
3. Write an essay in which you summarize how you would use specific personnel management techniques to select, train, motivate, and appraise employees.
4. Explain the impact of HRM on employee commitment.
5. Discuss HRM's role in strategic planning.

HUMAN RESOURCE MANAGEMENT SIMULATION

Setting and pursuing organizational goals are an integral part of *The Human Resources Simulation*. Your instructor may require you to formalize these goals. There are instructions and forms for this purpose in Chapter 3. Although you have wide latitude in this area, the CEO has instructed you to "get this organization moving." Ultimately, you will be judged by the success or failure of your organization to achieve the goals you select, whether the goals are formalized or not.

Your team's performance will be judged against the goals you have (formally or informally) set in terms of your ability to manage a budget, unit labor cost, quality, morale, grievances, absenteeism, accident rate, and turnover. As in the real world, you do not have enough budget to do everything. Your team must make choices as to what is most important to you and concentrate your budget on those factors. You will, in a sense, be competing with all other teams on the items mentioned above. However, in terms of direct competition, you are competing only with other firms in the local labor market for new employees. The other firms (teams) in your class comprise the local labor area.

NOTES

1. This is based on Edward E. Lawler III, "Human Resources Management: Meeting the New Challenges," *Personnel* (January 1988), pp. 24–25. See also Judith Waldrop, The Baby Boomers Turn 45," *American Demographers,* January 1991, pp. 22–26. Charlene Solomon, "Managing the Baby Busters," *Personnel Journal,* Vol. 71, No. 3, pp. 52–59.
2. This section is based on ibid., pp. 24–27; Michael Driver, Robert Coffey, and David Bowen, "Where is HR Management Going?" *Personnel* (January 1988), pp. 28–31; Eric G. Flamholtz et al., "Personnel Management: The Tone of Tomorrow," *Personnel Journal* (July 1987), pp. 43–48; and Laura Herren, "The New Game of HR: Playing to Win," *Personnel* (June 1989), pp. 19–22.
3. Thomas Paine, "Benefits in the 1990's," *Personnel Journal,* March 1988, p. 8.
4. Peter Drucker, *Wall Street Journal*, January 20, 1988.
5. See ibid.
6. Herren, "The New Game of HR," p. 20.
7. See ibid., p. 22.
8. Two writers point out that it is important not to fall in the trap of assuming that HRM is involved only in strategic planning to the extent of matching personnel activities with strategies, forecasting labor power requirements and supplies, and presenting means for integrating HRM into the overall effort to match corporate strategy. Instead, they say, there is a "reciprocal interdependence between a firm's business strategy and its human resources strategy." In other words, the company's human resources (and

therefore human resource management department) can be among other things a way to gain an improved competitive position. See Cynthia Lengnick-Hall and Mark Lengnick-Hall, "Strategic Human Resources Management: A Review of the Literature and a Proposed Typology," *Academy of Management Review* (July 1988), pp. 454–470; see also Peg Anthony and Lincoln Norton, "Link HR to Corporate Strategy," *Personnel Journal* April 1991, pp. 75–86. See also Peter Boxall, "Strategic Human Resource Management: Beginnings of a New Theoretical Sophistication?", *Human Resource Management Journal,* Vol. 2, No. 3, Spring 1992, pp. 60–79; Jeffrey Arthur, "The Link Between Business Strategy and Industrial Relations Systems in American Steel Minimills," *Industrial and Labor Relations Review,* Vol. 45, No. 3, April 1992, pp. 488–506.

9. This is based on Robert Burg and Brian Smith, "Restructuring Compensation and Benefits to Support Strategy," Part I, "Executive Compensation," *Compensation and Benefits Review* (November–December 1987), pp. 15–22.
10. Ibid., p. 17.
11. Sue Ellen Thompson, *Encyclopedia of Personnel Policies,* Business and Legal Reports, 1983, p. 1.02.
12. These are based on Margaret Magnus, "Personnel Policies in Partnership with Profit," *Personnel Journal* (September 1987), pp. 102–109.
13. Ibid.
14. For a recent discussion along these lines, see Joel Lapointe and Jo Ann Verdin, "How to Calculate the Cost of Human Resources," *Personnel Journal* (January 1988), pp. 34–45.
15. This is based on Bruce R. Ellig, "Improving Effectiveness Through an HR Review," *Personnel* (June 1989), pp. 56–64.
16. Ellig, "Improving Effectiveness Through an HR Review," p. 57.
17. For a discussion of employees as a competitive advantage see, for example, Anthony and Norton, "Link HR to Corporate Strategy." Several studies suggest that personnel policies do tend to cluster, indicating that HR policies flow in a consistent manner from a firm's strategy. In one study six policy areas—job design, promotions, recruiting, training, grievance procedures, and communication clustered into "high-commitment" versus "rigid, formalized" HR systems. In a second study, Arthur found that HR systems in a steel mill could be categorized as emphasizing either cost reduction or employee commitment. Personal correspondence with Professor Casey Ichniowski, Graduate School of Business Administration, Columbia University, Uris 713, New York, NY 10027, April 1990; Jeffrey Arthur, "The Link Between Business Strategy and Industrial Relations Systems," *Industrial and Labor Relations Review,* Vol. 45, no. 3 (April 1992), pp. 488–506.

VIDEO CASE 5

—Conclusion—

DRINKING AND FLYING

In the Introduction to Video Case 5 on page 591, we asked several important questions that you should now refer to.

Whether it's an airline or a dry cleaning store, reducing accidents at work comes down to reducing unsafe conditions and unsafe acts. In some respects, reducing unsafe conditions is the easier of the two tasks: Guard rails can be placed around machines, floors can be swept, and safety goggles can be supplied. Reducing unsafe *acts,* however, is not always so simple. As the video makes vividly clear, employees can and will break the company's safety rules, even if the consequences for themselves and their colleagues and customers (in this case, passengers) are extremely severe. Employee testing and selection can certainly play a role in reducing unsafe acts. References can be carefully checked, and tests can help to identify and screen out potentially dangerous employees, for example. Training, propaganda, and continuous reinforcement are some other ways to reduce accidents at work. As in the case of the airline flight crew, once troubled employees are identified, then discipline and counseling or discharge can be prescribed. Furthermore, when a company takes steps to reduce unsafe acts, top management's values impact all aspects of employee behavior. A top management commitment to employee safety, in fact, is one sure way to guarantee that unsafe conditions and acts are minimized.

In Part 5 we're also reminded that top management's values mold a lot more than worker safety. Guaranteed fair treatment, employee job security, and the trust on which two-way communication depends also flow from top management's values.

Finally, human resource management plays an important role in strategic planning. The firm's human resource management department does this, in part, by helping top management identify external opportunities and threats and internal strengths and weaknesses. In addition, the human resources management department should be heavily involved in the successful execution of the company's strategic plan. This department can help to eliminate weaknesses that might inhibit the plan and institute employee commitment-building practices that foster the high levels of quality, service, and flexibility that today's strategies increasingly require.

INTERNATIONAL ISSUES IN HUMAN RESOURCE MANAGEMENT

APPENDIX

▸ INTRODUCTION

You don't have to look very far to see how important international business has become to companies here and abroad. In the United States, exports are expected to increase by over 74% in the next 10 years, a rate of growth that's over twice that of any other component of the Gross National Product.[1]

This rapid growth of exports reflects the fact that many more U.S.-based companies are focusing their marketing efforts not only here, but abroad. Huge "global" companies like Procter & Gamble, IBM, and Citibank have long had extensive overseas operations, of course. However, with the European market unification in 1992, the opening up of Eastern Europe, and the rapid development of demand in other areas of the world, more and more companies are finding that their success (and perhaps their survival) depends on their ability to market and manage overseas. And, of course, to foreign companies the United States is "overseas" and tens of thousands of foreign firms already have thriving operations on (and beyond) our U.S. shores.

As a result of this internationalization, companies must increasingly be managed globally, even though such globalization confronts managers with some herculean challenges. Market, product, and production plans must often now be coordinated on a worldwide basis, for instance, and organization structures capable of balancing centralized home–office control with adequate local autonomy must be created.

Some of the most pressing challenges facing employers concern the impact of globalization on a company's human resource management system. These challenges range from (1) general issues like how to select, train, and compensate managers who must be sent to foreign posts, to (2) dealing with country-specific differences which demand corresponding country-specific fine tuning of a firm's human resource management policies. These two sets of challenges are addressed next.

▸ GENERAL INTERNATIONAL ISSUES IN HRM

As we have already touched on at several points in this book, there are at least three major HRM issues a global company has to address: selecting managers for overseas assignments, orienting and training these people, and then compensating them.

SELECTION FOR MULTINATIONAL MANAGEMENT

The thing you have to remember about selecting multinational managers is that you must be as careful to define the job demands and human requirements as you would for any domestic job. Many companies make the mistake of evaluating only the technical (such as manufacturing knowledge) demands of the overseas job, while ignoring the cultural demands and need for adaptability that characterize such overseas jobs. Thus, as one vice-president for international human resources puts it: "There is too much emphasis on executives' technical abilities and too little on their cultural skills and family situations . . . when international executive relocations fail, they generally fail either because expatriates can't fathom the customs of the new country or because their families can't deal with the emotional stress that a company's relocation entails."[2] In the same vein, one expert on Japanese multinational enterprises argues that Japanese multinationals have had better success rates with the employees they send overseas than do U.S. firms; she argues that this is largely a product of superior selection and training.[3]

As is often the case with employee selection, the best rule is often that past experience is the best predictor of future success. Companies like Colgate-Palmolive therefore look for overseas candidates whose work and nonwork experience, education, and language skills already demonstrate a commitment to and facility in living and working with different cultures.[4] Even several successful summers spent traveling overseas or participating in foreign student programs would seem to provide some concrete basis for believing that the potential transferee can accomplish the required adaptation when he or she arrives overseas.

Realistic previews at this point are also crucial. Both the potential transferee and his or her family need to have all the information you can provide on the problems to expect in the new job (such as mandatory private schooling for the children) as well as any information obtainable on the cultural benefits, problems, and idiosyncrasies of the country in question. International human resource managers speak about avoiding "culture shock" in much the same way as we discussed using realistic previews to avoid "reality shock" amongst new employees. In any case, the golden rule here is to "spell it out ahead of time" as Ciba-Geigy does for its international transferees.[5]

The question arises as to whether there are paper-and-pencil tests that can be used to more effectively select employees for overseas assignments and here the answer seems to be "yes." Generally speaking, of course, the development and use of any such test should ideally be company-specific and validated as a tool for placing candidates overseas. However, companies have developed and validated general-purpose tests that focus on the aptitudes and personality characteristics of successful overseas candidates. One such assessment tool is called the Overseas Assignment Inventory. Based on 12 years of research involving more than 7,000 cases the test's publisher indicates that it is useful in identifying characteristics and attitudes such candidates should have.[6]

ORIENTING AND TRAINING EMPLOYEES FOR INTERNATIONAL ASSIGNMENTS

When it comes to providing the orientation and training required for success overseas, the practices of most U.S. firms reflect more form than substance. One consultant (who admittedly is in the business of providing training for overseas assignments) says that despite many companies' claims there is generally little or no systematic selection and training for assignments overseas. One relevant survey concluded that a sample of company presidents and chairpersons agreed that international business was growing in importance and required employees firmly grounded in the economics and practices of foreign countries. However, few of their companies actually provided such overseas-oriented training to their employees.[7]

What sort of special training do overseas candidates need? One firm specializing in such programs prescribes a four-step approach.[8] Level 1 training focuses on the impact of cultural differences, and on raising trainees' awareness of such differences and the impact on business outcomes of these cultural differences. Level 2 focuses on attitudes and aims at getting participants to understand how attitudes (both negative and positive) are formed and how they influence behavior. (For example, unfavorable stereotypes may subconsciously influence how a new manager responds to and treats his or her new foreign subordinates.) Finally, Level 3 training provides factual knowledge about the target country, while Level 4 provides skill building in areas like language and adjustment and adaptation skills. (Additional guidelines for developing international executives—such as "brief candidates fully and clearly on all relocation policies," and "provide all relocating executives with a mentor to monitor their overseas careers and help them secure appropriate jobs with the company when they repatriate"—were discussed in Chapter 8.)

Beyond these special training practices there is also the need for more traditional training and development of your overseas employees. At IBM, for instance, such development involves using a series of rotating assignments that will permit overseas IBM managers to grow professionally. At the same time, IBM and a number of other major firms have established management development centers around the world where executives can come to hone their skills. Beyond that, classroom programs (such as those at the London Business School, or at INSEAD in Fountainebleu, France) provide overseas executives the sorts of opportunities to hone their functional skills that similar programs stateside do for their U.S.-based colleagues.

INTERNATIONAL ISSUES IN COMPENSATION MANAGEMENT

Generally speaking, the whole area of international compensation management presents some tricky problems. On the one hand, there is a certain logic in maintaining companywide pay scales and policies so that, for instance, divisional marketing directors throughout the world are all paid within the same narrow range. This reduces the risk of perceived inequities and dramatically simplifies the job of keeping track of disparate country-by-country wage rates.

And yet not adapting pay scales to local markets can present an HR manager with more problems than it solves. The fact is that it can be enormously more expensive to live in some countries (like Japan) than others (like Greece), and if these cost-of-living differences aren't considered it may be almost impossible to get managers to take "high cost" assignments.

Yet even here the answer is usually not just to pay, say, marketing directors more in one country than in another. For example, you could thereby elicit resistance when telling a marketing director in Japan who's earning $2,000 per week to move to your division in Spain, where his or her pay for the same job (cost of living notwithstanding) will drop by half. One way to handle this problem is to pay a similar base salary companywide and then add on various allowances according to individual market conditions.[9]

The problem here is that determining what equitable wage rates should be in many countries is no simple matter. As we explained in Chapter 12, there is a wealth of "packaged" compensation survey data already available in the United States, but such data are not so easy to come by overseas. As one expert on the matter has said, "Unfortunately, local sources of compensation information in foreign countries are hard to find, and often only compound the problem rather than help to bridge the gap."[10] As a result, he says that "one of the greatest difficulties in managing total compensation on a multinational level is establishing a consistent compensation measure between countries that builds credibility both at home and abroad."

Some multinational companies deal with this problem by conducting their own annual compensation surveys. For example, Kraft conducts an annual study of total compensation in Belgium, Germany, Italy, Spain, and the United Kingdom. Kraft tries to maintain a fairly constant sample group of study participants (companies) in its survey. It then focuses on the total compensation paid to each of 10 senior management positions held by local nationals in these firms. The survey covers all forms of compensation including cash, short- and long-term incentives, retirement plans, medical benefits, and perquisites.[11] The company then uses these data to establish a competitive value for each element of pay. This information in turn becomes the input used for annual salary increases and proposed changes in the benefit package.

One international compensation trend of growing importance concerns the awarding of long-term incentive pay to overseas managers. While it may not seem particularly logical, many U.S. multinationals only permit the top managers at corporate headquarters to participate in long-term incentive programs like stock option plans.[12] Equally problematical is the fact that many of the multinationals that do offer overseas managers long-term incentives (32 out of 40 were in one survey) use only overall corporate performance criteria when awarding incentive pay. Since the performance of the company's stock on a U.S. stock market may have little relevance to, say, a West Berlin manager in a German subsidiary, the incentive value of such a reward is highly suspect. This is particularly so in that, as one expert writes, "Regardless of size, a foreign subsidiary's influence on its parent company's stock price (U.S. dollars) is more likely to result from exchange rate movements than from management action."[13]

The answer here, more multinationals are finding, is to formulate new long-term incentives specifically for overseas executives. More and more U.S. multinationals are thus devising performance-based long-term incentive plans that are tied more closely to performance at the subsidiary level. These can help build a sense of ownership among key local managers while providing the financial incentives needed to attract and keep the people you need overseas.

Global HRM

Managing Intercountry Differences in Human Resource Management

There are two basic sets of issues in international HRM management. One, as previously explained, is the more general set of issues regarding how to select, train, and compensate managers, given the unique demands that dealing with new and different cultures places on international transferees. The second set of thorny international HRM issues derives from the fact that there are wide-ranging differences in legal systems, labor availability, and so on among countries. As a result, multinationals must, to some extent, fine tune their HRM policies to the unique needs of each country in which they do business. We turn now to a closer examination of these sorts of intercountry differences and their impact on HRM.

INTERCOUNTRY DIFFERENCES IMPACTING HRM

To a large extent companies operating only within the borders of the United States enjoy the luxury of dealing with a relatively limited set of economic, cultural, and legal variables. Notwithstanding the range from liberal to conservative, for instance, America's is basically a capitalist competitive society. And while a multitude of cultural and ethnic backgrounds are represented in America's work force, various shared values (such as an appreciation for democracy) help to blur the otherwise sharp cultural differences. While the different states and municipalities (as explained in Chapter 2) certainly have their own laws affecting HRM, a basic legal framework as laid down by federal law also helps to produce a fairly predictable set of legal guidelines regarding matters such as employment discrimination, labor relations, and safety and health.

A company operating multiple units abroad is generally not blessed with such relative homogeneity. For example, minimum legally mandated holidays may range from none in the United Kingdom to five weeks per year in Luxembourg. And, while there are no formal requirements for employee participation in Italy, employee representatives on boards of directors are required in companies with more than 30 employees in Denmark. The point is that the management of the human resource function in multinational companies is complicated enormously by the need to adapt personnel policies and procedures to the differences among countries in which each subsidiary is based. Here are some intercountry differences which demand such adaptation.[14]

Cultural Factors

There are wide-ranging cultural and ethnic differences from country to country which demand corresponding differences in personnel practices among a company's foreign subsidiaries. We might generalize, for instance, that given the cultural background of the Far East and the importance there of the patriarchal system, the typical Japanese worker's view of his or her relationship to an employer has an important impact on how that person works. Human resource incentive plans in Japan therefore tend to focus on the work group while in the West the more usual prescription is to focus on individual worker incentives.[15]

In addition to arguing for differences in HR practices, these sorts of cultural differences also suggest that HR staff in a foreign subsidiary is best comprised of citizens of the subsidiary's host country. A high degree of sensitivity and empathy for cultural and attitudinal demands of coworkers is always important when selecting employees to staff overseas operations, as we have explained. However, such sensitivity is especially important when the job is HRM and the work involves "human" jobs like interviewing, testing, orienting, training, counseling, and (if need be) terminating. As one expert puts it, "An HR staff that shares the employee's cultural background is more likely to be sensitive to the employee's needs and expectations in the work place—and is thus more likely to manage the company successfully."[16]

Economic Factors

Differences in economic systems among countries also influence the role played by HRM. In free enterprise systems, for instance, the need for efficiency tends to favor HR policies that value productivity, efficient workers, and staff cutting where market forces dictate it. Moving along the scale toward more socialist systems, on the other hand, HR practices tend to shift more toward preventing unemployment, even at the expense of sacrificing efficiency.

Labor Cost Factors

Differences in labor costs may also produce corresponding differences in HR practices. High labor costs can require a focus on efficiency, for instance, and on all those HR practices aimed at improving employee performance. On the other hand, the lower labor costs associated with some less developed countries may make it cost effective to spend less on employee productivity-boosting activities.

Industrial Relations Factors

Industrial relations (and particularly the relationship between the worker, the union, and the employer) vary dramatically from country to country and have an enormous impact on human resource management practices. In the Federal Republic of Germany, for instance, "co-determination" is the rule. Here employees have the legal right to have a voice in setting company policies. In this and several other countries workers elect their own representatives to the supervisory board of the employer, and there is also a vice-president for labor at the top management level.[17] On the other hand, in many other countries the state interferes very little in the relations between employers and unions. In the United States, for instance, HR policies on most matters such as wages and benefits are set not by the state but by the employer or by the employer in negotiations with its labor unions. In Germany, on the other hand, the various laws on co-determination including the Works Constitution Act (1972), the Co-Determination Act (1976), and the ECSC Co-Determination Act (1951) largely determine what HR policies will be in many German firms.

Europe 1992[18]

The 12 separate countries of the European community are now unified into a common market for goods, services, capital, and even labor. Generally speaking, tariffs for goods moving across borders from one EC country to another disappeared, and employees (with some exceptions) found it easier to move relatively freely between jobs in various EC countries.

Figure A.1 summarizes current employment practices and policies among EC countries. The figure underscores two things. First (in line with our discussion of intercountry differences), you can see that there are some wide-ranging differences in HR practices among EC countries. Thus Figure A-1 shows that many countries have minimum wages while others do not, and maximum hours permitted in the workday and workweek vary from no maximum in the United Kingdom to 48 per week in Greece and Italy. Similar differences are apparent in matters like minimum annual holidays, minimum notice to be given by employer, termination formalities, and employee participation.

Figure A.1 Current Employment Practices and Policies Among EC Countries

Country	*Employment Formalities*	*Minimum Pay*	*Max. Hours (Including overtime)*	*Minimum Annual Holiday*	*Minimum Notice to Be Given by Employer*	*Termination Formalities*	*Employee Participation*
Belgium	Certain terms must be in writing.	Yes	8 per day; 40 per week	4 weeks.	Workers: 14–28 days. Others: 3 months for up to 5 years' service + 3 mos. for every 5 years' service. Higher paid employees notice period agreed on when notice given or decided by Court.	Can terminate without notice for gross misconduct (but this does not include all instances of incompetence). Redundancy payments.	Work councils.
Denmark	Contracts usually oral.	No, but must conform to one of 2 compulsory wage systems.	Depends on collective agreement.	2½ days per month.	Workers depends on collective agreement. Others: 1–6 months.	Can terminate without notice for gross misconduct; unfair dismissal and redundancy payments.	Employee representatives on board of directors where there are more than 30 employees.
France	Contracts in writing. Collective agreements may be generally binding.	Yes	10 per day. 39 per week.	2½ days per month (includes 5 Saturdays).	1 month after 6 months' service; 2 months after 2 years' service.	Unfair dismissal. Redundancy payments. Authorization of redundancies required.	Employee and union representatives. Works councils.
Germany	Fixed-term agreements restricted; collective agreements may be generally binding.	No, but if a collective agreement, this must make provision.	8 per day. 48 per week.	18 days.	Workers: 2 weeks to 3 months. Others: 6 weeks to 6 months from end of calendar-year quarter.	Unfair dismissal. Prior consultation on redundancies or dismissals with works council and in some cases the labor authorities.	Works councils.
Greece	No substantial formalities.	Yes	48 per week.	4 weeks (after 1 year's employment).	Workers: none. Others: 1 month to 2 years.	Severance payments of 5–52 days' pay for workers or 1–24 months' pay for other employees. If notice given, only ½ payable.	Employee committees.

FIGURE A.1 **(continued)**

Ireland	Employees may require employers to supply written statements of terms of employment.	No	No generally applicable statutory maximum.	3 weeks.	1–8 weeks.	Unfair dismissal. Redundancy payments.	No formal requirements.
Italy	Contracts in writing. National collective agreements.	Collective agreement.	48 per week. 8 per day.	Collective agreement.	Collective agreement.	Severance payments. Can dismiss only for redundancy or good cause.	No formal requirements.
Luxembourg	Written contracts must be provided. Agreements may be binding on a sector.	Yes	40 per week, 8 per day.	25 working days (5 days' holiday equals one week).	4 weeks to 6 months, depending on category of worker and length of service.	Severance payments, 1–12 months. Prior notification of redundancy and redundancy payments.	Employees' representatives. Joint works councils. Employee directors.
The Netherlands	No substantial formalities.	Yes	48 per week. 8½ per day. 5½ days per week.	4 weeks.	Interval of payment (usually 2 weeks or 1 month) or a period of up to 13 weeks (26 weeks for older employees) based on length of service, whichever is longer.	Authorization of labor office usually required to dismiss with notice. May need to go to the Court; either procedure can take several months.	Works council in undertakings with 35 or more employees.
Portugal	Fixed-term contracts must be in writing.	Yes	Office workers: 42 hours per week. Others: 48 per week; 8 per day.	Not less than 21 days nor more than 30 days.	Redundancy-notice period fixed when conditions of redundancy established.	Can dismiss only for "just cause" or redundancy. Prior notification of redundancies.	Workers' commissions and registered trade unions.
Spain	No substantial formalities.	Yes	40 per week. 9 per day	2½ days per month.	1 month after 1 year's service, 3 months after 2 years.	Only for specified causes. Dismissal for other causes: compensation to 45 days pay per year of service.	Employee delegates and committees, employee directors.
United Kingdom	Written statement of terms of employment.	No	No	No	1–13 weeks.	Unfair dismissal. Redundancy payments. Prior notification of redundancies.	No formal requirements.

Source: Sedel, Rae, "Europe 1992: HR Implications of the European Unification," *Personnel,* October 1989, p. 22. (reprinted with the permission of the publisher from *Personnel Today,* April 4, 1989).

Second, the impact of "1992" will be to gradually reduce these sorts of differences among member countries. However, these changes will be gradual, not all-at-once. Social legislation and examinations by the European Commission are at the present time slowly harmonizing some of these differences. However, even if all of these differences summarized in the figure are eventually eliminated, HR practices will still differ from country to country; cultural differences will require that, no doubt. Even into the far-distant future, in other words, managing human resources multinationally will present some tricky problems for HR managers.

NOTES

1. "The Gross National Product," *Occupational Outlook Quarterly* (Fall 1989), U.S. Department of Labor; see also Ellen Brandt, "Global HR," *Personnel Journal*, March 1991, pp. 38–44.
2. Paul Blocklyn, "Developing the International Executive," *Personnel* (March 1989), p. 44.
3. Rosalie L. Tung, "Human Resource Planning in Japanese Multinationals: A Model for U.S. Firms?" *Journal of International Business Studies*, Vol. 15, no. 2 (Fall 1984), pp. 139–149. See also Mooke Banai, "Human Resource Management Problems in American Multinational Corporations," *Business & The Contemporary World,* Vol. 3, No. 4, Summer 1991, pp. 113–120.
4. See, for example, Blocklyn, "Developing the International Executive," p. 45.
5. Ibid,. p. 45.
6. Discussed in Madelyn Callahan, "Preparing the New Global Manager," *Training and Development Journal* (March 1989), p. 30. The publisher of the inventory is the New York consulting firm Moran, Stahl & Boyer; see also Jennifer Laabs, "The Global Talent Search," *Personnel Journal* (August 1991), pp. 38–44 for a discussion of how firms such as Coca-Cola recruit and develop international managers.
7. Callahan, "Preparing the New Global Manager," pp. 29–30.
8. This is based on ibid., p. 30. See also Daniel Feldman, "Repatriate Moves as Career Transitions," *Human Resource Management Review,* Vol. 1, No. 3, Fall 1991, pp. 163–178.
9. James Stoner and R. Edward Freeman, *Management*, 4th ed. (Englewood Cliffs, NJ: Prentice Hall, 1989), p. 783.
10. Hewitt Associates, "On Compensation," (May 1989), p. 1 (Hewitt Associates, 86-87 East Via De Ventura, Scottsdale, Arizona 85258).
11. Hewitt Associates, "On Compensation," p. 2.
12. This is based on Brian Brooks, "Long-Term Incentives: International Executives Need Them, Too," *Personnel* (August 1988), pp. 40–42. See also James Ward and Mark Blumenthal, "Localization: A Study in Cost Containment," *Innovations in International Compensation,* Vol. 17, No. 4, Nov. 1991, pp. 3–4.
13. Brooks, "Long-Term Incentives," p. 41.
14. These are based on Eduard Gaugler, "HR Management: An International Comparison," *Personnel* (August 1988), pp. 24–30.
15. For a discussion of this see ibid., p. 26; see also George Palmer, "Transferred to Tokyo—A Guide to Etiquette in the Land of the Rising Sun," *Multinational Business*, no. 4 (1990/1991), pp. 36–44.
16. Gaugler, "HR Management," p. 27. See also Simcha Ronen and Oded Shenkar, "Using Employee Attitudes to Establish MNC Regional Divisions," *Personnel* (August 1988), pp. 32–39.
17. This is discussed in Gaugler, "HR Management," p. 28.
18. This is based on Rae Sedel, "Europe 1992: HR Implications of the European Unification," *Personnel* (October 1989), pp. 19–24.

GLOSSARY

"9,9" managers A manager with this rating is highly concerned with people and with production.

action learning A training technique by which management trainees are allowed to work full time analyzing and solving problems in other departments or government agencies.

adverse impact The overall impact of employer practices that result in significantly higher percentages of members of minorities and other protected groups being rejected for employment, placement, or promotion.

affirmative action Steps that are taken for the purpose of eliminating the present effects of past discrimination.

Age Discrimination in Employment Act of 1967 The act prohibiting arbitrary age discrimination and specifically protecting individuals over 40 years old.

agency shop A form of union security in which employees who do not belong to the union must still pay union dues (on the assumption that union efforts benefit all workers).

Albemarle Paper Company* v. *Moody Supreme Court case in which it was ruled that the validity of job tests must be documented and that employee performance standards must be unambiguous.

alternation ranking method Ranking employees from best to worst on a particular trait.

American Federation of Labor and Congress of Industrial Organizations (AFL-CIO) A voluntary federation of 190 national and international labor unions formed by the merger of the AFL and CIO in 1955.

Americans with Disabilities Act (ADA) The act requiring employers to make reasonable accommodations for disabled employees, it prohibits discrimination against disabled persons.

annual bonus Plans that are designed to motivate short-term performance of managers and are tied to company profitability.

application form The application that provides information on education, prior work record, and skills.

appraisal interview A discussion following a performance appraisal in which supervisor and employee discuss the employee's rating and possible remedial actions.

aptitudes These include intelligence, numerical aptitude, mechanical comprehension, and manual dexterity, as well as talents such as artistic, theatrical, or musical ability that play an important role in career decisions.

arbitration The most definitive type of third-party intervention, in which the arbitrator usually has the power to determine and dictate the settlement terms.

authority The right to make decisions, direct others' work, and give orders.

authorization cards In order to petition for a union election, the union must show that at least 30% of employees may be interested in being unionized. Employees indicate this interest by signing authorization cards.

bargaining unit The group of employees the union will be authorized to represent.

behavior modeling A training technique in which trainees are first shown good management techniques (in a film), are then asked to play roles in a simulated situation, and are then given feedback and praise by their supervisor.

behaviorally anchored rating scale (BARS) An appraisal method that aims at combining the benefits of narrative critical incidents and quantified ratings by anchoring a quantified scale with specific narrative examples of good or poor performance.

benchmark job A job that is used to anchor the employer's pay scale and around which other jobs are arranged in order of relative worth.

benefits Any supplements to wages given to employees. They may include health and life insurance, vacation, pension, education plans, and discounts on company products, for instance.

bias The tendency to allow individual differences such as age, race, and sex affect the appraisal rates these employees receive.

bona fide occupational qualification (BFOQ) Requirement that an employee be of a certain religion, sex, or national origin where that is reasonably necessary to the organization's normal operation. Specified by the 1964 Civil Rights Act.

boycott The combined refusal by employees and other interested parties to buy or use the employer's products.

bumping/layoff procedures Detailed procedures that determine who will be laid off if no work is available; generally allow employees to use their seniority to remain on the job.

burnout The total depletion of physical and mental

resources caused by excessive striving to reach some unrealistic work-related goal.

business necessity Justification for an otherwise discriminatory employment practice, provided there is an overriding legitimate business purpose.

candidate-order error An error of judgment on the part of the interviewer due to interviewing one or more very good or very bad candidates just before the interview in question.

capital accumulation programs Long-term incentives most often reserved for senior executives. Six popular plans include stock options, stock appreciation rights, performance achievement plans, restricted stock plans, phantom stock plans, and book value plans.

career anchors A concern or value that you will not give up if a choice has to be made.

career cycle The stages through which a person's career evolves.

career planning and development Giving employees the assistance to form realistic career goals and the opportunities to realize them.

case study method A development method in which the manager is presented with a written description of an organizational problem to diagnose and solve.

central tendency A tendency to rate all employees the same way, such as rating them all average.

citations Summons informing employers and employees of the regulations and standards that have been violated in the workplace.

Civil Rights Act of 1991 (CRA 1991) It places burden of proof back on employers and permits compensatory and punitive damages.

Civil Rights Act This law makes it illegal to discriminate in employment because of race, color, religion, sex, or national origin.

classes Dividing jobs into classes based on a set of rules for each class, such as amount of independent judgment, skill, physical effort, and so forth, required for each class of jobs. Classes usually contain similar jobs—such as all secretaries.

classification (or grading) method A method for categorizing jobs into groups.

closed shop A form of union security in which the company can hire only union members. This was outlawed in 1947 but still exists in some industries (such as printing).

collective bargaining The process through which representatives of management and the union meet to negotiate a labor agreement.

comparable worth The concept by which women (who are usually paid less than men) can claim that men in comparable (rather than strictly equal) jobs are paid more.

compensable factor A fundamental, compensable element of a job, such as skill, effort, responsibility, or working conditions.

computerized forecast The determination of future staff needs by projecting a firm's sales, volume of production, and personnel required to maintain this volume of output, with computers and software packages.

content validity A test that is "content valid" is one in which the test contains a fair sample of the tasks and skills actually needed for the job in question.

criterion validity A type of validity based on showing that scores on the test ("predictors") are related to job performance ("criterion").

critical incident method Keeping a record of uncommonly good or undesirable examples of an employee's work-related behavior and reviewing it with the employee at predetermined times.

Davis-Bacon Act A law passed in 1931 that sets wage rates for laborers employed by contractors working for the federal government.

day-to-day collective bargaining The process of grievance resolution through which the collective bargaining agreement's clauses are interpreted (but *not* renegotiated).

decline stage The period during which many people are faced with the prospect of having to accept reduced levels of power and responsibility.

deferred profit-sharing plan A plan in which a certain amount of profits is credited to each employee's account, payable at retirement, termination, or death.

defined benefit A plan that contains a formula for determining retirement benefits.

defined contribution A plan in which the employer's contribution to employees' retirement or savings funds are specified.

Department of Labor job analysis Standardized method for rating, classifying, and comparing virtually every kind of job based on data, people, and things.

directive interview An interview following a set sequence of questions.

discipline A procedure that corrects or punishes a subordinate because a rule or procedure has been violated.

dismissal Involuntary termination of an employee's employment with the firm.

disparate impact Means there is an unintentional disparity between the proportion of a protected group applying for a position and the proportion getting the job.

disparate rejection rates One test for adverse impact, in which it can be demonstrated that there is a discrepancy between rates of rejection of members of a protected group and of others.

disparate treatment Means there is an intentional disparity between the proportion of a protected group and the proportion getting the job.

downsizings Refers to the process of reducing, usually dramatically, the number of people employed by the firm.

early retirement window A type of "golden offering" by which employees are encouraged to retire early, the incentive being liberal pension benefits plus, perhaps, a cash payment.

economic strike A strike that results from a failure to agree on the terms of a contract.

Employee Assistance Program (EAP) A formal employer program for providing employees with counseling and/or treatment programs for problems such as alcoholism, gambling, or stress.

Employee Retirement Income Security Act (ERISA) Signed into law by President Ford in 1974, this law provides government protection of pensions for all employees with company pension plans. It also regulates vesting rights (employees who leave before retirement may claim compensation from the pension plan).

Employee Stock Ownership Plan (ESOP) This plan usually involves having a corporation contribute shares of its own stock to a trust in which additional contributions are made annually. The trust distributes the stock to employees on retirement or separation from service.

employee compensation All forms of pay or rewards going to employees and arising from their employment.

employee orientation A procedure for providing new employees with basic background information about the firm.

Equal Employment Opportunity Commission (EEOC) The commission, created by Title VII, is empowered to investigate job discrimination complaints and sue on behalf of complainants.

Equal Pay Act of 1963 An amendment to the Fair Labor Standards Act designed to require equal pay for women doing the same work as men.

Equal Pay Act of 1963 The act requiring equal pay for equal work, regardless of sex.

establishment stage The period, roughly from ages 24 to 44, that is the heart of most people's work lives.

exit interview Interviews, usually conducted by the human resource department, with any and all employees who are leaving the firm for any reason and which are aimed at eliciting information about the job or related matters that might give the employer a better insight into what is right or what is wrong about the company.

expectancy chart A graph showing the relationship between test scores and job performance for a large group of people.

experimentation Formal methods for testing the effectiveness of a training program, preferably with before and after tests and a control group.

exploration stage The period from around ages 15 to 24 during which a person seriously explores various occupational alternatives, attempting to match these alternatives with his or her interests and abilities.

fact-finder A neutral party who studies the issues in a dispute and makes a public recommendation for settlement.

factor comparison method A widely used method of ranking jobs according to a variety of skill and difficulty factors, then adding up these rankings to arrive at an overall numerical rating for each given job.

Fair Labor Standards Act Congress passed this act in 1936 to provide for minimum wages, maximum hours, overtime pay, and child labor protection. The law has been amended many times and covers most employees.

fair day's work Frederick Taylor's observation that haphazard setting of piecework requirements and wages by supervisors was not sufficient, and that careful study was needed to define acceptable production quotas for each job.

federal agency guidelines Guidelines issued by federal agencies charged with ensuring compliance with equal employment federal legislation that explain recommended employer procedures in detail.

flexible benefits program Individualized plans allowed by employers to accommodate employee preferences for benefits.

flexiplace A flexible work arrangement in which employees are allowed or encouraged to work at home or in a satellite office closer to home.

flextime A plan whereby employees build their workday around a core of midday hours.

forced distribution method Similar to grading on a curve; predetermined percentages of ratees are placed in various performance categories.

four-day workweek An arrangement that allows employees to work four ten-hour days instead of the more usual five eight-hour days.

functional control The authority exerted by a personnel manager as coordinator of personnel activities.

functional job analysis A method for classifying jobs similar to the Department of Labor job analysis, but additionally taking into account the extent to which instructions, reasoning, judgment, and verbal facility are necessary for performing job tasks.

gainsharing An incentive plan that engages employees in a common effort to achieve productivity objectives and share the gains.

golden offerings Offers to current employees aimed at encouraging them to retire early—perhaps even with the same pensions they would expect if they retired at, say, age 65.

good faith bargaining A term that means both parties are communicating and negotiating. Also, that proposals are being matched with counterproposals and that both parties are making every reasonable effort to arrive at agreements. It does not mean that either party is compelled to agree to a proposal.

good faith effort strategy Employment strategy aimed at changing practices that have contributed in the past to excluding or underutilizing protected groups.

grade description Written descriptions of the level of, say, responsibility and knowledge required by jobs in each grade. Similar jobs can then be combined into grades or classes.

grades A job classification system synonymous with class. Grade descriptions are written based on compensable factors listed in classification systems, such as the federal classification system. Grades often contain dissimilar jobs, such as secretaries, mechanics, and firefighters.

graphic rating scale A scale that lists a number of traits and a range of performance for each. The employee is then rated by identifying the score that best describes his or her level of performance for each trait.

grid training A formal approach to team building designed by Black and Mouton.

grievance Any factor involving wages, hours, or conditions of employment that is used as a complaint against the employer.

grievance procedure An orderly system whereby employer and union determine whether or not the contract has been violated.

Griggs* v. *The Duke Power Company Case heard by the Supreme Court in which the plaintiff argued that his employer's requirement that coal handlers be high school graduates was unfairly discriminatory. In finding for the plaintiff, the Court ruled that discrimination need not be overt to be illegal, that employment practices must be related to job performance, and that the burden of proof is on the employer to show that hiring standards are job related.

group life insurance Provides for lower rates for the employer or employee and includes all employees, including new employees, regardless of health or physical condition.

group pension plan A plan in which the employer and/or employee makes a set contribution to a pension fund.

growth stage Period from birth to age 14 during which the person develops a self-concept by identifying with and interacting with other people such as family, friends, and teachers.

guaranteed fair treatment Employer programs that are aimed at ensuring that all employees are treated fairly, generally by providing formalized, well-documented and highly publicized vehicles through which employees can appeal any eligible issues.

guaranteed piecework plan The minimum hourly wage plus an incentive for each piece produced above a set number of pieces per hour.

halo effect In performance appraisal, the problem that occurs when a supervisor's rating of a subordinate on one trait biases the rating of that person on other traits.

health maintenance organization (HMO) A prepaid health care system that generally provides routine round-the-clock medical services as well as preventive medicine in a clinic-type arrangement for employees, who pay a nominal fee in addition to the fixed annual fee the employer pays.

John Holland The career-counseling expert who carried out research with his Vocational Preference Test.

illegal bargaining items Items in collective bargaining that are forbidden by law; for example, the clause agreeing to hire "union members exclusively" would be illegal in a right-to-work state.

impasse A situation in which the parties cannot reach settlement, usually because one party is demanding more than the other will offer.

implied authority The authority exerted by a personnel manager by virtue of others' knowledge that he or she has access to top management (in areas like testing and affirmative action).

in-house development centers A company-based method for exposing prospective managers to realistic exercises to develop improved management skills.

individual retirement accounts (IRA) Pension plans qualified under tax laws to receive favorable tax treatment; established individually by employees

insubordination Willful disregard or disobedience of the boss's authority or legitimate orders; criticizing the boss in public.

insurance benefits Include worker's compensation benefits, life insurance plans, and hospitalization, medical, and disability insurance.

job analysis The procedure for determining the duties and skill requirements of a job and the kind of person who should be hired for it.

job description A list of a job's duties, responsibilities, reporting relationships, working conditions, and supervisory responsibilities—one product of a job analysis.

job evaluation A systematic comparison done in order to determine the worth of one job relative to another.

job instruction training (JIT) Listing of each of a job's basic tasks, along with a "key point" for each, in order to provide step-by-step training for employees.

job posting Posting notices of job openings on company bulletin boards is an effective recruiting method.

job rotation A management training technique that involves moving a trainee from department to department to broaden his or her experience and identify strong and weak points.

job sharing A concept that allows two or more people to share a single full-time job.

job specification A list of a job's "human requirements," that is, the requisite education, skills, personality, and so on—another product of a job analysis.

junior board A method of providing middle-management trainees with experience in analyzing company problems by inviting them to sit on a junior board of directors and make recommendations on overall company policies.

Landrum-Griffin Act The law aimed at protecting union members from possible wrongdoing on the part of their unions.

layoff A situation in which there is a temporary shortage of work so that employees are told there is no work for them but that management intends to recall the employee when work is again available.

leader match training A program that identifies types of leaders and teaches them how to fit their leadership style to their situation.

lifetime employment without guarantees Refers to a commitment on the part of firms like Toyota and Saturn to do all that is reasonably possible to avoid layoffs and non-performance-based dismissals while recognizing that ultimately the employment relationship must be "at-will."

line manager A manager who is authorized to direct the work of subordinates and responsible for accomplishing the organization's goals.

lockout A refusal by the employer to provide opportunities to work.

maintenance of membership arrangement A form of union security in which employees do not have to belong to the union; however, union members employed by the firm must maintain membership in the union for the contract period.

maintenance stage The period from about ages 45 to 65 during which the person secures his or her place in the world of work.

management assessment centers A situation in which management candidates are asked to make decisions in hypothetical situations and are scored on their performance. It usually also involves testing and the use of management games.

management by objectives (MBO) Involves setting specific measurable goals with each employee and then periodically reviewing the progress made.

management development Any attempt to improve current or future management performance by imparting knowledge, changing attitudes, or increasing skills.

management game A development technique in which teams of managers compete with one another by making computerized decisions regarding realistic but simulated companies.

management process The five basic functions of planning, organizing, staffing, leading, and controlling.

managerial grid A matrix that represents different possible leadership styles.

mandatory bargaining items Items in collective bargaining that a party must bargain over if they are introduced by the other party—for example, pay.

mediation Intervention in which a neutral third party tries to assist the principals toward reaching agreement.

merit pay Any salary increase awarded to an employee based on his or her individual performance.

merit raise Merit raise is another term for merit pay.

Meritor Savings Bank, FSB* v. *Vinson U.S. Supreme Court's first decision on sexual harassment. Held that existence of a hostile environment even without economic hardship is sufficient to prove harassment, even if participation was voluntary.

midcareer crisis substage The period occurring between the mid-thirties and mid-forties during which people often make a major reassessment of their progress relative to their original career ambitions and goals.

modern operating agreements A type of labor contract designed to give workers a greater say in how their jobs are performed through inclusion of work teams, fewer job classifications, and pay-for-knowledge systems.

National Labor Relations (or Wagner) Act This law banned certain types of unfair labor practices and provided for secret ballot elections and majority rule for determining whether or not a firm's employees want to unionize.

National Labor Relations Board (NLRB) The agency created by the Wagner Act to investigate unfair labor practice charges and to provide for secret ballot elections and majority rule in determining whether or not a firm's employees want a union.

national emergency strikes Strikes that might "imperil the national health and safety."

nondirective interview An unstructured conversational-style interview. The interviewer pursues points of interest as they come up in response to questions.

Norris-LaGuardia Act This law marked the beginning of the era of strong encouragement of unions and guaranteed to each employee the right to bargain collectively "free from interference, restraint, or coercion."

Occupational Safety and Health Act The law passed by Congress in 1970 "to assure so far as possible every working man and woman in the nation safe and healthful working conditions and to preserve our human resources."

Occupational Safety and Health Administration (OSHA) The agency created within the Department of Labor to set safety and health standards for almost all workers in the United States.

occupational market conditions The Bureau of Labor Statistics of the U.S. Department of Labor publishes projections of labor supply and demand for various occupations, as do other agencies.

occupational orientation The theory developed by John Holland that says there are six basic personal orientations that determine the sorts of careers to which people are drawn.

occupational skills The skills needed to be successful in a particular occupation. According to the Dictionary of Occupational Titles, occupational skills break down into three groups depending on whether they emphasize data, people, or things.

Office of Federal Contract Compliance Programs (OFCCP) This office is responsible for implementing the executive orders and ensuring compliance of federal contractors.

on-the-job training (OJT) Training a person to learn a job while working at it.

open shop Perhaps the least attractive type of union security from the union's point of view, the workers decide whether or not to join the union; and those who do not do not pay dues.

open-door program IBM's fair-treatment program, which gives every IBM employee the right to appeal the actions of his or her supervisor by taking the concern to successively higher levels of management.

opinion surveys Communication devices that use questionnaires to regularly ask employees their opinions about the company, management, and work life.

organizational development (OD) A program aimed at changing the attitudes, values, and beliefs of employees so that employees can improve the organization.

organizing committee Employees of a firm, identified by union officials as good prospects, who are established as a committee to be educated about the benefits of forming a union.

outplacement counseling A systematic process by which a terminated person is trained and counseled in the techniques of self-appraisal and securing a new position.

paired comparison method Ranking employees by making a chart of all possible pairs of the employees for each trait and indicating which is the better employee of the pair.

panel interview An interview in which a group of interviewers questions the applicant, a method similar to a press conference.

participant diary/logs Daily listings, made by workers, of every activity in which they engage, along with times.

pay grade A pay grade is comprised of jobs of approximately equal difficulty.

Pension Benefits Guarantee Corporation (PBGC) Established under ERISA to assure that pensions meet vesting obligations; also insures pensions should a plan terminate without sufficient funds to meet its vested obligations.

pension plans Plans that provide a fixed sum when employees reach a predetermined retirement age or when they can no longer work due to disability.

people-first values Values that emphasize putting employees first in all decisions because it is believed that employees are the firm's most important assets and deserve respect and trust.

performance analysis Careful study of performance to identify a deficiency and then correct it with new equipment, a new employee, a training program, or some other adjustment.

personnel management The concepts and techniques one needs to carry out the "people" or human resource aspects of a management position, including recruiting, screening, training, rewarding, and appraising.

personnel replacement charts Company records showing present performance and promotability of inside candidates for the most important positions.

piecework A system of pay based on the number of items processed by each individual worker in a unit of time, such as items per hour or items per day.

plant closing law The Worker Adjustment and Retraining Notification Act, which requires notifying employees in the event an employer decides to close its facility.

point method The job evaluation method in which a number of compensable factors are identified and then the degree to which each of these factors is present on the job is determined.

policies Guides to action that assure consistency under a particular set of circumstances and within the framework of the company's plan.

position analysis questionnaire (PAQ) A questionnaire used to collect quantifiable data concerning the duties and responsibilities of various jobs.

position replacement card A card prepared for each position in a company to show possible replacement candidates and their qualifications.

pre-retirement counseling Counseling provided to employees who are about to retire, and which covers matters such as benefits advice, second careers, and so on.

Pregnancy Discrimination Act (PDA) An amendment to Title VII of the Civil Rights Act that prohibits sex discrimination based on "pregnancy, childbirth, or related medical conditions." It requires employers to provide benefits—including sick leave and disability benefits and health and medical insurance—the same as for any employee not able to work because of disability.

profit-sharing plan A plan whereby most employees share in the company's profits.

programmed learning A systematic method for teaching job skills involving presenting questions or facts, allowing the person to respond, and giving the learner immediate feedback on the accuracy of his or her answers.

qualifications inventories Systematic records, either manual or computerized, listing employees' education, career and development interests, languages, special skills, etc., to be used in forecasting inside candidates for promotion.

quality circle A group of five to ten specially trained employees who meet on a regular basis to identify and solve problems in their work area.

quota strategy Employment strategy aimed at mandating the same results as the good faith effort strategy through specific hiring and promotion restrictions.

ranking method The simplest method of job evaluation that involves ranking each job relative to all other jobs, usually based on overall difficulty.

rate ranges A series of steps or levels within a pay grade, usually based upon years of service.

ratio analysis A forecasting technique for determining future staff needs by using ratios between sales volume and number of employees needed.

reality shock That state which results from the discrepancy between what the new employee expected from his or her new job, and the realities of it: may occur at the initial career entry when the new employee's high job expectations confront the reality of a boring, unchallenging job.

reliability The characteristic which refers to the consistency of scores obtained by the same person when retested with the identical or equivalent tests.

restricted policy Another test for adverse impact, involving demonstration that an employer's hiring practices exclude a protected group, whether intentionally or not.

retirement The point at which a person gives up one's work, usually around the age of 60–65, but increasingly earlier today due to firms' early-retirement incentive plans.

retirement benefits Provide the employee with an income upon retirement.

reverse discrimination Claim that due to affirmative action quota systems, white males are discriminated against.

right-to-work laws Legislation that outlawed labor contracts that made union membership a condition for retaining employment.

rings of defense An alternative layoff plan in which temporary supplemental employees are hired with the understanding that they may be laid off at any time.

role playing A training technique in which trainees act out the parts of people in a realistic management situation.

salary survey A survey aimed at determining prevailing wage rates. A good salary survey provides specific wage rates for specific jobs. Formal written questionnaire surveys are the most comprehensive, but telephone surveys and newspaper ads are also sources of information.

savings plan A plan in which employees contribute for their retirement a fixed percentage of their weekly wage, usually matched by a certain percentage by the employer.

Scanlon plan An incentive plan developed in 1937 by Joseph Scanlon and designed to encourage cooperation, involvement, and sharing of benefits. Plan involves attitudes, suggestions by workers, and benefits formulas.

scatter plot A graphical method used to help identify the relationship between two variables.

Edgar Schein Based on his research at the Massachusetts Institute of Technology, he identified five career anchors: creativity, managerial, security, technical, autonomy/independence.

School Board of Nassau County* v. *Arline U.S. Supreme Court ruling that persons with contagious diseases are covered by the Vocational Rehabilitation Act of 1973.

scientific management Implies careful, "scientific" study of all the factors that go into work and includes workers' motivation and job satisfaction, as well as optimum production.

self-actualization The full utilization of one's skills to become "all that one can be."

self-directed teams Highly trained work groups that use consensus decision making and broad authority to "self-direct" their activities.

sensitivity training A method for increasing employees' insights into their own behavior by candid discussions in groups led by special trainers.

serialized interview An interview in which the applicant is interviewed sequentially by several supervisors and each rates the applicant on a standard form.

severance pay A one-time payment some employers provide when terminating an employee.

sexual harassment Harassment, on the basis of sex, that has the purpose or effect of substantially interfering with a person's work performance or creating an intimidating, hostile, or offensive work environment.

sick leave Provides pay to an employee when he or she is out of work because of illness.

situational interview A series of job-related questions with "preferred" answers that are asked of all job applicants.

skip-level interview Also known as the executive interview, this is an IBM program in which employees are periodically invited to speak to a manager one or more levels above that of their manager for the purpose of ensuring more fair, open communications throughout the firm.

Social Security Provides three types of benefits: retirement income at the age of 62 and thereafter; survivor's or death benefits payable to the employee's dependents, regardless of age at time of death; and disability benefits payable to disabled employees and their dependents. These benefits are payable only if the employee is insured under the Social Security Act.

speak up! programs Communications programs that allow employees to register questions, concerns, and complaints about work-related matters.

special awards Individual bonuses, such as TVs, paid on the basis of performance ratings.

special management development techniques Techniques like leader match that develop leadership ability, increase sensitivity to others, and reduce interdepartmental conflicts.

stabilization substage The period, roughly from age 30 to 40, during which firm occupational goals are set and more explicit career planning is made to determine the sequence for accomplishing these goals.

staff (service) function The function of a personnel manager in assisting and advising line management.

staff manager A manager who assists and advises line managers.

standard hour plan A plan by which a worker is paid

a basic hourly rate but is paid an extra percentage of his or her base rate for production exceeding the standard per hour or per day. Similar to piecework payment but based on a percent premium.

stock option The right to purchase a stated number of shares of a company stock at a stated price during a stated period of time. An executive is given the right to purchase shares in the future at today's price. If the company grows, share prices may rise and the executive may benefit, assuming the economy is stable.

straight piecework plan Under this pay system each worker receives a set payment for each piece produced or processed in a factory or shop.

strategic plan Course of action the firm plans to pursue in becoming the sort of enterprise it wants to be, given the firm's external opportunities and threats and its internal strengths and weaknesses.

stress interview An interview in which the applicant is made uncomfortable by a series of often rude questions. This technique helps identify hypersensitive applicants and those with low or high stress tolerance.

strictness/leniency The problem that occurs when a supervisor has a tendency to rate all subordinates either high or low.

strike Refusal by employees to work until their demands are met by the employer.

succession planning A process through which senior-level openings are planned for and eventually filled.

supplemental pay benefits Benefits for time not worked such as unemployment insurance, vacation and holiday pay, and sick pay.

supplemental unemployment benefits Provisions for a "guaranteed annual income" in certain industries where employers must shut down to change machinery or due to reduced work. These benefits are paid by the company and supplement unemployment benefits.

survey feedback A method which involves surveying employees' attitudes and providing feedback to department managers so that problems can be solved by the managers and employees.

sympathy strike A strike that takes place when one union strikes in support of the strike of another.

System I The organizational system, described by Rensis Likert, in which managers mistrust subordinates and thus feel compelled to coerce them to work. (Corresponds to Theory X.)

System IV Likert's alternative system in which managers have confidence in workers and purposely involve them in decision-making processes. (Corresponds to Theory Y.)

Taft-Hartley Act Also known as the Labor–Management Relations Act, this law prohibited union unfair labor practices and enumerated the rights of employees as union members. It also enumerated the rights of employers.

task analysis A detailed study of a job to identify the skills required, so that an appropriate training program may be instituted.

Frederick Taylor Father of the scientific management movement, according to which a fair day's work should depend on a careful, formal process of inspection and observation.

team building Improving the effectiveness of teams such as corporate officers and division directors through use of consultants, interviews, and team-building meetings.

team or group incentive plan A plan in which a production standard is set for a specific work group, and its members are paid incentives if the group exceeds the production standard.

termination at will The idea, based in law, that the employment relationship can be terminated "at will" by either the employer or the employee for any reason.

termination interview The interview in which an employee is informed of the fact that he or she has been dismissed.

Theory X The set of assumptions which holds that workers cannot be trusted and must be coerced into doing their jobs.

Theory Y McGregor's alternative theory that people do not have an aversion to work and are capable of self-control in the work situation.

third-party involvement Interventions by a third party used to overcome an impasse, such as mediation, fact-finding, and arbitration.

Title VII of the 1964 Civil Rights Act The section of the act that says you cannot discriminate on the basis of race, color, religion, sex, or national origin with respect to employment.

top-down programs Communications activities including in-house TV centers, frequent roundtable discussions, and in-house newsletters that provide continuing opportunities for the firm to let all employees be updated on important matters regarding the firm.

training The process of teaching new employees the basic skills they need to perform their jobs.

transactional analysis (TA) A method for helping two people communicate and behave on the job in an adult manner by understanding each other's motives.

trend analysis Study of a firm's past employment needs over a period of years to predict future needs.

trial substage The period from about age 25 to 30 during which the person determines whether or not the chosen field is suitable and if it is not, attempts to change it.

unclear performance standards An appraisal scale that is too open to interpretation; instead, include descriptive phrases that define each trait and what is meant by standards like "good" or "unsatisfactory."

unemployment insurance Provides weekly benefits if a person is unable to work through some fault other than his or her own.

unfair labor practice strike A strike aimed at protesting illegal conduct by the employer.

unfair labor practices Under the Wagner Act, it is unfair for management to "interfere with, restrain, or coerce employees" in exercising their legally sanctioned right of self-organization.

union security Unions' desire to establish security for themselves by gaining the right to represent a firm's workers.

union shop A form of union security in which the company can hire nonunion people but they must join the union after a prescribed period of time and pay dues. (If they do not, they can be fired.)

union unfair labor practices The Taft-Hartley Act banned unions from restraining or coercing employees from exercising their guaranteed bargaining rights; prohibited unions from causing an employer to discriminate in any way against an employee in order to encourage or discourage membership in a union; prohibited a union from refusing to bargain "in good faith" with the employer about wages, hours, and other employment conditions; and prohibited a union from engaging in "feather-bedding."

United Steel Workers of America v. Weber Supreme Court case in which the plaintiff claimed being a victim of reverse discrimination.

unsafe acts Behavior tendencies and undesirable attitudes that cause accidents.

unsafe conditions The mechanical and physical conditions that cause accidents.

validity The accuracy with which a test, interview, etc. measures what it purports to measure or fulfills the function it was designed to fill.

value-based hiring An exhaustive selection process that seeks to match not only the person's skills with the job but also his or her values with those of the company.

variable compensation Financial rewards paid as one-time awards that do not permanently increase fixed payroll costs.

vestibule or simulated training Training employees on special off-the-job equipment, as in airplane pilot training, whereby training costs and hazards can be reduced.

vesting Provision that money placed in a pension fund cannot be forfeited for any reason.

Vocational Rehabilitation Act of 1973 The act requiring certain federal contractors to take affirmative action for disabled persons.

voluntary bargaining items Items in collective bargaining, over which bargaining is neither illegal nor mandatory—neither party can be compelled against its wishes to negotiate over those items.

voluntary reduction in pay plan An alternative to layoffs in which all employees agree to reductions in pay to keep everyone working.

voluntary time off An alternative to layoffs in which some employees agree to take time off to reduce the employer's payroll and avoid the need for a layoff.

Vroom-Yetton leadership training A development program for management trainees that focuses on decision making with varying degrees of input from subordinates.

wage curve Shows the relationship between the value of the job and the average wage paid for this job.

Walsh-Healey Public Contract Act A law from 1936 that requires minimum wage and working conditions for employees working on any government contract amounting to more than $10,000.

Wards Cove v. Atonio U.S. Supreme Court decision that makes it difficult to prove a case of unlawful discrimination against an employer.

wildcat strike An unauthorized strike occurring during the term of a contract.

work samples Actual job tasks used in testing applicants' performance.

work sampling technique A testing method based on measuring performance on actual, basic job tasks.

work sharing A temporary reduction in work hours by a group of employees during economic difficulties to prevent layoffs.

worker involvement programs Programs that aim to boost organizational effectiveness by getting employees to participate in the planning, organizing, and managing of their jobs.

worker's compensation Provides employer-funded income and medical benefits to work-related accident victims or their dependents, regardless of fault.

wrongful discharge An employee dismissal that does not comply with the law or does not comply with the contractual arrangement stated or implied by the firm via its employment application forms, employee manuals, or other promises.

PHOTO CREDITS

CHAPTER 1:

3 Andy Levin/Photo Researchers
10 Charles Gupton/Stock Market
12 Ken Straiton/Stock Market
18 Stacey Pick/Stock Boston
19 Alex Quesada/Matrix
20 Rhoda Sidney

CHAPTER 2:

34 Paul Fetters/Matrix
44 Stacey Pick/Stock Boston
64 Karen Kasmauski/Woodfin Camp & Associates

CHAPTER 3:

82 Charles Westerman/Gamma Liaison
91 Nita Winter/The Image Works
98 Bob Daemmrich/Stock Boston
102 IBM

CHAPTER 4:

117 Chris Gierlich/SABA
118 Delta Airlines
120 Delta Airlines
122 Bob Daemmrich/The Image Works
140 Gillette International
141 Joseph Giannetti/Stock Boston

CHAPTER 5:

158 Bob Daemmrich/Stock Boston
177 W.B. Spunbarg/Picture Cube
184 Laima Druskis/Stock Boston

CHAPTER 6:

212 Jim Pickerell/Stock Boston
217 Grant LeDuc/Stock Boston
222 Jack McKigney/Picture Group

CHAPTER 7:

235 Miro Vintoniv/Stock Boston
237 Saturn
244 L. Skoogfors/Woodfin Camp & Associates
249 The Roach Organization
250 Jeff Greenberg/Picture Cube
253 Lindsay Hebberd/Woodfin Camp & Associates
256 Peter Vadnai/Stock Market

CHAPTER 8:

268 M. Richards
275 Tim Davis/Photo Researchers
279 Bob Gomel/Stock Market
291 Charles Gupton/Stock Market
292 Carole Lee/Picture Cube

CHAPTER 9:

306 Will & Deni McIntyre/Photo Researchers
311 U.S. Department of Commerce
317 Jim Harrison/Stock Boston
318 Louis Psihoyos/Matrix
319 Saturn

CHAPTER 10:

346 Gabe Palmer/Mugshots/Stock Boston
354 Richard Paisley/Stock Boston
358 Edward L. Miller/Stock Boston

CHAPTER 11:

373 Lisa Quinones/Black Star
377 Gabe Palmer/Mugshots/Stock Boston
381 Frank White/Gamma-Liaison
382 D. Aubert/Sygma
384 Mark Richards
388 Randy Taylor/Sygma

CHAPTER 12:

403 Ogust/The Image Works

423 William Strobe/Woodfin Camp & Associates
425 Dan Lamont/Matrix
427 Sygma
434 Robert Reichert/Gamma-Liaison
435 Bob Daemmrich/Tony Stone Images

CHAPTER 13:

465 Bob Daemmrich/Stock Boston
471 Thomas Craig/Picture Cube
476 Ted Streshinsky/Photo 20-20
478 Mark Richards

CHAPTER 14:

490 John Giordano/SABA
496 Andree Abescassis/Photo 20-20
500 John Ficara/Woodfin Camp & Associates
508 Arnold Zahn/Black Star
514 Richard Palsey/Stock Boston
517 Robbie McClaran

CHAPTER 15:

529 Archive Photos
531 UPI/Bettmann
544 Charles Gupton/Stock Boston

CHAPTER 16:

571 Andrew Holbrooke/Stock Boston
579 Skjold/The Image Works
582 Rick Brown/Stock Boston

CHAPTER 17:

593 Comstock
597 Mark Katzman
603 UPI/Bettmann
607 David Sams/Stock Boston
611 Patrick Pfister/Picture Group

CHAPTER 18:

622 Joe Carini/The Image Works
633 John Elk III/Stock Boston
637 Frank Fisher/Gamma-Liaison

CHAPTER 19:

668 Blair Seitz/Photo Researchers
678 Henry Horenstein/Picture Cube

APPENDIX:

687 Eiji Miyazawa/Black Star

INDEX

NAME AND ORGANIZATION

SUBJECT

D

Q

V

W

Y